RATANLAL & DHIRAJLAL

THE

LAW OF EVIDENCE

First Edition	1916
Second Edition	1919
Third Edition	1923
Fourth Edition	1926
Fifth Edition	1928
Sixth Edition	1932
Seventh Edition	1935
Eighth Edition	1939
Ninth Edition	1944
Tenth Edition	1946
Eleventh Edn.	1949
Twelfth Edition	1953
Thirteenth Edn.	1958
Fourteenth Edn.	
Fifteenth Edn.	1968
Sixteenth Edn.	1973
Seventeenth Edn.	1987
Reprint	1988, 1989, 1990, 1991
Eighteenth Edn.	1992
Reprint	1993, 1994, 1995, 1996
Nineteenth Edn.	1997
Reprint	1999, 2000, 2001, 2002
Twentieth (Enlarged) Edn.	2002
Reprint	2003
Twenty First (Eco. P/B) Edn.	2004
Reprint	2006, 2007, 2008, 2009, 2010
Twenty Second (Enl.) Hindi Edn.	2009
Twenty Third (Enlarged) Edn.	2010
Twenty Fourth (Eco. P/B) Edn.	2011
Reprint	2011, 2012, 2013
Twenty Fifth Edn.	2013
Reprint	2014, 2015, 2016, 2017
Twenty Sixth Edn.	2017
Reprint	2019
Twenty Seventh Edn.	2019
Reprint	2019
Reprint	2020
Reprint	2021
Reprint	2021
Reprint	2021
Reprint	2021
Reprint	2021
Reprint	2021
Reprint	2021
Reprint	2021
Reprint	2021
Reprint	2022
Reprint	2022
Reprint	2022
Reprint	2022
Reprint	**2022**

RATANLAL & DHIRAJLAL

THE LAW OF EVIDENCE

27th Edition

Editorial Board

K Kannan
Chairman, Railway Claims Tribunal
Former Judge, Punjab & Haryana High Court

Anjana Prakash
Advocate, Supreme Court of India
Former Judge, Patna High Court

in collaboration with Specialist Editors

LexisNexis

This book is a publication of **LexisNexis**
(A Division of RELX India Pvt Ltd)
14th floor, Building No 10, Tower–B, DLF Cyber City, Phase-II,
Gurgaon–122002, Haryana, India.
Tel: + 91 124 4774444 Fax: + 91 124 4774100
Website: www.lexisnexis.co.in / E-mail: help.in@lexisnexis.com

---

Ratanlal & Dhirajlal The Law of Evidence, 27th Edition, 2019

ISBN: 978-93-8854-852-6

Printed by: Sai Printo Packs Pvt. Ltd., A-102/4, Okhla Industrial Area, Phase-II, New Delhi: 110 020

Publisher's Note

It gives us immense pleasure to place before you the 27th edition of *Ratanlal & Dhirajlal's* seminal work on the law of evidence. A leading commentary on the subject for over ten decades, this celebrated work on the law of evidence enjoys the reputation of being one of the most authoritative publications on the subject. The work explains the complex rules of evidence in a lucid, comprehensive and systematic manner.

The last edition of this classic commentary on the Indian Evidence Act was published in July, 2017 and its revision became indispensable after the enactment of Criminal Law (Amendment) Act, 2018 and a few very important pronouncements by the Supreme Court of India. Authenticity, originality and reliability have always been the hallmarks of this publication and every possible care has been taken in this edition to maintain the excellence, style and quality of the work.

The law relating to sexual offences was last amended drastically *vide* the Criminal Law (Amendment) Act, 2013. The 2013 Amendment Act was enacted in the wake of brutal gang rape and murder in December, 2012 which led to a nationwide protest and outcry. The Criminal Law (Amendment) Act, 2018 has further amended the law relating to sexual offences in India. The Amendment Act of 2018 replaces the Ordinance promulgated by the President in April, 2018 in the wake of public outcry over abduction, rape, and murder of an 8-year-old girl in Kathua in the State of Jammu and Kashmir and the rape of another woman at Unnao in Uttar Pradesh. The Amendment Act of 2018 which came into force with effect from 21 April, 2018 has amended the relevant sections of the Indian Penal Code, the Indian Evidence Act, the Code of Criminal Procedure and the Protection of Children from Sexual Offences Act, 2012 to provide for stringent punishment for perpetrators of rape particularly of girls below 12 and 16 years. Rape on a woman under 12 years of age is now made punishable with rigorous imprisonment for a term which shall not be less than 20 years, but which may extend to imprisonment for life, and with fine or with death. Gang rape on a woman under 12 years of age is now made punishable with imprisonment for life, and with fine, or with death.

The first edition of this leading commentary was published in 1916 and the commentary had grown voluminous over the years. In order to rationalise the size of the book, many topics have been rewritten and existing comments have been carefully pruned but the commentary remains pithy and concise. Just like the previous versions, the current edition will offer great help to students and professionals, when they require a quick overview in the form of summary to bolster their preparations.

We are confident that this new edition will be valued by students, teachers, lawyers, judges, judicial and police training academies (national and state), police departments, CBI officials, researchers and scholars.

Due caution has been exercised in bringing out the present work, yet human fallibility cannot be discounted as a matter of guarantee. Therefore, readers' feedback is welcome and will be very useful for improving the future editions.

August, 2019 — Editorial Board

Preface to the Twenty Sixth Edition

The names of Ratanlal and Dhirajlal popularly known as R&D are amongst the pioneer authors of India in the field of law. They have been favourites of the devotees of law and one will hardly find a person in the field of law who has not come across one or the other of their commentaries on the most important subjects such as the Indian Penal Code, the Code of Criminal Procedure, the Indian Evidence Act and the like. Their commentaries have been favourites not only of the students of law and the new entrants as legal practitioners but of the Magistrates/Judicial Magistrates particularly at the stage of framing of charges against the accused.

This commentary i.e. the Law of Evidence was first published in 1916, thus covering an era much before our independence when the hierarchy of the Courts of Law was to a great extent different from that of ours today. To remain standing on the high pedestal for more than a century as a favourite itself speaks volumes of the credibility and usefulness of this commentary.

Owing to the general applicability of the law of evidence with the exception of special provisions made in the special enactments and fields like domestic inquiries, it acquires a unique place among all the laws. A legal practitioner has to master over the provisions of the law of evidence as they apply to all of cases with a very few exceptions as already mentioned above where the principle of '*generalibus specialia derogant*' applies. One has to after all prove one's case as per the provisions of the law of evidence to get the matter decided in one's favour by the Court of Law.

Ratanlal & Dhirajlal's the Law of Evidence has a very long coverage though selectively as everything cannot be summed up in an Edition particularly meant for the law students and the beginners as legal practitioners. However, almost all important cases have been covered in this very handy volume. For the sake of convenience the whole matter has been divided under various headings and sub-headings. Thus, all the important rulings on a particular point can very easily be traced.

To have a grasp over the subject, this Edition adds about more than fifty such headings/sub-headings and that further adds to its usefulness and suitability. All the important rulings of the Supreme Court and that of the High Courts in respect of the law of evidence have been incorporated with the help of the judgments reported in the SCC, AIR, CrLJ and AIR CC from the year 2014 to the almost quarter of 2017.

A summary of the whole matter given at the end of the Book makes it even more useful to the students of law and the detailed Subject Index makes the search for the rulings on a particular point much easier.

Nothing would be more gratifying to us than its still remaining a favourite of all those concerned and retaining its past grandeur.

Lucknow
June 29, 2017

Shakil Ahmad Khan

Preface to the Twenty Fifth Edition

The law of evidence is a vehicle which enables the justice dispensation mechanism to catch up with fast paced rapid changes in the world. It also requires fast paced evolution and subject-specific tailoring so as to take care of new situations, new offences and new modes of committing these offences. The promotion of accuracy in the decision making process is the primary target meant to be achieved through the law of evidence.

However, in an adversarial form of litigation, which we have in our country, one of the problems vexing the system is the extent to which it is possible to mould trial procedures, be it in a civil or a criminal case, in consistence with human rights norms, so as to expedite the fact-finding quest of a court of law. While it is a cardinal rule in the law of evidence that the best available evidence should be brought before the court, experience shows that delay very often results in such best available evidence getting washed off and the courts keep on waiting.

As a result, in the recent past, we have seen new legislative changes with specific situations and goals. A separate set of laws to deal with the recent growth of offences against women is the latest legislative exercise depicting the need to maintain pace with society. Apparently, the Legislature as well as the Judiciary have used every occasion to give flexibility and a dynamic character to the law of evidence.

In *Sky Land International Pvt Ltd v Kavita Lawani*,[1] it was observed by the Delhi High Court as under:

> … Section 165 casts a duty on the Judge to discover truth to do complete justice and empowers him to summon and examine or recall and re-examine any such person if his evidence appears to be essential to the just decision of the case. The Judge has to play an active role to discover the truth. He is expected, and indeed it is his duty, to explore all avenues open to him in order to discover the truth and, to that end, question witnesses on points which the lawyers for the parties have either overlooked or left obscure or willfully avoided. The Court can also invoke section 30 of the Code of Civil Procedure to ascertain the truth.

Shri Arun Mohan, an eminent jurist and Senior Advocate, is of the view that if courts, with the assistance of lawyers, were to formulate precise questions as part of a formal order under section 30 CPC and direct filing affidavits in answer at the earliest stage of any case, there will be little need for viva-voce examination. But if that survives, then by resort to section 30 CPC and section 165 Evidence Act the parties can be examined. So done, the time taken by civil litigation will cut down to one-half.

In view of these contentious issues, being associated with this prestigious work namely *Ratanlal and Dhirajlal's Law of Evidence* was indeed a proud but humbling experience. While revising this 25th Edition, our earnest effort was to follow in the footsteps of the previous illustrious authors so that this edition reaches as close as possible to the high standards set by them in its previous editions. It is for the legal fraternity—the Hon'ble Judges, the lawyers as also those in academics, who use this for their professional or academic pursuit, to examine how far we have succeeded in achieving our goal.

---

1. Justice JR Midha in RFA 697 of 2010 decided by the Delhi High Court on 25 May, 2012.

We are thankful to Shri Sidharth Luthra (Addl. Solicitor General), Shri Arun Mohan, Shri Rakesh Munjal, Shri Sunil Kumar and Shri Neeraj Kr Jain, all Senior Advocates, with whom we were in constant touch and who were ever ready with their valuable suggestions and guidance.

Family support was always forthcoming in the form of Mr U S Prasad, Ms Anita Mohan, Mr Umang Shankar and Ms Kaveri Mohan in logistics, research and their respective professional experiences.

We are also grateful to colleagues, Ms Priya Hingorani, Ms Ketaki Goswami, Mr CD Singh, Mr Nagendra Kumar, Mr Pramod Dubey, Mr Rajiv Shukla, Ms Anita Pandey, Mr Chandra Bhushan Prasad, Mr Anshuman Ashok, Mr Ardhendumauli Kr Prasad, Mr Aditya Shankar, Mr Aditya Singla, Mr Parveen Kumar, Mr Aditya Pratap Singh and Ms Rohini Prasad, Advocates for their assistance as and when required.

Special mention in this regard is due to Ms Neha Srivastava, an Asstt. Professor at the Amity Law School, Noida and also to Ms Shaliza Katoch, Advocate. As an intern, Ms Deepti Dayal (Campus Law Centre, Delhi University) also contributed her bit in ensuring that this Edition book attains its present form.

Our thanks are also due to the entire editorial team of publishers, LexisNexis, for conceiving and bringing out this edition of the book in its present form, as also in affording an opportunity to us to contribute in taking this treatise forward and joining the list of legal luminaries who were earlier part of this work.

We hope that the book is useful not only for the Bar, the Bench, students and researchers of law but also to those who are subjected to the Code of Criminal Procedure and those who invoke it upon being a victim in any manner whatsoever.

Suggestions for the improvement of this book would be highly appreciated, as they can be a useful source for improvement in the future editions as also in the evolution of law on the subject.

New Delhi
20 October, 2013

Binod Mohan Prasad
Manish Mohan

Preface to the Twenty Fourth Edition

During the period between the preceding and the present editions, the statutory contribution to the development of the subject has been the amendments in the Act brought in by the changes made in the Information Technology (Amendment) Act, 2009. The changes are of a technical nature. The words 'digital signature' are to be replaced by the words 'electronic signature'. A new provision, namely section 45-A, has been added. It provides for 'relevancy of opinion of examiner of electronic evidence'.

As is usual with this subject, the role of the judiciary in explaining and developing the scope of provisions of the Evidence Act has always been much more than anything else. A number of decisions of the Supreme Court have shown how to use the testimony of relatives and that circumstantial evidence must establish an unbroken chain up to the point of the incident, and to what extent an evidence illegally obtained can be used. Points relating to DNA test have been explained in quite a number of cases and also the extent to which an FIR can become a substantive evidence. Identification by voice has not been given evidentiary status. Evidence cannot be given of the recovery of a weapon of offence which has no nexus with the types of injury caused to the deceased. A conviction cannot generally be founded on a retracted confession. In the case of multiple dying declarations, each has to be considered independently of others on its own merit as to their evidentiary value. One cannot be rejected because of the contents of the other. A dying declaration by a woman committing suicide spoke of torture for dowry by the husband. It led to the husband's conviction. Letters written by wife before her killing were taken to be dying declarations because they revealed the circumstances which led to her death. Interaction between decisions of civil and criminal courts over the same cause of action came up for clarification in some cases.

An expert opinion should be definite and not just what appears to be the case. An expert was considered to be competent to express opinion on voice of the party to an oral agreement and also on value of the property. Evidence on live television link and video conferencing was considered under section 62. A PIL can be supported by a newspaper report. Secondary evidence of call records of cellular telephones has been allowed. The effect of second illegal marriage on the right of succession has been considered. The value of provisions relating to dowry death has become all the more noticeable. The presumption of marriage arising from a live-in-relationship has prevented it from being considered as being a walk-in and walk-out relationship. An exemption granted under a taxing statute which was not permissible would not constitute any estoppel.

All these developments and valuable opinions have been considered at their respective places in the text.

12 April, 2011 — Editors

'Ram Navmi Day'

Preface to the Twenty First Edition

The Law of Evidence occupies a unique position in the field of substantive and procedural laws. The existence of substantive rights can only be established by relevant and admissible evidence. The law of evidence plays a pivotal role in the effective functioning of the judicial system. With rapid advances in diverse fields of life, human relations have undergone an unforeseen transformation, generating new conflicts and controversies. The law of evidence had to groom itself up for facing the emerging developments which pose unprecedented problems in the collection of evidence and proof of facts. Significant changes have taken place between the publication of the last edition and the present edition of this time-honoured commentary on the subject by Ratanlal and Dhirajlal. The present edition has had to face the vast ramification of the subject during the period intervening between the preceding and present editions. Legal pronouncements, scholarly views on the provisions of the Act and on judicial decisions, and statutory amendments reflecting the legislative response to the existing and emerging social challenges have not only developed the subject out of its narrow contours but have given to it new dimensions. Capturing all the strands of the changing scenario, integrating them into the existing text, examining them from the point of view of their success or failure in the context of the socio-economic and legal problems which brought about the statutory provisions and legal decisions and, shaping the comments accordingly, have been the main tasks that the present edition set before itself. In shaping the comments and reporting the decisions of the period, the traditional style of the book, namely, sorting out the principles in the form of comments on the one hand, and giving the facts and decisions under the heading "Cases", on the other, has been maintained.

Fair trial is the essence of all judicial proceedings. More often than not, it is matters of evidence which prejudice a fair trial. In the application of the various provisions of the Act to a trial process, due attention has been paid to human rights and fair trial.

The changes brought about in the Evidence Act by its amendment by the Information Technology Act, have been noted and discussed at appropriate places.

We are thankful for the assistance given ungrudgingly by several scholars in the preparation of this edition. We have also benefited by the help of the editiorial staff of Wadhwa and Company. We are grateful for their support in making the book worthwhile.

Mumbai
4 October, 2003
'Vijaya Dashmi' Day

Y V Chandrachud
Chief Editor

Preface to the Nineteenth Edition

The Law of Evidence occupies a unique position between substantive and procedural laws. The assertion of Substantive rights can only be established by evidence, relevant and admissible. Therefore, the law of evidence plays a pivotal role in the effective functioning of judicial system. With rapid advances in diverse fields of life, human relationship has undergone an unforseen transformation, presenting new kinds of conflicts and controversies. The law of evidence has to groom itself for the emerging developments which pose unprecedented problems in the collection of evidence and the proof of facts. Naturally, significant changes have taken place between the publication of the last edition and the present edition of this book on evidence. In some interesting cases, courts have had to examine anew whether the statements contained in the First Information Report can be ascribed evidentiary value in an exceptional class of cases. A number of judgments of the Supreme Court have thrown light upon the assessment and appreciation of the testimony of police witnesses, chance witnesses, interested witnesses, child witnesses and so forth. Considerable light has been thrown by these decisions and the High Court decisions upon questions relating to standard of proof and appreciation of evidence. Clarifications have been provided in a number of judgments on the conflict between ocular, circumstantial and technical evidence. Special rules of evidence are being developed in the appreciation of evidence of victims of sexual assault. The doctrine of "*res gestae*" has been elaborated to lend a liberal touch to cases in which the victim can be the sole witness. The strict rule of corroboration has been softened and freed from its hackenyed shackles, to meet new forms of human ingenuity. Significant developments have also taken place in the field of "without prejudice communications". The effect of presumptions in cases of dowry deaths has occupied the minds and concerns of courts to meet a growing social evil of desperate dimensions. A set of new rules has been devised to deal effectively with cases requiring a person to be subjected to blood test for determining paternity or drunkenness. The frontiers of the doctrine of estoppel have been widened to meet the challenge of novel contentions. The scope of the theory of privilege as to documents is being constantly narrowed, one of the latest and one of the thorniest questions being whether a Commission of Enquiry can enter upon and decide the question of privilege claimed by the State and its agencies.

These and many other developments have been noticed in this edition to enrich the text of the commentaries.

Mumbai
3 April, 1997

YV Chandrachud
Chief Editor

Preface to the Eighteenth Edition

Appearing, as it does, five years after the preceding edition, the present edition has had to face and harness the vast growth of the subject during the period. Legal pronouncements, in the shape of a large body of case-law, scholarly views on the provisions of the Act and also on judicial decisions under those provisions and statutory amendments showing legislative responses to the existing and emerging social problems have not only developed the subject out of its existing bounds but also imparted to it certain new trends and directions. Capturing all the strands of the changing scenario, integrating them into the existing text, examining them from the point of view of their success or failure in the context of the socio-economic and legal problems which brough about the statutory provisions and legal decisions and shaping the comments accordingly have been the main tasks that the present edition set before itself. In shaping the comments and reporting the decisions of the period, the traditional style of the book, namely, sorting out the principles in the form of comments, on the one hand, and giving the facts and decisions under the heading "Cases", on the other, has been maintained.

This edition witnesses the explanation of the status of family courts; the growing recognition of the utility and value of circumstantial evidence, rethinking about the appreciation of the evidence of victims of sexual assault; the use of evidence obtained by unlawful means; the extent to which domestic inquiries have to follow the principles of this subject; the extent to which the Supreme Court can interfere in concurrent findings; a liberalisation of the view about statements which can be regarded as parts of the transaction, (*res gestae*); the expanded meaning of the word "conduct" in reference to persons and parties whose conduct is relevant; the methods of ascertaining the identity of wrongdoers; a new dimension to the meaning of the expression "reasonable ground to believe" in the context of evidence in cases of conspiracies; expansion of the scope of the expression "without prejudice negotiations"; the accused using in his favour his statements to police which amount to confession; viewing the dying declarations of women sacrificed at the altar of dowry; probative element in the statements as to facts of public nature in Acts and notifications, and acceptance of the opinion of experts about the identity of type script. These developments have been recorded in the field of relevancy of facts.

In reference to the scope of the expression "direct evidence" computerised information and videotaping of a happening have been taken out of the "hearsay" exclusion, but not newspaper reports of similar happenings. In the matters of burden of proof, the matters relating to election petitions and *alibi* pleas have attracted comments from the Supreme Court. The maxim *res ipsa loquitur* has also invited Supreme Court comments as to the scope of its application. The newly created presumptions about suicide by married women and absence of consent in certain rape cases have had their share of cases explaining the scope of the expressions used in creating these presumptions. The rapid expansion of the varied applications of the doctrine of estoppel, which were likely to have cripping effects on the functioning of the Government and educational institutions, the same has now been subjected to the requirement of the balancing process of equities on both sides.

The extent of police privilege in not disclosing their sources of information, and the legal professional privilege and how it becomes affected if a privileged document happens to fall in the hands of a third person, have been examined anew in the light of demands of public interest.

Mumbai
31 August, 1992
"Ganesh Chaturthi"

M Hidayatullah
Manohar VR

Preface to the Sixteenth Edition

This edition has undergone a through and careful revision and the case law has been brought down to December 1972.

The Commentary under each section is divided into two parts: Comment and Cases. In the Comment, the object, principle, and meaning of the provisions of the Act are carefully explained and elucidated in the light of leading Indian and English decisions. Under the heading Cases, the facts of important decision have been given to illustrate the meaning of the provisions.

A critical study of this book will enable a student to acquire a sound knowledge of the law of evidence. A complete mastery of the principles of the law of evidence is a *sine qua non* to one who seriously aspires to rise in the profession.

The Summary of the provisions of the Act at the end of the book will give to the beginner a bird's eye view of the whole Act.

This Commentary will be useful to the Bench and the Bar as a handy reference book on the subject, as it incorporates all the important decisions of the Supreme Court and the High Courts.

November, 1973 MRV

Contents

THE INDIAN EVIDENCE ACT

(Act 1 of 1872)

Arrangement of Sections

PART I
RELEVANCY OF FACTS

CHAPTER I
PRELIMINARY

CHAPTER II
OF THE RELEVANCY OF FACTS

CHAPTER XI

OF IMPROPER ADMISSION AND REJECTION OF EVIDENCE

The Indian Evidence Act, 1872

(1 of 1872)

List of Amending Acts

1. The Indian Evidence Amendment Act, 1872 (18 of 1872).
2. The Indian Evidence Act, 1872 Amendment Act, 1887 (3 of 1887).
3. The Indian Evidence Act, 1872 Amendment Act, 1891 (3 of 1891).
4. The General Clauses Act, 1897 (10 of 1897).
5. The Indian Evidence Act, 1899 (5 of 1899).
6. The Repealing and Amending Act, 1914 (10 of 1914).
7. The Repealing and Amending Act, 1819 (18 of 1919).
8. The Indian Evidence (Amendment) Act, 1926 (31 of 1926).
9. The Repealing and Amending Act, 1927 (10 of 1927).
10. The Repealing Act, 1927 (12 of 1927).
11. The Amending Act, 1934 (35 of 1934).
12. The Government of India (Adaptation of Indian Laws) Order, 1937.
13. The Repealing Act, 1938 (1 of 1938).
14. The Indian Independence (Adaptation of Central Acts and Ordinances) Order, 1948.
15. The Repealing and Amending Act, 1949 (40 of 1949).
16. The Adaptation of Laws Order, 1950.
17. The Part B States (Laws) Act, 1951 (3 of 1951).
18. The Criminal Law (Amendment) Act, 1983 (43 of 1983).
19. The Criminal Law (Second Amendment) Act, 1983 (46 of 1983).
20. The Terrorist Affected Areas (Special Courts) Act, 1984 (61 of 1984).
21. The Dowry Prohibition (Amendment) Act, 1986 (43 of 1986).
22. The Information Technology Act, 2000 (21 of 2000).
23. The Indian Evidence (Amendment) Act, 2002 (4 of 2003).
24. The Criminal Law (Amendment) Act, 2005 (2 of 2006).
25. The Information Technology (Amendment) Act, 2008 (10 of 2009).
26. The Criminal Law (Amendment) Act, 2013 (13 of 2013).
27. The Criminal Law (Amendment) Act, 2018 (22 of 2018).

Table of Cases

A

B

C

D

E

I

J

L

M

N

Q

T

U

V

THE LAW OF EVIDENCE

THE INDIAN EVIDENCE ACT

(Act I of 1872)[1]

[*Received the Governor General's assent on March 15, 1872*]

Preamble.—WHEREAS it is expedient to consolidate, define and amend the law of Evidence; it is hereby enacted as follows:—

COMMENT

The object of the preamble of an Act is to indicate what, in general terms, was the object of the Legislature in passing the Act. The preamble here shows that the Indian Evidence Act is not merely a fragmentary enactment, but a consolidatory one.

The Act reduces the English law of evidence to the form of express propositions arranged in their natural order with some modifications rendered necessary by the peculiar circumstances of India. It is in the main, drawn on the lines of the English law of evidence.

The word "evidence" is derived from the Latin word *evidens* or *evidere*, which means "to show clearly; to make clear to the sight; to discover clearly; to make plainly certain; to ascertain; to prove".

Before the passing of the Indian Evidence Act, the principles of English law of evidence were followed by the courts in India in presidency-towns. In the mofussil, Mohammedan law of evidence was followed for some time by British Courts, but subsequently various regulations, dealing with principles of evidence, were passed for the guidance of mofussil courts. Act II of 1855 partially codified the law of evidence. But it did not affect the practice in vogue in mofussil courts. In 1868, Mr Maine (afterwards Sir Henry Sumner) prepared a Draft Bill of the Law of Evidence, but it was abandoned as it was not suited to the country. In 1871, Mr Stephen (afterwards Sir James Fitz-James) prepared a new draft which was passed as Act I of 1872.

One great object of the Evidence Act is to prevent laxity in the admissibility of evidence, and to introduce a more correct and uniform rule of practice than was previously in vogue. The Act is not intended to do more than prescribe rules for the admissibility or otherwise of evidence on the issues as to which the courts have to record findings.

---

1. For Statement of Objects and Reason, see the Gazette of India, 1868, p 1574.

The main principles which underlie the law of evidence are—

(1) evidence must be confined to the matter in issue;

(2) hearsay evidence must not be admitted; and

(3) best evidence must be given in all cases.

The Indian Evidence Act is not exhaustive of the rules of evidence.[2] For the interpretation of the sections of the Act the court can look to the relevant English common law,[3] but the law of evidence which is a complete Code does not permit the importation of any principle of English Common Law relating to evidence in criminal cases to the contrary.[4]

Once a statute is passed, which purports to contain the whole law of evidence applicable in India, it is imperative. It is not open to any Judge to exercise a dispensing power, and admit evidence not admissible by the statute, because it appears to him that the irregular evidence would throw light upon the issue. The principles of exclusion of evidence adopted by the Act must be applied strictly and cannot be relaxed at the discretion of the court.[5]

The Evidence Act has no application to enquiries by Tribunals, even though they may be judicial in character. And the law only requires that rules of natural justice should be observed in the conduct of enquiries and if they do so the decisions of Tribunals are not liable to be impeached.[6]

The law of evidence is an adjective law, and, as such, has retrospective effect.[7]

---

2. *Re Rudolf Stallmann,* (1911) 39 Cal 164; *King-Emperor v Tun Hlaing,* (1923) 1 Ran 759 FB; *Re Annavi Muthiriyan,* (1915) 39 Mad 449.

3. *State of Punjab v SS Singh,* AIR 1961 SC 493 : (1961) 2 SCR 371.

4. *HH Advani v State of Maharashtra,* AIR 1971 SC 44 : 73 Bom LR 112 : 1971 Cr LJ 5.

5. *Sris Chandra Nandy v Rakhalananda,* (1940) 43 Bom LR 794 : 68 IA 34 : (1941) 1 Cal 468; *Emperor v Parbhoo,* (1941) All 843 (FB).

6. *UOI v TR Varma,* (1958) SCJ 142.

7. *Data Xiva v State,* AIR 1967 Goa 4.

PART I
RELEVANCY OF FACTS

CHAPTER I

PRELIMINARY

[s 1] Short title, extent and commencement.—This Act may be called the Indian Evidence Act, 1872.

It extends to the whole of India[s 1.1] [1][except the State of Jammu and Kashmir[2]] and applies to all judicial proceedings[s 1.2] in or before any Court,[s 1.3] including Courts martial, [3][other than Courts-martial convened under the Army Act], [4][the Naval Discipline Act] [5][***] or the Indian Navy (Discipline) Act, 1934, [6][or the Air Force Act] but not to affidavits[s 1.4] presented to any Court or officer, nor to proceedings before an arbitrator;[s 1.5]

And it shall come into force on the first day of September, 1872.

SYNOPSIS

COMMENT

The Indian Evidence Act applies to all judicial proceedings before (a) any court, or (b) a court-martial (other than the courts-martial held under the specified Acts). It does not apply to (a) affidavits, and (b) proceedings before arbitrators.

"The law of evidence is the *lex fori* which governs the Courts. Whether a witness is competent or not; whether a certain matter requires to be proved by writing or not; whether certain evidence proves a certain fact or not; that is to be determined by the law of the country where the question arises, where the remedy is sought to be enforced, and where the Court sits to enforce it."[7] The law of evidence is a part of the law of procedure.

---

1. Subs. by Act 3 of 1951, section 3 and Schedule, for "except Part B States".
2. The Act now extends to the Union Territories of (1) Dadra and Nagar Haveli (*vide* Regulation 6 of 1963); (2) Goa, Daman and Diu (*vide* Regulation 11 of 1963); (3) Pondicherry (*vide* Regulation 7 of 1963) and (4) Lakshdweep (*vide* Regulation 8 of 1965).
3. Ins. by Act 18 of 1919, section 2 and Sch. I. See section 127 of the Army Act (44 and 45 Vict., c. 58).
4. Ins. by Act 35 of 1934, section 2 and Schedule
5. The words "that Act as modified by" omitted by the A.O. 1950.
6. Ins. by Act 10 of 1927, section 2 and Sch. I.
7. *Bain v Whitehaven and Furness Junction Railway Co*, (1850) 3 HLC 1, 19.

[s 1.1] "India".—"India" means the territory of India excluding the State of Jammu and Kashmir.[8]

[s 1.2] "Judicial proceedings".—An inquiry is judicial if the object of it is to determine a jural relation between one person and another, or a group of persons; or between him and the community generally; but, even a Judge, acting without such an object in view, is not acting judicially.[9] An enquiry in which evidence is legally taken is included in the term judicial proceeding.[10] An inquiry about matters of fact, where there is no discretion to be exercised and no judgment to be formed but something is to be done in a certain event as a duty, is not a judicial but an administrative inquiry. Similarly, proceedings before a Magistrate not authorised to conduct any inquiry,[11] or before a Collector under the Land Acquisition Act[12] or an inquest proceeding before the Coroner under the Coroners Act, 1871,[13] are not judicial proceedings.

[s 1.3] "Court".—This word includes Judges and Magistrates and all persons, except arbitrators, legally authorised to take evidence (Section 3). A family court is a court within the meaning of this expression.[14] The court said:[15] "In order to constitute a court, a State's sovereign judicial powers must be conferred on it by a statute for deciding a dispute in the judicial manner so as to decide the rights of the parties in a definitive judgment. To decide a dispute in a judicial manner and to declare the rights of the parties in a definitive judgment is essential *sine qua non* of a court. The decision in a judicial manner contemplates that parties are entitled as of right (i) to be heard in support of their claim; (ii) and to adduce evidence in proof of it, and (iii) to decide the matter on consideration of evidence in accordance with the law." The court of the Lokayukta is a civil court and, therefore, the protection of section 132 is available to a witness before it who has been compelled to answer a question.[16]

[s 1.4] "Affidavits".—Affidavits are confined to such facts as the deponent is able of his own knowledge to prove. Matters to which affidavits are confined are regulated by O XIX, rules 1, 2 and 3, etc. of the Code of Civil Procedure, and by section 297 etc. of the Code of Criminal Procedure, 1973. An affidavit filed by a party *suo motu* and not under directions from the court could not be termed as evidence. As action under the Penal Code could not be taken against the deponent.[17]

---

8. Act III of 1951, section 3.

9. *Queen-Empress v Tulja,* (1887) 12 Bom 36, 42. Section 3(4) of the Code of Criminal Procedure, 1973.

10. *Ibid*

11. *Queen-Empress v Bharma,* (1886) 11 Bom 702 FB.

12. *Ezra v The Secretary of State,* (1902) 30 Cal 36.

13. *Tanajirao v HJ Chinoy,* (1969) 71 Bom LR 732.

14. *Munna Lal v State of UP,* AIR 1991 All 189: 1991 Cr LJ 1838.

15. *Ibid,* at p 192.

16. *Rajendra Manubhai Patel v State of Gujarat,* AIR 1992 Guj 10 : (1992) 1 GLR 223.

17. *Delhi Lotteries v Rajesh Aggarwal,* AIR 1998 Del 332 : 1999 97 Comp Cas 758 Delhi : 69 (1997) DLT 543 : 1997 (43) DRJ 448.

A declaration in the shape of an affidavit cannot be received as evidence of the facts stated in it.[18] An affidavit cannot be used as evidence unless the law specifically permits certain matters to be proved by affidavit. The reason is that the deponent of an affidavit is not available to be cross-examined in respect of his declarations in the affidavit.[19]

Where the party denied execution of documents alleged to have been stated in the affidavit, the deponent can be cross-examined only if the party seeking cross-examination shows reasons and prejudice if such relief is not granted. An application for cross-examination which seemed to the court to have been filed only to delay proceedings was held to be something which ought to be rejected.[20]

[s 1.5] "Arbitrator".—The provisions of the Evidence Act do not apply to proceedings before an arbitrator. Arbitrators are bound to conform to the rules of natural justice. They are unfettered by technical rules of evidence.[21]

[s 2] **Repeal of enactments.**—***[Rep. by the Repealing Act, 1938 (1 of 1938), sec. 2 and Sch.]***

[s 3] **Interpretation clause.—In this Act the following words and expressions are used in the following senses, unless a contrary intention appears from the context:—**

"Court".—"Court" includes all Judges and Magistrates, and all persons, except arbitrators, legally authorized to take evidence.

COMMENT

[s 3.1] Court.—This definition is not meant to be exhaustive.[22] The word "Court" means not only the Judge in a trial by a Judge with a jury, but includes both Judge and jury.[23] A Magistrate holding a preliminary inquiry under section 164 of the Code of Criminal Procedure in a police investigation does not exercise the functions of a Court;[24] but a Magistrate committing a case to the Court of Session is a "Court".[25] An Industrial Tribunal set up under section 7 of the Industrial Disputes Act is a "Court".[26] Authorities under the MP Madhyastham Adhiniyam, 1983 have been held to be a court.[27]

"Fact."—"Fact" means and includes—

(1) any thing, state of things, or relation of things, capable of being perceived by the senses;

(2) any mental condition of which any person is conscious.

---

18. *Re Iswar Chunder Guho,* (1887) 14 Cal 653.
19. *Nirmala v Hari Singh,* AIR 2001 HP.
20. *Veer Singh Kothari v State Bank of India,* AIR 2009 Ori 29 (DB).
21. *Suppu v Govindacharyar,* (1887) 11 Mad 85, 87; *Municipal Corporation of Delhi v Jagan Nath Ashok Kumar,* AIR 1987 SC 2316 : (1987) 4 SCC 497.
22. *MV Rajwade v Dr SM Hasan,* (1954) Nag 1.
23. *Empress v Ashootosh Chuckerbutty,* (1878) 4 Cal 483 FB; Jury stands abolished.
24. *Queen-Empress v Bharma,* (1886) 11 Bom 702 FB.
25. *Atchayya v Gangayya,* (1891) 15 Mad 138 FB.
26. *Raghu Singh v Burrakur Coal Co Ltd,* AIR 1966 Cal 504.
27. *State of MP v Anshuman Shukla,* AIR 2008 SC 2454 : (2008) 7 SCC 487.

ILLUSTRATIONS

(a) That there are certain objects arranged in a certain order in a certain place, is a fact.

(b) That a man heard or saw something, is a fact.

(c) That a man said certain words, is a fact.

(d) That a man holds a certain opinion, has a certain intention, acts in good faith or fraudulently, or uses a particular word in a particular sense, or is or was at a specified time conscious of a particular sensation, is a fact.

(e) That a man has a certain reputation, is a fact.

COMMENT

[s 3.2] Fact.—Clause (1) refers to external facts which can be perceived by the five senses. See illustrations (a), (b) and (c). Clause (2) refers to internal facts which are the subject of consciousness. Thus, facts are either physical or psychological. See illustrations (d) and (e).

A misrepresentation as to the intention of a person is a misrepresentation of a "fact".[28] See illustration (d). The state of a man's mind is as much a fact as the state of his digestion.[29]

Facts and events which have neither occurred in the past, nor are occurring *in presenti* but are likely to occur in future do not fall within the definition of a fact.[30]

"Matter of fact" is anything which is the subject of testimony. "Matter of law" is the general law of the land, of which the courts will take judicial cognizance. Denning LJ stated the distinction between "Law" and "Fact" in the following words:[31] "Primary facts are facts which are observed by witnesses and proved by oral testimony or facts proved by the production of a thing itself, such as original documents. Their determination is essentially a question of fact for the tribunal of fact, and the only question of law that can arise on them is whether there was evidence to support the finding. The conclusions from primary facts are, however, inference deducted by a process of reasoning from them. If, and insofar as those conclusions can as well be drawn by a layman (properly instructed on the law) as by a lawyer, they are conclusions of fact for the tribunal of fact; and the only questions of law that can arise on them are whether there was a proper direction in point of law and whether the conclusion is one that could reasonably be drawn from the primary facts. If, and insofar as the correct conclusions to be drawn from the primary facts requires, for its correctness, determination by a trained lawyer, the conclusion is a conclusion of law."

"Relevant".—One fact is said to be relevant to another when the one is connected with the other in any of the ways referred to in the provisions of this Act relating to the relevancy of facts.

---

28. *Re Jaladu*, (1911) 36 Mad 453; *The Crown v Mussammat Soma*, (1916) PR No. 17 of 1916 (Cr); *Saleh v Mussammat Bakhtawar*, (1916) PR No. 3 of 1917 (Civil).
29. Per Bowen, LJ, in *Edgington v Fitzmaurice*, (1885) 29 Ch D 459, 483.
30. *Dueful Laboratory v State*, 1998 Cr LJ 4534 (Raj) : 1999 (1) WLC 498.
31. *British Launderers' Assn. v Hendon Rating Authority*, (1949) 1 KB 462 at pp 471-472.

SYNOPSIS

COMMENT

[s 3.3] Relevant fact.—The word "relevant" means that any two facts to which it is applied are so related to each other that, according to the common course of events, one, either taken by itself or in connection with other facts, proves or renders probable the past, present or future existence or non-existence of the other. "Relevant", strictly speaking, means admissible in evidence. Erroneous admission of any evidence does not make it relevant.

The word "relevant" is used in the Act with two distinct meanings: (a) as admissible, (b) as connected.[32]

Of all rules of evidence, the most universal and the most obvious is this—that the evidence adduced should be alike directed and confined to the matters which are in dispute, or which form the subject of investigation. The theoretical propriety of this rule never can be a matter of doubt, whatever difficulties may arise in its application. The Tribunal is created to determine matters which either are in dispute between contending parties, or otherwise require proof; and anything which is neither directly nor indirectly relevant to those matters ought at once to be put aside as beyond the jurisdiction of the Tribunal, and as tending to distract its attention and to waste its time. Evidence may be rejected as irrelevant for one or two reasons: First, that the connection between the principal and evidentiary facts is too remote and conjectural. Second, that it is excluded by the state of the pleadings, or what is analogous to the pleadings; or is rendered superfluous by the admissions of the party against whom it is offered.[33]

Questions which may be put in cross-examination may not always be determinative of the suit of the accused person, but they may be relevant to the guilt in question.[34]

[s 3.4] Drawing of inference of "*particeps criminis*"

[s 3.4.1] Factors relevant.—In a case of bride burning the mother-in-law and the husband were accused of murdering the deceased-wife in the matrimonial home and the possibility of presence of the accused-husband at the time of occurrence was not ruled out as no one else was present in the house. On the facts and circumstances, it was impossible for the mother-in-law of the deceased alone to commit the crime. The conduct of the husband was also unnatural and inculpatory. It was inferred that the accused-husband was "*particeps criminis*"[35] and was convicted.

---

32. *Lala Lakmi Chand v Sayid Haidar Shah,* (1899) 4 Cal WN 82 PC.
33. *Best,* 12th Edn, sections 215, 252, p 232.
34. *Jesu Aeir Singh v State,* AIR 2007 SC 3015 : (2007) 12 SCC 19.
35. *Sarojini v State of MP,* 1993 Supp (4) SCC 632 : 1993 Cr LJ 1648 (SC).

[s 3.4.2] Proof of drunkenness.—Blood or urine test is not a must for proving the charge of drunkenness. Drunkenness is a question of fact and smelling of alcohol, unsteady gait, dilation of pupils, incoherent speech would all be relevant considerations.[36]

"Facts in issue".—The expression "facts in issue" means and includes—any fact from which, either by itself or in connection with other facts, the existence, non-existence, nature or extent of any right, liability, or disability, asserted or denied in any suit or proceeding, necessarily follows.

***Explanation.*—Whenever, under the provisions of the law for the time being in force relating to Civil Procedure, any Court records an issue of fact, the fact to be asserted or denied in the answer to such issue is a fact in issue.**

ILLUSTRATIONS

A is accused of the murder of *B*.

At his trial the following facts may be in issue:—

That *A* caused *B*'s death;

That *A* intended to cause *B*'s death;

That *A* had received grave and sudden provocation from *B*;

That *A*, at the time of doing the act which caused *B*'s death, was, by reason of unsoundness of mind, incapable of knowing its nature.

SYNOPSIS

COMMENT

[s 3.5] Facts in issue—Defined.—"Facts in issue" are facts out of which some legal right, liability, or disability, involved in the inquiry, necessarily arises, and upon which, accordingly, decision must be arrived at. Matters which are affirmed by one party to a suit and denied by the other may be denominated facts in issue; what facts are in issue in particular cases, is a question to be determined by the substantive law or in some cases by that branch of the law of procedure which regulates the law of pleadings, civil or criminal.[37]

[s 3.5.1] Criminal cases.—As regards criminal cases, the charge constitutes and includes "facts in issue". See Chapter XVII of the Code of Criminal Procedure, 1973.

[s 3.5.2] Civil cases.—As regards civil cases, "facts in issue" are determined by the process of framing issues. See O XIV, rules 1-7, Code of Civil Procedure.

"Document."—"Document" means any matter expressed or described upon any substance by means of letters, figures or marks, or by more than one of those

36. *George Kutty v State of Kerala*, 1992 Cr LJ 1663 (Ker).

37. *STEPHEN'S INTRODUCTION TO THE EVIDENCE ACT*, pp 12, 13.

means, intended to be used, or which may be used, for the purpose of recording that matter.

ILLUSTRATIONS

A writing is a document;

Words printed, lithographed or photographed are documents;

A map or plan is a document;

An inscription on a metal plate or stone is a document;

A caricature is a document.

COMMENT

[s 3.6] **Document.**—This definition is similar to the definition in section 29 of the Indian Penal Code.

Under the term "document" are properly included all material substances on which the thoughts of men are represented by writing, or any other species of conventional mark or symbol. Thus the wooden score on which bakers, milk-men, etc., indicate by notches, the number of loaves of bread or quarts of milk supplied to their customers are documents as much as the most elaborate deeds.[38]

Compact disc is a document.[39] Articles like Memory Card, Hard Disc, CD, Pen-drive, etc. containing relevant data in electronic form are also documents.[40]

[s 3.6.1] Photograph, evidentiary value of.—If the court is satisfied that there is no trick photography and the photograph is above suspicion, the photograph can be received in evidence. But the evidence of photographs to prove writing or handwriting can only be received if the original cannot be obtained and the photographic reproduction is faithful and not faked or false.[41]

"Evidence."—"Evidence" means and includes—

(1) all statements which the Court permits or requires to be made before it by witnesses, in relation to matters of fact under inquiry; such statements are called oral evidence;

(2) [42][all documents including electronic records produced for the inspection of the Court;]

such documents are called documentary evidence.

---

38. *Best,* 12th Edn, sections 215, 216, pp 199, 200.

39. *Shamsher Singh Verma v State of Haryana,* 2016 Cr LJ 364, para 14 (SC) : 2016(1) Ren CR (Crim)167.

40. *K Ramajayam v Inspector of Police, Chennai,* 2016 Cr LJ 1542, para 8 (Mad-DB) : 2016 (2) Mad LJ (Crl) 715.

41. *L Choraria v State of Maharashtra,* AIR 1968 SC 938 : (1967) 70 Bom LR 575 : 1968 Cr LJ 1134.

42. Subs. by Act 21 of 2000, section 92 and Sch. II–1(a), for "all documents produced for the inspection of the Court" (w.e.f. 17-10-2000).

SYNOPSIS

COMMENT

[s 3.7] Evidence.—The word "evidence", considered in relation to law, includes all the legal means, exclusive of mere argument, which tend to prove or disprove any matter of fact, the truth of which is submitted to judicial investigation. This term and the word *proof* are often used as synonyms, but the latter is applied by accurate logicians rather to the effect of evidence than to evidence itself. "Evidence" has been defined to be any matter of fact, the effect, tendency, or design of which is to produce in the mind a persuasion, affirmative or disaffirmative, of the existence of some other matter of fact. "'Evidence" means the testimony, whether oral, documentary or real, which may be legally received in order to prove or disprove some fact in dispute."[43] It also includes the content of that testimony.

The definition of evidence provided under section 3 of the Evidence Act, 1872 is an exhaustive definition. Wherever the words "means and includes" are used, it is an indication of the fact that the definition "is a hard-and-fast definition", and no other meaning can be assigned to the expression other than that is laid down in the definition. It indicates an exhaustive explanation of the meaning which, for the purposes of the Act, must invariably be attached to these words or expression.[44]

The juristic conception of the term "evidence" in the case of the oral testimony of witnesses is that the party against whom it is used has had the right and opportunity of cross-examining the witnesses. So long as the accused is not allowed the right and opportunity of cross-examining the witnesses, any statements made by them can only be described as statements but cannot be dignified with the name of evidence.[45]

Evidence is "the means from which an inference may logically be drawn as to the existence of a fact. It consists of proof by testimony of witnesses, on oath, or by writing or records."[46]

The definition of "evidence" covers (a) the evidence of witnesses,[47] and (b) documentary evidence. "... evidence can be both oral and documentary and electronic records can be produced as evidence. This means that evidence, even in criminal matters, can also be by way of electronic records. This would include video-conferencing".[48] The word "evidence" does not cover everything that a court has before it. There are certain other media of proof; e.g., the statements of the parties, the result of local investigation, facts of which the court takes judicial notice, and any real or personal property, the inspection of which may be material in determining the question at issue, such as weapons, tools or stolen property.[49] A newspaper report as to prices of property in the neighbourhood has been held to be no evidence of the value of property for the purposes of the Land Acquisition Act, 1894.[50] The definition of "evidence" is considered to be incomplete as it does not include the whole material on which the decision of the Judge may rest.[51] Electronic record can also be received as evidence.[52]

---

43. *PHIPSON ON EVIDENCE*, 15th Edn, 2000, p 2.

44. *Hardeep Singh v State of Punjab*, (2014) 3 SCC 92, para 63 : AIR 2014 SC 1400.

45. *Syed Mohammad Husain Afqar Mohani v Mirza Fakhrullah Beg*, (1932) 8 Luck 135.

46. *TOMLIN'S LAW DICTIONARY*, Vol 2, p 1811.

47. The employees of a company are not identifiable with the legal person of the company, when they appear as witness against the company the constitutional protection against self-incrimination as contained in Article 20(3) of the Constitution *Godrej Soap Ltd v State of WB*, 1991 Cr LJ 828 (Cal).

48. *State of Maharashtra v Dr Praful B Desai*, AIR 2003 SC 2053 at p 2059 : 2003 Cr LJ 2033. The police had recorded evidence by video conferencing.

49. *FIELD*, 8th Edn, p 17. Evidence of a voluntary witness cannot be ignored for that reason alone. *Ladies Corner v State of Karnataka*, 1987 Cr LJ 2078 (Karn). Evidence of a police officer cannot be rejected for that reason alone. *Jagdamba Pd Tewari v State of UP*, 1991 Cr LJ 1883 (All), a police report is not an evidence for the purposes of S. 138 Cr PC; *Raju Parshad Gupta v State of UP*, 1991 Cr LJ 2899 (Del) no reliance on police witnesses. *Mahadeo v State*, 1990 Cr LJ 858 : 1989 All LJ 475, no presumption that police officers are liars. *State of Assam v Muhim Barkatali*, 1987 Cr LJ 152 : AIR 1987 SC 98. *Asst. Collector of Central Excise v Duncan Agro Industries*, 1992 Cr LJ 231, statements of witnesses recorded by excise officers is not evidence.

50. *Ratan Kumar Tandon v State of UP*, AIR 1996 SC 2710 : (1997) 2 SCC 161.

51. *Arun Dube v State of MP*, 1991 Cr LJ 840 (MP), meaning of "evidence" in section 319, CrPC and this section taken together.

52. *KK Velusamy v N Palanisamy*, (2011) 11 SCC 275.

A person who has not been charge-sheeted, has to be summoned on the basis of evidence available on record. The word "evidence" includes the statement of witness who has not been tested on cross-examination. However, the court should exercise such power in rarest of rare cases.[53]

Hence, the word "evidence" in its relation to law includes all the legal means exclusive of mere arguments which tend to prove or disprove any fact the truth of which is submitted to judicial investigation. This term and the word "proof" are often used as synonymous, but the latter is applied by accurate logicians rather to the effect of evidence, than to evidence itself.[54]

[s 3.7.1] Speeches of Ministers and Members.—Speeches delivered by members and Ministers in the Legislative Assembly are not admissible in a court of law when the court is considering the provisions of the enactment in question.[55]

[s 3.7.2] Investigation.—The result of an investigation is not a legal evidence.[56] A finding of guilt cannot be based on the result of police investigation. The evidence produced at the trial as a result of an investigation constitutes evidence for the purposes of formulating judicial conclusions.[57]

While the services of a sniffer dog may be taken for the purpose of investigation, its faculties cannot be taken as evidence for the purpose of establishing the guilt of an accused.[58]

[s 3.7.3] Statements made in court in an attempt for conciliation.—The statements made in the court in the attempt for conciliation are not evidence before the court and will not be used as such.[59]

[s 3.8] Circumstantial evidence.—It is one of the established principles of law that a witness may lie but not the circumstances. Direct ocular evidence is not necessary for proving the person behind the crime. The guilt of a person can be proved by circumstantial evidence also.[60] However, the court must adopt a cautious approach while basing its conviction purely on circumstantial evidence.[61] As evidence there is no difference between direct and circumstantial evidence. The only difference is in that as proof, the former directly establishes the commission of the offence whereas the latter does so by placing

---

53. *Sivrani v Suryanarain,* 1994 Cr LJ 2026 (All).
54. *TAYLOR ON EVIDENCE,* 1 (11th Edn), cited by the MP High Court in *Phoolchand Garg v Gopaldas Agarwal,* AIR 1990 MP 135, 137.
55. *SR Mehrotra (Dr.) v State of HP,* AIR 1997 HP 51.
56. *Kaptan Singh v State of MP,* AIR 1997 SC 2485 : 1997 Cr LJ 2987.
57. *Vijender v State of Delhi,* (1997) 6 SCC 171.
58. *Dinesh Borthakur v State of Assam,* (2008) 5 SCC 697.
59. *Mayank Pathak v State (Government of NCT of Delhi),* (2015) 11 SCC 798, para 5.
60. *Vilas Pandurang Patil v State of Maharashtra,* (2004) 6 SCC 158 : AIR 2004 SC 3562.
61. *State of Haryana v Ved Prakash,* AIR 1994 SC 468 : 1994 Cr LJ 140; *State of Karnataka v Hanumantha,* 2002 Cr LJ (NOC) 254 (Kant), weak link of circumstances, the witness ran away on seeing the accused, leaving the victim alone, last seen together not conclusively proved, recovery of the instrument was also inconclusive. *Bodh Raj v State of J&K,* 2002 Cr LJ 4664 (SC), circumstantial evidence can be the sole basis of conviction. The court stated the conditions to be satisfied. *Dharyashil v State of Maharashtra,* 2003 Cr LJ 317 (Bom), circumstantial evidence, the accused was last seen with the deceased, motive also proved, conviction, the entire testimony of a hostile witness was not thrown away.

circumstances which lead to irresistible inference of guilt.[62] Circumstantial evidence is an indirect mode of proof by drawing inference from facts closely connected to the fact in issue.[63] The standard of proof required to convict a person on circumstantial evidence is well-established by a series of decisions of the Supreme Court. According to that standard the circumstances relied upon in support of the conviction must be fully established[64] and the chain of evidence furnished by those circumstances must be so far complete as not to leave any reasonable ground for a conclusion consistent with the innocence of the accused[65] and further it must be such as to show that within all human

---

62. *Makbul Ahammad v Abdul Rahaman Akand,* (1953) 1 Cal 348; *Debar Kundu Rama Krishna Rao v State of WB,* 1988 Cr LJ 345 (Cal), conviction of husband for strangulating his wife, evidence circumstantial. *Narayan Chandra Dey v State of WB,* 1988 Cr LJ 387 (Cal), conviction of father for drowning his 2½ year old child, evidence circumstantial. *Dayaram v State,* 1988 Cr LJ 865 : AIR 1988 SC 615, accused apprehended by passers-by with knife in hand and blood-stained clothes, circumstances admitted hypothesis of guilt only. *Nanahau Ram v State of MP,* 1988 Cr LJ 936 : AIR 1988 SC 912, proper identification of the accused by the deceased in his dying declaration and by his son and wife. *Sardar Hussain v State of UP,* 1988 Cr LJ 1807 : AIR 1988 SC 1766, where the circumstantial evidence fell short of required standards. *Nanak Chand v State of Delhi,* 1992 Cr LJ 55, no member of public produced as a witness, even when available, charge doubtful. *Mananiga Digal v State of Orissa,* 2002 Cr LJ (NOC) 152 (Ori) : (2001) 20 OCR 594, the deceased and the accused were last seen together, the witnesses heard groaning sounds, the ornaments worn by her were recovered at the instance of the accused. The court said that even if the extra-judicial confession was excluded from evidence, other evidence pointed towards the guilt of the accused.

63. *Liyakat v State of Uttaranchal,* AIR 2008 SC 1537 : (2008) 16 SCC 148. *Kusuma Ankama Rao v State of AP,* AIR 2008 SC 2819 : (2008) 13 SCC 257, conditions precedent for acting on circumstantial evidence stated. *Ram Singh v Sonia,* AIR 2007 SC 1218 : (2007) 3 SCC 1, chain of circumstances found to be complete. *Harish Chandra Ladaku Thange v State of Maharashtra,* AIR 2007 SC 2957 : (2007) 11 SCC 436, chain of circumstances was not complete because of missing links *e.g.* body lying undetected at the adjoining field for 5 days, recovery of weapon unreliable.

64. *Govinda Reddy v State of Mysore,* AIR 1960 SC 29 : 1960 Cr LJ 137.

65. *Deonandan Mishra v The State of Bihar,* (1955) 2 SCR 570 : 1955 Cr LJ 1647 : AIR 1955 SC 801. **Followed** in *Laxman Naik v State of Orissa,* AIR 1995 SC 1387 : 1995 Cr LJ 2692, also **relied on** *Sharad v State of Maharashtra,* AIR 1984 SC 1622 : 1984 Cr LJ 1738 and *Dhananjaya Chatterjee v State of WB,* (1994) 1 JT (SC) 33 : (1994) 2 SCC 200. An example of a chain of circumstances indicative of guilt was found in *R. v George,* 2002 EWCA Crimes 1923 (CA Crimes Div.). The accused was charged with the murder of a journalist and television presenter. The eye-witness was able to make only a qualified identification at the identification parade. The court said: "In the instant case there was evidence, other than the qualified identification, to support the prosecution's case, including a particle of firearm discharge in the coat, a fibre on the victim consistent with the accused's clothing, his association with firearms, his obsession with the victim and other female television presenters, lies, he had told in questioning, and his flawed alibi statement. The evidence was compelling and therefore the conviction safe. *Arun Bhakta v State of West Begal,* AIR 2009 SC 1228 : (2008) 17 SCC 367, burden lies on the prosecution to show that the chain of circumstances is complete. Conviction permissible only when all the circumstances lead to the hypothesis of guilt of the accused. *Mohd Azad v State of WB,* AIR 2009 SC 1307 : (2008) 15 SCC 449, all the circumstances to be incompatible with innocence of accused, if two views are possible, one favouring the accused has to be accepted, false defence pleas cannot cure infirmities in the prosecution case, time gap between last seen together and incident should not be large; *Vithal Eknath Adlinge v State of Maharashtra,* AIR 2009 SC 2087 : (2008) 12 SCC 701; *Raju v State,* AIR 2009 SC 2171 : (2009) 11 SCC 111, circumstances must be closely connected with the principal fact. *Baldev Singh v State of Haryana,* AIR 2009 SC 963, earlier rulings as stated above reiterated *State of Goa v Pandurang Mohite,* AIR 2009 SC 1066 : (2008) 16 SCC 714, another ruling of the same kind, *KT Palanisami v State of Tamil Nadu,* AIR 2008 SC 1095 : (2008) 3 SCC 100, the deceased, on the advice of the appellant performed *puja* by the river side. He did not return home. One of the circumstances was that he was last seen with the appellant from whom his gold chain was recovered. Dead body was

(Footnote No. 65 contd.)

probability the act must have been done by the accused.[66] Some of these principles were applied by the Supreme Court in *Hanumant Govind Narjundkar v State of MP*.[67] The court said: In dealing with circumstantial evidence the rules specially applicable to such evidence must be borne in mind. In such cases there is always the danger that conjecture or suspicion may take the place of legal proof and, therefore, it is right to recall the warning addressed by BARON ALDERSON to the jury in *Reg v Hodge*,[68] wherein his Lordship said: "The mind was apt to take a pleasure in adapting circumstances to one another and even in straining them a little, if need be to force them to form parts of one connected whole; and more ingenious the mind of the individual, the more likely was it, considering such matters, to overreach and mislead itself, to supply some little link that is waiting to take for granted some fact consistent with its previous theories and necessary to render them complete."[69]

(Footnote No. 65 contd.)

not recovered. All witnesses were relatives. No report of missing was lodged. Conviction of the accused was not proper. *Kusuma Ankama Rao v State of AP*, AIR 2008 SC 2819 : (2008) 13 SCC 257, the gap between the point of time when the accused and deceased were seen•together and deceased found dead should not be large; *Roopsena Khatoon v State of West Bengal*, 2011 Cr LJ 3597 (SC), where deceased was last seen with accused one day earlier and the body of deceased was found next day, since prosecution had not fixed time of death it was held that there was no proximity between time when deceased was last seen together with accused and time of death. Circumstance, even if incriminating, was insignificant to hold the accused guilty.

66. *Bakshish Singh v State of Punjab*, AIR 1971 SC 2016 : 1971 Cr LJ 1452. See *Ganpat v State*, 1987 Cr LJ 6 (Del), where circumstantial evidence was contrary to medial evidence, hence acquittal. From the circumstantial evidence there should be inevitable conclusion of the guilt of the accused beyond reasonable doubt and the facts so established should be consistent only with the hypothesis of the guilt of the accused. If two views are possible, the court should adopt the view favourable to the accused. *State of HP v Diwana*, 1995 Cr LJ 3002 (HP); *Bishikeshan Nag. v State of Orissa*, 2001 Cr LJ (NOC) 76 (Ori) : (2000) 19 OCR 276, circumstantial evidence, alleged killing of the owner by the domestic servant for robbing him of cash and ornaments, the servant did not run away, other missing links in the chain of circumstances, acquittal. *Panchanan Muduli v State*, 2001 Cr LJ (NOC) 81 (Ori). *G Parshwanath v State of Karnataka*, AIR 2010 SC 2914 : (2010) 8 SCC 593, each circumstance must be fully established individually, cumulative effect of all the proved facts must be inference of guilt, this does not mean that each and every hypothesis suggested by the accused must be excluded by proved facts. *Shivaji v State of Maharashtra*, AIR 2009 SC 56 : (2008) 15 SCC 269, conviction is justified when all incriminating facts and circumstances are proved beyond reasonable doubt and are found incompatible with innocence of the accused or guilt of any other person. *Asraf Sk v State of West Bengal*, AIR 2009 SC 271 : (2008) 15 SCC 597, circumstances to be proved beyond reasonable doubt and shown to be connected with the principal fact, conviction can be based. *Mula Devi v State of Uttarakhand*, AIR 2009 SC 655 : (2008) 14 SCC 511, conviction possible on the basis of circumstantial evidence if the requirements laid down by the Supreme Court from time to time are satisfied; *Raju v State*, AIR 2009 SC 2171 : (2009) 11 SCC 111. *Krishna Ghosh v State of WB*, AIR 2009 SC 2279 : (2009) 12 SCC 413, circumstances connecting with the principal fact have to be proved beyond reasonable doubt, cruelty and murder of wife, injuries on person noted by witnesses, dead body in husband's home, husband's plea of *alibi* found to be false, absconding after the incident was a further inculpating circumstances, doctor's opinion death due to asphyxia resulting from throttling, conviction. *Gamparai Hrudayaraju v State of AP*, AIR 2009 SC 2364 : (2009) 13 SCC 740, circumstances to be incompatible with the innocence of the accused. No circumstances which could fasten guilt on the accused.

67. *Hanumant Govind Narjundkar v State of MP*, AIR 1952 SC 343 : 1953 Cr LJ 129.

68. *Reg v Hodge*, (1838) 2 Lewin 227.

69. These principles have been restated in *Sudama Pandey v State of Bihar*, (2002) 1 SCC 679 : AIR 2002 SC 293 : AIR 2001 SCW 5012 : 2002 Cr LJ 582 : AIR Jhar. HCR 451 and *Subhash Chand v State of Rajasthan*, (2002) 1 SCC 702 : AIR 2001 SCW 4209 and **followed** in *Ashish Batham v State of MP*, AIR 2002 SC 3206 : 2002 Cr LJ 4676.

The crime scene has to be scientifically dealt with, without any error. In criminal cases, especially based on circumstantial evidence, forensic science plays a pivotal role, which may assist in establishing the element of crime, identifying the suspect, ascertaining the guilt or innocence of the accused. One of the major activities of the investigating officer at the crime scene is to make thorough search for potential evidence that have probative value in the crime. The investigating officer may be guided against potential contamination of physical evidence, which can grow at the crime scene during collection, packing and forwarding. Proper precaution has to be taken to preserve evidence and also against any attempt to tamper with the material or causing any contamination or damage.[70]

It is not necessary that every one of the proved facts must in itself be decisive of the complicity of the accused or point conclusively to his guilt. Therefore, when deciding the question of sufficiency, what the court has to consider is the total cumulative effect of all the proved facts each one of which re-enforces the conclusion of guilt.[71] In such cases, the court must guard against the danger of allowing conjecture or suspicion to take the place of legal proof.[72] There is this basic rule of criminal jurisprudence that if two views are possible on the evidence adduced in a case of circumstantial evidence, one pointing to the guilt of the accused and the other to his innocence, the court should adopt the view favourable to the accused.[73]

In reference to cases where there is no direct evidence and the decision has to rest on circumstantial evidence, the Supreme Court in a line of decisions has consistently held that such evidence must satisfy the following tests:

(1) the circumstances from which an inference of guilt is sought to be drawn must be cogently and firmly established;

(2) those circumstances should be of a definite tendency unerringly pointing towards the guilt of the accused;

---

70. *Dharam Deo Yadav v State of UP*, (2014) 5 SCC 509 (para 27) : 2014 (2) Mad LJ (Crl) 435.

71. *State of AP v IBSP Rao, AIR 1970 SC 648* : 1970 Cr LJ 733. Again emphasised in *State of UP v Ashok Kumar Srivastva,* AIR 1992 SC 840 : 1992 Cr LJ 1104 : 1992 AIR SCW 640 : 1992 All LJ 1115, which was a circumstances linked story of wife-burning, nobody helping her at the moment, all of them disappearing afterwards, preceding ill-treatment and torture for dowry, conviction under sections 302/34, IPC. *Sooraj v State of Kerala,* 1994 Cr LJ 1155 (Ker), considering only one or two sentences from deposition not sufficient. *State of Maharashtra v Vilas Pandurang,* 1999 Cr LJ 1062, where at pp 1065-1066 the court presented a similar version of the points which have to be kept in mind in processing circumstantial evidence. *Gade Lakshmi Mangraju v State of AP,* AIR 2001 SC 2677 at p 2681, one circumstance cannot be called out of the rest to give a different meaning to it because every circumstance has to be taken as a part of the rest of circumstances and what has to be watched is the cumulative effect.

72. *Charan Singh v State of UP,* AIR 1967 SC 520 : 1967 Cr LJ 525; Insufficient circumstantial evidence, benefit of doubt, *State of UP v Sukhbasi,* AIR 1985 SC 1224 : 1985 Supp SCC 79 : 1985 Cr LJ 1479; *Hukam Singh v State of Rajasthan,* AIR 1977 SC 1063 : 1977 Cr LJ 639; *Mahmood v State of UP,* AIR 1976 SC 69 : 1976 Cr LJ 10, explains the requirements as to circumstantial evidence.

73. *Harendra Narain Singh v State of Bihar,* AIR 1991 SC 1842, 1845 : 1991 Cr LJ 2666. Only those accused ought to be convicted in reference to whom evidence is clear, the rest are entitled to benefit of doubt. *Budhwa v State of MP,* 1990 Cr LJ 2597 : AIR 1991 SC 4.

(3) the circumstances, taken cumulatively, should form a chain so complete that there is no escape from the conclusion that within all human probability the crime was committed by the accused and none else;[74] and

(4) the circumstantial evidence in order to sustain conviction must be complete and incapable of explanation on any other hypothesis than that of the guilt of the accused and such evidence should not only be consistent with the guilt of the accused but should be inconsistent with his innocence.[75]

Where a case is to be proved solely on circumstantial evidence, the court said that the presumption of innocence of the accused must have a dominant role. The facts evolving out of the proven circumstances must not admit any inference except that of guilt of the accused.[76]

---

74. *Lakshmi Kirsani v State,* 2001 Cr LJ 3648 (Ori) : (2001) 91 Cut LT 223, the circumstances did not form a complete chain in a murder case, death was alleged to have been caused by hitting with an arrow, medical examination report was that neither the arrow nor the clothes of the deceased were stained with blood, witnesses gave contradictory account *Pabitra Pradhan v State of Orissa,* 2001 Cr LJ 3798 (Ori), doubtful circumstances. *Manjunath Chennabasappa Madalli v State of Karnataka,* AIR 2007 SC 2080 : (2007) 9 SCC 160, husband charged of killing his wife at night at in-law's place, prosecution relied upon two circumstances, unnatural death and dying declaration, the tehsildar stated that the dying declaration could not be recorded because the doctor opined that the victim was not in fit state to make statement. Conviction not maintained. *Abubucker Siddiqui v State and State v MP Rafiq Ad,* AIR 2011 SC 91 : (2011) 2 SCC 12, case registered against the accused persons for blasting a Hindu Organisation, the bomb was supposed to be made of material of which no trace was found at the sight, no circumstantial link-up.

75. As summarised by S Ratnavel Pandian J in *Ashok Kumar v State of MP,* AIR 1989 SC 1890 at 1896 : 1989 Cr LJ 2124. Reiterated in *State of UP v Ravindra Prakash Mittal,* AIR 1992 SC 2045 : 1992 Cr LJ 3693. See also *Kartik Sahu v State of Orissa,* 1994 Cr LJ 102 (Ori), *Ashoke Gavade v State of Goa,* 1995 Cr LJ 943 (Bom) and *Ganpat Kisan v State of Maharashtra,* 1995 Cr LJ 792 (Bom). The court cited the following authorities: *Rama Nand v State of Himachal Pradesh,* AIR 1981 SC 738; *Gambhir v State of Maharashtra,* AIR 1982 SC 1157 : 1982 Cr LJ 1243; *Prem Thakur v State of Punjab,* AIR 1983 SC 61 : 1983 Cr LJ 155; *Earabhadrapa v State of Karnataka,* AIR 1983 SC 446 : (1983) 2 SCC 330 : 1983 Cr LJ 846 : 1983 SCC (Cri) 447; *Gian Singh v State of Punjab,* AIR 1987 SC 1921 : 1987 Cr LJ 1918; *Balbir Singh v State of Punjab,* 1991 Cr LJ 3286 : AIR 1991 SC 2231; *Balwinder Singh v State of Punjab,* AIR 1987 SC 350 : 1986 Cr LJ 329; *Sharad v State of Maharashtra,* AIR 1984 SC 1622 : 1984 Cr LJ 1738; *Prakash Sen v State,* 1988 Cr LJ 1275 Cal, last seen together, not sufficient in itself. Where testimony of the eye-witness for invoking the principle of "last seen" together was not considered trustworthy, *Lal Chand v State of HP,* 1992 Cr LJ 1946 (HP). Witnesses stating that they saw the accused taking away deceased child to the backyard of house, whereafter the child went missing and was found dead next morning, and no explanation offered by the accused for his taking away the child. Besides, he confessed to crime and incriminating articles were recovered at his insistences. He was held guilty, *Ramesh v State,* AIR 2014 SC 2852, para 16 : 2014 (9) SCJ 496. *State of Maharashtra v Champalal Panjaji Shah,* AIR 1981 SC 1675 : 1981 Cr LJ 1273 : (1981) 3 SCC 610, an unreasonable suggestion or explanation on the part of the defence would not be acceptable or disprove the guilt of the accused where circumstances clearly prove the guilt of the accused, *Yedlapati v Raghavendra Prasad v State of AP,* 2002 Cr LJ (NOC) 77 (AP) : (2001) 2 Andh LD 720, failure on the part of the prosecution to prove its case. *Niranjan Mallick v State of Orissa,* 2002 Cr LJ 108 (Ori) : (2000) 18 OCR 203, unreliable prosecution witness, *Gurucharan Dusadh v State of Bihar,* 2002 Cr LJ 1459 (Pat), prosecution failure to prove its case. Links in chain of circumstances not established, conviction reversed, *Durga Burman Roy v State of Sikkim,* (2014) 13 SCC 35 (paras 19 and 20) : 2014 (8) SCJ 217. See also *Vijay Thakur v State of HP,* (2014) 14 SCC 609 (paras 18 to 21) : 2014 AIR SCW 5625.

76. *Musheer Khan v State of MP,* AIR 2010 SC 762 : (2010) 2 SCC 748; *Vithal Eknath Adilinge v State of Maharashtra,* AIR 2009 SC 2067 : (2009) 11 SCC 637, conditions for conviction on basis

(Footnote No. 76 contd.)

Abscondence of the accused is not a circumstance which can be taken as a conclusive proof of guilt. The fact that the *panchayat* was held after the incident and it had pardoned the accused was held by the Supreme Court to be not a circumstance charging him with the crime.[77]

[s 3.8.1] Last seen together.—Last seen together by itself is not a conclusive proof but along with other circumstances surrounding the incident, may lead to the inference of guilt of the accused.[78] The doctrine of "last seen together" shifts the burden of proof on the accused, requiring him to explain how the incident had occurred. Failure on the part of the accused to furnish any explanation in this regard, would give rise to a very strong presumption against him.[79]

[s 3.8.2] False defence pleas.—False pleas raised by the accused can be taken as a circumstance against the accused. False and inconsistent defences taken by the accused charged of murder were held to be additional circumstances against him strengthening the chain of circumstances already firmly established.[80] Infirmity or lacuna in the prosecution case cannot be cured by false defence pleas.[81]

[s 3.9] Affidavit.—An affidavit is not evidence within the meaning of this section. It cannot be used as evidence unless the court has ordered under the Code of Civil Procedure any particular facts to be proved by such affidavit.[82] Where the contents of an affidavit were not assailed at the time when they were tendered in evidence, they were deemed to have been admitted by the accused.[83]

An affidavit is not "evidence" within the meaning of section 3 of the Evidence Act, 1872. Affidavits are, therefore, not included within the purview of the definition of "evidence" as has been given in section 3 of the Evidence Act, and the same can be used as "evidence" only if, for sufficient reasons, the court passes an order under Order 19 of the Code of Civil Procedure, 1908. Thus, the filing of an affidavit of one's own statement, in one's own favour, cannot be regarded as sufficient evidence for any court or tribunal, on the basis of which it can come to a conclusion as regards a particular fact situation.

However, in a case where the deponent is available for cross-examination, and opportunity is given to the other side to cross-examine him, the same can be relied

---

(Footnote No. 76 contd.)

of circumstantial evidence restated. Where two views are possible, the view which goes in favour of the accused should be accepted. *Chattar Singh v State of Haryana*, AIR 2009 SC 378 : (2008) 14 SCC 667, the point of time at which the accused and deceased were seen together alive and the time of death must be small according to the circumstances of the case. *Venkatesan v State of TN*, AIR 2008 SC 2369 : (2008) 8 SCC 456, conditions precedent for acting on circumstantial evidence stated.

77. *Paramjeet Singh v State of Uttarakhand*, AIR 2011 SC 200 : (2010) 10 SCC 439.
78. *Ashok v State of Maharashtra*, 2015 Cr LJ 2036 (para 13) (SC) : (2015) 4 SCC 393.
79. *Rohtash Kumar v State of Haryana*, 2013 Cr LJ 3183 (para 25) (SC) : 2013 (7) Scale 472. See also *Ram Kumar v State of Chhattisgarh*, 2014 Cr LJ 2679 (paras 16 and 17) (Chh-DB) : 2014 (2) CGLJ 393.
80. *G Parshwanath v State of Karnataka*, AIR 2010 SC 2914 : (2010) 8 SCC 593.
81. *Arun Bhakta v State of West Bengal*, AIR 2009 SC 1228 : (2008) 17 SCC 367; *Vithal Eknath Adlinge v State of Maharashtra*, AIR 2009 SC 2067 : (2009) 11 SCC 637.
82. *Federal India Assurance Co Ltd v Anandrao*, AIR 1944 Nag 161: (1944) Nag 436.
83. *Krishan Lal v State of Haryana*, 1996 Cr LJ 1401 (P&H).

upon. Such view, stands fully affirmed particularly, in view of the amended provisions of O XVIII, rules 4 and 5 CPC.[84]

[s 3.10] Evidentiary value of FIR.—In *Gulshan Kumar v State,* it was held that though an FIR is not a substantive piece of evidence, it can be used to corroborate or contradict the statement of maker thereof and also to judge trustworthiness of the prosecution story.[85] For the purpose of summoning a person whose name is mentioned in the FIR but has not been charge-sheeted, the FIR can be taken into consideration because it is evidence at that stage.[86] Where the FIR was registered on the basis of a written complaint submitted to the police and there was no mention of the presence of some persons as eye-witnesses in it, it was held that the presence of those eye-witnesses was rightly disbelieved.[87]

[s 3.11] Inquest Report.—Omission to mention in the inquest report the crime number, names of accused, penal provisions applicable to the offence has been held to be not fatal to the prosecution case. Such omissions do not lead to the inference that the FIR was ante-timed. The evidence of eye-witness could not be discarded if their names did not figure in the inquest report. Inquest report being not a substantive evidence, it may be used to contradict the witnesses of inquest.[88]

[s 3.11.1] Report of scientific officer.—The report of a junior scientific officer on the point whether the material seized was *charas* was held to be of no evidentiary value unless the signatory was examined.[89]

[s 3.11.2] Confessions of co-accused whether evidence.—The confession of an accused person against a co-accused is not evidence in the ordinary sense of the term. It does not come within the meaning of evidence contained in this section inasmuch as it is not required to be given on oath, nor in the presence of the accused, and cannot be tested by cross-examination. It is a much weaker type of evidence than the evidence of an approver which is not subject to any of these infirmities. Such a confession can only be used to lend assurance to other evidence against a co-accused. The proper way to approach a case of this kind is, first, to marshal the evidence against the accused excluding the confession altogether from consideration and see whether if it is believed, a conviction could safely be based on it. If it is capable of belief independently of the confession, then it is not necessary to call the confession in aid. But cases may arise where the Judge is not prepared to act on the other evidence as it stands even though, if believed, it would be sufficient to sustain a conviction. In such an event the Judge may call in aid the confession and use it to lend assurance to the other evidence and thus fortify himself in believing what without the aid of the confession he would not be prepared to accept.[90]

[s 3.11.3] Written statement of accused.—A statement of an accused in the written statement filed by him is not strictly evidence, even though the court may consider it.[91]

---

84. *Ayaaubkhan Noorkhan Pathan v State of Maharashtra,* AIR 2013 SC 58 : (2013) 4 SCC 465.
85 *Gulshan Kumar v State,* 1993 Cr LJ 1525 (Del) : (1993) ILR 2 Del 168.
86. *Sivrani v Suryanarain,* 1994 Cr LJ 2026 (All).
87. *Bhimappa Jinnappa Naganur v State of Karnataka,* AIR 1993 SC 1469 : 1993 Cr LJ 1801.
88. *Brahm Swaroop v State of MP,* AIR 2011 SC 280 : (2010) 11 JT 437 : 2011 Cr LJ 306.
89. *State of HP v Edward Samual Chareton,* 2001 Cr LJ 1356 (HP) : 2001 (3) RCR (Criminal) 129.
90. *Kashmira Singh v State of Madhya Pradesh,* (1952) SCR 526 : 1952 Cr LJ 839 : AIR 1952 SC 129.
91. *Emperor v Tuti Babu,* AIR 1946 Pat 373 : (1945) 25 Pat 33.

[s 3.11.3.1] *Statement of accused under section 313, CrPC*—The statement of the accused recorded under section 313, CrPC, cannot be treated as evidence. Further the entire prosecution evidence need not be put to the accused.[92]

In a case under the Narcotic Drugs and Psychotropic Substances Act, 1985, there was recovery of huge quantity of "*charas*" that was concealed in a car in which two persons were travelling. In the trial, accused took the plea that he had taken lift in the car and, therefore, he could not be said to be in conscious possession of the contraband. Once possession of the contraband is established, the person who claims that it was not in conscious possession must establish it, because how he came into possession is within his special knowledge. However, in the above case, the accused's statement under section 313 CrPC was that he had taken a lift in the car. It was held by the Supreme Court that statement under section 313 of the CrPC is taken into consideration to appreciate the truthfulness or otherwise of the prosecution case, but it is not evidence.[93]

[s 3.11.4] Evidence taken in another case.—The evidence given in one case upon the issues raised in that case cannot be taken into consideration in another case in which other issues arise but parties may agree that evidence taken in one suit shall be treated as evidence in another.[94]

[s 3.11.5] Unregistered deed.—Unregistered lease deed, though not allowed to be produced in evidence, it could be used by the carrier to explain the character of the possession.[95]

[s 3.11.6] Evidence of Judge.—If, in a case, a Judge wishes to give evidence and intends the court to act on his statement of facts, he should make that statement in the same manner as any other witness and not merely introduce it in his judgment. A Judge cannot, without giving evidence as a witness, import into a case his own knowledge of particular facts.[96]

[s 3.12] Police witness.—Credibility of.—When independent evidence is not available for any reason, the court will have to examine the evidence of police witnesses carefully and scrutinise the same and, if found reliable, conviction can be based on such evidence. In the instant case, other witnesses had become hostile.[97] The mere fact that police personnel belong to the police department cannot be a ground to reject their testimony if it otherwise inspires confidence and no hostility of the police with the accused is shown.[98] A witness is normally considered to be independent unless he springs from sources which are likely to be tainted and this usually means that the said witness has caused to bear such enmity against the accused so as to implicate him falsely. Therefore, there can be no prohibition to the effect that a policeman cannot be a

---

92. *Sidharth Vashist @ Manu Sharma v State (NCT of Delhi),* AIR 2010 SC 2352 : (2010) 6 SCC 1.

93. *Dehal Singh v State of Himachal Pradesh,* AIR 2010 SC 3594 : (2010) Cr LJ 4715 : (2010) 9 SCC 85.

94. *Re Lubeck,* (1905) 7 Bom LR 894 : 32 IA 217 : 33 Cal 151.

95. *Kousalya Ammal v Valli,* AIR 1988 Mad 287.

96. *Hurpurshad v Sheo Dyal,* (1876) 3 IA 259.

97. *Rifakatalikhan v State of Maharashtra,* 1993 Cr LJ 3844 (Bom).

98. *Prithvi Nath Pandey v State of UP,* 1994 Cr LJ 3623 (All). *Girja Prasad v State of MP,* AIR 2007 SC 3106 : (2007) 7 SCC 625, a police witness is not always to be disbelieved. The presumption of honest behaviour applies equally to police officials. A conviction can be based on such testimony.

witness or that his deposition cannot be relied upon if it inspires confidence.[99] Evidence of police witnesses cannot be discarded merely on the ground that they belong to police force and are interested in the investigation and desire to see the success of the case. Prudence however requires that the evidence of police officials who are interested in the outcome of the case, needs to be carefully scrutinized and independently appreciated. Mere fact that they are police officials does not by itself give rise to any doubt about their creditworthiness.[100] Where weapons of assault were recovered pursuant to the statement of the accused and there was no animosity between the accused and the police nor any suggestion was made that the police foisted the recoveries, it was held that it would be safe to believe uncorroborated statement of the Police Inspector, the solitary witness, in respect of recoveries.[101] Where there was discrepancy in the depositions of the two police officers as to the number of cartridges recovered and independent witnesses though available were not examined, such discrepancy would not inspire confidence about reliability of the prosecution case.[102] The accused fired at the victim and the police party escorting him. Some of the policemen also received injuries. They were thus the eye-witnesses to the incident. The court said that they could not be regarded as official witnesses who were interested in the success of the investigation or prosecution. Their testimony was worthy of credence and, therefore, could be acted upon.[103] The court noted the observations of the Supreme Court in *Pradeep Narayan Madgaonhar v State of Maharashtra,*[104] which were to the effect that prudence dictates that their (police personnel) evidence needs to be subjected to strict scrutiny and as far as possible corroboration of their evidence in material particulars should be sought. Their desire to see the success of the case requires greater care in appreciating their testimony. Where a police witness does not have any grudge or rancour against the accused, the presumption that a person acts honestly would equally apply to such a witness.[105] There is no principle of law that the testimony of police personnel cannot be relied upon without independent corroboration. The presumption that every person acts honestly applies in favour of police personnel also. It would not be a proper judicial approach to distrust them and hold them in suspicion without any good grounds.[106]

[s 3.12.1] ***Associates of Accused as Circumstance.***—The close nature of association of the accused with certain persons is a very important piece of evidence where the

---

99. *Madhu v State of Karnataka,* AIR 2014 SC 394 : 2014 (2) Kant LJ 158.

100. *Baldev Singh v State of Haryana,* 2016 Cr LJ 154, para 10 (SC).

101. *Bhimsha Subanna Pawar v State of Maharashtra,* 1996 (1) Bom CR 212 : 1996 AIHC 1 (Bom).

102. *Megha Singh v State of Haryana,* AIR 1995 SC 2339 : 1995 Cr LJ 3988.

103. *Ravindra Shantaram Sawant v State of Maharashtra,* AIR 2002 SC 2461 : (2002)5SCC 604 : [2002] 3 SCR 881.

104. *Pradeep Narayan Madgaonhar v State of Maharastra,* AIR 1995 SC 1930 : 1995 Cr LJ 3213 : AIR 1995 SCW 2088 : (1995) 4 SCC 255.

105. *Gopal Mahadeo Tambada v State of Maharashtra,* 1997 Cr LJ 2425 (Bom) ; *Ram Kumar v State (NCT) of Delhi,* AIR 1999 SC 2259 : 1999 Cr LJ 3522, the accused fired at and killed his victim outside the village no witness was present at the spot. Evidence was collected through police search and seizures and was found to be reliable. The evidence was not allowed to be discarded on the ground that no independent witness was examined.

106. *Karamjit Singh v State (Delhi Admn),* AIR 2003 SC 1311 : 2003 Cr LJ 2021. The evidence in this case under TADA (now replaced) was that of search and seizure by police of which the testimony was also that of the raiding party only.

case is based upon circumstantial evidence. Evidence of phone calls made by various accused to one another was held to be very relevant and admissible piece of evidence.[107]

[s 3.12.2] ***Naturality of Conduct.***—In a case of multiple murders, the witness was one amongst those who were abducted, taken to the riverside, where they were killed and thrown into the river one by one. The witness, though seriously injured, survived and swam to side. This was a sheer miracle. The accused were members of an upper caste. The witness remained in hiding to save his life. That was a normal human instinct. The delay in giving his statement was therefore quite natural for him. The court said that the testimony of such a witness could not be disbelieved. His evidence was that of an eye-witness. He filed the FIR. This evidence was supported by that of the head constable who told that he met the accused some hours before the incident and was told that they were going to the village of the deceased. This was held to be sufficient for conviction.[108]

[s 3.13] Official witness.—In the trial of an offence under the Prevention of Food Adulteration Act, the evidence was that of the Food Inspector. It was held that such evidence could not be rejected on the ground that the official witness was interested in the success of his case. It would have to be proved for rejecting his evidence that he acted in a *mala fide* manner against the party who was facing the charge.[109]

[s 3.13.1] ***Institutional witness.***—It was held to be not necessary that persons appearing as witnesses on behalf of a bank in a suit filed by it, should carry a power of attorney or written authorisation.[110]

[s 3.14] Being witness against oneself.—Where some strands of hair of the assailant were found in the hands of the deceased and an objection was raised to the taking of sample of hair of the accused for comparison, it was held that by mere taking of sample of hair the accused did not become a witness and he was not furnishing evidence against himself.[111]

[s 3.15] Independent witness.—In a case of suicide of a newly-wed wife, evidence about physical and mental torture of the deceased was given by the mother, elder brother and other close relations, it was held that such depositions need not be discarded simply on the score of absence of corroboration by independent witness.[112] Where two persons

---

107. *Sidharth Vashist @ Manu Sharma v State (NCT of Delhi)*, AIR 2010 SC 2352 : (2010) 6 SCC 1.

108. *State of UP v Ram Sajivan*, AIR 2010 SC 1738 : (2010) 1 SCC 529. *Balasaheb Appa Rao Patil v State of Maharashtra*, AIR 2009 SC 1461 : (2008) 17 SCC 425, the eye-witness, instead of reporting to police, went to the house of his uncle, conduct not unnatural, so impairment.

109. *Gautam v State of MP*, 1999 Cr LJ 3104 (MP).

110. *Central Bank of India v Tarseema Compress Wood Mfg Co*, AIR 1997 Bom 225 : 1997 (2) Bom CR 267.

111. *Neeraj Sharma v State of UP*, 1993 Cr LJ 2266 (All). The court **referred** to *State of Bombay v Kathi Kalu*, AIR 1961 SC 1808 : (1961) 2 Cr LJ 856 where the Apex Court explained the expressions "furnishing evidence" and "to be a witness".

112. *State of West Bengal v Orilal Jaiswal*, AIR 1994 SC 1418 : 1994 Cr LJ 2104 : (1994) 1 SCC 73 : 1994 SCC (Cri) 107. Non-examination of independent eye-witness, not a ground to reject the testimony of interested eye-witnesses, *State of Punjab v Nazar Singh*, 1992 Cr LJ 1796 (P&H). Evidence of independent eye-witness corroborated by medical evidence, conviction sustained, *Dharam Deo Singh v State of UP*, AIR 1993 SC 2654 : 1993 Cr LJ 3676. *Abdulla Hafiz v State of Maharashtra*, 1998 Cr LJ 1422 : AIR 1998 SC 1451 : (1998) 1 SCC 526, witness not shown to be interested in the prosecution of criminal to accused person, naturally disinterested and independent witness, evidence accepted. *Balram Singh v State of Punjab*, AIR 2003 SC 2213 : 2003 (1) ALD (Cri) 1032, independent witnesses were not considered necessary in a family feud where one person lost life. Evidence of the injured children of the deceased served the purpose. *State of Karnataka v Vishwanatha S Anchan*, 2003 Cr LJ 2743 (Kant) : 2003 (3) Kant LJ 215, testimony of injured eye-witness found to be reliable.

boarded the last trip of the bus and therefore became acquainted with the conductor and the next morning one of them came back and told the conductor that his companion had been murdered, the bus conductor was held to be an independent witness, neither connected with the accused, nor the deceased. The court said that his evidence could not be doubted.[113] In a case involving raid and search under the Prevention of Corruption Act, 1947, the fact that the independent witness had an acquaintance with the police or that he had helped police action, would not by itself discredit his evidence.[114]

Where the evidence of an independent witness fully corroborated the evidence of eye-witnesses, its veracity could not be doubted only on the ground that the brother of the accused had lost an election against the independent witnesses.[115] The fact that an independent witness turned hostile was held to be not a ground in itself for acquittal.[116]

Where a case involved police raid and search, the fact that the independent witness was acquainted with the police or that he had helped police action was held as not sufficient to discredit his evidence.[117] Where the incident occurred inside the house in the late hours of the night, the court said that it could not be expected of the prosecution that they would be able to produce any independent witnesses.[118] Prosecution version cannot be discarded merely on ground of lack of independent witness.[119]

[s 3.16] Chance witness.—Where the eye-witness was inimical towards the accused and he was also a chance-witness, it was necessary to have had a closer scrutiny of his evidence.[120]

Where all the three eye-witnesses, who were villagers belonging to the same village, gave reasons as to why they were in the town of occurrence, it was held that they were

---

113. *Kothakalava Naga Subba Reddy v Public Prosecutor,* AIR 2000 SC 3480 : 2000 Cr LJ 3452 (SC). *State of MP v Sardar,* 2001 Cr LJ 3984 (SC), statement of independent witnesses who first went to the spot and saw the doors broken open by the accused aggressors accused, **relied upon**. *Kasam Abdullha Hafiz v State of Maharashtra,* AIR 1998 SC 1451 : (1998) 1 SCC 526 : 1998 Cr LJ 1422, an independent witness because he was not related either way, nor anything could be shown against him, nor it was shown that any other witnesses were there who were not examined.

114. *State of UP v Zakaullah,* AIR 1998 SC 1474 : (1998) 1 SCC 557 : 1998 Cr LJ 863.

115. *Leela Ram v State of Haryana,* AIR 1999 SC 3717 : (1999) 9 SCC 525.

116. *Bhola Ram Kushwaha v State of MP,* AIR 2001 SC 229. *Sanjay v State (NCT of Delhi),* AIR 2001 SC 979 : 2001 (3) SCC 193, the fact that the accused was not immediately after the independent witness made a statement before the police was held to be immaterial to his testimony. *State of UP v Man Singh,* AIR 2003 SC 62, the fact of murder proved through testimony of witnesses, but at the High Court stage the theory of fog was introduced which was supposed to have prevented the witnesses from observing the identity of the killers, theory found to be wrong, reversal of acquittal by the High Court set aside.

117. *State of UP v Zakaullah,* 1998 Cr LJ 863 : AIR 1998 SC 1474 : (1998) 1 SCC 557 (SC).

118. *Naresh Yadav v State of Bihar,* 2000 Cr LJ 2041 (Pat).

119. *Yogesh Singh v Mahabeer Singh,* 2017 Cr LJ 291, para 50 (SC) : 2016 (10) JT 332, **relying on** *Darya Singh v State of Punjab,* AIR 1965 SC 328 : [1964] 3 SCR 397.

120. *Patel Chela Viram v State of Gujarat,* AIR 1994 SC 1250 : 1994 Cr LJ 2252; see also *Bhagwati Prasad v State,* 1994 Cr LJ 2310 (All). Evidence of a chance-witness which is reliable corroborated reliable, cannot be discarded on the sole ground of being a chance witness, *Parappurath Cholayil Beeran v State of Kerala,* 1992 Cr LJ 2225 (Ker). *Baldev Singh v State of MP,* AIR 2003 SC 2098 : 2003 Cr LJ 880, both eye-witnesses to a murder were chance witnesses. The circumstances did not justify their presence at the spot, not relied upon.

not chance-witnesses as it is a matter of common knowledge that villagers belonging to the same village move together when they visit town.[121]

The evidence of a chance witness requires a very cautious and close scrutiny. He must adequately explain his presence at the place of occurrence.[122] Deposition of a chance witness whose presence at the place of incident remains doubtful should be discarded.[123] The conduct of the chance witness subsequent to the incident may also be taken into consideration particularly as to whether he informed anyone else in the village about the incident.[124]

Where the presence of the witnesses was natural at the place where they professed to be, the court said that they could not be dubbed as chance witnesses.[125] Where the incident happened during broad day light and the witnesses being residents of the locality, their presence at the place of occurrence could not be considered unnatural. They had no cause to give false evidence. Their testimony could not be disregarded by treating them as chance witnesses.[126]

The expression "chance witnesses" is borrowed from countries where every man's home is considered his castle and every man must have an explanation for his presence elsewhere or in another man's castle. It is a most unsuitable expression in a country, where people are less formal and more casual. To discard the evidence of street hawkers and street vendors on the ground that they are "chance witnesses" even where murder is committed in a street, is to abandon good sense and take a shallow view of the evidence.[127]

[s 3.16.1] Witness bringing in unrelated things.—In a prosecution for rape and murder, it was held that the case of the prosecution could not be discarded on the mere ground that the prosecution witnesses brought into evidence other circumstances which were not related with the cause of death in question.[128]

[s 3.17] Natural witnesses.—The Supreme Court observed on the facts of a case:[129] "The consistency in the evidence of the eye-witnesses is also understandable in the facts of this case. The witnesses were known to each other and they also knew the appellants and their victims. The occurrence took place in the morning and there was sufficient light to enable the witnesses to identify the appellants and the deceased. The assault on the victims was not simultaneous. They were shot dead one after the other. The witnesses were only 10 to 15 steps behind the assailants, and had therefore the opportunity to notice the manner in which the occurrence took place and the

---

121. *Lakhbir Singh v State of Punjab*, AIR 1994 SC 1029 : 1994 Cr LJ 1374 : 1994 Supp (1) SCC 524.

122. *Jarnail Singh v State of Punjab*, AIR 2010 SC 3699 : (2009) 9 SCC 719, citing on this point *Satbir v Surat Singh*, (1997) 4 SCC 192: 1997 AIR SCW 1170 : AIR 1997 SC 1160; *Harjinder Singh v State of Gujarat*, (2004) 11 SCC 253 : 2004 AIR SCW 4356 : AIR 2004 SC 3962; *Acharaparambath Pradeepan v State of Kerala*, (2006) 13 SCC 643 : 2007 AIR SCW 6843.

123. *Ibid*, citing *Sarvesh Narain Shukla v Daroga Singh* (2007) 13 SCC 360 : 2007 AIR SCW 3437 : AIR 2008 SC 320.

124. *Jarnail Singh v State of Punjab*, AIR 2010 SC 3699 : (2009) 9 SCC 719, citing *Thangiya v State of Tamil Nadu*, (2005) 9 SCC 650 : 2005 AIR SCW 761 : 2005 Cr LJ 684.

125. *Vikram Singh v State of Punjab*, AIR 2010 SC 1007 : (2010) 3 SCC 56.

126. *Ramvir v State of UP*, AIR 2009 SC 3185 : (2009) 15 SCC 254; *Sarvesh Narain Shukla v Daroga Singh*, AIR 2008 SC 320 : (2007) 13 SCC 360.

127. *Venkatesha v State of Karnataka*, 2016 Cr LJ 501, para 16 (Kar).

128. *Shyam Singh Hada v State*, 2002 Cr LJ 1437 (Raj) : RLW 2003 (3) Raj 1918, 2002 (1) WLC 382.

129. *Ram Anup Singh v State of Bihar*, AIR 2002 SC 3006.

role played by the appellants. There was therefore no scope for any confusion in the mind of the witnesses. Their statements were recorded immediately after the arrival of the investigating officer. In these circumstances the case of the prosecution cannot be disbelieved merely because the testimony of the eye-witnesses is consistent by raising a suspicion that they may be got up or tutored witnesses."

"In order to appreciate evidence, the court is required to bear in mind the set up and environment in which the crime is committed and the level of understanding of the witnesses. There is often over jealousness on the part of some of near relations to ensure that everyone even remotely connected with the crime be also convicted. Everyone has the different way of narration of same facts. These are only illustrative instances. Bearing in mind these broad principles, the evidence is required to be appreciated to find out what part out of the evidence represents the true and correct state of affairs. It is for the courts to separate the grain from the chaff."[130]

[s 3.18] Injured eye-witness.—The evidence of an injured eye-witness cannot be discarded *in toto* on the ground of inimical disposition towards the accused particularly where his evidence, when tested in the light of broad probabilities, it can be concluded that he was a natural eye-witness, and had no reason to concoct a case against the accused.[131]

The court should not discriminate injured witnesses as against those who were not injured as to their capacity for identifying the accused persons while in action.[132] The injuries of a witness may best assure of his presence at the spot but his truthfulness has to be demonstrated. He should not have any reason to falsely implicate the

---

130. *Ganesh K Gulve v State of Maharashtra,* AIR 2002 SC 3068 at 3071; *Shanker Mahto v State of Bihar,* AIR 2002 SC 2987, Children in the home who saw three members of their family being killed were considered to be the most natural witnesses and it was immaterial that the fact of their being also injured in the incident was neither on record nor mentioned in the FIR. *Rachhpal Singh v State of Punjab,* AIR 2002 SC 2710, witnesses found to be present naturally at the roof of the house of the deceased where he was shot dead. *Podapati v State of AP,* AIR 2002 SC 2724, village witnesses, contradictions in their statement as to the distance from where they saw the incident was considered to be not material, reliable otherwise. *State of UP v Hari Mohan,* AIR 2001 SC 142 : 2001 Cr LJ 170, letters written by the deceased married woman to her brother asking him to take her away otherwise she would be killed by her in-laws, the fact that other letters were also written but not produced and the fact that the accused did not ask for testing of handwriting nor it was otherwise tested, was immaterial. *Sewa Kaur v State of Punjab,* AIR 1997 SC 1843 : 1997 Cr LJ 1833, the victim was killed by his wife and her paramour. The son of the victim was produced as a natural eye-witness. His version was corroborated by medical evidence and recovery of dead body. Evidence and conviction was found to be proper. *Gajula Venkateswara Rao v State of AP,* 2000 Cr LJ 3565 (SC) witnesses naturally there, presence established their evidence not to be discarded only because they belonged to or connected with the party of the victim.

131. *Suresh Sitaram Surve v State of Maharashtra,* AIR 2003 SC 344 at 346. *Dalip Singh v State of Punjab,* AIR 1997 SC 2985 : 1997 Cr LJ 3647, there was an incident of assault in a dispute about the construction of a channel, eye-witnesses included persons who were injured on the spot. Their presence being natural, their testimony was found to be believable. *Rukona v Jala,* AIR 1997 SC 3907 : 1997 Cr LJ 4641 (SC), an explanation of the circumstances in which injured eye-witnesses should be trusted. Their testimony in this case was in the content of the right of private defence.

132. *Binay Kumar Singh v State of Bihar,* AIR 1957 SC 322 : 1997 Cr LJ 362; *Pyara v State,* 1997 Cr LJ 1065 (Raj), non-explanation of injuries on the person of the prosecution witness did not affect the prosecution case. *Veeran v State,* 2002 Cr LJ (NOC) (MP), injured eye-witness is best witness, he would not substitute wrong persons for his actual assailant, he should not be disbelieved for minor discrepancies.

accused person.[133] His testimony cannot be doubted merely because he is related to the informant.[134] But, there is no immutable rule that the evidence of an injured eye-witness should be mechanically accepted.[135] Where the eye-witness is also an injured person, due credence to his version needs to be accorded.[136] The testimony of an injured witness holds more credence.[137] Some of the eye-witnesses were injured in the incident. Their presence thus became established beyond all doubt. The court said that their testimony could not be rejected just only because they were inimical to the accused. Enmity is a double-edged weapon. It could as much be a motivation for falsity as compulsive to see that the real culprits should not escape.[138]

Where the testimony of the injured witnesses was natural, cogent and trustworthy, non-examination of the other two injured witnesses, did not in any way affect the prosecution case.[139]

[s 3.18.1] *Injured Accused.*—Failure on the part of the prosecution to explain injuries on the person of the accused is not always fatal.[140]

[s 3.19] Interested, relative or partisan witnesses.—A close relative who is a natural witness cannot be regarded as an interested witness having a direct interest in having the accused somehow or the other convicted.[141] Relationship can never be a factor to

---

133. *Sujit Gulab Sohatre v State,* 1997 Cr LJ 454 (Bom). *Ramesh Bhagwan Manjrekar v State,* 1997 Cr LJ 796 (Bom), natural injuries on the person of a witness assure his presence at the spot.

134. *Muttaicose v State of Tamil Nadu*, AIR 2017 SC 3117 : 2017 8 SCC 598.

135. *Narayan Ranu Datavale v State,* 1997 Cr LJ 1788 (Bom).

136. *Baleshwar Mahto v State of Bihar,* AIR 2017 SC 873 : 2017 (1) Scale 443 : 2017(1) crimes 26 (SC).

137. *Vijay Shankar Shinde v State of Maharashtra,* AIR 2008 SC 1198 : (2008) 2 SCC 670.

138. *State of Maharashtra v Tulshiram Bhanudas, Kamble,* AIR 2007 SC 3042 : 2007 Cr LJ 4319. *Brahm Swaroop v State of UP,* AIR 2011 SC 280 : 2011 Cr LJ 306, witness to the occurrence was also injured in the occurrence. His presence at the spot could not be doubled. Immediately after lodging FIR, he was put through grueling cross-examination but nothing could be elicited to his discredit.

139. *Balwan v State of Haryana,* AIR 2014 SC 3644 (para 16) : 2014 Cr LJ 4321.

140. *Ram Sunder Yadav v State of Bihar,* AIR 1998 SC 3117 : 1998 Cr LJ 4558. *Chandrappa v State of Karnataka,* AIR 2008 SC 2323 : (2008) 11 SCC 328, non-explanation of insignificant injury on the person of only one accused, does not dislodge the prosecution story.

141. *Kartik Malhar v State of Bihar,* 1996 Cr LJ 889 : 1996(1) SCC 614. See also *SG Gundegowda v State of Karnataka,* 1996 Cr LJ 852 (Kant). *Kailash v State of UP,* 1997 Cr LJ 3511 : (1997) 11 SCC 525 : AIR 1997 SC 2835, prosecution witness had no enmity with the accused, his testimony not to be brushed aside simply because of relationship with the family of the deceased. *Harpal Singh v Devinder Singh,* (1997) Cr LJ 3561 (SC) : AIR 1997 SC 2914 : (1997) 6 SCC 660, testimony of the partisan witness was corroborated by other evidence, relied upon for reversing order of acquittal. *Dharampal Singh v State,* 1998 Cr LJ 3372 (Raj), eye-witnesses, close relative of the deceased, not a ground in itself for rejecting their evidence unless some serious infirmity is found which raises considerable doubt in the mind of the judge. *Rizan v State of Chhatisgarh,* AIR 2003 SC 976, relationship is not a factor to affect credibility of a witness. *Shyam Sunder v State of Chhatisgarh,* AIR 2002 SC 2292, strained relationship, criminal litigation pending testimony of interested witnesses to be subjected to close scrutiny. *Ravishwar Manjhi v State of Jharkhand,* AIR 2009 SC 1262 : (2008) 16 SCC 561, a witness is not to be disbelieved only for being a relative *Paramjit Singh v State of Punjab,* AIR 2008 SC 441 : (2007) 13 SCC 530, eye-witness was son of the deceased, the fact that he could not spell out accurately the situs of injuries on the dead body, did not make his presence at the spot doubtful. The presence of the witnesses could not be doubted by reason of the fact that, they did not make any attempt to rescue the deceased. *Gali Venkataiah v State of AP,* AIR 2008 SC 462, relationship does not affect credibility, foundation has to be laid for suggesting falsehood. *D Sailu v State of AP,* AIR 2008 SC 505 : (2008) Cr LJ 686, relative witnesses are more particular in assuring that real culprits

(Footnote No. 141 contd.)

affect the credibility of the witness as it is always not possible to get an independent witness.[142] The evidence of witnesses cannot be discarded for the mere fact that he was an interested witness. The relationship or the partisan nature of the evidence only puts the court on its guard to scrutinise the evidence more carefully.[143] The relative of the deceased cannot be regarded as an untruthful witness. The Supreme Court said that some reason has to be shown if the plea of partiality is raised.[144]

Where the sole eye-witness was a close relative of the deceased and his conduct was unnatural and his evidence contradictory to medical evidence, it was held that his testimony could not be relied upon without some independent corroboration.[145]

[s 3.19.1] ***Enmity.***—Where the witness stood in a state of hostile relations with the accused, the Supreme Court said that the testimony of such a witness needs to be subjected to careful scrutiny.[146]

(Footnote No. 141 contd.)

do not escape. *Kapildeo Mandal v State of Bihar*, AIR 2008 SC 533 : (2008) Cr LJ 730, credibility of a witness is not to to be judged merely on the basis of his relationship with the deceased and strained relations with the accused. *Ponnam Chandraiah v State of AP*, AIR 2008 SC 3209 : (2008) 11 SCC 640, relationship does not affect credibility. More often than not a relative would not conceal the actual culprit and inculpate an innocent person. *Ashok Kumar Chaudhary v State of Bihar*, AIR 2008 SC 2436 : (2008) 12 SCC 173, relative witness is not the something as an interested witness, producing public witnesses is not a compulsory requirement. Injured witness in the case was found to be reliable. *Kalegura Padma Rao v State of AP*, AIR 2007 SC 1299 : (2007) 12 SCC 48, relationship is not a factor to affect credibility of the witness. *Boddu Satyavathi v Boddu Ramakrishna Rao*, AIR 2007 NOC 220 (AP), a suit for specific performance, no enmity between the plaintiff's witness and defendant, testimony could not be rejected merely because he was a classmate of the plaintiff. *Amit Singh Bhikam Sing Thakur v State of Maharashtra*, AIR 2007 SC 676 : (2007) 2 SCC 310, servant going back from the shop with his master, master, attacked with gunshot and killed, master identified the culprit at the TI parade also, evidence not to be discarded because of the relationship.

142. *Sudhakar v State*, AIR 2018 SC 1372 : LNIND 2018 SC 105.

143. *State of AP v Punati Ramulu*, AIR 1993 SC 2644 : 1993 Cr LJ 3684. To the same effect, *Bolineedi Venkataramaiah v State of AP*, AIR 1994 SC 76 : 1994 Cr LJ 61. Evidence of interested witness is to be scrutinised with care, *Shaukat v State of UP*, 1996 AIHC 634 (All). *Karuppiah v State of Tamil Nadu*, 1993 Cr LJ 1688 (Mad), to be weighed in golden scale before being relied upon. See also, *Jai Narain v State of UP*, 1995 Cr LJ 2333 (All). Hostility or interestedness does not require outright rejection of evidence, only deeper scrutiny is necessary, *Kulamani Sahu v State of Orissa*, 1994 Cr LJ 2245 (Ori); *Jayalal Sahu v State of Orissa*, 1994 Cr LJ 2254; *Raju v State of MP*, 1994 Cr LJ 2167; *Sher Singh v State of Haryana*, AIR 1994 SCC (Cr) 783 : 1994 Cr LJ 1980; *Brijpal Singh v State of UP*, AIR 1994 SC 1624 : 1994 Cr LJ 2082; *DD Suvarna v State of Maharashtra*, 1994 Cr LJ 3602. *Raj Kumar Yadav v State of UP*, 2003 Cr LJ 2075 (All), there is no rule of law that the testimony of interested witnesses cannot be believed. *Bur Singh v State of Punjab*, AIR 2009 SC 157 : (2008) 16 SCC 65, relationship is not a factor to affect credibility, the only thing is that the court has to adopt a careful approach and examine cogency. Also to the same affect, *Bhupendra Singh v State of UP*, AIR 2009 SC 3265 : (2009) 12 SCC 447. *Sudhakar v State*, AIR 2018 SC 1372 : LNIND 2018 SC 105, In such cases the Courts have to be cautious while evaluating the evidence to exclude the possibility of false implication.

144. *Rajesh Kumar v State of UP*, AIR 2009 SC 1. *Murugan v State*, AIR 2009 SC 72 : (2008) 16 SCC 40, reliable eye-witnesses, they had gone with the person (injured) to the village well for morning bath, they arranged taxi for taking him to hospital, hence could not be false. *State v Sarvanan*, AIR 2009 SC 152 : (2008) 17 SCC 587, relatives would not generally conceal actual culprit and rope in an innocent person. Also to the same effect: *Ganapathi v State of Tamil Nadu*, AIR 2018 SC 1635 : LNIND 2018 SC 162, foundation has to be laid if plea of false implication is made.

145. *Anil Phukan v State of Assam*, AIR 1993 SC 1462 : 1993 Cr LJ 1796.

146. *Shyam Sunder v State of Chhattisgarh*, 2002 Cr LJ 4315 (SC) : (2002) 8 SCC 39.

[s 3.20] Delay in reporting.—Where the eye-witness was spared by the accused only on an assurance that he would not reveal about the incident to anybody but the witness mustered strength to approach the investigating officer only after the CBI took up the investigation and revealed the facts pertaining to the incident, his evidence cannot be eschewed from consideration only on the ground that there was delay in reporting his version to the investigating officer.[147]

[s 3.21] Child witness.—Testimony of child witness is not to be rejected outright, but it is to be scrutinised with greatest caution.[148]

Where the children of the deceased figured as eye-witnesses and their evidence was recorded after putting to them preliminary questions to satisfy whether they could answer intelligently and fearlessly and they gave all details of occurrence and withstood the test of cross-examination, it was held that their evidence was acceptable.[149] Failure to hold preliminary examination to ascertain the level of understanding of a minor child does not necessarily introduce a fatal infirmity in his evidence.[150]

A child witness who testified to the ghastly honour killing of several persons, an event which he witnessed several years ago in his tender years, could not be disbelieved on the ground that he could not recapitulate details of such old incident. One of the witnesses was the youngest member of the family which was subjected to the honour killings. He was sleeping in the same room in which other members were killed. The court said that his evidence was not to be discarded because his elder brother and sister

---

147. *Dharam Pal v State of Haryana,* AIR 2017 SC 3720.

148. *State of Maharashtra v Prabhu Barku Gade,* 1995 Cr LJ 1432 (Bom). The following cases were **referred**, *State of Bihar v Kapil Singh,* AIR 1969 SC 53 : 1969 Cr LJ 279; *Ratna Munda v State of Orissa,* 1986 Cr LJ 1363 (DB—Ori) and *Abbas Ali Shah v Emperor,* AIR 1933 Lah 667 (DB): (1933) 34 Cr LJ 606. See also *Mangoo v State of MP,* AIR 1995 SC 959 : 1995 Cr LJ 1461. *Narayan Kanu Datavale v State,* 1997 Cr LJ 1788 (Bom), evidence of child witness to be accepted with greatest caution and circumspection. *National Commission for Women v State of UP,* 1998 Cr LJ 4044 : AIR 1998 SC 2726 : (1998) 7 SCC 177, evidence of a child witness cannot be rejected if it is otherwise reliable. *Zafar v State of UP,* 2000 Cr LJ 3786 (All), testimony to be scrutinised with great caution, where there was no likelihood of tutoring no corroboration of his statement was considered necessary. *Balram Singh v State of Punjab,* AIR 2003 SC 2213, evidence of the injured children of the deceased who were eye-witnesses was found reliable in all respects.

149. *Baby Kandayanathil v State of Kerala,* AIR 1993 SC 2275 : 1993 Cr LJ 2605. *Nandeshwar v State of Maharashtra,* 2001 Cr LJ 4351 (Bom), the minor son of the couple saw how his father beat up his mother to death, abandoned her in a forest and went away with the son to the place of a person whose daughter he intended to marry. Evidence was found to be reliable. It was corroborated with the proof of motive. *State of MP v Bhagwan Singh,* 2002 Cr LJ 3169 (MP), murder of the mother of the child, assailants surrounded here and set her on fire. The child got afraid and retreated to the cot. But his evidence was quite clear. **Relied upon** *Jhunka Sao v State of Bihar,* 2002 Cr LJ 4230 (Jhar), child accompanying her mother and aunt to river for water, on the way the accused attacked and killed the mother. The child was found by the court to be competent witness. *Dalbir Singh v State of Haryana,* 2003 Cr LJ 1878 (P&H), a child witness of 8 years & sole eye-witness to the murder of his mother, reliable, giving full details and verified by other evidence. Testimony accepted.

150. *JV Wagh v State of Maharashtra,* 1996 Cr LJ 803 (Bom). *Sudesh Dhaku v KCJ,* 1998 Cr LJ 2428 (Delhi), a child witness, victim of sexual assault, the court stated the precautions to be taken in recording statements of such witnesses. *State of HP v Prem Chand,* 2003 Cr LJ 872 : AIR 2003 SC 708, clear and cogent of child witness, he already knew the accused as his uncle. *Panchhi & National Commission for Women v State of UP,* AIR 1998 SC 2726, the evidence of a child witness was not rejected because the evidence was found to be reliable.

were not examined by the prosecution. Corroboration of his testimony was considered to be not necessary because he narrated things in a simple manner.[151]

In the case of child witnesses of rape and murder, the trial court had the opportunity of watching demeanour and conduct of the witnesses and found them to be truthful. They also stood the test of cross examination. Their evidence was also supported by circumstances like recovery of articles with blood stains of the victim's blood at the instance of the accused. The Supreme Court restored the conviction recorded by the trial court and said that it was not proper for the High Court to ignore such evidence and disbelieve the evidence of child witnesses.[152]

[s 3.22] Defence witnesses.—The issue of credit and trustworthiness of defence witnesses is to be tested by the standards as are applicable to prosecution witnesses. A lapse on the part of a defence witness cannot be treated differently from any such lapse on the part of a prosecution witness.[153]

[s 3.22.1] Character of witness not material.—The fact that a witness is, in his personal life, a person of easy virtue, does not constitute a ground to throw overboard his testimony, if otherwise it is found to be believable.[154]

[s 3.23] Rustic witnesses.—The evidence of rustic witnesses must be read bearing their simple background in mind. Their evidence cannot be rejected on minor inconsistencies.[155]

[s 3.23.1] *Allegation of second marriage.*—Divorce was sought on the ground of cruelty. The wife levelled the charge of second marriage against the husband placing reliance on the voter's list. The court said that an electoral roll could not be cogent evidence to prove the charge of second marriage. Electoral roll is hearsay evidence. It cannot be accepted as conclusive evidence.[156]

[s 3.24] Panch witness or stock witness.—Because of appearing as police witnesses in number of cases and they being pliable and untrustworthy, their evidence cannot be relied upon.[157]

[s 3.25] Contradictions and discrepancies in depositions of witnesses.—Criminal courts should not expect set reactions from eye-witnesses on seeing an incident like a murder.[158] Unless the discrepancies and contradictions are so material and substantial and they are also in respect of the vitally relevant aspects of the facts deposed, the witnesses cannot be straightway condemned and their testimony discarded in its entirety.[159]

---

151. *State of UP v Krishna Master*, AIR 2010 SC 3071 : (2010) 12 SCC 324.

152. *State of Maharashtra v Bharat Fakira Dhiwar*, AIR 2002 SC 16 : (2002) 1 SCC 622 : 2002 (1) Crimes 164 (SC).

153. *Munshi Prasad v State of Bihar*, AIR 2001 SC 3031 at 3033. *State of Haryana v Ram Singh*, 2002 Cr LJ 987 (SC), a defence witness is entitled to an equal treatment with prosecution witnesses.

154. *Shyam Sunder v State*, 1997 Cr LJ 35 (Del).

155. *Sukhwinder Singh v State of Punjab*, 2014 Cr LJ 446 (para 9) (SC).

156. *Raj Kumari Jaiswal v Ramesh Kumar Jaiswal*, AIR 2007 Cal 94 : [LNIND 2006 Cal 679].

157. *State of Gujarat v KP Singh*, 1995 Cr LJ 3623 (SC).

158. *State of Karnataka v K Varappa*, 2000 Cr LJ 400 : AIR 2000 SC 185 : (1998) 8 SCC 715.

159. *Joseph v State of Kerala*, 2000 Cr LJ 2467 : AIR 2000 SC 1608; *Narayan Chetanram Chaudhury v State of Maharashtra*, 2000 Cr LJ 4640 : (2000) 8 SCC 457, minor contradictions in statements of witness under section 161, CrPC, and deposition made by him before the investigating officer and in the court were held to be not fatal to his testimony. No material improvement was made by him in his testimony.

The post event conduct of a witness could not be predicted on specified lines. It varied from person to person as different person reacted differently under different situations.[160] Where the witnesses were villagers and they differed as to the distance from which the shots were fired and they saw the incident, the same was considered to be immaterial. There was nothing against their evidence otherwise.[161]

[s 3.25.1] ***Material and normal discrepancies.***—In the exercise of appreciation of evidence, the court has to distinguish between normal and material discrepancies. While normal discrepancies do not corrode the credibility of a party's case, material discrepancies would do so. The maxim *falsus in uno falsus in omnibus* is not a rule of law. It is only a rule of caution. The maxim has no application in India.[162] Where the evidence of a witness was not accepted in reference to some of the accused persons, the court did not accept the argument that his testimony should be rejected against all accused persons. A witness cannot be taken to be false in all respects when he has been shown to be false in one respect.[163] It is therefore not required that the entire testimony of a witness be disregarded because one portion of such testimony is found to be false. Thus, the court can separate the truth from the false statements in the witnesses' testimony.[164]

Even where a major portion of the evidence is found to be deficient, if the residue is sufficient to prove the guilt of the accused, his conviction can be sustained notwithstanding the acquittal of a number of his co-accused.[165]

[s 3.25.2] ***Improvements made by witness in his testimony.***—Improvements made by the witness in his testimony related to irrelevant details. The court said that such improvements could not be labelled as omissions or contradictions.[166]

[s 3.26] Accomplice witness.—Where the testimony of an approver was not accepted in respect of one of the co-accused for want of independent corroboration, it was held that this did not have the effect of introducing any infirmity in her evidence or creating any doubt regarding her reliability as a witness.[167] Where the evidence of an approver implicated several accused persons, there should have been corroboration not only generally but also *qua* each accused. But corroboration from independent source of each and every circumstance was not necessary.[168]

---

160. *State of Orissa v Dibakar Naik*, 2002 Cr LJ 2826 : AIR 2002 SC 2148.

161. *Podapati Malakondaiah v State of AP*, 2002 Cr LJ 3555 : AIR 2002 SC 2724.

162. *Jayaseelan v State of TN*, AIR 2009 SC 1901 : (2009) 12 SCC 275.

163. *Ponnam Chandraiah v State of AP*, AIR 2008 SC 3209 : (2008) 11 *SCC 640. Dinesh Kumar v State of Rajasthan*, AIR 2008 SC 3259 *: (2008) 8 SCC 270, the evidence of was f*ound to be exaggerated against the co-accused. But his testimony was cogent, truthful and credible against the other accused (appellant). The court said that the appellant could be convicted on the basis of his evidence.

164. *Prabhu Dayal v State of Rajasthan*, AIR 2018 SC 3199 : 2018 (104) ACC 630.

165. *Kalegura Padma Rao v State of AP*, AIR 2007 SC 1299 : (2007) 12 SCC 48; *Kulesh Mondal v State of WB*, AIR 2007 SC 3228 : (2007) 8 SCC 578, a discrepancy not expected of a normal person are material discrepancies. Witnesses were close relatives of the deceased, no ground for rejection of testimony. *Kulwinder Singh v State of Punjab*, AIR 2007 SC 2868 : (2007) 10 SCC 455, the maxim "*falsus...*" does not apply.

166. *State of Rajasthan v Om Prakash*, AIR 2007 SC 2257 : (2007) 12 SCC 381.

167. *Ranadhir Basu v State of West Bengal*, 2000 Cr LJ 1417 : AIR 2000 SC 908 : (2000) 3 SCC 161.

168. *A Deivendran v State of Tamil Nadu*, AIR 1998 SC 2821 at p 2834 : (1997) 11 SCC 720 : 1998 Cr LJ 814.

[s 3.26.1] ***Failure of witness to appear.***—The police in its charge sheet enlisted the name of a person amongst its witnesses. He was summoned for examination. But he could not appear because he was shifted to Hong Kong and not staying in India. The court held that it could not be said that the prosecution did not deliberately examine him.[169]

[s 3.27] Witness failing at identification.—Where the incident took place during the broad day light and an identification parade was held within a gap of 20 days where the witness could not identify the accused, it was held that no sanctity could be attached to the fact that the witness named the accused in his statement in the trial court.[170] The court said that such failure considerably distracts from the value to be attached to their evidence.

The incident happened in court premises. The eye-witness informant claimed that he knew the murderer by name. But even so the name was not given in the FIR lodged immediately after the incident. He failed to identify at TI parade also. A court constable identified him but he had seen the culprit when he was produced in the court. The third witness identified by the scar on the forehead and no such person was put up in the line. The testimony of the eye-witnesses was held to be not reliable.[171]

[s 3.28] Non-examination of immaterial witness.—The non-examination of the investigating officer was held to be of no consequence where the defence had failed to shake the credibility of the eye-witnesses or to point out any material contradiction in the prosecution case.[172]

[s 3.28.1] Belated examination.—Where there was sufficient cause to explain delay in examination of witnesses in whose presence the dying declaration was recorded, their evidence was not rejected on the ground of delay.[173]

Delay in the examination of a witness is not a ground to throw out his testimony.[174] Where witnesses were examined after a gap of five years from the date of the incident and were subjected to lengthy cross-examination, number of persons were involved including injured witnesses, assailants and the deceased, the court said that some discrepancy as to injuries and weapons of offence in the statement of witnesses was likely. They could not be disbelieved unless the discrepancies were very serious, vital and significant.[175]

[s 3.29] Panchnama.—Persons summoned as witnesses during a police investigation are called *panchas*. A panchnama is merely a record of what a *panch* sees. The only use to which it can properly be put is that when the *panch* goes into the witness box and swears to what he saw, the *panchnama* can be used as a contemporary record to refresh

---

169. *Sidharth Vashisht @ Manu Sharma v State (NCT of Delhi)*, AIR 2010 SC 2352 : (2010) 6 SCC 1.

170. *Suresh Pandurang Tigare v State of Maharashtra*, (1997) Cr LJ 157 (Bom).

171. *Siddanki Ram Reddy v State of AP*, AIR 2010 SC 3000 : (2010) 7 SCC 697; *Musheer Khan v State of MP*, AIR 2010 SC 762 : (2010) 2 SCC 748, presence of eye-witness at the spot doubtful because the star witness testified that he saw no body around.

172. *Bahadur Naik v State of Bihar*, 2000 Cr LJ 2466 : AIR 2000 SC 1582 : (2000) 9 SCC 153.

173. *Malik Ram Bhoi v State of Orissa*, 1993 Cr LJ 984 (Ori).

174. *Sidhartha Vashisht@Manu Sharma v. State (NCT of Delhi)*, AIR 2010 SC 2352 : (2010) 6 SCC 1; *Abuthagir v. State*, AIR 2009 SC 2797 : 2009 Cr LJ 3987, plausible explanation offered for delayed examination, no ground for doubting veracity of prosecution case, witnesses were independent, neither anti-accused nor pro-prosecution, revealing truth long time after seeing photographs of accused, no ground to discard evidence.

175. *BK Channappa v State of Karnataka*, AIR 2007 SC 432 : (2006) 12 SCC 57.

his memory. If the police want to rely on a panchnama they must call a *panch* to prove it.[176] The *panchnama* of a search of premises is not evidence of what was found on the search unless the *panchas* are examined as witnesses.[177]

No statutory provision requires taking the signature of the accused on the recovery *panchnama*. Absence of his signature on it does not make it inadmissible.[178]

Where a recovery memo is prepared at the police station,[179] or where the panch witnesses are found to have signed the recovery memo at the police station,[180] it loses its sanctity.

[s 3.30] Tape-recording.—Tape recorded conversation is admissible provided the conversation is relevant to the matters in issue, there is identification of the voice and the accuracy of the tape recorded conversation is proved by eliminating the possibility of erasing the tape record.[181] Tape recordings can be legal evidence by way of corroborating the statements of a person who deposes that the other speaker and he carried on that conversation or even of the statement of a person who may depose that he overheard the conversation between the two persons and what they actually stated had been tape recorded.[182] The time, place and accuracy of the recording must be proved by a competent witness and the voices must be properly identified.[183] A previous statement made by a person and recorded on tape, can be used not only to corroborate the evidence given by the witness in court but also to contradict the evidence given before the court, as well as to test the veracity of the witness and also to impeach his impartiality.[184] For the tape-recorded evidence to be acceptable, the tape must have been sealed at the earliest point of time and not opened except under orders of the court.[185]

A tape record of speeches (election) has been held to be a document. Tapes are more easily susceptible to tampering than any other documentary evidence. The standard of proof about their authenticity and accuracy has to be more stringent.[186]

[s 3.31] Dog tracking.—Evidence of dog tracking, even if admissible, is not ordinarily of much weight.[187] In a case of alleged murder of the wife by the accused-husband, the dogs of the police dogs squad pointed towards the husband. It was held that it was not a circumstance compatible only with the hypothesis of the guilt of the accused husband.[188]

---

176. *Emperor v Mohanlal Bababhai*, (1940) 43 Bom LR 163.

177. *Emperor v Rustom Lam*, (1931) 34 Bom LR 267.

178. *Kishore Bhadke v State of Maharashtra*, AIR 2017 SC 279, paras 22 and 23 : 2017 (1) Scale 270.

179. *Varun Chaudhary v State of Rajasthan*, AIR 2011 SC 72.

180. *Mustkeem v State of Rajasthan*, AIR 2011 SC 4920 : AIR 2011 SC 2769.

181. *RM Malkani v State of Maharashtra*, AIR 1973 SC 157 : 1973 Cr LJ 228 : (1973) 1 SCC 471 : 1973 SCC (Cri) 399. *All India Anna Dravida Munnetra Kazhagam v LK Tripathi*, AIR 2009 SC 1314 : (2009) 5 SCC 417, tests for determining admissibility of tape recorded evidence explained.

182. PER RAGHUBAR DAYAL AND MUDHOLKAR JJ in *Pratap Singh v State of Punjab*, AIR 1964 SC 72 : 1964(4) SCR 733.

183. *Yusufalli v State of Maharashtra*, (1967) 70 Bom LR 76 SC : [1967] 3 SCR 720.

184. *Rama Reddy v VV Giri*, AIR 1971 SC 1162 : 1970(2) SCC 340.

185. *CR Mehta v State of Maharashtra*, 1993 Cr LJ 2863 (Bom).

186. *Tukaram S Dighole v Manikrao Shivaji Kokate*, AIR 2010 SC 965 : (2010) 4 SCC 329.

187. *Abdul Razak v The State*, (1969) 72 Bom LR 646 SC; *Jit Singh v State of Punjab*, 1988 Cr LJ 39 (P&H), where the evidence of the dog in tracing the accused was rejected because there was no evidence to show whether the dog was earlier taken to the scenting points.

188. *Surinder Pal Jain v Delhi Administration*, AIR 1993 SC 1723 : 1993 Cr LJ 1871.

Evidence relating to the movements of the tracker dogs is admissible as its reliability depends upon the acceptability of testimony of persons who manned the dog and those who witnessed its movements and conduct.[189] In *Babu Maqbul Shaikh v State of Maharashtra*,[190] it was held that tracker dog's evidence must pass the test of scrutiny and reliability as in the case of any other evidence. The following guidelines must be borne in mind:

(a) There must be a reliable and complete record of the exact manner in which the tracking was done and a *panchnama* in respect of the dog tracking evidence will have to be clear and complete. It will have to be properly proved and will have to be supported by the evidence of the handler.

(b) There must be no discrepancies between the version as recorded in the *panchnama* and the evidence of the handler as deposed before the court.

(c) The evidence of the handler will have to pass the test of cross-examination independently.

(d) Some material will have to be placed before the court by the handler, such as the type of training imparted to the dog, its past performance, achievements, reliability, etc. supported, if possible, by documents. In a case of murder, the chappal and knife were found near the place of the incident. Both the articles were wrapped in a paper to preserve original scent. Identification parade was held within twenty four hours and after smelling the chappal and knife the police dog immediately picked up the two accused from amongst the persons in the parade. It was held that the evidence provided by the dog was sufficient to link those two items with the accused.[191]

Genuineness of dog tracking evidence need not necessarily be tested in restricted terms of availability or non-availability of a drawn *panchnama* supported by testimony of dog handler.[192]

In its decision in *Gade Lakshmi Mangaraju v State of AP*,[193] the Supreme Court again emphasised that the evidence based on sniffer dogs has inherent frailties. The possibility of error on the part of a dog or its master is the first among them. The possibility of misunderstanding between the dog and its master is close to its heels. The possibility of a wrong inference from the behaviour of the dog could not be ruled out.

The services of a sniffer dog may be taken for purposes of investigation. But its faculties cannot be taken as evidence for the purpose of establishing the accused's guilt.[194]

The High Court of Delhi has observed that the fact a dog squad has been called does not necessarily lead to the inference that perpetrators of the crime were not identified.[195]

[s 3.31.1] ***Restraint expected of court towards witness.***—A witness committed some mistake in his narration. The court said that that part could be disbelieved by the court

---

189. *Bhadran v State of Kerala*, 1995 Cr LJ 676 (Ker).

190. *Babu Maqbul Shaikh v State of Maharashtra*, 1993 Cr LJ 2808 (Bom) : Mah LJ 1118.

191. *Pandian K Nadar v State of Maharashtra*, 1993 Cr LJ 3883 (Bom). The court discussed the Evidentiary Value of Dog Tracking Evidence at length.

192. *Ashok Gavade v State of Goa*, 1995 Cr LJ 943 (Bom).

193. *Gade Lakshmi Mangaraju v State of AP*, AIR 2001 SC 3677 : 2001 Cr LJ 3317.

194. *Dinesh Borthakur v State of Assam*, AIR 2008 SC 2205 : (2008) 5 SCC 697.

195. *Vishnu v State (NCT of Delhi)*, 2001 Cr LJ 4006 (Delhi).

below. But only for that reason alone, the court should not have made disparaging remarks that there was falsehood on the part of the witness.[196]

"Proved".—A fact is said to be proved when, after considering the matters before it, the Court either believes it to exist, or considers its existence so probable that a prudent man ought, under the circumstances of the particular case, to act upon the supposition that it exists.

SYNOPSIS

196. *Kishan Singh v State of Punjab*, AIR 2008 SC 233 : (2007) 14 SCC 204.

COMMENT

[s 3.32] Standard of proof.—The word "proof" seems properly to mean anything which serves, either immediately or mediately, to convince the mind of the truth or falsehood of a fact or proposition; and the proofs of matters of fact in general are our senses, the testimony of witnesses, documents, and the like. "Proof does not mean proof to rigid mathematical demonstration, because that is impossible; it must mean such evidence as would induce a reasonable man to come to the conclusion."[197] Proof beyond reasonable doubt does not mean perfect proof, which may sound artificial.[198] "A reasonable doubt is that quality or kind of doubt which when you are dealing with matters of importance in your own affairs allow to influence you one way or another."[199] Doubts are reasonable if they are free from zest for abstract speculation. Reasonable doubt is not an imaginary, trivial or merely a possible doubt, but a fair doubt based upon reason and common sense. What degree of probability amounts to proof is an exercise particular to each case.[200] There is no absolute standard of reasonable doubt. A reasonable doubt is a fair doubt based on reason and common sense and must grow out of evidence in the case. The concept of probability cannot by expressed with mathematical precision. It involves subjective element and rests on common sense.[201] The degree of certainty which must be arrived at before a fact is said to be proved is that described in this section.[202] In human affairs everything cannot be proved with mathematical certainty and the law does not require it.[203] The definition of "proof" centres round probability.[204] The court said in this case that the preponderance of probability and normal human behaviour is to be kept in mind drawing reasonable inference from other facts established by evidence. Such inferences cannot be termed as surmises and conjectures.[205] What is required is production of such materials on which the court can reasonably act to reach the supposition that a fact exists. Proof of a fact depends upon the degree of probability of its having existed. The standard required for reaching the supposition is that of a prudent man acting in any important matter

---

197. *Hawkins v Powells Tillery Steam Coal Co Ltd,* (1911) 1 KB 988, 995; *Emperor v Shafi Ahmed,* (1925) 31 Bom LR 515; *Bhano v Babu Singh,* 1998 Cr LJ 4768 (Raj), facts must be proved by the best evidence available.

198. *Inder Singh v State (Delhi Admn.),* AIR 1978 SC 1091 : 1978 Cr LJ 766; Doubt must be real, not fanciful. *Gurbachan Singh v Satpal Singh,* AIR 1990 SC 209; 1990 Cr LJ 562 : (1990) 1 SCC 445 : 1990 SCC (Cri) 151. The court pointed out that the same standards of proof are applicable in reference to crimes against women and the provisions of S. 498A of IPC and S. 113A of the Evidence Act. *Vijayee Singh v State of UP,* AIR 1990 SC 1459 : 1990 Cr LJ 1510.

199. *Walters v R,* (1969) 2 AC 26 (PC). *Ram Bihari Yadav v State of Bihar,* AIR 1998 SC 1850 : (1998) 4 SCC 517 : 1998 Cr LJ 2515, the Supreme Court explains concepts like probative value of evidence which means the weight to be given to it and the legal implications of relevancy and admissibility.

200. *State of Goa v Pandurang,* AIR 2009 SC 1066 : (2008) 16 SCC 714; *State of Punjab v Sukhchain Singh,* AIR 2009 SC 1542 : (2008) 16 SCC 629.

201. *State of MP v Dharkole,* AIR 2005 SC 44 : (2004) 13 SCC 308 : 2005 Cr LJ 108.

202. *Abdul Karim v The Crown,* (1879) PR No. 32 of 1878 (Cr).

203. *Emperor v Shafi Ahmed,* (1925) 31 Bom LR 515, 516.

204. *Tej Bahadur Singh v State of UP,* AIR 1990 SC 431; 1990 Cr LJ 611 : 1990 Supp SCC 125 : 1990 SCC (Cri) 627. *Sevaka Perumal v State of TN,* 1991 Cr LJ 1845 : AIR 1991 SC 1863 : (1991) 3 SCC 471, a murder can be proved by direct or circumstantial evidence though there may be no trace of the body of the deceased.

205. *Devendra Bhai Shankar Mehta v Ramesh Chandra Vithaldas Sheth,* AIR 1992 SC 1398 : (1992) 3 SCC 473.

concerning him.[206] Thus an accused in establishing his plea of private defence may discharge his burden by evidence satisfying the jury of the probability of his defence.[207] "It is necessary to occasionally remind ourselves of this interpretation clause in the Evidence Act lest we act on artificial standard of proof not warranted by the provisions of the Act".[208] The law requires for a conviction proof beyond reasonable doubt and not conclusive proof.[209] The falsity of a plea taken by the accused person cannot prove his guilt, though it may be an additional circumstance against him.[210] "The criminal jurisprudence no doubt requires a high standard of proof for imposing punishment on an accused, but it is equally important that on hypothetical grounds and surmises prosecution evidence of a sterling character should not be brushed aside and disbelieved to give undue benefit of doubt to the accused."[211] Where neither the dead body of the victim of murder was recovered nor post-mortem performed, it was held that factum of murder in such a case must be proved by strongest possible evidence.[212]

The proof of a fact depends upon the degree of probability of its existence. The standard required for reaching the supposition is that of a prudent man acting in any important manner concerning him.[213]

The Supreme Court observed in the matter of a custodial death that an exaggerated adherence to and insistence upon proof beyond every reasonable doubt may result in miscarriage of justice. Courts should therefore deal with such cases in realistic manner and with sensitivity.[214]

[s 3.33] Allegation of murder in Civil Action.—Where there is an allegation of murder in a civil action, the standard of proof for the plaintiff would to be establish a *prima facie* case if the defendant offers no evidence in defence. In the appreciation of evidence of witnesses in civil cases, hyper-technical approach should be avoided. The litigant should not be allowed to suffer for the lawyer's default.[215]

Where a plaintiff established a *prima facie* case against the defendant, who then chose not to give evidence in his defence, the case had to be regarded as proved on a balance of probabilities. In the instant case, given that the plaintiff had shown that the defendant was obsessed with the victim, that he had been violent towards her in

---

206. *M Narsinga Rao v State of AP,* 2001 Cr LJ 515 : AIR 2001 SC 318.

207. *Government of Bombay v Samuel,* (1946) 48 Bom LR 746 (SB); *Yogendra Morarji v State of Gujarat,* AIR 1980 SC 661 : 1980 Cr LJ 459; *Naval Kishore Somani v Poonam Somani,* AIR 1999 AP 1, a fact not proved does not necessarily mean that it is a false fact.

208. *Murarilal v State of MP,* AIR 1980 SC 531 at 535: 1980 Cr LJ 393. Further vividly explained by the Supreme Court in *Yogendra Morarji v State of Gujarat,* AIR 1980 SC 660 : 1980 Cr LJ 459 and again in *State of UP v Krishna Gopal,* AIR 1988 SC 2154 : (1988) 4 SCC 302 : 1988 SCC (Cri) 928. There can always be two views. But the alternative view should be totally ignored unless it carries some degree of plausibility. *State of UP v Chet Ram,* AIR 1989 SC 1543 : 1989 Cr LJ 1785 : (1989) 2 SCC 425 : 1989 SCC (Cr) 388.

209. *State of Kerala v Bahueyan,* AIR 1987 SC 482 : 1988 Cr LJ 1579 : 1986 4 SCC 124.

210. *Shankarlal Gyarasill Lal Dixit v State of Maharashtra,* AIR 1981 SC 765 : 1981 Cr LJ 325 : (1981) 2 SCC 35.

211. *State of UP v Ram Sewak,* AIR 2003 SC 2141 at p 2147.

212. *Ramua v State of UP,* 1992 Cr LJ 3972 (All).

213. *M Narsinga Rao v State of AP,* AIR 2001 SC 318, the case was under the prevention of Corruption Act, 1988.

214. *Dalbir Singh v. State of U.P.,* AIR 2009 SC 1674 : (2009) 11 SCC 376.

215. *Central Bank of India v Ashran Degraj Rathi,* AIR 2007 NOC 277 (Gau).

the past, that he had no explanation for where he was on the day she died and that he had lied to the police when questioned, it was unbelievable that the defendant had failed to adduce any evidence that he was innocent. That converted a *prima facie* case into an extremely strong case, which permitted the court to conclude that assault and battery, effectively murder, had been proved.[216]

[s 3.33.1] Suspicion.—The rules of evidence cannot be departed from, because there may be a strong moral conviction of guilt; for a Judge cannot set himself above the law which he has to administer or make it or mould it to suit the exigencies of a particular occasion.[217] Punishment of an accused person on the basis of suspicion alone has been held to be not permissible. Burden is always on the prosecution to prove its case beyond reasonable doubt. The graver the offence, the stricter should be the degree of proof.[218] Suspicion cannot give probative force to testimony which in itself is insufficient to establish or to justify an inference of a particular fact.[219] Suspicion, though a ground for scrutiny, cannot be made the foundation of a decision.[220] The gravest suspicion against an accused will not suffice to convict him of a crime unless evidence establishes it beyond doubt.[221] "The sea of suspicion has no shore and the Court that embarks upon it is without rudder and compass".[222]

In cases based on circumstantial evidence that evidence should be so strong as to point unmistakably to the guilt of the accused. The fundamental rule by which the effect of the circumstantial evidence is to be estimated is that in order to justify the inference of guilt the inculpatory facts must be incompatible with the innocence of

---

216. *Francisco v Diedrick, The Times,* April 3, 1998 (QBD).

217. *Barindra Kumar Ghose v Emperor,* (1909) 37 Cal 467, 508; *Lakhwinder Singh v State,* 1998 Cr LJ 468 (P&H), proving of guilt of the accused is the burden of the prosecution. Mere conjectures or surmises or picking up some sentences from here and there would not be enough to establish the guilt of the accused.

218. *Mousam Singha Roy v State of WB,* (2003) 12 SCC 377 : 2003 (3) Crimes 321 (SC).

219. *Ibid.* Also *Padala Veera Reddy v State of AP,* 1989 BBCJ 121 : 1990 Cr LJ 605 : AIR 1990 SC 79 : 1989 Supp (2) SCC 706; *Abdulla Mohammed Pagarkar v State,* AIR 1980 SC 499 : (1980) 1 SCR 604 : 1980 Cr LJ 220; *Vindo Samuel v Delhi Admn,* AIR 1992 SC 465 : 1991 Cr LJ 3359, the fact that a person getting down from a bus walked away fastly might create suspicion that he was the chain snatcher of lady passenger, but not proof. *Jagga Singh v State of Punjab,* AIR 1995 SC 135 : 1994 Supp (3) SCC 463, suspicion.

220. *Mohammad Mehdi Hasan Khan v Mandir Das,* (1912) 39 IA 184 : 190 34 All 511 : 14 Bom LR 1073, quoted in *Hari Krishna v King-Emperor,* (1935) 11 Luck 327, 335.

221. *Hawaldar Singh v King-Emperor,* (1932) 7 Luck 623.

222. *Ibid.* See also observations to the same effect in *Sharad Birdhichand Sarda v State of Maharashtra,* AIR 1984 SC 1622; 1984 Cr LJ 1738 : (1984) 4 SCC 116 : 1984 SCC (Cri) 487 ; *Bhugdomal Gangaram v State of Gujarat* (1984) 1 SCC 319 : AIR 1983 SC 906 : 1984 SCC (Cri) 67 : 1983 Cr LJ 1276. Suspicion is not a substitute for proof. *Varkey Joseph v State of Kerala,* AIR 1993 SC 1892 : 1993 Cr LJ 2010 : 1993 Supp (3) SCC 754. See also *State of Maharashtra v Prabhu Barku Gade,* 1995 Cr LJ 1432 (Bom). On mere suspicion, however strong, conviction cannot be based, *Babuda v State of Rajasthan,* AIR 1992 SC 2091 : 1992 Cr LJ 3451. See also *State of Maharashtra v Sukhdev Singh,* AIR 1992 SC 2100 : 1992 Cr LJ 3554 : (1992) 3 SCC 700. Mere suggestion or suspicion of defence cannot discredit the eye-witness, *Kirtan Bhuyan v State of Orissa,* AIR 1992 SC 1579 : 1992 Cr LJ 2325. Where the testimony of the eye-witness was clouded with grave suspicion and serious doubts, it was quite unsafe to act upon his evidence. *Jagdish Prasad v State of MP,* AIR 1994 SC 1251 : 1994 Cr LJ 1106; *Pabitra Pradhan v State of Orissa,* 2001 Cr LJ 3798 (Ori), conflicting version with regard to time and place of occurrence, recovery of weapon and its identification was doubtful, doctor also had difference of opinion, prosecution case rejected.

the accused and incapable of explanation upon any other reasonable hypothesis than that of his guilt.[223]

In cases depending largely upon circumstantial evidence, there is always a danger that the conjecture or suspicion may take the place of legal proof. Such suspicion, however strong, cannot be allowed to take the place of proof. The court has to be watchful and ensure that conjectures and suspicions do not take the place of legal proof.[224] Suspicion, however strong, cannot be a substitute for legal proof. Graver the charge, the greater has to be the standard of proof. The court must keep in mind that there lies a long mental distance between "may be true" and "must be true".[225]

[s 3.33.2] **"Matters before it".**—The expression "matters before it" includes matters which do not fall within the definition of "evidence" in section 3. Therefore, in determining what is evidence other than evidence within the phraseology of the Act, the definition of "evidence" must be read with that of "proved". It would appear, therefore, that the Legislature intentionally refrained from using the word "evidence" in this definition, but used instead the words, "matters before it". For instance, a fact may be orally admitted in court. The admission would not come within the definition of the word "evidence" as given in this Act, but still it is a matter which the court before whom the admission was made would have to take into consideration in order to determine whether the particular fact was proved or not.[226] Therefore, the word "matters" in section 3 of the Act is of a wide connotation. It not only includes evidence but also the surrounding circumstances.[227]

Similarly, the result of a local investigation under the Code of Civil Procedure must be taken into consideration by the court though not "evidence" within the definition given by the Act. The result of a local enquiry by a presiding judicial officer, although it does not come under clauses (1) and (2) of the definition of the word "evidence", falls within the meaning of the word "proved" which comes immediately after.[228]

Where certain letters were not produced before the court by any known procedure of law, nor any affidavit filed for using some of them in evidence, use of any one of those letters was held to be not proper.[229] The use of the word "proved" does not

---

223. *Ibid*, Appreciation of circumstantial evidence cannot create presumption of guilt. *Naresh Kumar v State of Maharashtra*, AIR 1980 SC 1168 : 1980 Cr LJ 920; *State (Delhi Admn) v VC. Shukla*, AIR 1980 SC 1382 : 1980(2) SCC 665. Standard of proof in incidental matters is the same as in others. *State (Delhi Admn.) v Sanjay Gandhi*, AIR 1978 SC 961 : 1978 Cr LJ 952. Requirements of "proved" are the same whether the evidence is direct or circumstantial. *State of Maharashtra v Mohd. Yakub*, AIR 1980 SC 1111; 1980 Cr LJ 793.

224. *Jaherlala Das v State of Orissa*, (1991) 3 SCC 27 : AIR 1991 SC 1388 : (1991) 2 Crimes 268 : *Swinder Singh v State of Punjab*, AIR 1992 SC 669 : 1992 Cr LJ 606, suspicion, however strong, cannot take the place of proof. *State v Bhanudas Sommanna Sangolkar*, 1997 Cr LJ 3205 (Bom), *motive* may create a very strong suspicion but cannot take the place of proof.

225. The Supreme Court following this line of reasoning in *State (NCT) of Delhi v Navjot Sandhu*, (2005) 11 SCC 600 : 2005 Cr LJ 3950 : (2005) 122 DLT 194, and observed that there was a serious suspicion as to complicity of the accused, SAR Gilani, in the conspiracy to attack Parliament House, the court could not condemn him in the absence of sufficient evidence pointing unmistakably to his guilt.

226. *Joy Coomar v Bundhoo Lall*, (1882) 9 Cal 363, 366.

227. *Govindan v P Mahendran*, AS No. 569 of 2006, decided on 27 April 2017 (Madras High Court).

228. *Joy Coomar v Bundhoo Lall*, (1882) 9 Cal 363, 366.

229. *Charidrakant Anna Patil v State*, 1998 Cr LJ 369 (SC).

enable the court to take into consideration matters including statements whose use is absolutely barred.[230]

[s 3.33.3] Difference between evidence in civil and criminal proceedings.—The rules of evidence are in general the same in civil and criminal proceedings, and bind alike State and citizen, prosecutor and accused, plaintiff and defendant, counsel and client. There are, however, some exceptions, e.g. the doctrine of estoppel applies to civil proceedings only;[231] the provisions relating to confessions (Sections 24-30), character of persons appearing before courts (Sections 53, 54), and incompetence of parties as witnesses (Section 120), are peculiar to criminal proceedings.

In a civil case, a Judge of fact must find for the party in whose favour there is a preponderance of proof, though the evidence is not entirely free from doubt. In a criminal case no weight of preponderant evidence is sufficient, short of that which excludes all reasonable doubt. Unbiased moral conviction is no sufficient foundation for a verdict of guilty unless it is based on substantial facts leading to no other reasonable conclusion than that of guilt. In cases dependent on circumstantial evidence, the incriminating facts must be incompatible with the innocence of the accused and incapable of explanation on any other reasonable hypothesis than that of his guilt. Circumstantial evidence not furnishing conclusive evidence against an accused, though forming a ground for grave suspicion against him, cannot sustain a conviction. To justify the inference of guilt from circumstances, the inculpating facts must be shown to be incompatible with the innocence of the accused and incapable of explanation on any other reasonable hypothesis than that of guilt.[232] No man can be convicted of an offence where the theory of his guilt is no more likely than the theory of his innocence.[233]

In a criminal trial the degree of probability of guilt has got to be very much higher—almost amounting to a certainty—than in a civil proceeding, and, if there is the slightest reasonable or probable chance of innocence of an accused, the benefit of it must be given to him. But that is quite a different thing from contending that even where the burden of proof, say of proving an exception, is on the accused, the term "proved" should be differently and more liberally construed than when the burden of proof is on the prosecution. The Evidence Act does not contemplate and does not lay down that the satisfaction which is required to be caused in the mind of a prudent man before acting on or accepting the prosecution story is to be of a different kind or degree from the satisfaction which is required when the accused has to discharge the burden which is cast upon him by law.[234] The standard of proof required in election matters in proving corrupt practices is the same as that for a criminal offence.[235]

---

230. *Hazarilal v State (Delhi Admn.),* AIR 1980 SC 873 : 1980 Cr LJ 564.

231. *Best,* 12th Edn, section 94, p 81.

232. *Emperor v Kangal Mali,* (1905) 41 Cal 601; *Emperor v Parbhoo,* (1941) All 843 FB; *Pritam Singh v Tilok Singh,* (1953) 2 Patiala 187. Circumstances which throw suspicion about the genuineness of a will for civil purposes may not be enough to sustain a criminal charge. *Arjun Singh v Hazara Singh,* 1979 Cr LJ 1029 : AIR 1979 SC 1236.

233. *Emperor v Shivdas Omkar,* (1912) 15 Bom LR 315.

234. *State v Harprasad Ghashiram Gupta,* (1951) 53 Bom LR 938.

235. *C Subba Rao v K B Reddy,* AIR 1967 AP 155. *Jahed v State of WB,* 1995 Cr LJ 3451 (Cal), in a criminal trial degree of proof is stricter than what is required in a civil proceeding.

The onus of proof in criminal cases never shifts to the accused, and they are under no obligation to prove their innocence or adduce evidence in their defence or make any statement.[236]

In a civil case, it is the duty of the parties to place their case before the court as they think best, whereas in a criminal case it is the duty of the court to bring all relevant evidence on the record and to see that justice is done.[237]

In a criminal trial, it is for the court to determine the question of the guilt of the accused and it must do this upon the evidence before it, independently of decisions in a civil litigation between the same parties. A judgment or decree is not admissible in evidence in all cases as a matter of course, and, generally speaking, a judgment is only admissible to show its date and legal consequence.[238]

The rules regulating the admissibility of evidence are, in general, the same in civil as in criminal proceedings. When dealing with the serious question of the guilt or innocence of persons charged with crime, the following general rules have been suggested for the guidance of Tribunals:—

1. The onus of proving everything essential to the establishment of the charge against the accused lies on the prosecutor.
2. The evidence must be such as to exclude, to a moral certainty, every reasonable doubt of the guilt of the accused.
3. In matters of doubt it is safer to acquit than to condemn, since it is better that several guilty persons should escape than that one innocent person should suffer.
4. There must be clear and unequivocal proof of the *corpus delicti* (substance of the offence).
5. The hypothesis of delinquency should be consistent with all the facts proved.[239]

[s **3.33.3.1**] ***Corpus delicti*.**—In cases of homicide, death as a fact must be proved. Where the dead body of the deceased was not recovered, and no piece of mortal remains of the deceased was found, and no evidence was brought on record to show that there was no possibility of recovery of dead body, it having been washed away in the river, the Supreme Court held that *corpus delicti* has not been proved.[240] In *Sevaka Perumal v State of Tamil Nadu*, the Supreme Court held that there may be cases where *corpus delicti* is not possible to be traced or recovered, such as the dead body was thrown into the river stream or washed away or burnt. But where no such circumstance exists or has been brought on record, *corpus delicti* must be established like any other fact.[241]

---

236. *Binayendra Chandra Pande v Emperor,* (1936) 63 Cal 929.

237. *Emperor v Janki Prasad,* (1920) 43 All 283; *Hema Reddy v Rakesh Reddy,* AIR 2002 AP 228, wife pleaded and produced evidence that her husband contemplated marrying a girl from among his close relationship but she could not prove it. A false allegation may amount to evidence of cruelty.

238. *Trailokyanath Das v Emperor,* (1931) 59 Cal 136.

239. *Best,* 12th Edn, sections 439, 440, 441-451, pp 372-382.

240. *KT Palanisamy v State of Tamil Nadu,* AIR 2008 SC 1095 : (2008) 3 SCC 100 : (2008) 1 SCC (Cri) 627.

241. AIR 1991 SC 1463, (1991) 3 SCC 471.

[s 3.33.3.2] ***Balance of Probability.***—Civil cases are decided on the basis of preponderance of evidence, while in criminal case, the entire burden lies on the prosecution, and proof beyond reasonable doubt has to be given. Findings recorded in one proceeding have no binding effect on another proceedings. The evidence in one case and arguments presented in it might have been different from those in the other.[242]

[s 3.34] Appreciation of Evidence.—The court has to decide on the basis of the evidence adduced before it by the parties whether the guilt of the accused is made out beyond a reasonable doubt[243] and whether, in a civil case, on a balance of probabilities the plaintiff has made out a case for relief.[244] The prosecution case has to rest on its own strength, and not on absence of any explanation by the accused person or his inability to raise any plausible defence. The governing principle is known as that of "standard of proof". But here under the Evidence Act all such cases are reported under the caption "appreciation of evidence".[245] Absolute standard of proof does not exist. For a proof to be beyond reasonable doubt, the standard of reasonable man must be adopted.[246] This is a very delicate task. The higher courts have often to reject or remand cases because the evidence was not properly appreciated. A testimony without a fringe or embroidery of untruth is rare. The court can reject it only when it is tainted to the core, that is, where falsehood and truth are inextricably intertwined.[247] If this is not so the court must separate the grain from the chaff.[248] Where the story told by the witnesses in the court was consistent and also fitted into medical evidence and contents of FIR, it warranted implicit reliance notwithstanding different statements obtained by the police under section 162, CrPC.[249] In *Kanwar Pal Singh v State of Haryana,*[250] the Supreme Court

---

242. *Iqbal Singh Marwah v Meenakshi Marwah,* AIR 2005 2119 : (2005) 4 SCC 370 : (2005) 3 Mah LJ 530 : 2005 Cr LJ 2161.

243. *Chhotanney v State of UP,* AIR 2009 SC 2013 : (2009) 11 SCC 71, doubts would be called reasonable if they are free from zest for abstract speculation.

244. *Toran Singh v State of MP,* AIR 2002 SC 2807 : (2002) 6 SCC 494.

245. *Balbir Singh v State of Haryana,* 1987 Cr LJ 853 : AIR 1987 SC 1053 : (1987) SCC 533 : 1987 SSC (Cri) 193, a prosecution under Terrorist and Disruptive Activities Act, 1985 (now repealed) suffering from incredibility and infirm evidence, no proof of alleged facts. See also *Mohd. Iqbal M Shaikh v State of Maharashtra,* 1998 Cr LJ 2537 : AIR 1998 SC 2864 : (1998) 4 SCC 494.

246. *State of WB v Orilal Jaiswal,* AIR 1994 SC 1418 : (1994) 1 SCC 73, 89, 90 : 1994 Cr LJ 2104.

247. The Supreme Court observed on the facts of a case before it that the conduct of a responsible officer should not have been doubted on the basis of a mere suspicion. *Lila Krishan v Maniram Godara,* AIR 1985 SC 1073 : 1985 Supp SCC 179. In *Forest Range Officer v Aboobacker,* 1989 Cr LJ 2038 Ker, the testimony of a forest range officer was accepted without corroboration. *State of Kerala v Kuttan,* 1988 Cr LJ 453 (Ker), the testimony of the owner of articles stolen from him not rejected only because he had not reported the crime.

248. *State of UP v Shanker,* AIR 1981 SC 897 : 1981 Cr LJ 23 : 1980 Supp SCC 489; *Biswambar Meher v State of Orissa,* 1989 Cr LJ 271 Orissa, evidence of a sole tribal eye-witness to a ghastly murder, **relied**.

249. *Gurnam Kaur v Bakshish Singh,* AIR 1981 SC 631 : 1981 Cr LJ 34. Minor discrepancies in the statements of witnesses and those in the FIR are generally ignored because no one can expect an FIR to be perfect in its minute details. See *Ram Udgar Jha v State of Bihar,* 1987 Cr LJ 113 (Pat); *Gajanand v State of Gujarat,* 1987 Cr LJ 374 (Guj). A person who was injured by gun fire, his failure to note that the accused was taking out the empty cartridge manually, did not cast any reflection upon his testimony, he being concerned with his injury, *Ved Prakash v State of Haryana,* AIR 1996 SC 2795 : 1996 Cr LJ 4156 .

250. *Kanwar Pal Singh v State of Haryana,* AIR 1994 SC 1045 : 1994 Cr LJ 1392.

held that, though the statement of the witnesses recorded under section 164 CrPC is to be viewed with some initial distrust, it is not a rule of law and such evidence cannot be discarded in all cases. The court cannot proceed on the hypothesis that eye-witnesses are implicitly reliable. Every piece of evidence has to be subjected to the test of objectivity.[251] Fabric of truth should be the guiding factor, and not the village or rustic background of the witness.[252]

The question of weight to be attached to a particular piece of evidence is a matter on which decided cases cannot be of much help.[253] The weight of the testimony of a witness does not depend upon his social strata. The Supreme Court did not approve the rejection of the evidence of a poor teacher or a peon.[254] A previous convict can testify.[255] It was shown of a witness that he was convicted 43 years ago. His testimony was not allowed to be rejected on that ground alone.[256] Where all the witnesses gave a consistent account of the happening which was sufficient in itself to convict, it was immaterial that there were slight discrepancies in examination-in-chief and cross-examination or that there was one more witness who was not produced,[257] or that the articles connected with the crime were not seized.[258] Witness showed slight discrepancies as to the number of blows and whether the victim was at the time in a standing or lying posture. The Supreme Court observed:[259]

> Such discrepancies in matters of detail may occur even in the evidence of truthful witnesses. Such variations creep in because there are always natural differences in the faculties of different individuals in the matter of observation, perception and memorisation of details.

---

251. *Hallu v State of MP,* AIR 1974 SC 1936 : 1974 Cr LJ 1385.

252. *Shivaji v State of Maharashtra,* AIR 1973 SC 2622 : 1973 Cr LJ 1783; *Kondamuri Anasuyamma v Dist Judge,* AIR 1991 AP 47, no adverse presumption about a rustic witness who appeared to testify about a document particularly when the document itself was not produced.

253. *Charan Singh v State of Punjab,* AIR 1975 SC 246 : 1974 Cr LJ 1253.

254. *Sat Paul v Delhi Admn.* AIR 1976 SC 294 : 1976 Cr LJ 295, though it was a trap case and the court said that evidence of trap witnesses should be scrutinised with extra care. See also *Gurdial Singh v Biru,* AIR 1976 SC 449 : 1976 Cr LJ 346; *R.P Arora v State of Punjab,* AIR 1973 SC 498 : 1972 Cr LJ 1214. It is not proper to disbelieve a witness merely because the police had not examined him as a witness. *Fizabai v Nemichand,* AIR 1993 MP 79, relying on *Varadamma v H Mallapa Gowda,* 1972 ACJ 375 (Mys).

255. *Varghese Thomas v State of Kerala,* AIR 1977 SC 701 : 1977 Cr LJ 343.

256. *Arumuga Nadar v State of TN,* AIR 1976 SC 2588 : 1976 Cr LJ 1998.

257. *State of Maharashtra v Krishnamurti,* AIR 1981 SC 617 : 1981 Cr LJ 9. **Followed** in *State of Orissa v Dilip Kumar Chand,* 1987 Cr LJ 1242 (Ori), presumption against prosecution only when there is deliberate suppression of evidence; effect of discrepancies also considered. *Baskar Re,* 1991 Cr LJ 535 (Mad), one witness turning hostile, testimony of others not affected. *Thunincharam Re,* 1991 Cr LJ 1319 (Mad), minor variations in the statements of a relative eye-witness ignored: *Babarali Ahmedali Sayed v State of Gujarat,* 1991 Cr LJ 1269 (Guj), prosecution for accepting bribe, minor discrepancies in the statements of the witness creeping in because of lapse of time, ignored. *Rakka Dineshan v State of Kerala,* 1990 Cr LJ 1361 (Ker), evidence of a witness not to be discarded only because his name was not listed in the FIR. *Rachpal Singh v State of Punjab,* 2002 Cr LJ 3540 (SC), death by gunshot injuries, discrepancy regarding nature of injury as to whether the wound edges were averted or inverted, not material, the presence of the accused persons at that place with those weapons was established, ballistic examination, proof good.

258. *Santosh Kumar Sarkar v State of WB,* 1988 Cr LJ 1828 (Cal). This is so because such articles are only of corroborative value and in this case corroboration was not needed.

259. *ST Shinde v State of Maharashtra,* AIR 1974 SC 791 : 1974 Cr LJ 674.

That is hardly a ground for rejecting their evidence when there is consensus as to the substratum of the case.[260]

Deficiencies, drawbacks and infirmities in evidence need not be evaluated to find out whether they go against the general tenor of evidence, rendering it unworthy of belief. Discrepancies normally exist in oral evidence. They are due to errors of observation, mental disposition, shock and horror at the time of incident. Unless they go to the root of the matter, such discrepancies do not make the evidence unreliable. A rustic witness was subjected to gruelling cross-examination for many days. Inconsistencies are bound to occur in his narration of the event. They should not be blown out of proportion. The court deprecated the practice of confusing witnesses by lengthy cross-examinations.[261] A person who witnessed a murder was so upset and shocked that he could not speak anything on reaching home until he recovered his breath. This did not destroy the value of his testimony.[262] Improvements made by a witness in his testimony and variations in earlier and later statements do not by itself make his testimony infirm.[263]

Where a witness is not successfully contradicted with reference to his earlier statement recorded by the IO under section 161(3) of CrPC, he cannot be said to be an unreliable witness.[264]

The fact that a witness improves his testimony at the trial or that he was not reliable at one point does not ruin the value of his testimony in its entirety.[265]

---

260. See also *Boya Gaganna v State of Maharashtra,* AIR 1976 SC 1541 : 1976 Cr LJ 1158, Minor contradictions in the testimony of illiterate and ignorant women who were eye-witnesses were held to be not material; *Narpal Singh v State of Haryana,* AIR 1977 SC 1066 : 1977 Cr LJ 642, accused bent upon murder, killed 5, accuracy could not be expected from witnesses as to the number of injuries, shots, etc. But unexplained discrepancies in the statement of witnesses would give benefit of doubt. See *Ajmer Singh v State of Punjab,* AIR 1977 SC 1078; *Bava Hajee v State of Kerala,* AIR 1974 SC 902 : 1974 Cr LJ 755. Minor contradictions in the evidence of the victim of an assault can be ignored. *Appabhai v State of Gujarat,* 1988 Cr LJ 848 : AIR 1988 SC 696; *Martin v State of Kerala,* 1991 Cr LJ 2391 (Ker). Non-compliance with the formality of the presence of a gazetted officer or magistrate at search or seizure, the accused being told of his right but did not insist upon it, evidence not vitiated. *Om Prakash v State,* 1991 Cr LJ 2980 Delhi, under the Narcotic Drugs etc. Act, 1985. *State of UP v Krishna Master,* AIR 2010 SC 3071 : (2010) 12 SCC 324, minor discrepancies not touching the core of the case, not a ground for rejection of evidence in entirety. Minor omissions in police statements, never considered to be fatal.

261. *State of UP v Krishna Master,* AIR 2010 SC 3071 : (2010) 12 SCC 324.

262. *Narayan Singh v State of MP,* AIR 1985 SC 1678 : (1985) 4 SCC 26 : 1985 SCC (Cri) 460; *Ram Avtar v Delhi Admn.,* AIR 1985 SC 1692 : 1985 Cr LJ 1865. Where a witness contradicted himself, his statement first in time should be preferred. See *Mohan Lal v State of Maharashtra,* AIR 1982 SC 839 : (1982) 1 SCC 700 : 1982 SCC (Cri) 334 : 1982 Cr LJ 630 (2). Adivasi woman showed some discrepancies in her evidence but even so accepted. *Boti Pedia v State of Orissa,* AIR 1981 SC 1163 : 1981 Cr LJ 626. Minor discrepancies, *Jagdish v State of MP,* AIR 1981 SC 1167 : 1981 Cr LJ 630.

263. *Maqsoodan v State of UP,* AIR 1983 SC 126 : (1983) 1 SCC 218 : 1983 Cr LJ 218 : 1982 All LJ 1524 : 1983 SCC Cr LJ 176; *Rangi Lal v State of UP,* 1991 Cr LJ 916 (All), improvements in testimony; *Kapil Singh v State of Bihar,* 1990 Cr LJ 1249 (Pat), a chance witness improving his testimony, even then found reliable.

264. *Mani v State, Represented by Inspector of Police,* 2010 Cr LJ 4151 (Mad)(DB).

265. *Bhimrao v State of Maharashtra,* AIR 1980 SC 1322 : 1980 Cr LJ 958. See also *Kuleshwar v State UP,* AIR 1980 SC 1534 where the court said that acquittal of all the accused because prosecution case is unreliable but convicting one on the ground that there injuries on his person was wrong. *Bhagwan v MP,* AIR 1980 SC 1873 on appreciation of evidence. Where the witness improved his testimony to make it conform with the medical opinion, his testimony was rejected. See *Mahendra Singh v State of Rajasthan,* 1989 Cr LJ 886 : AIR 1989 SC 982.

[s 3.35] Credibility of direct testimony of witness (Eye-witness).—Direct testimony of witnesses which is in general agreement as to material circumstances cannot be discarded for not being in strict conformity with medical evidence. Minor discrepancies are not material since they occur due to individual differences.[266] Where minor discrepancies, not going to the root of the matter, are found in the evidence of natural and probable witnesses, the discrepancies should not be over-emphasised.[267] Where the presence of eye-witness could not be secured at all, that would not prevent the prosecution from relying on the evidence, though circumstantial in nature, and, if such evidence is sufficient to bring home the guilt, the conviction should follow.[268]

The Supreme Court held in *PS Rao v State of AP,* that the evidence of the employees of the concerned branch of the bank could not be rejected merely on the ground that they were working under the accused.[269] Credibility of a witness should not be accepted merely because it is corroborated by the evidence of other witnesses but credibility should be tested in the touchstone of the broad probabilities of the case. If doubt arises with regard to any material fact, the accused is always entitled to benefit of such doubt.[270] The fact of failure of a witness's married life with her

266. *State of Rajasthan v Ganesh Das,* 1995 Cr LJ 25 (Raj), the court **referred** to Shivaji Sah*ebrao Bobade v State of Maharashtra,* AIR 1973 SC 2622 at 2634 : 1973 Cr LJ 1783 at pp 1794-95 and *Kishan Narain v State of Maharashtra,* AIR 1973 SC 2751 : (1973 Cr LJ 1839). *Ram Bhukan v State of UP,* AIR 1994 SC 561 : 1994 Cr LJ 596, one witness turning hostile, testimony of others not to be rejected. *State of UP v Man Singh,* 2003 Cr LJ 82 (SC), evidence of eye-witnesses to murder rejected by the High Court on the subsequently introduced theory of fog. The Supreme Court considered this to be improper.

267. *Qaiyum Mian v State of Bihar, 1993* Cr LJ 1756 (Pat). *Balbir Singh v State of Punjab,* AIR 1994 SC 969 : 1994 Cr LJ 1206, minor inconsistencies as to the time of occurrence in the corroborated testimony of the eye-witnesses ignored.

268. *Jagjit Singh v State of Himachal Pradesh,* 1994 SCC (Cr) 176 : 1994 Cr LJ 233; *State of Karnataka v Md Nazeer,* AIR 2003 SC 999, statement of the witness that a blow was given by the accused on a particular part of the body. It is enough for sake of evidence. The witness is not bound to explain whether the blow was intended or directed to a particular part.

269. AIR 1994 SC 1407 : 1994 Cr LJ 2102. *See also Nonappa Poojari v State of Karnataka,* AIR 1994 SC 1581 : 1994 Cr LJ 2185. *Govind v State of MP,* AIR 1994 SC 826 : 1994 Cr LJ 938, reliable eye-witness but not giving many details, evidence not to be rejected. *Gurdev Singh v State of Punjab,* AIR 1992 SC 1924 : 1992 Cr LJ 3447, testimony of eye-witness belonging to one faction, not discarded. Testimony of the witness truthful, could not be discarded on the ground of long delay in recording his statement, *Ganeshlal v State of Maharashtra,* (1992) 3 SCC 106 : 1992 Cr LJ 1545 (SC). A remote possibility of innocence in favour of the accused, to let him escape punishment would not be legally justifiable, *Hans Raj v State of Rajasthan,* 1995 Cr LJ 1004 (Raj), *Arjun Singh v State of Rajasthan,* AIR 1995 SC 2507 : 1995 Cr LJ 410, benefit of doubt to some accused does not entitle others to automatic acquittal. To the same effect, *Ram Narain v State of Haryana,* 1993 Cr LJ 1343 (P&H).

270. *Mangulu Kanhar v State of Orissa,* 1995 Cr LJ 2036 (Ori); *Bijaya Ananda v State of Orissa,* 1992 Cr LJ 3293 (Ori), the claim of a witness that he heard the conversation from a distance 355 feet was held to be doubtful. *Harpal Singh v Devinder Singh,* AIR 1997 SC 2914 : 1997 Cr LJ 3561, the eye-witness made the injured to reach hospital. His clothes became soaked with blood. The failure of the investigating agency to seize his clothes was not a ground for holding that the eye-witness must not have seen the incident. *Sarjerao Sahadeo Gaikwad v State,* 1997 Cr LJ 3839 (Bom), there was a lacerated wound on the head of the deceased which was bleeding when he was medically examined. This was not explained by the witnesses. Such witnesses not creditable. *Pandit Ram Prakash Sharma v Khairatilal,* 1998 Cr LJ 1410 : AIR 1998 SC 2820, eye-witnesses

(Footnote No. 270 contd.)

husband and her subsequent living with another man cannot be a ground to discard her evidence.[271] The credibility of the prosecution case is not affected by the fact that the FIR was lodged at the police station of the place to which the injured was being brought for treatment and he died on the way and not at the place of occurrence. The court also held that non-production of the weapon of offence had no effect on the prosecution case.[272]

[s 3.35.1] ***Eye-witness's account vis-à-vis medical opinion.***—Where the eye-witnesses' account is found credible and trustworthy, a medical opinion pointing to the alternative possibilities cannot be accepted as conclusive.[273]

[s 3.35.2] ***Demeanour of witness.***—The court cannot disbelieve evidence of one witness and believes that of the other merely on the basis of demeanour without giving reasons or grounds for the same. The demeanour can only be an additional factor to be taken into account.[274]

[s 3.35.3] ***Multiple eye-witnesses.***—Where a case involved a large number of eye-witnesses, the Supreme Court said that there must be a string running through the evidence of all of them satisfying the test of consistency.[275]

[s 3.35.4] ***Status of witness.***—It has been held that respectability and veracity of a witness does not necessarily depend upon his status in life. Merely because the respondent is a school teacher, it could not be presumed that whatever he has deposed was a gospel truth and to dismiss the plaintiff's case on that basis.[276]

[s 3.36] Sole witness.—The court may and can act on the testimony of a sole witness though uncorroborated. But corroboration should be insisted upon where nature of the testimony itself requires. Hence, no general rule can be laid down.[277]

(Footnote No. 270 contd.)

did not disclose names of two accused in their initial version to the police or to the doctor though all the accused were known to them. They also did not explain 8 injuries on the body of the deceased. *Jayasena Pradhan v State,* 2000 Cri PC 1953 (Ori), testimony bristled with infirmities and improbabilities, it could not be relied upon. *Cherlopalli Cheliminabi Saheb v State of AP,* 2003 Cr LJ 1246 (SC), four assailants killed one man, only one weapon recovered, improbable that they used a single weapon, the injured accused and the deceased reached the hospital at the same time and the prosecution failed to explain injuries on the person of the accused, other witnesses turned hostile, acquittal.

271. *Vishnu Naraya Moger v State of Karnataka,* 1996 Cr LJ 1121 (Kant). *Ram Sunder Yadav v State of Bihar,* 1998 Cr LJ 4558 : AIR 1998 SC 3117, failure by the prosecution injuries on the person of the accused was held to be not fatal to their case. *Inder Singh v State of HP,* 2003 Cr LJ 1482 (HP), conviction on the basis of proper evidence of identification and other evidence.

272. *Shashidhar Singh v State,* 1998 Cr LJ 2676 (MP). *State of Punjab v Jugraj Singh,* 2002 Cr LJ 1503 (SC) eye-witnesses could not speak of the total number of injuries because they ran away after witnessing two gun-shot injuries, eye-witness account prevailed. *Bhim Singh v State of Haryana,* 2003 Cr LJ 857 (SC), there was variation in evidence as to time of death, evidence of prosecution witnesses was sought to be corroborated by stomach contents of the deceased as found in the post-mortem report. The court said that this could not be relied on as conclusive evidence, there should be some other evidence, for example, as to when the deceased had taken his last meal.

273. *Vijay Pal v State (GNCT) of Delhi,* 2015 Cr LJ 2041 (para 13) : AIR 2015 SC 1495.

274. *Navaneetham v S.S. Jayarama Pillai,* 1996 AIHC 1849.

275. *C Magesh v State of Karnataka,* AIR 2010 SC 2768 : (2010) 5 SCC 645.

276. *Soev Bhimabai Eknath Shejwal v Suresh Dayanand Kasab,* AIR 1999 Bom 379.

277. *Vithal Pundalik Zendge v State of Maharashtra,* AIR 2009 SC 1110 : (2008) 17 SCC 239.

[s 3.36.1] Mass killing by mob.—A deep-seated enmity between two communities resulted in the annihilation of 9 human lives and serious injury to 4 persons. Proof of motive was available. The trial judge adopted this guiding principle that out of 51 accused persons whom he was trying he would convict only those against whom some *overt act* was proved and there were at least three eye-witnesses to establish participation or *overt act* of each one of the accused persons, was held to be proper.[278]

[s 3.36.2] Motive not established.—Failure to prove motive in a case resting entirely on circumstantial evidence is not fatal in itself to the prosecution case. However, courts are to be more careful and circumspect in scrutinising the evidence to ensure that suspicion does not take the place of proof while finding the accused guilty.[279]

[s 3.37] Conclusive Proof.—Mere matching of blood group of the deceased in the wearing apparel of the accused cannot be said to be a conclusive proof to fasten the accused with culpability.[280] In a case of murder, weapon of the crime was seized at the instance of the accused from a room of his house occupied by all members of his family, it was not a conclusive proof that the accused himself kept the weapon in the room under his exclusive possession and the seizure of the weapon was not a piece of incriminating evidence.[281] Where out of six accused persons, two were given benefit of doubt on certain grounds which were available to two more accused also whose participation in crime was not established beyond reasonable doubt, it was held that they also were entitled to benefit of doubt.[282]

[s 3.38] Non-examination of Investigating Officer.—Where there is no contradiction in the statements of the prosecution witnesses given in the court and their earlier statements, the non-examination of the investigating officer like other witnesses cannot be said to be fatal for the prosecution.[283]

[s 3.38.1] *Failure of Investigating Officer to point out spot on site plan.*—A failure on the part of the investigating officer to point out on the site plan the spot at which the eye-witnesses had seen the occurrence taking place was held to be not

---

278. *State of UP v Ram Bharat*, 2002 Cr LJ 1529 (All).
279. *Sunil Rai @ Pauna v Union Territory of Chandigarh*, AIR 2011 SC 2545 : (2011) 12 SCC 258.
280. *Binder Munda v State of Orissa*, 1992 Cr LJ 3508 (Ori), blood found on the apparel of the accused matching with that of the deceased, not a conclusive proof.
281. *Binder Munda v State of Orissa*, 1992 Cr LJ 3508 (Ori); *Chandar Singh v State of MP*, 1992 Cr LJ 3947 (MP), pre-existing enmity, whole family charge-sheeted, benefit of doubt. *Mohar v State of UP*, 2002 Cr LJ 4310 (SC), misspelling the name of the witness in the FIR and in the court proceedings could not be used as a ground for doubting his presence at the stop.
282. *Pulla Reddy v State of AP*, AIR 1993 SC 1899: 1993 Cr LJ 2246. *Chinnasamy v State of TN*, 1994 Cr LJ 882 (Mad), all but one accused acquitted, the sole one could not be convicted by making a new case. *Leelason Breweries Ltd v Beemireddy*, AIR 2002 AP 253, appointment of guardian of the infirm plaintiff, contents of medical certificate showed his infirmity, such certificate can be taken into consideration in deciding the question of infirmity.
283. *Hakru v State of Rajasthan*, 1994 Cr LJ 2141 (Raj). In another case of non-examination of the IO which caused no prejudice to the accused, other reliable and trustworthy evidence was not allowed to be discarded, *Shyam Narayan Singh v State of Bihar*, 1993 Cr LJ 772 (Pat). *Bahadur Naik v State of Bihar*, AIR 2000 SC 1582 : (2000) 9 SCC 153 : 2000 Cr LJ 2466, non-examination of the investigating officer was held to be of no consequence when the defence failed to shake the credibility of the eye-witnesses or to point out any material contradiction in the prosecution case.

material. The court said that it could not be said that the evidence was hit by section 162, CrPC.[284]

[s 3.39] Non-examination by ballistic expert.—The testimony of eye-witnesses was that the accused was armed with a double barrel gun. He fired two gun shots which hit the victim who died. The statement of the investigating officer was that the gun seized was not in working condition and that no purpose would be served in sending it for examination by ballistic expert. It was held that non-examination by ballistic expert could not be said to have affected the credit-worthiness of the version put forth by eye-witnesses.[285]

[s 3.40] Non-examination of one doctor.—Where the postmortem report was prepared jointly by two doctors, examination of one of them who had done major work was held to be sufficient.[286]

[s 3.41] Appreciation of question of law.—A wrong appreciation of facts, even if it results in a concurrent finding of facts, is liable to be set aside.[287] As against this, the Supreme Court did not interfere in the order of conviction for bride burning on the basis of proper appreciation of circumstantial evidence and extra judicial confession.[288]

[s 3.41.1] Appreciation of the testimony of victim of sexual assault.—In a prosecution under section 377 for unnatural offence on a minor girl, the court explained the matter of appreciation of her testimony in these words.[289]

The evidence of the victim girl as described by her is satisfactory even in its minutest details, and nothing has been shown to me that she had falsely implicated the accused at the cost of her own dignity. Where the eye-witness' account is credible and trustworthy, medical opinion pointing to alternative possibilities is not accepted as conclusive. Witnesses are the eyes and ears of justice, said Bentham. Eye-witnesses' account should not be adversely evaluated and other evidence including medical evidence should not outweigh the former in the scales of credibility. Similar observations were made by the Apex Court in *State of UP v Krishna Gopal*.[290]

[s 3.42] Right to maintenance.—Evidence.—Where the mother of an illegitimate child claimed maintenance from the alleged father of the child, it was held that the evidence of the mother could not be accepted as a proof of paternity of the said child without proper corroboration.[291] In another case for maintenance, it was held that factum of marriage could not be based on the few statements given in support of the same.[292] In a case the mother of an illegitimate child claimed maintenance from the alleged father of the said child. There were no allegations regarding moral lapses on

---

284. *Pyara v State,* 1997 Cr LJ 1065 (Raj).

285. *State of Punjab v Jugraj Singh,* AIR 2002 SC 1083. The court also said that the doctor was not bound to explain the origin or cause of injuries in the post-mortem report.

286. *State of Gujarat v Anirudh Singh,* AIR 1997 SC 2780 : 1997 Cr LJ 3397.

287. *Mahabir Prashad v State of MP,* 1991 Cr LJ 3325 : AIR 1991 SC 2296.

288. *Baldev Raj v State of Haryana,* 1990 Cr LJ 2643 : AIR 1991 SC 37 : 1991 Supp (1) SCC 14.

289. *Mihir v State of Orissa* , 1992 Cr LJ 488 (Ori).

290. *State of UP v Krishna Gopal,* AIR 1988 SC 2154 : 1989 Cr LJ 288 : (1988) 4 SCC 302 : 1988 SCC (Cri) 928.

291. *Chaya v KG Channappa Gowda,* 1993 Cr LJ 767 (Kant).

292. *Shibsankar Samanta v Sobhana Samanta,* 1992 Cr LJ 2196 (Cal).

the part of the mother and the *panchayatdars* corroborated the evidence of mother, it was held that the child would be entitled to maintenance from the alleged father.[293]

[s 3.42.1] Medical opinion about husband's conduct towards wife dying of burns.—Where a man was prosecuted for killing his wife by setting her on fire and he tried to defend himself by saying that he rather tried to save her and sustained burn injuries, the court preferred the medical opinion which was to the effect that the nature of injuries on the person of the accused showed that he tried to hold her by his hands and prevented her from going out of the room.[294]

[s 3.42.2] Duty to come with clean hands.—Where neither the prosecution nor the accused person came with clean hands and, therefore, the court was not able to put reliance on either side, it was under no duty to make out a third situation. The accused would be entitled to acquittal.[295] The court said[296] that if the versions of both the sides were found to be incorrect, it had no option but to acquit the accused persons. The infirmities of the prosecution case may lead the case to acquittal but the infirmities of the defence put up by the accused cannot lead to his conviction.

[s 3.42.3] Appreciation of evidence.—Normally the Supreme Court would not subject the evidence to a reappreciation particularly against a concurrent finding of fact by the courts below.[297]

[s 3.43] Disciplinary Proceedings.—A case before the Supreme Court involved the removal of a bus conductor for not collecting fare from certain passengers. The court held that strict rules of the Evidence Act were not applicable to a domestic inquiry. Unrecorded statements of passengers reproduced by the inspector of the flying squad were held to be sufficient.[298] The Supreme Court has also held that rules of evidence are not applicable to inquiries under Article 311 of the Constitution.[299]

The Supreme Court upheld the removal from service of a police inspector who had attempted to force a woman in her hut to submit to him. Only direct evidence was the statement of the woman though that was supported by the evidence of the circumstances generated by the inspector's unsuccessful attempt to convert the incident into resistance being offered to a prohibition raid. The Supreme Court regarded the woman's evidence to be acceptable though she was described in the judgment as an "unchaste woman" for the fact that she was keeping a friend in addition to her husband.[300]

In a case of bribery, corroboration of the evidence of the complainant need not be direct. It can be by circumstantial evidence also.[301]

[s 3.43.1] Disciplinary proceedings, illegally obtained evidence.—The Professional Conduct Committee of the General Medical Council (GMC) found a doctor to be

---

293. *Chaya v KG Channappa Gowda*, 1993 Cr LJ 767 (Kant).
294. *Rajendra Kumar v State of UP*, 1998 Cr LJ 3293 : AIR 1998 SC 2379 : (1998) 5 SCC 690.
295. *State of UP v Bhagat Singh*, 1999 Cr LJ 2333 (All).
296. At p 2337.
297. *C Chenga Reddy v State of AP*, AIR 1996 SC 3390 : 1996 Cr LJ 3461 : 1996 AIR SCW 3461. See also *Dharam Pal v State of Haryana*, AIR 2017 SC 3720.
298. *State of Haryana v Rattan Singh*, AIR 1977 SC 1512 : (1977) 2 SCC 491.
299. *KL Shinde v State of Mysore*, AIR 1976 SC 1080 : (1976) 3 SCC 76.
300. *State of Maharashtra v Madhukar N Mardikar*, (1991) 1 SCC 57 : AIR 1991 SC 207, AHMADI J.
301. *Ramesh Kumar Gupta v State of MP*, AIR 1995 SC 2121 : 1995 Cr LJ 3656.

guilty of serious professional misconduct and suspended her registration for 12 months following her failure to return to her duties as a Senior House Officer, her failure to give any or any adequate notice of her intention to leave her post or any subsequent explanation. Her defence to the complaints made against her was based upon medical grounds. She appealed against the decision contending that, whilst she had given her consent to the partial disclosure of her medical records, the committee had overstepped that consent and as such the information relied upon by the committee in reaching the decision had been obtained illegally and was, therefore, inadmissible. Her appeal was dismissed.

The court said[302] that the admissibility of evidence in disciplinary proceedings was not dependent upon it having been obtained legally.[303] The principle in *Khan* was not restricted to criminal proceedings and in any event the Rules of the GMC permitted wider admissibility than is generally allowed in English criminal proceedings.

[s 3.44] Mode of obtaining evidence, irrelevant.—The Supreme Court in its decision in *Pushpadevi M Jatia v ML Wadhawan*,[304] endorsed the already established principle that relevant evidence can be taken into account irrespective of the method by which it was obtained. The court cited the observation of Sir Lawrence Jenkins in *Barindra Kumar Ghose v Emperor*[305] to the effect that evidence which would otherwise be relevant does not become irrelevant because it was discovered in the course of a search or seizure in violation of the statutory enactments.[306] The court also cited the observation of Lord Diplock in *R v Sang*[307] to the effect that however much the judge may dislike the way in which a particular piece of evidence was obtained, if it is admissible evidence probative of the accused's guilt, it is no part of his judicial function to exclude it on the ground that it was obtained by improper or unfair means. The court is not concerned with how it was obtained. The court may, however, exclude such evidence where its prejudicial effect would be out of proportion to its evidential value.[308]

Wrongs committed by the investigating officer were not allowed to affect that part of the evidence which was trustworthy.[309] There is of course always a word of caution. It is that the judge has the discretion to disallow evidence in a criminal case if non-

302. *Idenburg v General Medical Council*, (2000) 55 BMLR101, Cly, PC.

303. The court **followed** *R. v Khan*, (*Sultan*), 1997 SC 558 : (1997) 2 SCC 664.

304. *Pushpadevi M Jatia v ML Wadhawan*AIR 1987 SC 1748 : 1987 Cr LJ 1888 : (1987) 3 SCC 367 : 1987 SCC (Cri) 526 : (1987) 12 ECC 356.

305. *Barindra Kumar Ghose v Emperor*, ILR (1910) 37 Cal 467

306. Citing also the observation to the same effect of Goddard LJ in *Kuruma v Reginam*, (1955) 1 All ER 236, 239, saying that the principle is applicable to civil as well as criminal proceedings.

307. *R v Sang*, (1979) 2 All ER 1222, 1230-31.

308. The following authorities were relied upon: *Megraj Patodia v RK Borla*, AIR 1971 SC 1295 : (1971) 2 SCR 118; *R M Malkani v State of Maharashtra*, (1973) 2 SCR 417 : 1973 Cr LJ 228 and *Pooran Mal v Director Inspection (IT)*, (1974) 2 SCR 764: (1974) 93 ITR 505 : (1974) 1 SCC 345 : 1994 SCC (Tax) 114.

309. *Jai Narain v State of UP*, 2000 Cr LJ 3806 (All) *State of Punjab v Baldev Singh*, AIR 1999 SC 2378 : (1999) 6 SCC 172 : 1999 Cr LJ 3672, a search and seizure was made under the Narcotic Drugs and Psychotropic Substances Act, 1985, which was in violation of the provisions of the Act. The court said that the contraband seized could not by itself be used as evidence of proof of unlawful possession. Presumption under section 50 of that Act could not be applied. *Pon Adithan v Deputy Director, Narcotic Control Bureau*, AIR 1999 SC 2355 : (1999) 6 SCC 1 : 1999 Cr LJ 3663 statement of the Intelligence Officer that the accused was informed of his rights, the fact that 10 years earlier he was involved in a corruption case could not be said to damage testimony here.

observance of the strict rules of admissibility would operate unfairly against the accused. That caution is the golden rule in criminal jurisprudence.[310]

Objections as to incompetency of the inquiring officer must be raised at the earliest opportunity. The court said that such incompetence does not vitiate the entire proceedings. The right to object becomes waived if not exercised in time. It cannot be raised for the first time before superior courts.[311]

Where in an appeal against certification as a terrorist under the Anti Terrorisms, Crime and Security Act, 2001, the question was whether the evidence obtained by torture was admissible, the House of Lords were of the opinion that if the accused has created a suspicion about torture, the fact of it should be probed first and the evidence so obtained, even if it remains admissible, it may lose its weight. The provisions relating to certification were repealed by the Prevention of Terrorism Act, 2005.[312]

[s 3.45] DNA test.—A woman was under the charge of adultery. She had undergone termination of pregnancy. Slides relating to the operation were preserved in the hospital. The husband applied for testing his DNA for examining whether he was father of the foetus. The court ordered it in accordance with the law. It was held that such evidence could not be taken to be collected at the behest of the court.[313]

In a dispute about the paternity of a child, the husband sought divorce on the ground that the child was the result of the adulterous life of his wife. It was held that the High Court had the inherent power to compel parties to undergo DNA test to find out the truth and clear misunderstanding between the parties.[314] The property in dispute was the self-acquired property of the mother. The suit for partition was filed by the plaintiff (daughter). The son was defendant. He stated that the plaintiff and her brother were destitutes and not born to his mother. As such they had no right of inheritance. The court said that the maternity of the parties was thus disputed. The court directed both the parties to undergo DNA test.[315]

[s 3.45.1] *Order of DNA test by Women's Commission.*—A woman sought declaration that she was the legitimate wife of her husband and the female child is his legitimate daughter. The court said that if the DNA test came out to be positive, it would redeem the woman and her child of their trauma which they had been undergoing for several years. The order of DNA test by Women's Commission was proper.[316]

[s 3.46] Domestic Inquiry.—The standards of proof in domestic inquiries other than those involved in disciplinary proceedings are also the same, namely, proof by preponderance of probability. Strict rules of evidence are not applicable to departmental proceedings or proceedings before domestic tribunals. But there must be relevant evidence whether direct or circumstantial to support necessary inference as to the

310. *State (NCT) of Delhi v Navjot Sandhu*, (2005) 11 SCC 600 : 2005 Cr LJ 3950 : (2005) 122 DLT 194.
311. *HV Nirmala v Karnataka State Financial Corpn.*, AIR 2008 SC 2440 : (2008) 7 SCC 639.
312. *A v Secretary of State for the Home Deptt. (No. 2)*, (2006) 1 All ER 575 HL : 2005 UKHL 71.
313. *"X" Mrs v Z*, AIR 2002 Del 217.
314. *Buridi Vanajakshmi v Buridi Venkata Satya Varha Pd Gangadhar Rao*, AIR 2010 AP 172.
315. *Mavada Venkateswara Rao v Oleti Vana Lakshmi*, AIR 2008 AP 195 : 2008 (4) RCR (Civil) 155.
316. *Joseph v State of Kerala*, AIR 2006 Ker 191.

existence of the alleged facts. Applying these principles to the facts of a case before it, the Supreme Court came to the conclusion that where the marks awarded by a moderator were tampered with in favour of the candidate, the probability would suggest, and it would have to be taken as a proof, that the tampering must have been in league with either the candidate or his parent/guardian etc.[317]

The court proceeded to explain the position as follows: "Strict rules of the Evidence Act, and the standard of proof envisaged therein do not apply to departmental proceedings or domestic tribunal. It is open to the authorities to receive and place on record all the necessary, relevant, cogent and acceptable material facts though not proved strictly in conformity with the Evidence Act. The material must be germane and relevant to the facts in issue. In grave cases like forgery, fraud, conspiracy, mis-appropriation, etc. seldom direct evidence would be available. Only the circumstantial evidence would furnish the proof. Inference from the evidence and circumstances must be carefully distinguished from conjectures or speculation. The mind is prone to take pleasure to adapt circumstances to one another and even in straining them a little to force them to form parts of one connected whole. There must be evidence, direct or circumstantial, to deduce necessary inferences in proof of the facts in issue. There can be no inferences unless there are objectively proved facts, direct or circumstantial from which to infer the other fact which it is sought to establish. The standard of proof is not proof beyond reasonable doubt but the preponderance of probabilities tending to draw an inference that the fact must be more probable. Standard of proof, however, cannot be put in a strait-jacket formula. The probative value could be gauged from facts and circumstances in a given case. The standard of proof is the same both in civil cases and domestic enquiries".

"Unless either the examinee or parent or guardian approached the fabricator; gave the number and instructed him/them to fabricate the marks, it would not be possible to know their number to fabricate. The act of fabrication is an offence. Merely that is done in one subject or more than one, makes little difference. Its gravity is not mitigated if it is committed in one subject alone. This is not an innocent at or a casual mistake during the course of performance of the official duty. It was obviously done as a concerted action. In view of the admitted facts and above circumstances the necessary conclusion that could unerringly be drawn would be that either the examinee or the parent or guardian obviously was a privy to the fabrication and that the forgery was committed at his or her or parent's or guardian's instance. It is, therefore, clear that the conclusion reached by the standing committee that the fabrication was done at the instance of either the examinees or their parents or guardians is amply borne out from the record."[318]

[s 3.46.1] Interference in concurrent findings.—The Supreme Court laid down in *Balak Ram v State of UP*,[319] "that the powers of the Supreme Court under Article 136 of the Constitution are wide enough but in criminal appeals, this court does not interfere with the concurrent findings of fact save in exceptional circumstances. The [question] of the scope of interference arose in *Arunachalam v PSR Setharathnam*[320]

---

317. *Maharashtra State Board of Secondary and Higher Education v KS Gandhi,* (1991) 2 SCC 716 : (1991) 1 SCR 772.

318. *Ibid.*

319. *Balak Ram v State of UP,* AIR 1974 SC 2165, at 2170 : (1975) 3 SCC 219 at 227.

320. *Arunachalam v PSR Setharathnam,* AIR 1979 SC 1284 : (1979) 2 SCC 297.

wherein the Supreme Court held that ... the very nature of the power has led the court to set limits. It is now the well established practice of this court to permit the invocation of the power under Article 136 only in very exceptional circumstances, as when a question of law of general public importance arises or a decision shocks the conscience of the court. But within the restrictions imposed by itself, this court has the undoubted power to interfere even in findings of facts making no distinction between judgments of acquittal and conviction, if the High Court in arriving at those findings has acted perversely or otherwise improperly."[321]

[s 3.46.2] Prior enmity.—Where prior enmity of the accused with the deceased and the witnesses was duly established and the presence of the accused at the place of occurrence was highly doubtful, it was held that it was not safe to place reliance on the evidence of such witnesses.[322]

The courts have said time and again that the post-event conduct of a person varies from person to person. There cannot be a cast-iron reaction to be followed as a model by everyone witnessing such event. Different persons would react differently on seeing any violence and their behaviour and conduct would, therefore, be different.[323]

[s 3.46.3] Omission to state material facts.—When a solitary witness omits to state the material facts of the actual incident in his first disclosure before the investigating officer, then his evidence becomes doubtful and is to be pushed out of the arena of trustworthiness.[324]

[s 3.46.4] Non-explanation of injuries on person of accused.—The significance of non-explanation of injuries on the person of the accused was explained by the Supreme Court in *Dhananjay Shanker Shetty v State of Maharashtra.*[325] In this case four incised injuries on non-vital parts of the person of the accused were found which were caused by sharp edged weapon and the prosecution completely failed to explain the same. The court said: "It cannot be laid down as a matter of law or invariably a rule that whenever accused sustained an injury in the same occurrence, the prosecution is obliged to explain it and on its failure to do so the prosecution case should be disbelieved." But non-explanation of injuries assumes significance when there are material circumstances which make the prosecution case doubtful. Reference in this connection may be made to decisions of this court in the cases of *Takhaji Hiraji v*

---

321. Citing *State of Madras v A Vaidyanatha Iyer,* 1958 SCR 580 : AIR 1958 SC 61 and *Himachal Pradesh Admn v Om Prakash,* AIR 1972 SC 975 : (1972) 1 SCC 249.

322. *Dharam Singh v State of Punjab,* AIR 1993 SC 319 : 1993 Cr LJ 150 : 1993 Supp (3) SCC 532.

323. *Rammi v State of MP,* AIR 1999 SC 3544 : (1999) 8 SCC 649 : 1999 Cr LJ 4561. *Leela Ram v State of Haryana,* AIR 1999 SC 3717 : (1999) 9 SCC 525, discrepancy *in the evidence of eye-wi*tnesses cannot affect credibility of their evidence and corroboration of evidence with mathematical niceties cannot be expected in criminal cases.

324. *Bilaluddin v State of Assam,* 1992 Cr LJ 161 (Gau). *Prem v State of Maharashtra,* 1993 CrLJ 1608 (Bom), failure to disclose the names of all the assailants, does not destroy the case against the accused. Absence of particulars in complaint regarding weapons used, not a material omission to make the testimony incredible, *Manoj Wasudeo Ingley v State of Maharashtra,* 1992 Cr LJ 1970 (Bom). Eye-witnesses not speaking truth but suppressing material facts, other evidence contradictory and improbable, acquittal, no interference, *Biri Singh v State of UP,* 1992 Supp (2) SCC 264 : 1992 Cr LJ 1510 (SC).

325. *Dhananjay Shanker Shetty v State of Maharashtra,* AIR 2002 SC 2787 at p 2789.

Thakore Kubersing Chamansingh,[326] and *Kashiram v State of MP*.[327] In the present case, non-explanation of injuries on the appellant by the prosecution assumes significance as there are circumstances which make the prosecution case, showing complicity of appellant with the crime, highly doubtful.

[s 3.47] Hostile witness.—The testimony of such a witness is acceptable to the extent to which it is corroborated by the evidence of a reliable witness.[328] The evidence of a hostile witness is not to be totally discarded. The admissible parts of his statement can be used by the prosecution or defence.[329] Where the prosecution witness supported the defence side but even so the prosecution did not get him declared as a hostile witness, it was held that the accused could rely on such evidence.[330]

[s 3.48] FIR as evidence.—An FIR does not constitute substantive evidence. It can only be used as a previous statement for purposes of either corroborating its maker or for contradicting him. In such a situation, previous statement cannot be used unless attention of the witness has first been drawn to those parts by which it is proposed to contradict him.[331]

[s 3.48.1] Newspaper report.—The court has to react, with extreme caution on a newspaper report, which has not been substantiated in adversarial litigation. It would be a perilous piece of evidence to find the State Government to be guilty of fraud and perjury.[332]

[s 3.48.2] Variance between statements in FIR and in deposition.—An FIR need not contain an exhaustive account of the incident. In this case the court found that all the essential and relevant details of the incident were given in the FIR. The witness who had dictated the FIR gave a few more details in her evidence. The court said that her evidence could not discarded by saying that there was an improvements in her testimony.[333]

[s 3.48.3] Variance between medical evidence and ocular evidence.—In case of variance between medical evidence and ocular evidence, unimpeachable evidence of

---

326. *Takhaji Hiraji v Thakore Kubersing Chamansingh*, AIR 2001 SC 2328 : (2001) 6 SCC 145 : AIR 2001 SCW 2077.

327. *Kashiram v State of MP*, AIR 2001 SC 2902 : AIR 2001 SCW 4350 : (2002) 1 SCC 71.

328. *State v Harishchandra Tukaram Awatade*, 1997 Cr LJ 612 (Bom). For a full account of hostile witnesses see section 154.

329. *C Muniappan v State of Tamil Nadu*, AIR 2010 SC 3718 : (2010) 9 SCC 567, citing *Gagan Kanojia v State of Punjab*, (2006) 13 SCC 516 : 2007 (2) Crimes 81 (SC); *Radha Mohan Singh v State of UP*, AIR 2006 SC 951 : 2006 AIR SCW 421 : (2006) 2 SCC 450; *Subbu Singh v State* (2009) 6 SCC 462 : 2009 AIR SCW 3937 : 2009 Cr J 3433.

330. *Javed Masood v State of Rajasthan*, AIR 2010 SC 979. *Sarvesh Narain Shukla v Daroga Singh*, AIR 2008 SC 320 : (2007) 13 SCC 360, both parties are entitled *to rely on such part of his evidence* as assists their case. *Paramjeet Singh v State of Uttarakhand*, AIR 2011 SC 200 : (2010) 10 SCC 439, evidence not to be rejected, *to be considered with caution*, court should look for *corroboration*.

331. *Utpal Das v State of WB*, AIR 2010 SC 1894 : (2010) 6 SCC 493.

332. *Kunal Saha v State of WB*, AIR 2016 (NOC) 308 (Cal).

333. *Om Prakash v State of Uttaranchal*, 2003 Cr LJ 483 (SC), the domestic servant killed three members of the family, the fourth (the witness) managed to save herself by locking herself in the bathroom. She heard voices which clinchingly showed the involvement of the domestic servant. Her evidence, though not direct, was that of circumstances surrounding the transaction. It was relevant and sufficient to support conviction.

eye-witnesses should be accepted in preference to hypothetical answers given by medical officer.[334]

Doctors are usually confronted with questions on different possibilities and probabilities about the consequences of injuries. Their response depends upon the manner of questioning. But their answers are not the last word on such possibilities. The court said that the evidence of eye-witnesses cannot be discarded on the basis of possibilities so suggested.[335]

[s 3.48.4] Variance between ballistic evidence and eye-witness account.—The eye-witness deposed that the accused fired the fatal shot from mouser rifle and that the other accused who fired at the son of the deceased with a 12-bore gun missed him and hit the wall. The report of a ballistic expert was that the discharged empties of the cartridge which was found near the dead body was not fired from mouser rifle. The bullets recovered from the wall were mouser bullets. The eye-witnesses were relatives of the deceased. Their statements also suffered from *inter se* contradictions. This raised doubts about their presence at the spot.[336]

"Disproved".—A fact is said to be disproved when, after considering the matters before it, the Court either believes that it does not exist, or considers its non-existence so probable that a prudent man ought, under the circumstances of the particular case, to act upon the supposition that it does not exist.

COMMENT

This is merely the converse of the definition of "proved".[337]

"Not proved".—A fact is said not to be proved when it is neither proved nor disproved.

COMMENT

[s 3.49] Not Proved.— The definition of "proved" is the embodiment of a sound rule of common sense. It describes what degree of certainty must be arrived at before a fact can be said to be proved. Proof means anything which serves, either immediately or mediately, to convince the mind of the truth or falsehood of a fact or proposition. It is apparent from the definitions of the words "proved" "disproved" and "not proved" in this section that the Act applies the same standard of proof in all civil cases.[338] The term "not proved" indicates a state of mind between two states of mind ("proved" and "disproved") when one is unable to say precisely how the matter stands.[339]

---

334. *Kedar Behera v State,* 1993 Cr LJ 378 (Ori). *State of Maharashtra v Vithal,* 1993 Cr LJ 2285 (Bom), direct evidence cogent, reliable and unimpeachable, medical evidence not to override it. *Bhim Singh v State of Haryana,* AIR 2003 SC 693, variation in medical evidence and that of other witnesses as to time of death, medical evidence not relied upon as conclusive in the absence of some other evidence as to when the deceased had last meal and attended call of nature.
335. *Ram Swaroop v State of Rajasthan,* AIR 2008 SC 1747 : (2008) 13 SCC 515.
336. *Brijpal Singh v State of MP,* 2003 Cr LJ 2533 : AIR 2003 SC 2460.
337. *Emperor v Shafi Ahmed,* (1925) 31 Bom LR 515.
338. *Gulabchand v Kudilal,* AIR 1966 SC 1734 : (1966) 3 SCR 623.
339. *Emperor v Shafi Ahmed,* (1925) 31 Bom LR 515 : AIR 1925 PC 305.

[340]["India".—"India" means the territory of India excluding the State of Jammu and Kashmir.]

[341][the expression "certifying Authority", [342]["electronic signature"], [342]["Electronic Signature Certificate"], "electronic form", "electronic records", "information", "secure electronic record", "secured digital signature" and "subscriber" shall have the meanings respectively assigned to them in the Information Technology Act, 2000 (21 of 2000)]

COMMENT

[s 3.50] India.—This definition was inserted by section 92 of the IT Act, 2000 to give credence to documents and evidences which were in electronic and digital form. However, initially the reference was to "digital signature" and "digital signature certificate", till before the same was changed in 2008 to the present form.

Vide Information Technology (Amendment) Act, 2008,[343] section 3 was amended so as to substitute the following words—

"digital signature" was substituted by *"electronic signature"*

"Digital Signature Certificate" was substituted by *"Electronic Signature Certificate"*.

A digital signature (standard electronic signature) is technology specific and an electronic "fingerprint" of the signatory. It is supposed to be irreversibly unique to both the document and the signer and binds both of them together. It ensures the authenticity of the signer and any change made into the document after it has been digitally signed invalidates the sanctity of the document, thereby protecting the document against signature forgery and information tampering.

An electronic signature is technology neutral and generic in nature. It has a proprietary format (there is no standard for electronic signatures) such as even a typed name or a digitized image of a handwritten signature. Consequently, the integrity, sanctity and security of electronic signatures are a big issue since nothing prevents one individual from typing another individual's name. Due to this practical problem, an electronic signature that does not incorporate additional measures of security (the way digital signatures do) is considered an insecure way of signing documentation.

Since an electronic signature is vulnerable to copying and tampering, and invites forgery, there was a debate in the United States on the legally binding nature of the generic electronic signatures and whether only a technology specific digital signature should form the basis of electronic commerce. This debate finally resulted in the enactment of the Electronic Signatures in Global and National Commerce (E-SIGN) Act, 2000. This Act aimed at creating sanctity for the electronic signatures by providing

---

340. Subs. by Act 3 of 1951, section 3 and Schedule, for the definitions of "State" and "States". Earlier the definitions of "State" and "States" were inserted by the A.O. 1950.

341. Ins. by Act 21 of 2000, section 92 and Sch. II–1(b) (w.e.f. 17-10-2000).

342. Subs. by Act 10 of 2009, section 52(a), for "digital signature" and "Digital Signature Certificate" respectively (w.e.f. 27-10-2009).

343. Amended by the Information Technology (Amendment) Act, 2008 (10 of 2009), section 51 (w.e.f. 27-10-2009 *vide* Notification No. S.O. 2689(E), dated 27-10-2009).

that a signature may not be denied legal effect solely because it is in electronic form or because it did not fit or follow a prescribed technological process.

This substitution is a part of the entire scheme under which digital signature regime is being switched over to electronic signature regime in the field of e-commerce and e-governance. This switching over of regime is meant to broaden the spectrum and follow the global trend.

[s 4] "May presume".—Whenever it is provided by this Act that the Court may presume a fact, it may either regard such fact as proved, unless and until it is disproved, or may call for proof of it.

"Shall presume".—Whenever it is directed by this Act that the Court shall presume a fact, it shall regard such fact as proved, unless and until it is disproved.

"Conclusive proof".—When one fact is declared by this Act to be conclusive proof of another, the Court shall, on proof of the one fact, regard the other as proved, and shall not allow evidence to be given for the purpose of disproving it.

SYNOPSIS

COMMENT

[s 4.1] ***Conclusive proof.***—The term "presumption", in its largest and most comprehensive signification, may be defined to be an inference, affirmative or disaffirmative of the truth or falsehood of a doubtful fact or proposition, drawn by a process of probable reasoning from something proved or taken for granted.[344]

A presumption means a rule of law that courts and Judges shall draw a particular inference from a particular fact, or from particular evidence, unless and until the truth of such inference is disproved. A presumption is a legal or factual assumption drawn from the existence of certain facts. They are raised in terms of the Evidence Act. A presumption raised under the provisions of a statute carries only evidentiary value. Presumption drawn on the basis of a fact may constitute an evidence for presumption in respect of another fact.[345]

A court, where it "may presume" a fact, has a discretion to presume it as proved, or to call for confirmatory evidence of it, as the circumstances require. In such a case the presumption is not a hard and fast presumption, incapable of rebuttal, *a presumptio juris et de jure.*[346] In cases in which a court shall presume a fact, the presumption is not conclusive but rebuttable.

---

344. *Best,* 12th Edn, section 299, p 267. *Babukhan v State of Rajasthan,* AIR 1997 SC 2960 : 1997 Cr LJ 3567; *Mayank Rajput v State,* 1998 Cr LJ 2797 (All).
345. *MS Narayana Menon v State of Kerala,* (2006) 6 SCC 39: (2006) 3 Ker LT 404 : (2006) 5 Mah LJ 676 : (2006) 4 MPLJ 97 : AIR 2006 SC 3366.
346. *Emperor v Shrinivas,* (1905) 7 Bom LR 969. For the clarification of expressions "may presume" and "shall presume" see *Haradhan Mahatha v Dukhu Mahatha,* AIR 1993 Pat 129.

Presumptions of fact or natural presumptions are inferences which are naturally and logically drawn from experience and observation of the course of nature, the constitution of human mind, the springs of human action, the usages and habits of society. These presumptions are generally rebuttable.[347] Clause (1) of the section appears to point at presumptions of facts.

Where the statute prescribes for a rebuttable presumption, it has been held by Supreme Court that it is not just any evidence, howsoever shaky and nebulous, that would satisfy the test of preponderance of probability to rebut the statutory presumption but evidence that can by proper and judicial application of mind be said to be fairly and reasonably showing that the real fact is not as presumed. In other words the evidence required to rebut a statutory presumption ought to be clear and convincing, no matter that the degree of proof may not be as high as proving the fact to the contrary beyond a reasonable doubt. Thus, the evidence intended to rebut the statutory presumption ought to be clear and convincing evidence showing that what is presumed under the provision is not the real fact.[348]

Presumptions of law are based, like presumptions of fact, on the uniformity of deduction which experience proves to be justifiable; they differ in being vested by the law with the quality of a rule, which directs that they *must* be drawn; they are not permissive like natural presumptions, which *may* or *may not* be drawn; and presumptions of law again differ in their force, according as they are rebuttable or irrebuttable. As to the former, the presumption shall stand good only until it is disproved. The latter class, or irrebuttable presumptions, the law holds conclusive.[349] See sections 79 to 90 and section 105, *infra*, as to presumptions of fact and rebuttable presumptions of law.

Clause 3 of the section points at irrebuttable presumptions of law and the number of such presumptions is very few (see sections 41, 112, 113, *infra* and section 82 of the Indian Penal Code). The certificate issued by the Director of Central Food Laboratory is conclusive proof of facts stated therein. Examination of the Director as witness is not permissible.[350]

Where husband and wife were in love and led an amorous life for about eight years before their marriage, both were sound in health and mind and after marriage lived together in a room for months together and had privacy, the presumption was conclusive that consummation of marriage was an accomplished fact.[351]

---

347. *Amal Chandra Datt v Second Addl. DJ,* 1988 ALR 794 : AIR 1989 SC 255 : (1989) 1 SCC 1. Reiterated in *Gitika Bagechi v Subhabrota Bagechi,* AIR 1996 Cal 246, a comparison has been drawn between this section and section 114.

348. *Heinz India Pvt Ltd v State of UP,* (2012) 5 SCC 443.

349. Norton on Evidence, sections 97-98. See also *Syad Akbar v State of Kant,* AIR 1979 SC 1848; 1979 Cr LJ 1374 where the difference between the operation of a presumption of law and that of fact is explained; *Yogendra Morarji v State of Gujarat,* AIR 1980 SC 660 : 1980 Cr LJ 459 the court presumes the absence of circumstances which justify the right of private defence.

350. *KV Baby v Food Inspector, Wadakkanchery,* 1994 Cr LJ 3421 (Ker) :1994 (2) ILR (Ker) 502.

351. *Gitika Bagechi v Subhabrota Bagechi,* AIR 1966 Cal 246. See the decision of the Supreme Court in *Sodhi Transport Co v State of UP,* AIR 1986 SC 1099 : (1986) 2 SCC 486 : 1986 Tax LR 2347, where the effect on burden of proof of all the kinds of presumption has been explained. The court further said that these presumptions are not peculiar to the Evidence Act. They are generally used wherever facts are to be ascertained by a judicial process. For details see under section 114.

Where the plaintiff claimed to be a partner in a firm and it was shown that the application for registration of the firm showed his signature as a partner, the court said that he could thus be regarded as a partner in the firm and the plea that he was only nominally shown to be a partner was not tenable.[352]

Dealing with the use of phrases *"until the contrary is proved"* in section 118 and *"unless the contrary is proved"* in section 139 of Negotiable Instruments Act, 1881 read with definitions of *"may presume"* and *"shall presume"* as given in section 4 of Evidence Act, it has been explained by Supreme Court that presumptions to be raised under both the provisions are rebuttable. When a presumption is rebuttable, it only points out that when the party against whom the presumption is drawn produces evidence fairly and reasonably tending to show that real fact is not as presumed, the purpose of the presumption is over.[353]

Where it was alleged against an eighteen year old student that he had passed a fake note of Rs 100 to a shop keeper and 13 more such notes were recovered from him, it was held by the Supreme Court that the presumption thus created was not sufficient to prove the *mens rea* requirement under section 489-B, IPC, that he knew or had reason to believe that the notes in question were forged or counterfeit.[354]

[s 4.2] Marriage Certificate.—A marriage certificate issued under the Special Marriage Act, 1954 is a conclusive evidence of the solemnisation of marriage under the Act and also of compliance of formalities and signatures of parties and witnesses. The genuineness of the compliance procedure is a different question. It remains questionable.[355]

In a matrimonial dispute, the marriage was said to have been performed according to Hindu customs. Thereafter they married as per Japanese Custom and the registration certificate showing their marriage under section 17 of the Foreign Marriage Act, 1969 was issued. It was held by Bombay High Court that upon the factum of registration of marriage, the solemnisation of the marriage becomes a conclusive fact under section 14(2) of the Foreign Marriage Act, 1969. Thus, under section 4 of the Evidence Act, no evidence with regard to the fact that marriage was also solemnised under the Hindu Marriage Act, 1955 can be allowed.[356]

---

352. *Shivraj Reddy & Bros v S Raghu Raj Reddy*, AIR 2002 NOC 120 (AP).
353. *Kumar Exports v Sharma Carpets*, (2009) 2 SCC 513.
354. *Umashanker v State of Chhattisgarh*, AIR 2001 SC 3074 : 2001 Cr LJ 4696.
355. *Nirmal Das Bose v Mamta Gulati*, AIR 1997 All 401.
356. *Minoti Anand v Subhash Anand*; AIR 2011 Bom 61 : 2011 (2) Mah LJ 812 : 2011 (5) Bom CR 624.

CHAPTER II

OF THE RELEVANCY OF FACTS

[s 5] Evidence may be given of facts in issue and relevant facts.—Evidence may be given in any suit or proceeding of the existence or non-existence of every fact in issue and of such other facts as are hereinafter declared to be relevant,[s 5.5] and of no others.[s 5.6]

***Explanation.*—This section shall not enable any person to give evidence of a fact which he is disentitled to prove by any provision of the law for the time being in force relating to Civil Procedure.[1]**

ILLUSTRATIONS

(a) *A* is tried for the murder of *B* by beating him with a club with the intention of causing his death.

At *A*'s trial the following facts are in issue:—

A's beating *B* with the club;

A's causing *B*'s death by such beating;

A's intention to cause *B*'s death.

(b) A suitor does not bring with him and have in readiness for production at the first hearing of the case, a bond on which he relies. This section does not enable him to produce the bond or prove its contents at a subsequent stage of the proceedings, otherwise than in accordance with the conditions prescribed by the Code of Civil Procedure.

SYNOPSIS

COMMENT

[s 5.1] Evidence of facts in issue and relevant facts only.—Section 3 says that one fact is relevant to another when the one is connected with the other in any of the ways referred to in this chapter. Relevancy is thus fully explained in sections 6 to 11. "These sections enumerate specifically the different instances of the connection between cause

1. See the Code of Civil Procedure, 1908 (Act No. 5 of 1908).

and effect which occur most frequently in judicial proceedings. They are designedly worded very widely, and in such a way as to overlap each other. Thus a motive for a fact in issue (section 8) is part of its cause (section 7); subsequent conduct influenced by it (section 8) is part of its effect (section 7). Facts relevant under section 11 would, in most cases, be relevant under the other sections."[2]

The object of this Chapter is to point out in what cases collateral facts are relevant.

[s 5.2] Object.—The object of this section is to restrict the investigation made by courts within the bounds prescribed by general convenience.

[s 5.3] Principle.—Of no fact can evidence be given unless it be either a fact in issue or one declared relevant under the following sections. Thus evidence of all collateral facts, which are incapable of affording any reasonable presumption as to the principal matters in dispute, is excluded to save public time.

Where the entire evidence of eyewitnesses was not accepted by the High Court, it was held by Supreme Court that the accused cannot be convicted for an offence under section 302 IPC merely on the basis of the post-mortem report. The post-mortem report should be in corroboration with the evidence of eyewitnesses and cannot be an evidence sufficient to reach the conclusion for convicting the accused.[3]

[s 5.4] Scope.—This section excludes everything not covered by the purview of some other succeeding section. The last four words of the section "and of no others" preclude a party from proving any facts not in issue or not declared relevant by any of the remaining sections of this Chapter. To establish the relevancy of any fact, it must be shown that it is a fact in issue or fact such as is declared to be relevant. Evidence is to be confined strictly to the issue.

[s 5.5] "Facts ... declared to be relevant".—The relevant facts are all those facts which are in the eye of the law so connected with or related to the facts in issue that they render the latter probable or improbable.

[s 5.6] "And of no others".—The section excludes everything which is not covered by the purview of some other section which follows in the Statute.[4] There must be a specific provision before facts can be treated as relevant and facts must also be proved as laid down in the Act.[5] Anyone who wants to give evidence on a particular fact must show that it is admissible under someone or other of the following sections. The words "and of no others" impliedly impose a duty on the court to exclude evidence of irrelevant facts, irrespective of objections by the parties. In criminal proceedings this duty is expressly imposed by the Code of Criminal Procedure, section 298 (omitted by the Code of 1973). In civil proceedings, see the Code of Civil Procedure, 1908, O XIII, rule 3.[6]

[s 5.7] Admissibility of evidence.—The court is to decide the question of admissibility of evidence (section 136, *infra*). It should be decided as it arises and

---

2. *Stephen's Introduction*, p 72.
3. *Balaji Gunthu Dhule v State of Maharashtra*, (2012) 11 SCC 685.
4. *The Collector of Gorakhpur v Palakdhari Singh*, (1889) 12 All 1, 43, FB; *Mt Khedia v Mt Turea*, AIR 1962 Pat 420.
5. *Hasan Abdulla v State of Gujarat*, AIR 1962 Guj 214.
6. *Stokes' Anglo Indian Codes*, Vol II, p 854, fn 1.

should not be reserved until judgment in the case is given. The moment a witness commences giving evidence which is inadmissible, he should be stopped by the court. A party objecting to a question must do so as soon as it is stated and before the answer is given. When an irrelevant document is tendered an objection should be made at that time. If it is not taken in time, it is considered to be waived.

A party filing a document cannot urge its inadmissibility when the opposite party seeks to use it against him.[7]

Where no objection is taken in the court of first instance to the reception of a document in evidence, it is not within the province of the appellate court to raise or recognise it in appeal.[8] The appellate court, however, has a perfect right to attach such weight to the document as it thinks proper, or to say whether it ought to be treated as evidence as against particular parties to the suit.[9] The Gujarat High Court has held that an objection that a piece of evidence which was considered by the trial judge was irrelevant can be taken for the first time in appeal. If the evidence is irrelevant the consent of parties cannot make it relevant.[10]

The fact that a document was procured by improper or even illegal means will not be a bar to its admissibility if it is relevant and its genuineness proved. But while examining the proof given as to its genuineness the circumstances under which it came to be produced into court have to be taken into consideration.[11]

[s 5.8] Inadmissibility of evidence.—While the services of a sniffer dog may be taken for the purpose of investigation, its faculties cannot be taken as evidence for the purpose of establishing the guilt of an accused.[12]

[s 5.9] Explanation.—The Explanation appended to the section prohibits a party from claiming any relief upon facts or documents not stated or referred to by him in his pleadings. Illustration (b) elucidates the meaning of the Explanation.

[s 5.10] Admissibility of new evidence after trial.—When what is pleaded is not proved, or what is stated in the evidence is contrary to the pleadings, the dictum that no amount of evidence, howsoever cogent, can be relied upon if it is contrary to the pleadings, would apply.[13]

An issue which has been finally settled and therefore attracts the bar of *res judicata*, an evidence led on such issue in a later part of the proceedings has been held to be not admissible.[14]

[s 6] Relevancy of facts forming part of same transaction.—Facts which, though not in issue, are so connected with a fact in issue as to form part of the same

---

7. *Raman v Secretary of State for India in Council*, (1901) 24 Mad 427.
8. *Chimnaji Govind Godbole v Dinkar Dhondev Godbole*, (1886) 11 Bom 320.
9. *Akbur Ali v Bhyea Lal Jha*, (1880) 6 Cal 666, 670.
10. *Nathubhai v Chhotubhai*, AIR 1962 Guj 68.
11. *Magraj Patodia v RK Birla*, AIR 1971 SC 1295 : (1970) 2 SCC 888. For a study of this subject see Shah Ashok Damodar, *Relevancy and Admissibility*, AIR 2001 Journal 232.
12. *Dinesh Borthakur v State of Assam*, (2008) 5 SCC 697.
13. *Janak Dulari Devi v Kapildeo Rai*, (2011) 6 SCC 555.
14. *Amarendra Komalam v Usha Sinha*, AIR 2005 SC 2758 : (2005) 11 SCC 251.

transaction, are relevant, whether they occurred at the same time and place or at different times and places.

ILLUSTRATIONS

(a) *A* is accused of the murder of *B* by beating him. Whatever was said or done by *A* or *B* or the by-standers at the beating, or so shortly before or after it as to form part of the transaction, is a relevant fact.

(b) *A* is accused of waging war against the [15][Government of India] by taking part in an armed insurrection in which property is destroyed, troops are attacked, and gaols are broken open. The occurrence of these facts is relevant, as forming part of the general transaction, though *A* may not have been present at all of them.

(c) *A* sues *B* for a libel contained in a letter forming part of a correspondence. Letters between the parties relating to the subject out of which the libel arose, and forming part of the correspondence in which it is contained, are relevant facts, though they do not contain the libel itself.

(d) The question is, whether certain goods ordered from *B* were delivered to *A*. The goods were delivered to several intermediate persons successively. Each delivery is a relevant fact.

SYNOPSIS

COMMENT

[s 6.1] Principle.—*res gestae*.—This section admits those facts the admissibility of which comes under the technical expression *res gestae* [i.e. the things done (including words spoken) in the course of a transaction], but such facts must "form part of the same transaction". If facts form part of the transaction which is the subject of enquiry, manifestly evidence of them ought not to be excluded. The question is whether they do form part or are too remote to be considered really part of the transaction before the court. A transaction is a group of facts so connected together as to be referred to by a single legal name, as a crime, a contract, a wrong or any other subject of inquiry which may be in issue.[16] Roughly, a transaction may be described as any physical act, or a series of connected physical acts, together with the words accompanying such act or acts.[17] Every fact which is part of the same transaction as the fact in issue is deemed to be relevant to the fact in issue although it may not be actually in issue, and although if it were not part of the same transaction it might be excluded as hearsay.[18] Illustration (b) indicates that acts done at different places and times may form part of the same transaction. Thus, a transaction consists both of the physical acts and the words accompanying such physical acts, whether spoken by the person doing such acts,

---

15. Subs. by the A.O. 1950, for "Queen".
16. Stephen's Digest of Evidence, Article 3.
17. Phipson on Evidence, 51-79.
18. *Chain Mahto v Emperor,* (1906) 11 Cal WN 266, 270. See also *Thakur Das v State of HP,* 1992 Cr LJ 2415 (HP).

the person to whom they were done or any other person or persons. Such words are admissible in evidence as parts of a transaction [*vide* Illustration (a)]. The expression "bystanders" used in illustration (a) means the persons who are present at the time of the occurrence and not those who gather on the spot after the occurrence. The remarks made by persons other than the eye-witnesses could only be hearsay because they must have picked up the news from others.[19]

The statement as that in Illustration (a) is relevant only if it is that of a person who has seen the actual occurrence and who uttered it simultaneously with the incident or so soon thereafter as to make it reasonably certain that the speaker is still under the stress of the excitement caused by his having seen the incident.[20] "[T]he statement uttered or act done must be a spontaneous reaction of the person witnessing the crime and forming part of the transaction. The bystanders' declaration must relate only to that which came under their observation. The declaration must be substantially contemporaneous with the fact and not merely the narration of a prior event."[21] Applying this to the facts of a case before it in which the witnesses rushed to the scene of the crime on hearing the sound of an explosion and heard from the mouth of the bystanders as to what had happened, the Kerala High Court has held that the statement was not a part of the transaction.[22] What is admissible under this section is a fact which is connected with the fact in issue as "part of the same transaction". A transaction may consist of a single incident occupying a few minutes or it may be spread over a variety of facts, *etc.*, occupying a much longer time and occurring on different occasions or at different places. Where the transaction consists of different acts, in order that the chain of such acts may constitute the same transaction, they must be connected together by proximity of time, proximity or unity of place, continuity of action and community of purpose or design.[23] Where the witness deposed that immediately after the occurrence, his niece told him that his wife was shot by the accused, it was held that his statement was admissible under section 6, Illustration (a) and so also his statement that the accused was threatening persons on the spot that he would kill them too.[24]

Explaining this aspect of the doctrine of *res gestae* in *Rattan v Reginam*,[25] and trying to lay down a more rational formula, Lord Wilberforce said: "The test should not be the uncertain one whether the making of the statement was in some sense part of the event or transaction. This may often be difficult to establish; such external matters as the time which elapses between the events and the speaking of the words (or *vice versa*) and differences in location being relevant factors but not, taken by

---

19. *Nasir Din v Crown,* (1944) 25 Lah 461.

20. Thus an FIR lodged soon after the incident by persons who witnessed it becomes a part of the happening. *Shayam Nandan Singh v State of Bihar,* 1991 Cr LJ 3359. Description of the assault by the victim at a police station on the same day, the victim dying subsequently of injuries developing infection, held, a part of the transaction. *Kulamani Sandha v State of Orissa,* 1991 Cr LJ 599 (Ori). See also *Jadumani Khanda v State,* 1993 Cr LJ 2701 (Ori).

21. *Bhaskaran v State of Kerala,* (1985) Ker LT 122; (1985) Cr LJ 1711 (DB).

22. *Rajan v State of Kerala,* 1992 Cr LJ 575 Ker.

23. *Hadu v State,* (1950) Cut 509.

24. *Mohd. Islam v State of UP,* 1993 Cr LJ 1736 (All). *Mahender Singh Dhaiya v State (CBI),* 2003 Cr LJ 1908 (Del), letters of deceased wife to her husband (wife alleged to be murdered by him), the court said that the contents of such letters were not relevant under section 6 or section 11 as they did not fall within the domain 32, i.e. did not amount to a lying declaration.

25. *Rattan v Reginam* (1971) 1 WLR 801.

themselves, decisive criteria. As regards statements made after the event it must be for the judge to satisfy himself that the statement was so clearly made in circumstances of spontaneity or involvement in the event that the possibility of concoction can be disregarded. Conversely, if he considers that the statement was made by way of narrative of a detached prior event so that the speaker was disengaged from it as to be able to construct or adapt his account, he should exclude it". In this case a man was prosecuted for the murder of his wife. His defence was that the shot went off accidentally. There was evidence to the effect that the deceased telephoned to say: "Get me the police please". Before the operator could connect the police, the caller, who spoke in distress, gave her address and the call suddenly ended. Thereafter the police came to the house and found the body of a dead woman. Her call and the words she spoke were held to be relevant as a part of the transaction which brought about her death. Her call in distress showed that the shooting in question was intentional and not accidental for no victim of an accident could have thought of getting the police before the happening.

Lord Wilberforce said:

> There was ample evidence of the close and intimate connection between the statement ascribed to the deceased and the shooting which occurred very shortly afterwards. They were closely associated in place and in time. The way in which the statement came to be made (in a call for the police) and the tone of voice used, showed intrinsically that the statement was being forced from the deceased by an overwhelming pressure of contemporary event. It carried its own stamp of spontaneity.

This aspect of the doctrine was applied by the Supreme Court in *Rattan Singh v State of HP*,[26] The accused intruded into the courtyard of the victim's house at night and inflicted gun-shot injury on her. She was able to identify him. She stated before her death that the accused was standing with a gun before her. She explained the time and space proximity between her and the assailant. The statement was held to be a part of the transaction and relevant as such under section 6.

The eye-witness spontaneously told the persons reaching the place immediately after the occurrence that the accused killed the deceased. Such persons derived knowledge about the incident spontaneously with the happening from the eye-witness. Their evidence was held to be relevant under section 6 as forming part of the same transaction.[27]

A transaction in its ordinary sense is some business or dealing which is carried on or transacted between two or more persons.[28]

This and the following sections deal with circumstantial evidence. Sections 7, 8 and 9 explain and illustrate this section.

[s 6.2] CASES

[s 6.2.1] Facts forming part of same transaction.—Statements of bystanders witnessing a transaction are relevant if they are made while the transaction is in progress or so shortly before or after it as to form part of the same transaction.[29] Where A was

---

26. *Rattan Singh v State of HP*, AIR 1997 SC 768 : 1997 Cr LJ 833.
27. *Om Singh v State*, 1997 Cr LJ 2419 (Raj).
28. *Gujju Lall v Fatteh Lall*, (1880) 6 Cal 171 (FB).
29. *Chain Mahto v Emperor*, (1906) 11 Cal WN 266, 271.

tried for the murder of B by shooting him, the facts that the person, then in the room, with B, saw a man with a gun in his hand pass a window opening into the room where B was shot, and thereupon exclaimed "there's Butcher" (a name by which A was known), were held to be relevant.[30] The only evidence against an accused charged with having voluntarily caused grievous hurt was a statement made in the presence of the accused by the person injured to a third person, immediately after the commission of the offence. The accused did not, when the statement was made, deny that she had done the act complained of. It was held that the evidence was admissible under this section and section 8, Illustration (g).[31] A husband, his father and mother were prosecuted for the murder of his wife. She cried out for help as soon as she was pushed into the room. Her children who were playing outside in the verandah exclaimed at the same time that their mother was being killed. The exclamations of children were received through the evidence of persons who heard them.[32]

[s 6.2.2] Facts not so connected as to form part of same transaction.—The statements of persons who were injured by burns by the act of the accused in setting fire to the bus in which they were travelling, though recorded by a Magistrate under expectation of death, were held to be not relevant there being a gap of time between the incident and the recording of the statements.[33]

In a case involving murder by a man of his wife and daughter, evidence was offered to show that the wife's father received a phone call from the father of the accused that his son had caused the deaths in question. This was held to be not relevant under section 6 because there was nothing to show that the communication had taken place so soon after the crime as the form a part of the same transaction.[34]

The prosecution of the husband was for torture of his wife for non-fulfillment of his demand. The witnesses testified to what the deceased told them about torture and harassment. The court said such deposition had no connection with any of the circumstances of the transaction which resulted in her death. Their evidence was also not admissible under section 32.[35]

[s 6.2.2.1] *Newspaper report.*—A newspaper report can be relied on by the Election Commission while deciding a petition in connection with repolling. In similar circumstances the High Court can also rely on newspaper reports.[36]

[s 7] Facts which are the occasion, cause or effect of facts in issue.—Facts which are the occasion, cause or effect, immediate or otherwise, of relevant facts, or facts in issue, or which constitute the state of things under which they happened, or which afforded an opportunity for their occurrence or transaction, are relevant.

---

30. *Fowkes,* (1856) *Stephen's Digest,* 12th Edn, (1946).

31. *Re Surat Dhobni,* (1884) 10 Cal 302.

32. *Sawaldas v State of Bihar,* AIR 1974 SC 778 : 1974 Cr LJ 664.

33. *Gentela V Rao v State of AP,* AIR 1996 SC 2791 : 1996 Cr LJ 4151; *State of Gujarat v Anirudhsing,* AIR 1997 SC 2780 : 1997 Cr LJ 3397, evidence of police officer that the accused made confession to someone, not covered by section 6. It was wholly a hearsay and in no way a part of the transaction.

34. *Vasa Chandra Sekhar v Ponna Satyanarayana,* 2000 Cr LJ 3175 : AIR 2000 SC 2138 : (2000) 6 SCC 286.

35. *Bhairon Singh v State of MP,* AIR 2009 SC 2603 : (2009) 13 SCC 80.

36. *All India Anna Dravida Munnetra Kazhagam v State Election Commission,* AIR 2007 NOC 1801 (Mad—FB).

ILLUSTRIATIONS

(a) The question is, whether *A* robbed *B*.

The facts that, shortly before the robbery, *B* went to a fair with money in his possession, and that he showed it or mentioned the fact that he had it, to third persons, are relevant.

(b) The question is, whether *A* murdered *B*.

Marks on the ground, produced by a struggle at or near the place where the murder was committed, are relevant facts.

(c) The question is, whether *A* poisoned *B*.

The state of *B*'s health before the symptoms ascribed to poison, and habits of *B*, known to *A*, which afforded an opportunity for the administration of poison, are relevant facts.

COMMENT

This section admits a very large class of facts connected with facts in issue or relevant facts, though not forming part of the transaction. Facts forming part of the same transaction are admissible under the preceding section. Evidence relating to collateral facts is admissible when such facts will, if established, establish reasonable presumption as to the matter in dispute and when such evidence is reasonably conclusive. The section provides for the admission of several classes of facts which are connected with the transaction under inquiry in particular modes, viz. (1) as being the occasion or cause of a fact; (2) as being its effect; (3) as giving opportunity for its occurrence; and (4) as constituting the state of things under which it happened.

A fact in issue cannot be proved by showing that facts similar to it, but not part of the same transaction, have occurred at other times. Thus, when the question is, whether a person has committed a crime, the fact that he had committed a similar crime before, is irrelevant.

Illustration (a) is an instance of facts relevant as giving occasion or opportunity, (b) of facts constituting an effect, (c) of facts constituting the state of things under which an alleged fact happened.

[s 7.1] Tape-recording.—A contemporaneous tape record of a relevant conversation is a relevant fact and is admissible under this section but such evidence must be received with caution.[37] Where the tape recorded conversation carried music before and after the recorded conversation and the same could not be explained, the court said that the only plausible explanation was that the tape was tampered.[38] A contemporaneous tape-

37. *Yusufalli v State*, (1967) 70 Bom LR 76 (SC). See also *Mahabir Pd Verma v SurinderKaur*, AIR 1982 SC 1043 : (1982) 2 SCC 258, where a tape-recorded matter was rejected because there was no proof of the conversation which it could have been used to corroborate. The court said that a tape-recorded conversation could only be relied upon as corroborative evidence of conversation deposed by any of the parties to the conversation. In the absence of evidence of any such conversation, the tape is no proper evidence and could not be relied upon. In this case there was no evidence of any such conversation between the tenant and the husband of the landlady. In such case, tape-recorded conversation could be no proper evidence. See also *Sunil Panchal v State of Rajasthan*, 2016 Cr LJ 4238, para 40 (Raj-DB).

38. *State of Maharashtra v Ramdas Shankar Kurtekar*, 1999 Cr LJ 196 (Bom).

record of a relevant conversation is a relevant fact and is admissible under section 7. The manner and mode of its proof and its use in a trial is a matter of detail. It can be used for the purpose of confronting a witness with his earlier tape-recorded statements. It may also be legitimately used for the purpose of shaking the credit of a witness.[39]

For the use of an earlier tape-recorded statement, the identification of the taped voices is a crucial matter and indeed such proper identification is a *sine qua non* for the use of the earlier tape recording. Where the voice is denied by the alleged maker thereof, a comparison of the same becomes inevitable and proper identification of the voices must be proved by a competent witness. The recording of the voice of a witness for the purposes of a comparison with and identification of his earlier recorded voice can, therefore, be allowed by the court and such comparison is neither expressly nor impliedly prohibited under any statute.[40]

[s 8] Motive, preparation and previous or subsequent conduct.—Any fact is relevant which shows or constitutes a motive or preparation for any fact in issue or relevant fact.

The conduct of any party,[s 8.4] or of any agent to any party, to any suit or proceeding, in reference to such suit or proceeding, or in reference to any fact in issue therein or relevant thereto, and the conduct of any person an offence against whom is the subject of any proceeding, is relevant, if such conduct influences or is influenced by any fact in issue or relevant fact, and whether it was previous or subsequent thereto.

***Explanation 1.*[s 8.5]—The word "conduct" in this section does not include statements, unless those statements accompany and explain acts other than statements; but this explanation is not to affect the relevancy of statements under any other section of this Act.**

***Explanation 2.*[s 8.6]—When the conduct of any person is relevant, any statement made to him or in his presence and hearing, which affects such conduct, is relevant.**

ILLUSTRATIONS

(a) *A* is tried for the murder of *B*.

The facts that *A* murdered *C*, that *B* knew that *A* had murdered *C*, and that *B* had tried to extort money from *A* by threatening to make his knowledge public, are relevant.

(b) *A* sues *B* upon a bond for the payment of money. *B* denies the making of the bond.

The fact that, at the time when the bond was alleged to be made, *B* required money for a particular purpose, is relevant.

(c) *A* is tried for the murder of *B* by poison.

The fact that, before the death of *B*, *A* procured poison similar to that which was administered to *B*, is relevant.

(d) The question is, whether a certain document is the will of *A*.

The facts that, not long before the date of the alleged will, *A* made inquiry into matters to which the provisions of the alleged will relate, that he consulted vakils in reference to making

39. *Dial Singh Narain Singh v Rajapal Jagan Nath*, AIR 1969 P&H. 350 : 1969 Cr LJ 1422.
40. *Nirmala v Ashu Ram*, 2000 Cr LJ 2001 (Raj).

the will, and that he caused drafts of other wills to be prepared of which he did not approve, are relevant.

(e) *A* is accused of a crime.

The facts that, either before or at the time of, or after the alleged crime, *A* provided evidence which would tend to give to the facts of the case an appearance favourable to himself, or that he destroyed or concealed evidence, or prevented the presence or procured the absence of persons who might have been witnesses, or suborned persons to give false evidence respecting it, are relevant.

(f) The question is, whether *A* robbed *B*.

The facts that, after *B* was robbed, *C* said in *A*'s presence—"the police are coming to look for the man who robbed *B*," and that immediately afterwards *A* ran away, are relevant.

(g) The question is, whether *A* owes *B* rupees 10,000.

The facts that *A* asked *C* to lend him money, and that *D* said to *C* in *A*'s presence and hearing—"I advise you not to trust *A*, for he owes *B* 10,000 rupees," and that *A* went away without making any answer, are relevant facts.

(h) The question is, whether *A* committed a crime.

The fact that *A* absconded after receiving a letter warning him that inquiry was being made for the criminal, and the contents of the letter, are relevant.

(i) *A* is accused of a crime.

The facts that, after the commission of the alleged crime, he absconded, or was in possession of property or the proceeds of property acquired by the crime, or attempted to conceal things which were or might have been used in committing it, are relevant.

(j) The question is, whether *A* was ravished.

The facts that, shortly after the alleged rape, she made a complaint relating to the crime, the circumstances under which, and the terms in which the complaint was made, are relevant.

The fact that, without making a complaint, she said that she had been ravished is not relevant as conduct under this section, though it may be relevant as a dying declaration under section 32, clause (1), or as corroborative evidence under section 157.

(k) The question is, whether *A* was robbed.

The fact that, soon after the alleged robbery, he made a complaint relating to the offence, the circumstances under which, and the terms in which, the complaint was made, are relevant.

The fact that he said he had been robbed without making any complaint, is not relevant, as conduct under this section, though it may be relevant as a dying declaration under section 32, clause (1), or as corroborative evidence under section 157.

SYNOPSIS

COMMENT

[s 8.1] Principle.—Under this section the motive which induces a party to do an act, or the preparation which he makes in its commission, will be taken into account. Evidence of motive or preparation becomes important when a case depends upon circumstantial evidence only.

This section embodies the rule that the testimony of *res gestae* is allowable when it goes to the root of the matter concerning the commission of a crime. Consequently, a verbal statement to a police officer during the time of recovery of articles upon the information of an accused in custody is admissible in evidence.[41]

[s 8.2] Motive.—Motive is that which moves a man to do a particular act. There can be no action without a motive, which must exist for every voluntary act. Generally speaking the voluntary acts of sane persons have an impelling emotion or motive. Motive in the correct sense is the emotion supposed to have led to the act. It is often proved by the conduct of a person. "The ordinary feelings, passions and propensities under which parties act, are facts known by observation and experience; and they are so uniform in their operation that a conclusion may be safely drawn that, if a party acts in a particular manner, he does so under the influence of a particular motive".[42] Previous threats, previous altercations, or previous litigations between parties are admitted to show motive.[43] The mere existence of motive is by itself not an incriminating circumstance.[44] Motive, however strong, cannot take place of proof.[45] The motive for commission of an offence is of particular importance only in cases of purely circumstantial evidence for, in such cases, motive itself would be a circumstance which the court would have to consider.[46] However, absence of motive is not sufficient to disregard circumstantial evidence.[47]

[s 8.3] Preparation.—Preparation consists in devising or arranging the means or measures necessary for the commission of a crime. Preparations on the part of the accused to accomplish the crime charged, or to prevent its discovery, or to aid his escape, or to avert suspicion from himself are relevant on the question of his guilt. Where the question is whether A has committed an offence, the fact of his having procured the instruments, which are used in its commission, is relevant. Illustrations (c) and (d) refer to preparation.

---

41. *Kali Jeeban Bhattacharjya v Emperor,* (1936) 63 Cal 1053.
42. *Com. v Webster,* 5 Cuch 295, 316. *State of UP v Babu Ram,* 2000 Cr LJ 2457 : AIR 2000 SC 1735 : 2000(4) SCC 515, an explanation of the role of motive, the accused asked for partition of landed property which the deceased was resisting. False explanations by accused persons are relevant.
43. *Chhotka v State of West Bengal,* AIR 1958 Cal 482.
44. *Hadu v State,* (1950) Cut 309. *Tara Devi v State of UP,* AIR 1991 SC 342 : 1991 Cr LJ 434, motive of a woman to get rid of husband not enough to convict particularly when her paramour acquitted.
45. *State of Punjab v Sucha Singh,* AIR 2003 SC 1471.
46. *State v Dinkar Bandu,* (1969) 72 Bom LR 405. Motive provides a strong link. Losing job because of the conduct of the deceased was held to be a strong provocating cause for the accused to act as he did. *Re Baskar,* 1991 Cr LJ 535 (Mad). *Brahm Swaroop v State of UP,* AIR 2011 SC 280 : 2011 Cr LJ 306, the eye-witness account was trustworthy and believable, no proof of motive was irrelevant. *Varun Chaudhary v State of Rajasthan,* AIR 2011 SC 72, evidence of motive becomes one of the circumstances where there is no direct evidence.
47. *Sher Singh Nawab Singh v State of Rajasthan,* 2017 Cr LJ (NOC) 1 (Raj).

But no inference of guilt will arise where the preparations may have been innocent, or for the execution of something different, though illegal; or where the crime for the execution of which the preparations were made may have been subsequently frustrated or voluntarily abandoned. A is indicted for murdering B by poisoning him. It appears that shortly before A purchased a quantity of poison. This raises an inference of guilt. But it appears that A had purchased the poison to kill vermin. This overthrows the inference of guilt. A prepares poison with which he intends to kill B. Before he uses it he repents of his crime and abandons the idea of killing B. This overthrows the inference arising from the purchase of poison.

[s 8.4] "Conduct of any party".—The conduct of any party or his agent in reference to a suit or proceeding will be scanned under this section. A fact can be proved by conduct of a party and by surrounding circumstances. The production of articles by an accused person is relevant as evidence of conduct. Statements accompanying or explaining conduct are also relevant as part of the conduct itself. Conversation over telephone for settling details for passing bribe-money was recorded by secret instruments. This was held to be evidence of conduct.[48] The court cited from *R v Leatham*:[49] "It matters not how you get it, if you steal it even, it would be admissible in evidence." If such statements do not appear on record, the evidence remains incomplete or imperfect.[50]

In the case of documents the courts very often interpret them by evidence of the mode in which property dealt with by them has been held and enjoyed. SUGDEN LC, in a case said:

Tell me what you have done under such a deed, and I will tell you what that deed means.[51]

The word "party" includes the plaintiff and defendant in a civil suit as well as the accused in a criminal prosecution.

The conduct of an accused in absconding when the police gets suspicious of his complicity in the offence of murder is relevant under this section and might well be indicative to some extent of guilty mind. But this is not the only conclusion to which it must lead the court. Such is the instinct of self-preservation in an average human being that even innocent persons may, when suspected of grave crimes, be tempted to evade arrest.[52] Explaining the meaning of the term "absconder", the Supreme Court[53] said:

> To be an absconder, in the eye of law, it is not necessary that a person should have run away from his home, it is sufficient if he hides himself to evade the process of law even if the hiding place be in his own home.

"To abscond" means, go away secretly or illegally and hurriedly to escape from custody or avoid arrest. In the instant case, the accused had told others that they were going from their place of work to their home in another district, from where they

---

48. *M Malkani v State of Maharashtra*, AIR 1973 SC 157 : 1973 Cr LJ 228.

49. *R v Leatham*, (1861) 8 Cox CC 198.

50. *Emperor v Rafique-ud-din Ahmad*, (1934) 62 Cal 572; *Neharu v Emperor*, (1937) Nag 268.

51. *The Attorney-General v Drummond*, (1842) I Dru & War 353, 368 on appeal, (1849) 2 HLC 837.

52. *Thimma v State of Mysore*, AIR 1971 SC 1871 : 1971 Cr LJ 1314; *Rahman v State of UP*, AIR 1972 SC 110 : 1972 Cr LJ 23; *Ramnathan v Tamil Nadu*, AIR 1978 SC 1204: 1978 Cr LJ 1137.

53. *Kartarey v UP*, AIR 1976 SC 76 : 1976 Cr LJ 13.

were admittedly taken into custody (from their respective houses only) on the third day of the incident. The Supreme Court observed that it was difficult to hold that they had been absconding. Even assuming for the argument's sake that they were not seen at their workplace after the alleged incident, it cannot be held that by itself an adverse inference is to be drawn against them.[54] The suspect was secretly squatting in a chappar. The conduct of an official on being questioned immediately after taking bribe was allowed to be cited.[55] Refusal to appear in identification parade and to give specimen foot-prints is indicative of guilt.[56]

The presence of the accused before and after the incident in the vicinity of the village in which dacoity look place was held to be evidence of conduct admissible under the section.[57]

[s 8.5] Conduct accompanying or explaining statements—*[Explanation 1]*.—The conduct of a party interested in any proceeding at the time when the facts occurred out of which the proceeding arises is extremely relevant. According to this Explanation the word "conduct" does not include statements, unless those statements accompany and explain acts other than statements; and it is on such a statement that the significance of the act, which it accompanies, in many cases, wholly depends. Mere statements, as distinguished from acts, do not constitute conduct. A statement by a retiring partner, made immediately after his retirement, as the reason for his refusing to continue to guarantee the firm's account with a bank, may be admissible to explain his conduct.[58]

The conduct of the wife of the deceased in putting off relatives and others on a wrong track by telling them that the deceased had left the village and had not returned was held to be relevant under this section.[59]

Acts of parties cannot be allowed to affect the construction of written instruments if that construction be in itself ambiguous;[60] otherwise, the conduct of the party is very important in the construction of documents. In criminal cases all the circumstances of the case in every part of the conduct of the accused may be taken into consideration for the purpose of showing the presence of crime by negativing the operation of every natural agency.

Illustration (d) refers to previous conduct; illustration (e), to previous and subsequent conduct of the accused. Illustrations (j) and (k) make statements of a person against

---

54. *Durga Burman Roy v State of Sikkim*, (2014) 13 SCC 35 (para 41). See also *Sunil Kundu v State of Jharkhand*, (2013) 4 SCC 422 (para 28) and *Sk. Yusuf v State of West Bengal*, (2011) 11 SCC 754.

55. *Prakash Chand v State (Delhi Admn.)*, (1979) 2 SCR 330 : (1979) 1 SCJ 512 : (1979) Mad LJ (Cr) 419 : 1979 Cr LJ 329 : AIR 1979 SC 400. See also *Malkhan Singh v State of UP*, AIR 1975 SC 12 : 1975 Cr LJ 32, where the suspect was seen holding pistol immediately after shooting and also running away, the finding of fact was not disturbed by the Supreme Court. See also *Mohan Lal v UP*, AIR 1974 SC 1144 : 1974 Cr LJ 800, hiding with blood stained clothes.

56. *Mulkh Raj v Delhi Admn.*, AIR 1976 SC 1721 : 1 (977) 1 SCC 46.

57. *Sunil v State of Rajasthan*, 2001 Cr LJ 3063 (Raj), the prosecution had strengthened its case through TI parade of four accused and through voice of one accused, delay in holding TI parade was also explained.

58. *Pramathachandra Kar v Bhagwandas Madanlal*, (1931) 59 Cal 40.

59. *Basanti v State of HP*, 1987 Cr LJ 1869 : AIR 1987 SC 1572 : (1987) 3 SCC 227 : 1987 SCC (Cri) 473.

60. *Re Purmanandas Jeewandas*, (1882) 7 Bom 109.

whom an offence has been committed, relevant. Illustration (j) is an example of the admissibility of a complaint in a case of rape as evidence of conduct.

[s 8.6] Statements Affecting Conduct—*[Explanation 2].*

The conduct must be such as has a close nexus with a fact in issue or a relevant fact. The conduct of the accused in this case pointing out to the police the place of hiding the weapon of offence or articles connected with it was held to be a relevant conduct, whether it was contemporaneous with the event or otherwise.[61] The exhumation of the dead body from the place of burial as pointed out by the accused was held to be a relevant conduct even if it was not covered by section 27 because no statement was recorded.[62] The name and address of the shop had become known to the police from the packets of seized articles; this fact was pointed out by the accused; it was not relevant under section 27. But the conduct of pointing out the shop and its proprietor was relevant under section 8.[63]

[s 8.7] Section 8 and Domestic Violence Act.—Conduct of the parties even prior to the commencement of the Protection of Women from Domestic Violence Act, 2005 can be taken into consideration while passing an order under sections 18, 19 and 20 of the said Act.[64]

[s 9] Facts necessary to explain or introduce relevant facts.—Facts necessary to explain or introduce a fact in issue or relevant fact, or which support or rebut an inference suggested by a fact in issue or relevant fact, or which establish the identity of any thing[s 9.2] or person[s 9.3] whose identity is relevant, or fix the time or place at which any fact in issue or relevant fact happened, or which show the relation of parties by whom any such fact was transacted, are relevant in so far as they are necessary for that purpose.

ILLUSTRATIONS

(a) The question is, whether a given document is the will of *A*.

The state of *A*'s property and of his family at the date of the alleged will may be relevant facts.

(b) *A* sues *B* for a libel imputing disgraceful conduct to *A*; *B* affirms that the matter alleged to be libellous is true.

The position and relations of the parties at the time when the libel was published may be relevant facts as introductory to the facts in issue.

The particulars of a dispute between *A* and *B* about a matter unconnected with the alleged libel are irrelevant, though the fact that there was a dispute may be relevant if it affected the relations between *A* and *B*.

(c) *A* is accused of a crime.

---

61. *State (NCT) of Delhi v Navjot Sandhu (2005)* 11 SCC 600 : 2005 Cr LJ 3950 : (2005) 122 DLT 194.

62. *AN Venkatesh v State of Karnataka,* (2005) 7 SCC 714 : 2005 Cr LJ 3732. *Peerappa v State of Karnataka,* (2005) 12 SCC 461, unrecorded statement, not made in the presence of any witnesses, not relevant either under section 8 or 27.

63. *State (NCT) of Delhi v Navjot Sandhu,* (2005) 11 SCC 600 : AIR 2005 SC 3820.

64. *Saraswathy v Babu, (2014) 3 SCC* 712 (para 23), **following** *VD Bhanot v Savita Bhanot,* (2012) 3 SCC 183 and **affirming** *Savita Bhanot v Lt Col VD Bhanot,* (2010) 168 DLT 68.

The fact that, soon after the commission of the crime, *A* absconded from his house, is relevant under section 8, as conduct subsequent to and affected by facts in issue.

The fact that, at the time when he left home he had sudden and urgent business at the place to which he went, is relevant, as tending to explain the fact that he left home suddenly.

The details of the business on which he left are not relevant, except in so far as they are necessary to show that the business was sudden and urgent.

(d) *A* sues *B* for inducing *C* to break a contract of service made by him with *A*. *C*, on leaving *A*'s service, says to *A*—"I am leaving you because *B* has made me a better offer." This statement is a relevant fact as explanatory of *C*'s conduct, which is relevant as a fact in issue.

(e) *A*, accused of theft, is seen to give the stolen property to *B*, who is seen to give it to *A*'s wife. *B* says as he delivers it—"A says you are to hide this." *B*'s statement is relevant as explanatory of a fact which is part of the transaction.

(f) *A* is tried for a riot and is proved to have marched at the head of a mob. The cries of the mob are relevant as explanatory of the nature of the transaction.

SYNOPSIS

COMMENT

Section 7 deals with the admissibility of facts which are the occasion, cause, or effect of facts in issue. Section 8 similarly makes admissible facts showing motive or preparation for any fact in issue or relevant fact. This section makes admissible facts which are necessary to explain or introduce relevant facts, such as place, name, date, identity of parties, circumstances and relations of the parties. Thus, evidence of other offences committed by the accused is admitted in order to establish his identity or to corroborate the testimony of a witness in a material particular. Identity can also be established by technical evidence like medical report.[65] Section 11 is like the present section.

Illustrations (a) and (b) are examples of *introductory fact*.[66]

---

65. *Hardayal v State of UP*, AIR 1976 SC 2027 : 1976 Cr LJ 1563, the report showed that the body was not decomposed beyond recognition.

66. *State of Tamil Nadu v T Thulasingam*, 1994 SCC (Cri) 1504, evidence relating to the period prior to the commencement of a conspiracy could not be looked into in regard to the criminal conspiracy itself, it can be relevant as a fact introductory to the facts in issue, i.e., criminal conspiracy.

Illustrations (d) and (e) indicate that explanatory statements are admitted under this section irrespective of the fact whether the person against whom it is made heard it or was present when it was made. Under this section it is not necessary that the person against whom the statement is made should be present when it is made.

[s 9.1] Importance of identity evidence.—The principles governing Test Identification Parade (TI parade) have been succinctly summed up by P Sathasivam J (as His Lordship then was) in following words:[67]

"The identification parades are not primarily meant for the court. They are meant for investigation purposes. The object of conducting a test identification parade is twofold. First is to enable the witnesses to satisfy themselves that the accused whom they suspect is really the one who was seen by them in connection with the commission of the crime. Second is to satisfy the investigating authorities that the suspect is the real person whom the witnesses had seen in connection with the said occurrence. Therefore, the following principles regarding identification parade emerge:

(1) an identification parade ideally must be conducted as soon as possible to avoid any mistake on the part of witnesses;

(2) this condition can be revoked if proper explanation justifying the delay is provided; and

(3) the authorities must make sure that the delay does not result in exposure of the accused which may lead to mistakes on the part of the witnesses".

[s 9.2] "Identity of any thing".—A superimposed photograph of the deceased over the skeleton of a human body was held admissible by the Supreme Court to prove the fact that the skeleton was that of the deceased.[68]

[s 9.2.1] *Identity of Motor Vehicle.*—In order to prove that the recovered motor cycle was used in the offence, the prosecution has to show that the tyre marks found at the place of offence were that of the recovered motor cycle. For that purpose the tyre marks have to be lifted from the place and compared with the marks of the recovered motor cycle. The fact that the home-guard and police constable had seen one digit of the registration number of the motor cycle was held to be not sufficient to establish the identity even if the same digit was there in the recovered vehicle also.[69]

[s 9.3] Identity of Accused: Test Identification (TI) Parade.—One of the methods of establishing the identity of the accused is "test identification parade". Its evidence is received under this section. The idea of the parade is to test the veracity of the witness on the question of his capability to identify, from among several persons made to stand in a queue, an unknown person whom the witness had seen at the time of the occurrence.[70] It is only an aid to investigation. The practice is not borne out of

---

67. *Mulla v State of UP,* (2010) 3 SCC 508.

68. *Ram Lochan v State of West Bengal,* AIR 1963 SC 1074 : (1963) 2 Cr LJ 170.

69. *Varun Chaudhary v State of Rajasthan,* AIR 2011 SC 72.

70. *Kanan v State of Kerala,* 1979 Cr LJ 919; *Chonampra v State of Kerala,* AIR 1979 SC 1761 : 1979 Cr LJ 1335. The statement of the witness that he identified the accused in the light of torch flashed by him and in the court that it was in the light of a lantern, held not reliable. *Basudev Yadaw v State of Bihar,* 1988 Cr LJ 1408 (Pat). The evidence of identity given by the inmates of the house cannot be rejected for the fact that they are interested witnesses. *Ram Deo Yadaw v State of Bihar,* 1988 Cr LJ

(Footnote No. 70 contd.)

procedure but out of prudence.[71] The purpose is to test and strengthen the substantive evidence of the witness in court. Such evidence is used for corroboration.[72] The TI Parade, even if it is held may not be considered in all cases as trustworthy evidence on which the conviction of the accused can be sustained.[73]

The main object of holding TI parade during investigation is to test the memory of the witness based upon the first impression and also to enable the prosecution to decide whether all the witnesses or any of them could be called as an eye-witness to the crime.[74]

The relevant factors to be taken into consideration in connection with identification are whether there was opportunity for the witnesses to see the accused at the time of the incident, whether they could remember by face the accused persons and whether

---

(Footnote No. 70 contd.)

1431 (Pat). Identification by voice not accepted. *Pramahans Traders v Collector,* 1988 Cr LJ 506 (Ori); *Kalipadu Gope v State of Bihar,* 1987 Cr LJ 1320, proper identification of dacoits on test identification parade, conviction on such evidence, good. *Raj Kumar Singh v State of Bihar,* 1988 Cr LJ 1273 (Pat), unreliable evidence of identity of dacoits. *Tain Singh v State,* 1987 Cr LJ 53 (Del), refusal of the accused to stand in the line-up saying that he had been exposed to the witnesses, held strict proof of the allegation not needed. *Sher Singh v State,* 1991 Cr LJ 2612 (Del), where there was no evidence to show that the accused in a robbery case was shown to the witnesses, his refusal to appear in the line-up created presumption against him; *Govinda Pradhan v State of Orissa,* 1991 Cr LJ 269 (Ori), accused made to walk on several occasions to and from between court and jail, possibility of witnesses having seen them not ruled out. *Mahendra Singh v State of UP,* 1991 Cr LJ 1381 (All), no evidence that the accused was not shown to the witness before TI parade. *Pramod Kumar v State,* 1991 Cr LJ 68 (Del), accused taken out for recovery of the weapon of offence, possibility of being seen by the accused, subsequent identification ruled out. *Chaman v State of UP,* AIR 1992 SC 601 : 1993 Supp (1) SCC 403 : 1993 SCC (Cri) 212, face of the accused and those of others in the line covered with too many paper patches, held, identification parade a wasted effort, *State of Orissa v Pravarkar Babera,* 1991 Cr LJ 745 (Ori); *Ahmad Sayeed v State of UP,* 1991 Cr LJ 991 (All), delay not fatal by itself; if the dacoits came with covered faces in TI parade, they should be similarly covered. *Satrughana v State of Orissa,* 1991 Cr LJ 846 (Ori), separate for each accused not necessary; effect of delay. *Suraj Pal v State of Haryana,* (1995) 2 SCC 64 : 1995 SCC (Cri) 313, the Supreme Court explained the reasons for and the utility of the practice of the test identification parade. *Har Pal Singh v State of UP,* 2000 Cr LJ 4552 (All), test of veracity of witness as to identification without which not safe to believe the witness. *Kapporchand Chaudhary v State of Bihar,* 2002 Cr LJ 1424 (Pat), looting of passengers in a bus, the miscreants were strangers to the victims, they had not covered their faces, the victims had the opportunity to see them in the light of the vehicle which was on, evidence of identification by the victims in the court and in TI parade was held to be reliable. *Lakhwinder Singh v State of Punjab,* AIR 2003 SC 2577, eye-witness not knowing assailants who committed murder. Not holding a test identification parade to enable the witnesses to identify them was a serious lapse and was fatal to the prosecution case. *Bachan v State of UP,* 2003 Cr LJ 2060 (All), the accused was seen by the witnesses during transit, identification evidence of such witness was not relied upon. *Heera v State of Rajasthan,* AIR 2007 SC 2425 : (2007) 10 SCC 175, purpose explained and also emphasising that the parade should be paid at the earliest after arrest.

71. *Sidharth Vashisth @ Manu Sharma v State (NCT of Delhi),* AIR 2010 SC 2352 : (2010) 6 SCC 1.
72. *Latesh v State of Maharashtra,* AIR 2018 SC 659 : (2018) 3 SCC 66 : LNIND 2018 SC 36; *Ram Babu v State of UP,* AIR 2010 SC 2143 : (2010) 5 SCC 63. *Ankush Maruti Shinde v State of Maharashtra,* AIR 2009 SC 2609 : (2009) 6 SCC 667, object of TI parade stated. *Md Kalam v State of Rajasthan,* AIR 2008 SC 1813 : (2008) 11 SCC 352, purpose of TI parade stated.
73. *Latesh v State of Maharashtra,* AIR 2018 SC 659 : (2018) 3 SCC 66 : LNIND 2018 SC 36.
74. *Mahabir v State of Delhi,* AIR 2008 SC 2343 : 2008 Cr LJ 3036, the purpose is to test and strengthen trustworthiness of the evidence. It is accordingly considered as a safe rule of prudence to generally look for corroboration of sworn testimony of the witness in the court. *Mahabir v State of Delhi,* AIR 2008 SC 2343 : 2008 Cr LJ 3036, TI parade belongs to the stage of investigation. There is nothing in CrPC obliging the investigating agency to hold it or conferring right on the accused to demand it.

they could identify them by such memory in the court.[75] Where a parade of this kind was held within two days of arrest under the supervision of a Judicial Magistrate and with all the necessary precautions, the evidence so obtained, the Supreme Court held, should not have been rejected on the accused telling the court that he was shown to the witnesses beforehand. All this is for the accused to prove.[76] The Magistrate has to satisfy himself that the accused was not shown to the witnesses and that the parade was otherwise fair[77] and not a farce.[78] Evidence of identity so obtained can in circumstances be the sole basis of conviction.[79] But generally such evidence is only of supporting nature. It can be used as corroborative evidence.[80] The identification parade must be

---

75. *State of Karnataka v Rajan,* 1994 Cr LJ 1042 (Kant). *Vilas Vasatrao Patil v State of Maharashtra,* 1996 Cr LJ 1854 (Bom), non-compliance of the provisions of the Criminal Manual issued by the High Court in respect to identification parade, makes it unacceptable. *Ahmed Bin Salam v State of AP,* 1999 Cr LJ 2281 : AIR 1999 SC 1617, where the accused persons were shown to the witness and he identified them, this was held to be no identification parade.

76. *Sone Lal v State of UP,* AIR 1978 SC 1142: 1978 Cr LJ 1122; *Ramanathan v State of TN,* AIR 1978 SC 1204 : 1978 Cr LJ 1137. See also *Ashok Narhari Nath v State of Maharashtra,* 1980 Cr LJ 205 : (1980) 2 SCR 628 : AIR 1980 SC 727, the witness identifying two out of several accused, namely, one who assaulted him and one who inflicted fatal injuries on his complainant, held, TI good evidence; delay of 44 hours was not so material as to convince the court that the memory of the witness must have become blurred. *Digambar Singh v State of UP,* 1990 Cr LJ 489 : 1989 All LJ 180, dacoit identified in moonlight and lantern light and also in TI parade, good evidence.

77. *Somappa V Madar v State of Mysore,* AIR 1979 SC 1831 : 1979 Cr LJ 1358. Prosecution has to show that the accused was carried for remand *ba parda.*

78. *Yeshwant v State of Maharashtra,* AIR 1973 SC 337 : 1972 Cr LJ 1254; *State of MP v Samaylal,* 1994 Cr LJ 3407 (MP), the accused shown to the witness. Such chances should be eliminated, *RB Gupta v State of Maharashtra,* 1995 Cr LJ 4048 (Bom). *Anoop Singh v State,* 1994 Cr LJ 3442 (Delhi), conducting TI parade one day after the accused was shown to the complainant, farce. *Juglal Mehto v State (Delhi Admn.),* 1995 Cr LJ 1618 (Del), the witness had earlier occasion to see the assailants, not reliable. Accused as well as police officials present at police station for photographs, possibility of being seen, TI parade held after more than one month of the arrest, conviction could not be based on such identification, *Kabul v State of Rajasthan,* 1992 Cr LJ 1491 (Raj). Rejection of evidence obtained by identification parade was upheld by the Supreme Court because the make up of the persons standing in the line-up was overdone making the parade a farcical exercise. Moles, and scars on the face of the accused covered to a large extent with pieces of paper and similar covering done on faces of others in the line up. Held not safe to convict on such evidence. *Chaman v State of UP,* 1992 Cr LJ 524 SC : AIR 1992 SC 601.

79. *Jugal Gopal v State of Bihar,* (1979) 3 SCC 272 : 1981 Cr LJ 4 : AIR 1981 SC 612. But where the parade was held after inordinate delay, such conviction was not sustained. *Avtar Singh v State of MP,* AIR 1979 SC 1188 : 1979 Cr LJ 715.

80. *ST Shinde v State of Maharashtra,* AIR 1974 SC 791 : 1974 Cr LJ 674. The value of such evidence depends upon many things particularly the fact whether at the time of occurrence the circumstances were such as to enable a witness to have a clear perception of the assailant. See *Wakil Singh v State of Bihar,* AIR 1981 SC 1392 : 1981 Supp SCC 28 : 1981 Cr LJ 1014; *State of UP v Boota,* AIR 1978 SC 1770 : (1979) 1 SCR 298 : 1978 All LJ 1156 : 1979 Mad LJ (Cr) 290; *Ram Deo Rao Yadav v State of Bihar,* AIR 1990 SC 1180 : 1990 Cr LJ 1183. *Danu v State of Orissa,* 1996 Cr LJ 2107 (Ori), the accused were detained for a long period of 7 to 10 days with a view to be shown to the witnesses, identification parade conducted thereafter was held to be unreliable. *Dana Yadav v State of Bihar,* AIR 2002 SC 3325, the accused denied the fact that he was known to the prosecution witness from before. He challenged the identification by filing a petition and praying for holding test identification parade. The court explained the procedure to be followed in such a case. The court said that identification of accused for the first time in the court should not ordinarily be the basis of conviction unless corroborated by identification previously in identification parade, though it may in exceptional circumstances form the basis of conviction, for example, where the solitary witness named the accused in the FIR and also in the court and correctly identified him in the deck the accused persons were known to him. Their identification by such a witness could form the basis of conviction. The evidence was also consistent and found to be credible. Where the accused was not named in the FIR his identification in the court could not be relied upon.

held by the investigating agency with reasonable despatch.[81] The identifying witness has to appear personally to depose.[82] It is not necessary for him to tell what role was played by the person whom he identified.[83] Where TI is not held, identification in the court for the first time does not serve much purpose.[84] The trial court as well as the High Court has found various legal infirmities in the holding of test identification parade as such no reliance has been placed thereon. Moreover, as the appellant was a named accused person, his so-called identification in the test identification parade could not be of any avail to the prosecution as it was meaningless."[85]

[s 9.3.1] Joint test identification parade.—There is no invariable rule that two accused persons cannot be made part of the same test identification parade. The joint test identification parade, in no manner, affects the validity of the test identification parade.[86]

---

81. *Dana Yadav v State of Bihar*, AIR 2002 SC 3325.

82. *CP Fernandes v UT Goa*, AIR 1977 SC 135 : 1977 Cr LJ 167, otherwise the accused misses the opportunity to cross-examine him.

83. *State of AP v KV Reddy*, AIR 1976 SC 2207 : 1976 Cr LJ 1723.

84. *State v UC Shukla*, AIR 1980 SC 1382 : 1980 Supp SCC 249; *Mohd Abdul Hafeez v AD*, AIR 1983 SC 367 : 1983 Cr LJ 689; names and descriptions of the 4 accused were not given in the FIR and no TI parade was held, identification of accused after 4 months was held to be of no use for connecting the accused persons with the crime. *Pravakar Bahera v State*, 1997 Cr LJ 3291 (Ori), dacoity, TI parade after 3½ months, no material to show that the accused persons were shown to the witnesses before the parade. Evidence of identification was relied upon. See also *Siri Ram Sharma v State*, 1995 Cr LJ 1116 (Del), no identification parade held, witness identified the accused for the first time in court, not to serve as basis for conviction. *Rampal Pithwa Rahidass v State of Maharashtra*, 1994 Supp (2) SCC 73 : 1994 Cr LJ 2320 (SC), dacoity, no identification parade held, accused unknown to witnesses, identification in court not sufficient to base conviction. *Ramnath Naik v State of Orissa*, 1995 Cr LJ 2255 (Ori), identification for the first time during trial, weak evidence. *State of Maharashtra v Sukhdev Singh*, AIR 1992 SC 2100 : 1992 Cr LJ 3454 : (1992) 3 SCC 700, TI parade not held, no satisfactory explanation, accused identified in the court, no corroboration, not reliable. *Earabhadrappa v State of Karnataka*, AIR 1983 SC 446 : (1983) 3 SCC 330 : 1983 Cr LJ 846, conviction cannot be based on the identification by a single witness. *Wakil Singh v State of Bihar*, AIR 1981 SC 1392 : 1981 Supp SC 628 : 1981 Cr LJ 1014 : 1981 SCC (Cri) 634. In *Hari Nath v State of UP*, (1988) 1 SCC 14 : AIR 1988 SC 345 : 1988 Cr LJ 422 : 1988 CCC (Cri) 149, the Supreme Court cited the following passage from HALSBURY'S LAWS OF ENGLAND: "It is undesirable that witnesses should be asked to identify a defendant for the first time in the dock at his trial; and as a general practice it is preferable that he should have been placed previously on a parade with other persons, so that potential witnesses can be asked to pick him out [para 363, Vol II, 4th Edn]. See also, *Sheikh Habib v State of Bihar*, AIR 1972 SC 283: (1972) Cr LJ 233: (1972) 2 SCC 773; *Rameshwar Singh v State of J&K*, AIR 1972 SC 102: (1971) SCC (Cr) 638: (1971) 2 SCC 715. *Parasnath Singh v State of Bihar*, (1988) 2 SCC 96 : AIR 1988 SC 863 : 1988 Cr LJ 925, identification of the accused by two witnesses in the witness-box, held to be useless when one of them had failed to identify in TI parade. Failure to identify in the court after identification in TI parade is likely to be equally fatal. See *Ramadhar Thakur v State of Bihar*, 1988 Cr LJ 264 Pat; *Khan Singh v State*, 1997 Cr LJ 2305 (All), dacoity, looting of arms, evidence not adduced to show that the accused persons were not shown to the witnesses. Conviction based on identification by witnesses without TI parade was held to be not proper. No recovery from one of the accused. Recovery from the other was not connected with the present dacoity. *Kishore Amarsingh Maheshkar v State of Maharashtra*, 1998 Cr LJ 4059 : AIR 1998 SC 3031 : (1998) 6 SCC 609, photographs of accused persons shown to witnesses, parade held in the lock-up of the investigating agency, evidence rejected *Asifkhan Haiderkhan Pathan v State*, 1998 Cr LJ 4458 (Guj), the witness and the accused were present at the police station before the parade, failure of the prosecution to rule out the accused being seen. Evidence of TI parade not reliable.

85. *Dhananjay Shankar Shetty v State of Maharashtra*, AIR 2002 SC 2787, at p 2789.

86. *Sheikh Sintha Madhar v State*, AIR 2016 SC 1844, para 16.

[s 9.3.2] Delay in holding TI parade.—The test identification parade should be held at the earliest-possible opportunity, but there is no hard-and-fast rule that can be laid down in this regard. If the delay is inordinate and there is evidence probabilising the possibility of the accused having been shown to the witnesses, the court may not act on the basis of such evidence. Moreover, cases where the conviction is based not solely on the basis of identification in court, but on the basis of other corroborative evidence, such as recovery of looted articles, stand on a different footing and the court has to consider the evidence in its entirety.[87] Where the identification parade was held four months after the incident, the Supreme Court held that it was not a reliable evidence. Its weakness further appeared from the fact that the accused and the witness belonged to adjoining villages and had also been students in one and the same school and, therefore, must have known each other even before the parade.[88] The dacoity in this case had been committed at night. The court was of the view that the evidence of identification in such cases should be examined more carefully. Venkatachaliah J relied

---

87. *Md. Sajjad v State of West Bengal*, AIR 2017 SC 642 : (2017) 11 SCC 150 : LNIND 2017 SC 21.

88. *Hari Nath v State of UP*, (1988) 1 SCC 14 : AIR 1988 SC 345 : 1989 Cr LJ 842. Other cases involving four months delay: *Subash v State of UP*, 1987 Cr LJ 991 : AIR 1987 SC 1282; *Habal Shaikh v State of WB*, 1991 Cr LJ 1258 (Cal); *Khalak Singh v State of MP*, 1992 Cr LJ 1151 MP, 57 days' of unexplained delay in conducting identification parade, hence no evidentiary value. *Mohd. Isa Khan v State of UP*, 1992 Cr LJ 3987 (All), ocular witness saw the accused for the first time at the time of incident, identified after seven years, not reliable. *Adithela Immanuel Raju v State of Orissa*, 1992 Cr LJ 243 (Ori), encashment of drafts by accused lasting only for few minutes, identification after nearly five months, not plausible. Identification parade after three and a half months, identification not proper, *Banifas Samad v State of Orissa*, 1992 Cr LJ 2271 (Ori), the court **relied on** *Satrughana v State of Orissa*, 1990 (2) Ori LR 324. *Brij Mohan v State of Rajasthan*, AIR 1994 SC 739 : 1994 Cr LJ 922 : (1994) 1 SCC 413, TI parade within twenty four hours of the arrest but after three months from the occurrence, can't be rejected on the grounds of delay. *Ganpat Singh v State of Rajasthan*, 1994 Cr LJ 1565 (Raj), 14 days delay, not fatal. For another case of prior knowledge, see *Bali Ahir v State of Bihar*, AIR 1983 SC 289: (1984) Supp SCR 625: 1983 SCC (Cr) 312; *Soni v State of UP*, (1982) 3 SCC 368: (1983) SCC (Cr) 49, another case of weak evidence of identification and consequential benefit of doubt. *Bollavaram Pedda Narsi Reddy v State of AP*, AIR 1991 SC 1468 : (1991) 3 SCC 434 : (1991) Cr LJ 1833, misconducted identification parade; *Manne Subbaro v State of AP*, AIR 1980 SC 2113 : 1980 Cr LJ 1476, and *Rahimal v State of UP*, 1992 Cr LJ 3819 (All), question of sufficiency of light.*Munna v State*, 1993 Cr LJ 3719, broad day light dacoity, T.I. after six months, not fatal and *Kasu Bhai v State of HP*, 1992 Cr LJ 3251 (HP), house, breaking, a long struggle of the accused with the victim lady in well lighted house, identification parade after the release of the victim from the hospital, legal. *Sukumar Jena v State of Orissa*, 1993 Cr LJ 1354 dacoity, sufficient light, identification corroborated by seizures of articles, reliable. *Abdul Waheed Khan v State of AP*, AIR 2002 SC 2961, where the witnesses were not available on the date on which TI parade was organised and, therefore, it had to be rescheduled and some delay which took place was sufficiently explained, the evidence thus generated was held to be relevant. *Surendra Singh Rautela v State of Bihar*, AIR 2002 SC 260 : 2002 Cr LJ 555, accused fired at inmates of a car, the witness stated in the FIR that he could not identify the assailant, his identification at TI parade was held to be a farce *Prakash Dhawal v State of Maharashtra*, AIR 2002 SC 540, plea that the confessional statement should not be admissible because he was acquitted of the main offence, held not tenable because there was also the confessional statement of the co-accused who was jointly tried. *Kanwar Lal v State of MP*, 1999 Cr LJ 3632 (MP) in a dacoity cum murder case, there was an unexplained delay of 2½ months in holding the test identification parade. There was no proof also that no opportunity was given to the witnesses to see the accused persons. The court did not put corroborative value upon such a parade. *State v Ramesh*, 2000 Cr LJ 2855 (All), the identification of the accused took place 2½ years after the incident. The court said that the testimony of the identifying witnesses could not be relied upon. *Ganpat Singh v State of Rajasthan*, (1997) 11 SCC 565 : 1998 SCC (Cr) 201, accused shown to the witness, TI parade wasted.

upon authorities as to the value of and disservice by, identification evidence. He said: The one area of criminal evidence susceptible of miscarriage of criminal justice is the error in the identification of the criminal.

The utility of the evidence created by an identification parade was explained by the Supreme Court in *Ramanathan v State of Tamil Nadu,*[89] Shinghal J said: Identification parades have been in common use for a very long time for the object of placing suspect in a line-up with other persons for identification. The purpose is to find out whether he is the perpetrator of the crime. This is all the more necessary where the name of the offender is not mentioned by those who claim to be eye-witnesses of the incident, but they claim that although they did not know him earlier, they could recall his features in sufficient details and would also be able to identify him if and when they happen to see him again. Such identification is in the interest of both, the accused and the investigating agency. It enables the investigating officer to ascertain whether the witnesses had really seen the perpetrator of the crime and test their capacity to identify him and thereby to fill the gap in the investigation regarding the identity of the culprit. The line-up of the accused in a test identification parade is therefore a workable way of testing the memory and veracity of the witnesses and has worked well in actual practice. In the present case where there was satisfactory evidence to prove that at least two of the witnesses emphatically claimed that they had noticed the culprit and had in fact described him and claimed that they could identify him, the holding of a test identification parade was absolutely necessary. The fact that such parade was held within two days of the arrest and was supervised by a Judicial Magistrate with all the necessary precautions and arrangements, leaves no room for doubt that the evidence was of considerable importance.

The accused persons were hired criminals and not residents of the locality. There was street light. But they were fleeing on scooter. Except for a fleeting glance, the witness must have had a very limited chance of observing properly. The court had to take this fact into the account. The accused were kept in open police custody for four days prior to identification. The parade was held three months after the incident and one month

---

89. *Ramanathan v State of Tamil Nadu,* AIR 1978 SC 1201, at pp 1211-12 : (1978) 1 SCC 632; *Shiv Charan v State of Haryana,* AIR 1987 SC 1 : (1978) 1 SCC 27 : 1978 Cr LJ 1. See *Somappa Vamanappa Madar v State of Mysore,* (1980) 1 SCC 479, 485 : AIR 1975 SC 1831 : 1979 Cr LJ 1358, where the SC points out that the witnesses ought to be questioned as to whether the accused had not been shown to them and in the absence of such questioning by the Magistrate or the accused, the evidence is not reliable; *Ashok Narhari v State of Maharashtra,* (1980) 3 SCC 91 : 1980 SCC (Cr) 538, accused not shown to witnesses. *Ramesh Kumar v State of Punjab,* (1993) Cr LJ 1800 (SC) there is no need for identification parade where the witnesses already knew who the assailants were. *Ahmed Bin Salam v State of AP,* 1999 Cri 2281 : AIR 1999 SC 1617 : (1999) 4 SCC 111, police inquired from the witness as to whether he could identify the persons who were on scooter and who threw bombs towards the deceased. The accused persons were then shown to him and he identified them. The Supreme Court said that such an exercise could not be described as a test identification parade; *Matru v State of UP,* (1971) 2 SCC 75 : AIR 1971 SC 1050; *Raj Kishore Singh v State of Bihar,* AIR 1971 SC 1058; *Jadunath Singh v State of UP,* AIR 1971 SC 363. Where norms as to organising a parade are not observed, it becomes a wasted exercise. *Musheer Khan v State of MP,* AIR 2010 SC 762 : (2010) 2 SCC 748, evidence not of substantive nature. The identifying witness said that persons in the line were covered up to neck those who organised the parade testified that there was no such cover, because of this contradiction the court regarded identification as doubtful.

after arrest. No explanation was offered for the delay. The court said that no reliance could be placed on such identification.[90]

[s 9.4] Corroborative, not substantive evidence.—The evidence generated through TI parade has been described by the Supreme Court to be corroborative only. It is used only to corroborate the evidence recorded in the court. It is not substantive evidence. The actual evidence is what is given by the witness in the court. The TI parade provides an assurance that the investigation is proceeding in the right direction. It enables the witnesses to satisfy themselves that the accused whom they suspect is really one who was seen by them at the time of commission of the offence. The accused should not be shown to any of the witnesses after arrest. Up to the time of parade, he must be kept "*baparda*", (with face covered). It was alleged in this case that the parade was conducted in undue haste, but the magistrate was not examined on this point. Hence, the plea was of no significance.[91]

[s 9.5] Identification inside the Court.—In the decision in *Suresh Candra Bahri v State of Bihar*,[92] it is well settled that statement of the witness in the court is his evidence but when the accused person is not previously known to the witness concerned then identification of the accused by the witness soon after his arrest is of great importance because it furnishes an assurance that the investigation is proceeding on right lines in addition to furnishing corroboration of the evidence to be given by the witness later in the court at the trial. From this point of view it is a matter of great importance both for the investigating agency and for the accused and a fortiori for the proper administration of justice that such identification is held without avoidable and unreasonable delay after the arrest of the accused and that all the necessary precautions and safeguards were effectively taken so that the investigation proceeds on correct lines for punishing the real culprit. It would, in addition, be fair to the witness concerned also who was a stranger to the accused because in that event the chances of his memory fading away are reduced and he is required to identify the alleged culprit at the earliest possible opportunity after the occurrence. It is in adopting this course alone that justice and fair play can be assured both to the accused as well as to the prosecution. But the position may be different when the accused or a culprit who stands trial had been seen not once but for quite a number of times at different points of time and places which fact may do away with the necessity of a TI parade.

Where the accused was not named in the FIR, nor was any identification parade conducted to identify him by the witnesses, it was held by Supreme Court that it is rather impossible to identify the accused person when he is produced for the first time in the court, i.e., after 10 years since he was unknown to the witnesses.[93]

---

90. *Musheer Khan v State of MP*, AIR 2010 SC 762 : (2010) 2 SCC 748, *Mahabir v State of Delhi*, AIR 2008 SC 2343 : 2008 Cr LJ 3036, fleeting glimpse of an accused who was stranger, not reliable identification possible.

91. *C. Muniappa v State of Tamil Nadu*, AIR 2010 SC 3718 at pp 3729, 3730 : (2010) 9 SCC 567; *Mahabir v State of Delhi*, AIR 2008 SC 2343 : 2008 Cr LJ 3036, evidence of identification can be used only as corroborative of statement in the court.

92. AIR 1994 SC 2420 : 1994 Cr LJ 3271. *Thankayyan v State of Kerala*, 1994 SCC (Cri) 1751, the accused was not previously known to the witness, identified for the first time in court, no reliance on such evidence.

93. *Oma v State of TN*, (2013) 3 SCC 440. Accused stranger, first seen briefly, no TI parade, identification in court after a gap of 4$^1/2$ years, did not inspire confidence, *Prakash v State of Karnataka*, (2014) 12 SCC 133 (paras 17 and 18).

Identification in court is an evidence of weak character. It could have derived strength if identification had taken place in a parade. Holding of TI parade being not obligatory, its absence does make the evidence of identification in court as inadmissible.[94]

It has consistently been held by the Supreme Court that what is substantive evidence is the identification of the accused in the court by a witness and that the prior identification in a test identification parade is used only to corroborate the identification in court. Holding the test identification parade is not the rule of law but rule of prudence. Normally, the identification of the accused in a test identification parade lends assurance, so that the subsequent identification in court during trial could be safely relied upon. However, even in the absence of such a test identification parade, the identification in court can in a given circumstance be relied upon, if the witness is otherwise trustworthy and reliable as in the instant case, wherein the victim of a broad daylight rape identified her assailant in court and was relied on.[95]

In the absence of identification in court at the time of tendering evidence, the result of TI parade would be of little value.[96]

In the case of *Sidhartha Vashisht @ Manu Sharma v State (NCT of Delhi)*,[97] one witness who was said to be present at the scene of crime at the time of murder, had left for Kolkata. One police officer went to Kolkata to get the identification of the accused done by showing photographs to the witness. The witness identified the accused by his photograph in the presence of Police Officer, though he refused to sign the same. Holding the factum of photo identification as admissible in evidence, it was held by Supreme Court that the factum of photo-identification as witnessed by the concerned Officer is a relevant and admissible piece of evidence.

In the case relating to the murder of a Christian Missionary Graham Staines, the question of identification from photographs arose, and it was held by Supreme Court that showing photographs of the miscreants and identification for the first time in the trial court without being corroborated by TI parade held before a Magistrate or without any other material may not be helpful to the prosecution case. It was further held that the evidence of witness given in the court as to the identification may be accepted only if he identified the same person in a previously held TI parade in jail. The identification of the accused during trial for the first time was considered to be of an inherently weak character, and therefore, it was held to be desirable to look for corroboration of the sworn testimony of witnesses in court as to the identity of the accused who are strangers to them, in the form of earlier TI parade.[98]

The court may appreciate the dock identification even if there is no previous TI parade. In the case at hand, the informant, apart from identifying the accused who had made themselves available in the TI parade, has also identified all of them in court.

---

94. *Heera v State of Rajasthan*, AIR 2007 SC 2425 : (2007) 10 SCC 175.

95. *S v Sunil Kumar*, (2015) 8 SCC 478, paras 11 and 12, **following** *Ashok Debbarma v State of Tripura*, (2014) 4 SCC 747.

96. *Umesh Kumar v State of Bihar*, AIR 2005 SC 726 : (2005) 9 SCC 200 : 2005 Cr LJ 908.

97. *Sidhartha Vashisht @ Manu Sharma v State (NCT of Delhi)*, AIR 2010 SC 2352, para 107 at p 2414, (2010) 6 SCC 1, P Sathasivam, J, speaking for the Bench.

98. *Rabindra Kumar Pal @ Dara Singh v Republic of India*, AIR 2011 SC 1436, para 12 at pp 1445-1446, (2011) 1 Scale 615, (2011) 1 SCC (Cr) 706, P Sathasivam J.

The dock identification by the informant deserved acceptance and could be accepted as reliable identification.[99]

[s 9.6] Refusal to submit for parade.—The effect of such refusal was explained by the Supreme Court in the following words:[100] In the present case, the prosecution was anxiously taking steps to hold the test identification parade but the appellants declined to submit themselves for that purpose. It is true that they could not have been compelled to line up for test parade and so if they refused to submit for it they did so at their own risk. The prosecution could not be blamed for not holding the test parade. The reason given out by the appellants for declining to stand the test of identification was that they were shown by the police to the witnesses. This allegation was found to be baseless and unfounded by both the courts below. There was absolutely no basis to say that the appellants or any of them were shown to the witnesses. If the appellants had, in exercise of their own volition, chosen not to stand the test of identification without any reasonable cause, they did so at their own risk for which they could not be heard to say that in the absence of test parade, dock identification was not proper and should not be accepted, if it was otherwise found to be reliable.

There was nothing on record to show that newspapers in question had shown the photograph of the accused. The photograph which was taken when surrendered before the police was with muffled face. It was held that the refusal of the accused to appear in TI parade on the ground that his photograph had appeared in newspapers was unjustified. An adverse inference could be drawn against him.[101]

Where the plea that the accused had refused to participate in the test identification parade because their faces were shown to the prosecution witness at the police station after their arrest, was raised for the first time before the Supreme Court, the same was not entertained.[102]

[s 9.7] Identification by voice, gait etc.—Known persons can be recognised by the timbre of their voice and gait.[103] Where the accused persons were close relatives of the witnesses, it was held that they could be recognised even in the absence of light by gait, timbre of voice etc.[104] There can be identification by the shape of the body, gait, manner of walking, or even by voice.[105] Where the witnesses were not closely acquainted with the accused, yet they claimed to have identified the accused from short replies given by him, the evidence of identification was held to be unreliable.[106] The evidence of an expert witness or of a non-expert witness who is capable, is admissible to identify the voice of a defendant.[107] The facts involved the kidnapping of a wealthy businessman. Ransom demands and other telephone calls were tape recorded. The court held that

---

99. *Mukesh v State for NCT Delhi*, AIR 2017 SC 2161 : (2017) 6 SCC 1 : LNIND 2017 SC 252.

100. *Suraj Pal v State of Haryana*, (1995) 2 SCC 64.

101. *Sidharth Vashisht @ Manu Sharma v State (NCT of Delhi)*, AIR 2010 SC 2352 : (2010) 6 SCC 1.

102. *Pargan Singh v State of Punjab*, (2014) 14 SCC 619 (para 23) : AIR 2014 SC 3790.

103. *State v Harishchandra Tukaram Awatade*, 1997 Cr LJ 612 (Bom); *Shyamrao Vishnu Patil v State*, 1998 Cr LJ 3446 (Bom), incident at 8.30 p.m. Light was not there. But that was not necessary, because known persons could be identified by their gait and voice.

104. *Shankar Sridhar Kavale v State*, 1998 Cr LJ 4491 (Bom); *Shivaji Ganu Naik v State of Maharashtra*, 1999 Cr LJ 471 (Bom).

105. *Kedar Singh v State of Bihar*, 1999 Cr LJ 601 : AIR 1999 SC 1481.

106. *Inspector of Police v Palaniswamy*, AIR 2009 SC 1012 : 2009 Cr LJ 788.

107. *R v Robb*, (1991) 93 Cr App R 161 (CA).

the expert was well qualified through training and experience to express the opinion that the voice on the recordings and that of the defendant was the same and that the police officers were entitled to give evidence, not of opinion, but of recognition as a matter of fact.

[s 9.8] Identification of public figure.—In a case of fraud and misappropriation, the person accused was a public figure in the locality. The witnesses identified him in the court. Their testimony was found to be reliable. The court said that no identification parade was necessary.[108]

[s 9.9] Identification by footprints.—Where the incident of murder took place in a ploughed field and many people visited the site before the arrival of the investigating officer and moulds were prepared from the alleged footprints of the accused and from that of the seized foot wears, not shown to have been asked to wear when specimen was taken, it was held that no reliance could be placed on the result of identification.[109]

[s 9.10] Crime by several persons.—The Supreme Court laid down in *Chandra Shekhar v State of Bihar*,[110] that where a large number of persons participated in a crime, two witness theory could be adopted for identification of the accused persons. Benefit of doubt was given to the accused who could not be identified by more than one witness. Other accused persons who were identified by at least two witnesses, their conviction was maintained.[111]

[s 9.11] Identification by finger prints.—In a murder case before the Supreme Court, two accused persons were involved. Finger prints of one of them were found in the scene of occurrence. The other accused was not allowed to raise the plea that the prosecution had failed to prove that the finger prints used for comparison were those of the proper accused. The evidence was not challenged by the accused whose finger-prints were found there.[112]

[s 9.12] Photofits.—The Supreme Court in *Ram Lochan v State of West Bengal*,[113] held that the superimposed photograph of the deceased over the skeleton of a human

---

108. *Arun Parshuram Sutar v State of Maharashtra*, 1999 Cr LJ 438 (Bom).

109. *Niranjan Lal v State of Haryana*, 1995 Cr LJ 248 (P&H).

110. *Chandra Shekhar v State of Bihar*, 2001 Cr LJ 4693 (SC).

111. The court referred to its own earlier decisions in *Binay Kumar Singh v State of Bihar*, AIR 1997 SC 322 : 1997 Cr LJ 3621 : 1997 AIR SCW 78 : (1997) 1 SCC 283 and *Masalti v State of UP*, AIR 1965 SC 202 : 1965 Cr LJ 226 in both of which the two-witness theory was adopted in cases of crimes in which several persons are involved.

112. *Gade Lakshmi Mangraju v State of AP*, AIR 2001 SC 2677 : 2001 Cr LJ 3317. Absence of the fingerprints was not sufficient to establish his absence from the scene of occurrence.

113. *Ram Lochan v State of West Bengal*, AIR 1963 SC 1074 : (1964) 1 SCJ 82 : (1963) SCD 638 : (1963) 2 Cr LJ 170. *Har Dayal v State of UP*, AIR 1976 SC 2055 : 1976(2) SCC 812 : 1976 Cr LJ 1578, where the clothes and shoes of a deceased child were held to be good marks for his identification. *State of Kerala v Baby Joseph*, 1992 Cr LJ 2257 (Ker). The identity of a person established through hair left behind by him in the fingers of the deceased and also on the knife. Report of an expert on analysis of the hair is an acceptable form of evidence, citing. *Kanbi Karsan Jadawa v State of Gujarat*, AIR 1996 SC 821 : 1966 Cr LJ 605, TAYLOR'S MEDICAL JURISPRUDENCE, 122 (1965) where some cases are given showing that hairs were identified as belonging to a particular person; *Moghar Singh v State of Punjab*, AIR 1975 SC 1320 : 1975 Cr LJ 1102, blades of hair of the deceased stuck to the Kirpan used by the accused; *Ravindra Laxman v Maharashtra*, 1997 Cr LJ 3833 (Bom), crime at night, 9 : 30 p.m., not sufficient light for identification, single witness, not

(Footnote No. 113 contd.)

body recovered from a tank was admissible to prove the fact that the skeleton was that of the deceased. Ayyanger J, explained the basic principles:

The question at issue in the case is identity of the skeleton. The identity could be established by its physical or visual examination with reference to any peculiar features in it which would mark it out as belonging to the person whose bones or skeleton it is stated to be. Similarly, the size of the bones, their angularity or curvature, the prominences or the recessions would be features which any examination and comparison might serve to establish "the identity of a thing" within the meaning of section 9. What we have in the present case is a photograph of that skull. That the skull would be admissible in evidence for establishing the identity of the deceased was not disputed and similarly a photograph of that skull. That a photograph of the deceased was admissible in evidence to prove his facial features, where these are facts in issue or relevant facts, is also beyond controversy. (What the witnesses have done) is to combine these two. The outlines of the skull which is seen in the superimposed photograph show the nasion prominences, the width of the jaw bones, and their shape, the general contours of the cheek bones, the position of the eye cavity and the comparison of these with the contours, etc., of the face of the deceased as seen in the photograph serve to prove that the features found in the skull and the features in the bones of the fact of the deceased are identical or at least not dissimilar. It appears to us that such evidence would clearly be within section 9 of the Evidence Act.

[s 9.13] Weight of identity evidence.—The Supreme Court in its decision in *Kanta Prasad v Delhi Admn.*[114] observed that "the weight to be attached to such identification would be a matter for the court of fact and it is not for this court to reassess the evidence unless exceptional grounds were established necessitating such a course." Following this in *Ramdeo Rai Yadav v State of Bihar,*[115] the Supreme Court laid down that "in the present case, both the trial court and the appellate court have assessed the evidence in the proper perspective and attached much importance to the evidence in regard to the identification of the appellant in finding him guilty. Before this court no exception ground has been established necessitating reassessment of that evidence."[116]

(Footnote No. 113 contd.)

sufficient to found conviction. *Umar Abdul Shakoor Sorathia v Intelligence Officer, Narcotic Control Bureau,* AIR 1999 SC 2562, evidence of identification by a witness by photograph outside the court was accepted for framing a charge, but not as substantive evidence unless he appeared before the court to testify on the matter. *Mohd. Iqbal M Shaikh v State of Maharashtra,* (1998) 4 SCC 494, accused shown to the witness before identification parade, evidence useless, identification in court subsequently was also inconsequential. *Prahlad Singh v State of MP,* (1997) 8 SCC 515 : AIR 1997 SC 3442 : 1997 Cr LJ 4078 : *Ganpat Singh v State of Rajasthan,* (1997) 11 SCC 565 : 1998 SCC (Cr) 201 were also to the same effect.

114. *Kanta Prasad v Delhi Admn,* 1958 SCR 1218 : 1958 Cr LJ 698.

115. *Ramdeo Rai Yadav v State of Bihar* , 1990 Cr LJ 1183.

116. Ibid, p 1186, per S Ratnavel Pandian J See also *Sheonath Bhar v State of UP,* 1990 Cr LJ 2423 All, where a perfectly executed TI parade was disbelieved. Proper identification is substantive evidence, *Ram Nath Mahto v State of Bihar,* AIR 1996 SC 2511 : 1996 Cr LJ 3585; *Praveen Kumer Kailashchandra Shukla v State,* 1997 Cr LJ 577 (Bom), Criminal Manual II, magistrate entitled to put questions to the witness to know whether he had seen the suspect after the incident. No serious defect in identification parade. Identification and conviction. *Ali Bahadur v State,* 1998 Cr LJ 2871 (All), accused persons were known to witnesses as they were residing in a village within a radius of two miles. No weight was given to their evidence of identification. Identification memo was also not proved by any of the witnesses or by the magistrate. *Ramesh Jogi v State,* 1998 Cr LJ 3861 (All), the

(Footnote No. 116 contd.)

The identification of the accused made in the court is substantive evidence, whereas identification at the test identification parade, though a primary evidence, is not substantive. It can be used only to corroborate the identification of the accused by the witness in the court.[117] Evidence of identification cannot be rejected on mere suspicion that the accused might have been shown to the witnesses. The fact that the witnesses identified the accused during the identification parade itself is a strong corroborative circumstance to the identification of the accused made by them in the court.[118]

[s 10] Things said or done by conspirator in reference to common design.—Where there is reasonable ground to believe[s 10.3] that two or more persons have conspired together to commit an offence or an actionable wrong, anything said, done or written by any one of such persons in reference to their common intention,[s 10.4] after the time when such intention was first entertained by any one of them, is a relevant fact as against each of the persons believed to be so conspiring, as well for the purpose of proving the existence of the conspiracy as for the purpose of showing that any such person was a party to it.

ILLUSTRATION

(i) Reasonable ground exists for believing that *A* has joined in a conspiracy to wage war against the [119][Government of India].

(ii) The facts that *B* procured arms in Europe for the purpose of the conspiracy, *C* collected money in Calcutta for a like object, *D* persuaded persons to join the conspiracy in Bombay, *E* published writings advocating the object in view at Agra, and F transmitted from Delhi to *G* at Cabul the money which *C* had collected at Calcutta, and the contents of a letter written by *H* giving an account of the conspiracy, are each relevant, both to prove the existence of the conspiracy, and to prove *A*'s complicity in it, although he may have been ignorant of all of them, and although the persons by whom they were done were strangers to him, and although they may have taken place before he joined the conspiracy or after he left it.

(Footnote No. 116 contd.)

accused resided in the same locality as the witness with a gap of only 2½ furlong. But the witness did not know him, nor he had the opportunity to see the face of the accused at the time of the incident. Evidence of identification, held unacceptable. *Ramesh Jogi v State*, 1998 Cr LJ 3861 (All), the witness ran away from the attacking accused to save his life, he did not tell the investigating officer that he turned back subsequently. He had no opportunity to identify the accused. The name of the accused was known for about two months before his arrest. Thus the witness might have known him before he identified him at the parade. The evidence was held to be of zero value.

117. *Dana Yadav v State of Bihar*, AIR 2002 SC 3325.

118. *Radha Ballabh v State of UP*, (1995) Supp 1 SCC 119 : 1995 SCC (Cri) 797; *Karam Singh v State*, AIR 1992 SC 1438 : 1992 Cr LJ 2333, no test identification parade conducted, conviction on the basis of identification in court, not safe, particularly where no overt act was attributed to him. *Rajesh Govind Jagesda v State of Maharashtra*, 2000 Cr LJ 350 : AIR 2000 SC 160, the witnesses said that one of the miscreants was sporting long hair and beard. No such person was there in the parade, possibly he could have shorn off. But even so the witnesses identified him. The court felt that because of the gap of 5 weeks between the arrest and identification, the possibility could not be ruled out that the culprit was shown to the witnesses in the meantime. The court did believe upon the explanation for the delay that no magistrate was available. The court said that it was not believable that in a city like Bombay there should be dearth of magistrates particularly when no magistrate was specifically designated for identification purposes. *Ganga Din v State of UP*, 2001 Cr LJ 1762 (All), robbery at night, FIR mentioned of only one torchlight, subsequently more torchlight mentioned, identification not reliable.

119. Subs. by the A.O. 1950, for "Queen".

Synopsis

COMMENT

This section refers to things said or done by conspirators in reference to the common design. To attract the applicability of this section, the court must have reasonable ground to believe that two or more persons had conspired together for committing an offence and then the evidence of action or statement made by one of the accused could be used as evidence against the other.[120]

[s 10.1] Principle.—The principle on which the acts and declarations of other conspirators, and acts done at different times, are admitted in evidence against the persons prosecuted, is, that, by the act of conspiring together, the conspirators have jointly assumed to themselves, as a body, the attitude of individuality, so far as regards the prosecution of the common design; thus rendering whatever is done or said by any one in furtherance of that design, a part of the *res gestae* and therefore the act of all. This section has been deliberately enacted in order to make such acts and statements of a co-conspirator admissible against the whole body of conspirators because of the nature of the crime. A conspiracy is hatched in secrecy, and executed in darkness. Naturally, therefore, it is not feasible for the prosecution to connect each isolated act or statement of one accused with the acts or statements of the others, unless there is a common bond linking all of them together.[121]

[s 10.2] Scope.—The operation of this section is strictly conditional upon there being reasonable ground to believe that two or more persons have conspired together to commit an offence.[122] There must be reason to believe that there was a conspiracy and the accused persons were members of that conspiracy.[123] The section refers to things said or done by a conspirator in reference to the common intention. Anything said, done or written "in reference to the common intention" is admissible, and therefore the contents of letters written by one in reference to the conspiracy is relevant against the others even though not written in support of it or in furtherance of it.[124] The expression "in reference to their common intention" in this section is very comprehensive with the result that anything said, done or written by a co-conspirator, after the conspiracy was formed, will be evidence against the other before he entered the field of conspiracy or after he left it. It cannot be used in favour of

---

120. *State of Karnataka v Selvi J Jayalalitha,* 2017(2) Scale 375 : (2017) 6 SCC 263 : LNIND 2017 SC 72.

121. *Badri Rai,* (1958) Pat 1504 SC: (1959) SCR 1141 : AIR 1958 SC 953 : 1958 Cr LJ 1434.

122. *Barindra Kumar Ghose v Emperor,* (1909) 37 Cal 467, 504; *Natwarlal v State of Bombay,* (1963) 65 Bom LR 660 SC.

123. *Chandrattan v Crown,* (1945) Kar 129.

124. *Emperor v Bhola Nath,* (1939) All 736.

the other party or for the purpose of showing that such a person was not a party to the conspiracy.[125]

However, where prosecution fails to substantiate the allegation of conspiracy against an accused, that accused cannot be called a co-conspirator so as to attract the provisions of section 10 of the Evidence Act, for the purposes of roping in the other accused persons.[126]

"An *overt act* committed by any one of the conspirators is sufficient on the general principles of agency to make it the act of all."[127]

[s 10.3] "Reasonable ground to believe".—The fact that the accused and the person who shot dead the deceased were together at a social gathering sometime before the shooting and having isolated themselves at the house top, were seen talking and avoided questions as to what they were talking about, was held by the Supreme Court to be sufficient to create a reason to believe that they might be conspiring about something. The accused was accordingly sentenced to death along with those who actually caused death though he was no where there at the place of shooting.[128]

[s 10.4] "Common intention"—[*Effect when common intention ceases*].—These words signify a common intention existing at the time when the thing was said, done or written by one of them. Things said, done or written while the conspiracy was on foot are relevant as evidence of the common intention, once reasonable ground has been shown to believe in its existence. Hence, any narrative or statement or confession made to a third party after the common intention or conspiracy was no longer operating and had ceased to exist, is not admissible against the other party. There is then no common intention of the conspirators to which the statement can have reference.[129] Lord Wright said:

> The words 'common intention' signify a common intention existing at the time when the thing was said, done or written by the one of them. Things said, done or written while the conspiracy was on foot are relevant as evidence of the common intention. But it would be very different matter to hold that any narrative or statement or confession made to a third party after the common intention or conspiracy was no longer operating and had ceased to exist is admissible against the other party. There is then no common intention of the conspirators to which the statement can have reference. In their lordships' judgment section 10 embodies this principle. That is the construction which has been rightly applied to section 10 in India, for instance, in *Emperor v Ganesh Raghunath*,[130] and *Emperor v*

125. *Bhagwan Swarup v State of Maharashtra*, AIR 1965 SC 682 : (1965) 1 Cr LJ 608; *Abhay Tuli v Lt Governor*, 1998 Cr LJ 3217 (Del), the petitioners who were not being prosecuted but only detained under COFEPOSA, section 10 was held not applicable to them. *Ram Narayan Popli v CBI*, (2003) 3 SCC 641 : AIR 2003 SC 2748 **followed in** *K Hashim v State of TN*, AIR 2005 SC 128 : (2005) 11 SCC 600 : 2005 Cr LJ 3950.

126. *S Arul Raja v State of TN*, (2010) 8 SCC 233.

127. Roscoe's Criminal Evidence, 482 (16th Edn), cited by Jagannath J in *Sardul Singh v State of Bombay*, AIR 1957 SC 747 at p 765 : 1957 Cr LJ 1325.

128. *Kehar Singh v State (Delhi Admn)*, AIR 1988 SC 1883 : 1989 Cr LJ 1 : (1988) 3 SCC 609 : 1988 SCC (Cri) 711. The court doubted on this point the ratio of the decision in *Sardar Sardul Singh v State of Maharashtra*, AIR 1965 SC 681 : (1965) 2 Cr LJ 8 : (1965) 1 SCR 65 : (1965) Cr LJ 608.

129. *Mirza Akbar v Emperor*, (1940) 43 Bom LR 20 PC : AIR 1940 PC 760.

130. *Emperor v Ganesh Raghunath*, AIR 1932 Bom 56 : 55 Bom 839 : 33 Bom LR 1150.

Abani.[131] In these cases the distinction was rightly drawn from communications between conspirators while the conspiracy was going on the statement made after arrest or after the conspiracy had ended, by way of description of events then past.

The agreement to conspire may be inferred from circumstances which raise a presumption of a concerted plan to carry out an unlawful design.[132] A conspiracy need not be established by proof which actually brings the parties together; but may be shown, like any other fact, by circumstantial evidence.

In the Bombay terror attack case, the appellant was apprehended while he was on a killing spree in execution of the objects of the conspiracy. The transcripts of the phone conversation of the other terrorists, who were associates of the appellant and their foreign collaborators, related to a time when the speakers were not only free but were actively involved in trying to fulfil the objects of their conspiracy. Therefore, it was held by Supreme Court that the transcripts were by no means any confessional statements made under arrest and they were fully covered by the provisions of section 10 of the Indian Evidence Act for the purposes of proving the factum of conspiracy amongst them.[133]

Under section 34 of the Indian Penal Code, when a criminal act is done by several persons, in furtherance of the common intention of all, each of such persons is liable for that act in the same manner as if it were done by him alone. This section makes admissible in evidence things said or done by a conspirator in reference to the common design. It applies to crimes as well as torts, i.e., to joint offenders as well as joint tort-feasors. It has no bearing on the question as to how far a conspiracy to commit an offence or actionable wrong is an offence under the Indian Penal Code. It is based upon the principle that, when several persons conspire to commit a crime or a tort, each makes the rest his agent to carry the plan into execution.[134]

[s 10.5] Confession.—A confession by a conspirator made to a Magistrate after arrest disclosing the existence of a conspiracy, its objects and the names of its members, is not admissible under this section against the co-conspirators jointly tried with him, but only under section 30.[135] When a person accused along with others voluntarily comes into the witness-box and deposes as a witness for defence, he is in the same position as an ordinary witness, and is, therefore, subject to cross-examination.[136]

---

131. *Emperor v Ganesh Raghunath*, (1911) 38 Cal 189 : 81 C 779 : 15 Cal WN 25. *Sidharth v State of Bihar*, AIR 2005 SC 4352 : (2005) 12 SCC 545, confession made after the common intention was no longer there, not admissible against others.

132. *Barindra Kumar Ghose v Emperor*, (1909) 37 Cal 467; *State of Kerala v P Sugathan*, 2000 Cr LJ 4584 : (2000) 8 SCC 203, intention to cause death under conspiracy not proved.

133. *Mohd. Ajmal Amir Kasab v State of Maharashtra*, (2012) 9 SCC 1.

134. *State of Delhi (NCT) v Navjot Sandhu*, (2005) 11 SCC 600 : AIR 2005 SC 3820, the principle on the basis of which hearsay evidence is made admissible is that there is mutual agency amongst the conspirators. *Jayendra Saraswathi Swamigal v State of TN*, AIR 2005 SC 716 : (2005) 2 SCC 13, statements made after their arrest, not admissible statements made or acts done after completion of conspiracy are not evidence against each other.

135. *Emperor v Abani Bhushan Chuckerbutty*, (1910) 38 Cal 169 (SB).

136. *People's Ins. Co v Sardul*, AIR 1962 Panj 101 and *Jibatch Shan v State of Bihar*, AIR 1965 Pat 331.

Once his evidence as a witness for the defence is on record and it speaks of a communication between one conspirator and the other during the existence of the conspiracy and relates to its implementation, it becomes relevant.[137]

The confessional statement of an accused who is not alive would not be of any use. It is not every statement of an accused person, whether amounting to confession or not, which can fall within the scope of section 10.[138]

In an enquiry into removal for misbehaviour of a member of the Public Service Commission, the evidence given by an official of the PSC was sought to be corroborated by a confessional statement made earlier by such official. The court said that even if the confessional statement was not evidence under section 10, it could not be totally discarded while considering the acceptability of his evidence on the point of misbehaviour.[139]

[s 10.6] Agreement but not direct meeting necessary.—"Though to establish the charge of conspiracy there must be agreement, there need not be proof of direct meeting or combination, nor need the parties be brought into each other's presence; the agreement may be inferred from circumstances raising a presumption of a common concerted plan to carry out the unlawful design. So again it is not necessary that all should have joined in the scheme from the first; those who come in at a later stage are equally guilty, provided the agreement be proved".[140]

[s 10.7] CASES.— From the evidence of conspiracy to assassinate the Prime Minister of India, Mr Rajiv Gandhi, the court said that it could not be inferred that the conspirators intended to disrupt the sovereignty of India.[141] Where four accused persons were alleged to have conspired together to commit offences of abduction and murder of children, a confession by one of them in respect of what the other accused persons did in reference to their common intention was admissible as evidence as much against the confessing accused as against the others.[142]

[s 11] When facts not otherwise relevant become relevant.—Facts not otherwise relevant are relevant—

(1) if they are inconsistent with any fact in issue[s 11.2] or relevant fact;

(2) if by themselves or in connection with other facts they make the existence or non-existence of any fact in issue or relevant fact highly probable or improbable.[s 11.3]

---

137. *Tribhuvan Nath v State of Maharashtra,* AIR 1973 SC 450 : 1972 Cr LJ 1277.

138. *State of Gujarat v Mohd. Atik,* 1998 Cr LJ 2251 : AIR 1998 SC 1686. *CBI v VC Shukla,* 1998 Cr LJ 1905 : AIR 1998 SC 1406, entries in books of account were alleged to be showing conspiracy among all the accused persons.

139. *Re Sayalee Sanjeev Joshi, Member, Maharashtra Public Service Commission,* AIR 2007 SC 2809 : (2007) 11 SCC 547.

140. Per Jenkins CJ, in *Barindra Kumar Ghose v Emperor,* (1909) 37 Cal 467, 507.

141. *State of TN v Nalini,* AIR 1999 SC 2640 : 1999 Cr LJ 3124 (SC) at p 3143-3144.

142. *State of Maharashtra v Damu Gopinath Shinde,* 2000 Cr LJ 2301 : AIR 2000 SC 1691 : (2000) 6 SCC 260.

ILLUSTRATIONS

(a) The question is, whether *A* committed a crime at Calcutta on a certain day. The fact that, on that day *A* was at Lahore is relevant.

The fact that, near the time when the crime was committed, *A* was at a distance from the place where it was committed, which would render it highly improbable, though not impossible, that he committed it, is relevant.

(b) The question is, whether *A* committed a crime.

The circumstances are such that the crime must have been committed either by *A, B, C* or *D.* Every fact which shows that the crime could have been committed by no one else and that it was not committed by either *B, C* or *D,* is relevant.

SYNOPSIS

COMMENT

[s 11.1] Principle.—In order that a collateral fact may be admissible as relevant under this section there are two requirements:

(1) that the collateral fact must itself be established by reasonably conclusive evidence; and

(2) that it must, when established, afford a reasonable presumption or inference as to the matter in dispute.[143]

Under certain circumstances, in certain cases, the judgment in a previous suit, to which one of the parties in the subsequent suit was not a party, may be admissible in evidence for certain purposes and with certain objects in the subsequent suit.[144] Except where they are judgments *in rem*, or where they relate to public matters, judgments not *inter partes* have been always held to be not *res judicata*, but they cannot be wholly excluded for other purposes insofar as they explain the nature of possession, or throw light on the motives or conduct of parties or identify property.[145] Evidence recorded by one forum cannot be read in relation to proceedings emanating from another forum.[146]

[s 11.2] "Inconsistent with any fact in issue".—*Plea of Alibi.*—The usual theory of essential inconsistency is that a certain fact cannot co-exist with the doing of the act in question, and, therefore, that if that fact is true of a person of whom the act is alleged, it is impossible that he should have done the act. Thus the fact of presence

---

143. *Khaver Sultan v Rukha Sultan,* (1904) 6 Bom LR 983.

144. *Tepu Khan v Rajani Mohun Das,* (1898) 25 Cal 522 FB, holding that *Gujju Lall v Fatteh Lall,* (1880) 6 Cal 171 FB, is materially qualified by the decisions of the Privy Council in *Ram Ranjan Chuckerbutty v Ram Narain Singh,* (1894) 22 IA 60: 22 Cal 533, and *Bitto Kunwar v Kesho Pershad,* (1897) 24 IA 10, 19 All 277.

145. Per Ranade J, in *Lakshman v Amrit,* (1900) 24 Bom 591, 599 : 2 Bom LR 386, 393.

146. *Sangeeta Balkrishna Kadam v Balkrishna Ramchandra Kadam,* AIR 1994 Bom 1.

elsewhere is essentially inconsistent with the presence at the place and time alleged, and therefore with personal participation in the act (theory of *alibi*).[147] The plea of "alibi" has to be weighed against the positive evidence led by the prosecution, i.e., not only the substantive evidence of the witness and the dying declarations, but also against the scientific evidence, viz., the DNA analysis, finger print analysis and bite marks analysis, the accuracy of which is scientifically acclaimed.[148] The Supreme Court has observed that it is well settled that the plea of *alibi* must be proved with absolute certainty so as to completely exclude the possibility of the presence of the person concerned at the place of occurrence.

[s 11.3] "Highly probable or improbable".—These words point out that the connection between the facts in issue and the collateral facts sought to be proved must be so mediate as to render the co-existence of the two *highly* probable.[149]

[s 11.4] CASES

[s 11.4.1] *Highly probable.*—Where the plaintiffs and some of the defendants were co-owners of certain properties, the question at issue being whether there was a partition between them, and whether under that partition the defendants came to be in possession of a specific property in lieu of their shares in all the properties, a petition and a written statement filed by the defendants in certain previous suits admitting the partition and the exclusive acquisition of the specific property were put in, but

147. *Dhananjoy Chatterjee v State of West Bengal*, (1994) 2 SCC 220, the plea of *alibi* must be proved by cogent and satisfactory evidence completely excluding the possibility of the presence of the accused at the scene of occurrence at the relevant time. The court found that the belated and vague plea of *alibi* was only an afterthought.

State of UP v Mukunde Singh, (1994) 2 SCC 191, evidence regarding was adduced for the first time in the High Court during pendency of appeal, found to be very unsatisfactory, on the basis of such *alibi* the testimony of eyewitnesses among whom there were two injured witnesses, could not be brushed aside. *Gurcharan Singh v State of Punjab*, 1994 Supp (1) SCC 515 : 1994 SCC (Cri) 512, the accused pleaded that he had been away from the scene of crime and had gone to purchase a thresher. The thresher dealer testified to that and showed a book but that was in an irregular shape with blank pages, no good evidence. *Rajesh Kumar v Dharamvi*, AIR 1997 SC 3769 : 1997 Cr LJ 2242, the accused claimed to have gone to an Advocate for consultation at the time when the occurrence took place. No contemporaneous document was produced by the Advocate showing the fact and timing of his visit. The plea of *alibi* was not accepted. *Binay Kumar Singh v State of Bihar*, AIR 1997 SC 322 : 1997 Cr LJ 362, strict proof is required for establishing plea of *alibi*. There was a finding of fact by the court below disbelieving the plea of *alibi*. The founding was based upon strong and sturdy reasons. The Supreme Court did not interfere. *CBI v VC Shukla*, 1998 Cr LJ 1905 : AIR 1998 SC 1406, entries in books of account alleged to be showing conspiracy among all the accused persons. The evidence of the prosecution witness was that one of the accused persons was known to the other and visited him on formal occasions. The witness did not speak even a word about the other accused persons. Held, section 10 could not be pushed into service for holding that a conspiracy existed. *State of Gujarat v Chavda Manaji Chelaji*, 2000 Cr LJ 1091 (Guj), where the presence of the accused at the scene of occurrence was satisfactorily established by the prosecution, the court would be slow to believe any counter evidence. *Jayanthbhai Bhenkarbhai v State of Gujarat*, 2002 Cr LJ 4734 (SC), proved that the accused was at some other place for quite some time during the day when the deceased was assaulted.

148. *Mukesh v State for NCT Delhi*, AIR 2017 SC 2161 : (2017) 6 SCC 1 : LNIND 2017 SC 252.

149. *Empress v MJ Vyapoory Moodeliar*, (1881) 6 Cal 655, 662. An application by the co-accused that the police had already arrested the accused and were then trying to implicate him falsely, was allowed to be taken along with his similar statement to the police under section 342 CrPC as making his allegation probable. *Satbir v State of Haryana*, AIR 1981 SC 2074; 1981 Cr LJ 1702 : (1981) 4 SCC 508 : 1981 SCC (Cri) 860.

objected to as inadmissible in evidence; it was held that the documents were admissible against those defendants as they made the existence of the partition, which was the fact in issue, highly probable. They were also admissible under section 21, clause (3).[150]

In a case where the previous suit was to recover a two-thirds share of the property in question, and the subsequent suit was by a different plaintiff to recover the remaining one-third share of the same property, it was held in the subsequent suit that the judgment in the previous suit was not admissible in evidence, the subject-matter in the two suits not being identical.[151]

In respect of the alleged hidden loss to a company in previous years, the finding of the Board for Industrial and Financial Reconstruction under Sick Industrial Companies (Special Provisions) Act, 1985 was that there was no prior period loss, it was held that the finding was relevant under section 11 read with section 43, though it was not conclusive and binding.[152] A rectified trust deed pursuant to the order of the court would certainly make the rectification order relevant under the provisions of section 11.[153]

In a suit for recovery of possession of a plot and declaration of title, the defendant denied the existence of the plot. The sale deed of the adjacent plot acknowledged the existence of the plot and the plaintiff's possession over it. This was held to be admissible in evidence under sections 11 and 13(a).[154]

[s 12] In suits for damages, facts tending to enable Court to determine amount are relevant.—In suits in which damages are claimed, any fact which will enable the Court to determine the amount of damages which ought to be awarded, is relevant.

COMMENT

[s 12.1] Principle.—This section enables the court to admit any facts which will help it to determine the amount of damages which ought to be awarded to a party. When damages are claimed in a suit, the amount of damages is a fact in issue. "Damages" are the pecuniary satisfaction which the plaintiff may obtain by success in an action. They are limited to the loss which the plaintiff has actually sustained.

Under this section it may be laid down generally that evidence tending to determine, i.e., to increase or diminish the damages, is admissible though not expressly involved in issue. Thus, in an action for breach of promise of marriage, the plaintiff may give evidence of the defendant's fortunes; for it obviously tends to prove the loss sustained by the plaintiff; but not in an action for adultery; nor for malicious prosecution. But the evidence of the amount of damages, which is the necessary and obvious result of

---

150. *Gyannessa v Mobarakannessa,* (1897) 25 Cal 210; *Nana v Shanker,* (1901) 3 Bom LR 465; *Naro Vinayak Patvardhan v Narharibin Raghunath,* (1891) 16 Bom 125; *Malkiat Singh v State of Punjab,* (1991) 4 SCC 341 : 1991 SCC (Cri) 976.

151. *Tepu Khan v Rajani Mohun Das,* (1898) 25 Cal 522 FB; *Mahender Singh Dhaiya v State (CBI),* 2003 Cr LJ 1908 (Del) husband charged with killing his wife, her letters to him were not taken to be relevant under this section as they did not indicate any probability.

152. *AK Khosla v TS Venkatesan,* 1992 Cr LJ 1448 (Cal).

153. *IT Commr., Kanpur v Kamla Town Trust,* AIR 1996 SC 619 : (1995) 4 SCC 151; *Sadhurajan v Sriramulu Naidu,* AIR 1999 Mad 377, recitals of boundaries in deeds not *inter partes* were held to be inadmissible in evidence unless the executants were examined.

154. *Kantilal v Shanti Devi,* AIR 1997 Raj 230.

the defendant's breach of contract, or of his tort, may be proved, though only alleged generally in the plaint.[155]

Where the plaintiff failed to adduce the best available evidence and this caused difficulty in assessing damages, this was held to be no ground for refusing damages or fixing nominal damages. It is for the court to determine the quantum of damages.[156]

Section 73 of the Indian Contract Act lays down the rule governing damages in actions on contract.

Section 55 of the Evidence Act lays down the conditions under which evidence of character may be given in civil cases with a view to the award of damages.

In a claim for damages for employment injury, fresh evidence as to the plaintiff's credibility was held to be inadmissible.[157]

[s 13] Facts relevant when right or custom is in question.—Where the question is as to the existence of any right[s 13.2] or custom,[s 13.3] the following facts are relevant.

(a) any transaction[s 13.4] by which the right or custom in question was created, claimed,[s 13.5] modified, recognized,[s 13.7] asserted or denied, or which was inconsistent with its existence.

(b) particular instances in which the right or custom was claimed, recognized or exercised, or in which its exercise was disputed, asserted or departed from.

ILLUSTRATION

The question is, whether *A* has a right to a fishery. A deed conferring the fishery on *A*'s ancestors, a mortgage of the fishery by *A*'s father, a subsequent grant of the fishery by *A*'s father, irreconcilable with the mortgage, particular instances in which *A*'s father exercised the right, or in which the exercise of the right was stopped by *A*'s neighbours, are relevant facts.

SYNOPSIS

COMMENT

[s 13.1] Principle.—The cases this section is intended to meet are those in which the right or custom in question is regarded as capable of surviving repeated instances of its assertion and denial, where transactions may be supposed to have gone on modifying, asserting, denying, creating, recognizing it, or being inconsistent with its existence,

155. Norton, 124.

156. *Shaikh Gafoor v State of Maharashtra*, AIR 2008 NOC 1637 (Bom), digging cannal caused damage to the crops on the plaintiff's adjoining land.

157. *Owens v Redpath Offshore (South) Ltd*, 1998 CLY p 92 (323). The court **followed** *Mulholland v Mitchell*, (1971) AC 666 : (1971) CLY 3232 and *Coghlan v Cumberland*, (1898) 1 Ch 704.

leaving it, after all that has been given in evidence, fair matter for judicial consideration, as to whether the court should or should not decree it.[158]

[s 13.2] "Right".—The rights contemplated by this section are plainly conceived as admitting of proof by cumulative instances and transactions, and not by a single and decisive and final way, namely the terms of a document. The whole context indicates that the section is dealing with continuing rights which may be interrupted without being necessarily destroyed. The term "right" comprehends every right known to the law.[159] It includes both corporeal and incorporeal rights including "a right of ownership".[160] This is the view of the Bombay, the Madras and the Allahabad High Courts. The Calcutta High Court has, however, held that the term "right" includes only incorporeal rights.[161] But its decisions are conflicting.[162] The Patna High Court agreed with the Bombay, the Madras and the Allahabad High Courts in one case,[163] but, in a subsequent case, a single Judge has adopted the view of the Calcutta High Court.[164]

The section is not confined to public rights but covers private rights also, e.g., see the illustration to the section. The way in which a property and its income have been treated has been held relevant to consider whether it is secular or religious.[165] Right to perform Kali puja can be proved by showing that it was reasonable, ancient, and exercised openly and peaceably. It is not necessary to prove exercise of the right since time immemorial.[166] The court cited the opinion of the Privy Council that the true legal basis of such right lies in custom, and customary right can be claimed only in respect of the inhabitants of a district, and not of the public at large.[167]

The court also cited the opinion of the Supreme Court as to what is meant by an immemorial custom:[168] A phenomenon is said to be happening from time immemorial when the date of its commencement is shrouded in the merits of antiquity.

"Having regard to the circumstances under which local customs have arisen, and do arise in India, both with reference to Muslims and Hindus and the case and frequency with which people migrate from one district or province to another, it would, in their Lordships' opinion, create great perplexity in the already uncertain character of

---

158. *Mahamad v Hasan,* (1906) 31 Bom 143 : 9 Bom LR 65.

159. Per Beaman J, in *Mahamad v Hasan,* (1906) 31 Bom 143, 154, 155 : 9 Bom LR 65, 75.

160. *The Collector of Gorakhpur v Palakdhari Singh,* (1889) 12 All 1 FB; *Ranchhoddas Krishnadas v Bapu Narhar,* (1886) 10 Bom 439; *Lakshman v Amrit,* (1900) 24 Bom 591, 599 : 2 Bom LR 386; *Ramasami v Appavu,* (1887) 12 Mad 9; *Venkatasami v Venkatreddi,* (1891) 15 Mad 12; *Vythilinga v Venkatachala,* (1892) 16 Mad 194.

161. *Gujju Lall v Fatteh Lall,* (1880) 6 Cal 171 FB; *Kalidhun Chuttapadhya v Shiba Nath Chuttapadhya,* (1882) 8 Cal 483, 505 FB.

162. See *Tepu Khan v Rajani Mohun Das,* (1898) 25 Cal 522 FB, and the judgment of Mitter J, in *Gujju Lall v Fatteh Lall,* (1880) 6 Cal 171 FB.

163. *Sabran Sheikh v Odoy Mahto,* (1922) 1 Pat 375.

164. *Ram Kishun v Niranjan Pande,* (1932) 12 Pat 285.

165. *Phani Bhusandas v Kenaram Bhaniya,* AIR 1980 Cal 255.

166. *Purna Chandra v Durlav Chandra,* AIR 1980 Cal 11. *Radha Krishna Kandolkar v Tukaram,* AIR 1991 Bom 119, use of a right (drawing water) for 30 years does not by itself create a customary right.

167. *Lakshmidhar Misra v Rangalal,* AIR 1950 PC 56. Their Lordships held in this case that the villagers acquired a customary right in respect of a portion of the land for cremation purposes.

168. *Patneedi Rudrayya v Velu Gubantala,* AIR 1961 SC 1821.

customary law to require that, in every case the antiquity of a custom must be carried back to a period which is beyond the memory of man."[169]

Previous judicial determination of the basis of valuation of land can be cited in a subsequent acquisition matter.[170]

[s 13.3] "Custom".—A custom is a rule which in a particular family or in a particular district, has from long usage obtained the force of law.[171] The English rule that "a custom, in order that it may be legal and binding, must have been used so long that the memory of man runneth not to the contrary" does not apply to conditions in India. A custom observed in a particular district derives its force from the fact that it has, from long usage, obtained in that district the force of law. It must be ancient, but it is not of the essence of this rule that its antiquity must in every case be carried back to a period beyond the memory of man. It will depend upon the circumstances of each case what antiquity must be established before the custom can be accepted. What is necessary to be proved is that the usage has been acted upon in practice for such a long period and with such invariability as to show that it has, by common consent, been submitted to as the established governing rule of the particular district.[172]

A custom to be recognized by a court should be—

(1) Ancient,

(2) continuous and uniform,

(3) reasonable

(4) certain,

(5) compulsory and not optional,

(6) peaceable, and

(7) not immoral.

The customs which will be recognized under the Act will be—

(1) general, e.g., customs common to a class of people living in the same district or belonging to the same caste or community;

(2) public, i.e., any custom which is a matter of public interest;

(3) private, e.g., family customs and usages. The burden of proving a custom lies on the party setting it up.

In order to prove a custom—

(1) The evidence should be such as to prove the uniformity and continuity of the usage and the conviction of those *following it that they were acting in accordance with law,* and this conviction must be inferred from the evidence. Oral evidence of witnesses who depose to having heard of the custom from their deceased ancestors is admissible.[173]

169. For another Privy Council decision see *Baba Narayan v Sabossa,* AIR 1943 PC 111.
170. *State of Bihar v Mosafir Thakur,* AIR 1980 Pat 40.
171. *Hurpurshad v Sheo Dyal,* (1876) 3 IA 259, 285.
172. *Subhani v Nawab,* (1940) 43 Bom LR 432: (1941) 22 Lah 154: 68 IA 1.
173. *Sri Krishan Datt v Ahmadi Bibi,* (1934) 57 All 588.

(2) Evidence of acts of the kind, acquiescence in those acts, their publicity, decisions of courts, or even of panchayats upholding such acts, the statements of experienced and competent persons of their belief that such acts were legal and valid will all be admissible, but it is obvious that, although admissible, evidence of this latter kind will be of little weight if unsupported by actual examples of the usage asserted.[174]

It is incumbent on a party setting up a custom to allege and prove the custom on which he relies and it is not any theory of custom or deductions from other customs which can be made a rule of decision but only any custom applicable to the parties concerned that can be the rule of decision in a particular case. Custom cannot be extended by analogy and it cannot be established by a *priori* methods.[175]

The rule of custom should prevail in all cases and if any aberrations have to be corrected such correction must take the court in the direction of re-establishing the rule of custom.[176]

A trade usage or custom may be proved in the same way as a family custom, except that it is unnecessary to show that such a custom is either ancient or continuous. A trade usage may be still in course of growth; it may require evidence for its support in each case; but in the result it is enough if it appears to be so well known and acquiesced in, that it may be reasonably presumed to have been an ingredient tacitly imported by the parties into their contract.[177]

There was a custom of appointing the senior most trustee as the President of a trust, in absence of any other provision, it was held that the senior most trustee would be entitled to assume the office of President, even though the custom was not of a sufficiently long standing.[178]

[s 13.4] "Transaction".—A transaction, in the ordinary sense of the word, is some business or dealing which is carried on or transacted between two or more persons.

The term "transaction" is not confined to a dealing with property between two persons *inter vivos*, but includes a testamentary dealing with the property.[179]

Whether judgments not *inter partes* (between the same parties) are admissible in evidence under this section as "transactions" [clause (a)] or "particular instances" [clause (b)] gave rise to conflicting decisions,[180] but, in view of subsequent pronouncements

---

174. *Gopalayyan v Raghupatiyyan*, (1873) 7 Mad HCR 250, 254.

175. *Saraswathi Ammal v Jagadambal*, AIR 1953 SC 201 : 1953 SCR 939.

176. *Rajendra Ram v Devendra Doss*, AIR 1973 SC 268 : (1973) 1 SCC 14, approving *Annasami Pillai v Ramakrishna Mudaliar*, (1900) 24 Mad 219.

177. *Juggomohun Ghose v Manickchund*, (1859) 7 Moo Ind App 263, 282. See also *Rajendra Ram v Devendra Das*, AIR 1973 SC 268 : (1973) 1 SCC 14, as to proof of customs.

178. *Homi P Ranina v Eruch B Desai*, AIR 1996 Bom 141, following *Harihar Prasad v Balmiki Prasad*, AIR 1975 SC 733 : (1995) 1 SCC 212 and *Gokal Chand v Pravin Kumari*, AIR 1952 SC 231, 234 : 1952 SCR 825.

179. *Chandrakant v Sharatchandra*, (1954) MB 123.

180. *Gujju Lall v Fatteh Lall*, (1880) 6 Cal 171 FB; approved of in *Surender Nath Pal Chowdhry v Brojo Nath Pal Chowdhry*, (1886) 13 Cal 352 FB; *Subramanyan v Paramaswaran*, (1887) 11 Mad 116; *Nilakanta v Imamsahib*, (1892) 16 Mad 361; *Ranchhoddas Krishnadas v Bapu Narhar*, (1886) 10 Bom 439; *Ram Kishun v Niranjan Pande*, (1932) 12 Pat 285; *Indar Singh v Fateh Singh*, (1920) 1 Lah 540; *Shankar v Kesheo*, (1929) 26 NLR 33 FB. Not approved of in the *Collector of Gorakhpur v Palakdhari Singh*, (1889) 12 All 1 FB; *Tepu Khan v Rajani Mohun Das*, (1898) 25 Cal 522 FB; *Lakshman v Amrit*, (1900) 24 Bom 591: 2 Bom LR 386; *Govindji v Chhotalal*, (1900) 2 Bom LR 651; *Mahamad v Hasan*, (1906) 31 Bom 143: 9 Bom LR 65; *Devidatt v Shriram Narayandas*, (1931) 56 Bom 324: 34 Bom LR 236; *Shreemati Purnima Debya v Nand Lal Ojha*, (1931) 11 Pat 50.

of the Judicial Committee, under certain circumstances, in certain cases, the judgment in a previous suit, to which one of the parties in a subsequent suit was not a party, may be admissible in evidence for certain purposes and with certain objects in the subsequent suit.[181]

Police orders made under the provisions of the Code of Criminal Procedure to prevent breaches of the peace, in cases of dispute as to immovable property are held admissible in evidence under this section to show the fact that such orders were made. This necessarily makes them evidence of the facts appearing on the orders themselves, *viz.*, who the parties to the dispute were; what the land in dispute was; and who was declared entitled to retain possession. For this purpose and to this extent such orders are admissible in evidence for and against anyone, when the fact of possession at the date of the order has to be ascertained.[182]

Judgments not *inter partes* might be admissible in evidence as establishing a particular transaction, if any, by which the relevant right was asserted, recognised, claimed or denied, but in no case the reasons and the findings of fact arrived at in them would be admissible in evidence.[183]

The judgment of a court is a document which usually contains both a description of the litigation and the adjudication, with the reasons for the adjudication. The narrative given in a judgment not *inter partes* of the nature of the litigation, the names of the parties and witnesses, the rival assertions or claims, and the character of the evidence oral and documentary is admissible under section 35 to prove those facts, if relevant under this or any other section. The court's written judgment is often the most convenient means of proof, and, in the case of an old proceeding, sometimes the only available proof of these matters. Thus a statement in a decree that a certain pedigree table had been put in evidence by one of the parties was admitted in evidence of that fact under section 35 in a subsequent suit between other parties.[184]

In the case of an adjudication not *inter partes* its existence alone is admissible under section 43, and only in cases where such existence is relevant. Its correctness or incorrectness is not admissible, nor are the reasons on which it is based. Although a judgment (an adjudication) in a proceeding A *v* B may perhaps be used in a subsequent proceeding A and B *v* C as evidence that there was a decision on a certain point, it cannot be used as evidence that there was an accurate decision based on true facts.[185]

A finding of fact arrived at on the evidence in one case is not evidence of that fact in another case between different parties.[186] So far as regards the truth of the matter

---

181. *Ram Ranjan Chuckerbutty v Ram Narain Singh,* (1984) 22 IA 60: 22 Cal 533; *Bitto Kunwar v Kesho Pershad,* (1897) 24 IA 10: 19 All 277.

182. *Dinomoni Chowdhrani v Brojo Mohini Chowdhrani,* (1901) 29 IA 24, 33: 4 Bom LR 167: 29 Cal 187.

183. *Gajanfar Ali Khan v Province of Assam,* (1944) 1 Cal 203. See also *Hira Lal v Hari Narain,* AIR 1964 All 302, where it is held that it is inherent in the scheme of this section that only a judgment which has become final can be said to be a transaction or an instance for the purposes of this section.

184. *Collector of Gorakhpur v Ram Sundar Mal,* (1934) 61 IA 286: 36 Bom LR 867: 56 All 468.

185. *Gobinda Narayan Singh v Sham Lal Singh,* (1931) 58 IA 125, 136: 33 Bom LR 885: 58 Cal 1187; *Devidatt v Shriram Narayandas,* (1931) 56 Bom 324: 34 Bom LR 236.

186. *Gopika Raman Roy v Atal Singh,* (1929) 56 IA 119: 31 Bom LR 734: 56 Cal 1003, followed in *Shankar v Kesheo,* (1929) 26 NLR 33 FB.

decided, a judgment is not admissible as evidence against one who is a stranger to the suit. In a suit for possession of land a judgment in a previous suit, though admissible as evidence of assertion of a right to the land, is not evidence of the right as against a stranger.[187] Where the right of a party has been concluded by a judgment that judgment is admissible to prove that fact.[188]

The original owner (mortgager) bequeathed the property under a will in favour of the plaintiff. The legal heirs of the original owner could not assail the validity of the will. The title became declared in favour of the plaintiff. The judgment was held to be admissible in the subsequent suit for redemption of the mortgage even though the mortgagee was not a party to the earlier suit. The judgment had the effect of being a part of the transaction of will.[189]

[s 13.5] "Claimed".—This word indicates that the right is asserted to the knowledge and in the presence of the person whose right will be affected by the establishment of the claim. The mere assertion of a right in a document to which the person against whom the right is asserted is not a party and of which he knows nothing is not to claim the right.[190]

[s 13.6] Judgment.—"It may be taken to be fairly settled that the judgment in a previous suit though not *inter partes* is admissible in proof of a transaction or a particular instance in which the relationship was asserted and recognised or denied. A judgment in the previous suit though not conclusive is admissible in evidence like any other fact to be weighed in the balance. It is not the correctness of the previous decision but the fact that there has been a previous decision that is established by the judgment".[191] The court reviewed earlier authorities.[192]

In a Calcutta case[193] a question arose whether a judgment not *inter partes* was admissible under section 13 and Garth CJ expressed the view that the former judgment was not a transaction and that the right claimed in the particular suit was not a right within the meaning of section 13. A Full Bench of the Allahabad High Court[194] came to a different conclusion and held that such judgments were admissible under section 13. Their Lordships observed that the majority view of the Calcutta decision had put too narrow a construction on the word "right" as used in section 13 and that the term includes not only incorporated rights, but also right of ownership. It was further held that though the judgment itself was not a transaction, the suit or the litigation in which it was pronounced might be treated as a transaction or an instance in which a

187. *Kesheo Prasad v Bhagjogna Kuer,* (1937) 39 Bom LR 731: 16 Pat 258 PC.
188. *Maroti v Jagannathdas,* (1940) Nag 699.
189. *Sohan Singh v Murti Rani,* AIR 2008 P&H 129 : (2008) 2 PLR 591.
190. *Raja Sri Sri Jyoti Prasad Singh Deo v Bharat Shah Babu,* (1935) 15 Pat 260.
191. *Rama Chandra v Gadhadhar Mohapatra,* AIR 1980 Ori 54 citing *Gopika Raman Roy v Satpal Singh,* AIR 1929 PC 99; *Gobinda Narayan Singh v Sham Lal Singh,* AIR 1931 PC 89; *Kesho Pd. Singh v Bhagjogna,* AIR 1937 PC 69. The Calcutta High Court in *Gujja Lal v Fatteh Lal* (1881) ILR 6 Cal 171 had held a judgment not relevant under section 13; The Allahabad High Court had held otherwise : *Collector ofGorakhpur v Palakdhari Singh,* (1890) ILR 12 All 1 FB The Supreme Court in *Sital Das v Sant Ram,* AIR 1954 SC 606 has held a judgment on the right to be Mohunt to be relevant.
192. At p 56, AIR 1980 Ori.
193. *Gujja Lal v Fatteh Lal,* (1881) ILR 6 Cal 171.
194. *Collector of Gorakhpur v Palakdhari Singh,* 1890 ILR 12 All 1.

right may have been asserted, acknowledged or denied. In the case of *Sital Das v Sant Ram,*[195] the Supreme Court held that in a dispute as to the succession to the office of a Mohunt, a previous judgment in a suit by the former Mohunt is admissible as a transaction in which a person from whom one of the parties purported to derive his title, asserted his right as a spiritual collateral of the former Mohunt and on that footing got a decree. Their Lordships also observed that although the judgment in the previous suit was not conclusive and had to be weighed and appraised for what it is worth, it could be used in support of the oral evidence adduced in the case. The Andhra Pradesh High Court[196] held that a previous judgment was admissible under section 13 to show that the right of the plaintiff as the son of the sixth defendant was claimed and recognised. In one of the cases[197] a judgment not *inter partes* in a previous case in which an adoption was upheld was held to be a relevant piece of evidence under section 13. In still another case[198] section 13 was held applicable to the class of cases where the alleged relationship admitted of assertion, denial and recognition. A judgment in which the illegitimacy of a person was recognised was held to be admissible under section 13,[199] where the question of his legitimacy was in issue in a subsequent suit.

In view of these authorities, it may be taken to be fairly settled that the judgment in a previous suit though not *inter partes*, is admissible in evidence like any other fact to be weighed in the balance. It is not the correctness of the previous decision but the fact that there has been a previous decision that is established by the judgment. The finding of fact arrived at on the evidence of one case cannot be evidence of that fact in another case.[200]

A judgment, not *inter partes*, and mentioning a fact not relevant in that case, is inadmissible in evidence to prove that fact in a subsequent case. Thus the previous decision not *inter partes*, in which it was mentioned that N took F in adoption, when the fact of adoption was not relevant in that case is inadmissible to prove F's adoption to N in a subsequent case.[201]

In a case of sale of property which was under attachment, the District Court gave the finding that the decree in respect of some other portion of the property was vitiated by fraud. In a suit for permanent injunction in respect of the other portion, it was held that the earlier finding might not operate as *res judicata* but it was admissible under section 13 as the transaction was the same and section 43 was no bar.[202]

A judgment is relevant if it is earlier to the case even though the case was filed subsequently.[203] The plaintiff filed a suit in his capacity as a lessee of the suit property

---

195. *Sital Das v Sant Ram,* AIR 1954 SC 606.

196. *Ajjarrapu Subbarao v Pallavenkata Rama Ras,* AIR 1964 AP 58.

197. *Yamunabai v Dhannalal,* (1929) 114 IC 616.

198. *Secy. of State for India v Subraya,* 115 Mad WN 962; *Tirumala Tirupati Devasthanam v KM Krishnaiah,* AIR 1998 SC 1132 : (1998) 3 SCC 331, a judgment was produced in evidence to prove title to the suit property, it was held to be admissible in evidence though the plaintiff was not a party to the suit.

199. *Raj Fateh Singh v Baldeo Singh,* (1928) 109 IC 310 (Oudh).

200. *Ajjarrapu Subbarao v Pallowenkata Rawa Rao,* AIR 1964 AP 58.

201. *Dalu v Juhar Mal,* (1951) 1 Raj 166.

202. *N Subbhakaran v K Rajmany,* 1996 AIHC 1024 (Ker), **following** *Sital Das v Sant Rams,* AIR 1954 SC 606.

203. *Qazi Sharaf v Dau Singh,* AIR 1996 Raj 227.

for mandatory injunction for protection of his possession. The defendant claimed that he was in possession of the property. An earlier judgment was cited by the plaintiff in which the lessor's (temple) proceedings for recovery of possession were dismissed. He also cited another judgment in which his right to possession was decreed and the temple was restrained from interfering with his possession. The court said that these judgments could not be said to be irrelevant. They could not be said to be irrelevant only because they were not *inter-partes*, particularly when the defendant was claiming to be in possession of the property.[204]

Judgments which support a plea of *res judicata* under section 11, Code of Civil Procedure, or that of *autrefois acquit* under section 300, Code of Criminal Procedure, 1973, judgments in *rem,* and judgments which refer to matters of public nature, are expressly made relevant by the Act. But other judgments are irrelevant, unless their existence is either a fact in issue or relevant under some other section of the Act. That there are cases where the existence of a judgment might become a fact in issue or a relevant fact under some other section of the Act, is perfectly clear from the illustrations to section 43.

[s 13.7] "Recognized".—Judicial recognition of a custom is relevant under this section as an instance of the custom being recognised.[205] But a judicial decision is far from having the same importance as a clear-cut instance of custom recognised by the parties themselves.[206]

[s 13.8] Will.—The validity of a will was directly in question in an earlier proceedings in which its validity was upheld. It was held that such fact could not be discarded by the court in subsequent proceedings. This was particularly so because all the reasons on which wills are generally discarded were found to be missing in the earlier proceedings. The validity of a will which has been determined in an earlier proceedings has a high probative content. It is a valid document to be considered as a sound piece of evidence under section 13.[207]

[s 14] Facts showing existence of state of mind, or of body, or bodily feeling.—Facts showing the existence of any state of mind, such as intention, knowledge, good faith, negligence, rashness, ill-will or good-will towards any particular person, or showing the existence of any state of body or bodily feeling, are relevant, when the existence of any such state of mind or body or bodily feeling is in issue, or relevant.

[208]**[*Explanation* 1.—A fact relevant as showing the existence of a relevant state of mind must show that the state of mind exists, not generally, but in reference to the particular matter in question.**

***Explanation* 2.—But where, upon the trial of a person accused of an offence, the previous commission by the accused of an offence is relevant within the meaning of this section, the previous conviction of such person shall also be a relevant fact.]**

---

204. *S Govindarasu Udayar v Pattu,* AIR 1999 Mad 435.
205. *Mst Janat Bibi v Ghulam Hussain,* (1934) 16 Lah 307.
206. *Dewan Singh v Mst. Santi,* (1936) 17 Lah 809.
207. *Ajmer Singh v Gurdev Singh,* AIR 2010 NOC 700 (P&H).
208. Subs. by Act 3 of 1891, section 1, for Explanation.

ILLUSTRATIONS

(a) A is accused of receiving stolen goods knowing them to be stolen. It is proved that he was in possession of a particular stolen article.

The fact that, at the same time, he was in possession of many other stolen articles is relevant, as tending to show that he knew each and all of the articles of which he was in possession to be stolen.

(b) [209][A is accused of fraudulently delivering to another person a counterfeit coin which, at the time when he delivered it, he knew to be counterfeit.

The fact that, at the time of its delivery, *A* was possessed of a number of other pieces of counterfeit coin is relevant.

The fact that *A* had been previously convicted of delivering to another person as genuine a counterfeit coin knowing it to be counterfeit is relevant.]

(c) *A* sues *B* for damage done by a dog of *B*'s, which *B* knew to be ferocious.

The facts that the dog had previously bitten X, Y and Z, and that they had made complaints to *B*, are relevant.

(d) The question is, whether *A*, the acceptor of a bill of exchange, knew that the name of the payee was fictitious.

The fact that *A* had accepted other bills drawn in the same manner before they could have been transmitted to him by the payee if the payee had been a real person, is relevant as showing that *A* knew that the payee was a fictitious person.

(e) A is accused of defaming *B* by publishing an imputation intended to harm the reputation of *B*.

The fact of previous publications by *A* respecting *B*, showing ill-will on the part of *A* towards *B* is relevant as proving *A*'s intention to harm *B*'s reputation by the particular publication in question.

The facts that there was no previous quarrel between *A* and *B*, and that *A* repeated the matter complained of as he heard it, are relevant, as showing that *A* did not intend to harm the reputation of *B*.

(f) A is sued by *B* for fraudulently representing to *B* that *C* was solvent, whereby *B*, being induced to trust *C*, who was insolvent, suffered loss.

The fact that at the time when *A* represented *C* to be solvent, *C* was supposed to be solvent by his neighbours and by persons dealing with him, is relevant, as showing that *A* made the representation in good faith.

(g) A is sued by *B* for the price of work done by *B*, upon a house of which *A* is owner, by the order of *C*, a contractor.

A's defence is that *B*'s contract was with *C*.

The fact that *A* paid *C* for the work in question is relevant, as proving that *A* did, in good faith, make over to *C* the management of the work in question, so that *C* was in a position to contract with *B* on *C*'s own account, and not as agent for *A*.

(h) A is accused of the dishonest misappropriation of property which he had found, and the question is whether, when he appropriated it, he believed in good faith that the real owner could not be found.

---

209. Subs. by Act 3 of 1891, section 1, for Illustration (b).

The fact that public notice of the loss of the property had been given in the place where *A* was, is relevant, as showing that *A* did not in good faith believe that the real owner of the property could not be found.

The fact that *A* knew, or had reason to believe, that the notice was given fraudulently by *C*, who had heard of the loss of the property and wished to set up a false claim to it, is relevant as showing that the fact that *A* knew of the notice did not disprove *A*'s good faith.

(i) A is charged with shooting at *B* with intent to kill him. In order to show *A*'s intent the fact of *A*'s having previously shot at *B* may be proved.

(j) *A* is charged with sending threatening letters to *B*. Threatening letters previously sent by *A* to *B* may be proved, as showing the intention of the letters.

(k) The question is, whether *A* has been guilty of cruelty towards *B*, his wife.

Expressions of their feeling towards each other shortly before or after the alleged cruelty are relevant facts.

(l) The question is, whether *A*'s death was caused by poison.

Statements made by *A* during his illness as to his symptoms are relevant facts.

(m) The question is, what was the state of *A*'s health at the time when an assurance on his life was effected.

(n) Statements made by *A* as to the state of his health at or near the time in question are relevant facts.

(o) *A* sues *B* for negligence in providing him with a carriage for hire not reasonably fit for use, whereby *A* was injured.

The fact that *B*'s attention was drawn on other occasions to the defect of that particular carriage is relevant.

The fact that *B* was habitually negligent about the carriages which he let to hire is irrelevant.

(p) *A* is tried for the murder of *B* by intentionally shooting him dead.

The fact that *A* on other occasions shot at *B* is relevant as showing his intention to shoot *B*. The fact that *A* was in the habit of shooting at people with intent to murder them is irrelevant.

(q) *A* is tried for a crime.

The fact that he said something indicating an intention to commit that particular crime is relevant.

The fact that he said something indicating a general disposition to commit crimes of that class is irrelevant.

SYNOPSIS

COMMENTS

[s 14.1] Principle.—This section declares that facts which show the existence of any state of (1) mind, *viz.*, intention, knowledge, good faith, negligence, rashness, ill-will, good-will or (2) body or (3) bodily feeling are relevant when such state of mind or body or bodily feeling is in issue or relevant.

Intention, knowledge, and similar other states of mind, are matters of cogent inquiry in criminal cases; in some civil cases they are very material, e.g., in cases of malicious prosecution, fraud, negligence etc.

Where the question is as to knowledge, intent, motive, or any bodily or mental state, evidence of other acts done, showing the existence of such knowledge, intent, motive, or bodily or mental state, are admissible, even though it involves the proof of other crimes. Evidence admitted for such purpose must be confined within the limits for which it is admitted.

See the illustrations. Illustrations (e), (i) and (j) deal with intention; (a), (b), (c) and (d) with knowledge; (f), (g) and (h), with good faith; (n) with negligence and knowledge; (k), (l) and (m), with mental and bodily feeling. To explain states of mind evidence is admissible though it does not otherwise bear upon the issue to be tried.

The principle on which evidence of similar acts is admissible is not to show that because the defendant has committed one crime therefore he would be likely to commit another, but to establish the *animus* of the act and rebut, by anticipation, the obvious defences, of ignorance, accident, mistake or other innocent state of mind.[210]

What is "intended" is a matter of the mind. Therefore, unless actions speak for themselves, no presumption can be drawn on the "intent" of a party. When a party expresses its design repeatedly in writing, no contrary assumption should normally be drawn. No one can be presumed or deemed to be intending something, which is contrary to law. Obviously therefore, "intent" has its limitations also, confining it within the confines of lawfulness.[211]

Where a man is prosecuted for making speeches promoting hatred and enmity between different communities (section 153A, Indian Penal Code), previous speeches made by him are admissible in evidence against him to show his intention in making the speeches which are the subject-matter of the proceedings.[212]

[s 14.2] Scope.—The conduct of each individual co-conspirator including his acts, writings and statements irrespective of the time to which it relates can be relied on by the prosecution to show the criminality of the intention of the individual accused with reference to his proved participation in the alleged conspiracy to rebut a probable defence that the participation, though proved, was innocent. Such evidence is admissible under this section.[213]

Jagannath Das J said: There can be no doubt that such conduct can be relied on by the prosecution to show the criminality of the intention of the individual accused with reference to his proved participation in the alleged conspiracy, that is, to rebut a probable defence *viz.*, that the participation was innocent.

[s 14.3] Specific state of mind, not general.—*[Explanation 1]*.—Illustrations (n), (o) and (p) explain the purport of this Explanation. Under this Explanation evidence of general reputation is excluded. The evidence relating to the state of mind of a person must show that the state of mind exists not generally but in reference to the

210. *Phipson*, 7th Edn, p 167.
211. *Sahara India Real Estate Corp Ltd v SEBI*, (2013) 1 SCC 1, at para 291-292.
212. *Jagannath Prasad v Crown*, (1942) Nag 62.
213. *Sardul Singh Caveeshar v State of Bombay*, (1958) SCR 161.

particular matter in question. Evidence of general disposition, habit or tendencies is inadmissible.[214] Anything having a distinct and immediate reference to the particular matter in question is admissible.[215] See illustrations (a) and (b).

[s 14.4] Previous convictions—*[Explanation 2]*.—This Explanation distinctly states that, where the previous commission of an offence is relevant, the previous conviction of such person should also be a relevant fact. The Explanation is a particular application of the general rule contained in the section itself. Previous convictions become relevant when the existence of any state of mind, or body, or bodily feeling, is in issue or relevant.[216] See illustrations (e) and (f) to section 43.

[s 15] Facts bearing on question whether act was accidental or intentional.—When there is a question whether an act was accidental or intentional, [217][or done with a particular knowledge or intention], the fact that such act formed part of a series of similar occurrences, in each of which the person doing the act was concerned, is relevant.

ILLUSTRATIONS

(a) A is accused of burning down his house in order to obtain money for which it is insured.

The facts that *A* lived in several houses successively, each of which he insured, in each of which a fire occurred, and after each of such fire, *A* received payment from a different insurance office, are relevant, as tending to show that the fires were not accidental.

(b) *A* is employed to receive money from the debtors of *B*. It is *A*'s duty to make entries in a book showing the amounts received by him. He makes an entry showing that on a particular occasion he received less than he really did receive.

The question is, whether this false entry was accidental or intentional.

The facts that other entries made by *A* in the same book are false, and that the false entry is in each case in favour of *A*, are relevant.

(c) *A* is accused of fraudulently delivering to *B* a counterfeit rupee. The question is, whether the delivery of the rupee was accidental.

The facts that, soon before or soon after the delivery to *B*, *A* delivered counterfeit rupees to *C*, *D* and *E* are relevant, as showing that the delivery to *B* was not accidental.

COMMENT

[s 15.1] Principle.—Where it is uncertain, whether an act was done with a guilty knowledge or intention or whether it was innocent or accidental, proof that it formed one of a series of similar acts raises the presumption that the act in question and the others, together forming a series, were done upon system, and were therefore not innocent or accidental. This section is an application of the general rule laid down in section 14, and the words of the section as well as of Illustration (a) show that it is not necessary that all the acts should form parts of one transaction, but that they

---

214. See *Emperor v Gangaram,* (1920) 22 Bom LR 1274; *Emperor v Haji Sher Mahomed,* (1921) 25 Bom LR 214: 46 Bom 958.

215. *Emperor v Debendra Prosad,* (1909) 36 Cal 573.

216. *Emperor v Alloomiya Husan,* (1903) 28 Bom 129, 135, 5 Bom LR 805. See *Wazir v Queen Empress,* (1895) PR No. 7 of 1895 (Cr).

217. Ins. by Act 3 of 1891, section 2.

should be parts of a series of similar occurrences.[218] For example under Illustration (a) the fact that the shops of the same person insured against fire were successively burnt down on different occasions is relevant to prove that the incidents were not accidental but part of a design.[219]

Section 14 provides that the facts showing the existence of any state of mind, such as intention or knowledge, are relevant, when the existence of any such state of mind is in issue or relevant; and this section provides specifically for allowing evidence of similar occurrences, in each of which the person doing the act was concerned, whenever there is a question whether an act is done with a particular knowledge or intention.[220] In this section, as in section 14, the intention of the party, is taken into account. But if there is no common link between the fact to be proved and the evidentiary fact, they cannot form a series. A regular system worked by the common intention should be proved.

Evidence tending to show that the accused has been guilty of criminal acts other than those covered by the indictment is not admissible unless upon the issue whether the acts charged against the accused were designed or accidental, or unless to rebut a defence otherwise open to him.

Whenever it is necessary to rebut, even by anticipation, the defence of accident, mistake or other innocent condition of mind, evidence may be given to prove that the accused has been concerned in a systematic course of conduct of the same specific kind and proximate in time to the conduct in question.[221]

[s 16] Existence of course of business when relevant.—When there is a question whether a particular act was done, the existence of any course of business,[s 16.2] according to which it naturally would have been done, is a relevant fact.

ILLUSTRATIONS

(a) The question is, whether a particular letter was despatched.

The facts that it was the ordinary course of business for all letters put in a certain place to be carried to the post, and that that particular letter was put in that place, are relevant.

(b) The question is, whether a particular letter reached *A*. The facts that it was posted in due course, and was not returned through the Dead Letter Office, are relevant.

---

218. *Emperor v Debendra Prosad,* (1904) 36 Cal 573. See also *Emperor v Panchu Das,* (1920) 47 Cal 671 FB; *Gandhi v King,* (1941) Ran 566. Where it was not shown that the director of a company was instrumental in the late posting of the notice of a shareholders' meeting, this section was not attracted. There was no question of the delay being intentional or accidental. *Needle Industries (India) Ltd v Needle Industries Newey (India) Holding Ltd,* AIR 1981 SC 1298 : (1981) 3 SCC 333 : (1981) 3 SCR 698 : (1981) 51 Com Cas 743.

219. *Nural Amin v Emperor,* (1939) 1 Cal 511. Repeated violation of Stock Exchange bye-laws by not paying in time, declaration as defaulter legal. *Akhileshwar Upadhyaya v Magadh Stock Exchange Assn,* AIR 1992 Pat 61.

220. *Emperor v Harjivan Valji,* (1925) 50 Bom 174, 182 : 28 Bom LR 115.

221. *Amrita Lal Hazara v Emperor,* (1915) 42 Cal 957; *Emperor v Harjivan Valji,* (1925) 50 Bom 174: 28 Bom LR 115.

SYNOPSIS

COMMENT

[s 16.1] Principle.—Under this section when the ordinary course of a particular business is proved, the court is asked to presume that, on the particular occasion in question, there was no departure from the ordinary and general rule. For instance, if letters properly directed to a gentleman be left with his servant it is only reasonable to presume *prima facie* that they reached his hands. Section 114, illustration (f), lays down that the court may presume that the common course of business has been followed in particular cases. This presumption is an application of the general maxim *omnia proesumuntur rite esse acta* (all acts are presumed to be rightly done), and is based on the fact that the conduct of men in official and commercial matters is, to a great extent, uniform. In such cases there is a strong presumption that the general regularity will not, in any particular instance, be departed from. This, however, is a rebuttable presumption.

[s 16.2] "Course of business".—This must mean the ordinary course of a professional avocation or mercantile transaction or trade or business. The section covers both private and public offices.[222] Illustration (a) relates to the former; illustration (b), to the latter, *viz.*, the post office. Illustration (b) only means that each one of the facts mentioned therein is relevant; it cannot be read as indicating that without a combination of these facts no presumption can arise.[223] The usage in a private house, however methodical, cannot convey the same weight as the ordinary routine of an office.

[s 16.3] CASES

[s 16.3.1] Registered letters.—A person refusing a registered letter sent by post cannot afterwards plead ignorance of its contents.[224] Similarly, if a letter is put into a post office, that is *prima facie* evidence, till rebutted, that the addressee received it in due course. The post marks on letters are considered as evidence of the dates and places mentioned therein.

A detenu under COFEPOSA contended that he posted a letter under certificate of posting withdrawing his statement. He filed a photo copy of the certificate of posting but not of the letter itself. The letter was also not traceable in the Department. No presumption of posting was raised.[225] See also comment under Illustration (f) of section 114.

Where a representation against preventive detention was sent by registered post but the acknowledgement receipt which was produced in proof of service was not signed on behalf of the Central Government, np question of considering the representation arose.[226]

---

222. *Ningawa v Bharmappa*, (1897) 23 Bom 63, 66.
223. *Mobarik Ali Ahmed v State of Bombay*, AIR 1957 SC 857 : (1957) Cr LJ 1346.
224. *Loolf Ali Meah v Pearce Mohun Roy*, (1871) 16 WR (Civil) 223; *Budha v Bedariya*, AIR 1981 MP 76.
225. *LMS Uma Saleema v BB Gujral*, AIR 1981 SC 1191 : 1981 Cr LJ 889.
226. *Abdul Shakur Khan v RD Tyagi*, 1999 Cr LJ 1524 (Bom).

ADMISSIONS

[s 17] Admission defined.—An admission is a statement, [227][oral or documentary, or contained in electronic form] which suggests any inference as to any fact in issue or relevant fact, and which is made by any of the persons, and under the circumstances, hereinafter mentioned.

SYNOPSIS

COMMENT

An "admission" is a statement of fact which waives or dispenses with the production of evidence by conceding that the fact asserted by the opponent is true. Admissions are admitted because the conduct of a party to a proceeding, in respect to the matter in dispute, whether by acts, speech, or writing, which is clearly inconsistent with the truth of his contention, is a fact relevant to the issue. Admissions are very weak kind of evidence and the court may reject them if it is satisfied from other circumstances that they are untrue.[228]

Admission of a party in the proceedings either in the pleadings or oral is the best evidence and the same does not need any further corroboration.[229]

The Supreme Court has observed: Admissions as defined in sections 17 and 20 and fulfilling the requirements of section 21 are substantive evidence, *propio vigore*. An admission is the best evidence against the party making it and, though not conclusive, shifts the onus to the maker on the principle that what a party himself admits to be true may be reasonably presumed to be true so that until the presumption is rebutted the fact admitted must be taken to be true.[230] An assessee cannot resile from his admission made in tax return even at appellate stage.[231]

There is this observation in Phipson on Evidence[232] "Subject to certain exceptions, the general rule, then both in civil and criminal cases, is that any relevant statement made

---

227. Subs. by Act 21 of 2000, section 92 and Sch. II–2, for "oral or documentary" (w.e.f. 17-10-2000).

228. *Latafat Husain v Lala Onkar Mal,* (1934) 10 Luck 423; *Raja Partab Bahadur Singh v Raja Rajgan Maharaja Jagatjit Singh,* (1936) 12 Luck 371 : (1977) 3 SCC 540; *UOI v Roop Narain,* AIR 1977 Raj 123, in a claim against railway for loss of goods in transit, the railway receipt contained the remark : "said to contain" held, this was not admission on the part of the railway as to what were the contents of the consignment. Other records would have to be examined to see what was the real state of the consignment at the starting point and terminus.

229. *Ahmedsaheb v Sayed Ismail,* (2012) 8 SCC 516.

230. *Thiru John v Returning Officer,* AIR 1977 SC 1724, admission of age by the returned candidate.

231. *Federal Bank Ltd v State,* AIR 1995 Ker 62.

232. *Phipson on Evidence*, 9th Edn, 1952, p 231.

by a party is evidence against himself. *R v Erdheim.*[233] The weight of the declaration is, of course, a totally different matter; this may vary with the circumstances and will not doubt, be greater if against interest at the time, than the contrary."

In *ECT Farming Society* case,[234] Beg J of the Supreme Court observed:

> It is well settled that the effect of an admission depends upon the circumstances in which it was made.

A statement to be used as an admission must be clear, specific and unambiguous and in the own words of the person making it and has to be proved to be so. It is not an inference drawn by anybody which should be taken as an admission. An admission to be worthy of being received in evidence, considered and relied upon, it should firstly be the clear-cut and accurate statement of that very person in his own works. It has to be proved to be the statement of the person who made it.[235]

An admission must be examined as a whole and not in parts.[236] "It is settled law that an admission of any party has to be read in its entirety and no statement out of context can constitute admission of any fact."[237] Statements in pleadings are admissions against the party making them. He cannot be heard to rely upon favourable parts and throw the rest by oral evidence.[238] In *UOI v Moksh Builders etc,*[239] the Supreme Court cited a statement from its own earlier decision[240] to the effect that an admission is substantive evidence of the fact admitted and when properly proved is relevant irrespective of the fact whether the maker approved in the witness-box or not and when he appears, whether he was confronted with those statements or not in case he made a statement contrary to his admissions. The court cited a statement from Wigmore on Evidence[241] to the effect that an admission need not be contrary to the maker's interest. Thus it is not necessary before admitting the evidence of an admission that it should be brought to the notice of the party who made it.[242]

An admission in so far as facts are concerned would bind the maker of the admission but not in so far as it relates to a question of law.[243]

It is immaterial to whom an admission is made.[244] The word "confession" has not been defined anywhere. A confession is an admission made at any time by a person

---

233. *R v Erdheim,* (1986) 2 QB 260.

234. *ECT Farming Society* case (1974) 2 SCC 319 at 321 : AIR 1974 SC 1121.

235. *HG Ramachandra Rao v Master Srikantha,* AIR 1997 Kant 347.

236. *Mohammad Koya v Muthuboya,* (1979) 1 SCR 664 : AIR 1979 SC 154 .

237. *Dharamwati Bai v Shiv Singh,* AIR 1991 MP 18. Accordingly a statement of the claimant that her personal estate arising before 1956 Hindu Succession Act was in the management of the Court of Wards could not be taken as an admission that the property in question was not her estate.

238. *Sunil Chandra v Hemendra,* AIR 1985 Cal 233.

239. *UOI v Moksh Builders etc.,* AIR 1977 SC 408 : 1977 Cr LJ 376.

240. *Bharat Singh v Bhagrathi,* AIR 1977 SC 408 : 1977 Cr LJ 376.

241. Vol 4, p 1048.

242. *Maimunna Bibi v Rasool Mian,* AIR 1991 Pat 203.

243. *Banarsi Das v Kanshi Ram,* AIR 1963 SC 1165 : (1964) 1 SCR 316.

244. *Rakesh Wadhawan v Jagdambha Industrial Corpon.,* AIR 2002 SC 2004, : (2002) 5 SCC 440, the value of an admission depends upon the circumstances in which it is made and to whom it is made. Failure to object to wrong averment as to rate of rent made in a partition suit. This was held to be nothing more than an admission. It could not outweigh admissions made by tenants as to rate of rent in lease deed and letters written by them to the landlord.

charged with a crime, stating or suggesting the inference that he committed the crime.[245] Statement is a genus, admission is the species and confession is the sub-species. A confession, therefore, is a statement made by an accused admitting his guilt.[246] When a party accepts his statement made in earlier proceedings, it amounts to admission.[247]

[s 17.1] Prior statement.—A prior statement in one's own interest may not be evidence, but a prior statement adverse to one's interest would be evidence.[248]

[s 17.2] Admissions in criminal proceedings.—Every admission made by an accused person is not, in the view of the law, a confession, nor can it be held that admissions mean only statements made by parties to civil proceedings, and do not include statements made by parties in criminal proceedings. Every statement, oral or documentary, which suggests any inference as to any fact in issue or relevant fact made by an accused person is an admission under sections 17 and 18, and under section 19 an admission may be proved as against the person who makes it unless, under some provision of the Evidence Act or other law, it is rendered inadmissible. Under sections 24 to 26 statements made by accused persons are inadmissible, subject to the provisions of sections 27 to 29, when such statements are confessions.[249] A confession which is inadmissible may yet for other purposes be admissible as an admission under section 18 against the person who makes it in civil matters.[250] Thus, admission of guilt by a person to a police officer, though not receivable in evidence in a criminal trial, may be proved in civil proceedings as an admission under this section and sections 18 and 21.[251] In *Sashidhara Kurup v UOI*, it was held that the admissibility of plea of guilt can be determined only if the plea is recorded in the words used by the accused. The accused simply said that he was guilty of the charge. This did not constitute an admission of guilt.[252]

[s 17.3] Admissions in publication.—The court said that statements made in a book, though cannot be regarded as conclusive admissions, they can be taken as an additional circumstance along with the other circumstances for determining whether the conduct of the appellant amounted to waiver and/or abandonment of the right in respect of the articles in question.[253]

[s 17.4] Oral or documentary.—Judicial or extra-judicial.—Admissions may be oral or contained in documents, e.g., letters, depositions, affidavits, plaints, written statements, deeds, receipts, horoscopes. Admissions in pleadings are judicial admissions.

---

245. *Queen-Empress v Babu Lal*, (1884) 6 All 509, 539 FB; *Sahoo v State of UP*, AIR 1966 SC 40 : 1966 Cr LJ 68.

246. *Sahoo v State of UP*, AIR 1966 SC 40 : 1966 Cr LJ 68.

247. *Alpana v Mohanlal*, 1993 Cr LJ 1008; *Krishan Mohan v Balkrishna Chaturvedi*, AIR 2001 All 334, a plea that the admission was not accepted just by itself. No proof of that fact was offered either in evidence or in written statement. Bare argument without any basis was held to be not tenable.

248. *Satrucharla Vijaya Rama Raju v Nimmaka Jaya Raju*, (2006) 1 SCC 212 : AIR 2006 SC 543.

249. *Ilahi Baksh v The Empress*, (1886) PR No. 16 of 1886 (Cr); *Raj Mal v Empress*, (1879) PR No. 3 of 1880 (Cr); *Shree Singh v The Empress*, (1881) PR No. 21 of 1881 (Cr).

250. *Queen-Empress v Tribhovan Manekchand*, (1884) 9 Bom 131, 134.

251. *Bishen Das v Ram Labhaya*, (1915) PR No. 106 of 1915 (Civil). Where a woman stated that she caused death to save herself from being raped, since this did not amount to a confession, it was admissible under this section as an admission of the fact, *State of Orissa v Nirupama*, 1989 Cr L J 621 (Ori).

252. *KK Chari v RM Sheshadri*, 1994 Cr LJ 375 (Gau).

253. *Karan Singh (Dr) v State of J&K*, (2004) 5 SCC 698 : AIR 2004 SC 2480.

They can be made the foundation of rights.[254] In *KK Chari v RM Sheshadri,*[255] Dua J said:

> If the tenant in fact admits that the landlord is entitled to possession on one or the other of the statutory grounds mentioned in the Act, it is open to the Court to act on that admission and make an order for possession in favour of the landlord without further enquiry.

The material for the satisfaction of the court "may take the shape either of evidence recorded or produced in the case, or it may partly or wholly be in shape of an express or implied admission made in the compromise agreement itself."[256]

Explaining the weight of a judicial admission as compared with informal or casual admissions, Sarkaria J said:

> Admissions, if true and clear, are by far the best proof of the facts admitted. Admissions in pleadings or judicial admissions, admissible under s. 58, made by the parties or their agents at or before the hearing of the case, stand on a higher footing than evidentiary admissions. The former class of admissions are fully binding upon the party that makes them and constitutes a waiver of proof. They by themselves can be the foundation of the rights of the parties. On the other hand, evidentiary admissions which are receivable at the trial as evidence, are by themselves not conclusive. They can be shown to be wrong.

A post-dated cheque in satisfaction of debts amounts to acknowledgment of liability irrespective of the fact whether the cheque is honoured or not.[257] Admissions may be implied from the acquiescence of a party.[258] Admissions in the written statement filed in some other case have been held by the Supreme Court to be an important piece of evidence and, therefore, entitled to its due weight, though like all other admissions, it is neither conclusive nor irrebutable.[259] The general rule is that admissions are admissible against the party making them and not against any other party. The exceptions to this rule are mentioned in sections 18 to 20.

A statement by an applicant for old age pension in her cross-examination that she was getting old age pension and that her form was filled by the pradhan of the village was held not to have the effect of an admission in respect of the contents of her application.[260]

[s 17.5] Voluntary.—For an admission to have the effect of substantive evidence it must be voluntary. An examinee gave undertaking that if he did not file his employer's permission, the university might do anything it liked. That did not put him out of court. "It is well settled that admission made in ignorance of legal rights or under duress cannot bind the maker." The examinee submitted the undertaking under the constraint of not being permitted. The consequences of the University's failure to scrutinise his

254. *Satish Mohan v State of UP,* AIR 1986 All 126.
255. *KK Chari v RM Sheshadri,* (1973) 1 SCC 761, at p 774 : AIR 1973 SC 1311.
256. *Nagindas Ramdas v Dalpatram,* (1974) 1 SCC 242, at p 252 : AIR 1974 SC 471.
257. *Rajpati Pd. v Kaushalya Kaur,* AIR 1981 Pat 187.
258. *Kehar Singh v State (Delhi Admn.),* (1998) 3 SCC 609, allegations against the accused made by police is application for extension of remand were held as not amounting to admissions on the part of the accused only for his failure to object to them.
259. *Shankarrao Dajisaheb Shinde v Vithalrao Ganpatrao Shinde,* AIR 1989 SC 879 : 1989 Supp (2) SCC 162.
260. *Twatku v Surti,* AIR 1997 HP 76.

form and to find out the fraud, if any, cannot be visited upon the candidate.[261] Similarly, an admission made by a party in a previous criminal proceeding in order to get rid of the chances of conviction was held to be *in terrorem* and, therefore, of very little significance.[262] In a suit for eviction, vague allegations about the ownership of the premises by the tenant, could not be treated as his admission about the contract of tenancy with the landlord.[263]

[s 17.6] Admissions as hearsay.—Examining the nature of the evidence of an admission and distinguishing it from hearsay, PARKE B said:[264]

> The rule as to the production of the best evidence is not at all infringed. It does not apply to the present case (oral admissions as to the contents of a document). That rule is founded on the supposition that a party is going to offer worse evidence than the nature of the case admits. But what is said by a party to the suit is not open to that objection. We, therefore, think it is a sound rule that admissions made by a party to a suit may be received against him.

There is no general agreement on admissions as hearsay. A learned commentator says:

> Whether an admission is an exception to the hearsay rule depends upon one's definition of hearsay. If we define hearsay as an extra-judicial statement offered as tending to prove the truth of the matter stated, an admission clearly falls within it. It must be conceded that the rule which makes admissions receivable is older than the hearsay rule and is a necessary concomitant of the accepted doctrine that evidence of any relevant conduct of a party is admissible against him.[265]

A passage in Wigmore on Evidence,[266] has been adopted by the Allahabad High Court,[267] and the Supreme Court.[268] "The theory of the hearsay rule is that an extra-judicial assertion is excluded unless there has been a sufficient opportunity to test the grounds of assertion and the credit of the witness by cross-examination by the party against whom it is offered, e.g., if Jones had said out of court, "The party-opponent Smith borrowed this fifty dollars." Smith is entitled to an opportunity to cross-examine Jones upon that assertion. But if it is Smith himself who said out of court, "I borrowed this fifty dollars", certainly Smith cannot complain of lack of opportunity to cross-examine himself before his assertion is admitted against him. Such a request would be absurd. Hence the objection of the hearsay rule falls away, because the very basis of the rule is lacking *viz.*, the need and prudence of affording an opportunity for cross-examination."

[s 17.7] Persons whose admissions are relevant.—List of persons whose admissions are relevant is to be found in the provisions of sections 18 to 20. Admissions made by any other persons are not receivable in evidence. Thus, the statements of some officers admitting their guilt that lesser number of persons were shown on records of

---

261. *Shri Krishan v Kurukshetra University*, AIR 1976 SC 376 : (1976) 1 SCC 311.
262. *Mohd v Mohd*, AIR 1976 SC 1569 : (1976) 4 SCC 780.
263. *Anurag Misra v Ravindra Singh*, AIR 1994 All 174.
264. *Shatleric v Pooley*, (1840) 151 ER 579.
265. *Morgan, Basic Principles of Evidence*, 265 cited by *Edwards, Cases on Evidence in Australia*, 507 (1968).
266 Vol 4, section 1048.
267. *Ayodhaya Prasad Bhargava v Bhawani Shankar Bhargava*, AIR 1957 All 15 : ILR (1956) 2 All 399.
268. *UOI v Mokshi Builders*, (1977) 1 SCC 60 at p 68 : AIR 1977 SC 409.

the factory so as to keep it out of the application of the Central Excise was held to be not an admission against the owner.

Failure to prove the defence does not amount to an admission, nor does it reverse or discharge the burden of proof of the plaintiff.[269]

Legally enforceable admission has to be made by adversary against whom a relief is claimed, not by a person who asserts a claim.[270]

[s 18] Admission by party to proceeding or his agent.—Statements made by a party to the proceeding, or by an agent to any such party, whom the Court regards, under the circumstances of the case, as expressly or impliedly authorized by him to make them, are admissions.

by suitor in representative character.—Statements made by parties to suits suing or sued in a representative character, are not admissions, unless they were made while the party making them held that character.

Statements made by—

(1) party interested in subject-matter.—persons who have any proprietary or pecuniary interest in the subject-matter of the proceeding, and who make the statement in their character of persons so interested, or

(2) person from whom interest derived.—persons from whom the parties to the suit have derived their interest in the subject-matter of the suit,

are admissions, if they are made during the continuance of the interest of the persons making the statements.

COMMENT

Sections 18 and 19 indicate the persons by whom an admission must be made.

Statements by the accused are admissions under section 18.[271]

Section 18 lays down five classes of persons who can make admissions—

(1) Party to the proceeding.

(2) Agent authorized by such party.

(3) Party suing or sued in a representative character making admissions while holding such character.

(4) Person who has any proprietary or pecuniary interest in the subject-matter of the proceeding during the continuance of such interest.

(5) Person from whom the parties to the suit have derived their interest in the subject-matter of the suit during the continuance of such interest.

269. *LIC v Ram Pal Singh Bisen*, (2010) 4 SCC 491.
270. *N Murali Krishna v South Central Railway, Secunderabad*, AIR 2014 AP 100 (para 10) (DB).
271. *Azimuddy v Emperor*, (1926) 54 Cal 237.

(1) Party to the proceedings.—What is admitted by a party to be true must be presumed to be true unless the contrary is shown;[272] but before this proposition can be invoked, it must be shown that there is a clear and unambiguous statement by the party such as will be conclusive unless explained.[273] A statement made by a party in a former suit between the same or different parties is admissible. The proceeding may be civil or criminal.[274] A statement made by a party in a pleading cannot be evidence in subsequent proceedings before a court of law unless it amounts to an admission.[275]

"When several persons are *jointly* interested in the subject-matter of the suit, the general rule is that the admissions of any one of these persons are receivable against himself and fellows, whether they be all jointly suing or sued, or whether an action be brought in favour of or against one or more of them separately, provided the admissions relate to the subject-matter in dispute, and be made by the declarant in his character of a person jointly interested with the party against whom the evidence is tendered."[276] Admissions made by a party's witness cannot be treated as admissions made by the party. Such admissions do not bind the party.[277]

When a fact pleaded in a plaint is not specifically denied but mere ignorance about its existence is pleaded, it amounts to admission unless by necessary implication it amounts to denial.[278]

(2) Agent.—The admissions of an agent are admissible because the principal is bound by the acts of his agent done in the course of business and within the scope of his authority. A statement made by an agent whom the court regards, under the circumstances of the case, as expressly or impliedly authorized to make it, is admissible though not on oath,[279] e.g., a statement by an agent before a settlement officer that his principal was a bastard.[280] Before the statements of an agent can be relevant as admissions, the fact of agency must be proved. Where there is no such relationship, the statement in question would not qualify for relevancy. Thus, where over a matter of sub-letting, the tenant's brother stated on affidavit before Income-tax Authorities that he was the tenant, there being no agency relationship between the two brothers,

---

272. *Nathoo Lal v Durga Prasad,* AIR 1954 SC 355 : (1955) 1 SCR 51.

273. *Nagubai v B Shama Rao,* AIR 1956 SC 593 : (1956) SCR 451; *Special Land Acquisition Officer v Pari Keshaulal Jamnadas,* (1987) 3 SCC 306, a concession on a question of fact should not be disregarded.*Jagdish Parshad v Sarwan Kumar,* AIR 2003 P&H 3, the person in question who had since died, signed and stated in the *bahi* of visitors maintained by the *Panda* of a temple that the person claiming a share in his property was not his brother. This admission was held to be relevant for showing absence of relationship.

274. *Dattatraya Shripati v Shankar,* (1959) 61 Bom LR 792.

275. *Raj Kumar v Gopi Nath,* AIR 1971 All 273.

276. *Taylor,* 12th Edn, section 743, p 475; *Meajan Matbar v Alimuddi Mia,* (1916) 44 Cal 130, 143, 144. *Dulal Chandra Adnk v Gunadhar Patra,* AIR 1998 Cal 150, statements of a party to the proceeding are of a binding nature. The dispute was about the genuineness of a gift deed. The suit was for declaring it as a forged document. Statements made by co-plaintiff admitting the claim of the defendant. They bound the plaintiff also. The court also said that averments made in the plaint also have a binding effect. They cannot be allowed to be abandoned unless explained by cogent evidence.

277. *Krishna Mohan v Bal Krishna Chaturvedi,* AIR 2001 All 334.

278. *Roopi Bai v Mahaveer,* AIR 1994 Raj 133, **relying on** *Jahuri Sah v Dwarka Prasad Jhunjhunwala,* AIR 1967 SC 109 : 1966 Supp SCR 280.

279. *Govindji v Chhotalal,* (1900) 2 Bom LR 651.

280. *Raj Fateh Singh Thakur v Baldeo Singh Thakur,* (1928) 3 Luck 416.

nor there being signature of the tenant, the Supreme Court held that the statement was not admissible against the tenant.[281]

Counsel, pleader, attorney.—Admissions of facts made by a pleader in the conduct of a suit on his client's behalf are binding on the client.[282] But a party is not bound, generally speaking, by a pleader's admission in argument on what is a pure question of law.[283] Generally, admissions of fact made by a counsel are binding upon their principals (clients)as long as they are unequivocal, where, however, doubt exists as to a purported admission, the court should be vary to accept such admissions until and unless the counsel or the advocate is authorised by his principal to make admissions. Furthermore, a client is not bound by a statement or admission which he or his lawyer was not authorised to make. A lawyer generally has no implied or apparent authority to make an admission or statement, which would directly surrender or conclude the substantial legal rights of the client, unless such an admission or statement is clearly a proper step in accomplishing the purpose for which the lawyer was employed. Neither the client nor the court is bound by the lawyer's statements or admissions as to matters of law or legal conclusions. Thus, according to the generally accepted notions of professional responsibility, the lawyers should follow their client's instructions rather than substitute their judgment for that of the client. In some cases the lawyers can make decisions without consulting the client, while in others, the decision is reserved for the client. The lawyers can make decision as to tactics without consulting the client, while the client has a right to make decisions that can affect his rights.[284] The admissions of a party's solicitors before the commencement of litigation are not relevant. Observation of formalities is, however, something different. The testimony of counsel that the thumb impression taken as a specimen was that of his client cannot be excluded on the ground that a counsel cannot admit facts on client's behalf.[285] The counsel of a tenant admitted, against the stand taken by the tenant, that the landlord was a public charitable institution and it needed the premises for its purposes. The court said such statement could not be admitted in evidence as an admission made by the party. The Additional Rent Controller could not record his satisfaction on the basis of such statement. The order of eviction was held to be without justification.[286]

Admission by defendant.—The defendant sought declaration that she was the only legally married wife of her deceased husband. The court said that it was a clear admission by the defendant that she was the legally married wife of the deceased. No evidence was produced to show divorce between them. Under such circumstances, it was held that the order of the first appellate court accepting the admission as a substantive evidence in support of the marriage was proper.[287]

Co-defendants.—An admission or a confession of judgment by one of several defendants in a suit is no evidence against another defendant. No defendant can, by an admission or consent, convey the right, or delegate the authority to one, for more

---

281. *Sri Chand Gupta v Gulzar Singh,* (1992) 1 SCC 143 : AIR 1992 SC 123.

282. *Khajah Abdool Gunee v Gour Monee Debia,* (1868) 9 WR (Civil) 375; *Mahadev v Sundrabai,* (1901) 3 Bom LR 467; *Emperor v Bansilal Gangaram,* (1928) 30 Bom LR 646 : 52 Bom 686.

283. *Narayan v Venkatacharya,* (1904) 6 Bom LR 434 : 28 Bom 408.

284. *Himalayan Cooperative Group Housing Societyv. Balwan Singh,* (2015) 7 SCC 373, para 32.

285. *Raghunath v State of UP,* AIR 1973 SC 1100 : (1973) 1 SCC 564.

286. *Sri Swami Krishnanand v MD Oswal Hosiery,* AIR 2002 SC 1162.

287. *Damayanti Nahak v Kalpana Bhatacharya,* AIR 2007 NOC 294 (Ori) : (2006) 2 CutLR 395.

than his own share in property.[288] Thus, the admissions by one defendant will not be relevant against a co-defendant, because it would be unjust to bind a co-defendant by the admission of another whom he has had no opportunity to answer or cross-examine; it would afford to the plaintiff opportunities of defeating his opponent by unfair means. Even a confession of judgment by one of several defendants is no evidence against another defendant.[289]

Co-owners.—Admission by one of the co-owners that the other co-owner had one-third share in the joint properties, can be relied upon.[290]

Partner.—Partners are agents of one another so far as the business of partnership is concerned. Where several persons are engaged in one common business or dealing, a statement made by one of them with reference to any transaction which forms part of their joint business, has always been held admissible as evidence against the others.[291] Each member of a firm, being the agent of the others for all purposes within the scope of the partnership business, admissions by one member are binding on all. Admissions by a partner of a dissolved firm are binding on the other partners when they have an identical interest in the subject-matter of the suit.[292]

Principal and surety.—"The admissions of a *principal* can sometimes (but only seldom) be received as evidence in an action *against the surety* upon his collateral undertaking. In these cases the main inquiry is whether the declarations of the principal were made during the transaction of the business for which the surety was bound, so as to become part of the *res gestae.* If so, they are admissible; otherwise, they are not."[293]

Guardian.—The admissions of a guardian *ad litem*, or next friend, do not bind the minor. The guardian of an infant has no power to bind him by admissions. According to the Bombay and the Madras High Courts, a guardian appointed under the Guardians and Wards Act can sign an acknowledgment of liability in respect of, or pay in part the principal of, a debt, so as to extend the period of limitation against his ward, provided the guardian's act was for the benefit of the ward's property.[294]

(3) Party suing or sued in a representative character.—This means trustees, executors, administrators, managers in the character of an executor or administrator, or the assignee of a bankrupt.

It is important that such persons must make "the statement in their character of persons so interested". A statement made by a trustee, executor or administrator, is not admissible against him when sued as trustee, *etc.*, if it was made before he became trustee, *etc.* This principle is grounded on the fact that a statement against the interest of a person making it will not be made unless truth compelled it. But the fact that

---

288. *Lachman Singh v Tansukh,* (1884) 6 All 395; *Azizullah Khan v Ahmad Ali Khan,* (1885) 7 All 353.
289. *Aumirtolall Bose v Rajoneekant Mitter,* (1874-75) 2 IA 113 : (1875) 23 WR 214.
290. *Raj Kumar v Official Receiver, Chiranji Lal Ram Chand,* AIR 1996 SC 941 : (1996) 2 SCC 288.
291. *Kowsulliah Sundari Dasi v Mukta Sundari Dasi,* (1885) 11 Cal 588.
292. *Sohanlal v Gulab Chand,* AIR 1966 Raj 229.
293. *Taylor,* 12th Edn, Vol I, section 785, p 494.
294. *Annapagauda v Sangadyapa,* (1901) 3 Bom LR 817: 26 Bom 221, FB; *Kailasa Padaiachi v Ponnukannu Achi,* (1894) 18 Mad 456. See, Limitation Act, 1963, section 20(1).

two persons have a common interest in the subject-matter does not entitle them to make admissions, respecting it, as against each other.[295]

(4) Person who has any proprietary or pecuniary interest.—When several persons are jointly interested in the subject-matter of a suit, an admission of any one of these persons is receivable not only against himself but also against the other defendants, whether they be all jointly suing or sued, provided that the admission relates to the subject-matter in dispute and be made by the declarant in his character of a person jointly interested with the party against whom the evidence is tendered.[296] In a suit for declaration of title, a statement by the suitor's father that the defendant was in possession was admitted.[297] Admissions made by a person about his ownership of property after he had transferred it are not relevant to the prejudice of the buyer's interest. After transfer he no longer had any interest in the property.[298] In a tenancy matter, an admission made by the tenant's brother was not relevant because he had no pecuniary or proprietary interest in the matter of the tenancy.[299] Admission by a party is not possible after parting with his interest in the property.[300]

An admission made by one of several parties in fraud of the others jointly interested will not bind the others.

(5) Persons from whom the parties to the suit have derived their interest in the subject-matter of the suit.—Statements made either by parties interested or by persons from whom the parties to the suit have derived their interest are admissions only if they are made during the continuance of the interest of the persons making the statement. The admissions of a former owner of property after he has ceased to have any interest in it are not evidence against the party in possession.[301] A, a landowner, filed a suit for ejectment against B, a tenant. B alleged that he was a permanent tenant at a fixed rent under an agreement with the original owner of the land, who was dead, and put in evidence, statements made by the original owner after he had transferred his interest. It was held that the statements were inadmissible.[302] Where the deceased father of the plaintiff admitted that the defendant was his second legally wedded wife and her children were his legitimate children, the admission was binding on the plaintiff.[303]

This clause indicates that there ought to be a privity, i.e., mutual or successive relationship to the same right of property. Privies are of three kinds:—

(1) Privies in blood, as an heir, an ancestor, and coparceners.

(2) Privies in law, as executor and testator, administrator and a person dying intestate.

(3) Privies in estate or interest, as vendor and purchaser, lessor and lessee, mortgagor and mortgagee, donor and donee.

---

295. *Stephen's Dig*, Article 17.

296. *Meajan Matbar v Alimuddi Mia*, (1916) 44 Cal 130, 143; Taylor, 12th Edn, section 743, p 475; *Ambika Devi v Balmukand Pandey*, AIR 1981 Pat 111, a matter of family partition.

297. *Sahdeo v Board of Rev.*, AIR 1980 All 408.

298. *Hardatt Sharma v Jaikishan*, AIR 1983 J&K 29.

299. *Sri Chand Gupta v Gulzar Singh*, AIR 1992 SC 123 : (1992) 1 SCC 143.

300. *Chironjilal v Khatoon Bi*, AIR 1995 MP 238.

301. *Khenum Kuree Chowdhrain v Gour Chunder Mojoomdar*, (1866) 5 WR 267.

302. *Shwe Yat Aung v Da Li*, (1916) 9 LBR 27.

303. *Nirmala v Rukminibai*, AIR 1994 Kant 247.

The grounds upon which admissions are evidence against those in privity with the party making them are that they are identified in interest. Where it was proved that an agreement sued on was made by the plaintiff on behalf of himself and the other proprietors of a theatre, evidence of the declarations of one of such other proprietors was held admissible on the part of the defendant.[304] But where a gift deed executed by father contained certain admissions, it did not bind the sons because they were claiming not through him, but in their own right as coparceners.[305]

[s 19] Admissions by persons whose position must be proved as against party to suit.—Statements made by persons whose position or liability it is necessary to prove as against any party to the suit, are admissions, if such statements would be relevant as against such persons in relation to such position or liability in a suit brought by or against them, and if they are made whilst the person making them occupies such position or is subject to such liability.

ILLUSTRATION

A undertakes to collect rents for *B*.

B sues *A* for not collecting rent due from *C* to *B*.

A denies that rent was due from *C* to *B*.

A statement by *C* that he owed *B* rent is an admission, and is a relevant fact as against *A*, if *A* denies that *C* did owe rent to *B*.

SYNOPSIS

COMMENT

The admission of a third person against his own interest when it affects his position or liability and when that position or liability has to be proved as against a party to the suit, is relevant against the party. Ordinary statements by strangers to a proceeding are not relevant as against the parties.

[s 19.1] Object.—The object of this section is not to lay down that certain statements are relevant or admissible but merely to add to the category of persons by whom a statement may be made before it can be considered to be an admission within the terms of the Act.

[s 19.2] Principle.—This section forms an exception to the rule that statements made by strangers to a proceeding are not admissible as against the parties. Thus, in an action by the trustees of a bankrupt, the latter's admissions, made before the act of bankruptcy, are admissible in proof of the petitioning creditor's debt.[306]

---

304. *Kemble v Farren*, (1829) 3 C&P 623; Taylor, 12th Edn, Vol I, section 743, p 475.

305. *Avtar Singh v Atma Singh*, AIR 1982 J&K 141.

306. *Appavu Chettiar v Nanjappa Goundan*, (1913) 25 Mad LJ 329; *Taylor*, 12th Edn, section 759, Vol I, p 484.

The illustration exemplifies that when the liability of a person who is one of the parties to a suit depends upon the liability of a stranger to the suit, then an admission by the stranger in respect of his liability amounts to an admission on the part of that person. Where a landlord died and the tenant questioned the title of the lady living with him saying that she was not the wife of the deceased landlord, a thirty three year old registered deed was produced which showed the landlord's admission about the lady to be his wife, it was held that the right of the lady was conclusively proved by the admission.[307]

Execution of a will cannot be doubted merely because of delay in applying for letters of administration which was satisfactorily explained, more so when due execution of the will was admitted by preferential heirs to the estate of the testatrix against their own interest.[308]

[s 19.3] Scope.—The statements referred to in this section become admissible only provided that they satisfy the requirements of section 17 as regards their nature and section 21 or any of the following sections as regards their liability.

[s 20] Admissions by persons expressly referred to by party to suit.—Statements made by persons to whom a party to the suit has expressly referred for information[s 20.2] in reference to a matter in dispute are admissions.

ILLUSTRATION

The question is, whether a horse sold by *A* to *B* is sound.

A says to *B*—"Go and ask *C*, *C* knows all about it." *C*'s statement is an admission.

SYNOPSIS

COMMENT

This section forms another exception to the rule that admissions by strangers to a suit are not relevant. Under it the admissions of a third person are also receivable in evidence against, and have frequently been held to be in fact binding upon, the party who has expressly referred another to him for information in regard to an uncertain or disputed matter.[309]

[s 20.1] Principle.—If a reference is made over a disputed matter to a third person, not in the nature of a submission to arbitration, but rather as an aid to the settlement of the differences existing between the parties and to enable the parties themselves to effect a settlement on the information, in such cases the party is bound by the declaration of the person referred to in the same manner and to the same extent as if it was made by himself.[310]

---

307. *Sivalingam v Sakthivel*, AIR 1989 Mad 252.

308. *Laxmi Bai v A Chandravati*, AIR 1995 Ori 131.

309. *Taylor*, 12th Edn, section 760, p 484.

310. *Sloman v Herne*, (1799) 2 Esp. 695; *Williams v Bridges*, (1817) 2 Stark 42.

[s 20.2] "Expressly referred for information".—There must be an express reference for information in order to make the statement of the person referred to admissible. Such admissions come very near to the case of arbitration. In the application of this principle, it matters not whether the question referred be one of law or of fact, whether the person to whom reference is made have or have not any peculiar knowledge on the subject, or whether the statements of the referee be adduced in evidence in an action on contract, or in an action for tort.[311]

If one party in a cause offers to the other party to settle it, provided that a witness makes a statement on oath as to a certain fact in dispute, and the statement is made, it shall bind the party making the offer.[312] Where the defendant said, "If C will say that he did deliver the goods, I will pay for them," it was held that C's statement was admissible and the defendant was bound by it.[313] Explaining the term "information", the Supreme Court has said: "The word "information" occurring in section 20 is not to be understood in the sense that the parties desired to know something which none of them had any knowledge of. Where there is a dispute as regards a certain question and the court is in need of information regarding the truth on that point, any statement that the referee may make is nevertheless information within the meaning of section 20".[314] The court accordingly regarded the report of an assessor "information" within the meaning of the section. The court said that it would also include reference to arbitration. Explaining the point of information, the court proceeded as follows: Section 20 is the second exception to the general rule laid down in section 18. It deals with one of the classes of vicarious admissions. Where a party refers to a third person for some information or an opinion on a matter in dispute, the statements made by the third person are receivable as admissions against the person making the reference. The word "Information" occurring in section 20 is not to be understood in the sense that the parties desired to know something of which none of them had any knowledge. Where there is a dispute as regards a certain question and the court is in need of information regarding the truth on that point, any statement which the referee may make is nevertheless information within the purview of section 20 and is admissible. The reason behind admissibility of the statement is that when a party refers to another person for a statement of his views, the party approves of his utterance in anticipation and adopts that as his own. The principle is the same as that of reference to arbitration. The reference under section 20 may be by express words or by conduct, but in any case there must be a clear intention to refer and the statements made by the referee are generally conclusive. Admissions so obtained may operate as an estoppel and they do so where parties had agreed to abide by them. In the present case though the concerned Minister had deputed a Town Planning Officer to assess the valuation of the disputed land but he did not make any commitment on behalf of the State Government that whatever assessment was made by him would be binding on the Government. The Government never agreed to abide by the valuation made by the assessor.

Where in a suit for eviction, one of the tenants on the basis of power of attorney from other tenants, admitted in his statement before the court the liability as regards the arrears of rent, such a statement would bind the tenants as their own admission within the

311. *Taylor*, 12th Edn, section 761, p 485.
312. *Lloyd v Willan*, (1794) 1 Esp. 178.
313. *Daniel v Pitt*, (1806) 1 Camp 366n.
314. *Hirachand Kothari v State of Rajasthan*, AIR 1985 SC 998, at 1000-1 : 1985 Supp SCC 17.

meaning of section 20 of the Evidence Act.[315] A suit was filed for a declaration that the resignation tendered by the plaintiff from his post was involuntary having been extracted by fraud, coercion, threat, etc. In the course of the proceedings, the plaintiff filed an application that if the two named persons stated on special oath, one in Gurdwara, and the other in temple, that the resignation was not extracted as alleged, he would withdraw that aspect of the matter. An oath commissioner was appointed to record the respective statements. They went against the plaintiff. He was held bound by the statements.[316]

[s 21] Proof of admissions against persons making them and by or on their behalf.—Admissions are relevant and may be proved as against the person who makes them,[s 21.2] or his representative in interest;[s 21.3] but they cannot be proved by or on behalf of the person who makes them or by his representative in interest, except in the following cases:—

(1) An admission may be proved by or on behalf of the person making it, when it is of such a nature that, if the person making it were dead, it would be relevant as between third persons under section 32.

(2) An admission may be proved by or on behalf of the person making it, when it consists of a statement of the existence of any state of mind or body, relevant or in issue, made at or about the time when such state of mind or body existed, and is accompanied by conduct rendering its falsehood improbable.

(3) An admission may be proved by or on behalf of the person making it, if it is relevant otherwise than as an admission.

ILLUSTRATIONS

(a) The question between *A* and *B* is, whether a certain deed is or is not forged. *A* affirms that it is genuine, *B* that it is forged.

A may prove a statement by *B* that the deed is genuine, and *B* may prove a statement by *A* that the deed is forged; but *A* cannot prove a statement by himself that the deed is genuine, nor can *B* prove a statement by himself that the deed is forged.

(b) *A*, the captain of a ship, is tried for casting her away.

Evidence is given to show that the ship was taken out of her proper course.

A produces a book kept by him in the ordinary course of his business showing observations alleged to have been taken by him from day to day, and indicating that the ship was not taken out of her proper course. *A* may prove these statements, because they would be admissible between third parties, if he were dead, under section 32, clause (2).

(c) *A* is accused of a crime committed by him at Calcutta.

He produces a letter written by himself and dated at Lahore on that day, and bearing the Lahore post mark of that day.

The statement in the date of the letter is admissible, because, if *A* were dead, it would be admissible under section 32, clause (2).

(d) *A* is accused of receiving stolen goods knowing them to be stolen. He offers to prove that he refused to sell them below their value.

---

315. *Ram Sahai v Jai Prakash*, AIR 1993 MP 147.
316. *KM Singh v Secretary, Assn. of Indian Universities*, (1992) 3 SCC 129 : AIR 1992 SC 1536.

A may prove these statements, though they are admissions, because they are explanatory of conduct influenced by facts in issue.

(e) *A* is accused of fraudulently having in his possession counterfeit coin which he knew to be counterfeit.

He offers to prove that he asked a skilful person to examine the coin as he doubted whether it was counterfeit or not, and that that person did examine it and told him it was genuine.

A may prove these facts for the reasons stated in the last preceding *illustration*.

SYNOPSIS

COMMENT

This section lays down as a general rule that admissions are relevant and may be proved against the person who makes them or his representative in interest. Admissions must be clear if they are to be used against the person making it. Admissions are substantive evidence by themselves, in view of section 17 and this section, though they are not conclusive proof of the matters admitted. Admissions duly proved are admissible evidence irrespective of whether the party making them appeared in the witness-box or not and whether that party when appearing as witness was confronted with those statements in case he made a statement contrary to those admissions.[317] In certain circumstances an admission may operate as an estoppel.[318] The effect usually given to admissions proved against persons who make them is destructive, not constructive. Whether they are true or not does not matter. The effective point is that they destroy the force of inconsistent statements made later.

What a party himself admits to be true may reasonably be presumed to be so, and until that presumption is rebutted, the fact admitted should be taken to be established.[319] A contractor's final bill expressly stating that it would be a final settlement of his claim under the contract was allowed to be proved against him as an admission of finality. He could get rid of it by showing something else, like a mistake etc.[320] The person against whom an admission is proved is at liberty to show that it was mistaken or untrue. When an admission is duly proved and the person against whom it is proved does not satisfy the court that it was mistaken or untrue, the court may decide the case

317. *Bharat Singh v Bhagirathi,* AIR 1966 SC 405 : (1966) 1 SCR 606. Followed in *Mudaliar Bapuji Valve v Yallappa Lalu Chaugule,* AIR 1994 Bom 358.

318. *KS Srinivasan v UOI,* AIR 1958 SC 419 : 1958 SCR 1295.

319. *Revappa v Madhava Rao,* AIR 1960 Mys. 97; *Sardar Tota Singh v Gold Field Leather Works,* AIR 1985 SC 507 : (1985) 1 SCC 414, admission as to the lawful nature of a sub-tenancy in an eviction proceeding.

320. *Central Coalfields Ltd v Mining Construction and Multi Contract Pvt Ltd,* (1982) 1 SCC 415.

in accordance with it. An erroneous admission does not bind the person making such admission. Admission must be considered as a whole;[321] but the court is not bound to believe or disbelieve the statement as a whole.[322]

An admission made by a party in a plaint signed and verified by him may be used against him in other suits. In other suits, this admission cannot be regarded as conclusive, and it is open to the party to show that it is not true.[323] If an admission in a pleading is made subject to a condition it must be either accepted subject to that condition or not accepted at all.[324] The value of an admission depends upon the circumstances in which it was made. Where those circumstances had not been properly investigated, the court was not able to determine the value of the alleged admission.[325] An admission is distinct from the former statement of a witness which is cited to contradict him. An admission can be proved without confronting the maker with his earlier statements.[326] Krishna Iyer J said in this case:[327] "There is a cardinal distinction between a party who is the author of a prior statement and a witness who is examined and is sought to be discredited by the use of his prior statement. In the former case in admission by a party is a substantive evidence if it fulfils the requirement of section 21; in the latter case a prior statement is used to discredit the credibility of the witness and does not become substantive evidence. In the former there is not necessary requirement of the statement containing the admission having to be put to the party because it is evidence *proprio vigore;* in the latter case the court cannot be invited to disbelieve a witness on the strength of the prior contradictory statement unless it has been put to him, as required by section 145."

This distinction was clearly made out in *Bharat Singh v Bhagirathi,*[328] where the court disposed of a similar argument with the following observation: "Admissions are substantive evidence by themselves, in view of sections 17 and 21 of the Act, though they are not conclusive proof of the matters admitted. We are of opinion that admissions duly proved are admissible evidence irrespective of whether the party making them appeared in the witness-box or not and whether he was confronted with these statements in case he made a statement contrary to those admission. An admission is a substantive evidence of the fact admitted while a previous statement used to contradict a witness does not become substantive evidence and merely serves the purpose of throwing doubt on the veracity of the witness."

Admissions cannot be proved by or on behalf of the person who makes them, or by his representative in interest, except

(1) when it is of such a nature that, if the person making it were dead, it would be relevant as between third persons under section 32;

---

321. *Mahendra v Sushila,* AIR 1965 SC 364 : (1964) 7 SCR 267; *Abida Khatoon v State of UP,* AIR 1963 All 260.

322. *Shiv Ram v Shiv Charan,* AIR 1964 Raj 126.

323. *Basant Singh v Janki Singh,* AIR 1967 SC 341 : (1967) 1 SCR 1.

324. *Calcutta National Bank v Rangaroon Tea Co,* AIR 1967 Cal 294.

325. *Prem Ex-servicemen Co-operative Society v State of Haryana,* AIR 1974 SC 1121 : (1974) 2 SCC 319; *State of Orissa v Ghanshyam Mohanty,* 1987 Cr LJ 1008 Orissa, a statement before a Magistrate, before investigation, allowed to be proved as an admission, though not a confession under section 164 CrPC.

326. *Biswanath Pd. v Dwarka Pd,* AIR 1974 SC 117 : (1974) 1 SCC 78.

327. *Ibid,* p 81.

328. AIR 1966 SC 405 : (1966) 1 SCR 606 : (1966) 2 SCJ 53.

(2) when it consists of a statement of the existence of any state of mind or body made at or about the time when such state of mind or body existed, and is accompanied by conduct rendering its falsehood improbable;

(3) when it is relevant otherwise than as an admission.

[s 21.1] Scope.—There is nothing in sections 18 to 21 to suggest that they apply to civil cases only; they apply also to admissions in criminal cases.[329] The accused went to a police station and lodged a FIR of murder, narrating the events preceding the commission of the offence and stating further how the offence was committed. It was held that the narrative of the antecedent events was admissible as admissions not amounting to confessions.[330] Illustration (a) exemplifies this rule.

The principle laid down in this section must be taken subject to sections 24, 25 and 26 of this Act and sections 164 and 201 of the Code of Criminal Procedure.[331] A confession made to a Magistrate but not recorded by him, under section 164 of the Code of Criminal Procedure, cannot be proved by tendering the oral evidence of the Magistrate.[332]

The scheme of sections 21 to 27 shows that this group of sections relate to admissions of which a confession made by an accused is a species and to certain circumstances which may prohibit the proof of such confessions or admissions. A confession is a kind of admission and there is no clear-cut line of demarcation between the two. Again, admissions may be relevant in civil as well as in criminal cases, and admissions that might be proved in civil cases are not inadmissible in criminal cases as such.[333]

[s 21.2] "As against the person who makes them".—The rule as regards statements made by a person is that they may be proved only when they are against him; otherwise a party may manufacture any amount of evidence in his own favour.[334] Where the statements are against the interest of the person making them there is a natural presumption of truth, and they may be proved. An admission is not conclusive as to the truth of the matters stated therein. It is only a piece of evidence, the weight to be attached to which must depend on the circumstances under which it is made. It can be shown to be erroneous or untrue, so long as the person to whom it was made has not acted upon it to his detriment, when it might become conclusive by way of estoppel.[335]

In a transaction for sale of property, the vendors admitted in the agreement, affidavits and other papers that the delivery of possession was made on the date of the agreement itself. It was held that there was a heavy burden on the vendor to prove that the statement in the agreement was not correct. The admission was coupled with the fact that a very big amount was paid to the vendors on the date of the agreement for vacating the property immediately. This was a strong circumstance in support of the fact of

---

329. *Md Baksh v Crown,* (1914) Kar 257.

330. *Legal Remembrancer v Lalit Mohan Singh Roy,* (1921) 49 Cal 167; *Pakala Narayana Swamy v King-Emperor,* (1937) 17 Pat 15.

331. *Queen-Empress v Bhairab Chunder Chuckerbutty,* (1898) 2 Cal WN 702.

332. *Nazir Ahmad v The King-Emperor,* (1936) 63 IA 372, 38 Bom LR 987 : 17 Lah 629.

333. *Ramchandran,* (1960) Mad 224; *Salil Kumar Roy v Banu Devi Bhansali,* AIR 1999 Cal 270, a letter was tendered in evidence by the earlier defendant. It was not necessary to show that letter to the substituted defendant before calling upon him to make a statement on the point.

334. *Ramani Pershad Narain Singh v Mahanth Adaiya Gossain,* (1903) 31 Cal 380; *Mahendra v Sushila,* AIR 1965 SC 364 : (1964) 7 SCR 267.

335. *Nagubai v B Shama Rao,* AIR 1956 SC 593 : (1956) SCR 451.

admission. The vendors could not turn around and say that the recital regarding delivery of possession in the agreement was made for the sake of completing the papers only.[336]

An admission by a plaintiff of her marriage with a person made before there was any dispute about such marriage may be proved by or on behalf of her under clause (1) of this section read with section 32.[337]

A receipt is nothing but an admission by the party making it that he has received the amount specified in the document. It is an admission against his own interest and he is of course bound by it, and so are those who claim through or under him.[338]

[s 21.3] "Representative in interest".—This expression will include those who are privies in blood, law or estate. The purchaser at an ordinary execution sale is in privy with, and is the representative-in-interest of the judgment-debtor so as to be bound by the latter's admission.[339] There is a distinction between the position of a purchaser in a private sale and in a public sale in execution of a decree. In the former he derives his title through, and cannot acquire a better title than, the vendor: in the latter he acquires his title by operation of law adversely to the judgment-debtor and so freed from all alienations and encumbrances effected by the debtor subsequently to the attachment of the property sold in execution.[340] But the purchaser in a public or a private sale acquires only the right, title and interest of the judgment-debtor with all its defects and the creditor takes the property subject to all equities which would affect it in the debtor's hands.

[s 21.4] Exceptions.—Admissions cannot be proved by, or on behalf of, the person who makes them, because a person will always naturally make statements that are favourable to him. Thus the opinion of a person as to the valuation of his property which is under acquisition is not relevant.[341] To this principle three Exceptions are laid down in the section:—

[s 21.4.1] Statements of deceased person relevant in dispute between third parties.—[*Exception 1*].—This exception enables a person to prove his own statement where the circumstances are such that if he were dead, the statement would have been relevant in a dispute between third parties.[342]

[s 21.4.2] Explanation of state of mind or body or mental or bodily feeling.—[*Exception 2*].—The state of a man's mind or body is relevant under section 14; and

---

336. *Chetak Constructions Ltd v Om Prakash,* AIR 2003 MP 145.

337. *Musammat Bashiran v Mohammad Husain,* (1941) 16 Luck 615.

338. *Akal Sahu v King-Emperor,* (1947) 26 Pat 49; *Idandas v Anant Ramchandra Phadke,* AIR 1982 SC 127 : (1982) 1SCR 1197 : (1982) 1 SCC 27 : 1982 Mah LJ 328, entries in counterfoils are not admissions against the opposite party of the maker of the entries. *State of Rajasthan v Vinod Malhotra,* 1997 Cr LJ 1488 (Raj), statements which do not amount to admissions or confessions are outside the scope of the section . They are provable like any other relevant statement. In this case a police officer received information on telephone which was probably conveyed by the accused. The information led to discovery of dead bodies, which fact was also admissible under section 27.

339. *Ishan Chunder Sirkar v Beni Madhub Sirkar,* (1896) 24 Cal 62 FB; *Mahomed Mozuffer Hossein v Kishori Mohun Roy,* (1895) 22 Cal 909 : 22 IA 129.

340. *Dinendronath Sannyal v Ramcoomar Ghose,* (1880) 8 IA 65, 75: 7 Cal 107. See, *Thakur Bhim Singh v Thakur Kan Singh,* AIR 1980 SC 727: (1980) 2 SCR 628, admission in 1955 about a transaction in 1940 admitted against the legal representative of the maker.

341. *Mariam v State of Kerala,* AIR 1980 Ker 176.

342. See Illustrations (*a*) and (*b*).

statements narrating such facts indicating the state of mind or body may be proved on behalf of a person narrating them. But such statements should have been made at or about the time when such state of mind or body existed; see illustrations (d) and (e). Section 14 merely declares that such statements are relevant. This clause shows that such facts or statements may be proved on behalf of the person making them, notwithstanding the general rule that persons cannot make evidence for themselves by what they choose to say.

[s 21.4.3] Facts otherwise relevant.—[*Exception 3*].—This Exception lays down that facts which are relevant under sections 6 to 13 will not be rendered inadmissible because they may be proved on behalf of the person making them. Illustrations (d) and (e) refer to this Exception.[343] A person who sought exemption from the application of the Urban Land Ceiling Act of his land was not taken thereby to have admitted that the Act was applicable to his land, the application of the Act to a given situation being a question of law.[344] Where an injured accused person was examined by a doctor and in the course of such examination he explained the cause of his injuries, it was held by the Supreme Court that the statement was not an admission and was a relevant evidence under section 3 otherwise than as an admission. He could prove his own statement.[345]

A "yadi" being a contemporaneous document prepared by a prosecution witness was held to be something which could be relied upon.[346]

[s 22] When oral admissions as to contents of documents are relevant.—Oral admissions as to the contents of a document are not relevant, unless and until the party proposing to prove them shows that he is entitled to give secondary evidence of the contents of such document under the rules hereinafter contained, or unless the genuineness of a document produced is in question.

COMMENT

[s 22.1] Principle.—The contents of a document which is capable of being produced must be proved by the instrument itself and not by oral evidence.

Oral admissions as to contents of a document are excluded under this section. They are, however, admissible when the party is entitled to give secondary evidence of the contents of such document under sections 65 and 66. Such admissions are also admissible when the genuineness of the document produced is in question.

As to the validity of a gift deed, one of the donors stated that he was minor at the time of its execution. But in the gift deed itself he admitted his age to be 22. This admission was contained in the registered deed. This was held to be binding on him unless he could show any vitiating circumstance like fraud, coercion, etc.[347]

---

343. See, *Basanti v State of HP,* 1987 Cr LJ 1869 : AIR 1987 SC 1572 : (1987) 3 SCC 227 : 1987 SCC (Cri) 473, where the statement outside the court by the wife of the deceased that she and other named persons had committed the murder was held to be not provable under this section.

344. *Dilipsinh Mohansinh v SJ Mansha,* AIR 1995 Guj 1.

345. *Ammini v State of Kerala,* 1998 Cr LJ 481 (SC).

346. *Subhash Maruti Avasare v State of Maharashtra,* (2006) 10 SCC 631 : 2006 (4) Crimes 304 (SC).

347. *Patel Prabhudas Hargovandas v Heirs of Patel Babubhai Kachrabhai,* AIR 2007 Guj 148.

[348]**[s 22A] When oral admission as to contents of electronic records are relevant.—Oral admissions as to the contents of electronic records are not relevant, unless the genuineness of the electronic record produced is in question].**

COMMENT

[s 22A.1] Information Technology Act.—Section 22A has been inserted into the Evidence Act by the Information Technology Act, 2000. The purpose of this section is to provide for the circumstances in which an oral admission could be proved as to the contents of an electronic record. The section disallows the evidence of oral admission as to the contents of an electronic record. It then talks of an exceptional situation, which is that when the genuineness of the electronic record produced before the court is itself in question. The section says that oral admissions as to the contents of an electronic record may be proved in evidence when the genuineness of the record has been questioned.

[s 23] Admissions in civil cases when relevant.—In civil cases no admission is relevant, if it is made either upon an express condition that evidence of it is not to be given,[s 23.2] or under circumstances from which the Court can infer that the parties agreed together that evidence of it should not be given.[s 23.3]

***Explanation*.—Nothing in this section shall be taken to exempt any barrister, pleader, attorney or vakil from giving evidence of any matter of which he may be compelled to give evidence under section 126.**

SYNOPSIS

COMMENT

[s 23.1] Principle.—This section lays down that in civil cases an admission is not relevant when it is made (1) upon an express condition that evidence of it is not to be given, or (2) under circumstances from which the court can infer that the parties agreed together that evidence of it should not be given. The section gives effect to the maxim, *interest reipublicae ut sit finis litium* (it is for the interest of the State that there should be an end of litigation). "The law relating to communications without prejudice is of course familiar. As a matter of policy, the law has long excluded from evidence admissions by words or conduct made by parties in the course of negotiations to settle litigation. The purpose is to enable parties in an attempt to compromise litigation to communicate with one another freely and without the embarrassment which the liability of their communications to be put in evidence subsequently might impose upon them. The law relieves them of this embarrassment so that their negotiations to

348. Ins. by Act 21 of 2000, section 92 and Sch. II–3 (w.e.f. 17-10-2000).

avoid litigation or to settle it may go unhampered...The privilege covers admissions by words or conduct. For example, neither party can use the readiness of the other to negotiate as an implied admission."[349]

[s 23.2] "Express condition that evidence of it is not to be given".—This section protects communications made "without prejudice". Confidential overtures of pacification and any other offers or propositions between litigating parties, expressly or impliedly made without prejudice are excluded on grounds of public policy. For, if parties were to be prejudiced by their efforts to compromise it would be impossible to attempt any amicable arrangement of differences.[350] The expression "without prejudice" means without prejudice to the writer of the letter if the terms he proposes are not accepted. It means this: "I make you an offer which you may accept or not, as you like; but if you do not accept it, my having made it is to have no effect at all".[351] If the terms proposed in the letter are accepted, a complete contract is established, and the letter, although written without prejudice, operates to alter the old state of things and to establish a new one.[352] If letters marked "without prejudice" are tendered in evidence and the other party admits them, the admission implies that the privilege is withdrawn and the letters are free to be used as evidence in a judicial proceeding. Letters so marked show the writer's desire as to the privilege, but unless there are circumstances from which it can be inferred that the other party agreed to respect the privilege, the letters cannot be excluded under this section.[353]

The reply to a letter written "without prejudice" cannot be admitted in evidence even though not guarded in a similar manner. The words once used will exclude an entire correspondence. Thus, where "without prejudice" negotiations led to an agreed settlement between two parties engaged in litigation, the content of those negotiations was not discoverable to another party in the litigation, nor would it be admissible evidence.[354]

The rule which excludes documents marked "without prejudice" has no application unless some person is in dispute or negotiation with another and terms are offered for the settlement of the dispute or negotiation.[355] Thus, where letters were written without reference to any dispute, they were held to be not privileged though they were marked "without prejudice."[356] The fact that the document is headed "without prejudice" does not conclusively or automatically render it privileged from admission in evidence in any subsequent proceedings, and if a claim for such privilege of the document is challenged the court will look at the document to determine its nature. However, all documents which form part of negotiations between the parties are *prima facie* privileged from admission in

349. Dixon CJ in *Field v Commissioner for Railways,* (1957)99 CLR 285, cited Edward's *Cases on Evidence in Australia,* 519 at p 520 (1968).

350. *Hoghton v Hoghton,* (1852) 15 Beav 278.

351. *Re River Steamer Co,* (1871) LR 6 Ch 822, 832.

352. *Walker v Wilsher,* (1889) 23 QBD 335.

353. *The Lucknow Improvement Trust v PL Jaitly & Co,* (1929) 5 Luck 465.

354. *Rush and Tompkins v Greater London Council,* The Independent, Nov 4, 1988 HL; 1988 CLY 2956; without prejudice correspondence between the parties about their claims as to costs were not allowed to be disclosed without their consent. *Simaan General Contracting Co v Pilkington Glass Ltd,* (1987) 1 All ER 345 (QBD).

355. *Madhavrav v Gulabbhai,* (1898) 23 Bom 177, 180.

356. *Dentrey Re, ex p Holt,* (1893) 2 QB 116, 119-20.

evidence if they are marked "without prejudice" even if the document in question merely initiates the negotiations and even if the document does not itself contain an offer.[357]

An admission made to a stranger, under whatever terms as to secrecy, is not protected by law from disclosure.

[s 23.3] "Under circumstances from which the Court can infer that the parties agreed together that evidence of it should not be given".—Such circumstances must be of such a character that the court must naturally come to the conclusion that the parties agreed together that evidence of it should not be given. In a suit for rent, there was a talk of settlement between the plaintiff's pleader and one of the defendants when the suit was about to be instituted. It was held that the mere fact of the conversation taking place when the parties were contemplating that a suit might be instituted was not in itself sufficient to prevent the conversation from being put in evidence.[358]

[s 23.4] Use of "without prejudice" material by one party.—Where one party used "without prejudice" material for the purpose of a freezing injunction which had been issued against it, the court said that the other party also become entitled to demand production of the documents containing that materials. The court observed that it would be unfair to allow one party to rely on without prejudice material on an interlocutory application which concerned the merits of a case without also allowing the other party to use that material at the trial. Since the merits of the case had been relevant for the purpose of the opponent's application for a freezing injunction, the plaintiff would be permitted to rely on the without prejudice discussions at the trial.[359]

[s 23.5] Restraint of use of without prejudice material in subsequent connected proceedings.—It has been held that the use of without prejudice documents in subsequent connected proceedings with the same subject matter is restrained. It is likely that the without prejudice document are subject to an implied condition that they would not be used in litigation and, unless protection extended to subsequent litigation, the public policy aim of allowing without prejudice documents to be drawn up freely would be defeated.[360] The court followed *Unilever Plc v Proctor and Gamble Co.*[361]

[s 24] Confession caused by inducement, threat or promise, when irrelevant in criminal proceeding.—A confession[s 24.2] made by an accused person[s 24.3] is irrelevant in a criminal proceeding, if the making of the confession appears to the Court to have been caused by any inducement, threat or promise[s 24.4] having reference to the

---

357. *South Shropshire District Council v Amos,* (1987) 1 All ER 340 CA; applying *Holt Ex p.,* (1891-4) All ER Rep 209 and *Cutts v Head,* (1984) 1 All ER 611.

358. *Meajan Matbar v Alimuddi Mia,* (1916) 44 Cal 130; *Uybl Ltd v British Railways Board,* (2000) 97 (42) LSG 45 (CA), negotiations concerning the settling of disputes which were made without prejudice to any forthcoming litigation, and thus at a future trial "without prejudice" documents could not be referred to. Counsel had not cited any authorities and therefore the issue was a difficult one, although *Rush & Tompkins Ltd v Greater London Council,* (1989) AC 1280 : (1989) CLY 1701 approved the principles of the without prejudice rule set out in *Cutts v Head,* (1984) Ch. 290 : (1984) CLY 2608 which acknowledged that unless a without prejudice letter was marked "without prejudice save as to costs", it was not admissible on the costs hearing following trial. The draft report was a draft and the figures enclosed were wholly different to those in the final report.

359. *Somatra Ltd v Sinclair Roche & Temperley; Sinclair Roche & Temperley v Somatra Ltd,* (2000) 1 WLR 2453 (CA).

360. *Instance v Denny Bros Printing Ltd (interim injunction)* (2000) FSR 869.

361. *Unilever Plc v Proctor and Gamble Co,* 2000 FSR 344 (UK) : (1999) 2 All ER 691 : (1999) LWLR 1630 (Ch D).

charge against the accused person,[s 24.5] proceeding from a person in authority[s 24.6] and sufficient, in the opinion of the Court, to give the accused person grounds which would appear to him reasonable[s 24.7] for supposing that by making it he would gain any advantage or avoid any evil of a temporal nature[s 24.8] in reference to the proceedings against him.

SYNOPSIS

COMMENT

The substantive law of confession is contained in sections 24 to 30 of the Evidence Act and the adjective law, in sections 164, 281 and 463 of the Code of Criminal Procedure, 1973. Confessions are received in evidence in criminal cases upon the same principle on which admissions are received in civil cases, namely, the presumption that a person will not make an untrue statement against his own interest. A man of sound mind and full age, who makes a statement in ordinary simple language and has not been the victim of malpractices, threat or inducement in making such statement, must be bound by the language of the statement and by its ordinary plain meaning and the act spoken of must be given its legal consequence.[362] This section does not require positive proof as defined in section 3 of improper inducement. A well-grounded conjecture reasonably based upon circumstances disclosed in the evidence, is sufficient to exclude a confession.[363]

The confession of an accused is only relevant against himself, though section 30 is an exception to this rule.

[s 24.1] Principle.—According to this section a confession by an accused is irrelevant if it is caused by (1) inducement; (2) threat; or (3) promise. The inducement, threat, or promise should have (a) reference to the charge against the accused, (b) proceeded from a person in authority, and (c) sufficiently given the accused person reasonable grounds for supposing that by making the confession he would gain any advantage or avoid any evil of a temporal nature in reference to the proceedings against him.

---

362. Per Mears CJ, in *Raggha v Emperor,* (1925) 23 A LJR 821, 826 FB.
363. *Bhukin v King-Emperor,* (1948) Nag 147; see generally *Kamlesh v State,* 1997 Cr LJ 3191 (All) : *State of HP v Prakash Chand,* 1997 Cr LJ 1979 (HP); *Rajan Johnsonhai Christy v State,* 1997 Cr LJ 3702 (Guj).

A confession is relevant—

(1) if it is made after the impression caused by any such inducement, threat or promise has been fully removed (section 28);

(2) if it is not made to a police officer (section 25); or

(3) if it is made in the presence of a Magistrate when the accused is in the custody of a police officer (section 26).

[s 24.2] "Confession".—The word "confession" has not been defined anywhere in the Act. A "confession" is an admission made at any time by a person charged with a crime, stating or suggesting the inference that he committed that crime.[364] This definition was adopted by Lord Atkin in *Pakala Narain Swami v Emperor*,[365] His Lordship said: "A confession must either admit in terms the offence, or at any rate substantially all the facts which constitute the offence. An admission of a gravely incriminating fact, even a conclusively incriminating fact, is not in itself a confession, for example, an admission that the accused is the owner of and was in recent possession of the knife or revolver which caused death with no explanation of any other man's possession. The definition is not contained in the Evidence Act, 1872; and in that Act it would not be consistent with the natural use of language to construe confession as a statement by an accused suggesting the inference that he committed the crime."

In order to decide whether a statement is confessional or not, it must be read as a whole.[366] A statement which might, at the most, be described as suggesting an inference that the accused committed the crime does not amount to confession.[367] An admission of a gravely incriminating fact is not of itself a confession.[368] Where the accused admitted his complicity in crime merely by stating that he was in the company of the other accused who strangulated the deceased, it was held that such statement could not be construed as confession of his involvement in the crime, hence it was inadmissible in evidence.[369]

---

364. *Stephen's Dig*, 12th Edn, Article 22; *Queen-Empress v Babu Lal*, (1884) 6 All 509, 539 FB; *Queen Empress v Nana*, (1889) 14 Bom 260 FB; *Superintendent and Remembrancer of Legal Affairs, Bengal v Bhaju Majhi*, (1929) 57 Cal 1062; *Shankar v State of Tamil Nadu*, (1994) 4 SCC 478 : 1994 Cr LJ 3071, a confession is a form of admission consisting of direct acknowledgement of guilt in a criminal charge. It must be an admission in express words by the accused person of the truth of the guilty fact charged or some essential part of it. A statement that contains a self-exculpatory matter cannot amount to a confession. The confession should be a voluntary one, that is to say, not caused by inducement, threat or promise. Whether a confession is voluntary or not is essentially a question of fact. *Mahabir Biswas v State of WB*, (1995) 2 SCC 25 : 1995 SCC (Cr) 308, a confession should be proved to be voluntary and true, before it should be acted upon : *State of Karnataka v Thangaraj*, AIR 1995 SC 2134, a confession confirmed by circumstances. *Ganesh Traders v District Collector, Karimnagar*, 2002 Cr LJ 1108 (AP), confession must relate to the offence in question. If the purported admission makes out no offence, the provisions relating to confession would not come into play.

365. *Pakala Narain Swami v Emperor*, AIR 1939 PC 47.

366. *Lokeman Shah v State of West Bengal*, 2001 Cr LJ 2196 : AIR 2001 SC 1760.

367. *Om Prakash v State of UP*, AIR 1960 SC 409 : 1960 Cr LJ 544. See further, *Pandru Khadia v State of Orissa*, 1992 Cr LJ 762 (Ori), where it was pointed out that a confessional statement must be addressed to some person and that, therefore, the accused going round the village and shouting that he had killed his wife did not amount to confession.

368. *Palvinder Kaur v State of Punjab*, AIR 1952 SC 354 : 1953 Cr LJ 154 : 1953 SCR 94.

369. *Valiyaveetil Ashraf v State of Kerala*, 1994 Cr LJ 555 (Ker); *Shankar v State of Tamil Nadu*, 1994 Cr LJ 3071, a statement containing self-exculpatory matter cannot amount to a confession. *Suresh Bhudarmal Kalani v State of Maharashtra*, 1998 Cr LJ 4592 : AIR 1998 SC 3258 : (1998) 7 SCC 337, a self-exculpatory statement by an accused person was held to be not an admissible confession.

Merely because one of the witnesses to the confessional statement did not support the confession in its entirety, the entire confession should not be brushed aside as unreliable, even though an independent witness had supported the recording of conviction. However, the conviction of the accused was not based merely on the confessional statements but also on other substantial evidence relied upon by the prosecution viz. recovery of the dead body, post-mortem report matching with confessional statements, evidence of other independent witnesses, who corroborated the recording of confessional statement in their presence and thus do not create doubt about the credibility of the prosecution case, so as to discard the same. The Supreme Court found no infirmity in the judgment and order of the High Court, holding the accused guilty.[370]

The principles governing admissibility of an extra-judicial confession capable of forming the basis of conviction of an accused have been summed up by Supreme Court[371] as follows:

(i) The extra-judicial confession is a weak evidence by itself. It has to be examined by the court with greater care and caution.

(ii) It should be made voluntarily and should be truthful.

(iii) It should inspire confidence.

(iv) An extra-judicial confession attains greater credibility and evidentiary value if it is supported by a chain of cogent circumstances and is further corroborated by other prosecution evidence.

(v) For an extra-judicial confession to be the basis of conviction, it should not suffer from any material discrepancies and inherent improbabilities.

(vi) Such statement essentially has to be proved like any other fact and in accordance with law.

An extra-judicial confession can be relied upon only if the same is voluntary and true and made in a fit state of mind. The value of evidence as to the confession like any other evidence depends upon the veracity of the witness to whom it has been made. The value of the evidence as to the confession depends on the reliability of the witness who gives the evidence. But is not open to any court to start with the presumption that extra-judicial confession is insufficient to convict the accused, even though it is supported by the other circumstantial evidence and corroborated by independent witness, as is the position in the instant case and the courts cannot be unmindful of the legal position, that if the evidence relating to extra-judicial confession is found credible after being tested on the touchstone of credibility and acceptability, it can solely form the basis of conviction.[372] Extra-judicial confession is a weak piece of evidence and the courts are to view it with greater care and caution. For an extra-judicial confession to form the basis of a conviction, it should not suffer from any material discrepancies and inherent improbabilities.[373] The accused was suspected of committing the rape and murder of the victim only after the Investigating Officer found it was affirmed with a witness, that he was seen close to the place of occurrence. Thereafter, he made an extra-judicial confession to the Village

---

370. *Baskaran v State of TN*, (2014) 5 SCC 765 (paras 18 and 19), **affirming** *Baskaran v State*, Criminal Appeal No. 9 of 2005, decided on 9.11.2006 (Mad).

371. *Sahadevan v State of TN*, (2012) 6 SCC 403.

372. *Baskaran v State of TN*, (2014) 5 SCC 765 (para 17).

373. *Vijay Shankar v State of Haryana*, (2015) 12 SCC 644, para 19.

Administrative Officer who was an unrelated person both to the complainant and the accused. The non-recording of the extra-judicial confession over a long period of time was held to be of no consequence. Further, the Village Administrative Officer was not inimical to the accused. The extra-judicial confession was relied on.[374]

Before a confession can be accepted in evidence, it must be established by cogent evidence what were the exact words used by the accused.[375] Even if so much is established, prudence and justice demand that such evidence cannot be made the sole ground of conviction. It may be used only as a corroborative piece of evidence.[376] The rule of prudence does not require that each and every circumstance mentioned in the confession with regard to the participation of the accused person in the crime must be separately and independently corroborated, nor is it essential that the corroboration must come from facts and circumstances discovered after the confession was made.[377] An extra-judicial confession may or may not be a weak evidence. Each case has to be examined on the basis of its own facts and circumstances.[378] Deliberate and voluntary confessions of guilt, if clearly proved, are among the most effectual proofs in law.[379] The court should not start with the presumption that extra-judicial confession is a weak type of

---

374. *Kadamanian @ Manikandan v State,* AIR 2016 SC 4266, paras 12 and 15 : (2016) 9 SCC 325.

375. *State of Assam v Manik Chandra Dey,* 1989 Cr LJ 1495 Gau, stereotype recording of confession not showing the words used by the accused and what was his rational motive in confessing, evidence rejected. To the same effect, *Arjun Sahu v State of Orissa,* 1988 Cr LJ 1086 (Ori), **following** *Rahim Beg v State of UP,* AIR 1973 SC 343 : 1972 Cr LJ 1260 and *Heramba Brahma v State of Assam,* AIR 1982 SC 1595 : 1983 Cr LJ 149 : (1982) 3 SCC 351 : 1983 SCC (Cri) 40. Prosecution witness deposing that the accused told him that he strangled the woman to rob her, but not telling the words spoken by the accused, confession not reliable. *Santosh v State of Kerala,* 1991 Cr LJ 570 Ker.

376. *Sahoo v State of UP,* AIR 1966 SC 40 : 1966 Cr LJ 68. See, *Chandrakant Chimanlal Desai v State of Gujarat,* (1992) 1 SCC 473 : 1992 Cr LJ 2757, where the Supreme Court laid that the same principles should be followed as were enunciated in *Kashmira Singh v State of MP,* AIR 1952 SC 159 : 1952 SCR 526 : 1952 Cr LJ 839, namely, such evidence should be used only to lend assurance to other evidence. The Supreme Court has observed that a confession can be acted upon without corroboration for the purpose of entering conviction. The confession in this case was recorded by a judicial magistrate. Its voluntariness, therefore, was not in doubt. It explained the circumstances in which a prisoner died in custody. *Lokeman Shah v State of WB,* 2001 Cr LJ 2196 : AIR 2001 SC 1760.

377. *Balbir Singh v State of Punjab,* AIR 1957 SC 216 : 1957 Cr LJ 481. Confession corroborated by circumstantial evidence, *Lavji Mona v State of Gujarat,* 1993 Cr LJ 3148 : 1994 SCC (Cri) 53 : AIR 1993 SC 2480.

378. *Sivakumar v State,* (2006) 1 SCC 714 : AIR 2006 SC 653 : 2006 Cr LJ 536.

379. *Emperor v Narayen,* (1907) 9 Bom LR 789, 801: 32 Bom 111 FB *Kishan Lal v State,* 1991 Cr LJ 742 (Del), confession as to rape, neither commanding belief nor supported by medical evidence, conviction quashed, the court **relying** upon *State of UP v MK Anthony,* AIR 1985 SC 48 : 1985 Cr LJ 493 : (1985) 1 SCC 505 : 1985 SCC (Cri) 105; *Pyara Singh v State of Punjab,* AIR 1977 SC 2274 : 1977 Cr LJ 1941, weak evidence; *Heramba Brahma v State of Assam,* AIR 1982 SC 1595 : 1983 Cr LJ 149 : (1982) 3 SCC 351 : 1983 SCC (Cri) 40; *Rahim Beg v State of UP,* AIR 1973 SC 343 : 1972 Cr LJ 1260, exact words of confession not reproduced; *Kishore Chand v State of HP,* 1990 Cr LJ 2289 SC : 1990 JT SC 662 : (1991) 1 SCC 286 : 1991 SCC (Cri) 172 : AIR 1990 SC 2140. See, *Manjit Singh v State of Punjab,* 1991 Cr LJ 2265 (P&H), confession before a respectable person of the town followed by recovery of dead body and weapon at the instance of the accused in the presence of the Sarpanch, motive also established, proper evidence, conviction confirmed. *Balkar Singh v State of UP,* 1991 Cr LJ 77 (All), the circumstances should show the reasons for the desire to confess and that it was natural for him to confess to the person appearing as a witness. This cannot happen in reference to a perfect stranger.

evidence.[380] The court should apply two tests: Is it voluntary? Is it true?[381] The Supreme Court prescribed this guideline in a case where it held that the evidentiary value of a confession was not destroyed by the facts that the accused was taken from one place to another because of the non-availability of a Magistrate there and that a police station was not in the vicinity of the judicial lock-up. If it appears that the confession has been improperly induced, then the court is bound to exclude it, no matter how true it may be.[382] An extra-judicial confession is in the very nature of things a weak evidence.[383] the acceptability of an extra-judicial confession will depend upon the reliability of the evidence of the person to whom such confession is said to have been made.[384]

The accused, while in police custody, was produced before the magistrate on three different occasions. He was then remanded to judicial custody and made a confession after being in such custody for seven days. He admitted in full length the role played by him along with the other accused. The magistrate certified that in his opinion the accused made the confession voluntarily. The Supreme Court held that it could not be said that the accused was pressurised by the police or was prevailed upon by any extraneous influences to make the confession.[385]

It is the duty of the court to inquire very carefully into all the circumstances under which the confession was made, and particularly as to the length of time during which the accused was in custody.[386] Where the Magistrate while recording a confession elicited answers by questioning the accused, it could not be said that the answers given were voluntary statements of the accused.[387] A statement made under section 164 of the Code of Criminal Procedure, which does not amount to a confession, can be used against the maker as an admission within the purview of sections 18 to 21.[388]

A confession which has not been retracted even up to the last stage of the trial and also accepted by the accused in examination under section 313, CrPC, can be fully relied upon.[389]

---

380. *Narayan Singh v State of MP,* AIR 1985 SC 1678 : 1985 Cr LJ 1862 : (1985) 4 SCC 26 : 1985 SCC Cri 460. But, see, *Akanman Bora v State of Assam,* 1988 Cr LJ 573 (Gau), extra-judicial confession not disclosing the name of the victim, held not reliable.

381. *Shankaria v State of Rajasthan,* AIR 1978 SC 1248 : 1978 Cr LJ 1251. **Followed** in *Ganesh Prasad Singh v State of Orissa,* 1987 Cr LJ 1345 (Ori), confession recorded by Magistrate, but no corroboration, rejected; *State of Orissa v Adiknanda,* 1987 Cr LJ 603, another uncorroborated confession.

382. *Emperor v Bhagi,* (1906) 8 Bom LR 697, 699.

383. *Makhan Singh v State of Punjab,* AIR 1988 SC 1705 : 1988 Supp SCC 526 : 1988 SCC (Cri) 916, where the confession was made to a person who was harassing the accused and the motivation was only to get rid of the harassment, held, confession not reliable though the person causing harassment had no official status.

384. *State of Kerala v Thomas,* (1986) 2 SCC 411 at p 414 : 1986 SCC (Cr) 176.

385. *State of TN v Kutty,* AIR 2001 SC 2778 : 2001 Cr LJ 4168.

386. *Queen-Emp. v Narayan,* (1901) 3 Bom LR 122, 124 : 25 Bom 543.

387. *Lingiah,* (1954) Mys 27; *State of MP v Dayaram Hansraj,* AIR 1981 SC 2007 : 1981 Cr LJ 1688 : 1981 Supp SCC 14 : 1981 SCC (Cri) 601.*Bhagwati Singh v State of MP,* AIR 2003 SC 1088, accused produced before the magistrate hand-cuffed in police custody, record of the statement did not show what questions were put to see whether he was mentally or physically pressurised, the record was also not in proper form. The statement was also retracted by the accused. Not sufficient to prove his guilt.

388. *Ghulam Hussain v King,* (1949) 52 Bom LR 508 : 77 IA 65.

389. *Bishnu Prasad Sinha v State of Assam,* AIR 2007 SC 848 : (2007) 11 SCC 467.

[s 24.2.1] Confession of the co-accused.—Confession of the co-accused cannot be treated as substantive evidence.[390] [See further under section 30].

[s 24.2.2] Recording of confession.—Giving warning that it will be used against the person making it, is fundamental basic principle of Criminal Jurisprudence.[391] Where confessional statement of the accused could be recorded only by Judicial Magistrate, the same recorded by Executive Magistrate was not admissible in evidence.[392]

A confessional statement recorded under section 108 of the Customs Act, 1962 was held to be admissible in evidence although the requirements of section 164 CrPC, regarding recording of confessions were not complied with, this provision being not applicable to recording of confessions under the Customs Act.[393]

Where the accused was produced before the magistrate hand cuffed from police custody and he recorded the confession without ascertaining the possibility of pressurisation by police, the confession was held to be wasted.[394]

[s 24.2.3] To be accepted as a whole or rejected as a whole.—It is a well accepted rule regarding the use of confessions and admissions that these must be accepted as a whole or rejected as a whole and that the court is not competent to accept only the inculpatory part while rejecting the exculpatory part as inherently incredible.[395] A statement that contains self-exculpatory matter cannot amount to a confession, if the exculpatory matter includes some fact, which if true would negative the offence alleged to be confessed. A confession must either admit in terms the offence or at any rate substantially all the facts that constitute the offence.[396] However, where the exculpatory part of a confessional statement is not only inherently improbable but is contradicted by other evidence, the court can accept the inculpatory part and piecing the same with the other evidence convict the accused.[397] Thus exculpatory part may be excluded where the evidence on record disproves it[398] or where it is apparently false.[399] When a statement, treated as a confessional statement, contains both exculpatory as well as inculpatory statements, it is possible for the court to reject the exculpatory part of such a confessional statement, which stands belied by the other evidence on record, and rely

---

390. *Balbir Singh v State of Orissa,* 1995 Cr LJ 1762 (Ori); *Haricharan Kurmi v State of Bihar,* AIR 1964 SC 1184.

391. *NSR Krishna Prasad v Directorate of Enforcement LBK Market,* 1992 Cr LJ 1888 (AP).

392. *State of Haryana v Parmanand,* 1995 Cr LJ 396 (P&H).

393. *Gulam Husain Shaikh Chougule v S Reynolds, Suptd.of Customs, Marmgoa,* AIR 2001 SC 2930 : 2001 Cr LJ 4755.

394. *Bhagwan Singh v State of MP,* 2003 Cr LJ 1262. *Gurdeep Singh v State (Delhi Admn.),* AIR 1999 SC 3646 : (2000) 1 SCC 498 : 1999 Cr LJ 4573.

395. *State of TN v Kutty,* 2001 Cr LJ 4168 : AIR 2001 SC 2778, confession to be read as a whole. So read it became clear that the accused had clearly described the role played by him along with others in murdering two ladies. Confession admissible. It was immaterial that he did not say that he too had inflicted a stab injury.

396. *Palvinder Kaur v State of Punjab,* 1953 SCR 94 : 1953 Cr LJ 154 : AIR 1952 SC 354. Followed in *Kasim Babamiya Shaikh v, State of Maharashtra,* 1996 AIHC 18 (Bom); *Hanumant Govind Nargundkar v State of MP,* AIR 1952 SC 343 : 1953 Cr LJ 129.

397. *Nishi Kant v State of Bihar,* AIR 1969 SC 422 : 1969 Cr LJ 671; *Jamuram v State of Rajasthan,*1995 Cr LJ 1333 (Raj), exculpatory part false, inculpatory part can be accepted.

398. *Mohan Lal v Ajit Singh,* AIR 1978 SC 1183 : 1978 Cr LJ 1107.

399. *Keshoram Bora v Assam,* AIR 1978 SC 1096: 1978 Cr LJ 1089. **Followed** in *Rajesh Thakur v State of WB,* 1988 Cr LJ 1477 (Cal).

upon that inculpatory part of the confessional statement, which is proved to be true by the evidence on record.[400]

[s 24.2.4] Points of difference between confession and admission.—A confession differs from an admission:

(1) A confession is a statement made by an accused person which is sought to be proved against him in a criminal proceeding to establish the commission of an offence by him; while an admission usually relates to a civil transaction and comprises all statements amounting to admissions as defined in section 18.

(2) A confession if deliberately and voluntarily made may be accepted as conclusive in itself of the matters confessed;[401] an admission is not a conclusive proof of the matters admitted, but may operate as an estoppel.

(3) A confession always goes against the person making it; an admission may be used on behalf of the person making it under the Exceptions provided in section 21.

(4) The confession of one of two or more accused jointly tried for the same offence can be taken into consideration against the co-accused (section 30). But an admission by one of several defendants in a suit is no evidence against another defendant.

See Comment on section 17, *supra.*

[s 24.3] "By an accused person".—The expression "accused person" describes the person against whom evidence is sought to be led in a criminal proceeding. This expression has the same connotation as the expression "a person accused of any offence" in the following section.[402] If a person makes a statement when he is a suspect but not an accused person and subsequently becomes an accused, his statement will be regarded as a confession.[403] When a person states that he has done certain acts which amount to an offence, he accuses himself of committing the offence, and the statement is, therefore, a confession by an "accused person" within the meaning of this section.[404]

[s 24.4] "Appears to the Court to have been caused by any inducement, threat or promise".—Going by the prescriptions contained in section 164, CrPC, 1973, what is to be ensured is that the confession is made voluntarily by the offender, that there was no external pressure particularly by the police, that the concerned person's mindset while making the confession was uninfluenced by any external factors, that he was fully conscious of what he was saying, that he was also fully aware that based on his statement there is every scope for his suffering the conviction, which may result in the imposition of extreme punishment of life imprisonment and even capital punishment of death, that prior to the making of the confession he was in a free state of mind and was not in the midst of any persons who would have influenced his mind in any manner for making the confession, that the statement was made in the presence of the Judicial Magistrate and none else, that while making the confession there was no other person present other than the accused and the Magistrate concerned and that if he

---

400. *Irshad Alam v State of Bihar*, 2014 Cr LJ 2107 (para 89) : 2015 (1) Pat LJR 368 (Pat—DB).

401. *Queen-Empress v Sangappa,* (1889) Unrep. Cr C 463, Cr R No. 22 of 1896; *Emperor v Narayen,* (1907) 9 Bom LR 789, 801 : 32 Bom 111 FB.

402. *State of UP v Deoman,* AIR 1960 SC 1125 : 1960 Cr LJ 1504.

403. *Emperor v Bhagwandas Bisesar,* (1940) 42 Bom LR 938: (1941) Bom 27.

404. *Santokhi Beldar v King-Emperor,* (1932) 12 Pat 241 FB.

expressed his desire not to make the confession after appearing before the Magistrate, the Magistrate should ensure that he is not entrusted to police custody. All this is to ensure that the confession was recorded at the free will of the accused and was not influenced by any other factor. The trial Judge has to analyse the confession carefully and if while making such analysis, he develops an iota of doubt, the same will be rejected at the very outset. However, in the instant case, there was no such doubt as to its veracity.[405] Protection against self-incrimination is available even at the stage of investigation. Such protection ensures reliability of the statement and of its voluntary nature. Police powers of investigation cannot override constitutional protection.[406]

The appropriate meaning of the word "appears" is "seems". It imports a lesser degree of probability than proof. The standard of a prudent man is not completely displaced, but the stringent rule of proof is relaxed. Even so, the laxity of proof permitted does not warrant a court's opinion based on pure surmise. A *prima facie* opinion based on evidence and circumstances may be adopted as the standard laid down.[407] The word "appears" is not so strong as the expression "proved".[408]

[s 24.5] "Having reference to the charge against the accused person".—Charge" means a criminal charge or a charge of an offence in a criminal proceeding. The inducement, threat, or promise, must be with reference to the offence, with which the accused is charged.

[s 24.6] "Person in authority"—Where a confession was made to a tahsildar who was a person of some influence in the village, but had no interest in the prosecution of the accused other than the interest which every citizen has in the maintenance of law and order, and the confession was made in consequence of questions put, and a promise made by him, it was held that the tahsildar not being a person empowered to examine the accused or one who could legitimately influence the course of proceeding, the confession was not excluded by this section.[409] Customs Officers[410] as well as Excise Officers[411] are persons in authority.

But a confession made by a person while he was in the custody of customs officials for the purposes of an enquiry on the orders of a magistrate was held to be not barred.[412]

---

405. *Mohd Jamiludin Nasir v State of West Bengal,* (2014) 7 SCC 443 (para 21) :AIR 2014 SC 2587.

406. *Selvi v State of Karnataka,* AIR 2010 SC 1974 : (2010) 7 SCC 263.

407. *Pyare Lal v State of Rajasthan,* AIR 1963 SC 1094 and *Percy Rustomji Basta v State of Maharashtra,* AIR 1971 SC 1087 : 1971 Cr LJ 933, followed in *Budhwara Bai v State of MP,* 1991 Cr LJ 354 MP, the lady in this case confessed because of threats.

408. *Khiro Mandal v The Emperor,* (1929) 57 Cal 649.*State (NCT) of Delhi v Navjot Sandhu,* (2005) 11 SCC 600 : AIR 2005 SC 3820 : 2005 Cr LJ 3950, the extent of proof of vitiation of voluntariness of confession has to be of *prima facie* nature, creating a reasonable belief.

409. *Santokhi Beldar v King-Emperor,* (1932) 12 Pat 241 FB. In *Taula v King-Emperor,* (1929) 5 Luck 91, it was held that a ziladar serving under a big estate was a person in authority. *Gura Munda v State of Orissa,* 2002 Cr LJ (NOC) 24 (Ori), extra-judicial made to a ward member who was not a person in authority, held admissible.

410. *Vallabhdas v Asst. Collector, Customs,* (1964) 66 Bom LR 482 (SC); *SK Modi v State of Maharashtra,* AIR 1979 SC 705: 1979 Cr LJ 645; *State of Maharashtra v PK Pathak,* AIR 1980 SC 1224. See also, *Banshidhar Maharana v State of Bihar,* 1993 Cr LJ 1310.

411. *Harbansingh v State,* (1968) 71 Bom LR 599.

412. *CCE v C. Fernandez,* (1982) 3 SCC 512 : 1983 SCC (Cr) 109.

[s 24.7] "Grounds which would appear to him reasonable".—The Supreme Court has held that the mere existence of the threat, inducement or promise is not enough, but, in the opinion of the court, the said threat, inducement or promise shall be sufficient to cause a reasonable belief in the mind of the accused that by confessing he would get an advantage or avoid any evil of a temporal nature in reference to the proceedings against him: while the opinion is that of the court the criterion is the reasonable belief of the accused.[413]

[s 24.8] "Temporal nature".—The inducement must be of a temporal kind, i.e., not spiritual or religious. Confessions obtained by spiritual exhortations are admissible in evidence. A merely moral exhortation to tell the truth is not objectionable.[414]

[s 24.9] Retracted confessions.—As to this see notes under section 30.

[s 24.10] Extra-judicial confessions.—[For notes *see* under section 26].

[s 24.11] Panchayat.—In *Kansa Bahera v State of Orissa*,[415] the Supreme Court held a confession to be irrelevant which was made by the accused before the village *Pradhan*, (President) on the assurance that he would not be handed over to the police.

[s 24.12] Intelligence Officer of NCB—Where the confessional statement was recorded by Intelligence Officer of Narcotics Control Bureau, he being not a police officer, such statement was held to be admissible in evidence.[416]

[s 24.13] Confessional statement following assault and beating.—An extra-judicial confession made by the accused person following assault and beating was not taken to be either voluntary or natural. It was not relied upon for any purpose whatsoever.[417]

[s 24.14] Exculpatory statement.—Where the statement made by the accused contained an admission that she had placed the dead body of her husband in a trunk and had carried it in a jeep and thrown it into a well, but with regard to the cause of the death the statement made by her was that her husband had accidentally taken a poisonous substance which was meant for washing photos erroneously thinking it to be a medicine, it was held that the statement read as a whole was exculpatory in character and that the whole statement was inadmissible in evidence.[418]

[s 24.15] Corroboration.—Judicial confession were made both by the accused and his co-accused. The High Court rejected the confession made by the co-accused and acquitted him. This position remained undisturbed for some other reasons. The Supreme Court held that no part of such a confession could be used for the purpose of corroborating the confession of the accused.[419]

---

413. *Pyare Lal v State of Rajasthan*, AIR 1963 SC 1094 : (1963) 2 Cr LJ 178.
414. *King-Emperor v Akhileshwari Prasad*, (1925) 4 Pat 646.
415. AIR 1987 SC 1507; 1987 Cr LJ 1857.
416. *Nandi Francis Nwazor v Narcotics Control Bureau*, 1995 Cr LJ 665 (Del).
417. *Param Hans Yadav v State of Bihar*, AIR 1987 SC 955 : 1987 Cr LJ 789 : (1987) 2 SCC 197.
418. *Palvinder Kaur v State of Punjab*, AIR 1952 SC 354 : 1953 Cr LJ 154 : 1953 SCR 94. See further, *Keshroam Bora v State of Assam*, AIR 1978 SC 1096: 1978 Cr LJ 1089; *Mohan Lal v Ajit Singh*, AIR 1978 SC 1183: 1978 Cr LJ 1107; *Bhagwan Singh v State of Haryana*, AIR 1976 SC 1797 : 1976 Cr LJ 1379, noted elsewhere under this section.
419. *State of Tamil Nadu v Kutty*, AIR 2001 SC 2778 : 2001 Cr LJ 4168.

Extra-judicial confession is by its very nature, a rather weak type of evidence and requires appreciation with great deal of care and caution. Where an extra-judicial confession is warranted by suspicious circumstances, its credibility becomes doubtful and it loses its importance. It is for this reason that court generally looks for an independent reliable corroboration before placing any reliance upon such a confession. However, in the instant case, the extra-judicial confession was reliably corroborated and was relied upon.[420] Extra judicial confession can form basis for conviction if supported by other substantive evidence, which is lacking in this case.[421]

[s 25] Confession to police officer not to be proved.—No confession[s 25.4] made to a police-officer[s 25.5] shall be proved as against a person accused of any offence.[s 25.6]

SYNOPSIS

COMMENT

[s 25.1] Principle.—The Supreme Court explained the effect of provisions in these words.[422]

The fascicule of sections 24 to 30 aim to zealously protect the accused against becoming the victim of his own delusion or the mechanisation of others to self-incriminate in crime. The confession, therefore, is not received with an assurance, if its source be not *omni suspicious mojes,* above and free from the remotest taint of suspicion. The mind of the accused before he makes a confession must be in a state of perfect equanimity and must not have been operated upon by fear or hope or inducement. Hence, threat or promise or inducement held out to an accused makes the confession irrelevant and excludes it from consideration. A confession made to a police officer while the accused is in the custody or made before he became an accused, is not provable against him in any proceeding in which he is charged to the commission of an offence. Equally a confession made by him, while in the custody of the police officer, to any other person is also not probable in a proceeding in which he is charged with the commission of the offence unless it is made in the immediate presence of a Magistrate. Police officer is inherently suspect of employing coercion to obtain confession. Therefore, the confession made to a police officer under section 25 should totally be excluded from evidence. The reasons seem to be that the custody of police officer provides easy opportunities of coercion for extorting confession. Section 25 rests upon the principle that it is dangerous to depend upon a confession made to a police officer which cannot extricate itself from the suspicion that it might have been produced by the exercise of coercion. The legislative policy and practical reality

420. *Pargan Singh v State of Punjab,* AIR 2014 SC 3790 : (2014) 14 SCC 619 (para 24), **relying on** *Balwinder Singh v State of Punjab,* 1995 Supp (4) SCC 259 : 1996 SCC (Cri) 59.

421. *State of Karnataka v P Ravikumar,* AIR 2018 SC 3993 : (2018) 9 SCC 614.

422. *Kartar Singh v State of Punjab,* 1994 Cr LJ 3139, *per* K Ramaswamy J.

emphasise that a statement obtained, while the accused is in police custody, truly be not the product of his free choice.

Section 162 of the Code of Criminal Procedure enacts that neither statement made by any person to a police-officer in the course of an investigation shall, if taken down in writing, be signed by the person making it, nor shall such writing be used as evidence.

[s 25.2] Object.— Under the next section a confession made to a private person by a person in custody of the police is inadmissible in evidence.

[s 25.3] Scope.—This section covers a confession made by the accused when he was free and not in police custody, as also a confession made before any investigation has begun.[423] No part of a first information report lodged by the accused with the police could be admitted into evidence if it was in the nature of a confessional statement. The statement can, however, be admitted to identify the accused as the maker of the report.[424]

Where in a case of murder, the FIR given by the accused contained confession as well as incriminating facts, it was held to be not admissible in evidence.[425]

The confessional part of the FIR cannot be used in evidence against the accused except to the limited extent allowed by section 27. But the non-confessional part can be used against him as an evidence of conduct under section 8.[426] A confessional statement in the FIR was used for the purpose of examining whether the case fell within Exception 1 of section 300, IPC and for throwing light on the origin of the quarrel which resulted in the attack.[427]

A confession contained in a letter written and signed by the accused and addressed to a police-officer was held to be admissible as the letter was not written in presence of the police-officer.[428]

[s 25.4] "Confession".—A confession must either admit in terms the offence, or at any rate substantially all the facts which constitute the offence. No statement that contains self-exculpatory matter can amount to a confession, if the exculpatory statement is of some fact which if true would negative the offence alleged to be confessed.[429] An

---

423. *Pakala Narayana Swami v King-Emperor,* (1939) 66 IA 66 : 41 Bom LR 428 : 18 Pat 234 : (1941) Ran 789n; *A Nagesia v State of Bihar,* AIR 1966 SC 119 : 1966 Cr LJ 100.

424. *A Nagesia v State of Bihar,* AIR 1966 SC 119 : 1966 Cr LJ 100, **followed** in *KH Amulakh v State of Gujarat,* AIR 1972 SC 922.

425. *Metropolitan SJ, Vijayawada v B Srinivasa Rao,* 1992 Cr LJ 3027 (AP).

426. *Bheru Singh v State of Rajasthan,* (1994) 1 Crimes 630 : (1994) 2 SCC 467. The statements showing the relationship of the accused with the deceased, the motive for multiple murders, presence of the sister-in-law at the scene, were not in the nature of confessions, hence relevant under sections 7 and 8.

427. *Murli v State of Rajasthan,* AIR 1994 SC 610 : 1994 Cr LJ 1114.

428. *Sita Ram v State of UP,* AIR 1966 SC 1906 : 1966 Cr LJ 1519. Statement of an accused made to police officer during investigation is inadmissible and it does not become admissible merely because the accused is dead. *Amar Singh v State of MP,* 1996 Cr LJ 1582 (MP).*Murli v State of Rajasthan,* 1995 Supp. (1) SCC 39 : 1995 SCC (Cri) 57 : AIR 1994 SC 610 : 1994 Cr LJ 1114. A confessional FIR cannot be used for any purpose in favour of the prosecution and against the accused, such a statement can be taken into account to examine whether the case fell under Exception 1 to section 300, IPC particularly when there was no evidence disclosing as to how the quarrel ensued and attack took place.

429. *A Nagesia v State of Bihar,* AIR 1966 SC 119 : 1966 Cr LJ 100.

admission of a gravely incriminating fact, even a conclusively incriminating fact, is not of itself a confession, e.g., an admission that the accused is the owner of and was in recent possession of the knife or revolver which caused a death with no explanation of any other man's possession.[430] The accused can insist that the entire admission including the exculpatory part must be tendered in evidence.[431]

Communication to another is not a necessary ingredient of the concept of confession.[432] The word "statement" includes both oral and written statement. If the statement is an admission of guilt, it would amount to a confession whether it is communicated to any one or not.[433]

This section does not exclude all statements by an accused to the police but only confessions. There is a distinction between mere admission and confessions which are statements either directly admitting guilt or suggesting the inference of guilt of the crime charged. The general rule in the section is further subject to that which admits statements leading to discovery whether they amount to confessions or not.

[s 25.5] "Police-officer".—The term cannot be construed in so wide a sense as to include persons on whom only some of the powers exercised by the police are conferred.[434] It applies to everypolice-officer and is not restricted to officers in a regular police force. Thus a Chowkidar,[435] a Police Patel,[436] a village headman,[437] an excise peon,[438] and an excise officer, according to the Calcutta[439] and Bombay[440] High Courts, are police-officers. A home-guard has been held by the Orissa High Court to be a police personnel for the purposes of this section.[441] But a member of a village defence party constituted under Assam Village Defence Organisation Act, 1966 has been held to be not a police officer.[442] A grama rakhi has been held to be a police officer.[443] The Supreme Court has held that the test for determining whether a person is a police-officer for purposes of this section would be whether

430. *Pakala Narayana Swami v King-Emperor,* (1939) 66 IA 66, at p 81 : 41 Bom LR 428 : 18 Pat 234 : (1941) Ran 789n.

431. *A Nagesia v State of Bihar,* AIR 1966 SC 119 : 1966 Cr LJ 100.

432. *Sahoo v State of UP,* AIR 1966 SC 40 : 1966 Cr LJ 68. See also, *Luku Paike v State of Orissa,* 1995 Cr LJ 1207 (Ori).

433. *Shiv Karam Payaswami Tewari v State of Maharashtra,* AIR 2009 SC 1692 : (2009) 11 SCC 262.

434. *Raj Kumar Karwal v UOI,* (1990) 2 SCC 409 : AIR 1991 SC 45 : (1990) 48 ELT 496; 1990 SCC (Cr) 330 : 1991 Cr LJ 97, an officer invested with some of the powers analogous with those of an investigating police officer. (Narcotic Drugs and Psychotropic Substances Act, 1985).

435. *Queen-Empress v Salemuddin Sheik,* (1899) 26 Cal 569; *King-Emperor v Pancham,* (1933) 8 Luck 410; *Emperor v Deokinandan,* (1937) All 85, FB; *Budha Majhi,* (1962) Cut 366. In the Punjab a village chaukidar is held to be not a "police-officer": *Khuda Bakhsh v The Crown,* (1917) PR No. 42 of 1917 (Cr).

436. *Empress v Rama Birapa,* (1878) 3 Bom 12; *Queen-Empress v Bhima,* (1892) 17 Bom 485.

437. *Lu Bein v Queen-Empress,* (1889) SJLB 479; *Po Sin v King-Emperor,* (1907) 3 LBR 283.

438. *Emperor v Dinshaw Driver,* (1928) 31 Bom LR 49.

439. *Ibrahim Ahmad v King-Emperor,* (1931) 58 Cal 1260, dissenting from *Ah Foong v Emperor,* (1918) 46 Cal 411; *Ameen Sharif v Emperor,* (1934) 61 Cal 607 FB.

440. *Emperor v Nanoo,* (1926) 28 Bom LR 1196, 51 Bom 78 FB; **overruling**, *Pereira v Emperor,* (1926) 28 Bom LR 674.

441. *State of Orissa v Dubuga Tubud,* 1989 Cr LJ 1556 (Ori).

442. *Akanman Bora v State of Assam,* 1988 Cr LJ 573 (Gau). A Kotwar has been held to be not a police officer. *State of MP v Premlal,* 1987 Cr LJ 204 MP FB *Alluri Ramayya v State of Maharashtra,* 1987 Cr LJ 1172, confession to crowd, among whom a police patil was also present, relevant.

443. *Pandru Khadia v State of Orissa,* 1992 Cr LJ 762 (Ori).

the powers of a police officer which are conferred on him or which are exercisable by him establish a direct or substantial relationship with the prohibition enacted by this section, that is relating to the recording of a confession.[444] A Central Excise Officer who has the powers of a police-officer for investigation but not the power to frame a charge-sheet under section 173 of the Code of Criminal Procedure is not a police-officer for the purposes of this section.[445] A Customs Officer is not a police-officer.[446] The Supreme Court held that a confessional statement made by an accused person to the Superintendent of Excise under the provisions of the Bihar and Orissa Excise Act, 1915 was inadmissible in evidence, since an Excise Officer was a police officer within the meaning of section 25.[447]

The Supreme Court in *Gulam Hussain Shaikh Chougule v S Reynolds*[448] cited the effect of some earlier authorities as follows: "We hold that a statement recorded by Customs Officers under section 108 of the Customs Act, 1962 is admissible in evidence. The court has to test whether the inculpating portions were made voluntarily or whether it is vitiated on account of any of the premises envisaged in section 24 of the Evidence Act."[449] The court also said that the provisions of section 16 CrPC are not applicable to the recording of such confessions. The members of the Railway Protection Force constituted under the Railway Protection Force Act, 1957, are not Police Officers.[450] A constable of the Rajasthan Armed Constabulary has been held to be not a police officer. The FIR was lodged after a confessional statement was made before him. The provisions of section 25 were not attracted.[451] Confessional statements made to Customs Officers have been held by the Supreme Court not to come within the inhibitions of sections 24 and 25 because they are

---

444. *Raja Ram v State of Bihar,* AIR 1964 SC 828 : 1964 Cr LJ 705.

445. *Badaku Joti v State of Mysore,* AIR 1966 SC 1746 : 1966 Cr LJ 1353. See, however, *Rajendra Kumar v State of UP,* AIR 1966 All 42.

446. *State of Punjab v Barkat Ram,* AIR 1962 SC 276 : (1962) 1 Cr LJ 217. See, *Maylavahanam,* (1947) Mad 788; *Ramesh Chandra v State of West Bengal,* (1968) 72 Bom LR 787 (SC); *Deputy Director ED Madras v P Mansoor Md Ali Jinnah,* 1989 Cr LJ 2138 (Mad); *UOI v Ashok Sukhadeo Singh,* 1991 Cr LJ 2359 (Bom). Also see, *Supdt. of Customs and Central Excise, Nagercoil v R Sunder,* 1993 Cr LJ 956, customs personnel, not to be construed as police personnel, though powers are akin; *Bashidhar Maharana v State of Bihar,* 1993 Cr LJ 1310.

447. *Abdul Rashid v State of Bihar,* AIR 2001 SC 2422 : 2001 Cr LJ 3290. The court also held that a conviction based only on the fact that the accused was found together with the co-accused from whom the offending article was recovered and on the basis of the confession of the co-accused was liable to be set aside.

448. *Gulam Hussain Shaikh Chougule v S Reynolds,* 2001 Cr LJ 4755 : AIR 2001 SC 2930.

449. A summarised version of the effect of the following authorities : *Percy Rustomji Bosta v State of Maharashtra,* (1971) 1 SCC 847 : AIR 1971 SC 1087 : 1971 Cr LJ 933 and the three judge Bench decision in *Harbansingh Sardar Lenasingh v State of Maharashtra,* AIR 1972 SC 1224 : 1972 Cr LJ 759; *Veera Ibrahim v State of Maharashtra,* (1976) 2 SCC 302 : AIR SC 1167 : 1976 Cr LJ 2761 and *Poolpandi v Suptd. Central Excise,* (1992) 3 SCC 259 : AIR 1992 SC 1795 : 1992 AIR SCW 2012 : 1992 Cr LJ 2761.

450. *Hari Rachu v The State,* (1971) 73 Bom LR 891. *Balkishan A Devidayal v State of Maharashtra,* 1980 Cr LJ 1424: (1980) 17 ACC 300, **following**, *Badku Joti Savant v State of Mysore,* (1966) 3 SCR 698 : AIR 1966 SC 1746 : 1966 Cr LJ 1353.*Salim Mohamed Babul Miniyar v State of Maharashtra,* 2001 Cr LJ 58 (Bom), the accused confessed to RPF officer that he had purchased stolen railway property. The confession was held to be relevant. Conviction on its basis was not illegal. *Santosh Kumar Karmakar v State of WB,* 2001 Cr LJ 3828 (Cal) theft of railway property, free and voluntary confession before RPF personnel, not ruled out from evidence.

451. *Ramesh Kumar v State of Rajasthan,* 1999 Cr LJ 871 (Raj).

not police officers.[452] An officer under the FERA is not an officer in charge of a police station, though he has certain powers which are similar to the powers of a police officer. The Act does not confer upon him the power to lodge a report under section 173 CrPC. He can only file a complaint. He is not competent to submit a report. Powers of investigation are not conferred upon him. Hence he cannot be said to be a police officer.[453] Accordingly the statement of an accused person recorded by an officer under the Act is not excluded.

A Reserve Police Force Officer has been held to be a police officer appointed under the State Reserve Police Force Act and an officer-in-charge of a police station under the Bombay Police Act. But he is not a police officer for the purposes of Chapter XII of CrPC. Hence, section 25 of the Evidence Act would not be attracted.[454] A forest officer under an Orissa legislation has been held to be not a police officer though certain powers of police officers have been conferred on him. A confession made to such an officer was held to be admissible in evidence.[455]

Officers empowered under the Narcotic Drugs and Psychotropic Substances Act, 1985 have been held to be not police officers. Hence, a confessional statement made to them was held to be admissible against the person making the confession.[456]

[s 25.6] "Accused of any offence".—This expression covers a person accused of an offence at the trial whether or not he was accused of the offence when he made the confession.[457]

The concept was thus explained by the Supreme Court in *Bheru Singh v State of Rajasthan*:[458] By virtue of the provisions of section 25 of the Evidence Act, a confession made to police officer is not admissible in evidence under any circumstances. A confession made to a policeman even before investigation had begun is also ruled out. The expression "accused of any offence" in section 25 would cover the case of an accused who has since been put on trial, whether or not at the time when he made the confessional statement, he was under arrest or in custody as an accused. Inadmissibility of a confessional statement made to a police officer under section 25 is based on the

---

452. *P Rustomji v State of Maharashtra,* AIR 1971 SC 1087 : 1971 Cr LJ 933; *Hazari Singh v UOI,* AIR 1973 SC 62 : 1974 Cr LJ 391; *Asst. Collector of Customs v Vallabhdas,* (1965) 3 SCR 854 : AIR 1965 SC 481 : 1965 Cr LJ 490 and *R.C. Mehta v West Bengal,* (1969) 2 SCR 461 : AIR 1970 SC 940; *Balkrishna v West Bengal,* AIR 1974 SC 120 : 1974 Cr LJ 280; *Assistant Collector, Central Excise v C Fernandes,* (1982) 3 SCC 512 : 1983 SCC (Cr) 109; *Balkrishana Naik v State of MP,* 2000 Cr LJ 4797 (MP), the Central Excise Officer under the Narcotic Drugs and Substances Act, 1985 is not a police officer. A statement made to him could be proved in evidence in accordance with the provisions of that Act.

453. *PS Barkathali v Director, Enforcement,* AIR 1981 Ker 81. *Deputy Director ED Madras v P Mansoor Md Ali Jinnah,* 1989 Cr LJ 2138, 2151. The same is the position of the officers recording statements under the Narcotic Drugs and Psychotropic Substances Act (61 of 1985). See *MB Rathod v State of Gujarat,* 1989 Cr LJ 460 (Guj); *Abdul Razak v Sudip,* 1989 Cr LJ 2007 (Cal); *Raj Kumar Karwal v UOI,* 1991 Cr LJ 97 SC : AIR 1991 SC 45 : (1990) 2 SCC 405 : 1990 SCC (Cri) 330; *R.N Kaker v Shabir Fidahusein,* 1990 Cr LJ 144 (Bom).

454. *State of Gujarat v Anirudhsing,* AIR 1997 SC 2780 : 1997 Cr LJ 3397.

455. *Matia Patel v State of Orissa,* 2001 Cr LJ 1897 (Ori).

456. *Nathubhai Babarbhai Patel v State of Maharashtra,* 2001 Cr LJ 536 (Bom).

457. *A Nagesia v State of Bihar,* AIR 1966 SC 119 : 1966 Cr LJ 100.

458. *Bheru Singh v State of Rajasthan,* (1994) 2 SCC 467 : (1994) 1 Crimes 630.

ground of public policy. The section excludes all statement of incriminating nature made to a police officer whether made before or after becoming an accused person.

[s 25.7] FIR in form of confession.—The FIR written at the instance of a person who is accused of an offence is inadmissible under section 25 unless some recovery in pursuance to the statement is made and only that part is admissible.[459] A confessional FIR cannot be used against the accused himself or against his co-accused whom he implicated in it. If he offers himself as a witness at the trial, the statements in the FIR can be used to contradict or corroborate his testimony.[460]

[s 25.8] Confession under NDPS Act.—A statement of the accused under section 67 of the Narcotic Drugs and Substances Act, 1985 is not the same as a statement under section 161, CrPC. It can be used as a confession against him. It is excluded from the operation of sections 24-27 of the Evidence Act. A conviction can be based on it.[461] The Supreme Court has added this note of caution that such confession should be subjected to close scrutiny.[462]

[s 25.9] Confession in Departmental proceedings.—A confession was made by the delinquent to the police in the course of Departmental proceedings. This was held to be admissible. The court said that the embargo placed on admissibility of confessions under section 25 does not apply to Departmental proceedings.[463]

[s 26] Confession by accused while in custody of police not to be proved against him.—No confession made by any person whilst he is in the custody[s 26.2] of a police-officer,[s 26.3] unless it be made in the immediate presence of a Magistrate,shall be proved as against such person.

[464][*Explanation.*—In this section "Magistrate" does not include the head of a village discharging magisterial functions in the Presidency of Fort St. George [465][***] or elsewhere, unless such headman is a Magistrate exercising the powers of a Magistrate under the Code of Criminal Procedure, 1882.]

SYNOPSIS

---

459. *Ram Beti v State of UP,* 1996 Cr LJ 1512 (All); *Naresh v State of MP,* 2003 Cr LJ (NOC) 19 (MP), the accused lodged FIR with the police that he killed the victim with a knife wound in the abdomen, not allowed to be used as evidence because it was in the nature of a confession.

460. *Bandlamuddi Atchuta Ramaiah v State of AP,* AIR 1997 SC 496 : (1996) 11 SCC 133 : 1996 Cr LJ 4463.

461. *Kanhaiyalal v UOI,* AIR 2008 SC 1044 : (2008) 4 SCC 668, there was corroboration by other evidence.

462. *Francis Stanly v Intelligence Officer, Narcotic Central Bureau,* AIR 2007 SC 794 : 2007 Cr LJ 1157.

463. *Commissioner of Police v Narender Singh,* AIR 2006 SC 1800 : (2006) 4 SCC 265 : (2006) 128 DLT 801 : (2006) 3 Serv LR 31. The provisions of the Evidence Act are not applicable to departmental proceedings.

Note—A Coroner has been declared to be a Magistrate for the purposes of this section, see the Coroners Act, 1871 (4 of 1871), section 20.

464. Ins. by Act 3 of 1891, section 3.

465. The words "or in Burma" omitted by the A.O. 1937.

COMMENT

[s 26.1] Principle.—Under this section no confession made by a person in custody to *any person* other than a police-officer, shall be admissible, unless made in the immediate presence of a Magistrate. Section 25 excludes confessions to police-officers under any circumstances. This section excludes confessions to anyone else, while the person making it is in a position to be influenced by a police-officer. The presence of the Magistrate secures the free and voluntary nature of the confession and the confessing person has an opportunity of making a statement uncontrolled by any fear of the police.[466] Thus, this section is a further extension of the principle laid down in section 25. Section 25 applies to all confessions made to police-officers, this section to confessions made to persons other than police-officers but made while in police custody. A confession made to a police-officer would, however, be admissible in evidence under section 26 if it is made in the presence of a Magistrate and it is recorded by him in the manner prescribed by section 164, Code of Criminal Procedure, 1898.[467]

[s 26.2] "Custody".— Where the accused was in police custody regarding a different case on the date when he was first brought before the Magistrate for recording his confession, the Magistrate, being aware of the procedure, instead of recording his confession on that date, sent him to a correctional home and recorded his confession the next day. He also certified that during the recording of the confession, no police personnel were present in his chamber. It was held that the accused was not in police custody, when his confession was recorded.[468]

The words "in custody" which are to be found in this and other sections of the Act only denote surveillance or restriction on the movements of the persons concerned, which may be complete as, for instance, in the case of an arrested person, or may be partial.[469]

[s 26.3] "Police-officer".—A Jailor is not a police-officer, and a confession made to him may be given in evidence.[470]

[s 26.4] Extra-judicial confessions.—These are made by the party elsewhere than before a Magistrate or in court. The words used by the accused in confessing are very much important and, therefore, the same words would be necessary to give to the

---

466. *Hiran Miya,* (1877) 1 CLR 21.

467. *Zwinglee Ariel v State of MP,* AIR 1954 SC 15 : 1954 Cr LJ 230. *Sarkar Mardi v State of WB,*1992 Cr LJ 367 (Cal), where a confession so recorded inspired all round confidence, it being immaterial that no counsel was made available to the indigent accused at that time. *Hemant Kumar v State of UP,* 1991 Cr LJ 3239 (All), not recorded by observing the requirements of section 164 CrPC, no good confession.

468. *Mohd. Jamiludin Nasir v State of WB,* (2014) 7 SCC 443 (paras 27 to 30) : AIR 2014 SC 2587.

469. *Harban Singh v State,* (1968) 71 Bom LR 599.*Ram Singh v Sonia,* AIR 2007 SC 1218 : 2007 Cr LJ 1642 : (2007) 3 SCC 1, the accused in hospital at the time of his statement. There was nothing to show any custody established on him by the police.

470. *Queen-Empress v Bhima,* (1892) 17 Bom 485; *Queen-Empress v Tatya,* (1895) 20 Bom 795; *State of Gujarat v Anirudhsing,* AIR 1997 SC 2780 : 1997 Cr LJ 3397, confession to a Reserve Police Force Officer who was on duty at the place of occurrence. There was evidence of another police officer who stated that a confession was made to someone. This was held to be hearsay. The statement in FIR could not be used to corroborate it. The statement to the RPF personnel was not on record.

court an impression of what the true confession was.[471] The law in regard to extra-judicial confessions may be stated thus: An extra-judicial confession, if voluntary, can be relied upon by the court along with other evidence in convicting the accused.[472] In examining the value of an extra-judicial confession one factor is whether the accused was a free man while making his confession. The second factor is that the value of the confession as an evidence on veracity of the witness to whom it was made.[473] A conviction can be founded on an extra-judicial confession. It should be clear, specific and unambiguous. But it should not be expected that the witness, in order to establish his credibility, should be able to reproduce the statement in its word for word original version.[474]

An extra-judicial confession can be made to or before a private individual. It can also be made before a magistrate who is not especially empowered to record confessions under section 164 of CrPC or who receives the confession at a time when section 164 is not applying. The court also added that every inducement, threat or promise does not vitiate a confession.[475]

---

471. *Bhanwar Singh v State of Rajasthan,* 1988 Cr LJ 1054 (Raj). See further, *Sudhir Sarkar v State of Tripura,* 1992 Cr LJ 13 (Gau), where what the accused said was not produced and he was kept chained till arrival of police, confession unreliable. Extra-judicial confession must be free from suspicion and must be within reasonable time and corroborated by circumstantial evidence. *Chandraiahgari Ananthareddi v State of AP,* 1996 Cr LJ 2109 (AP). *Balvinder Singh v State of Punjab,* 1996 Cr LJ 883 : AIR 1996 SC 607 : 1995 Supp (4) SCC 259, confession to a socialworker, suspicious, because the accused remained with the police even though for some other crime. *Kailash v State of Rajasthan,* 1995 Cr LJ 3111 (Raj), witness did not tell the police about the confession during confession, doubtful. Extra-judicial confession made in the custody of police cannot be made the basis of conviction as the same cannot be said to be voluntary. *Kausar Ali Gazi v State of WB,* 1996 Cr LJ 1745 (Cal). *State of HP v Diwana,* 1995 Cr LJ 3002 (HP), confession to the inimical village pradhan, unbelievable.

472. *Mulk Raj v State of UP,* AIR 1959 SC 902 : 1959 Cr LJ 1219; *Francis Stanly v Intelligence Officer, Narcotic Control Bureau,* AIR 2007 SC 794 : 2007 Cr LJ 1157, value of extra-judicial confession explained. *Farid Khan v State of J&K,* 2000 Cr LJ 2680 (J&K), the conviction was based on a voluntary confession by the accused, no infraction or violation of any rule of substantive or procedural law was made out. Conviction was held to be legal. The trial was under the Ranbir Penal Code (12 of 1989).*Jaswant Gir v State of Punjab,* (2005) 12 SCC 438, extra-judicial confession found to be not reliable. *State (NCT) of Delhi v Navjot Sandhu,* (2005) 11 SCC 600 : AIR 2005 SC 3820 : 2005 Cr LJ 3950, retracted confession requires corroboration, extent of requisite corroboration explained. The court also explained the effect of delay in retraction and inconsistent grounds of retraction. Statements made to TV and press reporters by the accused in immediate presence of and while in police custody, held, inadmissible. Relationship between confession and admission explained.

473. *Chattar Singh v State of Haryana,* AIR 2009 SC 378 : 2009 Cr LJ 319. *Kusuma Ankama v State of AP,* AIR (2008) SC 2819 : 2008 Cr LJ 3502 : (2008) 13 SCC 257, the accused should be a free man at the time.

474. *Shiva Karam Payaswami Tewari v State of Maharashtra,* AIR 2009 SC 1692 : (2009) 11 SCC 262; *Kusuma Ankama Rao v State of AP,* AIR 2008 SC 2819 : 2008 Cr LJ 3502 : (2008) 13 SCC 257, conviction on its basis when the witness passes the rigorous test of credibility; *Ajay Singh v State of Maharashtra,* AIR 2007 SC 2188 : (2007) 12 SCC 341 exact words need not be reproduced, but there should not material or vital difference.

475. *State of Punjab v Harjagdev Singh,* AIR 2009 SC 2693 : (2009) 16 SCC 91. The confession was made in this case to a village resident, but proper procedure for recording the same was not followed.

Usually, and as a matter of caution, courts require some material corroboration to an extra-judicial confessional statement.[476] Extra-judicial confessions, voluntarily made and fully consistent with circumstantial evidences establish the guilt of the accused.[477] Where the version of the accused as per the extra-judicial confession was inconsistent with the medical evidence besides the same being retracted, conviction of the accused solely on the basis of such extra-judicial confession was highly unsafe.[478] A confession should be clear and unequivocal whether it is a judicial or extra-judicial confession. The confession in this case which was made before a large number of persons in the *panchayat* was more in general and vague terms. The court said that no reliance could be placed on it.[479] An extra-judicial confession was made before a witness who was the close relative of the accused. The testimony of the witness was found to be realistic and truthful. There was a delay of 20 days in recording his statement which was sufficiently explained by the investigating officer. A conviction on the basis of the confession was held to be proper.[480] A confession was supposed to have been made to the former president of the Village Panchayat almost a week after the occurrence. The president neither reduced it into writing nor produced the accused before the police. Information was given to the police after many hours. The confession was held to be unreliable.[481] It was alleged that the accused assaulted the deceased with a piece of stone. The extra-judicial confession made before the Village Administrative Officer did not find any corroboration on any general particulars. Withholding of information as to the time at which the material record was prepared also created doubt. The applicable procedure was also not followed. Confession was not acceptable.[482]

The accused must be a freeman while making his confession. The evidentiary value of the confessional statement depends on the credibility of the witness to whom it is made.[483]

---

476. *Ratan Gonda v State of Bihar,* AIR 1959 SC 18 : 1959 Cr LJ 108. *Piara Singh v State of Punjab,* AIR 1977 SC 2274 : 1977 Cr LJ 1941, followed in *Jarinakhatun v State of Assam,* 1992 Cr LJ 733, 735 (Gau), where the extra-judicial confession was testified to the court by as many as six independent witnesses; *Badhna Kharia v State of Assam,* 1988 Cr LJ 1412 (Gau), where the court added that where such a confession is spoken by a person having no reason to state falsely against the accused, it is of material value. *Nirmal Singh v State of HP,* 1987 Cr LJ 1644 (HP), confession made several days after the incident and that too to a person living 80 to 90 miles away from the residence of the accused, rejected.

477. *Gokaraju Venkatanarasa Raju v State of AP,* (1993) 3 Crimes 235 : 1993 Supp (4) SCC 191. Extra judicial confession corroborated by circumstantial evidence, held, could not be brushed aside as unreliable, *State of Kerala v Mani,* 1992 Cr LJ 1682 (Ker). *Chhinder Singh v State of Rajasthan,* 1993 Cr LJ 1616 (Raj), can be used for corroboration of other material on record. *S.V Chalke v State of Maharashtra,* 1993 Cr LJ 3364 (Bom), requires sufficient and reliable corroboration. Extra-judicial confession, no corroboration, cannot be relied upon, *Naga Reddy v State of AP,* 1994 Cr LJ 2545.

478. *Chhittar v State of Rajasthan,* AIR 1994 SC 214 : 1994 Cr LJ 245 : (1995) Supp 4 SCC 519.

479. *Kishan Lal v State of Rajasthan,* AIR 1999 SC 3062 : (2000) 1 SCC 310 : 1999 Cr LJ 4070.

480. *Ram Khilari v State of Rajasthan,* 1999 Cr LJ 1450 : AIR 1999 SC 1002.

481. *Inspector of Police v Palanisamy,* AIR 2009 SC 1012 : 2009 Cr LJ 788.

482. *State of TN v Manmatharaj,* AIR 2009 SC 1757 : (2008) 16 SCC 61.

483. *Mohd. Azad v State of WB,* AIR 2009 SC 1307 : (2008) 15 SCC 449.

It is a well settled law that confession must be addressed to somebody. It has been observed for the making of a confessional statement, communication to another person is not necessary. Utterances made in soliloquy are also statements.[484] Extra-judicial confession made before stock witness who was casually knowing the accused, was held to be not acceptable.[485] Where it was alleged that the accused made extra-judicial confession to a doctor and another person, both strangers and the same was tape-recorded as if it was anticipated and the tape-recorder kept ready. It was held that evidently it denoted influence and involuntariness.[486] Where extra-judicial confession was made to a stranger and exact words were not recorded and *corpus deliciti*, i.e., substance or foundation of an offence was also not available, it was held that the confession could not be relied upon.[487] It was wholly unlikely that the accused would have made an extra-judicial confession to a person whom they never know.[488]

In *Sakharam Shankar Bansode v State of Maharashtra*,[489] the Supreme Court held that conviction could not be based solely on retracted extra-judicial confession. Where details of alleged retracted extra-judicial confession were not extracted and there was no corroborative evidence, the fact that the accused persons and the deceased were together on the night of occurrence, might raise suspicion but it would not be sufficient to hold the accused persons guilty.[490]

The Supreme Court considered the position of extra-judicial confession in *State of Karnataka v MN Ramdas*.[491] In this case, the accused killed his companion in a room in a lodge where they were staying and was then supposed to have confessed to a stranger just only because he was a friend of the owner of the lodge. The court surveyed authorities on extra-judicial confession in order to support the relevancy of the confession in this case[492]: "With regard to the extra judicial confession, the trial court neither discarded nor relied upon it apparently for the reason that according to the decision cited before him—*Rahim Beg v State of UP*.[493] Such confession is a weak evidence especially when it is made before a person with whom the accused had no previous contacts. The learned Sessions Judge observed that even if the extra judicial confession is eschewed from consideration the other circumstances referred to supra are sufficient to establish the guilt of the accused."

---

484. *Ajay Singh v State of Maharashtra*, AIR 2007 SC 2188 : (2007) 12 SCC 341.

485. *Tarseem Kumar v Delhi Administration*, 1995 Cr LJ 470 : AIR 1994 SC 2585 : 1994 Supp (3) SCC 374.

486. *State of Haryana v Ved Prakash*, AIR 1994 SC 468 : 1994 Cr LJ 140.

487. *Palani v State of TN*, 1993 Cr LJ 1679 (Mad); *Sandeep v State of Haryana*, AIR 2001 SC 1103 : 2001 Cr LJ 1456 the reason for the accused persons to go to the residence of the witness for the purpose of confessing to their crimes not made clear; that person did not have the status of influence in the society so as to be of any help; the statement of the witness was that only one of the accused persons confessed. All this made the statement unreliable.

488. *Sunny Kapoor v State (UT) of Chandigarh*, AIR 2006 SC 2242 : (2006) 10 SCC 182 : 2006 Cr LJ 2920.

489. *Sakharam Shankar Bansode v State of Maharashtra*, AIR 1994 SC 1594 : 1994 Cr LJ 2189.

490. *Uttam Sadda v State of Punjab*, 1993 Cr LJ 2597 : 1993 SCC (Cri) 1020.

491. *State of Karnataka v MN Ramdas*, AIR 2002 SC 3109

492. *Ibid*, pp 3111-3112.

493. *Rahim Beg v State of UP*, (1972) 3 SCC 759 : AIR 1973 SC 343 : 1972 Cr LJ 1260. See also *State of Karnataka v AB Nagaraj*, AIR 2003 SC 666, allegation that the girl was killed by her father and step-mother in the national park, confession made by them during detention in forest office. This was not mentioned in the report given to the police, nor any witness was present at that time, confession not relied upon.

Going further the court said: "We deem it appropriate to refer to a recent decision of this court in *Gura Singh v State of Rajasthan,*[494] wherein the evidentiary value to be attached to the extra-judicial confession has been explained thus: 'It is settled position of law that extra-judicial confession, if true and voluntary, it can be relied upon by the court to convict the accused for the commission of the crime alleged. Despite inherent weakness of extra-judicial confession as an item of evidence, it cannot be ignored when shown that such confession was made before a person who has no reason to state falsely and to whom it is made in the circumstances which tend to support the statement. Relying upon an earlier judgment in *Rao Shiv Bahadur Singh v State of Vindhya Pradesh*[495] this court again in *Maghar Singh v State of Punjab*[496] held the evidence in the form of extra-judicial confession made by the accused to witness cannot be always termed to be a tainted evidence. Corroboration of such evidence is required only by way of abundant caution. If the court believes the witness before whom the confession is made and is satisfied that the confession was true and voluntarily made, then the conviction can be founded on such evidence alone. In *Narayan Singh v State of MP*[497] this court cautioned that it is not open to the court trying the criminal case to start with a presumption that extra-judicial confession is always a weak type of evidence. It would depend on the nature of the circumstances, the time when the confession is made and the credibility of the witnesses who speak for such a confession. The retraction of extra-judicial confession which is a usual phenomenon in criminal cases would itself not weaken the case of the prosecution based upon such a confession. In *Kishore Chand v State of HP*[498], this court held that an unambiguous extra-judicial confession possesses high probative value force as it emanates from the person who committed the crime and is admissible in evidence provided it is free from suspicion and suggestion of any falsity. However, before relying on the alleged confession, the court has to be satisfied that it is voluntary and is not the result of inducement, threat or promise envisaged under section 24 of the Evidence Act or was brought about in suspicious circumstances to circumvent sections 25 and 26. The court is required to look into the surrounding circumstances to find out as to whether such confession is not inspired by any improper or collateral consideration or circumvention of law suggesting that it may not be true. All relevant circumstances such as the person to whom the confession is made the time and place of making it, the circumstances in which it was made have to be scrutinized.'"

In *Piara Singh v State of Punjab,*[499] the Supreme Court explained the value of an extra-judicial confession and observed that the law does not require that the evidence of an extra-judicial confession should in all cases be corroborated. In the instant case, the

---

494. *Gura Singh v State of Rajasthan,* (2001) 2 SCC 205 : AIR 2001 SC 330 : AIR SCW 4439 : 2001 Cr LJ 487.

495. *Rao Shiv Bahadur Singh v State of Vindhya Pradesh,* AIR 1954 SC 322 : 1954 Cr LJ 910.

496. *Maghar Singh v State of Punjab,* AIR 1975 SC 1320 : 1975 Cr LJ 1102.

497. *Narayan Singh v State of MP* AIR 1985 SC 1678 at p 1680 : 1985 Cr LJ 1862.

498. *Kishore Chand v State of HP,* AIR 1990 SC 2140 : 1990 Cr LJ 2289.

499. *Piara Singh v State of Punjab,* (1977) 4 SCC 452 at p 459 : AIR 1977 SC 2274 : 1977 Cr LJ 1941. *Polyami Sukada v State of MP,* AIR 2010 SC 2977 : 2010 Cr LJ 4273 : (2010) 12 SCC 142, an extra-judicial confession need not be corroborated in all cases. Conviction can be based solely on such confession. In this case, the witnesses of confession did not inspire confidence. Their evidence was slippery. Conviction was not proper even if there was recovery of weapon on the basis of confession.

extra-judicial confession was proved by an independent witness (Sarpanch) who was a responsible officer and who bore no animus against the appellants and was corroborated by the recovery of an empty cartridge from the place of occurrence.

The Supreme Court held that minor discrepancies should be ignored in appreciating the evidentiary value of an extra-judicial confession..[500] In this case, the confession was made inside the police station but its contents were disclosed to a witness a long before they were reduced to writing. The bar of section 26 was not attracted.[501]

The principles which would make an extra-judicial confession an admissible piece of evidence capable of forming the basis of conviction of an accused have been thus summed up by Supreme Court:[502]

(i) The extra-judicial confession is a weak evidence by itself. It has to be examined by the court with greater care and caution.

(ii) It should be made voluntarily and should be truthful.

(iii) It should inspire confidence.

(iv) An extra-judicial confession attains greater credibility and evidentiary value if it is supported by a chain of cogent circumstances and is further corroborated by other prosecution evidence.

(v) For an extra-judicial confession to be the basis of conviction, it should not suffer from any material discrepancies and inherent improbabilities.

(vi) Such statement essentially has to be proved like any other fact and in accordance with law.

A confession to an under-trial co-prisoner was not allowed to be proved.[503] Where the accused whilst in police custody made a statement before the doctor that the injury on his person was caused by the murdered person, as the statement does not amount to a confession, it is not barred under this section but can be relied upon as an admission under section 21 of the fact that he was in the deceased's room.[504]

[s 27] How much of information received from accused may be proved.—Provided that, when any fact is deposed to as discovered in consequence of information[s 27.5] received from a person accused of any offence,[s 27.6] in the custody of a police-officer,[s 27.7] so much of such information, whether it amounts to a confession or not, as relates distinctly to the fact thereby discovered, may be proved.

---

500. *State of AP v Gangula Satya Murthy,* AIR 1997 SC 1585 : 1997 Cr LJ 774. *State of MP v Nisar,* AIR 2007 SC 2316 : (2007) 5 SCC 658, an extra-judicial confession made even before the FIR was lodged, but not mentioned in the FIR, reliability doubtful, improbable that the informant must have forgotten, recovery of the weapon on the basis of confession but blood stain on it matched with that of the deceased, not acceptable.

501. *Ibid*

502. *Sahadevan v State of Tamil Nadu,* (2012) 6 SCC 403.

503. *Heramba Brahma v State of Assam,* AIR 1982 SC 1595 : 1983 Cr LJ 149 : (1982) 3 SCC 351 : 1983 SCC (Cri) 40.

504. *K Padayachi v State of Tamil Nadu,* AIR 1972 SC 66 : 1972 Cr LJ 11.

SYNOPSIS

COMMENT

[s 27.1] Principle.—This section is founded on the principle that if the confession of the accused is supported by the discovery of a fact it may be presumed to be true and not to have been extracted. It comes into operation only:

(1) if and when certain facts are deposed to as discovered in consequence of information received from an accused person in police custody; and

(2) if the information relates distinctly to the fact discovered.

The broad ground for not admitting confessions made under inducement, threat or promise to a police-officer is the danger of admitting false confessions, but the necessity for the exclusion disappears in a case provided for by this section when the truth of the confession is guaranteed by the discovery of facts in consequence of the information given.[505]

Section 27 starts with the word "provided". Therefore, it is a proviso by way of an exception to sections 25 and 26 of the Evidence Act.[506] This section is based on the view that if a fact is actually discovered in consequence of information given, some guarantee is afforded thereby that the information was true and accordingly can be safely allowed to be given in evidence. But clearly the extent of the information admissible must depend on the exact nature of the fact discovered to which such information is required to relate.[507]

It is proper for the prosecution if they want to adduce evidence under this section to prove by production of written record only so much of the statement as led to

---

505. *Bulaqi v The Crown,* (1928) 9 Lah 671, 675. For another case of the same kind see, *State of Kerala v Ammini,* 1988 Cr LJ 107 : AIR 1988 Ker 1; the evidence discovered under this section is not important where there is direct evidence. *Parduman Sinh v State of Gujarat,* AIR 1992 SC 881 : 1992 Cr LJ 1111, communal violence. *Shivaji Gana Naik v State of Maharashtra,* 1999 Cr LJ 471 (Bom), the accused stated that injuries on his person were due to dog bite, but only one such injury was found, evidence not admissible because it was not supported by any discovery.

506. *Musheer Khan v State of MP,* (2010) 2 SCC 748.

507. *Ramkishan Mithanlal Sharma v State of Bombay,* (1955) SCR 903 : 1955 Cr LJ 196 : AIR 1955 SC 104. *Mahendra Mandal v State of Bihar,* 1991 Cr LJ 1030, information is usable only against the accused giving it.

the discovery of the article.. An oral statement, without corroboration by any written record of any such statement contemporaneously made, even if admissible, is unsafe to rely on.[508]

[s 27.1.1] ***Doctrine of Confirmation.***—In the light of section 27, whatever information given by the accused, in consequence of which a fact is discovered, only would be admissible in evidence, whether such information amounts to a confession or not. The basic idea embedded under this section is the doctrine of confirmation by subsequent events. The doctrine is founded on the principle that if any fact is discovered in a search made on the strength of any information obtained from a prisoner, such a discovery is a guarantee that the information supplied by the prisoner is true. The information might be confessional or non-inculpatory in nature, but if it results in discovery of a fact, it becomes a reliable information.[509]

[s 27.2] Object.—The Supreme Court has held that in order that this section may apply the prosecution must establish that the information given by the accused led to the discovery of some fact deposed to by him. The discovery must be of some fact which the police had not previously learnt from other sources and that the knowledge of the fact was first derived from information given by the accused.[510]

[s 27.3] Scope.—The Supreme Court has held that this section controls sections 24, 25 and 26.[511] This section is applicable only if confessional statement leads to discovery of some new fact.[512]

It is fallacious to treat the "fact discovered" in this section as equivalent to the object produced: the fact discovered embraces the place from which the object is produced and the knowledge of the accused as to this, and the information given must relate distinctly to this fact. Information as to the past user, or the past history of the object produced is not related to its discovery in the setting in which it is discovered. Information supplied by a person in custody that "I will produce a knife concealed in the roof of my house" does not lead to the discovery of a knife. It leads to the discovery of the fact that a knife is concealed in the house of the informant to his knowledge; and if the knife is proved to have been used in the commission of the offence, the fact discovered is very relevant. But if to the statement the words be added "with which I stabbed *A*", these words are inadmissible since they do not relate to the discovery of the knife in the house of the informant.

---

508. *Panchu Gopal v State of WB,* AIR 1968 Cal 38; *State of Karnataka v David Rozario,* 2002 Cr LJ 4127 : AIR 2002 SC 3272 the Supreme Court explains the extent of information which is admissible and the principle behind the section and also the anomalous effect of the requirement that the statement of disclosure should occur while the accused person is in custody. The Supreme Court also explained whether the evidence of recovery could be the sole basis of conviction.

509. *State of Maharashtra v Damu Gopinath Shinde,* (2000) 6 SCC 269 : AIR 2000 SC 1691, See also *Pawan Kumar v State of UP,* (2015) 7 SCC 148, para 29; *Raja v State of Haryana,* (2015) 11 SCC 43, paras 15 to 18.

510. *Jaffer Hussein Dastagir v State of Maharashtra,* AIR (1969) 73 Bom LR 26 : AIR 1970 SC 1934 : 1970 Cr LJ 1659. Recoveries are not a material evidence where there is direct evidence. *Pradumansinh Kalubha v State of Gujarat,* (1992) Cr LJ 1111 : AIR 1992 SC 881 : 1992 AIR SCW 650

511. *A Nagesia v State of Bihar,* AIR 1966 SC 119 : 1966 Cr LJ 100; *Mathura v King-Emperor,* (1945) 24 Pat 671.

512. *Navaneethakrishnan v State by Inspector of Police,* AIR 2018 SC 2027.

The difficulty, however great, of proving that a fact discovered on information supplied by the accused is a relevant fact can afford no justification for reading into this section something which is not there, and admitting in evidence a confession barred by section 26. Except in cases in which the possession or concealment of an object constitutes the gist of the offence charged, it can seldom happen that information relating to the discovery of a fact forms the foundation of the prosecution case. It is only one link in the chain of proof, and the other links must be forged in manner allowed by law.[513]

The information becomes admissible only to the extent of the part leading to the discovery of a fact. The facts discovered should be such which are in exclusive knowledge of the accused and none else. If the Investigating Officer, after recording information under section 27 of the Act from an accused in his custody, recovers some incriminating article from an open place accessible to all and sundry, the information and the discovery lose significance. Likewise, if the fact discovered is known to the Investigating Officer in advance, then the discovery made in furtherance of the subsequent information recorded under section 27 at the instance of the accused would be inconsequential.[514]

The information given by an accused person to a police-officer leading to the discovery of a fact which may or may not prove incriminating has been made admissible in evidence by the section unless compulsion has been used in which case it will be an infringement of Article 20(3) of the Constitution.[515] Where the fact is discovered not at the instance of the accused but on the basis of information supplied by him, the Supreme Court said that such information is admissible so long as it is the immediate and proximate cause of discovery. The fact that the informant accused was not taken to the spot of recovery would have no bearing on admissibility but it might be one of the aspects that goes into evaluation of the particular piece of evidence.[516] Signing of the information statement by the accused in contravention of section 162(1), CrPC, has been held by the Supreme Court to be not detracting from its admissibility to the extent to which it is otherwise relevant.[517] Simultaneous disclosure by more than one accused also does not render it inadmissible but it may go towards evaluation.[518]

Where the participation of the accused persons in the incident has been proved by unimpeachable ocular evidence, the fact that no incriminating materials were recovered from them was held to be not a ground in itself for their acquittal.[519]

Where the discovery is otherwise reliable, its evidentiary value has been held to be not diluted by the fact that the provisions of section 100(4) or (5), CrPC were not complied with.[520]

---

513. *Pulukuri Kottaya v Emperor,* (1946) 49 Bom LR 508 : 74 IA 65 : AIR 1947 PC 67 : 1947 Cr LJ 533. See also, *Udai Bhan v State of UP,* AIR 1962 SC 1116 : (1962) 2 Cr LJ 251 and *Prabhoo v State of UP,* AIR 1963 SC 1113 : 1963 Cr LJ 341; *Joseph,* (1951) TC 417; *Kuruvila Joseph,* (1952) TC 261; *Raghava Nadar Reghu v State of Kerala,* 1988 Cr LJ 1364 (Ker).

514. *State of Rajasthan v Mangal Singh,* AIR 2017 Raj 68 : 2017 (1) RLW 716 (Raj).

515. *State of Bombay v Kathi Kalu,* AIR 1961 SC 1808 : 64 Bom LR 240 : (1961) 2 Cr LJ 856.

516. *State (NCT) of Delhi v Navjot Sandhu,* (2005) 11 SCC 600 : AIR 2005 SC 3820.

517. *Ibid*

518. *Ibid*

519. *Krishna Mochi v State of Bihar,* 2002 Cr LJ 2645 (SC).

520. *Musheer Khan v State of MP,* AIR 2010 SC 762 : (2010) 2 SCC 748.

[s 27.3.1] ***Signature upon statement.***—It is not obligatory on the part of the investigating officer to get the signature of the accused on a confessional statement recorded under section 27.[521]

[s 27.4] Sections 25, 26, 27.—The scope and effect of the provisions of these sections are as follows[522]:—

(i) No confession made to a police-officer by an accused person whether in custody or not can be proved against the accused unless it be made in the immediate presence of a Magistrate.

(ii) So much of the information received from a person accused of an offence in custody of a police-officer as relates distinctly to the fact thereby discovered is admissible under section 27 and can be proved against him; but any statement made to a police-officer which connects the fact discovered with the offence charged is inadmissible.

(iii) The statement of the accused while in police custody regarding the concealment of any article or the accused's knowledge of its whereabouts and the discovery in consequence of the said statement is admissible in evidence.[523]

[s 27.5] "When any fact is deposed to as discovered in consequence of information".— The "fact" must be a "relevant fact" (section 5). The fact said to have been discovered in consequence of information received from a person accused of an offence must be of a kind which such information really helps to bring to light and which it would be difficult to find out otherwise before it can be treated as of any substantial probative value.[524] The fact must be the consequence, and the information the cause of its discovery. The information and the fact should be connected with each other as cause and effect. The fact discovered must be in consequence of the information received from the accused, and the fact should not have been already within the prior knowledge of the police. The information should be free from any element of compulsion.[525] If any portion of the information does not satisfy this test, it should be excluded.[526] In order to utilise the provisions of this section against an accused person an ordinary recovery

---

521. *Natarajan v UT of Pondicherry,* 2003 Cr LJ 2372 (Mad), following the Supreme Court decision in *State of Rajasthan v Teja Ram,* 1999 Cr LJ 2588 (SC). The contrary opinion expressed in 1998 Cr LJ 2479 (Kant) and (2002) 1 Mad LW (Cri) 145 is no longer good law. A statement leading to recoveries becomes an informative statement.

522. For a full discussion of the law relating to confession contained in sections 24 to 30, see, *A Nagesia v State of Bihar,* AIR 1966 SC 119 : 1966 Cr LJ 100.

523. *Narayan,* (1953) Hyd 32.

524. *Nga Shwe Tat v Queen-Empress,* (1897) 1 UBR (1897-1901) 152.*Murugan v State of TN,* AIR 2008 SC 2876 : (2008) 11 SCC 610, shopkeeper's servant killed his wife after closing the shop from inside, runaway after opening and seeing owner arrived, blood-stained clothes recovered at his instance, relevant.

525. *State (NCT) of Delhi v Navjot Sandhu,* (2005) 11 SCC 600 : AIR 2005 SC 3820.

526. *Sukhan v Crown,* (1929) 10 Lah 283, 293 FB; *King-Emperor v Ramanujam,* (1934) 58 Mad 642 *FB Vinod Kumar Vaidh v State,* 1992 Cr LJ 3674 (Del), disclosure statement must lead to discovery. *Anter Singh v State of Maharashtra,* AIR 2004 SC 4197 : (2004) 7 SCC 779, the expression "fact discovered" explained, and also the various requirements of the section restated in point form. The concept of statement which distinctly relates to discovery also explained. Dead body was recovered from an open place after 25 days, a pistol was recovered from near about the same place. The whole evidence was regarded as a doubtful.

cannot be turned into a discovery.[527] That portion of the information which merely explains the material thing discovered is not admissible under this section and cannot be proved.[528] Where a suspect in the custody of police makes a statement that he committed murder and removed ornaments which he produced later, the first part of the statement does not fall under this section because it is not a statement required to lead up to the production of the property.[529] In a case of burglary a statement made by the accused in police custody that he would show the place where he had hidden the ornaments when that statement leads to the discovery of the ornaments is admissible.[530] Where recovery of the dead bodies of the victims from covered gutters and their personal belongings from other places disclosed by the accused stood fully established, it cast a duty on the accused to explain as to how they alone had the information leading to the recoveries, which was admissible under this section. Failure of the accused to give an explanation or giving of false explanation is an additional circumstance against the accused.[531]

In order that a "discovery" may come under the provisions of this section, the place from which the incriminating article was recovered must be a place of concealment which would be difficult or impossible for the police to discover without some assistance from the accused.[532] The discovery of a pistol, the murder weapon at the instance of the

527. *Amin v State of UP,* AIR 1958 All 293. Thus, where the accused spoke nothing but only showed the way to the place from where a few personal articles of the deceased were recovered, section 8 was held to apply and not this section. *Amar Layek v State of West Bengal,* 1988 Cr LJ 1293 (Cal). *Sambhu Bora v State of Assam,* 1987 Cr LJ 1027 (Gau), where the statement which was supposed to have brought about the discovery was not cited, hence evidence rejected. *Dadasaheb Patalu Misal v State of Maharashtra,* 1987 Cr LJ 1512 (Bom), nothing to connect the thing recovered with the crime in question. Where the disclosure statement did not bear the signatures or thumb impression of the accused and the *punch* witnesses were also not examined at trial to testify its authenticity, the statement could not be relied upon, *Jackaran Singh v State of Punjab,* AIR 1995 SC 2345 : 1995 Cr LJ 3992.

528. *HP Administration v Om Prakash,* AIR 1972 SC 975 : 1972 Cr LJ 606; *Dhananjay Chatterjee v State of WB,* (1994) 2 SCC 220, fact discovered includes the discovery of the object found, the place from which it is produced and the knowledge of the accused as to its existence. *Suresh Chandra Bahri v State of Bihar,* AIR 1994 SC 2420 : 1994 Cr LJ 3271, articles used in wrapping the dead body and pieces of saree belonging to the deceased were seized from a place of hiding at the instance of the accused. Discovery was made soon after the arrest of the accused. The articles were identified by the witnesses. No public witness was produced. The IO also did not record the disclosure statements. Even so, the evidence was held to be good. *Mohibur Rahman v State of Assam,* 2000 Cr LJ 4725 (Gau) recovery of dead body and wearing apparels at the instance of the accused.

529. *Emperor v Bhikha Gober,* (1943) 45 Bom LR 884 : (1944) Bom 25.

530. *Chinnaswamy v State of Andhra Pradesh,* AIR 1962 SC 1788 : (1963) Cr LJ 1.

531. *Suresh v State of Haryana,* AIR 2015 SC 518 (para 8) : 2015 Cr LJ 661.

532. *Sadhu Singh v State,* AIR 1967 P&H. 14; *Amin v State of UP,* AIR 1958 All 293. See also, *Mohd. Inayatullah v State of Maharashtra,* AIR 1976 SC 461 : (1977) 1 SCC 669, discovery from an open platform; *SV Chalke v State of Maharashtra,* 1993 Cr LJ 3364, article discovered from an open place. Articles recovered on information of the accused from open place, not in his occupation, held, section 27 not attracted, *Kabul v State of Rajasthan,* 1992 Cr LJ 1491 (Raj), *Ganpat Kisan v State of Maharashtra,* 1995 Cr LJ 792 (Bom), weapon recovered from open space on footpath. But the *Ghuraiyha v State of MP,* 1990 Cr LJ 1129 (MP), recovery of articles connected with rape from a place of concealment on information given by the accused held relevant: *Pandru Khadia v State of Orissa,* 1992 Cr LJ 762 (Ori), discovery of the instrument from place known only to the accused, relevant; **following** *Pohalya Motya Vlavi v State of Maharashtra,* AIR 1979 SC 1949 : 1979 Cr LJ 1310, authorship of concealment is the important fact discovered. *Aftab Ahmad Ansari v State of Uttaranchal,* AIR 2010 SC 773 : (2010) 2 SCC 583, the accused stated that he was ready to disclose the place where he had concealed the clothes of the deceased, the same were recovered from that very place, held admissible evidence.

accused from a place which was a public thoroughfare was held to be not relevant.[533] Recovery of the wearing apparel of the deceased more than three weeks after the occurrence from a public place, a burrow pit nearby the place of murder, was held to be irrelevant.[534] Recovery of dead bodies three months after the incident from an open field which was surrounded by other fields did not constitute any evidence under this section. It was not such a place of concealment about which exclusive knowledge could have been attributed to the accused.[535]

The accused from outside the State were arrested within the limits of some other police station, without following the procedure laid down under section 166, CrPC, 1973. Recovery on their alleged voluntary disclosure statement, was not admissible.[536]

Where the disclosure statement of the accused led to the recovery of crime articles from a concealed place, it was held that prosecution should lead the best possible evidence instead of escaping its responsibility by pleading lapse of memory on account of passage of time or contending that no question was put to the prosecution witness.[537]

Disclosure statement is not a substantive evidence to convict the accused persons but it is only a corroborative evidence.[538]

[27.5.1] Failure of Investigating Officer to state details of information.—The failure of the Investigating Officer to state the details of the information given by the accused, makes the information inadmissible.[539]

[27.5.1.1] *Fact discovered.*—The "fact discovered" as envisaged under section 27 embraces the place from where the object was produced, the knowledge of the accused as to it, but the information must relate distinctly to that object.[540] The facts need not be self-probatory and the word "fact" as contemplated in section 27 is not limited to "actual physical material object".[541]

---

533. *Dudh Nath Pandey v State of UP,* AIR 1981 SC 911 : (1981) 2 SCC 166 : 1981 SCC (Cri) 379 : 1981 Cr LJ 618 : (1981) 2 SCR 711 : 1981 All LJ 328.

534. *Abdul Sattar v UT, Chandigarh,* AIR 1986 SC 1438 : 1986 Cr LJ 1072 : 1985 Supp SCC 599 : 1985 SCC (Cri) 505, See further, *Balkar Singh v State of UP,* 1990 Cr LJ 77, articles recovered which cannot be identified as those belonging to the accused, not relevant. The court also pointed out that stage-managed recoveries would serve no purpose.

535. *Makhan Singh v State of Punjab,* AIR 1988 SC 1705 : 1988 Supp SCC 526 : 1988 SCC (Cri) 916. See also *Kora Ghasi v State of Orissa,* AIR 1983 SC 360; 1983 Cr LJ 69(2) : (1983) 2 SCC 251 : 1983 SCC (Cri) 387, recovery from an open place does not carry much weight; *State of Rajasthan v Sukhpal Singh,* (1983) 1 SCC 393 : 1983 Cr LJ 1923 : AIR 1984 SC 207 : 1983 SCC (Cri) 213, recovery of heavy stolen object abandoned on chase. *Jit Singh v State of Punjab,* 1988 Cr LJ 39 (P&H), recovery of earrings about which there was no proof that they were on the person of the deceased at the material time. As against this in *Santosh v State of Kerala,* 1991 Cr LJ 570 (Ker), where proof was available that the ornaments discovered at the instance of the accused were on the person of the deceased at the material time, the discovery was relevant under the section.

536. *Thimmareddy v State of Karnataka,* (2014) 13 SCC 408 (para 14) : 2014 Cr LJ 2495.

537. *Kartar Singh v State of Punjab,* AIR 1993 SC 341 : 1993 Cr LJ 183.

538. *Dharam Pal v State of HP,* 2015 Cr LJ 4598, para 20 (HP) (DB).

539. *Aladdin v State of Rajasthan,* 2016 Cr LJ 3173, para 30 (Raj).

540. *Pawan Kumar v State of UP,* (2015) 7 SCC 148 para 30.

541. *Asar Mohammad v State of UP,* AIR 2018 SC 5264; *Charandas Swami v State of Gujarat,* AIR 2017 SC 1761.

Mere recovery of incriminating articles at the instance of the accused is not enough to incriminate the accused unless it is also established that the recovered articles connect the accused with the alleged crime.[542]

[27.5.1.2] ***Discovery in consequence of information given by another person.***—In the instant case, a scooter was recovered pursuant to the statement made by another person (investigation witness) and not on the basis of any disclosure statements made by the accused persons, given in the form of confessional statements. Hence, section 27 was not attracted.[543]

[27.6] "Information received from a person accused of any offence".—The Patna High Court has held that the statement must be of a person who was then an accused. If at the time when the confession was made, the person making it was not an accused person, the statement would not be admissible. A husband who had fatally assaulted his wife immediately went to the police-station and stated, "I went into the west facing room and finding my wife sitting, wounded her and she became senseless". In consequence of this information the Sub-Inspector went to the house of the informant and found the corpse of the woman in that room. It was held that as the informant had not, up to the time of making the statement, been in the custody of a police officer, the statement was not admissible.[544]

The expression "accused of any offence" is descriptive of the person against whom evidence relating to information alleged to be given by him is made provable by this section. It does not predicate a formal accusation against him at the time of making the statement sought to be proved, as a condition of its applicability.[545] Statement leading to recovery must be proved. Where recovery took place twenty three days after the statement, the informant being still not charged, and ultimately charged only as an abettor, the Supreme Court upheld the exclusion of the evidence.[546] Where there was no statement on the part of the accused, recoveries were held to be useless.[547]

---

542. *Prakash v State of Karnataka*, (2014) 12 SCC 133 (paras 38 to 45).

543. *Indra Dalal v State of Haryana*, AIR 2015 SC (Supp) 1428: (2015) 11 SCC 31 , para 33.

544. *Deonandan Dusadh v King-Emperor*, (1928) 7 Pat 411; *Sarabjit Singh v State*, 1998 Cr LJ 2231 (P & H), recovery made in consequence of disclosure statement made at a time when the maker of the statement was neither accused of any offence nor under arrest, the statement and recovery were held to be not admissible.

545. *State of UP v Deoman*, AIR 1960 SC 1125 : 1960 Cr LJ 1504.

546. *Chandran v State of TN*, AIR 1978 SC 1574 : 1978 Cr LJ 1693.

547. *Bahadul v State of Orissa*, 1979 Cr LJ 1075: AIR 1979 SC 1262. Recovery by itself cannot sustain conviction. The accused produced the weapon of offence and handed it over to the police but said nothing, evidence excluded. *State of Punjab v Gurnam Singh*, AIR 1984 SC 1799(1) : 1984 Supp SCC 502 : 1985 SCC (Cri) 616. *Kheraj Ram v State of Rajasthan*, 1995 Cr LJ 3113(Raj), *Bhagat Bahadur v State*, 1996 Cr LJ 2201 (Del) statement that the blood stain belonged to himself and the co-accused, not admissible. Where incriminating articles were alleged to have been recovered from the house of the accused at his instance 10 to 12 days after his statement whereas those articles were not recovered in the two searches made previously, the recoveries did not inspire confidence. *Jackaran Singh v State of Punjab*, AIR 1995 SC 2345 : 1995 Cr LJ 3992. Absence of the signature and the thumb impression of the accused on the disclosure statement and non-examination of the *panch* witnesses, would render the statement unreliable. *State of Haryana v Sher Singh*, AIR 1981 SC 1021 : 1981 Cr LJ 714 : (1981) 2 SCC 307, mere failure on the part of police to interrogate the accused person at whose instance the weapon was recovered was not regarded as a justification for concluding that the recovery was fake.

The words "accused of any offence" have been held to be descriptive of the person making the statement. It cannot be said that section 27 would operate only after formal arrest under section 46(1), CrPC. Recoveries were made on the basis of their statements a day before their formal arrest but they were in police custody. Their statements were not regarded as inadmissible under the section. Most of the recoveries made in the presence of the grand-father of the deceased and the investigating sub-inspector. The court said that their evidence could not be disbelieved only on the ground that they were interested in the success of the prosecution. No circumstance of materially adverse nature was brought forth.[548]

[27.7] "In the custody of a police-officer".—"Custody" does not necessarily mean detention or confinement. A person who makes a statement to a police-officer voluntarily confessing that he had committed an act which the penal law regards as an offence, submits himself to the custody of the said officer is within the meaning of this section.[549]

The statement of an accused person in custody to a police officer as a result of which the murder weapon and a blood-stained bed sheet were recovered was held to be admissible in evidence even though it was taken by the officer without the presence of any witnesses.[550]

[s 27.8] Witnesses of Discovery.—Where there was no evidence of the discovery statement and, therefore, it could not be proved, the consequential recovery at the instance of the accused was not taken into evidence.[551] There was recovery of dead body, weapon and blood stained soil from the house of the accused. The witness of recovery was not resident in the immediate proximity of the house of the accused. Persons in the proximity were not joined though available. There was also discrepancy over the fact whether the witness was called or himself chanced to be there. The evidence of recovery was held to be doubtful.[552]

[s 27.9] Disclosure under duress, pressure or threat, etc.— The information which the accused furnishes to the police officer and which leads to the discovery of a fact is admissible in evidence. But admissibility by itself is not enough. The court has to see whether disclosure was of voluntary origin.[553]

[s 28] Confession made after removal of impression caused by inducement, threat or promise, relevant.—If such a confession as is referred to in section 24 is made after

---

548. *Vikram Singh v State of Punjab*, AIR 2010 SC 1007 : (2010) 3 SCC 56.

549. *Wirsa Singh*, (1953) Patiala 711; *Ashish Batham v State of MP*, AIR 2002 SC 3206 : 2002 Cr LJ 4676, recovery of blood-stained knife and clothes alleged to be recovered on disclosure made by the accused person, but because the recovery was delayed and was made only after the second remand, doubtful evidentiary value.

550. *Masang Kishti v State of Orissa*, 2001 Cr LJ 1633 (Ori).

551. *Rattan Chand v State of HP*, 2002 Cr LJ 1598 (HP).

552. *State of UP v Arun Kumar Gupta*, 2003 Cr LJ 894 : AIR 2003 SC 801. *Lakhwinder Singh v State of Punjab*, AIR 2003 2577, the supposed independent witness to recovery and seizure not examined, the police inspector's presence was also disproved, recoveries doubtful. *Salim Akhtar v State of UP*, 2003 Cr LJ 2302 (SC), recovery of arms and ammunition, place of recovery very near to a locality, no witness was summoned from the locality, recovery witnessed by a photographer who was a frequent visitor to the police station and was also under police obligations, recovery became doubtful.

553. *Rammi v State of MP*, AIR 1999 SC 3544 : (1999) 8 SCC 649 : 1999 Cr LJ 4561.

the impression caused by any such inducement, threat or promise has, in the opinion of the Court, been fully removed it is relevant.

COMMENT

[s 28.1] Principle.—A confession is admissible after the impression caused by an inducement, threat, or promise, has been fully removed because it becomes free and voluntary. The impression caused by inducement, promise, or threat, should have been fully removed before the confession is admissible by lapse of time or by caution given by a person holding an authority superior to that of person holding out the inducement, or by any intervening act. In determining whether an inducement has ceased to operate, the nature of such inducement, the time and circumstances under which it was made, the situation of the person making it, will be taken into consideration by the court.

[s 29] Confession otherwise relevant not to become irrelevant because of promise of secrecy, etc.—If such a confession is otherwise relevant it does not become irrelevant merely because it was made under a promise of secrecy, or in consequence of a deception practised on the accused person for the purpose of obtaining it, or when he was drunk, or because it was made in answer to questions which he need not have answered, whatever may have been the form of those questions, or because he was not warned that he was not bound to make such confession, and that evidence of it might be given against him.

COMMENT

[s 29.1] Principle.—A relevant confession does not become irrelevant because it was made—

(1) under a promise of secrecy; or

(2) in consequence of a deception practised on the accused; or

(3) when the accused was drunk; or

(4) in answer to questions which the accused need not have answered; or

(5) in consequence of the accused not receiving a warning that he was not bound to make it and that it might be used against him.

This section applies to criminal cases and is to be read along with section 24.

[s 30] Consideration of proved confession affecting person making it and others jointly under trial for same offence.—When more persons than one are being tried jointly[s 30.3] for the same offence, and a confession made by one of such persons affecting himself and some other of such persons[s 30.4] is proved, the Court may take into consideration such confession[s 30.5] as against such other person as well as against the person who makes such confession.

[554] **[*Explanation.*—"Offence", as used in this section, includes the abetment of, or attempt to commit, the offence.]**

---

554. Ins. by Act 3 of 1891, section 4.

ILLUSTRATIONS

(a) *A* and *B* are jointly tried for the murder of *C*. It is proved that *A* said—"*B* and I murdered *C*". The Court may consider the effect of this confession as against *B*.

(b) *A* is on his trial for the murder of *C*. There is evidence to show that *C* was murdered by *A* and *B*, and that *B* said—"*A* and I murdered *C*".

This statement may not be taken into consideration by the Court against *A*, as *B* is not being jointly tried.

SYNOPSIS

COMMENT

[s 30.1] Object and evidentiary value.—The object of this section is that where an accused person unreservedly confesses his own guilt, and at the same time implicates another person who is jointly tried with him for the same offence, his confession may be taken into consideration against such other person as well as against himself, because the admission of his own guilt operates as a sort of sanction, which, to some extent, takes the place of the sanction of an oath and so affords some guarantee that the whole statement is a true one.[555]

"The confession may be considered by the court, but the section does not say that the confession is to amount to proof; clearly there must be other evidence. The confession is only one element in the consideration of all the facts proved in the case; it can be put into the scale and weighed with the other evidence." The Supreme Court accepted this observation about the effect of the section. The case before the court was *Kashmira Singh v State of Madhya Pradesh*.[556]

Bose J emphasised this aspect: "In our opinion, the matter was put succinctly by Sir Lawrence Jenkins in *Emperor v Lalit Mohan*,[557] where he said that such a confession can only be used "to lend assurance to other evidence against an accused," or to put it in another way as Reilly J did in *Periyaswami Moopan*[558] the proviso goes no further than this—where there is evidence against the co-accused sufficient, if believed, to support his conviction, then the kind of confession described in section 30 may be thrown into the scale as an additional reason for believing that evidence."

Translating these observations into concrete terms, Bose J continued: "They come to this: "The proper way to approach a case of this kind is, first to marshal the evidence against the accused excluding the confession altogether from consideration and see

555. *Queen-Empress v Jagrup*, (1885) 7 All 646, 648.
556. *Kashmira Singh v State of Madhya Pradesh* AIR 1952 SC 159 : 1952 Cr LJ 839.
557. 38 Cal 559 at p 588.
558. 54 Mad 75 at p 77.

whether, if it is believed, conviction could safely be based on it. If it is capable of belief independently of the confession, then of course it is necessary to call the confession in aid. But cases may arise where the judge is not prepared to act on the other evidence as it stands even though, if believed, it would be sufficient to sustain a conviction. In such an event the Judge may call in aid the confession and use it to lend assurance to the other evidence and thus satisfy himself in believing that which without the aid of the confession he would not be prepared to accept."

[s 30.2] Principle.—Where more persons than one are jointly tried for the same offence, the confession made by one of them, if admissible in evidence at all, should be taken into consideration against all the accused, and not against the person alone who made it.[559] This section is an exception to the rule that the confession of one person is entirely inadmissible against another. The policy of the law in allowing a confession by one accused to be considered against another who is being jointly tried for the same offence, seems to rest on the recognition of the palpable fact that such a confession cannot fail to make an impression on the Judge's mind, which it was therefore better to control within limits than to ignore altogether.[560] Where confessions were made by the accused and also by his co-accused, but the High Court rejected the confession made by the co-accused and acquitted him, which acquittal remained undisturbed for other reasons also, the Supreme Court held that no part of the confession of the co-accused could be used for the purpose of corroborating the confession of the accused.[561]

The Supreme Court has observed that the confession of a co-accused cannot be elevated to the status of substantive evidence which can form the basis of conviction of co-accused.[562]

Under this section a confession by one person may be taken into consideration against another—

(1) if both of them are tried jointly;

(2) if they are tried for the same offence; and

(3) if the confession is legally proved.[563]

[s 30.3] "Tried jointly".—There should be a joint trial of the accused. The joint trial should be legal. If from any cause the accused who made the confession cannot be legally tried with the accused against whom the confession is to be used, the court should not attach any value to the confession.

[s 30.4] "Confession made by one of such persons affecting himself and some other of such persons".—The Supreme Court has held that a confession must implicate the maker substantially to the same extent as the other accused person against whom it

---

559. *Empress v Rama Birapa,* (1878) 3 Bom 12.

560. *Re Ganganmull,* (1924) 20 LW 202, 205; *Pradeep Kumar Jain v State of UP*, 2003 Cr LJ 682 (All), where no other evidence could be collected than that of the confession of the co-accused, it was held that any further continuation of the proceedings on the basis of such evidence only would be an abuse of the process of the court.

561. *State of Tamil Nadu v Kutty,* 2001 Cr LJ 4168 : AIR 2001 SC 2778.

562. *State (NCT of Delhi) v Navjot Sandhu,* (2005) 11 SCC 600 :AIR 2005 SC 3820, in the content of retracted confession.

563. *Mohan Singh Patel v State of MP,* 2002 Cr LJ (NOC) 145 (MP) : (2001) 4 Crimes 357, hearsay evidence of a witness cannot be relied upon in proof of a confession of co-accused.

is sought to be taken into consideration.[564] Thus the test is that the confessing accused must tar himself and the person or persons he implicates with one and the same brush.[565]

[s 30.5] "The Court may take into consideration such confession".—The section provides that the court may take the confession into consideration and thereby make it evidence on which the court may act, but it does not say that the confession is to amount to proof. There must clearly be other evidence. The confession is only one element in the consideration of all the facts proved in the case; it can be put into the scale and weighed with the other evidence. The confession of a co-accused can be used only in support of other evidence and cannot be made the foundation of a conviction.[566]

The confession of a co-accused cannot be treated as a substantive evidence to convict other than the person who made the confession on the evidentiary value of it. It is, however, well established and reiterated in several decisions of the Supreme Court that based on the consideration of the other evidence on record and if such evidence sufficiently supports the case of the prosecution and if requires further support, the confession of a co-accused can be pressed into service and reliance can be placed upon it. In other words, if there are sufficient materials to reasonably believe that there was concert and connection between the persons charged with the commission of an offence based on a conspiracy, it is immaterial even if they were strangers to each other and were ignorant of the actual role played by them of such acts, which they committed by their joint efforts. In terms of section 30 of the Evidence Act, 1972, when more than one person are being tried jointly for the same offence and a confession made by one of such persons is found to affect the maker as well as the co-accused and it stands sufficiently proved, the court can take into consideration such confession as against other persons and also against the person who made such a confession.[567]

[s 30.6] Retracted confession.—The rules regarding a confession, which is subsequently retracted, are: (1) that a confession is not to be regarded as involuntary merely because it is retracted;[568] (2) as against the maker of the confession the retracted confession may form the basis of a conviction if it is believed to be true and voluntarily made;[569] (3) as against the co-accused, both prudence and caution require the court not to rely on a retracted confessional without independent corroborative evidence.[570] (4) retraction should not be ambiguous vague or imaginary.[571] The corroboration should

---

564. *Balbir Singh v Punjab State,* AIR 1957 SC 216 : 1957 Cr LJ 481.

565. *Empress of India v Ganraj,* (1879) 2 All 444, 446; *Gul Hassan v The King-Emperor of India,* (1910) PR No. 24 of 1910 (Cr); *Jai Nand v Rex,* (1947) All 658; *Ammini v State of Kerala,* 1998 Cr LJ 481 : AIR 1998 SC 260, confession by one of the accused persons. There was reasonable ground to believe that the accused persons had conspired together for committing murder. The confession could be used against the other accused also.

566. *Bhubani Sahu v. The King,* (1949) 51 Bom LR 955 : 76 IA 147.

567. *Mohd Jamiludin Nasir v State of WB,* (2014) 7 SCC 443 (para 144).

568. *Phatik Chandra Gagoi v State of Assam,* 1988 Cr LJ 24 (Gau).

569. *Shrishail Nageshi Pare v State of Maharashtra,* AIR 1985 SC 866; 1985 Cr LJ 1173 : (1985) 2 SCC 341 : 1985 SCC (Cri) 235.

570. *Ibid.* Also see, *Vinayak v State of Maharashtra,* AIR 1984 SC 1793 : (1984) 4 SCC 441 : 1984 SCC (Cri) 605, where the accused persons were not typically co-accused, being charged under one common and one different section and the confession was also retracted.

571. *Taj Md Khan v State,* 1998 Cr LJ 2312 (Kant). *Sube Kireem v Asst. Collector of Customs,* 1998 Cr LJ 3052 (Bom), confession under section 108 of the Custom Act was retracted after nearly 5 years on the ground that it was made because of torture by Customs Authorities. But there was no satisfactory explanation of belated retraction. This was held to be not a genuine retraction.

not only confirm the general story of the alleged crime, but must also connect the accused with it.[572] The Supreme Court observed.[573]

As, however, the confession was a retracted one it could be acted upon only if substantially corroborated by independent circumstances. It is not necessary that retracted confession should be corroborated in each material particular, it is sufficient that there is a general corroboration of the important incidents mentioned in the confession.

The Supreme Court has held that there can be no absolute rule that a retracted confession cannot be acted upon unless it is corroborated materially. But as a matter of prudence and caution which has sanctified itself into a rule of law, a retracted confession cannot be made solely the basis of conviction unless it is corroborated. It is not necessary that each and every circumstance mentioned in the confession regarding the complicity of the accused should be separately and independently corroborated nor is it essential that the corroboration must come from facts and circumstances discovered after the confession was made. It would be sufficient if the general trend of the confession is substantiated by some evidence which would tally with what is contained in the confession.[574] It has also held that a voluntary and true confession made by an accused, though it was subsequently retracted by him, can be taken into consideration against a co-accused, but as a matter of prudence and practice the court should not act upon it to sustain a conviction of the co-accused without full and strong corroboration in material particulars both as to the crime and as to his connection with that crime. The amount of credibility to be attached to a retracted confession would depend upon the circumstances of each particular case.[575] However, such retracted confession cannot be used to support the evidence of the other accomplices.[576] It has further held that a retracted confession must be looked upon with greater concern unless the reasons given for having made in the first instance (not for retraction as erroneously stated in some cases) are on the face of them false. Once the confession is proved satisfactorily any admission made therein must be satisfactorily withdrawn or the making of it explained as having proceeded from fear, duress, promise or the like from someone in authority.[577]

[s 31] Admissions not conclusive proof, but may estop.—Admissions are not conclusive proof of the matters admitted, but they may operate as estoppels under the provisions hereinafter contained.

---

572. *Emperor v Bhagwandas Bisesar,* (1940) 42 Bom LR 938 : (1941) Bom 27.

573. *State of UP v Boota Singh,* AIR 1978 SC 1770 at p 1775 : (1979) 1 SCC 31.

574. *Subramania Goundan v The State of Madras,* (1958) SCR 428 : 1958 Cr LJ 238 : AIR 1958 SC 1958; *Pyare Lal v State of Rajasthan,* AIR 1963 SC 1094 : (1963) 2 Cr LJ 178; *Abdul Ghani v State of UP,* AIR 1973 SC 264 : 1973 Cr LJ 280; *Kehar Singh v State (Delhi Admn.),* AIR 1988 SC 1883; 1989 Cr LJ 1 : (1988) 3 SCC 609 : 1988 SCC Cri 711. where at p 44 RAY J surveyed some cases so as to come to the same conclusion which has all along been accepted as the right notion as to the evidentiary value of retracted confessions. But, see, *Puran v State of Punjab (I),* AIR 1953 SC 459 : 1953 Cr LJ 1925, at p 462, where it is stated: "It is a settled rule of evidence that unless a retracted confession is corroborated in material particulars, it is not prudent to base a conviction in a criminal case on its strength alone." *Kartar Singh v State of Punjab,* 1994 Cr LJ 3139, conviction can be founded on a voluntary confession and also on a retracted confession if it is corroborated generally. *Shankar v State of TN,* 1994 Cr LJ 3071 : (1994) 2 Crimes 1 : (1994) 2 Andh LT (Cri) 429, dead body discovered at the instance of the accused, even if not relevant under section 27, the fact could be used to corroborate the retracted confession of the accused.

575. *Ram Prakash v The State of Punjab,* (1959) SCR 1219.

576. *Hussain Umar v Dalipsinghji,* AIR 1970 SC 45 : 1970 Cr LJ 9.

577. *Haroom Haji v State of Maharashtra,* AIR 1968 SC 832 : 1968 Cr LJ 1017.

SYNOPSIS

COMMENT

[s 31.1] Admission may operate as estoppel.—This section declares that admissions are not conclusive proof of the matters admitted, but that they may operate as estoppels. "Admission" is defined in section 17, *supra*; "estoppel", in section 115, *infra*. Unless admissions are contractual or unless they constitute an estoppel they are not conclusive, but are open to rebuttal or explanation. Admissions being declarations against an interest are good evidence but they are not conclusive and a party is always at liberty to withdraw admissions by proving that they are either mistaken or untrue. But estoppel creates an absolute bar.[578] Admissions, whether written or oral, which do not operate by way of estoppel, constitute a kind of evidence, which may be rebutted, against their makers and those claiming under them, as between them and others. A party is not bound by his own representations, where they have not been acted upon by the opposite party. If treated as admission not acted upon, the party who made them may prove that they were not true or were mistaken. A mere admission is conclusive only where it has been acted on by the party to whom it was made. An estoppel, i.e., a representation acted on by the other party, by creating a substantive right, does oblige the estopped party to make good his representation, in other words, it is conclusive. A heavy burden of proof lies on the party who wants to get rid of his admissions.[579]

Admissions operating as estoppels are not the only kind of admissions that will either be relevant to or conclude the matter in issue. Two other kinds of admissions equally, if not more, effective, are

(1) admissions contained in the pleadings in a case which would circumscribe the issues and avoid the necessity for proof, and

(2) admissions made by the parties to a suit on earlier occasions either in prior proceedings in a court of law, or in statements made out of court. What a party himself admits to be true may reasonably be presumed to be so.[580]

An estoppel differs from an admission, for it cannot generally be taken advantage of by strangers. It binds only parties and privies. An estoppel is generally said to be only a rule of evidence, for an action cannot be founded upon it. As a defence it has been held to have the effect of rule of substantive law. Where the question was as to the existence of an arbitration agreement, the court said that the matter was to be decided by ascertaining the parties' intention from the language used by them and not on the basis of admissions of one of the parties.[581]

---

578. *Chhaganlal Keshwlal Mehta v Patel Narandas Haribhai*, AIR 1982 SC 121 : (1982) 1 SCC 223.

579. *Chetak Constructions Ltd v Om Prakash*, AIR 2003 MP 145. In a contract for sale of property the vendors stated that the possession was handed over at the time of agreement itself and a big amount was paid to them for vacating the property immediately. The vendors were not allowed to say subsequently that there was no surrender of possession.

580. *Avira v Varkey*, (1951) TC 209.

581. *Garg Builders and Engineers v UP Rajkiya Nirman Nigam*, AIR 1995 Del 111.

The section says that an admission is not *conclusive* proof; it does not say that an admission is not sufficient proof without corroboration. It deals with the effect as to conclusiveness of an admission. The express admissions of a party to the suit, or admissions implied from his conduct, are strong evidence against him.[582]

The expression "conclusive proof" is defined in section 4, and when a fact is declared to be conclusive proof of another, a court cannot allow evidence to be given for the purpose of disproving the fact conclusively proved. All that this section provides is that an admission, unless it operates as an estoppel, is not conclusive. What a party himself admits to be true may reasonably be presumed to be so. The person against whom it is proved is at liberty to show that it was mistaken or untrue. An admission does not estop the party who makes it; he is still at liberty to disprove it by evidence so far as regards his own interest. The rule that admissions are not conclusive is applicable to mistakes in respect of legal liability as well as to those in respect of fact. A plaintiff is not bound by an admission on a point of law, nor precluded from asserting the contrary in order to obtain the relief to which, upon a true construction of the law, he may appear to be entitled.[583] But, if the admission is duly proved and if the person against whom it is proved does not satisfy the court that it was mistaken or untrue, there is nothing in this Act, and there is no general principle or rule of law to prevent the court from deciding the case in accordance with it.[584]

The provisions of this section are not restricted to admissions made at any particular time or place, but are wide enough to include admissions made in pleadings. Where an admission was made by the predecessor in title and the successor in interest confirmed it, he became bound by it.[585]

[s 31.2] Facts admitted need not be proved.—Section 58 declares that the facts admitted need not be produced. The effect is that facts admitted are presumed to be true. The Supreme Court has therefore declared the law to be that unless the presumption created by an admission is rebutted, the facts admitted must be taken to be established. A person, who first admits a fact and then goes back upon it, has to disprove his admission with the help of evidence of clinching nature. It was accordingly held that the Consumer Forum should not have allowed a party to resile from his admission without adequate rebuttal.[586]

STATEMENTS BY PERSONS WHO CANNOT BE CALLED AS WITNESSES

[s 32] Cases in which statement of relevant fact by person who is dead or cannot be found, etc., is relevant.—Statements, written or verbal, of relevant facts[s 32.10] **made by a person who is dead, or who cannot be found, or who has become incapable of giving evidence, or whose attendance cannot be procured without an amount of delay or**

582. *Narayan v Gopal,* AIR 1960 SC 100 : (1960) 1 SCR 773.

583. *Juttendromohun Tagore v Ganendromohun Tagore,* (1872) LR Sup IA 47; *Jagwant Singh v Silan Singh,* (1899) 21 All 285; *Rani Chandra v Chaudhuri,* (1906) 9 Bom LR 267 : 29 All 184 : 34 IA 27; *Shri Dolatsinghji Jaswantsinghji v Khachar Mansur Rukhad,* (1936) 63 IA 248 : 38 Bom LR 690 : 60 Bom 634. See, *Messrs Jetmull Bhojraj v State of Bihar,* AIR 1967 Pat 287.

584. *Maung Mya v Ma Tha Ya,* (1899) 2 UBR (1897-1901) 377.

585. *Avadh Kishore Das v Ram Gopal,* AIR 1979 SC 861 : (1979) 4 SCC 790. Admission made by a party in a previous suit binds the successors in interest and legal representatives in subsequent suit, *Modgi Krishna v Modgi Krishna Bai,* AIR 1994 AP 16.

586. *United India Insurance Co Ltd v Samir Chandra Chaudhury,* (2005) 5 SCC 784 : (2005) 3 CPJ 2 SC.

expense which, under the circumstances of the case, appears to the Court unreasonable, are themselves relevant facts in the following cases:—

(1) when it relates to cause of death.—When the statement is made by a person as to the cause of his death, or as to any of the circumstances of the transaction which resulted in his death, in cases in which the cause of that person's death comes into question.

Such statements are relevant whether the person who made them was or was not, at the time when they were made, under expectation of death, and whatever may be the nature of the proceeding in which the cause of his death comes into question.

(2) or is made in course of business—When the statement was made by such person in the ordinary course of business, and in particular when it consists of any entry or memorandum made by him in books kept in the ordinary course of business, or in the discharge of professional duty; or of an acknowledgement written or signed by him of the receipt of money, goods, securities or property of any kind; or of a document used in commerce written or signed by him; or of the date of a letter or other document usually dated, written or signed by him.

(3) or against interest of maker.—When the statement is against the pecuniary or proprietary interest of the person making it, or when, if true, it would expose him or would have exposed him to a criminal prosecution or to a suit for damages.

(4) or gives opinion as to a public right or custom, or matters of general interest.—When the statement gives the opinion of any such person, as to the existence of any public right or custom or matter of public or general interest, of the existence of which, if it existed, he would have been likely to be aware, and when such statement was made before any controversy as to such right, custom or matter has arisen.

(5) or relates to existence of relationship.—When the statement relates to the existence of any relationship by blood, marriage or adoption between persons as to whose relationship [587][by blood, marriage or adoption] the person making the statement had special means of knowledge, and when the statement was made before the question in dispute was raised.

(6) or is made in will or deed relating to family affairs.—When the statement relates to the existence of any relationship [588][by blood, marriage or adoption] between persons deceased, and is made in any will or deed relating to the affairs of the family to which any such deceased person belonged, or in any family pedigree, or upon any tombstone, family portrait or other thing on which such statements are usually made, and when such statement was made before the question in dispute was raised.

(7) or in document relating to transaction mentioned in section 13, clause (a).—When the statement is contained in any deed, will or other document which relates to any such transaction as is mentioned in section 13, clause (a).

---

587. Ins. by Act 18 of 1872, section 2.
588. Ins. by Act 18 of 1872, section 2.

(8) or is made by several persons and expresses feelings relevant to matter in question.—When the statement was made by a number of persons, and expressed feelings or impressions on their part relevant to the matter in question.

ILLUSTRATIONS

(a) The question is, whether *A* was murdered by *B*; or

A dies of injuries received in a transaction in the course of which she was ravished. The question, is whether she was ravished by *B*; or

The question is, whether *A* was killed by *B* under such circumstances that a suit would lie against *B* by *A*'s widow.

Statements made by *A* as to the cause of his or her death, referring respectively to the murder, the rape and the actionable wrong under consideration are relevant facts.

(b) The question is as to the date of *A*'s birth.

An entry in the diary of a deceased surgeon regularly kept in the course of business, stating that on a given day he attended *A*'s mother and delivered her of a son, is a relevant fact.

(c) The question is, whether *A* was in Calcutta on a given day.

A statement in the diary of a deceased solicitor, regularly kept in the course of business, that on a given day the solicitor attended *A* at a place mentioned, in Calcutta, for the purpose of conferring with him upon specified business, is a relevant fact.

(d) The question is, whether a ship sailed from Bombay harbour on a given day.

A letter written by a deceased member of a merchant's firm, by which she was chartered to their correspondents in London, to whom the cargo was consigned, stating that the ship sailed on a given day from Bombay harbour, is a relevant fact.

(e) The question is, whether rent was paid to *A* for certain land.

A letter from *A*'s deceased agent to *A* saying that he had received the rent on *A*'s account and held it at *A*'s orders, is a relevant fact.

(f) The question is, whether *A* and *B* were legally married.

The statement of a deceased clergyman that he married them under such circumstances that the celebration would be a crime, is relevant.

(g) The question is, whether *A*, a person who cannot be found, wrote a letter on a certain day. The fact that a letter written by him is dated on that day is relevant.

(h) The question is, what was the cause of the wreck of a ship.

A protest made by the captain, whose attendance cannot be procured, is a relevant fact.

(i) The question is, whether a given road is a public way.

A statement by *A*, a deceased headman of the village, that the road was public, is a relevant fact.

(j) The question is, what was the price of grain on a certain day in a particular market.

A statement of the price, made by a deceased banya in the ordinary course of his business, is a relevant fact.

(k) The question is, whether *A*, who is dead, was the father of *B*. A statement by *A* that *B* was his son, is a relevant fact.

(l) The question is, what was the date of the birth of *A*.

A letter from *A*'s deceased father to a friend, announcing the birth of *A* on a given day, is a relevant fact.

(m) The question is, whether, and when, *A* and *B* were married.

An entry in a memorandum book by *C*, the deceased father of *B*, of his daughter's marriage with *A* on a given date, is a relevant fact.

(n) *A* sues *B* for a libel expressed in a painted caricature exposed in a shop window. The question is as to the similarity of the caricature and its libellous character. The remarks of a crowd of spectators on these points may be proved.

SYNOPSIS

COMMENT

This and the following section are exceptions to the general rule that hearsay evidence is not admissible. Hearsay evidence is excluded on the ground that it is always desirable in the interest of justice to get the person, whose statement is relied upon, into court for his examination in the regular way in order that many possible sources of inaccuracy and untrustworthiness can be best brought to light and exposed, if they exist, by the test of cross-examination. Section 60 lays down that oral evidence must be direct.

The exceptions to the hearsay evidence have been directed by necessity. This rule excluding the hearsay evidence is relaxed so far as the statements contained in sections 32 and 33 are concerned. The general ground of admissibility of the evidence referred to in these sections is that no better evidence could be produced. The phrase "hearsay evidence" is not used in the Act; because it is inaccurate and vague. Before such evidence is let in, the court must arrive at a finding on evidence formally and regularly taken and recorded that one or other of the grounds specified in the section exists. The admission of such deposition in evidence without such finding is illegal.[589]

[s 32.1] Principle.—Under this section written or verbal statements of relevant facts made by a person—

(a) who is dead;

(b) who cannot be found;

(c) who has become incapable of giving evidence; or

(d) whose attendance cannot be procured without unreasonable delay or expense;

are relevant under the following circumstances:—

(1) When it relates to the cause of his death.

(2) When it is made in the course of business, such as, entry in books, or acknowledgment or the receipt of any property, or date of a document.

(3) When it is against the pecuniary or proprietary interest of the person making it or when it would have exposed him to a criminal prosecution or to a suit for damages.

(4) When it gives opinion as to a public right or custom or matters of general interest and it was made before any controversy as to such right or custom has arisen.

(5) When it relates to the existence of any relationship between persons as to whose relationship the maker had special means of knowledge and was made before the question in dispute arose.

(6) When it relates to the existence of any relationship between persons deceased and is made in any will or deed or family pedigree, or upon any tomb-stone on family portrait, and was made before the question in dispute arose.

(7) When it is contained in any deed, will, or other document.

(8) When it is made by a number of persons and expresses feelings relevant to the matter in question.

---

589. *Satish Chandra Seal v Emperor,* (1944) 2 Cal 76; *P Bikshapathi v State of AP,* 1989 Cr LJ 1186 AP, dowry death, the court explaining the rationale of these exceptions.

Section 30 does not limit the operation of this section, but section 118 does.

The words "dying declaration" mean a statement written or verbal of relevant facts made by a person who is dead.[590] A dying declaration is not complete unless the full names and addresses of the persons involved are given in it. Therefore, only because the deceased in his dying declaration uttered first names similar to that of the accused, it was not proper to accept the prosecution version based on such incomplete dying declaration.[591] Evidence of dying declaration is admissible not only against the person actually causing death but also against other persons participating in causing death.[592]

Dying declaration is an exception to the general rule against hearsay. The grounds of admission are firstly, the victim is generally the only principal eye-witness to the crime; secondly, sense of impending death creates a sanction which is equal to obligation of an oath. A man would not like to meet his maker with a lie in his mouth. The requirements of oath and cross-examination are dispensed with.[593] Though a dying declaration is not recorded in the court and nor is it put to strict proof of cross-examination by the accused, still it is admissible in evidence against the general rule that hearsay evidence is not admissible in evidence.[594]

[s 32.2] Relevancy of a dying declaration.—A statement by a person made before his death to be relevant, the following ingredients are to be satisfied:

(i) The statement is made by a person who is conscious and believes or apprehends that death is imminent.

(ii) The statement must pertain to what the person believes to be the cause or circumstances of his/her death.

(iii) What is recorded must be a statement made by the person concerned, since it is an exception to the rule of hearsay evidence.

(iv) The statement must be confidence bearing, truthful and credible.[595]

In *Mallella Shyamsunder v State of AP*,[596] the Supreme Court added two more ingredients as under:

(v) the statement should not be one made on tutoring or prompting.

(vi) The court may also scan the statement to see whether the same is prompted by any motive of vengeance.[597]

---

590. *Sant Gopal v State of UP,* 1995 Cr LJ 312 (All).

591. *Kajal Sarkar v State of Assam,* 1993 Cr LJ 3869 (Gau).

592. *Sant Gopal v State of UP,* 1995 Cr LJ 312 (All); *Arjun Kushwah v State of MP,* 1999 Cr LJ 2538 (MP), the maxim of law is that a man will not like to meet his maker with a lie in his mouth. A dying declaration made by the victim in a fit mental state but on the verge of death has a special sanctity of the solemn moment.

593. *Dashrath v State of MP*, AIR 2008 SC 316 : (2007) 12 SCC 487, can be the sole basis of conviction, requiring corroboration is merely a rule of prudence.

594. *Umakant v State of Chhattisgarh*, AIR 2014 SC 2943 (para 18).

595. *Laxman v State of Maharashtra*, (2002) 6 SCC 710.

596. *Mallella Shyamsunder v State of Andhra Pradesh*, (2015) 2 SCC 486.

597. *Mallella Shyamsunder v State of AP*, (2015) 2 SCC 486.

[s 32.3] Form or procedure for recording dying declaration.—There is no particular form or procedure prescribed for recording a dying declaration nor is it required to be recorded only by a Magistrate. As a general rule, it is advisable to get the evidence of the declarant certified from a doctor. In appropriate cases, the satisfaction of the person recording the statement regarding the state of mind of the deceased would also be sufficient to hold that the deceased was in a position to make a statement. It is settled law that if the prosecution solely depends on the dying declaration, the normal rule is that the courts must exercise due care and caution to ensure genuineness of the dying declaration, keeping in mind that the accused had no opportunity to test the veracity of the statement of the deceased by cross-examination. The law does not insist upon the corroboration of dying declaration before it can be accepted. The insistence of corroboration to a dying declaration is only a rule of prudence. When the court is satisfied that the dying declaration is voluntary, not tainted by tutoring or animosity, and is not a product of the imagination of the declarant, in that event, there is no impediment in convicting the accused on the basis of such dying declaration.[598]

[s 32.4] Dying declaration recorded by Magistrate.—The dying declaration was recorded by Special Executive Magistrate who deposed that he had satisfied himself that the deceased was in a perfectly fit condition to make statement which was supported by the Police Officer. The statement was not vitiated by interpolations or apparent inconsistencies and was consistent with two earlier dying declarations. It was held that the dying declaration could be relied on and accepted even in absence of the certificate from the doctor that the deceased was in a fit condition to make statements.[599] Where the dying declaration was recorded by the Special Magistrate who was not entrusted with the duty of recording it, it was held that it could not be discarded as all precautions were taken before recording it and it inspired confidence.[600] Where the dying declaration was recorded by the Magistrate which was neither signed by the deceased, nor contained date and time of its recording and the prosecution failed to give any explanation that the deceased was not in a position to sign it, it was held that such dying declaration

---

598. *Ashabai v State of Maharashtra,* (2013) 2 SCC 224.

599. *Pandian K Nadar v State of Maharashtra,* 1993 Cr LJ 3883 (Bom); *Prem Chand v State of UP,* 1993 Supp. 4 SCC 214 : 1994 SCC (Cri) 11, dying declaration recorded by magistrate, no discrepancies, consistent with statement of eye-witnesses, reliable. *Bolem Bhaskara Rao v State of AP,* 1995 Supp 4 SCC 211 : 1996 SCC (Cri) 49, magistrate recording the statement verified that he was fully satisfied that the injured person was in good mental condition, the declaration was held to be relevant though no question was put to the injured person about his fitness. *Rafat Mian v State of UP,* 2000 Cr LJ 3039 (All), deceased admitted to hospital in an unconscious state after two hours of burn injuries of first and second degree she regained consciousness during night and made a statement. Her dying declaration was recorded by a magistrate and the same was regarded by the court as authentic. *Ram Bihari Yadav v State of Bihar,* AIR 1998 SC 1850 : 1998 Cr LJ 2515 : (1998) 4 SCC 517, recorded by magistrate after being satisfied as to the identity of the maker as well as her fitness to make the statement signature of the trainee nurse was taken because of the non-availability of doctor. Concurrent findings as to the value of the declaration upheld. *Harjit Kaur v State of Punjab,* AIR 1999 SC 2571 : 1999 Cr LJ 4055 : (1999) 6 SCC 545, recorded by a sub-Divisional Magistrate, who was an IAS officer, relatives of the deceased were not present, agitation by relatives did not make the recording to be under their pressure. Thumbs were burnt, but medical evidence did not disclose that she could not have her thumb impression.

600. *Amir Jamal Khan v State of Maharashtra,* 1995 Cr LJ 1956 (Bom).

which was impregnant with so many suspicious circumstances which created doubt about its genuineness and it was not safe to base conviction on it.[601]

There is no requirement of law that a dying declaration must necessarily be made to a Magistrate.[602] What evidentiary value or weight has to be attached to such statement, must necessarily depend on the facts and circumstances of each particular case. In a proper case, it may be permissible to convict a person only on the basis of a dying declaration in the light of the facts and circumstances of the case.

In this case the dying declaration was properly proved; no question was put during cross-examination regarding the condition of the victim at the relevant time; medical evidence was not adverse and statement was corroborated. Hence conviction based on such dying declaration could not be said to be improper.[603]

[s 32.5] Form of dying declaration.—*Question-answer form.*—The mere fact that a dying declaration is not in a question-answer form does not destroy its value.[604] Merely because the dying declaration is not in a question-answer form, the sanctity attached to it, as it comes from the mouth of a dying person, cannot be brushed aside and its reliability cannot be doubted.[605] A dying declaration cannot be discarded only on the ground that it was not recorded in question-answer form. A statement recorded in a narrative form may be more natural and may give a true version of the incident as perceived by the injured person.[606]

A dying declaration was recorded by the magistrate in narrative form in his own language and not in question-answer form. This was held to be not a ground for

---

601. *State of UP v Shishupal Singh,* AIR 1994 SC 129 : 1994 Cr LJ 617 : 1992 Supp (3) SCC 60. *Subhash v State of Haryana,* AIR 2011 SC 349 : 2011 (1) Crimes 62 (SC), the magistrate recorded the statement without trying to know whether the hospital was located within his jurisdiction, fitness was endorsed by the doctor after recording of the statement, the Supreme Court regarded the declaration as suspicious.

602. *Kulwant Singh v State of Punjab,* (2004) 9 SCC 257 : AIR 2004 SC 2875, not necessary to be recorded in the presence of a magistrate.

603. *Ramawati Devi v State of Bihar,* (1983) 1 SCC 211 : AIR 1983 SC 164 : 1983 Cr LJ 221; *Surinder Paul v State,* 1991 Cr LJ 745 (P&H), the magistrate must record dying declaration in accordance with prescribed rules. *State v Sita Devi,* 1997 Cr LJ 2210 (P&H), High Court Rules required recording by Judicial Magistrate, no explanation as to why recorded by executive magistrate. Even then he did not record it in his own handwriting. No indication of time of recording of state of health. Rejected. *Raj Kumar v State of Punjab,* 2000 Cr LJ 3218 (P&H), Punjab Police Rules, 1934, dying declaration to be recorded by Judicial Magistrate, if possible. A dying declaration recorded otherwise was not excluded from consideration.

604. *Sant Gopal v State of UP,* 1995 Cr LJ 312 (All). A dying declaration not recorded in question and answer form is not inadmissible on that ground when it is complete, *Surjeet Kaur v State of MP,* 1994 Cr LJ 1886 (MP). See also, *Ganpat Mahadeo Mane v State of Maharashtra,* AIR 1993 SC 1180 : 1993 Cr LJ 298 : 1993 Supp (2) SCC 242. *Rajendra Singh v State of Rajasthan,* 1996 Cr LJ 1560 (Raj), **distinguishing** *Rabi Chandra Pradhan v State of Orissa,* AIR 1980 SC 1738 : (1980) 1 SCC 240 and referring to *Padmaben Shamabhai Patel v State of Gujarat,* 1991 CLR (SC) 162 : (1991) 1 SCC 744 : 1991 SCC (Cri) 275. *State of Karnataka v Shariff,* AIR 2003 SC 1074, a statement cannot be discarded for the reason that it was not recorded in question-answer form. A statement in narrative form may be more natural and may give a version of the incident as it was perceived by the victim.

605. *Prem Kumar Gulati v State of Haryana,* (2014) 14 SCC 646 (para 16) : 2015 Cr LJ 159.

606. *State of Karnataka v Shariff,* 2003 Cr LJ 1254 (SC). *Ram Bihari Yadav v State of Bihar,* AIR 1998 SC 1850 : 1998 Cr LJ 2515, should preferably be in question-answer form; the fact that it consists of a few sentences in the actual words of the maker, not a ground against its reliability.

discarding it. The maker of the statement was in fit condition. The magistrate had no reason to record a false statement. Failure to mention time was not material. Presence of relatives at the time of recording did not have the effect of tutoring. The deceased also had no enmity with the accused so as falsely implicate him. The dying declaration was accepted as good piece of evidence.[607]

The witness who recorded the dying declaration categorically stated that the deceased gave replies to questions. But the declaration produced was not in question—answer from. The court said that such fact was not material.[608]

A dying declaration should be short concise and to the point. It is not desirable to have a dying declaration in a cyclostyled form.[609]

[s 32.6] Oral dying declaration.—An oral dying declaration means a statement which was not recorded and is reproduced by the witnesses out of memory. The Supreme Court has laid down that the exact words of such statement must be reproduced. Any variance in statements of the witnesses with regard to the exact words would materially affect the value of the oral dying declaration. Even though an oral dying declaration can form basis of conviction in a given case, but such a dying declaration has to be trustworthy and free from every blemish and inspire confidence. The reproduction of the exact words of the oral declaration in such cases is very important. The difference in the exact words of the declaration in the present case detracted materially from the value of the oral dying declaration.[610]

---

607. *Rajendra Singh v State*, 1997 Cr LJ 2668 (All).

608. *Amarsingh Munnasingh Suryawanshi v State of Maharashtra*, AIR 2008 SC 479 : 2008 Cr LJ 705.

609. *Adevappa Nagappa Anaglokar v State of Karnataka*, 1998 Cr LJ 584 (Kant).

610. *Darshana Devi v State of Punjab*, 1995 Supp (4) SCC 126 : 1996 SCC (Cri) 38. *Ramesh Bhagwan Manjrekar v State*, 1997 Cr LJ 796 (Bom), it was highly doubtful whether the injured person was in state of consciousness at the time of declaration. There were discrepancies in the FIR and statements in the court. Oral declaration not accepted *Subramanian v State*, 1997 Cr LJ 3540 (Mad), oral statement made before the head-constable, thumb impression obtained on blank paper which was subsequently filled up with the contents of the statement, held not reliable. *Ram Bihari Yadav v State*, 1998 Cr LJ 2515 : AIR 1998 SC 1862 : (1998) 4 SCC 517, recording should be in question answer form. But the fact that the statement was in the form of a few sentences in the actual words of the maker was held to be not a ground against its reliability. Recording was by the magistrate after satisfying himself about the identity of the maker and her fitness. Signature was that of the trainee-nurse because of non-availability of doctor. Concurrent-finding about admissibility of the statement was upheld. *Paras Yadav v State of Bihar*, 1999 Cr LJ 1122 : AIR 1999 SC 644, oral statement made by the injured person to the police and other witnesses at the place where he was lying injured. The statement was taken to be a dying declaration because of the death of the declarant. The witnesses testified that the injured person was in a fit state of health. The statement was corroborated by medical report. Non-recording in regular form was held to be not material. *State v Surya Prasad Verma*, 2001 Cr LJ 2481 (All), immediately prior to his death, the victim said that he and another person were administered poison by the accused, it was corroborated by other evidence, no positive reason was found to disbelieve the oral dying declaration, held, conviction on its basis was proper. *S Tripat Patra v State of Orissa*, 2003 Cr LJ 1591 (Ori), oral declaration was supposed to have been made by a poison victim, she could not reach hospital, was brought back home. Circumstances showed that she was not in position to make any statement. *Kishanlal v State of Rajasthan*, AIR 1999 SC 3062, oral declaration made before her father, uncle and grand-mother, mentioning the names of accused persons. In her second dying declaration made before the Magistrate she did not name any persons, nor could speak of their identity because of smoke. The court did not act upon the declaration.

It is well settled that an oral dying declaration can form the basis of conviction, if the deponent is in a fit condition to make the declaration and if it is found to be truthful. The courts as a matter of prudence look for corroboration to an oral dying declaration. In the instant case the dying declaration did not inspire the confidence of the court.[611]

[s 32.7] Fitness of declarant.—The court should be satisfied that the deceased was in a fit state of mind and capable of making a statement at the time when it was recorded.[612] Where the parents of the deceased woman stated that she was not mentally sound, it was held that this fact should not have been ignored by the court.[613]

Certificate from the doctor and endorsement from him that the victim was not only conscious but also in a fit condition to make statements is a must. In the absence of such a certificate the declaration may be rendered heavily suspect.[614] The Supreme Court has also laid down that the absence of the medical certificate of fitness does not render a dying declaration to be unacceptable. What is essentially required is that the person who records it must be satisfied that the injured person was in a fit state of mind. The medical certificate is a rule of caution. Truthful dying declaration can be assured even otherwise.[615]

---

611. *Balbir v Vazir*, (2014) 12 SCC 670 (para 20).

612. *Laxmi v Om Prakash*, 2000 Cr LJ 3302 : AIR 2001 SC 2383. *Sabbita Saryavathi v Bandala Srinivasarao*, (2004) 10 SCC 620 : 2004 Cr LJ 3337, grave injuries in the heart and lungs region, should have gone unconscious as indicated by medical opinion earlier than two years and, therefore, the injured could not have made any statement after two years, dying declaration not reliable.

613. *Dandu Lakshmi Reddy v State of AP*, AIR 1999 SC 3255 : 1999 Cr LJ 4287, the court also noted that there were divergent versions in the statement and the same could not have been ignored.

614. *Vithal Sadashiv Gaikwad v State of Maharashtra*, 1994 Cr LJ 2035 (Bom). *Amar Singh v State of MP*, 1996 Cr LJ 1582 (MP), without proof of mental or physical fitness, not reliable. *Vinay Kumar v State of MP*, AIR 1994 SC 830 : 1994 Cr LJ 942, dying declaration recorded by doctor after verification that the victim was not tutored, nor assisted by anyone present there and also that he was in a proper state of mind to make the statement. The declaration was regarded as good evidence. *Panna v State of Rajasthan*, 1994 SCC Cri 1140, head injury, the doctor observed that generally in such cases, the victim should have died or rendered unconscious from which he would not recover. The doctor, however, did not rule out the possibility of the victim being able to speak. His dying declaration was held to be relevant. *Sita Ram v State*, 1998 Cr LJ 287 (Raj) a dying declaration not bearing the certificate that the deceased was in a fit state of mind to make the statement could not make the basis of conviction. *Rajendra Singh v State*, 1998 Cr LJ 2126 (Raj), there was no certificate of the scribe that he had recorded the true statement or that of the doctor that the injured person was in a fit state to make the statement. No attempt seemed to have been made to get the statement recorded by a magistrate. The language of the statement did not seem to be that of the deceased. The manner of recording was also doubtful. The declaration was rejected. *Mange Ram v State (Delhi Admn.)* 1998 Cr LJ 2269 (SC), dying declaration before the investigating officer and the doctor was found to be consistent and reliable. Medical certificate was that the injured person was in full senses when brought to the hospital and fit for making the statement. The statement of the witness that he was under the influence of drink could not be relied upon. Order of conviction was upheld. *Jai Karan v State (NCT) Delhi*, AIR 1999 SC 3512 : 1999 Cr LJ 4512 : (1999) 8 SCC 161, doctor recorded the statement in hospital, did not read it over to her, nor taken her signature or thumb impression, not attested by any other person, medical incharge of the ward stated that the injured woman was not fit enough to make any statement, declaration not relied upon. *State of Karnataka v Shariff*, AIR 2003 SC 1074, the doctor recorded in the accident register of the hospital that the patient was conscious, her orientation was good and she answered well the questions put to her. Declaration not to be discarded because the injury report and post-mortem report stated that she must not have been in a position to make the statement.

615. *Laxman v State of Maharashtra*, 2002 Cr LJ 4095 (SC).

[s 32.7.1] ***Dying declaration and medical certificate of fitness.***—Overruling some earlier cases to the contrary effect a Constitution Bench of the Supreme Court in *Laxman v State of Maharashtra*,[616] speaking through PATTANAIK J adopted the view that the absence of the certificate of the doctor as to fitness of mind of the injured person would not render his dying declaration to be unacceptable. The court said that what is essentially required is that the person who records the statement must be satisfied that the injured person was in a fit state of mind. Certification by the doctor is only a rule of caution. But voluntary and truthful nature of the statement can be established otherwise.

[s 32.8] More than one dying declarations.—When there are more than one dying declarations of the same person, they have to be read as one and the same statement for proper appreciation of the value and, if they differ from each other on material aspects. effort should be made to see if they could be reconciled. If no assumption could explain the difference, the statements might become unworthy of credit but if one is possible, the position may be different. If there was a reasonable explanation for the difference, the statement may be taken at par with an omission covered by explanation to section 161, CrPC and be considered as a matter of fact in each case on its own strength.[617] The Supreme Court has suggested that the first statement in point of time made by the injured person must be preferred to any of his subsequent statements.[618] A mere omission on the part of the prosecutrix to state the entire factual details of the incident in her very first statement does not make her subsequent statements unworthy, especially when her statements are duly corroborated by other prosecution witnesses including the medical evidence.[619] The Supreme Court has also observed that the fact there are more than one and apparently consistent dying declarations is not in itself sufficient to persuade the court to act thereon.[620] Consistency is a very relevant factor. Where contradictory and inconsistent stand is taken by the deceased, the Supreme Court said that corroboration from other sources would become necessary. If it is then found to be true and voluntary, conviction can be based on it.[621]

---

616. *Laxman v State of Maharashtra*, AIR 2002 SC 2973.

617. *Radhey Shyam v State of UP*, 1993 Cr LJ 3709 (All); *Jose v State of Kerala*, 1994 Supp 3 SCC 1 : 1994 SCC (Cri) 1659, dying declaration recorded in the question-answer-form by a doctor in the presence of another doctor, subsequently another statement recorded by a police officer in his own words under section 161, CrPC, this was also corroborated by witnesses. The dying declaration recorded by the doctor could not be ignored just only on the ground that they were two declarations with variations. *Harijit Kaur v State of Punjab*, AIR 1999 SC 2571 : 1999 Cr LJ 4055 : (1999) 6 SCC 545, endorsement by doctor as to fitness was made not on the dying declaration but on the application, not rendering the declaration suspicious in any manner *Shashidhar Singh v State*, 1998 Cr LJ 2676 (MP), the victim suffered multiple gunshot injuries. A statement immediately after the incident and the last statement varied in the sense that only names of the accused persons were given in the last statement and not other details. Such variation could not be said to be impossible.

618. *Gangaram Gehani v State of Maharashtra*, (1982) 1 SCC 700 : AIR 1982 SC 839 : 1982 Cr LJ 630.

619. *Mukesh v State for NCT Delhi*, AIR 2017 SC 2161 : : (2017) 6 SCC 1 : LNIND 2017 SC 252.

620. *Laxmi v Om Prakash*, 2001 Cr LJ 3302 : AIR 2001 SC 2383.

621. *Samadhan Dhudaka Koli v State of Maharashtra*, AIR 2009 SC 1059 : (2008) 12 SCC 705; *Rajendra v State of Maharashtra*, (2006) 10 SCC 759 : (2007) 1 SCC (Cri) 158, three dying declarations were consistent, there could no objection that the second one was not recorded by a magistrate, there is no law which mandates recording by magistrate. *Ravi Kumar v State of TN*, AIR 2006 SC 1448 : (2006) 9 SCC 240 : 2006 Cr LJ 1625, the dying declaration was in contradiction with the accident register, held not fatal when it was explained away in the face of two dying declarations.

[s 32.9] Whether a conviction can be based on the sole basis of a dying declaration.—The law on the issue of dying declaration can be summarised to the effect that in case the court comes to the conclusion that if the dying declaration is true and reliable, has been recorded by a person at a time when the deceased was physically and mentally fit to make the declaration and it has not been made under any tutoring/duress/prompting; it can be the sole basis for recording conviction. In such an eventuality no corroboration is required. In case there are multiple dying declarations and there are inconsistencies between them, generally, the dying declaration recorded by the higher officer like a Magistrate can be relied upon, provided that there is no circumstance giving rise to any suspicion about its truthfulness. In case there are circumstances wherein the declaration had been made, not voluntarily and even otherwise, it is not supported by the other evidence, the court has to scrutinise the facts of an individual case very carefully and take a decision as to which of the declarations is worth reliance.[622] In the absence of any kind of infirmity or inherent contradiction or inconsistency or any facet that would create a serious doubt on the dying declaration, it cannot be discarded. Conviction indisputably can be based on dying declaration, if it is found totally reliable.[623]

[s 32.9.1] ***Admissibility/relevancy of a dying declaration as to cause of death of other person.***—The dying declaration is admissible about the cause of death or the circumstances of the transaction which resulted in the death of the person making it. However, when two deaths have taken place in the same transaction and circumstances of the transaction resulting in one death are closely inter-connected with the other death, the situation is different; such a statement may not by itself be admissible to determine the cause of death of anyone other than the person making the statement. However, when the circumstances of the transaction which resulted in the death of the person making the statement as well as death of any other person are part of the same transaction, the same will be relevant also about the cause of death of such other person. Thus, a dying declaration relating to circumstances of the transaction which resulted in the death of a person making the declaration are integral part of the circumstances resulting in death of any other person, such a dying declaration has relevance for the death of such other person also.[624]

[s 32.10] "Statements, written or verbal, of relevant facts".—"Verbal" means by words. It is not necessary that the words should be spoken. The words of another person may be adopted by a witness by a nod or shake of the head.[625] If the significance of the signs made by a deceased person in response to questions put to her shortly before her death is established satisfactorily to the mind of the court, then such questions, taken with her assent or dissent to them, clearly proved, constitute a verbal statement as to the cause of her death.[626] In a trial upon a charge of murder, it appeared that the deceased shortly before her death was questioned by various persons as to the circumstances in which the injuries had been inflicted on her; that she was at that time unable to speak,

---

622. *Lakhan v State of MP,* (2010) 8 SCC 514.

623. *Vutukuru Lakshmaiah v State of AP*, (2015) 11 SCC 102, paras 20 and 21.

624. *Tejram Patil v State of Maharashtra*, (2015) 8 SCC 494, paras 18 and 21 : 2015 (2) SCJ 710.

625. *Queen-Empress v Abdullah,* (1885) 7 All 385, 397 FB; *Chandrasekera v The King,* (1937) AC 220 : (1936) 39 Bom LR 359.

626. *Queen-Empress v Abdullah, sup.*; *Emperor v Sadhu Charan Das,* (1921) 49 Cal 600; *Chandrika Ram Kahar v King-Emperor,* (1922) 1 Pat 401; *Ranga v The Crown,* (1924) 5 Lah 305; *Emperor v Motiram Raisingh,* (1936) 38 Bom LR 818 : (1937) Bom 68.

but was conscious and able to make signs. Evidence was offered by the prosecution, and admitted by the Sessions Judge, to prove the questions put to the deceased, and the signs made by her in answer to such questions. It was held that the questions and the signs taken together might properly be regarded as "verbal statements" made by the person as to the cause of her death within the meaning of this section, and were, therefore, admissible in evidence under this section.[627] Statement of the deceased to a police officer on the basis of which investigation was commenced was described by the Supreme Court as capable of serving as a dying declaration.[628]

The questions put to the injured person who is unable to speak and the signs made by him in reply taken together amount to "verbal statements" within the meaning of this section.[629]

Where the deceased stated in her dying declarations that the accused molested her and she immolated herself after such incident, it was held that the dying declaration was a relevant fact and was admissible in evidence and to hold it otherwise would be negation of justice and clear misrepresentation of the provisions of section 32(1).[630]

[s 32.11] Cause of death [Clause 1].—The word "death" appearing in section 32 is inclusive of suicidal or homicidal death.[631] Statement by a person as to the cause of his death becomes relevant when the cause of his death comes into question even if the person was not under expectation of death at the time of making the statement.[632] The statement must be as to the cause of the declarant's death, or as to any of the circumstances of the transaction which resulted in his death, that is the cause and circumstances of the death;[633] but such details which fall outside the ambit of this are not strictly within the permissible limits laid down by this sub-section.[634] The statement is admissible although it is made before the cause of death has arisen, or before the deceased has any reason to anticipate being killed. The circumstances must be circumstances of the transaction: general expressions indicating fear or suspicion whether of a particular individual or otherwise and not directly related to the occasion of the death are not admissible.[635] An information lodged by a person who died subsequently,

---

627. *Queen-Empress v Abdullah, sup.*: *Chandrasekera v The King, sup. Pandian K Nadar v State of Maharashtra,* 1993 Cr LJ 3883 (Bom), the deceased indicated to the accused through gestures, relied upon.

628. *State of Assam v Bhelu Sheikh,* AIR 1989 SC 1097 : 1989 Cr LJ 879 : 1989 Supp (2) SCC 1 : 1989 SCC (Cri) 643; *State of Punjab v Amarjit Singh,* AIR 1988 SC 2012 : 1989 Cr LJ 95 : 1988 Supp SCC 709, statement before FIR recorded by ASI but in the presence of doctor.

629. *Sudama v King-Emperor,* (1949) Nag 301.

630. *Deepak v State of MP,* 1994 Cr LJ 767 (MP).

631. *Ibid. Kans Raj v State of Punjab,* 2000 Cr LJ 2993 : AIR 2000 SC 2324.

632. *Thakur Das v State of HP,* 1992 Cr LJ 2415 (HP); *Ram Bihari Yadav v State,* 1998 Cr LJ 2269 (SC), an explanation about relevancy and admissibility of dying declarations. *Ram Kumar v State,* 1998 Cr LJ 952 (MP), in a prosecution for abetment of suicide, it was held that letters written by the deceased wife to her relatives disclosing the circumstances which led to her suicide were admissible in evidence. *State of Haryana v Mange Ram,* 2003 Cr LJ 830 (SC), it is not necessary that the maker of the statement should at the time be under shadow of death or entertain a belief that his death was imminent. The injured person in this case was fully conscious and stated the circumstances in detail. Evidence admitted.

633. *Venkatasubba Reddi,* (1931) 54 Mad 931; *MF Rego Mrs v Emperor,* (1933) 29 NLR 251.

634. *Bakhshish Singh v The State of Punjab,* AIR 1957 SC 904 : 1957 Cr LJ 1459.

635. *Pakala Narayana Swami v The King-Emperor,* (1939) 66 IA 66 : 41 Bom LR 428 : (1941) Ran 789n : (1939) 18 Pat 234 : AIR 1939 SC 47.

relating to the cause of his death, is admissible in evidence under this clause.[636] It is not necessary that there should be a direct nexus between the "Circumstances" and death. Where the victim uttered before her death that the accused was standing before her with a gun, this was held to be a part of the circumstances which resulted in her death and, therefore, admissible under sub-section (1).[637] The statement may be oral or written. It is relevant whatever may be the nature of the proceeding in which the cause of the death of the person who made the statement comes into question. A complaint in writing made by a person who dies sometime thereafter, expressing apprehension of death at the hands of a person is admissible in evidence under this clause, when the person whose conduct is the source of the apprehension is charged with the offence of murder of the person making the complaint. The deceased had submitted a written complaint against her husband, to the Commissioner of Police, which stated that she was afraid she would be killed by her husband. It was held that the statement showing apprehension of death on account of the conduct of the husband was admissible under this clause.[638] A woman was injured by her husband. Her statements were recorded while she was in hospital. She died two months after the incident and 21 days after her discharge from the hospital, from what cause, not known. Her statements in the hospital were not admitted as dying declaration.[639]

A statement made by a person since deceased, as to the cause of the death of another, is inadmissible in evidence. The statement of one dead person is not a relevant fact with respect to the question about the death of another person.[640]

The section is not confined to any particular kind of death, e.g. homicide. It includes suicidal death also. The circumstances which may be relevant to prove a case of suicide would be equally relevant under the section.[641]

[s 32.12] "Circumstances of the transaction".—This phrase conveys some limitations. It is not as broad as the analogous use in "circumstantial evidence" which includes evidence of all relevant facts. It is narrower than *res gestae*. Circumstances must have some proximate relation to the actual occurrence and must be of the transaction which resulted in the death of the declarant. The condition of the admissibility of the evidence is that the cause of the declarant's death comes into question. It is not necessary that the statement must be made after the transaction has taken place or that the person making it must be near death or that the "circumstances" can only include the acts done when and where the death was caused.[642]

---

636. *Emperor v Mohammad Shaikh,* (1942) 2 Cal 144. See also, *Kulamanji Sandha v State of Orissa,* 1991 Cr LJ 599 (Ori), description of injured at the police station, dying subsequently of infection in injuries, held relevant under the section. The court cited *Motisingh v State of UP,* AIR 1964 SC 900 : 1963 All LJ 647; *Chandrabhan Singh v State,* 1971 Cr LJ 94 and *Abdul Gani Bandukchi v Emperor,* AIR 1943 Cal 465 : 1945 Cr LJ 71.

637. *Rattan Singh v State of HP,* AIR 1997 SC 768 : 1997 Cr LJ 833.

638. *Allijan Munshi,* (1959) 61 Bom LR 1620.

639. *Satwa Wakode v State of Maharashtra,* 1996 Cr LJ 4028 (Bom).

640. *Emperor v Kunwarpal Singh,* (1948) All 122.

641. *Sharad Birdichand Sarda v State of Maharashtra,* AIR 1984 SC 1622 : (1984) 4 SCC 116.

642. *Pakala Narayana Swami v The King-Emperor,* (1939) 66 IA 66 : 41 Bom LR 428 : (1941) Ran 789n : (1939) 18 Pat 234. See further, *Tellu v State,* 1988 Cr LJ 1062 (Del) following *Tehal Singh v State of Punjab,* AIR 1979 SC 1347 : 1979 Cr LJ 1031; *Sharad Birdichand Sarda v State of Maharashtra,* 1984 Cr LJ 1738 : AIR 1984 SC 1622, at 1630 : (1984) 4 SCC 116 : 1984 SCC (Cri) 487;

(Footnote No. 642 contd.)

The Supreme Court has emphasised the need for effort by courts, as far as possible, to include a statement within the scope of the section 32(1). Hence, statements as to any of the circumstances of the transaction which resulted in the death should be included.[643]

The Supreme Court[644] examined the scope of the words "statement as to any of the circumstances of the transaction which resulted in his death" and said that these words expand the scope of admissibility on the facts of the case.

In order to test the reliability of a dying declaration, the court has to keep in view, the circumstances like the opportunity of the dying man for observation, (e.g.), whether there was sufficient light if the crime was committed at night; whether the capacity of the man to remember the facts stated had not been impaired at the time of making the statement; that the statement has been consistent throughout if he had several opportunities of making a dying declaration apart from the official record of it; and that the statement had been made at the earliest opportunity and was not the result of tutoring by interested parties.[645]

A brief statement ("save me, a person has stabbed me") made to relatives half an hour before death was followed by a detailed version in the presence of the medical officer, the Supreme Court attached value to the statement.[646]

(Footnote No. 642 contd.)

Rajindra Kumar v State of Punjab, AIR 1960 Punj 310 : 1960 Cr LJ 851; *State of UP v Kanchan Singh,* AIR 1954 All 153 : 1954 Cr LJ 264, in all of which it was reemphasised that it is not necessary that the statement should be made at a time when the person making it was at the point or in danger of death. *Saraswathi Swamigal v State of TN,* (2005) 2 SCC 13 : AIR 2005 SC 716 : 2005 Cr LJ 883, telephonic conversation of the deceased with one of the witnesses did not refer to the circumstances of death.

643. *Patel Hiralal Jottaram v State of Gujarat,* AIR 2001 SC 2944, wife burning, original statement gave wrong name of the father of the accused, the mistake was rectified by further questioning, even this process was held to be a part of the transaction.

644. *Patel Hiralal Jottaram v State of Gujarat,* AIR 2001 SC 2944 at 2949.

645. *Khushal Rao v State of Bombay,* (1958) SCR 552 : 1958 Cr LJ 106 : AIR 1958 SC 22; *Pompiah v State of Mysore,* AIR 1965 SC 939 : (1965) 2 Cr LJ 31; *Bijoy Kumar Sen v State of WB,* 1988 Cr LJ 1818 (Cal). A dying declaration from the very nature of things should be closely scrutinised :*Kishen Singh v State of Punjab,* AIR 1963 Punj 170. *Jorubha Juzer Singh v State of Gujarat,* AIR 1980 SC 358 : 1980 Cr LJ 314, dying declaration found to be reliable, it was made first to the constable who reached the spot, repeated before Taluk Magistrate and again to the PSI, doctor's certificate of conscious state, no tutoring and no motivation against accused. *Suraj Mal v State of Punjab,* AIR 1992 SC 559 : 1992 Cr LJ 520 : 1993 Supp (1) SCC 639, dying declaration found reliable despite different opinion of police officer. *Girdhar Shankar Tawade v State of Maharashtra,* 2002 Cr LJ 2814 : AIR 2002 SC 2078, corroboration, though not necessary, if it is there it will strengthen the evidence. Independent witnesses may not be there, but there should be proper care and caution in accepting the evidence and relying upon it.

See generally, *Rawal Singh v State,* 1997 Cr LJ 1195 (Del); *Batto v State,* 1997 Cr LJ 1201 (Del); *Public Prosecutor, High Court of AP, Hyd, v Jangili Nirmala,* 1997 Cr LJ 1420 (AP); *Baijnath v State,* 1997 Cr LJ 1691 (All); *Kale Mian v State,* 1997 Cr LJ 1848 (Pat); *Naguloncha Krishna v State,* 1997 Cr LJ 2834 (AP); *Virendra Singh v State,* 1997 Cr LJ 3098 (Del); *Re Basith,* 1997 Cr LJ 3232 (Mad); *Kartar Singh v State,* 1997 Cr LJ 4376 (P&H).

646. *Habib Usman v State of Gujarat,* AIR 1979 SC 1181 : 1979 Cr LJ 711; *Jayaraj v State of TN,* AIR 1976 SC 1519.

This court, a decade later in *Munnu Raja v State of Madhya Pradesh*,[647] stated the law to the effect that though the dying declaration must be approached with caution for the reason that the maker of the statement cannot be subjected to cross examination, there is neither a rule of law nor a rule of prudence which has hardened into a rule of law that a dying declaration cannot be acted upon unless it is corroborated. This court went up to observe that the court must not look out for corroboration unless it comes to the conclusion that a dying declaration suffered from any infirmity.

[s 32.13] Proximity between time of statement and that of Death.—The problem of proximity was for the first time raised before the Supreme Court in *Sharad v State of Maharashtra*.[648] The court held that the statements were not so remote in time as to lose their proximity with the cause of death. Fazal Ali J conducted a vast survey of authorities and picked up the following propositions: 1. A declaration will be relevant whether death is homicide or suicide, provided it relates to the cause of death or exhibits circumstances leading to death. 2. The test of proximity cannot be literally pursued and practically reduced to a cut and dried formula of universal application. Distance of time would depend on or vary with the circumstances of each case. For example, where death is a logical consequence of a continuous drama long in process and in a way a finale to the story, the statement regarding each step directly connected with the end of the drama would be admissible because the entire statement would have to be read as an organic whole and not torn from the context. Where death takes place within short time of the marriage or the distance of time is not spread over more than three to four months, the statement may be admissible under section 32.[649] Where the finding of the court was that dying declaration were acceptable, it was held that the declarations would not lose their value on the ground that the maker died long after making the statements. This question has to be considered on the facts of each case.[650]

The Supreme Court stated in a case: "The prosecution had not examined the doctor who made the endorsement on the dying declaration that "the patient was in a fit state of mind to depose". No other witness was examined to prove the certificate of the doctor either. The non-production of the doctor to prove his certificate and subject himself to be cross-examined by the appellants, when considered in the light of the testimony of the mother of the deceased, who specifically stated that the condition of the patient was "*not good and that she was not in a fit condition*", created a doubt as to

647. *Munnu Raja v State of Madhya Pradesh*, AIR 1976 SC 2199 : 1976 Cr LJ 1718.

648. *Sharad v State of Maharashtra*, AIR 1984 SC 1622 : 1984 Cr LJ 1738. A similar case *Mithailal v State of Maharashtra*, 1993 Cr LJ 3580 (Bom), death of victim-wife due to starvation, cruelty and ill-treatment, letters written to her brother, held, admissible. See also, *Suresh Raghunath Kochare v State of Maharashtra*, 1992 Cr LJ 2455 (Bom), the court **relied on** *Wazir Chand v State of Haryana*, AIR 1989 SC 378 : 1989 Cr LJ 809 and **referred** to *Sharad Birdhichand Sarda v State of Maharashtra*, AIR 1984 SC 1622 : 1984 Cr LJ 1738 : (1984) 4 SCC 116 : 1984 SCC (Cri) 487.

649. Followed in *Padmabai v State of MP*, 1987 Cr LJ 1573 (MP), where also letters were written by the deceased wife to her sisters within a time reasonably close in proximity of time to the incident in which she lost her life, admissible. **Distinguished** in *Tapan Pal v State of WB*, 1992 Cr LJ 1017 (Cal), where isolated statements made six months before the suicide by the married woman were held to be not relevant as dying declaration. The court relied upon statements of law at pp 94-95 of this book, Reprint Edn of 1982.

650. *Najjam Faraghi v State of WB*, 1998 Cr LJ 866 : AIR 1998 SC 682; *Kans Raj v State of Punjab*, 2000 Cr LJ 2993 AIR 2000 SC 2324, it is not required that the statement as to death to have been made in imminent expectation of death.

whether the patient was actually in a proper mental condition to make a consciously truthful statement. This infirmity rendered it unsafe to rely on the dying declaration."[651]

When a dying declaration is recorded voluntarily, pursuant to a fitness report of a certified doctor, nothing much remains to be questioned unless, it is proved that the dying declaration was tainted with animosity and a result of tutoring.[652]

The, Supreme Court[653] summed up the legal principles governing a dying declaration as follows:

(i) Dying declaration can be the sole basis of conviction if it inspires the full confidence of the court.

(ii) The court should be satisfied that the deceased was in a fit state of mind at the time of making the statement and that it was not the result of tutoring, prompting or imagination.

(iii) Where the court is satisfied that the declaration is true and voluntary, it can base its conviction without any further corroboration.

(iv) It cannot be laid down as an absolute rule of law that the dying declaration cannot form the sole basis of conviction unless it is corroborated. The rule requiring corroboration is merely a rule of prudence.

(v) Where the dying declaration is suspicious, it should not be acted upon without corroborative evidence.

(vi) A dying declaration which suffers from infirmity such as the deceased was unconscious and could never make any statement cannot form the basis of conviction.

(vii) Merely because a dying declaration does not contain all the details as to the occurrence, it is not to be rejected.

(viii) Even if it is a brief statement, it is not to be discarded.

(ix) When the eyewitness affirms that the deceased was not in a fit and conscious state to make the dying declaration, medical opinion cannot prevail.

(x) If after careful scrutiny, the court is satisfied that it is true and free from any effort to induce the deceased to make a false statement and if it is coherent and consistent, there shall be no legal impediment to make it the basis of conviction, even if there is no corroboration.

---

651. *Kanchy Komuramma v State of AP*, 1995 Supp (4) SCC 118 : 1996 SCC (Cri) 31. *Goverdhan Raoji Ghyare v State of Maharashtra*, 1993 Supp 4 SCC 316 : 1994 SCC Cri 15, minor discrepancies in the two declarations of the injured bride (deceased), but both were similar in material particulars, one was taken down by a police officer and the other by the taluka magistrate, minor discrepancies inconsequential. *Satya Narayan v State*, 2003 Cr LJ (NOC) 185 (MP) : 2002 CLR (SC & MP) 820, death of wife by burn injuries in oral statements to her parents and in a letter to them, she complained of cruelty by husband, did not fall within the purview of section 32 because they did not relate to cause of death the husband was acquitted under section 306, IPC on the basis of the dying declaration that she sustained burn injuries accidentally from stove. Acquittal under section 498-A also. *Kamalakar Nandram Bhavasar v State of Maharashtra*, AIR 2004 SC 503 : (2004) 10 SCC 192, no dying declaration because of extensive burns.

652. *Mukesh v State for NCT Delhi*, AIR 2017 SC 2161 : (2017) 6 SCC 1 : LNIND 2017 SC 252.

653. *Atbir v Govt (NCT of Delhi)*, (2010) 9 SCC 1.

[s 32.14] Where the declarant survives.—The statement of a person as to the cause of his injuries becomes a dying declaration relevant under section 32 if he subsequently dies. Should he survive his injuries, his statement cannot be proved under section 32. It may become relevant under section 21(1) or under section 157.[654] Such statement is not a declaration under section 32. It becomes a statement under section 164, CrPC. It can be used under section 157 for the purpose of corroboration and under section 155 for the purpose of contradiction.[655] Such statement has to be taken as of a superior quality and of a higher value than that recorded under section 161, CrPC. It can also be used under section 157 as the former statement of witnesses for corroboration purposes.[656]

[s 32.15] Statements in course of business [Clause 2].—This clause contemplates a statement by a person whose duty it was to make such a statement or whose business was such that statements of the kind were to be expected in the ordinary course of things.[657] "The considerations which have induced the courts to recognize this exception appear to be principally that, in the absence of all suspicion of sinister motives, a fair presumption arises that entries made in the ordinary routine of business are correct, since the process of invention implying trouble, it is easier to state what is true than what is false; that such entries usually form a link in a chain of circumstances, which mutually corroborate each other: that false entries would be likely to bring clerks into disgrace with their employers: that, as most entries made in the course of business are subject to the inspection of several persons, an error would be exposed to speedy discovery; and that, as the facts to which they relate are generally known but to few persons, a relaxation of the strict rules of evidence in favour of such entries may often prove convenient, if not necessary, for the due investigation of truth".[658]

Clause (2) provides that a written statement of a relevant fact made by a person who is dead is itself a relevant fact, when the statement was made by such person in

---

654. *Maqsoodhan v State of UP,* AIR 1983 SC 126 : 1983 Cr LJ 218. Section 21(1) covers cases in which a person can use his own statement where that would have been relevant in a dispute between third parties if he had died. Section 157 would permit a former statement of the witness to be proved in support of his present statement in the court. *Ram Prasad v State of Maharashtra,* 1999 Cr LJ 2889 : AIR 1999 SC 1969, where the person making a dying declaration survives, his statement cannot be treated as a dying declaration. But it is capable of being used to corroborate his testimony or to contradict it. *Heera Lal (Dr) v State of UP,* 2001 Cr LJ 2849 (All), the accused committed murder of wife and three children and attempted to kill himself. He made a statement before the magistrate under section 164, CrPC. It could not be treated as dying declaration because he survived, nor it was relevant as a confession. *Biswanatha Jena v State,* 2002 Cr LJ (NOC) 37 (Ori), victim with multiple injuries, doctor recorded statement, but the victim survived, the statement not allowed to be used as a substantive evidence. *Shrawan Bhadaji Bhirad v State of Maharashtra,* 2003 Cr LJ 398 (SC), unlawful assembly, several injured, but some survived, statements recorded then and there under fear of death might occur, conviction on the basis of such statements was not disturbed. *Ram Singh v Sonia,* AIR 2007 SC 1218 : (2007) 3 SCC 1, admission into hospital because of suspected poisoning, as against her dying declaration, it was not allowed to be contended that as the victim survived, no dying declaration must have been recorded.

655. *State of UP v Veer Singh,* (2004) 10 SCC 117 : 2004 Cr LJ 3835.

656. *Ranjit Singh v State of MP,* AIR 2011 SC 255 : 2010 (4) Crimes 280 (SC).

657. *Soney Lal Jha v Darabdeo Narain Singh,* (1935) 14 Pat 461 FB, approving *Ningawa v Bharmappa,* (1897) 23 Bom 63, on the interpretation of this clause, but differing on the interpretation of clause 3.

658. *Taylor,* 12th Edn, section 697, p 446; *Lakha Singh v State,* 1997 Cr LJ 3638 (Raj), report of injuries and postmortem report which were proved to be in the handwriting of the doctor who prepared them, held to be relevant and could be used in evidence against the accused.

"the ordinary course of business". The expression "course of business" occurs in more than one place in the Act. See sections 16, 34, 47, 114.

The phrase "in the ordinary course of business" is apparently used to indicate the current routine of business which was usually followed by the person whose declaration it is sought to introduce. The rule laid down in this clause extends only to statements made during the course, not of any particular transaction of an exceptional kind such as the execution of a deed of mortgage, but of business or professional employment in which the declarant was ordinarily or habitually engaged. The particulars set out in this clause, though not exhaustive, may fairly be taken as indicating the nature of the statements made in the course of business. The expression "in the ordinary course of business" must mean in the ordinary course of a professional avocation.[659] The business referred to may be of a temporary character.[660] See Illustrations (b), (c), (d), and (g).

The entries should have been made by the deceased person himself. Entries made by another person at his instance are not admissible under this section.[661] Entries in registers prepared by an Amin who is dead are admissible for proving the nature of the tenancy.[662]

[s 32.15.1] Account books.—Entries in account books should, in order to be relevant, be regularly kept in the course of business.[663] Where accounts are kept in loose sheets of paper they do not have the probative force of a book of accounts regularly kept in the course of business.[664]

A book of accounts may be said to be regularly kept although the book is not entered up from day to day or from hour to hour as the transactions take place.[665]

[s 32.15.2] Difference between section 32, clause (2), and section 34.—The plaintiff relied on entries in the handwriting of her deceased husband kept in the ordinary course of his business. It was held that entries in accounts relevant only under section 34 are not alone sufficient to charge any person with liability, corroboration is required. But where accounts are relevant also under this clause, they are in law sufficient evidence in themselves, and the law does not, as in the case of accounts admissible only under section 34, require corroboration. Entries in accounts may in the same suit be relevant under both sections, and where this is so, the necessity of corroboration prescribed by section 34 does not arise. Though accounts which are relevant under this clause do not as a matter of law require corroboration, the Judge is not bound to act on them without corroboration; that is a matter on which he must exercise his own judicial discretion as a judge of fact.[666] Clause (2) does not make the account books conclusive proof of the facts stated therein. Under section 34, liability cannot be fastened on any person merely because in the account books of the opposite party,

---

659. *Ningawa v Bharmappa,* (1897) 23 Bom 63, 67.

660. *Sheonandan Singh v Jeonandan Dusadh,* (1908) 13 Cal WN 71.

661. *Mussamat Naina Koer v Gobardhan Singh,* (1916) 2 PLJ 42.

662. *Abinas Chandra Majhi v Pratul Chandra Ghose,* (1928) 55 Cal 1070.

663. *Ibid.*

664. *Ganesh Prasad v Narendra Nath,* AIR 1953 SC 431.

665. *Deputy Commissioner ofBara Banki v Munshi Ram Parshad,* (1899) 26 IA 254: 27 Cal 118, overruling *Munchershaw Bezonji v New Dhurumsey S & W Co,* (1880) 4 Bom 576; *Chandreshwar Prasad Narain Singh v Bisheshwar Pratap Narain Singh,* (1926) 5 Pat 777.

666. *Rampyarabai v Balaji Shridhar,* (1904) 28 Bom 294: 6 Bom LR 50.

there are certain entries adverse to him. Taking section 32(2) and section 34 together, it is clear that even if the account books may be treated as relevant it is discretionary for the court to require additional proof of any particular entry.[667] The material difference as between an entry relevant under section 34 and one relevant under section 32(2) is that in the former case the person who made the entry may be available as a witness while in the latter case he is not.

[s 32.15.3] CASES

[s 32.15.3.1] *Samadaskat book.*—Entries of payments made by a creditor in the ledger (*samadaskat* book) belonging to a debtor fall within this clause, and although they are admissions in his own favour they are not excluded by section 21.[668]

[s 32.15.4] Record of identification parade.—Such record by a Magistrate cannot be regarded as a statement made by a Magistrate in the ordinary course of business. It cannot be admitted under clause (2). Proceedings of parades can only be proved by the oral deposition of the Magistrate who held them and who could then be subjected to cross-examination.[669]

[s 32.15.5] Registered letter returned.—An endorsement on the cover of a letter by a postal peon that the cover tendered to the addressee on a certain date was refused, is at best a record of a statement by the peon and must be proved by calling him as a witness.[670]

[s 32.15.6] Balance-sheet.—Facts stated in the balance-sheet of a company have to be proved like any other fact.[671]

[s 32.15.7] *Bahi* (logbook) of *Panda* of Temple.—A *panda* of a temple was maintaining a *bahi* incorporating the list of persons who visited the temple. This was held to be admissible in evidence. The page in question was signed by the visitor and for that reason the court said that it was immaterial whether the *bahi* was maintained in the course of business or whether the entries were regularly made.[672]

[s 32.16] "Statement against interest of maker" [Clause 3].—A statement of a deceased person in order to be admissible under this clause must be a statement of a relevant fact and must be against the proprietary or pecuniary interest of the person making it.[673] This clause makes declarations against interest admissible in evidence. The principle upon which such statements are regarded as admissible in evidence is that in the ordinary course of affairs a person is not likely to make a statement to his own detriment unless it is true.[674] The clause is based upon knowledge of human nature. Self-interest induces a man to be cautious in saying anything against himself. When one makes a declaration in disparagement of one's own rights or interests, it is

---

667. *Kachrulal v Nandilal,* (1955) Nag 618.
668. *Jethibai v Putlibai,* (1912) 14 Bom LR 1020.
669. *Roshan,* (1956) Pun 140.
670. *Shreepad v Kanhaiyalal,* (1955) MB 352.
671. *Petlad Turkey RD Works v Workers' Union,* AIR 1960 SC 1006.
672. *Jagdish Parshad v Sarwan Kumar,* AIR 2003 P&H. 3, the entry was relevant against the visitor because it carried a statement that a particular person was not his brother. The visitor had since died.
673. *Soney Lal Jha v Darabdeo Narain Singh,* (1935) 14 Pat 461 FB.
674. *Dal Bahadur Singh v Bijai Bahadur Singh,* (1929) 32 Bom LR 487: 57 IA 14: 52 All 1.

generally true, and because it is so, the law has deemed it safe to admit evidence of such a declaration. Illustrations (e) and (f) apply to this clause.

Before a statement can be admissible under this clause it must be shown that the person making it knew that it was against his pecuniary or proprietary interest. In most cases such knowledge would have to be inferred from the surrounding circumstances.[675] A statement by a person having proprietary interest in the suit property about *benami* holding which was against his own interest was held to be provable.[676]

This clause comprises three classes of declarations against interest: where they affect the declarant's (1) pecuniary interest; (2) proprietary interest; and (3) personal liberty or property by tending to charge him with a crime or to subject him to payment of damages. A statement made by a person, against whom there is, already, in existence evidence which would lead to his prosecution and conviction, is inadmissible in evidence under this clause.[677]

Under this clause, the previous statements of a dead witness (e.g., approver) in a previous trial implicating not only himself but also an absconding accused, cannot be admitted for convicting such absconding accused in a subsequent trial. A man cannot by his statement expose himself to criminal proceedings when such criminal proceedings have already started. As soon as criminal proceedings have started against a person making a statement exposing himself to a criminal prosecution, the words of this clause cease to have application or force as they cannot be stretched or extended so as to cover statements made after proceedings have been instituted.[678]

The form of the declaration is immaterial; it may be verbal or written, in a deed or a will, or any other document.

In *Taylor v Witham*,[679] The question was whether a person (deceased) had lent money to another. He maintained a book and there was an entry in it saying: "*B* (the borrower) paid me three months' interest". A few other entries also referred to the same loan. "The Court held that the entry was against the interest of the maker and, therefore, all the entries became admissible although some of them were in his favour" Jeesel, MR explained the reason in the following passage:

"It is, no doubt, an established rule in the courts of this country that an entry against the interest of the man who made it is receivable in evidence after his death for all purposes. Of course, if you can prove *aliundi* that the man had a particular reason for making it, and that it was fit for this interest, you may destroy the value of the evidence altogether, but the question of admissibility is not a question of value. The entry may be utterly worthless when you get it, if you show any reason to believe that he had a motive for making it, and that though apparently against his interest, yet really was for it; but that is a matter for subsequent consideration when you estimate the value of the testimony."

---

675. *Ramrati Kuer v Dwarika Prasad,* AIR 1967 SC 1134 : (1967) 1 SCR 153.
676. *Bhim Singh v Kan Singh,* AIR 1980 SC 727 : 1980 (3) SCC 72.
677. *Achhailall v King-Emperor,* (1945-46) 25 Pat 347.
678. *Janu Kadir v Crown,* (1946) Kar 79.
679. *Taylor v Witham,* (1876) 3 Ch D 605 : 45 LJ Ch 798 : 24 WR 877.

[s 32.16.1] *Declaration exposing the maker to criminal or civil liability.*— Declarations against interest should, to be admissible, have been against interest at *the time they were made,* and it is no answer that they might possibly turn out to be so subsequently.[680] The confession of an accused person who is dead implicating himself and an accomplice in a crime is admissible under this clause and is not excluded by Illustration (b) to section 30.[681] The question of admissibility is not a question of value.

Clause (3) also declares relevant any statement which would have the effect of exposing the declarant to a criminal prosecution or a suit for damages. Where a woman died after telling her lover that she had witnessed a murder, the statement was held to be relevant because if she were alive she could have been prosecuted for not informing the police. It is the duty of every person witnessing a crime to inform the authorities.[682] Such a statement is probably not relevant under English Law. It is observed in *Cockel's Cases and Statutes on Evidence*:[683]

"It should be observed that statements, in order to be admissible must be against either pecuniary or proprietary interest. It is not sufficient for instance, that the statement was made in circumstances which show that the person making it would be liable to criminal prosecution. (*Sussex Peerage case*).[684] Although that would seem to be a case in which he would be liable to a pecuniary penalty, by way of fine, or to something admittedly worse, i.e., imprisonment."

[s 32.16.2] *Admissible against those who derive title from maker of statement.*— Such statements are admissible only against any person who has derived his title from the maker of the statement.

The declaration of a deceased tenant of the farm to the effect that he was not entitled to common pasture in respect of the farm, was held to be not admissible against the landlord.[685] Lord Campbell CJ remarked: "You cannot receive in evidence a declaration of tenant which derogates from the title of the landlord. Such evidence, if receivable, would be most mischievous, because a tenant might thus destroy a valuable easement or be enabled to impose a servitude".

A letter from the co-respondent to the petitioner in a divorce suit admitting adultery with the respondent was held to be admissible in evidence as it would expose the co-respondent to a criminal prosecution.[686]

[s 32.16.3] Inadmissible statements.—A statement made by a deceased person in his will that he had spent a certain amount in effecting repairs to his house was held to be not admissible in evidence as it was not a statement made against his pecuniary or proprietary interest.[687]

A Hindu widow purported to adopt her brother's grandson, fifty-four years after the death of her husband, in pursuance of a power to adopt conferred on her by her

680. *Ex parte Edwards: Re Tollemache,* (1884) 14 QBD 415.
681. *Nga Po Yin v King-Emperor,* (1906) UBR (Evi) (1904-06) 3.
682. *Ajodhi v Emperor,* 56 IC 582.
683. Page 205 (11th Edn 1972).
684. (1844) 11 Ct. f. 85.
685. *Pofendick v Bridgwater,* (1855) 24 LJ QB 289 : 119 ER 443.
686. *Cockman v Cockman,* (1933) 56 All 570.
687. *Narhari v Ambabai,* (1919) 22 Bom LR 57: 44 Bom 192.

husband. The widow obtained mutation of the name of the adopted boy in place of her own in revenue registers. In her evidence in the mutation proceedings she stated that she had her husband's authority to adopt in a suit by the reversioners against the adopted boy to recover the property it was held that the evidence of the widow in the mutation proceedings was not admissible either under this clause or under section 33.[688]

[s 32.17] "Opinion ... as to ... public right or custom" [Clause 4].—The admissibility of declarations of deceased persons in cases of public right or custom, or matters of public or general interest, is allowed, as these rights or customs are generally of ancient and obscure origin, and may be acted upon only at distant intervals of time; direct proof of their existence is not, therefore, demanded.[689]

The principle on which the exception of reputation regarding public rights rests in this—that the reputation can hardly exist without the concurrence of many parties interested to investigate the subject, and such concurrence is presumptive evidence of the existence of an ancient right, of which direct proof cannot be given in most cases.[690]

The admissibility of the declarations of deceased persons in such cases is sanctioned, because in local matters, in which the community are interested, all persons living in the neighbourhood are likely to be conversant; because, common rights and liabilities being naturally talked of in public, what is dropped in conversation respecting them may be presumed to be true; because conflicting interests would lead to contradiction from others if the statements were false; and thus a trustworthy reputation may arise from the concurrence of many parties unconnected with each other, who are all interested in investigating the subjects.[691]

[s 32.17.1] Public and general rights.—Public rights are those common to all members of the State, *e.g.*, rights of highways or of ferry or of fishery. General rights are those affecting any considerable section of the community, *e.g.*, disputes as to the boundaries of a village. The right must have been one of whose existence the declarant should be aware. If the declaration is made otherwise than upon the declarant's own knowledge it will be rejected.

This clause is inapplicable to a document purporting to deal with the rights of a private individual as against the public, in which the interests of the individual form the subject matter of the statement.[692] A map prepared by a person, who is dead, in a previous case not *inter partes,* showing the limits of a particular district, is not admissible as it is not a matter of public right or public or general interest within the meaning of this clause.[693]

Illustration (i) exemplifies this clause.

[s 32.17.2] Statement before any controversy had arisen.—The declarations should have been made *ante litam motam*, i.e., before the beginning of any controversy and

---

688. *Dal Bahadur Singh v Bijai Bahadur Singh,* (1929) 32 Bom LR 487: 57 IA 14: 52 All 1.
689. *Queen v Inhabitants of Bedfordshire,* (1855) 4 E&B 535.
690. *Wright v Tatham,* (1838) 5 clause & F 670.
691. Per Lord Campbell CJ, in *The Queen v Inhabitants of Bedfordshire,* (1855) 4 E&B 535, 542.
692. *Heiniger v Droz,* (1900) 3 Bom LR 1: 25 Bom 433.
693. *Kesho Prasad v Bhagjogna Kuer,* (1937) 39 Bom LR 731: 16 Pat 258 PC.

not simply before the commencement of any suit involving the same subject-matter. The operation of bias is thus excluded.[694]

To render a statement inadmissible as having been made *post litam motam* the same thing must be in controversy both before and after it is made.[695]

The recitals in the document are admissible under this section. The history dealing with the founding of a temple is a matter of general interest and when a statement about it is made by a deceased person at a time when there was no controversy on this question, that statement would clearly come within the scope of this clause.[696]

[s 32.18] Statement as to existence of relationship [Clause 5].—Statements relating to the existence of any relationship between persons alive or dead as to whose relationship the declarant has *special means* of knowledge are admissible if they are made before the question in dispute was raised. Four conditions must be fulfilled for the application of this clause: firstly, the statements, written or verbal, of relevant facts must have been made by a person who is dead or cannot be found etc., as mentioned in the initial part of the section; secondly, the statements must relate to the existence of any relationship by blood, marriage or adoption; thirdly, the person making the statement must have special means of knowledge as to the relationship in question; and lastly, the statements must have been made before the question in dispute was raised.[697] A special knowledge is to be presumed in the case of members of the family.[698] A Hindu Brahmin has a special means of knowledge of the names and relationship of the members of his family including collaterals up to at least seventh degree.[699] Statements made by deceased members of a family are admissible in evidence to prove pedigree if they are made before there was anything to throw doubt upon them.[700]

In *State of Bihar v Radha Krishna Singh*,[701] the Supreme Court explained the approach to be adopted in evaluating evidence regarding genealogy or pedigree:

In considering the oral evidence regarding a pedigree, a purely mathematical approach cannot be adopted because where a long line of descent has to be proved spreading over a century, it is obvious that the witnesses who are examined to depose to the genealogy would have to depend on their special means of knowledge which might have come to them through their ancestors. But, at the same time, there is a great risk and a serious danger involved in relying solely on the evidence of witnesses given from pure memory because the witnesses who are interested normally have a tendency to draw more from their imagination or turn and twist the facts which they may have heard from their ancestors in order to help the parties for whom they are deposing. The court therefore,

---

694. *Berkeley Peerage Case*, (1811) 4 Camp 401, 417; *Amina Khatun Musammat v Khalil-ur-Rahman Khan*, (1933) 8 Luck 455; *State of Bihar v Radha Krishna Singh*, AIR 1983 SC 684 : 1983(3) SCC 118.

695. *Kalka Parshad v Mathura Parshad*, (1908) 35 IA 166: 10 Bom LR 1088 : 30 All 510.

696. *KCM Harichandan v Commissioner of Endowments*, (1961) Cut 109.

697. *Dolgobinda v Nimai Charan*, AIR 1959 SC 914 : 1959 Supp (2) SCR 814; *Musammat Biro v Atma Ram*, (1937) 64 IA 92: 39 Bom LR 726. These requirements were restated by the Supreme Court in *State of Bihar v Radha Krishna Singh*, AIR 1983 SC 684 : 1983 (3) SCC 118.

698. *Prabhakar v Sarubai*, (1943) Nag 779.

699. *Gobardhan Mandal v Janaki Nath Mukharjee*, (1953) 2 Cal 199.

700. *Abdul Ghafur v Hussain Bibi*, (1930) 33 Bom LR 420: 58 IA 188: 12 Lah 336; *Gokhul Pande v Baldeo Sukul*, (1927) 7 Pat 90.

701. *State of Bihar v Radha Krishna Singh*, AIR 1983 SC 684 : (1983) 3 SCC 118.

must take this safeguard that the evidence of such evidence may not be accepted as is based purely on imagination or an imaginary or illusory source of information rather than special means of knowledge as required by law. Oral testimony of the witnesses on this matter is bound to be hearsay and their evidence is admissible as an exception to the general rule where hearsay evidence is not admissible. In order to appreciate the evidence of such witnesses, the principles to be kept in mind are:

(1) The relationship or the connection which the witness bears to the persons whose pedigree is sought to be deposed by him;

(2) the nature and character of the special means of knowledge through which the witness has come to know about the pedigree;

(3) the state of interest of the witness concerned;

(4) the precaution which must be taken to rule out any false statement made by the witness *post litem motam* or a statement which is derived not by means of any special knowledge but purely from his imagination; and

(5) the evidence of the witness must be substantially corroborated as far as time and memory are concerned.

The Act does not contain any express provision making evidence of general reputation admissible as proof of relationship. It is necessary to put forward evidence of the kind described in clauses (5), (6) and (7) and section 50 to prove the existence of relationship between persons deceased whenever the question is in issue.[702]

A statement of one's age made by a deceased person having special means of knowledge is admissible under this clause.[703] It is not necessary that the statement should have been made in a judicial proceeding.[704] Entries made in books of priests (*pande's bahis*) if made by persons who are dead or cannot be found are relevant only under this clause and clause (6) read with section 90 and are admissible only if all the requirements laid down therein are proved, and among other things, the identity of the maker of those statements is established.[705] As the question as to the existence of any relationship also includes the question as to the commencement of that relationship, declarations of deceased competent declarants are admissible to prove a person's date of birth, and, consequently, his age, minority or majority or the order in which the members of the family are born. Such declarations are also admissible to prove parentage, names of relations or the date of death of a member of the family as death implies termination of a relationship, just as birth implies its commencement.[706] Where the executant of the deed is dead, a statement therein that the donee is his legally married wife, is admissible under this section.[707] Where the deed of adoption contained the statement of the adoptive widow that she had taken a person in adoption and the widow being

---

702. *Shivlal v Jootha,* (1952) 2 Raj 231.

703. *Abdul Subhan Khan alias Khalilur-Rahman v Nusrat Ali Khan,* (1936) 12 Luck 606; *Madan Singh v State of Rajasthan,* (1952) 2 Raj 775. *State of Punjab v Mohinder Singh*, AIR 2005 SC 1868 : (2005) 3 SCC 702 : (2005) 4 Serv LR 683, for proof of date of birth, horoscope has been held to be weak kind of evidence, and may be considered on if authenticity is established.

704. *Musammat Biro v Atma Ram,* (1937) 64 IA 92: 39 Bom LR 726.

705. *Hazura Singh v Mohindar Singh,* (1937) 18 Lah 732, disapproving *Jahangir v Sheoraj Singh,* (1915) 37 All 600.

706. *Mahadeo Prasad v Ghulam Mohammad,* (1946) All 649.

707. *Subarna Bissoiani v Arjuno Bissoi,* (1949) Cut 527.

dead could not be called as a witness, the statement as it related to the relationship by adoption could be admitted under this clause.[708]

The statement, as to heirship in the family, of a person who had been the housekeeper of the family for 24 years was rejected. Explaining the reason, BEST CJ said:[709] "Facts must be spoken of which took place many years before the trial, and of these, traditional evidence is often the only evidence which can be obtained; but evidence of that kind must be subject to limitation, otherwise it would be a course of great uncertainty, and the limitation hitherto pursued, namely, the confining of such evidence to the declarations of relations of the family, affords a rule at once certain and intelligible. If the admissibility of such evidence were not so restrained, we should on every occasion before the testimony could be admitted have to enter upon a long inquiry as to the degree of intimacy or confidence that subsisted between the party and the deceased declarant...If we look into the cases we shall find that the rule has always been confined to the declaration of kindred."

Evidence of this kind is relevant only when the relationship is in question and not merely the date of birth. Where a person refused to pay for the goods supplied to him on the ground that he was minor, he offered evidence of his late father's declaration in an affidavit in an earlier case as to the date of his birth, the evidence was rejected.[710] BRETT MR said:

> It is obvious that in this case the question of family is immaterial, that the question whose son the defendant was, is immaterial, and so were all such questions as whether he was a legitimate or a natural son, an elder or a younger son, or as to what relation he occupied with regard to the rest of the family. There was, therefore, no question which could be called a question of family the only question is, what was the date of birth…?

[s 32.18.1] "Before the question in dispute was raised".—These words do not necessarily mean before the dispute was raised in the particular litigation in which such a statement is sought to be adduced in evidence, that is the declarations are required to have been made not merely before the commencement of legal proceedings but before even the existence of any actual controversy concerning the subject-matter of the declarations.[711]

Illustration (k) exemplifies this clause. See also, Illustration (l)

[s 32.18.2] Marriage.—Strict proof of marriage is necessary in certain criminal offences, e.g., bigamy, adultery, enticing away a married woman. This clause had no application in such cases.[712] Otherwise general reputation of marriage is admissible. An admission by a plaintiff of her marriage with a person made before there was any dispute about such marriage may be proved by or on her behalf under section 21(1) read with this clause.[713]

---

708. *Punjabrao Deorao,* (1959) 62 Bom LR 726.

709. *Johnson v Lauson,* (1824) 2 Bing 86 : 136 ER 257.

710. *Haynes v Guthrie,* (1884) 13 QBD 818 : 53 LJ QB 521 : 31 LT 645.

711. *KV Subbaraju v C. Subbaraju,* AIR 1968 SC 947 : 1968 (3) SCR 137; *Kalka Parshad v Mathura Parshad,* (1908) 35 IA 166: 10 Bom LR 1088: 30 All 510.

712. *Empress v Pitambur Singh,* (1879) 5 Cal 566 FB.

713. *Mussammat Bashiran v Mohammad Husain,* (1941) 16 Luck 615.

Where an entry in a family register maintained in accordance with Rules showed that the name of the first wife of the person in question was deleted on the basis of divorce deed and the name of the second wife was entered, it was held that the entry in the register made at the instance of the husband was very much relevant under section 32(5) to prove that the person mentioned in the entry had married the second time.[714]

Evidence of competent witnesses as to their having heard the names of the ancestors recited by members of the plaintiff's family on ceremonial and other occasions was held to be admissible evidence in support of the pedigree on which the plaintiff based his claim. Such evidence is not open to criticism merely on the ground that the witnesses are relatives.[715]

The oral evidence in a case consisted of statements made by the plaintiffs as to their descent, the information as to which they had received from their ancestors. Objection was taken that such of those statements as were made since 1847 were inadmissible in evidence under clauses (5) and (6) as being *post litam.* The Privy Council held that they were admissible, the heirship of the then claimants not being really in dispute at that time.[716]

A statement as to the age of a member of a family made by a sister[717] or a statement as to his age made by a testator in his will[718] was held admissible after her death. Statements of the father (since deceased) in his written statement in a maintenance case filed by the mother of the child, denying the paternity of the child, were not within this clause or section 33 and were not admissible in evidence as against the child. The judgment of the Magistrate in the same proceedings, holding that the child was not the child of that father, was not binding upon the child and was inadmissible in evidence. Statements by the mother that the child was begotten by a person other than her husband were inadmissible against the child.[719]

For the purpose of the decision of a question of limitation, it was necessary to prove the date of the plaintiff's birth. The plaintiff and one of his witnesses each spoke to statements made to them by relatives of the plaintiff, who were since deceased, relating to the date of the plaintiff's birth. It was held that such statements were admissible in evidence.[720] A plaint in a former suit verified by a deceased member of the family, and as such having special means of knowledge, was held admissible under this clause to prove the order in which certain persons were born and their ages.[721] In an action to recover the amount due upon certain mortgages, the defendant pleaded that he was an infant when he executed them. As evidence in support of this plea there was tendered at the trial an entry, recording the date of the defendant's birth made by the defendant's deceased father in a book in which he made similar entries with regard to

---

714. *Twarku v Surti,* AIR 1997 AP 76.

715. *Debi Pershad Chowdhry v Rani Radha Chowdhrain,* (1904) 31 IA 160: 32 Cal 84.

716. *Bahadur Singh v Mohar Singh,* (1901) 29 IA 1: 4 Bom LR 233: 24 All 94.

717. *Oriental Government Security Life Assurance Co Ltd v Narasimha Chari,* (1901) 25 Mad 183.

718. *KV Subbaraju v C. Subbaraju,* AIR 1968 SC 947 : 1968 (2) SCR 292.

719. *Karapaya Servai v Mayandi,* (1933) 12 Ran 243: 36 Bom LR 394 (PC).

720. *Ram Chandra Dutt v Jogeswar Narain Deo,* (1893) 20 Cal 758; *Bipin Behary Daw v Sreedam Chunder Dey,* (1886) 13 Cal 42 may be considered as **overruled**.

721. *Dhanmull v Ram Chunder Ghose,* (1890) 24 Cal 265, 268; *Gokhul Pande v Baldeo Sukul,* (1927) 7 Pat 90; *Mauladad Khan v Abdul Sattar,* (1917) 39 All 426.

his family. It was held under an Ordinance exactly similar to the Evidence Act that having regard to Illustration (l) to this section the entry was admissible in evidence.[722]

[s 32.19] Difference between clauses (5) and (6) [Clause 6].—Clause (5) refers to statements relating to the existence of any relationship between persons alive or dead, and the statement is to be made by a person who had special means of knowledge, that is, it imposes the restrictions that the person making the statement should have special means of knowledge. See Illustration (k). Clause (6) refers to the existence of relationship between deceased persons only; and it imposes no such restriction as under clause (5). It is enough if the statement is made in a will or deed relating to the affairs of the family or in any family pedigree, *etc.*, no matter by whom it was made.

Clause (6) also refers to pedigree, but differs from clause (5) in this—that in clause (5) the evidence is the declaration of the person deceased or otherwise unproduceable, in clause (6) the evidence is that of things, such as genealogical trees, tomb-stones, etc.

The statements in clause (5) may be either written or verbal; the statement in clause (6) must always be written as the evidence therein is that of things.

In order to be admissible the statement relied on must be made *ante litem motam* by persons who are dead i.e. before the commencement of any controversy actual or legal upon the same point.[723]

[s 32.19.1] Statement as to relationship in will or deed.—Under this clause statements relating to the existence of relationship between deceased persons made before the question in dispute was raised are admissible when they are contained in a will or a deed or in a family pedigree,[724] or upon a tomb-stone. It is not necessary as in clause (5) that the statements should have been made by a person who had special means of knowledge, simply because it is not probable that a person would insert in a will or a solemn deed any matter the truth of which he did not know. The statement should not have been made in the testator's own interest or in view of contemplated litigation.[725] The statement of testator in his will that the defendant No. 1 was his adopted son was held to be relevant to show the fact but not conclusive of it.[726]

The word "verbal" used in the beginning of this section has no application to this clause.

Illustrations (l) and (m) exemplify this clause.

[s 32.19.2] CASES.—Horoscope.—In a suit to recover possession of immoveable property, the plaintiff tendered in evidence a horoscope which, he said, had been given to him by his mother and had been seen by members of his family and used on the occasion of his marriage. He was unable to say by whom the horoscope, or an endorsement on it, which purported to state what his name was, had been written. It

722. *Mahomed Syedol Ariffin v Yeoh Ooi Gark*, (1916) 43 IA 256: 19 Bom LR 157: (1916) 2 AC 575.

723. *Kalidindi Venkata Subbaraju v Chintalpati Subbaraju*, AIR 1968 SC 947, p 953 : [1968] 2 SCR 292. See also *Om Prakash Sharma v Rajendra Prasad Shewda*, (2015) 15 SCC 556, para 22 : 2016 (2) SCJ 90.

724. *Jang Bahadur Singh Thakur v Arjun Singh Thakur*, (1927) 3 Luck 256.

725. *Chandreshwar Prasad Narain Singh v Bisheshwar Pratap Narain Singh*, (1926) 5 Pat 777.

726. *Banwari Lal v Trilok Chand*, AIR 1980 SC 419 : 1980(1) SCC 349.

was held that the horoscope was not admissible.[727] This case has been distinguished in a Madras case where the defendants relied on a horoscope produced by the plaintiff's mother and which had been a public record from a period *ante litam motam* and was put in as an admission under sections 17 and 18.[728]

[s 32.19.2.1] Pedigree table.—In a suit for inheritance claimed by the plaintiffs, alleging themselves to be collateral relations and heirs of the last male owner, through an ancestor common to him and to them, a pedigree table was put in evidence. The persons from whose statements at no distant date the pedigree had been drawn up were absent, and it had not been shown that this had been for any one or other of the reasons contained in this section. It was held that the pedigree table was inadmissible.[729] A family pedigree was sought to be proved by the books kept by the family chronicler prepared by the chroniclers from time to time from the information supplied by members of the family. It was held that the pedigree would be admissible under this clause and also under clause 2.[730]

[s 32.20] Statements as to Customs or Rights [Clause 7].—A statement contained in any deed, will, or other document which relates to a transaction by which a right or custom in question was created, modified, recognized, asserted, or denied, is admissible under this clause. A statement in any relevant document, however recent, and though not more than thirty years old, is admissible. Statements of facts contained in a will of a deceased person tending to show that the properties are his self-acquisitions are admissible.[731]

The word "verbal" used in the beginning of this section naturally does not apply to this clause as well. This clause does not allow introduction of parole evidence.[732]

Under this clause the word "right" will include both public and private rights.

[s 32.21] General Remarks [Clause 8].—When a number of persons assemble together to give vent to one common statement, which statement expresses the feelings or impressions made in their minds at the time of making it, that statement may be repeated by the witnesses, and is evidence.[733] Thus, where a person was charged with raising a seditious mob, expressions of alarm by persons in the neighbourhood were admitted in evidence to show the feelings produced by the gathering;[734] evidence that a plaintiff was publicly laughed at in consequence of a libel was admitted to prove that the libel referred to the plaintiff.[735] Illustration (n) is intended to exemplify this clause.

---

727. *Ram Narain Kallia v Monee Bibee,* (1883) 9 Cal 613; *Satis Chunder Mukhopadhya v Mohendro Lal Pathuk,* (1890) 17 Cal 849.
728. *Raja Goundan v Raja Goundan,* (1893) 17 Mad 134.
729. *Surjan v Sardar,* (1900) 2 Bom LR 942: 27 IA 183: 23 All 72.
730. *Mohansingh v Dalpatsingh,* (1921) 24 Bom LR 289: 46 Bom 753.
731. *Venkataramayya v Seshamma,* (1937) Mad 1012; *Chandrakant v Sharat Chandra,* (1954) MB 123; *Kuldeep Sharma v Satyandra Kumar Sharma,* AIR 2001 All 366, in a dispute as to title to property, there was a recital in a gift deed of 1945 as to the matter of title of that property. The court did not accept this as evidence of title and, therefore, said that the question of title would have to be decided on the basis of other evidence.
732. *Dwarka Nath v Lalchand,* AIR 1965 SC 1549 : 1965(3) SCR 27.
733. *The Queen v Ram Dutt Chowdhry,* (1874) 23 WR (Cr) 35, 38.
734. *Redford v Birley,* (1822) 1 St. Tr NS 1071, 3 Stark 76.
735. *Cook v Ward,* (1830) 4 M&P 99.

[s 33] Relevancy of certain evidence for proving, in subsequent proceeding, the truth of facts therein stated.—Evidence given by a witness in a judicial proceeding,[s 33.2] or before any person authorised by law to take it,[s 33.3] is relevant[s 33.4] for the purpose of proving, in a subsequent judicial proceeding, or in a later stage of the same judicial proceeding, the truth of the facts which it states, when the witness is dead,[s 33.5] or cannot be found,[s 33.6] or is incapable of giving evidence,[s 33.7] or is kept out of the way by the adverse party,[s 33.8] or if his presence cannot be obtained without an amount of delay or expense which, under the circumstances of the case, the Court considers unreasonable:[s 33.9]

Provided—

that the proceeding was between the same parties[s 33.10] or their representatives in interest;[s 33.11]

that the adverse party in the first proceeding had the right and opportunity to cross-examine;[s 33.12]

that the questions in issue were substantially the same in the first as in the second proceeding.[s 33.13]

***Explanation.*—A criminal trial or inquiry shall be deemed to be a proceeding between the prosecutor and the accused within the meaning of this section.**

SYNOPSIS

COMMENT

[s 33.1] Principle.—Evidence of depositions in former trials is admissible as it forms an exception to the hearsay rule. Depositions are in general admissible only after proof that the persons who made them cannot be produced before the court to give evidence. It is only in cases where the production of the primary evidence is beyond the party's power that secondary evidence of oral testimony is admissible. Non-compliance with the provisions of this section is not cured by the fact that counsel for the accused gives his consent thereto.[736]

It is an elementary right of an accused person or a litigant in a civil suit that a witness who is to testify against him should give his evidence before the court trying the case which then has the opportunity of seeing the witness and observing his demeanour and can thus form a better opinion as to his reliability than is possible from reading a statement or deposition given by that witness in a previous judicial proceeding or in an early stage of the same judicial proceeding.

Where a statute (e.g., the Evidence Act, 1872), makes provision for exceptional cases where it is impossible for the witness to be before the court, the court must be careful to see that the conditions on which the statute permits previous evidence given by the witness to be read are strictly proved. Previous statement of a witness not appearing in court should not be taken on record under this section without strict proof of the conditions justifying it being taken so.[737]

In a civil case a party can, if he chooses, waive the proof; but in a criminal case strict proof ought to be given that the witness is incapable of giving evidence, and even the consent of the accused's counsel cannot do away with the necessity of the court being satisfied by proof of that fact.

It is not necessary in every case where a witness is unable to attend the court on the ground of physical incapacity that there must be evidence of a medical man. There may be many cases in which the facts are such that the incapacity can be proved by a lay witness.[738]

The section enumerates the cases in which the evidence given by a witness (a) in a judicial proceeding, or (b) before any person authorized by law to take it, is relevant in a subsequent judicial proceeding or a later stage of the same proceeding. Such cases are five in number, *viz.*

(a) when the witness is dead;

(b) when he cannot be found;

(c) when he is incapable of giving evidence;

(d) when he is kept out of the way by the adverse party; and

(e) when his presence cannot be obtained without an amount of delay or expense which the court considers unreasonable.

The use of such secondary evidence is limited by three provisions. Such evidence will be only admissible—

(1) if the proceeding was between the same parties, or their representatives in interest;

(2) if the adverse party in the first proceeding had the right and opportunity to cross-examine; and

(3) if the questions in issue were substantially the same in the first as in the second proceeding.

---

736. *Ghulam Haidar v The Crown,* (1929) 10 Lah 837.

737. *Hari Prasad v State of UP,* (1955) 1 All 749.

738. *Chainchal Singh v Emperor,* (1945) 48 Bom LR 284 : 72 IA 270.

Evidence given on a different occasion is also admissible to contradict a witness (section 155) or to corroborate him (section 157).

[s 33.2] "Evidence given... in a judicial proceeding".—"It must be proved that the witness was *duly sworn* in some judicial proceeding, to the authority of which the party, against whom his testimony is offered, was legally bound to submit, and in which he might have exercised the *right of cross-examination*".[739] Evidence of a witness in a proceeding subsequently pronounced to be *coram non judice* is not admissible if the witness is dead, on a re-trial before a competent court.[740] An affidavit is not "evidence given by a witness" within the meaning of this section and cannot therefore be admitted in evidence.[741]

[s 33.3] "Before any person authorised by law to take it".—A deposition is inadmissible unless it was taken by an officer or other person authorised by law.[742]

[s 33.4] "Is relevant".—Depositions which satisfy the conditions laid down in this section are relevant for the purpose of proving the truth of the facts which they state. They are, however, open to all the objections which might have been raised if the witness himself had been present during the trial. Leading and other illegal questions are, therefore, not allowed to go in.

The burden of proving that the conditions essential to the admissibility of depositions under this section have been complied with lies on the person who tenders the evidence. The depositions of witnesses given in a counter-case may be used as evidence against them on their trial as accused persons, but such depositions can only be evidence against the persons making them.[743]

Objections as to the admissibility of evidence should be raised at the trial and at any rate in the court of first appeal, and will not as a general rule be entertained by the High Court if raised for the first time in second appeal.[744]

[s 33.5] "When the witness is dead".—The death of the witness whose evidence is to be admitted should first be strictly proved unless it is admitted on the other side.[745] The deposition of a witness taken before one Magistrate is admissible in evidence at a re-trial before another Magistrate if the witness was dead at the time of re-trial.[746]

The deposition of a witness, who was not cross-examined before the committing Magistrate and who died before the trial, was held admissible because the accused had the right and opportunity of cross-examining him notwithstanding the omission of

---

739. *Taylor*, 12th Edn, section 465, p 320.

740. *Rami Reddi*, (1881) 3 Mad 48, 51; *Buta Singh v The Crown*, (1926) 7 Lah 396; *Sankappa Rai v Koraga Pujary*, (1930) 54 Mad 561.

741. *Malik Jaindkhan v Province of Sind*, (1947) Kar 273.

742. *K Venkatappa v Uday Shanker*, AIR 1981 AP 34.

743. *Queen-Empress v Ganu Sonba*, (1888) 12 Bom 440.

744. *Radha Kishan v Kedar Nath*, (1924) 46 All 815.

745. *Sajan Singh v The Crown*, (1925) 6 Lah 437.

746. *Lekal v The Crown*, (1927) 8 Lah 570; *Nirmal Singh v State of Haryana*, 2000 Cr LJ 1803 : AIR 2000 SC 1416, evidence was recorded in the absence of the accused, there was sufficient material to show that the accused was absconding, summons had come back unserved, in the meantime time the witnesses died, the court said that the requirements of the section were satisfied, the deposition of the witnesses could be used to convict the accused.

their pleader to avail himself of that right.[747] But if a witness under examination by a court dies before his cross-examination is completed, no part of his evidence can be made use of.[748] The applicant was the beneficiary of the will along with his mother who was given life estate. During the trial of testamentary proceedings the attesting witness was examined on commission and later he died. His evidence was not taken in any previous proceedings or at the earlier stage of the same proceedings. Thus, the provisions of section 33 were not attracted. There was opportunity to cross-examine but the same was not used. In the absence of cross-examination, the evidence recorded in-chief became acceptable.[749]

[s 33.6] "Cannot be found".—Proof of a diligent search is necessary before tendering the evidence of a witness who cannot be found. A Sessions Judge, finding that the witnesses, who had been summoned to give evidence for the prosecution, did not appear on the date fixed, adjourned the case for eighteen days and ordered fresh summonses to be issued. On the adjourned date, the witnesses were again absent. Thereupon the Sessions Judge made use of the evidence, which those witnesses had given before the committing Magistrate, purporting to do so under this section. It was held that the evidence could not be so used; the Sessions Judge ought to have directed to issue warrants to enforce the attendance of the prosecution witnesses and compelled their attendance in court.[750]

Section 299 of the Code of Criminal Procedure, 1973 supersedes this section to a certain extent. It provides that if it is proved that an accused person has absconded, and that there is no immediate prospect of arresting him, the court competent to try or commit for trial such person for the offence complained of may, in his absence, examine the witnesses (if any) produced on behalf of the prosecution, and record their depositions, and that such depositions may be used at the subsequent trial of the absconder, if the witnesses are dead or otherwise incapable of appearing.

[s 33.7] "Incapable of giving evidence".—The incapacity contemplated by the section is not necessarily a permanent one and something short of permanent incapacity might satisfy the words of the section.[751] The fact of incapacity must be strictly proved.[752]

Precise evidence should be given as to the nature of the illness and the incapacity to attend. When a witness is shown to be insane, his evidence, given in a former judicial proceeding, is relevant in a subsequent judicial proceeding.

[s 33.8] "Kept out of the way by the adverse party".—The evidence given by a witness who is kept out of the way by the adverse party is admissible upon the broad principle of justice which will not permit a party to take advantage of his own wrong.

---

747. *Queen-Emp. v Baswanta,* (1900) 2 Bom LR 761: 25 Bom 168.

748. *Narsingh Das v Gokul Prasad,* (1927) 50 All 113; *Nirmal Singh v State of Haryana,* AIR 2000 SC 1416, the witnesses deposed in the absence of the accused who remained absconding, subsequently the witnesses also died, conviction could be recorded on the basis of the evidence of deceased witnesses.

749. *Shyamal Kumar Chatterjee v Rabindra Narayan Banerjee,* AIR 2007 NOC 1430 (Cal-DB).

750. *Emperor v Dost Muhammad,* (1905) 28 All 98.

751. In the matter of the Petition of *Asgur Hossein,* (1881) 6 Cal. 774.

752. *Chainchal Singh v Emperor,* (1945) 48 Bom LR 284: 72 IA 270.

[s 33.9] "Presence cannot be obtained without an amount of delay or expense, *etc.*".— It is only in extreme cases of expense or delay that the personal attendance of a witness is dispensed with, and his evidence given in a former inquiry referred to.[753] The Judge must satisfy himself that the presence of the witness cannot be obtained without an amount of delay or expense which he considers to be unreasonable. Mere consent of the prosecutor and the accused's pleader to that effect is not sufficient.[754] Inconvenience to witnesses or amount of expense is no ground where the entire case rests on the evidence of those witnesses.[755]

[s 33.10] "Proceeding...between the same parties".—The two suits must be brought by, or against, the same parties, or their representatives in interest, at the time when the suits are proceeding and the evidence is given.[756] This proviso is based on the grounds of reciprocity, because the right to use evidence being co-extensive with the liability to be bound thereby, the adversary in the second suit has no power to offer evidence in his own favour which, had it been tendered against him, would have been clearly inadmissible. R charged A with breach of trust, and S gave evidence in support of the charge. A being acquitted, R was tried for making a false charge and S for perjury. It was held that the depositions given by witnesses in the first case could be used against R in the second case, but not against S under this section.[757]

[s 33.11] "Representatives in interest".—This proviso requires that the party to the first proceeding should have represented in interest the party to the second proceeding in relation to the question in issue in the first proceeding to which the facts which the evidence states were relevant. It covers not only cases of privity in estate and succession of title, but also cases where both the following conditions exist, *viz.* (1) the interest of the relevant party to the second proceeding in the subject-matter of the first proceeding is consistent with and not antagonistic to the interest therein of the relevant party to the first proceeding, and (2) the interest of both in the answer to be given to the particular question in issue in the first proceeding is identical. If both the above conditions are fulfilled, the relevant party to the first proceeding in fact represented in the first proceeding the relevant party to the second proceeding in regard to his interest in relation to the particular question in issue in the first proceeding, and may rightly be described as a "representative in interest" of the party to the second proceeding within the wider meaning of those words as laid down above.[758]

Partners and joint contractors who are each other's agents for the purpose of making admissions against each other in relation to partnership transactions or joint contracts are regarded as privies in estate, and are included in the term "representatives in interest".[759]

[s 33.12] "Adverse party...had the right and opportunity to cross-examine".— The term "adverse party" occurring in the 2nd proviso of section 33 is the party in

---

753. *Empress of India v Mulu,* (1880) 2 All 646.
754. *Re Annavi Muthiriyan,* (1915) 39 Mad 449; *Emperor v Savlimiya Miyabhai,* (1944) 46 Bom LR 589; *Emperor v Gajendra Mohan Kar,* (1943) 1 Cal 405.
755. *Queen-Empress v T Burke,* (1884) 6 All 224.
756. *Sitanath Dass v Mohesh Chunder Chuckerbati,* (1886) 12 Cal 627.
757. *Rami Reddi,* (1881) 3 Mad 48, 51. See, *Emperor v Kadhe Mal,* (1919) 42 All 24. See, *Phool Chand v Amrit Lal,* AIR 1980 P&H 122, where the earlier proceeding was *ex parte* and, therefore, not between the same parties.
758. *Krishnayya Rao v Venkata Kumara Mahipati,* (1933) 35 Bom LR 1076: 60 IA 336: 57 Mad 1.
759. *Chandreshwar Prasad Narain Singh v Bisheshwar Pratap Narain Singh,* (1926) 5 Pat 777.

the previous proceeding against whom the evidence adduced therein was given against his interest, thus having right and opportunity to cross-examine. It does not protect the rights of the party producing a witness.[760] The court explained in this case as to what the section means to lay down as follows: "The section lays down as to when the evidence of a witness in a previous judicial proceeding is relevant. It consists of two parts, the main section and the *proviso*. The main section lays down the conditions which are required to be satisfied for the previous statement of a witness in a judicial proceeding to be admitted in evidence in the later proceeding. The question of party having the right and opportunity to cross-examine will arise, if he is an adverse party in the first proceeding. The second *proviso,* which is an exception to the main part of the section, operates only if the adverse party in the first proceeding did not have the right and opportunity to cross-examine the witness examined therein. The term "adverse party" connotes that party which has a right and opportunity to cross-examine in the first proceeding. This proviso, therefore, obviously protects the rights of the adverse party in the first proceeding and not the party who produced the witness. The party against whom the witness is produced in the previous proceeding is the adverse party and not the person who produced the witness and had the advantage of having examined the witness. He had the right and opportunity to cross-examine the witness in the previous proceeding. Take an instance where *ex parte* proceedings were taken against the defendant; he had no right and opportunity to cross-examine the witness. If the same evidence is sought to be used, he is certainly an adverse party in the previous proceeding and since he had no right and opportunity to cross-examine that witness, the same evidence cannot be used against the defendant in the subsequent proceeding. In other words, the proviso lays down the acid test that statement of a particular witness should have been tested by both parties by examination and cross-examination in order to make it admissible in the later proceeding. Thereby it seeks to protect the rights against whom the previous proceeding might have gone *ex parte* who had no right and opportunity to cross-examine the witness. For the same reason, it would also protect the co-plaintiffs and co-defendants who may have a right but no opportunity to cross-examine the witness since it was produced by one of the co-plaintiffs or co-defendants on their side but that evidence went against their interest. It is, therefore, clear that a person who examined the witness should not be permitted, in the subsequent proceeding between the same parties, to raise the objection that the statement which was recorded in the previous proceeding on his behalf should not be admissible because he had no right and opportunity to cross-examine him. It would also be unfair that the person producing a witness in the previous proceeding should be able to utilise the evidence recorded in his favour in the previous proceeding as evidence in the subsequent proceeding, while the adverse party should be denied of the same right of using the same statement favourable to him which went against the party producing the witness in the previous proceeding."[761]

760. *VM Mathew v VS Sharma,* AIR 1996 SC 109 : 1995(6) SCC 122 : (1995) 6 SCC 122.

761. *VM Mathew v VS Sharma,* (1995) 6 SCC 122 : AIR 1996 SC 109. *Sasdi Jena v Khadal Swain,* AIR 2004 SC 1492 : (2004) 4 SCC 236 : 2004 Cr LJ 1394, the accused had no right and opportunity to cross-examine any prosecution witness at the stage of enquiry under section 202, CrPC, held such statement would not be relevant and admissible under section 33 at a later stage of the proceedings at which conviction was recorded.

The adverse party must have both the right and the opportunity to cross-examine. The word "and" cannot be read as "or".[762] The word "right" means a legal right. Consequently, when a witness is not produced for cross-examination after charge in a warrant case, his evidence should not be taken into consideration, even if the accused was given the option to cross-examine him before charge, but he did not do so.[763] Where a case in respect of adulteration of milk was instituted on a private complaint by a Food Inspector and conviction was based on his evidence alone, though he was not cross-examined by the accused and his cross-examination was not possible due to his accidental death, it was held that the conviction could not be based merely on his evidence which was recorded before framing the charge and particularly when panch witnesses did not support his evidence. But the accused could not say that he having not exercised his right to cross-examine the Food Inspector the uncross-examined evidence of the Food Inspector could not be relied upon, by referring to section 33.[764] This proviso is based on the fundamental principle in the administration of justice that every man should have an opportunity of cross-examining witnesses whose evidence is to be used against him. If the adverse party has had liberty to cross-examine and has not chosen to exercise it, the case is then same in effect as if he had cross-examined. It is not necessary that the opponent should have exercised his right of cross-examining, for the depositions will be relevant if he deliberately forbore from, or waived the absence of, an opportunity for cross-examining.[765] Upon the allegation that the accused had induced the complainant to part with money under false representation, the complainant started a prosecution against the accused. The complainant was examined and charge was framed. The complainant thereafter died before he could be cross-examined. It was held that the complainant's deposition before charge was inadmissible in evidence.[766]

The Allahabad High Court has held that the evidence of a witness, who has been examined in open court, is not inadmissible in the course of the same judicial proceeding merely because it is impossible to cross-examine him on account of his having died between his examination-in-chief and his cross-examination, but the weight to be attached to his testimony depends on the circumstances of each case.[767]

[s 33.13] "The questions in issue were substantially the same in the first as in the second proceeding".—It is not necessary that all the questions in issue in the two proceedings should be substantially the same, it is sufficient if the principal question in issue in both the proceedings is identical.[768] The principle involved in requiring identity

---

762. *Dal Bahadur Singh v Bijai Bahadur Singh,* (1929) 32 Bom LR 487: 57 IA 14: 52 All 1.

763. *SC Mitter v State,* (1951) 1 Cal 480. See, however, *State v Baldev Kishan,* (1952) Patiala 543.

764. *Nandram Khemraj v State of MP,* 1995 Cr LJ 1270 (MP). *Turner Morrison & Co, Bombay v KN Tapuria,* 1993 Cr LJ 3384 (Bom), witness examined before the framing of charge, not available for cross-examination after framing the charge, cautious approach required.

765. *M'Combie v Anton,* (1843) 6 M&G 27; *Gurudin v Emperor,* (1934) 31 NLR 276; *Queen-Empress v Ramchandra Govind Harshe,* (1895) 19 Bom 749; *Sadu v The Empress,* (1885) PR No. 26 of 1885 (Cr); *State v Hazura Singh,* (1952) Patiala 48; *Mulkh Raj v Delhi Admn.,* AIR 1974 SC 1723 : 1974 Cr LJ 1171, where opportunity of cross-examination was not made use of. *VM Mathew v VS Saramma,* 1996 AIHC (Ker), dissenting from *Poonamchand v Motilal,* AIR 1955 Raj 179, where the plaintiff had no right or opportunity to cross-examine.

766. *Brahmachari Ajitananda v Ananth Bandhu Dutt,* (1955) 2 Cal 19; *State v Hazura Singh,* (1952) Patiala 48.

767. *Ahmad Ali v Joti Prasad,* (1944) All 241.

768. *Krishnayya Rao v Venkata Kumara Mahipati,* (1933) 35 Bom LR 1076: 60 IA 336: 57 Mad 1.

of the matter in issue is to secure that in the former proceeding the parties were not without the opportunity of examining and cross-examining to the very point upon which their evidence is adduced in the subsequent proceeding. And though separate proceedings may involve issues, of which some only are common to both, the evidence to those common issues given in the former proceeding may be given in the subsequent proceedings. Thus, "if in a dispute respecting lands, any fact comes directly in issue, the testimony given to that fact is admissible to prove the same point in another action between the same parties or their privies though the last suit relates to other lands".[769]

Whether the questions at issue are substantially the same, depends upon whether the same evidence is applicable, although different consequences may follow from the same fact.[770] Where the same question is substantially in issue in both the proceedings, it does not matter that they relate to different transactions or properties.[771] A prosecution was instituted by S against N at the instance and on behalf of F for criminal trespass in respect of a certain house, and on his own behalf for assault and insult. S gave evidence at the trial in support of those charges. F subsequently brought a civil suit against N for possession of the same house under section 9 of the Specific Relief Act. S died before the institution of the civil suit. At the trial of the civil suit, the deposition of S in the criminal court was tendered by F as evidence on the issue of possession. It was held that S being dead and the proceedings being between the same parties and the issues being substantially the same, the deposition of S was admissible.[772]

[s 33.14] Criminal trial or inquiry, deemed proceeding—*[Explanation]*.—The Explanation is intended to do away with the objection that, in criminal cases, the State is the prosecutor.[773] The effect of the Explanation is that the deposition taken in criminal proceedings may be used in a civil suit, and *vice versa*.

The deposition of a witness taken in the course of an enquiry before the Coroner cannot, in the event of death of the witness, be taken in evidence at the trial of the case in the High Court, because the enquiry before the Coroner is not a proceeding between the prosecutor and the accused.[774]

The introduction and use of depositions taken in criminal cases in bulk in a subsequent civil suit for the purpose of either contradicting or discounting the evidence of witnesses given in the suit, are illegitimate, unless the particular matter or point had been placed before the witness as one for explanation in view of its discrepancy with the evidence then being tendered.[775]

[s 33.15] Expression of opinion on oral evidence.—Where an opinion was expressed on oral evidence even before it was analysed and assessed by the criminal court, the court said that such opinion amounted to an inference in the functioning of the court inasmuch as it was likely to cause prejudice to the judicial mind. There was also no case yet that the witness was not available within the meaning of section 33.[776]

---

769. *Rami Reddi,* (1881) 3 Mad 48, 52; Taylor, 12th Edn, para 467, p 321.
770. In the matter of the Petition of *Rochia Mohato,* (1881) 7 Cal 42.
771. *Llanover v Homfray: Phillip v Llanover,* (1881) 19 Ch D 224.
772. *Foolkissory Dasee v Nobin Chunder Bhujno,* (1895) 23 Cal 441.
773. *Soojan Bibee v Achmut Ali,* (1874) 14 Beng LR (Appx.) 3.
774. *Emperor v Mohomed Yusuf,* (1932) 35 Bom LR 1020.
775. *Bal Gangadhar Tilak v Shri Shrinivas Pandit,* (1915) 17 Bom LR 527: 42 IA 135: 39 Bom 441.
776. *DP Anand v State,* 1998 Cr LJ 724 (Mad).

STATEMENTS MADE UNDER SPECIAL CIRCUMSTANCES

[s 34] [777]**[Entries in books of account including those maintained in an electronic form] when relevant.—**[777]**[Entries in the books of account, including those maintained in an electronic form], regularly kept in the course of business, are relevant whenever they refer to a matter into which the Court has to inquire, but such statements shall not alone be sufficient evidence to charge any person with liability.**

ILLUSTRATION

A sues *B* for Rs. 1,000, and shows entries in his account books showing *B* to be indebted to him to this amount. The entries are relevant, but are not sufficient, without other evidence, to prove the debt.

SYNOPSIS

COMMENT

[s 34.1] Principle.—This section is based upon the principle that entries made regularly in the course of business are sure to be accurate. In all such entries the writer has full knowledge, no motive to falsehood, and there is the strongest improbability of untruth.

This section provides (1) that entries in books of account regularly kept in the course of business are relevant and therefore admissible whenever they refer to a matter into which the court has to enquire; and (2) that such entries though admissible are not alone sufficient to charge a person with liability unless corroborated by other evidence.[778] Account books are admissible in evidence without any formal proof that they were regularly kept in the course of business.[779]

The entries in books of account, regularly kept in the course of business, are relevant in all proceedings in a court of law but these entries are not by themselves sufficient to charge any person with liability.[780] Even correct and authentic entries cannot fix liability upon any person in the absence of some independent evidence of their trustworthiness.[781] In a suit for eviction on the ground of non-payment of rents, the tenants produced his books which showed payment. It was held that such

---

777. Subs. by Act 21 of 2000, section 92 and Sch. II–4, for "Entries in the books of account" (w.e.f. 17-10-2000).

778. *Gopeswar Sen v Bejoy Chand Mahatab*, (1928) 55 Cal 1167.

779. *Emperor v Narbada Prasad*, (1929) 51 All 864.

780. *State of Andhra Pradesh v Ganeswara Rao*, AIR 1963 SC 1850 : 1963(2) Cr LJ 671. See also *Chandrakantaben v VB Modi*, AIR 1989 SC 1269 : 1989(2) SCC 630, mere entries in *Khatabandis*, (Ledger A/c) without support of the evidence of any witness or of cash book, were held to be not reliable. *Rukmanand Ajitsaria v Usha Sales Pvt Ltd*, AIR 1991 NOC 108 Gau, such entries are not sufficient to charge any person with liability. Certified copy of ledger account maintained in the regular course of business, admissible, *State Bank of India v Ramayanapu Krishna Rao*, AIR 1995 Ori 244. *Guru Amarjit Singh v Rattan Chand*, AIR 1994 SC 227 : 1993(4) SCC 349, entries in Jamabandi are not proof of title and the parties have to establish their title to the property.

781. *CBI v VC Shukla*, 1998 Cr LJ 1905 : AIR 1998 SC 1406.

entries would neither create liability nor discharge anybody's liability.[782] In a suit for recovery of money advanced by way of a loan, entries in the register of the lender were held not sufficient to charge the alleged borrower.[783] A book of account should be foolproof. A bundle of sheets detachable and replaceable at pleasure cannot be characterised as a book of account. Spiral pads, and spiral notebooks have been held to be books within the meaning of section 34. The court also said that loose sheets of papers contained in files would not be in the category of books.[784]A ledger by itself is also not a proof. There must be supporting evidence.[785] The general ledger entries cannot be the basis for accepting that cash transactions mentioned therein are correct, unless there is authentic supporting material.[786] Where the question was whether money had been entrusted, it was held that an entry in books of account could not be given much weight. The court has to examine the whole state of accounts at the material time.[787]

Such books may be admissible under section 32(2) as statements made by a person in the ordinary course of business or entries made by him in books kept in the ordinary course of business. Such books are also relevant under section 159 to refresh the memory of the writer.[788]

In account books regularly kept in due course of business usually the pages are interconnected, and particularly in daily accounts, the balance of one day or one page is carried over to the other day or the other page so that interpolation or replacement of a particular page becomes very difficult and sanctity is to be attached to such books. Where the credit register is not a bound book but a stitched one, the pages can be replaced or interpolated. No importance can be attached to the entries made in such a register and they cannot be taken to be accounts regularly kept in the course of business.[789]

[s 34.2] "Regularly kept in the course of business".—The Privy Council has laid down that the admissibility of books of account regularly kept in the course of business is not restricted to books in which entries have been made from day to day, or from hour to hour, as transactions have taken place. The time of making the entries may affect the value of them but should not, if they have been made regularly in the course of business afterwards made them irrelevant.[790] The Privy Council has also held that

---

782. *Suresh Kumar v Mewa Ram,* AIR 1991 P&H 254.

783. *Ajit Chandra Bagchi v Harishpur Tea Co P Ltd,* AIR 1991 Gau 92.

784. *CBI v VC Shukla,* 1998 Cr LJ 1905 : AIR 1998 SC 1406. The spiral notebook in this case recorded monetary transactions, i.e., entries of receipt of money from certain persons on left side of the page and payment to certain persons on the right page, the entries were totalled and balances taken.

785. *Zenna Sorabji v Mirabe,* AIR 1981 Bom 446; *Mohan Lal v Dwarkanath,* AIR 1985 J&K 86. *Dharam Chand Joshi v Satya Narayana Bazaz,* AIR 1993 Gau 35, a book of account is only a corroborative evidence.

786. *Subrata Roy Sahara v UOI,* (2014) 8 SCC 470 (para 150) : 2014 (8) SCJ 240.

787. *Dadarao v State of Maharashtra,* AIR 1974 SC 389 : 1974 Cr LJ 447.

788. *Bhoy Hong v Ramnathan,* (1902) 4 Bom LR 378: 29 IA 43: 29 Cal 34.

789. *Hira v Birbal,* (1957) Cut 437. *Dharam Chand Joshi v Satya Narayan Bazaz,* AIR 1993 Gau 35, unbound sheets, interpolations and overwriting, no credibility. *R. v Sunders (Gurmit Singh),* 1998 CLY 314 (892) (CA), insurance claim forms have been held to be no such documents as are required for an accounting purpose.

790. *The Deputy Commissioner of Bara Banki v Ram Parshad,* (1899) 27 Cal 118: 26 IA 254, overruling *Munchershaw Bezonji v The New Dhurumsey S&W Co,* (1880) 4 Bom 576; *Emperor v Narbada Prasad,* (1929) 51 All 864; *Gulab Chand Lala v Manni Lal Lala,* (1940) 16 Luck 302; *Pannalal v Labhchand,* (1954) MB 237. See, however, *Balmukund v Jagan Nath,* AIR 1963 Raj 212.

books of account professing to record facts relating only to the particular transaction in question are less reliable than a book in which the same is recorded in common with other transactions in the ordinary course of business.[791] The *prima facie* evidentiary value is attached to a banker's books under the *Bankers' Books Evidence Act*. Such evidence is admissible under section 16 as well as under this section. It has been held that paid cheques and paying-in-slips which are retained by a bank after the conclusion of a banking transaction to which they relate are not "bankers' books" and accordingly cannot be the subject of an inspection order.[792]

Where the question was whether records of meetings constituted *bankers books* for the purposes of disclosure, the court said that on the true construction of section 9(2) of the 1879 Act [English] the words "other records" were not apt to cover records kept by a bank of conversation between its employees, however senior, and its customers. Rather, they covered records of the same kind as ledgers, day books, cash books and account books, which were the means by which a bank recorded day-to-day financial transactions. In the instant case, the records sought were essentially records of meetings. As such, they could not be properly regarded as entries in books kept by a bank for the purpose of its ordinary business within the definition in section 9(2). Accordingly, the registrar was not entitled to order disclosure of those classes of documents under the 1879 Act.[793]

Account books containing entries not made by, nor at the dictation of, a person who had a personal knowledge of the truth of the facts stated, if regularly kept in the course of business, are admissible as evidence under this section.[794]

The books of accounts maintained in the regular course of business should not be rejected without any kind of rebuttal or discarded without any reason.[795]

However, entries in an account book which is not regularly kept in the course of business are not admissible in evidence under this section.[796]

Trip sheets were produced by a taxi driver showing movements of the vehicle, distance covered, consumption of fuel, etc. They were in loose sheet form and not in a bound book. They were held to be not relevant under the section.[797]

In the absence of evidence that the books produced were account books regularly kept in the ordinary course of business, the account books should not be admitted. In such a case, however, it is essential that objection should be taken as soon as the books of account are sought to be admitted in evidence. However, even if no objection could be taken in appeal to the admissibility of the evidence, their reliability and weight to

---

791. *Bhoy Hong Kong v RMMSP Ramanathan Chetty,* (1902) 6 Cal WN 401.

792. *Williams v Williams,* (1987) 3 All ER 257 CA *Canara Bank v Eastern Mechanical Works,* AIR 2008 Bom 188, recovery on the basis of documents made from banker's books under the Bankers Books Evidence Act, 1891.

793. *Re Howglen Ltd,* (2001) 1 All ER 376 : (2001) BCC 245 : (2001) 2 BCLC 695. The court applied the principle laid down in *Williams v Williams; Tucker v Williams,* (1987) 3 All ER 257.

794. *Reg v Hanmanta,* (1877) 1 Bom 610.

795. *Gian Chand and Bros. v Rattan Lal,* (2013) 2 SCC 606.

796. *Vithu v Thakurdas,* (1949) Nag 307.

797. *State of Kerala v Thomas,* (1986) 2 SCC 411, 413 : 1986 SCC (Cri) 176. See also *Common Cause (A Registered Society) v UOI,* AIR 2017 SC 540, para 20 : 2017 (1) Scale 573.

be given to the account books have still to be considered.[798] It is not necessary that an entry in a book of account should have been made at or at about the same time as the transaction concerned took place so as to pass the test of "a book regularly kept".[799]

The words "regularly kept" do not necessarily mean kept in a technically correct manner. No particular set of rules or system of keeping accounts is prescribed under this section. Even the roughest memoranda of accounts kept by petty shop-keepers are admissible if they are authentic. The crucial question for consideration is whether the entries are honest or whether there are any conscious attempts at falsification. Account books will be discredited if some of the entries therein are proved to be bogus by independent evidence which precludes the possibility of error or accident.[800]

The word "business" for this purpose has been taken to mean activities carried on continuously in an organised manner with a set purpose (be it illegal) to augment one's own resources.[801]

[s 34.3] Hotel Register.—A hotel register kept at its counter was not taken to be a book of account for the purposes of this section. It could have been so regarded if it were shown that the register also pertained to pecuniary transactions relating to customers.[802]

[s 34.4] "Such statements shall not alone be sufficient evidence".—Entries in accounts relevant only under this section are not by themselves alone sufficient to charge any person with liability. Corroboration is required. The section does not mean that there should be independent evidence to prove each and every transaction entered in a book of account. What is necessary to be seen in each case is whether besides the entries in a book of account, there is any evidence to prove that the transactions referred to in those entries actually took place. Such corroboration will be best afforded by the evidence of the person who wrote the books of account and in whose presence the transactions took place.[803] Corroborated entries in the bank's books of account are sufficient proof of loan transaction, more so when the loanee had admitted the loan.[804] Where there was no evidence to prove the receipt of goods by the purchaser, liability for the payment of those goods could not be fastened on him solely on the basis of entries in the books of account, though regularly maintained.[805] There has to

---

798. *Ramaji v Manohar,* AIR 1967 Bom 169 : 62 Bom LR 329; *Kulamani Mohanty v Industrial Development Corpn. of Orissa Ltd,* AIR 2002 Ori. 38, entries in books of account were proved by official staff. There were no objections, nor any evidence to doubt correctness of the entries, held to be admissible in evidence.

799. *CBI v VC Shukla,* 1998 Cr LJ 1905 : AIR 1998 SC 1406.

800. *Thomas v Govinda Gurukkal,* (1960) Kerala 51. An exercise book produced, contained some slips of paper, pages not numbered and entries were not proved by any witness, the book was held to be not admissible; its production without objection would not prevent the court from examining its evidentiary value, *State of Meghalaya v JN Giri,* AIR 1995 Gau 23.

801. *CBI v VC Shukla,* 1998 Cr LJ 1905 : AIR 1998 SC 1406.

802. *Manish Dixit v State of Rajasthan,* AIR 2001 SC 93 : (2001) Cr LJ 133. The court said that even otherwise an entry in the register would not have been sufficient to charge anybody with liability.

803. *Ramgobind Prasad v Gulab Chand Sahu,* (1940) 20 Pat 273; *Dwarka Doss v Baboo Jankee Doss,* (1855) 6 Moo Ind App 88, 98; *Lachmi Narain v Musaddi Lall,* (1941) 17 Luck 327; *Himmat Mal v Shah Magaji Khubaji,* (1953) 3 Raj 815; *Laxmi Sahu v Ganeshi Sahu,* AIR 1990 Pat 201, "jamabandi" records, held not sufficient to bind anybody by themselves.

804. *State Bank of India v Yumnam Gouramani Singh,* AIR 1994 SC 1644 : 1993(3) SCC 631.

805. *Hada Steel Products Ltd v Engineering Enterprises,* AIR 1995 P&H 327. *Vaiyapuri Mudaliar & Sons v Arunodhaya Textiles, Erode,* AIR 1996 Mad 19, regularly maintained accounts of a firm.

be evidence to prove payment of the money which may appear in the books of account in order that the person may be charged with liability thereunder, except where the person to be charged accepts the correctness of the books of account and does not challenge them.[806] Where accounts are relevant also under section 32(2), they are in law sufficient evidence in themselves, and the law does not, as in the case of accounts admissible only under this section, require corroboration. Entries in account may, in the same suit, be relevant under both the sections; and in that case the necessity for corroboration does not arise.[807] In a suit for breach of contract relating to a sales transaction, it was held that entries in account books were not sufficient in themselves to charge any person with liability. Some independent evidence would have to be produced showing the genesis of the entries reflecting the transaction which brought about the entries.[808]

One party, by merely producing his own books of account, cannot bind the other.[809] But the plaintiff's own testimony on oath in support of the entries in his books could be sufficient to fix the defendant with liability.[810] For the purpose of showing whether the amount referred to in the regularly maintained books of account was actually paid by the party, a clerk keeping the accounts or somebody competent to speak about the facts should be called so that he may testify to the fact that the books were regularly kept and that their entries were accurate.[811]

There should be some corroborative evidence in support of the record. The section does not prescribe any particular kind of corroboration. Such evidence may be oral or documentary. In this case, the court said that the plaintiff's (seller) own testimony on oath in support of the entries in his books of account could be treated as sufficient corroboration to charge the defendant with liability.[812]

[s 34.5] Books of account in electronic form.—Books of account maintained in electronic form have also become relevant under the section by reason of the addition of these words to the section under the amendments introduced by the Information Technology Act, 2000. The Act has introduced similar changes in the Bankers' Books Evidence Act, 1891. The amendment was necessary to accommodate the present practice of keeping only computerised accounts.

---

806. *Chandradhar v Gauhati Bank*, AIR 1967 SC 1058 : 1967(1) SCR 898.

807. *Rampyarabai v Balaji*, (1904) 6 Bom LR 50: 28 Bom 294.

808. *Mettur Beardsell Ltd v Salem Textiles Ltd*, AIR 2001 Mad 466.

809. *Hira Bhagat v Gobind Ram* (1897) PR No. 63 of 1897 (Civil); *Abdul Ali v Puran Mal*, (1914) PR No. 82 of 1914 (Civil); *Bichha Lal v Jai Pershad*, (1899) PR No. 45 of 1899 (Civil); *Gopeswar Sen v Bejoy Chand Mahatab*, (1928) 55 Cal 1167; *Radha Agencies v Vijaya Bank*, AIR 2002 AP 91, in a suit for recovery of bank loan, the court said that mere entries in books of account were not sufficient to prove the fact of loan. Some independent evidence would be necessary to prove the transaction of loan and actual disbursement of the loan amount. In this case the borrower admitted the loan and, therefore, the account was relevant. *Advani LK v CBI*, 1997 Cr LJ 2559 (Delhi), entries in the diary of the accused showing receipt of money, neither mentioning date of payment nor purpose, they were held to be not akin to books of account, such diary or loose sheets were held to be not relevant.

810. *Kaka Ram v Firm Thakar Das Mathura Das*, AIR 1962 Punj 27.

811. *Arakkan Narayanan v Indian Handloom Tenders*, AIR 1999 Ker 279.

812. *Fateh Lal v Bhagwati Lal*, AIR 2008 NOC 725 (Raj).

[s 35] Relevancy of entry in public [813][record or an electronic record] made in performance of duty.—An entry in any public or other official book, register[s 35.3] or [813][record or an electronic record] stating a fact in issue or relevant fact, and made by a public servant in the discharge of his official duty, or by any other person in performance of a duty specially enjoined by the law of the country in which such book, register or [813][record or an electronic record] is kept, is itself a relevant fact.

SYNOPSIS

COMMENT

[s 35.1] Principle.—This section is based upon the circumstance that in the case of public documents entries are made in discharge of public duty by an officer who is an authorized and accredited agent appointed for the purpose. The law reposes such a confidence in public officers that it presumes they will discharge their several trusts with accuracy and fidelity.

The section is applicable to entries in public records of a former Indian State or a foreign country.[814]

[s 35.2] Scope.—In a case the Calcutta High Court held that the section is confined to that class of cases where a public officer has to enter in a register or other books some actual fact which is known to him.[815] But this case has not been approved of in a subsequent case in which it is held that certified copies of entries in a register kept by a public servant under a statute are admissible in evidence.[816] However, the privilege given to public record under this section does not extend to entries which the public officer is not expected to, and is not permitted to, make.[817]

To render a document admissible under this section three conditions are necessary:—

(1) the entry that is relied upon must be one in any public or other official book, register or record;

---

813. Subs. by the Act 21 of 2000, section 92 and Sch. II–5, for "record" (w.e.f. 17-10-2000).

814. *Maharaj Bhanudas v Krishnabai,* (1926) 28 Bom LR 1225: 50 Bom 716.

815. *Saraswati Dasi v Dhanpat Singh,* (1882) 9 Cal 431.

816. *Shoshi Bhooshun Bose v Girish Chunder Mitter,* (1893) 20 Cal 940; *Raj Dirgaj Deo v Beni Mahto,* (1917) 20 Bom LR 712 PC. Also see, *Anita v Atal Bihari,* 1993 Cr LJ 549 (MP).

817. *Ali Nasir Khan v Manik Chand,* (1902) 25 All 90 FB.

(2) it must be an entry stating a fact in issue or a relevant fact; and,

(3) it must be made by a public servant in the discharge of his official duty, or by any other person in the performance of a duty specially enjoined by the law.[818]

In a subsequent decision the Supreme Court added one more point to these requirements, namely that "all persons concerned indisputably must have an access to the public record or register."[819]

[s 35.3] "Public or other official book, register or record".—*Age, birth, death.*—Section 74 specifies what public documents are. Statements in public documents are receivable to prove the facts stated on the general grounds that they were made by the authorised agents of the public in the course of official duty and respecting facts which were of public interest or required to be recorded for the benefit of the community.[820] A register of births and deaths kept by village officials under the orders of a Board of Revenue is a public document within the meaning of this section, and an entry in such register recording the death of a person is evidence of the actual date of his death.[821] In a case of alleged kidnapping, birth register extract from the Municipality was held to be a valuable piece of evidence as regards the age of the victim.[822] Where the victim's date of birth was entered in the birth register but there was no evidence as to who was the author when the entry was made and the copy of the birth entry was obtained after six months of the occurrence, it was held that in these suspicious circumstances, entry of birth cannot be relied upon.[823] Where the employer was retiring an employee on the basis his date of birth unsupported by any document, the date of birth given in school leaving certificate adduced by the employee was relied upon.[824] A birth certificate of a respectable person is not relevant because he is under no statutory duty.[825] A certificate of guardianship is not a public or other official book, register or record within the meaning of this section, and an entry therein relating to the age of the minor is not in itself admissible in evidence to

---

818. *Samar Dasadh v Juggul Kishore Singh,* (1895) 23 Cal. 366. Restated by the Supreme Court in *State of Bihar v Radha Krishna Singh,* AIR 1983 SC 684 : 1984 Cr LJ 613; *State v Kamruddin,* (1956) Nag 282; *Birad Mal Singhvi v Anand Purohit,* AIR 1988 SC 1796 : 1988 Supp SCC 604.

819. *Ravinder Singh Gorkhi v State of UP,* AIR 2006 SC 2157 : (2006) 5 SCC 584.

820. *Ghulam Rasul Khan v Secretary of State,* (1925) 6 Lah 269: 52 IA 201; *Secretary of State v Chimanlal Jamnadas,* (1941) 44 Bom LR 295: (1942) Bom 357; *Barikrao v Crown,* (1943) Nag 358; *Chitru Devi v Ram Dei,* AIR 2002 HP 59, entry in Birth and Death Register maintained under Birth and Death Registration Act, 1969, by competent authority showing birth of a male child, admissible to prove parentage and date of birth. Voters' list was also held to be admissible for the same purpose. Such list is prepared by competent officers in Election Deptt. in discharge of their official duty. See generally, *Bishnudas Behera v State,* 1997 Cr LJ 2207 (Ori).

821. *Ramalinga Reddi v Kotayya,* (1917) 41 Mad 26.

822. *Goverdhan v State of MP,* 1995 Cr LJ 632 (MP). *Kanji Bibi v Md. Siddique,* 1996 AIHC 3912 (Cal) entry in birth register, supported by other evidence, not to be ignored. *Fulmatia v Sub Divisional Officer,* AIR 2008 NOC 1136 (All), entry of birth or death in the *Parivar* register is not conclusive proof, it is merely a piece of evidence.

823. *State of HP v Dharam Dass,* 1992 Cr LJ 1758 (HP).

824. *Mahendra Prasad Singh v State of Bihar,* AIR 1995 Pat 162.

825. *Raj Rani v Chief Settlement Commr.,* AIR 1984 SC 1236 : (1984) 3 SCC 619. See, further, *Raj Rani v Chief Settlement Commr, Delhi,* AIR 1984 SC 1234, where a certificate of death authenticated by certain respectable persons of the locality where the accused resided was held to be not relevant. They were neither under a duty to prepare a public record, nor they testified to the place of death from personal knowledge.

prove the age.[826] An entry in a School Admission Register with regard to the age of a pupil is admissible in evidence to prove the age of the person concerned.[827] Where for the proof of age, school leaving certificate was produced but in the said certificate the name of the original school from which the student was transferred was not mentioned, it was held that such school certificate could not be relied upon for proving the age of the accused.[828] The Supreme Court observed that the admissibility of an evidence and its probative value are two different things. An entry in a school leaving certificate would have to be proved in the same manner as required in civil and criminal matters.[829] For the purposes of the Juvenile Justice Act, 2000, the age of the accused as shown by school admission register which was corroborated by medical opinion was given effect to.[830] Entry in school register has evidentiary value, though it may not be conclusive. The entry was supported by the parents. The court said that the father's statement as to her age should not have been rejected.[831] To determine the age of a person, in the first place, what will have to be seen is the primary document such as a birth certificate or a school admission register. That will be credible evidence. For in law, there is presumption about the correctness of those documents, unless rebutted. It was held that it was a manifest error to rely merely on the medical certificate.[832] Where an employee failed to mention the alleged correct date of birth in the option forms and while filing the provident fund withdrawal form and made representation for correction three decades after joining the service, he was not entitled to relief due to unexplained and inordinate delay in making representation and the proof adduced being also unreliable.[833] Entertainment by High Courts of writ applications made by employees of Government or its instrumentalities for correction of date of birth at the fag end of their services has been viewed as unwarranted.[834] A Matriculation certificate is also admissible in evidence.[835] An entry made by a teacher in a private school in his admission register or transfer certificate cannot come within the scope of this section.[836] The Rangoon High Court held that if the school is not a Government School such entry

826. *Said-un-nissa Bibi v Ruqaiya Bibi,* (1930) 53 All 428; *Manikrao v Deorao,* (1954) Nag 709. But, see **Contra**, *Rajkumar v Vijaya Kumar,* AIR 1969 All 162.

827. *Manikchand v Krishna,* (1931) 28 NLR 127; *Mohd. Ikram Hussain v State of UP,* AIR 1964 SC 1625 : 1964(2) Cr LJ 590; *Bhim Mandal v Magaram,* AIR 1961 Pat 21; *Sahib Singh v State,* 1991 Cr LJ 687 (Del), medical evidence and primary school certificate, sufficient evidence of age.

828. *Jagtar Singh v State of Punjab,* AIR 1993 SC 2448 : 1993 Cr LJ 2886 : 1994 Supp (1) SCC 65. *Kedar Nath Singh v State,* 1995 Cr LJ 4121 (Del), evidence from school admission register accepted for proving age of the victim of rape. *Raghunath Behera v Balaram Behera,* AIR 1996 Ori 38, relying on *L Debi Prasad (dead) by LRs. v Smt. Tribeni Devi,* AIR 1970 SC 1286 : (1970) 1 SCC 677. Entry in admission register is a very important piece of evidence.

829. *Madan Mohan Singh v Rajni Kant,* AIR 2010 SC 2933 : (2010) 9 SCC 209. Birth certificate preferred to school leaving certificate, *Iswarlal Mohanlal Thakkar v Paschim Gujarat Vij Co Ltd,* (2014) 6 SCC 434 (para 19) : 2014 (5) Scale 285. See also *Satish Kumar Jayanti Lal Dabgar v State of Gujarat,* (2015) 7 SCC 359, para 11 : 2015 (5) SCJ 135.

830. *Ram Suresh Singh v Prabhat Singh,* AIR 2009 SC 2005 : (2009) 4 SCC 504. Date of birth shown in school certificate accepted as correct to disentitle candidate to contest election, *Dimpal v Rajesh Baluni,* AIR 2016 Uttr 17, para 9 : 2016 132 RD 47.

831. *State of Chhatisgarh v Lekhram,* AIR 2006 SC 1746 : (2006) 5 SCC 736, rape case.

832. *Neeta Jain v State of MP,* AIR 2016 MP 81, paras 7 and 8.

833. *UOI v Kantilal Hematram Pandya,* AIR 1995 SC 1349 : 1995 (3) SCC 17, following *UOI v Harnam Singh,* (1993) 2 SCC 162 : 1993 AIR SCW 1241 : AIR 1993 SC 1367.

834. *Burn Standard Co Ltd v Dinabandhu Majumdar,* AIR 1995 SC 1499 : 1995(4) SCC 172, overruling *Pramath Nath Choudhury v State of West Bengal,* (1981) 1 Serv LR 570 (Cal).

835. *Vaidyanath v Rambadan,* AIR 1966 Pat 383.

836. *Rajappan,* (1960) Kerala 481.

has but little probative value.[837] Thus in a service matter the Supreme Court held that in the absence of the material on the basis of which the school register was prepared, the entry in it as to the age of the person in question was not of much evidentiary value.[838] Where the mother who is otherwise the best person to testify to her child's age, failed to tell her son's date of birth and the elder brother said that the entry in the school register was not correct, the court said that it would be very difficult to accept age of minority on the basis of such school certificate.[839]

It has been held that an entry in the voter's list carries more evidentiary value than an entry in a school admission register.[840] There is a presumption that age certified by the High School Certificate is correct. The burden lies on the other side to prove it to be otherwise.[841] Where the age of prosecutrix had to be determined in a charge of rape and the age shown in the school register was different from that shown in birth register, the court rejected the contention that both entries should be discarded. The birth entry in the High School Certificate or school record was held to prevail being the conclusive evidence.[842] The court had to determine age for the purposes of Juvenile Justice Act, 2000. The court said that medical board's opinion based on radiological examination is a useful guiding factor. But the opinion is not *per se* a conclusive proof of age. The matriculation certificate was not filed. The entry in the voters' list could not be taken mechanically. Its probative value has to be examined. The medical board's reports showed the age to be 17-18 years. No member of the board was examined. The Juvenile Board on the basis of physical appearance placed him to be of 18 years. The court did not approve it and set aside the order based on such determination of age.[843]

Where the doctor certified the age of the accused to be admittedly more than 20 years and less than 25, the court said that the statement of the doctor was no more than an opinion. The court has to base its conclusions upon all the facts and circumstances disclosed on the examination of the physical features of the person whose age is in question in conjunction with such oral testimony as may be available. An X-ray ossification test may provide a surer basis for determination of age than the opinion of a medical expert but it can by no means be so infallible and accurate test as to indicate the exact date of birth of the person concerned. Too much reliance cannot be placed upon text books on medical jurisprudence and toxicology while determining the age

---

837. *Hoak Saing v Moung E Hla*, (1940) Ran 481.

838. *Birad Mal Singhvi v Anand Purohit*, AIR 1988 SC 1796 : 1988 Supp SCC 604. In a rape case, the father of the prosecutrix made an admission that she was the eldest of his three children and his son had completed 18 years, the school certificate showing her minor was held to be suspicious and unreliable, *Annakodi v State*, 1995 Cr LJ 3387 (Mad).

839. *Shubhendra Nath Bakshi v Sekhar nath Bakshi*, AIR 2007 NOC 1714 (Cal—DB).

840. *Nazir Hossain Halder v State*, 1998 Cr LJ 1720 (Cal).

841. *Mayank Rajput v State*, 1998 Cr LJ 2979 (All). *Sumitra Bai v State of MP*, 1999 Cr LJ 2541 (MP), entry in school register regarding age of child is a relevant and admissible piece of evidence. The girl in question was induced and taken away by the accused.

842. *Mohandas Suryavanshi v State of MP*, 1999 Cr LJ 3451.

843. *Babloo Pasi v State of Jharkhand*, AIR 2009 SC 314 : (2008) 13 SCC 133; *Ravinder Singh Gorkhi v State of UP*, AIR 2006 SC 2157 : (2006) 5 SCC 584 : (2006) 4 All LJ 269 : 2006 Cr LJ 2791, school certificate for proving age of the accused, copy of the certificate 26 years after he left school, head-master had no personal knowledge, there was no register of the school was produced, not accept in proof of age. The standard of proof under the section in civil and criminal cases same, not different. Entry should be authentic in nature. It should not be of mechanical nature so as to be merely a piece of evidence.

of an accused person. In this vast country with varied latitude, heights, environments, vegetation and nutrition, the height and weight cannot be expected to be uniform.[844]

Entry in a municipal register of deaths[845] or Land Record Register[846] is admissible. Entries in village crime notebook are admissible in evidence.[847] The register of births and deaths is a public document. Though it can be admitted into evidence without formal report, entry in it must be proved. No presumption as to correctness could be drawn.[848] A statement in a decree that a certain pedigree was filed by the parties thereto, and reciting the full pedigree, is admissible.[849] An Indian Court's written judgment and decree are public records within the meaning of this section. Official record evidencing public affairs like the Gazetteer is admissible in evidence. Statements contained in it can be taken into account to discover historical material. Facts stated are evidence under section 45.[850] Letters forming part of a chain of correspondence and official record were tendered in evidence without objection from the opposite party, documents were taken to be proved and their contents could be read in evidence.[851]

[s 35.4] Correction of age.—The petitioner claimed that the entry of his age in the school record was wrong. He produced the hospital and municipal records to show his correct date of birth. The school authorities corrected the age accordingly. The correction of the age by the Board of Education was nothing but removal of a typographical error. A mandamus was issued to the CBSE to issue a new certificate with corrected age.[852]

[s 35.5] Revenue Record.—Entries in revenue record as to possession are presumed to be true. A finding of fact without taking them into account can be interfered with.[853]

---

844. *Ram Deo Chauhan v State of Assam,* 2001 Cr LJ 2902 : AIR 2001 SC 2230 at pp 2919-2920 : *Dhobedhar Naik v State,* 2002 Cr LJ 113 (Ori) : (2001) 1 Ori LR 122, birth register is a conclusive evidence, but in its absence, the court has to base its decision upon physical features and other oral evidence, ossification test invariably needs to be carried out whenever possible and it is a sure test for ascertaining age.

845. *Anis-ul-Rehman Khan v Beni Ram,* (1901) PR No. 59 of 1901 (Civil).

846. *Po Gaung v Ma Shwe Bwin,* (1908) 4 LBR 231; *Gangabai v Fakirgowda,* (1929) 57 IA 61: 32 Bom LR 368: 54 Bom 336; *State of Punjab v Subhash Chander,* AIR 1991 P&H 134, entries in record of right maintained under Punjab Land Revenue Act, 1887 not showing that brick-earth would vest in the State, presumption that it vested in the owner. *Maniyamkandi Kunhiraman v Machil Parambath,* AIR 1998 Ker 24, minor members of a family challenged the alienation of family property. Original copy of the school admission register was produced in proof of age. The evidence of age was held to be proper.

847. *Amdumiyan v Crown,* (1937) Nag 315; *Shrikisan v Jagoba,* (1937) Nag 382.

848. *Ranjan Acharya v Arjun Rout,* AIR 2010 Ori 76.

849. *Collector of Gorakhpur v Ram Sunder,* (1934) 36 Bom LR 867: 61 IA 286: 56 All 468. *Seethapati Rao Dora v Venkanna Dora,* (1922) 45 Mad 332 FB, not correct in view of this decision. *Tara Devi v Sudesh Chaudhary,* AIR 1998 Raj 59, in an election petition, the lower court called upon the elected candidate to prove her age and was also relying upon her school record for proof of age without trying to ascertain its probative value, the court said that it was an error apparent on the face of the award. As to the school record the court said that entries are circumstantial evidence. It is necessary to consider their probative value. A failure to prove that the entry is correct does not increase its evidentiary value.

850. *Pattakal Cheriyakoya v Aliyathammuda B Muthukoya,* AIR 2008 NOC 1421 (Ker—DB).

851. *Food Corpn. of India v Assam State Co-op Marketing & Consumer Federation Ltd,* (2004) 12 SCC 360.

852. *Rajesh Kumar Jain v Secretary, CBSE,* AIR 1999 Delhi 395.

853. *Sant Ram v Faquiroo,* AIR 1985 HP 10; *Gurcharan Singh v Prithi Singh,* AIR 1974 SC 223 :1974 (1) SCC 138; *Avadh Kishore Das v Ram Gopal,* AIR 1979 SC 861 : 1979(4) SCC 790 about Wajibulzar paper, a village admn. paper, *Vishwa Vijay v F Hasan,* AIR 1976 SC 1485 : 1976(3) SCC 642, bogus entries.

But they are not taken to be proof of an ownership or title by themselves.[854] In a case before the Gauhati High Court,[855] there was a suit for a declaration that the property in question dedicated by the Maharani to the deity and that the plaintiff was successor to the line of shebiats. There was no proof of the fact of dedication or of shebiatship. There were only entries in revenue records. It was held that reliance could not be placed on such entries for proof of title. The court further said that by virtue of the provisions of section 101 relating to burden of proof, advantage could not be taken of the weakness of the defendant's title for proving the plaintiff's title.

Explaining the reason why entries in revenue records are not taken to be evidence of ownership, the Supreme Court said:[856] "Entries in revenue records are the paradise of the *Patwari*. The tiller of the soil is rarely concerned with the same. So long as his possession and enjoyment are not interdicted by the due process and course of law, he is least concerned with entries. It is common knowledge in rural India that a *raiyat* always regards the lands he ploughs as his dominion and generally obeys with moral fibre, the commands of the intermediary so long as his possession is not disturbed. Therefore, the creation of records may be a camouflage to defeat the just and legal right or claim and interests of the *riyat,* the tiller of the soil on whom the Act confers title to the land he tills."

An entry in revenue record creates a presumption in favour of the person whose name is entered. Burden lies on the party who challenges the entry to establish by unimpeachable evidence that the entry in question was erroneous. A concurrent finding by courts below that the party challenging the entry had signally failed to lead any credible evidence to destroy the presumption, could not be interfered with.[857] Cultivation register showing cultivation of land by different persons can be proved by producing copies.[858] Entries in the record of rights are presumed to be correct unless it is shown by evidence that they are not correct.[859] *Khasra* is a record of right. Its entries are presumed to be true. The court should not have discarded them on the basis of statements in the plaint.[860] *Khasra* entries do not convey any title. They are relevant for the purposes of paying land revenue and have nothing to do with ownership.[861] Where the details of the manner, mode, time *etc.* of the *Khasra* entry of sub-tenancy

---

854. *Gurunath Manohar Pavaskar v Nagesh Siddappa Navalgund,* AIR 2008 SC 901 : (2007) 13 SCC 565, revenue record is not a document of title, it merely raises a presumption of possession.

855. *RK Madhuryyajit Singh v Takhellamban Abung Singh,* AIR 2001 Gau 181.

856. *Baleshwar Tewari v Sheo Jatan Tewari,* AIR 1997 SC 2889 at p 2094 : (1997) 5 SCC 112.

857. *Anwar Hussain Sheikh v Santi Kumar Mondal,* AIR 1997 Cal 120.

858. *Puran Singh v Ram Lok,* AIR 1983 P&H 162; *Tahzibunissa v SA Rehman,* AIR 1980 Pat 89; *Musa Jena v PC Naik,* AIR 1980 Ori 183, evidence of public records.

859. *Motilal Lakhotia v Mewang Tobgyal Wangehuk Tenzing Namgyal,* AIR 1994 Sikkim 6, following *Prem Chden Bhutiani v Richen Dorjee,* AIR 1986 Sikkim 22 and *Sita Ram v Ramchandra,* AIR 1977 SC 1712 (para 20) : 1977(2) SCC 49. Entries in Bandobast *Missal* and *Khasra* taken to be true, *Jayaprakash v State of Maharashtra,* 1996 AIHC 1328 (Bom).

860. *Shikharchand v DJP Karini Sabha,* AIR 1974 SC 1178 : 1974(1) SCC 675. Such entries have been held to be of very little probative value for the purpose of proving genealogy. *State of Bihar v Radha Krishna Singh,* AIR 1983 SC 684 : 1983(3) SCC 118. *Digambar Adhar Patil v Davram Girdhar Patil,* AIR 1995 SC 1728 : 1995 Supp (2) SCC 428, entries in record of rights regarding factum of partition, a relevant piece of evidence.

861. *Municipal Corp, Gwalior v Puran Singh,* AIR 2014 SC 2665 (para 30) : 2015 (5) SCJ 673.

made by the *Patwari* was not shown and the *Patwari* was not examined to prove that entry, the entry was not admissible.[862]

The dismissal of a suit challenging deletion of a person's name from revenue records has been held to be not an act conferring title on anybody in respect of the property in question.[863]

[s 35.6] Land record.—An entry in Government Land Register of the Cantonment Board that the disputed land area as Mohammadan Graveyard was regarded as conclusive proof of the plaintiff's claim that it was Wakf property. The land in question was declared to be the graveyard of Muslims.[864]

A map prepared by a person, who is dead, in a previous case not *inter partes*, showing the limits of a particular district is not admissible as it cannot be called a public map offered generally for public sale or made under the authority of Government.[865]

Entries made by a police officer in site inspection map and site inspection of a memo of a motor vehicle accident were held to be record made in discharge of his official duties. They were relevant under the section. They were also in the category of public documents.[866]

[s 35.7] Register of marriages, etc.—As far as the entries in the register of births or deaths or marriages are concerned, evidence must be produced to connect the entries with the persons whose births or deaths or marriages have to be established.[867] Entries in Death Register maintained by Gram Panchayat under the Bihar Panchayat Raj Act, 1948 are admissible in proof of a person's date of death.[868] Certified extracts from electoral rolls and the family register of a village, which are public documents, are admissible.[869] The Bombay High Court did not rely upon the extract from the register of marriages maintained by the Gram Panchayat without the informant or Gram Sewak being produced.[870]

[s 35.8] Gazette.—The Gazette of The Bombay Presidency, Vol III published in 1879, being official record evidencing public affairs, is admissible under section 35

---

862. *Sitaram v Ram Charan,* AIR 1995 MP 134; *Jattu Ram v Hakam Sing,* (1993) 4 SCC 403, *Jamabandi* entries are not evidence of title. *Major Pakhar Singh Atwal v State of Punjab,* AIR 1995 SC 2185 : 1995 Supp (2) SCC 401, mutation entries, not relevant evidence for the purpose of showing the neighbouring land value for the purposes of acquisition. *Shivraya v Bakkappa,* 1995 Supp. 3 SCC 400. Panchayat register entries could not be exclusively relied on to determine title to land. *Jagdeshwar Ramasahay Ahir v Parmeshwar Ramprasad Yadav,* AIR 2000 MP 223, *Khasra* entries in remarks column, no presumption arises as to rights, possession.

863. *E Parashuraman v V Duraiswamy,* (2006) 1 SCC 658 : AIR 2006 SC 376.

864. *All Muslim Residents at Ranikhet Cantonment v Mathura Nath,* AIR 2008 NOC 182 (Utr).

865. *Kesho Prasad v Bhagjogna Kuer,* (1937) 39 Bom LR 731: 16 Pat 258 (PC).

866. *Rajasthan State Road Transport Cropn. v Nand Kishore,* AIR 2001 Raj 334.

867. *Paryanibai v Bajirao,* (1961) 64 Bom LR 86; *Brij Lal v Board of Revenue,* (1993) 2 SCC 544 : AIR 1994 SC 1128, rejection of school certificate as well as medical certificate in proof of age of majority for purposes of allotment of land was held to be improper. The onus was on the authorities to show that the applicant was misrepresenting his age which they failed to discharge. Their decision was not tenable.

868. *Manni Devi v Ramayan Singh,* AIR 1985 Pat 35. For an entry as to birth in an official record, see, *Harpal Singh v HP,* AIR 1981 HP 361.

869. *Aina Devi v Bachan Singh,* AIR 1980 All 174, at 177.

870. *Baby v Jayant,* AIR 1981 Bom 283.

read with section 81 of the Evidence Act and the court may presume their contents as genuine. The statement therein can be taken into account to discover the historical material contained therein and the facts stated therein are evidence under section 35. Though not conclusive, the court may consider such evidence in conjunction with other evidence.[871] Electoral roll being a public document is admissible in evidence and the person preparing it need not be examined.[872]

[s 35.9] Mutation not evidence of title.—Mutation of names in the revenue record are not evidence of title.[873] Where mutation was done in compliance to the orders of the SDO without placing and proving the said order, the mutation entry could not be relied upon.[874] Mutation of a land in the revenue records does not create or extinguish the title over such land nor it has any presumptive value on the title. It only enables the person in whose favour mutation is ordered to pay the land revenue in question.[875] Entries in revenue records do not create or extinguish title. A widow got the lands mutated in favour of her adopted son. The Supreme Court held that neither the adopted sons acquired any title nor the widow's title in the property was extinguished thereby. Since no title could pass under the alleged mutation gift, the widow's right in the property became enlarged on the coming into force of the Hindu Succession Act, 1956. Alienation made by her by way of gift could not be said to be without authority.[876]

Mutation is not a proof of title. the guiding principle in recording mutation is possession. A suit based on title was held to be not adversely affected by mutation of the suit property in favour of the defendant. The plaintiff's failure to file objections to mutation proceedings was considered to be of no consequence.[877] Where the mutation of water rights from a well was surreptitiously changed behind the back of the owner, the question of raising objections could not arise at all in such circumstances. Such a change could not confer any right even after a long lapse of time.[878]

[s 35.10] Electronic Record.—The scope of the word "record" has been expanded by the Information Technology Act, 2000 by inserted into section 35 the words "electronic records". Thus, paperless material would also be regarded as a record. The material produced before the court would, of course, be in the shape of a paper print out.

---

871. *Bala Shankar Maha Shankar Bhattjee v Charity Commissioner, Gujarat,* AIR 1995 SC 167 . 1995 Supp (1) SCC 485 : (1995) 1 (Cri) LR 711. *Kerala Pattika Jathi Samrekshana Samithy v State of Kerala (FB),* AIR 1995 Ker 337. As an entry of name, date of birth and religion can be corrected on the ground of wrong entry or subsequent changes, Government direction permitting to correct a wrong entry of caste, was valid.

872. *Raghunath Behera v Balaram Behera,* AIR 1996 Ori 38.

873. *Nawalshankar Ishwarlal Dave v State of Gujarat,* AIR 1994 SC 1496 : 1994 Cr LJ 2170, following *Mohinder Singh v State of Punjab,* (1978) 1 SCR 177: AIR 1977 SC 2012 and *Vatticherukuru Village Panchayat v Nori Venkatarama Deekshithulu,* (1991) 2 SCR 531 : 1991 AIR SCW 1303 : 1991 Supp (2) SCC 228.

874. *Akshara Nand v State of HP,* 1996 AIHC 1894 (HP).

875. *Bhimabai Mahadeo Kambekar v Arthur Import and Export Company,* AIR 2019 SC 719; *Balwant Singh v Daular Singh,* AIR 1997 SC 2719.

876. *Balwant Singh v Daular Singh,* AIR 1997 SC 2719 : (1997) 7 SCC 137.

877. *Talat Fitima Hasan v His Highness Nawab Syed Murtaza Ali Khan Sahib Bahadur,* AIR 1997 All 122; *Purshottam Das Tandon v Military Estate Officer,* AIR 2000 All 127, writ court refused to interfere in mutation matters. Mutation of property does not create or extinguish title, nor it has a presumptive value of title.

878. *Bhoguji Bayaji Pokale v Kantilal Baban Gunjawale,* AIR 1998 Bom 114.

[s 35.11] Official Reports.—The reports of public officials made in the discharge of their official duties are admissible under this section with reference to statements therein of relevant facts or facts in issue. But a distinction has to be made between the statements contained therein relating to relevant facts and the opinions expressed therein as to such relevant facts. So far as mere opinions are concerned while they are admissible, the value to be attached to them is comparatively less. No such broad proposition can be laid down that the report of a public official which has been merely submitted to the higher authorities for the latter's information or guidance and which itself does not bear the stamp of finality on it, or a report made in compliance with the order of the higher authorities and submitted to them is not admissible in evidence.[879] BHAGWATI J (later CJ) observed in *Kanwar Lal v Amarnath*:[880] "There can be no doubt that these reports (election meetings) were made by public servants in discharge of their official duty and they were relevant under the first part of section 35, since they contained statements showing what were the public meetings held by the first respondent.[881] It is difficult to see how, barring any observations or notings made by officers by way of comment or opinion, the rest of the reports containing factual bio-data could possibly be regarded as privileged". An official report on Bihar blindings by police prepared at the behest of the State was relevant to the cases arising out of the blindings and, therefore, the State Government was not allowed to keep back the report.[882]

Facts in the communication between the RBI and Capital Issues Controller about the sterling value of a company's assets are relevant without producing the author. But it is generally a weak evidence. On author being produced, it becomes strong. Hearsay rule has no place in reference to public documents.[883]

Entries in the Record of Rights regarding the factum of partition, maintained in the official course of business is a relevant piece of documentary evidence.[884]

In *State of Bihar v Radha Krishna Singh*,[885] the document in question was a report written by a Serishetedar in due discharge of his official duty for ascertaining the actual possession of lands by various landlords. Its recitals and the fact that it was kept in a purely Government department, *viz.*, the Collectorate, from where it was produced before the trial court, clearly and conclusively proved that the report was made by an official *Serishetedar* appointed by a very high governmental authority. Since the report mentioned a number of persons through whom the plaintiffs claimed their title it related to a relevant fact. Thus all the conditions of section 35 were fully satisfied and

---

879. *Maheshwar Naik v Tikayet Sailendra Narayan*, (1949) Cut 312.

880. *Kanwar Lal v Amarnath*, AIR 1975 SC 308 : 1975(3) SCC 804.

881. Citing *PC Purushottama Reddiar v S Perumal*, (1972) 2 SCR 646; AIR 1972 SC 608.

882. *Khatri (IV) v State of Bihar*, AIR 1981 SC 1068 : (1981) 3 SCR 145 : 1981 Cr LJ 597 : (1981) 2 SCC 493 : 1981 Mad LJ (Cri) 456 : (1981) 29 BLJR 425. A report by a Tahsildar on spot inspection has been held to be not a public document. *Radhey v Board of Revenue*, AIR 1990 All 176.

883. *Octavious Steel Co v Endogram Tea Co*, AIR 1980 Cal 83.

884. *Digambar Adhar Patil v Devram Girdhar Patil*, AIR 1995 SC 1728 : 1995 Supp (2) SCC 428. *Pakhar Singh Atwal v State of Punjab*, AIR 1995 SC 2185 : 1995 Supp (2) SCC 401, mutation entries. *Durga Das v Collector*, AIR 1996 SC 2786 : 1996 (5) SCC 618, a person not allowed to claim compensation under the Land Acquisition Act, 1894 merely on the basis of mutation entries. *Sawrni v Inder Kaur*, AIR 1996 SC 2823 : 1996 (6) SCC 223, mere mutation entry in favour of defendant, not sufficient proof of ownership.

885. *State of Bihar v Radha Krishna Singh*, AIR 1983 SC 684 : 1983 (3) SCC 118.

the document was admissible in evidence. However, admissibility of a document and its probative value are two distinct and separate aspects and cannot be combined together. A document may be admissible and yet may not have any probative value. Where a report is given by a responsible officer, which is based on evidence of witnesses and documents and has a statutory flavour in that it is given not merely by an administrative officer but under the authority of a statute, its probative value would indeed be very high so as to be entitled to great weight. The probative value of a document, however ancient it may be, is reduced to the minimum where there is no evidence to disclose the nature of the instructions given to the author of the document tendered in evidence, or the source or knowledge or information on which the report is based or has achieved sufficient notoriety. Though a document may be admissible because its author was no longer alive, much value cannot be attached to it if it contains information which is based on hearsay. In the present case the report had no probative value at all. It did not disclose the source from which the facts or materials mentioned therein were gathered. Nor did it show that the author of the report consulted either contemporary or previous records or entries there in order to satisfy himself regarding the correctness or various statements made pertaining to the genealogy of landlords who were in possession of the lands, as stated in the report. The author of the report had to depend on some unknown persons, who were not even mentioned in the document, to gather his facts. There was no evidence to indicate as to what happened after the author had submitted his report to the Government and whether or not any follow-up action was taken on the basis of his report or it was just filed and kept on the record lying lifeless and mute. There was no evidence to corroborate the recitals in the document by any contemporary or subsequent Government record. No proper verification was made by the author of the report regarding the facts stated in his report from any source and it did not form part of a revenue entry or record which was ever referred to by any Executive, Judicial or statutory authority subsequent to the filing of the report. The report, after it was submitted, was shrouded in mystery and was obliviated until the present suit was filed, when a person from the Collectorate merely produced the document but he had no knowledge about its contents or about its being acted upon. Moreover, even if the document was taken into consideration it, being a report regarding possession of the properties, was not any evidence of title with which the present litigations were mainly concerned. If there was no probative value of the report, it could not be corroborated by any other document which would have to be judged and examined on its own merits.[886] The report prepared by the process server in due discharge of his official duties may safely be admitted in evidence even without examining the process server.[887]

The survey record was prepared after the passing of the decree in the partition suit. The report was held to be subject to the decree passed in the suit. Unless the decree is set aside or declared as a nullity, no one can look into that document purporting to be a partition by ignoring the decree.[888]

[s 35.12] Post-office delivery stamp.—In a case before the Supreme Court the petitioner was selected for admission to MBBS course. A letter dated 19 July 1990 was sent asking him to join by 25 July 1990. The letter reached him on 4 August

886. *State of Bihar v Radha Krishna Singh*, AIR 1983 SC 684 : (1983) 3 SCC 118.
887. *Sawagat Ali Mullick v Sk. Akbar Ali*, AIR 2016 Cal 93, para 16 :(2016) 4 WBLR (Cal) 607.
888. *Marchai Naw Sharma v State of Bihar*, AIR 2007 NOC 335 (Pat—DB).

1990. He could not join in time. He was denied admission. The petitioner produced the letter before the Supreme Court. It was found that the date of delivery was missing and same was filled in hand within the postal seal. Declaring this to be an improper procedure, the court said: "The petitioner would have been well-advised to file envelope in the condition it was received by him and should have produced a certificate from the post office about actual date of delivery. This was not done. The petitioner did not even explain the circumstances in which the dates were supplied later by hand within the postal seal. The places meant for indicating the month appear to have originally contained some marks. He may be right that originally it was not possible to read the date and month but in view of attempt to supply the same in hand without disclosing as to how and in what situation that was done, no reliance could be placed on it."[889]

[s 35.13] Income tax return.—In a motor vehicle accident claim case, to determine the annual income of the claimant, a self-employed person, the income tax return filed by him was relied upon.[890]

[s 35.14] Copy of average sale of land for one year.—The District Judge awarded compensation for the acquired land by relying on the copy of average sale of land for one year, which was proved as per the testimony of the *Patwari* and was prepared by a public official in discharge of his official duty. The said document was admissible under section 35. Besides, no evidence was produced in rebuttal of the same.[891]

[s 36] Relevancy of statements in maps, charts and plans.—Statements of facts in issue or relevant facts, made in published maps or charts generally offered for public sale, or in maps or plans made under the authority of [892][the Central Government or any State Government], as to matters usually represented or stated in such maps, charts or plans, are themselves relevant facts.

COMMENT

This section mentions two kinds of maps or charts, viz., (1) maps or charts generally offered for public sale; (2) maps or plans made under the authority of Government. The admissibility of the first kind of maps rests upon the ground that they contain the result of enquiries made under competent authority concerning matters in which the public are interested. The Supreme Court has held that such private maps offered for public sale though not irrelevant do not get the benefit of presumption of accuracy under section 83 of the Act.[893] The admissibility of the second class rests on the ground that, being made and published under the authority of Government, they must be taken to have been made by, and to be the result of, the study or inquiries of competent persons.

---

889. *Jasbir Singh Dhanda v Dean, Mahatma Gandhi Institute of Medical Sciences,* 1991 Supp (2) SCC 528 : AIR 1991 SC 330.

890. *Sanjay Verma v Haryana Roadways,* (2014) 3 SCC 210 (para 12) : 2014 (4) SCJ 128.

891. *State of HP v. Roshan Lal,* 2015 AIR CC 2174, para 9 (HP).

892. Subs. by the A.O. 1948, for "any Government in British India."

893. *Ram Kishore v UOI,* AIR 1966 SC 644 : 1966 (1) SCR 430.

To render inquisitions, reports, surveys, and other similar documents admissible in evidence as *public documents,* it must appear that they were made so that the public might make use of them and be able to refer to them, for the fact that the public are interested in the documents, and are in a position to challenge or dispute them, if inaccurate invests them with a certain amount of authority.[894]

Neither this section nor section 83 has any application to maps prepared for private purposes, that is, for the purpose of any particular suit or by any Government officer for any special purpose. Thus, a map made by a Deputy Collector for the purpose of the settlement of land forming the silted bed of a river is not one which is admissible in evidence under this section and section 83 of the Act; but it is a map the accuracy of which must be proved before it can be admitted in evidence.[895] But maps printed by Government of different wards of a city are admissible in evidence.[896]

[s 37] Relevancy of statement as to fact of public nature contained in certain Acts or notifications.—When the Court has to form an opinion as to the existence of any fact of a public nature, any statement of it made in a recital contained in any Act of Parliament [897][of the United Kingdom] or in any Central Act, Provincial Act or [898][a State Act] or in a Government notification or notification by the Crown Representative appearing in the Official Gazette or in any printed paper purporting to be the London Gazette or the Government Gazette of any Dominion, colony or possession of His Majesty, is a relevant fact.

[899][***]

COMMENT

Acts of Parliament of the UK or of the Central Government or of Provincial or State Government are admissible in evidence when the court has to form an opinion as to the existence of any fact of a public nature stated therein. Under section 81 the court "shall presume" the genuineness of these documents. These documents, as well as all others of a public nature, are generally admissible in evidence, although their authenticity be not confirmed by the usual test of truth, namely, the swearing, and the cross-examining, of the persons who prepared them. The relevancy factor stated in the section is fortified by the presumption of genuineness created by section 81, but neither provision compels the court to take for granted the truth of the matter stated in the records enumerated in the section. This is so because the court has to find out the relationship between the facts officially and those which are in dispute and also whether the fact in dispute is of public nature. Accordingly, the Supreme Court did not agree

---

894. *Taylor,* 12th Edn, section 1769 A, p 1113. *Rahmat Ulla Khan v Secretary of State for India,* (1913) PR No. 63 of 1913 (Civil).

895. *Kanto Prashad Hazari v Jagat Chandra Dutta,* (1895) 23 Cal 335.

896. *Secretary of State v Chimanlal,* (1941) 44 Bom LR 295: (1942) Bom 357.

897. Ins. by the A.O. 1950.

898. Subs. by Act 3 of 1951 sec. 3 and Sch., for "an Act of the Legislature of Part A State or a Part C State".

899. The last para omitted by Act 10 of 1914, sec. 3 and Sch. II. Earlier it was added by Act 5 of 1899, section 2.

to the proposition that the statement in the Indore State Gazette that some Dhangar families of Mathura in UP had migrated to Maharashtra and settled in Ahmednagar should be taken to create a proof that every Dhangar family residing in Ahmednagar is a migratory family.[900] The court cited a passage from *Phipson on Evidence*[901] to the effect that Government Gazettes...are admissible evidence, (and sometimes conclusive) evidence of the public, but not of the private matters contained therein. K Ramaswamy J surveyed some earlier authorities.[902] "In *Rajah Muttu Ramalinga v Perianayagum*[903] the Judicial Committee, while considering the reliability of a report sent by the District Collector to the Commissioner about the management of a temple, held that when the reports express opinions on the private rights of parties, such opinions are not to be regarded as having judicial authority or force. But being the reports of public officers made in the course of duty, and under statutory authority, they are entitled to great consideration so far as they supply information of official proceedings and historical facts, and also insofar as they are relevant to explain the conduct and acts of the parties in relation to them, and the proceedings of the Government founded on them. Same view was reiterated in *Martand Rao v Malhar Rao*,[904] on the question of reliability of official reports relating to succession to a zamindari. "Their Lordships consider it necessary at the outset to point out that though such official reports are valuable and in many cases the best evidence of facts stated therein, opinions therein expressed should not be treated as conclusive in respect of matters requiring judicial determination, however eminent the authors of such reports may be."[905] In *Arunachalam Chetty v Vekatachala-pathi Guruswamigal*[906] it was held that while their Lordships do not doubt that such a report (Inam register) would not displace actual and authentic evidence in individual cases; yet the Board, when such is not available, cannot fail to attach the utmost importance, as part of the history of the property, to the information set forth in the Inam register. "[907]

[s 38] Relevancy of statements as to any law contained in law-books.—When the Court has to form an opinion as to a law of any country, any statement of such law contained in a book purporting to be printed or published under the authority of the Government of such country and to contain any such law, and any report of a ruling of the Courts of such country contained in a book purporting to be a report of such rulings, is relevant.

---

900. *Vimla Bai v Hiralal Gupta*, (1990) 2 SCC 22 at 27 : 1989 Supp (2) SCR 759. The dispute was about private temples and the same could also not be regarded as a fact of public nature.

901. 510, para 25.07 (13th Ed, Common Law Library).

902. *Supra.*

903. *Rajah Muttu Ramalinga v Perianayagum*, (1873-74) IA 238; 3 Suther 7.

904. *Martand Rao v Malhar Rao*, (1927-28) 55 IA 45 at 48; AIR 1928 PC 10.

905. Italicised by the Supreme Court.

906. *Arunachalam Chetty v Vekatachala-pathi Guruswamigal*, (1919) 46 IA 204; AIR 1919 PC 62

907. **Followed** by the Supreme Court in *Narayan Bhagwantrao Gosavi Balajiwale v Gopal Vinayak Gosavi* (1960) 1 SCR 773, 788; AIR 1960 SC 100; *Poohari Fakir Sadavarthy of Bondilipuram v Commissioner, Hindu Religious and Charitable Endowments*, (1962) Supp 2 SCR 276; AIR 1963 SC 510. Both the cases were on Inam register. *Mahant Shri Srinivasa Ramanuj Das v Surajnarayan Dass*, (1966) Supp SCR 436 at 447: AIR 1967 SC 256, where it was held that the statements in the Gazetteer can be consulted on matters of public history. *VS Nagraja Shetty v MN Krishna*, 1996 AIHC 2904 (Kant), documentary evidence will prevail over oral evidence.

COMMENT

When it is necessary to form an opinion as to the law of any country, statements of such law in a book published under the authority of Government of that country and reports of cases decided by courts of that country and contained in books purporting to be reports of such rulings, are relevant, that is, may be referred to by the court. A statement contained in an unauthorized translation of the Code Napoleon as to what the French law is on a particular matter, is not relevant.[908] Statements in books of law and in law reports are admissible on grounds similar to those stated in sections 35, 36 and 37. The opinion of an expert on foreign law can be received under section 45. Strictly speaking, under this section the report of a case in a newspaper does not appear to be relevant, because a newspaper cannot be regarded as a book purporting to be a report of the rulings of the court.[909]

Production of a copy of a foreign Government Gazette attested as true copy by a seal of the court is not the mode approved by this Act for proving a foreign law and the court cannot take notice of such copy for the purpose.[910]

No court takes judicial notice of the laws of a foreign country, but they must be proved as facts.

HOW MUCH OF A STATEMENT IS TO BE PROVED

[911]**[s 39] What evidence to be given when statement forms part of a conversation, document, electronic record book or series of letters or papers.—When any statement of which evidence is given forms part of a longer statement, or of a conversation or part of an isolated document, or is contained in a document which forms part of a book, or is contained in part of electronic record or of a connected series of letters or papers, evidence shall be given of so much and no more of the statement, conversation, document, electronic record book or series of letters or papers as the Court considers necessary in that particular case to the full understanding of the nature and effect of the statement, and of the circumstances under which it was made.**

COMMENT

[s 39.1] Principle.—When evidence is given of a statement which forms part of (a) a longer statement or (b) a conversation, or (c) an isolated document, or (d) a document contained in a book, or (e) a series of letters of papers, the court has discretion as to how much evidence should be given of the statement, conversation, document, book, or series of letters or papers for the full understanding of the nature and effect of the statement and the circumstances under which it was made. The principle on which this section is based is that it would not be just to take part of a conversation, letter, *etc.*, as evidence against a party without giving to the party at the same time the benefit of the entire residue of what he wrote or said on the same occasion.[912] Thus, the rule enacted in this section will not warrant the reading of distinct entries in an account

---

908. *Christien v Delanney,* (1899) 26 Cal 931.
909. *State v Sardar Bahadur,* AIR 1969 Cal 451.
910. *Raman Lal v Ram Gopal,* (1954) 4 Raj 262.
911. Subs. by Act 21 of 2000, section 92 and Sch. II–6, for section 39 (w.e.f. 17-10-2000).
912. *The Queen's Case,* (1820) 2 Br & B 284, 302.

book, or distinct paragraphs in a newspaper, unconnected with the particular entry or paragraph relied on by the opponent.

Statements made in books about ownership of property were held by the Supreme Court to be something which could not be relied upon unless there were some contemporaneous records showing or supporting the basis for statements in the books.[913]

Amendment.—The section has been totally substituted because of the amendment introduced under the Information Technology Act, 2000. The recasting of the section became necessary because a few new words had to be put into the section, such as "electronic record", "forms part of electronic record."

JUDGMENTS OF COURTS OF JUSTICE, WHEN RELEVANT

[s 40] Previous judgments relevant to bar a second suit or trial.—The existence of any judgment, order or decree which by law prevents any Court from taking cognizance of a suit or holding a trial, is a relevant fact when the question is whether such Court ought to take cognizance of such suit or to hold such trial.

COMMENT

Sections 40 to 43 deal with the subject of relevancy of judgments. Judgments *qua* judgments or adjudications are admissible as *res judicata* under this section and as relating to matters of public nature under section 42. Judgments other than those mentioned in sections 40, 41 and 42 may be relevant under section 43, if their existence is a fact in issue or is relevant under some other provision.

[s 40.1] Principle.—Under this section the existence of a judgment, decree, or order, is a relevant fact, if, by law, it has the effect of preventing any court from taking cognizance of a suit, or holding a trial. It is intended to include all cases in which a general law relating to *res judicata inter partes* applies. The main object of the doctrine of *res judicata* is to prevent multiplicity of suits and interminable disputes between litigants. *Res judicata* means, by its very words, a thing upon which the court has exercised its judicial mind. Section 11 of the Code of Civil Procedure lays down the law as to *res judicata*. A resident in a Council house sued the Council for ill-health caused by disrepair and dampness. Subsequently, her dependent daughter brought an action for her disability on the same facts. The suit was held to be maintainable, the earlier suit being not between the same parties. The court said that she being not a party to the earlier proceedings, the doctrine of *res judicata*, even in its widest sense, had no application. The court restated the general principle to be as follows: The doctrine of *res judicata* in its wider sense, which includes a bar on the subsequent litigation not only of all issues resolved in the earlier proceedings but also of every point which properly belongs to the subject-matter of the litigation, applies only when the cause of action or issue is or remains between the same parties or their predecessors in title and does not extend to those not themselves party to the earlier proceedings. The expression "a

913. *Karnataka Wakf Board v State of Karnataka*, AIR 2003 SC 2467.

party to earlier proceedings" would not include a disabled and dependent child of one of the parties.[914]

Where a proceeding was instituted by a landowner for conversion of his agricultural land and the same was dismissed by a reasoned order which was confirmed by a Division Bench on cogent and convincing reasons thus attaining finality, a writ petition subsequently filed by a legal heir with the same prayer was held to be barred by *res judicata.* The earlier decision was relevant because the same issue was directly and substantially involved in the earlier proceeding.[915]

This section has nothing to do with questions of evidence beyond the admissibility of the judgments, because a plea of *res judicata* is not a plea as a matter of evidence, but only a plea barring the action as a matter of procedure as distinguished from the rules of evidence.[916]

In a judgment *inter partes* in a suit for title, it was held that recitals made in the judgment between the predecessors of the plaintiff and those of the defendant regarding rights in the suit property, were admissible for deciding the title to the property between the plaintiff and the defendant.[917] Referring to authorities the court said:[918] "In *Srinivas Krishnarao Kango v Narayan Devji Kango,*[919]*AYYAR J held that a judgment not inter partes* is admissible in evidence under section 13 of the Evidence Act as evidence of an assertion of a right to property in dispute. A contention that judgments other than those falling under sections 40 to 44 were not admissible in evidence was expressly rejected. In *Sital Das v Santa Ram,*[920] *it was held that a previous judgement not inter partes* was admissible in evidence under section 13 as a transaction in which a right to property was asserted and recognised."

The principle of this section applies to criminal courts as well. The plea of *autrefois convict* or *autrefois acquit,* that is, of a previous lawful conviction or lawful acquittal, has always been held to be a good plea. See section 403, Code of Criminal Procedure.

The judgment of a criminal court that a person did or did not commit an offence, does not operate as *res judicata* to prevent a civil court from determining such questions for purposes of a suit.[921] The judgment of acquittal of a co-accused rendered in an earlier trial arising out of the same transaction was held to be wholly irrelevant in the case of the present accused who was tried separately. It was not admissible under sections 40 to 44. The case of the co-accused leading to his acquittal was decided on the basis of evidence produced in that case whereas the case of the present accused was decided on the basis of evidence adduced in his trial.[922] Similarly, the judgment of a civil court is

---

914. *C (a minor) v Hackney London Borough Council,* (1996) 1 All ER 973 (CA), their Lordships observed that the Judge was not entitled to find that the mother's dependants had a sufficient nexus between them so as to be regarded as effectively the same party. *Shamlata v Vishweshwar Tukaram Giripunje,* AIR 2008 Bom 155 : (2008) 3 Bom CR 166, the defendant in the present suit was not a party to the earlier suit. The judgement in that suit neither fell within the scope of section 40, nor the doctrine of *res judicata* as enshrined in section 11, CPC was attracted.

915. *Udit Gopal Beri v State of Rajasthan,* AIR 2001 Raj 147.

916. *The Collector of Gorakhpur v Palakdhari Singh,* (1889) 12 All, 1 44 FB.

917. *Raman Pillai v Kumaran Parameswaran,* AIR 2000 Ker 133.

918. *Ibid,* at p 143.

919. *Srinivas Krishnarao Kango v Narayan Devji Kango* AIR 1954 SC 379 : (1955) 1 SCR 1.

920. *Sital Das v Santa Ram,* AIR 1954 SC 606 (Bench of 4 Judges).

921. *Ram Lal v Tula Ram,* (1881) 4 All 97. See *Bishen Das v Ram Labhaya,* (1915) PR No. 106 of 1915 (Civil). *Raja Ram Garg v Chhanga Singh,* AIR 1992 All 28, simultaneous criminal and civil proceedings in an accident case, neither to be stayed.

922. *Rajan Rai v State of Bihar,* AIR 2006 SC 433 : (2006) 1 SCC 191 : 2005 Cr LJ 163.

not admissible in a criminal prosecution to prove the innocence of the accused.[923] In a criminal trial, it is for the court to determine the question of the guilt of the accused and it must do this upon the evidence before it, independently of decisions in civil litigation between the same parties. A judgment or a decree is not admissible in evidence in all cases as a matter of course and, generally speaking, a judgment is only admissible to show its date and legal consequences.[924] A judgment of a civil court other than one *in rem* cannot finally decide a matter subsequently dealt with in a criminal court even though the facts in dispute in the civil suit govern the only question that can arise in the criminal proceedings.[925] To hold that when a party has been able to satisfy a civil court as to the justice of his claim and has in the result succeeded in obtaining a decree which is final and binding upon the parties, it would not be open to criminal courts to go behind the findings of the civil courts, is to place the civil court, without any valid reason, in a much higher position than what it actually occupies in the system of administration in this country and to make it the master not only of cases which it is called upon to adjudicate but also of cases which it is not called upon to determine and over which it has really no control.[926]

Where a civil suit for compensation was filed and at the same time criminal proceedings were also instituted on the same cause of action and the civil suit was dismissed, it was held that criminal proceedings were not required to be dropped for that reason alone.[927]

It is a well-recognised principle of law that a conviction in a criminal case is no evidence of the facts on which that conviction was based in a civil case in which those facts are in issue or form the subject-matter of the suit. But the authorities are clear that, when the conviction is based on a plea of guilty, that plea is relevant and to prove in the judgment in the criminal case is admissible in evidence in the subsequent civil suit in which the facts giving rise to the charge are in issue or form the subject-matter of the suit.[928] A judgment *in personam* which is not *inter partes* has been held to be not admissible in evidence.[929]

[s 41] Relevancy of certain judgments in probate, etc., jurisdiction.—A final judgment, order or decree of a competent Court,[s 41.2] **in the exercise of probate, matrimonial, admiralty or insolvency jurisdiction, which confers upon or takes away from any person any legal character, or which declares any person to be entitled to any such character, or to be entitled to any specific thing, not as against any specified**

---

923. *Ramanamma v Appalanarasayya,* (1931) 55 Mad 346. In Bombay a judgment of a civil court dismissing a suit to recover moneys was held relevant in a prosecution for criminal breach of trust for some of the items covered by the civil suit : *Markur,* (1914) 41 Bom 1: 18 Bom LR 185. *Narayanan v Mathan Mathai,* AIR 1982 Ker 239. *Nawab Deen v Sohan Singh,* AIR 2002 HP 143, a finding of fact recorded by a criminal court, is not relevant in a suit before civil court except for the purpose of showing whether the accused was acquitted or convicted. The civil court has to reach its own conclusions as to commission or non-commission of the act in question which gave rise to the claim put forth in the suit.

924. *Trailokyanath Das v Emperor,* (1931) 59 Cal 136.

925. *Maung Po Nwe v Ma Pwa Chone,* (1940) Ran. 163.

926. *BN Kashyap v The Crown,* (1944) 25 Lah 408 FB : AIR 1945 Lah 231 : 1945 Cr LJ 296.

927. *KG Premshankar v Inspector of Police,* 2002 Cr LJ 4343 : AIR 2002 SC 372.

928. *B Meenakshisundaram Cheety v Kuttimalu,* (1958) Ker 39.

929. *Nagarathnamma v Halamma,* AIR 2010 NOC 1084 (Kar).

person but absolutely, is relevant when the existence of any such legal character, or the title of any such person to any such thing, is relevant.

Such judgment, order or decree is conclusive proof—

that any legal character, to which it confers accrued at the time when such judgment, order or decree came into operation;

that any legal character, to which it declares any such person to be entitled, accrued to that person at the time when such judgment, order or decree declares it to have accrued to that person;

that any legal character which it takes away from any such person ceased at the time from which such judgment, order or decree declared that it had ceased or should cease;

and that anything to which it declares any person to be so entitled was the property of that person at the time from which such judgment, [930][order or decree] declares that it had been or should be his property.

SYNOPSIS

COMMENT

[s 41.1] Judgments *in rem*.—This section consists of two parts. The first part makes the final judgment, order or decree of a competent court in the exercise of probate, matrimonial, admiralty or insolvency jurisdiction relevant; the second part makes the judgments conclusive proof in certain matters.

The section deals with what are usually called judgments *in rem*, i.e. judgments which are conclusive not only against the parties to them but also against all the world. "A judgment *in rem* has been defined to be "an adjudication pronounced, as its name indeed denotes, upon the *status* of some particular subject-matter, by a tribunal having competent authority for that purpose" [931] "This rule appears to rest, partly, upon the ground that...every one who can possibly be affected by the decision is entitled, if he thinks fit, to appear and assert his own rights, by becoming an actual party to the proceedings; partly, upon the ground that judgments *in rem* not merely declare the *status* of the subject-matter adjudicated upon, but, *ipso facto*, render it such as they declare it to be; and, partly, if not principally, upon the broad ground of public policy, it being essential to the peace of society, that the social relations of every member of the community should not be left doubtful, but that, after having been clearly defined by one solemn adjudication, they should conclusively be set at rest".[932] The judgments referred to under section 41 are known as judgments *in rem,* binding the whole world.

---

930. Ins. by Act 18 of 1872, section 3.
931. *Taylor*, 12th Edn, section 1674, p 1050.
932. *Taylor*, 12th Edn, section 1676, p 1054.

But the judgment of that kind must have done something positive, onwards. This provision is indicative of the quality of matrimonial jurisdiction.[933]

Intention in judgment *in rem* may be to give benefit to all similarly situated persons, whether they approached the court or not. With such a pronouncement the obligation is cast upon the authorities to itself extend the benefit thereof to all similarly situated persons. Such a situation can occur when the subject-matter of the decision touches upon the policy matters, like scheme of regularisation and the like.[934]

A judgment *in rem* can only be impeached if it can be shown—

(1) that the court has no jurisdiction; or

(2) that the judgment was obtained by fraud or collusion; or

(3) that it was not given on the merits; or

(4) that it was not final, e.g., interlocutory.

There is no distinction between a judgment *in rem* and a judgment *in personam*, excepting that in the one the point adjudicated upon, which is always as to the status of the *res*, is conclusive against all the world as to that status, whereas in the other the point is only conclusive between parties and privies. The term "privy" means a partaker who is not a party.[935] A judgment in *personam* is the ordinary judgment between parties in cases of contract, tort, or crime. It is no proof of the truth either of the decision or of its grounds as between strangers, or a party and a stranger.

If the judgment of the court is *in personam* and states expressly its intention or it can be impliedly found out from the tenor and language of the judgment that the benefit of the said judgment shall accrue only to the parties before the court, then those who want to get the benefit of the said judgment extended to them, shall have to satisfy that their petition does not suffer from *laches* and delay or acquiescence.[936]

Once a judgment falls within the section law dispenses with the proof of the legal character which it confers or declares together with the declarations of property arising from that legal character.[937] A judgment *in rem* is conclusive only as regards status but not as regards the ground on which it is based.[938]

Under this section a judgment, order or decree, given by a competent court in the exercise of (1) probate, (2) matrimonial, (3) admiralty, or (4) insolvency jurisdiction, will be conclusive proof as to the legal character conferred on, or taken away from, any person or to which any person is declared to be entitled.

[s 41.2] "Competent Court".—The word "Court" is not limited to courts in India. The expression "competent Court" means the court of any country which is competent to pass such judgment as is referred to in this section, that is to say, a judgment *in*

---

933. *Chand Dhawan v Jawaharlal Dhawan,* (1993) 3 SCC 406, 416 : 1993 SCC (Cri) 915 : 1993 Cr LJ 2930.

934. *State of UP v Arvind Kumar Srivastava,* (2015) 1 SCC 347 (para 22.3) :(2015)1SCC347.

935. *Ashan Hussain v Maina,* (1938) Nag 431.

936. *State of UP v Arvind Kumar Srivastava,* (2015) 1 SCC 347 (para 22.3) :(2015)1SCC347.

937. *Viswanathan v Abdul Wajid,* AIR 1963 SC 1.

938. *DG Sahasrabudhe v Kilachand Deochand& Co,* (1947) Nag 85.

rem.[939] No court can pronounce a judgment *in rem* binding outside the State in which the court exercises jurisdiction unless such judgment affects either a thing situate, or a person domiciled, within such State. Thus it was held that a judgment of the Supreme Court of His Britannic Majesty at Alexandria as to the validity or otherwise of a will made by a person domiciled at Aden would be binding on the parties so far as the properties in Egypt are concerned; but it had no effect as a judgment *in rem* in respect of assets outside Egypt.[940] A person married in India and had two children from the marriage. He went abroad for his studies but settled there. Five years after that his wife filed a suit for maintenance. He cited in defence, a divorce decree of the court of the place where he was in service. The Supreme Court following its own decision in *R Viswanathan v Ruk-ul-Mulk Syed Abdul Majid*[941] held that a judgment of a foreign court to be conclusive must be by a competent court, as contemplated by section 13, IPC, in an international sense and not merely by the law of the foreign State. Such judgments can be challenged on the ground of fraud.[942] An Indian couple had gone to Brazil where they obtained judicial separation from a competent court by mutual consent. On returning to India, they prayed for confirmation of their consensual divorce and the same was granted as the grounds of divorce were not opposed to public policy in India and the judgment was pronounced by the court of competent jurisdiction. It was held that presumptions as to the conclusiveness of the judgment were available to the parties.[943]

[s 41.2.1] Probate jurisdiction.—The grant of probate under the Indian Succession Act (XXXIX of 1925) is conclusive proof of the title of executors and of the genuineness of the will admitted to probate. The conclusiveness of the probate rests upon the declared will of the Legislature as expressed in sections 227 and 273 of the Indian Succession Act, 1925. The grant of probate is the method which the law specially provides for establishing a will.

The section is not applicable to the judgment of the Probate Court refusing probate.[944] A judgment of a Court of Probate is conclusive proof that the person to whom letters or probate have been granted has been clothed with the powers and the responsibilities of the deceased and of nothing else and a question of status decided by a Court of Probate can be raised again.[945]

[s 41.2.2] Matrimonial jurisdiction.—This jurisdiction is conferred on courts by the following Acts:—

(a) The Indian Divorce Act (IV of 1869) relating to the divorce of persons professing the Christian religion.

(b) The Parsi Marriage and Divorce Act (III of 1936) relating to marriage and divorce among the Parsis.

(c) The Native Converts' Marriage Dissolution Act (XXI of 1866).

---

939. *Messa v Messa,* (1938) 40 Bom LR 571: (1938) Bom 529.

940. *Messa v Messa, ibid.*

941. *R Viswanathan v Ruk-ul-Mulk Syed Abdul Majid* (1963) 3 SCR 22, 42: AIR 1963 SC 1, 14

942. *Satya v Teja Singh,* AIR 1975 SC 105 : 1975 Cr LJ 52.

943. *Roy Andre Sales de Andrade v State of Goa,* 1996 AIHC 99 (Bom).

944. *Kalyanchand v Sitabai,* (1913) 16 Bom LR 5 : 38 Bom 309 FB.

945. *Mi Ngwe Zan v Mi Shwe Taik,* (1910) 1 UBR (1910-13) 61, 63; *Mali Muthu Servay v King Emperor,* (1926) 4 Ran 251.

(d) The Indian Christian Marriage Act (XV of 1872).

(e) The Dissolution of Muslim Marriages Act, 1939.

(f) The Special Marriage Act, 1954.

(g) The Hindu Marriage Act, 1955.

A judgment of a Matrimonial Court, decreeing divorce or nullity of marriage is binding as to the status of the parties concerned. It is conclusive upon all persons that the parties have been divorced and that they are no longer husband and wife. But a judgment in a suit for restitution of conjugal rights is in a purely private suit between two persons, and such a judgment is not a judgment *in rem* within the meaning of this section.[946]

Execution proceedings were launched for realisation of maintenance. An order was passed attaching the husband's movable property. His mother objected. The judgment was held to be a judgment *in rem* binding on the whole world. But the attachment could be challenged only by the party and not by the husband's mother.[947]

[s 41.2.3] Admiralty jurisdiction.—Admiralty jurisdiction is conferred on several High Courts by Letters Patent. It was also conferred on mofussil courts by 12 & 13 Vic. c. 88. The decision of a Prize Court is conclusive upon all the world. A judgment delivered in an ordinary suit in an Admiralty Court is not a judgment *in rem* binding strangers. Explaining the effect and purpose of this jurisdiction the Bombay High Court stated as follows:[948]

"It is further to be seen here that section 51 of the Merchant Shipping Act, 1958 makes a specific provision for recovery of the mortgage money by the mortgagee by sale of the vessel, which is mortgaged. Perusal of the provisions in Part III of the Rules and Forms of the High Court of Judicature at Bombay on the Original Side, shows that when a person has a claim against a vessel, he can bring in an action *in rem* and there is a special and effective procedure provided for recovering the claim of the person in such a suit. It is further to be seen here that the rules provide a special procedure for sale of a ship or vessel pursuant to its arrest. It provides for determination of various claims that may be lodged against the vessel and distribution of the sale proceeds amount the claimants, with the result any person who buys a vessel sold in the admiralty jurisdiction gets a clear title and he gets the vessel free from all encumbrances. By virtue of the provisions of section 41 of the Evidence Act, the sale certificate issued by this court in favour of the purchaser is a conclusive proof of his title to the ship and any person who may have a claim against that vessel cannot make any claim against the purchaser or the vessel in his hand. On the contrary, when a vessel would be sold in execution of a certificate issued by the DRT [Debt Recovery Tribunal] the sale certificate issued by DRT may not confer a clear title on the purchaser. It is further to be seen that in admiralty jurisdiction, the plaintiff can proceed against the vessel itself and can get the vessel arrested in the first instance and the court can proceed to sell the vessel after its arrest immediately unless within a stipulated time, the owner appears and furnishes

946. *Ma Po Khin v Ma Shin,* (1933) 11 Ran 198.

947. *Hemalata Sahu v Sugyani Sahu*, AIR 2010 Ori 35 (DB) : 2009 (Supp) Ori LR 1117. The fact of marriage and the right to maintenance whether valid or not, was not to be examined in the execution proceedings.

948. *ICICI Ltd v MFV Shilpa,* AIR 2002 Bom 371 at p 381.

security and gets the vessel released. Thus, in admiralty jurisdiction, the claim of the plaintiff is secured firstly by arrest of the ship and secondly, when the ship is released from arrest by the security furnished. Thus, the procedure that is followed by this court in its admiralty jurisdiction is efficacious and effective procedure than the procedure provided by the DRT Act. It is clear from the preamble of that Act that Act has been enacted for providing speedy recovery of the claims of banks and financial institutions. Thus, it cannot be said that in enacting the DRT Act, it was the intention of the Legislature to deprive banks and financial institutions of an existing more effective and efficacious remedy. Therefore, requiring banks and financial institutions to go to the DRT for recovering of their claims against the vessels would defeat the purpose for which the DRT Act has been enacted and, therefore, it cannot be said that the suit of the plaintiffs is not maintainable."

An order in an admiralty suit emphatically stated that all the authorities concerned would be bound by the order. The order being an order *in rem,* the court said that a finding in such an order was conclusive against the whole world. Disputes in such a suit could not be referred to arbitration by invoking the arbitration clause in the insurance cover of the vessel in question.[949]

[s 41.3] CASES

The executors named in a will, executed in the mofussil, applied for probate of the will. The court refused probate on the ground that the testator was not of a sound disposing mind at the time of execution. The testator's widow filed a regular suit against the defendants, as executors *de son tort,* to recover possession of the testator's property. The defendants again set up the will and claimed to be invested under it with all the legal character of executors. It was held that this section was not applicable to the judgment of the Probate Court, for the finding of the court that an attempted proof had failed was not a judgment such as was contemplated in this section. The only kind of negative judgment which was contemplated was that which expressly took away from a person the legal character which had up to that time subsisted.[950] In order to attract section 41 it is necessary that the judgment should have been pronounced. The mere pendency of proceedings whether civil or criminal is not sufficient in itself to enable anyone to seek the benefit of the section.[951]

[s 41.3.1] Judgment based on compromise.—A previous judgment passed on a compromise is not a judgment *in rem* within the meaning of this section and is therefore no bar to a subsequent suit.[952]

[s 42] Relevancy and effect of judgments, orders or decrees, other than those mentioned in section 41.—Judgments, orders or decrees other than those mentioned in section 41 are relevant if they relate to matters of a public nature relevant to the enquiry; but such judgments, orders or decrees are not conclusive proof of that which they state.

---

949. *Osprey Underwriting Agencies Ltd v Oil & National Gas Corporation Ltd,* AIR 1999 Bom 173.

950. *Kalyanchand v Sitabai,* (1913) 16 Bom LR 5 : 38 Bom 309 FB

951. *Syed Askari Hadi Ali Augustine Imam v State (Delhi Admn),* AIR 2009 SC 3232 : (2009) 5 SCC 528.

952. *Rahmat Ali Khan (Pir) v Musammat Babu Zuhra,* (1911) PR No. 14 of 1912 (Civil).

ILLUSTRATION

A sues *B* for trespass on his land. *B* alleges the existence of a public right of way over the land, which *A* denies.

The existence of a decree in favour of the defendant, in a suit by *A* against *C* for a trespass on the same land, in which *C* alleged the existence of the same right of way, is relevant, but it is not conclusive proof that the right of way exists.

COMMENT

[s 42.1] Principle.—Under this section judgments relating to matters of a public nature are declared relevant, whether between the same parties or not. It also forms an exception to the general rule that no one shall be affected or prejudiced by judgments to which he is not a party or privy. The exception just stated is allowed in favour of verdicts, judgments, and other adjudications upon subjects of a *public nature*, such as customs, prescriptions, tolls, boundaries between parishes, counties, or manors, rights of ferry, liabilities to repair roads, or sea-walls, moduses, and the like. In all cases of this nature, as evidence of reputation will be admissible, adjudications—which for this purpose are regarded as a species of reputation—will also be received, and this, too, whether the parties in the second suit be those who litigated the first, or be utter strangers. The effect, however, of the adjudication, when admitted, will so far vary that, if the parties be the same in both suits, they will be bound by the previous judgment but, if the litigants in the second suit be strangers to the parties in the first, the judgment, though admissible, will not be conclusive.[953] Under this section the decrees of competent courts are good evidence in matters of public interest, such as the existence of a custom of succession in a particular community,[954] or of a custom under which a tenure is held.[955] An appointment to a post in a temple has been held to be a matter of public importance. A suit was filed for recovery of *math* property by the *Padadayya* (*Mathadhipati*) by virtue of his appointment as successor. There was a claim that some other person had been appointed and installed and that appointment was found to be valid by the Privy Council in an earlier litigation initiated by another person. It was held by the Supreme Court that the judgement of the Privy Council did not have the effect of *res judicata*. It was not binding on the appellant in the present case but it was relevant under section 42.[956] A judgment in a criminal case is not a matter of a public nature and is not admissible in evidence in civil proceedings under this section.[957] A Coroner's inquisition is not relevant under any of the provisions of this Act and is, therefore, inadmissible in evidence. It is not a judgment, nor can it be treated as an opinion.[958]

Section 40 admits as evidence all judgments *inter partes* which would operate as *res judicata* in a second suit. Section 41 admits judgments *in rem* as evidence in all subsequent suits where the existence of the right is in issue, whether between the same parties or not. And this section admits all judgments not as *res judicata*, but as evidence,

---

953. *Taylor*, 12th Edn, section 1683, p 1058.
954. *Bai Baiji v Bai Santok*, (1894) 20 Bom 53.
955. *Dalglish v Guzuffer Hassain*, (1896) 23 Cal 427.
956. *Virupakshayya Shankarayya v Neelakanta Shivacharaya Pattadadevaru*, AIR 1995 SC 2187.
957. *Bishen Das v Ram Labhaya*, (1915) PR No. 106 of 1915 (Civil).
958. *Emperor v Bhagwandas Tulsidas (No. 2)*, (1945) 47 Bom LR 997.

although they may not be between the same parties, provided they relate to matters of public nature relevant to the enquiry.[959]

Whether judgments, orders or decrees of a court are transactions within the meaning of section 13 has been much disputed. A court adjudication is obviously not a transaction, and that part of the written judgment which describes the litigation may be admissible to prove the transaction under section 35.

[s 43] Judgments, etc., other than those mentioned in sections 40 to 42, when relevant.—Judgments, orders or decrees, other than those mentioned in sections 40, 41 and 42, are irrelevant, unless the existence of such judgment, order or decree is a fact in issue or is relevant under some other provision of this Act.[s 43.4]

ILLUSTRATIONS

(a) *A* and *B* separately sue *C* for a libel which reflects upon each of them. *C* in each case says that the matter alleged to be libellous is true, and the circumstances are such that it is probably true in each case, or in neither.

A obtains a decree against *C* for damages on the ground that *C* failed to make out his justification. The fact is irrelevant as between *B* and *C*.

(b)*A* prosecutes *B* for adultery with *C*, *A*'s wife.

B denies that *C* is *A*'s wife, but the Court convicts *B* of adultery.

Afterwards, *C* is prosecuted for the bigamy in marrying *B* during *A*'s life-time. *C* says that she never was *A*'s wife.

The judgment against *B* is irrelevant as against *C*.

(c) *A* prosecutes *B* for stealing a cow from him. *B* is convicted.

A afterwards sues *C* for the cow, which *B* had sold to him before his conviction. As between *A* and *C*, the judgment against *B* is irrelevant.

(d) *A* has obtained a decree for the possession of land against *B*. *C*, *B*'s son, murders *A* in consequence.

The existence of the judgment is relevant, as showing motive for a crime.

(e) [960][*A* is charged with theft and with having been previously convicted of theft. The previous conviction is relevant as a fact in issue.

(f) *A* is tried for the murder of *B*. The fact that *B* prosecuted *A* for libel and that *A* was convicted and sentenced is relevant under section 8 as showing the motive for the fact in issue.]

SYNOPSIS

959. *Gujju Lall v Fatteh Lall*, (1880) 6 Cal 171 FB.
960. Ins. by Act 3 of 1891, section 5.

COMMENT

[s 43.1] Principle.—The section declares that judgments, orders and decrees, other than those mentioned in sections 40, 41 and 42, are of themselves irrelevant, that is, in the sense that they can have any such effect or operation as mentioned in those recited sections, *qua* judgments, orders and decrees but it must not be taken to make them absolutely inadmissible when they are the best evidence of something that may be proved *aliunde*.[961] A judgment is generally speaking admissible to show its date and its legal consequences.[962] So far as regards the truth of the matter decided, a judgment is not admissible evidence against one who is a stranger to the suit.[963]

What, however, would be admissible is the admission made by a party in a previous proceeding.[964]

To have the effect of *res judicata*, a judgment *inter partes* alone can be admitted in evidence, but for other purposes where judgments are sought to be used to show the conduct of the parties, or show particular instances of the exercise of a right, or admissions made by ancestors, or how the property was dealt with previously, they may be used under section 11 or section 13 as exceptions recognised under this section, as relevant evidence. That is to say, their existence, though not their correctness, might be proved. Except where they are judgments *in rem* or where they relate to public matters, judgments not *inter partes* have been always held to be not *res judicata*, but they cannot be wholly excluded for other purposes in so far as they explain the nature of possession, or throw light on the motives or conduct of parties or identify property.[965]

[s 43.2] Scope.—This section expressly contemplates cases in which judgments would be admissible under other sections of the Act, which are not admissible under section 40, 41 or 42. The cases contemplated by this section are those where a judgment is used not as *res judicata* or as evidence more or less binding upon an opponent by reason of the adjudication which it contains. But the cases referred to in this section are such as the section itself illustrates, *viz.*, when the fact of any particular judgment having been given is a matter to be proved in the case. As for instance, if A sued B for slander, in saying that he had been convicted forgery and B justified upon the ground that the alleged slander was true, the conviction of A for forgery would be a fact to be proved by B like any other fact in the case, and quite irrespective of whether A had been actually guilty of the forgery or not. This would be one of the many cases alluded to in this section.[966]

---

961. *The Collector of Gorakhpur v Palakadhari Singh,* (1889) 12 All 1 FB. *A Munuswami v R Sethuraman,* AIR 1995 Mad 375, the judgment was not a fact in issue. Also see, *Seth Ramdayal Jat v Laxmi Prasad,* (2009) 11 SCC 545.

962. *Trailokyanath Das v Emperor,* (1931) 59 Cal 136; *Raghunath Singh v King-Emperor,* (1935) 15 Pat 336.

963. *The Natal Land & Colonisation Co v Good,* (1868) LR 2 PC 121, 133; *Maroti v Jagannathdas,* (1940) Nag 699.

964. *Seth Ramdayal Jat v Laxmi Prasad,* (2009) 11 SCC 545.

965. *Lakshman v Amrit,* (1900) 24 Bom 591 598, 599: 2 Bom LR 386.

966. *Gujju Lall v Fatteh Lall,* (1880) 6 Cal 171, 192 FB See *Secretary of State v Syed Ahmad Badsha,* (1921) 44 Mad 778 FB; *Indar Singh v Fateh Singh,* (1920) 1 Lah 540. *V Shankarayya v NS Pattadadevaru,* AIR 1995 SC 2187 : AIR 1976 Kant 103 : 1995(3) JT 513, reversed. An issue finally determined by the highest court, could not be re-examined.

Explaining the reason for the rule in the *Duchees of Kingston's*[967] case "As a general principle a transaction between two parties, in judicial proceedings, ought not be binding upon a third : for it would be unjust to bind any person who could not be admitted to make a defence, or to examine witness, or to appeal from a judgment he might think erroneous; and therefore the depositions of witnesses in another cause in proof of a fact, the verdict, of a jury finding the fact, and the judgment of the court upon, the facts found, although evidence against the parties, and all claiming under them, are not, in general, to be used to the prejudice of strangers."

Explaining further in this case as to why a civil judgment is not relevant in a criminal trial though both cases arose out of the same set of facts, the court said: "First, because the parties are not the same; for the King, in whom the trust for prosecuting public offences is vested and which is not party to such (civil) proceedings, and cannot be admitted to defend, examine witnesses, in any manner intervene or appeal; secondly, such doctrines would tend to give the civil courts, which are not permitted to exercise any judicial cognizance in matters of crime, an immediate influence upon trials for offences."

[s 43.3] Admissibility of judgments in civil and criminal matters.—A judgment in a criminal case cannot be received in a civil action to establish the truth of the facts upon which it is rendered.[968] The Privy Council observed that the findings in a civil proceeding are not binding in a subsequent prosecution founded upon the same or similar allegations.[969] Technically, it is inadmissible as it is not between the same parties, the parties in the prosecution being the State on the one hand, and the accused on the other, and in the civil suit the accused and some third party; but the substantial ground is that the issues in a civil and a criminal proceeding are not identical and the burden of proof rests in each case on different shoulders.[970] Trial and conviction for murder is not relevant in a succession suit for excluding the convict from succession though it is relevant for showing the fact of it.[971] A previous acquittal can be cited in a fresh prosecution over the same matter, but it cannot be used to prevent a new trial.[972]

The ruling of the Privy Council in *Emperor v Khwaja Nazir Ahmad*[973] has been applied by the Supreme Court in *KG Premshanker v Inspector of Police.*[974] In this case a civil suit for damages was also filed against the person accused in a criminal proceeding. The suit was dismissed. The court observed that criminal proceedings are not required to be dropped on that ground. The court also felt that it was bound by the decision of the *Constitution Bench in MS Sheriff v State of Madras*[975] which was to the effect

967. *Duchees of Kingston's,* (1776) 20 St Tr 355 at p 357 : 168 ER 175. See generally, *Gopal v State,* 1997 Cr LJ 2162 (Raj).

968. *Anil Behari v Latika Bala Dasi,* AIR 1955 SC 566 : 1955(2) SCR 270; *Raj Kumari Debi v Bama Sundari Debi,* (1896) 23 Cal 610, 613; *Ram Lal v Tula Ram,* (1881) 4 All 97.

969. *Emperor v Khwawaja Nazir Ahmad,* AIR 1945 PC 18.

970. *Gogun Chunder Ghose v The Empress,* (1880) 6 Cal 247, 248.

971. *Biro v Banta Singh,* AIR 1980 P&H 164. An acquittal in a prosecution for rash and negligent driving was held to be not relevant to a civil suit for compensation arising out of the same accident. *APSRT Corpn. v Sravaji Aruna,* AIR 1990 AP 162.

972. *S.PE Madras v KV Sundravelu,* AIR 1978 SC 1017: 1978 Cr LJ 775; *Brijbasi L Shrivastava v MP,* 1979 Cr LJ 913.

973. *Emperor v Khwaja Nazir Ahmad,* AIR 1945 PC 18 : 46 Cr LJ 413.

974. *KG Premshanker v Inspector of Police,* AIR 2002 SC 3372.

975. *MS Sheriff v State of Madras,* AIR 1954 SC 397 : 1954 Cr LJ 1019.

that no hard and fast rule could be laid down and that the possibility of conflicting decisions in civil and criminal courts was not a relevant consideration. The law envisaged "such an eventuality when it expressly refrained from making the decision of one court binding on another court or even relevant except for limited purposes such as sentence or damages. The court overruled the decision in *VM Shah v State of Maharashtra.*[976] An opinion was expressed in this case that a finding recorded by a criminal court becomes superseded when a finding is recorded by a civil court in a parallel civil case. In Kharkan v State of UP,[977] it was observed that the "earlier judgment could only be relevant if it fulfils the conditions laid down by the Evidence Act in sections 40 to 43. The earlier judgment is no doubt admissible to show the parties and the decision but it is not admissible for the purpose of relying upon the appreciation of evidence."

A decision on a point of law may affect all the pending cases on the same point of law, for example, a decision that the effect of an amendment of an Act is that a certain kind of restriction has become lifted with retrospective effect. It would affect all other proceedings then pending on the same subject.[978]

In a charge for criminal mis-appropriation, there was a finding on the point in a departmental inquiry; the court said that it was irrelevant in the criminal proceeding. Hence, the finding could not be used to show that no *prima facie* case was made out against the accused.[979]

An agreement to sell property was executed in favour of two different persons. An FIR was lodged by one of the purchasers alleging that he was cheated by forged signatures of the seller. The other purchase had filed a civil suit for specific performance of the agreement and the same was pending. It was held that a finding of fact by the civil court would not have any bearing on the criminal case and *vice versa*. The FIR was not to be quashed on the basis of a finding in the civil suit.[980]

A settlement in a civil proceeding for recovery of a loan was held to be not of much relevance in a subsequent criminal proceeding arising out of the same cause. The court said that a civil and criminal proceedings can proceed simultaneously over the same cause of action.[981]

An admission made by a party in a previous criminal proceedings has been held to be admissible in a subsequent civil proceedings.[982]

A decision by a criminal court does not bind the civil court but a civil court decision has a binding effect in a criminal proceeding to the extent of civil aspects. An order passed by an executive magistrate in proceedings under sections 145/146, CrPC has been held an order of a criminal court and that two based on a summary enquiry. At the final stage, it would only be a piece of evidence.[983] The evidence and the finding recorded by the criminal courts in a criminal proceeding cannot be conclusive proof

---

976. *VM Shah v State of Maharashtra*, AIR 1996 SC 339 : 1995 SCW 4140 : (1995) 5 SCC 767.
977. *Kharkan v State of UP*, (1964) 4 SCR 673 : AIR 1965 SC 83 : 1965 Cr LJ 116.
978. *Karam Chand Ganga Prasad v UOI*, AIR 1971 SC 1244 : (1970) 3 SCC 6941 : (1971) Cr LJ 1072.
979. *Jagdhish Chandra Soni v State*, 1998 Cr LJ 1902 (Raj).
980. *Kishan Singh v Gurpal Singh*, AIR 2010 SC 3624 : 2010 Cr LJ 4710.
981. *Rumi Dhar v State of WB*, AIR 2009 SC 2195 : (2009) 6 SCC 364.
982. *Seth Ram Dayal Jat v Laxmi Prasad*, AIR 2009 SC 2463 : (2009) 11 SCC 545.
983. *Shanti Kumar Panda v Shakuntala Devi*, AIR 2004 SC 115 : (2004) 1 SCC 438.

of existence of any fact, particularly, the existence of agreement to grant a decree for specific performance without an independent finding recorded by the civil court.[984]

[s 43.4] "Or is relevant under some other provision of this Act".—These words clearly show that there are other provisions in this Act, under which the existence of judgments not *inter partes* are relevant; for instance, under sections 8, 11, 13, 14 and section 54, Explanation (2), judgments not *inter partes* are relevant.[985] Illustrations (d), (e), and (f) explain the meaning of the last words of this section and are examples of judgments being relevant otherwise than under sections 40, 41, and 42.

A judgment not *inter partes* is admissible in evidence, *quantum valeat,* if its existence is a relevant fact.[986] The Supreme Court has laid down that in the matter of valuation of land under acquisition, a judgment about valuation of land fairly adjoining to the land in question is relevant. The party against whom such evidence is admitted must be informed so as to invite his comments.[987]

[s 43.5] CASES.—In deciding a suit for damages arising from a malicious prosecution, the Judge treated the judgment of the Magistrate and evidence given before the Magistrate, in the prosecution complained of, as evidence in the case. And looking at the judgment of the Magistrate, as being a record of the facts found, the Judge came to the conclusion that the plaintiff was not present at the time when the alleged offence was committed; and decreed the plaintiff's claim. It was held that it was not permissible to the Judge to utilize the judgment of the Magistrate in the way he did; and that this section or section 13 or section 11 did not apply to the case.[988] The court found in this case: "In deciding a suit for damages arising from a malicious prosecution the judge treated the judgment of the magistrate and the evidence given before him, as evidence in the civil case for damages. Looking at that evidence the judge came to the conclusion that the plaintiff was not present when the offence in question was committed and, therefore, he was maliciously prosecuted." In respect of the alleged hidden loss to a company in previous years, the finding of the Board for Industrial and Financial Reconstruction under Sick Industrial Companies (Special Provisions) Act, 1985 was that there was no prior period loss. It was held that the finding was relevant under section 11 read with section 43, though it was not conclusive and binding.[989]

The findings in a judgment as to legal heirship are relevant in a tenancy-landlord matter where legal heirs are supposed to become the new landlords.[990]

[s 44] Fraud or collusion in obtaining judgment, or incompetency of Court, may be proved.—Any party to a suit or other proceeding may show that any judgment, order or decree which is relevant under section 40, 41 or 42, and which has been

---

984. *K Nanjappa v RA Hameed,* (2016) 1 SCC 762, para 31 : 2015 (9) SCJ 704.

985. See *Wazir v Queen Empress,* (1895) PR No. 7 of 1895 (Cr.); *Narayanan v Mathan Mathai,* AIR 1982 Ker 239.

986. *Babui Shamsunder Kuer v Ramkhelawan Sah,* (1929) 8 Pat 783.

987. *City Improvement Trust v H Narayanaiah,* AIR 1976 SC 2403 : 1976(4) SCC 9. To the same effect, *State of Bihar v Mosafir Thakur,* AIR 1984 Pat 40. But the Kerala HC had held that such a judgment is in *personam* and not relevant to valuation of adjoining land. *Mariam v State,* AIR 1980 Ker 176.

988. *Gulabchand v Chunilal,* (1907) 9 Bom LR 1134; *Onkarmal v Banwarilal,* AIR 1962 Raj 127.

989. *AK Khosla v TS Venkatesan,* 1992 Cr LJ 1448 (Cal).

990. *Gopikrishan v Bajrang,* 1996 AIHC 4064 (Raj).

proved by the adverse party,[s 44.2] was delivered by a Court not competent to deliver it,[s 44.3] or was obtained by fraud or collusion.[s 44.4]

SYNOPSIS

COMMENT

[s 44.1] Principle.—A party to a suit or other proceeding may show that a judgment, order, or decree, which is relevant under section 40, that is, which would, as a judgment *inter partes*, operate as *res judicata*, or which is relevant under section 41, that is, which is evidence as a judgment *in rem*, or which is relevant under section 42, that is, which is evidence as a judgment relating to a public matter, and which is proved by the adverse party, was passed by a court, which had no jurisdiction to pass it or was obtained by fraud or collusion.[991] It is not necessary for the party against whom such judgment, order or decree is sought to be used to bring a separate suit to have it set aside, but it is open to such party in the same suit in which such judgment, order or decree is sought to be used against him, to show, if such be the case, that the judgment, order or decree relied upon by the other side was delivered by a court not competent to deliver it, or was obtained by fraud or collusion.[992]

The section lays down not only a rule of law relating to evidence, but also a rule of procedure. There are many sections of this Act, such as sections 66 to 73, 130, 135, 136 and 150, which relate more or less to matters of procedure.

The right of a party to set aside by a suit a judgment or decree on the ground of fraud, exists independently of the provisions of this Act.[993]

The Allahabad High Court has held that this section does not prevent a minor from adducing evidence of negligence of his guardian, if he has a substantive right to prove such negligence and thereby to avoid the judgment. It does not enumerate and exhaust the grounds upon which a decree or order may be attacked.[994] Similarly, the Calcutta High Court has held that a decree against a minor can be set aside in a subsequent suit by him if the decree was passed against the minor as a result of gross and culpable negligence of the next friend or guardian-*ad-litam*.[995] The Madras[996] and the Patna[997] High Courts are of the same view. A Full Bench of the Bombay High

---

991. *Rajib Panda v Lakhan Sendh Mahapatra,* (1899) 27 Cal 11, 20. Also see *Keepattel Bappu v Kizhakke Valappi Muhammad,* AIR 1993 Ker 272.

992. *Bansi Lal v Dhapo,* (1902) 24 All 242; *Rajib Panda v Lakhan Sendh Mahapatra,* (1899) 27 Cal 11, 20; *Bhagwandas Narandas v Patel & Co,* (1939) 42 Bom LR 231.

993. *Venkatappa Naick v Subba Naick,* (1905) 29 Mad 179.

994. *Siraj Fatma v Mahmud Ali,* (1932) 54 All 646 FB; *Desari Venkanna v Desari,* AIR 1980 NOC 82 (AP).

995. *Mahesh Chandra Bayan v Manindra Nath Das,* (1941) 1 Cal 477.

996. *Punnayah v Viranna,* (1921) 45 Mad 425.

997. *Kumar Ganganand Singh v Maharaja Sir Rameshwar Singh Bahadur,* (1927) 6 Pat 388; *Mathura Singh v Ram Rudra Prashad Sinha,* (1935) 14 Pat 824.

Court has held that gross negligence, apart from fraud or collusion, on the part of the next friend or guardian-*ad-litam*, does not afford the basis of a suit to set aside a decree obtained against a minor.[998] The Patna High Court has held that a decree passed against a minor can be avoided by him on attaining majority on the ground of gross negligence on the part of his next friend or guardian-*ad-litam* by bringing a subsequent suit even if he has not succeeded in proving fraud or collusion on the part of such next friend or guardian.[999]

[s 44.2] "Which has been proved by the adverse party".—The judgment or decree which the section allows a party to impeach on the ground of fraud must be one which has been proved by the adverse party.[1000] A party can impeach a decree even if he was a party to the suit in which the decree was passed.[1001]

[s 44.3] "Delivered by a Court not competent to deliver it".—Every species of judgment will be rendered inadmissible in evidence on proof given that the court which pronounced it had no jurisdiction.

The "competency" of a court and its "jurisdiction" are synonymous terms. They mean the right of a court to adjudicate in a given matter. They do not mean, in a case where that right exists, the coming to a correct conclusion upon any question of law or fact arising in that matter.[1002] The words "not competent" refer to a court acting without jurisdiction.[1003] This section does not apply to cases where a decree is passed by a court having no territorial jurisdiction but applies only to cases where there is inherent lack of jurisdiction.[1004] Either party or a stranger against whom a previous judgment is used in a subsequent suit may impeach it on the ground of want of jurisdiction.

[s 44.4] "Obtained by fraud or collusion".—This section allows a party to prove a fraud or collusion in order to avoid a judgment or order.[1005] The section is not applicable in cases of gross negligence.[1006] The fraud contemplated in this section must be a fraud practised on the court itself. "Fraud" is an extremely collateral act which vitiates the most solemn proceedings of courts of Justice.[1007] The term "fraud" is defined in section 17 of the Indian Contract Act. There must be actual or positive fraud, that is, there must be an intention to cheat or deceive another person to his injury.

998. *Krishnadas Padmanabhrao v Vithoba Annappa,* (1939) Bom 340: 41 Bom LR 59 FB.

999. *RB Kamakshya N Singh v Baldeo,* (1948) 27 Pat 441; *Kungammal v Muthukumar,* 2001 AIHC 3134 : AIR 2001 NOC 106 (Mad), the son of the property owner filed a suit to exclude the property from partition, but lost it. His wife filed a second suit on the basis of a will and lost it. Her children, on attaining majority, filed the third suit saying that first their father and then their mother conducted the litigation negligently and, therefore, they were not bound by decrees in such suits. No proof was offered of the fact of negligence or of lack of diligence. Hence, the findings in the earlier suits operated as *res judicata.* The sons were not entitled to avoid the decree of partition.

1000. A decree holder or one claiming through him can avoid the decree under section 44. *Ibne Hasan v Hasina Bibi,* AIR 1984 All 216.

1001. *Nachittar Singh v Jagir Kaur,* AIR 1984 P&H 197; *Joginder Singh v Nirmal Naini Mehta,* AIR 1986 Del 305.

1002. *Sardarmal v Aranvayal Sabhapathy,* (1896) 21 Bom 205.

1003. *Ketliamma v Kelappan,* (1887) 12 Mad 228.

1004. *Beerappa v Yeshwantrao,* AIR 1972 Mys 338.

1005. *Siraj Fatma v Mahmud Ali,* (1932) 54 All 646 FB

1006. *Venkata Seshayya v Kotiswara Rao,* (1936) 39 Bom LR 317 : 64 IA 17 : (1937) Mad 263.

1007. *Meadows v Duchess of Kingston,* (1775) 2 Amb 756.

"Collusion" means an agreement or contract between two or more persons to do some act in order to prejudice a third person, or for some improper purpose. It may be of two kinds: (1) when the facts put forward as the foundation of the sentence of the court do not exist; (2) when they exist, but have been corruptly preconcerted for the express purpose of obtaining the sentence.[1008]

A judgment or decree obtained by fraud upon a court does not bind such court or any other, and its nullity upon this ground, though it has not been set aside or reversed, may be alleged in a collateral proceeding.[1009] In applying this rule it matters not whether the impeached judgment has been pronounced by an inferior tribunal or by the highest court of Judicature in the realm; in all cases alike it is competent for every court, whether superior or inferior, to treat as a nullity any judgment which can be clearly shown to have been obtained by manifest fraud.[1010] A court of inferior jurisdiction is competent to declare a decree of a superior court to be a nullity on the ground of fraud, if otherwise it has jurisdiction to entertain the suit.[1011]

It is always competent to any court to vacate any judgment or order, if it be proved that such judgment or order was obtained by manifest fraud.[1012] A distinction exists between those cases in which the fraud is only attempted but not carried into effect and those in which it has actually been carried into effect. In the former case a party attempting to commit fraud is not precluded from maintaining an action to set aside the fraudulent transaction; but in the latter case he is not allowed to take advantage of his own wrong and is precluded from maintaining an action to set aside the fraudulent transaction actually carried into effect.[1013]

On the slightest of doubt or even *prima facie* proof of fraud, the matter must be thoroughly investigated by the court to arrive at the truth. Judicial order must be based on strong fundamental facts free from any doubt as regards the corrections and authenticity thereof.[1014]

Where both parties to a suit practise fraud on court and obtain a collusive decree, it is not open to either of them to impeach the judgment of the court on the ground that it was collusively procured.[1015] Where an inference of fraud or collusion can be drawn from the negligence or gross negligence of the next friend of a minor, it would be permissible for the minor to avoid the judgment or decree passed in the earlier proceeding by invoking section 44.[1016]

1008. *Wharton*, 14th Edn, p 212.

1009. *The Queen v Saddlers Co*, (1863) 10 HLC 404, 431.

1010. *Nistarini Dassi v Nundo Lall Bose*, (1899) 26 Cal 891, 908.

1011. *Sarthakram Maiti v Nundo Ram Maiti*, (1906) 11 Cal WN 579.

1012. *Paranjpe v Kanade*, (1882) 6 Bom 148, 153; *Bhikaji v Balvant*, (1927) 29 Bom LR 1046; *Mahomed Golab v Mahomed Sulliman*, (1894) 21 Cal 612.

1013. See *Goberdhan Singh v Ritu Roy*, (1896) 23 Cal 962; *Banka Behary Dass v Raj KumarDass*, (1899) 27 Cal 231; *Govinda Kuar v Lala Kishun Prosad*, (1900) 28 Cal 370; *Honapa v Narsapa*, (1898) 23 Bom 406; *Sham Lall Mitra v Amarendra Nath Bose*, (1895) 23 Cal 460.

1014. *State of Orissa v Fakir Charan Sethi*, (2015) 1 SCC 466 (para 18) : 2014 (9) SCJ 654, **relying on** *State of Orissa v Harapriya Bisoi*, (2009) 12 SCC 378 : [2009] 7 SCR 34.

1015. *Shripadchuda Venkangauda v Govindgouda Narayangouda*, (1940) 42 Bom LR 1185 : (1941) Bom 160. See *Parameswaran v Aiyappan Pillai*, AIR 1959 Ker 206.

1016. *Asharfi Lal v Koili*, AIR 1995 SC 1440 : 1995(4) SCC 163 : 1995 All LJ 1154.

The Supreme Court said in this case:

> The judgement of a competent Court is normally binding on the parties to the proceeding and it operates as *res judicata* in a subsequent proceeding between the same parties. An exception to the said rule is engrafted by s. 44 of the Evidence Act. The effect of the said provision is that a judgment delivered by a Court not competent to deliver it or a judgement which is obtained by fraud or collusion does not operate as *res judicata* and is not binding on the parties to the said proceedings. A judgment can be avoided in a subsequent proceeding by a party which is able to show that it was delivered by a Court not competent to deliver it or it was obtained by fraud or collusion. Since such a judgment does not operate as *res judicata* it is not necessary to institute a proceeding for setting it aside. A party to a proceeding against whom a judgment in an earlier suit is relied can successfully avoid the said judgment if he can establish in the subsequent proceeding that the said judgment was delivered by a Court not competent to deliver it or that it was obtained by fraud or collusion.

No doubt, if a fraud is alleged and proved, it can be sufficient to get rid of most solemn of proceedings including court proceedings. But in case of an order of a court of competent jurisdiction, this must be done only by throwing a direct challenge to the proceedings by instituting a suit for that purpose or through any appropriate legal proceedings, which may permit such direct challenge. Judgment of courts cannot be ignored by another court in a collateral proceeding and that also on mere suspicion of fraud or collusion, as was done in the instant case.[1017] So far as the alleged decree obtained by fraud or collusion is concerned, the principle of public policy requires that the court will not lend its aid to a man, who founded his cause of action upon an immoral or illegal act. It is well known that no polluted hand shall touch the pure fountain of justice.[1018]

"It is permissible for a minor to file a separate suit for setting aside a decree, in an earlier suit in which he was a party, on ground of gross negligence on the part of his next friend. Apart from that it is also permissible for a minor to avoid a decree, if relied upon in a subsequent proceeding, on the ground that the said decree was obtained on account of gross negligence on the part of his next friend in the previous suit. This would be permissible only if section 44 of the Evidence Act can be invoked. The court cannot treat negligence, or gross negligence, as fraud or collusion, unless fraud or collusion is the proper inference from the facts. In cases where an inference of fraud or collusion can be drawn from the negligence or gross negligence of the next friend it would be permissible for a minor to avoid the judgment or decree passed in the earlier proceeding by invoking section 44 of the Evidence Act without taking resort to a separate suit for setting aside the decree or judgment."

"In the present case if a judgment falls within the ambit of section 44 of the Evidence Act it can be avoided in the proceedings in which it is sought to be relied upon and it is not necessary to have it set aside by instituting independent proceedings in a competent court. What was required to be considered was whether

---

1017. *Embassy Hotels Pvt Ltd v Gajraj*, (2015) 14 SCC 316, para 17 : 2015 (1) Ren CR (Civil) 310.

1018. *Prabhatai Shankarrao Bodhankar v Chimote and Sons, Amravati*, 2017 AIR CC 210, para 65 : 2017 (2) BomCR 207 (Bom-DB).

the judgment in the earlier declaratory suit fell within the ambit of section 44 of the Evidence Act and for that purpose it was necessary to examine whether an inference of fraud or collusion could be drawn from the gross negligence on the part of the next friend of the appellant. Since the matter has not been examined from this aspect, it is appropriate that the matter be remitted to the Deputy Director (Consolidation) for considering whether in view of the finding recorded by him there was gross negligence on the part of the next friend of the appellant in prosecuting the earlier declaratory suit filed, an inference of fraud or collusion can be drawn so as to attract the provisions of section 44 of the Evidence Act. If he finds that such an inference can be drawn he would not be bound by the judgment in the earlier declaratory suit but if he finds that such an inference cannot be drawn he would be bound by the said judgment till it is set aside by the competent court in an appropriate proceeding."[1019]

[s 44.5] Challenge by stranger.—A decree passed by a foreign court was not allowed to be challenged by a person who was a stranger to the proceedings which culminated in the decree. It is necessary for a person to be able to challenge that he had a pre-existing interest in the subject-matter of the decree and that was adversely affected by the decree. Events happening subsequently to the passing of the decree could not clothe the stranger with a right to maintain an action against the decree. A person marrying a woman was trying to challenge that the decree of divorce passed in a proceeding between the woman and her first husband was illegal.[1020]

[s 44.6] Challenge to criminal conviction.—The defendant in a civil proceeding sought permission to adduce evidence to challenge his conviction in an earlier criminal proceedings. The court said that he could adduce evidence which challenged his convictions. To do otherwise would be manifestly unfair under section 11 of the Civil Evidence Act, 1968, a conviction was *prima facie* evidence that a person did commit the offence of which he was convicted, but, unlike under section 13 it is not conclusive evidence, and a defendant to civil proceedings is allowed under section 11 to prove, if he can, that he did not commit the offence. The position of a defendant in civil proceedings who sought to re-open a criminal matter which had previously been decided against him is to be distinguished from that of a plaintiff in the same situation.[1021]

Where the plaintiff sued the defendant for compensation for injury caused in a road traffic accident and cited a criminal conviction of the defendant in a road traffic offence, it was held that the defendant could challenge the conviction. The court said: "A plaintiff who brought a civil action in respect of injuries sustained in a road traffic accident and sought to rely on the defendant's conviction of driving without due care and attention was not entitled to summary judgment under the Rules of the Supreme Court O XIV where the defendant admitted the conviction but wished to contend, on the basis of an expert's report, that he was wrongly convicted. It was clear from the Civil Evidence Act, 1968 section 11(2) that it was open to such a defendant to

---

1019. *Asharfi Lal v Koili,* (1995) 4 SCC 163 : AIR 1995 SC 1440 : 1995 All LJ 1154 : 1995 RD 390.

1020. *J v Oyston,* [1999] 1 WLR 694, QBD, the court **followed** *Deva Prasad Reddy v Kamini Reddy,* AIR 2002 Kant 356.

1021. *Nawrot v Chief Constable of Hampshire,* The Independent, Jan. 7 1992 : 1992 CLY 3346.

challenge his conviction if he had good reason to do so and could satisfy the onus of proof to the civil standard. In such circumstances, since there were serious issues to be tried, the O XIV procedure (summary) was not appropriate."[1022]

Dealing with a case in which defective buildings were provided, the court said: "It would be unjust to disregard the new evidence which demonstrated that her account was credible. The case illustrated the need to ensure that affidavits were not used by solicitors as a means of putting across complex legal arguments. Affidavits and statements of truth were statements of evidence in the words of the witness and should not contain anything on which the witness could not be cross examined.[1023]

OPINIONS OF THIRD PERSONS, WHEN RELEVANT

[s 45] Opinions of experts.—When the Court has to form an opinion upon a point of foreign law, or of science, or art, or as to identity of handwriting [1024][or finger impressions], the opinions upon that point of persons specially skilled in such foreign law, science or art,[s 45.5] [1025][or in questions as to identity of handwriting[s 45.8]] [1024][or finger impressions] are relevant facts.

Such persons are called experts.

ILLU.STRATIONS

(a) The question is, whether the death of *A* was caused by poison.

Opinion of evidence

The opinions of experts as to the symptoms produced by the poison by which *A* is supposed to have died, are relevant.

(b) The question is, whether *A*, at the time of doing a certain act, was, by reason of unsoundness of mind, incapable of knowing the nature of the act, or that he was doing what was either wrong or contrary to law.

The opinions of experts upon the question whether the symptoms exhibited by *A* commonly show unsoundness of mind, and whether such unsoundness of mind usually renders persons incapable of knowing the nature of the acts which they do, or of knowing that what they do is either wrong or contrary to law, are relevant.

(c) The question is, whether a certain document was written by *A*. Another document is produced which is proved or admitted to have been written by *A*.

The opinions of experts on the question whether the two documents were written by the same person or by different persons, are relevant.

1022. *McCauley v Hope; sub nom, McCauley v Vine,* (1999) 1 WLR 1977 (CA).

1023. *Alex Lawrie Factors Ltd v Morgan,* The Times, August 18, 1999 (CA).

1024. Ins. by Act 5 of 1899, section 3. For discussion in Council as to whether "finger impressions" include "thumb impressions", see Gazette of India, 1898, Part VI, p. 24.

1025. Ins. by Act 18 of 1872, section 4.

SYNOPSIS

COMMENT

This section is an exception to the rule as regards the exclusion of opinion evidence. Opinions of experts are relevant upon a point of (a) foreign law, (b) science, (c) art, (d) identity of handwriting and (e) finger impressions.

Both under this section and section 47 the evidence is of an opinion, in the former by a scientific comparison and in the latter on the basis of familiarity resulting from frequent observations and experience. In either case the court must satisfy itself by such means as are open that the opinion may be acted upon.[1026] Expert opinion is only opinion evidence and is not helpful to the court in interpretation of the law.[1027]

[s 45.1] Principle.—It is "a general rule that the opinion of witnesses possessing peculiar skill is admissible, whenever the subject-matter of enquiry is such that inexperienced persons are unlikely to prove capable of forming a correct judgment

1026. *Fakhruddin v State of MP,* AIR 1967 SC 1326 : 1967 Cr LJ 1197.
1027. *Forest Range Officer v P Mohammed Ali,* AIR 1994 SC 120.

upon it without such assistance. In other words, this is so when it so far partakes of the character of a science or art as to require a course of previous habit or study to obtain a competent knowledge of its nature."[1028] The need to hear an expert opinion is the first and foremost requirement.[1029]

The opinion of an expert witness on technical aspects has relevance but the opinion has to be based upon specialised knowledge and the data on which it is based, has to be found acceptable by the court.[1030] The duty of an expert is to furnish the court his opinion along with all the materials. It is for the court thereafter to see whether the basis of the opinion is correct and proper and then form its own conclusion, unlike a witness of facts where facts are facts and they remain and have to remain as such for ever and he does not give his opinion on facts but presents the facts as such. However, the expert gives an opinion on what he has tested or on what has been subjected to any process of scrutiny. The inference drawn thereafter is still an opinion based on his knowledge. In case, subsequently, he comes across some authentic material, which may suggest a different opinion, he must address the same, lest he should be branded as intellectually dishonest. Objective approach and openness to truth actually form the basis of any expert opinion.[1031] Merely because an expert has tendered an opinion while furnishing the basis of the opinion and that too without being conclusive and definite, it cannot be said that he has committed perjury, so as to help somebody. And, mere rejection of the expert evidence by itself may not also warrant institution of proceedings under section 340, CrPC, 1973.[1032] The opinions of skilled witnesses cannot be received when the inquiry relates to a subject which does not require any peculiar habits or course of study to qualify a man to understand it,[1033] e.g., similarity of fraudulent trademark.[1034] In all other cases witnesses must speak only of facts and not of opinion or inferences.[1035]

The reason for the rule is thus explained by Report on Cross Evidence:[1036]

> An artist's views concerning the components of a chemical compound or the law of a South American State, would not assist the English Court in coming to the conclusion with regard to these matters for the simple reason that they do not warrant an inference to the probable existence of the facts to which he deposes.

Goddard LJ, in the decision of the court of Appeal in *Hollington v Hewthorn*,[1037] in a civil proceeding dismissed the judgment of a criminal court on the same facts as irrelevant being only the opinion of the criminal court. "It frequently happens that a bystander has a full and complete view of an accident. It is beyond question that while he may inform the court of everything that he saw, he may not express any opinion on

---

1028. *Taylor*, 12th Edn, section 1418, p 902.
1029. *Ramesh Chandra Agarwal v Regency Hospital Ltd*, AIR 2010 SC 806 : (2009) 9 SCC 709.
1030. *Sultan Singh v State of Haryana*, (2014) 14 SCC 664 (para 13) : 2015 Cr LJ 259.
1031. *Prem Sagar Manocha v State (NCT of Delhi)*, (2016) 4 SCC 571, para 20 : 2016 (1) Scale 220.
1032. *Prem Sagar Manocha v State (NCT of Delhi)*, (2016) 4 SCC 571, para 22 : 2016 (1) Scale 220.
1033. *Ibid*, section 1419, p 902. *Nagina Sharma v State of Bihar*, 1991 Cr LJ 1195 (Pat), an expert has to appear personally, Government's duty to issue personal appearance of Government doctors emphasised.
1034. *Swadeshi Mills Co Ltd v Juggi Lal Kamlapat Cotton Mills Co Ltd*, (1926) 49 All 92.
1035. *Babuli v State of Orissa*, AIR 1974 SC 775 : 1974 Cr LJ 510.
1036. 328 (1958).
1037. *Hollington v Hewthorn*, (1943) KB 507 at p 595 (CA).

whether either or both of the parties were negligent. The reason commonly assigned is that this is the precise question the court has to decide, but in truth, it is because his opinion, is not relevant. Any fact that he can prove is relevant but his opinion is not."

The Supreme Court of India in *Mobarik Ali Ahmed v State of Bombay,*[1038] preferred to rely upon the reason that if a witness was permitted to express his opinion, it would amount to delegation of judicial function. "A witness has to state the facts which he has seen, heard or perceived and not the conclusion which he has formed on observing or perceiving them (Section 60). The function of drawing inference is a judicial function and must be performed by the Court."

[s 45.2] Who is an expert.—An "expert" witness is one who has devoted time and study to a special branch of learning, and thus is specially skilled on those points on which he is asked to state his opinion.[1039] His evidence on such points is admissible to enable the tribunal to come to a satisfactory conclusion.[1040] The section does not refer to any particular attainment, standard of study or experience, which would qualify a person to give evidence as an expert. Generally, a witness is considered as an expert if he is skilled in any particular art, trade or profession, and possessed of peculiar knowledge concerning the same. He must have made a special study of the subject or acquired a special experience therein. In such cases, the question is: Is he peritus? Is he skilled? Does he possess adequate knowledge?[1041] The question of competency of fitness of a witness as an expert is to be decided by the judge.[1042] Experts cannot act as judges or jury. The court has to assess their opinion and decide finally.[1043] An expert, in order to be competent as a witness, need not have acquired his knowledge professionally. It is sufficient, so far as the admissibility of the evidence goes, if he has acquired special experience therein.[1044] The opinion of an expert must be given orally and a mere report or certificate by him is not evidence.[1045] Senior Scientist (Chemistry), Central Forensic Science Laboratory was held to be an expert in science, though not falling in the category of officers mentioned section 293, CrPC. His opinion would be a relevant piece of evidence in view of section 45.[1046] In *MS Reddy v State Inspector of Police, ACB, Nellore,*[1047] it was held that, in the case of an alleged fraud committed on large scale by Officers of Irrigation Department in carrying out work of jungle clearance, an engineer working in that department entrusted to assist the investigation agency could not be said to be an "expert" because of special knowledge acquired by him while in service. All persons who practise a business or profession which requires them to possess a certain knowledge of the matter in hand are experts, so far as expertness is required. It is the duty of the Judge to decide whether the skill of any person in the matter on

---

1038. *Mobarik Ali Ahmed v The State of Bombay,* 1958 SCR 328 at p 342 : AIR 1957 SC 857.

1039. *Ramesh Chandra Agarwal v Regency Hospital Ltd,* AIR 2010 SC 806 : (2009) 9 SCC 709, it has to be shown that he has made a special study of the subject or acquired special experience in that field of study.

1040. *Powell,* 10th Edn, p 39.

1041. The quotation is from *R. v Silverlock,* (1874) 2 QB 766, 771 per LORD RUSSEL

1042. MR Zafer, *Scientific Evidence : Expert Witnesses,* (1962) JILI (Special Issue) 56.

1043. *Law Society of India v Fertilizers & Chemicals Travancore Ltd,* AIR 1994 Ker 308.

1044. *Collector, Jabalpur v AY Jahagir Khan,* AIR 1971 MP 32.

1045. *Perumal Mudaliar v South Indian Railway Co Ltd,* (1937) Mad 764; *Ahmedabad Municipality v Shantilal,* AIR 1961 Guj 196.

1046. *Amarjit Singh v State (Delhi Admn),* 1995 Cr LJ 1623 (Del).

1047. *MS Reddy v State Inspector of Police, AC.B, Nellore,* 1993 Cr LJ 558 (AP).

which evidence of his opinion is offered, is sufficient to entitle him to be considered as an expert. The opinion (prediction as to duration of pregnancy) of an experienced obstetrician cannot be rejected merely because she is not specialised in gynaecology.[1048] Where a handwriting expert was not in practice since 1950 and also expressed opinions beyond his natural field, his evidence was rejected.[1049] A person who is not well-versed with a particular language cannot testify as an expert as to handwriting.[1050] Whether an expert is competent to speak on the matter of handwriting can be discovered by cross examination.[1051] The opinion of a goldsmith can be relied upon. "They are able to find out whether a piece of metal is gold or not by the colour of the streak produced by rubbing on a touchstone though their assessment of purity may not be exact."[1052] An Excise Inspector who had put in twenty-one years of service, tested countless samples of liquor, and whose competence to test the contents and strength of seized liquor had not been questioned at all, was an expert within the meaning of the section.[1053] Where an expert had given no reasons in support of his opinion, nor was it shown that he possessed special skill, knowledge and experience in the science of identification of fingerprints, the Supreme Court did not consider it safe to rely upon his opinion even if it was supposed to be admissible under section 45.[1054]

A government scientific expert certainly stands on a different footing as compared to others i.e. those called by a party.[1055]

Where the evidence of a dumb witness required interpretation, the Principal of the Government Residential School for Deaf was held to be an expert interpreter. The testimony of the prosecutrix with the help of the interpreter proved not only the commission of rape but also the identity of the offender. The court said that her testimony could be relied upon.[1056] A police officer who was trained to handle guns was considered an expert for the purpose of certifying whether the gun in question was in a working condition.[1057]

A caddie was held to be not an expert for the purpose of expressing opinion whether a golf player, who had caused death of a caddie hitting him by a stroke of the stick, had acted rashly and negligently.[1058] Where a person was charged with the theft of railway raw coal and the question was whether the coal found in his possession belonged to that category of railway property, the court rejected the opinion of a person about whom there was no evidence on record to show that he had acquired any special knowledge or still to give his opinion as an expert in the matter of raw coal belonging to railways.[1059]

1048. *Baldev Raj Miglani v Urmila Kumari Smt.*, AIR 1979 SC 879 : 1979(3) SCC 782. See *Chatt Ram v State of Haryana,* AIR 1979 SC 1890 : 1979 Cr LJ 1411, generally on the meaning of "expert".

1049. *Lakshmi Chand v Ishroo Devi,* AIR 1977 SC 1694 : 1977(2) SCC 501.

1050. *Gulab Chand v Satya Vrat,* AIR 1983 All 54.

1051. *Balkrishna Das v Radha Devi,* AIR 1989 All 133.

1052. *Assistant Collector of Central Excise v VP Syed Mohd.*, AIR 1983 SC 168, 169 : 1983 Cr LJ 225. : (1983) 1 SCC 370.

1053. *SC Batra v VP,* AIR 1974 SC 639 : 1974 Cr LJ 590. *Huding Singh v State of Orissa,* 1995 Cr LJ 1128 (Ori), conviction can be maintained on the evidence of officials of Excise Department.

1054. *Mahmood v State of UP,* AIR 1976 SC 69, 73 : 1976 Cr LJ 10.

1055. *Prem Sagar Manocha v State (NCT of Delhi),* (2016) 4 SCC 571, para 19 : 2016 (1) Scale 220.

1056. *Public Prosecutor, HC of AP v Lingisetty Sreena,* 1997 Cr LJ 4003 (AP).

1057. *Jarnail Singh v State of Punjab,* 1999 Cr LJ 453 : AIR 1999 SC 321 : (1998) 8 SCC 126.

1058. *M Shafi Goroo v State,* 2000 Cr LJ 2172 (Delhi).

1059. *Sahdeo Ram v State,* 2002 Cr LJ 1090 (Pat.).

[s 45.3] Nursing staff, whether expert psychiatric stress.—S, a nurse manager of patients with learning disabilities, brought an action for stress at work against his employer, alleging that he was overworked and not provided with sufficient support. He disclosed an expert report from another nurse manager, then the general manager of learning disabilities service with a different NHS Trust, who purported to give evidence in relation to liability and causation. The employer applied for an order debarring the witness from giving either expert evidence or evidence as a witness of fact, on the basis that he failed to recognise his duty to the court and purported to give expert evidence on matters for which he had no expertise. It was held that the experience of the witness should be such as to make him capable of giving evidence as to management practice, but that he was not qualified to give expert evidence on the issues of causation of psychiatric injury or foreseeability in relation to psychiatric injury. He wrongly (1) made reference to published material which post-dated the period of alleged negligence; (2) raised issues that predated the period of alleged negligence and which were not pleaded in the particulars of claim, and (3) made findings of fact and expressed an opinion on the issue of liability, thereby trespassing on the function of the judge. As a result, and due to the intemperate language employed in the report, the report could not be said to be the objective and unbiased evidence of an expert of the court. The evidence was wholly discredited. The employer also intended to call at trial the manager of another home for patients with learning disabilities as a witness of fact, which was a further relevant consideration when debarring the witness from giving evidence, either as an expert or of fact at the trial.[1060]

[s 45.4] Role of expert opinion.—The court is bound to defer to the opinion of an expert where skill and experience alone render a person a competent Judge. In the case of an expert witness there exists the tendency to support the view which is favourable to the side which employs him so that it is difficult to get from him an independent opinion. An expert may revise his opinion if he finds cogent reason and his evidence need not be disbelieved on this ground.[1061] The court, normally would look at an expert evidence with a greater sense of acceptability, but it is equally true that the courts are not absolutely guided by the report of the experts, especially if such reports are perfunctory and unsustainable. The purpose of expert opinion is primarily to assist the court in arriving at a final conclusion but such report, is not a conclusive one.[1062]

An expert's evidence as to the handwriting is opinion evidence and it can rarely, if ever, take the place of substantive evidence. Before acting on such evidence it is usual to see if it is corroborated either by clear direct evidence or by circumstantial

---

1060. *Storey v Dorset Community NHS Trust,* Oct. 18, 1999, Judge Overend, CC (Plymouth). [*Ex. rel* Robert Weir, Barrister, Devereux Chamber, Devereux Court, London] CLY 2000.

1061. *Subodh Kumar v Soshi Kumar,* AIR 1958 Cal 264. Expert evidence based on notes prepared by him in the exercise of his official duty but copies of notes not supplied to the accused, the notes could not be relied upon. *Vithal Mahadev Patil v State of Karnataka,* 1996 Cr LJ 1796 (Kant).

1062. *Tomaso Bruno v State of UP,* (2015) 7 SCC 178, para 40 : 2015 (2) SCJ 328; *Paramesh Chandra Sen v Sanjukta Mukherjee,* AIR 2017 Cal 254, the court should not merely go by the *"ipse dixit"* of the report of the handwriting expert to form its conclusive opinion. The facts revealed in the said report may be relevant facts but cannot be a sole determinant fact either to impinge the document or to uphold the same.

evidence.[1063] Expert evidence can be used to corroborate other evidence.[1064] Opinion as to handwriting was accepted for corroboration of professional statements.[1065] Credibility and competence of an expert are material questions. Where the High Court did not believe an expert the Supreme Court did not interfere.[1066]

Where an expert was instructed by both sides, the court debarred him from evidence. There was hardly any chance left with him to prepare an unbiased report.[1067] Where the claim was against a Housing Society by its tenant for personal injury caused by disrepaired state of the premises and for specific performance, the court said that the fact that the designated expert was employed by the Authority did not disqualify him as an expert provided that he was actually qualified for the job. The court, however, stressed the need for independent experts whose credentials were not in dispute.[1068]

Documents need to be referred for an expert opinion, only in absence of other means to prove the same.[1069]

[s 45.4.1] Court not *functus officio* because of expert opinion.—The opinion of an expert may not have any binding effect on the court. The court does not become *functus officio* because of an expert opinion. It is not the province of the expert to act as judge or jury.[1070] The ultimate opinion has to be formulated by the court.[1071] Expert

---

1063. *Shashi Kumar v Subodh Kumar,* AIR 1964 SC 529; *Balkrishna Das v Radha Devi,* AIR 1989 All 133, 141.

1064. *Awadesh v State of MP,* (1988) 2 SCC 557 : AIR 1988 SC 1158, where the opinion of medical experts was used to corroborate the finding that the eye-witnesses must not have been present at the scene of the occurrence.

1065. *UP v Boota Singh,* (1979) 1 SCR 298; AIR 1978 SC 1770. A conviction can also be founded on expert opinion. *Kartar Singh v State of Punjab,* AIR 1977 SC 349 : 1977 Cr LJ 214.

1066. *Kanchan Singh v State of Gujarat,* (1979) 2 SCJ 260: 1979 Cr LJ 889 : AIR 1979 SC 1011; *Prem Ballab v State,* AIR 1977 SC 56 : 1977 Cr LJ 12, evidence of food inspector, corroboration considered not necessary. Direct evidence satisfactory and reliable, it could not be rejected on the basis of opinion evidence (here medical evidence) *S.G Gundegowda v State,* 1996 Cr LJ 852 (Kant), **relying on** *Punjab Singh v State of Haryana,* AIR 1984 SC 1233 : 1984 Cr LJ 921 : 1984 Supp 233 : 1984 SCC (Cri) 484. Expert evidence weak, not safe without corroboration, handwriting, *S Gopal Reddy v State of AP,* AIR 1996 SC 2184 : 1996 Cr LJ 3237; *Girish Vinayakrao Naik v Shivamurthappa,* AIR 2001 Kant 210, request for appointment of handwriting expert made at the appellate stage after 10 years, from the date of appeal, genuineness of the suit document was denied, delay was not explained, application rejected. *Krishna S v State,* 1998 Cr LJ 785 (Kant), expert turned hostile, he had certified as a Government doctor that the prosecutrix was the victim of rape. In the court he tried to protect the accused. Serious view was taken because it was nothing short of perjury concerned authorities were advised to take appropriate disciplinary proceedings against him.

1067. *Dunne v Kierggroup Plc.,* April 7, 2000 Devereur Court, London, 2000 CLY 103. The matter had arisen out of construction site accident.

1068. *Field v Leeds City Council,* (2001) CPLR 129 (CA); *Hugher v Wrexhamanaclor Hospital NHS Trust,* April 7, 2000, 2000 CLY 1, an application for instructing additional expert was rejected because the issue in question was not a new issue. *Hari Singh v State of MP,* AIR 2010 SC 3630 : (2010) 12 SCC 108, evidence of eye-witnesses that the shut was fixed from close range was fully corroborated by medical evidence. *Sarvesh Narain Shukla v Daroga Singh,* AIR 2008 SC 320 : (2007) 13 SCC 360, ocular evidence and expert opinion consistent on the point that different fire arms were used.

1069. *Sayed Moinuddin v Md Mehaboob Alam,* AIR 2016 SC 192, para 13.

1070. *Ramesh Chandra Agarwal v Regency Hospital Ltd,* AIR 2010 SC 806 : (2009) 9 SCC 709.

1071. *Thyssen Stahhunion GmbH v SAIL,* AIR 2002 Delhi 255. *Vishnu v State of Maharashtra,* AIR 2006 SC 508 : (2006) 1 SCC 283 : 2006 Cr LJ 303, expert medical evidence is not binding against ocular evidence. The opinion of the medical officer is for assistance of the court. He is not a witness of fact. The evidence of a witness of fact may prevail over it.

opinion is merely an aid to the court to arrive at a conclusion. Such an opinion is not binding. It is optional for the court to accept or reject it.[1072] However, interpretation by a technical body in regard to purely technical matters deserves acceptance and will not be interfered with, unless it is arbitrary or unreasonable.[1073]

The Calcutta High Court observed as follows:[1074] "The duty of an expert is to depose and not to decide. The only function of the expert is to furnish the data with necessary scientific criteria so as to enable the judge to come to an independent conclusion."

The guiding principle for courts dealing with expert opinion has been succinctly summed up by the Supreme Court in the following words:

The possibility of some variations in the exhibits, medical and ocular evidence cannot be ruled out. But it is not that every minor variation or inconsistency would tilt the balance of justice in favour of the accused. Where contradictions and variations are of a serious nature, which apparently or impliedly are destructive of the substantive case sought to be proved by the prosecution, they may provide an advantage to the accused. The courts, normally, look at expert evidence with a greater sense of acceptability, but courts are not absolutely guided by the report of the experts, especially if such reports are perfunctory, unsustainable and are the result of a deliberate attempt to misdirect the prosecution. Where the eyewitness account is found credible and trustworthy, medical opinion pointing to alternative possibilities may not be accepted as conclusive. The expert is not only to provide reasons to support his opinion but the result should be directly demonstrable. The court is not to surrender its own judgment to that of the expert or delegate its authority to a third party, but should assess his evidence like any other evidence. The purpose of expert testimony is to provide the court with useful, relevant information. The purpose of an expert opinion is primarily to assist the court in arriving at a final conclusion. Such report is not binding upon the court. The court is expected to analyse the report, read it in conjunction with the other evidence on record and then form its final opinion as to whether such report is worthy of reliance or not.[1075]

A medical witness called in as an expert to assist the court is not a witness of fact and the evidence given by the medical officer is really of an advisory character given on the basis of the symptoms found on examination. The expert witness is expected to put before the court all materials inclusive of the data which induced him to come to the conclusion and enlighten the court on the technical aspect of the case by explaining the terms of science so that the court although not an expert may form its own judgment on those materials after giving due regard to the expert's opinion because once the expert's opinion is accepted it is not the opinion of the medical officer but of the court.[1076]

1072. *Ajoy Kumar Das v Kalpana Das*, AIR 2007 NOC 897 (Cal—DB). Signature on the will was compared by the court with admitted signature and was found to be genuine. Of the two attesting witness, appeared and testified to the signature of the other witness.

1073. *Grid Corpn. of Orissa Ltd v Eastern Metals & Ferro Alloys*, (2011) 11 SCC 334.

1074. *Ibid* at p 268.

1075. *Dayal Singh v State of Uttaranchal*, AIR 2012 SC 3046 : (2012) 8 SCC 263.

1076. *Madan Gopal Kakkad v Naval Dubey*, (1992) 3 SCC 204, 221 :1992 SCC (Cri)598. To the same effect, *Ramesh Chandra Agarwal v Regency Hospital Ltd*, AIR 2010 SC 806 : (2009) 9 SCC 709, credibility of the expert witness depends on the reasons stated by him in support of his conclusions, and date and material furnished by him for that purpose. A patient who suffered from medical negligence filed an application for reconsideration of the expert opinion. Rejection of his application was held to be not proper. The order of rejection was quashed.

Medical evidence is only an evidence of opinion. It cannot be decisive.[1077] If the medical and ocular evidence is contrary then the ocular evidence must prevail.[1078] The story recited by eye-witness can be verified by medical evidence.[1079] The court said in this case:

> You must remember this particular point of view that if you believe the eye-witnesses, then there is no question of having it supported by medical evidence...But if you do not believe the eye-witnesses then consideration of the medical evidence in any manner becomes unnecessary.

An expert should be an independent person. Where an assessee company produced an expert witness to prove that an item being produced by the company was covered by an exemption entry, the opinion was held to have been rightly rejected by the Tribunal because the expert belonged to the company itself and was not an independent person.[1080]

The opinion of Forensic Science Laboratory that the substance recovered from the accused was "opium" was not accepted. The court said that the opinion was not binding on the court. The court considered the evidence and the relevant provisions of the NDPS Act and came to the conclusion that the substance in question was an "opium derivative" intoxicants.[1081]

Without scientific report, the court is not competent to opine with regard to the physical disability of the witness, more particularly when other witnesses deposed that he was little hard of hearing and not totally deaf.[1082]

[s 45.5] "Science or art".—These words include all subjects on which a course of special study or experience is necessary to the formation of an opinion.[1083] The following is an oft quoted passage from FIELD: "The words "science" or "art" are to be broadly construed, the term "science" not being limited to higher sciences, and the term "art" not being limited to fine arts but having its original sense of handicraft, trade, profession and skill in work which, with the advance of culture has been carried beyond the sphere of the common pursuits of life into that of artistic and scientific action."[1084]

The study of certain customs and manners of tribes and castes, of the areas occupied by them and of other connected matters comes within the meaning of "science or art" in this section. The words "science or art" are to be broadly construed, the term "science" not being limited to the higher sciences and the term "art" not being limited to fine arts but having its original sense of handicraft, trade, profession and skill in work, which, with the advance of culture, has been carried beyond the sphere of common pursuits of life into that of "artistic" and "scientific" action. The tests which may be applied in determining whether a particular question is one of scientific nature and consequently whether skilled witnesses may pass their opinions upon it are: Is the subject-matter of enquiry such that inexperienced men are unlikely to prove

1077. *Mani Ram v State of Rajasthan*, AIR 1993 SC 2453 : 1993 Cr LJ 2530.
1078. *Umesh Singh v State of Bihar*, (2013) 4 SCC 360.
1079. *Sunil Chandra v State*, AIR 1954 Cal 315, at p 318.
1080. *Novapan India Ltd v CCE&C*, (1994) 73 ELT 769.
1081. *Amarsingh Ramjibhai Barot v State of Gujarat*, (2005) 7 SCC 550 : AIR 2005 SC 4248.
1082. *Hema Majhi v Dubraj Majhi*, AIR 2016 NOC 477 (Ori).
1083. *Stephen's Dig*, 12th Edn, (1946) Article 49.
1084. *Field, Evidence*, 2442 (9th Edn).

capable of forming a correct judgment upon it without the assistance of experts; that is, does it so far partake of the character of a science or art as to require a course of previous habit or study in order to obtain a competent knowledge of its nature. Books dealing with customs and manners of different castes and tribes are admissible in evidence to prove them.[1085]

Adulteration is a matter of science. The opinion of an expert was not allowed to be rejected only because the sample taken was less than the statutory requirement because it was otherwise sufficient for test purposes.[1086] Microscopic evidence cannot be interfered with only because some further superior method, such as "photo", was not adopted.[1087] The opinion of an expert on narcotic substances was not allowed to be rejected for the fact that he did not know the difference between narcotic drugs and psychotropic substances, the court saying that a medical officer is not expected to know the differences in the legal parlance.[1088]

Soil erosion is also a matter of science. In the matter of the renewal of a mining lease, refusal of renewal was based on the ground of the expert opinion that constant mining operations would result in accelerated soil erosion in the leased area. The court refused to substitute the opinion of the expert body with its own opinion.[1089]

An expert has to be skillful and has to show that he has adequate knowledge of the subject. In this case, the Government had to acquire on payment from the growers diseased apples and to destroy them. There was a complaint that the growers had submitted false claims as to quantity. The expert who was appointed to report on the fruit bearing capacity of the orchards, visited the orchards in the subsequent year when the apple season was over. He had not made any scientific study on research on the subject nor was he offered any such job earlier. He prepared his report on the basis of surmises and conjectures. His report was not relied upon.[1090]

The word "science" occurring in section 45 includes experts in type-writers and type-writing has to be read within the meaning of the word "handwriting".[1091]

Where experts are called to pronounce their opinions on scientific questions, they may refresh their memory by referring to professional treatises. The word "science" is comprehensive enough to include the opinion of an expert in footprint.[1092]

[s 45.6] Age.—A doctor's opinion as to age of a person based on his or her height, weight and teeth, does not amount to legal proof of the age of that person.[1093] But

---

1085. *Mahadeo v Vyankammabai,* (1947) Nag 781.

1086. *Kisan v Maharashtra,* AIR 1979 SC 1824 : 1980 Supp SCC 390.

1087. *Ramanathan v State of TN,*1978 Cr LJ 1137.

1088. *Durand Didier v UT of Goa,* AIR 1989 SC 1966 at 1970 : 1990(1) SCC 95.

1089. *T Veerabhadrappa v Minister of Mines and Steel,* AIR 1998 Kant 412.

1090. *State of HP v Jai Lal,* AIR 1999 SC 3318 : 1999 Cr LJ 4294 : (1999) 7 SCC 280.

1091. *State v SJ Choudhary,* 1996 Cr LJ 1713 : AIR 1996 SC 1491, **overruling** *Hanumant v State of Madhya Pradesh,* AIR 1952 SC 343 : 1952 SCR 1091 : 1952 Cr LJ 129 and reversing Criminal Revision No. 105 of 1987 (Delhi). *Arulmighu Sadayappasamy Temple v State of Tamil Nadu,* (2017) 4 Mad LJ 230, the expression "science or art", occurring in section 45 includes handwriting expert as well as a typewriting expert.

1092. *Basudeo Gir,* (1959) Pat 69. Exceptional cases cited in treatises cannot overrule clear evidence before the court, *Baldev Raj Miglani v Urmila Kumari Smt,* AIR 1979 SC 879 : 1979(3) SCC 782.

1093. *Emperor v Qudrat,* (1939) All 871.

such evidence is relevant. In a charge of kidnapping and rape, the age of the victim was in question. The lady doctor certified that it was on the basis of the X-ray plate examination that she formed her opinion that the age of the prosecutrix was 15 years. She cited passage on the point from Modi's *Medico-Legal Jurisprudence.* The court said that her evidence was not liable to be rejected.[1094] In *Anita v Atal Bihari,*[1095] it was held that in ascertaining date of birth, opinion of radiologist cannot be preferred over the entry in the register of births and deaths maintained under the provisions of an Act. In an alleged case of kidnapping of a girl, the medical evidence showed her age between 17 and 18 years and the documentary evidence showed her to be above 18 years. It was held that medical evidence was not a conclusive proof of age.[1096]

Where determination of age for purpose of the Juvenile Justice Act, 1986 was necessary and where two certificates issued by respective schools where the accused had been a student conflicted with each other, it was held that the evidence of age contained in the medical Board opinion and radiological examination was to be preferred.[1097]

It has been held that ossification test to determine the age of a person is not a conclusive test.[1098] In another case, where the age of the rape victim had to be known, to the court that the age determined by the doctor only on clinical examination was based on fragile premises. He had not performed ossification test or other pathological tests.[1099]

[s 45.6.1] ***Rigor Mortis.***—*Time of death.*—*Rigor mortis* is an important factor for assessing time of death.[1100]

In the determination of time of death *Rigor 'mortis* is only rough guide. The doctor who had held post-mortem examination had occasion to see the injuries of the deceased quite closely. No evidence that he had deliberately given wrong report. His evidence could not be discarded. Opinion of the doctor holding post-mortem examination is to be preferred to expert opinion based on basis of post-mortem report and notes on post-mortem report and also taking into consideration the presence of *rigor mortis,* lividity, coolness and the report of injuries found on the person of the deceased.[1101]

1094. *Ram Swaroop v State of UP,* 1989 Cr LJ 2435 All. See also *Mangat Ram v State,* 1987 Cr LJ 224 Delhi, rough estimate of age given by illiterate relatives was accepted because it was supported by medical opinion. *Jitmohan Lohar v State,* 1997 Cr LJ 2842 (Ori), difference of opinion between ossification test and school admission certificate about the age of the rape victim. Ossification test could not be relied upon documentary evidence was found to be more reliable.

1095. 1993 Cr LJ 549 (MP).

1096. *SK Belal v State of Orissa,* 1994 Cr LJ 467 (Ori). *Abdul Razzak v State,* 2000 Cr LJ 3921 (All), medical opinion as to age, radiological that, margin of error in such test two years on either side. The court said that this margin could not be given where otherwise there is conclusive and decisive evidence of age.

1097. *Dayachand v Sahib Singh,* AIR 1991 SC 930 : 1991 Cr LJ 1370; *Sunil Kumar v State of UP,* 2000 Cr LJ 4687 (All), entry in school register did not appear to be genuine, medical certificate prevailed over school register.

1098. *Prem Chand v State of HP,* 2000 Cr LJ 951 (HP), age had to be determined in this case for the purposes of charge of rape.

1099. *Kamal Kishore v State of HP,* 2000 Cr LJ 2292 : AIR 2000 SC 1920.

1100. *Indradeo Rai v State of Bihar,* 1992 Cr LJ 4005 (Pat).

1101. *Tanviben Pankajkumar Divetia v State of Gujarat,* 1997 Cr LJ 2535 (SC) : AIR 1997 SC 2193.

A doctor's evidence can never be absolutely certain on point of time so far as the duration of injuries is concerned.[1102]

[s 45.7] Medical opinion.—Opinion of medical officer cannot be taken as contradicting the positive evidence of the witness to the facts.[1103]

Doctor's version as to the time of rape and that of the prosecution showed a gap of some hours. It was held that medical evidence would not be rejected on that ground alone.[1104] Where the medical witness, who had examined the rape-cum-murder accused, stated that the accused had not had intercourse within one hour of his examination, his evidence carried conviction with the court. It also fits with the other circumstances attending the case.[1105] Between the opinion of two doctors the opinion which supports direct evidence should be accepted.[1106] Where the direct evidence about assault by a

---

1102. *Ram Swaroop v State of UP,* 2000 Cr LJ 806 at p 810 : AIR 2000 SC 715.

1103. *Basappa Bhimappa v State of Mysore,* AIR 1961 Mys 21. *Salimzia v State of UP,* AIR 1979 SC 391: (1979) 2 SCR 394 : 1979 Cr LJ 323, exit wound cannot be smaller. *Nanhau Ram v State of MP,* AIR 1988 SC 912 : 1988 Cr LJ 936 : 1988 Supp SCC 152 : 1988 SCC (Cri) 342, direct evidence that the deceased was alive upto half an hour after the incident and did make the statement, not wiped out by the medical opinion that the gun shot injuries which he sustained would not leave him alive upto that time. *State of UP v Krishna Gopal,* 1989 Cr LJ 288 : AIR 1988 SC 2154 : (1988) 4 SCC 302 : 1988 SCC (Cri) 928, medical opinion suggesting alternative possibilities not allowed to prevail upon positive eye-witness account; *Amar Singh v State of Punjab,* 1987 Cr LJ 706 : AIR 1987 SC 726, where medical report differed from injuries described by witnesses, medical evidence prevailed. *Radha Kant Yadav v State of Jharkhand,* 2003 Cr LJ 13 (Jhar), medical opinion that death was homicidal and not suicidal, prevailed.

1104. *Pratap Misra v State of Orissa,* AIR 1977 SC 1307 : 1977 Cr LJ 817. The Supreme Court remarked in another case that medical evidence as to the time of death should not be viewed with mathematical accuracy. *Pattipati Venkaiah v State of AP,* AIR 1985 SC 1715 : 1985 Cr LJ 2012 : (1985) 4 SCC 80 : 1985 SCC (Cri) 484. Medical opinion that injuries were caused with a sharp weapon was not negatived by the fact that the prosecution failed to produce the weapon in question. *BV Danny Mao v State of Nagaland,* 1989 Cr LJ 226 (Gau). Contradiction between medical evidence and eye-witness account as to the fatal injury brought about acquittal. *Ashim Das v State of Assam,* 1987 Cr LJ 1533 Gau; *Ramesh Kumar v State (Delhi Admn.),* 1990 Cr LJ 255 (Del). For an example where the medical evidence was preferred to the ocular, see *Rajgopal Panda v State of Orissa,* 1990 Cr LJ 1848 (Ori).

1105. *Jaharlal Das v State of Orissa,* 1991 Cr LJ 1809 : AIR 1991 SC 1388 : (1991) 3 SCC 27 : 1991 SCC (Cri) 527. Weapon of offence, if available, should be shown to the medical witness and his opinion invited as to whether all or any of the injuries on the victim could be caused with that weapon. *K Mallikarjuna v State of AP,* 1995 Cr LJ 3100 (AP). *State Govt of NCT of Delhi v Sunil,* 2001 Cr LJ 504 (SC), medical report in a case of rape and murder preferred.

1106. *Piara Singh v State of Punjab,* AIR 1977 SC 2274 : 1977 Cr LJ 1941; *Purna Palai v State of Orissa,* 1987 Cr LJ 1406 (Ori). Again, in a rape case where the doctors differed, it was held that the evidence of expert witness which supported the direct evidence should be accepted. *Ram Antony Danasekaran v State of TN,* 1992 Cr LJ 475 (Mad). Medical opinion being an evidence of only corroborative nature, it cannot be used to rule direct eye witness account. *R Jagdish Murty v Balaram Mohanty,* 1992 Cr LJ 996 (Ori), where the court explained the importance of witnesses to the judicial process by citing Bentham as saying that the witnesses are the eyes and ears of justice. Medical evidence not to be made the sole touch-stone and following *State of UP v Krishna Gopal,* AIR 1988 SC 2154 : 1989 Cr LJ 288 : (1988) 4 SCC 302 : 1988 SCC (Cri) 928 and *Solanki Chimanbhai Ukabhai v State of Gujarat,* AIR 1983 SC 484 : 1983 Cr LJ 822 : (1983) 2 SCC 174 : 1983 SCC (Cri) 379. *State v Rangaswamy,* 2003 Cr LJ 607 (Kant), there was a pro accused medical report in the case of rape or sexual assault, the court said that it was evidence of the fact that there was misconduct on the part of doctors in public hospitals resulting in 94% acquittal in such cases. The court appealed to the conscience of the medical profession and directed the State Government to ensure stoppage of illegalities in hospitals.

particular person is satisfactory and reliable, medical evidence cannot override that because the latter is hypothetical.[1107] In case of discrepancy between medical evidence and ocular evidence, the latter will prevail because medical evidence is only an opinion as regards the nature of death.[1108] The High Court should not substitute its opinion as to the murder weapon for that of the expert.[1109] Weapon must be shown to the expert so as to enable him to comment whether all or any of the wounds would have been caused with it.[1110] A doctor's opinion about weapon, though theoretical, cannot be totally wiped out.[1111] A medical leave certificate cannot be questioned on the ground that it did not mention the condition of the patient in detail such as whether he was able to move or not.[1112] Whether a book advocating the use of cocaine tended to deprave and corrupt has been held to be a technical matter entitling medical men to speak.[1113]

[s 45.7.1] Medical evidence *vis-à-vis* oral evidence.—Evidentiary value of medical evidence is only corroborative and not conclusive and hence, in case of a conflict between the oral evidence and the medical evidence, the former is to be preferred unless the medical evidence completely rules out the oral evidence.[1114]

[s 45.7.2] Serologist's report.—Where the Serologist's report stated that blood on two of the clothes belonging to the accused was human blood, it was held that it connect the accused with crime.[1115]

The serological report with negative inference is not fatal to the prosecution case because at a considerable period, the blood gets disintegrated in natural course.[1116]

1107. *Punjab Singh v State of Haryana*, AIR 1984 SC 1233 : 1984 Cr LJ 921 : 1984 Supp SCC 233 : 1984 SCC (Cri) 484. *Dharamvir v State of UP*, 1990 Cr LJ 839 : 1989 All LJ 454, medical evidence not ruling out eye-witness version.

1108. *Arjun Naik v State of Orissa*, 2002 Cr LJ 2785 (Ori).

1109. *State of UP v Shanker*, AIR 1981 SC 897 : 1981 Cr LJ 23. See also *Munir Ad v State of Rajasthan*, AIR 1989 SC 705; 1989 Cr LJ 845 : 1989 Supp (1) SCC 377 : 1989 SCC (Cri) 455, where the Supreme Court specifically recognised that the doctor preparing the post mortern report was competent to express opinion about the nature of the weapon used in the assault.

1110. *Ishwar Singh v State of UP*, AIR 1976 SC 2423 : 1976 Cr LJ 1883. For evidence of age by radiological test see *Jaya Mala v Home Secy., J&K*, AIR 1982 SC 1297 : 1982 Cr LJ 1777; *State of Maharashtra v Lahu Laxman Pabale*, 2003 Cr LJ 1174 (Bom), nothing was brought out in the cross-examination of the doctor to contradict his expert opinion that the punctured wounds on the body of the deceased could have been caused with a wooden stick and an iron rod. The Supreme Court said that the rejection of such opinion by the court was not proper.

1111. *Anwarul Haq v State of UP*, (2005) 10 SCC 581 : AIR 2005 SC 2382 : 2005 Cr LJ 2602.

1112. *Nityananda v Sipra*, AIR 1986 or 102, seeking adjournment on medical basis.

1113. *R v Skirving*, (1985) 2 All ER 705. See All ER Annual Review 1985 at p 157. On sifting of expert evidence in personal injury cases. See *Sullivan v West Yorkshire Passenger Transport Executive*, (1985) 2 All ER 134; medical opinion preferred as against eye-witnesses. *Purshottam v State of MP*, AIR 1980 SC 1873 : 1980 Cr LJ 1298; *MD Jadhav v State of Maharashtra*, AIR 1976 SC 2327 : 1976 Cr LJ 1873, medical report as charred bodies found reliable. *Manguli Dei v State of Orissa*, AIR 1989 SC 483; 1989 Cr LJ 823 : 1989 Supp (1) SCC 161 : 1989 SCC (Cri) 322, where the body in a highly decomposed state and the difference between the medical version that there was only injury and that of the accused that he administered four axe injuries on the head was ignored, being not relevant.

1114. *Yogesh Singh v Mahabeer Singh*, 2017 Cr LJ 291, para 43 (SC) : 2016 (10) JT 332. See also *Sadhu Saran Singh v State of UP*, 2016 Cr LJ 1908, para 21(iii) : (2016) 4 SCC 357.

1115. *Boddu Murali v State of AP*, 1993 Cr LJ 2077 (AP).

1116. *Amar Mondal v State of WB*, 2016 Cr LJ 5036, para 46 (Cal-DB).

A medical officer is not a ballistic expert. He was not expected to answer whether the injury in question could have been caused by bullet alone.[1117]

[s 45.7.3] Polygraph Test.—The test is administered for finding out whether the statements being made by the person and his responses are correct or not. If he tells lies his responses are of a different kind. Foreign courts have subjected such a test to limitations in criminal cases.[1118]

[s 45.7.4] Narco analysis.—This test does not have absolute success rate.[1119]

[s 45.7.5] Brain Electrical Activation Profile Test.—This test is used for crime detection. Its reliability depends.[1120]

[s 45.7.6] Brain mapping test.—The admissibility of the result of a scientific test depends upon its authenticity. Whether the brain mapping test is so developed that the report would have probative value depends upon further consideration after submission of the report. The prosecution itself did not rely upon. So did the High Court. The Supreme Court also did not place any reliance upon it.[1121]

[s 45.7.7] Medical evidence of Chronic alcoholism.—The court said that the evidence of mental infirmity was relevant to the question of the capacity of the accused for self control. As the medical reports had only been available a few days before the trial, they could not be considered by the court of Appeal. A retrial was ordered.[1122]

[s 45.7.8] Chemical analyser.—In *Shatrughan v State of MP*,[1123] it was held that an unexhibited report of the chemical examiner did not require to be formally proved by any witness. It was a document which proved itself under section 293, CrPC. Where the samples taken out from the seized contraband remained with the police officer for three days without being noted down anywhere in records and thereafter they were sent to the chemical analyser and the prosecution gave no satisfactory explanation to exclude the possibility of tampering during that period, it was held that the certificate of the chemical analyser that the samples examined by him contained heroin must be discarded.[1124] Where the doctor failed to give his opinion about the nature of injury, the court cannot substitute its opinion assuming the role of an expert.[1125] Medical evidence is not sacrosanct and when the court is insistent on authenticity of some relevant particulars, it can ask for the same by way of clarification from the concerned physician in the witness box.[1126]

1117. *Mahmood v State of UP*, AIR 2008 SC 515 : 2008 Cr LJ 698.

1118. *Selvi v State of Karnataka*, AIR 2010 SC 1974 : (2010) 7 SCC 263.

1119. *Ibid*

1120. *Ibid*

1121. *Ranjitsing Brahamajeetsing Sharma v State of Maharashtra*, AIR 2005 SC 2277 : (2005) 5 SCC 294 : 2005 Cr LJ 2533.

1122. *R. v Parker*, (Philip) [CA (Crim Div)] 1997 CLY 435 (1127).

1123. 1993 Cr LJ 120 (MP).

1124. *Mohd. Hussain B Ramzan v State of Maharashtra*, 1994 Cr LJ 1020 (Bom).

1125. *Babloo v State of MP*, 1995 Cr LJ 3534 (MP), relying on *Gambhir v State of Maharashtra*, AIR 1982 SC 1157 : 1982 Cr LJ 1243.

1126. *Archana Devi v Kaji Majibur Rahaman*, AIR 1996 Cal 118. *Sree Vijayakumar v State*, (2005) 10 SCC 737 : 2005 Cr LJ 3085, found to be not reliable because there was no assurance that the sample was preserved and protected as originally submitted.

[s 45.7.9] Nautical assessors' opinion.—The advice given by nautical assessors is expert evidence, admissible in Admiralty Courts, on all issues of fact about seamanship.[1127] The decision of the case, however, rests entirely with the court and even in purely nautical matters the court is not bound to follow the advice of assessors, but on questions of nautical science and skill great attention must obviously be paid to the opinion of assessors since they are the only source of information on these points and some reasons should be given for disregarding them.[1128]

[s 45.7.10] Injury certificate.—Entries in injury certificate need not carry the names of the actual assailants.[1129]

[s 45.8] "Handwriting".—The science of handwriting is not an exact science and great care and caution should be exercised by the court in determining the genuineness of handwriting.[1130] A handwriting expert can certify only probability and not 100% certainty.[1131] It is necessary for the admission of the evidence of a handwriting expert, that the writing with which the comparison is made should be admitted or proved beyond doubt to be that of the person alleged, and that the comparison should be made in open court in the presence of such person.[1132] The evidence of handwriting expert is only an opinion evidence and is not conclusive and cannot be relied upon unless corroborated by clear direct evidence or by circumstantial evidence.[1133] Opinion of the handwriting expert can be sought for determining the age of the disputed handwriting.[1134]

Though the opinion of a handwriting expert on the question of the handwriting of a person is relevant it is not conclusive and the handwriting of the person can be proved by other means also.[1135] The court said: A court is competent to compare the disputed writing of a person with others which are admitted or proved to be his writings. It may not be safe for a court to record a finding about a person's writing in a certain document merely on the basis of comparison, but a court can itself compare the writings in order to appreciate properly the other evidence produced before it.

1127. *The Clan Lemont,* (1946) 79 Lloyd LR 521, at p 524.

1128. *Asiatic S.N Co v Arabinda,* AIR 1959 SC 597 : 1959 Supp (1) SCR 979.

1129. *P Babu v State of AP,* 1993 Cr LJ 3547.

1130. *Vandavasi Karthikeya v S Kamalamma,* AIR 1994 AP 102; *Ameer Mahammed v Harkat Ali,* AIR 2002 Raj 406, the opinion of an expert cannot be rejected only on the ground that he is a remunerated witness or that it is based on imperfect science. The court followed the decisions in *Judah v Isolyrie Shrojbashini Bose,* AIR 1945 PC 174; *Murailal v State of MP,* AIR 1980 SC 531 : 1980 Cr LJ 396.

1131. *MK Usman Koya v CS Santha,* AIR 2003 Ker 191.

1132. *Suresh Chandra Sanyal v Emperor,* (1912) 39 Cal 606.

1133. *SPS Rathor v CBI,* AIR 2016 SC 4486, para 27 : 2016 (10) SCJ 232.

1134. *Uppu Jhansi Lakshmi Bai v J Venkateswara Rao,* AIR 1994 AP 90.

1135. *State of Gujarat v Vinaya Chandra,* AIR 1967 SC 778 : 1967 Cr LJ 668. The opinion of an expert about the handwriting in a will is relevant but it would require corroboration. *Joseph v Aleyamma,* AIR 1991 NOC 28 (Ker). Evidence of the handwriting expert must be received with great caution. *Bhargava K Salunkhe v State of Maharashtra,* 1996 Cr LJ 1228 (Bom), **relying on** *Magan Bihari Lal v State of Punjab,* AIR 1977 SC 1091 : 1977 Cr LJ 711. *Mohd. Asadullah v State,* 2003 Cr LJ 2355 (J&K), mere opinion of handwriting expert without any corroborative evidence was held to be not sufficient for recording conviction on a charge of forgery and cheating. *Rajinder Bajaj v Indian Tanning Industries,* AIR 2008 Del 62 : (2008) 100 DRJ 534, appointment as commission agent, the court found glaring discrepancy in the signature on the appointment letter and those on the written statement and affidavit. Expert opinion was not necessary. The documents was fabricated.

The conviction of a guard for forging a railway receipt only on the evidence of handwriting expert was set aside.[1136] It is open to the court to rely upon other evidence than upon the opinion of expert that a document is executed by a particular person.[1137] Where the court's opinion agreed with the expert as to handwriting, a conviction was upheld.[1138] Where the question was whether a pronote was forged, it was held that expert opinion could not prevail over the evidence of eye-witnesses.[1139]

[s 45.8.1] ***Competence of handwriting expert.***—In case there is no expert opinion to assist the court in respect of handwriting available, the court should seek guidance from some authoritative textbook and the court's own experience and knowledge, however even in the absence of the same, it should discharge its duty with or without expert, with or without any other evidence.[1140]

[s 45.9] Palm impression.—Under this section the reasons as well as the opinion given by a finger-print expert as to the identity of a palm impression are admissible in evidence.[1141]

[s 45.10] Thumb impression.—The court cannot compare by itself the thumb impression on a document. Such comparison is to be made by an expert.[1142] Where it could not be proved that the thumb impression on the sole receipt was that of the deceased alone, it was held that comparison of finger prints of the deceased with that of the thumb impression on the sale receipt was of no consequence.[1143]

[s 45.11] Fingerprints.—The evidence given by a fingerprint expert need not necessarily be corroborated; but the court must satisfy itself as to the value of the evidence of the expert in the same way as it must satisfy itself of the value of other evidence.[1144]

Where the court had to determine the credibility of a fingerprint expert, it found that he was working in the Fingerprint Bureau as Fingerprint Researcher since 1971. He had passed All India Fingerprint Expert Examination conducted by the Central Fingerprint Bureau. He was given promotion as a fingerprint expert and also as fingerprint inspector. He had deposed in a number of civil and criminal cases as an expert. The court observed

---

1136. *Magan Bihari Lal v State of Punjab,* AIR 1977 SC 1091 : 1977 Cr LJ 711.

1137. *Srichand v Ramrati Devi,* AIR 1980 All 294. See also *VS Abdul Sattar v SP CBI,* 1987 Cr LJ 1670 (Ker), where there is other evidence, the opinion of expert can be sidelined.

1138. *Ram Pyarelal v State of Bihar,* AIR 1980 SC 1523 : 1980 Cr LJ (NOC) 175.

1139. *Brij Basi v Moti Ram,* AIR 1982 All 323.

1140. *Ajay Kumar Parmar v State of Rajasthan,* (2012) 12 SCC 406; Approved *Muraru Lal v State of MP,* (1979) 3 SCC 612 : AIR 1981 SC 363.

1141. *Emperor v Babulal Behari,* (1928) 30 Bom LR 321: 52 Bom 223; *Bhaluka Behera v State,* (1957) Cut 200. Thumb impression of one was disputed by the other. The court was competent to ask for specimen impression for self-comparison. *Sheo Narain v Raisat,* AIR 1986 P&H 174.

1142. *Inum Beevi v KS Syed Ahamed Kabir,* AIR 2001 NOC 25 (Mad) : 2001 ALHC 756. *Thiruvengada Pillai v Navaneethammal,* AIR 2008 SC 1541 : (2008) 4 SCC 530, the court recorded finding about authenticity of thumb impression without the benefit of any expert opinion merely by casual perusal, held illegal.

1143. *Sadashio Mundaji Bhalerao v State of Maharashtra,* AIR 2007 SC 1028 : (2007) 15 SCC 421.

1144. *Emperor v Fakir Mahomed,* (1935) 38 Bom LR 160 : 60 Bom 187, *differing from Jassu Ram v The Crown,* (1923) 4 Lah 236; *Keshavlal v State of MP,* AIR 2002 SC 1221, examination by finger print expert in order to connect the accused with the weapon of offence, the allegation that the accused had stabbed his mistress, the weapon was handled by many people before its seizure. Non examination of the finger print expert was held to be not material.

that he was duly qualified and experienced and therefore his opinion could not be discarded.[1145] Where the fingerprints evidence was obtained in a suspicious manner, the Supreme Court said that a conviction could not be sustained on the basis of such evidence though otherwise the expert opinion was free from any infirmity.[1146]

Where the court had to examine the reliability of finger-print evidence and it was found that specimen of the finger prints were not taken before the magistrate and the seized articles were neither produced nor exhibited, a conviction on the basis of such an evidence was held to be not proper.[1147] In this case, the glass on which finger impressions were found was seized from the house of the accused when he was in custody but the glass was neither produced nor exhibited, the evidence was held to be not reliable.[1148]

Where the photographic impressions of fingers which were taken earlier were not good enough to enable the expert to come to any definite conclusion and, therefore, second impressions were taken, it was held that raising suspicions about the second impressions without cross-examining the photographer was not proper.[1149]

In a case involving robbery, non-examination of the photographer, who lifted the finger prints and also non-production of the negatives of the photographs of the finger prints lifted by chance, could not be a ground for acquittal of the accused.[1150]

Where the weapon of offence with which the accused servant was supposed to have caused the death of his mistress was handled by several persons before its seizure, it was held that it was of no consequence that the weapon was not got examined by a finger print expert.[1151]

The evidence of a fingerprint expert is not a substantive evidence. It can only be used to corroborate some items of substantive evidence, which are otherwise on record. In this case, the accused, hired criminals, had shot dead their victim at point blank range. His body fell half inside and half outside the car. There was no evidence to show that the killers had any reason to touch the car and that too with the ring finger. The evidence of finger prints on the car ceased to have any relevance.[1152]

[s 45.11.1] ***Factors to be kept in mind in considering Fingerprint Evidence.***—The admissibility of fingerprint evidence is dependent upon (1) the expertise and experience of expert witnesses, whose evidence should be qualified with a jury direction that such evidence is not in itself conclusive of guilt; (2) the number of ridge characteristics matching the fingerprints of the accused with the fingerprints found at the scene of the crime. Where there were less than eight matching ridge characteristics, a judge would rarely exercise his discretion to allow the admission of such evidence and, in the absence of exceptional circumstances, the prosecution should not attempt to introduce it; (3) whether there were any dissimilar characteristics; (4) the size of print relied upon, and

1145. *State v M Krishna Mohan,* AIR 2008 SC 368 : (2007) 14 SCC 667.

1146. *Chandiran v State of Kerala,* AIR 1990 SC 2148 : 1990 Cr LJ 2296.

1147. *Babu Khan v State of Rajasthan,* AIR 1997 SC 2960 : 1997 Cr LJ 3567.

1148. *Ibid*

1149. *Ammini v State of Kerala,* 1998 Cr LJ 481 : AIR 1998 SC 260.

1150. *Ajay Kumar Singh v Flag Officer, Commanding-in-Chief,* AIR 2016 SC 3528, para 14 : 2016(6) Scale 785.

1151. *Keshavalal v State of MP,* 2002 Cr LJ 1776 (SC).

1152. *Musheer Khan v State of MP,* AIR 2010 SC 762 : (2010) 2 SCC 748.

(5) the quality and clarity of the print relied upon, which could involve consideration of any finger injuries.[1153]

[s 45.12] Footprints.—The science of identification is a rudimentary science and not much reliance can be placed on the result of such identification. The track evidence, however, can be relied upon as a circumstance which, along with other circumstances, would point to the identity of the culprit though by itself it would not be enough to carry conviction in the minds of the court.[1154]

The Supreme Court observed that the science of identification of footprints is not a fully developed science. Evidence of footprints for the purpose of proving identity of the accused can be used to reinforce the other evidence.[1155]

[s 45.13] Ear print comparison.—The accused appealed against his conviction for the murder of an elderly lady in her home. The prosecution relied, *inter alia*, on the evidence of two experts on ear print comparison, ear prints having been found on the glass of the window which the intruder had forced open to gain entry to the victims home. The accused argued that the jury should not have heard the expert evidence because the evidence of three forensic scientists, all of whom cast doubt on the evidence given by the experts instructed by the prosecution. It was held that the expert evidence relied on by the prosecution was admissible.[1156]

[s 45.14] Voice.—In a divorce petition, the husband tapped the conversation of his wife with others and sought to produce the disc in the court to substantiate his case. The court said that the act of recording conversation without knowledge of the wife was illegal and amounted to infringement of her right to privacy. Such tapes, even if true, were not admissible in evidence.[1157]

[s 45.15] Psychological autopsies on levels of well-being.—The accused was convicted for the murder of his heavily pregnant wife, she was found hanging in the garage of their home. At his trial the accused did not adduce any evidence. His original appeal was dismissed in 1995 on the ground that defence counsel had made a reasoned decision not to call expert evidence. The accused sought to adduce fresh evidence, *inter alia*, from a distinguished psychologist relating to the state of mind of his wife at the time of her death. His appeal was dismissed. The court said that while psychological evidence relating to the state of mind of a victim or defendant that fell short of mental illness could be admitted in certain cases if derived from medical records or established criteria, the existing academic standing of psychological autopsies is not sufficient to allow their admittance as expert evidence. While not alone fatal to the case, it was

1153. *R v Buckley (Robert John)*, (1999) 163 JP 561, [CA (Crim Div)].

1154. *Pritam Singh v State of Punjab*, AIR 1956 SC 415 : 1956 Cr LJ 805. *Shankaria v State of Rajasthan*, AIR 1978 SC 1248 : 1978 Cr LJ 1251. The expert may tell whether the evidence is usable and what degree of identification it can afford. *Mohan Lal v Ajit Singh*, AIR 1978 SC 1183 : 1978 Cr LJ 1107. Where the expert was not called by the either party, the matter could not be raised in appeal. *Phool Kumar v Delhi Admn.*, AIR 1975 SC 905 : 1975 Cr LJ 778.

1155. *Babu Khan v State of Rajasthan*, AIR 1997 SC 2960 : 1997 Cr LJ 3567; *Mohd. Aman v State of Rajasthan*, AIR 1997 SC 2960 : 1997 Cr LJ 3567 : (1997) 10 SCC 44.

1156. *R v Dallagher*, (2002) EWCA Crimes 1903, *The Times*, August 21, 2002 CA (Crim Div). The accused was, however, acquitted for other reasons.

1157. *Rayala v N Rayala*, AIR 2008 AP 98. The wife could not be compelled to undergo voice test and an expert could not be appointed to make comparison.

apparent that the psychologist, while an expert in his field, had not previously attempted the task required of him in the instant case. The psychological reports are speculative and could not be validated quantitatively or by previously established research. The opinions within the expert evidence were based upon biased information mainly provided by the accused and his family, who has not previously given evidence. It was likely that a jury would be capable by themselves of assessing levels of well-being and would not require an expert in order to do so.[1158]

[s 45.16] Typewritten documents.—The opinion of an expert that a particular letter was typed on a particular machine is not admissible as it does not fall within the ambit of this section.[1159] Opinion of a person who is claimed to be an expert on typewritten documents to prove that two different documents were typed on the same typewriter is not admissible under this section. Such a person cannot also be permitted to point out the similarities between the documents in respect of their typing or the defects which might enable the court to come to a conclusion as to whether the documents were or were not typed on the same typewriter. It is not permissible for a court to compare photographic enlargements and measurements of the letters in two documents and to arrive at a conclusion as to whether they were typed on the same typewriter or not.[1160] Such categorical exclusion is not likely to stand any longer. The Supreme Court has observed that the opinion of those who are capable of knowing the origin of a typescript should fall, in view of the scientific advances, within the meaning of expert opinion.[1161]

[s 45.17] Tracker dog.—In *Abdul Razak v State of Maharashtra,*[1162] the Supreme Court has expressed the opinion that in the present state of scientific knowledge evidence of dog tracking, even if admissible, is not ordinarily of much weight.

[s 45.18] Ballistic expert.—It cannot be laid down as a general proposition that in every case where a fire-arm is alleged to have been used by an accused person, in addition to the direct evidence, prosecution must lead the evidence of a ballistic expert, however good the direct evidence may be and though on the record there may be no reason to doubt the said direct evidence.[1163] Where those observed the incident stated that two persons independently fired at their victim and the expert stated that probably both the

---

1158. *R v Gilfoyle (Appeal Against Conviction)*, (2001) 2 Cr App R 5, CA (Crim Div).

1159. *Hanumant v State of MP,* AIR 1952 SC 343 : 1953 Cr LJ 129.

1160. *Chelaji Gomaji v Jashodharabai,* (1958) 60 Bom LR 251; *Emperor v Jhabwala,* (1933) 55 All 1040.

1161. *State v SJ Chowdhary,* 1990 Cr LJ 1112 : AIR 1990 SC 1050 : (1990) 2 SCC 1050.

1162. *Abdul Razak v State of Maharashtra,* AIR 1970 SC 283 : 1970 Cr LJ 373.

1163. *Gurcharan Singh v State of Punjab,* AIR 1963 SC 340 : 1963(1) Cr LJ 323; *Mohan Singh v State of Punjab,* AIR 1975 SC 2161 : 1975 Cr LJ 1865, where the technical evidence was full of doubts. *Ram Narayan v State of Punjab,* AIR 1975 SC 1725 at p 1726 where ballistic evidence was against the prosecution case. See also,*Ramanathan v State of TN,* AIR 1978 SC 1204 at 1213 : 1978 Cr LJ 1137, evidence not rejected only because the ballistic expert had not taken photographs. *State of MP v Surpa,* AIR 2001 SC 2408, death due to gunshot injuries, bullet removed from chest cavity of deceased by doctor, not sent to ballistic expert for examination. The case became weakened and in the light of other weaknesses acquittal upheld. *Dhula v State.* Forensic Science Laboratory report in regard to bloodstains present on the weapon of offence, could not be used against the accused unless it was put to accused in his statements under section 313, CrPC and accused was given an opportunity to explain it. *State of Punjab v Jugraj Singh,* 2002 Cr LJ 1504 (SC), the eye-witness account of gun-shot injuries was controverted by the investigating officer by saying that guns were not in working condition. He did. not send the guns for ballistic examination. The eye-witness account prevailed.

fires were from the same gun, it was held that the expert opinion shaky and, therefore, eye-witness account would prevail.[1164] It is not necessary for an expert for expressing his opinion for the firing capacity of a firearm that he should have it test-fired.[1165] In a case of murder it was held that till the guns were sent for ballistic examination and a report was obtained that they were in working order, mere recovery of guns could not connect the accused with the crime.[1166] Where the ballistic expert was not examined and, neither did the accused request for his cross-examination nor did the court find it necessary to summon him, it was held that the report of the ballistic expert was admissible in evidence without calling him as witness.[1167] Where the witnesses had identified the assailants who had fired gun shots and the firing was corroborated by the report of ballistic expert, the conviction of the accused was confirmed.[1168] Where the ballistic expert mentioned that he had fired six live cartridges from the rifle in question before recording his opinion that the empty cartridge recovered from the spot was fired from the said rifle and his opinion was not challenged in the trial court, the opinion of the expert could not be disbelieved at the appellate stage.[1169] The opinion of the ballistic expert about pin marks of the cartridges could not be rejected merely on the ground that no photographs of the cartridges concerned were taken.[1170]

The view of the ballistic expert as to the distance from which gun shots were fired at the deceased was preferred over that of medical expert.[1171] Where the question was

---

1164. *Anvaruddin v Shakoor,* 1990 Cr LJ 1269 : AIR 1990 SC 1242.

1165. *Sukhpal v State of Haryana,* AIR 1995 SC 578 : 1995(1) SCC 10.

1166. *Lakhasingh v State of Rajasthan,* 1994 Cr LJ 2952 (Raj). *Bhani Ram v State of Rajasthan,* 1995 Cr LJ 3165 (Raj) without ballistic report, recovery of cartridges is useless. *State of MP v Supra,* 2001 Cr LJ 3292 (SC), matters of death by gunshot injuries, not referred to ballistic expert, other evidence also weak.

1167. *Balak Ram v State of Rajasthan,* 1994 Cr LJ 2451 (Raj).

1168. *Bhola Singh v State of Punjab,* AIR 1993 SC 137 : 1993 Cr LJ 3904. *Lakhbir Singh v State of Punjab,* AIR 1994 SC 1029 : 1994 Cr LJ 1374, the opinion of the ballistic expert was that the cartridges recovered could not have been fired from the weapon seized. The positive eye-witness account and the medical opinion prevailed over that of the ballistic expert. The witnesses had seen the country made pistols being wielded by the accused persons. The doctor verified that injuries were caused by gun shots. *SS Ajmer Singh v State of Punjab,* 1993 SCC Cri 1113, delay in sending the pistol to the expert for finding out whether it was in working condition, not fatal in the circumstances of the case. *Mani Ram v State of Rajasthan,* AIR 1993 SC 2453 : 1993 Cr LJ 2530, inordinate delay in sending empty cartridges to ballistic expert, not material because the possibility of substitution was ruled out on the facts.

1169. *Surat Singh v State of AP,* 1995 Cr LJ 3189 (AP), explaining and distinguishing. In Re, *K Thimma Reddy,* AIR 1957 AP 758 : 1957 Cr LJ 1091; *Fakruddin v State of Madhya Pradesh,* AIR 1967 SC 1326 : 1967 Cr LJ 1197 and *Santosh Kumar v State of Madhya Pradesh,* 1988 Cr LJ 1583 and *Gopal Singh Gorkha v State of Uttar Pradesh,* 1991 Cr LJ 1235 : 1991 All LJ 374.

1170. *SG Gundegowda v State of Karnataka,* 1996 Cr LJ 852 (Kant), **following** *Ramnathan v State of TN,* 1978 CLR (SC) 318 : 1978 Cr LJ 1137; *S.G Gundegowda v State of Karnataka,* 1996 Cr LJ 852 (Kant). Delay of one month in sending the gun to the ballistic expert for examination is inconsequential if the seals are found to be intact. *Baldev Singh v State of Punjab,* (1990) 4 SCC 692 : AIR 1991 SC 31, delay in sending the crime articles to the laboratory created doubt about the connection of the cartridges with the crime. The pistol and fired cartridges were seized on Jan. 15 but sent to the Forensic Science Lab only on Jan. 27. *Bal Shanta v UOI,* 2001 Cr LJ 2152 (Guj), an application for testing the range of fire made after 27 years of the incident was not allowed.

1171. *Raza Pasha v State of MP,* AIR 1983 SC 575 : 1984 Mad LJ (Cri) 1; *Vinod Kumar v State of UP,* AIR 1991 SC 300 : 1991 Supp (1) SCC 353, view of the ballistic expert that the gun could not have been triggered of accidentally in the process of snatching; two shots were fired, which could not have happened accidentally. *Prem Kumar v State of Bihar,* 1995 Cr LJ 2634, failure to send the cartridges recovered from the body of the deceased to the ballistic expert was held to be not fatal particularly when the rifles alleged to have been used in the incident were not recovered.

whether a fatal gun-shot injury was suicide or homicide, the plea that the deceased was a schizophrenic patient and committed suicide was ruled out because of the noting in the medical opinion that there was absence of tattooing and blackening of skin surrounding the wound. This ruled out the theory of suicide as the shot must not have been fired from point blank range.[1172]

[s 45.19] Explosives expert.—The evidence of the explosives expert to the effect, that ammonium nitrate along with other articles recovered from the accused were sufficient for preparation of bombs for explosion, was relied upon.[1173]

[s 45.20] Expert evidence on valuation of Property.—The general opinion of the plaintiff vendor or of an advocate related to him that the valuation of the property was much higher was held to be unworthy of reliance particularly when concrete instances of other sales by the plaintiff were available and when neither of them was an expert on the subject of valuation of immovable property.[1174]

When the valuation report is available, it was held that the High Court committed an error in resorting to a guess estimate for reducing the value of the building.[1175]

[s 45.21] Oral agreement, identification of voice.—A suit for specific performance of a sale of property was based upon an oral agreement. The plaintiff (purchaser) produced a tape recorded conversation between him and the seller showing the existence of the oral agreement. At his instance, the court issued a direction to the parties to appear before the court to have their voice recorded for identification by expert opinion at the cost of the plaintiff. The court said that no prejudice to the defendant or miscarriage of justice was likely to result from such procedure.[1176]

[s 45.22] Corroboration not necessary.—The Supreme Court has laid down that although the approach has to be one of caution, there is no rule of law that the evidence of an expert should not be acted upon unless substantially corroborated.[1177]

Chinnappa Reddy J said in this case:[1178] "We begin with the observation that the expert is no accomplice. There is no justification for condemning his opinion to the same class of evidence as that of an accomplice and insist upon corroboration. It has occasionally been said on very high authority that it would be hazardous to base a conviction solely on the opinion of a handwriting expert. But the hazard in accepting the opinion of any expert, is not because experts, in general, are unreliable witnesses—the equality of credibility or incredibility being one which an expert shares with all other witnesses—but because all human judgment is fallible and an expert may go wrong because of some defect of observation, some error of premises or honest mistake of conclusion. The more developed and more perfect a science, less is the chance of an

---

1172. *Santokh Singh v State of Punjab*, AIR 2010 SC 3274 : (2010) 8 SCC 784.
1173. *Chandra Prakash v State of Rajasthan*, (2014) 8 SCC 340 (para 67) : 2014 (5) SCJ 1.
1174. *Uday Chand Dutt v Saibal Sen*, (1987) Supp SCC 506 : AIR 1988 SC 367.
1175. *Rajesh Valel Puthuvalil v Inland Waterways Authority of India*, (2014) 16 SCC 394, para 4 : 2014 (8) Scale 592.
1176. *Pustimargiya Tritiya Peeth Pranyas Shri Dwarkadheesh Mandir v Addl. DJ*, AIR 2009 Raj 9.
1177. *Murarilal v State of MP*, AIR 1980 SC 531 : 1980 Cr LJ 396. Citing Lord President Cooper in *Decei v Edinburgh Magistrate*, (1953) SC (Scotland) 34 on the importance of expert evidence, and *Ram Chandra v State of UP*, AIR 1957 SC 381 and *Fakhrudin v State of MP*, AIR 1967 SC 1326 : 1967 Cr LJ 1197.
1178. *Murari Lal v State of MP*, AIR 1980 SC 531 at p 534 : (1980) 1 SCC 704 : 1980 Cr LJ 396.

incorrect opinion and converse if the science is less developed and imperfect. The science of identification of finger prints has attained near perfection and the risk of incorrect opinion is practically non-existent. On the other hand, the science of identification of handwriting is not so perfect and the risk is, therefore, higher. But that is far from doubting the opinion of a handwriting expert as an invariable rule and insisting upon substantial corroboration in every case, however the opinion may be backed by the soundest of reasons. It is hardly fair to an expert to view his opinion with initial suspicion and to treat him as an inferior sort of witness. His opinion has to be tested by the acceptability of the reasons given by him. An expert deposes and does not decide. His duty is to furnish the Judge with the necessary scientific criteria for testing the accuracy of his conclusion, so as to enable the Judge to form his own independent judgment by the application of those criteria to the facts proved in evidence."[1179]

After reviewing all the earlier Supreme Court decisions, the learned judge concluded: "We are firmly of the opinion that there is no rule of law, nor any rule of prudence which has crystallised into a rule of law, that the opinion evidence of a handwriting expert must never be acted upon, unless substantially corroborated. But, having due regard to the imperfect nature of the science of identification of handwriting, the approach should be one of caution. Reasons for the opinion must be carefully probed and examined. All other relevant evidence must be considered. In appropriate cases corroboration must be sought. In cases where the reasons for the opinion are convincing and there is no reliable evidence throwing a doubt, the uncorroborated testimony of a handwriting expert may be accepted."

[s 45.23] Motor vehicle inspector.—In a case of death by negligent driving, the report of the motor vehicles inspector was placed on record with the consent of the parties. The court did not allow the report to be questioned subsequently on the ground that the inspector was not examined.[1180]

[s 45.24] Scheduled Tribe Certificate Scrutiny Committee.—The conclusions recorded by the Scheduled Tribe Certificate Scrutiny Committee about the caste of the petitioners, which were reasonable and fully supported by the material placed on record and affirmed by the High Court, were found to be neither perverse nor based on no evidence. The Supreme Court declined to interfere.[1181]

[s 45.25] Cost factor in calling expert.—In a claim for intimidation, the court said that the cost of relying on psychiatric evidence would be disproportionate to the potential advantage to be gained by its use. The court felt that the trial judge, having seen the witnesses would be in a position to assess the merits of the employee's allegations and decide whether the conditions described by the employee amounted to intimidation or not.[1182]

1179. The learned Judge cited Lord Cooper in *Derie v Edinburgh Magistrate,* 1953 SC 34 (Scotland) as cited by Cross Evidence, from earliest times the courts have received the opinion of experts as shown in *Buckley v Rice Thomas,* (1554) 1 Plowd 118. The court considered the earlier Supreme Court decisions in *Ram Chandra v UP State,* AIR 1957 SC 381 : 1957 Cr LJ 559.

1180. *Keshavamurthy v State,* 2002 Cr LJ 103 (Kant).

1181. *Pournima Suryakant Pawar v State of Maharashtra,* (2013) 3 SCC 690 (para 13) : AIR 2013 SC 1508.

1182. *Gumpo v Church of Scientology Religious Education College Inc.*, 2000 CP Rep 38 (QBD).

[s 45.26] Solicitor's professional negligence, evidence from another solicitor.— The plaintiff brought an action for professional negligence against his former solicitor concerning his advice and dealings with a mortgage. A sought to adduce expert evidence from a senior solicitor at another firm as to how a reasonably competent solicitor should have approached an enquiry of the type posed by the plaintiff. The plaintiff took out the mortgage to assist her brother establish a solicitor's practice. The solicitor objected to the evidence on the basis that it usurped the judicial function.

It was held that it assisted the court which lacked the relevant experience and was properly admitted in terms of the Civil Evidence Act, 1972, section 3.[1183]

[s 45.27] Conflict of interest and expert witnesses.—Guidance notes by Court of Appeal[1184]**.**— In the judgment of the court on this appeal and application to adduce new evidence, delivered by Sir Mark Potter P but to which all of its members contributed, the court of Appeal made the following observations and gave the following guidance relating to conflict of interest and expert witnesses:

> **[100]** We start with the point of principle. Does the presence of a conflict of interest automatically disqualify an expert? In our judgment, the answer to that question is No: the key question is whether the expert's opinion is independent. It is now well established that the expert's expression of opinion must be independent of the parties and the pressures of the litigation. Authority for this can be found in paras 1 and 2 of the guidance which Cresswell J gave in *National Justice Cia Naviera SA v Prudential Assurance Co Ltd, The Ikarian Reefer*,[1185]as summarised on pp. 938-939 (para 35.3.1) of the White Book (Civil Procedure (2006 Edn)) Vol 1:
>
> 1. Expert evidence presented to the court should be, and should be seen to be, the independent product of the expert uninfluenced as to the form or content by the exigencies of litigation.[1186]
>
> 2. An expert witness should provide independent assistance to the court by way of objective unbiased opinion in relation to matters within his expertise.[1187] An expert witness in the High Court should never assume the role of an advocate...
>
> **[101]** Moreover, CPR 35.3 sets out the overriding duty of an expert witness. His duty is to assist the court in relation to matters which fall within his expertise. The need for the expert to give an independent opinion flows also from this duty, which is stated to override any duty which the expert may owe to his client:
>
> (1) It is the duty of an expert to help the court on the matters within his expertise. (2) This duty overrides any obligation to the person from whom he has received instructions or by whom he is paid.
>
> **[102]** However, while the expression of an independent opinion is a necessary quality of expert evidence, it does not always follow that it is sufficient condition in itself. Where an expert has a material or significant conflict of interest, the court is likely to decline

---

1183. *Archer v Hickmotts* [1997] PNLR 318. [CC (County Court)].
1184. *Toth v Jarman*, (2006) 4 All ER 1276 : 2006 EWCA Civ 1028.
1185. (1993) 2 Lloyd's Rep 68 at 81-82.
1186. *Whitehouse v Jordan*, (1981) 1 All ER 267 at 276 : (1981) 1 WLR 246 at 256-257 per Lord Wilberforce.
1187. See *Polivitte Ltd v Commercial Union Assurance Co plc*, (1987) 1 Lloyd's Rep 379 at 386 per Garland J and *Re J (Child Abuse: Expert Evidence)*, (1991) 1 FCR 193 per Cazalet J.

to act on his evidence, or indeed to give permission for his evidence to be adduced. This means it is important that a party who wishes to call an expert with a potential conflict of interest should disclose details of that conflict at as early a stage in the proceedings as possible...

[113] The obligation to disclose the existence of a conflict of interest in our judgment stems from the overriding duty of an expert, to which we have already referred and which is clearly laid down in CPR 35.3, and also from the duty of the parties to help the court to further the overriding objective of dealing with cases justly (CPR 1.3). The court needs to be assisted by information as to any potential conflict of interest so that it can decide for itself whether it should act in reliance on the evidence of that expert.

[114] We note that the practice of the court as set out in the CPR and practice directions, the valuable new Protocol for the Instruction of Experts to give evidence in civil claims (set out at pp 966-977 of *Civil Procedure*), and the commentaries in *Civil Procedure* and *Civil Court Practice* (the Green Book), do not refer in terms to the need for disclosure by an expert of a conflict or potential conflict of interest. We also note that the standard form of order used by Master Ungley and Master Yoxall, to whom clinical negligence matters in the Queen's Bench Division in London are assigned, requires the production of an expert's curriculum vitae (cv) but this is only where the court has directed a single expert, and the parties cannot agree on who it should be. As already stated, in our judgment, an expert should produce his CV when he provides his report, and that CV should give details of any employment or an activity which raises a possible conflict of interest. This may indeed already be best practice.

[115] The practice direction supplementing CPR Pt 35 provides that an expert must verify his expert's report by a statement of truth in the following form:

I confirm that insofar as the facts stated in my report are within my own knowledge I have made clear which they are and I believe them to be true, and that the opinions I have expressed represent my true and complete professional opinion.

[116] In addition, the practice direction also requires the expert's report to state any qualification, if the expert is not able to give his opinion without qualification, and that the expert understands his duty to the court and has complied and will continue to comply with the duty.

[117] An expert will often make a declaration at the end of his report which not only contains the statement of truth required by the practice direction but also contains other matters designed to meet other requirements of the CPR or practice directions, or other issues which have arisen in practice. No doubt, in principle these declarations serve the valuable purpose of focusing the mind of the expert on all these matters...

[119] In our judgment, the Civil Procedure Rules Committee should consider extending the requirement for an expert's declaration at the end of his report. Its present form is directed to ensuring that the contents of the report represent the independent and unvarnished opinion of the expert making the report. But, as we have explained above, there is another side to independence. The expert should not leave undisclosed any conflict of interest which might bring into question the suitability of his evidence as the basis for the court's decision. The conflict of interest could be of any kind, including a financial interest, a personal connection, or an obligation, for example, as a member or officer of some other body. But ultimately, the question of what conflicts of interest fall within this description is a question for the court, taking into account all the circumstances of the case.

[1188]**[s 45A] Opinion of Examiner of Electronic Evidence.—When in a proceeding, the court has to form an opinion on any matter relating to any information transmitted or stored in any computer resource or any other electronic or digital form, the opinion of the Examiner of Electronic Evidence referred to in section 79A of the Information Technology Act, 2000 (21 of 2000), is a relevant fact.**

***Explanation*.—For the purposes of this section, an Examiner of Electronic Evidence shall be an expert.]**

COMMENTS

This section was inserted *vide* Information Technology (Amendment) Act, 2008.[1189]

The *Explanation* to this section explains the purpose behind the insertion of this section, i.e. to extend the status of an "expert" to the statutory office of Examiner of Electronic Evidence, created under section 79 of Information Technology Act, 2000.[1190]

Electronic or digitalized documents form a distinct category of documents, different from the traditional documents, and a different form of expertise is required for the purpose of giving an expert's opinion regarding such electronic or digitalized documents. It has been therefore provided that in a judicial proceeding, when either electronic or digitalized document which constitutes part of any information transmitted or stored in any computer resource, is the subject-matter for a court to form an opinion, then the opinion given by Examiner of Electronic Evidence shall be admissible as a relevant fact under this newly inserted section.

Only if the electronic record is duly produced in terms of section 65-B of the Evidence Act, 1872, would the question arise as to the genuineness thereof and in that situation, resort can be made to section 45-A, i.e., the opinion of the Examiner of Electronic Evidence.[1191]

[s 46] Facts bearing upon opinions of experts.—Facts, not otherwise relevant, are relevant if they support or are inconsistent with the opinions of experts, when such opinions are relevant.

ILLUSTRATIONS

(a) The question is, whether *A* was poisoned by a certain poison.

The fact that other persons, who were poisoned by that poison, exhibited certain symptoms which experts affirm or deny to be the symptoms of that poison, is relevant.

(b) The question is, whether an obstruction to a harbour is caused by a certain sea-wall.

1188. Ins. by Act 10 of 2009, section 52(b) (w.e.f. 27-10-2009).

1189. (10 of 2009), section 51 (w.e.f. 27.10.2009, *vide* Notification No. SO 2689(E), dated 27-10-2009).

1190. (21 of 2000).

1191. *Anvar PV v PK Basheer*, (2014) 10 SCC 473 (para 13) : AIR 2015 SC 180.

The fact that other harbours similarly situated in other respects, but where there were no such sea-wall, began to be obstructed at about the same time, is relevant.

SYNOPSIS

COMMENT

[s 46.1] Principle.—The opinion of an expert is open to corroboration or rebuttal. The illustrations indicate that for this purpose *res inter alia acta* is receivable.

An exception to the general rule, which lays down that evidence of collateral facts cannot be received, arises "where the question is a *matter of science*, and where the facts proved, though not directly in issue, tend to illustrate the opinions of scientific witnesses. Thus, where the point in dispute was, whether a sea-wall had caused the choking up of a harbour, and engineers were called to give their opinions as to the effect of the wall, proof that other harbours on the same coast, where there were no embankments, had begun to be chocked up about the same time as the harbour in question, was admitted, as such evidence served to elucidate the reasoning of the skilled witnesses."[1192]

Where the ocular evidence was that a number of assailants surrounded the person and continuously subjected him to injuries and the medical report showed some knife injuries, it was held that the eye-witness account stood nullified.[1193]

[s 46.2] Toxicologist's report.—Where the accused was convicted of driving with excess blood alcohol and he produced expert evidence from a toxicologist questioning the reliability of the blood alcohol test results. That contention was rejected on the basis that the toxicological evidence had been purely theoretical, that the expert had not actually carried out his own analysis and that the evidence as to the amounts of blood tested had come from a rough estimate by the police officer involved. It was held that the evidence of the toxicologist was admissible evidence that raised significant doubt as to the accuracy of the blood alcohol tests undertaken. The evidence was not merely theoretical but was opinion evidence based on certain uncontroversial facts. That evidence could not be rejected without some logical basis for doing so which did not exist. Given that the accused was found to be only four mg over the prescribed limit, the doubts raised by the toxicologist meant that it could not be said that the prosecution had discharged its burden of proof.[1194]

[s 46.3] Application for fresh expert evidence.—An accused appealed against his conviction for murder contending that expert evidence which was subsequently discovered and which was admissible was capable of casting a doubt on the safety of his conviction and, therefore, should be allowed to be admitted. The court allowed the appeal and ordered retrial.[1195] It said that when considering whether fresh evidence

1192. *Taylor*, 12th Edn, section 337, p 234; *Folkes v Chadd*, (1782) 3 Doug. 157. See generally *Murarilal v State of MP*, AIR 1980 SC 531 at 535 : 1980 Cr LJ 396.

1193. *Ram Karan Mal v State*, 1990 Cr LJ 846 : 1989 All LJ 463.

1194. *Gregory v DPP*, (2002) EWHC 385, (2002) 166 JP 400, QBD (Admin Ct).

1195. *R v Cairns*, The Times, March 8, 2000 (CA Crimes Div.).

should be admitted on appeal, regard has to be paid as to whether there was a reasonable explanation for the failure to adduce the evidence at trial. However, that is not decisive and the court should also consider other factors, including the effect of the evidence if it is received and whether in the light of those findings, it is necessary or expedient in the interests of justice to do so. In the instant case, the evidence was from two reliable experts and was capable of belief. Although there was no satisfactory explanation for the failure to adduce the evidence at the trial, it clearly had the potential to afford grounds for allowing an appeal against conviction.

[s 47] Opinion as to handwriting when relevant.—When the Court has to form an opinion as to the person by whom any document was written or signed,[s 47.2] the opinion of any person acquainted with the handwriting of the person by whom it is supposed to be written or signed that it was or was not written or signed by that person, is a relevant fact.

***Explanation.*—A person is said to be acquainted with the handwriting of another person when he has seen that person write, or when he has received documents purporting to be written by that person in answer to documents written by himself or under his authority and addressed to that person, or when, in the ordinary course of business, documents purporting to be written by that person have been habitually[s 47.3] submitted to him.**

ILLUSTRATION

The question is, whether a given letter is in the handwriting of *A*, a merchant in London.

B is a merchant in Calcutta, who has written letters addressed to *A* and received letters purporting to be written by him. *C* is *B*'s clerk, whose duty it was to examine and file *B*'s correspondence. *D* is *B*'s broker, to whom *B* habitually submitted the letters purporting to be written by *A* for the purpose of advising him thereon.

The opinions of *B*, *C* and *D* on the question whether the letter is in the handwriting of *A* are relevant, though neither *B*, *C* nor *D* ever saw *A* write.

SYNOPSIS

COMMENT

[s 47.1] Principle.—When the court has to form an opinion as to the handwriting of any person, the opinion of a person acquainted with the handwriting of such person is admissible in evidence. This section indicates one of the methods of proving handwriting. The handwriting of a person may be proved in the following ways:—

(1) By the evidence of the writer himself.

(2) By the evidence of a person who has seen the person, whose handwriting is in question, write.[1196]

1196. *In the matter of a First Grade Pleader*, (1914) PR No. 18 of 1915 (Civil).

(3) By the evidence of a person acquainted with such handwriting either by receiving letters purporting to be written by the person in answer to documents written by the witness or under his authority and addressed to that person or when, in the ordinary course of business, documents purporting to be written by that person have been habitually submitted to him. The wife can be regarded as a person acquainted with the handwriting of her husband. A letter written by her husband to another woman acknowledging marital relationship with her was in question.[1197] Evidence as to handwriting of a witness who did not say he was familiar with the handwriting in question was rejected.[1198]

In this category may be included cases where a person having custody of family records obtains familiarity with the handwriting of persons who are dead and gone.[1199]

(4) By the evidence of an expert in comparing handwriting. The court must satisfy itself by such means as are open to it that the opinion may be acted upon.[1200]

(5) By the court comparing the document in question with any others proved to the satisfaction of the court to be genuine.

(6) The court may also direct any person present in court to write any words or figures for the purpose of enabling the court to compare the words or figures so written with any words alleged to have been written by such person.

A witness need not state in the first instance how he knows the handwriting, since it is the duty of the opposite party to explore on cross-examination the sources of his knowledge, if he be dissatisfied with the testimony as it stands. It is within the power of the presiding Judge and often it may be desirable to permit the opposing advocate to intervene and cross-examine so that the court may at that stage be in a position to come to a definite conclusion on adequate materials as to the proof of the handwriting.[1201]

A document wholly in the handwriting of a party is said to be an autograph or holograph; where it is in the handwriting of another person, and is only signed by the party, the signature may be called "onomastic"; where it is signed by a cross or other symbol, "symbolic".[1202]

[s 47.2] "Signed".—Signing includes signature by stamping.[1203]

[s 47.3] "Habitually".—This word means "usually", "generally", or "according to custom". It does not refer to the frequency of the occasions but rather to the invariability of the practice. A record-keeper, who in the course of his official duty has to file papers

---

1197. *Shankeappa v Sushilabai,* AIR 1984 Kant 112.

1198. *Rahim Khan v Khurshid Ad.,* AIR 1975 SC 290 : 1994(2) SCC 660.

1199. *Pusaram v Manmal,* (1951) 1 Raj 764.

1200. *Fakhruddin v State of MP,* AIR 1967 SC 1326 : 1967 Cr LJ 1197; *Alamgir v State (NCT Delhi),* 2003 Cr LJ 456 : AIR 2003 SC 282, the accused alleged to have killed his wife in a guest house room and left after locking the room. Two slips of paper were recovered from the room. A handwriting expert gave the opinion that the handwriting on the slips was that of the accused. The court said that the opinion could be relied upon if it was supported by other items of evidence and also as corroborating circumstantial evidence. The chain of circumstances was found to be complete.

1201. *Shankar v Ramji,* (1903) 5 Bom LR 663 : 28 Bom 58.

1202. *Best,* 12th Edn, section 232, p 217.

1203. *Shyamsunder v Kurpasindhu,* (1962) Cut 501.

sent to him, is competent to testify to the handwriting of a person whose papers are so filed, though the number of such papers may not be numerically great.[1204]

[s 47.4] Evidentiary value.—Where the dead body of a woman was recovered from a room in a guest house, where she stayed along with her husband, and two slips also recovered from the room showed under expert opinion the handwriting and signature of her husband, the Supreme Court said that the opinion of the expert could be relied upon when supported by other items of evidence and could be used as corroborative circumstantial evidence.[1205] Where the handwriting expert was not examined the Bombay High Court held that no value or weightage could be given to his opinion.[1206] In this case the letters of the deceased to his brother were shown to the wife of the deceased in cross-examination and she stated that they were in the handwriting of her husband. She was not cross-examined on this point. Her opinion as to handwriting became relevant.

[1207][s 47A] Opinion as to electronic signature when relevant.—When the court has to form an opinion as to the [1208][electronic signature] of any person, the opinion of Certifying Authority which has issued the [1209][Electronic Signature Certificate] is a relevant fact.]

COMMENT

[s 47A.1] Opinion as to digital signature.—A new section has been added so as to provide for relevancy of expert opinion on the genuineness of a digital signature. The new provision says that when the court has to form an opinion as to the digital signature of any person, the opinion of the certifying authority which has issued the Digital Signature Certificate is a relevant fact. A "certifying authority" means an authority who has been granted a licence to issue a digital signature certificate under section 24 of Information Technology Act, 2000.

The purpose behind the insertion of this section is to extend the status of an "expert" to the statutory office of the Certifying Authority which has issued the Digital Signature Certificate.

In 2008, an amendment[1210] was made to this section, whereby the word "digital" was substituted with the word "electronic".

After the entire regimen of "digital signature" having been substituted by "electronic signature", the Office of Certifying Authority of electronic signature has been made the

---

1204. *Emperor v Ponde (No. 2),* (1925) 27 Bom LR 1031.

1205. *Alamgir v State, (NCT) Delhi,* AIR 2003 SC 282.

1206. *Bapurao v State of Maharashtra,* 2003Cr LJ 2181 (Bom) following *State of Maharashtra v Damu Gopinath Shinde,* AIR 2000 SC 1691 : 2000 Cr LJ 2301 where the expert was the Assistant State Examiner of Documents but no value was attached to his opinion without his appearing as a witness.

1207. Ins. by the Information Technology Act (Act 21 of 2000), section 92 and Second Schedule (w.e.f. 17-10-2000).

1208. Subs. by the Information Technology (Amendment) Act, 2008 (10 of 2009), section 52(c), for "digital signature" (w.e.f. 27-10-2009).

1209. Subs. by the Information Technology (Amendment) Act, 2008 (10 of 2009), section 52(c), for the words "Digital Signature Certificate" (w.e.f. 27-10-2009).

1210. (10 of 2009), section 52 (w.e.f. 27.10.2009 *vide* Notification No. S.O 2689(E) dated 27.10.2009).

statutory regulator who issues electronic signature certificate. By the insertion of this new section, the said statutory regulator, i.e. the Certifying Authority which has issued the electronic signature certificate, has been conferred the status of an "expert" meaning thereby that whenever the court has to form an opinion regarding the electronic signature of any person, the opinion given by Certifying Authority of electronic signature shall be admissible as a relevant fact under this newly inserted section.

[s 48] Opinion as to existence of right or custom, when relevant.—When the Court has to form an opinion as to the existence of any general custom[s 48.2] or right, the opinions, as to the existence of such custom or right, of persons who would be likely to know of its existence if it existed, are relevant.

***Explanation.*—The expression "general custom or right" includes customs or rights common to any considerable class of persons.**

ILLUSTRATION

The right of the villagers of a particular village to use the water of a particular well is a general right within the meaning of this section.

SYNOPSIS

COMMENT

[s 48.1] Principle.—Opinions of persons who are in a position to know of the existence of a custom or usage in their locality are admissible. For example, a person, who had been in the habit of writing out deeds of sale, or one who had been seeing transfers frequently made, would certainly be in a position to give his opinion whether there was a custom or usage in that particular locality, and the opinion of such persons would be admissible.[1211] The witness in question should, however, possess experiential qualification before his evidence gathers any credibility. If he does not have this qualification he should show the grounds on which his opinion is based. But if his opinion is not based on reliable information, his mere repetition of hearsay would not carry any weight.[1212]

This section read with section 60 requires that the person who holds the opinion should be called as a witness.[1213]

The section deals with oral evidence given in court by the person expressing the opinion. Section 13 applies to all rights and customs, public or private, and refers to specified facts which may be given in evidence. Under section 32, clause (4), opinion as to public right or custom of a person, who is dead or who had become incapable of giving evidence, or whose attendance cannot be procured without unreasonable delay or expense, is admissible. The statements made by deceased persons after the controversy

---

1211. *Sariatullah Sarkar v Pran Nath Nandi,* (1898) 26 Cal 184.
1212. *Daniraiji Vrajlalji v VM Chandraprabha,* AIR 1971 Guj 188.
1213. *Amina Khatun Musammat v Khalil-ur-Rahman Khan,* (1933) 8 Luck 445.

had arisen, and therefore inadmissible under section 32, are not admissible under this section and section 49. They cannot be admitted under clause (7) of section 32 either.[1214]

[s 48.2] "Custom".—As to "custom", see Comment on section 13. "Custom" is an unwritten law established by usage. "Custom" should be distinguished from "usage". "Usage" is a fact and "custom" is a law. There can be usage without custom, but not custom without usage.

A custom could properly be proved by general evidence given by members of the family or tribe without proof of special instances.[1215] Judicial decisions recognising customs are relevant evidence.[1216] When a custom has been repeatedly brought to the notice of the courts and has been recognised by them regularly in a series of cases, it attains the force of law.[1217] The question of private customary divorce among Jat Sikhs of Punjab arose before the High Court of Delhi.[1218] The court said: The witness must be a person likely to know of the custom. His testimony must be based upon personal knowledge. The weight of his evidence would naturally depend upon his position and character and of persons on whose statements he formed his opinion, but he cannot be confined to instances in which he had personally known the usage or custom exercised as a matter of fact. The court cited the following observation of the Privy Council:[1219] A tribal or family custom excluding a daughter or sister from inheritance in favour of collaterals may be proved by general evidence as to its existence by members of the tribe or family who would naturally be cognizant of its existence and its exercise without controversy. No specific instances need be proved.[1220]

Explanation.—The Explanation indicates that private rights are excluded from the operation of the section. Such rights must be proved by facts such as acts of ownership. The word "general" is an equivalent of the term "public".

[s 49] Opinion as to usages, tenets, etc., when relevant.—When the Court has to form an opinion as to—the usages,[s 49.1] and tenets[s 49.2] of any body of men or family, the constitution and governance of religious or charitable foundation, or the meaning of words or terms used in particular districts or by particular classes of people, the opinions of persons having special means of knowledge[s 49.3] thereon, are relevant facts.

SYNOPSIS

1214. *Amina Khatun Musammat v Khalil-ur-Rahman Khan,* (1933) 8 Luck 445.

1215. *Ahmad Khan v Channi Bibi,* (1925) 52 IA 379: 6 Lah 502. See *Rahimatbai v Hirabai,* (1877) 3 Bom 34. *Radha Krishna Kandolkar v Tukaram,* AIR 1991 Bom 119, not only that right to draw was used for 30 years, recognition by the community is also necessary.

1216. *Tulshiram v Chunilal,* (1940) Nag 149.

1217. *Suganchand Bhikamchand v Mangibai Gulabchand,* (1941) 44 Bom LR 358 : (1942) Bom 467.

1218. *Balwinder Singh v Gurpal Kaur,* AIR 1985 Del 14.

1219. *Ahmad Khan v Channi Bibi,* AIR 1925 PC 267.

1220. Reference was also made to *Gururadhwaja Pd v SP Singh,* (1900) 10 Mad LJ 267 in which it was held by PC that the opinion of a witness as to the existence of a family custom based upon information derived from deceased persons in relevant. See further, *Munshi Das v R Mal Singh,* AIR 1977 SC 2002, where evidence of opinion was not satisfactory.

COMMENT

The opinions of persons who have special means of knowledge as to (a) usages, (b) tenets, of any body of men or family, (c) constitution of any religious foundation, (d) meanings of words or terms used in a district, are admissible in evidence. "Such persons are, so to speak, the depositaries of customary law, just as the text books are the depositaries of the general law".[1221]

This section must be read with section 51.

[s 49.1] "Usages".—These will include usages of trade and agriculture, mercantile usage and any usage common to a body of men or family. Usages of a family will include, for instance, the custom of primogeniture, or any peculiar course of descent.

[s 49.2] "Tenets".—This will include any opinion, principle, dogma, or doctrine which is held or maintained by a body of men. It will apply to religion, politics, science, etc.

[s 49.3] "Special means of knowledge".—All that is meant by this expression is that the person must have had opportunities for acquiring knowledge of a usage or custom and that he had acquired the necessary knowledge.

Evidence relating to works that are technical is also admissible under this section.

[s 50] Opinion on relationship, when relevant.—When the Court has to form an opinion as to the relationship of one person to another, the opinion,[s 50.1] expressed by conduct, as to the existence of such relationship, of any person who, as a member of the family or otherwise, has special means of knowledge on the subject, is a relevant fact:

***Provided* that such opinion shall not be sufficient to prove a marriage in proceedings under the Indian Divorce Act, 1869 (4 of 1869) or in prosecutions under section 494, 495, 497 or 498 of the Indian Penal Code (45 of 1860).**

ILLUSTRATIONS

(a) The question is, whether *A* and *B* were married.

The fact that they were usually received and treated by their friends as husband and wife, is relevant.

(b) The question is, whether *A* was the legitimate son of *B*.

The fact that *A* was always treated as such by members of the family, is relevant.

SYNOPSIS

COMMENT

When the court has to ascertain the relationship of one person to another, the opinion of any person having special means of knowledge, as expressed by conduct, is admissible

1221. *Jugmohandas Mangaldas v Sri Mangaldas Nathubhoy,* (1886) 10 Bom 528, 543.

in evidence. The opinion may be of a member of the family or an outsider, but he must have special means of knowledge. Evidence of general reputation, which is an accumulation of perception testimonies, heard and gathered and reduced to an assertion to court, is not admissible, but the opinion or belief of a person specially competent in this respect, as expressed by his conduct in outward behaviour, is relevant. It is this conduct, which can be tendered in evidence, and the court is to examine whether such conduct is based on the opinion held by the person.[1222] The word "conduct" is not necessarily limited to the conduct of the relations of the person, whose relationship is in dispute, but is wide enough to include the conduct of the witness who was giving his opinion about the existence of such relationship.[1223]

A member of the family can speak in the witness box of what he has been told and what he has learned about his own ancestors, provided what he says is an expression of his own independent opinion (even though it is based on hearsay derived from deceased, not living, persons) and is not merely repetition of the hearsay opinion of others, and provided the opinion is expressed by conduct. His sources of information and the time at which he acquired the knowledge (for example, whether before the dispute or not) would affect its weight but not its admissibility.[1224] On a question of pedigree, family conduct is admissible to prove relationship; and the treatment of friends and neighbours may be received as presumptive proof of marriage. The opinion on behalf of a family regarding relationship; may be inferred from the family conduct, e.g., distribution of family property; tacit recognition of relations.

[s 50.1] "Opinion".—Opinion means something more than mere retailing of gossip or of hearsay; it means judgment or belief, that is, a belief or a conviction resulting from what one thinks on a particular question. Now, the "belief" or conviction may manifest itself in conduct or behaviour which indicates the existence of the belief or opinion.[1225] In *Sitaram Nai v Puranmal Sonar*,[1226] the Supreme Court explained the meaning of the term "opinion" in this connection. The court said that it was laid down in *Dolgobinda v Nimai Charan Misra*,[1227] that what is relevant is the opinion expressed by conduct and opinion means something more than mere relating of gossip or of hearsay; it means judgment or belief, that is, a belief or conviction resulting from what one thinks on a particular question. The section does not make the evidence of mere general reputation admissible as a proof of relationship. It is the conduct or outward behaviour which must be proved in the manner laid down in section 60. A family barber's statement that he knew a particular person to be a son is not relevant. The statement that the chief of the family used to call him as son was held to be within ambit. The witness admitted in cross-examination that the family had no fixed barber.

1222. *Chandu Lal Agarwala v Khalilar Rahman*, (1942) 2 Cal 299.

1223. *Nidhiram v Munei*, (1954) Cut 547; *Sm. Fulkalia v Nathuram*, (1960) Pat 891; *Shriram Sardarmal v Gourishankar*, AIR 1961 Bom 136. *Jagdish Parshad v Sarwan Kumar*, AIR 2003 P&H 3, the deceased father of the plaintiff had visited a temple where he made a signed entry in the *bahi* maintained by the *Panda* of the temple to the effect that a particular person (the defendant) was his nephew. This was held to be relevant to show that he was not the son so as to claim any inheritance.

1224. *Sitaji v Bijendra Narain*, AIR 1954 SC 601.

1225. *Doigobinda v Nimai Charan*, AIR 1959 SC 914 : 1959 Supp (2) SCR 836. Such opinion can be substantiated by the person holding the opinion or by the evidence of any other person. *Champa Devi v MS Singh*, AIR 1981 Pat 103.

1226. *Sitaram Nai v Puranmal Sonar*, AIR 1985 SC 171 at 176.

1227. *Dolgobinda v Nimai Charan Misra*, AIR 1959 SC 914 : 1959 Supp (2) SCr 836.

In *Dolgobinda*[1228] *case, SK Das, J said:*

> Opinion means something more than mere retailing of gossip or of hearsay; it means judgment or belief, that is a belief, that or a conviction resulting from what one thinks on a particular question. Now, the belief or conviction may manifest itself in conduct or behaviour which indicates the existence of the belief or opinion. What the section (s. 50) says is that such conduct or outward behaviour as evidence of the opinion held is relevant and may therefore be proved.

We also accept as correct the view that section 50 does not make evidence of mere general reputation (without conduct) admissible as proof of relationship.

Where the plaintiff claimed to be the daughter of one of the head members of the genealogical branches of the family and there was evidence of witnesses on the point of the claimed relationship of which they had knowledge as relatives and neighbours, the claim of the plaintiff was held to be allowable. Contradictions of trifling nature in the testimony of the witnesses was held to be not material.[1229]

The opinion of Karna Guru as to relationship was admitted because he was holding that respect in the family for fifty years.[1230] Where there was no documentary evidence to show that the women whose legal representatives were claiming shares in the land, were the daughters of the land owner, oral evidence of an old co-villager was not sufficient to infer their relationship particularly because he had no relationship with the family of the owner of the land.[1231]

The newly created offences of dowry death (section 304B, IPC) and dowry harassment (section 498A, IPC) also require proof of marriage. In a case before the AP High Court,[1232] the accused admitted the deceased to be his wife, the relatives, including the father of the deceased girl acknowledged marriage by exchange of garlands, living together and termination of a pregnancy. The court held that this was sufficient evidence within the meaning of section 50 of the fact of marriage.

A second marriage was proved with the help of circumstantial evidence, witnesses were not present at the marriage, but they deposed to the fact of second marriage and living with the second wife. The father of the second wife admitted that fact. The court's finding on the preponderance of probability that the fact of second marriage was proved was held to be not improper.[1233]

Over the question of marriage for the purposes of succession to the wife's estate, the sister and friend of the husband and eye-witnesses deposed to the fact of marriage. They had the special means of knowledge of the relationship. The relationship was kept secret because the parties belonged to different castes. The evidence was held to give a strong support to the presumption of marriage under section 50.[1234]

1228. *Supra,* AIR 1959 SC 914 at 918 : 1959 Supp (2) SCR 814.
1229. *Gourhari Das v Sanilata Singh,* AIR 1999 Ori 61.
1230. *Gobinda Das v B Rout,* AIR 1958 NOC 154 (Ori).
1231. *Sankhali Dhal v Nilamani Dei,* AIR 1994 Ori 298.
1232. *Vadde Rama Rao v State of AP,* 1990 Cr LJ 1666 AP.
1233. *Ajay Chandrakar v Ushabai,* AIR 2000 NOC 32 (AP), the suit was by the first wife for declaration of nullity of the second marriage.
1234. *Bhagwandas Yadav v Rohit Tiwari,* AIR 2010 NOC 589 (MP).

[s 50.2] Opinion as to relationship—[*Proviso*].—The proviso indicates that opinion on relationship cannot be sufficient to prove a marriage in proceedings under the Indian Divorce Act, or in prosecutions for bigamy, adultery and enticing away a married woman. In such cases the fact of the marriage must be strictly proved in the regular way.[1235]

Where the evidence is that a man and a woman lived and were treated as husband and wife for a number of years, in the absence of any material pointing to the contrary conclusion, a presumption might have been drawn that they were lawfully married. But the presumption which may be drawn from long cohabitation is rebuttable, and if there are circumstances which weaken or destroy that presumption the court cannot ignore them. The long cohabitation of a person's mother with his father was established by oral as well as documentary evidence. This was sufficient to record a finding of lawful wedlock. Examination of relatives or of persons having special knowledge was not necessary.[1236] Where the cumulative effect of the other circumstances warrants the conclusion that the man failed to prove the factum of his marriage with the woman, his claim to succeed to her estate as her heir under the customary law of Punjab must fail.[1237]

Where the marriage in question was celebrated several years ago, the court said that oral evidence might be the only available evidence.[1238] In a case for maintenance, the husband denied marriage. The claimant (wife) led evidence to show that both of them were living together as husband and wife. Their daughter corroborated this statement and said that she always received money from him. The court said that the presumption became applicable that they were legally married. He could not prove that the claimant was married to any other person or that he himself was married to some other person.[1239]

[s 51] Grounds of opinion, when relevant.—Whenever the opinion of any living person is relevant, the grounds on which such opinion is based are also relevant.

ILLUSTRATION

An expert may give an account of experiments performed by him for the purpose of forming his opinion.

1235. *Empress v Pitambur Singh,* (1879) Cal 566, FB; *Wadhawa v Fatteh Muhammad,* (1893) PR No.5 of 1894 (Cr). *B Chandra Manikyamma v B Sudarsana Rao,* 1988 Cr LJ 1849 (AP), strict proof of second marriage needed; second marriage and then both parties converting into Islam, not for conviction but for convenience, marriage held invalid. *Hazura Singh v Tej Kaur,* AIR 2002 P&H 162, a widow not allowed to succeed to the estate of her deceased husband because there was evidence that she was living with another person and had also borne his children and also that she was living in adultery.

1236. *Milkhi Ram v Milkhi Ram,* AIR 1996 HP 116.

1237. *Gokal Chand v Parvin Kumari,* (1952) SCJ 331.

1238. *Lakshmamma v Kamalamma,* AIR 2001 Kant 120 at p 121.

1239. *Pradeep Kumar Gupta v Kanti Devi,* 2003 Cr LJ 1350 (Jhar).*KK Thankappan v KS Jayan,* AIR 2003 Ker 114, there was no proof, documentary or oral of the fact of marriage nor any witnesses of opinion as to relationship produced. There was only one fact and that was that the woman lived with the man in his house till her death and the court said that this did not confer the status of wife on her. *Bant Singh v Niranjan Singh,* AIR 2008 SC 2512 : (2008) 4 SCC 75, suit for property, the plaintiff disputed that the defendant's mother was his sister, witness of 80 years was brother-in-law of defendant's mother, he had knowledge about family affairs, attended mother's marriage, acquainted with genealogy of the family, the court agreed that he had special means of knowledge about the family.

COMMENT

Where the opinion of an expert is receivable, the grounds or reasoning upon which such opinion is based may also be inquired into. Opinion is no evidence, without assigning the reason for such opinion. The correctness of the opinion can better be estimated in many instances when the reasons upon which it is based are known. If the reasons are frivolous or inconclusive the opinion is worth nothing.

Where reasons for the support of opinion were introduced at the time of evidence, it was held that the grounds so introduced formed part of the relevant testimony, for the opposite was not thereby deprived of their opportunity to cross-examine the expert nor it was otherwise prejudiced.[1240]

CHARACTER WHEN RELEVANT

[s 52] In civil cases character to prove conduct imputed, irrelevant.—In civil cases the fact that the character of any person concerned is such as to render probable or improbable any conduct imputed to him is irrelevant, except in so far as such character appears from facts otherwise relevant.

SYNOPSIS

COMMENT

In civil cases evidence of the character of any party to the suit to prove the probability or improbability of any conduct imputed to him is irrelevant.

"In respect of the character of a party, two distinctions must be drawn, namely between the cases when the character is in issue and is not in issue and when the cause is civil or criminal. When a party's general character is itself in issue, whether in a civil or criminal proceeding, proof must necessarily be received of what that general character is, or is not. But when general character is not in issue but is tendered in support of some other issue it is, as a general rule, excluded. So in civil proceedings evidence of character to prove conduct imputed is declared by the Act to be irrelevant (section 52). The two exceptions to this rule are, that in civil proceedings evidence of character as affecting *damages*, is admissible (section 55); and in criminal proceedings...the fact that the person accused is of a good character is relevant, but the fact that the has a bad character is, except in certain specified cases, irrelevant (sections 53 and 54.)"[1241]

[s 52.1] Principle.—The general exclusion of character evidence is based on grounds of public policy and fairness, since its admission would surprise and prejudice the parties by raking up the whole of their careers, which they could not possibly come into court prepared to defend.[1242] The business of the court is to try the case, and not the man; and a very bad man may have a very righteous cause.[1243]

1240. *Adithela Immanual Raju v State of Orissa,* 1992 Cr LJ 243 (Ori).
1241. *Woodroffe and Ameer Ali's Evidence,* 10th EdnVol II, p 718.
1242. *The Queen Rowton,* (1865) 34 LJ (MC) 57.
1243. Wigmore on Evidence, 135.

[s 52.2] Scope.—This section refers to the character of parties to the suit, and not to the character of witnesses. It excludes evidence of character from being given only for the purpose of rendering probable or improbable any conduct imputed to the party. But when the facts which are relevant otherwise than for the purpose of showing character are proved, and those facts raise inferences concerning the character of a party to the suit, such facts become relevant not only to prove the facts for which they were directly tendered, but also for the purpose of showing the character of the party concerned. In such a case it is open to the court to form its own conclusion as to the character of the party, and as to the effect of such character on the conduct imputed to the party.[1244]

[s 52.3] "Character".—The word "character" occurring in this section and sections 53 and 54 has been defined in the Explanation to section 55. "Character" is a combination of the peculiar qualities impressed by nature or by habit of the person, which distinguish him from others.[1245]

The evidence of character relates either (a) to character of witnesses, or (b) to character of parties. Character of a witness affects his credit and is always material as it helps the court to come to the conclusion whether his evidence should be treated as trustworthy. Questions touching the character of a witness are allowed to be put to a witness who comes to give evidence in a case.

[s 53] In criminal cases previous good character relevant.—In criminal proceedings the fact that the person accused is of a good character is relevant.

COMMENT

[s 53.1] Principle.—The principle upon which good character may be proved is that it affords a presumption against the commission of crime. This presumption arises from the improbability, as a general rule as proved by common observation and experience, that a man who has uniformly pursued an honest and upright course of conduct will depart from it and do an act so inconsistent with it. Such a person may be overcome by temptation and fall into crime, and cases of that kind often occur; but they are exceptions. The rule is otherwise; the influence of this presumption from character will necessarily vary according to the circumstances of different cases.[1246] Character evidence is a very weak evidence; it cannot outweigh positive evidence in regard to the guilt of a person.[1247]

The following passage in the judgment of Dixon CJ in *Attwood v R*,[1248] explains matters about such evidence in respect of the weight which ought to be attached to it: The history of the admission of evidence of good character, as given in Stephen's *History of the Criminal Law of England*, shows that such evidence does not stand on precisely the same plane as the concerning the relevant facts going to prove or disprove the issue. This is made abundantly clear by the following statement by Lord Ellenborough CJ in *Davison*. "This is the whole of the evidence on the substance of the charge. What follows is evidence, highly important if the case be at all doubtful, if it hangs in even

1244. Norton, 230.
1245. Webster.
1246. Wigmoreon Evidence, 123.
1247. *Bhagwan Swarup v State of Maharashtra*, AIR 1965 SC 682 : 1965 (1) Cr LJ 608.
1248. (1960) 102 CLR 353 at p 157.

scales. If you do not know what way to decide, character should have an effect; but it is otherwise in cases which are clear...If the evidence were in even balance, character should make it preponderate in favour of the defendant;...". In *Frost,* Tindal CJ, thus expresses himself on evidence of good character called on behalf of the defendant : "If the evidence which goes to the fact is sufficiently strong to convince you that the act of criminality which is imputed to him was actually committed, then it is no more than weighing probability against fact. If the scales are hanging even, and you feel a doubt whether the party is guilty or not of the act charged against him, then undoubtedly you will give him the full benefit of such testimony of general character which he may have earned by his previous conduct in life. You are to weigh it not as direct evidence in the case, not as positive evidence contradicting any that has been brought on the other side, but as testimony, probably, to induce you to doubt whether the other evidence is correct, and not to discard that evidence if you think it is so."

[1249][s 53A] Evidence of character or previous sexual experience not relevant in certain cases.—In a prosecution for an offence under section 354, section 354A, section 354B, section 354C, section 354D, section 376, [1250][section 376A, section 376AB, section 376B, section 376C, section 376D, section 376DA, section 376DB] or section 376E of the Indian Penal Code (45 of 1860) or for attempt to commit any such offence, where the question of consent is in issue, evidence of the character of the victim or of such person's previous sexual experience with any person shall not be relevant on the issue of such consent or the quality of consent.]

COMMENT

[s 53A.1] Principle.—This section was inserted *vide* the Criminal Law (Amendment) Act, 2013[1251] on the basis of recommendation given by Justice JS Verma Committee report in the aftermath of the Nirbhaya Rape incident. The Criminal Law (Amendment) Act, 2018 has further amended section 53A of the Indian Evidence Act, 1872. In section 53A of the Indian Evidence Act, 1872, for the words, figures and letters "section 376A, section 376B, section 376C, section 376D", the words, figures and letters "section 376A, section 376AB, section 376B, section 376C, section 376D, section 376DA, section 376DB" have been substituted. Section 53A required amendment to bring sections 376AB, 376DA and 376DB of the Indian Penal Code within its purview.

This section bars the leading of evidence of the character of the victim or her previous sexual experience with any person on the issue of consent given by the victim or the quality of consent, by making it not relevant. Therefore, now, during the course of trial for the offences specified in this section, namely the offences under section 354, section 354-A, section 354-B, section 354-C, section 354-D, section 376, section 376-A, section 376AB, section 376-B, section 376-C, section 376-D, section 376DA, section 376DB or section 376E of the Indian Penal Code or for attempt to commit any of these offence, the defence is barred from either leading any evidence or putting questions in cross-examination, which relates to or is suggestive of the victim's past

1249. Ins. by the Criminal Law (Amendment) Act, 2013 (13 of 2013), section 25 (w.e.f. 3-2-2013).
1250. Subs. by Act 22 of 2018, sec. 8, for "section 376A, section 376B, section 376C, section 376D" (w.r.e.f. 21-4-2018).
1251. Act 13 of 2013, section 25, (w.e.f. 03.02.2013).

previous sexual experience with any other person, in order to show that the victim was a consenting party to the offence which is being tried.

[1252][[s 54] **Previous bad character not relevant, except in reply.—In criminal proceedings the fact that the accused person has a bad character is irrelevant, unless evidence has been given that he has a good character,**[s 54.2] **in which case it becomes relevant.**

***Explanation* 1.—This section does not apply to cases in which the bad character of any person is itself a fact in issue.**

***Explanation* 2.—A previous conviction is relevant as evidence of bad character.**]

SYNOPSIS

COMMENT

[s 54.1] Principle.—Evidence of bad character of an accused person (of whose good character evidence has not been given) is not relevant under this section for the purpose of raising a general inference that the accused is likely to have committed the offence charged. Such evidence is irrelevant and cannot be legally admitted in evidence whether elicited by the prosecution or by the defence.[1253] This description of the accused as a law-breaker amounted to evidence of character. The Supreme Court excluded it.[1254] A man's guilt is to be established by proof of the facts alleged and not by proof of his character; such evidence might create prejudice but not lead a step towards substantiation of guilt.[1255] The prohibition does not in any way affect evidence which is required to prove a motive for the crime or which is otherwise relevant.[1256] But in assessing punishment the court may take into consideration the accused's character and antecedents or the state of crime in the country or locality.[1257]

If evidence is otherwise relevant, it is not rendered inadmissible under this section, merely because it shows bad character or the commission of offences other than the offence with which the accused is charged.[1258]

[s 54.2] "Unless evidence has been given that he has a good character".—Where the accused has attempted to show his good character in his own aid under the preceding section, the prosecution may in rebuttal offer evidence of his bad character. The accused by going into his own character gives a challenge to the prosecution. The prosecution,

---

1252. Subs. by Act 3 of 1891, section 6, for section 54..

1253. *Mi Myin v King-Emperor,* (1908) 5 LBR 4; *Emperor v Gangaram,* (1920) 22 Bom LR 1274.

1254. *Ram Lakhan v State of UP,* AIR 1977 SC 1936 : 1977 Cr LJ 1566.

1255. *Amrita Lal Hazra v Emperor,* (1915) 42 Cal 957.

1256. *Jagwa Dhanuk v King-Emperor,* (1925) 5 Pat 63.

1257. *King-Emperor v Nga Ba Shein,* (1928) 6 Ran 391 FB.

1258. *Sarojekumar Chakrabarti v Emperor,* (1932) 59 Cal 1361.

therefore, is at liberty to refute his claim that he has a good character, otherwise the court would be misled.

The bad conduct cannot be taken into consideration as laid down in this section, unless and until the defence is taken that the accused had good character.[1259]

Where a murder accused had tendered no evidence to show that he was a person of good character, it was held that the prosecution could not be allowed to adduce evidence tending to show that he was a person of bad character.[1260]

[s 54.3] Where bad character in issue—*[Explanation 1]*.—Where the bad character of any person is itself a fact in issue, then the principle of this section does not apply. See section 110(f) of the Code of Criminal Procedure. Therefore, evidence can be given of particular trait of bad character which may be in issue.[1261]

[s 54.4] Previous convictions—*[Explanation 2]*.—A previous conviction is not admissible in evidence against the accused, except where he is liable to enhanced punishment under section 75 of the Penal Code on account of previous conviction or unless evidence of good character be given, in which case the fact that the accused has been previously convicted of an offence is admissible as evidence of bad character.[1262]

As to evidence of previous convictions Lord Denning said:[1263]

> I do not accept (this) argument. I think that previous convictions are admissible. They stand in a class by themselves. They are the raw material upon which bad reputation is built up. They have taken place in open Court. They are matters of public knowledge. They are accepted by people generally as giving the best guide to his reputation and standing. They must, of course, be relevant, in the sense, that they must be convictions in the relevant sector of his life and have taken place within a relevant period such as to affect his current reputation. They are very different from previous instance of misconduct, for those have not been tried out or resulted in convictions, or come before a Court of law. To introduce these might lead to endless disputes, whereas previous convictions are virtually indisputable.[1264]

It has been held that the Crown could rely on attested copies of a foreign court's conviction records in order to rebut accused's claim of good character. Under the Evidence Act, 1851, section 7, the Crown could rely on "examined copies" or "authenticated copies" of a foreign court's records of conviction. Fingerprint evidence and the evidence of the police officer had been admissible since it had the objective of establishing that the person convicted in the foreign court and accused were one and the same person.[1265]

1259. *Divesh Vaidya v State of HP,* 2016 Cr LJ 1935, paras 52 and 53 (HP-DB).

1260. *Prithvi Singh v State of UP,* 2001 Cr LJ 4424 (All).

1261. *Bai Chaturi v State of Gujarat,* AIR 1960 Guj 5.

1262. *Emperor v Duming,* (1903) 5 Bom LR 1034; *Teka Ahir v The King-Emperor,* (1920) 5 PLJ 706. See also, *R v Powell,* (1988) 1 All ER 193 CA, where the accused had put his own character in issue, he was allowed to be cross-examined on his previous conviction on grounds of allowing his premises to be used for purposes of prostitution. The accused was presently charged with living wholly or in part on the earning of prostitution contrary to section 30 of Sexual Offences Act, 1956 [English].

1263. *Goody v Odhams Press Ltd,* (1967) 1 QB 333 (CA).

1264. It was a great train robbery case. The defendants commented upon the person who was convicted for the same saying that because his previous record of convictions he had become a dangerous menace to the society. He filed a civil suit for defamation. He contended that the defendants should not be allowed to adduce evidence of his previous convictions.

1265. *R v Mauricia,* [2002] EWCA Crimes 676, The Times, March 11, 2002, CA (Crim Div).

A previous conviction may also be relevant under section 8 as showing motive. It may also become relevant within the meaning of section 14, Explanation 2, when the existence of any state of mind, or body, or bodily feeling, is in issue or relevant.[1266] It may also be relevant under section 43. See illustration (e).

[s 55] Character as affecting damages.—In civil cases the fact that the character of any person is such as to affect the amount of damages which he ought to receive, is relevant.

***Explanation*.—In sections 52, 53, 54 and 55, the word "character" includes both reputation and disposition; but, except as provided in section 54, evidence may be given only of general reputation and general disposition, and not of particular acts by which reputation or disposition were shown.**

SYNOPSIS

COMMENT

[s 55.1] Principle.—*Evidence to be confined to general reputation and general disposition.*—It is in civil cases, where the question of amount of damages to be awarded to the plaintiff is concerned, that the character of the plaintiff becomes relevant.[1267]

In civil cases good character, being presumed, may not be proved in aggravation of damages, but bad character is admissible in mitigation of damages, provided that it would not, if pleaded, amount to a justification. For example, in cases of defamation the general bad reputation of the plaintiff may be proved. In cases of breach of promise of marriage the plaintiff's general character for immorality is relevant. In cases of seduction evidence of the general character for immorality on the part of the person seduced is relevant. The argument in favour of considering reputation is that the person should not be paid for the loss of that which he never had.

The evidence of the plaintiff's character was held to be receivable in a case in which a journalist had sued a woman drama artist who had said that he was abusing his position as a journalist for making money.[1268] Cave J said: "He complains of an injury to his reputation, and seeks to recover damages for that injury, and it seems most material that the jury who have to award those damages should know, if the fact is so, that he is a man of no reputation. "To deny this would", as is observed in *Starkie on Evidence,* "be to decide that a man of the worst character is entitled to the same measure of damages with one of unsullied and unblemished reputation. A reputed thief would be placed on the same footing with the most honourable merchant, a virtuous woman with the

1266. *Emperor v Alloomiya,* (1903) 5 Bom LR 805: 28 Bom 129.
1267. *D Shastri v KB Sahay,* (1953) 32 Pat 276.
1268. *Scott v Sampson,* (1882) 8 QBD 49 : 51 LJ QB 382 : 46 LT 412.

most abandoned prostitute. To enable the jury to estimate the probable quantum of injury sustained, knowledge of the party's previous character is not only material, but seems to be absolutely essential..."

In an action for breach of promise of marriage, the defendant was allowed to cite evidence of the plaintiff's bad character in mitigation of damages.[1269] In an action for damages, for seduction or rape, evidence of bad character of the plaintiff was allowed as it was likely to affect the damages that the plaintiff ought to receive.[1270]

The evidence of character is required to be confined only to "general evidence of reputation". This was laid down in *Scott v Sampson.*[1271] "If these rumours and suspicions have, in fact, affected the plaintiff's reputation, that may be proved by general evidence of reputation. If they have not affected it, they are not relevant to the issue. Unlike evidence of reputation, it is particularly difficult for the plaintiff to meet and rebut such evidence.[1272] Referring to the evidence of disposition, the learned judge said that "evidence of facts and circumstances tending to show the disposition of the plaintiff, both principle and authority seemed equally against its admission."

Explaining Lord Denning observed:[1273] "The reason is no doubt that the words "character" and "reputation" have various meanings. A man's "character", it is sometimes said, is *what he in fact is* whereas his reputation is *what other people think he is.*"

"Evidence of a person's good or bad character can be given only by those who know him and have had dealings with him, for his character is the esteem in which he is held by others who know him and are in a position to judge his worth.[1274] In *R v Rowton,*[1275] a witness as to character said: "I know nothing of the neighbourhood's opinion, because I was only a boy at school when I knew him". "The witness then expressed his own opinion about the character of the accused. This was held to be irrelevant. The court said: "The evidence must be of the man's general reputation, and not the individual opinion of the witness. The witness who acknowledged that he knew nothing of the general character, and had no opportunity of knowing it in the sense of reputation, would not be allowed to give an opinion as to a man's character."

Evidence of reputation or disposition must be confined to the particular traits which the charge is concerned about. Thus, it would be useless to offer evidence of a prisoner's reputation for honesty on a charge of cruelty, or of his mild disposition on a charge of theft. Reputation for honesty would be relevant on a charge of theft, and a merciful disposition on a charge of cruelty.[1276]

[s 55.2] "Character" includes reputation and disposition—*[Explanation].*—The word "character" includes both reputation and disposition. "Reputation" means what is thought of a person by others, and is constituted by public opinion. "Disposition" respects the whole frame and texture of the mind. It comprehends the springs and motives of actions. "Temper" influences the action of the moment, "disposition" is

---

1269. *Jefferson v Paskell,* (1916) 1 KB 57 at p 68 (CA).
1270. *Verry v Watkins,* (1836) 7 C&P 308.
1271. (1882) 8 QBD 491 : 51 LJ QB 380 : 40 LT 412.
1272. Cave J at p 504.
1273. *Plato Films Ltd v Spide,* (1961) AC 1090 at 1137.
1274. Lord Denningin *Plato Films Ltd v Spidel,* (1961) AC 1090 at 1137.
1275. *R. v Rowton,* (1865) 169 ER 1497 : 11 LT 745.
1276. Norton, 234.

permanent and settled; "temper" may be transitory and fluctuating. It is possible to have a good disposition with a bad temper, and *vice versa*.[1277]

[s 55.3] Who is qualified as witness of character.—Since there is no formal qualification for this purpose, all that is necessary is that the witness must expressly appear to be qualified. There is the following statement of law in *Wigmore on Evidence*:

When the character of a party or of a witness is to be evidenced by reputation, the reputation must itself be proved by a witness qualified by an opportunity to obtain knowledge of it. The first step here consists in an application of the general principle that a witness must *expressly appear to have had the means of knowledge,* before his testimony can proceed.[1278]

[s 55.4] Knowledge of the witness must be based on residence in the place of repute, not on mere inquiry.—The admissible reputation is that which is built up in the neighbourhood of a man's domicile or in the circle where his livelihood is followed and it is of slow formation. It is the sum of all that is said or not said for or against him. Consequently, it used to be ruled that a reputation can be adequately learned only by the *witness' residence* in the place, not by a mere visit of inquiry, or by a casual sojourn, or by a conversation with a resident who reports the reputation. How long this residence must have been, or how near to the place of domicile or occupation, was not defined by fixed rule—the qualification varied according to circumstances and it should be left entirely to the trial court. But in modern days of organized investigation and research it is easy to see that this original common law rule is too strict. Systematic inquiry by a person coming from outside will often be a better source of knowledge than the causal opportunities of a neighbour or a friend; the only reason for distrust exists when the inquirer is a paid partisan agent who seeks evidence of one person only.

1277. Crabb's Synonyms, p 323; See *Bhagwan Swarup v State of Maharashtra,* AIR 1965 SC 682 : 1965(1) Cr LJ 608. For distinction between "reputation" and "rumour", see *Harbhajan Singh v State of Punjab,* AIR 1961 Punj 215, at p 226.

1278. *Teese v Huntington,* 23 How. 2 (1859); *Shewitz v United States,* 293 Fed. 581 (6th Cir. 1923); *Gage v United States,* 167 F. 2d 122 (9th Cir. 1948) (reputation as of twelve years previously excluded for remoteness in discretion of court. *McClellan v State,* 117 Ala, 140, 145, 23 So. 653, 655 (1898) ("ordinarily" the witness means of knowledge will not be inquired into, if he says that he knows); *Elmore v State,* 216 Ala. 298, 113 Soo 32 (1927). *Crabtree v Kile,* 21 Ill. 180 (1859); *Crabtree v Hagenbaugh,* 25 Ill. 214 (1861); *Spies v People,* 122 Ill. 1, 12 NE 865 (1887); *People v Lyons,* 4 Ill.2d 396, 122 N.E.2d 809 (1954) (witness who testifies on direct examination to reputation admits on cross-examination that his testimony is based on his own personal opinion; motion to strike granted); *People v Wendt,* 104 Ill. App. 2d 192, 244 N.E. 2d 384 (1968) (witness had opinion based on specific encounters but no knowledge of reputation). *Brown v State,* 196 Ind. 77, 147 N.E. 136 (1925) (merely having heared only one complaint does not exclude a witness otherwise qualified). *Commonwealth v Rogers,* 136 Mass. 158 (1883) (the judge may inquire whether the witness has any knowledge, but not into its means or extent); *State v Barnard,* 176 Minn. 349, 223 N.W. 452 (1929) (trial court's discretion); *State v Palmersten,* 210 Minn. 476, 299 N.W. 669 (1941) (witness should first be asked whether he is acquainted with reputation); *State v Boswell,* 2 Dev. 210 (1829); *State v Parks,* 3 Ired. 296 (1843) (the witness must profess to know the general reputation before testifying); *State v O'Neale,* 4 Ired. 88, 89 (1843) ("the regular mode is to inquire whether have the means of knowing the general character); *State v Speight,* 69 N.C. 72, 75 (1873) "whether he knew the general character of the witness, and the means by which he had acquired that knowledge" must be asked; *State v Ellis,* 243 N.C. 142, 90 S.E.2d 255 (1955) (witness who did not know reputation in the community of residence not qualified, though knew of reputation where crime committed. *Gomez v State,* 145 Tex. Crimes 168, 171, 166 S.W.2d 699, 700 (1942) "If appellant sought to show that the deceased's reputation as a quarrelsome and dangerous man was bad, he should first have shown by the witness that he knew the reputation. *People v Dunham,* 344 Ill. 268, 274, 176.

PART II
ON PROOF

CHAPTER III

FACTS WHICH NEED NOT BE PROVED

[s 56] Fact judicially noticeable need not be proved.—No fact of which the Court will take judicial notice[s 56.1] need be proved.

COMMENT

Part I dealt with what facts may, and what facts may not, be proved in a civil or criminal case. Part II deals with the question what sort of evidence must be given of a fact which may be proved. This Part shows the manner in which a fact in issue or relevant fact must be proved.

All facts in issue and relevant facts must be proved by evidence, either oral or documentary. To this rule there are two exceptions: (a) facts judicially noticeable; and (b) facts admitted.

In the case of the facts dealt with by this section, the judge's belief in their existence is induced by the general knowledge acquired otherwise than in particular proceedings before the court and independently of the action of the parties therein. The meaning of the section will, however, be apparent, if we consider together with this section the last words of section 57. What these two provisions really come to is this: With regard to the facts enumerated in section 57, if their existence comes into question, the parties who assert their existence, or the contrary, need not in the first instance produce any evidence, in support of their assertions. They need only ask the judge to say whether these facts exist or not, and if the judge's own knowledge will not help him, then he must look the matter up; further, the judge can, if he thinks proper, call upon the parties to assist him. But in making this investigation the judge is emancipated entirely from all the rules of evidence laid down for the investigation of facts in general. He may resort to any source of information which he finds handy and which he thinks will help him. Thus, he may consult any book or obtain information from a bystander.[1]

[s 56.1] "Take judicial notice".—This expression means recognition without proof of something as existing or as being true.[2] Judicial notice is based upon very obvious reasons of convenience and expediency; and the wisdom of dispensing with proof of matters within the common knowledge of every one has never been questioned. Taking judicial notice of the scarcity of dwellings, the Calcutta High Court held that a dwelling

---

1. Markby 49.
2. For example, the court taking judicial notice that the law and order situation has deteriorated over the years and continues to be worsening fast and, therefore, it is an importune time to think of reconsidering death penalty. *Shashi Nayar v UOI,* AIR 1992 SC 395 : 1992 Cr LJ 514.

house cannot be acquired without providing alternative accommodation.[3] The Supreme Court has held that the court can take judicial notice of alternative sources.[4] The court can take judicial cognizance of the fact that a certain area is terrorist-stricken.[5] The court can take judicial notice of the fact that many blind persons have acquired great academic distinction.[6]

The court can take judicial notice of the fact that the system of education in the State has virtually crumbled and serious allegations are made frequently about the manner in which the system is being worked.[7]

[s 57] Facts of which Court must take judicial notice.—The Court shall take judicial notice of the following facts:—

[8][(1) All laws in force in the territory of India;]

(2) All public Acts passed or hereafter to be passed by Parliament [9][of the United Kingdom], and all local and personal Acts directed by Parliament [9][of the United Kingdom] to be judicially noticed:

(3) Articles of War for [10][the Indian] Army, [11][Navy or Air Force];

[12][(4) The course of proceedings of Parliament of the United Kingdom, of the Constituent Assembly of India, of Parliament and of the Legislatures established under any laws for the time being in force in a province or in a State;]

(5) The accession and the sign manual of the Sovereign for the time being of the United Kingdom of Great Britain and Ireland;

(6) All seals of which English Courts take judicial notice: the seals of all the [13][Courts in [14][India]], and all Courts out of [12][India] established by the authority of [15][the Central Government or the Crown Representative]: the seals of Courts of Admiralty and Maritime Jurisdiction and of Notaries Public, and all seals which any person is authorised to use by [16][the Constitution or an Act of Parliament of the United Kingdom or an] Act or Regulation having the force of law in [14][India];

---

3. *Bamandas Mukherjee v State of West Bengal,* AIR 1985 Cal 159.
4. *Assistant Collector of Central Excise v Dunlop India Ltd,* AIR 1985 SC 330 : 1985(1) SCC 260.
5. *Abdul Malik v State of UP,* AIR 1994 All 376. *Kesho Ram v Joga Ram,* AIR 2009 Del 157, death due to bomb explosion in bus, Sikh related violence was in full swing in Northern India, the court took judicial notice of this fact. Claim petition under MV Act maintainable.
6. *Jai Shankar Prasad v State of Bihar,* AIR 1993 Pat 22.
7. *Managing Committee of Rajo Sidheshwar High School v State of Bihar,* AIR 1996 Pat 19.
8. Subs. by the A.O. 1950, for para (1).
9. Ins. by the A.O. 1950.
10. Subs. by the A.O. 1950, for "Her Majesty's".
11. Subs. by Act 10 of 1927, section 25 and Sch I, for "or Navy".
12. Subs. by the A.O. 1950, for para 4.
13. Subs. by the A.O. 1948, for "Courts of British India".
14. Subs. by Act 3 of 1951, section 3 and Schedule, for "the States".
15. Subs. by the A.O. 1937, for the "the G.G. or any L.G. in Council".
16. Subs. by the A.O. 1950, "any Act of Parliament or other".

(7) The accession to office, names, titles, functions and signatures of the persons filling for the time being any public office in any State if the fact of their appointment to such office is notified in [17][any Official Gazette];

(8) The existence, title and national flag of every State or Sovereign recognised by [18][the Government of India];

(9) The divisions of time, the geographical divisions of the world, and public festivals, fasts and holidays notified in the Official Gazette;

(10) The territories under the dominion of [18][the Government of India];

(11) The commencement, continuance and termination of hostilities between [18][the Government of India] and any other State or body of persons;

(12) The names of the members and officers of the Court and of their deputies and subordinate officers and assistants, and also of all officers acting in execution of its process, and of all advocates, attorneys, proctors, vakils, pleaders and other persons authorized by law to appear or act before it;

(13) The rule of the road [19][on land or at sea].

In all these cases, and also on all matters of public history, literature, science or art, the Court may resort for its aid to appropriate books or documents of reference.

If the Court is called upon by any person to take judicial notice of any fact, it may refuse to do so unless and until such person produces any such book or document as it may consider necessary to enable it to do so.

SYNOPSIS

COMMENT

The list of facts of which the court shall take judicial notice and which are enumerated in this section is not exhaustive. It is for the sake of convenience that the courts are allowed to take judicial notice of certain facts which are so clearly established that evidence of their existence is unnecessary. The Supreme Court has held that the court can take judicial notice of circumstances in August–September, 1947 (communal disturbances after partition) in certain parts of the country.[20]

---

17. Subs. by the A.O. 1937, for "the Gazette of India, or in the Official Gazette of any L.G.".
18. Subs. by the A.O. 1950, for "the British Crown".
19. Ins. by Act 18 of 1872, section 5.
20. *Shiv Nath v UOI*, AIR 1965 SC 1666.

The section does not appear to have the effect of absolving the parties from any rules governing the proof of facts on which they desire to rely. The section does not say how any fact, historical or otherwise, is to be proved by the parties, but gives the court liberty to resort for its aid to appropriate books or documents of reference on matters of public history.[21]

[s 57.1] "All Laws in force"—*[Clause 1]*.—Under clause (1) of this section the court should take judicial notice of all Indian laws. "Indian law" is defined by the General Clauses Act, section 3(29), and includes any law, ordinance, order, bye-law, or regulation passed or made at any time by any competent legislature, authority, or person in India.[22] The expression "All laws" includes statutory law as well as unwritten law whether of personal or of a local nature. A report made by an officer containing customary law applicable to a particular community is admissible in evidence.[23] See Constitution of India, Article 13(3)(b). The factual background of a statutory enactment as stated in the statute itself is judicially noticeable.[24] Multi-storeyed Building Regulations were held to be judicially noticeable, they being statutory instruments made in public interest.[25]

A Government Order on conversion of agricultural land was held to be judicially noticeable.[26] Courts are bound to take judicial notice of statutory regulations even if they are not pleaded.[27]

Regulations made under the Act became part of the law and a tribunal takes judicial notice of the law, being at liberty to refresh memory by referring to the text of the regulations which, if there is any doubt about it, can be established by reference to a copy printed by the Government printer.[28] The Supreme Court pointed out that the court should have taken judicial notice of the fact that a notification had been issued concerning the land of an intermediary[29] the fact that the Life Insurance Corporation, a statutory corporation, has adopted varying ages of retirement for different services,[30] the fact of Government's white paper on Punjab agitation and information in it about

---

21. *"The Englishman", Ltd v Lajpat Rai,* (1910) 37 Cal 760.

22. *Public Prosecutor v Thippayya,* (1949) Mad 371; *S Nagarajan v Vasantha Kumar,* 1988 Cr LJ 1217. Foreign law is a matter of fact. It has to be proved the same way as any other fact, *Attorney General of South Australia v Brown,* (1960) AC 432 (PC).

23. *Tula Ram Sah v Shyam Lal Sah,* (1924) 49 All 848.

24. *J Kumar v UOI,* AIR 1982 SC 1064 : (1982) 2 SCC 116 : 1982 SCC (L&S) 177.

25. *3 ACES, Hyderabad v MC of Hyderabad,* AIR 1995 AP 17, judicial notice taken, demolition not stayed because the contractor prevented the Municipality from issuing public notice cautioning investors. Municipal Regulations as to construction of buildings were held to be judicially noticeable. The court followed *Pratibha Co-op Housing Society Ltd v State of Maharashtra,* AIR 1991 SC 1453 : (1991) 3 SCC 341. *Ramilal v Ghisa Ram,* (1996) 7 SCC 507 : AIR 1996 SC 3338; judicial notice of change in law under which the party's right of preemption was defeated. To the same effect, *Karan Singh v Bhagwan Singh,* (1996) 7 SCC 559 : AIR 1996 SC 2249. See JW Every-Burns, *Regulations Judicially Noticed,* (1957) 3 Aust LJ 458 at p 460.

26. *Udit Gopal Beri v State of Rajasthan,* AIR 2001 Raj 147; *State of UP v Pista Devi,* (1986) 4 SCC 251 : AIR 1987 SC 2055, the Court could take judicial notice of the fact that there was national urgency for acquisition of land for housing.

27. *Rajasthan State Electricity Board v Laxman Lal,* 1991 Supp 2 SCC 531.

28. *Yan Omerion v Bowick,* (1809) 2 Camp 42 : 170 ER 1073; *Mc Quaker v Goddard,* (1940) 1 KB 607, at 700.

29. *UOI v Nihar Kanta Jha,* AIR 1987 SC 1713 : (1987) 3 SCC 465.

30. *LIC of India v SS Srivastva,* AIR 1987 SC 1527 : 1988 Supp SCC 1.

Bhindranwale.[31] The courts also take judicial notice of general customs.[32] The general lien of bankers is part of the law merchant, and is to be judicially noticed like the negotiability of bill of exchange or days of grace allowed for their payment. When a general usage has been judicially ascertained and established, it becomes a part of the law merchant which courts of justice are bound to know and recognise.

[s 57.2] Public Acts—*[Clause 2]*.—Statutes are either public or private, general or special. A *public or general* Act is a universal rule applied to the whole community, which the courts must notice judicially and *ex officio*, although not formally set forth by a party claiming an advantage under it. But *special or private* Acts are rather exceptions than rules, since they only operate upon particular persons and private concerns, and the courts are not bound to take notice of them, if they are not formally pleaded, unless an express clause is inserted in them that they shall be deemed public Acts, and shall be judicially noticed as such without being specially pleaded—which provision is now usually introduced.[33]

Where the Hindi version of an Act contained a wrong entry in a schedule of the Act, the Supreme Court said that the English version should be taken into judicial notice being an authoritative text of the Act.[34]

[s 57.3] Articles of War—*[Clause 3]*.—Articles of War for officers, soldiers, *etc.*, are contained in the Army Act (XLVI of 1950).

[s 57.4] Parliamentary proceedings—*[Clause 4]*.—The court is bound to take judicial notice of the prorogation of a State Legislative Assembly,[35] so also of the budget speech of the Finance Minister.[36] Refusal to take judicial notice of statutory notification has been held to be an error which is of patent nature justifying review.[37]

[s 57.5] Accession to office, etc.—*[Clause 7]*.—Judicial notice of the signatures of the Secretaries to the Government on any instrument can be taken under this clause.[38] A true copy of a Gazette notification can be received in evidence if the other party does not object to its admissibility as secondary evidence.[39]

[s 57.6] Flags—*[Clause 8]*.—All courts must take judicial notice of the existence and title of every State or Sovereign recognised by the Government of India.

[s 57.7] Divisions of time, etc.—*[Clause 9]*.—The phrase "divisions of time" includes also Indian eras. Thus, Samvat, Shaka, Hindi, Bengali, Hizari and Jalus eras will be judicially noticed. The court is bound to take judicial notice of the holidays

---

31. *Sukh Deo Singh v Union Territory*, AIR 1967 P&H 5.
32. Lord Campbell in *Brando v Barnet*, (1846) 12 CLF 787 (HL). *Jiwan Singh v Des Raj*, AIR 1982 Punj (NOC) 306, the Court took judicial notice of the fact that agricultural land devolved upon sister's sons and not upon distant collaterals. This custom was found to be universal in Punjab. This was also known to all the agricultural communities there. Citing *Ujagar Singh v Mst. Jeo*, AIR 1959 SC 1041.
33. Field, 8th Edn, p 418.
34. *Nityanand Sharma v State of Bihar*, AIR 1966 SC 2306.
35. *State of Punjab v Satya Pal*, AIR 1969 SC 903 : 1969(1) SCR 478.
36. *State of UP v Anupam Traders*, 1989 SCC (Cr) 701 : 1989 Supp (2) SCC 88.
37. *State Bank of Travancore v K Vinayachandran*, AIR 1989 Ker 302.
38. *Kali Pada Upadhya v King-Emperor*, (1944) 23 Pat 475.
39. *State of Kerala v Enadeen*, AIR 1971 Ker 193 FB.

notified in the Official Gazette of any Local Government.[40] Where an incident took place at 7 a.m. in the month of April, it was held that the court could take judicial notice of the fact that it was not dark at that time.[41] A Magistrate ordering demolition of a dilapidated house taking judicial notice of incessant rains in the area was held to be justified.[42]

[s 57.8] "The rule of the road on land or at sea"—*[Clause 13]*.—This means the rule that horses and vehicles of all description should keep to the left side of the road. At sea, the rule is that ships and steamboats, on meeting, should port their helms, so as to pass on the port or left side of each other; steamboats should keep out of the way of sailing ships; and every vessel overtaking another should keep out of its way.

[s 57.9] Matters of common knowledge.—On all matters of public history, literature, science, or art, the court may sort for its aid to appropriate books or documents of reference. Thus, ancient facts of public nature and published works of history can be relied upon for finding the meaning of a "math".[43]

Under the last paragraph the court is given the discretion to refuse to take judicial notice of any fact unless the person calling upon the court to take judicial notice of such fact produces any such book or document as may be necessary to enable it to do so.[44]

The court can take judicial notice of the fact that an all-India railway strike was imminent on a particular day and that it actually commenced on a certain day.[45]

The only guiding principle, apart from statute, as to judicial notice which emerges from the various recorded cases, appears to be that wherever a fact is so generally known that every ordinary person may be reasonably presumed to be aware of it, the court noticed it, either simpliciter if it is at once satisfied of the fact without more, or after such information or investigation as it considers reliable and necessary in order to eliminate any reasonable doubt.[46] The basic essential is that the fact is to be of a class that is so generally known as to give rise to the presumption that all persons are aware of it. This excludes from the operation of judicial notice what are not "general" but "particular" facts. As to "particular" facts, even the judge's own personal knowledge is not to be imported into the case: *Hurpurshad v Sheo Dayal*,[47] and *Meethun Bebee v Busheer Khan*.[48] To import knowledge of a particular fact in issue would be to import evidence in the strict sense regarding a matter as to which the court is supposed to have no knowledge whatsoever of its own.

The court cannot be called upon to take judicial notice of facts published in a newspaper. The presence of the newsman who personally perceived the reported facts

---

40. *Gyan Singh v Budha*, (1932) 14 Lah 240. *Mannsingh v Commissioner of Police*, 1989 Cr LJ 1573 (Guj), (judicial notice of holidays).
41. *Balwan v State*, 1989 Cr LJ 2475 (Del).
42. *Tejmal v State of Maharashtra*, 1992 Cr LJ 379 (Bom).
43. *Swami Harbans Chari Ji v MP*, AIR 1981 MP 82; *Vimla Bai v Hiralal Gupta*, (1990) 2 SCC 22 : 1989 Supp (2) SCR 759 statements in the Gazette of Indore.
44. *Public Prosecutor v Thippayya*, (1949) Mad 371.
45. *Onkar Nath v Delhi Admn.*, AIR 1977 SC 1108 : 1977 Cr LJ 940 : (1977) 2 SCC, at p 614.
46. *Holland v Jones*, (1917) 23 CLR 49 (Australia).
47. Particular' facts, even the judge's own personal knowledge is not to be imported into the case: *Hurpurshad v Sheo Dayal*, (1876) 3 IA 259, 286.
48. *Meethun Bebee v Busheer Khan*, 11 *Moore Indian Appeals* 213, 221.

would be necessary.[49] The court did not take judicial notice of prices prevailing in different parts of the country at a given time and context.[50]

In a petition against calling of *bandh* by a political party, the Kerala High Court said that it could take judicial notice of what actually happens when a call for *bandh* is enforced.[51]

The court also pointed out that the list is not exhaustive. The court can also take notice of the enormous and manifold increase of rents throughout the country particularly in the urban areas[52] and, in a matter of acquisition, of the fact that land prices in the area have risen,[53] but not of the fact whether alternative accommodation is available for the purposes of evicting a tenant. This has to be proved as a fact.[54] Judicial notice was taken of the fact of the existence of followers of Islam in India and their belief in Koran as of divine origin through their Prophet.[55] The question whether a particular village was granted to a particular person by a former Ruler is not a matter of public history within the meaning of this section.[56]

In the absence of any evidence the court cannot take judicial notice of the practice that sale deeds are generally undervalued.[57]

The court could take judicial notice of the fact that the requirement of land by the Government for providing housing accommodation was a matter of national urgency;[58] that the police and jail authorities were using handcuffs and other fetters indiscriminately and without any justification.[59] The court can take notice of illegal immigration.[60] The court can take judicial notice of customs.[61]

Judges cannot and do not act within "ivory towers". Not to take notice of matters which are notorious is to shut one's eyes in the face of reality. It is true that judges cannot act on their own private knowledge or belief regarding the facts of a particular case but they are entitled to use the knowledge of the common affairs of life which men of ordinary intelligence possess. There are matters which are so notorious or clearly established that evidence of their existence is unnecessary. Speaking of this State (the State of Bihar) I have no doubt that the usufruct derived by usufructuary mortgages of agricultural lands is at least twice (and in many cases even thrice) the legally permissible rate of interest for secured creditors.[62]

---

49. *Laxmi Raj Shetty v State of Tamil Nadu,* AIR 1988 SC 1274 : (1988) 3 SC 319.
50. *State of AP v Bathu P Rao,* (1976) 3 SCC 301 : AIR 1976 SC 1845 : 1976 Cr LJ 1387.
51. *Bharat Kumar K Paticha v State of Kerala,* AIR 1997 Ker 291 (FB).
52. *Rattan Arya v State of Tamil Nadu,* AIR 1986 SC 1444 : 1986(3) SCC 385 : 1986 All LJ 1168.
53. *Puran v State of Maharashtra,* AIR 1986 P&H 305. *Baldev Singh v State of Punjab,* AIR 2007 P&H 129, percentage of increase in the matter of acquisition has to be worked out on evidence.
54. *Bhagwandas v Jiley Kaur,* AIR 1991 SC 266 : 1991 Supp (2) SCC 300.
55. *Chandmal Chopra v State of West Bengal,* 1988 Cr LJ 739 Cal.
56. *Kishanlal v Sohanlal,* (1955) 5 Raj 191. Facts reported in newspapers are not judicially noticeable. *Luxmi Raj Shetty v State of Tamil Nadu,* AIR 1988 SC 1274 : 1988 Cr LJ 1783.
57. *Tata Chemicals Ltd, Bombay v Sadhu Singh,* AIR 1994 All 66 : LNIND 1993 All 196.
58. *State of UP v Pista Devi,* AIR 1986 SC 2025 : (1986) 4 SCC 251.
59. *Citizens for Democracy v State of Assam,* (1995) 3 SCC 743.
60. *MDK Immigration Consultant v UOI,* 2000 Cr LJ 252 (P&H).
61. *Atluri Brahmanandan v Anne Sai Bapuji,* AIR 2011 SC 545 : (2011) 1 Mad LJ 742 (SC), judicial notice of the fact that in a particular community there was a custom to adopt a person as a son even when he was of more than 15 years of age.
62. *Fatehchand Himantlal v State of Maharashtra,* AIR 1977 SC 1825 : (1977) 2 SCC 670.

The court can take judicial notice of the fact that the Governments, whether at the Centre or States, cannot by themselves take effective measures for imparting education to the country's children.[63]

It is the discretion of the State Government to create new Districts. This action of the Government cannot be challenged. But the court can take judicial notice of the fact that the essential infrastructure for the new District has not been provided. If no judicial authorities are functioning in the new District it will be causative of great public inconvenience. The Government can be asked to focus its attention towards creation of judicial and administrative complexes.[64]

In the matter of determination of value of land for the purposes of the Land Acquisition Act, 1894, the court said that judicial notice could be taken of the fact that there is upward trend in prices of land and a continuously rising inflation.[65]

In a case arising out of the right of a woman to family pension, the court took note of the fact that human experience shows that it is very rare that a woman with children would claim that she was the wife of a person who was not her husband.[66]

The courts can take judicial notice of a custom which has been repeatedly recognised by the courts. Proof of such a custom would then not be necessary.[67]

[s 57.9.1] ***Subsequent events.***—The circumstances in which and the riders subject to which the court can take judicial notice of subsequent events were thus explained by the Supreme Court[68] in a case in which there was a current finding of the authorities below as to the landlord's personal need which became belied by some events taking place during the pendency of the proceedings:

> The power of the Court to take note of subsequent events is well-settled and undoubted. However, it is accompanied by three riders; firstly, the subsequent event should be brought promptly, to the notice of the Court; secondly, it should be brought to the notice of the Court consistently with rules of procedure enabling Court to take note of such events and affording the opposite party an opportunity of meeting or explaining such event; and thirdly, the subsequent event must have a material bearing on right to relief of any party.

[s 57.10] Consultation of books and references.—Matters in respect of which the court may take judicial notice, the court may call upon the party concerned to provide help by producing expert guidance and books and journals. Where a camel in a zoo bit a visitor and, in a tort action against the authorities, the court could have taken notice of the fact whether the camel is a domestic or wild animal, but even so

---

63. *Debasish Kar Gupta v State of West Bengal,* AIR 1999 Cal 300.
64. *District Bar Association v State of Haryana,* AIR 1997 P&H 231 : (1998) 118 PLR 265.
65. *Gulabi v State of HP,* AIR 1999 HP 9.
66. *Laxmi Kom Venkanna Nayak v Govt of India,* AIR 2002 Kant 54 : 2002 (6) Kar LJ 310
67. *Ass Kaur v Kartar Singh,* AIR 2007 SC 2369 : (2007) 5 SCC 561.
68. *Atma S Berar v Mukhtiar Singh,* AIR 2003 SC 624 at p 630, the court did not find the subsequent event to be relevant because no court has the right to tell the landlord how and where he should live. See also *Ram Nibas Gagau v Debojyoti Das,* AIR 2003 SC 632. The court said here that subsequent events could be taken into account to mould relief. But notice was not taken of such events in this case because there was no explanation for the failure on the part of the tenant to bring the events to the notice of the trial Court and why the application was moved belatedly for the first time before the Appellate Court.

consulted witnesses.[69] Glauson LJ explained matters as follows: The judges take judicial notice of the ordinary course of nature and in this particular case of the ordinary course of nature—in regard to the position of camels among other animals. The reasons why the evidence was given was for the assistance of the judge in forming his view as to what the ordinary course of nature in this regard in fact is, a matter of which he is supposed to have complete knowledge. The point is best explained by reading a few lines from that great work, the late Mr Justice Stephen's *Digest of the Law of Evidence*. In the 12th edition, Article 62 is as follows:

> No evidence of any fact of which the court will take judicial notice need be given by the party alleging its existence; but the judge, upon being called upon to take judicial notice thereof, may, if he is unacquainted with such fact, refer to any person or to any document or book of reference for his satisfaction in relation thereto, or may refuse to take judicial notice thereof unless and until the party calling upon him to take such notice produces any such document or book of reference". From the statement it appears that the document or book of reference only enshrines the knowledge of those who are acquainted with the particular branch of natural phenomena; and, in the present, case, owing to some extent to the fact that there appears to be a serious flaw in a statement in a well-known book of reference on the matter here in question, the learned judge permitted oral evidence to be given before him by persons who had, or professed to have, special knowledge with regard to this particular branch of natural history. When that evidence was given and weighed up with the statements in the books of reference the facts became perfectly plain; and the learned judge was able without any difficulty whatever to give a correct statement of the natural phenomena material to the matter in question of which he was bound to take judicial notice.[70]

The Supreme Court in a case discussed not only the evidence adduced before the trial court but also referred to textbooks and other materials and concluded on that basis that the custom in question was prevalent in a certain community. The court said that such material could be relied upon without much evidence.[71]

[s 58] Facts admitted need not be proved.—No fact need be proved in any proceeding which the parties thereto or their agents agree to admit at the hearing, or which before the hearing, they agree to admit by any writing under their hands, or which by any rule of pleading in force at the time they are deemed to have admitted by their pleadings:

***Provided* that the Court may, in its discretion, require the facts admitted to be proved otherwise than by such admissions.**

SYNOPSIS

69. *Mc Quaker v Goddard,* (1940) 1 KB 687 : (1940) 1 All ER 471 (CA).

70. In *Turner v Coates,* (1917) 1 KB 670, evidence in its strict sense was admitted as to the habit of Colts.

71. *Gurubasawwa v Irawwa,* AIR 1997 Kant 87. The case referred to was *Shakuntala Bai v LV Kulkarni,* AIR 1989 SC 1359 : (1989) 2 SCC 526 : ILR 1989 Kant 2323.

COMMENT

Admissions by parties before suit are dealt with in section 17, *et seq.* This section deals with admissions at or before the hearing.

[s 58.1] Principle.—No proof need be given of facts which the parties or their agents agree to admit at the hearing, or which, before the hearing, they agree to admit by writing under their hands, or which, by any rule of pleading in force at the time, they are deemed to have admitted by their pleadings.[72] Every allegation of fact in the plaint, if not denied specifically or by necessary implication, or stated to be not admitted in the pleading of the defendant, shall be taken to be admitted. The court may in its discretion require any fact so admitted to be proved otherwise than by such admission (O VIII, rule 3, Code of Civil Procedure). Where a document is not admitted in the pleadings but only at the trial in evidence, the document must be proved.[73] Where at the initial stage of eviction proceedings, execution of agreement of tenancy showing the other party as landlord/owner was admitted by the tenant, he subsequently could not take the plea that the agreement was obtained by fraud.[74] A party is bound by its initial admission and its legal consequences.[75]

The law on admissions can be summarised to the effect that admission made by a party though not conclusive, is a decisive factor in a case unless the other party successfully withdraws the same or proves it to be erroneous. Even if the admission is not conclusive it may operate as an estoppel. Law requires that an opportunity be given to the person who has made admission under cross-examination to tender his explanation and clarify the point on the question of admission. Failure of a party to prove its defence does not amount to admission, nor can it reverse or discharge the burden of proof of the plaintiff. Section 58 deals with admissions during trial i.e. at or before the hearing, which are known as judicial admissions or stipulations dispensed with proof. Documents are necessarily either proved by witness or marked on admission. Section 58 provides that a fact may not need to be proved in any proceeding which the parties thereto agreed to admit at the hearing or which, before the hearing, they agreed to admit by any writing under their hands or which they admitted by their pleading, even in that case the court may, in its discretion, even if such an admission has been made by the party, require the fact admitted to be proved otherwise than by such admission. In fact, admission by a party may be oral or in writing. Admission is the best piece of substantive evidence that an opposite party can rely upon, though not conclusive, is decisive of the matter, unless successfully withdrawn or proved erroneous.[76]

A court, in general, has to try the questions on which the parties are at issue, not those on which they are agreed. Admissions which have been deliberately made for the purposes of the suit, whether in the pleading or by agreement, will act as an estoppel to the admission of any evidence contradicting them.[77] It is with the object of doing

---

72. Markby, 50. **See** *Maung Po Kin v Maung Shwe Bya,* (1923) 1 Ran 405.
73. *Maung Wala v Maung Shwe Gon,* (1923) 1 Ran 472.
74. *Narendra Kumar v Vishnu Kr. Nayyar,* AIR 1994 Del 209.
75. *Zonal General Manager Ircon International Ltd v Vinay Heavy Equipments,* (2015) 13 SCC 680, para 10 : 2015 (6) Scale 103.
76. *UOI v Ibrahim Uddin,* (2012) 8 SCC 148.
77. *Burjorji Cursetji Panthaki v Muncherji Kuverji,* (1880) 5 Bom 143, 152.

away with the necessity of proving documents or facts admitted that admission are obtained, and the party unreasonably refusing or neglecting to admit any documents or facts when called upon to do so may be ordered to pay the costs of proof. Where the defendant admitted in his written statement that his father was married to the plaintiff's mother according to Henga custom, he was not allowed subsequently to contradict it.[78] A consent decree for possession which was based upon a compromise in a previous case and which showed the existence of a statutory ground of eviction, it was held that it could take the shape of evidence or an admission which is the best proof of facts and can be made the foundation of the rights of parties.[79]

Sarkaria J said in this case:

> Admissions in pleadings or judicial admissions, admissible under section 58 of the Evidence Act, made by the parties or their agents at or before the hearing of the case, stand on a higher footing than evidentiary admission. The former class of admissions are fully binding on the party that makes them and constitute a waiver of proof. They by themselves can be made the foundation of the rights of parties. On the other hand, evidentiary admissions which are receivable at the trial as evidence, are by themselves not conclusive. They can be shown to be wrong.[80]

This decision was relied on in *Raman Pillai v Kumaran Parameswarn.*[81] In this case the facts in question were admitted in written statement. In a suit for title, admissions were made by the predecessor-in-interest of the plaintiffs in their written statement in earlier judicial proceedings to the effect that the rights in the suit property were lost by adverse possession and limitation and that the predecessors of the respondents had perfected their title. Certified copy of the written statement was held to be relevant under section 58. Admissibility could not be discarded on the ground that the statement in question was not a public document.

Where the question was if possession had indeed been taken over from the lessee pursuant to the termination of the lease, it was noticed by Supreme Court that lessee had written a letter in which an unequivocal and unconditional admission was made that possession had indeed been taken over by the appellant Port Trust and lessee had asked for refund of the amount paid by her towards instalments and in case such a refund was not possible to return the plot to her. It was held that such an unequivocal admission as is contained in the letter cannot be wished away or ignored in a suit where the question was of dispossession of lessee pursuant to the termination of the lease. It was accordingly held on the basis of said admission contained in the letter of lessee that dispossession of the lessee had taken place pursuant to the termination of the lease deed in terms of panchnama.[82]

Where averments made in a writ petition were not controverted by the respondent, the court said that they should be presumed to have been admitted.[83]

---

78. *Rasamani Das v Patrabalo Devi,* AIR 1981 Gau 42.

79. *Nagindas v Dalpatram,* AIR 1974 SC 471 : 1974(1) SCC 242. Admission must be possible facts. *Sita Kumari v Basisth Narain,* AIR 1985 Pat 158.

80. *Ibid* at p 252.

81. *Raman Pillai v Kumaran Parameswarn.*, AIR 2002 Ker 133. *Rasu v Pandidurai,* AIR 2002 NOC 155 (Mad), marking of sale deed required for a collateral purposes. The case of the applicant was that he gained title and possession on the basis of the document. The document was not registered though it required registration. The court said that marking was not allowed.

82. *Kandla Port v Hargovind Jasraj,* (2013) 3 SCC 182.

83. *Naseem Bano v State of UP,* AIR 1993 SC 2592 : 1993 Supp (4) 46.

An admission must be clear and unambiguous in order that such an admission should relieve the opponent of the burden of proof of the fact said to have been admitted.[84]

Formal proof of a document even when it is required to be proved in a certain way (e.g., by calling a person who have attested it, see section 68, *infra*) may be waived by any of the parties whose interest it may affect, although such waiver does not affect the legal character of the document or its validity.[85] When a document is marked on admission without reservation, the contents are not only evidence, but are taken as admitted and cannot be challenged; but where documents are marked on admission dispensing with formal proof, the contents are evidence although the party admitting is free to challenge the contents.[86] If an agreement of discharge or satisfaction be admitted in the pleadings and hence no question of proof by oral or documentary evidence arises by virtue of this section, such compromise cannot be said to be inadmissible for want of registration.[87]

In divorce cases the court does not usually decide merely on the basis of admissions in the pleadings or the petition. Where, however, there is no room for supposing that parties are colluding, there is no reason why the admissions of parties should not be treated as evidence just as they are treated in other civil proceedings.[88]

The plaintiff was the registered proprietor of the trade mark "Atul". The defendant was using the trade name "Atul" since the birth of his son. The court said that the fact that the word "Atul" is a common proper name used in naming persons and things need not be proved.[89]

In the Code of Civil Procedure provision has been made for admission of facts by parties or their pleaders before the hearing (O XII, rules 1–9). In order that an admission may give rise to an inference of the title of another person, it has to be clear and explicit. Admissions, generally, cannot create any title.[90] Failure to prove a defence does not amount to an admission, nor does it reverse or discharge the burden of proof.[91] For admission in criminal cases, see the authors' *Code of Criminal Procedure*, 11th Edn.

A written statement has to be read as a whole. Evasive denials and non-specific denials may constitute an implied admission. Lawyer's incorrect instructions, omissions or failures lead to making of an implied admission. Though it may not be allowed to be withdrawn by an amendment of the written statement, the plaintiff can be allowed to prove his case.[92]

---

84. *Joshna Gouda v Brundaban Gouda*, (2012) 5 SCC 634.

85. *Baijanth Singh v Mussammat Biraj Kuer*, (1922) 2 Pat 52; *Arjun Sahu v Kelai Rath*, (1922) 2 Pat 317. A tenant admitting in his pleadings the buyer of his original landlord's interest as his new landlord, the latter need not produce any document in proof of this fact, *Gopi Kishan v Bajrang*, 1996 AIHC 4064 (Raj) parties admitted that the gift deed in question was executed with their consent, no formal proof needed, *Mada Rama Krishna Reddy v NP Reddy*, 1996 AIHC 3946 (AP).

86. *Lionel Edwards Ltd v State of WB*, AIR 1967 Cal 191.

87. *Ramchandra Sau v Kailashchandra Patra*, (1930) 58 Cal 532.

88. *Mahendra v Sushila*, AIR 1965 SC 364 : 1964(7) SCR 267.

89. *Atul Products Ltd v VP Mehta*, AIR 2009 Bom 84 : 2009 (111) Bom LR 796.

90. *Wakf Board v Subhan Shah*, (2006) 10 SCC 696 : (2006) 10 SCC 696.

91. *Manager, RBI v S Mani*, AIR 2005 SC 2179 : (2005) 5 SCC 100 : (2005) 3 Mah LJ 758.

92. *Uttam Chand Kothari v Gauri Shankar Jalan*, AIR 2007 Gau 20.

[s 58.2] Admission that one was partner and retired.—The court said that an admission made in an affidavit, unless explained otherwise, furnishes best evidence. The defendant in his affidavit sworn before Notary Public made an unequivocal admission that he was a member of the partnership in question and he retired from it. This was held to be a conclusive proof of the existence of the partnership and his retirement from it.[93]

[s 58.3] Unproved documents produced by the prosecution.—The documents produced by the prosecution, though not formally proved, can be relied upon by the defence to falsify the prosecution version.[94]

[s 58.4] Admission made in pleadings.—A categorical admission made in the pleadings, cannot be permitted to be withdrawn by way of an amendment.[95]

[s 58.5] When further evidence may be required—*[Proviso]*.—If the court is satisfied that the admission has been obtained by fraud or that there is other good and sufficient cause, it will be in its discretion, under the proviso, to require the fact to be proved otherwise than by such admission.[96]

---

93. *Broadway Centre v Gopaldas*, AIR 2002 Cal 78. The Court **followed** *Ramji Dayawala & Sons Pvt Ltd v Invest Import*, AIR 1981 SC 2085 : (1981) 1 SCC 80.

94. *Ramaiah v State of Karnataka*, (2014) 9 SCC 365 (para 14) : AIR 2014 SC 3388.

95. *Ram Niranjan Kajaria v Sheo Prakash Kajaria*, (2015) 10 SCC 203, para 23, to this extent proposition of law that even an admission can be withdrawn as held in *Panchdeo Narain Srivastava v Jyoti Sahay*, 1984 Supp SCC 594 was **overruled.**

96. *Oriental Govt Security Life Assurance Co Ltd v Narasimha Chari*, (1901) 25 Mad 183, 205. *Ammarukunhi Amma v State of Kerala*, AIR 2003 Ker 33, further proof required of the fact whether half of the private land was really acquired.

CHAPTER IV

OF ORAL EVIDENCE

[s 59] Proof of facts by oral evidence.—All facts, except the [1][contents of documents or electronic records], may be proved by oral evidence.

COMMENT

Oral evidence has been defined by the Act to be all statements which the court permits or requires to be made before it by witnesses in relation to matters of fact under inquiry (section 3). All facts except the contents of documents may be proved by oral evidence. This section is not happily worded. Contents of documents may be proved by oral evidence under certain circumstances, viz., when evidence of their contents is admissible as secondary evidence.

Oral evidence, if worthy of credit, is sufficient without documentary evidence to prove a fact or title.[2] It is a cardinal rule of evidence that where written documents exist, they must be produced as being the best evidence of their own contents.[3] Where oral testimony is conflicting, much greater credence is to be given to men's acts than to their alleged words, which are so easily mistaken or misrepresented.[4]

Where a body was recovered from a well, but the evidence of the witnesses to the fact of recovery could not be accepted because of the absence of their signature on the inquest and they also did not support the recovery, it was held that in such circumstances, the investigating officer himself becomes a direct witness and his evidence could not be disbelieved unless there was evidence that he had a motive to create a false evidence.[5]

An affidavit is not "evidence" within the meaning of section 3 of the Evidence Act, 1872. Affidavits are, therefore, not included within the purview of the definition of "evidence" as has been given in section 3 of the Evidence Act, and the same can be used as "evidence" only if, for sufficient reasons, the court passes an order under O XIX of the Code of Civil Procedure, 1908. Thus, the filing of an affidavit of one's own statement, in one's own favour, cannot be regarded as sufficient evidence for any Court or tribunal, on the basis of which it can come to a conclusion as regards a particular fact situation. However, in a case where the deponent is available for cross-examination,

---

1. Subs. by Act 21 of 2000, section 92 and Sch. II–8, for "contents of documents" (w.e.f. 17-10-2000).
2. *P Ram Reddy v Land Acquisition Officer,* (1995) 2 SCC 305 : (1995) 1 JT 593, oral evidence as to value of land produced by claimants in the context of acquisition, witnesses were not cross-examined or not effectively cross-examined, was not accepted particularly when it was based upon unbelievable probabilities.
3. *Dinomoyi Debi v Roy Luchmiput Singh,* (1879) 7 IA 8.3.
4. *Meer Usd Oalah v Mussumat Beeby Imaman,* (1836) 1 Moo Ind App 19, 42, 43.
5. *Radha Kant Yadav v State of Jharkhand,* 2003 Cr LJ (NOC) 13 (Jhar) : (2002) 3 JLJR 135.

and opportunity is given to the other side to cross-examine him, the same can be relied upon. Such a view, stands fully affirmed particularly, in view of the amended provisions of O XVIII, rules 4 and 5 CPC.[6]

[s 60] Oral evidence must be direct.—Oral evidence must, in all cases whatever, be direct; that is to say—

If it refers to a fact which could be seen, it must be the evidence of a witness who says he saw it;

If it refers to a fact which could be heard, it must be the evidence of a witness who says he heard it;

If it refers to a fact which could be perceived by any other sense or in any other manner, it must be the evidence of a witness who says he perceived it by that sense or in that manner;

If it refers to an opinion or to the grounds on which that opinion is held, it must be the evidence of the person who holds that opinion on those grounds:

Provided that the opinions of experts expressed in any treatise commonly offered for sale, and the grounds on which such opinions are held, may be proved by the production of such treatises if the author is dead or cannot be found, or has become incapable of giving evidence, or cannot be called as a witness without an amount of delay or expense which the Court regards as unreasonable:

Provided also that, if oral evidence refers to the existence or condition of any material thing other than a document, the Court may, if it thinks fit, require the production of such material thing for its inspection.

SYNOPSIS

COMMENT

This section says that oral evidence must be direct, that is, if it refers to

(1) a fact which could be seen,
the evidence must be of a witness who says he saw it;

(2) a fact which could be heard,
the evidence must be of a witness who says he heard it;

---

6. *Ayaaubkhan Noorkhan Pathan v State of Maharashtra,* (2013) 4 SCC 465 : AIR 2013 SC 58.

(3) a fact which could be perceived by any other sense or manner,
the evidence must be of a witness who says he perceived it by that sense or that manner;

(4) an opinion, or the grounds on which that opinion is held,
the evidence must be of a person who holds that opinion on those grounds.

This section, subject to the proviso excludes opinions given at second-hand. The use of the word "must" in the first clause of the section imposes a duty on the court to exclude all oral evidence that is not "direct", whether the party against whom it is tendered objects or not.[7] The word "direct" is opposed to mediate or derivative or "*hearsay*".

[s 60.1] Direct oral evidence.—Where a person is a witness of fact, his testimony is regarded as direct evidence, even if he is not able to recollect the facts with precision and has to rely upon his "belief" as to what he saw or heard. "A witness who perceived an event with his senses is not confined, when giving an account of it, to what he can swear to with complete certainty or with complete precision. He may swear to the substance or effect of the words used.[8] And it has long been established that, in giving evidence of what he saw or heard, he may swear, "to the best of his belief", if his recollection does not enable him to be more positive and precise.[9] Unless there is some indication to the contrary he may be taken, when he expresses his evidence in that way, to be stating his recollection but conceding that its quality does not enable him to swear with complete certainty and precision. But, of course, if the context or circumstances show that the reference to "belief" means that the witness is speaking from conjecture, from deduction or from information regarding what was perceived by others, then the evidence will ordinarily be rejected.[10]"

The reason for the laxity is that the law cannot afford to help to hold the social and psychological reality out of the court room. People's memories are fragile and short. Details fall out of mind rapidly with time. Subsequent publicity, discussions and suggestive questioning all exert their influence. This may lead to the exclusion of evidence which is superior in trustworthiness to evidence which is freely admitted. To minimise such chances, the courts have modified the rigid rule as to direct evidence by a number of exceptions.

The testimony of persons who saw the pitiable condition of a young woman in her in-laws' home where she met her death was held to be relevant.[11]

The doctrine of dying declaration is enshrined in section 32 of the Evidence Act, 1872 as an exception to the general rule contained in section 60 of the Evidence Act,

---

7. *Stokes' Anglo-Indian Codes*, Vol II, 889, fn 7.
8. *Hylife v Murray*, (1740) 2 All 58 at 60 : 26 ER 433, 434.
9. *Lord Melvillie's* case, (1806) 29 St. Tr. 549 at p 740 : *Taylor on Evidence*, 1st Edn, p 94; 12th Edn, p 899; *Starkie on Evidence*, 4th Edn, p 172; Kenny, *Outlines of Criminal Law*, 19th Edn, p 482; *Wigmore on Evidence*, 3rd Edn, sections 685, 726, 728, 729, 1280.
10. See *Phipson on Evidence*, 10th Edn, section 1528. The quotation is from judgment of Smith J at p 852 in *Atherton v Jackson Corio Meat Packing*, Supreme Court of Victoria, Australia, (1967) UR 850. *Achutananda Baidya v Prafullya Kumar Gayen*, AIR 1997 SC 2077 (SC) : (1997) 5 SCC 76, witnesses saying that they had heard talks between the parties but not that they had seen any agreement being made, was held to be not direct evidence.
11. *Birdichand Sarda v State of Maharashtra*, AIR 1984 SC 1622 : (1984) 4 SCC 116 : 1984 Cr LJ 1738.

which provides that oral evidence in all cases must be direct i.e. it must be the evidence of a witness, who says he saw it. The dying declaration is, in fact, the statement of a person, who cannot be called as witness and, therefore, cannot be cross-examined. Such statements themselves are relevant facts in certain cases.[12]

[s 60.2] Meaning of *hearsay* evidence.—The term *hearsay* is used with reference to what is *done or written,* as well as to what is *spoken,* and, in its legal sense, it denotes that kind of evidence which does not derive its value solely from the credit given to the witness himself, but which rests also, in part, on the veracity and competence of some other person. That this species of evidence is not given upon oath, that it cannot be tested by cross-examination, and that in many cases it supposes some better testimony which might be adduced in the particular case, are not the sole grounds for its exclusion. Its tendency to protract legal investigations to an embarrassing and dangerous length, its intrinsic weakness, its incompetency to satisfy the mind of the existence of the fact, and the frauds which may be practised with impunity under its cover, combine to support the rule that hearsay evidence is 'inadmissible.'[13] "The word '*hearsay*' is used in various senses. Sometimes it means whatever a person is heard to say; sometimes it means whatever a person declares on information given by someone else; sometimes it is treated as nearly synonymous with 'irrelevant'."[14]

The expressions "saw it", "heard it", and "perceived it", in clauses 2, 3 and 4 of the section mean "saw the fact deposed to", "heard the fact deposed to", and "perceived the fact deposed to".[15]

"Derivative or second-hand proofs are not receivable as evidence in *causa*.... Instead of stating as maxim that the law requires all evidence to be given *on oath* we should say that the law requires all evidence to be given *under personal responsibility;* i.e., every witness must give his testimony, under such circumstances as expose him to all the penalties of falsehood, which may be inflicted by any of the sanctions of truth...The true principle therefore appears to be this—that all second-hand evidence, whether of the contents of a document or of the language of a third person, which is not connected by *responsible* testimony with the party against whom it is offered, is to be rejected."[16] The witnesses deposed that they had personally seen and observed that the deceased wife was extremely unhappy and complained of incessant cruelty and that they had also seen injury marks on her person. They referred to the statements made to

---

12. *Lakhan v State of MP,* (2010) 8 SCC 514 : (2010) 8 SCC 514.

13. *Taylor,* 12th Edn, section 570, p 363.

14. Stephen's Introduction.

15. See *Shard Birichand Sarda v State of Maharashtra,* AIR 1984 SC 1622 : 1984 Cr LJ 1938, evidence of witnesses who spoke from personal knowledge of the mental state of the deceased housewife was allowed, but not their opinion as to her nature etc. *Muni Lal Gupta v State,* 1988 Cr LJ 627 (Del), evidence of what the witness heard on the spot the accused saying to his wife, held direct. *Satish Chandra v State of UP,* AIR 1986 SC 313 : 1985 Supp SCC 596 : 1985 Cr LJ 1921, the fact that after filing the FIR at the instance of the deceased's companion, the witness went to the spot and heard people talk the same thing as was scribed in the FIR was held to be not a direct evidence.

16. *Best,* 12th Edn, sections 493, 494, pp 415, 416. See *Sharad Birdichand Sarda v State of Maharashtra,* AIR 1984 SC 1622 : 1984 Cr LJ 1738 : (1984) 4 SCC 116 : 1984 SCC (Cri) 487, where the evidence of a person who was never mentioned by the deceased housewife in her letters, nor she had written any letter to him, but who heard her tales of woe from other only, was rejected. *Munir Ad. v State of Rajasthan,* 1989 Cr LJ 845 : AIR 1989 SC 705 : 1989 Supp (1) SCC 377 : 1989 SCC (Cri) 455, living person to give evidence by personal appearance unless exempted by lower court order.

them personally and not to third parties. Her letters beseeched the witnesses for their help in order to save herself from committing suicide. It was held that such evidence is admissible and not hit by the rule of hearsay.[17] The father of the accused made a statement to the *Sarpanch* that his son had informed him that the deceased had died after consuming pesticide. The medical report disclosed a different cause of death. The statement of the father of the accused was held to be not admissible.[18]

The court has jurisdiction to order examination of an overseas witness by means of a live-television link.[19]

[s 60.2.1] Rationale behind exclusion of hearsay.—Derivative or second-hand evidence is excluded owing to its infirmity as compared with its original source. Thus, where a witness told a material fact to another but himself resolved from it in the witness box, narration of the other was rejected as hearsay.[20]

[s 60.2.2] Select Committee report.—The Select Committee in their Report observed: This provision taken in connection with the provisions of relevancy contained in Chapter II will, we hope, set the whole doctrine of hearsay in a perfectly plain light, for their joint effect is that:—(1) the sayings and doings of third persons are, as a rule, irrelevant, so that no proof of them can be admitted; (2) in some excepted cases they are relevant; (3) every act done or word spoken which is relevant on any ground must (if proved by oral evidence) be proved by someone who saw it with his own eyes or heard it with his own ears.

[s 60.2.3] Written or newspaper information.—A written information is not evidence. If it is desired to make the matter contained in it evidence, a person who can directly testify to such matter must be produced.[21] A news item without any further proof of what had actually happened through witnesses is of no value. It is at best a second-hand secondary evidence. Such news item cannot be said to prove itself although it may be taken into account with other evidence if the other evidence is forcible.[22]

[s 60.2.4] Statements in public documents.—Statements in Acts of Parliament, official books and registers, can be proved by the production of the document and it is not necessary to produce before the court the draftsmen of the document. Lord Ellenborough observed[23]:

> Public Acts of Parliament are binding upon every subject, because every subject is, in the judgment of law, privy to the making of them, and, therefore, supposed to know them.

---

17. *State of Maharashtra v Vasant Shankar Mhasane,* 1993 Cr LJ 1134 (Bom); *Mukul Rani Varshnei v DDA,* (1995) 6 SCC 120 : 1995 SCC (Cri) 1049, rejection of hearsay evidence, a witness who could have been called but not called, fatal to the prosecution case.

18. *State of AP v Patnam Anandam,* AIR 2005 SC 764 : (2005) 9 SCC 237 : 2005 Cr LJ 894; *Ram Kishan v State of UP,* AIR 2004 SC 4678 : (2005) 2 SCC 736 : 2004 Cr LJ 4236, evidence of investigating officer based on the evidence of another witness recorded u/s 161, CrPC, not-admissible.

19. *Garcin v Amerindo Investment Advisors,* (1991) 1 WLR 1140.

20. *Yasin Gulam Haider v State of Maharashtra,* (1979) 4 SCC 600 : AIR 1980 SC 878.

21. *Mi Hauk v King Emperor,* (1907) 4 LBR 121; *Lal Singh v The Crown,* (1924) 5 Lah 396.

22. *SN Balakrishna v Fernandez,* AIR 1969 SC 1201 : 1969(3) SCC 238; *Luxmi Raj Shetty v State of TN,* AIR 1988 SC 1274 : 1988 Cr LJ 1783; *Ramesh v UOI,* AIR 1988 SC 775 : (1988) 1 SCC 668 : 1988 SCC (Cri) 266, newspaper report of an interview with the author of a book (Tamas). See also under section 63.

23. *R v Sutton,* (1816) 4 MNS 532.

Similarly, the Calcutta High Court observed:[24] The rule of hearsay may not stand in the way of proving public documents because once it is proved that the documents are official records or official correspondence, the court has to raise the presumption under section 114.

[s 60.2.5] Computerised information.—"One of the great revolutions of our generation has been brought about by computer use. Today a great deal of information is processed and stored by computers. Computer printouts containing factual statements fall foul, however, of the hearsay prohibition. But, as Steyn J has observed in *R v Minors*[25] if 'computer output cannot relatively readily be used as evidence in criminal cases, much crime ... will in practice be immune from prosecution."'[26] The court held in this case that a computer record was *hearsay* and, therefore, was not relevant all by itself. Either the person feeding the information must appear in person to testify to his sources of information or it must be proved that the supplier of information was unavailable for one of the reasons recognised by the law of evidence for admitting absentee statements or cannot reasonably be expected to have any recollection of the matter. This decision has been described as logically sound. "If it were otherwise, all *hearsay* will become admissible provided it has been entered into a computer. For instance, it would be admissible for the prosecution to adduce evidence of what witnesses told the police provided that the police entered the witnesses' statements into a word processor."[27]

[s 60.3] Opinions expressed in treatises—*[Proviso 1]*.—The first proviso is a departure from the rule of English law, under which medical and other treatises are not admissible, whether the author is alive or not. Any scientific textbook commonly offered for sale is admissible in evidence under the circumstances mentioned in the proviso. Section 45 refers to the evidence of expert witnesses who may be examined in court. Section 38 refers to books on law.

The quality of the literary work which can be relied upon was thus explained by Kirpal J of the Supreme Court:[28]

> Every article published or a book written cannot *ipso facto* be regarded as conclusive or worthy of acceptance. What is stated therein may only be a view of the author and may not be based on a data which is scientifically collected from a reliable source.

[s 60.4] Production of material thing may be required—*[Proviso 2]*.—This proviso enables the court to require the production of a material thing for its inspection. Under section 165 the court has power to direct the production of any document or thing in order to discover or to obtain proper proof of relevant facts.

---

24. *Octanious Steel Co v Enlegram Tea Co,* AIR 1980 Cal 83, in this case certain papers were produced from the custody of CBI which contained communications between RBI and Controller of Capital Issue (CCI, now replaced by SEBI). The information was necessary for ascertaining the value of the property of a sterling company. The court **relied** upon *Kanwar Lal Gupta v Amarnath Chawla,* AIR 1975 SC 308 : (1975) 3 SCC 646.

25. *R v Minors,* (1989) 2 All ER 208 at 210.

26. See comment by AAS Zuckerman in 1989 All ER Annual Review, 140.

27. *Ibid* at p 141.

28. *Hashamatullah v State of MP,* (1996) 4 SCC 391 at 401 : AIR 1996 SC 2076 : (1996) Supp 2 SCR 755.

CHAPTER V

OF DOCUMENTARY EVIDENCE

[s 61] Proof of contents of documents.—The contents of documents may be proved either by primary or by secondary evidence.

SYNOPSIS

COMMENT

Documentary evidence means all documents produced for the inspection of the court (section 3). Documents are of two kinds: public and private. Section 74 gives a list of documents which are regarded as public documents. All other documents are private. The production of documents in courts is regulated by the Code of Civil Procedure and the Code of Criminal Procedure.

[s 61.1] Principle.—The contents of documents must be proved either by the production of the document which is called primary evidence, or by copies or oral accounts of the contents, which are called secondary evidence. Where there is documentary evidence oral evidence is not entitled to any weight.[1]

Where a document was not required to be registered, it was admissible in evidence, even though unregistered.[2]

An *ex parte* affidavit without affording an opportunity to the other party to test the veracity of its contents by cross-examination, cannot be a proof of its contents.[3] Where the executant of a document admitted its execution, the same could be received in evidence.[4] Where the execution of a promissory note was denied, it was held that proof would be needed through the scribe and also that of an expert as to the thumb impression.[5] Where the truth of the facts stated in a document is in issue, the mere proof of the handwriting and execution of the document would not furnish evidence of the truth of the facts stated in the document or its contents. The truth or otherwise

1. *Murarka Properties Pvt Ltd v Beharilal Murarka*, AIR 1978 SC 300 : 1978(1) SCC 109.
2. *Purnabashi Mishra v Raj Kumari Mishra*, AIR 1995 Ori 284.
3. *Kripa Shankar v Gurudas*, AIR 1995 SC 2152.
4. *DB Thakur v State of Gujarat*, 1995 Cr LJ 3751 (Guj).
5. *PM Veeravu v K Moiudeen*, 1996 AIHC 3847 (Ker); *Shail Kumari v Saraswati Devi*, AIR 2002 NOC 167 (Del), questions of and objections to admissibility of documents or any other evidence should be decided before the case is put up for final arguments. The order of the trial judge that the matter of admissibility would be decided along with the final arguments was held to be not proper. *Mulji Mehta and Sons v C Mohan Krishna*, AIR 1997 AP 153, under stamp duty, admissibility of unstamped assignment of promissory note.

of the facts or contents so stated would have to be proved by admissible evidence, i.e. by the evidence of persons who can vouchsafe for the truth of the facts in issue.[6]

Primary evidence is evidence which the law requires to be given first. Secondary evidence is evidence which may be given in the absence of the better evidence which the law requires to be given first, when a proper explanation is given of the absence of that better record. Primary evidence is defined in section 62 and secondary evidence in section 63. Certified copy of a written statement has been held to be admissible under section 63(1).[7]

Mere marking of an exhibit does not dispense with the proof of document.[8]

[s 61.2] Admissibility of documents.—*Generalia specialibus non derogant.*— Where there is a specific provision covering the admissibility of a document, it is not open to the court to call into aid other general provisions in order to make a particular document admissible. If a judgment is not admissible as not falling within the ambit of sections 40–42, it must fulfil the conditions of section 43 otherwise it cannot be relevant under section 13 of the Evidence Act. The words "some other provision of this Act" cannot cover section 13 because this section does not deal with judgments at all. Therefore, section 13 cannot be used to aid the admissibility of a judgment as coming under the provisions of section 43. A judgment in *rem,* like judgments passed in probate, insolvency, matrimonial or guardianship or other similar proceedings, is admissible in all cases whether such judgments are *inter partes* or not. But a judgment *in personam* which is not *inter partes* is inadmissible in evidence except for the limited purpose of proving as to who the parties were and what was the decree passed and the properties which were the subject-matter of the suit. Therefore, the recitals in a judgment, like finding given in appreciation of evidence made or arguments or genealogies referred to in the judgment, would be wholly inadmissible in a case where neither the plaintiffs nor the defendants were parties.[9] A document produced by the Electricity Board was regarded as one produced by an organised establishment and therefore enjoying the presumption that the Board must have kept its documents in regular course. The allegation of fabrication was held to be not tenable in the absence of any supporting evidence.[10]

Where none of the documents on record was self-explanatory, nor explained by any competent witness on either side, it was not open to the special court to come up with its own explanations and decide the suit on the basic of its own inference based on

---

6. *Ramji Dayawala & Sons Pvt Ltd v Invest Import,* AIR 1981 SC 2085 : (1981) 1 SCR 899.
7. *Raman Pillai v Kumaran Parameswaran,* AIR 2002 Ker 133. The court noted that this was a common practice in suits and **distinguished** the case from the decision to *Kannu Asan v Trav Forward Bank Ltd,* 1956 Ker LT 203.
8. *Somappa v Mahadevappa,* 2016 AIR CC 929, para 15 : 2016 (2) KCCR 1389 (Kar).
9. *State of Bihar v Radha Krishna Singh,* AIR 1983 SC 684 : (1983) 3 SCC 118; *Pammi v Govt of MP,* 1998 Cr LJ 1617 : AIR 1998 SC 1185 : (1998) 2 SCC 700, a copy of the deposition of a witness in another case was relied upon to disbelieve the presence of an eyewitness at the place of occurrence in the present case. The person whose deposition was relied on was not examined. It was held that this was not proper for the purpose of disbelieving an eyewitness in the present case. *R Venkatakrishnan v CBI,* AIR 2010 SC 1812 : (2009) 11 SCC 737, the Reserve Bank constituted a committee for the limited purpose of inquiring into a securities scam. It was held to be not a court but merely a fact finding authority. It did not render any decision. The contents of its report could not have been taken into without formal proof.
10. *Umiya Glass Industries v MPSEB,* AIR 2006 MP 105.

assumed explanations, especially when the inferences ran contrary to the oral evidence of a witness.[11]

A demand notice was held to be not admissible in evidence because they were photocopies of typed documents without signature of any advocate who might have issued it. Also, no evidence was produced to show either the despatch or receipt of the notice.[12]

[s 62] Primary evidence.—Primary evidence means the document itself produced for the inspection of the Court.

***Explanation 1.*—Where a document is executed in several parts,[s 62.1] each part is primary evidence of the document.**

Where a document is executed in counterpart,[s 62.2] each counterpart being executed by one or some of the parties only, each counterpart is primary evidence as against the parties executing it.

***Explanation 2.*—Where a number of documents are all made by one uniform process,[s 62.3] as in the case of printing, lithography or photography, each is primary evidence of the contents of the rest; but, where they are all copies of a common original, they are not primary evidence of the contents of the original.**

ILLUSTRATION

A person is shown to have been in possession of a number of placards, all printed at one time from one original. Any one of the placards is primary evidence of the contents of any other, but no one of them is primary evidence of the contents of the original.

SYNOPSIS

COMMENT

This section defines the meaning of primary evidence which means the document itself produced for the inspection of the court. Where a document is executed in several parts, each part is primary evidence of the document. Where a document is executed in counterpart, each counterpart is primary evidence, as against the party executing it. Where a number of documents are made by printing, lithography, or photography, each is primary evidence of the contents of the rest. Where they are copies of a common original they are not primary evidence of the contents of the original. Two wills in identical language were prepared by the process of typing in which the second copy was obtained by carbon impression. Both were duly executed and attested. Both were

11. *Standard Chartered Bank v Andhra Bank Financial Services Ltd,* (2006) 6 SCC 94 ; AIR 2006 SC 3626.
12. *Bank of Baroda v Shri Moti Industries,* AIR 2008 Bom 201. The plaintiff bank had not filed extracts of the bank account, nor any other document from which amount due could be ascertained, computerised extracts, though available, were not produced.

held to be original and not one a copy of the other. The fact that the testator inserted a remark on one of them "true copy" would not alter their character.[13]

Primary evidence is the evidence which the law requires to be given first.

[s 62.1] "Document is executed in several parts".—Sometimes each party to a transaction wishes for the sake of convenience to have a complete document in his own possession. To effect this, the document is written out as many times over as there are parties, and each document is executed, i.e., signed or sealed, as the case may be, by all the parties. Any one of them may be produced as primary evidence of the contents of the document. The duplicates of partition deed executed and registered along with it whereby properties are created in favour of several persons are to be treated as original itself having the same operation and effect as that of the other.[14]

[s 62.2] "Document is executed in counterpart" [*Explanation 1*].—Where a document is executed in counterpart, each counterpart being executed by one or some of the parties only, each counterpart is primary evidence as against the parties executing it, and secondary evidence as against other parties (see section 63, clause 4).

A document was executed in two parts. The plaintiff was left with the carbon copy which was executed in the very same process but was in fact a counterpart of the original. It was held that the carbon copy was to be regarded as a primary evidence under the section and produced as such. The party against whose interest the document was sought to be produced could challenge its genuineness or disprove the same.[15]

[s 62.3] One uniform process [*Explanation 2*].—Where a carbon copy was made by one uniform process of the certificate of a doctor (as to the condition of a rape victim) given in the performance of professional duty, it was held to be a primary evidence within the meaning of the Explanation 2.[16]

A police station diary contained duplicate pages. A carbon copy was prepared by the same process by which the first copy was prepared. Each was held to be the primary evidence of the contents of the rest.[17]

The accused was charged for allegedly giving fake visa after charging money, it was pleaded on behalf of the accused that he is entitled to discharge as the document of visa was a photocopy and thus secondary evidence. It was held by Delhi High Court that in a given case where photocopy is used as the primary offending article, the same would be a primary evidence for the purposes of trial of the said case.[18]

[s 62.4] Application for grant of probate.—Section 276 of the Succession Act, 1925 requires that an application for probate or letters of administration should be made with the "will" annexed. Since this does not necessarily mean the "original will", a copy certified by the sub-registrar was allowed to be annexed.[19]

---

13. *Kamala Rajamanikham v Sushila Thakur Das,* AIR 1983 All 90.
14. *State Bank of Travancore v Velayudhan Pillai Bhaskaran Nair,* AIR 1996 Ker 32.
15. *Bhagwanji and Kalyanji v Punjabhai Hajabhai Rathod,* AIR 2007 Guj 88.
16. *Prithi Chand v State of HP,* AIR 1989 SC 702 : 1989 Cr LJ 841.
17. *Rajesh Rai v State of Sikkim,* 2002 Cr LJ 1385 (Sik).
18. *Nakul Kohli v State,* 2010 Cr LJ 4536 (Delhi).
19. *Rajrani Sehgal v Parshottam Lal (Dr),* AIR 1992 Del 134.

[s 62.5] Video evidence.—The provision of copies, though the norm, is not an absolute entitlement of the defence, and it is not appropriate to draw a line between entitlement to copies as against facilities for and conditions of inspection. There is at most a strong presumption in favour of provision to the defence in good time of copies of all capable exhibits, which was for the prosecution to displace. That was especially so where the exhibits were an important part of the prosecution case and were likely to warrant close examination to enable the defence to prepare properly for trial. Furthermore, although Article 6 of the Convention referred only to the defendant's and not the prosecutor's right to a fair hearing, the notion demanded some consideration as to whether it could be achieved whilst nevertheless paying proper regard to the public interest in prosecuting serious offenders to conviction. It would be a matter for the trial judge, at an early stage after committal, to determine whether in the particular circumstances of each case a fair hearing could be achieved by the prosecution permitting the defence to inspect originals or copies of capable exhibits rather than providing it with copies. It could not be said, in the light of the present statutory and common law regime governing the prosecution of criminal offences, that the CPS's refusal to provide copies of the tapes and its offer to arrange inspection were unlawful as a matter of principle. Protection of the safety and future usefulness of undercover police officers was clearly a valid consideration in the making of such a decision. There was an onus on the CPS to justify its departure from the norm, but whether it could do so was a task for the trial judge and not for the High Court on an application for judicial review. It followed that the CPS's stance had not been irrational, unlawful or contrary to Article 6. and, accordingly, the application was dismissed.[20]

[s 62.5.1] CCTV footage.—The court has the power to view CCTV footage and video recordings, be it primary or legally admissible secondary evidence, in the presence of the accused for satisfying itself as to whether the individual seen in the footage is the accused in the dock.[21]

[s 63] Secondary evidence.—Secondary evidence means and includes—

(1) **certified copies given under the provisions hereinafter contained;**

(2) **copies made from the original by mechanical processes which in themselves ensure the accuracy of the copy, and copies compared with such copies;**

(3) **copies made from or compared with the original;**

(4) **counterparts of documents as against the parties who did not execute them;**

(5) **oral accounts of the contents of a document given by some person who has himself seen it.**

ILLUSTRATIONS

(a) A photograph of an original is secondary evidence of its contents, though the two have not been compared, if it is proved that the thing photographed was the original.

20. The court **distinguished** *R v Central Criminal Court, ex parte Behbehani,* (1994) Crimes LR 352.
21. *K Ramajayam v Inspector of Police, Chennai,* 2016 Cr LJ 1542, para 8 (Mad-DB).

(b) A copy, compared with a copy of a letter, made by a copying machine is secondary evidence of the contents of the letter, if it is shown that the copy made by the copying machine was made from the original.

(c) A copy transcribed from a copy, but afterwards compared with the original is secondary evidence; but the copy not so compared is not secondary evidence of the original, although the copy from which it was transcribed was compared with the original.

(d) Neither an oral account of a copy compared with the original, nor an oral account of a photograph or machine copy of the original, is secondary evidence of the original.

SYNOPSIS

COMMENT

This section describes what constitutes "secondary evidence". "Secondary evidence", evidence which may be given under certain circumstances in the absence of that better evidence which the law requires to be given first.

Secondary evidence means and includes—

(1) certified copies;

(2) copies made from the original by mechanical processes, and copies compared with such copies;

(3) copies made from or compared with the original;

(4) counterparts of documents as against the parties who did not execute them;

(5) oral accounts of the contents of a document by a person who has seen it.

Clauses 1 to 3 deal with copies of documents. Where a copy of a document is admitted in evidence in the trial court without objection, its admissibility cannot be challenged in the Appeal Court. Because omission to object to its admission implies that it is a true copy and, therefore, it is not open to the Appeal Court to say whether the copy was properly compared with the original or not.[22]

[s 63.1] Certified copies—*[Clause 1]*.—Section 76 defines the expression "certified copies". See also sections 77, 78, 79 and 86.

---

22. *Chimnaji Govind Godbole v Dinkar Dhondev Godbole,* (1886) 11 Bom 320; *Lakshman v Amrit,* (1900) 24 Bom 591 : 2 Bom LR 386; *Kishori Lal Goswami v Rakhal Das Banerjee,* (1903) 31 Cal 155; *Ram Lochan Misra v Pandit Harinath Misra,* (1922) 1 Pat 606.

The correctness of certified copies will be presumed under section 79; but that of other copies will have to be proved. This proof may be afforded by calling a witness who can swear that he has compared the copy tendered in evidence with the original or with what some other person read as the contents of the original and that such is correct.[23] Certified copies of money lenders licences are admissible in evidence.[24]

Certified copies of sale deeds were held to be admissible as secondary evidence. The court, however, said that they could not be relied upon unless the vendor or vendee was examined to prove the consideration for the transaction and other circumstances, such as nearness to land.[25]

[s 63.2] Copies made by mechanical process—*[Clause 2]*.—Reading clause 2 and illustrations (b) and (c) together it will appear that a copy of a copy, i.e. a copy, transcribed from, and compared with, a copy, is inadmissible unless the copy with which it was compared was a copy made by some mechanical process which in itself ensures the accuracy of such copy. See Illustration (b).

Copies of copies kept in a registration office, when signed and sealed by the registering officer, are admissible for the purpose of proving the contents of the originals (section 57(5), Act XVI of 1908). Letter-process copies and photographs of writings are secondary evidence (*vide* Illustration (a)). Photostatic copies of document should be accepted in evidence only after examining original records.[26] Photostatic copy of the power of attorney executed by competent authority and authenticated by a notary public and proved from original is admissible in evidence.[27] In absence of any evidence that the originals were delivered to the addressee, the copy of the letters carry little evidentiary value.[28]

A photostat copy of a rent note which was proved to be the photostat of the originals, though not compared with the original, was held to be admissible.[29]

While it is true that the xerox copy of a certificate may not be evidence by itself especially when the respondent producing the same had stated that the original was with

---

23. A copy of Municipal record not issued in accordance with the requirements of the Municipal Act is not relevant. *Ganesh Pd v Budhi Pd,* AIR 1980 All 361. Certified copy of a registered deed is provable, but not a copy which was prepared while the deed was presented for registration. *Kalyan Singh v Chhoti,* AIR 1990 SC 396; 1990 ALR 155 : 1990(1) SCC 266; *Land Acquisition Officer v N Venkata Rao,* AIR 1991 AP 31, copies issued by sub-registrar, secondary evidence.

24. *K Shivalingaiah v BV Chandrashekara Gowda,* AIR 1993 Kant 29 : 1992 (2) Kar LJ 536; *Bidhan Paul v Paresh Chandra Ghose,* AIR 2002 Gau 46, a power of attorney registered with the sub-registrar has been held to be not a public document. A certified copy of such record is secondary evidence.

25. *Kummari Veeraiah v State of AP,* (1995) 4 SCC 136. See also *Gopinath Educational and Welfare Society v Rajendra Singh Shekhawat* , AIR 2016 Raj 106, (para 12). *Manda Laxmi Rajam v Kanaparthi Laxmi Bai,* AIR 2008 AP 255, an unregistered and unstamped sale deed cannot be admitted even as a secondary evidence. *Sushila Devi v ADJ,* AIR 2007 Raj 241.

26. *Govt of AP v Karri Chinna Venkata Reddy,* AIR 1994 SC 591 : 1995 Supp (1) SCC 462.

27. *Northland Traders v Bank of Baroda,* AIR 1994 All 381.

28. *J Patel & Co v National Federation of Industrial Co-op Ltd,* AIR 1996 Cal 253; *Ramesh Verma v Sajesh Saxena,* AIR 1998 MP 46, on admissibility of photocopies. *Rajasthan Golden Transport Co v Amritlal,* AIR 1998 Raj 153, photocopy of an assessment order produced, neither any opportunity was given to the witness to prove the original, nor there was anything to show that the photocopy was made from the original, the order permitting photocopy to be produced was held to be not proper.

29. *Ratan Sharma (Smt) v Ambesedar Dry Cleaners,* AIR 1997 Raj 75.

him, but had chosen not to produce the same, yet the document was allowed to be marked at the trial. Strict rules of evidence, it is fairly well-settled, are not applicable to the proceedings before the Labour Court. That being so, it was held that the admission of the xerox copy of the certificate without any objection from the opposite party could not be faulted at that belated stage.[30]

[s 63.3] Copies made from original—*[Clause 3]*.—Copies made from the original or copies compared with the original are admissible as secondary evidence. A copy of a copy, when compared with the original, would be receivable as secondary evidence of the original [Illustration (b)].

Illustration (c) lays down in express language that "a copy transcribed from a copy, but afterwards compared with the original, is secondary evidence; but a copy not so compared is not secondary evidence of the original, although the copy from which it was transcribed was compared with the original". An entry in a deed-writer's register which contains all the essential particulars contained in the document itself and is also signed or thumb-marked by the person executing the document amounts to a copy and is admissible in evidence.[31] A copy of a certified copy of a document, which has not been compared with the original, cannot be admitted in evidence, such a copy being neither primary nor secondary evidence of the contents of the original.[32]

Documents which are merely copies of copies, the originals not having been satisfactorily accounted for, are inadmissible in evidence and must be rejected.[33]

An abstract translation or a complete translation of a document is not "copy made from and compared with the original" within the meaning of this clause.[34]

True copy of the document incorporating facts of amicable partition, supplied from the office of Sub-Registrar bearing his seal and signature can be relied upon for its contents.[35] Newspaper reports, advertisements or messages are not admissible in evidence unless the original manuscripts are produced or they are proved by the person concerned.[36]

A draft of a document cannot be treated as secondary evidence;[37] but the Kerala High Court has held that a draft can be accepted in evidence only if there is proof that the original has been prepared without any corrections and that it is

---

30. *Bhavnagar Municipal Corp v Jadeja Govubha Chhanubha,* (2014) 16 SCC 130, para 8 : AIR 2015 SC 609.
31. *Sant Ram v Ghasita Ram,* (1956) 9 Pun 193.
32. *Ram Prasad v Raghunandan Prasad,* (1885) 7 All 738, 743; *Narasimham v Babu Rao,* (1939) Mad 333. *Sattamma v Ch. Bhikshapati Goud,* AIR 2010 AP 166, in a suit for specific performance of an agreement to sell, original document containing the agreement was lost. Permission was granted for filing a photocopy of the agreement attested by Notary as secondary evidence, being covered by section 63(3), illustration (c).
33. *Mahadeva Royal v Virabasava Royal,* (1948) 50 Bom LR 638 PC; *Badrunnisa Begum v Mohamooda Begum,* AIR 2001 AP 394, a copy of a copy of a document not compared with the original document was held to be not admissible in evidence. A decree based on such a copy of a copy was held liable to be set aside.
34. *Muhammad Suleman v Hari Ram,* (1936) 21 Lah 363.
35. *Monoranjan Paul v Narendra Kumar Paul,* AIR 1994 Gau 64.
36. *Quamarul Islam v SK Kanta,* AIR 1994 SC 1733 : 1994 Supp (3) SCC 5.
37. *Devi Chand v Har Kishan Das,* (1954) 2 All 531.

exactly a true copy of the draft.[38] The Allahabad High Court has similarly held that section 63 is not exhaustive of all types of secondary evidence. It, therefore, allowed the draft notice from which the final notice was prepared to be produced as secondary evidence.[39] The statement as to the contents of a document by a witness, who has not himself read the document, is not secondary evidence of the contents of the document.[40]

A photograph is a copy prepared from the negative, the original document. Hence where neither the original was produced nor the photographer was examined, the eye-witnesses were not allowed to be contradicted by photographs of the happening.[41]

In a criminal proceeding for contempt of court, the contemnor was alleged to have made a speech calculated to scandalise judiciary in general and the order restraining the *bandh* in particular. The petitioner adduced evidence of xerox copies of newspapers and the tape of the edited version of his speech telecast on TV No primary evidence of the speech was produced. It was held that a charge under section 2(c) of the Contempt of Courts Act, 1971 could not be framed on the basis of such evidence.[42]

[s 63.4] Counterparts—*[Clause 4]*.—When a document is executed in counterpart, each party signing only the part by which he is bound, each counterpart is the best evidence against the party signing it and his privies. As to the other party it is only secondary evidence. A landlord's counterfoil was held to be not relevant for the purpose of showing that the arrangement was a month-to-month tenancy.[43]

[s 63.5] Oral statements—*[Clause 5]*.— But a written statement of the contents of a copy of a document, the original of which the person making the statement has not seen, cannot be accepted as secondary evidence.[44] This clause does not necessarily mean that a witness who is called to give evidence as to a lost document must have himself read the document. He would be a competent witness if, having physically seen the document, the contents thereof had been read out or explained to him.[45] Secondary evidence of a document which is lost or difficult to trace can be adduced in two ways; (1) by oral evidence of persons who were present when the document was executed; (2) by a certified copy of the original document.[46] Copies of registered documents are admissible as secondary evidence where the person in whose custody the original should be swears that they are not with him though there is no evidence as to the loss or otherwise of the original.[47] The original dying declaration was lost. A head constable who maintained a copy testified to its accuracy. This was allowed as

38. *P Kunhammad v V Moosankutty*, AIR 1972 Ker 76.
39. *Lachcho v Dwari Mal*, AIR 1986 All 303. **See also** *Balbir Singh v State of Haryana*, AIR 1987 SC 1053 : 1987 Cr LJ 853 : (1987) 1 SCC 533 : 1987 SCC (Cri) 193, where a police report was prepared on the basis of rough notes which were not produced, no importance given to the report.
40. *Dalu v Juhar Mal*, (1951) 1 Raj 166.
41. *State of Gujarat v Bharat*, 1991 Cr LJ 978 (Guj).
42. *All India Anna Dravida Munnetra Kazhagam v LK Tripathi*, AIR 2009 SC 1314 : (2009) 5 SCC 417.
43. *Idandas v Anant Ram Chandra*, AIR 1982 SC 127 : 1982 (1) SCC 27 : (1982) 1 SCR 1197; *Minati Sen v Kalipada Ganguly*, AIR 1997 Cal 386, counterfoil of a rent payment receipt did not show any sub-tenancy, even otherwise there was no proof of sub-tenancy.
44. *Kanayala v Pyarabai*, (1882) 7 Bom 139.
45. *Mehi Lal v Ramji Das*, (1924) 47 All 13.
46. *Veerappa v Md. Attavullah*, (1951) Hyd 74.
47. *Hutchegowda v Chenningegowda*, (1952) Mys 49.

corroborative evidence.[48] A taped conversation not compared with the voice was not allowed to be used as evidence.[49] The newspaper report of an interview with the author of a book is not admissible to prove the nature and contents of the book (on the basis of which Tamas serial was produced) but the court agreed to look at it in view of the urgency of deciding the case on a matter of public importance.[50] Letters written by a police officer to his administrative superior were not allowed to be proved. The writer of the letters should have appeared in person so as to enable the opposite party to cross-examine him as to the contents of the letter.[51]

Where the report of accidental electrocution was based on the information given by another person who was not examined nor original report was produced, no reliance could be placed on the version of that person and the said report.[52]

A witness can be shown xerox copy of a document which is already on record. The statements of the witness as to the document would not mean the admission of the document in evidence.[53]

[s 63.6] Repeat application for permitting secondary evidence.—An application was made by the plaintiff bank for permission for filing photocopy of the "acknowledgement of debt" as the original happened to be misplaced. The application was dismissed without hearing the plaintiff's contention. Neither party had argued the matter, nor was it decided by the court. It was held that the filing of another application for producing secondary evidence was not barred by *res judicata.*[54]

[s 63.7] List not exhaustive.—The Allahabad High Court[55] held that section 63 is not exhaustive of all the categories of secondary evidence. The court allowed evidence of draft notes from which the final notice was prepared. The court said:

> The scope of Sec. 63 is not restricted to its five clauses but leaves enough scope for cases, which do not strictly fall within any of those enumerated therein. The term 'includes' leaves some scope for a case like the present one. The court must, however, be satisfied that the document sought to be introduced as secondary evidence is a faithful and accurate reproduction or draft of the final document whose copy it purports to be.

[s 63.8] A document insufficiently stamped.—A document insufficiently stamped can be admitted in evidence on payment of penal stamp duty.[56]

[s 63.8.1] *Secondary evidence of document insufficiently stamped, unregistered or unstamped.*—An application seeking permission for producing secondary evidence was not allowed because the document was unstamped and was also not registered and, therefore, the original itself would not have been admissible. This approach was

---

48. *Aher Ram Goa v Gujarat,* 1979 Cr LJ 1081.
49. *Joginder Kaur v Surjit Singh,* AIR 1985 P&H 128.
50. *Ramesh v UOI,* AIR 1988 SC 912 : 1988 Cr LJ 936 : (1988) 1 SCC 668 : 1988 SCC (Cri) 266.
51. *Vinod Chaturvedi v State of MP,* AIR 1984 SC 911 : 1984 Cr LJ 814 : (1984) 2 SCC 350 : 1984 SCC (Cri) 250.
52. *Asa Ram v MCD,* AIR 1995 Del 164.
53. *Ahmedabad New Textile Mills v Rajubhai Dalechandbhai,* AIR 1999 Guj 148.
54. *Ram Pal Singh v Syndicate Bank,* AIR 2000 P&H 296 : (2000) 126 PLR 135.
55. *Lachcho v Dwari Mal,* AIR 1986 All 303, 306.
56. *Kundan Mal v Nand Kishore,* AIR 1994 Raj 1.

held to be not justified. It was premature for the trial court to go into that question at the application stage.[57]

[s 63.9] Recorded tape.—Where the cassette was carefully sealed and kept in judicial custody, voice of the parties were clearly audible and possibility of tampering was ruled out, the taped statements were admissible.[58]

In has been said that there is "no reason in principle why the recording in some permanent or semi-permanent manner of human voice (or other sounds) which are relevant to the issue to be determined, provided that it furnishes information, cannot be a document."[59] In reference to the reception into evidence of models, maps, diagrams and photos, it is observed in Wigmore[60] "that for evidentiary purposes they are nothing except so far as they have a human being's credit to support them. Then they become media of communication as a superior substitute for words." An Australian Court observed:[61] If it should be established by oral evidence that there was a mechanical electronic recorder in operation at a material time which was capable of and did record accurately sounds as they occurred, and other oral evidence of identification, and non-interference, it appears that the material containing such recording is properly admissible in evidence. There is no distinction in principle from the reception into evidence of a photograph of a street accident taken at the time of its occurrence which is sworn to by an eye-witness as being a true representation of the scene at the relevant time. In that case light waves, and in the case of a recording, sound waves, have been captured and preserved by scientific means.

These principles have been followed by the Supreme Court of India. Tape recorded conversations came before the Supreme Court mostly in cases of officials in receiving or attempting to receive bribes. In *RM Malkani v State of Maharashtra*,[62] The accused was the coroner of Bombay. A doctor operated upon a patient who afterwards died. Being a post-operation death, it became the subject of post-mortem and inquest. The coroner persuaded the doctor to pay him a sum of money if he wanted the report to be favourable to him. The payment was arranged to be made through another doctor and the date and timing of the final meeting was to be settled by telephone call from the house of the other doctor. The Police Commissioner was called with the tape recording mechanism. This was connected to the doctor's telephone and thus the most incriminating conversation was recorded in the presence of the police officer. The Bombay High Court held that the testimony of two doctors required corroboration and

57. *Swaran Singh v Narinder Kaur*, AIR 2002 P&H 40. A similar approach was adopted in *Bihari Lal v Ram Piari*, (1999) 2 Punj LJ 213 and *Sinnu v Pali*, (1992) 1 Punj LR 378 : 1992 Punj LJ 74; *Mukhtiar Singh v Baint Singh*, (1991) 1 Punj LR 15 : 1991 Punj LJ 143, a photocopy of the original will be permitted as secondary evidence. The same view was taken in *Raj Kumari v Shri Lal Chand*, (1994) 1 Punj LR 190. The decision in *Roman Catholic Mission v State of Madras*, AIR 1966 SC 1457 : (1966) 3 SCR 283 was held to be not applicable at this stage.
58. *KS Mohan v Sandhya Mohan*, AIR 1993 Mad 59.
59. Darling J in *R v Daye*, (1908) KB 333 and Humphreys J in *R v Hill*, (1945) KB 329, at p 334.
60. *Wigmore on Evidence*, para 790 (3rd Edn 1940,Vol 3).
61. Holt, Ch of QS in *Travers*, (1958) SR (NSW) 87 at p 96 : reported, in Edwards, *Cases on Evidence in Australia*, p 317 (1968). Also see *Harry Parker Ltd v Mason*, (1940) 5 KB 590; *R v Mills and Rose*, (1952) 1 WLR 1152 : 42 Cr. App. R. 336 and *R v Maqsood Ali*, (1966) 1 QB 686, in both these cases tape-recorded statements were received in evidence.
62. *RM Malkani v State of Maharashtra*, AIR 1973 SC 157 : (1973) 1 SCC 471.

that the tape amply corroborated it. This decision was upheld by the Supreme Court. Ray J (afterwards CJ) looked into the previous authorities.

This Court in *N Sri Rama Reddy v VV Giri,*[63] *Yusufalli Esmail Nagree v State of Maharashtra,*[64] and *Pratap Singh v State of Punjab,*[65] accepted conversion of dialogue recorded on tape-recording machine as admissible evidence. In *Nagree's* case,[66] the conversation was between Nagree and Sheikh Nagree and Nagree was accused of offering bribe to Sheikh.

In the *Presidential Election* case questions were put to a witness that he had tried to dissuade the petitioner from filing an election petition. The petitioner had recorded on tape the conversation that took place between the petitioner and the witness. The Court admitted the recording to contradict the witness. The tape itself becomes the primary and direct evidence of what has been said and recorded.[67] "Tape recorded conversation is admissible provided, first, the conversation is relevant to the matters in issue; secondly, there should be identification of the voice; and thirdly, the accuracy of the tape recorded conversation is proved by eliminating the possibility of erasing the tape record. A contemporaneous tape record of a relevant conversation is a relevant fact and is relevant under section 8 of the Act. It is also *res gestae* (part of the same transaction) and therefore, relevant under section 6. It is also comparable to a photograph of a relevant incident and is, therefore, a relevant fact under section 7 of the Act."[68]

In another case before the Supreme Court, the question was whether the tenant had granted a sub-tenancy. The finding of the Rent Controller was that there was sub-tenancy based upon a tape recorded conversation between the tenant and the husband of the landlady. The court said that the tape recorded conversation could be used in corroborating the deposition in the court by one of the parties. In the absence of any such deposition, the tape was not allowed to be used as evidence in itself.[69] The Supreme Court subsequently tightened the rule to this extent that it must be shown that the tape was kept in proper custody. In that case the Deputy Commissioner had left the tape with the stenographer. That was held to be sufficient to destroy its authenticity.[70] How the cassette came into existence has been held by the Supreme Court to be an important consideration. The Court rejected the tape recorded evidence of an election speech because the tape was prepared by a police officer who was not able to explain why he had done so. The candidate had denied that the tape was in his voice.[71]

[s 63.10] Newspaper reports.—In the words of the Supreme Court a newspaper report is a hearsay-secondary evidence. It cannot be relied upon unless proved by evidence *aliunde.* Even where nobody has opposed the report, the party citing the report would not be absolved of his obligation to prove the truth of its contents. The

---

63. *N Sri Rama Reddy v VV Giri* (1970) 2 SCC 340 : (1971) 1 SCR 339.

64. *Yusufalli Esmail Nagree v State of Maharashtra,* (1967) 3 SCR 720 : AIR 1968 SC 147 : (1968) 1 SCJ 51.

65. *Pratap Singh v State of Punjab,,* AIR 1964 SC 72 : (1964) 4 SCR 733.

66. *Nagree's* case, AIR 1968 SC 147 : (1967) 3 SCR 730 : (1968) 1 SCJ 51.

67. *Pratap Singh v State of Punjab,* AIR 1964 SC 72.

68. *Ibid*

69. *Mahabir Prasad v Surinder Kaur,* AIR 1982 SC 1043 : (1982) 2 SCC 258. To the same effect, *State v Ravi,* 2000 Cr LJ 1125 (Del).

70. *Ram Singh v Col Ram Singh,* (1985) Supp SCC 611 : AIR 1986 SC 3.

71. *Quammaral Islam v SK Kanta,* AIR 1994 SC 1733 : 1994 Supp (3) SCC 5.

court said: In the present case, no evidence has been let in proof of the statement of facts contained in the newspaper report. The absence of any denial by the maker of the statement, viz., the Minister, will not absolve the applicant from discharging his obligation of proving the statement of facts as appeared in the press report. The Minister in his counter-affidavit had taken a stand that the statements attributed to him based on the newspaper report are mere hearsay and cannot in law be relied upon for the purpose of initiating such proceeding. Therefore, in the absence of required legal proof, the court will not be justified in issuing a *suo motu* notice for contempt of court. Moreover, the news item does not spell out any reference to the case of corruption or its proceeding pending before the Supreme Court. In the alleged contemptuous statement only the view of the reporter was mentioned as if the Minister had been provoked about the proceedings of the case before the Supreme Court. There is no reason much less compelling reason to issue *suo motu* notice to the Minister for contempt of court.[72]

Where the death of a prisoner was alleged to be due to the negligence of jail authorities and the information to that effect was collected wholly from newspaper items, the court said that facts published by way of news could not *ex facie* be taken to be of such authenticity which could warrant initiation of proceedings under Article 226.[73]

A PIL can be entertained on the basis of newspaper report if the Chief Justice or his designate finds that the information reveals gross violation of fundamental rights guaranteed under the Constitution.[74]

[s 63.11] Matters to be decided by the judge recording evidence.—The matters of secondary evidence are to be decided by the judge who is recording evidence. Objections to the secondary evidence have also to be decided by him. In the case of evidence before a Commissioner, objections, if any, can only be recorded by him. The decision has to be made only by the judge.[75]

Proof by secondary evidence has been allowed to provide relief to a party who is genuinely unable to produce the original through no personal fault. The election candidate in question was not able to produce the original certificate issued to her by the Arya Samaj reaffirming her faith in the Hindu religion. It was lying with her uncle who had lost it. She had a copy. The Supreme Court said that the refusal for production of secondary evidence was not proper. The court must see that the secondary evidence actually produced is authenticated by foundational evidence that the copy is a true copy of the original.[76]

[s 64] Proof of documents by primary evidence.—Documents must be proved by primary evidence except in the cases hereinafter mentioned.

---

72. *SA Khan v Ch. Bhajan Lal,* (1993) 3 SCC 151 : 1993 Cr LJ 1042 : AIR 1993 SC 1348 : (1993) 1 Serv LR 392. *AV Amarnathan v HD Kumaraswamy,* AIR 2007 NOC 1382 (Kar) : (2007) 3 AIR Kar R 150, contempt proceedings not entertained on the basis of mere paper publication.
73. *Sudha Gupta v State of MP,* 1999 Cr LJ 1742 (MP).
74. *SP Anand v Registrar General, MP,* AIR 2009 MP 1 (FB).
75. *Indian Overseas Bank v Trioka Textiles Industries,* AIR 2007 Bom 24 : 2007 AIHC 437 : (6) Bom CR 85.
76. *M Chandra v M Thangmuthu,* AIR 2011 SC 146 : (2010) 9 SCC 712.

SYNOPSIS

COMMENT

[s 64.1] Principle.—A written document can only be proved by the instrument itself. It is a general rule that if a person wants to get at the contents of a written document the proper way is to produce it if he can. "Where the contents of *any document* are in question, either as a fact directly in issue or a subalternate principal fact, the document is the proper evidence of its *own contents*. But where a written instrument or document of any description is not a fact in issue, and is merely used as evidence to prove some fact, independent proof *aliunde* is receivable. Thus although a receipt has been given for the payment of money, proof of the fact of payment may be made, by any person who witnessed it... So, although where the *contents* of a marriage register are in issue, verbal or other evidence of those contents is not receivable, the *fact* of the marriage may be proved by the independent evidence of a person who was present at it."[77] Once a document is properly admitted, the contents of that document are also admitted in evidence, though those contents may not be conclusive evidence.[78] By the mere filing of a document, its contents do not stand proved. A certificate issued by an expert should be brought on record by examining him.[79] Where the report of the Central Forensic Science Laboratory expert was admitted in evidence without objection regarding its mode of proof, the same could not be objected to at any later stage of the case or in appeal.[80] For proving the contents of a sale deed, the executant was not examined, though proof of his signature was offered. The sale deed was not allowed to be admitted.[81] Where the witness merely identified the person who had allegedly signed the document but did not state that it was signed in his presence, it would not prove the contents of the document.[82] No materials, which are not spoken to by persons who are competent to speak about them and are subjected to cross-examination, can be relied upon. The executant of a document must be produced or his affidavit filed.[83]

Mere admission of a document in evidence does not amount to its proof. Therefore, it is the obligation of the court to decide the question of admissibility of a document in secondary evidence before making endorsement thereon.[84] It is the duty of the court

---

77. *Best*, 12th Edn, section 223, p 209; *Balbahadar Prasad v The Maharajah of Betia*, (1887) 9 All 351, 356; *K Anjaneya Setty v KH Rangiah Setty*, AIR 2002 Kant 387, where a document is not admissible for one reason or another, the court can decide at the final hearing as to whether it can be looked at for collateral purposes.

78. *PC Purushothama v S Perumal*, AIR 1972 SC 608 : 1972(1) SCC 9.

79. *Subhash Maruti Avasare v State of Maharashtra*, (2006) 10 SCC 631 : 2006 (4) Crimes 304 (SC).

80. *Amarjit Singh v State (Delhi Admn)*, 1995 Cr LJ 1623 (Del), following *Phool Kumar v Delhi Admn*, AIR 1975 SC 905 : 1975 Cr LJ 778 and **overruling** *Heera Lal v State (Delhi)*, (1994) 2 Chand Cri C 300 (HC), *Nizamuddin v The State*, 1994 IV AD (Delhi) 50, *Attar Singh v State (Delhi Admn)*, 1994 III AD (Del) 626 and *Islam v State (Delhi Admn.)*, 1994 III AD (Del) 1495.

81. *Prakash Cotton Mills v M Commr*, AIR 1982 Bom 387.

82. *Nandkishore Lalbhai Mehta v New Era Fabrics Pvt Ltd*, (2015) 9 SCC 755, para 40.

83. *Ram Jawai v Shakuntala Devi*, AIR 1993 Delhi 330.

84. *U Sree v U Srinivas*, (2013) 2 SCC 114. Also see, *Joseph John Peter Sandy v Veronica Thomas Rajkumar*, (2013) 3 SCC 801.

to examine whether the documents produced in the court or contents thereof have any probative value.[85]

Oral admissions as to the contents of a document are not relevant, unless and until the party proposing to prove them shows that he is entitled to give secondary evidence of the contents of such document, or unless the genuineness of a document produced is in question.[86]

The tape recorded conversation of wife was lodged as a proof of her mental disorder. She was sitting in the court as a respondent. No effort was made to compare her voice with the tape. The tape was not allowed to be used as evidence or for shaking her credit in cross-examination.[87] A deed of adoption was produced before the trial court without any objection by the opposite party as to its mode of proof. Objections cannot be raised in appeal.[88]

A matter of title was settled by a settlement which was entered into the revenue record. A copy of the settlement was produced in evidence. The Court rejected it. The settlement had to be proved either by its primary evidence which was the original document containing the settlement or by its secondary evidence wherever permissible. There was no permission in this case for production of a copy in evidence.[89]

The Supreme Court observed in a case:

> It is true that ordinarily if a party to an action does not object to a document being taken on record and the same is marked as an exhibit, he is estopped and precluded from questioning its admissibility at a later stage. But it is trite that a document becomes inadmissible in evidence unless the author is examined as to contents and also subjected to cross-examination.[90]

In the absence of original documents being produced, the plea that there was a mistake in respect of some particulars in the copy was rejected.[91]

[s 64.2] Carbon copy.—The carbon copy of a suicide note was sought to be produced as secondary evidence. The original copy was with the opposite party and he failed to produce the same. The suicide was not within the knowledge of the appellant prior to the receipt of carbon copy. The court said that the provisions of sections 64, 65 were complied with. The order of the court to allow the appellant to lead secondary evidence was proper.[92]

[s 64.3] Registered document preferred.—When the probative value of documents is to be assessed, especially those dealing with the creation of any interest in property or its transfer of a value exceeding Rs 100, obviously documents which have been

---

85. *H Siddiqui v A Ramalingam,* (2011) 4 SCC 240.

86. Where there is documentary evidence, oral evidence is not entitled to any weight, *Murarka Properties Pvt Ltd v Beharilal Murarka,* AIR 1978 SC 300 : 1978(1) SCC 109.

87. *Joginder Kaur v Surjit Singh,* AIR 1985 P&H 128.

88. *Amar Singh v Tej Ram,* AIR 1982 P&H 382.

89. *Butu Naik v Saraswati Devi,* AIR 1998 Ori 119. *Sunil Kumar v Anguri Choudhari,* AIR 2003 NOC 105 (MP) : 2002 AIHC 3869, the document was neither photocopy, nor true copy of the original, nor compared with the original, not a secondary evidence as defined in section 63.

90. *Malay Kumar Ganguly v Sukumar Mukherjee,* AIR 2010 SC 1162 : (2009) 9 SCC 221.

91. *Shivanandam Vivekanand Babu v State of Maharashtra,* (2005) 10 SCC 587.

92. *Mohit Batra v Balu,* AIR 2007 DOC 74 P&H : (2006) 4 Ren CR (Civil) 452.

duly registered regardless of whether or not that was legally mandatory, would score over others.[93]

The production of a registered sale deed is sufficient to prove it, unless its executor denies its execution.[94]

[s 65] Cases in which secondary evidence relating to documents may be given.— Secondary evidence may be given of the existence, condition or contents of a document in the following cases:—

(a) When the original is shown or appears to be in the possession or power—

of the person against whom the document is sought to be proved, or

of any person out of reach of, or not subject to, the process of the Court, or

of any person legally bound to produce it,

and when, after the notice mentioned in section 66, such person does not produce it;

(b) when the existence, condition or contents of the original have been proved to be admitted in writing by the person against whom it is proved or by his representative in interest;

(c) when the original has been destroyed or lost, or when the party offering evidence of its contents cannot, for any other reason not arising from his own default or neglect, produce it in reasonable time;

(d) when the original is of such a nature as not to be easily moveable;

(e) when the original is a public document within the meaning of section 74;

(f) when the original is a document of which a certified copy is permitted by this Act, or by any other law in force in [95][India], to be given in evidence;

(g) when the originals consist of numerous accounts or other documents which cannot conveniently be examined in Court and the fact to be proved is the general result of the whole collection.

In cases (a), (c) and (d), any secondary evidence of the contents of the document is admissible.

In case (b), the written admission is admissible.

In case (e) or (f), a certified copy of the document, but no other kind of secondary evidence, is admissible.

In case (g), evidence may be given as to the general result of the documents by any person who has examined them, and who is skilled in the examination of such documents.

93. *Maya Devi v Lalta Prasad*, (2015) 5 SCC 588, para 16.
94. *Syed Basheer Malik v Jameela Begum*, AIR 2016 NOC 395 (Kar).
95. Subs. by Act 3 of 1951, section 3 and Schedule, for "the States".

SYNOPSIS

COMMENT

[s 65.1] Scope.—This section enumerates the seven exceptional cases in which secondary evidence is admissible. Under it secondary evidence may be given of the contents of a document in civil as well as in criminal proceedings.

Secondary evidence of the contents of a document cannot be admitted without the non-production of the original being first accounted for in such manner as to bring it within one or other of the cases provided for in the section.[96] It is incumbent on the person who tenders secondary evidence to show that it is admissible; the question of admissibility is ordinarily for the court of first instance.[97] Secondary evidence cannot be accepted unless sufficient reason is given for the non-production of the original.[98]

"Document" means a document admissible in evidence. If a document is inadmissible in consequence of not being registered or not being properly stamped, secondary evidence cannot be given of its existence.[99] If the original document is inadmissible in evidence owing to it being unstamped or unregistered, secondary evidence is inadmissible. Secondary evidence cannot be given to establish a fact, proof whereof by primary evidence is forbidden. Under no circumstances can secondary evidence be admitted as a substitute for inadmissible primary evidence.

Where permission was sought for producing secondary evidence of certain receipts on ground that the original receipts were lost, the court said that two things would

96. *Krishna Kishori Chowdhrani v Kishori Lal Roy,* (1887) 14 Cal 486 : 14 IA 71.

97. *Abdul Rasack v Ma U* (1898) 2 UBR (1897-1901) 382. Secondary evidence was not allowed where the primary was on record. *Kirpal Singh v Kartaro,* AIR 1980 Raj 213. *Oriental Fire & General Ins Co v Chandrawali,* AIR 1989 P&H 300, a copy of the original policy produced without making out any exception, held liable to be rejected. *Hari Singh v Shish Ram,* AIR 2003 P&H 150, a photostat copy of the original deed of family settlement was filed. The Court said that it was *sine qua non* for party to show that the original was in existence and could not be produced and that photo evidence was allowable under one or the other exceptions.

98. *State Bank of India v Allibhoy Mohammed,* AIR 2008 Bom 81.

99. Stokes' Anglo-Indian Codes, Vol II, p 892 f.n. 2.

have to be proved: there must be evidence of the existence of original receipts and there must be evidence of their loss. In this case, there was no evidence on record even of the existence of the original receipts. The permission granted was held to be improper.[100]

Section 65 of the 1872 Act provide for permitting the parties to adduce secondary evidence. However, such a course is subject to a large number of limitations. In a case where the original documents are not produced at any time, nor has any factual foundation been laid for giving secondary evidence, it is not permissible for the court to allow a party to adduce secondary evidence. Thus, secondary evidence relating to the contents of a document is inadmissible, until the non-production of the original is accounted for, so as to bring it within one or other of the cases provided for in the section. The secondary evidence must be authenticated by foundational evidence that the alleged copy is in fact a true copy of the original. Mere admission of a document in evidence does not amount to its proof. Therefore, the documentary evidence is required to be proved in accordance with law. The Court has an obligation to decide the question of admissibility of a document in secondary evidence before making endorsement thereon. In this case, the main issue was that whether the power of attorney had been executed by the respondent in favour of Defendant No. 2 enabling him to alienate the suit property and even if there was such power of attorney whether the same had been proved in accordance with law. The trial court decreed the suit observing that as the parties had deposed that the original power of attorney was not in their possession, the question of laying any further factual foundation could not arise. It was held by Supreme Court that the trial court cannot proceed in such an unwarranted manner for the reason that the respondent had merely admitted his signature on the photocopy of the power of attorney and did not admit the contents thereof. The court should bear in mind that admissibility of a document or contents thereof may not necessarily lead to drawing any inference unless the contents thereof have some probative value. It was further held that it is the duty of the court to examine whether the documents produced in the court or contents thereof have any probative value.[101]

Where a party comes into court resting his claim on a written title which the law requires to be registered, he cannot, when he has failed to register, and is, in consequence unable to use his title deed, turn round and say that he could prove his title by secondary evidence. Therefore, the oral evidence of the terms of an unregistered deed of mortgage, required by law to be registered, is inadmissible.[102] Secondary evidence was allowed

---

100. *Gurdial Kaur v Registrar of Co-op Societies,* AIR 2000 P&H 82. The Court relied upon *Ved Prakash v Kartar Kaur,* (1994) 1 QRR 361 wherein it was held that in order to enable a party to produce secondary evidence it is necessary for the party to prove the existence and execution of the original document; *Krishna Kumar v Pal Singh,* (1989) 95 Pun LR 55 , it was incumbent refer the respondent to lead evidence to prove existence of the original civil petition; *Gurditta v Balkar Singh,* (1989) 95 Pun LR 418, where the agreement to sell was never pleaded in the written statement, an application to lead secondary evidence by way of photostat copy was filed after more than two years, there was no occasion for the trial court to allow the defendant to lead secondary evidence particularly when the existence of the original document was not proved.

Sobha Rani v Ravi Kumar, AIR 1999 P&H 21, permission for secondary evidence was sought on the ground of loss of the document, the existence of the original was proved from the fact stated in the plaint and reply of the defendant. Order was granted for filing secondary evidence.

101. *H Siddiqui v A Ramalingam,* (2011) 4 SCC 240, AIR 2011 SC 1492.

102. *Sawa v Kuka,* (1951) 1 Raj 69; *Champalal v Pannalal,* (1951) 1 Raj 190.

where the defendant did not deny the registered deed.[103] Where the defendant-petitioner sought to produce secondary evidence in respect of certain documents without showing his entitlement to produce it, the trial court committed no irregularity in rejecting his application.[104]

[s 65.1.1] ***Suit for permanent injunction.***—The plaintiff alleged that he was the *bhumidhar* owner of the land and in possession for more than 12 years. The Court said that these were crucial facts which were essential to prove ownership and possession. The certified copy of the sale deed which had been filed was admissible for that purpose. The plaintiff could not be non-suited for non-compliance of O VI, rule 2, CPC.[105]

The section deals with the proof of the contents of documents tendered in evidence.

[s 65.2] Original in possession of opposite party—*[Clause (a)]*.— When the original is shown or appears to be in the possession or power of the person against whom the document is sought to be proved and when, after notice mentioned in section 66, such person does not produce it, then, the secondary evidence relating to these documents can be permitted.[106] The document need not be in the actual possession of the party; it is enough if it is in his power. A tenant alleged that the original rent note was in the landlord's possession. He applied for leave for production of a copy of the note. It was held that the rejection of his application without giving him an opportunity to explain his justification for permission for production of secondary evidence was not proper.[107]

Where the original power of attorney was not produced by the defendant in whose possession the same was and the xerox copy of the said power of attorney was produced by the plaintiff in evidence and the signature and the contents of the said xerox copy of the power of attorney were admitted by the defendant, there was no question of proving the said document as required under the Evidence Act, 1872.[108]

This expression "not subject to" seems intended to include the case of a person not legally bound to produce the document, who refuses to produce it.[109]

---

103. *Ranjit Kumar v Kamal Kumar*, AIR 1982 Cal 493. See also *Shiola Singh v Shankar*, AIR 1984 Bom 19, where execution could not be proved.

104. *Dropadi v Mahagraha Bhagwat Singh*, AIR 1995 Raj 138.

105. *Ved Prakash Rastogi v Nagar Palika, Budaun*, AIR 2008 All 27.

106. *Rajendra Mahadev Todkar v Paranjpe Schemes (Construction) Co Ltd*, WP No. 1385 of 2017, decided on 5 January 2018 (Bombay High Court).

107. *Nawab Singh v Inderjit Kaur*, AIR 1999 SC 1668 : (1999) 4 SCC 413.

108. *Zarina Siddiqui v A Ramalingam*, (2015) 1 SCC 705 (para 22).

109. Stokes' Anglo-Indian Codes, Vol, II, p 892 fn 30. *LS Sadapopan v KS Sabarinathan*, AIR 2002 Mad 278, in an agreement to sell immovable property, the original deed was with the vendor whereas only a copy was given to the plaintiff vendee and that was also lost. Only a photocopy was produced in the suit for specific performance. The court admitted it as secondary evidence. The court said that clauses (a) and (c) of section 65 are independent of clause (f) and even an ordinary copy, not necessarily certified copy would be admissible. The court cited the following cases as making detailed interpretation of sections 63 and 65 : *Marwari Kumhar v Bhagwanpuri Guru Ganeshpuri*, AIR 2000 SC 2629 : (2000) 6 SCC 735; *Ratan Sharma v Ambesedar Drycleaners*, AIR 1997 Raj 75; *Harijiwan Sahu v Jairam Sahu*, AIR 1989 Pat 96; *Sabarna Barik v State*, AIR 1970 Ori 236; *Arunkumar v Ramanlal*, AIR 1975 Guj 73 and *Santanan Mohanty v Baldhar Rout*, AIR 1986 Ori 66; *Gopal Krishna Jeevan Kumar v Puran Singh*, AIR 1998 P&H 144, best evidence was in possession of the opposite party who had not produced it, secondary evidence was allowed.

[s 65.2.1] "Legally bound to produce it."—The wording of this clause has given rise to considerable doubt. Secondary evidence of a document is admissible when the original appears to be in the possession *of any person legally bound to produce it.* But if a person summoned to produce a document objects to do so and his objection is upheld by the court, it seems equally clear that such a document does not fall within the words of this section. It may be, however, that the courts will admit secondary evidence in such a case upon the general principles of the English law and the decisions, of the English Courts upon the subject.[110] Under this clause secondary evidence in the form of an authenticated copy of a document becomes admissible if a person cannot be legally compelled to produce the original in his possession and refuses to produce it.[111]

The provisions of section 65 of the 1872 Act provide for permitting the parties to adduce secondary evidence. However, such a course is subject to a large number of limitations. In a case where the original documents are not produced at any time, nor has any factual foundation been laid for giving secondary evidence, it is not permissible for the court to allow a party to adduce secondary evidence. Thus, secondary evidence relating to the contents of a document is inadmissible, until the non-production of the original is accounted for, so as to bring it within one or other of the cases provided for in the section. The secondary evidence must be authenticated by foundational evidence that the alleged copy is in fact a true copy of the original. Mere admission of a document in evidence does not amount to its proof. Therefore, the documentary evidence is required to be proved in accordance with law. The Court has an obligation to decide the question of admissibility of a document in secondary evidence before making endorsement thereon.[112]

Where the existence of the mortgage deed was not specifically denied by the mortgagee and therefore, it was not necessary for the plaintiff to call attesting witnesses and the defendant (mortgagee) was refusing to file the original deed in the court, it was held that the filing of a certified copy of the deed by the plaintiff as secondary evidence was a sufficient proof of the existence and execution of the deed.[113]

The documents in question were admittedly photocopies. There was no possibility of comparing them with the original as the same were with another person. Thus, the requirement of section 65(a) was not satisfied. The Court did not accept them as secondary evidence.[114] The original arrangement between the landlord and tenant was changed for reducing accommodation and rent. A new agreement was made to that effect. The landlord filed suit for eviction. The tenant applied for production of the original deed and the changed rent deed. The landlord did not produce the changed rent deed. The defendant sought permission for producing photocopy of the same. The

110. *Field,* 8th Edn, p 436.

111. *Muniammal v Govindarajan* (1958) Mad 415. *Hindustan Engineering Co v Bhagwanlal Agarwal,* AIR 2003 Raj 198, a civil suit was filed by the Electricity Board against its consumer. The latter sought permission to produce a photostat copy of the application filed by him before the Electricity Board. The Board denied the existence of any such application. It made no inquiry before expressing its denial. This was held to be not proper.

112. *H Siddiqui v A Ramalingam,* (2011) 4 SCC 240 : 2011 (1) CLR 761 : 2011 (3) Scale 290.

113. *Ishwar Das Jain v Sohan Lal,* AIR 2000 SC 426 : (2000) 1 SCC 434.

114. *J Yashoda v K Shobha Rani,* AIR 2007 SC 1721 : (2007) 5 SCC 730.

Court said that it could not be tendered in evidence without any revelation of the source from which it was obtained.[115]

[s 65.2.2] "When after the notice mentioned in section 66 such person does not produce it."—If a person who is legally bound to produce the document refuses to produce it notwithstanding notice to do so, the existence and contents of the original document can be proved under this clause by proof of the authenticated copy.[116] The original Will was in possession of the plaintiff. The defendant applied for permission for producing secondary evidence on the ground that the plaintiff was deliberately not producing the original. The trial court formed the opinion about the veracity of the document without giving an opportunity to the defendant to adduce his evidence on the point. This was held to be improper.[117]

[s 65.3] Documents admitted by opposite party—*[Clause (b)]*.—This clause must be read with section 22. Under it the written admission may always be proved. The oral admission can only be proved under the circumstances mentioned in clauses (a), (c) and (d). But secondary evidence by means of a written admission under this clause cannot be given of the contents of a document, which is inadmissible for want of registration[118] or of stamps.[119] Admission of documents amounts to admission of contents thereof but not its truth. Truth or correctness is to be ascertained from evidence.[120] Where the defendant himself admitted the payment under the cheque, absence of cheque as primary evidence would not vitiate the suit.[121]

[s 65.4] Original lost or destroyed—*[Clause (c)]*.—Secondary evidence is admissible when the party offering evidence of the contents of a document cannot for any reason not arising from his own default or neglect produce the original document in reasonable time.[122] Secondary evidence of the contents of a document cannot be admitted without the non-production of the original being first accounted for.[123]

Where an original book of accounts is in a very tottering condition and is also worm-eaten, secondary evidence of such accounts cannot be given.[124] It is not permissible to go to other evidence for the purpose of indicating what the contents of the document

---

115. *Haji Md Islam v Asgar Ali,* AIR 2007 MP 157 : LNIND 2001 AP 155.

116. *Muniammal v Govindarajan,* (1958) Mad 415.

117. *Rajesh Kumar Bhati v ADJ, Jodhpur,* AIR 2009 Raj 137.

118. *Varada v Krisnasami,* (1882) 6 Mad 117.

119. *Damodar Jagannath v Atmaram Babaji,* (1888) 12 Bom 443.

120. *Life Insurance Corp of India v Narmada Agarwalla,* AIR 1993 Ori 103.

121. *Sharda Talkies (Firm) v Madhulata Vyas,* AIR 1996 MP 68.

122. *Surendra Krishna Roy v Mirza Mahammad Syed Ali Matwali,* (1935) 63 IA 85. 38 Bom LR 330. *Akshara Nand v State of HP,* 1996 AIHC 1894 (HP).

123. *Muhammad Zafar v Zahur Husain,* (1926) 49 All 78; *Womesh Chunder Ghose v Shama Sundari Bai,* (1881) 7 Cal 98; *Mt Hana v Lokumal,* (1943) Kar 420; *Harshvardhan Singh v Ranveer Singh,* AIR 1997 Raj 211, an unstamped and unregistered document, containing family settlement, created rights in immovable property, the original was not produced before the court, nor its absence accounted for, order allowing a copy of the settlement to be filed was held to be illegal.

124. *Amrita Devi v Sripat Rai,* AIR 1962 All 111; *Chandan v Longabai,* AIR 1998 MP1, the document containing a will was shown to be eaten by rats, secondary evidence allowed. Loss and non-production of original will, reasonably explained, *Leela Rajagopal v Kamala Menon Cocharan,* 2014 (15) SCC 570 , para 15.

may prove to be if once it were examined.[125] There must be evidence on the record to show that the document has been lost.[126]

It must, therefore, be established that the party has exhausted all resources and means in search of the document which were available to him.[127] If a registered sale-deed is lost a certified copy can be put in as secondary evidence,[128] but the reception of other evidence must always be of a very weak character in place of registered document evidencing the transaction.[129] Where the loss of the original award was proved by examining one of the Arbitrators, its photocopy bearing not only that Arbitrator's signature but also of both the parties was admissible in evidence.[130]

Secondary evidence of a lost public document, other than a certified copy, is admissible upon proof of loss or destruction of the original, and further proof that no certified copy of the original is available to the party seeking to prove the contents of the original. So long as the original is in existence, no secondary evidence other than a certified copy is admissible.[131] Where the record in a case has been destroyed and is not available for the purpose of proving previous convictions, secondary evidence under this clause is admissible.[132] Secondary evidence was allowed where the plaintiff stated on affidavit that the original was lost,[133] and also where the sale deed was handed over to a patwari and the same was not returned by him.[134] In an election petition, the photocopy of the manuscript of a leaflet was not allowed because it was not shown where the original was. There must be some explanation as to the original.[135]

Secondary evidence of the contents of a document cannot be given by a party who is in custody of the original document.[136]

In a case before the P&H High Court,[137] a suit was filed for recovery of money on the basis of an agreement. The plaintiff produced only the photostat copy of the agreement and not the original. The defendant argued that the photocopy was produced deliberately to suppress the fact that the agreement was fabricated. The plaintiff pleaded that the original was in the custody of the defendant. He applied for permission to produce secondary evidence. It was held that a summary dismissal of such application was not proper. Opportunity should have been given to the plaintiff to make out his case. The Court then explained the basic principles as follows:

> A perusal of clause (c) of Section 65 of the Act would show that secondary evidence of existence, condition or contents of a document can also be adduced when the party offering evidence of its contents cannot produce the original in reasonable time. But such a delay in production of the document should not have arisen from the fault or neglect of the party who wish to adduce secondary evidence of the document. To succeed in getting permission to adduce secondary evidence it must be shown that the document

125. *KS Bonnerji v Sitanath,* (1921) 24 Bom LR 565 : 49 IA 46 : 49 Cal 325.
126. *Mohammad Khan v Sheo Bikh Singh,* (1929) 5 Luck 377.
127. *Parekh Bros. v Kartick Chandra,* AIR 1968 Cal 532.
128. *Entisham Ali v Jamna Prasad,* (1921) 24 Bom LR 675 : 48 IA 365.
129. *Nani Bai v Gita Bai,* AIR 1958 SC 706 : 1959 SCR 479.
130. *Om Prakash v Dev Raj,* AIR 1995 P&H 349.
131. *Syad Pir Shan v Gulab Shah,* (1878) PR No. 63 of 1878 (Civil).
132. *Pokar v Crown,* (1941) Kar 308.
133. *Sanatan Mohanty v Baidhar Rout,* AIR 1986 Ori 66.
134. *Krishna Devi v Gain Kaur,* AIR 1981 P&H 224.
135. *Ashok v Madhav Lal,* AIR 1975 SC 1748 : 1975(4) SCC 664.
136. *Hira Lal v Ganesh Prasad,* (1882) 4 All 406 PC.
137. *PK Gupta v Varinder Sharma,* AIR 2002 P&H 342.

was in existence which was capable of being proved by secondary evidence and secondly proper foundation must be laid to establish the right to adduce secondary evidence. This view has been taken by a Constitution Bench of the Supreme Court in the case of *Roman Catholic Mission v State of Madras.*[138]

Another well-known principle with regard to proof of facts is that the best evidence must come before the court because the best evidence which is, of course, the original document, would furnish an opportunity to the court to examine various surrounding facts attached with the original alone like the veraciousness of the signatures of the parties, the age of the document and other host of factors depending on the facts of each case. It is in the absence of the best evidence that the secondary evidence is allowed to be adduced because the object of judicial investigation by Court is to fathom the truth. Therefore, the law although insists upon production of the best evidence, i.e., the original document yet it permit with proper safeguards the production of the secondary evidence of the original if certain conditions are satisfied, namely, the existence of the document which might have been lost or destroyed or the party in whose possession the original is shown or appears to be—have refused to produce it before the court despite notice or its existence, condition or contents have been proved to be admitted in writing so on and so forth. The rule regarding secondary evidence is not an open rule allowing any piece of photostat copies or an oral account of the original and the likewise to be tendered as secondary evidence.

It is sufficient to say that the document in question is not available at the relevant time and its whereabouts were unknown. It is not necessary to plead that the document has been lost. The words "lost" or "not traceable" both enable invocation of secondary evidence.[139]

[s 65.5] Original not easily movable *[Clause (d)]*.—This clause covers things not easily moved, as in the case of things fixed in the ground or a building; for example, notices painted on walls, tablets in buildings, tombstones, monuments, or marks on boundary stones or trees. Secondary evidence is admissible on account of the great inconvenience and impracticability of producing the original.

The principle of law is that where you cannot get the best possible evidence, you must take the next.

[s 65.5.1] ***Rule Restricted to Written Documents.***—The courts have declined to extend the best evidence rule to documents consisting of film, tape and the like. There is little reason to burden these categories with a restrictive and formalistic rule conceived in the days before technology had begun to spawn new forms of storing information which give a new meaning to the term "original".

[s 65.6] Public document *[Clause (e)]*.—This clause is intended to protect the originals of public records from the danger to which they would be exposed by constant production in evidence. Secondary evidence is admissible in the case of public documents mentioned in section 74. What section 74 provides is that public records kept in any state of private documents are public documents, but private documents of which public records are kept are not in themselves public documents. A registered document, therefore, does not fall under either clause (e) or clause (f). The entry in the register

---

138. *Roman Catholic Mission v State of Madras,* AIR 1966 SC 1457; Referred to in *H Siddiqui v A Ramalingam,* (2011) 4 SCC 240.

139. *Prem Chandra Jain v Ram,* AIR 2010 NOC 424 (Del).

book is a public document, but the original is a private document. A certified copy of the original cannot be given in evidence. The Gujarat High Court held that a copy of a registered sale deed certified by the registration officer is a public document within the meaning of section 74 and is, therefore, admissible for the purpose of proving the contents of the original document.[140] No true copy or private copy of any public document is admissible as secondary evidence. The party has to produce a certified copy of the public document which should have been issued by the competent authority whose office is in possession of the original record.[141]

The rule that a certified copy is the only secondary evidence admissible when the original is a public document, does not apply where the original has been lost or destroyed.[142]

A charge was levelled against an election candidate alleging that he appealed to voters on communal lines. The petitioner produced a cassette to prove the charge. There was no cogent evidence regarding the source and manner of acquisition of the tape. The petitioner did not prove that cassette was true reproduction of the original speeches made by the candidate or his agent. The petition was rejected.[143]

The certified copy of a Will has been held to be not a public document within the meaning of section 74. It is not admissible in evidence *per se*. It cannot be accepted as primary evidence. It could be proved as secondary evidence under permission of the court by showing loss or destruction, etc. of the original.[144]

[s 65.7] Certified copies permitted by law *[Clause (f)]*.—Certified copies are admissible as secondary evidence under this clause. Sections 76, 78 and 86 may be read along with it. Where an original document cannot be given in evidence owing to a statutory ban, its certified copy cannot be admitted in evidence, e.g. certified copy of the income tax return.[145]

Where a case falls under clause (a) or clause (c) and also under clause (f) any secondary evidence may be received.[146]

Where both the original and the certified copy of a public document were proved to have been lost, the court allowed secondary evidence in the form of an ordinary copy.[147]

The entry of a private document i.e. a sale deed made in the book maintained by the registering authority, comes within the purview of a public document and the certified copy of the document is admissible in evidence.[148]

---

140. *Jagdishchandra Chandulal Shah v State of Gujarat,* 1989 Cr LJ 1724 (Guj), a copy of the plaint certified by the court where it is filed was also held to be a public document for purposes of evidence. *M Madasamy Thevar v AM Arjuna Raja,* AIR 2000 Mad 465, certified copies obtained from the office of the Registrar of Documents are secondary evidence and admissible as such. *Rekha Rana v Ratnashree Jain,* AIR 2006 MP 107, to the same effect. The court added that such document does not dispense with the need for proof of execution of the document.

141. *Chalasani Satyanarayana Murthy v Chalasani Rama Koteswara Rao,* AIR 2011 NOC 35 (AP).

142. *Chandreshwar Prasad Narain Singh v Bisheshwar Pratap Narain Singh,* (1926) 5 Pat 777.

143. *Tukaram S Dighole v Manikrao Shivaji Kokate,* AIR 2010 SC 965 : (2010) 4 SCC 329.

144. *Sampat Singh v Bhagwanti,* AIR 2010 NOC 701 (P&H).

145. *Devidatt v Shriram,* (1931) 34 Bom LR 236 : 56 Bom 324.

146. *In the Matter of a Collision between the "Ava" and the "Brenhilda",* (1879) 5 Cal 568, 573, approved by the Supreme Court in *Bibi Aisha v Bihar SSM Waqaf,* AIR 1969 SC 253 : 1969(1) SCR 417. A copy of the Municipal record not issued in accordance with the requirements of the Municipal Act is not relevant. *Ganesh Pd v Badri Pd,* AIR 1970 All 361.

147. *Marwari Kumhar v Bhagwanpuri Guru Ganeshpuri,* AIR 2000 SC 2629 : (2000) 7 SCC 333.

148. *Hemlata Devi v Ramautar Sao,* 2016 AIR CC 686 (Jhar).

Xerox copies certified by the designated Public Information Officer under the RTI Act are not certified copies as envisaged by section 65 of the Evidence Act. They are merely true copies of private documents in the records of a particular department. Only true copies of public documents certified by the said Officer can be taken as certified copies.[149]

An application for production of a particular document was filed after eight years of institution of the suit. The document sought to be produced was also a copy of the original document. The Court said that such a document could not be accepted in evidence without showing any of the exceptional situations.[150]

An instrument of partition was insufficiently stamped. It was therefore held not admissible in evidence. The Court said that once an original itself is not admissible, the question of taking xerox copy of the same into evidence does not arise.[151]

[s 65.8] Documents which cannot be conveniently examined *[Clause (g)]*.—This provision is meant for saving public time. Where the fact to be proved is the general result of the examination of numerous documents and not the contents of each particular document and the documents are such as cannot be conveniently examined in court, evidence may be given, under this section, as to the general result of the documents by a person who has examined them and who is skilled in the examination of those documents, although they may be public within the meaning of this section and section 74.[152]

[s 65.9] Call records of cellular telephones *[Clause (g)]*.—The call records of cellular phones are stored in large servers that cannot be easily moved and produced in court. The court allowed secondary evidence of such matter regardless of compliance with section 65B(4). It has to be shown that there was no misuse of the computer and that it was performing properly. Such evidence would vary from case to case. It will be very rarely necessary to call an expert. The burden can be discharged by calling a witness who is familiar with the operation of the computer concerned.[153]

[s 65.10] Objection to reception of secondary evidence in Appeal Court.—The objection as to admission of secondary evidence should be taken when it is tendered in evidence and not subsequently. Once the document is admitted without any objection, its contents are also taken to have been proved though not conclusively.[154] If a copy of a document is admitted in evidence in the first court without any objection no objection can be allowed to be taken in the appeal court as to its admissibility.[155] Where no objection was raised when the certified copy of the Will was admitted, non-production of the original Will cannot subsequently be urged as a ground to invalidate the Will.[156] When an

149. *Datti Kameshwari v Singam Rao Sarath Chandra,* AIR 2016 AP 112 , para 8.

150. *Arati Bhargawa v Ravi Kumar Bhargava,* AIR 1999 Del 280. *Ganpat Pandurang Ghongade v Nivrutti Pandurang Ghongade,* AIR 2008 NOC 2571 (Bom), it is well known that the process of making xrox copies is open to manipulations, hence it is not safe to act upon such copies.

151. *Obelisetty Ramanadhan v Oblesetti Bhaskar Rao,* AIR 2008 NOC 1154 (AP).

152. *Sundar Kaur v Chandreshwar Prasad Narain Singh,* (1907) 34 Cal 293.

153. *State (NCT of Delhi) v Navjot Sandhu,* (2005) 11 SCC 600 : AIR 2005 SC 3820.

154. *V Subramaniam v T Krishnan,* AIR 2007 NOC 1547 (Mad).

155. *Kishori Lal Goswami v Rakhal Das Banerjee,* (1903) 31 Cal 155; *Akbur Ali v Bhyea Lal Jha,* (1880) 6 Cal 666; *Bacharam Mundul v Peary Mohun Banerjee,* (1883) 9 Cal 813; *Narendra Narain Rai v Bishun Chundra Das,* (1885) 12 Cal 182; *Chimnaji Govind Godbole v Dinkar Dhondev Godbole,* (1886) 11 Bom 320; *Thet She v Moung Ba,* (1905) 3 LBR 49. *Amar Singh v Tej Ram,* AIR 1982 P&H 382. *Dayamathi Bai v KM Shaffi,* (2004) 7 SCC 107 : AIR 2004 SC 4082, objection to be taken at the stage of admission and not at a later stage.

156. *SA Quddus v S Veerappa,* AIR 1994 Kant 20 : 1993 (2) HinduLR 383 : LNIND 1993 Kant 64.

objection that the document which is sought to be proved is itself inadmissible in evidence, is raised, the court can give a tentative exhibit number to such a document and deal with the admissibility thereof at the final stage of judgment; however, where the objection which is raised does not dispute the admissibility of the document in evidence but is directed towards the mode of proof, alleging the same to be irregular or insufficient, such objection has to be decided at the same time when it is raised, as the same would enable the party tendering the evidence to cure the defect and resort to such mode of proof as would be regular.[157] The question of proof of a document is a question of procedure and can be waived. But a question of relevancy of document is a question of law, and can be raised at the appellate stage as well.[158] The object of the rule is obvious, for, if objection is taken in the first court, the party producing the copy can ask for an adjournment in order to get the original or else to give evidence justifying the admission of secondary evidence.

[s 65.11] Uncertified copies.—It is a basic principle of our jurisprudence that if any uncertified document is produced on record, then it should be self-attested as true copy and should be supported by an affidavit that it is a genuine document and need to be relied upon as such.[159]

[160]**[[s 65A] Special provisions as to evidence relating to electronic record.—The contents of electronic records may be proved in accordance with the provisions of section 65B.**

[160]**[s 65B] Admissibility of electronic records.—(1) Notwithstanding anything contained in this Act, any information contained in an electronic record which is printed on a paper, stored, recorded or copied in optical or magnetic media produced by a computer (hereinafter referred to as the computer output) shall be deemed to be also a document, if the conditions mentioned in this section are satisfied in relation to the information and computer in question and shall be admissible in any proceedings, without further proof or production of the original, as evidence or any contents of the original or of any fact stated therein of which direct evidence would be admissible.**

(2) The conditions referred to in sub-section (1) in respect of a computer output shall be the following, namely:—

(a) the computer output containing the information was produced by the computer during the period over which the computer was used regularly to store or process information for the purposes of any activities regularly carried on over that period by the person having lawful control over the use of the computer;

(b) during the said period, information of the kind contained in the electronic record or of the kind from which the information so contained is derived was regularly fed into the computer in the ordinary course of the said activities;

(c) throughout the material part of the said period, the computer was operating properly or, if not, then in respect of any period in which it

---

157. *Ramniklal Shivlal Bavishi v Tulsidas Chakubhai Gorvadiya,* AIR 2016 NOC 54 (Guj).
158. *Subbarao v Venkata Rama Rao,* AIR 1964 AP 53 : LNIND 1963 AP 63.
159. *Swati Abhishek Binaykia v Abhishek Madanlal Binaykia,* 2016 AIR CC 1730, para 46 (Guj).
160. Ins. by Act 21 of 2000, section 92 and Sch II–9 (w.e.f. 17-10-2000).

was not operating properly or was out of operation during that part of the period, was not such as to affect the electronic record or the accuracy of its contents; and

(d) the information contained in the electronic record reproduces or is derived from such information fed into the computer in the ordinary course of the said activities.

(3) Where over any period, the function of storing or processing information for the purposes of any activities regularly carried on over that period as mentioned in clause (a) of sub-section (2) was regularly performed by computers, whether—

(a) by a combination of computers operating over that period; or

(b) by different computers operating in succession over that period; or

(c) by different combinations of computers operating in succession over that period; or

(d) in any other manner involving the successive operation over that period, in whatever order, of one or more computers and one or more combinations of computers,

all the computers used for that purpose during that period shall be treated for the purposes of this section as constituting a single computer; and references in this section to a computer shall be construed accordingly.

(4) In any proceedings where it is desired to give a statement in evidence by virtue of this section, a certificate doing any of the following things, that is to say,—

(a) identifying the electronic record containing the statement and describing the manner in which it was produced;

(b) giving such particulars of any device involved in the production of that electronic record as may be appropriate for the purpose of showing that the electronic record was produced by a computer;

(c) dealing with any of the matters to which the conditions mentioned in sub-section (2) relate,

and purporting to be signed by a person occupying a responsible official position in relation to the operation of the relevant device or the management of the relevant activities (whichever is appropriate) shall be evidence of any matter stated in the certificate; and for the purposes of this sub-section it shall be sufficient for a matter to be stated to the best of the knowledge and belief of the person stating it.

(5) For the purposes of this section,—

(a) information shall be taken to be supplied to a computer if it is supplied thereto in any appropriate form and whether it is so supplied directly or (with or without human intervention) by means of any appropriate equipment;

(b) whether in the course of activities carried on by any official information is supplied with a view to its being stored or processed for the purposes of those activities by a computer operated otherwise than in the course of those activities, that information, if duly supplied to that computer, shall be taken to be supplied to it in the course of those activities;

(c) a computer output shall be taken to have been produced by a computer whether it was produced by it directly or (with or without human intervention) by means of any appropriate equipment.

***Explanation*.—For the purposes of this section any reference to information being derived from other, information shall be a reference to its being derived therefrom by calculation, comparison or any other process.]**

SYNOPSIS

COMMENT

[s 65B.1] Information Technology Act, 2000—Proof of contents of electronic records *[Sections 65A, 65B]*.—The new section, namely section 65A, says that the contents of electronic records may be proved in accordance with the provisions of section 65B. This section is also a new provision. It prescribes the mode for proof of contents of electronic records. The primary purpose is to sanctify proof by secondary evidence. This facility of proof by secondary evidence would apply to any computer output, such output being deemed as a document. A computer output is a deemed document for the purposes of proof. The section says in sub-section (1) that any information contained in an electronic record which is printed on a paper, stored, recorded or copied in optical or magnetic media produced by a computer and to be referred to as computer output, shall also be deemed to be a document. The section lays down certain conditions which have to be satisfied in relation to the information and the computer in question. Where those conditions are satisfied, the electronic record shall become admissible in any proceedings without further proof or production of the original as evidence of any contents of the original or of any fact stated in it.

With the advancement of information technology, scientific temper at the individual and the institutional level is to pervade the methods of investigation. With the increasing impact of technology in everyday life, and as a result, the production of electronic evidence in cases, has become relevant to establish the guilt of the accused or the liability of the defendant. Electronic documents *stricto sensu* are admitted as material evidence. Such evidence is of great help to the investigating agency and also to the prosecution.[161]

---

161. *Tomaso Bruno v State of UP*, (2015) 7 SCC 178, paras 24 and 25.

[s 65B.2] Conditions as to relevancy of computer output *[Section 65B(2)]*.—The conditions which have to be satisfied so as to make a computer output as evidence are stated in sub-section (2). They are as follows:

(a) the computer output containing the information was produced by the computer during the period over which the computer was used regularly to store or process the information for the purposes of any activities regularly carried on over that period by the person having lawful control over the use of the computer;

(b) the information contained in the electronic record is of the kind which was regularly fed into the computer in the ordinary course of its activities;

(c) the computer should have been operating properly during the period of the data feeding, or, if it was not operating properly during that period or was out of operation, that gap was not such as to affect the electronic record or the accuracy of its contents;

(d) the information contained in the electronic record was derived or is reproduced from the information fed into the computer in the ordinary course of its activities.

Where the information was processed or fed into the computer on interlinked computers or one computer after the other in succession, all the computers so used shall be treated as one single computer. The references to a computer have to be construed accordingly [section 65B(3)]:

When a statement has to be produced in evidence under this section, it should be accompanied by a certificate which should identify the electronic record containing the statement and describe the manner in which it was produced, give the particulars of the device involved in the production of the electronic record showing that the same was produced by a computer and showing compliance with the conditions of sub-section (2) of this section. The statement should be signed by a person occupying a responsible official position in relation to the operation or management of the relevant activities. Such statement shall be evidence of the matter stated in the certificate. It should be sufficient for this purpose that the statement is made to the best of knowledge and belief of the person making it [section 65B(4)].

For the purposes of this section an information shall be taken to be supplied to a computer, if it is done in any appropriate form whether this is done directly with or without human intervention by means of any appropriate equipment, or if the information is supplied by any official in the course of his activities with a view to storing or processing the information even if the computer is being operated outside those activities.

An explanation to the section declares that for the purposes of section 65B any reference to information being derived from other information is to be taken to mean derived by calculation, comparison or any other process [section 65B (*Explanation*)].

[s 65B.3] Proof of electronic record.—Any documentary evidence by way of an electronic record under the Indian Evidence Act, 1872, can in view of sections 59 and 65A, be proved only in accordance with the admissibility of the electronic record. The purpose of these provisions is to sanctify secondary evidence in electronic form, generated by a computer. Section 65B starts with a *non obstante* clause, viz. notwithstanding anything contained in the Evidence Act, any information contained in an electronic record which is printed on a paper, stored, recorded or copied in optical or magnetic media produced by a computer shall be deemed to be a document only if the conditions in sub-section (2) are satisfied, without further proof or production of the original.[162]

The Evidence Act does not contemplate or permit the proof of an electronic record by oral evidence, if the requirements under section 65B of the Evidence Act are not complied with.[163]

Proof of electronic record, is a special provision introduced by the Information Technology Act, 2000 amending various provisions of the Evidence Act, 1872. The very caption of section 65A of the Evidence Act read with sections 59 and 65B of the Evidence Act is sufficient to hold that the special provisions on evidence relating to electronic record shall be governed by the procedure prescribed under section 65B, which is a complete code in itself. Being a special law, the general law under sections 63 and 65 has to yield.[164]

[s 65B.4] Admissibility of electronic record.—The very admissibility of an electronic record which is called as computer output, depends upon the satisfaction of the four conditions under section 65B(2), enumerated as below:—

(i) The electronic record containing the information should have been produced by the computer during the period over which the same was regularly used to store or process information for the purpose of any activity regularly carried on over that period by the person having lawful control over the use of that computer;

(ii) The information of the kind contained in electronic record or of the kind from which the information is derived was regularly fed into the computer in the ordinary course of the said activity;

(iii) During the material part of the said period, the computer was operating properly and that even if it was not operating properly for some time, the break or breaks had not affected either the record or the accuracy of its contents; and

(iv) The information contained in the record should be a reproduction or derivation from the information fed into the computer in the ordinary course of the said activity.[165]

Where an electronic record is used as primary evidence the same is admissible in evidence, without compliance with the conditions in section 65B.[166]

Irrespective of the compliance with the requirements of section 65B, which a special provision dealing with admissibility of the electronic record, there is no bar in adducing secondary evidence under sections 63 and 65 of the Evidence Act, 1872, of an electronic record.[167]

---

162. *Anvar PV v PK Basheer,* 2014 (10) Scale 660 : (2014) 10 SCC 473 (para 14).
163. *Anvar PV v PK Basheer,* 2014 (10) Scale 660 : (2014) 10 SCC 473 (para 18).
164. *Anvar PV v PK Basheer,* 2014 (10) Scale 660 : (2014) 10 SCC 473 (para 20).
165. *Anvar PV v PK Basheer,* 2014 (10) Scale 660 : (2014) 10 SCC 473 (para 14).
166. *Vikram Singh v State of Punjab,* AIR 2017 SC 3227 : 2017 CriLJ 4305.
167. *Anvar PV v PK Basheer,* 2014 (10) Scale 660 : (2014) 10 SCC 473 (para 21).

[s 65B.5] Giving statement in any proceeding pertaining electronic record.—If it is desired to give a statement in any proceeding pertaining to an electronic record, it is permissible provided the following conditions enumerated under section 65B(4) are satisfied:—

(a) There must be a certificate which identifies the electronic record containing the statement;

(b) The certificate must describe the manner in which the electronic record was produced;

(c) The certificate must furnish the particulars of the device involved in the production of that record;

(d) The certificate must deal the applicable conditions mentioned under section 65B(2) of the Evidence Act; and

(e) The certificate must be signed by a person occupying a responsible official position in relation to the operation of the relevant device.[168]

It is further clarified that the person need only to state in the certificate that the same is to the best of his knowledge and belief. Most importantly, such a certificate must accompany the electronic record like computer printout, compact disc (CD), video compact disc (VCD), pen drive etc., pertaining to which a statement is sought to be given in evidence, when the same is produced in evidence. All these safeguards are taken to ensure the source and authenticity, which are the two hallmarks pertaining to electronic record sought to be used in evidence. Electronic records being more susceptible to tampering, alteration, transposition, excision, etc. without such safeguards, the whole trial based on proof of electronic records can lead to a travesty of justice.[169]

[s 65B.5.1] ***Electronic Evidence.***—Certain unlawful acts were alleged to have been committed by the petitioner by an illegal mining operation encroaching into forest area in violation of the conditions of lease agreement entered into with Forest Authorities. Satellite sketches based in support of the allegations were held to be admissible in evidence. But they had to be substantiated by evidence in the court. The petitioner could rebut the same.[170]

[s 65B.5.2] ***ATM***—Money was withdrawn from the account without there being sufficient balance. The bank filed a case for recovery. The claim was based on extracts of ATM machine and ledger entry. The bank admitted mal-functioning of the machine which snapped the link between the ATM and Ledger. The claim was not allowed. Ledger entries were supposed to be independent of ATM Certified copy of the ledger entries was held to be not admissible.[171]

[s 65B.5.3] ***Audio CD***—In a matrimonial proceeding for dissolution of marriage, the wife was alleged to have abused and threatened the husband on his cell-phone and the same was recorded in the phone. The husband re-recorded the matter in an audio CD. The cell-phone was not produced. Only the audio CD was exhibited. The wife objected that the audio CD was not admissible as it was fabricated. The audio CD was

---

168. *Anvar PV v PK Basheer,* 2014 (10) Scale 660 : (2014) 10 SCC 473 (para 15).
169. *Anvar PV v PK Basheer,* 2014 (10) Scale 660 : (2014) 10 SCC 473 (para 16).
170. *VS Lad & Sons v State of Karnataka,* 2009 Cr LJ 3760 : 2009 (6) Kar LJ 430.
171. *P Padmanabh v Syndicate Bank Ltd,* AIR 2008 Kar 42.

marked by the court as an exhibit with this condition that when it was displayed, an opportunity would be given to the wife for cross-examining the husband.[172]

[s 65B.5.4] ***Video-Conferencing.***—The facility of producing evidence by recording it through the process of video-conferencing has been permitted in criminal cases. The Court expressed the view that there cannot be any plausible objection for adopting the same procedure in civil cases also. But necessary precautions must be taken as to both identifying of witnesses and the accuracy of the equipment used.[173]

Where a witness or a party requests that the evidence of a witness may be recorded through video conferencing, the court should be liberal in granting such a prayer.[174]

[s 65B.5.5] ***Tape recorded evidence.***—A tape recorded cassette is clearly a primary and direct evidence of what has been said and recorded.[175]

[s 65B.5.6] ***Official website.***—In the instant case, the information as to the balance sheet of the party concerned available on its official website was relied upon.[176]

[s 65B.5.7] ***Voice recorder.***—Where the only evidence as to demand of bribe by the accused was the conversation recorded by the voice recorder, the same was sent to the Forensic Laboratory which stated that the conversation was not in an audible condition and hence, the same could not be considered for spectrographic analysis. It was submitted that the conversation was translated and verified by the *panch* witnesses. It was observed that admittedly the *panch* witnesses had not heard the conversation since they were not present in the room and as the voice recorder itself could not be subjected to analysis, there was no use in placing reliance on the translated version. Without source there is no authenticity for the translation. Source and authenticity are the two key factors for an electronic evidence.[177]

Where a husband had tape recorded the conversation of his wife with a third person for the purpose of seeking divorce on that ground, it was held that the submitted conversation was recorded without the knowledge of the wife, thus infringing her right to privacy, hence the tapes produced by the husband were not admissible in evidence.[178]

[s 65B.6] Non-production of electronic evidence.—Production of scientific and electronic evidence in court is of great help to the investigating agency and also to the prosecution, therefore, in a murder case non-production of CCTV footage, non-collection of call records (details) and SIM details of mobile phones seized from the accused cannot be said to be mere instances of faulty investigation but amount to withholding of best evidence. It is not the case of the prosecution that CCTV footage could not be lifted or a CD copy could not be made. Adverse inference was drawn against the prosecution.[179]

---

172. *G Shyamal Rajini v MS. Tamizhnathan,* AIR 2008 NOC 476 (Mad).

173. *Bodala Murali Krishna v Bodala Prathima,* AIR 2007 AP 43.

174. *International Planned Parenthood Federation v Madhu Bala Nath,* AIR 2016 Del 71, paras 14, 15 and 16.

175. *Sunil Panchal v State of Rajasthan,* 2016 Cr LJ 4238, para 39 (Raj-DB).

176. *Subrata Roy Sahara v UOI,* (2014) 8 SCC 470.

177. *Sanjaysinh Ramrao Chavan v Dattatray Gulabrao Phalke,* (2015) 3 SCC 123 (para 16), **relying on** *Anvar PV v PK Basheer,* (2014) 10 SCC 473.

178. *Anurima v Sunil Mehta,* AIR 2016 MP 112, para 6 and 7. See also *Preeti Jain v Kunal Jain,* AIR 2016 Raj 153, paras 8 and 9.

179. *Tomaso Bruno v State of UP,* 2015 Cr LJ 1690 (para 24 to 29) (SC).

[s 65B.7] Secondary evidence in the form of printed copy of call details of a cell phone *[Section 65B(4)]*.—Secondary evidence in the form of call details of a cell phone is inadmissible in evidence in the absence of production of the certificate under section 65B(4).[180]

[s 66] Rules as to notice to produce.—Secondary evidence of the contents[s 66.1] of the documents referred to in section 65, clause (a), shall not be given unless the party[s 66.2] proposing to give such secondary evidence has previously given to the party in whose possession or power the document is, [181][or to his attorney or pleader,] such notice to produce it as is prescribed by law; and if no notice is prescribed by law, then such notice as the Court considers reasonable under the circumstances of the case:

***Provided* that such notice shall not be required in order to render secondary evidence admissible in any of the following cases, or in any other case in which the Court thinks fit to dispense with it:—**

(1) when the document to be proved is itself a notice;

(2) when, from the nature of the case, the adverse party must know that he will be required to produce it;

(3) when it appears or is proved that the adverse party has obtained possession of the original by fraud or force;

(4) when the adverse party or his agent has the original in Court;

(5) when the adverse party or his agent has admitted the loss of the document;

(6) when the person in possession of the document is out of reach of, or not subject to, the process of the Court.

SYNOPSIS

COMMENT

This section lays down that a notice must be given before secondary evidence can be received under section 65(a). Notice to produce a document must be in writing. O XI, rule 15. of the Code of Civil Procedure , prescribes the kind of notice to produce a document.

Notice is required in order to give the opposite party a sufficient opportunity to produce the document, and thereby to secure the best evidence of its contents.[182] Such notice may be dispensed with if it is not necessary on the pleadings,[183] or the court thinks fit to dispense with it.[184]

---

180. *Harpal Singh v State of Punjab*, 2017 Cr LJ 551, para 11 (SC) **relying on** *Anvar PV v PK Basheer*, (2014) 10 SCC 473 : AIR 2015 SC 180. See also *Mohammad Akbar v Ashok Sahu*, 2016 AIR CC 1665, para 39 (Chh).

181. Ins. by Act 18 of 1872, section 6.

182. *Surendra Krishna Roy v Mirza Mahammad Syed Ali Matwali*, (1935) 63 IA 85 : 38 Bom LR 330. See also *Oriental Fire & General Ins. Co v Chandrawali*, AIR 1989 P&H 100, the insurer saying that the original policy was in possession of the other party but not requiring him to produce, held disentitled from producing the secondary evidence.

183. *Dinanath Rai v Rama Rai*, (1926) 6 Pat 102.

184. *Surendra Krishna Roy v Mirza Mahammad Syed Ali Matwali, supra.*

[s 66.1] "Secondary evidence of the contents".—"Secondary evidence of the contents" means apparently "not ... of the existence or condition" of the documents.[185]

[s 66.2] "Party".—This word means not only adversary in the cause, but also a stranger "legally bound to produce" the document.[186]

[s 66.3] Cases in which notice not required—*[Proviso]*.—The proviso enumerates six cases in which a notice is not required to be given to the party in whose possession or power the document is, in order to render secondary evidence admissible.

The procedure for the production of documents in criminal cases is laid down in sections 94-98 of the Code of Criminal Procedure.

Section 175 of the Indian Penal Code punishes the person who omits to produce a document required by a public servant.

[s 67] Proof of signature and handwriting of person alleged to have signed or written document produced.—If a document is alleged to be signed or to have been written wholly or in part by any person, the signature or the handwriting of so much of the document as is alleged to be in that person's handwriting must be proved to be in his handwriting.

SYNOPSIS

COMMENT

This section merely requires proof of signature and handwriting of the person alleged to have signed or written the document produced.[187] Mere admission of execution of a document is not sufficient. Proof that the signature of the executant is in his handwriting is necessary.[188]

Where merely the signature of a person to a type-written document was identified by a witness, it was held that what was formally proved was the signature and not the body of the document.[189]

The Evidence Act permits secondary evidence to be given with regard to the attestation of an attesting witness who is either dead or cannot be brought to Court. The signature of the attesting witness when proved in evidence is proof of everything on the face of the document and that he saw the executant make his mark.[190]

---

185. Stokes' Anglo-Indian Codes,Vol II, p 893, f.n. 6.

186. *Ibid,* fn 7.

187. *Abdool Ali v Abdoor Rushman,* (1874) 21 WR 429; *Madholal Sindhu v Asian. Assu. Co Ltd,* (1945) 56 Bom LR 147.

188. *Bulakidas v Shaikh Chhotu,* (1942) Nag 661; *Bhanwaria v Ramratan,* (1953) 4 Raj 145; *Ramkrishna Girischandra Dode v Anand Govind Kelkar,* AIR 1999 Bom 89, executants of rent receipt/receipts were not examined by the party about whom the court felt had launched obstructionist proceedings. An opportunity of examining the signatory was given to the party Refusal to admit the receipts in evidence was held to be proper. *Bank of India v Alibhoy Mohammed,* AIR 2008 Bom 81, a document produced either as a primary or secondary evidence, has to be proved in the manner laid down in sections 67 to 73.

189. In the matter of Mr *D & Mr S,* (1961) 68 Bom LR 228; but see contra the view expressed by Vimadalal J, in *Bhima Tima v Pioneer Chemicals,* (1967) 70 Bom LR 683. *Madholal v Asian Assu. Co Ltd,* (1945) 56 Bom LR 147.

190. *Ponnuswami Goundan v Kalyanasundara Ayyar,* (1934) 57 Mad 662.

As to the method of proof, see sections 47 and 73.

Besides the question which arises as to the contents of a document (see sections 61–66), there is always the question when the document is used in evidence—Is it what it purports to be? In other words, is it genuine? The evidence upon this point is dealt with in sections 67–73. The nature of the evidence will depend to a large extent on the nature of the document. If it is a mere memorandum, such as the entry in a diary mentioned in section 32(b), it must be proved that the diary was really that of the person whose statements it is said to contain. If it is a letter it must be shown who wrote it, or at any rate who signed it, for a signature to a document turns the whole document into a statement by the person who signs it. If it is an agreement it must be shown who executed it.[191] In the case of a money suit for goods sold on credit, the plaintiff examined his accountant who prepared the documents such as ledgers, challans, and corresponding bills, but who, in his cross-examination categorically stated that he did not know who prepared the documents. It was held that the documents in question could not be said to have been proved.[192] In the case of a document executed by the thumb impression of an illiterate person, the party putting forth the document has to prove that the document was read over and explained to the executant.[193]

[s 67.1] Execution of document.—Execution means signing, sealing and delivery of a document. The term may be defined as a formal completion of a deed. It is the last act or series of acts which completes it.[194]

Mere registration of a document is not in itself sufficient proof of its execution.[195] Where a mere photostatic copy of the registered sale deed was placed on record, it was held that the mere proof of registration was not the proof of due execution. Where there is a failure to produce the original sale deed or its certified copy and non-examination of an attesting witness or scribe of the document, it would have to be held that execution of the document was not proved.[196]

The mere production of a registered deed is not sufficient to prove it. The identity of the executant has to be established by oral evidence before the deed can be taken to have been proved.[197] In the case of a will, the burden lies upon its propounder to prove its genuineness, the deceased testator being no longer available to speak to its genuineness. Accordingly where the evidence produced by him was contradicting his claim and there was also inconsistency in the opinion of the handwriting expert, the will was held to be not proved.[198]

---

191. Markby 60.

192. *Rukmanand Ajitsaria v Usha Sales P Ltd,* AIR 1991 NOC 108 (Gau).

193. *Ramjan Khan v Baba Raghunath Das,* AIR 1992 MP 22; *Ram Singh v Col. Ram Singh,* AIR 1986 SC 3, a document the contents of which were not proved nor the maker of the document examined was held to be irrelevant.

194. *Bhawanji Horbhum v Devji Punja,* (1894) 19 Bom 635.

195. *Salimatul-Fatima Alias Bibi Hossaini v Koylashpoti Narain Singh,* (1890) 17 Cal 903; *Bulakidas v Shaikh Chhotu,* (1942) Nag 661. *KK Thankaappan v KS. Jayan,* AIR 2003 Ker 114, only a certified copy of the registered document of dissolution of marriage was available on record. There was no other evidence of due execution of the deed. Signature and handwriting on the deed were not proved to be that of the husband and wife. The Court said that the fact of dissolution of marriage was not proved.

196. *Khushi Ram v Findhi,* AIR 2003 HP 23.

197. *Prem Raj v Mishrimal,* (1959) 9 Raj 573.

198. *A Chandrabati v Laxmi Dei,* AIR 1991 Ori 289.

[s 67.2] CASES.—A deed of conveyance was tendered in evidence which purported to bear the mark of G, as vendor, and which was duly attested by four witnesses. G, however, denied that she had ever executed the deed, and said that the mark was not hers. All the attesting witnesses were dead. A witness was called who knew the handwriting of one of the attesting witnesses, and who swore that the signature of that witness to the attestation clause of the deed was genuine. It was held that the deed was admissible in evidence, its execution by G being sufficiently proved.[199]

A suit for recovery of loan amount was filed by a bank. The demand notice was sent by an advocate. The photocopy of the demand notice which was filed carried no signature of the advocate who was supposed to have issued it. Nobody proved the contents of the demand notice. There was no evidence showing despatch or receipt of the notice. The notice was held to be not admissible as legal evidence.[200]

Merely because the *mahzar*/recovery memo executed at the time of recovery, was attested by two independent witnesses, that would not lend credibility to the same. Such credibility would attach to it only if the said two independent witnesses are produced as witnesses and the accused is afforded an opportunity to cross-examine them, which was not done in the instant case.[201]

[s 67.2.1] ***Non-examination of Executant.***—Section 67 mandates that the signature and handwriting of a person on a written document can be proved only by examining the person concerned. When the person is very much available and alive, an attempt to prove his signature and handwriting by examining a third person as a witness would have its own drawback. An inference of the type indicated in section 114 [clause (e)] would become applicable.[202]

[203][s 67A] Proof as to [204][electronic signature].—Except in the case of a secure [204][electronic signature], if the [204][electronic signature] of any subscriber is alleged to have been affixed to an electronic record the fact that such [204][electronic signature] is the [204][electronic signature] of the subscriber must be proved.]

COMMENTS

This section was initially inserted *vide* Information Technology (Amendment) Act, 2000.[205]

Thereafter, in 2008, an amendment[206] was made in this section, whereby the word "digital signature" was substituted by the word "electronic signature" at three places in this section. This substitution is a part of the entire scheme under which the digital

---

199. *Abdulla Paru v Gannibai,* (1887) 11 Bom 690; *Babban v Shiv Nath,* AIR 1986 All 185, attesting witnesses duly produced. *Pankhothang Haokip v Dozakhup Paite,* AIR 2003 Gau 44, sale deed, execution by the seller proved by the buyer, the seller made no plea of cancellation that of denial of his signature. He was bound by the document.

200. *Bank of India v Alibhoy Mohammed,* AIR 2008 Bom 81.

201. *A Tajudeen v UOI,* (2015) 4 SCC 435 (para 31).

202. *Muddasani Savojana v Muddasami Venkat Narsaiah,* AIR 2007 AP 50.

203. Ins. by Act 21 of 2000, section 92 and Sch. II–10 (w.e.f. 17-10-2000).

204. Subs. by Act 10 of 2009, section 52(d), for "digital signature" (w.e.f. 27-10-2009).

205. Ins. by the Information Technology Act, 2000 (21 of 2000), section 52 & Schedule, (w.e.f. 17.10.2000).

206. (10 of 2009), section 52 [w.e.f. 27-10-2009 *vide* Notification No. S.O. 2689(E) dated 27-10-2009].

signature regime is being switched over to the electronic signature regime in the field of e-commerce and e-governance. This switching over of regime is meant to broaden the spectrum and follow the global trend.[207]

After the entire regimen of "digital signature" having been shifted to "electronic signature", a digital signature is treated as a secured electronic signature, whereas an electronic signature is a proprietary format with no standard for security. For example, even a typed name or a digitized image of a handwritten signature. Consequently, the integrity, sanctity and security of electronic signatures are a big issue since nothing prevents one individual from typing another individual's name. Therefore, a party to litigation, who asserts on the basis of an electronic signature of a subscriber, has been put under an obligation to prove before the court that the electronic signature actually belonged to that subscriber. A Court is no longer entitled to take an electronic signature on its face value without the party harping upon such electronic signature on a document having proved the same by leading cogent evidence.

[s 68] Proof of execution of document required by law to be attested.—If a document is required by law[s 68.2] to be attested,[s 68.3] it shall not be used as evidence[s 68.4] until one attesting witness at least has been called for the purpose of proving its execution,[s 68.5] if there be an attesting witness alive, and subject to the process of the Court and capable of giving evidence:

[208][Provided[s 68.6] that it shall not be necessary to call an attesting witness in proof of the execution[s 68.8] of any document, not being a will, which has been registered in accordance with the provisions of the Indian Registration Act, 1908, unless its execution by the person by whom it purports to have been executed is specifically denied.]

SYNOPSIS

COMMENT

This section applies to cases where an instrument required by law to be attested bears the necessary attestation. What the section prohibits is a proof of execution of a document otherwise than by the evidence of an attesting witness if available.[209]

---

207. For difference between "digital signature" and "electronic signature", please see section 3 (*ante*).

208. Ins. by Act 31 of 1926, section 2.

209. *Veerappa Kavundan v Ramasami Kavundan,* (1907) 30 Mad 251; *Ram Gopal Lal v Aipna Kunwar,* (1922) 44 All 495 : 49 IA 413.

This section applies only where the execution of a document has to be proved or when the allegation is that the executant was not in a fit state of mind to know the real nature of the document.[210] Where, however, the execution is not to be proved, it is not necessary to call any attesting witness, unless it is expressly contended that the attesting witness has not witnessed the execution of the document.[211]

The object of placing more attestations than one upon a document whether at the party's voluntary instance or by requirement of law, is ordinarily not to demand the combined testimony of all at the trial, but merely to provide by way of caution a number of witnesses; so that the contingencies of death, removal of residence, and the like, may be guarded against, and one witness at least may be available. But the main object in statutes requiring attestation as an element of validity is to surround the act of execution with certain safeguards; the object of securing evidence for litigation is a secondary one.[212]

A mere general denial of a mortgage or not admitting it cannot be regarded as a specific denial of its execution within the meaning of the proviso to this section. When there is only a general denial of execution and there is no cross-examination regarding attestation of a witness who comes forward to swear to execution then it can be presumed that there was due attestation.[213]

[s 68.1] Proof of Will.—This section is not permissive or enabling. It lays down the necessary requirements which the court has to observe in order that a document can be held to be proved. The principle underlying the section is that execution of the will must be proved by at least one attesting witness, that it is only an attesting witness who is entitled to prove the execution of the will. It is a concession that the legislature has made. If that concession does not result in complying with the mandatory requirements of this section the only proper method is to call the other attesting witness, so that both the attesting witnesses are before the court, and the due execution of the will is proved by the two attesting witnesses which are necessary before a will can become a valid document.[214] To prove a will it is not necessary that the attesting witness should depose that the other attesting witness had signed the will in the presence of the testator and after seeing the testator signing the will as both the attesting witnesses need not be present at the same time.[215] "A plain perusal of section 68 of the Evidence Act shows that the requirement of examining at least one

210. *Radhamohan v Haribandhu,* AIR 1991 NOC 109 (Ori).

211. *Komalsing Kuwarsing v Krishnabai,* (1945) 48 Bom LR 83 : (1946) Bom 146.

212. Wigmore, section 1304.

213. *Dashrath prasad v Laloosingh,* (1951) Nag 873.

214. *Bishnu Ram Krishan v Nathu Vithal,* (1948) 51 Bom LR 245. *Ram Rattan v Bittan Kaur,* AIR 1980 All 395, where the attesting witness though alive was not produced. *State of Haryana v Raj Kaur,* AIR 2001 P&H 322, the original will was not produced, only one attesting witness produced who stated that he was not aware whether the testator had executed any will or he had thumb marked any will. The testator had excluded his daughters from succession and preferred his nephews. The propounder of will did not produce any evidence to show that the testator was free from extraneous influence and used or was capable of using his free mind. The sub-Registrar who registered the will was not produced. The court said that the will was not proved to the satisfaction of the court so as to exclude natural heirs. *N Kamalam v Ayyaswamy,* AIR 2001 SC 2802, signature of the subscribe cannot be equated with that of an attesting witness. Attestation is a legal requirement. *Sundariya Bai Choudhary v UOI,* AIR 2008 MP 227 (DB), will shown to be properly executed and attested.

215. *KM Varghese v KM Oommen,* AIR 1994 Ker 85, **dissenting** from Road *Fromroze v Kanta Varjvandas,* AIR 1946 Bom 12, *Vishni Ram Krishna v Nathu Vithal,* AIR 1949 Bom 266, *K Nookaraju v P Venkatarao,* AIR 1974 AP 13 and *Pattammal v Kanniammal,* AIR 1981 Mad 252.

attesting witness is to be fulfilled "if there be an attesting witness alive". Where the attesting witnesses are dead the will can certainly be proved in the manner provided for proof of a document".[216] Where the executant and attesting witnesses of a will were not alive, identification of their signature by another witness, present at the time of its execution was not necessary to prove the will.[217] The mode of proving a will does not ordinarily differ from that of proving any other document except in the special circumstances as incorporated in section 63 of the Act.[218] Merely from the vague evidence of the attesting witness and without taking all circumstances into consideration, the court should not conclude that the will was not duly executed.[219] However, where the attesting witness had signed the document, without knowing its nature, as his evidence was that he only signed the document and went away and he was unable to say whether the document was a will or gift, in such circumstances, the will could not be said to be duly executed.[220]

The fact of the testator giving instruction for the making of a will was proved. He himself presented the will for registration and acknowledged its due execution. No vitiating circumstances were made out to rebut the presumption arising out of registration or to create any doubt about the presence of testators at the time of registration. The finding of the court below that the will was regularly executed did not call for any interference.[221] Where the scribe of the will had deposed on oath that he had scribed the Will and had read it over and explained to the testatrix under whose instructions it was so written and his evidence showed that the testatrix was clearly in a sound state of health and mind at that point of time, it was held that the due execution of the will was proved.[222] Where the attesting witness identified the thumb impression of the testatrix and also the scribe of the will and the other attesting witness and withstood the test of cross-examination; besides the will was not kept a secret from the beneficiaries. It was held that execution of the will was duly proved despite a minor discrepancy of variance in the date of dictation of will.[223]

---

216. *Balwant v Mainabai,* AIR 1991 MP 11; *A Chandrabati v Laxmi Dei,* AIR 1991 Ori 289.

217. *Haradhan Mahatha v Dukhu Mahatha,* AIR 1993 Pat 129.

218. *Bhagya Wati Jain v General Public,* AIR 1995 P&H 201, the court surveyed a large number of cases at pp 204-209.

219. *KM Varghese v KM Oommen,* AIR 1994 Ker 85; *Madhukar D Shende v Tarabal Aka Shedage,* AIR 2002 SC 637, the validity of a will could not be questioned on the basis of suspicion and conjectures with no foundation in evidence and having no relevance to the facts of the case. There was no challenge by any relative of the testatrix. The court set aside the finding. *C. Ananda Sundaraman v C. Thirupunasundari,* AIR 2008 NOC 2658 (Mad—DB) will proved by proper evidence, not allowed to be shaken off by mere allegations of undue influence, those who were supposed to have influenced were abroad.

220. *Laxminarayan Panigrahi v Panchanana Panda,* AIR 2016 NOC 20 (Ori).

221. *Baburajan v Parukutty,* AIR 1999 Ker 274, signature and attestation were put at the end of the document after the schedule of property. The failure of the testator to sign one of the pages was held as not making any difference. *S Kaliyammal v K Paliammal,* AIR 1999 Mad 40, execution of the will was not denied, but the allegation was that the execution was under fraud and under influence. No evidence was produced in support of the allegation. The court said that an inference of the validity of the will was warranted. *Janardan Badrinarayan Patel v Sheth Ambalal Himatlal,* AIR 1999 Guj 162, the propounders did not produce the draft of the will and there was no evidence to show the happenings prior to the finalisation of the will.

222. *P Arakhita Senapati v P Sabitri Senapati,* 2016 AIR CC 359 (Ori).

223. *Ved Prakash v Buta Singh,* 2016 AIR CC 1861, para 10 (P&H).

Where the execution of a Will is surrounded by suspicious circumstances, the propounder must offer reasonable explanation to remove such suspicious circumstances.[224]

An unprobated Will has been held to be admissible in evidence for collateral purposes in any other proceedings except probate proceedings.[225]

Where at the time of execution of the will, the thumb impression over the alleged will was taken by beneficiaries, the document writer was shown to be the scribe of the will, whereas the same was scribed by him and the defendant testatrix who expired during the litigation, did not whisper anything about its execution in her written statement though it was executed earlier, it was held that the will was not proved.[226]

The execution of a will being 30 years old does not absolve from the requirement of statutory proof. A presumption regarding documents being 30 years old under section 90 does not apply to a will.[227]

[s 68.2] "Required by law".—This means required by the law of the country where the property is situate. The rule as to the law of domicile is not extended to immovable property.

[s 68.3] "Attested".—"Attested" means that a person has signed the document by way of testimony to the fact that he saw it executed.[228] An attesting witness is one who signs the document in the presence of the executant after seeing the execution of the document or after receiving a personal acknowledgment of the execution of the document by the executant.[229] A document cannot be attested by a party to it. The object of attestation is that some person should verify that the deed was signed voluntarily. Knowledge of the contents of a document ought not to be inferred from the mere fact of attestation.[230]

"Attested", in relation to an instrument, means attested by two or more witnesses each of whom has seen the executant sign or affix his mark to the instrument, or has

---

224. *Bharpur Singh v Shamsher Singh,* AIR 2009 SC 1766 : (2009) 3 SCC 687; *Basanta Kumar Ghosh v Bimal Kumar Nayak,* AIR 2009 NOC 2677 (Cal—DB) suspicious circumstances about civil, not clarified. *Babu Singh v Ram Sahai,* AIR 2008 SC 2485 : (2008) 14 SCC 754, suspicious circumstances have to be clarified. Party has to take steps to bring forth attesting witnesses. *JT Surappa v Satchidhanandendra,* AIR 2008 NOC 2433 (Kar), will came into being six hours before testator's death, it could not be said that he must have been in proper state of time, signature on side margin of first two sheets, not at bottom, doubts about presence of attesting witnesses. *Afoline D'Souza v John D'Souza,* AIR 2007 SC 2219 : (2007) 7 SCC 225, 96 years old testatrix lady, many suspicious circumstances like nothing to show that the Will was read over to her and understood by her, not accepted. *Niranjan Umeshchandra Joshi v Mrudula Jyoti,* AIR 2007 SC 614 : (2006) 13 SCC 433, will executed while in ICU, one of his sons was attending doctor, whole legacy left to him, no reason stated, doubtful circumstances, denial of probate was held proper. *Sham Singh v Rano Devi,* AIR 2007 NOC 621 (HP), suspicious circumstances, not explained.

225. *Commr v Mohan Krishna Abrol,* AIR 2004 SC 2060 : (2004) 7 SCC 505.

226. *Dhannulal v Ganeshram,* AIR 2015 SC 2382 (para 20).

227. *Prem Devi v Bholanath Gattani,* AIR 2015 Raj 200, paras 10 and 12.

228. *Alagappa Chettiyar v Ko Kala Pai,* (1940) Ran 199; *Shamu Patter v Abdul Kadir Ravuthan,* (1912) 35 Mad 607 : 39 IA 218 : 14 Bom LR 1034.

229. *Lachman Singh v Surendra Bahadur Singh,* (1932) 54 All 1051 FB *Benga Behera v Braja Kishore Nanda,* AIR 2007 SC 1975 : (2007) 9 SCC 728, a person signing a Will in performance of a statutory duty is not an attesting witness. A certifying witness (an advocate in this case) was not treated as an attesting witness. The certificate was that the Will was dictated by him to his clerk.

230. *Nainsukhdas Sheonarayan Shop v Goverdhandas,* (1947) Nag 510.

seen some other person sign the instrument in the presence and by the direction of the executant, or has received from the executant a personal acknowledgment of his signature or mark or of the signature of such other person, and each of whom has signed the instrument in the presence of the executant; but it is not necessary that more than one of such witnesses should be present at the same time, and no particular form of attestation is necessary (see section 3 of the Transfer of Property Act, 1882 and section 63(c) of the Indian Succession Act, 1925).

Where a document is written, executed and attested in one ink the presumption of due attestation is permissible under the maxim *Omnia praesumuntur rite et solemniter esse acta donec probetur in contrarium.*[231]

"Personal acknowledgment" is not the equivalent of "express acknowledgment" by words and an acknowledgment may be inferred from gestures or conduct.[232]

According to the Allahabad, the Patna and the Bombay High Courts, the scribe of a mortgage deed cannot be counted as an attesting witness merely because he has signed the deed, even though the deed may in fact have been executed in his presence,[233] but the Madras[234] and Calcutta,[235] Orissa[236] and Punjab and Haryana[237] High Courts have held to the contrary. The Rangoon High Court has held that the writer of a document may perform a dual role; he may be an attesting witness as well as the writer. When a man places his signature upon a document and at the same time describes himself as the writer thereof, the inference is that he signs as the writer and nothing else, but, as a matter of fact, it can be shown that he signed not only as the writer but also as a witness of the fact that he saw the document executed or received a personal acknowledgment from the executant that he had executed it.[238] The Bombay High Court has further held that where the writer has signed not as a scribe but as an attesting witness the attestation is good.[239] Where the only available attesting witness to a mortgage deed denies his attestation, it is permissible to prove the deed by calling its writer under section 71 to depose to the execution of the deed by the mortgagor and to its attestation by the two witnesses.[240]

The direct evidence of the attestor will be "primary evidence". If there is no attesting witness alive, then the document must be proved in the manner provided by sections 47

231. *Rao Bhimsing v Fakirchand,* (1947) Nag 649.

232. *Amir Husain v Abdul Samad,* (1937) All 723.

233. *Badri Prasad v Abdul Karim,* (1913) 35 All 254; *Ram Bahadur Singh v Ajodhya Singh,* (1916) 20 Cal WN 699 (Patna); *Dalichand v Lotu,* (1919) 22 Bom LR 136 : 44 Bom 405; *Amardas Mangaldas v Haramanbhai Jethabhai,* (1942) 44 Bom LR 643.

234. *Paramasiva Udayan v Krishna Padhyachi,* (1917) 41 Mad 535.

235. *Jagannath Khan v Bajrang Das Agarwala,* (1920) 48 Cal 61; *Abinash Chandra Bidyanidhi Bhattacharya v Dasarath Malo,* (1928) 56 Cal 598.

236. *Dhruba Sahu v Nalumoni Sahu,* AIR 1983 Ori 24, the Court adding that it is not necessary for the attesting witness to add that he signed in the presence of the executant.

237. *Ujagar Singh v Parmesh Knitting Works,* AIR 1986 P&H 230.

238. *Alagappa Chettiyar v Ko Kala Pai,* (1940) Ran 199.

239. *Yacubkhan v Guljarkhan,* (1927) 52 Bom 219 : 30 Bom LR 565.

240. *Lakshman v Krishnaji,* (1927) 29 Bom LR 1425; *Thakkar Vrajlal Bhimjee v Thakkar Jamnadass Valjee,* (1994) 4 SCC 723, no attesting witness to a mortgage deed was produced. Its execution was not deemed to have been proved. The admission by the guarantor of his signature upon the mortgage deed was not a substitute for proof by attesting witnesses. The court followed *Kunwar Surendra Bahadur Singh v Thakur Behari Singh,* AIR 1939 PC 117.

and 73. Should there be any doubt about the genuineness of the signature of an attesting witness, the same can be resolved through the opinion of an expert under section 45.[241]

When attestation is not specifically challenged and when an attesting witness is not cross-examined regarding the details of attestation his evidence that the deed was attested by the other attesting witnesses and by him is sufficient proof of attestation under this section. The law will then assume that when the witness swears that it was attested the witness means that it was attested according to the forms required by law.[242]

[s 68.3.1] Documents requiring attestation.—(1) A will (sections 57 and 63 of the Indian Succession Act, 1925); (2) a mortgage, the principal money secured by which is Rs 100 or upwards (Transfer of Property Act, 1882, section 59); (3) a gift of immovable property (Transfer of Property Act, 1882, section 132). Any such document which is not attested is not valid.[243] Where the document was that of reconveyance, it did not require attestation.[244]

The proper mode of attesting is that the witness should either sign or affix his thumb impression himself. The section does not permit the delegation of that function, if he does so, he is not an attesting witness.

[s 68.4] "It shall not be used as evidence".—These words means that the document cannot be used in a suit for enforcement of the document, leaving the ordinary provisions of law in section 67 to apply where the document is to be used for any other purpose. Although a document cannot be used in evidence as a mortgage deed, which requires attestation, yet this section does not prevent it from being used in evidence for the purpose of proving it as an acknowledgment saving limitation.[245]

[s 68.5] "Until one attesting witness at least has been called for the purpose of proving its execution".—The word "called" means tendered for the purpose of giving evidence.[246] It is not used in the sense of summoned.[247] It is not necessary for the attesting person, in order to prove execution, to point to the signature or mark made by the executant. It does not therefore follow that because a witness is unable to point to the signature on a document of the person whose signature he purports to have attested, he has failed to prove that signature.[248]

This section provides that a document cannot be held to have been proved unless one of the attesting witnesses is called where it is not established that all of them are dead or were incapable of giving evidence.[249] The words "at least" presuppose that more evidence may be required and it can only be by reference to the circumstances of each case that the quantum of evidence necessary to discharge the onus of proof can be measured. A will duly signed by the testator and attested by two witnesses, who attest not in the presence of each other but at different times on the acknowledgment by the testator of his own signature, cannot be admitted to proof on the evidence of

241. *Sumangala T Pai v Sundaresa Pai,* AIR 1991 Ker 259.
242. *Kuwarlal v Rekhlal,* (1950) Nag 321.
243. *Chand Bee v Hameedunisa,* AIR 2007 AP 150.
244. *HS Rudrappa v HY Shivlingappa,* AIR 2000 NOC 42 : 1999 AI HC 4543.
245. *Shyam Lal v Lakshmi Narain,* (1939) All 366.
246. *Moti Chand v Lalta Prasad,* (1917) 40 All 256.
247. *Ruprao v Ramrao,* (1952) Nag 189.
248. *Raizulnisa Begam v Lala Puran Chand,* (1943) 19 Luck 443.
249. *Ananta Raghuram v Rajah Bommaderara,* AIR 1958 Andhra 418.

only one of the attesting witnesses.[250] There is no requirement that attesting witnesses should identify each other.[251] Where the attesting witnesses proved the execution, it was immaterial that their names were not mentioned in the will.[252] Where the sole evidence of title was a "will" and the attesting witness failed to prove it, it would not be said that the will had been legally proved.[253] It would not be necessary to call an attesting witness where execution of a deed was not denied, only its validity was questioned on the ground of undue influence.[254]

Where all the attesting witnesses had died, the Sub-Registrar, who had registered the will was examined on commission set out the circumstances in which the attesting witnesses as well as the testator had signed the document, the execution of the will was held to be proved.[255]

There is no legal bar in a scribe himself being an attesting witness, provided he has actually seen the executant signing or affixing his mark or has received a personal acknowledgement from the executant and consciously affixed his signature as an attesting witness, as a token of having witnessed the executants signing or affixing his mark. Evidence should prove that the scribe, apart from being so, had signed for the purpose of testifying to the signature of the executant and had the *animo attestandi*.[256] However, where the scribe puts his signature in the document in the discharge of his statutory duty, he cannot be treated as an attesting witness. His evidence cannot be taken as a substitute for the evidence of an attesting witness.[257] Simply because the signature of a person appeared on the will, the said person cannot be termed as an attesting witness, in absence of evidence to substantiate that he had put his signatures on the document for the purpose of attesting it.[258]

Where the opposite party took no steps to produce any attesting witness and he could not be cross-examined, it was held that his statement that he saw the executant sign the document and then he himself attested it remained unrebutted. The requirement of section 68 was satisfied. The Court further said that no qualification is prescribed for anybody being an attesting witness.[259]

[s 68.6] Registered documents—*[Proviso]*.—The proviso was added by Act XXXI of 1926. It simplifies the difficulty of calling attesting witnesses where the document to be proved is a registered one and is not a will and its execution is not specifically denied by the person executing it.[260] If the attestation is not specifically denied it is

---

250. *Roda Framroze v Kanta Varjivandas*, (1945) 47 Bom LR 709 : (1946) Bom 295; *Ruprao v Ramrao*, (1952) Nag 189.

251. *Krishna Kumar v Kayastha Pathsala*, AIR 1966 All 570.

252. *Beni Chand v Kamla Kunwar*, AIR 1977 SC 63 : 1977(4) SCC 554.

253. *Rameshwari Devi v Shyam Lal*, AIR 1980 All 292.

254. *Engineers (Overseas) Corpn. v WB Fin. Corp*, AIR 1986 Cal 132; *Chandrashekhar v Rahul Shikshan Prasarak Mandal Sansar Nagar*, 2017 (6) Andh LD 121, unless the execution of a document, not being a Will, is denied by the executant, it would not be necessary to call an attesting witness in proof of execution of any document which otherwise is required by law to be attested.

255. *Ved Mitra Verma v Dharam Deo Verma*, (2014) 15 SCC 578 para 13 : 2014 (9) Scale 219.

256. *CG Raveendran v C.G Gopi*, AIR 2015 Ker 250, para 17 (DB).

257. *Laxminarayan Panigrahi v Panchanana Panda*, AIR 2016 NOC 20 (Ori).

258. *Narotam v Laxmi Devi*, AIR 2016 HP 160, para 17, **relying on** *Punni v Sumer Chand*, AIR 1995 HP 74.

259. *Peddavandla Narayanamma v Peddasani Venkata Reddy*, AIR 2007 AP 137.

260. The **following** cases are affected by this proviso; *Veerappa Kavundan v Ramasami Kavundan*, (1907) 30 Mad 251; *Satish Chandra Mitra v Jogendranath Mahalanabis*, (1916) 44 Cal 345; *Rosammal Issethenammal Fernandez v Joosa Marlyan Fernandez*, AIR 2000 SC 2857 : (2000) 7 SCC 189, denial must not be vague, pleadings of the parties must also be considered while recording a finding as to denial.

not necessary to call any attesting witness.[261] What has to be specifically denied is the execution of the document and a mere denial of the genuineness of the document is not enough to indicate that the execution of the document was denied.[262]

The words "specifically denied" means specifically denied by the party against whom it is sought to be used and not only by the executant. Where, therefore, a party against whom a document is sought to be used denied its execution, even though the executant does not do so, it is necessary to call an attesting witness to prove it.[263] A third party who is a party to a mortgage suit but not to the mortgage deed can deny execution and require proof of attestation when the executant of the deed admits execution.[264] Where the plaintiff alleged that the executant of the gift deed was so old and infirm that he could not understand the nature of the document, the court said that it was not "a specific denial".[265] Where the execution of a registered gift deed was not denied by the executant, proviso to section 68 was not attracted.[266] The proviso to section 68 is not applicable to the sale deed of immovable property. Even if the sale deed has been attested by witnesses, they need not be examined.[267]

A registered deed of gift of immovable property was signed by the donor and attested by the witnesses. The donor also admitted execution of the gift in favour of the appellant. It was held that the deed was duly proved even if one of the attesting witnesses was not called upon to testify to the execution.[268]

The Madras High Court has held that the proviso has a retrospective effect as it relates to procedural law and not to substantive law. If the execution of a deed required to be attested by law is not denied by the executant, it need not be proved by any attesting witness, though it might have been executed before the enactment of the proviso.[269]

[s 68.7] Will.—To prove the execution of a will, mere examination of its writer or proof of his signature[270] or the fact that the will was registered one was held to be not sufficient.[271]

Examination of at least one attesting witness is mandatory. Where only one attesting was alive but he could not be produced despite best efforts and an application for filing additional evidence was made at the late stage of arguments, it was held that the

---

261. *Yacubkhan v Guljarkhan,* (1927) 52 Bom 219, 30 Bom LR 565; *Hari Nath Ghosh v Nepal Chandra Ray Chaudhuri,* (1937) 1 Cal 507, *Sheo Ratan Singh v Jagannath,* (1936) 12 Luck 681; *Bhagwandas Dhondidas v Basawwa,* (1956) 58 Bom LR 809.

262. *K Narasimhappa v Lokkanna,* AIR 1959 Mys 148.

263. *Chandra Kali v Bhabuti Prasad,* (1943) 19 Luck 365.

264. *Syed Zaharul Hussain v Mahadeo,* (1948) Nag 621.

265. *Chuttan Lal v Shanti Pd,* AIR 1981 All 50.

266. *Shyama Devi v Premvati,* AIR 1996 All 57.

267. *Hans Raji v Yosodanand,* AIR 1996 SC 761 : 1996 (7) SCC 122; *Bayanabai Kaware v Rajendra,* 2017 (13) Scale 644 : (2018) 1 SCC 585 : (2018)1 SCC 585, section 68 is not applicable to sale deed which is governed by section 54 of the Transfer of Property Act.

268. *Surendra Kumar v Nathulal,* AIR 2001 SC 2040 : (2001) 5 SCC 46.

269. *Thayammal v Mutukumaraswami Chettiar,* (1929) 53 Mad 119.

270. *Janki Narayan Bhoir v Narayan Namdeo Kadam,* AIR 2003 SC 761, when one attesting witness is produced, the examination of the other attesting witness can be dispensed with.

271. *Asia Bi v SA Abdul Gaffor,* 1996 AIHC 1332 (Mad); *Mohanlal Dungarmal Furmani v Vishanji Dungarmal Furmani,* AIR 2001 Cal 122, construction of an unprobated will has to be according to the agreement as it is and not by adding to or varying its terms.

application was to be allowed since proof of registered will was not possible without examining at least one attesting witness.[272] Even where the sole attesting witness produced denies the Will, it can be accepted if it is proved by other evidence that there was proper attestation. The requirement of proof that the Will was duly executed is on the propounder. The mere proof of the signature of the testator is not enough.[273] Proof of will stands in a higher degree in comparison to other documents. There must be clear evidence of the attesting witnesses or other witnesses, that the contents of the will were read over to the executant and he, after admitting the same to be correct, put his signature in the presence of witnesses. It is only after the executant puts his signature, that the attesting witnesses shall put their signatures in the presence of the executant.[274]

Where the will in question was a registered document and was more than 50 years old, and all the attesting witnesses and scribe were dead and, therefore, the question of their examination did not arise, it was held that, in the absence of any suspicious circumstances, the presumption of genuineness of the will prevailed.[275] Registration of a will is a piece of evidence confirming its genuineness and can confer it a higher degree of sanctity.[276]

The scribe of a will stated that the will was scribed by him at the instance of the testator who was in a fit state of health and mind and that the will was signed by him after it was read over to him. This statement of the scribe, the court said, amounted to the statement of an attesting witness. The marginal witness also corroborated the statement of the scribe. It was immaterial that the attesting witness did not say that he signed the will in the presence of the executant.[277]

The defendant categorically deposed that he was in possession of the suit property by virtue of the Will. It was held that he was estopped from disputing due execution of the Will as regards bequeathing of the suit property to the plaintiff. He was not allowed to say that no attesting witness was examined by the plaintiff.[278]

[s 68.7.1] ***Unregistered Partition and Will.***—It was a case of an unregistered partition deed and Will, but it was given the nomenclature of Will. The predecessor of the parties gave the suit properly by way of family partition to the plaintiff, defendant and their missing brother. The document required registration because the property apparently was

---

272. *Rajinder Singh v Hari Singh,* AIR 2000 P&H. 257. *Mathew Jacob v Salestine Jacob,* AIR 1998 Del 320, examination of only one witness is sufficient.
273. *Joseph v KV Ippunny,* AIR 2007 NOC 2517 (Ker—DB); *Josephrise Jerome v S. Santiago,* AIR 2007 NOC 2486 (Mad—DB).
274. *Dhannulal v Ganeshram,* (2015) 12 SCC 301, para 19.
275. *Kesarapu Manikyalu v Venna Pertimallaya,* AIR 2000 NOC 20 (AP).
276. *CG Raveendran v CG Gopi,* AIR 2015 Ker 250 DT, para 15 (DB).
277. *Dhyam Chand v Savitri Devi,* AIR 1998 HP 37. *Chandan Longa Bai,* AIR 1998 MP 1, attesting witness denied attestation by him. Other evidence became permissible. The scribe testified to scribing the will and attestation by two witnesses. The document was also registered. The statement of scribe comes under section 71. A subsequent will referred to the earlier will. The execution of the will was taken to be proved. *Madhab Bohora v Braja Kishore Nanda,* AIR 2003 Ori 107, attesting witnesses became hostile, the scribe was also avoiding but he was arrested and produced, he admitted he did the scribing service and attested the thumb impression of the executant. Evidence accepted that the will was duly attested in accordance with the law. One of the copies carried a certificate from the party's advocate which was not there on the original. Since there was no legal requirement of such endorsement, its absence on the original was immaterial. *Pt AK Misra v Pt Ram Chandra Sharma,* AIR 2003 All 96, of the two wills, the second was found to be genuine and natural.
278. *Minor Mani v Ammakannu,* AIR 2008 NOC 2434 (Mad).

of more than Rs 100 in value. The document being not admissible in evidence, it was held that decreeing the plaintiff's claim on the strength of such document was not valid.[279]

[s 68.8] "Execution".—"Execution" means not only signing by the person executing the document but also the attestation of his signature by witnesses where it requires such attestation.[280]

The expression "execution" does not merely mean signature. It also means that the executant or the person who puts the signature has done so after understanding the contents of the document. It has to be proved that the testator had put his signature after understanding the contents of the document. The fact of registration is not a conclusive evidence of due execution. Since official acts are presumed to be regularly done, the fact of registration creates the presumption of due execution.[281]

[s 68.8.1] ***Gift Deed.***—The attesting witnesses of the gift deed was not examined. The person examined denied that he was an attesting witness. He denied any knowledge about signature on the gift deed. The Court held that it could not be said that the gift deed was proved.[282]

Where the executant of the gift deed, an illiterate lady, pleaded that her signature on the gift deed was taken without explaining its contents to her and no evidence was given to prove that the same was read out and explained to her, besides its attestation was not proved, it was held that the gift deed was invalid.[283]

[s 68.9] Effect of non-denial of attestation and/or execution.—The prevalent view that the court will always insist on proof of will irrespective of a plea denying it specifically was itself put to challenge in Kerala High Court that was noticed by the Delhi High Court. This was by reading section 58 as overriding section 68 of the Evidence Act, 1872. In *Neelam Sahgal alias Nellu Sahgal v Seema Mehra,*[284] the Delhi High Court recounted:

> In *Thayyullathil Kunhikannan v Thayyullathil Kalliani,*[285] a Division Bench of the Kerala High Court held that section 58 of the Indian Evidence Act, 1872 has to be read as overriding section 68 and as obviating the necessity for calling an attesting witness, unless the execution of the will or the attestation is in dispute. Section 68 states that if a document is required by law to be attested, it shall not be used as evidence until one attesting witness at least has been called for the purpose of proving its execution, if there be an attesting witness alive. The proviso to the section which was introduced by the amending Act 31 of 1926 makes an exception in the case of any document, not being a will, which has been registered, unless its execution by the persons by whom it purports to have been executed, is specifically denied. The fact that the proviso is not applicable to wills, and that it does not make an exception in the case of registered wills, does not lead to any inference that a will cannot be acted upon or used as evidence, unless it has been proved by an attesting witness. The only effect of the proviso is that registration of the will by itself does not obviate the necessity of calling an attesting witness to prove it,

279. *Mohinder Lal v Tule Ram,* AIR 2008 HP 103.

280. *Hari Nath Ghosh v Nepal Chandra Ray Chaudhuri,* (1937) 1 Cal 507.

281. *J Mathew v Leela Joseph,* AIR 2007 NOC (Mad—DB).

282. *K Laxmanan v Thekkayil Padmini,* AIR 2009 SC 951 : (2009) 1 SCC 354.

283. *Sushama Rani Roy Chowdhury v Bani Roy,* AIR 2017 NOC 34 (Cal).

284. *Neelam Sahgal alias Nellu Sahgal v Seema Mehra,* 2017 SCC OnLine Del 8743 : (2017) 245 DLT 404 : (2018) 184 AIC (Sum 5) 2.

285. *Thayyullathil Kunhikannan v Thayyullathil Kalliani,* AIR 1990 Kerala 226 : (1990) 1 Hindu LR 235 : 1990 (1) KLJ 114.

if it is otherwise required to be proved. The proviso does not speak of a case where a will is not in dispute. Section 68 relates to those documents which require to be proved at the trial of a suit. If by any rule of law or of pleadings, such proof is not required, section 68 cannot operate to insist on formal proof by calling an attesting witness. Section 58 has to be read as overriding section 68 and as obviating the necessity for calling an attesting witness, unless the execution of the will or the attestation is in dispute. In the absence of any such plea in the written statement, it will be the height of technicality and waste of judicial time to insist on examination of an attesting witness, before a will could be used as evidence. Order VII rule 5 CPC deems the execution of the will to be admitted in the absence of any denial thereof in the written statement. Examination of an attesting witness is therefore unnecessary when the parties have not joined issue on the validity or genuineness of the will.

[s 69] Proof where no attesting witness found.—If no such attesting witness can be found, or if the document purports to have been executed in the United Kingdom, it must be proved that the attestation of one attesting witness at least is in his handwriting, and that the signature of the person executing the document is in the handwriting of that person.

COMMENT

An attesting witness, if available, should be called in evidence. If the attesting witness is dead, or is living out of the jurisdiction of the court or cannot be found after diligent search,[286] or if the document purports to have been executed in the UK of Great Britain and Ireland, two things must be proved:

(1) the signature of one attesting witness, and

(2) the signature of the executant.

Section 69 applies when no attesting witness is found. In the absence of any other provision dealing with cases wherein the presence of witnesses cannot be procured for various other reasons, like death of both the attesting witnesses, out of jurisdiction, physical incapacity, insanity, etc., this section should apply.[287]

Section 69 imposes a twin fold duty on the propounder. It provides that if no such attesting witness can be found, it must be proved that attestation of one attesting witness at least is in his handwriting and also that the signature of the person executing the document is in the handwriting of that person. Both of these will have to be cumulatively proved by the propounder. Evidently, the section demands proof of execution in addition to attestation and does not permit execution to be inferred from proof of attestation. However, section 69 presumes that once the handwriting of the attesting witness is proved, he has witnessed the execution of the document. The provings have to be in accordance with section 67 of the Act.[288]

Where the executant of, and all the marginal witnesses to, a mortgage deed were dead, it was held that the mortgage deed was sufficiently proved by evidence that the

---

286. *Mussammat Shahzamdi Begum v Sud Mahammad Qasim,* (1928) 7 Pat 312. In this case the effect of the proviso to section 68 was not brought to the notice of the Court.

287. *CG Raveendran v CG Gopi,* AIR 2015 Ker 250, para 18 (DB).

288. *CG Raveendran v CG Gopi,* AIR 2015 Ker 250, para 19 (DB).

signature of the mortgagor was in his handwriting and that the signatures of two of the marginal witnesses were in their handwriting.[289]

Where no attesting witness of a Will could be found, the court said that there must be proof of the signature of at least one attesting witness and that of the executant. Identification of the signature of the scribe would not be sufficient.[290]

Where none of the attesting witnesses is alive, the will can be proved by a person who is acquainted with the signature/handwriting of any attesting witness by giving evidence that the signature in the will is that of the attesting witness as was done in the instant case.[291]

[s 70] Admission of execution by party to attested document.—The admission[s 70.2] of a party to an attested document of its execution by himself shall be sufficient proof of its execution as against him, though it be a document required by law to be attested.

SYNOPSIS

COMMENT

This section serves as a proviso to section 68.

The effect of this section is to make the admission of the executant a sufficient proof of the execution of a document as against the executant himself,[292] even though it may be a document attestation of which is required by law.[293] The document is not for that reason binding on other persons.[294] An attested document means a duly attested one, and the execution that is contemplated in this section is a due execution or execution in accordance with what the law requires for a particular document; so, if a question of attestation is put in issue, it is incumbent on the plaintiff to prove that the document has been duly attested before this section can be relied on.[295]

[s 70.1] Scope.—This section operates only where the person relying on a document has not given any evidence at all of the due execution of the document by the executant but relies on an admission of execution by the latter. So that if a mortgagor admits execution of a document in the written statement, it is wholly unnecessary for the mortgagee to adduce any evidence as to the execution of the document. It is only in cases where it appears on the face of a document or it is positively made out by the evidence on record that a document required by law to be attested has not been attested in accordance with law that this section cannot be made applicable in spite of the admission of a party to an

---

289. *Uttam Singh v Hukam Singh,* (1916) 39 All 112.

290. *Giddamma v Venkatamma,* AIR 2010 NOC 626 (Kar).

291. *Silvy George v Anna Joseph,* 2014 AIR CC 2515, (paras 23 & 24) (Ker-DB).

292. *Jagannath v Ravji,* (1922) 24 Bom LR 1296 : 47 Bom 137; *Bhagwandas Dhondidas v Basawwa,* (1956) 58 Bom LR 809.

293. *Asharfi Lal v Musammat Nannhi,* (1921) 44 All 127; *Raja Ram v Thakur Rameshwar Bakhsh Singh,* (1936) 12 Luck 109.

294. *Arjun Sahu v Kelai Rath,* (1922) 2 Pat 317.

295. *Davood Rowther v Ramanathan Chettiar,* (1938) Mad 523.

attested document of its execution by himself for the simple reason that a court cannot shut its eyes to obvious facts appearing on the face of a document or on the record.[296]

[s 70.2] "Admission".—The admission here spoken of relates only to the execution. It must be distinguished from the admissions mentioned in sections 22 and 65B which relate to the contents of a document.

The Calcutta and the Allahabad High Courts have held that the word "admission" relates only to the admission of a party in the course of the trial of a suit, and not to the attestation of a document by the admission of the party executing it. In other words, it has no relation to any admission of execution made before an attesting witness without reference to any suit or proceeding.[297] But the Patna and the Rangoon High Courts have laid down that an admission under this section is admissible in evidence even though it be an admission not made in the course of legal proceedings pending before a court of Justice, but is an admission made antecedent to the institution of legal proceedings.[298] The Madras High Court has adopted the view of the Calcutta and the Allahabad High Courts and held that the admission within the meaning of this section must be an admission made for the purpose of or having reference to the cause either in the pleadings or during the course of the trial.[299]

[s 71] Proof when attesting witness denies the execution.—If the attesting witness denies or does not recollect the execution of the document, its execution may be proved by other evidence.

SYNOPSIS

COMMENT

[s 71.1] Principle.—Where an attesting witness has denied all knowledge of the matter, the case stands as if there was no attesting witness, and the execution of the document may be proved by other independent evidence.[300] This section only operates if the attesting witness denies or does not recollect the execution of the document or has turned hostile.[301] If the evidence of the witnesses produced by the propounder is inherently worthless and lacking in credibility, section 71 cannot be invoked to bail him (the propounder) out of the situation, to facilitate a roving pursuit. In the absence

296. *Raja Ram v Thakur Rameshwar Bakhsh Singh,* (1936) 12 Luck 109.

297. *Abdul Karim v Salimun,* (1899) 27 Cal 190; *Raj Mangal Misir v Mathura Dubain,* (1915) 38 All 1. **See** *Asharfi Lal v Musammat Nannhi,* (1921) 44 All 127.

298. *Nageshwar Prasad v Bachu Singh,* (1919) 4 PLJ 511, doubted in *Musammat Hira Bibi v Ramdhan Lal,* (1921) 6 PLJ 465; *Aung Rhi v Ma Aung Krwa Pru,* (1923) 1 Ran 557.

299. *Davood Rowther v Ramanathan Chettiar,* (1938) Mad 523, 532. Interpolation of words in a receipt for payment of rent does not make it inadmissible. *Kuri Lal Rungta v Banarsi Devi,* AIR 1986 All 94.

300. See *Lakshman v Krishnaji,* (1927) 29 Bom LR 1425. See also *Brundaban Nayak v Gobardhan Biswal,* AIR 1990 Ori 232, where the attesting witness denied that he attested the gift deed and other evidence was allowed.

301. *Chaitan Charan Parida v Maheshwar Parida,* AIR 1991 Ori 125. *Maria Sheilla v T Joseph Catherine,* AIR 2003 Mad 270, the propounder was allowed to prove execution of the will where either the attesting witness was not available or was unable to recollect facts. The will was proved by showing that the testatrix had admitted her signature in the presence of the witness who had deposed to that fact and also that she was in sound disposing state of mind.

of any touch of truthfulness and genuineness in the overall approach, this provision, which is not a substitute of section 63(c) of Indian Succession Act, 1925 and section 68 of the Evidence Act, 1872, cannot be invoked to supplement such failed speculative endeavour.[302] Under it execution of a document includes attestation.[303]

The attestation of a document does not amount to an admission of its contents by the attesting person unless it can be proved that the document was read over to him and that he made the attestation conscious of the statement made in the document.[304]

This section is a sort of a safeguard introduced by the legislature to the mandatory provisions of section 68, where it is not possible to prove the execution of the will by calling attesting witnesses, though alive. This section can only be requisitioned when the attesting witnesses who have been called fail to prove the execution of the will by reason of their either denying their own signatures, or denying the signature of the testator, or having no recollection as to the execution of the document. The section has no application when one attesting witness has failed to prove the execution of the will and other attesting witnesses are available who could prove the execution if they were called.[305] Section 71 cannot be so used to as to allow a party to give a go-buy to the mandate of section 68 *qua* the requirement of calling an attesting witness. Where one attesting witness could not recollect and the other attesting witness, though available, was not called, it was held that the will was not proved as the mandatory requirement of section 68 was not satisfied.[306]

[s 71.2] Principle as applied to will.—The requirement of calling at least one attesting witness to prove attestation is laid down under section 68 of the Evidence Act, 1872. This section constitutes an exception, as it were to section 68 but the conditions laid down for invoking the exception are strict. If the attesting witness denies or does not recollect the execution of the document, its execution may be proved by the other evidence. The interplay of the above statutory provisions and the underlying legislative objective would be of formidable relevance in evaluating the materials on record and recording the conclusions, as held in *Jagdish Chand Sharma v Narain Singh Saini*.[307] The two contingencies permitting the play of this provision, namely, denial or failure to recollect the execution by the attesting witness produced, thus *a fortiori* has to be extended a meaning to ensure that the limited liberty granted by section 71 of the 1872 Act does not in any manner efface or emasculate the essence and efficacy of section 63 of the Indian Succession Act,1925 and section 68 of the 1872 Act. The distinction between failure on the part of an attesting witness to prove the execution and attestation of a will and his or her denial of the said event or failure to recollect the same, has to be essentially maintained. Any unwarranted indulgence, permitting extra liberal flexibility to these two stipulations, would render the predication of section 63 of the Act and section 68 of the 1872 Act, otiose. The propounder can be initiated to the benefit of section 71 of the 1872 Act only if the attesting witness/witnesses, who is/are alive and is/are produced and in clear terms either denies/deny the execution of

---

302. *Jagdish Chandra Sharma v Narain Singh Saini*, (2015) 8 SCC 615, para 45.1.

303. *Laksman Sahu v Gokul Maharana*, (1921) 1 Pat 154. *Ram Ratan v Bittan Kaur*, AIR 1980 All 395.

304. *Roop Lal v Shanker*, (1951) 1 Raj 597.

305. *Vishu Ramkrishna v Nathu Vithal*, (1948) 51 Bom LR 245.

306. *Janki Narayan Bhoire v Narayan Namdeo Kadam*, AIR 2003 SC 761, evidence of other witnesses, for example, the person (respondent) who claimed the suit property and that of the scribe could have been considered if the requirement of section 68 had been satisfied.

307. *Jagdish Chand Sharma v Narain Singh Saini*, (2015) 8 SCC 615 : 2015 SCC OnLine SC 415.

the document or cannot recollect the said incident. Not only this witness/witnesses has/have to be credible and impartial, the evidence adduced ought to demonstrate unhesitant denial of the execution of the document or authenticate real forgetfulness of such fact. If the testimony evinces a casual account of the execution and attestation of the document disregardful of truth, and thereby fails to prove these two essentials as per law, the propounder cannot be permitted to adduce other evidence under cover of section 71 of the 1872 Act. Such a sanction would not only be incompatible with the scheme of section 63 of the Act read with section 68 of the 1872 Act but also would be extinctive of the paramountcy and sacrosanctity thereof, a consequence, not legislatively intended. If the evidence of the witnesses produced by the propounder is inherently worthless and lacking in credibility, section 71 of the 1872 Act cannot be invoked to bail him (the propounder) out of the situation to facilitate a roving pursuit. In absence of any touch of truthfulness and genuineness in the overall approach, this provision, which is not a substitute of section 63(c) of the Act and section 68 of the 1872 Act, cannot be invoked to supplement such failed speculative endeavour.

[s 72] Proof of document not required by law to be attested.—An attested document not required by law to be attested may be proved as if it was unattested.

COMMENT

[s 72.1] Principle.—Where the law does not require attestation for the validity of a document, it may be proved by admission or otherwise, as though no attesting witnesses existed.

[s 73] Comparison of signature, writing or seal with others admitted or proved.— In order to ascertain whether a signature, writing or seal is that of the person by whom it purports to have been written or made,[s 73.2] any signature, writing or seal admitted or proved to the satisfaction of the Court to have been written or made by that person[s 73.3] may be compared with the one which is to be proved, although that signature, writing or seal has not been produced or proved for any other purpose.

The Court may direct any person present in Court to write any words or figures[s 73.4] for the purpose of enabling the Court to compare the words or figures so written with any words or figures alleged to have been written by such person.

[308][This section applies also, with any necessary modifications, to finger impressions.]

SYNOPSIS

308. Ins. by Act 5 of 1899, section 3.

COMMENT

[s 73.1] Principle.—The provisions of this section will apply only when a matter is pending before the court and not otherwise.[309] The Court may compare the disputed signature, writing, or seal of a person with signatures, writings or seals which have been admitted or proved to the satisfaction of the court to have been made or written by that person. A Court may rely upon its own comparison of the signature, writing, or seal, unaided by expert evidence.[310] The rule of prudence is that comparison of signatures by Courts as a mode of ascertaining the truth should be used with great care and caution.[311] The dispute about the genuineness of handwriting or signature should not be decided by the court merely on the basis of its personal comparison.[312] This section does not infringe Article 20(3) of the Constitution of India.[313] Thus, it was pointed by the Bombay High Court in a case before it that where the prosecution had failed to prove that the handwriting and signature on a document were those of the accused, the court itself comparing the signature on the *vakalatnama* with the document would not constitute evidence of signature and much less of handwriting.[314] Though the court is competent to do so, it would not normally compare signature of its own.[315] The question as to whether a direction given by a court to an accused present in court to give his specimen writing and signature for the purpose of comparison under section 73 of Indian Evidence Act, 1872, infringes the fundamental right enshrined in Article 20(3) of the Constitution, has been referred to a three-judge bench of Supreme Court, in view of disagreement between the two judges constituting the Division Bench.[316]

In the case of dishonour of a cheque, the defence of the accused was that his signature on the cheque was forged. The cheque was not sent for forensic examination. The Court said that no credence could be given for comparison purposes to signature made by the accused on documents subsequent to the cheque, e.g., in this case signature on *vakalatnama* and acknowledgements card. Decision on the basis of such comparison was held to be not proper because subsequent signatures are only of self-serving value. The magistrate should have compared the signature with those available on earlier agreements and stamp paper.[317]

Two pronotes were alleged to have been executed for consideration. But neither the scribe nor the attesting witnesses cogently deposed about it. The ink used for signature was different from that used in scribing. The defendant denied execution. Evidence

---

309. *T Subbiah v Ramaswamy*, AIR 1970 Mad 85.

310. *Abdul Subhan Khan alias Khalilur-Rahman v Nusrat Ali Khan*, (1936) 12 Luck 606; *Pakala Narayana Swamy v King-Emperor*, (1937) 17 Pat 15. See *Tilakdhari v Jagat Rai*, AIR 1962 Pat 76; *Mathew Jacob v Salestine Jacob*, AIR 1998 Del 390, the Court is empowered to draw the comparison with an admitted signature.

311. *Nagappa Chendappa v Nannibu*, AIR 1960 Mys 220.

312. *Laxmi Bai v A Chandravati*, AIR 1995 Ori 131. *Ajit Savant Majagavi v State of Karnataka*, AIR 1997 SC 1255 : 1997 Cr LJ 3964 (SC), on the permissibility of this method of comparison. See generally, *Mukhtiar Singh v State*, 1997 Cr LJ 4544 (P&H).

313. *State of Bombay v Kathi Kalu*, (1961) 64 Bom LR 240 (SC).

314. *Vishwanath Mahadev Karkhania v State of Maharashtra*, 1991 Cr LJ 3146 (Bom).

315. *D Pandi v Dhanalakshmi Bank Ltd*, AIR 2001 Mad 243.

316. *Ritesh Sinha v State of UP*, (2013) 2 SCC 357.

317. *Ajithkumar v Rejinkumar*, AIR 2010 NOC 908 (Ker).

and statement were contradictory. The Court said that the comparison by experts was necessary. The comparison by the court in such circumstances was not proper.[318]

Where signature on a registered Will was disputed on the basis of a sale deed executed by the testator long back and the court rejected the prayer for sending the document to an expert and recorded a finding by itself comparing the signatures, it was held that the modality adopted by the court was improper.[319]

Signatures of the testators on the Will were disputed. The defendants produced a document which carried the undisputed signature of the testator. Neither party took any steps to have the signatures compared by an expert. It was held that comparison by the court in such circumstances was proper. The Court could do so without the assistance of any expert.[320]

Although section 73 specifically empowers the court to compare the disputed writings with the specimen or admitted writings shown to be genuine, prudence demands that the court should be extremely slow in venturing an opinion on the basis of mere comparison, particularly when the quality of evidence in respect of specimen or admitted writings is not of high standard or is not beyond doubt.[321]

Handwriting can be proved in the following ways:—

(1) By proof of signature and handwriting of the person alleged to have signed or written the document (section 67).

(2) By the opinion of an expert who can compare handwritings (section 45).[322]

(3) By a witness who is acquainted with the handwriting of a person by whom it is supposed to have been written and signed (section 47).

(4) By comparison of signature, writing or seal with others admitted or proved (section 73).

---

318. *Venkatachalam v Govindan Chettiar*, AIR 2010 NOC 698 (Mad); *VK Sridhar v CR Shankar*, AIR 2010 NOC 697 (Mad), execution of sale deed challenged only after death of a senior in the family when it was said that signature was fabricated. Challenge allowed, comparison to be made by expert, not court.

319. *Gaudiya Mission v Shobha Bose*, AIR 2008 SC 1012 : (2008) 17 SCC 714.

320. *SB Itligi v SV Salochana*, AIR 2007 NOC 424 (Kar).

321. *State of Maharashtra v Sukhdev Singh*, (1992) 3 SCC 700, 730 : 1992 SCC (Cri) 705 : AIR 1992 SC 2100. *A Neelalahtthadasan Nadar v George Mascrene*, (1994) Supp 2 SCC 619, the court did the comparison itself in a case of double voting, the Supreme Court said that it was necessary for the expeditious disposal of an election petition, but issued the advice that the court should be slow in adopting this procedure. *Tarak Nath Sha v Bhutoria Bros*, AIR 1988 Cal 31, the court should be slow to undertake the task of comparison itself. It should take the aid of an expert. *Booma Naicken v Chinna Gounde*, AIR 1998 Mad 375, thumb impression, the judge himself compared the disputed impression with the admitted impression and gave his finding. This was held to be not proper.

322. *KS Satyanaryana v VR Narayana Rao*, AIR 1999 SC 2544 : (1999) 6 SCC 104, this was a suit for recovery of amount from two defendants paid earlier as a sale consideration for property. The plaintiffs plea was that the defendant No. 1 authorised the defendant No. 2 for the purpose. But the defendant No. 1 denied his signature on any such paper as well as on *Vakalatnama* and written statement. Dismissal of the suit on this ground was held to be illegal. *Nallabothu Purnaiah v Garre Malikarjuna Rao*, AIR 2003 AP 201, the evidence of the handwriting expert was rejected by the court by reason of the fact that expert had no qualification, held, not proper because identification of handwriting being not a developed science. There was no formal qualification to be possessed. Direct and circumstantial evidence lent support to the expert opinion. Rejection of his opinion by the court was held to be not proper.

[s 73.2] "By whom it purports to have been written or made".—According to the Bombay High Court this expression means, by whom it is alleged to have been written or made.[323] The Calcutta High Court has construed it to mean that the writing which is in dispute must itself in terms express or indicate that it was written by the person to whom the writing is attributed. It has observed that the section "does not sanction the comparison of any two documents, but requires that the writing with which the comparison is to be made ... shall be admitted or proved to have been written by the person to whom it is attributed, and next the writing to be compared with the standard. must *purport* to have been written by the same person, that is to say, the writing itself must state or indicate that it was written by that person. a comparison of handwriting is at all times as a mode of proof hazardous and inconclusive, and especially when it is made by one not conversant with the subject and without such guidance as might be derived from the arguments of counsel and the evidence of experts."[324]

According to the Bombay view when an anonymous writing is produced and ascribed by the prosecution to a particular person, the case for the prosecution must be taken to be that having regard to the admitted documents, and the comparison between them and the disputed writing, the prosecution alleges that the disputed document purports to have been written or made by the accused.[325]

[s 73.3] "Signature, writing or seal admitted or proved to the satisfaction of the Court to have been written or made by that person".—Where such signature, writing or seal on a particular document is not proved or admitted to be genuine, it cannot be legitimately used for comparing it with the signature, writing or seal other documents.[326]

Specimen signatures and writings made by an accused person while he is in the custody of the police and while the police are investigating into the offence are admissible in evidence at the trial of the accused for the offence of forgery.[327]

[s 73.4] "Court may direct any person present in Court to write any words or figures".—This section limits the power of the court to direct a person present in court to write any words or figures only where the court itself is of the view that it is necessary for its own purposes to take such writing in order to compare the words or figures so written with any words or figures alleged to have been written by such person. The power does not extend to permitting one or the other party before the court to ask the court to take such writing for the purpose of its evidence or its own case.[328] The Court also cannot send such a document to an expert who is a prosecution

---

323. *Emperor v Ganpat Balkrishna,* (1912) 14 Bom LR 310. See *Mangubhai Mansukhram v Pranjivan,* AIR 1992 Guj 1, a promissory note which was proved to be in the handwriting of the dependant made him liable.

324. *Barindra Kumar Ghose v Emperor,* (1909) 37 Cal 467, 502, 503. See *Sarojini Dasi v Hari Das Ghose,* (1921) 49 Cal 235; *Khijiruddin Sonar v Emperor,* (1925) 53 Cal 372.

325. *Emperor v Ganpat Balkrishna,* (1912) 14 Bom LR 310; *Bhagirati Sahu v Akapati Bhaskar Patra,* AIR 2001 Ori 185, a suit for specific performance was based on an agreement of sale of the property in question, the defendant pleaded that the document was fabricated and that his signature was forged and, therefore, he asked for examination by a handwriting expert. The order rejecting the application was held liable to be set aside.

326. *Sri Prasad v Special Manager, Court of Wards, Balrampur Estate,* (1936) 12 Luck 400.

327. *Emperor v Ramrao Mangesh,* (1932) 56 Bom 304 : 34 Bom LR 598.

328. *Punamchand v State of MP,* (1957) 59 Bom LR 1165; *RB Khajotia v The State of Maharashtra,* (1972) 75 Bom LR 116.

witness, but it can call its own expert as a court-witness.[329] The writing obtained by the court under this section does not come within the expression "evidence".[330]

A direction to the accused to give a specimen writing can only be issued by the court holding inquiry under the Code of Criminal Procedure, 1974 or the court conducting the trial of the accused person. The person under investigation against whom no case is pending cannot be compelled to provide any specimen. The exercise of this power by anyone else, for example, as in this case, by the Tehsildar or the Executive Magistrate, will not be valid even if the accused failed to raise any objection.[331]

The words "any person present in Court" may not include an onlooker or a spectator who has come to Court for purpose of sightseeing or witnessing the proceedings in court. The words refer to persons who are parties to a "cause" pending before the court and may include the witnesses of the contesting parties in the cause.[332]

A Court can call upon the accused to give his writing in court and make it available for comparison by an expert.[333] Though, section 73 does not specifically say as to who could make such a comparison but reading section 73 as a whole, it is obvious that it is the court which has to make the comparison and it may form the opinion itself by comparing the disputed and the admitted writings or seek the assistance of an expert who will put before the court all the material, together with reasons, which induced the expert to come to a conclusion that the disputed and the admitted writings are of one and the same author so that the court may form its own opinion by its own assessment of the report of the expert based on the data furnished by the expert. The function of a handwriting expert is to express his opinion after a scientific comparison of the disputed writing with the admitted writing with regard to the points of similarity and dissimilarity in the two sets of writings.[334]

Where a person denied that he was married to the complainant and a letter supposed to have been written by him which had a bearing on the fact of marriage was also denied by him, the direction by the court requiring him to give a specimen of his handwriting was held to be proper.[335] Where in a case for enforcement of bank guarantee, the guarantor pleaded that his signature was forged, his specimen signatures which were admitted by him, were there on acknowledgement slip and summons, the court said that it was not necessary to ask him to give his specimen signature in the open Court.[336]

A person required by the court to give a specimen may refuse to do so. There is no element of compulsion in it. The only consequence of non-compliance is that the court

329. *Hiralal v State,* AIR 1958 Cal 123.

330. *Ram Swarup v The State of UP* , AIR 1958 All 119.

331. *Sukhvinder Singh v State of Punjab,* (1994) 5 SCC 152 : 1994 SCC (Cri) 1376.

332. *T Subbiah v Ramaswamy,* AIR 1970 Mad 85; *Sanjay Goel v State of UP,* 2002 Cr LJ 625 (All), the Court could compel the accused under section 164, CrPC to give his specimen handwriting to the investigating officer to enable him to get it compared with the note found at the scene of crime in which the accused confessed to his crime. Another Allahabad decision, *Guru Pal Singh v State of UP,* 2002 Cr LJ 1517 (All), is to the contrary effect. The Court said that it could not compel the accused to give his specimen writing to the police for comparison with disputed writings when the case was at the stage of investigation.

333. *State of Mysore v Gapala Rao,* (1953) Mys 697; *State v Parameswaran Pillai,* (1952) TC 447.

334. *Sukhvinder Singh v State of Punjab,* (1994) 5 SCC 152, 162, 163 : 1994 SCC (Cri) 1376.

335. *Kumaran Nair v Bhargavi,* 1988 Cr LJ 1000 Ker.

336. *New Bank of India v Sajitha Textiles,* AIR 1997 Ker 201.

is free to draw an adverse presumption under section 144.[337] Where the plaintiff refused to give his signature in court for comparison, the court refused to accept the prayer that a presumption should be drawn against him under section 114. The Court said a person could not be compelled to provide a specimen of his handwriting or signature because that would tantamount to asking him to become a witness against himself. It would be violative of Article 20(3) of the Constitution. The High Court did not accept this approach. It said that such approach can be adopted only in reference to persons accused of a crime and would not extend to parties and witnesses in a civil proceeding.[338]

The Court can direct even a stranger to the suit to write something. The son of a party was so directed in this case.[339] The Court cannot take specimen handwriting at the stage of investigation. There must be a case before it.[340]

Comparing of disputed signatures on the counter foils by the High Court judge without the aid of an expert or person conversant with disputed signatures was held to be illegal.[341] Where the trial court formed the opinion that the signature on the document in question was that of the plaintiff and, without considering any other evidence, based the decision on its own comparison, it was held that this approach was not proper.[342] Expert opinion should be obtained as a rule of prudence. The court should give cogent reasons for its conclusions.[343]

In order to secure evidentiary value to footmarks, it is not enough to show that the footmarks tally with the shoes of the accused. The evidence must go further and show that the marks have some peculiarity which is found in the shoes of the accused and will not be found in most other shoes.[344] The court cannot be told not to exercise the power under the section only because it is hazardous to do so. The court is not thereby assuming the role of an expert.[345] Chinappa Reddy J said at 537: The argument that the court should not venture to compare writings itself, as it would thereby assume to itself the role of an expert is entirely without force. Section 73 expressly enables the court to compare disputed writings with admitted or proved writings to ascertain whether the writing is that of the person by whom it purports to have been written. If it is hazardous to do so, we are afraid, it is one of the hazards to which judges and litigants must expose themselves whenever it becomes necessary. There may be cases where both sides call experts and the voices of science are heard. There are cases where neither side calls an expert, being unable to afford him. In all such cases it becomes the plain duty of the court to compare the writings and come to its own conclusion. The duty cannot

---

337. *Sashi Bhusan v S.BI,* AIR 1986 Ori 218.

338. *Shyam Sundar Chowkhani v Kajal Kanti Biswas,* AIR 1999 Gau 101.

339. *Dinanth v Sukhdeo,* AIR 1980 Pat 253.

340. *State of UP v Ram Babu Misra,* AIR 1980 SC 791 : 1980(2) SCC 343. Followed in *Harekrishna Patnaik v State of Orissa,* 1991 Cr LJ 462 (Ori), the court adding that if the specimen was taken by the investigating officer in the course of investigation, even if with some irregularities, the same can still be used.

341. *Bharathan v K Sudhakaran,* AIR 1996 SC 1140 : 1996(2) SCC 704, relying on *State (Delhi Admn.) v Pali Ram,* AIR 1979 SC 14 : 1979 Cr LJ 17.

342. *Shyam Sundar Chowkhani v Kajal Kanti Biswas,* AIR 1999 Gau 101.

343. *Ashok Kumar Uttamchand Shah v Patel Mohmad,* AIR 1999 Guj 108.

344. *Emperor v Bhika Gober,* (1943) 45 Bom LR 884 : (1944) Bom 25.

345. *Murarilal v State of MP,* AIR 1980 SC 531 at 537 : 1980 Cr LJ 396 citing *Shashi Kumar v Subodh Kumar,* AIR 1964 SC 529 and *Fakhruddin v State of MP,* AIR 1967 SC 1326 : 1967 Cr LJ 1197. where the Court itself had done the comparison.

be avoided by recourse to the statement that the court is no expert. Where there are expert opinions, they will aid the court. Where there is none, the court will have to seek guidance from some authoritative textbook and the court's own experience and knowledge. But it must, discharge the plain duty, with or without expert. We may mention that *Shashi Kumar v Subodh Kumar*[346] and *Fakhruddin v State of MP*[347] were cases where the court itself compared the writings. Section 73 does not make any difference between civil and criminal proceedings. In neither case does the section authorise the court to ask the prisoner to provide a specimen of his handwriting at the stage of investigation itself.[348]

[s 73.4.1] *Specimen handwriting of stranger.*—The Patna High Court[349] directed the defendant's son who was present in the court to give a sample of his handwriting, though he was not a party to the case. The Court said:

> The language (of the section) is wide in terms and empowers the court to give necessary directions to any person present in the Court and there does not appear to be any reason to limit the expression "any person" to parties to the litigation. If the authenticity of a writing by a stranger is necessary to be decided in a case, such a person must come within the sweep of the section. Even if the meaning of the provision be assumed to be ambiguous, the Court must construe it in a way which may advance the object of the section and the interest of justice.

[350]**[[s 73A] Proof as to verification of digital signature.—In order to ascertain whether a digital signature is that of the person by whom it purports to have been affixed, the Court may direct—**

(a) **that person or the Controller or the Certifying Authority to produce the Digital Signature Certificate;**

(b) **any other person to apply the public key listed in the Digital Signature Certificate and verify the digital signature purported to have been affixed by that person.**

***Explanation.*—For the purposes of this section, "Controller" means the Controller appointed under sub-section (1) of section 17 of the Information Technology Act, 2000].**

COMMENT

[s 73A.1] Information Technology Act, 2000—Proof of digital signature.— For the purpose of ascertaining whether a digital signature is that of the person by whom it purports to have been affixed, the court may direct that person or the controller or the certifying authority have to produce the digital signature certificate. The Court may also direct any other person to apply the public key listed in the digital signature certificate and verify the digital signature purported to have been affixed by that person. For this purpose the "controller" means the controller appointed under section 17(1) of the Information Technology Act, 2000.

---

346. *Shashi Kumar v Subodh Kumar,* AIR 1964 SC 529 : LNIND 1963 SC 402

347. *Fakhruddin v State of MP,* AIR 1967 SC 1326 : 1967 Cr LJ 1197.

348. *State of UP v Ram Babu Misra,* AIR 1980 SC 791 : (1980) 2 SCC 343. *Laxmi Shankar v Shyam Lal,* AIR 2006 All 171, comparison of signature by court on sale agreement of motor vehicles with signature on other documents and also supported by witnesses, finding of being genuine.

349. *Dinanath v Sukhdeo,* AIR 1980 Pat 253 : 1980 BJLR 398.

350. Ins. by Act 21 of 2000, section 92 and Sch. II-11 (w.e.f. 17-10-2000).

PUBLIC DOCUMENTS

[s 74] Public documents.—The following documents are public documents:—

(1) documents forming the acts or records of the acts.[s 74.1]**—**

(i) of the sovereign authority,

(ii) of official bodies and tribunals, and

(iii) of public officers, legislative, judicial and executive, [351][of any part of India or of the Commonwealth], or of a foreign country;

(2) public records kept [352][in any State] of private documents.[s 74.4]

SYNOPSIS

COMMENT

Documents are divided into two categories: public and private.

This section states what comes in the category of public documents. Section 75 states that all other documents are private.

Certain modes of proof are prescribed in regard to public documents as distinguished from private documents.

Sections 74–78 deal with (a) the nature of public documents, and (b) the proof which is to be given of them. Section 74 defines their nature; and sections 76–78 deal with the exceptional mode of proof applicable in their case. The proof of private documents is subject to the general provisions of the Act relating to the proof of documentary evidence contained in sections 71–73.

"There are several exceptions to the rule which requires primary evidence to be given.... The most important and conspicuous exception, however, is with respect to the proof of records, and other public documents of general concernment; the objection to producing which rests on the ground of *moral*, not physical inconvenience. They are, comparatively speaking, not liable to corruption, alteration, or misrepresentation—the whole community being interested in their preservation, and, in most instances, entitled to inspect them; while private writings, on the contrary, are the objects of interest but to few, whose property they are, and the inspection of them can only be obtained, if at all, by application to a court of justice. The number of persons interested in public documents also renders them much more frequently required for evidentiary

---

351. The original words "whether of British India, or of any other part of Her Majesty's dominions" have successively been amended by the A.O. 1948 and the A.O. 1950 to read as above.

352. Subs. by the A.O. 1950, for "in any province".

purposes; and if the production of the originals were insisted on, not only would great inconvenience result from the same documents being wanted in different places at the same time, but the continual change of place would expose them to be lost, and the handling from frequent use would soon ensure their destruction. For these and other reasons the law deems it better to allow their contents to be proved by derivative evidence, and to run the chance, whatever that may be, of errors arising from inaccurate transcription, either intentional or casual. But, true to its great principle of exacting the best evidence that the nature of the matter affords, the law requires this derivative evidence to be of a very trustworthy kind, and has defined, with much precision, the forms of it which may be resorted to in proof of the different sorts of public writings."[353]

Public documents form an exception to the *hearsay* rule and their admissibility rests on the ground that the facts contained therein are of public interest and the statements are made by authorised and competent agents of the public in the course of their official duty.

However, the statutory declaration that a particular document is conclusive proof of a particular fact or legal right by itself, does not oust the jurisdiction of the civil courts. The effect of such a statutory declaration is that in any enquiry regarding the existence of such fact or a legal right, Courts/tribunals are forbidden from entertaining any further evidence on such an issue the moment the document which is declared to be conclusive proof of such fact/legal rights is produced before the court or tribunal conducting such an enquiry. The ouster of the jurisdiction is altogether a different matter.[354]

[s 74.1] "Documents forming the acts or records of the acts".—"The word "acts" in the phrase "documents forming the acts or records of the acts" is used in one and the same sense. The act of which the record made in a public document must be similar in kind to the act which takes shape and form in a public document. The kind of acts which section 74 has in view is indicated by section 78. An electoral roll is a public document. It requires no formal proof. Certified copies are enough proof.[355] The acts there mentioned are all final completed acts as distinguished from acts of a preparatory or tentative character. The inquiries which a public officer may make, whether under the Code of Criminal Procedure or otherwise, may or may not result in action. There may be no publicity about them. There is a substantial distinction between such measures and the specific act in which they may result. It is to the latter only ... that section 74 was intended to refer."[356]

Statements recorded by police officers under section 161, CrPC are required by sections 115(5) and (7), read together, to be furnished to the accused. Hence all the earlier cases, before this provision was enacted in the CrPC, 1973, which regarded such statements as public documents entitled to the privilege against disclosure under section 123 of Indian Evidence Act, 1872, became out of date since then.[357]

A document which is brought into existence as a result of a survey, inquiry or inquisition carried out or held under lawful authority is not admissible in evidence as a public

---

353. *Best*, 12th Edn, sections 484, 485, pp 407-409. *Abanti Jena v Priyabada Jena*, AIR 2000 Ori 156, whenever a document of this kind (electoral roll in this case) in produced, opportunity should be given to the opposite party to lead rebuttal evidence.

354. *Achyutanand Choudhary v Luxman Mahto*, (2012) 2 SCC 76.

355. *Naladhar Mahapatra v Seva Dibya*, AIR 1991 Ori 166 : LNIND 1990 Ori 50.

356. *Queen-Empress v Arumugam*, (1897) 20 Mad 189, 197 FB.

357. *Ram Jethmalani v Director CBI*, 1987 Cr LJ 570 (Del) and the case law surveyed there.

document unless the inquiry was a judicial or quasi-judicial inquiry and the document is not only available for public inspection, but was brought into existence for that very purpose. The statements in a document tendered in evidence as a public document should be statements with regard to matters which it was the duty of the public officer holding the inquiry to inquire into and report on.[358] Records maintained by revenue officers relating to land revenue, survey and settlement, *etc.* are public documents, "*Pahanies*" and "*faisal patties*" are public documents.[359] The documents issued by the concerned Government Department indicating salary and allowances of a deceased employee, do not require corroboration or any evidence to prove them and can be received as additional evidence by the appellate court.[360] Records of a Development Authority are public documents. Certified copies of such records are admissible in evidence.[361]

A document which purports to be a letter or report of an executive official is not a public document.[362]

[s 74.1.1] ***Published Scheme under Statute.***—A scheme was published in the Official Gazette under the Electricity Supply Act, 1948. The scheme envisaged installation of overhead transmission lines. The scheme had thus become a public document. The Notification had the effect of law under the provisions of the Constitution. No adverse presumption could be drawn against a party for his failure to produce the document in the court.[363]

There is a statutory requirement under section 159 of the Companies Act, 1956 that every company having a share capital shall have to file with the Registrar of Companies an annual return which includes details of the existing Directors. The provisions of the Companies Act, 1956 require the annual return to be made available by a company for inspection (section 163) as well as section 610 which entitles any person to inspect documents kept by the Registrar of Companies. Therefore, a conjoint reading of sections 159, 163 and 610(3) of the Companies Act, 1956 read with sub-section (2) of section 74 of the Indian Evidence Act, 1872 makes it clear that a certified copy of annual return is a public document.[364]

[s 74.1.2] ***Orders of civil court, FIR, charge sheet.***—Certified copies of the orders of the civil court and FIR were allowed to be submitted because they are all public documents. They were admissible in evidence under section 77 of the Indian Evidence Act, 1872.[365] A charge sheet under section 120B, IPC, 1860 against an election candidate was held to be a public document and admissible in evidence without any proof.[366] An order of sanction for prosecution issued in the name of the Governor and authenticated by the secretary was regarded as a public document. It was held that its authenticity, if not challenged before the trial court, the same could not be challenged for the first time before the Appellate Court.[367]

---

358. *Thrasyvoulos Ioannou v Papa Christoford L Demetriou,* (1952) AC 84. A spot inspection report by a Tahsildar has been held to be not a public document. *Radhey v Board of Revenue,* AIR 1990 All 175.
359. *K Pedda Jangaiah v Mandal Revenue Officer, Moinabad,* 1996 AIHC 1006 (AP).
360. *Subhandra Kumari v Lallu Ram,* AIR 1996 Del 64.
361. *Roshan Lal Khandelwal v Dr Jagdish Chand,* AIR 2008 NOC 2043 (All).
362. *Fazl Ahmad v Crown,* (1913) PR No. 1 of 1914 (Cr).
363. *Vijay Kumar S Rajput v MC of Greater Bombay,* AIR 2000 Cal 97.
364. *Anita Malhotra v Apparel Export Promotion Council,* (2012) 1 SCC 520.
365. *Md Akbar v State of AP,* 2002 Cr LJ 3167 (AP).
366. *Kitab Singh v Deputy Commissioner,* AIR 2008 NOC 2310 (Raj).
367. *State v K Narasimhachary,* (2005) 8 SCC 364 : AIR 2006 SC 628.

Similarly, when a compromise becomes part of the decree which is passed by the court, it is a public document in terms of section 74 of the Indian Evidence Act, 1872 and certified copy of public document prepared under section 76 of the Act is admissible in evidence under section 77 of the said Act. A certified copy of a public document is admissible in evidence without being proved by calling witness.[368]

[s 74.2] Executive officer.—A school master comes within the purview of "executive officer" and a copy of a certificate given by him is admissible in evidence if properly certified.[369] The check memo which is required to be maintained by the officers in charge of the counting table is a document forming record of the acts of public officers and, therefore, a certified copy given by the collector in whose custody the document is kept can be admitted in evidence in proof of the contents of the original document.[370] The report of an officer who effected delivery of possession in the Land Restoration Register was held to be not a public document. But it happened to be admitted without objection at the trial stage having been marked as an exhibit. Its admissibility was not allowed to be challenged at any subsequent stage.[371]

[s 74.3] Marriage register.—Hindu Marriage Register has been held to be a public document. Its contents were, therefore, provable by producing certified copies.[372] Where the documentary evidence based in the official registration of marriage was produced, it was accepted as a proof of marriage for award of *interim* maintenance. The contrary evidence produced by the husband in the shape of Ration Card and the Voters' List did not show any date of marriage of the accused with any other person.[373]

A death certificate was issued by a police station. The death was not unnatural. A set of police officers, who prepared the panchanama, it could not be said of them that they did so in discharge of official duty enjoined upon them. No reasons were given for placing the matter on record. The certificate could not also be described as a part of a public record. Hence, the certificate was of weak evidentiary value. Its rejection from evidence was not improper.[374] A death certificate, though a public document, could not be accepted without considering circumstances. A decree passed against a dead person is a nullity and cannot be executed against his legal representatives.[375]

[s 74.4] "Public records kept in any state of private documents".—This clause refers to public records or original will and of registered documents.[376] According to the Bombay High Court an income-tax return is not a public document or a public record

---

368. *Jaswant Singh v Gurdev Singh,* (2012) 1 SCC 425 : 2011 (12) Scale 182.

369. *Maharaj Bhanudas v Krishnabai,* (1926) 28 Bom LR 1225, 50 Bom 716.

370. *Banamli Das v Rajendra Chandra,* AIR 1975 SC 1863 : 1976(1) SCC 54.

371. *Junul Surin v Surdas Munda,* AIR 2008 Jhar 82.

372. *Manjula v Mani,* 1998 Cr LJ 1476 (Mad).

373. *Kashi Nath Naskar v Aparupa Naskar,* 2003 Cr LJ 1201 (Cal).

374. *Hardayal v Aram Singh,* AIR 2001 MP 203. *New India Assurance Co Ltd v Krishma Sharma,* AIR 1998 Delhi 386, an insurance policy is not a public document.

375. *Nilamani Pradhan v Narottam Pradhan,* AIR 2008 Ori 185, the decree happened to be passed against a deceased person. The plea that the date of death was incorrect was raised after 15 years.

376. *Rekha Rana v Ratnashree Jain,* AIR 2006 MP 107, registered documents (deed of sale) is a private document registered in a public office. **Overruling** *Nawab Saheb v Firoz Ahmed,* (2002) 5 MPLJ 438 : 2003 AIHC 544. *Hussaini Mahto v Hulash Mahto,* AIR 2006 Jhar 87, certified copy of registered sale deed produced by way of additional evidence, held, admissible without further proof, the sale deed was not challenged.

of a private document.[377] Similarly, the Calcutta High Court has held that certified copies of assessment or dues and order sheets are inadmissible in evidence.[378] The Madras High Court has held that an income-tax return or a statement filed in support of it is a public document and certified copies will be admissible under section 65(c).[379] Memorandum of Association of a company is a public document within the meaning of this section.[380] Electoral roll prepared under the Representation of the People Act, 1951 is a public document.[381] A plaint or a written statement filed in a case is not a public document.[382] An agreement between a Maharaja and Government setting up a Gurudwara as a public trust and the Government setting a scheme of constituting a Temples' Board of Management including the Gurudwara, is a part of public records—a public document and, therefore, needs no formal proof.[383] So is true of a wakf deed[384] and a sale deed[385] which are private documents but are recorded with the sub-registrar.

In a case of this kind, a Division Bench of the Gauhati High[386] Court explained the status of such documents in these words: "Public records are those records which a Government unit is required by law to keep or which it is necessary to keep in discharge of duties imposed by law. A public record is one required by law to be kept, or necessary to be kept in the discharge of a duty imposed by law, or directed by law to serve as a memorial and evidence of something written, said or done. Therefore, a private document would be a "public record" within the meaning of section 74(2) if the private document is filed and the public official is required to keep it for a memorial or permanent evidence of something written, said or done."

The Gauhati High Court has held that a registered power of attorney is not a public document and, therefore, a certified copy cannot be admitted as equivalent to primary evidence. It would rank as secondary evidence and would be admissible only when any of the categories of admissibility under section 65 is proved to be available.[387] Explaining the reason, the court said in the above case that the Registration Act, 1908 provides for registration of documents and the method of registration is that the contents of documents are copies in a book maintained in the office of the sub-Registrar which is commonly called the "Volume Book". Thus, the book contains only copies of documents and not original documents. Documents so registered do not become

---

377. *Devidatt v Shriram,* (1931) 34 Bom LR 236, 56 Bom 324. Same is the view of the Rangoon High Court: *Anwar Ali v Tafozal Ahmed,* (1924) 2 Ran 391.

378. *Pramatha Nath Pramanik v Nirode Chandra Ghosh,* (1939) 2 Cal 394.

379. *Rama Rao v Venkataramayya,* (1940) Mad 969 FB.

380. *Binani Properties v GA Hossein & Co,* AIR 1967 Cal 390.

381. *Kirtan v Thakur,* AIR 1972 Ori 158.

382. *Gulab Chand v Sheo Karan Lall,* AIR 1964 Pat 45. But for a contrary view see *Jagdishchandra v State of Gujarat,* 1989 Cr LJ 1724 (Guj). *Bawa Singh v Harnam Singh,* AIR 2008 NOC 2574 (P&H), certified copy of written statement filed by plaintiff in earlier suit, not admissible in evidence *per se.* Those who signed them or made them would have to appear to be examined. *Shamlata v Visheshwara Tukaram Giripuriji,* AIR 2008 Bom 155, certificate copy of a plaint is not a public document. It requires proof.

383. *Kabul Singh v Ram Singh,* AIR 1986 All 75.

384. *Fazal Sheikh v Abdur Rahman,* AIR 1991 Gau 17.

385. *Jagdishchandra v State of Gujarat,* 1989 Cr LJ 1724 (Guj).

386. *Narattam Das v Md. Masadharali,* (1991) 1 Gau LR 197 (DB).

387. *Bidhan Paul v Paresh Chandra Ghose,* AIR 2002 Gau 46.

public documents. Only those public records which keep private documents and not copies of private documents are treated as public documents.[388]

A registered document has a lot of sanctity attached to it. Such sanctity can be demolished only by following proper procedure. The mere filing of a complaint against a registered power of attorney holder was held to be not sufficient to revoke the power of attorney.[389] A girl was rescued from flesh trade. She was prosecuted under the Immoral Traffic (Prevention) Act, 1956. The question was of her age. The police produced public documents showing her age. It was held that everything else, like statement in FIR, medical documents or even her supplementary affidavit would have to give way to the public record.[390]

[s 74.5] Sale/Lease deed.—A sale deed or a lease deed is undoubtedly a private document, but once it is registered and entered in the Book-I of the Registering Officer, the records maintained by such Registering Officer becomes a public document.[391]

[s 74.6] Medico-legal report.—In a medico-legal case, the medical officer prepares the (MLC) report as a public servant in discharge of his duties and the (MLC) report is a public document, the contents of which are admissible in evidence.[392] Neither the post-mortem report nor any certificate issued by the doctor regarding the date of death, is a public document and they must be proved by the doctor concerned.[393]

The document furnished to the Press Council of India by organisations in order to substantiate their claims to be recognised by the Press Council, are public documents and are open to inspection.[394]

[s 74.6.1] *School register.*—The age of the accused had to be determined for the purposes of the Juvenile Justice Act, 1986. There was a concurrent finding of courts below that he was of the age between 19 and 20 years and, therefore, not a juvenile. This finding was based upon the report of the Medical Board. The doctor who examined the accused was not produced as a witness. The school leaving certificate showed the age to be 15 years. No evidence was produced to show that the certificate was wrong. The school records could not be doubted for the fact that the admission register was not signed by the father of the accused.[395] A school leaving certificate is a document which falls within the ambit of section 74. It is admissible in evidence *per se* without the need for any formal proof.

[s 74.6.2] *Records of nationalised banks.*—Records of nationalised banks have been taken to be in the category of public documents. They are, therefore, admissible

---

388. The court referred to the following authorities, *Narattam Das v Md Masadharali Haribhuiyan,* (1991) 1 Gau LR 197 (DB) **overruling** the decision in *Md. Saimuddin Sheikh v Abejuddin Sheikh,* AIR 1979 Gau 14; *Manindra Kumar Dey v Mahendra Sukla Baidya,* (1999) 2 Gau LR 219 : AIR 1999 HC 2147. *State of Haryana v Ram Singh,* AIR 2001 SC 2532, certified copy of a registered sale deed of immovable property admitted in evidence for proving comparative land value without examining the parties to the document.

389. *Shanti Budhiya Vesta Patel v Nirmala Jayprakash Tiwari,* AIR 2010 SC 2132 : (2010) 5 SCC 104.

390. *State of Maharashtra v Mohd Sajid Hussain,* AIR 2008 SC 155 : (2008) 1 SCC 213.

391. *Gopinath Educational and Welfare Society v Rejendra Singh Shekhawat* , AIR 2016 Raj 106, para 12. See also *Hemlata Devi v Ramautar Sao,* 2016 AIR CC 686, para 15 (Jhar).

392. *Dalip Kumar v State,* 1995 Cr LJ 1742 (Del).

393. *State v Bhola Pal,* 1995 Cr LJ 3717 (Cal).

394. *Indian Federation of S. & M Newspapers v Press Council of India,* AIR 1996 Del 90.

395. *Prem Chand Sao v State of Jharkhand,* 2003 Cr LJ NOC 66 (Jhar).

without further proof. The examination of the person who prepared the document which is being offered in evidence is not necessary.[396]

[s 75] Private documents.—All other documents are private.

COMMENT

Documents which are not public documents are private documents, *e.g.*, contracts, leases, mortgage-deeds, *etc.*

[s 76] Certified copies of public documents.—Every public officer having the custody of a public document, which any person has a right to inspect, shall give that person on demand a copy of it on payment of the legal fees therefor, together with a certificate written at the foot of such copy that it is a true copy of such document or part thereof, as the case may be, and such certificate shall be dated and subscribed by such officer with his name and his official title, and shall be sealed, whenever such officer is authorised by law to make use of a seal, and such copies so certified shall be called certified copies.

***Explanation.*—Any officer who, by the ordinary course of official duty, is authorised to deliver such copies, shall be deemed to have the custody of such documents within the meaning of this section.**

COMMENT

This section provides the means of proof of public documents which any person has a right to inspect. There is a common law right of a person to take inspection of a document in which that person is interested for the protection of such interest.[397] The person claiming interest in the specified land cannot be refused certified copies of "*pahanies*" and "*faisal patties*" on the ground that the land in question is classified in the revenue records as Government land.[398]

The section requires that a copy of a public document given by a public officer should bear a certificate written at the foot of such copy that it is a true copy of such document. Where a copy bears no certificate and it is not supported by the evidence of the person who prepared it, it is not admissible in evidence.[399] But a carbon copy of the court order issued in official process but not marked as "true copy" was allowed in evidence.[400]

When a compromise becomes part of the decree which is passed by the court, it is a public document in terms of section 74 of the Evidence Act, 1872 and certified copy of public document prepared under section 76 of the Act is admissible in evidence under section 77 of the said Act. A certified copy of a public document is admissible in evidence without being proved by calling witness.[401]

---

396. *Gorantla Venkateshwarlu v B Demudu,* AIR 2003 AP 251 : 2003 (2) Andh LD 648.

397. *Shamdasani v Sir Hugh Cocke,* (1941) 43 Bom LR 961 : (1942) Bom 71.

398. *K Pedda Jangaiah v Mandal Revenue Officer, Moinabad,* 1996 AIHC 1006 (AP).

399. *Khadim Ali v Jagannath,* (1940) 16 Luck 230.

400. *Thatha v Peru,* AIR 1986 Ker 196. *Democratic Bar Assn, Allahabad v High Court, Allahabad,* AIR 2000 All 300, recommendation of screening committee, which was not a public document.

401. *Jaswant Singh v Gurdev Singh,* (2012) 1 SCC 425.

[s 76.1] ***Corrupt Practice in Election Speeches.***—An election petition alleged corrupt practice. It was alleged that the returned candidate had resorted to communal appeals. A certified copy of a cassette of video recording of the speeches was alleged to have been obtained by the petitioner from the office of the Election Commission. The court said that the mere fact of obtaining from the office of the Election Commission was not sufficient to show that the receipt was issued against payment made by the petitioner for obtaining a certified copy.[402]

[s 77] **Proof of documents by production of certified copies.—Such certified copies may be produced in proof of the contents of the public documents or parts of the public documents of which they purport to be copies.**

COMMENT

In reference to a claim for compensation before the Accident Claims Tribunal, the Rajasthan High Court held that the Tribunal has to follow summary procedure without insisting upon strict compliance of the provisions of the Evidence Act. The court said that certified copies of the FIR, inspection map, site inspection memo, panchanama, injury report or post mortem report and other relevant documents produced by police officer or doctor while discharging official duties should have been admitted in evidence without any formal proof.[403]

Even a compromise becomes part of the decree which is passed by the court, it is a public document in terms of section 74 of the Evidence Act, 1872 and certified copy of public document prepared under section 76 of the Act is admissible in evidence under section 77 of the said Act. A certified copy of a public document is admissible in evidence without being proved by calling witness.[404]

In a compensation claim for land acquisition, comparable sales method was adopted for working out the compensation amount. It was held that certified copy of a registered agreement of sale was admissible without examining the parties to the document.[405]

It has been held that *Khasra* (Revenue Record) is a public document. A mere production of a copy of the record would be sufficient for its proof under section 77. But a certificate given by the *Patwari* (village record keeper), being a private document, it has to be proved by examining the *Patwari*.[406]

A birth certificate issued by the appropriate Municipal Authority is an ultimate document for proof of date of birth. It carries presumption as to its genuineness and is admissible in evidence. The presumption holds good unless rebutted. Different handwriting in date of birth and name of child born can be explained. That by itself does not make the record suspicious or fabricated.[407]

---

402. *Tukaram S. Dighole v Manikrao Shivajee Kokate,* AIR 2008 NOC 1767 (Bom).
403. *Rajasthan State Road Transport Corpn. v Nand Kishore,* AIR 2001 Raj 334.
404. *Jaswant Singh v Gurdev Singh,* (2012) 1 SCC 425.
405. *State of Haryana v Ram Singh,* AIR 2001 SC 2532.
406. *Badri Prasad v State of MP,* AIR 2010 NOC 937 (MP).
407. *Vasudha Gorakmati Mandvikar v City and Industrial Development Corp of Maharashtra,* AIR 2008 NOC 2572 (Bom).

[s 77.1] ***Marriage Certificate.***—The registration of a marriage cannot be proof of a valid marriage *per se* and is also not a determinative factor regarding validity of a marriage. But it has a great evidentiary value in family matters. This is shown by the fact that a marriage can be denied where it is not registered nor otherwise ceremonially performed.[408]

[s 78] Proof of other official documents.—The following public documents may be proved as follows:—

(1) Acts, orders or notifications of [409][the Central Government] in any of its departments, [410][or of the Crown Representative] or of any State Government or any department of any State Government,—

by the records of the departments, certified by the heads of those departments respectively,

or by any document purporting to be printed by order of any such Government [410][or, as the case may be, of the Crown Representative];

(2) the proceedings of the Legislatures,—

by the journals of those bodies respectively, or by published Acts or abstracts, or by copies purporting to be printed [411][by order of the Government concerned];

(3) proclamations, orders or regulations issued by Her Majesty or by the Privy Council, or by any department of Her Majesty's Government,—

by copies or extracts contained in the London Gazette, or purporting to be printed by the Queen's Printer;

(4) the Acts of the Executive or the proceedings of the Legislature of a foreign country,—

by journals published by their authority, or commonly received in that country as such, or by a copy certified under the seal of the country or sovereign, or by a recognition thereof in some [412][Central Act];

(5) the proceedings of a municipal body in [413][a State],—

by a copy of such proceedings, certified by the legal keeper thereof, or by a printed book purporting to be published by the authority of such body;

(6) public documents of any other class in a foreign country,—

by the original, or by a copy certified by the legal keeper thereof, with a certificate under the seal of a notary public, or of [414][an Indian Consul] or diplomatic agent, that the copy is duly certified by the officer having the legal custody of the original, and upon proof of the character of the document according to the law of the foreign country.

---

408. *Seema v Ashwani Kumar,* (2006) 2 SCC 578 : AIR 2006 SC 1158 : (2006) 101 Cut LT 639 : (2006) 127 DLT 282 : (2006) 1 KLT 791.

409. Subs. by the A.O. 1937, for "the Executive Government of British India".

410. Ins. by the A.O. 1937.

411. Subs. by the A.O. 1937, for "by order of Government".

412. Subs. by the A.O. 1937, for "public Act of the Governor General of India in Council".

413. Subs. by the A.O. 1950, for "a Province".

414. Subs. by the A.O. 1950, for "a British Consul".

[s 78.1] STATE AMENDMENTS

West Bengal.—*New s. 78A, inserted by W.B. Act No. 20 of 1960, s. 3 (w.e.f. 5-1- 1961).*

"78-A. Copies of public documents, to be as good as original documents in certain cases.—Notwithstanding anything contained in this Act or any other law for the time being in force, where any public documents concerning any areas within West Bengal have been kept in Pakistan, then copies of such public documents shall, on being authenticated in such manner as may be prescribed from time to time by the State Government by notification in the Official Gazette, be deemed to have taken the place of, and to be, the original documents from which such copies were made and all references to the original documents shall be construed as including references to such copies".

COMMENT

This section specifies the various ways in which the contents of a public document can be proved.

The word "may" is used only as denoting a mode of proof other than the ordinary one, namely, the production of the original. For, when the original is a public document within the meaning of section 74, a certified copy of the document, but no other kind of secondary evidence, is admissible.[415]

This section does not appear to have the effect of absolving the parties from any rules governing the proof of the facts on which they desire to rely. It is to be observed that the section does not say how any fact, historical or otherwise, is to be proved by the parties, but gives the court liberty to resort for its aid to appropriate books or documents of reference on matters of public history.[416] The proceedings of Parliament may be proved under clause (2) by the Journals of the House of Commons or by copies purporting to be printed by order of the Government.[417] A carbon copy of a court order issued by official process, but not marked as "true copy" has been regarded as good evidence.[418] Cyclostyled copy of typed notification attested by Divisional Forest Officer is not an "authenticated copy" of the notification as a proof of a particular forest being a reserved one. In making an act of authentication, the officer who makes it, is to declare his authority to do so.[419] The landlord refused to receive the money sent by the tenant by money order. The post office issued a letter showing refusal. The letter is based on a public record and, therefore, relevant.[420] A copy of the post mortem report can be received in evidence for the purposes of a claim under the Motor Vehicles Act without calling the doctor.[421]

The Exhibit was a photostat copy of the passport and the same was an inadmissible document as it was not authenticated by the legal keeper as provided under section 78(6) of the Evidence Act. Based on such inadmissible document, it was argued on behalf of the accused that no prosecution could be launched and once it was to be held that

415. *Jagdishchandra v State of Gujarat,* 1989 Cr LJ 1724 (Guj), proof of registered sale deed and plaint filed in court by certified copies.

416. *"The Englishman" Ltd v Lajpat Rai,* (1910) 37 Cal 760.

417. *Ibid*

418. *Thatha v Peru,* AIR 1986 Ker 196 : 1985 Ker LT 1069.

419. *Chandra Naik v State of Orissa,* 1993 Cr LJ 2128 (Ori).

420. *Shiv Narain v Nag & Co,* AIR 1982 All 44.

421. *Raj SRTC v Devilal,* AIR 1991 Raj 29.

the said document was not admissible, the whole case of the prosecution collapsed like a pack of cards. The Supreme Court upheld the conclusion of the High Court that section 78(6) of the Indian Evidence Act, 1872 deals with public documents of any other class in a foreign country. In the present case, the original of Ext. P-50 is the passport issued by the competent authorities in this country and, therefore, section 78(6) has no application whatsoever to the facts of this case. The issuance of original of Ext. P-50, passport is clearly proved. It is based on that passport that the accused travelled abroad and entered Portugal for which she had to face a prosecution and suffer conviction and sentence. Accordingly, it was held that the prosecution cannot be held to be vitiated.[422]

The Calcutta High Court has held that a court is not bound to have recourse exclusively to the mode of proof in respect of public documents set out in this section. This is a permissive and not an exclusive section.[423] On a point of limitation it adopted the version contained in the published Act and not that contained in the Gazette.[424] The Lahore High Court has, on the other hand, held that the text published in the Gazette must be taken to be the authorized text of the Limitation Act, 1963, under clause (2) of this section.[425] Newspapers are not documents within the meaning of this section. Hence the privilege given by this section is not enjoyed by facts reported in a newspaper.[426]

PRESUMPTIONS AS TO DOCUMENTS

[s 79] Presumption as to genuineness of certified copies.—The Court shall presume [427][to be genuine] every document purporting to be a certificate, certified copy or other document, which is by law declared to be admissible as evidence of any particular fact and which purports to be duly certified by any officer [428][of the Central Government or of a State Government, or by any [429][officer in the State of Jammu and Kashmir] who is duly authorised thereto by the Central Government]:

Provided **that such document is substantially in the form and purports to be executed in the manner directed by law in that behalf.**

The Court shall also presume that any officer by whom any such document purports to be signed or certified, held, when he signed it, the official character which he claims in such paper.

SYNOPSIS

COMMENT

Sections 79–90 deal with certain presumptions as to documents.

---

422. *Monica Bedi v State of AP*, (2011) 1 SCC 284.

423. *Seodayal Khemka v Joharmull Manmull*, (1923) 50 Cal 549, 560.

424. *Ibid*

425. *Gobind Das v Rup Kishore*, (1923) 4 Lah 367; *Mathuradas v State*, (1954) Nag 578.

426. *Luxmi Raj Shetty v State of TN*, AIR 1988 SC 1274 : 1988 Cr LJ 1783. Newspaper report supported by documentary evidence, admitted, *Pvt Bus Operator Welfare Society v State of HP*, AIR 2016 NOC 138 (HP).

427. Ins. by the A.O. 1948.

428. The original word beginning from "in British India" and ending with the words "to be genuine" have been successively amended by the A.O. 1937, A.O. 1948 and A.O. 1950 to read as above.

429. Subs. by Act 3 of 1951, section 3 and Schedule, for "in a Part B State".

This section proceeds upon the maxim *omnia proesumuntur rite esse acta* (all acts are presumed to be rightly done). In fact all the following sections down to section 90 inclusive, are illustrations of, and founded upon, this principle. But though the courts are directed to draw a presumption in favour of official certificates, it is not a conclusive presumption; it is rebuttable. It is but a *prima facie* presumption, and if the certificate, *etc.* be not correct, its incorrectness may be shown. On the same maxim stands the last clause of this section. It is very old law that where a person acts in an official capacity it shall be presumed that he was duly appointed.[430]

This section applies to certificates, certified copies or other documents which are duly certified by an officer of the Central Government or of a State Government or by an officer in the State of Jammu and Kashmir who is authorised by the Central Government in that behalf, to be genuine. The section has also been held to apply to a carbon copy of a court order issued in official process though not certified as "true copy".[431]

Under this section a court is bound to draw the presumption that a certified copy of a document is genuine and also that the officer signed it in the official character which he claimed in the said document;[432] but if the original of a public document is sought to be tendered in evidence it must be proved in the manner required by law as any other document required to be proved under sections 67 and 68 of the Act.[433] This presumption is liable to be rebutted. This section imperatively directs the court to raise a presumption. The terms of section 114 are only permissive. The words "shall presume" indicate that if no other evidence is given the court is bound to find that the facts mentioned in the section exist. They occur in sections 79–85 and section 89. These sections are, therefore, mandatory.

[s 79.1] Presumption as to signing authority—*[Clause 2]*.—Where a letter purporting to be issued from the Chief Secretary to the Government of Bengal was signed by a Deputy Secretary, not in his official capacity, but "for the Chief Secretary," it was held that there was no legal proof that the Local Government had ordered or authorized a prosecution under section 196 of the Code of Criminal Procedure. The presumption under this section would have arisen if the letter had been signed by the Chief Secretary himself.[434]

[s 79.2] CASES.—In a suit for permanent injunction, the certified copy of the *Khasra* entry made by the Patwari showing the defendant as sub-tenant could not be presumed to be correct as no evidence was adduced to prove that entry and the Patwari who made the entry was not examined.[435] A certified copy of a registered sale deed is admissible in evidence without examining the vendors or vendees as witnesses.[436]

---

430. Norton, 260-261.

431. *Thatha v Peru,* AIR 1986 Ker 196.

432. *Binka v Charan Singh,* AIR 1959 SC 960 : 1959 Cr LJ 1223.

433. *CH Shah v Malpathak,* (1971) 74 Bom LR 505.

434. *Oziullah v Beni Madhab Chowdhuri,* (1922) 50 Cal 135.

435. *Sitaram v Ram Charan,* AIR 1995 MP 134.

436. *Tata Chemicals Ltd, Bombay v Sadhu Singh,* AIR 1994 All 66, **distinguishing** *Collector Kamrup v Prabati Phukhan,* AIR 1973 Gau 114; *Mohamedbhai Rasulbhai Malek v Amirbhai Rahimbhai Malek,* AIR 2001 Guj 37, certified copies of a judgment were produced in evidence, the copy did not bear signature of the judge, the final portion of the judgment was also missing, date of the judgment was also not appearing on the copy, held inadmissible in evidence, being incomplete.

[s 80] Presumption as to documents produced as record of evidence.—Whenever any document is produced before any Court, purporting to be a record or memorandum of the evidence, or of any part of the evidence, given by a witness in a judicial proceeding[s 80.1] or before any officer authorized by law to take such evidence or to be a statement or confession by any prisoner or accused person, taken in accordance with law, and purporting to be signed by any Judge or Magistrate,[s 80.2] or by any such officer as aforesaid, the Court shall presume—

that the document is genuine; that any statements as to the circumstances under which it was taken, purporting to be made by the person signing it, are true, and that such evidence, statement or confession was duly taken.

SYNOPSIS

COMMENT

The presumptions to be raised under this section are considerably wider than those under section 79. They embrace not only the genuineness of the document, but that it was duly taken and given under the circumstances recorded in the document. The presumptions under this section are not conclusive; they may be rebutted.

The section is applicable (a) to a document which purports to be a record or memorandum of the evidence given by a witness in a judicial proceeding or before any official authorised by law to take such evidence and (b) to a statement or confession by an accused person, taken in accordance with law, and signed by any Judge or Magistrate.

The section dispenses with the necessity for formal proof in the case of certain documents taken in accordance with law. If a document has not been taken in accordance with law, this section does not operate to render it admissible. The section merely gives legal sanction to the maxim "*Omnia praesumuntur rite esse acta*" with regard to documents taken in the course of a judicial proceeding.[437] The depositions and statements may be proved by the production of the document without any witness being called to prove it.[438] Where, for instance, a confession is reduced to writing by a Magistrate in accordance with the provisions of the Code of Criminal Procedure, the record is admissible in evidence without further proof.[439] The court will presume that a confession was duly recorded and that the circumstances under which the confession was recorded were such as had been set down in the record made by the Magistrate. It says nothing about there being any presumption regarding the voluntariness of the confession.[440] Statements in writing made soon after the incident are far more trustworthy than later denials or embellishments. Such statements are admissible in evidence and presumption of genuineness under section 80 attaches to such statements.[441] A dying declaration, which has been recorded

437. *Queen-Empress v Viran,* (1886) 9 Mad 224, 227. **See** *Hashim v The Empress,* (1900) PR No. 9 of 1900 (Cr).
438. *Emperor v Surajbali,* (1933) 56 All 750.
439. *Kheman v Crown,* (1924) 6 Lah 58; *Nga San Baw v The Crown,* (1902) 1 LBR 340 FB
440. *Emperor v Thakur Das Malo,* (1943) 1 Cal 487.
441. *Ramchit Rajbhar v State of WB,* 1992 Cr LJ 372 (Cal).

by a Magistrate, can be tendered in evidence without the Magistrate who recorded it being called.[442] When a deposition is taken in open Court or a confession is taken by a Magistrate, there is a degree of publicity and solemnity, which affords a sufficient guarantee for the presumption that everything was formally, correctly and honestly done.

[s 80.1] "Evidence ... given by a witness in a judicial proceeding".—See section 33. This section will not apply to any statement failing to satisfy the provisions of section 33.

A deposition given by a person is not admissible in evidence against him in a subsequent proceeding without it being first proved that he was the person examined and giving the deposition. A pardon was tendered to an accused, and his evidence was recorded by a Magistrate. Subsequently the pardon was revoked, and he was put on trial before the Sessions judge along with the other accused. At the trial the deposition given by him before the Magistrate was put in and used in evidence against him without any proof being given that he was the person who was examined as a witness before the Magistrate. It was held that the deposition was inadmissible without proof being given as to the identity of the accused with the person who was examined as a witness before the Magistrate.[443]

[s 80.2] "Taken in accordance with law, and purporting to be signed by any Judge or Magistrate".—If particular provisions of law in recording evidence are not fully complied with, this section does not operate. Thus, omission to read over to a witness his deposition, in accordance with O XVIII, rule 5, of the Code of Civil Procedure, renders the same inadmissible in evidence against him on his subsequent trial for perjury.[444] Where a confession, made before a Magistrate, did not bear his certificate, stating his belief that it was freely and voluntarily made, as required by section 164(3) of the Code of Criminal Procedure, it was held that it could not be admitted under this section without proof of its having been so made.[445]

By virtue of the provision in this section, statements recorded under section 164, CrPC are presumed to be genuine, but not a guarantee of truth.[446]

A confession made by an accused before a Magistrate in a former Indian State cannot be admitted in evidence under this section. The Magistrate recording the confession must be examined to prove all the confession before it can be used as evidence.[447] Where such is not the case, it is not necessary that the recorder of a confession should always be examined.[448]

[s 81] Presumption as to Gazettes, newspapers, private Acts of Parliament and other documents.—The Court shall presume the genuineness of every document

442. *Emperor v Surajbali*, (1933) 56 All 750.
443. *Queen-Empress v Durga Sonar*, (1885) 11 Cal 580.
444. *Emperor v Nabab Ali Sarkar*, (1923) 51 Cal 236, **following** *Jyotish Chandra Mukerjee v Emperor*, (1909) 36 Cal 955, and *Emperor v Jogendra Nath Ghose*, (1914) 42 Cal 240, **distinguishing** *Ramesh Chandra Das v Emperor*, (1919) 46 Cal 895, and **disapproving** *Elahi Baksh Kazi v Emperor*, (1918) 45 Cal 825.
445. *The Emperor v Radhe Halwai*, (1902) 7 Cal WN 220. See *Nadir v The Empress*, (1887) PR No. 36 of 1887 (Cr).
446. *Ramchit Rajbhar v State of WB*, 1992 Cr LJ 372 (Cal), statement of the prosecutrix who was the victim of a rape not recorded under section 164 CrPC, this did not detract from her testimony which was otherwise without any embellishment.
447. *Emperor v Dhanka Amra*, (1914) 16 Bom LR 261.
448. *Guja Majhi v The King-Emperor*, (1917) 2 PLJ 80.

purporting to be the London Gazette or [449][any Official Gazette, or the Government Gazette] of any colony, dependency of possession of the British Crown, or to be a newspaper or journal, or to be a copy of a private Act of Parliament [450][of the United Kingdom] printed by the Queen's Printer and of every document purporting to be a document directed by any law to be kept by any person, if such document is kept substantially in the form required by law and is produced from proper custody.

COMMENT

[s 81.1] Principle.—Government Gazettes or newspapers or journals or copies of private Acts of Parliament printed by the King's Printer are *prima facie* proof of their genuineness.

As to the meaning of the expression "proper custody", see the Explanation to section 90, *infra.*

As to the relevancy of statements in a Gazette, see section 37, and the Supreme Court decision in *Vimla Bai v Hiralal Gupta.*[451]

The second part of this section includes most of the documents which contain matters referred to in section 35 and which are declared to be public documents by section 74. Genuineness of the Gazette of Bombay Presidency published in 1879 was presumed. So far as the statements recorded showed the historical material on the matter in dispute, namely whether the temple in question which was of ancient origin was a public trust, it was considered to be an expert evidence under section 45 and also evidence from a public record under section 35.[452] A clause in a Government contract providing for arbitration was deleted and a notification to that effect was published in the Official Gazette. The court said that it attracted the presumption under section 23(5) of the General Clauses Act, 1897 and section 81 of the Evidence Act. It became binding on the parties in respect of their commercial transactions with the Government.[453] Statements contained in the Gazetteer can be taken into account to discover historical material contained in it. Facts stated in it are evidence under section 81.[454]

In the case of carriage of goods by sea the bill of lading is evidence to establish the fact that the goods were actually put on Board by the master of the ship. Unless proved otherwise, the contents of and details mentioned in the bill of lading are presumed to be true.[455]

[s 81.1.1] ***Newspaper reports.***—The presumption of genuineness attached under this section to a newspaper cannot be treated as proof of the facts reported therein, and the statement of a fact contained in a newspaper is merely hearsay and, therefore,

---

449. Subs. by A.O. 1937, for "the Gazette of India or the Government Gazette of any L.G., or".
450. Ins. by the A.O. 1950.
451. *Vimla Bai v Hiralal Gupta,* (1990) 2 SCC 22 : 1989 Supp (2) SCR 759, on the value of the statements in the Gazette of Indore relating to a certain migration. For full statement see under section 37.
452. *Bala Shankar Maha Shankar v Charity Commissioner, Gujarat State,* AIR 1995 SC 167 : 1995 Supp (1) SCC 485 : 1995 Supp (1) SCC 485 : (1995) 1 Guj LR 711.
453. *Shambhu Sharma v State of Bihar,* AIR 2009 Pat 161.
454. *Pattakal Cheriyakoya v Aliyathammuda B Muthunoya,* AIR 2008 Ker 1421 DB.
455. *SK Networks Co Ltd v Amulya Exports Ltd,* AIR 2007 Bom 15.

inadmissible in evidence.[456] The translated copies of the news item cannot be considered by the court as a document in the absence of the original newspaper. The newspaper as a whole must be filed before the court.[457]

Matters published in newspapers are not admissible in themselves.[458] The presumption of genuineness cannot be treated as a proof of the facts stated in the newspaper report. Such a statement of facts is only a hearsay.[459]

[460][s 81A] Presumption as to Gazettes in electronic forms.—The Court shall presume the genuineness of every electronic record purporting to be the Official Gazette or purporting to be electronic record directed by any law to be kept by any person, if such electronic record is kept substantially in the form required by law and is produced from proper custody.]

COMMENT

[s 81A.1] Information Technology Act, 2000—Presumption as to Gazettes in electronic form.—The court has to presume the genuineness of any electronic record purporting to be the Official Gazette or purporting to be the electronic record directed by law to be kept by a person. It is necessary that the electronic record is substantially kept in accordance with the form required by the law and is produced from proper custody.

[s 82] Presumption as to document admissible in England without proof of seal or signature.—When any document is produced before any Court, purporting to be a document which, by the law in force for the time being in England or Ireland, would be admissible in proof of any particular in any Court of Justice in England or Ireland, without proof of the seal or stamp or signature authenticating it, or of the judicial or official character claimed by the person by whom it purports to be signed, the Court shall presume that such seal, stamp or signature is genuine, and that the person signing it held, at the time when he signed it, the judicial or official character which he claims, and the document shall be admissible for the same purpose for which it would be admissible in England or Ireland.

COMMENT

This section enables the courts to recognise presumptions with regard to certain classes of documents which are recognised in English Courts. The court must presume (a) that the seal or stamp or signature is genuine; and (b) that the person signing the document held, at the time when he signed, the judicial or official character he claims.

---

456. *Harbhajan Singh v State of Punjab,* AIR 1961 Punj 215; *Luxmi Raj Shetty v State of Tamil Nadu,* AIR 1988 SC 1274 : 1988 Cr LJ 1783, where the court ruled out newspaper reports as against direct evidence substantiating the prosecution case. *Ramswaroop Bagari v State of Rajasthan,* AIR 2002 Raj 27, newspaper report not allowed to be the basis of filing a petition. Statement of facts in a newspaper is merely hearsay. It is inadmissible in evidence. The court followed the above cited decision.
457. *Binod Kumar Jain v Gauhati Municipal Corp,* AIR 1994 Gau 96. *Tulsi v Besar,* AIR 2002 HP 12, the possession of the plaintiff was shown to be recorded as co-sharer in *Khasra Girdwari* and *Jamabandi,* presumption of correctness attached to the entry, not rebutted, plaintiff was entitled to the injunction in respect of his possession. *B Singh (Dr) v UOI,* AIR 2004 SC 1923 : (2004) 3 SCC 363, newspaper reports do not *per se* constitute legally acceptable evidence.
458. *Krishnamma v Govt of Tamil Nadu,* 1999 Cr LJ 1915 (Mad).
459. *Ravinder Kumar Sharma v State of Assam,* AIR 1999 SC 3571 : (1999) 7 SCC 435.
460. Ins. by Act 21 of 2000, section 92 and Sch. II-12 (w.e.f. 17-10-2000)

Documents which, without proof of the seal or signature, or of the official character of the person by whom they purport to have been signed, are admissible in England, will be admissible in courts in India.

[s 83] Presumption as to maps or plans made by authority of Government.—The Court shall presume that maps or plans purporting to be made by the authority of [461][the Central Government or any State Government] were so made, and are accurate; but maps or plans made for the purposes of any cause must be proved to be accurate.

COMMENT

The presumption as to accuracy is limited only to maps or plans made under the authority of Government.[462] Such maps or plans contain the results of inquiries made under competent public authority. In all other cases proof of accuracy is needed. Where maps are prepared by private persons no presumption in favour of accuracy can be drawn under this section.[463] This section must be read with section 36, which deals with statements in maps, charts and plans. These are provable under Sections 77 and 79 by the production of certified copies.

Maps and surveys made in India for revenue purposes are official documents prepared by competent persons and with such publicity and notice to persons interested as to be admissible and valuable evidence of the state of things at the time they are made. They are not conclusive, and may be shown to be wrong; but, in the absence of evidence to the contrary, they may be properly, judicially received in evidence as correct when made.[464] Where the survey number in dispute was covered by the development plan of the municipal limits which was prepared in compliance with statutory provisions, its correctness will be presumed and mere collection of taxes by *Panchayat* did not disentitle the Municipal Corporation to levy octroi.[465]

Where the site plan and inventory prepared on behalf of a former ruler was not produced in its original state, the Supreme Court did not allow any objections to be raised about the matter in the Supreme Court.[466]

The section concludes by providing that maps, etc. made for any particular cause must be proved to be accurate. This can be done by examining persons who actually prepared them. Any defect or infirmity can be overcome by bringing before the court the maker of the map, etc. and testifying to the accuracy.[467]

[s 84] Presumption as to collection of laws and reports of decisions.—The Court shall presume the genuine ness of every book purporting to be printed or published

---

461. The original word "Government" has successively been amended by the A.O. 1937, A.O. 1948, Act 40 of 1949, A.O. 1950, to read as above.

462. *Rahmat-ulla Khan v Secretary of State for India,* (1913) PR No. 63 of 1913 (Civil); *Secretary of State v Chimanlal Jamnadas,* (1941) 44 Bom LR 295 : (1942) Bom 357.

463. *Ram Kishore v UOI,* AIR 1966 SC 644 : 1966(1) SCR 430.

464. *Jagudindra v Secretary of State,* (1902) 5 Bom LR 1 : 30 IA 44 : 30 Cal 291.

465. *Morvi Municipality v Arunodaya Mills Ltd,* AIR 1995 Guj 109.

466. *Adhunik Grah Nirman Sahakari Samiti Ltd v State of Rajasthan,* AIR 1989 SC 867 : 1989 Supp (1) SCC 656.

467. *Ranganath Ramchandra Suryavanshi v Mohan,* AIR 2008 NOC 2814 (Kar).

under the authority of the Government of any country, and to contain any of the laws of that country, and of every book purporting to contain reports of decisions of the Courts of such country.

COMMENT

This section should be read along with section 38, which makes relevant statements as to any law and rulings contained in officially printed books of any country. It dispenses with the proof of the genuineness of authorized books of any country containing laws and reports of decisions of courts. Section 57 authorizes the courts to take judicial notice of the existence of all laws and statutes in India and in the UK. Section 74 recognizes statutory records to be public records. Section 78 lays down the method of proving the statute passed by the legislature.

[s 85] Presumption as to powers-of-attorney.—The Court shall presume that every document purporting to be a power-of-attorney, and to have been executed before, and authenticated by, a notary public, or any Court, Judge, Magistrate, [468][Indian] Consul or Vice-Consul, or representative [469][***] of the [470][Central Government], was so executed and authenticated.

COMMENT

[s 85.1] Principle.—The court shall presume the due execution and authentication of a power-of-attorney when executed before and authenticated by a notary public, or any Court, Judge, Magistrate, Indian Consul or Vice-Consul, *etc.* The section does not exclude other legal modes of proving the execution of a power-of-attorney.[471] The court can presume that the Notary Public must have satisfied himself about competence of the executant.[472] The presumption applies not merely to local Notaries but also those functioning abroad.[473] A power of attorney in favour of a company's permanent delegate in Delhi authenticated by a judge of the foreign country, due execution and authentication was presumed.[474]

"Power-of-attorney includes any instrument (not chargeable with a fee under the law relating to court-fees for the time being in force) empowering a specified person to act for and in the name of the person executing it" [Indian Stamp Act, 1899, section 2(21)].

A "notary public" is an officer who takes notes of anything which may concern the public; he attests deeds or writings to make them authentic in another country; but is principally employed in mercantile affairs, to make protests of bills of exchange, *etc.*[475] Under section 138 of the Negotiable Instruments Act (XXVI of 1881), the Central

468. Subs. by the A.O. 1950, for "British".

469. The words "of Her Majesty, or" omitted by the A.O. 1950.

470. Subs. by the A.O. 1937, for "Government of India".

471. *Re Sladen,* (1898) 21 Mad 492; *Punjab National Bank v Parmesh Knitting Works,* AIR 1986 P&H 214.

472. *Citi Bank NA, New Delhi v JK Jute Mills,* AIR 1982 Del 487, 488; *Yogesh Singh Sohta v Niranjan Lal,* AIR 1981 Del 222, the objector could not offer any proof to the contrary. *Sandip Ghosh v Submal Chowdhury,* AIR 2010 NOC 979 (Cal), document not stamped as power of attorney cannot be attested as such by notary, it cannot be considered as power of attorney, the question of drawing presumption under the section did not arise.

473. *Abdul Zabbar v ADJ Orai,* AIR 1980 All 369, Pakistan Notary.

474. *Rudnap Export-Import v Eastern Associates Co,* AIR 1984 Del 20.

475. *Wharton's Law Lexicon,* 14th Edn, p 697.

Government is authorised to appoint notaries public within any local area. There can be no presumption without compliance of the formalities.[476]

The mere fact that the document had not been drafted or typed out by the executant before the Notary Public and the fact that the typed matter duly signed by the executant was presented before the Notary Public, did not in any way, make the execution and authentication doubtful.[477]

An application for regularisation of a building plan was filed through power of attorney which did not convey or confer any title or interest whether vested or contingent. The court said that the application was not liable to be rejected because of the fact that the power of attorney was not registered. The power of attorney was duly notarised and therefore carried the presumption of validity under section 85. The officer order insisting upon registered power of attorney had no legal sanctity.[478]

Presumption as to due execution and authentication is available in favour of the original power of attorney holder provided the mandate of section 85 is duly followed.[479]

[s 85.1.1] ***Foreign Power of Attorney.***—For creating the presumption about a foreign power of attorney, the document has to be authenticated by the Indian Counsel or the relevant Indian Authority. That was not done, nor was the relevant law in the United State about the power of a Notary Public cited. The presumption under the section was not attracted.[480]

[481][[s 85A] Presumption as to electronic agreement.—The Court shall presume that every electronic record purporting to be an agreement containing the [482][electronic signature] of the parties was so concluded by affixing the [482][electronic signature] of the parties.]

COMMENT

This section was initially inserted *vide* Information Technology (Amendment) Act, 2000.[483]

---

476. *EC & E Co v JE Works, Sisra,* AIR 1984 Del 363.

477. *Raj Kumar Gupta v Des Raj,* AIR 1995 HP 107. Power of attorney duly authenticated by a Notary Public would be presumed to be true. *Northern Traders v Bank of Baroda,* AIR 1994 All 381. *KA Pradeep v Branch Manager, Nedungadi Bank Ltd,* AIR 2007 Ker 269, the presumption applies both to execution and authentication by notary. The document bore the seal of notary. Unsatisfactory endorsement by notary was held to be immaterial. It is not necessary that there should be attestation by two witnesses.

478. *B Maragathammi v Member-Secretary, Chennai Metropolitan Development Authority,* AIR 2010 Mad 81 (DB).

479. *Bank of India v Allibhoy Mohammed,* AIR 2008 Bom 81. *Kamla Rani v Texmaco Ltd,* AIR 2007 Del 147, power of attorney presumed to be valid, an eviction petition filed.

480. *In the Goods of Pradeep Kumar Jalota,* AIR 2008 NOC 2318 (Cal), by the authorised person was held to be competent, it was not necessary that any high functionary of the company should have been examined as to authorisation.

481. Ins. by Act 21 of 2000, section 92 and Sch. II–13 (w.e.f. 17-10-2000).

482. Subs. by Act 10 of 2009, section 52(e), for "digital signature" (w.e.f. 27-10-2009).

483. Ins. by the Information Technology Act, 2000, section 92 & Schedule 2, (w.e.f. 17-10-2000).

In 2008, an amendment[484] was made in this section, whereby the word "digital signature" was substituted by the word "electronic signature" at three places in this section. This substitution is a part of the entire scheme under which the digital signature regime is being switched over to the electronic signature regime in the field of e-commerce and e-governance. This switching over of regime is meant to broaden the spectrum and follow the global trend.[485]

After this amendment, where an electronic record happens to be an agreement between the parties therein and it has been entered into in an electronic format with the electronic signatures of the parties, a party to litigation has to prove before the court that the electronic signature actually belonged to that party in terms of section 67A of this Act. Once this aspect is proved, the court is under an obligation to presume that the agreement was entered into by affixing of electronic signature by the parties. No further proof is to be required for the purposes of proving the execution of that agreement in the electronic format.

[481][[s 85B] Presumption as to electronic records and [486][electronic signatures]—(1) In any proceedings involving a secure electronic record, the Court shall presume unless contrary is proved, that the secure electronic record has not been altered since the specific point of time to which the secure statute relates.

(2) In any proceedings involving secure [486][electronic signature], the Court shall presume unless the contrary is proved that—

(a) **the secure [486][electronic signature] is affixed by subscriber with the intention of signing or approving the electronic record;**

(b) **except in the case of a secure electronic record or a secure [486][electronic signature], nothing in this section shall create any presumption, relating to authenticity and integrity of the electronic record or any [486][electronic signature].**

COMMENT

This section was initially inserted *vide* the Information Technology (Amendment) Act, 2000.[487]

In 2008, an amendment[488] was made in this section, whereby the word "digital signature" was substituted by the word "electronic signature" in the heading and at four places in this section. This substitution is a part of the entire scheme under which the digital signature regime is being switched over to the electronic signature regime in the field of e-commerce and e-governance. This switching over of regime is meant to broaden the spectrum and follow the global trend.[489]

---

484. (10 of 2009), section 52, [w.e.f. 27-10-2009 *vide* Notification No. S.O 2689(E), dated 27-10-2009].
485. For difference between "digital signature" and "electronic signature", please see section 3 (*ante*).
486. Subs. by Act 10 of 2009, section 52(f), for "digital signature" (w.e.f. 27-10-2009).
487. Ins. by the Information Technology Act, 2000, section 92 & Schedule 2 (w.e.f. 17-10-2000).
488. (10 of 2009), section 52, (w.e.f. 27-10-2009 *vide* Notification No. S.O 2689(E) dated 27-10-2009).
489. For difference between "digital signature" and "electronic signature", please see section 3 (*ante*).

This section intends to grant the sanctity of rebuttable presumption to secured electronic records and signatures.

Under sub-section (1), where a secure electronic record is involved, the court is under an obligation to presume that the secure electronic record has not been altered since the specific point of time to which the secure status relates, unless the contrary is proved by the party which wants to impeach the sanctity of such secure electronic record.

Under sub-section (2), clause (a) provides that where a secure electronic signature is involved, the court is under an obligation to presume that the secure electronic signature has been affixed by subscriber with the intention of signing or approving the electronic record. However, clause (b) explains that nothing in this section imposes any obligation upon the court to presume relating to authenticity and integrity of an ordinary electronic record or an ordinary electronic signature, except where it is a secure electronic record or a secure electronic signature. These statutory presumptions are rebuttable and the party which wants to impeach the sanctity of such secure electronic record or such secure electronic signature can prove the contrary by leading cogent evidence of the secure electronic record or the secure electronic signature having been tampered with.[490]

Secure system is defined in section 2(*ze*) of the IT Act as follows:

(*ze*) "secure system" means computer hardware, software, and procedure that—

(a) are reasonably secure from unauthorised access and misuse;

(b) provide a reasonable level of reliability and correct operation;

(c) are reasonably suited to performing the intended function; and

(d) adhere to generally accepted security procedures;

[481][[s 85C] Presumption as to [491][Electronic Signature Certificates].—The Court shall presume, unless contrary is proved, that the information listed in a [491][Electronic Signature Certificate] is correct, except for information specified as subscriber information which has not been verified, if the certificate was accepted by the subscriber.]

COMMENT

This section was initially inserted *vide* the Information Technology (Amendment) Act, 2000.[492]

In 2008, an amendment[493] was made in this section, whereby the word "digital signature" was substituted by the word "electronic signature" and the word "digital signature certificate" was substituted by the word "electronic signature certificate". This substitution is a part of the entire scheme under which the digital signature regime is being switched over to the electronic signature regime in the field of e-commerce and

490. For secure system, please see section 2 (ze) of the Information Technology Act, 2000.

491. Subs. by Act 10 of 2009, section 52(g), for "Digital Signature Certificates" (w.e.f. 27-10-2009).

492. Ins. by the Information Technology Act, 2000, section 92 & Schedule 2 (w.e.f. 17-10-2000).

493. (10 of 2009), section 52, [w.e.f. 27-10-2009 *vide* Notification No. S.O 2689(E), dated 27-10-2009].

e-governance. As mentioned earlier, this switching over of regime is meant to broaden the spectrum and follow the global trend.[494]

After this amendment, the court is under an obligation to presume that information listed in an Electronic Signature Certificate is correct, unless the party challenging to impeach the Electronic Signature Certificate leads positive evidence to shake its veracity. However, under the second limb of this section, the presumption is not applicable to information specified as subscriber information, which has not been verified, if the certificate was accepted by the subscriber. Therefore, the presumption is only valid up to the certification done by statutory regulator who has been empowered to issue certificate and not for subscriber's information, which is attributable to a subscriber which remains unverified.

[s 86] Presumption as to certified copies of foreign judicial records.—The Court may presume that any document purporting to be a certified copy of any judicial record of [495][[496][***] any country not forming part of India] or of Her Majesty's Dominions is genuine and accurate, if the document purports to be certified in any manner which is certified by any representative of [497][***] the [498][Central Government] [499][in or for] [500][such country] to be the manner commonly in use in [501][that country] for the certification of copies of judicial records.]

[502][An officer who, with respect to [503][***] any territory or place not forming part of [504][India or] Her Majesty's Dominions, is a Political Agent therefor, as defined in section 3, [505][clause (43)], of the General Clauses Act, 1897, shall, for the purposes of this section, be deemed to be a representative of the Central Government in and for the country comprising that territory or place.

COMMENT

[s 86.1] Principle.—If a copy of a foreign judicial record purports to be certified in a given way, the court may presume it to be genuine and accurate. It, however, does not exclude other proof, for, under Sections 65 and 66, secondary evidence may be given of public documents, without notice to the adverse party, when the person in possession of documents is out of the reach of, or not subject to, the process of the court.[506]

---

494. For difference between "digital signature" and "electronic signature", please see section 3 (*ante*).
495. Subs. by A.O. 1950, for "any country not forming part".
496. The words "a Part B State or of" omitted by Act 3 of 1951, section 3 and Schedule.
497. The words "Her Majesty or of" omitted by the A.O. 1950.
498. Subs. by the A.O. 1937, for "Government of India".
499 Subs. by Act 3 of 1891, section 8, for "resident in".
500. Subs. by Act 3 of 1951, section 3 and Schedule, for "such Part B State or country".
501. Subs. by Act 3 of 1951, section 3 and Schedule, for "that State or country".
502. Subs. by Act 5 of 1899, section 4, for the para added by Act 3 of 1891, section 3.
503. The words "a Part B State or" omitted by Act 3 of 1951, section 3 and Schedule. Earlier the words "a Part B State or" were insterted by the A.O. 1950.
504. Ins. by the A.O. 1950.
505. Subs. by the A.O. 1950, for "clause (40)".
506. *Haranund v Ram Gopal,* (1899) 2 Bom LR 562 : 27 IA 1 : 27 Cal 639; *Vallabhdass v Pranshankar* (1926) 30 Bom LR 1519.

A photostat copy of a decree of a foreign Court was held to be admissible and also capable of being acted upon by the court provided only that it was certified as required by the section.[507]

This section contains an instance of documents which section 65, Clause (f), seems to refer to. The provisions of this section are imperative and must be complied with.

[s 87] Presumption as to books, maps and charts.—The Court may presume that any book to which it may refer for information on matters of public or general interest, and that any published map or chart, the statements of which are relevant facts and which is produced for its inspection, was written and published by the person and at the time and place, by whom or at which it purports to have been written or published.

COMMENT

[s 87.1] Principle.—The court may presume that any book to which it may refer for information on matters of public or general interest or any published chart or map, was written and published by the person, and at the time and place by whom or at which it purports to have been written or published. See Sections 36 and 83.

A map is nothing but statements of the maker thereof regarding the state of configuration of a particular site and objects standing thereon, by lines and pictorial representations, instead of by words of mouth, and admitting such a map in evidence without calling the maker thereof is admitting statements by a third party who is not called as witness and amounts to admitting hearsay evidence. So mere proof of the map by itself is only proof of the fact of the preparation of the map and apart from independent proof about the correctness of its contents it cannot be said to have any bearing on the matters in issue and cannot be admitted into evidence unless shown to be admissible under any section of this Act. But a map and a *chitta* prepared under the orders of the defendants and filed along with collection papers showing collection on basis of the map and the *chitta* were held to be rightly admitted in evidence under section 13.[508]

[s 88] Presumption as to telegraphic messages.—The Court may presume that a message, forwarded from a telegraph office to the person to whom such message purports to be addressed, corresponds with a message delivered for transmission at the office from which the message purports to be sent; but the Court shall not make any presumption as to the person by whom such message was delivered for transmission.

COMMENT

[s 88.1] Principle.—The court may treat telegraphic message received, as if they were the originals sent, with the exception, that a presumption is not to be made as to the person,[509] by whom they were delivered for transmission and, unless the non-production of the originals is accounted for, secondary evidence of their contents is inadmissible. It must be proved that the message had been forwarded from the telegraphic office to

507. *Narasimha Rao v Venkata Lakshmi,* (1991) 3 SCC 451 : 1991 SCC Cri 626.
508. *Dwijesh Chandra Ray Chaudhuri v Naresh Chandra Gupta,* (1946) 1 Cal 149.
509. *Emperor v Abdul Gani,* (1925) 27 Bom LR 1373 : 49 Bom 878.

the person to whom such message purports to have been addressed. In the absence of such evidence, the telegram cannot be held to have been proved. A telegram is a primary evidence of the fact that the same was delivered to the addressee on the date indicated therein.[510]

The court is forbidden to make any presumption as to the person by whom the telegram was sent. Where the detenus sent a telegram conveying that they were illegally detained but the same was not taken into consideration, it was held that a telegram is not an authentic document. It is like an unsigned/anonymous communication. Unless a telegram is confirmed by a subsequent signed application, representation or an affidavit, the contents of telegram have no authenticity at all and the same cannot be taken into consideration.[511]

The section enables the court to accept the hearsay statement as evidence of the identity of the message delivered with that handed in.

[512]**[[s 88A] Presumption as to electronic messages.—The Court may presume that an electronic message, forwarded by the originator through an electronic mail server to the addressee to whom the message purports to be addressed corresponds with the message as fed into his computer for transmission; but the Court shall not make any presumption as to the person by whom such message was sent.**

***Explanation.*—For the purposes of this section, the expressions "addressee" and "originator" shall have the same meaning respectively assigned to them in clauses (b) and (za) of sub-section (1) of section 2 of the Information Technology Act, 2000.]**

COMMENT

[s 88A.1] Information Technology Act, 2000.—Presumption as to electronic messages.—The section provides that the court may presume that an electronic message forwarded by the originator through an electronic mail server to the addressee corresponds with the message as fed into his computer for transmission. The court is not authorised to make any presumption as to the person by whom such matter was sent.

The explanation to the section explains the meaning of the terms "addressee" and "originator". It says that these terms will have the same meaning as is assigned to them in clauses (*b*) and (*za*) of section 2(1) of the Information Technology Act, 2000. Section 2(1)(*b*) says that an addressee means a person who is intended by the originator to receive the electronic record but does not include any intermediary. Section 2(1)(*za*) says that an originator means a person who sends, generates, stores or transmits any electronic message or causes any electronic message to be sent, generated, stored or transmitted to any other person, but does not include an intermediary.

---

510. *Abba Astavans v Suresh*, AIR 1984 NOC 131 (Del).
511. *District Magistrate v G Jothisankar*, AIR 1993 SC 2633 : 1993 Cr LJ 3677.
512. Ins. by Act 21 of 2000, sec. 92 and Sch. II–13 (w.e.f. 17-10-2000).

[s 89] Presumption as to due execution, etc., of documents not produced.—The Court shall presume that every document, called for and not produced after notice to produce, was attested, stamped and executed in the manner required by law .

COMMENT

[s 89.1] Principle.—When a document is called for and not produced after proper notice so to do, the court shall presume that it was duly attested, stamped and executed in the manner prescribed by law. The section refers only to stamp, execution and attestation of documents. It is restricted to cases where notice to produce a document is given to a party. Where a document is shown to have remained unstamped for some time after its execution, the party who relied on it must prove that it was duly stamped. Where the defendant failed to produce mortgage deed despite notice, presumption that the mortgage deed was duly attested could be drawn.[513]

[s 90] Presumption as to documents thirty years old.—Where any document, purporting or proved to be thirty years old,[s 90.7] is produced from any custody which the Court in the particular case considers proper, the Court may presume[s 90.8] that the signature[s 90.9] and every other part of such document, which purports to be in the handwriting of any particular person, is in that person's handwriting, and in the case of a document executed or attested, that it was duly executed and attested by the persons by whom it purports to be executed and attested.

***Explanation.*—Documents are said to be in proper custody if they are in the place in which, and under the care of the person with whom they would naturally be; but no custody is improper if it is proved to have had legitimate origin, or if the circumstances of the particular case are such as to render such an origin probable.**

This explanation applies also to section 81.

ILLUSTRATIONS

(a) *A* has been in possession of landed property for a long time. He produces from his custody deeds relating to the land, showing his title to it. The custody is proper.

(b) *A* produces deeds relating to landed property of which he is the mortgagee. The mortgagor is in possession. The custody is proper.

(c) *A*, a connection of *B*, produces deeds relating to lands in *B*'s possession which were deposited with him by *B* for safe custody. The custody is proper.

[s 90.1] STATE AMENDMENTS

Uttar Pradesh.—*Amendments made by U.P. Act No. 24 of 1954, s. 2 and Sch. (w.e.f. 30-11-1954).*

In its application to the State of Uttar Pradesh, in Sec. 90—

(i) Renumber the existing section as sub-section (1) thereof, and

(ii) For the words "thirty-years', substitute the words 'twenty years', and

(iii) Insert the following as new sub-section (2):—

---

513. *Kodri Smt. v L Rs. of Fakira,* AIR 1994 NOC 182 (Raj).

"(2) Where any such document as is referred to in sub-section (1) was registered in accordance with the law relating to registration of documents and a duly certified copy thereof is produced, the Court may presume that the signature and every other part of such document which purports to be in the handwriting of any particular person, is in that person's handwriting, and in the case of a document executed or attested, that it was duly executed and attested by the person by whom it purports to have been executed or attested."

Section 90A.

New section 90-A, inserted by U.P. Act No. 24 of 1954.

"**90-A.**—(1) Where any registered document or duly certified copy thereof or any certified copy of a document which is a part of the record of a Court of Justice, is produced from any custody which the Court in the particular case considers proper, the Court may presume that the original was executed by the person by whom it purports to have been executed.

(2) The presumption shall not be made in respect of any document which is the basis of a suit or of a defence or is relied upon in the plaint or written-statement.[514]

(The explanation to sub-section (1) of section 90 will also apply to this section.)

SYNOPSIS

COMMENT

[s 90.2] Object.—The object of this section is not to make it too difficult for persons relying upon ancient documents to utilize those documents in proving their cases. It is intended to do away with the insuperable difficulty of proving the handwriting,

514. *Krishna Mohan v Bal Krishna Chaturvedi*, AIR 2001 AIR 334, the question of presumption as to execution of a document made in the auction sale of property, *dakhalnama* which was neither the basis of the suit nor defence, required no proof, presumption could be drawn in respect of it under the section.

execution, and attestation of documents in the ordinary way after the lapse of many years. It does away with the strict rule of proof of private documents.[515]

[s 90.3] Principle.—When a document is or purports to be more than 30 years old, if it be produced from what the court considers to be proper custody, it may be presumed (a) that the signature and every other part of such document, which purports to be in the handwriting of any particular person, is in that person's handwriting, and (b) that it was duly executed and attested by the person by whom it purports to be executed and attested.[516] Thirty-year-old document, produced from proper custody, not looking *ex facie* suspicious, presumption could be drawn in favour of the document.[517] Where the document relied on was not more than 30 years old, finding of the court based on no evidence could be interfered with.[518] It is not necessary that the signatures of the attesting witnesses or of the scribe be proved, for if everything was proved there would be no need to presume anything.[519] There can, however, be no presumption as to who the person who executed the document was and what authority he had to execute the document,[520] and whether he had the requisite authority,[521] or whether the contents of the document are true,[522] or that the document has the legal effect that it purports to have.[523] Presumption under section 90 in respect of 30 years' old document coming from proper custody relates to the signature, execution and attestation of a document i.e. to its genuineness but it does not give rise to presumption of correctness of every statement contained in it. That the contents of the document are true or it had been acted upon, have to be proved like any other fact.[524]

In *State of Bihar v Radha Krishna Singh*,[525] the Supreme Court said that the court relying on the genealogy of family must guard itself against falling into the trap laid by series of documents or labyrinth of seemingly old genealogies while deciding rival claims.

The presumption allowed by this section is not a presumption which the court is bound to make, and the court may require the document to be proved in the ordinary manner.[526]

---

515. *Lakhi Baruah v Padma Kanta Kalita,* AIR 1996 SC 1253 : 1996(8) SCC 357, the court stated the objects of this section. *Sesha Reddy v Managing Committee, Jame Masjid,* AIR 2002 NOC 164 (AP) : 2002 AIHC 1811, the presumption goes in favour of the contents of the document unless it is rebutted by adducing satisfactory evidence.

516. *Ekcowree Singh Roy v Kylash Chunder Mookerji,* (1873) 21 WR 45; *Hari Dhangar v Biru Dasru,* (1868) 5 BHC (ACJ) 135. Fifty year old registered deed of gift; burden was on those who alleged that the deed was fraudulent. *Fatima Bibi v Irfana Begam,* AIR 1980 All 394.

517. *Parkash Chand v Hans Raj,* AIR 1994 HP 144.

518. *State v Veerangouda Mallikarjunagouda,* AIR 1995 Kant 361 : 1994 (5) Kar LJ 266.

519. *Raghubir Singh v Thakurain Sukhraj Kaur,* (1938) 14 Luck 393.

520. *Sri Prasad v Special Manager, Court of Wards, Balrampur Estate,* (1936) 12 Luck 400.

521. *Ram Naresh Singh v Chirkut,* (1932) 8 Luck 18.

522. *Chandulal v Bai Kashi,* (1938) 40 Bom LR 1262 : (1938) Bom 97. Re-iterated in *Mohinuddin v President, Municipal Committee, Khargone,* AIR 1993 MP 5.

523. *Ramaji v Manohar,* AIR 1961 Bom 169 : 62 Bom LR 322. Ancient nature of the document is not sufficient in itself to prove the facts stated, genealogy in this case, *State of Bihar v Radha Krishna Singh,* AIR 1983 SC 684 : 1983(3) SCC 118. *Gangamma v Shivalingaiah,* (2005) 9 SCC 359, no presumption as to terms and authenticity or that recitals are correct.

524. *UOI v Ibrahim Uddin,* (2012) 8 SCC 148.

525. *State of Bihar v Radha Krishna Singh,,* AIR 1983 SC 684 : (1983) 3 SCC 118.

526. *Musammal Shafiq-un-nisa v Raja Shaban Ali Khan,* (1904) 6 Bom LR 750 : 26 All 581 : 31 IA 217; *Mansukj v Trikambhai,* (1929) 31 Bom LR 1279; *Anur v Nur Muhammad,* (1902) PR No. 82 of 1902 (Civil).

It is in the discretion of a court whether it will raise the presumption in favour of a document for which this section provides, but this discretion is not to be exercised arbitrarily; it must be governed by principles, which are consonant with law and justice. And while on the one hand great care is requisite in applying the presumption, on the other hand it is clear that very great injustice may be perpetrated, if an ancient document coming from proper custody is rejected by a court capriciously or for inadequate reasons. "Because a document purports to be an ancient document and to come from proper custody, it does not, therefore, follow that its genuineness, is to be assumed. If there are reasonable grounds for suspecting its genuineness and the party relying upon it fails to satisfy the court of its due execution, there is an end of it. But if no such grounds exist, and it satisfies the conditions prescribed by section 90 of the Indian Evidence Act, then proof of execution is dispensed with, and it is to be dealt with on the same footing as any other genuine instrument. If the authority or the title of the executant, for example, be not questioned, then, effect is to be given to it as though he had the requisite authority or title. If either be questioned, then of course the person on whom the burden of proof lies must adduce evidence to satisfy the court on the point, or he fails. When the genuineness of a document purporting to be an ancient document is put in issue, it appears to have been sometimes thought that any presumption in its favour is thereby excluded. But this would be to deprive the party producing it of the benefits of the presumption precisely in the circumstances in which he most stands in need of its aid. And there seems to be no difference in principle between cases in which due execution is traversed without more—those, that is, in which the party relying on the document is put to proof of it, and those in which it is alleged that the document is a forgery, except that in the latter case, the suspicions of the court may be aroused by the nature of the plea. But in the one case, as in the other, the presumption merely takes the place of the evidence which would, where modern document is concerned, be necessary for the purpose of proving due execution. The court may decline to raise the presumption, in which case the party producing the document must fail, unless he is provided with evidence in support of it. But where the court thinks proper to raise the presumption, it must be met and rebutted in the same way as direct evidence of the execution in the case of a modern document. The proper rule is ... well stated by Mr Taylor ... He says (page 587, 8th Edition)—

> An ancient deed, which has nothing suspicious about it, it presumed to be genuine without express proof, the witnesses being presumed dead, and if found in proper custody and corroborated by evidence of ancient or modern corresponding enjoyment or by other equivalent or explanatory proof, it will be presumed to have constituted part of the actual transfer of the property therein mentioned, because this is the usual course of such transaction.[527]

The Supreme Court observed that it should be produced at the earliest, so that it is not looked upon askance and with suspicion so far as its authenticity is concerned,[528] in the instant case.

Even if the document is purported or is proved to be 30 years old, the person seeking to rely on section 90 would not axiomatically receive a favourable presumption, the section 90 presumption being a discretionary one.[529]

---

527. Per Hill J, *in Govinda Hazra v Pratap Narain Mukhopadhya*, (1902) 29 Cal 740, 747.
528. *Om Prakash v Shanti Devi*, (2015) 4 SCC 601 (para 5) : AIR 2015 SC 976.
529. *Om Prakash v Shanti Devi*, (2015) 4 SCC 601 (para 10).

[s 90.4] Proper custody.—Before a court is justified in making a presumption in favour of the genuineness of an ancient document it should be satisfied *aliunde* that there is good ground for accepting it as a true document.[530] If there are circumstances in the case which throw great doubt on the genuineness of a document more than 30 years old, even if it is produced from proper custody, the court may exercise its discretion by not admitting that document in evidence without formal proof, and reject it when no such proof is given.[531]

[s 90.5] Presumption as to signature of executant.—The presumption permitted by this section in the case of a document purporting to be 30 years old, that it was duly executed by the party by whom it is purported to be executed, includes the presumption that when the signature of the executant purports to have been made by the pen of the scribe, the letter was duly authorised to sign for him.[532]

[s 90.6] Presumption as to seal.—Under this section the presumption does not apply to a seal and hence no such presumption can be drawn in favour of a document which bears only a seal but neither any signature nor purports to be in the handwriting of any particular person.[533]

[s 90.6.1] ***Presumption as to Caste.***—There was a dispute about the caste of an election candidate. His father's application for admission in a school was produced. It showed the caste. It carried the father's thumb impression. The document was more than 30 years old. It attracted the application of section 90. The mere fact that there was difficulty in reading one figure in the date was not considered by the court as a ground for rejecting the document.[534]

[s 90.7] "Document, purporting or proved to be 30 years old".—The period of 30 years is to be reckoned not from the date upon which the document is filed in court, but from the date on which, it having been tendered in evidence, its genuineness or otherwise becomes the subject of proof.[535]

A document dated 13 August 1888, was produced in court on 19 December 1917, and its genuineness was not called in question up to 12 August 1918, when the first court gave its judgment. It was only when the case came up to the appellate court that the defendants took objection that the document had not been proved. It was held that the period of 30 years should be reckoned from 12 August 1918, when the trial court gave its decision, and the due execution of the document could therefore be presumed.[536]

---

530. *Jesa Lal v Mussammat Ganga Devi,* (1913) PR No. 81 of 1913 (Civil).
531. *Musammat Shafiq-un-nisa v Khan Bahadur Raja Shaban Ali Khan,* (1904) 31 IA 217 : 6 Bom LR 750 : 26 All 581; *Charitar Raj v Kailash Bishari,* (1918) 3 PLJ 306.
532. *Haji Sheikh Bodha v Sukhram Singh,* (1924) 47 All 31 FB; *Balkaran Singh v Dulari Bai,* (1926) 49 All 55, contra, *Mohammad Azim v Special Manager, Court of Wards, Balrampur,* (1936) 12 Luck 98.
533. *Maheswar Naik v Tikayet Sailendra Narayan,* (1949) Cut 312.
534. *Desh Raj v Bodh Raj,* AIR 2008 SC 632 : (2008) 2 SCC 186.
535. *Minu Sirkar v Shedoy Nath Roy,* (1897) 5 CLR 135; *Surendra Krishna Roy v Mirza Mahammad,* (1935) 63 IA 85 : 38 Bom LR 330; *Bhanwaria v Ramratan,* (1953) 4 Raj 145; *Kesarapu Manikyalu v Venna Perumanayya,* AIR 2000 NOC 20 (AP) : 2000 AIHC 590 period of 30 years is to be computed from the date of execution of the document to the date on which the document was sought to be put into evidence.
536. *Ladha Singh v Mst Hukam Devi,* (1923) 4 Lah 233.

The plea for relaxation cannot be granted as the antiquity of the document is the very reason for it to be bestowed with the curial presumption that the signature and every other part of such document which purports to be the handwriting of any particular person, is in that person's handwriting, and in the case of a document executed or attested, that it was duly executed and attested by the person by whom it purports to be executed and attested. In the instant case the gift deed was only 29 years 5 months on the relevant date i.e. 30 years short by seven months.[537]

[s 90.7.1] Revenue records.—Entries in the revenue records made more than three decades before were presumed to be authentic.[538]

[s 90.7.2] Wills.—Presumption under this section extends to testamentary documents. A will purporting to be 30 years old and produced from proper custody may be presumed to have been duly attested and executed. The court must however act with extreme caution and utmost circumspection.[539] The period of 30 years will run from the date of the will and not from the death of the testator.[540]

[s 90.7.3] Copy of document.—The presumption under this section can be raised only with regard to the original document if produced before the court. It does not apply to a certified copy when the original document is not before the court. The section requires the production to the court of the particular document in regard to which the court may make the statutory presumption. If the document produced is a copy, admitted under section 65 as secondary evidence, and it is produced from proper custody and is over 30 years old, then the signature authenticating the copy may be presumed to be genuine, but the production of a copy is not sufficient to justify the presumption of the execution of the original under this section. The production which entitles the court to draw the presumption as to the execution and attestation of a will is of the original and not its copy.[541] Presumption of genuineness does not apply to a copy or a certified copy unless foundation is laid for admission of secondary evidence.[542]

[s 90.7.4] Gazette Notification.—A Gazette Notification issued 32 years prior to the suit was produced and marked in evidence. No circumstances were proved to justify the inference that it might not have been published as enjoined by law. The court said that the regularity of the issue of the Notification should have been presumed leaving it to the defendants to rebut that presumption.[543]

---

537. *Om Prakash v Shanti Devi,* (2015) 4 SCC 601 (para 8).

538. *Kartar Singh v Collector, Patiala,* 1996 AIHC 1538 (P&H).

539. *Dhanapal v Govindaraja,* AIR 1961 Mad 262. *Haradhan Mahatha v Dukhu Mahatha,* AIR 1993 Pat 129, executant and attesting witnesses not alive, execution and attestation may be presumed. *Kandadal Tirumalachari v Kandamal Venkatachari,* AIR 2008 NOC 2896 (AP), signature identified by witness and the Will being 30 years old, the signature and every other part of the Will was presumed to be in the testator's handwriting.

540. *Sarat Chandra Mondal v Panchanan Mondal,* (1955) 1 Cal 55; *Mahendra Nath Surul v Netai Charan Ghosh,* (1943) 1 Cal 392.

541. *Basant Singh v Kunwar Brij Raj Saran Singh,* (1935) 62 IA 180 : 37 Bom LR 805 : 57 All 494; *Seethayya v Subramanya Somayajulu,* (1929) 56 IA 146 : 31 Bom LR 756 : 52 Mad 453. See to the same effect; *Sital Das v Sant Ram,* AIR 1954 SC 606 and *Harihar Prasad v Deonarain Prasad,* AIR 1956 SC 305 : 1956 SCR 1; *KV Subbaraju v C. Subbaraju,* AIR 1968 SC 947 : 1968(2) SCR 292; *Shiolalsing v Shankar,* AIR 1984 Bom 19; *Dhirendra Singh v Dhanai,* AIR 1983 All 216.

542. *Lakhi Baruah v Padma Kanta Kalita,* AIR 1996 SC 1253 : 1996(8) SCC 357.

543. *Rohit Singh v State of Bihar,* AIR 2007 SC 10 : (2006) 12 SCC 734.

[s 90.8] "May presume".—The expression means that the trial court has a discretion either to presume a fact as proved or to call for proof of it.[544] The presumption is discretionary and not obligatory. Even if the elements mentioned in the section are satisfied, the court may require the document to be proved in the ordinary manner. It is necessary for the court to consider the evidence external and internal of the document in order to enable it to decide whether in any particular case it should or should not presume proper signature and execution. The court may, but is not bound to, make the presumption merely because of the alleged age of the document.[545] The presumption being based on the rule of expediency, unless the surrounding circumstances satisfied the court that the document was produced from proper custody it would be unsound to admit it.[546] Where the court chooses to raise the presumption, no further proof of the fact is necessary under section 69.[547]

The recorded statements of the members of a particular community regarding a custom prevailing in that community were produced in the shape of a document which was 30 years old. There was no mention that the declarants were the leaders of the community or that they had the authority to make the statement on behalf of the community. The designation of the officers before whom the statement was made was also not mentioned. The court did not accept the document as proving the fact stated. The presumption under the section applies only to genuineness and the fact of execution, attestation, etc.[548]

A private document produced from private custody, even if 30 years old, cannot have the same effect as a public document would have such a private document cannot be relied on to deny the paternity of a child.[549]

[s 90.9] "Signature".—Signature includes a mark, a mark being a sort of symbolic writing. The presumption of execution of a document under this section extends to a mark put on the document and it is taken to be the signature in the absence of proof to the contrary.[550] The section makes no provision for any presumption in regard to seals, nor can a seal be regarded as a signature within the definition of the word contained in the General Clauses Act, 1897.[551] Some High Courts have held that there is no presumption as to the truth of the contents though they constitute an estoppel against the executant and will be relevant against him under sections 17, 18, 21 and 32(2).[552]

Where a party leads evidence in proof of the due execution of the document, he cannot afterwards rely upon the presumption of genuineness of the document.[553]

---

544. *Rangu v Rambha,* AIR 1967 Bom 382 : 69 Bom LR 559. To the same effect is the decision of the Supreme Court in *Narendra Akash Maharaj Pelkar v Shahji Baburao Pelkar,* AIR 2009 Bom 165.

545. *Mansukh v Trikambhai,* (1929) 31 Bom LR 1279.

546. *Rudragouda v Basangouda,* (1937) 40 Bom LR 202.

547. *Mahendra Nath Surul v Netai Charan Ghosh,* (1943) 1 Cal 392; *Kirpal Singh v Aas Kaur,* AIR 1997 P&H 240, a gift-cum-will deed which was 30 years old and came from the custody of a proper person and was also registered, it was a presumptive evidence of its due execution and attestation.

548. *Mohmedbhai Basubhai Malek v Amirbhai Rahimbhai Malek,* AIR 2001 Guj 37.

549. *Pavitri Devi v Darbari Singh,* (1993) 4 SCC 392.

550. *Shailendranath Mitra v Girijabhushan Mukherji,* (1930) 58 Cal 686.

551. *Special Manager, Court of Wards, Balrampur v Tirbeni Prasad,* (1935) 11 Luck 35; *Sri Prasad v Special Manager, Court of Wards, Balrampur Estate,* (1936) 12 Luck 400.

552. *Bal Sakindabal v Gulam Rasul,* AIR 1981 Guj 142; *Ghurahu v Sheo Ratan,* AIR 1981 All 3.

553. *Chanda Bai v Anwar Khan,* AIR 1997 MP 238.

[s 90.9.1] ***Unregistered Partition Deed.***—A suit was filed for partition or separate possession. The division was effected by way of family arrangement recorded in City Survey Records after a lapse of 21 years. It was filed after 9 years from the date of the suit, and at Appellate stage. The document was unregistered. It was produced from the custody of the defendant. The author of the document and attesting witnesses were not available. The court said that no partition could be presumed on the basis of such document.[554]

[s 90.10] Proper Custody—*[Explanation]*.—"Proper custody" means the custody of any person so connected with the deed that his possession of it does not excite any suspicion of fraud.[555] It is not necessary that the document should be found in the best and the most proper place of deposit. The section insists only on a satisfactory account of the origin of the custody, and not on the history of the continuance. Possibly the origin of the custody was alone regarded as material because it is intelligible that ancient documents may be overlooked and left undisturbed notwithstanding a transfer of old, or creation of new, interests.[556] In illustrations (a) and (b) the documents are produced from their natural place of custody, in (c) A's custody is proper under the circumstances. The provisions of the section read with the Explanation insist on a satisfactory account of the origin of the possession being given by the party relying upon the documents. The custody might not be in the strictest sense legal custody, but, whether it originated in right or wrong, the origin must be explained. The court must, therefore, examine the surrounding circumstances tending to establish the connection of the party producing the document with the person with whom the documents should naturally have been.[557]

A document was produced by the plaintiff's witness which was in his custody and of which the plaintiff had no knowledge. It was held that there was no legal error in admitting such document in evidence in spite of the fact that there was no pleading about it.[558]

A copy of sale deed which was brought on record was only a photostat copy of a document which was not even registered. The sale deed was obtained from the court. It was held that such custody was not a proper custody. Refusal to place reliance on it was not improper.[559] Certain ancient letters written by the deceased to a third person were produced by the defendant. He failed to explain how the letters came to his custody. The court refused to draw the presumption under the section.[560] A person who was claiming title and possession of a property which was under mortgage and though he produced a redemption deed which was 90 years old, he was not able to show how it

---

554. *Roshanbi Shaikaji Attar v Usmansab Shaikaji Attar,* AIR 2006 NOC 1156 (Kant) : (2006) 4 AIR Kar. R 143.
555. *Doedem Neale v Samples,* (1838) 8 Ad & El 151.
556. *Tajudin v Govind,* (1902) 5 Bom LR 144 : 27 Bom 452.
557. *Rudragouda v Basangouda,* (1937) 40 Bom LR 202; *Chitru Devi v Ram Dei,* AIR 2002 HP 59, document executed in 1928 alleged to be showing marriage between the defendant and certain person and not being defendant and plaintiff's father, the plaintiff failed to prove that she was the proper custodian of the document, or how the document came to her custody, held that section 90 was not applicable.
558. *Jayadeb Swain v Santha Behera,* AIR 2007 Ori 15.
559. *Irshad Ali v Viresh Agarwal,* AIR 2009 NOC 197 (All).
560. *Narendra Akash Maharaj Petkar v Shahaji Baburao Petkar,* AIR 2009 Bom 165.

came into his custody and it also was not endorsed by the signature of the mortgagee. The evidence was held to be not admissible.[561]

[s 90.10.1] ***Presumption at any Stage.***—The presumption can be raised at any stage of the proceedings including the Appellate stage. A belated claim of presumption would not by itself confer any right on the other party to claim an opportunity to lead evidence in rebuttal.[562]

[563][[s 90A] Presumption as to electronic records five years old.—Where any electronic record, purporting or proved to be five years old, is produced from any custody which the Court in the particular case considers proper, the Court may presume that the [564][electronic signature] which purports to be the [564][electronic signature] of any particular person was so affixed by him or any person authorised by him in this behalf.

***Explanation.*—Electronic records are said to be in proper custody if they are in the place in which, and under the care of the person with whom, they naturally be; but no custody is improper if it is proved to have had a legitimate origin, or the circumstances of the particular case are such as to render such an origin probable.**

This *Explanation* applies also to section 81A]

COMMENT

[s 90A.1] Information Technology Act, 2000.—Where an electronic record purports to be or is proved to be five years old and is produced from any custody which the court considers proper in the particular case, the court may presume that the digital signature which purports to be the digital signature of any person was so affixed by him or by any person authorised by him in the behalf.

Defining the expression "proper custody" the explanation to the section says that electronic records are said to be in proper custody if they are in the place in which and under the care of the person with whom they would naturally be; but that no custody is improper if it is proved to have had a legitimate origin or the circumstances of the particular case are such as to render such an origin probable. This explanation also applies to the presumption under section 81A as to Gazettes in electronic forms.

---

561. *Harendra Rai v Chandrawati Devi,* AIR 2007 Pat 120.

562. *Hazarilal v Sh Shyamlal,* AIR 2007 NOC 323 (Raj—DB).

563. Ins. by the Information Technology Act (Act 21 of 2000), section 92 and Second Schedule (w.e.f. 17-10-2000).

564. Subs. by the Information Technology (Amendment) Act, 2008 (10 of 2009), section 52(h), for the word "digital signature" (w.e.f. 27-10-2009).

CHAPTER VI

OF THE EXCLUSION OF ORAL BY DOCUMENTARY EVIDENCE

[s 91] Evience of terms of contracts, grants and other dispositions of property reduced to form of document.—When the terms of a contract, or of a grant, or of any other disposition of property, have been reduced to the form of a document,[s 91.3] and in all cases in which any matter is required by law to be reduced to the form of a document,[s 91.4] no evidence shall be given in proof of the terms of such contract, grant or other disposition of property, or of such matter, except the document itself, or secondary evidence of its contents in cases in which secondary evidence is admissible under the provisions hereinbefore contained.

***Exception 1.*—When a public officer is required by law to be appointed in writing, and when it is shown that any particular person has acted as such officer, the writing by which he is appointed need not be proved.**

***Exception 2.*—Wills [1][admitted to probate in [2][India]] may be proved by the probate.**

***Explanation 1.*—This section applies equally to cases in which the contracts, grants or dispositions of property referred to are contained in one document and to cases in which they are contained in more documents than one.**

***Explanation 2.*—Where there are more originals than one, one original only need be proved.**

***Explanation 3.*—The statement, in any document whatever, of a fact other than the facts referred to in this section, shall not preclude the admission of oral evidence as to the same fact.**

ILLUSTRATIONS

(a) If a contract is contained in several letters, all the letters in which it is contained must be proved.

(b) If a contract is contained in a bill of exchange, the bill of exchange must be proved.

(c) If a bill of exchange is drawn in a set of three, one only need be proved.

(d) *A* contracts, in writing, with *B*, for the delivery of indigo upon certain terms. The contract mentions the fact that *B* had paid *A* the price of other indigo contracted for verbally on another occasion.

Oral evidence is offered that no payment was made for the other indigo. The evidence is admissible.

---

1. Subs. by Act 18 of 1872, section 7, for "under the Indian Succession Act".
2. Subs. by Act 3 of 1951, section 3 and Schedule, for "the States".

(e) *A* give *B* a receipt for money paid by *B*.

Oral evidence is offered of the payment.

The evidence is admissible.

SYNOPSIS

COMMENT

[s 91.1] Principle.—When a transaction has been reduced to writing either by agreement of the parties or by requirement of law, the writing becomes the exclusive memorial thereof, and no evidence shall be given to prove the transaction, except the document itself or secondary evidence of its contents where such evidence is admissible. This rule is based on the principle that *the best evidence, of which the case in its nature is susceptible,* should always be presented. This rule does not demand the greatest amount of evidence which can possibly be given of any fact, but its design is to prevent the introduction of any which, from the nature of the case, supposes that better evidence is in the possession of the party. It is adopted for the prevention of fraud, for, when better evidence is withheld, it is only fair to presume that the party has some sinister motive for not producing it, and that, if offered, his design would be frustrated. The rule thus becomes essential to the pure administration of justice.[3] The best evidence about the contents of a document is the document itself and it is the production of the document that is required by this section in proof of its contents.[4]

---

3. *Taylor*, 12th Edn, section 391, p 272. See *Entisham Ali v Jamna Prasad,* (1921) 24 Bom LR 675 : 48 IA 365, where secondary evidence of a sale-deed was admitted. *Roop Kumar v Mohan Thedani,* AIR 2003 SC 2418, the section embodies the best evidence rule, which becomes a doctrine of substantive law. Even a third party can prove a written contract by producing the writing.
4. *Hira Devi v Official Assignee, Bombay,* AIR 1958 SC 448 : 60 Bom LR 932 : 1958 SCC 1384. See also *National Insurance Co Ltd v Jugal Kishore,* AIR 1988 SC 719 : (1988) 63 Comp Cas 847 : 1988(1) SCC 626 : (1989) 3 SCC 346 : 1988 SCC (Cri) 633, stressing the duty of the party in possession to produce the document which would be helpful in arriving at a just solution of the problem.

The section lays down the best evidence rule but does not prohibit any other evidence where the writing is capable of being construed differently and which shows how the parties understood the document. By this process the parties were able to show that they intended to enter into a transaction of mortgage and not sale.[5] The surrounding and attending circumstances are relevant for the construction of a document only when some ambiguity exists in the document and not otherwise.[6]

Under this section:

(1) When the terms of (a) a contract, (b) a grant, or (c) any disposition of property have been reduced to the form of a document; or

(2) Where any matter is required by law to be reduced to the form of a document,

then (a) the document itself, or (b) secondary evidence of its contents, must be put in evidence.

The first provision refers to transactions voluntarily reduced to writing. The second refers to those cases in which any matter is required by law to be reduced to the form of a document, e.g., sale of immovable property of the value of Rs.100 and upwards, mortgage for an amount exceeding Rs 100, a lease of immovable property for a year at least, a trust of immovable property, a gift of immovable property,[7] *etc.*

There are two exceptions to these provisions:

(1) When a public officer is required by law to be appointed in writing, and any officer has acted as such, the writing need not be proved;

(2) Wills admitted to probate in India may be proved by the probate.

The general rule laid down in this section is also subject to the exceptions laid down in the following sections 95–99. The section has no application when the writing is not evidence of the matter reduced to writing.[8]

[s 91.2] Scope.—This section and section 92 define the cases in which documents are exclusive evidence of transactions which they embody. They only apply when the document evidencing a contract appears to contain all the terms thereof. The inference that a writing was intended to contain the whole agreement may be drawn from the document itself as well as from extrinsic evidence.[9] Sections 93–100 provide for the interpretation of documents by oral evidence.

---

5. *Tulsi v Chandrika Prasad,* AIR 2006 SC 3359 : (2006) 8 SCC 322.
6. *State Bank of India v Mula Sahakari Sakhar Karkhana Ltd,* (2006) 6 SCC 293 : AIR 2007 SC 2361, the document in question was a commercial document and did not exhibit any ambiguity on its face. The High Court itself said that *ex facie* the document appeared to be a contract of indemnity. Hence, reference by the High Court to oral evidence was not appropriate.
7. See *Chowgatta v Chattar Singh,* (1877) PR No. 18 of 1878 (Civil); *Fattesh Singh v Mian Singh,* (1883) PR No. 131 of 1883 (Civil).
8. *Javarasetty v Ningamma,* AIR 1992 Kant 160, there is nothing to compel the court to prefer documentary evidence over oral, or *vice versa.*
9. *Chimanram Motilal v Divanchand Govindram,* (1931) 56 Bom 180 : 34 Bom LR 26. These sections do not authorise the courts to prefer one kind of evidence over another. They only permit in some specific situations to exclude a certain type of evidence. *Jevarasetty v Ningamma,* AIR 1992 Kant 160.

A contract being a creature of an agreement between two or more parties, has to be interpreted giving literal meanings unless there is some ambiguity therein. The contract is to be interpreted giving the actual meaning to the words contained in the contract and it is not permissible for the court to make a new contract, however reasonable, if the parties have not made it themselves. It is to be interpreted in such a way that its terms may not be varied. The contract has to be interpreted without any outside aid. The terms of the contract have to be construed strictly without altering the nature of the contract, as it may affect the interest of either of the parties adversely.[10]

[s 91.3] "When the terms ... have been reduced to the form of a document".— The section prohibits the admission of oral evidence to prove the contents of the document.[11] If parties have reduced all the terms of a contract or of a grant or of any disposition of property into writing, then no parole evidence is admissible, but if they intended only to reduce to writing a portion of the terms of the contract, then they are entitled to give parole evidence of the terms which they did not intend to reduce to writing.[12] Where parties to a contract agree to substitute a written instrument for an oral contract the ultimate contract is deemed to be contained in the instrument alone and no oral evidence of its terms can be given thereafter.[13] This section excludes oral evidence as to the terms of a written contract. There is nothing to exclude oral evidence that there was no agreement between the parties and, therefore, no contract.[14] The expression "terms" in this section and section 92 relates to statements, assertions or representations contained in a written contract which relate to the subject-matter of the contract and to something to be done or not to be done *under* the contract, and has no application to a provision in the nature of a condition precedent to the very existence or formation of a contract.[15] The section does not preclude from proving that the real contract was different from what was found in the deed.[16]

Illustration (b) refers to the first part of the section.

A *wakf* can be created orally under Muhammadan law, but when the terms of a dedication are reduced to the form of a writing, no evidence can be given to prove the term except the document itself or secondary evidence thereof.[17]

Where a contract was signed by the defendant personally and he attempted to lead oral evidence to show that he was contracting as agent and that the name of his principal was disclosed at the time of the contract, it was held that such evidence was

---

10. *Rajasthan State Industrial Development & Investment Corp v Diamond & Gem Development Corp Ltd,* (2013) 5 SCC 470.

11. *Hira Devi v Official Assignee, Bombay,* AIR 1958 SC 448 : 60 Bom LR 932 : 1958 SCR 1384. *Y Ganganaidu v M Surkantam,* AIR 1993 AP 130, terms reduced to the form of a document, prohibition of oral evidence. *Kashiram v State of MP,* AIR 1996 MP 247, oral agricultural lease, subsequent entry in Government records, does not make it written lease.

12. *Jamna Doss v Srinath Roy,* (1889) 17 Cal 176, 177n. See *Sangam Lal v Mussammat Sikandar Jehan Begam,* (1889) PR No. 183 of 1889 FB (Civil); *Ram Gopal v Tulshi Ram,* (1928) 51 All 79 FB; *Ghasilal v Deobai,* (1953) MB 303.

13. *Nainsukhdas Sheonarayan Shop v Goverdhandas,* (1947) Nag 510; *Mohd. Daud v Abu Mohammad,* AIR 1961 Pat 310.

14. *Tyagaraja Mudaliyar v Vedathanni,* (1935) 63 10.IA 126 : 38 Bom LR 373 : 59 Mad 446.

15. *PB Bhatt v VR Thakkar,* (1971) 74 Bom LR 509.

16. *Arumoorthi v SE Committee,* AIR 1962 Mad 360.

17. *Shaikh Muhammad Ibrahim v Bibi Mariam,* (1928) 8 Pat 484; *Mohammed Khan v Sheo Bhikh Singh,* (1929) 5 Luck 377.

not admissible for the purpose of exonerating a contracting party from liability, for that would be substituting a different agreement from that evidenced by the writing.[18]

[s 91.4] "Any matter is required by law to be reduced to the form of a document".— Whereby any matter is required by law to be reduced to the form of a document, then the document itself must be put in evidence, *e.g.*, deeds, conveyances of land, mortgages, wills, *etc.* No other evidence can be substituted so long as the writing exists. But where the matter is not required by law to be reduced to the form of a document, this section does not apply, e.g., in 1866 an oral agreement with transfer of possession sufficed to create a mortgage and therefore a mortgage could be proved *aliunde* even if there was no registered document.[19] No oral evidence is admissible to prove the rent payable under a lease reduced to writing.[20] Where the document containing a transaction is inadmissible for want of registration no other evidence of its contents can be received. Where in a suit for redemption of land, the plaintiff alleged that possession was given to the defendant by way of security for a loan of Rs 100 or upwards but no registered deed was executed to evidence the transaction, oral evidence to prove the transaction was held inadmissible.[21]

[s 91.5] Appointment of public officer.—[Exception 1].—This Exception is partly based on the maxim *omnia praesumuntur rite esse acta.* "It is a general principle, that a person's acting in a public capacity is *prima facie* evidence of his having been duly authorised so to do; and even though the office be one the appointment to which must have been in writing, it is not, at least in the first instance, necessary to produce the document, or account for non-production".[22]

[s 91.6] Wills admitted to probate.—[Exception 2].—Probate means the copy of a will certified under the seal of a court of competent jurisdiction with a grant of administration to the estate of the testator.[23] Probate of a will is evidence of the contents of the will against all the parties interested thereunder. Probate is secondary evidence, but it is made admissible by this section.

[s 91.7] Transactions in one or more than one documents.—[Explanation 1].— Illustration (a) to the section exemplifies this Explanation. When parties negotiate at a distance by letters or telegrams, the entire mass of correspondence indicates the true nature of the agreement entered into by the parties.

[s 91.8] More than one original.—[Explanation 2].—Illustration (c) exemplifies the meaning of this Explanation. See section 62, Explanations 1 and 2. Bills of exchange and bills of lading have more originals than one.

[s 91.9] Extraneous facts in documents.—[Explanation 3].—Illustrations (d) and (e) exemplify this Explanation. When the contents of a document are in question, either as fact in issue or as a sub-alternate principal fact, the document is the proper evidence of its own contents, and all derivative proof is rejected until its absence is accounted

---

18. *Ebrahimbhoy Pabaney Mills Co Ltd, v Hassan Mamooji,* (1920) 23 Bom LR 767 : 45 Bom 1242.

19. *Narsi v Parshottam,* (1928) 30 Bom LR 1277 : 52 Bom 875; *Sir Sayaji Rao v Madhavrao,* (1928) 30 Bom LR 1463 : 53 Bom 12.

20. *Lal Rajendrasingh v Mahant Hulasdas,* (1944) Nag 704.

21. *Maung San Min v Maung Po Hlaing,* (1925) 4 Ran 1 FB

22. *Best,* 12th Edn, section 356, pp 313, 314.

23. The Indian Succession Act (XXXIX of 1925), section 2(f).

for. But when a written instrument or document of any description is not the fact in issue, and is merely used as evidence to prove some fact, independent proof *aliunde* is receivable. Thus, although a receipt has been given for the payment of money, proof of the fact of payment may be made by any person who witnessed it. A receipt for sums paid in part liquidation of a bond hypothecating immovable property must be registered to render it admissible as evidence. Under illustration (e) to this section such payments may nevertheless be proved by parole evidence, which is not excluded owing to the inadmissibility of the documentary evidence.[24]

In a suit, which was brought for the price of goods sold and delivered, the plaintiff swore to the fact of the sale and tendered in evidence a written admission of the defendant that the goods had been supplied to him. The writing was rejected, as unstamped, and the suit was dismissed. It was held that the judge should have allowed the plaintiff an opportunity of proving by oral testimony the delivery of the goods sold, and their value.[25] So, although where the contents of a marriage register are in issue, verbal evidence of those contents is not receivable, yet the fact of the marriage may be proved by the independent evidence of a person who was present at it.[26]

[s 91.10] Names on public record.—The name of a person entered in Municipal, sales tax and excise records can be brought before by oral evidence of an employee of the concerned department. But its evidentiary value would be worth very little unless accompanied by the record of the entry.[27]

[s 91.11] Suit on promissory note inadmissible in evidence.—The rulings of the Indian High Courts on the question where money is lent to a person who passes a promissory note, but the note is inadmissible in evidence for want of sufficient stamp or for any other reason, may be classified into two classes lucidly enunciated by Garth CJ, in *Sheikh Akbar v Sheikh Khan*,[28] in which the question was whether a copy of a lost promissory note, which was itself inadmissible as being insufficiently stamped, could be received in evidence. The court held that it could not be received in evidence. Garth CJ, said:

> When a cause of action for money is once complete in itself, whether for goods sold, or for money lent, or for any other claim, and the debtor then gives a bill or note to the creditor for payment of the money at a future time, the creditor, if the bill or note is not paid at maturity, may always, as a rule, sue for the original consideration, provided that he has not endorsed or lost or parted with the bill or note, under such circumstances as to make the debtor liable upon it to some third person. In such cases the bill or note is said to be taken by the creditor *on account of the debt*, and if it is not paid at maturity, the creditor may disregard the bill or note and sue for the original consideration...But when the original cause of action is the bill or note itself, and does not exist independently of it, as for instance, when, in consideration of A depositing money with B, B contracts by a promissory note to repay it with interest at six months' date, here there is no cause of action for money lent, or otherwise than upon the note itself, because the deposit is made upon the terms contained in the note and no other. In such a case the note is the

24. *Dalip Singh v Durga Prasad*, (1877) 1 All 442; *Sukh Dial v Mani Ram*, (1914) PR No. 29 of 1915 (Civil); *Sharaf Ali Khan v Jagandar Singh*, (1916) PR No. 98 of 1916 (Civil).

25. *Binja Ram v Rajmohun Roy*, (1881) 8 Cal 282.

26. *Balbhadar Prasad v The Maharajah of Betia*, (1887) 9 All 351, 356.

27. *Duli Chand v Jagmendar Das*, (1990) 1 SCC 169.

28. (1881) 7 Cal 256, 259; *Radhakant Shaha v Abhoychurn Mitter*, (1882) 8 Cal 721.

only contract between the parties, and if for want of proper stamp or some other reason the note is not admissible in evidence, the creditor must lose his money.

In a later case, however, the same High Court tried to explain away the above case and held in a suit brought on a *hatchitta* (promissory note) bearing an insufficient stamp and in which the defendant admitted the loan but pleaded payment, that the promissory note was not admissible in evidence but the plaintiff had a cause of action independently of it.[29] Subsequently, in another case it laid down that the question, whether, when a bill or note is found to be inadmissible in evidence, the payee can sue on the original consideration, depends upon whether the cause of action with regard to the original consideration is one, which is complete in itself, and the debtor then gives a bill or note to the creditor for payment of the money at a future time. If this be so, then the plaintiff may disregard the promissory note, if he chooses, and sue upon the original debt. Where, however, the original cause of action is a bill or a note itself and does not exist independently of it, then the plaintiff cannot disregard the note and sue for the original consideration.[30]

The Bombay High Court approved of the principle stated in *Sheikh Akbar v Sheikh Khan*[31] in a case in which the plaintiff sued to recover from the defendant the balance of a debt due on an unstamped note passed to him by the defendant for a consideration of Rs 38. The note recited that the defendant had received the amount, and would repay it after 3 months from the date of its execution. The defendant admitted, by his written statement, execution of the note and the receipt of Rs 37 in the shape of paddy, but alleged that he had paid off the debt. He also contended that the note being unstamped could not be admitted in evidence. It was held that the document sued on was a promissory note, and that the suit being brought on it as the original cause of action, the admission of its contents by the defendant did not avail the plaintiff, the document itself being inadmissible for want of a stamp and that the plaintiff could not recover irrespectively of the promissory note, as he did not seek to prove the consideration otherwise than by the note, which was inadmissible in evidence and the admission contained in the defendant's written statement did not amount to an admission of the claim as for money lent.[32] The distinction between cases in which a suit is brought solely on a promissory note or *hundi*, and cases in which there is and can be a claim to recover the original loan, has been acknowledged.[33] Where there is an independent admission of a loan, the holder of a *hundi*, bill or note, which is defective, and inadmissible in evidence for want of a stamp, may still sue on the consideration the person to whom he gave it, though he cannot use the bill in support of his suit.[34]

The Madras High Court has in a Full Bench case held that whether a suit lies on the debt apart from the instrument depends on the circumstances under which the

---

29. *Pramatha Nath Sandal v Dwarka Nath Dey,* (1896) 23 Cal 851, **following** *Golap Chand Marwaree v Thakurani Mohokoom Kooaree,* (1878) 3 Cal 314. It is dissented from by the Allahabad High Court in *Nazir Khan v Ram Mohan,* (1930) 53 All 114 FB.

30. *Ranendramohan Tagore v Keshabchandra Chanda,* (1934) 61 Cal 433.

31. *Sheikh Akbar v Sheikh Khan,* (1881) 7 Cal 256.

32. *Damodar Jagannath v Atmaram Babaji,* (1888) 12 Bom 443; *Jacob & Co v Vicumsey,* (1926) 29 Bom LR 432.

33. *Chenbasapa v Lakshman Ramchandra,* (1893) 18 Bom 369.

34. *Krishnaji v Rajmal,* (1899) 24 Bom 363 : 2 Bom LR 25; *Ranchhod v Ravjibhai,* (1925) 28 Bom LR 631; *Jacob & Co v Vicumsey,* (1926) 29 Bom LR 432; *Somabhai v Kalyanbhai,* (1937) 40 Bom LR 174.

instrument is executed. If the promissory note embodies all the terms of the contract and the instrument is improperly stamped no suit on the debt will lie. This section and section 35 of the Indian Stamp Act bar the way. But if it does not embody all the terms of the contract, the true nature of the transaction can be proved and, where an instrument has been given as a collateral security or by way of conditional payment, a suit on the debt will lie. The fact that the execution of the promissory note is contemporaneous with the borrowing cannot exclude the possibility of the instrument having been given as collateral security or by way of conditional payment. There is no presumption that the giving of a promissory note by a debtor to his creditor operates as a conditional payment only. A lender suing on the original consideration on the ground that the instrument was given by way of conditional payment must prove facts which warrant that inference.[35]

The Allahabad High Court has in a Full Bench case laid down that it is not open to a party who has lent money on terms recorded in a promissory note, which turns out to be inadmissible in evidence for want of proper stamp duty, to recover his money by proving orally the terms of the contract, in contravention of the provision of this section.[36] In a later Full Bench case it laid down that the entire terms of the contract were embodied in the promissory note in the above *Nazir's* case, but where all the substantial terms of the contract have not been embodied in the promissory note and where the promissory note is inadmissible in evidence for defect of proper stamp, it is open to the plaintiff to prove the terms of the contract. It is also pointed out by some of the judges that the distinction laid down in *Nazir's* case between cases where the money passed contemporaneously with the execution of the pro-note and where it was antecedent in time to the latter is unreal and artificial.[37] Where a loan was already existing, and part of it had been repaid and a promissory note was executed in favour of the creditor for the balance, it was held that the existence of the promissory note did not debar the creditor from resorting to his original consideration or exclude evidence of the oral acknowledgment of the debt.[38]

The Patna High Court has held that where the lending of money and the execution of a promissory note for repayment of it are contemporaneous, the plaintiff in a suit for recovery of the money is entitled to adduce evidence other than the promissory note itself, in order to prove the loan. Where, therefore, a hand note bore a one-anna stamp instead of a two-annas stamp and was therefore inadmissible in evidence, it was held that the plaintiff was entitled to prove the loan by other evidence.[39] Every loan carries with it a contract to repay and if a hand note, which forms the evidence of the transaction, cannot be accepted in evidence for some reason or other, there is nothing in law to prevent the plaintiff from giving other evidence as regards the loan and if he can satisfy the court as regards the truth of his version, he is entitled to a decree.[40] Where there is a partition deed which is inadmissible in evidence for want of registration it

---

35. *Perumal Chettiar v Kamakshi Ammal,* (1938) Mad 933 FB.

36. *Nazir Khan v Ram Mohan,* (1930) 53 All 114 FB. *Gopi Nath v Srimati Chameli,* (1938) All 741.

37. *Sheo Nath Prasad v Sarju Nanio,* (1943) All 610, 641 FB.

38. *Hira Lal v Datadin,* (1881) 4 All 135; *Benarsi Das v Bhikhari Das,* (1881) 3 All 717.

39. *Dhaneshwar Sahu v Ramrup Gir,* (1928) 7 Pat 845.

40. *Abdul Muhammad Khan v Mahananda Upadhyaya,* (1931) 11 Pat 135. See *Raja Lal Bahadursingh v Sheikh Gulam Yasin,* (1932) 29 NLR 131.

is open to the defendants to prove a previous partition by any other evidence and this section will not operate as a bar to the admissibility of such evidence.[41]

Where a promissory note is insufficiently stamped it is not admissible for any purpose and a suit based on it must fail,[42] but the suit can be decreed on money had and received.[43]

The Lahore High Court has held that where a negotiable instrument taken on account of pre-existing debt is inadmissible in evidence, the creditor may sue for the original consideration, but when the original cause of action is the instrument itself and does not exist independently of it, the plaintiff cannot sue except upon the instrument. Whether there is a cause of action independent of the instrument upon which independent evidence may be given, depends upon the question whether the plaintiff can allege any contract as the basis of his suit which is not the contract reduced to the form of a document. Where the money advanced a short time before the actual execution of a *hundi* was advanced on the security of the *hundi* and the agreement between the parties was that the loan should be made in consideration of the *hundi*, it was held that there was no cause of action independent of the *hundi*, and as the *hundi* was inadmissible in evidence on the ground that it was insufficiently stamped, and no secondary evidence could be given under this section, the plaintiff must fail.[44]

[s 91.12] CASES

[s 91.12.1] Confession.—A confession of an accused person made to a Magistrate holding an inquiry is a matter required by law to be reduced to the form of a document within the meaning of this section, and no evidence can be given of the terms of such a confession except the record, if any, made under section 364 of the Code of Criminal Procedure.[45]

[s 91.12.2] Deposition.—The omission to read over his deposition to the witness, in accordance with O XVIII, rule 5, of the Code of Civil Procedure, renders the same inadmissible in evidence against him on his subsequent trial for forgery and oral evidence of its contents is excluded by this section.[46]

[s 91.12.3] Unregistered Exchange Deed.—A deed of exchange involved property of more than Rs 100 in value. It being unregistered was held to be not admissible in evidence. No oral evidence was allowed to prove its contents.[47]

[s 91.12.4] Unregistered document may be looked into for collateral purpose.—Under the proviso now added to section 49 of the Indian Registration Act, an unregistered document affecting immovable property and required to be registered may be received as evidence of a contract in a suit for specific performance, or as evidence of part performance of a contract, or as evidence of any collateral transaction not required to be effected by a registered instrument. The proviso is declaratory of what

---

41. *Ramjugeshwar v Gajadhar*, (1950) 29 Pat 980.
42. *Chandra Sekhar v Gobinda Chandra*, AIR 1966 Ori 18. *Bollan Venkataiah v VV Ramana Reddy*, AIR 1985 AP 26.
43. *Mohd Jamal Saheb v Munwar Begum*, AIR 1964 AP 188.
44. *Chandra Singh v Amritsar Banking Co*, (1921) 2 Lah 330.
45. *Emperor v Gulabu*, (1913) 35 All 260.
46. *Emperor v Nabab Ali Sarkar*, (1923) 51 Cal 236; *Chenchian v King-Emperor*, (1919) 42 Mad 561; *Taj Mahmud v The Crown*, (1927) 15 Lah 407.
47. *Krishna Prasad v SN Prasad*, AIR 2006 Sikkim 25.

was previously the law. An unregistered document, though inadmissible as evidence of a transaction affecting immovable property, was admissible as evidence of collateral facts.[48] Such document is admissible in evidence to prove the nature of the possession of the person who holds under it.[49] In a suit to recover possession of certain property as joint undivided property the defendant relied on an earlier unregistered partition deed to show that the property in dispute was not joint but separate. It was held that the partition deed was admissible in evidence as it was not intended to prove its terms but all that the court had been concerned with was to find out whether particular properties claimed by the plaintiff to be joint family property were at the date of the suit joint or separate.[50]

Where a document, itself legally inadmissible in evidence, was subsequently referred to and partly incorporated in a second document of similar import duly executed between the same parties and registered according to law, it was held that the earlier document might be referred to for the purpose of explaining and amplifying the terms of the second, and of arriving at a correct conclusion as to the true nature of the transaction into which the parties had entered.[51]

The Madras High Court had held that where the instrument of partition, being unregistered, cannot be admitted as evidence of the transaction, oral evidence to prove the terms of the agreement is barred.[52] The Supreme Court has expressed the view in *Hriday Narain Choudhury v Shyam Kishore Singh*,[53] that where an unregistered partition deed is not admissible in evidence, other evidence may be adduced by a member to show the extent of his land holding and such evidence has to be considered. This would be more particularly so when the suit is not based on such a document. On the basis of other evidence, the lower Courts recorded a concurrent finding that the plaintiff's holding was less than 5 acres and, therefore, the relevant Bihar Act was not applicable. The Supreme Court found it to be improper for the High Court to interfere in the finding on the ground that the transaction was reduced to writing and the document being not admissible in evidence, oral evidence on the point could not have been looked into. An unregistered memorandum of the partition of a joint property, though inadmissible in evidence, can be used for collateral purpose of proving intention of partition. To prove partition, oral evidence is not hit by any bar contained in section 91 of the Evidence Act.[54]

---

48. *Ulfatunnisa Elahijan Bibi v Hosain Khan,* (1883) 9 Cal 520 FB.

49. *Haranchandra Chakrabarti v Kali Prasanna Sarkar,* (1931) 59 Cal 396; *Maharani Janki Kuer v Bir Bhikhan Ojha,* (1924) 3 Pat 349; *Thakore Fatesingji v Bomanji A Dalal,* (1903) 27 Bom 515 : 5 Bom LR 274; *Jhamplu v Kutramani,* (1917) 39 All 696; *Ata Muhammad v Shankar Das,* (1925) 6 Lah 319.

50. *Chhotalal v Bai Mahakore,* (1917) 19 Bom LR 322 : 41 Bom 466; *Maung Po Kin v Maung Shwe Bya,* (1923) 1 Ran 405; *Maung Tun Sein v Ko Tu,* (1928) 6 Ran 337; *Subramonian v Lutchman,* (1922) 50 Cal 338 : 25 Bom LR 582 : 50 IA 77.

51. *Moti Chand v Lalta Prasad,* (1917) 40 All 256.

52. *Subbu Naidu v Varadarajulu Naidu,* (1947) Mad 694; *Rasu v Pandidurai,* AIR 2002 NOC 155 (Mad), a sale deed was claimed to be required for collateral purposes, but the case of the applicant was that he gained title and possession of the property on the basis of the deed. The deed was unregistered though registration was compulsory. Marking of the document was not allowed.

53. *Hriday Narain Choudhury v Shyam Kishore Singh,* AIR 2002 SC 2526.

54. *Krishna Bai v Shivnath Singh,* AIR 1993 MP 65.

[s 91.12.5] Family arrangement/settlement.—There is no provision in law requiring family settlements to be reduced to writing and registered, though when reduced to writing, the question of registration may arise. Binding family arrangements dealing with immovable property worth more than Rs 100 can be made orally and when so made, no question of registration arises. If, however, it is reduced to the form of writing with the purpose that the terms should be evidence by it, it required registration and without registration it is inadmissible, but the said family arrangement can be used as a corroborative piece of evidence for showing or explaining the conduct of the parties.[55]

[s 91.12.6] Irrevocable Power of Attorney.—The petitioner executed a power of attorney for transferring the land in question. The power of attorney holder filed the application for restoration of writ petition against notification of acquisition which was dismissed for default. The attorney had been in possession of the land for long. The petitioners were not allowed to say that they never intended to transfer the land. Their oral contention against the written power could not be accepted because of the provisions of section 91.[56]

[s 92] Exclusion of evidence of oral agreement.—When the terms of any such contract, grant or other disposition of property,[s 92.5] or any matter required by law to be reduced to the form of a document,[s 92.6] have been proved according to the last section,[s 92.7] no evidence of any oral agreement or statement shall be admitted, as between the parties to any such instrument or their representatives in interest,[s 92.8] for the purpose of contradicting, varying, adding to, or subtracting from, its terms:

Proviso (1).—Any fact may be proved which would invalidate any document, or which would entitle any person to any decree or order relating thereto, such as fraud, intimidation, illegality, want of due execution, want of capacity in any contracting party, [57][want or failure] of consideration, or mistake in fact or law.

Proviso (2).—The existence of any separate oral agreement as to any matter on which a document is silent, and which is not inconsistent with its terms, may be proved. In considering whether or not this proviso applies, the Court shall have regard to the degree of formality of the document.

Proviso (3).—The existence of any separate oral agreement, constituting a condition precedent to the attaching of any obligation under any such contract, grant or disposition of property, may be proved.

Proviso (4).—The existence of any distinct subsequent oral agreement to rescind or modify any such contract, grant or disposition of property, may be proved, except in cases in which such contract, grant or disposition of property is by law required to be in writing, or has been registered according to the law in force for the time being as to the registration of documents.

---

55. *Subraya MN v Vittala MN*, (2016) 8 SCC 705, para 16 : AIR 2016 SC 3236.
56. *Najimmudin v UOI*, AIR 2009 SC 1429 : (2009) 2 SCC 720.
57. Subs. by Act 18 of 1872, section 8, "for want of failure".

Proviso (5).—Any usage or custom by which incidents not expressly mentioned in any contract are usually annexed to contracts of that description, may be proved:

Provided that the annexing of such incident would not be repugnant to, or inconsistent with, the express terms of the contract.

Proviso (6).—Any fact may be proved which shows in what manner the language of a document is related to existing facts.

ILLUSTRATIONS

(a) *A* policy of insurance is effected on goods "in ships from Calcutta to London". The goods are shipped in a particular ship which is lost. The fact that that particular ship was orally excepted from the policy cannot be proved.

(b) *A* agrees absolutely in writing to pay *B* Rs. 1,000 on the first March, 1873. The fact that, at the same time an oral agreement was made that the money should not be paid till the thirty-first March cannot be proved.

(c) An estate called "The Rampur Tea Estate" is sold by a deed which contains a map of the property sold. The fact that land not included in the map had always been regarded as part of the estate and was meant to pass by the deed cannot be proved.

(d) *A* enters into a written contract with *B* to work certain mines, the property of *B*, upon certain terms. *A* was induced to do so by a misrepresentation of *B*'s as to their value. This fact may be proved.

(e) *A* institutes a suit against *B* for the specific performance of a contract, and also prays that the contract may be reformed as to one of its provisions, as that provision was inserted in it by mistake. *A* may prove that such a mistake was made as would by law entitle him to have the contract reformed.

(f) *A* orders goods of *B* by a letter in which nothing is said as to the time of payment, and accepts the goods on delivery. *B* sues *A* for the price. *A* may show that the goods were supplied on credit for a term still unexpired.

(g) *A* sells *B* a horse and verbally warrants him sound. *A* gives *B* a paper in these words: "Bought of *A* a horse for Rs. 500". *B* may prove the verbal warranty.

(h) *A* hires lodgings of *B*, and *B* gives a card on which is written—"Rooms, Rs. 200 a month". *A* may prove a verbal agreement that these terms were to include partial board.

A hires lodgings of *B* for a year, and a regularly stamped agreement, drawn up by an attorney, is made between them. It is silent on the subject of board. *A* may not prove that board was included in the terms verbally.

(i) *A* applies to *B* for a debt due to *A* by sending a receipt for the money. *B* keeps the receipt and does not send the money. In a suit for the amount *A* may prove this.

(j) *A* and *B* make a contract in writing to take effect upon the happening of a certain contingency. The writing is left with *B*, who sues *A* upon it. *A* may show the circumstances under which it was delivered.

SYNOPSIS

COMMENT

[s 92.1] Principle.—When a transaction has been reduced into writing, either by requirement of law, or agreement of the parties, the writing becomes the exclusive memorial thereof; and no extrinsic evidence is admissible either to prove independently the transaction, or to contradict, vary, add to, or subtract from, the terms of the document, though the contents of such document may be proved by either primary or secondary evidence.[58]

The grounds of exclusion are: (1) that to admit inferior evidence when the law requires superior would be to nullify the law; and (2) that when the parties have deliberately put their agreement into writing, it is conclusively presumed between themselves and their privies that they intended the writing to form a full and final statement of their intentions, and one which should be placed beyond the reach of future controversy, bad faith, or treacherous memory.[59] All parole testimony of conversations held between parties, or declarations made by either of them, whether before, or after, or at the time of, the completion of a contract, will be rejected; because such evidence would tend to substitute a new and different contract for the one really agreed upon. Extrinsic evidence as to what transpired subsequent to a written contract is not admissible for ascertaining its terms.[60]

[s 92.2] Ingredients.—This section operates only as between, the parties to a deed or their representatives in interest. It has no application to strangers and does not therefore prevent a stranger from showing that a transaction which on the face of it purports to be one thing was in fact never intended by the parties to be that but was effected for some collateral purpose and that the real transaction between them was something different. But such a case must be pleaded and proved.[61]

Under this section:

(1) when the terms of (a) a contract, (b) a grant, or (c) any other disposition of property, have been reduced to the form of a document, or

(2) when any matter required by law to be reduced to the form of a document,

have been proved by the production of the document or by giving secondary evidence of its contents, no evidence of any oral agreement or statement shall be admitted as between the parties to any such document or their representatives in interest, for the purpose of (i) contradicting, (ii) varying, (iii) adding to, or (iv) subtracting from, its terms. There are six exceptions to this—

---

58. *Roop Kumar v Mohan Thedani,* AIR 2003 SC 2418. sections 91 and 92 are supplementary to each other and are based upon the "best evidence rule". The Supreme Court said:

"The two sections are, however, different in some material particulars. Section 91 applies to all documents, whether they purport to dispose of rights or not, whereas section 92 applies to documents which can be described as dispositive. Section 91 applies to documents which are both bilateral and unilateral, unlike section 92 the application of which is confined only to bilateral documents. (See *Bai Hira Devi v Official Assignee of Bombay,* AIR 1958 SC 448 : 1958 SCR 1384). Both these provisions are based on *"best evidence rule".* In *Bacon's Maxim Regulation* 23, Lord Bacon said: "The law will not couple and mingle matters of speciality, which is of the higher account, with matter of averment which is of the higher account, with matter of averment which is of inferior account in law. It would be inconvenient that matters in writing made by advice and on consideration, and which finally import the certain truth of the agreement of parties should be controlled by averment of the parties to be proved by the uncertain testimony of slippery memory."

59. *Phipson,* 7th Edn, p 552.

60. *Belapur Co v Mah, State Farming Corp,* (1968) 74 Bom LR 246.

61. *Rangubai v Govind,* (1949) Nag 78.

(1) Any fact which would (i) invalidate any document, or (ii) entitle any person to any decree or order relating thereto may be proved, such as fraud, intimidation, illegality, failure of consideration, mistake in fact or law.

(2) Any separate oral agreement (i) as to any matter on which the document is silent, and (ii) which is not inconsistent with its terms, may be proved.

(3) Any separate oral agreement, constituting a condition precedent to the attacking of any obligation under the document, may be proved.

(4) Any subsequent oral agreement to rescind or modify any such contract, grant, or disposition of property, may be proved, except when such contract of grant (i) is required to be in writing, or (ii) has been registered.

(5) Any usage or custom by which incidents not expressly mentioned in any contract are usually annexed to such contracts, may be proved if they are not repugnant to, or inconsistent with, its express terms.

(6) Any fact which shows in what manner the language of the document is related to existing facts, may be proved.

This section is supplementary to section 91 and is, to some extent, implied, in it. If the contract, grant or disposition has been reduced into writing, section 91 says no evidence shall be given of it, except the document itself, and this rule would be in vain, unless, as is said in this section, it was also forbidden to contradict, vary, add to, or subtract from, its terms.[62]

The bar of this section applies only when it is sought to be proved that the terms of the transaction were different and not that the transaction itself was different than what it purported to be.[63]

[s 92.3] Scope.—The section applies only where, upon the face of it, the written instrument appears to contain the whole contract.[64] If the parties have intended to reduce all the terms of the contract into writing, then no parole evidence is admissible; but if they intended only to reduce into writing a portion of the terms of the contract, then they are entitled to give parole evidence of the terms which they did not intend to reduce into writing.[65] This section is only applicable to cases as between parties to an instrument or their representatives in interest. Where, however, the dispute is between a stranger to an instrument and a party to it or his representative in interest, this section is inapplicable, and both the stranger and the party or his representative are at liberty to lead evidence of oral agreement notwithstanding the fact that such evidence, if believed, may contradict, vary, add to, or subtract from, its terms.[66] Where however a transaction is contained in more than one document the documents should be read and interpreted together and this section is not applicable.[67] A contract made on the

---

62. Markby, 73, *Bhawanbhai Premabhai v Bai Vahali*, (1954) 57 Bom LR 250.
63. *Heirs of Jatashanker v Heirs of Mavji*, AIR 1969 Guj 169.
64. *Cutts v Brown*, (1880) 6 Cal 328, 337.
65. *Jumna Doss v Srinath Roy*, (1886) 17 Cal 176n, 177.
66. *Bai Hira Devi v The Official Assignee of Bombay*, 1958 SCR 1384 : 60 Bom LR 932 : AIR 1958 SC 448.
67. *Chattanatha v Central Bank of India*, AIR 1965 SC 1856 : 1965(3) SCR 318 : (1965) 35 Com Cas 610.

basis of a tender is in writing. Additional terms were not allowed to be brought in either on oral basis or by the conduct of the officers of the authority making payments on a different basis.[68]

[s 92.4] *Benami* transaction.—This section applies only to the terms of a transfer and does not preclude the admission of any evidence to show the *benami* character of the transaction.[69] The Supreme Court allowed oral evidence to show that the real tenant was someone other than the ostensible tenant.[70] Oral evidence was allowed to show as to who were the parties to a *benami* transaction.[71]

[s 92.5] "When the terms of any such contract, grant or other disposition of property".—These words when read with the words "as between the parties to any such instrument" which follow them, refer to bilateral instruments only and not to unilateral instruments, such as wills and powers-of-attorney. Oral evidence as to the "terms" of a written contract is excluded. There is nothing to exclude oral evidence that there was no agreement between the parties and therefore no contract.[72] The recital in a sale deed that there are no encumbrances on the property sold is not a term of contract, and evidence to prove that the vendee was aware of certain liability on the property and purchased it subject to such liability is admissible.[73]

[s 92.6] "Or any matter required by law to be reduced to the form of a document".—These words, when read with the words "as between the parties" and "any oral agreement and statement," refer to bilateral contracts, grants or other dispositions of property, which the law requires to be reduced to writing and not to every matter which the law requires to be reduced to writing.

[s 92.7] "Have been proved according to the last section".—The provisions of the section come into force when the written instruments referred to in the section have been proved in accordance with the provisions of section 91, that is, either by the production of the document itself, or by the production of the secondary evidence of it.

[s 92.8] "No evidence of any oral agreement or statement shall be admitted as between the parties to any such instrument or their representatives in interest".—The section forbids the admission of evidence of an oral agreement for the purpose of contradicting, varying, adding to, or subtracting from, the terms of a written document as between the *parties* to such document or their representatives in interest.[74] The rule of exclusion laid down in the section does not apply to the case of a *third* party who is not a party to the document. On the contrary, section 99 distinctly provides that persons who are not parties to a document may give evidence tending to show a contemporaneous agreement varying the terms of the document.[75] Extraneous evidence

---

68. *TN Electricity Board v N Raju Reddiar,* AIR 1996 SC 2025 : 1996(4) SCC 551.
69. *Richard Taylor v Rajah of Parlakimedi,* (1909) 32 Mad 443, 454; *Pathammal v Syed Kalai Ravuthar,* (1903) 27 Mad 329.
70. *Niranjan Kumar v Dhyan Singh,* AIR 1976 SC 2400 : 1976(4) SCC 89.
71. *Raj Ballav Das v Haripada,* AIR 1985 Cal 2.
72. *Tyagaraja Mudaliyar v Vedathanni,* (1935) 38 Bom LR 373 : 63 IA 126 : 59 Mad 446.
73. *Munninarayan Reddi v Chinnaswamy Gownder,* (1953) Mys 29.
74. *Nibash Ch Saha v Champa Lal Ladhar,* AIR 2010 Gau 137 : 2010 (3) Gau LT 407, terms of an agreement of sale reduced to writing and registered under the Registration, subsequent oral agreement on those very terms held to be barred.
75. *Bageshri Dayal v Pancho,* (1906) 28 All 473.

to show that the parties to a sale deed had no intention of conveying a particular item of property included in the deed is admissible where the person challenging the transfer is not a party to the deed.[76]

The words "between the parties to any such instrument" do not preclude one of two persons in whose favour a deed of sale is purported to have been executed from proving by oral evidence in a suit by the one against the other, that the defendant was not a real but a nominal party only to a purchase, and that the plaintiff was solely entitled to the property to which it related. M conveyed certain houses and premises to plaintiff and defendant jointly by a sale deed. Plaintiff sued defendant for ejectment from the premises, alleging that he alone was the real purchaser, and that the defendant was only nominally associated with him in the deed. It was held that this section did not preclude the plaintiff from showing by oral evidence that he alone was the real purchaser, notwithstanding that the defendant was described in the sale deed as one of the two purchasers.[77] The plaintiff sued to recover money which he had been compelled to pay in virtue of a mortgage executed by his two half-sisters and himself. His claim was based on the plea that, though appearing in the bond as a co-obligor, he was in reality merely a surety. It was held that evidence was admissible to show that the plaintiff executed the mortgage bond as a surety only.[78] The Rangoon High Court has dissented from this view and held that oral evidence to show that one of the executants of a monetary bond to the knowledge of the money-lender signed it only as a surety is not admissible.[79] The Privy Council has held that oral evidence is inadmissible to show that the person who has signed a promissory note is not liable but someone else is.[80] Oral evidence was not allowed to contradict the contents of a written deed of liability to a bank.[81]

The section does not prevent proof of a fraudulent dealing with a third person's property or proof of notice that the property purporting to be absolutely conveyed in fact belonged to a third person who was not a party to the conveyance.[82] As between the parties to an absolute conveyance this section precludes the giving of oral evidence to prove that the transaction was intended to be a mortgage. But where the grantee took knowing that a third person was the owner of the property and the grantor was only a mortgagee, and that the intention of all parties was merely to transfer the mortgage, oral evidence of the third party's rights was admissible to prove the real nature of the transaction.[83]

The mere fact that both the parties have not signed a contract will not make the agreement oral within the meaning of sections 91 and 92, because these sections only require the terms to be reduced to writing and not the whole contract in the sense of signatures and dates and so forth. Even where signatures are absent on an agreement or

---

76. *Ram Sundar Mal v Collector of Gorakhpur,* (1930) 52 All 793.

77. *Mulchand v Madho Ram,* (1888) 10 All 421. **See** *Pokal Gungayah v Ismail Mohomed Madaree,* (1895) 2 UBR (1892-96) 354.

78. *Shamsh-ul-Jahan Begam v Ahmed Wali Khan,* (1903) 25 All 337; *Khudawand Karim v Narendra Nath,* (1935) 58 All 548; *Mohammad Husain v Lala Hanoman Prasad,* (1942) 18 Luck 81.

79. *Maung Ko Gyi v U Kyaw,* (1927) 5 Ran 168.

80. *National Bank of Upper India, Ltd v Bansidhar,* (1929) 5 Luck 1 : 32 Bom LR 136 : 57 IA 1; *Khumaji Gajaji & Co v Damaji,* (1933) 35 Bom LR 1197.

81. *Janki v Ganesh Ram,* AIR 1984 All 219. An altered deed cannot be put in evidence because it amounts to variation. *Suresh Chandra v Satish Chandra,* AIR 1983 All 81.

82. *Maung Kyin v Ma Shwe La,* (1911) 13 Bom LR 797 : 38 Cal 892 : 38 IA 146.

83. *Maung Kyin v Ma Shwe La,* (1917) 44 IA 236 : 20 Bom LR 278 : 45 Cal 320.

the proposal and acceptance are not entered in it, it would still be hit by sections 91 and 92 provided the "terms" meaning all the terms, are embodied in the written agreement. The absence of signatures could be used as good evidence of the fact that the document was not intended to be final and binding. But the mere absence of signatures would not prevent the document from being the final depository of the intention of parties, any more than the presence of signatures would operate to bind if it could be established that the signing was conditional.[84]

[s 92.9] "For the purpose of contradicting, varying, adding to, or subtracting from, its terms".—This is what the section forbids. But it does not prevent a party to a contract from showing by oral evidence that the consideration is different from that described in the contract. It is therefore open to a party to show that that part of the consideration as to rent payable in terms of a lease represented a past debt for rent and not a future liability arising under the contract.[85] Consideration is not a term. Oral evidence can be adduced as to what exactly was the nature of consideration.[86]

The recitals in a registered adoption deed clearly showed the date on which the adoption ceremony was held. It was held that no oral evidence could be allowed of any agreement to contradict the terms of the written document and to show that the adoption took place on a different date.[87]

[s 92.10] Evidence of intention, acts and conduct.—The Privy Council laid down in *Balkishen v Legge* that oral evidence of intention is not admissible for the purpose of construing a deed or ascertaining the intention of the parties to the deed. Oral evidence was not allowed, for example, to show whether a particular deed was intended by the parties to be a sale or lease.[88] A deed of sale of land for value was accompanied by a deed of agreement between the parties for purchase back by the vendor of the land on payment by him of money to the vendee on a future date fixed. The deeds were followed by transfer of possession to the vendee, and his receipt of the profits. The vendor did not exercise his right of re-purchase; but after many years, gave notice of his intention to redeem, and sued to enforce his right of redemption as upon a mortgage by conditional sale. The Privy Council held that oral evidence for the purpose of ascertaining the intention of the parties to the deeds was not admissible and that the case must be decided on a consideration of the contents of the documents themselves with such extrinsic evidence of surrounding circumstances as may be required to show in what manner the language of the document was related to existing facts.[89] Even after this pronouncement of the Judicial Committee there was a conflict of views between the Bombay and the Madras High Courts on the one hand and the Calcutta High Court on the other on the question whether oral evidence as to acts and conduct of parties subsequent to a deed was admissible to show that what on the face of it was a conveyance of sale was in reality a mortgage. The High Courts of Bombay[90] and

---

84. *Balram v Mahadeo,* (1949) Nag 849.

85. *Abdullakin v Maung Ne Dun,* (1929) 7 Ran 292.

86. *State Bank of India v Premco Saw Mills,* AIR 1984 Guj 93.

87. *MD Gopalaiah v Usha Priyadarshini,* AIR 2002 Kant 73 : 2002 (1) KCCR 185.

88. *Satyanarayan Shah v Star Co,* AIR 1984 Cal 399 : IR 1984 Cal 399.

89. *Balkishen v Legge,* (1899) 2 Bom LR 523 : 27 IA 58 : 22 All 149; *Maharu v Khandu,* (1924) 26 Bom LR 742 PC; *Vithoba v Narayan,* (1942) Nag 592; *Kesarbai v Rajabhau,* (1944) Nag 141.

90. *Dattoo v Ramchandra,* (1905) 30 Bom 119 : 7 Bom LR 669; *Abaji v Laxman,* (1906) 30 Bom 426 : 8 Bom LR 553.

Madras[91] were of opinion that such evidence was not admissible. The former Chief Court of Lower Burma[92] and the former Judicial Commissioner's Court of Upper Burma[93] followed this view. On the other hand, the Calcutta High Court[94] was of opinion that such evidence was admissible. The former Chief Court of the Punjab[95] had adopted the view of the Calcutta High Court. This conflict has been set at rest by the Privy Council in *Maung Kyin's* case, above referred to, in which it has expressly overruled the decisions of the Calcutta High Court and approved those of the Bombay and the Madras High Courts. It has held that as between the parties to an absolute conveyance this section precludes the giving of oral evidence to prove that the transaction was intended to be a mortgage.[96]

Though this section precludes oral evidence of intention for the purpose of construing deeds or proving the intention of the parties, it merely prescribes a rule of evidence, and does not fetter the court's power to arrive at the true meaning and effect of a document in the light of all the circumstances surrounding the transaction.[97] When it is said that a court should look into all the circumstances to find an author's intention, it is only for the purpose of finding out whether the words apply accurately to existing facts. But if the words are clear in the context of the surrounding circumstances the court cannot rely on them to attribute to the author an intention contrary to the plain meaning of the words used in the document.[98]

It is always permissible to look to the surrounding circumstances to see in what manner the language of a document was related to existing facts. A party is not precluded from showing that the writing was not the contract between the parties but was only a fictitious or colourable device which cloaked something else.[99]

Oral evidence was allowed to show that the transaction in question was actually intended to be a loan transaction and not as an agreement for sale of property.[100] In another similar case, the plaintiff contended that the sale deed of the property in question was executed not as a real sale deed but by way of security for the loan transaction between the parties and that the defendant would reconvey the property to the plaintiff after receiving back the amount of the loan and interest thereon. It was held that the plaintiff was entitled to prove these facts by oral evidence.[101]

---

91. *Achutaramaraju v Subbaraju,* (1901) 25 Mad 7.

92. *Maung Bin v Ma Hlaing,* (1906) 3 LBR 100 FB.

93. *Mi Gywe v, Kesha Ram,* (1908) 2 UBR (1907-1909) (Evi) 15.

94. *Preonath Shaha v Madhu Sudan Bhuiya,* (1898) 25 Cal 603 FB; *Khankar Abdur Rahman v Ali Hafez,* (1900) 28 Cal 256; *Mahomed Ali Hossein v Nazir Ali,* (1901) 28 Cal 289.

95. *Abdul Ghafur Khan v Abdul Kadir,* (1901) PR No. 72 of 1901 (Civil); *Bulaki Mal v CJ Floyd,* (1911) PR No. 27 of 1911 (Civil).

96. *Maung Kyin v Ma Shwe La,* (1917) 44 IA 236 : 20 Bom LR 278 : 45 Cal 320 : 9 LBR 114; *Maung Shwe Phoo v Maung Tun Shin,* (1927) 5 Ran 644.

97. *Baijnath Singh v Hajee Vally Mahomed,* (1924) 27 Bom LR 787 : 3 Ran 106 (PC).

98. *Kamla Devi v Takhatmal,* AIR 1964 SC 859 : 1964(2) SCR 152.

99. *Asaram v Lubdheshwar,* (1939) Nag 1.

100. *K Bhaskaran Nair v Habeeb Mohd.,* AIR 2002 Ker 308. *Balram Kirar v Ramkrishna,* AIR 2002 MP 139, statements of witnesses showed fraud in the making of the transaction. Concurrent finding of fact by courts below that the document was not a mortgage set aside. Document alleged to be sham, oral evidence permitted to show that the document executed was never intended, *Kashinath Yadeo Hiwarde v Osman Baig Sandu Baig,* AIR 2016 NOC 266 (Bom).

101. *Shankarlal Ganulal v Balmukund,* AIR 1999 Bom 260.

Evidence of subsequent conduct is not admissible for construing a document when the words used are plain.[102]

[s 92.11] CASES.—Intention, conduct, *etc.*—The plaintiff sued to recover possession of land contending that the document under which the defendants held the land, though in the form of an absolute conveyance, was intended to operate merely as a mortgage. The plaintiff's contention was based on the ground that the consideration was a previously existing debt and not money paid at the time; that the plaintiff's father, notwithstanding the execution of the deed, remained in possession until his death and that after his death his widow remained in possession for 3 years; that there was no transfer of the land into the *khata* of the transferee, and that the consideration was grossly inadequate. It was held that the transaction was an out-and-out sale and no evidence of the several circumstances relied on could be admitted to show that it was a mortgage.[103] Where in respect of an agreement to sell an agricultural land, the defendant contended he only intended usufructuary mortgage to secure advances of money made by the plaintiff who said that he would give up his possession if the money advanced was returned, the admission of the plaintiff could be used to invalidate the agreement to sell.[104] Where tenancy was granted for a limited period, the tenant, after expiry of the period, cannot make objection that the proceedings were camouflage and real intention was to create general tenancy.[105] The plaintiffs, who were agriculturists, brought a suit to redeem and the defendant contended that the transaction in suit was a sale out-and-out and not a mortgage. The lower Court held that the transaction was a mortgage and allowed redemption. It was held that evidence of intention could not be given for the purpose merely of construing a document which purported to be a sale out-and-out and not a mortgage.[106] A surgeon attached to a private hospital on honorary basis was allowed to occupy a cabin in the hospital. This kind of occupation was recorded on a stamped document. Oral evidence was not allowed to show that the occupation was on some other basis, like leave or licence. In support of the recorded fact the court admitted the testimony of the co-occupant, who deposed that the letting was not on leave or licence basis and that the basis was that the cabin was to be vacated whenever asked for. Though he was an interested party his evidence was not unnatural.[107] Oral evidence of the owners of the lands, adjoining the land sold, may be given to prove that the names of the adjoining owners were wrongly given.[108]

A deed of sale of immovable property and an agreement for resale to the vendor do not together constitute a mortgage unless it appears from the documents, in the light of surrounding circumstances, that the parties so intended. The intention of the

---

102. *Markandelal v Sitambharnath,* (1945) Nag 10.

103. *Dattoo v Ramchandra,* (1905) 7 Bom LR 669 : 30 Bom 119; *Keshavrao v Raya,* (1906) 8 Bom LR 287; *Bai Adhar v Lalbhai,* (1921) 24 Bom LR 239; *Talakchand v Atmaram,* (1923) 25 Bom LR 818; *Mathai v Thomas,* (1956) TC 411.

104. *Sitaram Lal v Jameswar Das,* AIR 1995 Ori 260.

105. *Sunil Puri v Modi Spinning & Weaving Mills Co Ltd,* AIR 1994 NOC 336 (Del).

106. *Abaji v Laxman,* (1906) 30 Bom 426, 8 Bom LR 553; *Achutaramaraju v Subbaraju,* (1901) 25 Mad 7.

107. *Vinod Chaturvedi v State of MP,* AIR 1984 SC 911 : 1984 Cr LJ 814 : (1984) 2 SCC 350 : 1984 SCC (Cri) 250.

108. *Mohan Rai v State of Bihar,* AIR 1994 Pat 42.

parties, which is the test in such a case, must be gathered from the language of the documents themselves.[109]

In a suit for specific performance on the basis of sale agreement, the defendant was allowed to contend that the parties never intended to act upon it and had a different contract altogether in mind. The bar of section 92 operates only if the defendant relies upon the agreement and also at the same time seeks to vary or contradict its terms.[110] It has also been held that oral evidence in departure from the terms of a deed is admissible to show that what was mentioned in the deed was not the real transaction but that was something different.[111]

[s 92.12] Oral evidence inadmissible to vary terms.—The executant of promissory note cannot be permitted to prove a separate agreement according to which the sum specified in the note was not, as expressed therein, payable on demand, but only after the adjustment of some accounts between the parties.[112] No oral evidence is admissible to vary the amount of price fixed in a registered sale deed,[113] or the terms of a cheque which is a negotiable instrument[114] or the rate of interest different[115] from that in the written contract. In the sale of the audio/CD rights in a movie, the agreement expressly stated that the sale consideration was Rs 12.50 lakhs and nothing more. Another clause of the agreement as to variation of terms would have no effect unless reduced to writing. The plea of a party that there was an oral agreement that the actual sale price would be Rs 1 crore was not allowed. A mortgage with possession was executed in plaintiff's favour for a term of 10 years. Possession was not, in fact, taken by the plaintiff, but by a second document of even date, the mortgaged land was leased to the mortgagor for the same term at an annual rent. The court of the Judicial Commissioner held that reading the mortgage with the lease of even date, and taking into account the fact that possession had remained all along with the mortgagor and that there had been other similar transactions between the parties, the mortgage should be construed only as a simple mortgage. The Privy Council held that this section forbade the admission or consideration of evidence as to the intention of the parties or to contradict the express terms of the document, and that the mortgage in question was, as it purported on the face of it to be, a possessory mortgage.[116]

An oral agreement not to execute a decree, entered into between the parties after the filing of the suit and before the passing of the decree, provided the defendant did not

109. *Jhanda Singh v Sheikh Wahid-ud-din,* (1916) 19 Bom LR 1 : 43 IA 284 : 39 All 570.
110. *Kanireddi Sattaraju v Kandanmuri Booleswari,* AIR 2007 NOC 540 (Mad—DB).
111. *Parvinder Singh v Renu Gautam,* AIR 2004 SC 2299 : (2004) 4 SCC 794.
112. *Sri Ram v Sabha Ram Gopal Rai,* (1922) 44 All 521. This case has been dissented from in a subsequent case in which the same High Court held that evidence to show that an instrument like a promissory note, the title to which generally passes by delivery, was delivered conditionally or for a special purpose only, and not for the purpose of transferring absolutely the property therein, is not only admissible but is precisely the class of evidence contemplated by section 46 of the Negotiable Instruments Act and this section; *Sheo Prasad v Gobind Prasad,* (1927) 49 All 464; *Bhogi Ram v Kishori Lal* (1928) 50 All 754.
113. *Adityam Iyer v Rama Krishna Iyer,* (1913) 38 Mad 514.
114. *Walter Mitchell v AK Tennent,* (1925) 52 Cal 677.
115. *Fitz-Holmes v Bank of Upper India Ltd,* (1923) 4 Lah 258.
116. *Feroz Shah v Sobhat Khan,* (1933) 35 Bom LR 877 : 14 Lah 466 : 60 IA 273.

contest the suit, is admissible in evidence as it does not vary the terms of the decree, and can be pleaded in bar of execution.[117]

Where a document purports to be an absolute sale, a contemporaneous unregistered agreement giving the vendor the right of redemption is inadmissible to prove that the deed of sale is in reality a mortgage.[118]

[s 92.13] Oral evidence inadmissible to contradict written terms.—In a suit for a declaration that an apparent sale deed executed by the plaintiff was a mortgage and for redemption, the lower Courts allowed the plaintiff to adduce evidence to prove that the defendant at the time of the execution of the sale deed represented to the plaintiff that the sale deed would not be enforced as such. It was held that no evidence of a contemporaneous agreement, or promise, or representation inconsistent with the written document could be admitted.[119] In a suit for a decree for sale for the mortgage amount due under an admittedly usufructuary mortgage the defendants contended that there was a contemporaneous oral agreement to treat the usufructuary deed as a simple mortgage and that transfer of possession was never intended. On the question whether evidence in support of the oral agreement could be allowed to be let in, it was held that the courts should give effect to the intention expressed in the document and that the contemporaneous oral agreement was inadmissible in evidence.[120] Where a registered document on the face of it without any ambiguity is a pure and simple mortgage, the parties to the transaction or their successors-in-interest cannot be allowed under section 92 to prove by parole evidence that it was intended to operate as a deed of sale.[121] The plaintiff's father conveyed the family properties to his sister's husband for a stated amount as consideration, the consideration being the obligation which the vendee undertook to discharge the family debts for that amount, and the vendee sold some of the properties and discharged the debts, and the plaintiff sued the vendee for the recovery of the properties left, and for an account of his management of the properties conveyed. It was held that the plaintiff was precluded from establishing an oral agreement to reduce an out-and-out sale into a trust so as to take away the right of the vendee to enjoy the properties, as such an agreement would be hit by this section.[122] Evidence in respect of an oral agreement to return the property which has been conveyed under a registered sale deed is inadmissible.[123]

[s 92.14] Oral evidence admitted where third party is concerned.—Plaintiff sued to recover one-fourth of the price of a house alleged to have been sold by the first defendant to the second defendant, the claim being based upon a local custom. The transaction between the defendants was ostensibly not a sale but a usufructuary mortgage. It was held that the plaintiff, not being a party to the transaction, was entitled

---

117. *Papamma v Venkayya,* (1935) 58 Mad 994 FB; **disapproving** *Rajah of Kalahasti v Venkatadri Rao,* (1927) 50 Mad 897; *Goseti Subba Row v Varigonda Narasimham,* (1903) 27 Mad 368; *Chidambaram Chettiar v Krishna Vathiyar,* (1916) 40 Mad 233 FB; *Laldas v Kishordas,* (1896) 22 Bom 463 FB. Contra *Benode Lal Pakrashi v Brajendra Kumar Saha,* (1902) 29 Cal 810; *Hassan Ali v Gauzi Ali Mir,* (1903) 31 Cal 179.

118. *Kondiram v Gundappa,* (1955) Hyd 440.

119. *Dagdu v Nama,* (1910) 12 Bom LR 972; *Namdev v Dhondu,* (1920) 22 Bom LR 979 : 44 Bom 961; *Ramlochan v Pradip Singh,* AIR 1959 Pat 230.

120. *Vasudevan Namboori v Devassi,* (1956) TC 704.

121. *Ram Narain v Manki Singh,* (1954) 33 Pat 638.

122. *Rakkiyana v Chinnu,* (1954) Mad 271.

123. *Thatha Rao v Jummarlal,* (1954) Hyd 373.

to give evidence to show that what purported to be a usufructuary mortgage was not in reality such, but was in fact a sale.[124]

The section is applicable only to parties to the instrument and not strangers to it. In a criminal proceedings arising out of a transaction, the prosecution is not a party to it. The bar applies to oral evidence to disprove the terms of the contract and not to disprove the contract itself. Thus, even a party to the instrument can show that the transaction contained in the instrument is itself sham or fictitious or nominal in the sense of being not intended to be acted upon. The prosecution could show that the transaction was fictitious because it was designed to offer an explanation for disproportionate wealth acquired by the accused.[125]

[s 92.15] Void or voidable.—[Proviso 1].—This proviso applies to cases where evidence is admitted to show that a contract is void, or voidable, or subject to re-formation, upon the ground of fraud, duress, illegality, *etc.*, in its inception.[126] See Illustrations (d) and (e). The instances given in the proviso are not exhaustive. They are set out by way of illustration only. If the validity of a written agreement is impeached, it is no defence to point to the apparent rectitude of the document and to claim protection from inquiry under a rule which exists against the contradiction and variance of the terms only of those instruments the validity of which is not in question. In such cases, the court is not bound by what has been described as the mere paper expressions of the parties, and is not precluded from inquiring into the real nature of the transaction between them. The proviso declares that any fact may be proved which would invalidate any document.[127] A party to an instrument may prove that it was a mere paper transaction, never intended to be given effect to or acted upon.[128]

The combined effect of this proviso and section 31 of the Specific Relief Act is to entitle either party to a contract, whether plaintiff or defendant, to protect his right by proving a mistake in a written contract i.e., a mistake in the description of the property sold by giving a wrong survey number to the same. Mistake in the belief of a party to a document may be pointed out under this proviso.[129] It is immaterial if the mistake is caused by innocent misrepresentation.[130] Evidence of mutual mistake is admissible under this proviso.[131]

---

124. *Bageshri Dayal v Pancho,* (1906) 28 All 473; *Rahiman v Elahi Baksh,* (1900) 28 Cal 70, dissented from *Ganu v Bhau,* (1918) 20 Bom LR 684 : 42 Bom 512; *Kumara v Srinivasa,* (1887) 11 Mad 213, 215; *Gurdial Singh v Raj Kumar Aneja,* AIR 2002 SC 1003, in a challenge to the validity of a lease deed, the question being whether the occupants were sub-tenants or tenants, they could raise the question whether the transaction between the owner and tenant was not what it appeared to be on reading the lease deed. They were not parties to the lease deed. Provisions of sections 91 and 92 were not attracted to their case.

125. *R Janakiraman v State,* AIR 2006 SC 1106 : (2006) 1 SCC 697.

126. Per Garth CJ, in *Cutts v Brown,* (1880) 6 Cal 328, 338.

127. *Beni Madhab Dass v Sadasook Kotary,* (1905) 32 Cal 437 FB; *Ma Thin Myaing v Maung Gyi,* (1923) 1 Ran 351; *General Court Martial v Anittej Singh Dhaliwal (Col),* 1998 Cr LJ 402 (SC), section 92 applies only when the execution of the document is admitted and there is no other infirmity in it. The oral evidence of witnesses to the proceedings of the Board was held to be admissible.

128. *Ram Sundar Mal v Collector of Gorakhpur,* (1930) 52 All 793.

129. *Tani Mahesha v Secretary of State for India in Council,* (1894) PR No. 67 of 1894 (Civil).

130. *Chimanram Motilal v Divanchand Govindram,* (1931) 56 Bom 180 : 34 Bom LR 26.

131. *Janardan v Venkatesh,* (1938) 41 Bom LR 191 : (1939) Bom 149.

The Privy Council has held that this section only excludes oral evidence to vary the terms of a written contract, and has no reference to the question whether the parties had agreed to contract upon the terms set forth in a particular document. Even if there were no provisos to sections 91 and 92 there is nothing in either section to exclude oral evidence that a document purporting to embody the terms of a contract was never intended to operate as an agreement but was brought into existence solely for the purpose of creating evidence on some other matter. Such oral evidence stands on the same footing as would evidence that the alleged signature of one of the parties was a forgery.[132]

Where parties enter into a sale deed, it is not competent to them to prove a contemporaneous oral agreement to reconvey the property sold on payment of the sum advanced, in the absence of fraud, misrepresentation, or failure of consideration, *etc.*, rendering the sale invalid.[133]

[s 92.15.1] Fraud.—Fraud in order to vitiate a document must have been committed in the execution of the document i.e. a document which was not intended to be executed must have been executed. In cases of fraud the important thing that has got to be proved is the intention to defraud. It would constitute fraud only where either there has been a promise made without any intention of performing it or where there has been an active concealment of fact by one having knowledge or belief of the fact.[134]

Where one party induces the other to contract on the faith of representations made to him any one of which is untrue, the whole contract is in a court of Equity considered as having been obtained fraudulently.[135]

In order to plead fraud effectively the particulars of fraud must be given by the party, and in the absence of such particulars, there cannot be any proper averment of fraud. The fraud which is alleged must be such as enters into the transaction itself and enables the party to avoid the transaction. It must be fraud within the meaning of the term as used in section 17(3) of the Indian Contract Act, 1872 and unless and until the allegations amount to that, there cannot be any valid plea of fraud which can be taken up by a party.[136]

It may be shown that the document is a sham. It was contended in this case that the mortgage deed in question was in fact intended to be a collateral security to the landlord-tenant relationship to enable the landlord to enforce eviction. But this fact was not proved as the document was found to be genuine. The mortgagee did not produce the original in the court. The judgment was based upon a certified copy filed by the plaintiff as secondary evidence.[137]

[s 92.15.2] Misrepresentation.—Where one party to a contract does not agree to any of its stipulations and the other party induces him, not indeed to agree to it, but to agree to its formal insertion in the written contract, by representing that the

---

132. *Tyagaraja Mudaliyar v Vedathanni,* (1935) 63 IA 126, 137 : 38 Bom LR 373 : 59 Mad 446.

133. *Sangira v Ramappa,* (1909) 11 Bom LR 1130 : 34 Bom 59.

134. *Thatha Rao v Jummarlal,* (1952) Hyd 373.

135. *Abaji v Laxman,* (1906) 30 Bom 426 : 8 Bom LR 553.

136. *Narsingdas Takhatmal v Radhakisan,* (1951) 54 Bom LR 492; *Raghunath Tiwari v Rama Kant Tiwari,* AIR 1991 Pat 145.

137. *Ishwar Dass Jain v Sohan Lal,* AIR 2000 SC 426 : (2000) 1 SCC 434.

stipulation in question would be in reality treated by him as a dead letter, it cannot be enforced because the party induced had never assented to it and its inclusion in the written contract was the result of misrepresentation.[138] Where, at the time of executing a document, a representation is made that the document though in form of a sale deed will not be enforced as against the executant as a sale deed, and where on the faith of that representation the executant executes the document, the sale deed cannot be upheld as a sale deed as against him.[139]

[s 92.15.3] Illegal or Sham.—Oral evidence is admissible to prove that the real object or consideration of an agreement in writing is unlawful and that therefore the agreement is void.[140] See section 23 of the Indian Contract Act.

Fraud would have to be proved by leading evidence and not by mere averments in pleadings. The High Court was not right in working on a mere suspicion of fraud or going merely by the allegations in the plaint. The material on record must be capable of spelling out at least a *prima facie* case of fraud.[141]

[s 92.15.4] Want of due execution.—The term "execution" means the last act or series of acts which completes a document. It is a formal completion of a document. Thus, execution of deeds is the signing, sealing and delivery of them in the presence of witnesses. Execution of a will includes attestation.[142] Writing, stamp, registration, attestation are all formalities necessitated by statutes.

[s 92.15.5] Want of consideration.—Want of consideration, or failure of consideration, or difference in the kind of consideration may be proved. But parole evidence to vary the consideration is not admissible.[143] The want or failure of consideration contemplated by the proviso is a complete want or failure of consideration.[144] Notwithstanding an admission in a sale deed that the consideration has been received, it is open to the vendor to prove that no consideration has actually been paid,[145] but was agreed to be paid in a different manner.[146] If this was not so, facilities would be afforded for the grossest frauds. It is no infringement of this section for a court to accept proof that by a collateral arrangement between the vendor and the purchaser the consideration money remained with the purchaser and under the conditions agreed upon between them.[147] The section does not say that no statement of fact in a written instrument

---

138. *Sangira v Ramappa,* (1909) 11 Bom LR 1130 : 35 Bom 59.

139. *Navalbai v Sivubai,* (1906) 8 Bom LR 761.

140. *Kashi Nath Chukerbati v Brindabun Chukerbati,* (1884) 10 Cal 649; *Anupchand Hemchand v Champsi Ugerchand,* (1888) 12 Bom 585.

141. *Svenska Handelsbanken v Indian Charge Chrome,* AIR 1994 SC 626 : (1994) 79 Comp Cas 589 : (1994) 1 Andh LT 37 (SC).

142. *Bhawanji Harbhum v Devji Punja,* (1894) 19 Bom 635, 638.

143. *Motilal Singh v Mt Fulia,* AIR 1958 Pat 61; *KS Narasimhachari v Indo-Commercial Bank,* AIR 1965 Mad 147; *Leelamma Ambika Kumari v Narayan Ramakrishnan,* AIR 1992 Ker 115, evidence that more consideration was given than that which was mentioned in the sale deed, evidence not allowed. The court distinguished the case from *Nabin Chandra v Shuna Mala,* AIR 1932 Cal 25, where evidence was allowed to show that a different kind of consideration was given than the one mentioned in the deed.

144. *Keshavrao v Raya,* (1906) 8 Bom LR 287.

145. *Radhamohan Thakur v Bipin Behari Mitra,* (1938) 17 Pat 318; *Savitri Devi v State of Bihar,* AIR 1989 Pat 327.

146. *Indrajit v Lal Chand,* (1895) 18 All 168.

147. *Irfanali Laskar v Jogendrachandra Das Patni,* (1932) 59 Cal 1111.

may be contradicted by oral evidence, but that the terms of the contract may not be varied.[148] Where a part of the sale consideration is on the face of the document still outstanding and to be paid by the vendee, it is not open to him to produce evidence to show that there was a separate contemporaneous oral agreement that this sum would not be payable and was merely fictitious.[149] The amount of sale consideration is a term of a deed of sale and no evidence of any oral agreement can be given for the purpose of varying the amount. An agreement made without consideration is void except in the three cases specified in section 25 of the Indian Contract Act, 1872. When it is brought to the notice of a court that the consideration for a contract which it is asked to enforce is, in whole or in part, an unlawful consideration, such Court is bound to give effect to the fact thus brought to its notice, notwithstanding that the contract may appear upon the face of it to be a perfectly legal contract, and that the unlawfulness of the consideration was never pleaded by the defendant.[150]

A suit for title and possession of property was based on a registered sale deed. The defendant pleaded that consideration was never paid to her. The original sale deed was produced by the defendant and not by the plaintiff. There were recitals in it that the entire consideration had already been paid. But there was no endorsement of the Registrar as to such payment on the sale deed. The suit was dismissed for non-payment of consideration.[151]

There is a presumption of execution of sale deed but there cannot be any presumption of actual payment of sale consideration even if it is mentioned in the sale deed that a particular amount towards full sale consideration has been paid. The contents in the sale deed with respect to payment of sale consideration are always a question of fact, which is required to be proved by leading evidence.[152]

[s 92.15.6] Value mentioned in loan application.—In a dispute about the adequacy of sale consideration for the suit, it was shown that the seller had applied for loan to a housing society in which he had mentioned the value of the property. The court said that such statement amounted to an admission about the value of the property and was relevant as such. The seller and the secretary of the society were examined for this purpose and the statement thus became verified.[153]

[s 92.15.7] Value Mentioned in Sale Deed.—It has been held that the section precludes a party who undervalued his property for the purposes of stamp duty from claiming that their own document did not reflect the correct market value. *Estoppel* arises under section 115 also.[154]

148. *Sah Lal v Indrajit,* (1900) 2 Bom LR 553 : 27 IA 93 : 22 All 370; *Lala Dholan Das v Ralya Shah,* (1899) PR No. 85 of 1898 (Civil); *Mussammat Zohra Jan v Mussammat Rajan Bibi,* (1915) PR No. 48 of 1915 (Civil).
149. *Muhammad Taqi Khan v Jang Singh,* (1935) 58 All 1 FB.
150. *Alice Mary Hill v William Clarke,* (1904) 27 All 266.
151. *Dhanbarti Koerin v Shyam Narain Mahton,* AIR 2007 Pat 52.
152. *Parmar Narmadaben v Amratlal Motibhai Prajapati,* 2017 AIR CC 540, para 6.1: (2016) 4 GLR 3205 (Guj-DB).
153. *KM Rajendran v Anil Prakasam,* AIR 1998 Mad 336.
154. *Krishi Utappadan Mandi Samiti v Bipin Kumar,* (2004) 2 SCC 283 : AIR 2004 SC 2895 : 2004 All LJ 665.

[s 92.15.8] CASES.—Where a deed of sale described the consideration to be Rs 100 in ready cash received, but the evidence showed that the consideration was an old bond for Rs 63 and 12 annas and Rs 36 and 4 annas in cash, it was held that there was no real variance between the statement in the deed and the evidence as to consideration, having regard to the fact that it is customary in India, when a bond is given wholly or partially in consideration of an existing debt, to describe the consideration as being "ready money received".[155] Plaintiffs sued for specific performance of an agreement in writing, which set forth, *inter alia*, that defendants had agreed to sell, *etc.*, under "certain conditions as agreed upon". The defendants alleged that the written agreement did not contain the whole of the agreement between the parties and offered parole evidence in support of their contention. It was held that the parole evidence was admissible to show what was meant by the clause "certain conditions as agreed upon."[156]

A Hindu widow, who signed a document evidencing the undivided status of her husband and his brother and making certain provision for the maintenance, alleged that she was induced to sign the document on the verbal assurance by the brother that the document was only intended to create evidence of the undivided status of the family and the provision for her maintenance was not final but was to be settled in future. In a suit for arrears of maintenance, it was held that oral evidence was admissible to establish that the provision for maintenance in the document was not to be acted upon and therefore there was no contract as to maintenance.[157]

[s 92.15.9] Mistake of fact.—Evidence may be admitted to prove that there was mutual mistake in the working of an agreement and to prove what the real intention of the parties was, and such evidence as to the alleged mistake may be given not only in a suit for the rectification of the mistake brought under section 31 of the Specific Relief Act, but also in a suit based upon the agreement itself.[158] It is open to the court to allow oral evidence of mutual mistake of fact to vary the terms of a deed. Oral evidence will be admissible even if the mistake is due to innocent misrepresentation.[159] Where a promissory note stated that the interest was payable at the rate of Rs 2 per mensem and in a suit on the promissory note the plaintiff contended that the interest agreed upon was two per cent. per mensem and that the words "per cent." had been omitted by mistake, it was held that oral evidence was admissible to prove that the rate of interest agreed upon was two per cent per month.[160] Where in an engineering contract the expression "sock" is typed for the term "rock", oral evidence for correcting such a typing mistake is admissible.[161]

A person who seeks to rectify a deed upon the ground of mistake must be required to establish, in the clearest and most satisfactory manner, that the alleged intention to which he desires it to be made conformable continued concurrently in the minds of all the parties down to the time of its execution, and also must be able to show exactly

---

155. *Hukumchand v Hiralal,* (1876) 3 Bom 159; *Sheikh Muhammad Bakhsh v Ramdat,* (1896) PR No. 5 of 1896 (Civil); *Le Hu v Elahi Bux,* (1900) 2 UBR (1897-1901) 400.

156. *Cutts v Brown,* (1880) 6 Cal 328.

157. *Tyagaraja Mudaliyar v Vedathanni,* (1935) 63 IA 126 : 38 Bom LR 373 : 59 Mad 446.

158. *S Narayanaswamy v James D Rodrigues,* (1906) 3 LBR 227; *Janardan v Venkatesh,* (1938) 41 Bom LR 191: (1939) Bom 149.

159. *Chimanram v Divanchand,* (1931) 34 Bom LR 26: 56 Bom 180.

160. *Kamla Prasad Pandey v Hasan Ali Khan,* (1939) All 329.

161. *Gujarat E Board v SA Jais & Co,* AIR 1972 Guj 192.

and precisely the form to which the deed ought to be brought.[162] The mistake referred to in proviso (1) refers to both unilateral as well as a mutual mistake.[163]

[s 92.15.10] Mistake of law.—Under the Indian Contract Act, 1872, an agreement is not voidable because it was caused by a mistake as to any law in force in India, but a mistake as to law not in force in India has the same effect as a mistake of fact (section 21). But Courts do relieve against mistakes in law as well as mistakes in fact, in cases where there is some circumstance which makes it inequitable that the party who has received the money of other party should retain it.

[s 92.16] Matters on which document is silent.—*[Proviso 2]*.—Under this proviso evidence of any collateral parole agreement which does not interfere with the terms of the contract may be given. See Illustrations (f), (g) and (h). Parties can prove that, either contemporaneously or as a preliminary measure, they entered into a distinct oral agreement on some collateral matter. The only case in which oral evidence will be admitted under this proviso is where the instrument is silent on the matter sought to be proved and the agreement to be proved is consistent with the terms of the document. It is allowable to urge an oral agreement which will have the effect of leaving matters otherwise than if they had depended on the written agreement alone, but such oral agreement must be clearly proved and the onus lies on him who sets it up.[164] Where the document does not record all the terms of the contract between the parties, oral evidence is admissible to explain the real nature of the transaction.[165] An incomplete agreement was entered into in terms of a court decree, external evidence was allowed to supply its missing links.[166] Proof of a separate oral agreement in respect of place of payment on which a promissory note is silent is admissible in evidence under this proviso.[167]

If there is a rule of law which requires the transaction to be in writing, any separate agreement must also be in writing.

The amount of the price agreed to be paid is an essential term of a contract of sale; and consequently no evidence of an oral agreement at variance with the provisions of a registered sale deed as to the amount of the price fixed for the sale is admissible.[168] Evidence that a sale deed was not intended by the parties thereto to be operative for the purpose of passing title is inadmissible.[169] The two vendees in a transaction can vary the contents as between themselves.[170]

[s 92.16.1] Consent Decree.—The consent decree did not cover the entire dispute between the parties and also some vagueness remained. The factual background as also

---

162. *Rajaram v Manik,* (1951) Nag 948.

163. *Sateri Shiddappa v Rudrappa,* (1953) 56 Bom LR 394.

164. *Motabhoy Mulla Essabhoy v Mujli Haridas,* (1915) 42 IA 103: 17 Bom LR 460: 39 Bom 399; *Badal Ram v Jhulai,* (1921) 44 All 53.

165. *Sir Mohammad Akbar Khan v Attar Singh,* (1936) 38 Bom LR 739: 17 Lah 557: 63 IA 279.

166. *Leena Roy v Indumati,* AIR 1980 Pat 120.

167. *JN Sahani v The State,* (1954) MB 343.

168. *Adityam Iyer v Rama Krishna Iyer,* (1913) 38 Mad 514.

169. *Lachman Das v Ram Prasad,* (1927) 49 All 680.

170. *Mohan Lal v Board of Rev.,* AIR 1982 All 273; *Anjali Das v Bidyut Sarkar,* AIR 1992 Cal 47, transfer of possession on payment in part of the consideration specified in an agreement to sell, held, provable. *BB Lohar v Prem Prakash Goyal,* AIR 1999 Sikkim 11, intention of the parties to a document can be drawn by the court by admitting and going into oral or other evidence.

the manner in which the existence of rights had been claimed by the parties had also to be considered. Evidence could be given of such matters. Section 92 was not attracted.[171]

[s 92.16.2] Degree of formality of document.—In a case before the Allahabad High Court[172] the document in question acknowledged the existence of a deed. It was on a stamp paper. It was silent about the interest payable. Oral evidence was offered on the point. The question was whether the document was so formal as to exclude oral evidence. The court allowed the evidence. Mehrotra J said: When the second proviso to section 92 speaks of the degrees of the formality of a document, it does not mean that every document should be treated as a formal one in case it is executed on a stamp paper and has stamps affixed to it. (The present document) cannot be treated to be of such formality that oral evidence regarding interest should be shut. Explaining when a document should be regarded as completely formal, the learned judge said:

> When the document is such that one may reasonably believe that the entire terms and conditions agreed to between the parties were sought to be put into the document, then oral evidence should not be allowed to creep in...Generally speaking, mere acknowledgment of debt, even though stamped in accordance with law of stamps, cannot be deemed to be such a formal document as to incorporate all the terms and conditions of the borrowing. It is basically an acknowledgment of liability not mentioning the terms and conditions on which the borrowing was contracted. In that sense, an acknowledgment of debt differs from a formal pronote which undoubtedly incorporates the terms and conditions of the loan.

[s 92.16.3] Contemporaneous oral agreement.—to pay interest on hundi.—Such an agreement is not admissible in evidence when there is no stipulation regarding interest on the *hundi* (promissory note). In such cases the payee of the *hundi* is entitled only to interest at the rate of six per cent per annum as provided by section 80 of the Negotiable Instruments Act, 1881.[173] If there is a collateral written agreement, fixing the rate of interest in accordance with the custom prevailing in the district, the interest is recoverable at the rate agreed upon between the parties.[174]

[s 92.16.4] Memorandum of Deposit.—Section 21 prohibits oral evidence only regarding the terms of the agreement or other evidence relating to terms. The section does not prohibit parties from leading oral evidence in respect of the nature of the contract or as it may be shown by a simultaneous oral agreement. It is well settled that if there is any ambiguity in the language employed or its recitals, the intention of the parties may be ascertained by adducing extrinsic evidence.[175]

[s 92.17] Condition precedent to obligation.—*[Proviso 3].*—This proviso presupposes that the contract, grant or disposition of property itself remains intact, but the condition precedent pleaded must in its very nature be extraneous to the contract, grant or disposition itself and as agreed must come into existence before the obligation

171. *Prayya Allayya Hittlamani v Prayya Gurulingayya Poojari,* AIR 2008 SC 241 : (2008) 2 Mad LJ 504 : (2007) 11 SCR 326 : (2007) 14 SCC 318.
172. *Brij Kishore v Lakhan Tiwari,* AIR 1978 All 314 at p 317. *MK Sethuramma Naidu v Poovammal,* AIR 2001 Mad 343 (Mad), tenancy granted, followed by the grants of simple mortgage. The terms of it were not allowed to be altered by a subsequent unregistered deed.
173. *Banwari Lal v Jagarnath Prasad,* (1916) 1 PLJ 71; *Fathuma Bivi v Hanumantha Row,* (1907) 17 Mad LJ 296; *Kishor Chand v Guram Ditta Mal,* (1911) PR No. 52 of 1911 (Civil). See, however, *Re Sowdamonee Debya v A Spalding,* (1882) 12 CLR 163.
174. *Goswami Sri Ghanshiam Lalji v Ram Narain,* (1906) 34 IA 6: 9 Bom LR 1: 29 All 33.
175. *Jayalakshmi Trading Co v Krishnamurthy,* AIR 2006 Mad 179.

attaches thereunder.[176] Under this proviso a contemporaneous oral agreement to the effect that a written contract was to be of no force or effect and that it was to impose no obligation at all until the happening of a certain event, may be proved. In a sale of property, payment of consideration was a condition precedent. Failure of consideration was allowed to be proved by independent evidence.[177] See Illustrations (i) and (j).

The true meaning of the words "any obligation" is any obligation whatever under the contract, and not some particular obligation which the contract may contain.[178] Where, at the time of the execution of a written contract, it is orally agreed between the parties that the written agreement shall not be of any force or validity until some condition precedent has been performed, parole evidence of such oral agreement is admissible to show that the condition has not been performed, and consequently that the written agreement has not become binding. This rule will not apply to a case where the written agreement had not only become binding, but had actually been performed as to a large portion of its obligations.[179] The distinction in point of law is that evidence to vary the terms of an agreement in writing is not admissible, but evidence to show that there is not an agreement at all is admissible. There is no rule of law to estop parties from showing that a paper, purporting to be a signed agreement, was in fact signed by mistake, or that it was signed on the terms that it should not be an agreement till money was paid or something else was done,[180] or that is was intended to be a sham and not operative.[181]

Evidence of a contemporaneous oral agreement to suspend the operation of a written contract of sale until an agreement for resale is executed is admissible.[182] A collateral oral agreement which is the condition of the execution of a promissory note would fall within this proviso, and evidence of it would therefore be admissible to prove it. Evidence of oral contract regarding the debt embodied in a promissory note was allowed. The note was taken as a collateral security for the debt.[183] A collateral agreement which alters the legal effect of a promissory note must be distinguished from an agreement that the instrument should not be an effective instrument until some condition is fulfilled or to put it in another form, an agreement in defeasance of the contract must be distinguished from an agreement suspending the coming into force of the contract contained in the promissory note. An agreement coming under the latter description is within this proviso. Where a promissory note is by its express terms payable on demand, the obligation under the note attaches immediately. But an oral agreement not to make a demand until some specified condition is fulfilled has the intention and effect of suspending the coming into force of that obligation which is the contract

---

176. *Chhaganlal Kalyandas v Jagjiwandas Gulabdas,* (1939) 41 Bom LR 1263.

177. *Ganesh Pd v Deo Nandan,* AIR 1985 Pat 94.

178. *Jugtanund Misser v Nerghan Singh,* (1880) 6 Cal 433; *Radhakissen Chamaria v Durga Prasad Chamaria,* (1931) 59 Cal 106.

179. *Jugtanund Misser v Nerghan Singh,* (1880) 6 Cal 433; *Walter Mitchell v AK Tennent,* (1925) 52 Cal 677; *CW Kinlock v Asa Ram,* (1877) PR No. 51 of 1877 (Civil); *Khuda Baksh v Budhar Mal,* (1882) PR No. 186 of 1882 (Civil).

180. *Pym v Campbell,* (1856) 6 El & Bl 370, 371.

181. *Gangabai v Chhababai,* AIR 1982 SC 20 : (1982) 1 SCC 4 : (1982) 1 SCR 1176 : 1982 Mah LJ 1. **Followed** in *Bimbadhar Rout v Kuna Senapati,* AIR 1995 Ori 258.

182. *Dada Honaji v Babaji Jagushet,* (1865) 2 BHC (ACJ) 38; *Ady v Administrator-General, Burma,* (1938) 40 Bom LR 1075: (1938) Ran 417 (PC).

183. *Khitish Chandra v Rajkishore Sahu,* AIR 1980 Ori 11.

contained in the promissory note. The oral agreement constitutes a condition precedent to the attaching of the obligation and is within the terms of this proviso.[184] Where the collateral agreement which was the condition of the execution of a promissory note was a written agreement it was held that it was outside this section.[185]

An oral agreement that the execution of a deed of reconveyance should be a condition precedent to the execution of the sale deed in pursuance of the written contract to sell immovable property can be proved under this proviso.[186]

[s 92.17.1] CASE.—Where the contract was to sell property for Rs 30,000 which sum was erroneously stated to have been paid, it was competent for the vendor, without infringing any provision of the Act, to prove a collateral agreement that the purchase-money should remain in the vendee's hands for the purposes and subject to the conditions alleged by the vendor;[187] because the section does not say that no statement of fact in a written instrument may be contradicted by oral evidence but the terms of the contract may not be varied, *etc.*

[s 92.18] Rescission or modification.—*[Proviso 4]*.—This proviso is based on the principle—"Nothing is so agreeable to natural equity as that a thing be unbound in the manner in which it was bound." Under this proviso a prior written contract may be varied by a subsequent verbal one, in cases in which the law does not require the contract to be in writing. Where the original contract is of such a nature as that the law requires it to be in writing or where its execution has been followed by the formality of registration, the only way of proving the rescission or modification of the original contract must be by proof of an agreement of the like formality and not by an oral agreement.

Only those agreements come within the proviso which affect the terms of the previous transaction directly by virtue of the consensus of those who alone are competent to rescind or modify the original contract, *viz.*, all the parties concerned or all their representatives.[188] The words of the proviso apply to any agreement whether executory or executed.[189]

The word "oral" is used in the sense of being not committed to writing, and the words "oral agreement" include all unwritten agreements, whether arrived at by word of mouth or otherwise, that is, by acts or conduct of parties.[190]

In a suit for redemption, the mortgagees pleaded that the mortgaged property was subsequently sold to them verbally for the mortgage debt and a further loan. It was held that the mortgage being by a registered deed, evidence of a subsequent oral agreement of sale was inadmissible under this proviso.[191]

---

184. *Narandas v Papammal,* AIR 1967 SC 333 : 1966 Supp SCR 88.

185. *Ady v Administrator-General, Burma,* (1938) 40 Bom LR 1075: (1938) Ran 417 PC; *Bhogi Ram v Kishori Lal,* (1928) 50 All 754; *Ali Jawad v Kulanjan Singh,* (1922) 44 All 421; *Dowlatram v Vasdeo,* (1942) Kar 516.

186. *Sahdeo v Namdeo,* (1948) Nag 900.

187. *Sah Lal v Indrajit,* (1900) 2 Bom LR 553: 27 IA 93: 22 All 370.

188. *Goseti Subba Row v Varigonda Narasimham,* (1903) 27 Mad 368, 370.

189. *Goseti Subba Row v Varigonda Narasimham, ibid.*

190. *Mayandi Chetti v Oliver,* (1889) 22 Mad 261.

191. *Maung Myat Tun Aung v Maung Lu Pu,* (1925) 3 Ran 243.

The Calcutta and the Madras High Courts have held that oral evidence is admissible to prove the discharge and satisfaction of a mortgage bond.[192] The Bombay and the Lahore High Courts have held that a subsequent agreement to take less than is due under a registered mortgage-bond is an agreement modifying the terms of a written contract and oral evidence is inadmissible in proof of it.[193] The Bombay High Court has subsequently held that where all that the defendant wants to prove is some fact tending to show that the obligation has been discharged, either by payment, or by remission of anything that was due, such fact may be proved as not amounting to a modification of the conditions of the mortgage but relating mainly to the discharge of the contract, and not involving any question of its terms.[194] A Full Bench of the Allahabad High Court has held that an agreement between parties to a mortgage deed cannot be proved by oral evidence to show that on payment of a sum of money less than what would be due on calculating the correct amount of principal and interest at the stipulated rate entered in the mortgage deed the debt would be discharged. Such evidence would be admissible to prove the satisfaction of the debt, as resulting from a mutual agreement by which the mortgagee accepted, in full discharge of the obligation, payment of a part of the sum due and remitted the balance. A plea of such agreement and satisfaction is not one setting up an agreement contradicting, varying, adding to or subtracting from the terms of the contract of mortgage and does not contravene the provisions of this section.[195] A debtor cannot prove that his creditor agreed verbally to take less, but he can prove that the creditor actually did accept less in full satisfaction.

A deed by which a property was settled by father upon his son was made in writing as required by law. Oral evidence was not allowed of any new arrangement which had the effect of modifying the deed of settlement.[196] Oral evidence was not allowed to show that the sale consideration for the property as agreed between the parties was more than that mentioned in the deed.[197]

[s 92.18.1] New contract.—This proviso does not exclude evidence of a subsequent oral agreement substituting a new contract for one reduced to writing and registered according to law, the said proviso only referring to a subsequent oral agreement to rescind or modify such contract.[198] The distinction between a substituted new agreement by novation and the mere alteration of an old contract is that in the former case the old contract is extinguished, while in the latter it remains binding subject to the alteration which the parties have agreed to.[199] According to the Rangoon, the Lahore and the Bombay High Courts a judgment-debtor can set up a new verbal agreement

---

192. *Ramlal Chandra Karmokar v Gobinda Karmokar,* (1900) 4 Cal WN 304; *Mahim v Ram Dayal,* (1925) 42 Cal LJ 582: 30 Cal WN 371; *Srimati Bhaba Sundari v Ram Kamal Dutta,* (1925) 44 Cal LJ 269; *Balasundra Naiker v Ranganatha Aiyar,* (1929) 53 Mad 127; *Munuswami Mudaliar v Govindaraja Chettiar,* (1934) 58 Mad 371.

193. *Jagannath v Shankar,* (1919) 44 Bom 55: 22 Bom LR 39; *Ghanaya Lal v Rallia Ram,* (1928) 9 Lah 597. But see *Sukhlal v Jetha,* (1928) 30 Bom LR 1455.

194. *Sukhlal v Jetha,* (1928) 30 Bom LR 1455, 1462.

195. *Collector of Etah v Kishori Lal,* (1930) 53 All 157 FB; *Jwala Prasad v Mohan Lal,* (1926) 48 All 705, **disapproved.**

196. *S Saktivel v M Venugopal Pillai,* AIR 2000 SC 2633 : (2000) 7 SCC 104.

197. *KM Rajendran v Anil Prakasam,* AIR 1998 Mad 336.

198. *Jaggat Singh v Devi Ditta Mal,* (1883) PR No. 169 of 1883 (Civil).

199. *Lakhu Ram v Amir Khan,* (1888) PR No. 14 of 1889 (Civil).

by the decree-holder to accept some variation or a new contract in substituting of the original decree,[200] but not according to the Allahabad High Court.[201]

[s 92.18.2] CASES.—Extraneous evidence admissible.—A receipt which purported to show that simple and not compound interest was to be charged (though the mortgage-bond contained provision for the payment of compound interest), was held to be admissible in evidence.[202] The receipt did not require registration and was therefore admissible in evidence. It operated as a waiver.

[s 92.18.3] Extraneous evidence when not admissible.—A lease contained a covenant for renewal of the lease whereby if the lessee desired to renew the lease he should give three months' notice in writing of his intention to do so. The lessee, however, failed to observe this covenant and relied on an oral agreement between himself and his lessors for renewal of the lease. It was held that evidence of such oral agreement was not admissible.[203] Oral evidence was similarly not allowed to show that another person than the one mentioned in the deed was intended to be the lessee.[204] Variation of rent fixed by a registered lease deed must be made by another registered instrument. The rent was increased under a separate agreement. It being a variation of the registered deed was not admissible.[205]

[s 92.19] Customs and usages.—*[Proviso 5]*.—Parole evidence of usage or custom is admissible in aid of the construction of a written instrument. Such evidence is received for explaining or filling up terms used in commercial contracts, policies of insurance, negotiable instruments, and other writings of a similar kind—when the language, though well understood by the parties, and by all who have to act upon it in matters of business, would often appear to the common reader scarcely intelligible, and sometimes almost a foreign language. The terms used in these instruments are to be interpreted according to the recognised practice and usage with reference to which the parties are supposed to have acted; and the sense of the words, so interpreted, may be taken to be the appropriate and true sense intended by the parties.[206] "But the rule for admitting evidence of usage must be taken always with this qualification, that the evidence proposed is not repugnant to, or inconsistent with, the written contract. It ought never to be allowed to vary or contradict the written instrument, either expressly or by implication...where the incident sought to be annexed to a contract is unreasonable or illegal, it cannot be annexed to the contract by evidence of usage."[207]

[s 92.20] Relationship with existing facts.—*[Proviso 6]*.—The proviso is a substantive provision laying down the law relating to the admissibility of extrinsic evidence as an aid to the construction of a document in cases in which it is necessary

200. *Ma Shwe Pee v Maung San Myo,* (1928) 6 Ran 573; *Abdul Karim v Hakam Mal-Tani Mal,* (1933) 14 Lah 688; *Kalyanji Dhana v Dharamsi Dhana & Co,* (1934) 37 Bom LR 230.
201. *Lachhman Das v Baba Ramnath Kalikamliwala,* (1921) 44 All 258.
202. *Kailash Chandra Nath v Sheikh Chhenu,* (1914) 42 Cal 546.
203. *Mark D'Cruz v Jitendra Nath Chatterjee,* (1919) 46 Cal 1079; *Karampalli Unni Kurup v Thekku Vittil Muthorakutti,* (1902) 26 Mad 195.
204. *Roshan Lal v Munshi Ram,* AIR 1981 P&H 73; *Ram Chandra v Manjal Singh,* AIR 1981 P&H 94.
205. *Raval & Co v KG Ramachandran,* AIR 1974 SC 818 : 1974(1) SCC 424.
206. Philips, 407.
207. *Best,* 12th Edn, section 228, p 213; *Lu Gale v Maung Mo,* (1904) 2 LBR 268; *KMPRNM Firm v Somasundaram Chetty & Co,* (1924) 48 Mad 275.

to find out how the document is related to the existing facts.[208] Where a document is a perfectly plain, straightforward document, no extrinsic evidence is required to show in what manner the language of the document is related to existing facts. But where the terms of the document themselves require explanation, then evidence can be led within the restrictions laid down in this proviso.[209] The language of this proviso is rather vague. It is true that evidence of the circumstances surrounding a document is admissible; but it is admissible only for the purpose of throwing light on its meaning. It is not permissible to consider the surrounding circumstances with a view to holding that a document which on the face of it is a sale deed is intended to operate as mortgage. There must be some limit to the suggestion that the surrounding circumstances can always be scrutinized so as to enable the court to alter or change the nature of a document to something different from what it purports to be. Otherwise, there can be no certainty as to the proper construction to be placed on a document which to all appearances is unambiguous.[210]

Extrinsic evidence is receivable of every material fact which will enable the court to ascertain the nature and qualities of the subject-matter of the instrument; that is, to identify the persons and things to which the instrument refers.[211] Previous correspondence between the parties for the purpose of explaining anything in a document before the court is admissible.[212] Subsequent conduct of the parties in reference to the subject-matter can also be taken into account. This proviso was used by the Supreme Court in a case where the grant of a *jagir* included the expression "part of the uncultivated *jagir*".[213] These words were found to be ambiguous in their setting and, therefore, "extrinsic evidence *aliunde* the grant became necessary to explain [their] coverage". The court took into account the past and subsequent history of the grant. Ahmadi J[214] cited a passage from an earlier Supreme Court decision which was adopted from *Halsbury's Laws of England*.[215] "The evidence of the conduct of the parties in this situation as to how they understood the words to mean can be considered in determining the true effect of the contract made between the parties. Extrinsic evidence to determine the effect of an instrument is permissible where there remains a doubt as to its true meaning. Evidence of acts done under it is a guide to the intention of the parties in such a case and particularly when acts are done shortly after the date of the instrument."[216]

---

208. *Belapur Co v Mah. State Farming Corpn.,* (1968) 74 Bom LR 246. See also *PB Bhat v VR. Thakkar,* (1971) 74 Bom LR 509.

209. *Ganpatrao v Bapu,* (1919) 22 Bom LR 831: 44 Bom 710; *The Punjab National Bank, Ltd v Mr SB Chaudhry,* (1943) 19 Luck 265. See *Firm Bolumal v Venkatachelapathi Rao,* AIR 1959 AP 612. Where the clauses of an agreement were clear and decisive, oral evidence was not allowed to deduce their meaning *Hindustan Lever v MRTPC.,* AIR 1977 SC 1285 : 1977(3) SCC 227.

210. *Martand v Amritrao,* (1925) 27 Bom LR 951: 49 Bom 662.

211. *Bank of New Zealand v Simpson,* (1900) AC 182. *NAS Ansari v T Ramalingam,* AIR 2003 SC 286, interpretation of power of attorney and a finding that the document was a general power of attorney.

212. *Simla Bank Corp, Ltd v HT Ball,* (1883) PR No. 2 of 1884 (Civil).

213. *Raj Kumar Rajinder Singh v State of HP,* (1990) 4 SCC 320 : AIR 1990 SC 1833. Followed in *Madalsa Devi v Mridula Chandra,* AIR 1994 Pat 91.

214. At p 339.

215. 274 (*Halsham,* Edn, Vol 10, para 343).

216. The passage was cited in *Abdulla Ahmed v Animendra Kissen Mitter,* AIR 1950 SC 15 : 1950 SCR 30.

On the basis of this authority, Ahmadi J observed:

> The object of admissibility of such evidence in such circumstances under the 6th proviso is to assist the court to get to the real intention of the parties and thereby overcome the difficulty caused by the ambiguity. In such a case the subsequent conduct of the parties furnishes evidence to clear the blurred area and to ascertain the true intention of the author of the document.[217]

Sections 91 and 92 do not come in the way of considering whether a particular trade practice is of restrictive nature or not. The decision in the *Telco* case did not proceed on an application of the principle embodied in section 92(6).[218] Correctness of facts stated in a document can be questioned. Section 92 does not prevent it.[219]

Section 92 read with sections 94 and 95 clearly suggests that proviso (6) of section 92 comes into play only when there is a latent ambiguity in a document, that is, when the language of the document is not *prima facie* consistent with the existing facts, or, in other words, when there is conflict in the plain meaning of the language used in the document and the facts existing or when put together they lead to an ambiguity. In a case, therefore, where the language used in a document is plain and not in any way ambiguous in reference to facts existing, there is no scope for coming into play of the rule of interpretation laid down in proviso (6) to section 92.[220]

This section makes evidence as to the intention of a document contrary to its express language inadmissible; but its proviso (6) lets in evidence to show in what manner the disputed transaction or the language of the document was related to existing facts.[221]

Evidence can be admitted to show whether a gift deed has been acted upon or not.[222]

[s 92.21] Deed of one kind may be shown to be deed of another kind.—Extrinsic evidence is admissible for purpose of showing that a document, which purports to be, and on the face of it is, a deed of sale, is in reality a deed of gift.[223] Oral evidence is admissible to show that a mortgage has been subsequently converted into a sale,[224] or that what ostensibly purported to be a sale with an agreement for a resale and repurchase at the same price at a certain date was a mortgage by conditional sale,[225] or that two deeds of sale were in reality a deed of exchange.[226] Where the parties professing to create a mortgage by deposit of title deeds, contemporaneously enter into a contractual agreement in writing, such a document would amount to mortgage by deposit of title deeds.[227]

---

217. [1990] 4 SCC at 339.
218. *Mahindra and Mahindra Ltd v UOI,* (1979) 49 Com Cas 419 : 1979 Tax LR 2064.
219. *Krishnabai v Appasaheb,* (1979) 4 SCC 60 : AIR 1979 SC 1880.
220. *Ram Narain v Manki Singh,* (1954) 33 Pat 638.
221. *Manindra Nath Bose,* (1956) 1 Cal 59; *Balachandran v Gopalan,* AIR 2001 Ker 337, construction of the document of tenancy.
222. *Gouranga Sahu v Magnu Dei,* AIR 1991 Ori 151.
223. *Hanif-un-nisa v Faiz-un-nisa,* (1911) 13 Bom LR 391: 39 IA 85: 33 All 340. **See** *Maung Kyin v Ma Shwe La,* (1911) 38 IA 146: 13 Bom LR 797; *Serajuddin Haldar v Isab Haldar,* (1921) 49 Cal 161.
224. *Badhawa Mal v Hira,* (1883) PR No. 30 of 1884 (Civil).
225. *Narasingerji Gyanagerji v Panuganti Parthyasaradhi,* (1924) 51 IA 305: 47 Mad 729: 27 Bom LR 4.
226. *Kishan Lal v Ram Lal,* (1927) 50 All 59.
227. *ST Industries, Surat v Chief Controlling Revenue Authority (SB),* AIR 1994 Guj 153.

There were certain recitals in the deed of a registered society. The court allowed oral evidence to show that the recitals were supposed to be only nominal or that they were not intended to be acted upon or that they were not meant to alter the existing state of affairs. Thus oral evidence was allowed to prove what was the dominant object of the society.[228]

Sections 93–97 partly develop and partly restrict the principle laid down by this proviso.

[s 93] Exclusion of evidence to explain or amend ambiguous document.—When the language used in a document is, on its face, ambiguous or defective, evidence may not be given of facts which would show its meaning or supply its defects.

ILLUSTRATIONS

(a) *A* agrees, in writing, to sell a horse to *B* for "Rs. 1,000 or Rs. 1,500." Evidence cannot be given to show which price was to be given.

(b) *A* deed contains blanks. Evidence cannot be given of facts which would show how they were meant to be filled.

COMMENT

Sections 93–98 deal with rules for construction of documents with the aid of extrinsic evidence. Sections 91 and 92 define the cases in which documents are exclusive evidence of the transactions which they embody. Sections 93–99 deal with the interpretation of documents by oral evidence.

There are two sorts of ambiguities of words—the one is *ambiguitas patens* and other *latens*. *Patens* is that which appears to be ambiguous upon the deed or instrument; *latens* is that which seems certain and without ambiguity, for anything that appears upon the deed or instrument; but there is some collateral matter out of the deed that breeds the ambiguity.[229] A good test of the difference is to put the instrument into the hands of an ordinary intelligent educated person. If, on perusal, he sees no ambiguity, but there is nevertheless an uncertainty as to its application, the ambiguity is latent; if he detects the ambiguity from merely reading the instrument it is patent. Thus, in illustration (b), the blanks would be patent ambiguities and they could not be filled in by parole testimony as to the intention of the parties, *etc.* In the illustration to section 95 no one could detect any ambiguity from merely reading the instrument. The ambiguity does not consist in the language, but is introduced by extrinsic circumstances.[230]

[s 93.1] Principle.—This section deals with patent ambiguities. If the language of a deed is, on its face, ambiguous or defective, no evidence can be given to make it certain.[231]

The duty of the court is always interpretation; to find out not what really was the intention of the parties, as distinguished from what mere words expressed but merely to

---

228. *Hindu Public v Rajdhani Puja Samithee*, AIR 1999 SC 964 : (1999) 2 SCC 583.
229. *Best*, 12th Edn, 226, p 211.
230. Norton, section 633, pp 351, 352.
231. *Deojit v Pitambar*, (1876) 1 All 275.

find out the meaning of the words used by them.[232] Under this section it is the language of the document alone that will decide the question and it would not be open to the parties or the court to attempt to remove the vagueness by relying upon any extrinsic evidence. Such an attempt would really mean the making of a new contract between the parties.[233] In a contract of transport made with the Food Corporation of India, the column for transport charges was left blank, the attempt of both sides to give evidence of the oral agreement on the point was not accepted, since blank spaces cannot be filled by oral agreements.[234] The charges for services rendered may be recovered under section 70 of the Contract Act.

Extrinsic evidence of every material fact which will enable the court to ascertain the nature and qualities of the subject matter of the instrument, or, in other words, to identify the person and things to which the instrument refers, is admissible.[235] Thus, where there is a written agreement to deliver a quantity of grain at a particular time, parole evidence is admissible under certain limitations to show what kind of grain the contracting parties had in their contemplation at the time the contract was made.[236]

[s 94] Exclusion of evidence against application of document to existing facts.—When language used in a document is plain in itself, and when it applies accurately to existing facts, evidence may not be given to show that it was not meant to apply to such facts.

ILLUSTRATION

A sells to *B*, by deed, "my estate at Rampur containing 100 bighas." *A* has an estate at Rampur containing 100 bighas. Evidence may not be given of the fact that the estate meant to be sold was one situated at a different place and of a different size.

COMMENT

[s 94.1] Principle.—The words of a written instrument must be construed according to their natural meaning, and no amount of acting by the parties can alter or qualify words which are plain and unambiguous. No principle has ever been more universally or rigorously insisted upon than those written instruments, if they are plain and unambiguous, must be construed according to the plain and unambiguous language of the instruments themselves.[237]

Under this section evidence to show that common words, whose meaning is plain, not appearing from the context to have been used in a peculiar sense, have been in fact so used, is not admissible.[238] Where the language in its ordinary sense properly applies

---

232. *Doe dem. Gwillim v Gwillim,* (1833) 5 B & Ad. 122, 129.

233. *Lallubhai Patel v Lalbhai Trikumlal Mills,* (1958) SCJ 866.

234. *Food Corp of India v Birendra Nath Dhar,* AIR 1989 NOC 119 (Cal).

235. *Valla Hataji v Sidoji Kondaji,* (1868) 5 BHC (ACJ) 87.

236. *Ibid. Pradeep Kumar v Mahaveer Pershad,* AIR 2003 AP 107, sections 93, 94, 95, 96, 97 are about patent and latent ambiguities and interpretation of documents. Sections 93 and 94 deal with patent ambiguity while sections 95, 96 and 97 deal with latent ambiguity.

237. *North Eastern Railway v Hastings (Lord),* (1900) AC 260, 263; *Babu v Sitaram,* (1901) 3 Bom LR 768; *Narayan v The Co-op Central Bank, Malkapur,* (1938) Nag 604.

238. Stephen's Dig., Article 91.

to the facts without any difficulty, evidence to show that it bears a different meaning will be rejected, as it contradicts the document.

Where in a lease agreement with the Government, payment of interest on arrears of rent was stipulated but mode of payment was not stipulated, the Collector was not prevented by section 94 from deciding the mode.[239] A promissory note was not allowed to be explained away as a deposit.[240]

This section applies only when the execution of the document is admitted and there are no vitiating circumstances against it. Oral evidence of witnesses in proceedings before the Board was admissible.[241]

[s 95] Evidence as to document unmeaning in reference to existing facts.—When language used in a document is plain in itself, but is unmeaning in reference to existing facts, evidence may be given to show that it was used in a peculiar sense.

ILLUSTRATION

A sells to *B*, by deed, "my house in Calcutta".

A had no house in Calcutta, but it appears that he has a house at Howrah, of which *B* had been in possession since the execution of the deed.

These facts may be proved to show that the deed related to the house at Howrah.

COMMENT

[s 95.1] Principle.—Where the language of a document is plain in itself but is unmeaning in reference to existing facts, evidence may be given to show that it was used in a peculiar sense. It is based upon the maxim *falsa demonstratio non necet* (a false description does not vitiate the document). Section 97 is a part of the rule in this section, and both the sections must be read together. The illustration to this section shows that if *A* sells to *B* "my house in Calcutta," and if *A* has no house in Calcutta but has a house in Howrah, of which *B* has been in possession since the execution of the deed, these facts may be proved to show that the deed related to the house in Howrah.[242] Where a sale deed describes the land sold by wrong survey numbers, extrinsic evidence is admissible to show that the lands intended to be sold and actually sold and delivered were lands bearing different survey numbers.[243] Where sufficient description of the premises is set forth by giving the name of the particular field or otherwise, a false description added thereto (*e.g.*, the mention of a wrong survey number) may be rejected.[244]

[s 96] Evidence as to application of language which can apply to one only of several persons.—When the facts are such that the language used might have been meant to apply to any one, and could not have been meant to apply to more than

---

239. *Tata Iron & Steel Co Ltd v State of Bihar,* AIR 1996 Pat 37.
240. *A Rangappa v P Krishnamurthy,* 1996 AIHC 4488 (Kant).
241. *General Court Martial v Col Anitej Singh,* AIR 1998 SC 983 : (1999) 3 SCC 60.
242. *Karuppa Goundan alias Thoppala Goundan v Periathambi Goundan,* (1907) 30 Mad 397, 399.
243. *Ibid.* See also *Basavapunnareddy v Krishnayya,* AIR 1966 AP 260.
244. *Santaya v Savitri,* (1902) 4 Bom LR 871; *Mahabir Prasad v Masiatulah,* (1915) 38 All 103.

one, of several persons or things, evidence may be given of facts which show which of those persons or things it was intended to apply to.

ILLUSTRATIONS

(a) *A* agrees to sell to *B*, for Rs. 1,000, "my white horse". *A* has two white horses. Evidence may be given of facts which show which of them was meant.

(b) *A* agrees to accompany *B* to Haidarabad. Evidence may be given of facts showing whether Haidarabad in the Dekkhan or Haidarabad in Sind was meant.

COMMENT

[s 96.1] Principle.—Where the description in the document applies equally to any one of two or more subjects, evidence to explain its language is admissible. Where the language of a document, though intended to apply to one person or thing only, applies equally to two or more, and it is impossible to gather from the context which was intended, an equivocation arises, e.g., when the same name or description fits two persons or things accurately; when the same name or description fits one exactly and the other but tolerably; when the same name or description fits two objects equally but subject to a common inaccuracy, provided that the inaccuracy be a mere blank or applicable to no other person or thing.

This section modifies the rule laid down in section 94 by providing that where the language of a document correctly describes two sets of circumstances but could not have been intended to apply to both, evidence may be given to show to which set it was intended to apply. Here the language is certain. The doubt as to which of similar persons or things the language applies has been introduced by extrinsic evidence.[245]

[s 97] Evidence as to application of language to one of two sets of facts, to neither of which the whole correctly applies.—When the language used applies partly to one set of existing facts, and partly to another set of existing facts, but the whole of it does not apply correctly to either, evidence may be given to show to which of the two it was meant to apply.

ILLUSTRATION

A agrees to sell to *B* "my land at *X* in the occupation of *Y*". *A* has land at *X*, but not in the occupation of *Y*, and he has land in the occupation of *Y*, but it is not at *X*. Evidence may be given of facts showing which he meant to sell.

COMMENT

This section is based upon the maxim *falsa demonstratio non necet.* It is only an extension of the provision of section 95. Sections 95, 96 and 97 all deal with latent ambiguity. "Where in a written instrument the description of the person or thing intended *is applicable with legal certainty to each of several subjects,* extrinsic evidence, including proof of declarations of intention, is admissible to establish which of such

---

245. *Doe D Hiscocks v Hiscoks,* (1839) 5 M&W 363; *Nga Cho v Mi Se Mt,* (1916) 2 UBR 110; Stephen's Dig., Article 91.

subjects was intended by the author."[246] The rule rejecting erroneous description not substantially important is applicable only where there is enough to show the intention clearly.

The illustration to this section shows that if A agrees to sell to B "my land at X in the occupation of Y", and A has land at X but not in the occupation of Y, and has land in the occupation of Y but it is not at X, evidence may be given to show which was intended to be sold. Another common case is where land within certain boundaries is sold and is wrongly described as containing a certain area, the error in area is regarded as a mere misdescription and does not vitiate the deed. The maxim *falsa demonstratio non necet* applies.[247]

[s 98] Evidence as to meaning of illegible characters, *etc.*—Evidence may be given to show the meaning of illegible or not commonly intelligible characters, of foreign, obsolete, technical, local and provincial expressions, of abbreviations and of words used in a peculiar sense.

ILLUSTRATION

A, a sculptor, agrees to sell to *B*, "all my mods". *A* has both models and modelling tools. Evidence may be given to show which he meant to sell.

SYNOPSIS

COMMENT

[s 98.1] Principle.—Evidence as to the meaning of illegible characters (e.g., shorthand-writer's notes) or of foreign obsolete, technical, local and provincial expressions and of words used in a peculiar sense may be given. In such cases the evidence cannot properly be said to vary the written instrument; it only explains the meaning of expressions used. Mercantile usage has given special meanings to many ordinary words. Evidence of the meaning which these words bear in mercantile transactions can be given under this section.

The principle upon which words are to be construed in instruments is very plain—where there is a popular and common word used in an instrument, that word must be construed *prima facie* in its popular and common sense. If it is a word of a technical or legal character it must be construed according to its technical or legal meaning. If it is a word which is of a technical and scientific character, then it must be construed according to that which is its primary meaning, namely, its technical and scientific meaning. But before you can give evidence of the secondary meaning of a word, you must satisfy the court from the instrument itself or from the circumstances of the case that the word ought to be construed, not in its popular or primary signification, but according to its secondary intention.[248]

---

246. *Taylor*, 12th Edn, section 1226, p 787.
247. *Karuppa Goundan alias Thoppala Goundan v Periathambi Goundan*, (1907) 30 Mad 397.
248. *Holt & Co v Collyer*, (1881) 16 Ch D 718, 720.

Where the point in dispute is as to the meaning of a particular word in the document, evidence may be admitted to show in what peculiar sense that particular word was used, and extrinsic evidence including the evidence regarding the subsequent conduct of the parties is admissible to determine the effect of the instrument as well as the intention of the parties.[249]

In a Government grant of land which involved questions of interpretation of the Government orders, that was held to be a question of fact.[250]

[s 98.2] Document in foreign language.—Where a document was written in an uncommon or foreign (Persian) language, it was held that the court could rely on ability and knowledge of the judge hearing the case to decipher such language and the meaning of words like *Huzoor, burzurgan, moris, biradari, minjoomle* requisite in the context.[251]

[s 99] Who may give evidence of agreement varying terms of document.—Persons who are not parties to a document, or their representatives in interest, may give evidence of any facts tending to show a contemporaneous agreement varying the terms of the document.

ILLUSTRATION

A and *B* make a contract in writing that *B* shall sell *A* certain cotton, to be paid for on delivery. At the same time they make an oral agreement that three months' credit shall be given to *A*. This could not be shown as between *A* and *B*, but it might be shown by *C*, if it affected his interest.

COMMENT

Section 92 forbids the admission of evidence of an oral agreement for the purpose of contradicting, varying, adding to, or subtracting from, the terms of a written document as between the parties to such document or their representatives in interest. The rule of exclusion laid down in the section does not apply to the case of a third party who is not a party to the document. On the contrary, this section distinctly provides that persons who are not parties to a document may give evidence tending to show a contemporaneous agreement varying the terms of the document.[252]

The principle of section 92 does not apply to third persons. If it were otherwise, third persons might be prejudiced by things recited in the writings, contrary to the truth, through the ignorance, carelessness, or fraud of the parties, and, therefore, ought not to be precluded from proving the truth, however contradictory it may be to the written statements of others.[253]

[s 99.1] Varying.—In this section the word "varying" only is used, while in section 92 the words are "contradicting, varying, adding to, or subtracting from". But it is difficult

---

249. *State of Rajasthan v Bundi Electric Supply Co*, AIR 1970 Raj 36; *State of Bihar v Radha Krishna Singh*, AIR 1983 SC 684 : (1983) 2 SCC 118, meaning of Persian words used in a document, reliance on the competence of the trial judge to find out the meaning.

250. *Anayatullah v Commissioner of Muslim Waqf of Jammu*, (1991) Supp 1 SCC 396.

251. *State of Bihar v Radha Krishna Singh*, (1983) 3 SCC 118 : AIR 1983 SC 684.

252. *Bageshri Dayal v Pancho*, (1906) 28 All 473, 474.

253. *Taylor*, 12th Edn, section 1149, p 735.

to see that in using the term "varying" only, anything less could have been meant than what is conveyed by the several expressions in section 92 and as every "contradicting", "adding to", or "subtracting from" would necessarily be a "varying" of the instrument, the legislature apparently used that expression as sufficient to convey all that is denoted by the other different expressions occurring in the earlier section.[254]

[s 99.1.1] CASES.—The plaintiff sued to recover one-fourth of the price of a house alleged to have been sold by the first defendant, the claim being based upon a local custom. The transaction between the defendants was ostensibly not a sale but a usufructuary mortgage. It was held that the plaintiff, not being a party to the transaction, was entitled to give evidence to show that what purported to be a usufructuary mortgage was not in reality such, but was in fact a sale.[255]

In the case of an alienation of land in which a document has been executed purporting to be a deed of gift or mortgage, it is open to a third party claiming to exercise a right of pre-emption to prove that the transaction was in reality one of sale, and that the document sought to be impugned was executed in order to conceal its real nature and to defraud him of his legal rights.[256]

[s 100] Saving of provisions of Indian Succession Act relating to wills.—Nothing in this Chapter contained shall be taken to affect any of the provisions of the Indian Succession Act (10 of 1865) as to the construction of wills.

COMMENT

Act X of 1865 is replaced by Act XXXIX of 1925.

254. *Pathammal v Syed Kalai Ravuthar,* (1903) 27 Mad 329, 331; *Tarachand v Baldeo,* (1890) PR No. 117 of 1890 FB (Civil).

255. *Bageshri Dayal v Pancho,* (1906) 28 All 473; *Rahiman v Elahi Baksh,* (1900) 28 Cal 70, dissented from *Pathammal v Syed Kalai Ravuthar,* (1903) 27 Mad 329.

256. *Tara Chand v Baldeo,* (1890) PR No. 117 of 1890 FB. (Civil); *Parmanand v Airapat Ram,* (1899) PR No. 20 of 1899 (Civil); *Megha Ram v Makhan Lal,* (1912) PR No. 67 of 1912 (Civil).

PART III
PRODUCTION AND EFFECT OF EVIDENCE

CHAPTER VII

OF THE BURDEN OF PROOF

[s 101] Burden of proof.—Whoever desires any Court to give judgment as to any legal right or liability dependent on the existence of facts which he asserts, must prove that those facts exist.

When a person is bound to prove the existence of any fact, it is said that the burden of proof[s 101.1] lies on that person.

ILLUSTRATIONS

(a) *A* desires a Court to give judgment that *B* shall be punished for a crime which *A* says *B* has committed.

A must prove that *B* has committed the crime.

(b) *A* desires a Court to give judgment that he is entitled to certain land in the possession of *B*, by reason of facts which he asserts, and which *B* denies, to be true.

A must prove the existence of those facts.

SYNOPSIS

COMMENT

The burden of proof lies on the party who substantially asserts the affirmative of the issue and not upon the party who denies it. This rule of convenience has been adopted in practice, not because it is impossible to prove a negative, but because the negative does not admit of the direct and simple proof of which the affirmative is capable. Moreover, it is but reasonable and just that the suitor, who relies upon the existence of a fact, should be called upon to prove his own case. In the application of this rule, regard must be had to the substance and effect of the issue, and not to its grammatical form, for in many cases the party, by making a slight alteration in the drawing of his pleadings, may give the issue a negative or affirmative form, at his pleasure.[1]

It is a settled law that parties are governed by their pleadings and the burden lies on the person who pleads to prove and further the plaintiff has to succeed on the strength of his case and cannot depend upon the weakness of the defendant's case.[2]

The party, on whom the onus of proof lies must, in order to succeed, establish a *prima facie* case. He cannot, on failure to do so, take advantage of the weakness of his adversary's case. He must succeed by the strength of his own right and the clearness of his own proof. He cannot be heard to say that it was too difficult or virtually impossible to prove the matter in question.[3] For example, a mere suspicion is not a proof of *benami*.[4] The initial burden is upon the claimant to establish that a person is his debtor.[5] Where a member of a family claims that a particular part of the joint property is his "personal", burden lies on him to prove that fact.[6] A person claiming through adoption has to prove the fact of it.[7] Burden of proof as to an oral will is heavily on the propounder.[8] The burden of proving his caste is upon the claimant.[9]

Where a party accepts the burden which is laid upon it by the trial court without any demur or protest and allows the case to proceed on that basis throughout the trial, it cannot, when it fails to discharge it, turn around and say in appeal that the burden should not have been placed upon it.[10]

The general rule that a party who desires to move the court must prove all facts necessary for that purpose (sections 101–105) is subject to two exceptions:—

(a) he will not be required to prove such facts as are especially within the knowledge of the other party (section 106); and he will not be required to prove so much of his allegations in respect of which there is any presumption of law (sections 107–113), or in some cases, of fact (section 114) in his favour. For example, a very old man donated

---

1. *Taylor*, 12th Edn, section 364, p 252.
2. *State of MP v Ushadevi*, (2015) 8 SCC 672, para 33.
3. *Shiv Charan Singh v Chandra Bhan Singh*, AIR 1988 SC 637 : 1988(2) SCC 12.
4. *Drigpal Singh v Wife of Laldhari Ojha*, AIR 1985 Pat 110.
5. *TS Kotagi v Tahsildar*, AIR 1985 Kant 365. See also *Avadesh Kumar v Sheo Shanker*, AIR 1985 All 104 which discusses the mode of proving whether a person has become a *Sanyasi*.
6. *Ram Kunwar Bai v Rani Bahu*, AIR 1985 MP 73.
7. *Madhusudan Das v Narayani Bai*, AIR 1983 SC 114 : 1983(1) SCC 35 : 1983 MahLJ 402.
8. *Shantilal v Mohan Lal*, AIR 1986 J&K 61.
9. *NB Rao v Principal, Osmania Medical College*, AIR 1986 AP 196.
10. *Raman Lal v Ram Gopal*, (1954) 4 Raj 262.

land and later sued for possession on the ground that the gift was not voluntary. The burden was upon the donee.[11]

[s 101.1] "Burden of proof".—This expression means two different things. It means sometimes that a party is required to prove an allegation before judgment can be given in its favour; it also means that on a contested issue one of the two contending parties has to introduce evidence. The burden of proof is of importance where by reason of not discharging the burden which was put upon it, a party must eventually fail.[12] This burden will, at the beginning of a trial, lie on one party, but during the course of the trial it may shift from one side to the other.[13] At the end of a case when both the parties have led evidence and the conflicting evidence can be weighed to determine which way the issue can be decided, the abstract question of burden of proof becomes academic.[14] Where in an eviction proceeding the fact of sub-tenancy was established and though the sub-tenant had left the ground it was not thereby wiped out, the court said that either party was free to prove his case and all questions as to burden of proof were no longer there.[15] The question of burden of proof also becomes irrelevant when the entire evidence on the matter is already on record.[16]

The term *onus probandi*, in its proper use, merely means that if a fact has to be proved, the person whose interest it is to prove it should adduce some evidence, however slight, upon which a court could find the fact he desires the court to find. It does not mean that he shall call all conceivable or available evidence. It merely means that the evidence he lays before the court should be sufficient, if not contradicted to form the basis of a judgment and decree upon that point in his favour.[17] Where there is

---

11. *Ajmer Singh v Atma Singh,* AIR 1985 P&H 315; *Mallo v Bakhtawari,* AIR 1985 All 160, gift by an old widow; *Clara Auroro de Branganca v SA Alvares,* AIR 1985 Bom 372, deed executed by a person of unsound mind. *Heirs Kantilal Purshottamdas Patel v Dahiben Jagdish Rathod,* AIR 2003 Guj 82, matters pleaded by the plaintiff and controverted by the defendant, the plaintiff has postively to prove those matters. It is not for the defendant to negatively disprove them.

12. *Narayan v Gopal,* AIR 1960 SC 100 : 1960(1) SCR 773; *Abdul Shukoor v Arji Papa Rao,* AIR 1963 SC 1150 : 1963 Supp (2) SCR 55; *Devadattam v UOI,* AIR 1964 SC 880 : 1964(4) SCR 191.

Reiterating these principles in *State of Maharashtra v Wasudeo Ram Chandra Kaidalwar,* AIR 1981 SC 1186 : 1981 Cr LJ 884 : (1981) 3 SCC 199 : (1981) 3 SCR 675, the court said: "The expression "burden of proof" has two distinct meanings, (1) the legal burden, i.e., the burden of establishing the guilt, and (2) the evidential burden, i.e. the burden of leading evidence. In a criminal trial, the burden of proving everything essential to establish the charge against the accused lies upon the prosecution, and that burden never shifts. Notwithstanding the general rule that the burden of proof lies exclusively upon the prosecution, in the case of certain offences, the burden of proving a particular fact in issue may be laid by law upon the accused. The burden resting on the accused in such cases is, however, not so onerous as that which lies on the prosecution and is discharged by proof of a balance of probabilities.

13. *Pannu Jeegania v Devi Prashad,* AIR 1963 MP 15. *Deena v UOI,* AIR 1983 SC 1155 : 1983 Cr LJ 1602 : (1983) 4 SCC 645 : 1983 SCC (Cri) 879, after looking at the entire material, the court can decide the question whether the respective burdens have been fully discharged.

14. *Narayan v Gopal,* AIR 1960 SC 100 : 1960(1) SCR 773. See also *MMB Catholicos v T Paulo Avira,* AIR 1959 SC 31; *Paras Nath v Mohani Das,* AIR 1959 SC 1204 : 1960(1) SCR 271; *Devadattam v UOI,* AIR 1964 SC 880.

15. *Raghunathi v Raju Ramappa,* AIR 1991 SC 1040 : 1991 Supp (2) SCC 267.

16. *Ram Saroop Rai v Lilavati,* 1980 All LJ 651; *Ramji Dayawala & Sons P Ltd v Invest Import,* AIR 1981 SC 2085 : (1981) 1 SCC 80; *Deena v UOI,* AIR 1983 SC 1155 : 1983 Cr LJ 1602.

17. *Unkar Nath v Mittu Lal,* (1898) 18 AWN 107.

an admission by a party the burden of proof shifts and it is for the party making the admission to explain it away.[18]

In the matter of proof, in a civil case, a defendant cannot take up the same stand as an accused in a criminal case. In civil cases, unlike criminal ones, it cannot be said that the benefit of reasonable doubt must necessarily go to the defendant. Even the preponderance of probabilities may serve as a good basis for decision.[19] The Supreme Court has held that in a civil case involving allegation of charges of criminal or fraudulent character insistence on proving charges clearly and beyond reasonable doubt is wrong.[20] In a tort action for malicious prosecution, the plaintiff failed to prove that the criminal complaint was lodged against him without any reasonable and probable cause. His suit failed.[21]

Deposit of money in wife's name does not amount to a gift. It is a resulting trust. If anybody says it was a gift he must prove it.[22] Where the question was of proving the corrupt practice of undue influence under the Representation of the People Act, 1951, the Supreme Court said,[23] "There is no ritualistic formula nor a cut and dried test to lay down as to how a charge of undue influence can be proved but if all the circumstances taken together lead to the irresistible inference that the voters were pressurised, threatened or assaulted at the instance of either candidate, that should be sufficient to vitiate the election while insisting on *standard of strict proof,* the court should not extend or stretch this doctrine to such an extent as to make it well-nigh impossible to prove an allegation of corrupt practice. Such an approach would defeat and frustrate the very laudable and sacrosanct object of the Act in maintaining purity of the electoral process." Where an assessee of property tax pleaded that the contractual rent should not be regarded as standard rent and that therefore rateable value had not been properly fixed, the onus of proof was on the assessee.[24] Where the person claiming tenancy produced a certified copy of admission of his tenancy given by landlord, burden of proof lay on the landlord to disprove the admission.[25] Where the tenant took the plea that the suit premises were not vacated by him, burden of proof to establish his plea would be on him.[26] In determining whether a temple/trust is public or private, the burden of proof lies on the person asserting that it is a private one.[27] Merely because a will is registered its genuineness cannot be presumed.[28]

In a claim of damages for breach of contract, the burden is on the complainant to show the basis on which the damages claimed by him have been quantified.[29]

---

18. *Chandra Kunwar v Narpat Singh,* (1906) 29 All 184: 34 IA 27: 9 Bom LR 267; *Dukh Haran Nath Zutshi v Commercial Credit Corp Ltd,* (1939) 15 Luck 191.

19. *Himmat Mal v Shah Magaji Khubaji,* (1953) 3 Raj 815.

20. *Gulabchand v Kudilal,* AIR 1966 SC 1734 : (1966) 3 SCR 623; *Latel v State of MP,* 1994 Cr LJ 1122, the accused has not to prove his defence plea beyond all reasonable doubt.

21. *Philip v Hindu Madhan Dharma Paripalana Sabha,* AIR 2003 Ker 205.

22. *P Narayana Menon v PB Amma,* AIR 1985 Ker 14.

23. *Ram Saran Yadav v Thakur Muneshwar Nath Singh,* AIR 1985 SC 24 at 25 : (1984) 4 SCC 649; *Takvi Devi v Rama Dogra,* AIR 1984 HP 11, proof of undue influence.

24. *Municipal Corp, Ahmedabad v Oriental F&G Insurance Co Ltd,* AIR 1994 Guj 167.

25. *Damu Ganu Bendale v Arvinda Dhondu Talekar,* AIR 1994 SC 1303 : 1995 Supp 1 SCC 182.

26. *Hardit Singh Chadha v Jagtar Singh Grover,* AIR 1994 Del 189.

27. *Kanteisuni Thakurani, Bije Rampur Kaitha v Babudhar Rout,* AIR 1995 Ori 197.

28. *Vattakam Purath Parambil Ananda Bhai v Kanaka Bhai,* AIR 1995 Ker 208.

29. *Usha Beltron Ltd v Nand Kishore Parasramka,* AIR 2001 Cal 137. The case required proof of market price for assessment of damages.

A party cannot be relieved from its burden of proving a fact only on the ground of hardship in the matter of proof. Where a sale deed was alleged to be forged and fabricated and, therefore, the party who made such allegation had to prove it, the court said that it was not proper for the court to shift the burden of proof because of hardship and require the other party to prove even to begin with that the allegation was false.[30]

[s 101.2] Criminal trial.—In a criminal trial the burden of proving the guilt of the accused beyond all reasonable doubts always rests on the prosecution and on its failure it cannot fall back upon the evidence adduced by the accused in support of his defence to rest its case solely thereon.[31] In criminal cases it is for the prosecution to bring the guilt home to the accused.[32] When two views are possible, the view favourable to the accused should be adopted.[33] It is not correct to say that when the prosecution has adduced such evidence as the circumstances and nature of the case require, it is for the accused to establish his innocence for the reason that there is no burden laid on the prisoner to prove his innocence and it is sufficient if he succeeds in raising a doubt as to his guilt.[34] Prosecution cannot succeed just by showing that the defence raised is suspicious.[35] Where the prosecution could not prove beyond a reasonable doubt that the accused was connected with the destruction of a film, the accused was given the benefit of doubt.[36]

Recovery of articles by itself does not connect anybody with the crime. Connection of the accused with the articles must be proved beyond a reasonable doubt.[37] Even total silence of the accused as to any defence on his part does not lighten the prosecution burden to prove its case satisfactorily.[38] More serious the crime, more strict proof would be requisite.[39]

---

30. *Anil Rishi v Gurbaksh Singh,* AIR 2006 SC 1971 : (2006) 5 SCC 558 : (2006) 6 Mah LJ 280.

31. *Jarnail Singh v State of Punjab,* AIR 1996 SC 755 : 1996 Cr LJ 1139; *Mahender Singh Dhayia v State (CBI),* 2003 Cr LJ 1908 (Del), the prosecution cannot take undue advantage of the defence put by the accused even if the same was found to be false and improbable.

32. *SD Soni v State of Gujarat,* AIR 1991 SC 917 : 1992 Supp (1) SCC 567; *State of UP v Krishna Gopal,* 1989 Cr LJ 288 : AIR 1988 SC 2154 : (1988) 4 SCC 302.

33. *State of Gujarat v Jayrajbhai Punjabhai Varu,* AIR 2016 SC 3218, para 13.

34. *Mangilal v The State of Rajasthan,* (1953) 3 Raj 706; Followed in *Nirmala v Rukminibai,* AIR 1994 Kant 247. For other cases, see *M Rangarajulu, Re,* AIR 1958 Mad 368; *Chottan v State of Bihar,* AIR 1959 Pat 326; *State of Rajasthan v Madho,* AIR 1991 SC 1065 : 1991 Cr LJ 1343. Proof that the accused was in possession of a forged note would not have the effect of shifting burden to the accused of proving his innocence. Knowledge reasonable to believe on the part of the accused that the note was forged must also be established. *Madan Lal Sarma v State of West Bengal,* 1990 Cr LJ 215 (Cal).

35. *JA Naidu v State of Maharashtra,* 1979 Cr LJ 962 SC : AIR 1979 SC 1537; *Jagdish v State of Rajasthan,* AIR 1979 SC 1010 : (1979) 3 SCR 428 : 1979 Cr LJ 888, where the prosecution could not explain injuries on the person of the accused which were caused at the time of occurrence; *Shanker Lal v State of Maharashtra,* AIR 1981 SC 765 : 1981 Cr LJ 325, falsity of defence does not establish prosecution case; *State of Punjab v Bhajan Singh,* AIR 1975 SC 258 : 1975 Cr LJ 282, suspicion, however strong, cannot take the place of proof. *State of Maharashtra v Champalal Punjaji Shah,* AIR 1981 SC 1675 : 1981 Cr LJ 1273 : (1981) 3 SCC 610 : 1981 SCC (Cri) 762, an unreasonable explanation by the defence of the facts established by the evidence for the prosecution.

36. *State (Delhi Admn.) v VC. Shukla,* AIR 1980 SC 1382 at 1390 : (1980) 2 SCC 665.

37. *Nagappa Dondiba v Kant,* AIR 1980 SC 1753 : 1980 Cr LJ 1270.

38. *Bishandas v State of Punjab,* AIR 1975 SC 573 at p 578 : 1975 Cr LJ 461.

39. *Paramjeet Singh v State of Uttarakhand,* AIR 2011 SC 200 : (2010) 10 SCC 410.

As against this heavy burden on the prosecution the accused can claim the benefit of his defence just by showing a balance of probabilities. He has not to prove his defence beyond a reasonable doubt. The prosecution proved in a case that an official had accepted a sum of money which was intended to be a bribe. The Supreme Court said that the accused must prove his justification and he can do so on a balance of probabilities and need not prove beyond reasonable doubt.[40] Prosecution cannot derive any advantage from falsity or other infirmities of the defence version, so long as it does not discharge its initial burden of proving its case beyond all reasonable doubt.[41]

Where the accused is under the burden of proving a fact for rebutting a statutory presumption, it should not be as heavy as on the prosecution but even so it would have to be of somewhat greater probability than the ordinary balance of probabilities.[42]

Where the accused claimed that he was acting in private defence of property and the sale deed showed transfer of possession in favour of the father of the accused, the court said that the possession of the accused had remained undisturbed.[43]

[s 101.3] Offence under NDPS Act.—The possession of a small quantity of psychotropic substance for personal use requires the prosecution to prove its allegation of commercial possession beyond reasonable doubt. It is enough for the accused in his defence to satisfy the judicial mind on a preponderance of probability.[44]

[s 101.4] Plea of Alibi.—Where the accused raises the plea of alibi (his presence elsewhere), burden lies on him to substantiate that fact at least to the extent of a reasonable probability. Even if the evidence produced is capable of creating a doubt whether the accused was there at the time of the happening, he becomes entitled to the benefit of doubt.[45] The court cited the decision of the Supreme Court in *Soma Bhai v State of Gujarat*[46] where it was taken to be a settled law that a plea of alibi has got to be proved to the satisfaction of the court. The court also noted the observation

---

40. *MP Gupta v State of Rajasthan,* AIR 1974 SC 773 : 1974 Cr LJ 509. See also *NP Lotlikar v CBI,* 1993 Cr LJ 2051 (Bom). *Kishore Chandra Patel v State of Orissa,* AIR 1993 Ori 259, section 16, Orissa Special Courts Act, 1992, burden upon the accused to show how he acquired property. *MS Narayana Menon v State of Kerala,* (2006) 6 SCC 39 : (2006) 3 KLT 404 : (2006) 5 Mah LJ 676 : (2006) 4 MPLJ 97, the accused has not to disprove the prosecution case in its entirety. The onus on the accused is not as heavy as on the prosecution; it may be compared with that on the defendant in a civil case. See further under section 106.

41. *Md. Alimuddin v State of Assam,* 1992 Cr LJ 3287 (Gau); *M Krishna Reddy v State Dy Supdt. of Police,* (1992) 4 SCC 45 : AIR 1993 SC 313, initial burden on prosecution, when this is fully discharged only then any sort of burden shifts to the accused person. *Ram Swarup v State of Haryana,* 1993 Supp 4 SCC 344 : 1994 SCC Cri 29, real onus on prosecution to prove its case which includes the manner of occurrence and the proof should be beyond all reasonable doubt. The accused has only to create a doubt about the prosecution case in the mind of the judge or to satisfy him that his version of the occurrence was probable. *Lakh Ram v State of Punjab,* 1993 Supp 4 SCC 361 : 1993 SCC Cri 1227, the burden of proving the prosecution case never shifts except to the extent to which shifting may take place under a presumption.

42. *Sanjay Dutt v State (through CBI),* (1994) 5 SCC 410 : 1994 SCC Cri 1433.

43. *Deepa v State of MP,* 1999 Cr LJ 413 (MP).

44. *Ouseph v State of Kerala,* (2004) 4 SCC 446.

45. *Jagarnath Giri v State of Bihar,* 1992 Cr LJ 648 Pat.

46. *Soma Bhai v State of Gujarat,* AIR 1975 SC 1453 : 1975 Cr LJ 1201.

of the Supreme Court in *State of UP v Sughar Singh*[47] to the effect that the burden of substantiating such a plea and making it reasonably probable is on him (the accused), and in *State of Maharashtra v Narsingarao Gangaram Pimple*[48] to the effect that "the plea of alibi must be proved with absolute certainty so as to completely exclude the possibility of the presence of the accused at the place of occurrence," and again in *Dudh Nath Pandey v State of UP*[49] that "the plea can succeed only if it is shown that the accused was so far away at the relevant time that he could not be present at the place where the crime (in question) was committed."

[s 101.5] Food Adulteration.—Where a person was charged under the Prevention of Food Adulteration Act, 1954 for selling sub-standard *Heeng*, and it was shown by him that the article was meant only for animal consumption, the pricing factor as well as report of the public analyst showed that it was being marketed for use of animals, the court said that the burden to show otherwise was upon the food inspector who had taken the sample from the accused.[50]

[s 101.6] Election Petition.—Where an election was challenged on the ground that the result was vitiated by the fact that the nomination of a candidate wrongly accepted, the Supreme Court held that the burden lay upon the petitioner to prove that the votes cast in favour of the wrongly accepted candidate would have gone in his favour to such an extent that he would have been returned and that though this fact is very difficult to prove the rules relating to burden of proof will remain whether it is difficult or virtually impossible to prove the fact in question.[51] Stating the effect of the Representation of the People Act, 1951, Singh J said:[52]

> Section 100(1)(d)(i) provides for setting aside the election of the returned candidate on the ground of improper acceptance of any nomination paper provided the result of the election of the returned candidate is materially affected by reason of such improper acceptance of nomination of a candidate other than the returned candidate. Improper acceptance of nomination of any candidate does not *ipso facto* render the election of the returned candidate void. [It must be] found that the result of the election of the returned candidate was materially affected on the ground of such improper acceptance. The burden of proving [this] is on the election petitioner. Unless this burden is discharged by [him], the result of the returned candidate cannot be declared void.[53]

---

47. *State of UP v Sughar Singh,* AIR 1978 SC 191 : 1978 Cr LJ 141.
48. *State of Maharashtra v Narsingarao Gangaram Pimple,*1984 Cr LJ 4 : (1984) 1 SCC 446 : AIR 1984 SC 63 : 1984 SCC (Cri) 109 : 1984 Mad LJ (Cri) 207. Plea of alibi not proved, conviction, held proper, *Surjit Singh v State of Punjab,* AIR 1992 SC 1389 : 1992 Cr LJ 1952 : 1993 Supp (1) SCC 208. See also *State v Balakrishnan,* 1992 Cr LJ 1872 (Mad).
49. *Dudh Nath Pandey v State of UP*AIR 1981 SC 911 : 1981 Cr LJ 618 : (1981) 2 SCC 166 : 1981 SCC (Cri) 379 : 1981 All LJ 228.
50. *Rajesh Kumar v State of UP,* 2001 Cr LJ 2093 (All).
51. *Shiv Charan Singh v Chandra Bhan Singh,* (1988) 2 SCC 12 : AIR 1988 SC 637.
52. *Ibid* at p 18.
53. The court followed *Vashist Narain Sharma v Dev Chandra,* AIR 1954 SC 513 : (1955) 1 SCR 509, where it was pointed out that there should be proof as to which way the wasted votes would have gone and that this question cannot be left to surmises, the court also considered *Paoki Hookip v Rishang,* AIR 1969 SC 663 : (1969) 1 SCR 637 where the election was set aside on proof of blatant violation of the Act.

Following an earlier case, the court said that in such a case it was impossible to foresee what the result would have been if the improperly nominated candidate had not been in the field. Since it was not possible to anticipate the result, the election petitioner must discharge the burden of proving that fact and on his failure to prove that fact the election of the returned candidate must be allowed to stand.

[s 101.7] Constitutionality.—In the petition challenging the constitutionality of a statute, the allegations regarding the violation of the constitutional provision should be specific, clear and unambiguous and burden of proof is on the person challenging its constitutionality.[54]

In *Gauri Shanker v UOI,*[55] The Supreme Court stated that:—

(a) there is always a presumption in favour of constitutional validity of an enactment and the burden is upon him who attacks it to show that there has been clear transgression of the constitutional principles;

(b) it must be presumed that the Legislature understands and correctly appreciates the need of its own people, that its laws are directed to problems made manifest by experience and that its discriminations are based on adequate grounds;

(c) in order to sustain the presumption of constitutionality the court may take into consideration matters of common knowledge, matters of common report, the history of the times and may assume every date of facts which can be conceived existing at the time of legislation.

[s 101.8] Reasonableness of restrictions.—Where the right to trade as guaranteed by Article 19(1)(g) of the Constitution is sought to be subjected to certain restrictions, such as, for example, prohibition on sale of sugarcane juice in Municipal Limits, the burden lies on the State to convince the court of the reasonableness of the restriction.[56]

[s 101.9] Matrimonial Cases.—In matrimonial cases principles of burden of proof relating to civil cases are applicable.[57]

[s 101.10] Blank Signature.—Where the defendant said that he had put his signature only on a blank paper, it was held that the evidence adduced by the plaintiff to the effect that the defendant had executed a document, if found reliable, would discharge the burden of the plaintiff and put the burden on the defendant to show that he had not executed any document.[58]

---

54. *Amrit Banaspati Co Ltd v UOI,* AIR 1995 SC 1340 : (1995) 3 SCC 335, relied on *VS Rice and Oil Mills v State of AP,* AIR 1964 SC 1781 and *R.K Garg v UOI,* AIR 1981 SC 2138 : (1981) 4 SCC 676.

55. *Gauri Shanker v UOI,* 1994 AIR SCW 4059. *Rakesh Bansal v State of Rajasthan,* AIR 2002 NOC 68 (Raj) : (2002) 2 Raj LR 153, a taxing statute imposing 4 times more fine than the amount of tax evaded, was held to be valid, the burden of proving otherwise was upon the person challenging it.

56. *Bhagwan Dass v MC of Delhi,* AIR 1995 Del 17.

57. *A v B* AIR 1985 Guj 121; *Dastane v Dastane,* AIR 1975 SC 1534 : (1975) 2 SCC 326.

58. *Kuttadan Velayudhan Re,* AIR 2001 SC 123.

[s 101.11] Whole evidence on record, burden irrelevant.—Where both parties have already produced whatever evidence they had, the question of burden of proof ceases to be of any importance.[59]

Where the motion is at the discretion of the court and both the parties have led evidence, the question of burden of proof would become relegated to the position of secondary importance.[60]

Burden of proof means that a party has to prove an allegation before he is entitled to a judgment in his favour. The one or the other of the contending parties has to introduce evidence on a contested issue. The question of onus is material only where the party on which it is placed would eventually lose if he failed to discharge the same. Where parties joined the issue, led evidence, such evidence could be weighed in order to determine the issue. The question of burden would become academic.[61]

It is always open to the defendant not to lead any evidence where the onus is upon the plaintiff but after having gone into evidence, he cannot ask the court not to look at and act on it. The question of burden of proof at the end of the case when both parties have tendered evidence is not of any great importance and the court has to come to a decision on the consideration of all materials. In examining the question whether the plaintiff had succeeded in proving the negative fact, it was open to the court to consider the entire evidence on record when both the parties have completed their evidence. No part of the evidence can be left out. A finding based on consideration of the whole of the evidence cannot be said to be vitiated.[62]

The question of burden of proof remains of no importance at the end of the case when both have already adduced the whole of the evidential material which they desired to produce.[63]

[s 101.12] Motive.—Where certain land was alienated shortly prior to the enforcement of the ceiling act, burden lay on the landlord to prove that the alienation was not done with a view to avoid the ceiling law.[83]

[s 101.13] Proof of good faith.—Where executant of the sale deed was an old, illiterate and blind woman and no consideration passed at the time of sale, onus lay

---

59. *Premlata v Arhant Kumar*, AIR 1973 SC 626 : (1973) 3 SCC 718; *Babban v Shiv Nath*, AIR 1986 All 185; In *M Equipment v N L Kanodia*, AIR 1986 Del 36. See also *Gangamma v Krishnappa*, 1996 AIHC 264 (Kant), **following** *Narayan Bhagwantrao Gosavi Balajiwale v Gopal Vinayak Gosavi*, AIR 1960 SC 100 : (1960) 1 SCR 773; *Kartick Pd. Gorai v Neami Pd Gorai*, AIR 1998 Cal 278, a sale deed was challenged, both parties had full knowledge of the respective cases and led evidence, question of burden of proof became a question of academic value only.

60. *Ramji Dayawala & Sons P Ltd v Invest Import*, AIR 1981 SC 2085 : (1981) 1 SCR 899 : 1981 1 SCC 80.

61. *Bala Shankar Maha Shanker Bhattjee v Charity Commr., Gujarat State*, AIR 1995 SC 167 : (1995) 1 Guj LR 711 : (1994) 2 GCD 830.

62. *Lakhan Sao v Dharamu Chaudhary*, (1991) 3 SCC 331 : (1991) 1 Guj LH 288 : (1991) 17 ALR 363.

63. *Revathinnal Balagopala Varma v Padmanabha Dasa Bala Rama Varma*, (1993) Supp 1 SCC 233. *Rebti Devi v Ram Dutt*, AIR 1998 SC 310 : (1997) 11 SCC 714, both sides led their respective evidence, the question of burden of proof paled into insignificance. *Arunmugham v Sundarambal*, AIR 1999 SC 2216 : (1998) 5 SCC 381, both parties adduced their oral as well documentary evidence, the question of burden of proof became insignificant.

on the purchaser to prove that the sale deed was not executed under undue influence.[64] Though in the execution of a gift deed by a "*pardanashin*" lady, fraud was not established, still onus was on the defendant to establish the fact that the document was read over and explained to her.[65]

Where a coal company's property was sold to the wife of a director and it was alleged that the sale was not a genuine transaction but a sham, it was held that the burden was upon the company to prove the *bona fides* of the transaction.[66] Those who wanted to take advantage under sale deeds executed by an illiterate person were put under the burden of proving the *bona fides* of the transaction by showing that the contents of the deed were read over and explained to the executant.[67]

[s 101.14] Presumption as to consideration.—Section 118, Negotiable Instruments Act, 1881, creates a number of presumptions, one of them being that every negotiable instrument shall be presumed to be transacted for consideration. This affects the position as to burden of proof. The party liable would have to show that there was no consideration. In this case, the party liable was not able to show absence of consideration. Therefore, the claimant was held to be entitled to the benefit of the presumption.[68]

[s 101.15] Suit for recovery of possession.—In a suit for recovery of possession based upon the plaintiff's possessory title, onus is on him to establish the fact of his possession within the preceding 12 years from the date of adverse possession. Once this fact was established, the onus would be shifted on to the defendant to show that he was entitled to retain his possession on the basis of a superior title.[69]

[s 101.16] Adverse possession.—The entire burden of proving that the possession is adverse to the plaintiff is on the defendant.[70]

[s 101.17] Burden of proving slum area as against landlord.—A tenant wanted to save himself from eviction on the ground that the property in question was located in a slum area which was protected against eviction under the TN Slum Area (Improvement and Clearance) Act, 1971. The landlady denied this fact. It was held that the burden of proving slum area situation was on the tenant. He failed to do so. The order that he was not entitled to the benefit of the Act was, therefore, proper.[71]

[s 101.18] Landlord's burden to prove personal need.—Where the proceeding was for eviction of the tenant on the ground of the landlord's personal need, the court said

64. *Sethani v Bhana*, AIR 1993 SC 956 : (1992) 2 JT 427.
65. *Kishore Ray Thakur Bije v Basanti Kumar Das*, AIR 1994 Ori 113; *Subhas Chandra Bhowmik v Kalyani Bhowmik*, AIR 1998 Gau 96, mother sold minor daughters' share of property to her sons for a very small amount. Burden upon the buyers to show good faith and legal necessity. DM's permission not taken. Burden not discharged. *Baban Girju Bangar v Namdeo Girju Bangar*, AIR 1999 Bom 46, the purchase of the suit property by the plaintiff was not disputed. The defendant alleged that the purchase price was paid out of joint family funds. The court said that the burden was on the defendant to prove that fact.
66. *Subhra Mukherjee v Bharat Coking Coal Ltd*, AIR 2000 SC 1203 : (2000) 3 SCC 312.
67. *Kartik Pd. Gorai v Neami Pd. Gorai*, AIR 1998 Cal 278. There were contradictory statements on their part. Failure to prove deeds inferred.
68. *TN Boopathy v TA Sattu*, AIR 2002 Mad 177.
69. *Kantilal v Shanti Devi*, AIR 1997 Raj 230.
70. *Janata Dal Party v Indian National Congress*, (2014) 16 SCC 731, para 17 : 2014 (1) Scale 533.
71. *Neelkantan v Mallika Begum*, AIR 2002 SC 827.

that a mere desire of the landlord to have his premises back from the tenant would not be sufficient to constitute a *bona fide* personal need. The need is to be tested objectively. The burden lies upon the landlord to convince the court that he genuinely requires the accommodation.[72]

[s 101.19] Dishonour of cheques [Special Statutory Provisions].—Section 118 of the Negotiable Instruments Act, 1881, lays special rules of evidence one of which is that every negotiable instrument shall be presumed to be supported by consideration. The same Act provides in sections 138 and 139 that a cheque shall be deemed to have been issued for the discharge of a debt or liability. On the basis of these provisions read with those of sections 101 and 104 of the Evidence Act, the Supreme Court held in *KN Beena v Muniyappan*[73] that where a cheque issued by a party has been dishonoured, the court has to presume that the cheque was issued for a consideration, namely for the discharge of a debt or liability and, therefore, burden of proof would be on the party issuing a cheque to show that there was no debt or liability for the discharge of which the cheque was issued.

It is the accused person who has to prove the absence of *mens rea*.[74]

[s 101.20] Gift deed.—A woman gifted her property to her grandson. The lady was more than 90 years, but she was fully intelligent and not infirm. The gift was due to the flow of a natural love as the donee had lost his mother and the step mother started torturing him. The suit was filed by the donor lady and her son. The burden of proof was held to be on the person who alleged that there was a fraud in the transaction.[75]

[s 101.21] Will.—Where the execution of a Will was surrounded by suspicious circumstances and there was also the allegation of coercion, the court said that the burden of proof was on the party who alleged coercion.[76]

[s 101.22] Title.—The plaintiff in a suit for declaration of title and possession could succeed only on the strength of its title and that could be done only by adducing sufficient evidence to discharge the onus on it, irrespective of the question whether the defendants have proved their case or not. Even if the title set up by the defendants is found against them, in the absence of establishment of the plaintiff's own title, the plaintiff must be non-suited.[77]

[s 101.23] Joint property.—The burden of proof that certain property was excluded from the partition of the joint property is on the party that alleges the same to be a joint property.[78]

[s 101.24] Caste Claim.—Where a candidate claimed that she belonged to a tribe which has been designated in the Scheduled Tribe Order, the court said that the burden of establishing such fact was upon the claimant.[79]

---

72. *SJ Ebenezer v Velayudhan*, AIR 1998 SC 746 : (1998) 1 SCC 633.
73. *KN Beena v Muniyappan*AIR 2001 SC 2895 : 2001 Cr LJ 4745.
74. *Sadhu Ram Singh v State*, 2002 Cr LJ 2760 (Del).
75. *Krishna Prasad v Gopal Prasad*, AIR 2001 Pat 1.
76. *Savithri v Karthyayani Amma*, AIR 2008 SC 300 : (2007) 11 SCC 621.
77. *UOI v Vasavi Cooperative Housing Society Ltd*, (2014) 2 SCC 269 (para 19).
78. *Kesharbai v Tarabai Prabhakarrao Nalawade*, (2014) 4 SCC 707 (para 22).
79. *Shilpa Vishnu Thakur v State of Maharashtra*, AIR 2009 NOC 2737 (Bom).

[s 101.25] Exercise of statutory power.—In cases where the exercise of a statutory power is subject to the fulfilment of a certain condition, then a recital in the order that the condition has been fulfilled, raises a presumption about fulfilment of such condition. The burden is on the person who challenges the validity of the order to show that the condition was not fulfilled. Where the order does not contain such a recital, the burden to prove that the condition was fulfilled would be on the authority passing the order.[80]

[s 101.26] Burden and onus.—The illustrations to the section show that the provision applies to civil as well as criminal cases. Viscount Dunedin explained in *Robins v National Trust Co*[81] the true function of "onus" in civil cases: "Onus is always on a person who asserts a proposition or a fact which is not self-evident. To assert that a man who is alive was born requires no proof. The onus is not on the person making the assertion, because it is self-evident that he had been born. But to assert that he was born on a certain date, if the date is material requires proof: the onus is on the person making the assertion. Now, in conducting any inquiry, the determining tribunal will often find that onus is sometimes on the side of one contending party, sometimes on the side of the other, or, as it is often expressed, that in certain circumstances onus shifts."

The same distinction has been further exemplified by the Gujarat High Court.[82] "There is an essential distinction between "burden of proof" and "onus of proof"; burden of proof lies on the person who has to prove a fact and it never shifts, but the onus of proof shifts.[83] Such a shifting of onus is a continuous process in the evaluation of evidence.[84] The court said: Burden of proof has two distinct meanings, namely, (i) the burden of proof as a matter of law and pleadings, and (ii) burden of proof as a matter of adducing evidence. Section 101 deals with the former and section 102 with the latter. The first remains constant, but the second shifts. In a claim application (as the present case was) the burden of proof, in the first instance, certainly lies on the claimant. If his evidence is found to be acceptable, the onus shifts to the tort-feasor to prove circumstances, if any, which disprove the assertions of the claimant. The victim of the accident died 7 months after the happening. The injuries sustained by him created urinary trouble from the very beginning and ultimately proved fatal. The defendant was not able to discharge the burden of showing that the death was due to some remote or isolated cause.

In a matter under the Prevention of Corruption Act, 1988, the Supreme Court again emphasized:[85] "The expression "burden of proof" has two distinct meanings: (1) the legal burden, i.e. burden of establishing the gift, and (2) the evidential burden, i.e., the burden of leading evidence. In a subsequent decision, the Supreme Court added one more point to the concept of burden; it said: A distinction exists between burden and onus of proof. The right to begin follows onus probandi. It assumes importance

80. *State of Haryana v Hari Ram Yadav*, AIR 1994 SC 1262 : (1994) 2 SCC 617.

81. *Robinsv National Trust Co*, (1927) AC 505 at p 510 (PC) See also *State Bank of India v Shyama Devi*, AIR 1978 SC 1263 : (1978) 3 SCC 399.

82. *Ranchodbhai Somabhai v Babubhai*, AIR 1982 Guj 308, 310.

83. The Supreme Court laid down in *Abdulla Mohammed v State*, (1980) 3 SCC 110 : AIR 1980 SC 499 : (1980) 1 SCR 604, that onus of proof of the existence of every ingredient of the charge is on the prosecution and never shifts on the accused.

84. Citing *Raghavamma v Chenchamma*, AIR 1964 SC 136 : (1964) 2 SCR 933.

85. *State of Maharashtra v Vasudeo Ramchandra Kaidalwar*, (1981) 3 SCC 199 : AIR 1981 SC 1186.

in the early stage of the case. The question of onus of proof has greater force where the question is as to which party is to begin. The concept of burden of proof is used in three ways:

(i) to indicate the duty of bringing forward evidence in support of a proposition at the beginning or later;

(ii) establishing a proposition as against all counter evidence, and

(iii) an indiscriminate use in which it may mean either or both of the others.[86]

In a criminal trial, the burden of proving everything essential to establish the charge against the accused lies upon the prosecution, and that burden never shifts. Notwithstanding the general rule that the burden of proof lies exclusively upon the prosecution, in the case of certain offences, the burden of proving a particular fact-in-issue may be laid by law on the accused. The burden resting on the accused in such cases is, however, not so onerous as that which lies on the prosecution and is discharged by a proof of balance of probabilities. Under the scheme of the Prevention of Corruption Act, burden lies upon the accused to account for his possessions."

[s 101.27] Benami transactions.—When a person purchases property in another person's name and also gets it registered in that person's name (*benami*), if subsequently he wishes to assert his ownership, the burden would be upon him to prove that fact. In a case of this kind, the Supreme Court observed as follows:[87]

> It is well settled that the burden of proving that a particular sale is *benami* and the apparent purchaser is not the real owner, always rests on the person asserting it to be so. The essence of a *benami* is the intention of the parties concerned; and not unoften such intention is shrouded in a thick veil which cannot be easily pierced through. But such difficulties do not relieve the person asserting the transaction to be a *benami* of the serious onus that rests on him, nor justify the acceptance of a mere conjecture or surmises, as a substitute for proof.

[s 101.28] Search and Seizure.—It is the burden of the prosecution to prove that the accused was informed under the Narcotic Drugs and Psychotropic Substances Act, 1985 of his rights under section 50(1) about search and seizures, compliance of those provisions being mandatory.[88]

[s 101.29] Burden of proving contempt of Court.—The common legal phraseology "he who asserts must prove" has the due application in the matter of the proof of the allegation that there has been contempt of court. As regards the standard of proof, a proceeding under the extraordinary jurisdiction of the court under the Contempt of Courts Act is of a quasi-criminal nature. The standard of proof required is that of a

---

86. *Anil Rishi v Gurbaksh Singh,* (2006) 5 SCC 558 : AIR 2006 SC 1971 : (2006) 6 Mah LJ 280.

87. *Jaydayal Poddar v Bibi Hazra,* AIR 1974 SC 171 : (1974) 1 SCC 3. This was followed, in *Janja Singh v Kuldeep Singh,* AIR 1978 : 276, 279 (Del); *Mushtaq Ahmad v Mohd. Shafi,* AIR 1983 J&K 44. *Rama Kanta Jain v MS Jain,* AIR 1999 281 (Del), wherein the person who claimed to be the owner and the registered owner to be only his *benamidar* could not prove that fact. *KR Sathyanarayana Rao v KR. Venkoba Rao,* AIR 1998 Mad 276, father and son carrying on business in partnership, property purchased in the name of the son, presumption that it was the son's property, burden upon father to show that purchase was for family purposes.

88. *Shanta Bai v State of MP,* 1999 Cr LJ 1945 (MP).

criminal proceeding. The offence would have to be established beyond all reasonable doubt.[89]

[s 101.30] Purchase of property in partner's name.—A person was carrying on business in partnership with his sons. A property was purchased in the name of his most senior son. There was no joint family nucleus. Consideration for the purchase was paid from the business. The court said that the presumption was that the property belonged to the partner in whose name it was purchased and a further presumption that payment was made from the share of the partner. The other partners who claimed that the purchase was for the benefit of all the partners had to prove that fact. It was their burden to show that the property was intended to belong to the firm.[90]

[s 102] On whom burden of proof lies.—The burden of proof in a suit or proceeding lies on that person who would fail if no evidence at all were given on either side.

ILLUSTRATIONS

(a) *A* sues *B* for land of which *B* is in possession, and which, as *A* asserts, was left to *A* by the will of *C*, *B*'s father.

If no evidence were given on either side, *B* would be entitled to retain his possession. Therefore the burden of proof is on *A*.

(b) *A* sues *B* for money due on a bond.

The execution of the bond is admitted, but *B* says that it was obtained by fraud, which *A* denies.

If no evidence were given on either side, *A* would succeed, as the bond is not disputed and fraud is not proved.

Therefore the burden of proof is on *B*.

SYNOPSIS

COMMENT

[s 102.1] Shifting of onus of proof.—The phrase "burden of proof" has two meanings—one, the burden of proof as a matter of law and pleading, and the other the burden of establishing a case; the former is fixed as a question on the basis of the pleadings and is unchanged during the entire trial, whereas the latter is not constant but shifts as soon as the party adduces sufficient evidence to raise a presumption in his favour.[91] This section lays down a test for ascertaining on which side the burden of proof lies. The section makes it clear that the initial onus is on the plaintiff. If he discharges that onus and makes out a case which entitles him to relief, the onus shifts

---

89. *Chhotu Ram v Urvashi Gulati*, 2001 Cr LJ 4204 (SC). To the same effect are observations of the Supreme Court in *All India Anna Dravida Munnetra Kazhagam v LK Tripathi*, AIR 2009 SC 1314 : (2009) 5 SCC 417.

90. *KR Sathyanaraynan Rao v KR Venkoba Rao*, AIR 1998 Mad 276.

91. *Kundan Lal v Custodian, Evacuee Property*, AIR 1961 SC 1316.

on to the defendant to prove those circumstances, if any, which would disentitle the plaintiff to the same. There is an essential distinction between burden of proof and onus of proof: burden of proof lies upon the person who has to prove a fact and it never shifts but the onus of proof shifts. Such a shifting onus is a continuous process in the valuation of evidence.[92]

The burden of proof lies upon the party, whether plaintiff or defendant, who substantially asserts the affirmative of the issue. This rule, derived from the maxim of Roman law, *ei qui affirmat, non ei qui negat, incumbit probatio,* is adopted partly because it is but just that he who invokes the aid of the law should be the first to prove his case; and partly because, in the nature of things, a negative is more difficult to establish than an affirmative.[93] The phrase "burden of proof" is used in two distinct meanings in the law of evidence, *viz.*, the burden of establishing a case and the burden of introducing evidence. The burden of establishing a case remains throughout the trial where it was originally placed; it never shifts. The burden of evidence may shift constantly as evidence is introduced by one side or the other.

One has to prove title by one's own evidence and not by any weakness in the case of the defendant.[94] A person who claims rights of reversion on genealogy basis has to prove that fact.[95]

In criminal cases the prosecution has to prove the ingredients of the offence.[96] In a criminal complaint for unauthorised construction, it was held that the onus was on the complaining authority to prove that the land belonged to it and the accused put up construction on it.[97] The value of goods and extent of damage have to be proved by the claimant because the railway certificate is not the final thing.[98] The burden of proving contributory negligence is on the defendant.[99] Where cheques were dishonoured, burden lay upon those issuing them to show that they were issued by mistake.[100] A debtor transferred his property. Creditors alleged and proved it to be a fraudulent transfer. The burden was now on him to show that the transfer was within any of the exceptions.[101]

To prove the validity of transfer of land of a member of scheduled tribe and perfection of title over it by adverse possession, the burden is on the transferee.[102] The plaintiff

---

92. *Raghavamma v Chenchamma,* AIR 1964 SC 136 : (1964) 2 SCR 933; *T Shesha Reddy v Managing Committee, Jame Masjid,* AIR 2002 NOC 164 (AP) : 2002 AHIC 1811, normally, the plaintiff has to prove his case *dehors* the averments of the defendant and the evidence adduced by him. But in the case of a suit and a cross-suit by the defendant being tried jointly, the principle of shifting of burden of proof would not apply. The matter has to be considered on the basis of materials and documents available on record.

93. *Phipson,* 10th Edn, p 92.

94. *Lalita James v Ajit Kumar,* AIR 1991 MP 15.

95. *State of Bihar v Radha Krishna Singh,* AIR 1983 SC 684 : (1983) 3 SCC 118.

96. *Tukaram v State of Maharashtra,* (1979) 1 SCR 810 : AIR 1979 SC 185 : 198 Cr LJ 1864.

97. *Special Development Area v Pooranlal,* 1997 Cr LJ 3484 (MP).

98. *UOI v Madan Mohan,* AIR 1981 Ori 9 : LNIND 1980 Ori 8.

99. *Krishana Goods Carriers v UOI,* AIR 1980 Del 92.

100. *J & KRT Co v 3 A Enterprises,* AIR 1981 J&K 64. Those who issued pronotes must show that they did so under undue influence. *Ram Raja Ram v Dhruba Charan Das,* AIR 1982 Ori 264.

101. *Basaregowda v S. Narayana Swamy,* AIR 1984 Kant 225.

102. *Trilochan Dandsena v State (FB),* AIR 1995 Ori 239.

would not succeed automatically without establishing his case on mere failure of the defendant to establish his case.[103]

[s 102.2] Illegal gratification.—The consistent view of the courts as well as the Apex Court from the beginning has been that the burden of proof under section 4(1) of the Prevention of Corruption Act, 1947 is cast on an accused person to rebut the presumption created by that section. This burden cannot be equated with the degree and character of proof which rests on the prosecution to prove the case, namely the receipt of money as bribe. The accused may rebut the presumption by showing a mere preponderance of probability in his favour. It is not necessary for him to establish his case beyond a reasonable doubt.[104]

[s 102.3] CASES.—In a suit on a bond, the plaintiff accounted for the non-production of the bond, by alleging that the defendant had stolen it. The defendant admitted the execution of the bond, but alleged he had paid it. It was held that the defendant was bound to begin and prove payment, either by the production of the bond or other evidence or by both.[105]

Where an unregistered document, the execution of which is admitted or proved, contains an admission of the payment of the consideration, the onus lies on the person executing the document to prove that what he himself admitted to be true was, as a matter of fact, false and that he did not receive the consideration.[106]

An insurance company pleaded breach of a term of the policy in that the driver did not have a valid licence, but produced no evidence of the lack of licence. The company's case failed.[107] Where a contract term provided that breach of any term by one would entitle the other party not to perform the contract, it was held that the party seeking to be relieved of the contract would have to show the breach of such term.[108] Where there was no direct evidence to prove that a person purchased ticket and boarded a train or that he died in the accident, the claim for compensation failed.[109] Where railways had to prove that the goods were not lost within seven days of the end of transit and offered no evidence, their case failed.[110] Where the landlord proved that the tenant was not in exclusive possession of the premises, it was held that the burden was upon the tenant to show what was the nature of the right of the person with whom he was sharing possession.[111] In a suit for eviction against a sub-tenant,

---

103. *Nirakar Das v Gourhari Das,* AIR 1995 Ori 270; *Surma Valley Saw Mills Pvt Ltd v Arati Das,* AIR 2002 Gau 108, the defendant contended in a title suit that the Court had shifted the burden of proving his title to the defendant. The Court rejected the argument because the impugned judgment did not reflect that the trial court had shifted the burden. The court also said that the shifting of onus of proof is a constant feature of any litigation and cannot be complained of unless there is an order against the provisions of the Act.

104. *Periyaswamy v Inspector, Vigilance and Anti-Corruption,* 1999 Cr LJ 2944 (Mad.)

105. *Chuni Kuar v Udai Ram,* (1883) 6 All 73.

106. *Ram Chand v Chhunnu Mal,* (1925) 6 Lah 470 (FB), **disapproving**; *Wazir Singh v Jai Gopal,* (1887) PR No. 17 of 1888 (Civil).

107. *NV Kamat v AAD Martina,* AIR 1985 SC 1281 : (1985) 2 SCC 574; *United India Insurance Co Ltd v O Jameela Beevi,* AIR 1991 Ker 380, insurer failing to prove wilful breach of terms of policy.

108. *Narchinva V Kamat v Alfredo, Antonio Doe Martins,* AIR 1985 SC 1281 : (1985) 2 SCC 574 : 1985 SCC (Cri) 274.

109. *Sudha Srivastva v Commr, NR,* AIR 1985 All 52.

110. *Raman & Co v UOI,* AIR 1985 Mad 37; *UOI v Ram Pd,* AIR 1982 Raj 253.

111. *Kishan Chand v Banarsi Dass,* AIR 1990 P&H 160.

the tenant did not contest the suit nor appeared as a witness. The landlord also did not appear but produced witnesses on his behalf. Decree was claimed on the basis of a document (*sulenama*) entered into between the landlord and the tenant. Contents of the *sulenama* were not proved. It was held that the *sulenama* could not be relied upon and the onus squarely lay on the landlord to prove sub-tenancy. Eviction decree was set aside.[112] Where a disputed property was proved to be a joint family property, the members who pleaded that it was purchased from the separate income of their father, onus was on them to prove that fact.[113] Where a person filed a petition for a declaration that a particular institution was a Sikh Gurudwara, it was held that the burden of proving the requirements of a Gurudwara and that the place in question satisfied those requirements was on the petitioner.[114] Where there was delay in filing a suit, onus was on the plaintiffs to show that their suit was within time.[115]

A party challenging an arbitration award must satisfy the court that the grounds contained in section 34(2) of the Arbitration and Conciliation Act, 1996 do exist. A very heavy onus lies on the party in this respect.[116]

[s 103] Burden of proof as to particular fact.—The burden of proof as to any particular fact lies on that person who wishes the Court to believe in its existence, unless it is provided by any law that the proof of that fact shall lie on any particular person.

ILLUSTRATION

A prosecutes *B* for theft, and wishes the Court to believe that *B* admitted the theft to *C*. *A* must prove the admission.

B wishes the Court to believe that, at the time in question, he was elsewhere. He must prove it.

SYNOPSIS

COMMENT

This section amplifies the general rule laid down in section 101. It differs from section 101. By section 101 the party has to prove the whole of the facts which he alleges to entitle him to judgment when the burden of proof is on him. This section provides for the proof of some one particular fact. The illustration sufficiently points out the meaning. All the facts, however numerous and complicated, which go to make up the accused's guilt, must be proved by the prosecution. If the accused wishes to prove a particular fact, his *alibi* for instance, he must prove it. If the prosecutor wishes

---

112. *Dibyeddu Bhowmik v Jogesh Chandra Nath,* 1996 AIHC 557 (Gau).

113. *Parkash Chand v Hans Raj,* AIR 1994 HP 144, *Murlidhar Bapuji Valve v Yellappa,* AIR 1994 Bom 358, section 19(b), Specific Relief Act, the onus to prove the exception is on the subsequent purchaser. *Kulwant Singh v Makhan Singh,* AIR 2003 P&H 142, the plea that an item of property owned by a member of the family was in fact a joint Hindu family property. The burden would rest upon him to prove that fact.

114. *Mahant Premdass v SGPC,* AIR 2003 NOC 127 (P&H) : 2002 AIHC 3594.

115. *Triro v Dev Raj,* AIR 1993 J&K 14.

116. *HPSIDC v R.P Verma,* AIR 2003 NOC 253 (HP) : (2003) 1 Sim LC 144.

to prove the case, not by independent oral testimony, but by the isolated fact of the accused's admission, or if he wishes to throw that in as an additional fact, he must prove it.[117] The plea of *alibi* must be substantiated by the accused. The trial court pointed out several suspicions throwing considerable doubts about the truth of the plea. The Supreme Court did not interfere.[118]

As an instance of provision of law that the proof of a particular fact shall be upon a particular person, see section 39 of the Code of Criminal Procedure, which says that all persons shall give information of the commission of certain offences to the nearest police officer or Magistrate, and throws upon such persons the burden of proving reasonable excuse for not doing so.

Where a person claims a right of way, he must prove that he acquired the right and it is not for the other party to show that he does not have any such right.[119] Where a person is protesting against nationalisation of a route, burden lies upon him to show that the scheme would not serve national purpose.[120] A person who claimed that his licence could not have been revoked without notice, the burden was held to be upon him to prove that fact.[121] Onus to prove payment of rent lies on the tenant and mere oral testimony is not sufficient for discharging the onus.[122]

Where the defendant alleged that the suit property was a public trust property, the plaintiff did not accept this fact throughout the proceedings. Thus, it became a fact which was asserted by the defendant and was denied by the plaintiff. The court said that the onus of proving the same was on the defendant.[123]

The burden of proving a particular fact lies on the party as indicated in the section irrespective of the fact whether it is an affirmative or negative of the issue. In the tort action of malicious prosecution, for example, the burden of proving that the plaintiff was prosecuted without reasonable and probable cause is on him although it is the negative of the issue.

[s 103.1] Examination of Party.—The plaintiff categorically averred in his plaint that the mortgage amount had been tendered to the defendant as also to her husband. The defendants denied it. The court said that having regard to the peculiar facts and circumstances of the case she should have supported her denial by getting herself examined.[124]

[s 103.2] Claim against carrier for damage to consignment.—In a claim against the railway for damage to consignment, it was contended by the railway that the damage was due to rainfall, i.e., an act of God. The court said that rain is normally an expected natural phenomenon against which precautions can be taken for saving property. Railway would have to prove what care and caution was taken and how it

---

117. Norton, 289.
118. *State of UP v Sughar Singh*, AIR 1978 SC 191: 1978 Cr LJ 141: 1978 All LJ 466.
119. *Mer Nagiam Asha v Punja Kana*, AIR 1981 Guj 141.
120. *Prakash Chandra v Managing Director*, ORTCO, AIR 1980 Ori 122.
121. *Sri Upendra Mandal v Sri Bhajahari Mandal*, AIR 1991 NOC 107 (Gau).
122. *Raghubir Prasad v Rajendra Kumar Gurdev*, AIR 1993 All 326.
123. *Champalal v Thakurji Shri Gopalji*, AIR 1998 Raj 220.
124. *Tulsi v Chandrika Prasad*, AIR 2006 SC 3359 : (2006) 8 SCC 322.

could be said that the operation of nature was irresistible.[125] In a claim against a carrier for non-delivery of goods, the court said that the burden was not on the plaintiff but on the defendant carrier to prove that there was no negligence on his part.[126]

[s 103.3] Claim for setting aside gift deed.—The plaintiff filed a suit for a declaration that the gift deed relating to his property was null and void because at the time of its execution he was a minor. His birth certificate was neither exhibited nor proved through other witnesses. It was for him to prove his age and not for the defendant. The suit was filed 3 years after attaining majority. He was held not entitled to the relief claimed.[127]

[s 104] Burden of proving fact to be proved to make evidence admissible.— The burden of proving any fact necessary to be proved in order to enable any person to give evidence of any other fact is on the person who wishes to give such evidence.

ILLUSTRATIONS

(a) *A* wishes to prove a dying declaration by *B*. *A* must prove *B*'s death.

(b) *A* wishes to prove, by secondary evidence, the contents of a lost document. *A* must prove that the document has been lost.

SYNOPSIS

COMMENT

[s 104.1] Principle.—Whenever it is necessary to prove any fact, in order to render evidence of any other fact admissible, the burden of proving that fact is on the person who wants to give such evidence. The illustrations explain the meaning of the section. A person seeking to recover possession has to prove that he was dispossessed within 12 years.[128] A father admitted that the girl whose legitimacy was in question was his daughter but that she was illegitimate. There being a presumption of legitimacy, burden lay upon father to prove otherwise.[129] In dealings with *pardanashin* women there is a presumption that the contract was the result of undue influence. Hence, the burden lies on the other party to prove that the transaction was fair and free.[130] A *pardanashin* woman transferred her lands to her son subject to certain conditions as to maintenance *etc.* But the deed was altered so as to remove the conditions, the burden to prove that the alteration was with the consent of the woman was upon those who were trying to take advantage of the deed.[131] An illiterate woman contended that the sale deed which she executed was not read over to her. It was held that the burden was upon the other party to prove that she was made fully aware of the

---

125. *General Manager, Southern Rly v Agarwal Traders*, AIR 2001 Kant 366.
126. *Karnataka Transport Corp v National Insurance Bank Ltd*, AIR 1999 Kant 233.
127. *Habib Ullah Bhat v Juna*, AIR 2003 J&K 32.
128. *Kalooram v Mangilal*, AIR 1984 MP 147.
129. *Hoovayya K Shetty v Renuka*, AIR 1984 Bom 229.
130. *Chaitan Charan Parida v Maheshwar Parida*, AIR 1991 Ori 125.
131. *Rankanidhi Sahu v Nandkishore Sahu*, AIR 1990 Ori 64 : LNIND 1989 Ori 156.

contents of the document.[132] Burden lies upon the plaintiff to prove all the points of the right of pre-emption.[133] A telegram by itself is not an authentic document. It is like an unsigned/anonymous communication. Unless a telegram is confirmed by a subsequent signed application, representation or an affidavit, contents of a telegram have no authenticity at all.[134]

Where the railways contention was that the person who died by falling from a train was not a *bona fide* passenger being without ticket, the court said that it was for the railways to prove that fact.[135] Where a vehicle was transferred prior to its accident, the fact that the insured failed to make an application for transfer of insurance was to be pleaded and proved by the insurer when the claimant is third party.[136] Where the rented premises were found to be in the possession of a stranger and not the tenant, the burden was upon the tenant to disprove the inference of sub-letting as he alone had the special knowledge of facts.[137] In a case of transfer of property by an ostensible owner, burden to prove that the ostensible owner under registered sale deed was only a *benamidar*, was upon the party who set up *benami*.[138] Burden of proof of material impairment to the value or the utility of the building as a result of unauthorised construction or alteration is on the landlord.[139] Where the guarantor alleged that the hypothecated goods were lost due to negligence of the creditor bank, onus to prove negligence was on the guarantor.[140]

[s 104.2] ***Res Ipsa Loquitur*.**—Where the vehicle suddenly went off the road, overturned and killed the victim, doctrine of *res ipsa loquitur* was attracted and onus was shifted from the claimant to the driver to prove his non-negligence or vigilance.[141]

This section should be read with clause 2 of section 136 and with the illustrations attached to that section.

[s 105] Burden of proving that case of accused comes within exceptions.—When a person is accused of any offence, the burden of proving the existence of circumstances bringing the case within any of the General Exceptions[s 105.2] in the Indian Penal Code, (45 of 1860), or within any special exception[s 105.6] or proviso contained in any other part of the same Code, or in any law defining the offence, is upon him, and the Court shall presume the absence of such circumstances.

ILLUSTRATIONS

(a) *A*, accused of murder, alleges that, by reason of unsoundness of mind, he did not know the nature of the act.

The burden of proof is on *A*.

---

132. *Sri Siya Ram v Lilawati*, AIR 1990 All 75.
133. *Pyare Mohan v Rameshwar*, AIR 1980 Raj 116.
134. *Distt. Magistrate v G Jothisankar*, AIR 1993 SC 2633.
135. *Mahaboob Sab v UOI*, AIR 2011 Kar 8.
136. *Oriental Insurance Co Ltd v Joshy*, 1996 AIHC 1150 (Ker).
137. *Gur Dayal Khanna v Malti Devi*, AIR 1993 All 90.
138. *Mirza Mahboob Baig v DV Narasimha Reddy*, 1996 AIHC 3070 (AP).
139. *Ratanlal Bansilal v Kishorilal Goenka (FB)*, AIR 1993 Cal 144, relying on *Om Pal v Anand Swaroop*, (1988) 4 SCC 545 : 1988 Supp (3) SCR 391.
140. *Gopal Chandra Bagaria v State Bank of India*, AIR 1994 Ori 329.
141. *Sumati Debnath v Sunil Kumar Sen*, AIR 1994 Gau 59.

(b) *A*, accused of murder, alleges that, by grave and sudden provocation, he was deprived of the power of self-control.

The burden of proof is on *A*.

(c) Section 325 of the Indian Penal Code provides that whoever, except in the case provided for by section 335, voluntarily causes grievous hurt, shall be subject to certain punishments.

A is charged with voluntarily causing grievous hurt under section 325.

The burden of proving the circumstances bringing the case under section 335 lies on *A*.

SYNOPSIS

COMMENT

In criminal cases the burden of proof, using the phrase in its strictest sense, is always upon the prosecution and never shifts whatever the evidence may be during the progress of the case. When sufficient proof of the commission of a crime has been adduced and the accused has been connected therewith as the guilty party, then the burden of proof, in another and quite different sense, namely in the sense of introducing evidence in rebuttal of the case for the prosecution is laid upon him.[142] The onus of establishing an exception shifts to the accused when he pleads an exception.[143] This onus can be discharged either by affirmatively establishing the plea taken by an accused person or by eliciting such circumstances which would create a doubt in the mind of the court that the reasonable possibility of the accused acting within the protection of the exception pleaded is not eliminated.[144] If on a consideration of the evidence as a whole a reasonable doubt is created in the mind of the court as to the guilt of the accused he would be entitled to acquittal.[145]

In a case where s. 84 was invoked by the accused, it was held that the burden of bringing his/her case under section 84 IPC lies squarely upon the person claiming the benefit of that provision. It was further held that the standard of proof which the accused has to satisfy for the discharge of the burden cast upon him under section 105 of the Evidence Act is not the same as is expected of the prosecution, which has to

142. The question of the accused being called upon to explain his defence arises only when the prosecution crosses the barrier of innocence. Where the allegation was that a mother simultaneously killed her four children and the prosecution did not bring out a medical report as to whether she was capable of entertaining a mental state essential for the alleged crime, the question of calling upon her to establish her defence did not arise. *Bai Ramilaben v State of Gujarat,* 1991 Cr LJ 2219 (Guj); See generally, *Khuraijam Somoi Singh v State of Manipur*, 1997 Cr LJ 1461 (Gau); *Ushman v State*, 1997 Cr LJ 2457 (Mad); *Solanki C.B v Srikanta Parashar*, 1997 Cr LJ 3050 (Kant).

143. The Court never presumes the existence of circumstances which entitle the accused to his defence. *Subodh Tiwari v State of Assam,* 1988 Cr LJ 223 (Gau). See also *Kuzhiyaramadiyil Madhavan v State of Kerala,* 1994 Cr LJ 450 (Ker).

144. *Babu Lal v State of UP,* AIR 1960 All 223. See also *State of Gujarat v Kolis Hira,* AIR 1961 Guj 8; *Lakshmanan v Lakshmanan,* AIR 1964 Mad 418; *Bhan Singh v State of MP,* 1990 Cr LJ 1861 (MP), thus the burden on the accused is of very light nature.

145. *Brindaban Prasad v State of Bihar,* AIR 1964 Pat 138.

prove the charges beyond reasonable doubt. Where the accused has led no evidence in defence to support the plea of legal insanity, it is open to an accused to rely upon the material brought on record by the prosecution to claim the benefit of the exception. Evidence in defence may be a surplusage in cases where the defence can make out a case for the acquittal of the accused based on the evidence adduced by the prosecution.[146]

The burden on the accused to prove his defence stands discharged by showing preponderance of probability in his favour.[147]

Where the plea of insanity is invoked by an accused it is for him to establish that fact.[148] But the burden of proof upon the accused is no higher than one which rests upon a party to civil proceedings.[149]

Where a part of a section of an Act has been held unenforceable by the court, it is for the prosecution to establish to the satisfaction of the judge that the case comes within the enforceable part; no onus is cast on the accused to prove that his case falls under that part of the section which has been declared unenforceable.[150]

The Supreme Court has laid down, in *Yogendra Morarji v Gujarat*[151] that the burden of proving defences arises only when the prosecution discharges its initial and traditional burden of establishing the complicity of the accused. Even under this section the standard of proof required for establishing a defence is that of a prudent man as laid down in section 3.[152] But within that standard there are degrees of probability. The nature of the burden on an accused person is not as onerous as the general burden of proving the charge beyond reasonable doubt. The accused may discharge his burden by establishing a mere balance probabilities in his favour with regard to the alleged crime.[153]

---

146. *Elavarasan v State,* (2011) 7 SCC 110. Also see *Surendra Mishra v State of Jharkhand,* (2011) 11 SCC 495 wherein it was held that the burden of proof in the face of S. 105 of the Evidence Act is on the accused. Though the burden is on the accused but he is not required to prove the same beyond all reasonable doubt, but merely satisfy the preponderance of probabilities. The onus has to be discharged by producing evidence as to the conduct of the accused prior to the offence, his conduct at the time or immediately after the offence with reference to his medical condition by production of medical evidence and other relevant factors. Even if the accused establishes unsoundness of mind, section 84 of the Penal Code will not come to his rescue, in case it is found that the accused knew that what he was doing was wrong or that it was contrary to law. In order to ascertain that, it is imperative to take into consideration the circumstances and the behaviour preceding, attending and following the crime. Behaviour of an accused pertaining to a desire for concealment of the weapon of offence and conduct to avoid detection of crime go a long way to ascertain as to whether, he knew the consequences of the act done by him.

147. *Rizam v State of Chhatisgarh,* 2003 Cr LJ 1227 : AIR 2003 SC 976.

148. *Bhikari v State of UP,* AIR 1966 SC 1 : 1966 Cr LJ 63; *Kannakunnummal v State of Kerala,* AIR 1967 Ker 92.

149. *Dahyabhai v State of Gujarat,* AIR 1964 SC 1563 : (1964) 2 Cr LJ 472.

150. *Behram Khurshid Pesikaka v State of Bombay,* (1954) 56 Bom LR 575 : AIR 1955 SC 123 : 1955 Cr LJ 215.

151. *Yogendra Morarji v Gujarat,* AIR 1980 SC 660, at 666 : 1980 Cr LJ 459.

152. See *Dahyabhai v State of Gujarat,* AIR 1964 SC 1563 : (1964) 2 Cr LJ 472. See also *Sankaran v State of Kerala,* 1994 Cr LJ 1173 (Ker).

153. Also to the same effect *Mohd. Ramzani v State of Delhi,* AIR 1980 SC 1341 : 1980 Cr LJ 1010; *Darshan Lal v State,* 1990 Cr LJ 2751 (Del), the accused failed to make out his right of private defence even to the extent of probability. See also *Valummel Thommachan v State of Kerala,* 1994 Cr LJ 1738 (Ker).

[s 105.1] Presumption of innocence.—In criminal cases, the rule is that the legal burden of proving every element of the offence and the guilt of the accused, lies from first to last on the prosecution. Where a fact is especially within the knowledge of the accused, burden lies upon him to prove that fact. Thus in a prosecution for *ticketless* travel, the fact whether a ticket was bought or not being especially within the knowledge of the accused, he must prove that fact. [see section 106 Illustration (b)]. This principle has been held to be not applicable to a case of a person who has lost his life in a railway accident. How can a dead person discharge any such burden. The presumption of innocence must prevail. Though the court would have to prove that he was without ticket and therefore not a *bona fide* passenger, the fact should remain that a person lost his life in the tragic circumstances of an accident for which railways cannot shirk blame and that the unfortunate person was there with the implicit railway permission. The opportunity to board trains without ticket is due to railway generosity.[154]

[s 105.2] "General Exceptions".—The General Exceptions here referred to are those applicable to all crimes, and are laid down in Chapter IV of the Indian Penal Code.

This section is a general provision which imposes the burden of bringing himself within an exception upon the person who relies upon the exception; and there is no distinction between a case in which the exception is contained in the body of the statute imposing the prohibition and a case in which it is not so included.[155]

[s 105.3] Burden of Proving Exception.—The basic principles underlying the subject of proving defence or exception were restated by the Supreme Court:[156] "The doctrine of burden of proof in the context of the plea of insanity may be stated in the following propositions: (1) the prosecution must prove beyond reasonable doubt that the accused had committed the offence with the requisite *mens rea*; and the burden of proving that always rests on the prosecution from the beginning to the end of the trial; (2) there is a rebuttable presumption that the accused was not insane when he committed the crime; the accused may rebut it by placing before the court all the relevant evidence oral, documentary or circumstantial, but the burden of proof upon him is no higher than that which rests upon a party to civil proceedings; (3) even if

---

154. *Asharani Das v UOI,* AIR 2009 Cal 205. *UOI v Hari Narayan Gupta,* AIR 2007 Raj 38, accidental fall from train, burden on railways to prove that he was without ticket.

155. *Emperor v Dahyabhai Savchand,* (1941) 43 Bom LR 519; *Government of Bombay v Samuel,* (1946) 48 Bom LR 746 (SB).

156. *Dayalbhai v State of Gujarat,* AIR 1964 SC 1563 at p 1568 : (1964) 2 Cr LJ 472 followed in *Periasami v State of TN,* (1996) 6 SCC 457 : 1997 Cr LJ 219. Followed in *Bhikari Singh v State of UP,* AIR 1966 SC 1; *Mohar Rai v State of* Bihar, (1968) 3 SCR 525 : AIR 1968 SC 1281. The court considered *Parbhoo v Emperor,* AIR 1941 All 402 : 1941 All LJ 619; *Rishi Kesh Singh v State,* AIR 1970 All 51; *Behram Khurshed Pesikaka v State of Bombay,* AIR 1955 SC 123 : 1955 CrL 215; *Vijayee Singh v State of UP,* AIR 1990 SC 1459 : (1990) 3 SCC 190 : 1990 Cr LJ 1510, where in the case of death in police custody, it was necessary for the police to prove that the accused was elsewhere at the time of death. *Partap v State of UP,* (1976) 2 SCC 798 : AIR 1976 SC 966; *KM Nanavati v State of Maharashtra,* AIR 1962 SC 605 at p 617 : 1962 Supp 1 SCR 567. *Siddhapal Kamala Yadav v State of Maharashtra,* AIR 2009 SC 97 : (2009) 1 SCC 124, burden of proving unsoundness of mind which is on the accused is no higher than that resting on the plaintiff or defendant in civil cases. *Surendra Mishra v State of Jharkhand,* AIR 2011 SC 627, the accused, who shot down a person, was running a medical shop. Afterwards he threatened the driver, ran away, threw the gun into a well. The court said all this showed that he understood the nature and consequences of his act. Also see, *Elavarasan v State,* (2011) 7 SCC 110.

the accused was not able to establish conclusively that he was insane at the time when he committed the offence, the evidence placed before the court may raise a reasonable doubt in the mind of the court as regards one or more of the ingredients of the offence, including *mens rea* and in that case the court would be entitled to acquit the accused."

The principles stated by the Supreme Court were restated by Fazal Ali J, in *Rabindra Kumar Dey v State of Orissa*:[157] In our opinion three cardinal principles of criminal jurisprudence are well settled, namely:—

(1) that the onus lies affirmatively on the prosecution to prove its case beyond reasonable doubt and it cannot derive any benefit from weakness or falsity of the defence version while proving its case;

(2) that in a criminal trial the accused must be presumed to be innocent unless he is proved to be guilty; and

(3) that the onus of the prosecution never shifts.

It is true that under section 105 of the Evidence Act the onus of proving exceptions mentioned in the Indian Penal Code lies on the accused, but the section does not at all indicate the nature and standard of proof required. The Evidence Act does not contemplate that the accused should prove his case with the same strictness and vigour as the prosecution is required to prove in a criminal charge. It is sufficient if the accused is able to prove his case by the standard of preponderance of probabilities envisaged by section 5 of the Evidence Act as a result of which he succeeds not because he proves his case to the guilt but because probability of the version given by him throws doubt on the prosecution case and, therefore, the prosecution cannot be said to have established the charge beyond reasonable doubt.[158]

Where the accused relies upon provocation in diminution of his responsibility, he has to prove that fact.[159]

The accused taking a plea in defence against the charge is not required necessarily to produce evidence in support of his plea. He can establish his plea by reference to circumstances as they emerge from the prosecution evidence itself.[160]

[s 105.4] Presumption of absence of exception.—The Supreme Court stated the effect of the provisions as follows:[161] From a combined reading of sections 105 and 4 of the Act, it may be inferred that where the existence of circumstances bringing the case within the exception is pleaded or is raised the court shall presume the absence of such circumstances as proved unless and until it is disproved. Taking section 105 as

---

157. *Rabindra Kumar Dey v State of Orissa*, (1976) 4 SCC 233 : AIR 1977 SC 170.

158. The Court relied upon *Harbhajan Singh v State of Punjab*, AIR 1966 SC 97 : (1966) Cr LJ 82; *State of UP v Ram Swaroop*, (1974) 1 SCC 764. To the same effect is *Pratap v State of UP*, (1976) 2 SCC 798; *Strong v Dowtry*, (1961) 1 WLR 841; *Man Singh v Delhi Admn.* AIR 1979 SC 1455 : 1979 Cr LJ 1118, *Chaturdas R. Lal v State of Gujarat*, AIR 1976 SC 1497 : 1976 Cr LJ 1180. The burden of proving that the case comes within any of the general exceptions can be discharged by showing a preponderance of probability. *Bhupendra Singh v State of Gujarat*, AIR 1997 SC 3790 : 1998 Cr LJ 57 : (1998) 2 SCC 603. *State of MP v Ramesh*, AIR 2005 SC 1186 : (2005) 9 SCC 705 : 2005 Cr LJ 652, the same principles restated.

159. *R v Padola*, (1860) 1 QB 325 (CCA) : *Bhikhari v State of UP*, AIR 1966 SC 1 : 1966 Cr LJ 63.

160. *Raghbir Singh v State of Haryana*, AIR 2009 SC 1223 : (2008) 16 SCC 33.

161. *Vijayee Singh v State of UP*, AIR 1990 SC 1459 : 1990 Cr LJ 1510 : (1990) 3 SCC 190.

a whole the "burden of proof" and the presumption have to be considered together. The accused may raise a plea of exception either by pleading the same specifically or by relying on the probabilities and circumstances obtaining in the case. He may adduce evidence in support of his plea directly or rely on the prosecution case itself or he can indirectly introduce such circumstances by way of cross-examination and also rely on the probabilities and the other circumstances. Then the initial presumption against the accused regarding the non-existence of the circumstances in favour of his plea gets displaced and on an examination of the material if a reasonable doubt arises, the benefit of it should go to the accused. The accused can also discharge the burden under section 105 by preponderance of probabilities in favour of his plea. In respect of the general exceptions, special exceptions, provisos contained in the Penal Code or in any law defining the offence, the accused by one of these processes would be discharging the burden contemplated under section 105 but in cases of the exceptions covered by special statutes and where the burden of proof is placed on the accused to establish his plea, he will be able to discharge the same by preponderance of probabilities and not by merely creating a doubt. In the case of general exceptions, special exceptions, provisos contained in the Penal Code or in any law defining the offence, the court, after due consideration of the evidence in the light of the above principle, if satisfied, would state, in the first instance, as to which exception the accused is entitled, then see whether he would be entitled to a complete acquittal of the offence charged or would be liable for a lesser offence. The court may convict him accordingly. These principles cannot be made applicable to a case where the accused sets up *alibi*. There the burden entirely lies on him and the plea of *alibi* does not come within the meaning of these exceptions. Circumstances leading to *alibi* are within his knowledge and as provided under section 106 of the Act he has to establish the same satisfactorily. Likewise, in the case where the statute throws special burden on the accused to disprove the existence of the ingredients of the offence, he has to discharge the burden, for example, in cases arising under Prevention of Food Adulteration Act, 1954, if the accused pleads a defence under section 19, the burden is on him to establish the same since the warranty on which he relies is a circumstance within his knowledge.

The plea of self-defence cannot be denied to an accused person on the ground that he did not specifically raise it in his statement under section 313, CrPC and because the injured accused did not enter the witness box.[162]

[s 105.5] Benefit of doubt.—The phrase "burden of proof" is not defined in the Act. In respect of criminal cases, it is an accepted principle of criminal jurisprudence that the burden is always on the prosecution and never shifts. This flows from the cardinal principle that the accused is presumed to be innocent unless proved guilty by the prosecution and the accused is entitled to the benefit of every reasonable doubt. Section 105 to some extent places the onus of proving any exception in a penal statute on the accused. The burden of proving the existence of circumstances bringing the case within the exceptions mentioned therein is upon him. The section further lays down that the court shall presume non-existence of circumstances bringing the case within an exception. The words "burden of proving the existence of circumstances" occurring

---

162. *Kashi Ram v State of MP*, AIR 2001 SC 2902, **following** *Vijayee Singh v State of UP*, AIR 1990 SC 1459 : 1990 Cr LJ 1510; *Bahadur Singh v State of Punjab*, (1992) 4 SCC 503 : AIR 1993 SC 70 : 1992 Cr LJ 3709.

in the section are very significant. "This burden" which rests on the accused does not absolve the prosecution from discharging its initial burden of establishing the case beyond all reasonable doubts. The accused need not set up a specific plea against the offence and adduce evidence.[163]

[s 105.6] "Special exception".—Special exceptions are those which are restricted to a particular crime.

Section 113A raises a presumption as to abetment of suicide by a married woman by her husband or his relatives. Similarly section 114A raises presumption of absence of consent in a rape case. Several statutes also provide for putting evidential burden on the accused.[164]

[s 106] Burden of proving fact especially within knowledge.—When any fact is especially within the knowledge of any person, the burden of proving that fact is upon him.

ILLUSTRATIONS

(a) When a person does an act with some intention other than that which the character and circumstances of the act suggest, the burden of proving that intention is upon him.

(b) *A* is charged with travelling on a railway without a ticket. The burden of proving that he had a ticket is on him.

SYNOPSIS

COMMENT

This section applies only to parties to a suit.[165]

[s 106.1] Principle.—Where the knowledge of the subject-matter of an allegation is peculiarly within the province of one party to a suit the burden of proof must lie there also. Thus, for example, sales of consignments entrusted to commission agents and particulars of those sales are matters which lie especially within their knowledge.[166]

---

163. *Vijayee Singh v State of UP,* (1990) 3 SCC 190 : AIR 1990 SC 1459 : 1990 Cr LJ 1510.
164. *PN Krishna Lal v Govt of Kerala,* 1995 Supp (2) SCC 187 : 1995 SCC (Cri) 466.
165. *Mahabir Singh v Rohini Ramanadhwaj Prasad Singh,* (1933) 35 Bom LR 500 (PC).
166. *Mayen v Alston,* (1893) 16 Mad 238, 245.

Similarly, in a case of a servant charged with misappropriation of goods of his master, if the failure to account was due to an accidental loss, the facts being within the servant's knowledge, it is for him to explain the loss.[167] In a claim for maintenance the claimant can quote a figure of income on guess work because the fact of exact income is especially within the knowledge of the other party.[168] Where a person was found in possession of gold with foreign markings, the Supreme Court held that burden lay upon him to account for his possession.[169] Where a shopkeeper had at his shop unmarked and unverified measure along with regular measures, it was held that an offence under the Weights and Measures law was made out unless he could show that they were not in use.[170] Burden lies upon the licensee to show that he used the goods for the licensed purpose. But it being a penalty matter, those seeking to impose penalties must give some evidence to show a different use.[171] In a prosecution under the Essential Commodities Act, the dealer accused has to show how broken rice came to be mixed with the whole rice, because that matter is especially within his knowledge.[172] Where the sample of *maida* taken from a grocery shop was found to be substandard and the accused took the plea that it was kept not for human consumption but for pasting purposes, it was held that it was a special knowledge of the accused and it was for him only to prove such a knowledge and having not done so it could not be said that the burden cast on him had been successfully discharged.[173] "The principle underlying section 106, which is an exception to the general rule governing burden of proof, applies only to such matters of defence which are supposed to be especially within the knowledge of the defendant. It cannot apply when the fact is such as to be capable of being known also by persons other than the defendant". In this case the carrying of voters free of charge was obviously known to many others too.[174]

It is the bounden duty of a party, personally knowing the whole circumstances of the case, to give evidence on his own behalf and to submit to cross-examination. His non-appearance as a witness would be the strongest possible circumstance going to discredit the truth of his case.[175] But in a criminal case even where the facts lie peculiarly within the knowledge of the accused the burden of proof lies on the prosecution though very slight evidence may be sufficient to discharge the burden.[176]

[s 106.2] Scope.—This section does not cast any burden on an accused person to prove that no crime was committed by proving facts especially within his knowledge; nor does it warrant the conclusion that if anything is unexplained which the court

167. *Krishan Kumar v UOI,* AIR 1959 SC 1390 : 1959 Cr LJ 1508.

168. *Maganbhai v Maniben,* AIR 1985 Guj 187.

169. *Shah Guman Mal v AP,* AIR 1980 SC 793 : 1980 Cr LJ 557; *Labhchand v Maharashtra,* AIR 1975 SC 182 : 1975 Cr LJ 246; *Collector of Customs v D Bhoormul,* AIR 1974 SC 859 : 1975 Cr LJ 545. Where goods are seized as a result of search or seizure, within or outside powers, the burden of showing that the possession was innocent would be upon the accused. *State of Maharashtra v Natwarlal Damodardas Soni,* (1980) 2 SCR 340: 1980 Cr LJ 429 : AIR 1980 SC 593.

170. *State of TN v Radhakrishnan,* 1989 Cr LJ 1161 (Mad).

171. *Polestar Electronics P Ltd v Additional CST,* 1978 Tax LR 1907.

172. *State of AP v B Prakash,* AIR 1976 SC 1845 : 1976 Cr LJ 1387.

173. *State of TN v Arunachalam,* 1992 Cr LJ 3930 (Mad).

174. *Razik Ram v JS Chauhan,* AIR 1975 SC 667 : (1975) 4 SCR 769, per Sarkaria J at 668.

175. *Gurbaksh Singh v Gurdial Singh,* (1927) 29 Bom LR 1392 PC.

176. *Provincial Govt, Central Provinces and Berar v Champalal,* (1946) Nag 504; *Gullegar Setty v State of Mysore,* (1953) Mys 298.

thinks the accused could explain, he ought therefore to be found guilty.[177] It does not affect the onus of proving the guilt of the accused. That onus rests on the prosecution and is not shifted on to the accused by reason of this section.[178] It is only in cases where the facts proved by the evidence give rise to a reasonable inference of guilt unless the same is rebutted and such inference can be negatived by proof of some fact which in its nature can be negatived by proof of some fact which in its nature can only be within the special knowledge of the accused that the burden of proving the fact is on the accused.[179] This section cannot be used to shift the onus of establishing an essential ingredient of the offence on the accused.[180]

So, section 106 of the Evidence Act is not intended to relieve the prosecution of its burden to prove the guilt of the accused beyond reasonable doubt, but it would apply only to cases where the prosecution has succeeded in proving facts from which a reasonable inference can be drawn regarding the existence of certain other facts, unless the accused by virtue of his special knowledge regarding such facts, failed to offer any explanation which might drive the court to draw a different inference.[181] It is designed to meet certain exceptional cases, in which, it would be impossible for the prosecution to establish certain facts which are particularly within the knowledge of the accused.[182]

A statute may impose limited onus on an accused person to prove matters especially within his knowledge. Such a statute does not violate Article 14 or 21 of the constitution.[183]

[s 106.3] Burden of proving negligence and *res ipsa loquitur*.—It has been considered by the Privy Council that the burden of proving negligence always rests with the plaintiff, even when the maxim *res ipsa loquitur* applies.[184] Once the initial burden of showing the setting of the mishap is discharged, this maxim will relieve the plaintiff of showing further evidence of negligence.

Acting upon this maxim and following the decision of the Supreme Court in *Sayed Akbar v State of Karnataka*[185] the Kerala High Court held that where a live wire was hanging on the road from an electric pole, it must be presumed that it must have been due to negligent management creating liability to the dependents of the pedestrian who was electrocuted.

---

177. *King-Emperor v U Damapala,* (1936) 14 Ran 666 FB; *Shewaram v Crown,* (1940) Kar 249; *Enamul Huq,* (1951) 1 Cal 204.

178. *Crown v Santa Singh,* (1945) 26 Lah 137.

179. *Narayan v Executive Officer, C.P Board,* AIR 1965 Ker 73. See also *Re Naina Mohamed,* AIR 1960 Mad 218 which was referred with approval in *State of Rajasthan v Kashi Ram,* AIR 2007 SC 144 : (2006) 12 SCC 254. Further referred with approval in *Sathya Narayanan v State,* (2012) 12 SCC 627.

180. *Jethalal v State of Gujarat,* AIR 1968 Guj 163.

181. *Tulshiram Sahadu Suryawanshi v State of Maharashtra,* (2012) 10 SCC 373.

182. *Prithipal Singh v State of Punjab,* (2012) 1 SCC 10.

183. *K Veeraswami v UOI,* (1991) 3 SCC 655 : 1991 SCC (Cr) 734. *A Jayaram v State of AP,* AIR 1995 SC 2128 : 1995 Cr LJ 3663. prosecution proved that the fertilisers were not transported by dealers as alleged by them. Burden was accordingly upon dealers to show the mode of transport which was different from that mentioned in their bills.

184. *Ng Chun Pui v Lec Chuen Tat,* The Times, May 25, 1988 PC; 1988 CLY 1582.

185. *Sayed Akbar v State of Karnataka,* AIR 1979 SC 1848 : 1979 Cr LJ 1374.

[s 106.4] Terminal tax.—Octroi duty was paid for bringing petroleum goods within the limits of a Municipal Corporation. Subsequently refund of the amount was claimed on the ground that the goods were brought within municipal limits only to be taken out. It was held that the burden lay upon the claimant to prove that he had not sold the goods locally and had taken them out.[186]

[s 106.5] Professional qualification.—Where a person was displaying on the signboard of his nursing home and on his professional papers certain qualifications about which the prosecution alleged that he did not possess, the burden was on him to show facts which justified him in the use of those qualifications, that fact being specially known only to him.[187]

[s 106.6] Taking away dead body.—Where the *corpus delicti* (dead body) was not found but there was the direct evidence of eyewitnesses that the victim was killed by accused persons before they took away the dead body. No explanation was offered by the accused persons as to what they had done with the dead body. The court said that they could be convicted by drawing the presumption that they had a reason to cause disappearance of the dead body and that reason must have been that the death was caused by them.[188]

[s 106.7] Spurious Liquor.—In a case of spurious liquor, the prosecution has the initial burden of suggesting of knowing that the accused person was involved in the business of illicit liquor and that he knew the nature thereof. It is only then that the burden would shift to the accused to prove that he had no means to know about the nature of the business or the fact that the liquor was being mixed with a noxious substance like methanol.[189]

[s 106.8] Dowry death.—Where the prosecution proved that there was a strong motive for the crime, that the deceased woman was last seen alive in the company of the accused and that the death was unnatural and homicidal, it was held that the burden to account for the circumstances of the death was shifted to the person in whose care the woman met her death. He alone must be in possession of the knowledge of those circumstances.[190]

[s 106.9] Death in custody.—When once it was established that the victim was taken into police custody it was their responsibility to show how the prisoner went out of their custody. There was not even a whisper from the side of the accused as to what happened to the deceased after he was taken into custody by them.[191] Due to lack of direct evidence in such cases, the Supreme Court stated the approach to be followed in such cases: Exaggerated adherence to and insistence upon requiring the truth to

---

186. *Indore Municipal Corpn. v Caltex (India) Ltd,* AIR 1991 SC 454 : 1991 Supp (2) SCC 707.

187. *State of Kerala v CK Bharathan (Dr),* 1989 Cr LJ 2025 (Ker).

188. *Ram Gulam Chaudhury v State of Bihar,* 2001 Cr LJ 4632 : AIR 2001 SC 2842.

189. *Chandran v State of Kerala,* (2011) 5 SCC 161.

190. *Amarjit Singh v State of Punjab,* 1989 Cr LJ (NOC) 13 (P&H). Compare with *Trilochan Panika v State of Orissa,* 1989 Cr LJ (NOC) 168 (Ori), where the prosecution was able to prove nothing more than this that the accused and deceased were last seen together and the special burden under section 106 did not arise.

191. *Dalip Singh v State of Haryana,* 1993 Supp. (3) SCC 336, 341 : 1943 SCC (Cri) 1005 : AIR 1993 SC 2119 : 1993 Cr LJ 2092.

be established by proof which is beyond every reasonable doubt would in such cases often result in miscarriage of justice and make the justice delivery system suspect and vulnerable. Torture in police custody receives encouragement by this type of unrealistic approach because it reinforces the belief in the police mind that no harm would come to them if one prisoner dies in the lockup because there would be hardly any evidence available to the prosecution to directly implicate them in the torture. Given the serious nature of the crime and its far reaching consequences, the court must deal with such cases in a realistic manner and with the sensitivity they deserve. The court suggested the rule of rebuttable presumption to be adopted.[192]

[s 106.10] Maintenance.—In a suit for maintenance, onus lies upon the husband to disclose his income.[193] The claim to interim maintenance of the child cannot be defeated merely by saying that he being an already married man, his marriage with the child's mother was void. He did not produce a copy of his income tax return from which the court presumed that he did not want to disclose his income. The wife was able to show that she was working nowhere. The award of Rs 5,000 a month for maintenance of the child and mother was held to be not excessive. Against the claim of a Hindu wife for maintenance the husband pleaded that he was already a married man and, therefore, his marriage with the claimant was void. It was held that the burden of proving his earlier marriage was upon the husband and he had failed to discharge his burden. The claim to maintenance was accordingly allowed.[194]

[s 106.11] Payment of rent.—In an eviction proceeding on the ground of default in payment of rent, the burden lies on the tenant to prove payment.[195]

[s 106.12] Land Acquisition.—Whenever acquisition of land is challenged on the ground that the notification has not been published as per the mandate of the statute, the authority defending acquisition is under an obligation to produce evidence in the form of documents to prove that requirement of publication has been complied with. In the absence of such evidence, the court cannot decide challenge to the acquisition proceedings by assuming that the particular notification had been published as per the requirement of law. In the given case, no material was produced before the High Court or before Supreme Court to show that the Notification issued under section 4(1) of the Land Acquisition Act, 1894, had been published in the Official Gazette. Therefore, it was held by Supreme Court that the High Court was not justified in declining relief to the land-owners/appellants by assuming that the said notification must have been published in the Official Gazette because other notifications including the one issued under section 6 were published in the Official Gazette.[196]

[s 106.13] Alibi.—Circumstances leading to *alibi* are within the knowledge of the accused and as provided in section 106 of the Act he has to establish the same satisfactorily. The burden of proving *alibi* rests on the accused.[197]

---

192. *Munshi Singh Gautam v State of MP*, AIR 2005 SC 402 : (2005) 9 SCC 631 : (2005) Cr LJ 320, court found evidence to convict the guilty officer.

193. *Anil Kumar v Laxmi Devi*, AIR 1994 NOC 61 (Raj).

194. *Vimla v Veerasamy*, (1991) 2 SCC 375 : (1991) 2 Ker LJ 162 : (1991) 1 Guj LH 380.

195. *Sukhanand v IV Additional District Judge, Bulandshahr*, AIR 1994 All 59.

196. *Lalrinvenga v State of Mizoram*, (2011) 13 SCC 190.

197. *Vijayee Singh v State of UP*, (1990) 3 SCC 190 : AIR 1990 SC 1459 : 1990 Cr LJ 1510.

[s 106.14] Last seen together.—The theory of "last seen alive" comes into play when the time gap between when the accused and the deceased were last seen together, and the deceased was found dead was so small, that the possibility of any other person committing the murder becomes impossible. Thus, on the principle that the person who is last found in the company of another is dead or missing, the person with whom he was last found alive has to explain the circumstances in which he parted company.[198]

In the case of "last seen together", the prosecution is exempted to prove the exact happening of the incident, as the accused himself would have special knowledge of the incident and thus, would have burden of proof as per section 106 of the Evidence Act, 1872. Therefore, "last seen together" itself is not a conclusive proof but along with other circumstances surrounding the incident, like relations between the accused and the deceased, enmity between them, previous history of hostility, recovery of weapon from the accused, etc. non-explanation of the death of the deceased, may lead to a presumption of guilt.[199]

[s 106.15] Knowledge about licenced firearm.—Where licenced pistol was alleged to have been used in a murder case, it was held that the onus would be on the accused to show where it was and in whose possession that being in his special knowledge. He failed to produce it and gave evasive answers. Adverse inference could be drawn against him under section 106.[200]

[s 106.16] Claim under Motor Vehicles Act.—The Supreme Court observed in a claim petition that it is not possible for a claimant to give a strict proof of the accident. The claimants have to establish their case merely on the touchstone of preponderance of probability. The standard of proof beyond reasonable doubt cannot be applied.[201]

[s 106.17] Industrial Dispute.—Whilst it is true that the provisions of the Evidence Act, 1872 per se are not applicable in an industrial adjudication, it is trite that its general principles do apply in proceedings before Industrial Tribunal or Labour Court, as the case may be. In any proceeding, the burden of proving a fact lies on the party that substantially asserts the affirmative of the issue, and not on the party who denies it. Therefore, it follows that where an employer asserts misconduct on the part of workman and dismisses or discharges him on that ground, it is for the employer to prove misconduct by workman before Industrial Tribunal or Labour Court, as the case may be, by leading relevant evidence before it and it is open to the workman to adduce evidence *contra*. In the first instance, a workman cannot be asked to prove that he has not committed any act tantamounting to misconduct. In the given case, since no enquiry was conducted before the service of a workman was terminated, the onus to prove that it was not possible to conduct the enquiry and that the termination was justified because of misconduct by the employee, was on management. It was for management to prove, by adducing evidence, that the workman was guilty of

---

198. *Kiriti Pal v State of WB*, (2015) 11 SCC 178, paras 16 and 17.

199. *Ashok v State of Maharashtra*, (2015) 4 SCC 393 (para 12), **relying on** *Rohtash Kumar v State of Haryana*, (2013) 14 SCC 434 and *Kanhaiya Lal v State of Rajasthan*, (2014) 4 SCC 715. See also *Paramasivam v State*, (2015) 13 SCC 300, para 35. Time gap not so small as to draw inference against accused, *Nizam v State of Rajasthan*, (2016) 1 SCC 550, para 17. See also *Rambraksh v State of Chhattisgarh*, AIR 2016 SC 2381, para 10.

200. *Sidhartha Vashisht @ Manu Sharma v State (NCT of Delhi)*, AIR 2010 SC 2352 : (2010) 6 SCC 1.

201. *Bimla Devi v Himachal Road Transport Corp*, AIR 2009 SC 2819 : (2009) 13 SCC 530.

misconduct and that the action taken by it is proper. Therefore, the order passed by the Labour Court, shifting the burden on the workmen was held to be fallacious is the inevitable conclusion.[202]

[s 107] Burden of proving death of person known to have been alive within thirty years.—When the question is whether a man is alive or dead, and it is shown that he was alive within thirty years, the burden of proving that he is dead is on the person who affirms it.

[s 108] Burden of proving that a person is alive who has not been heard of for seven years.—[203][Provided that when] the question is whether a man is alive or dead, and it is proved that he has not been heard of for seven years by those who would naturally have heard of him if he had been alive, the burden of proving that he is alive is [204][shifted to] the person who affirms it.

SYNOPSIS

COMMENT

Sections 107 and 108 must be read together because the latter is only a proviso to the rule contained in the former, and both constitute one rule when so read together.[205]

There is no presumption in law that a person was alive for seven years from the time when he was last heard of. These sections deal with the procedure to be followed when a question is raised before a court, as to whether a person is alive or dead, but do not lay down any presumption as to how long a man was alive or at what time he died. Assuming that the court could make a presumption that a person was alive for seven years after he was last heard of, it depends on the circumstances of each case, whether the court could draw such a presumption or not.[206]

[s 108.1] Presumption of survivorship—Burden of proving death [Section 107].—This section provides that if it appears that a person, whose present existence is in question, was alive within 30 years, and nothing whatever appears to suggest the probability of his being dead, the court is bound to regard the fact of his still being alive as proved. Dealing with the facts of a case the Supreme Court observed that in view of the fact that Sardul Singh was alive on 24 May 1960, it shall be presumed that he was not dead on 24 May 1970. The appellant has alleged that Sardul Singh

202. *Amar Chakravarty v Maruti Suzuki (I) Ltd,* (2010) 14 SCC 471.
203. Subs. by Act 18 of 1872, sec. 9, for "When".
204. Subs. by Act 18 of 1872, sec. 9, for "on".
205. *State of Punjab v Bachan Singh,* (1956) Pun 1232.
206. *Veeramma v Chenna Reddi,* (1021) 37 Mad 440. *Saroop Singh v Banto,* AIR 2005 SC 4407 : (2005) 8 SCC 330, there is no presumption that such person died seven years ago.

was dead on that date. The onus to prove that fact shall be on him.[207] But as soon as anything appears which suggests the probability of his being dead, the presumption disappears, and the question has to be determined on the balance of proof.[208]

The presumption is not a very strong one. It may be rebutted by slight evidence to the contrary, for example, seven years' absence. The court may not act upon it until positive proof of the person being still alive is offered.

[s 108.2] Presumption of death [Section 108].—If a person has not been heard of for seven years, there is a presumption of law that he is dead,[209] and the burden of proving that he is alive is shifted to the other side.[210] But at what time within that time he died is not a matter of presumption, but of evidence, and the onus of proving that the death took place at any particular time within the seven years lies upon the person who claims a right to the establishment of which that fact is essential.[211] The presumption of death does not extend to the date of death.[212]

The exact date of death after the expiry of 7 year period is not a matter of inference. This is a matter of evidence. Onus of proof lies on the person who claims a right which arises consequent upon death.[213]

Where only a period of 4½ years had elapsed since the mother of the missing person registering an FIR alleging abduction of her missing son, the Supreme Court declined to accept the presumption drawn by High Court against police.[214]

---

207. *Surjit Kaur v Jhujhar Singh*, AIR 1980 SC 274. *LIC of India v Anuradha*, AIR 2004 SC 2070 : (2004) 10 SCC 131 : (2004) 2 KLT 351, restating the import of the two provisions. Presumption arises on the completion of seven years up to the last day and not at any time earlier. Presumption arises only when the court, tribunal or when any other authority is called upon to decide whether a particular person was alive or dead. There is no presumption as to time of death.

208. Markby, 83.

209. *Ramrati Kuer v Dwarka Prasad*, AIR 1967 SC 1134.

210. *HJ Bhagat v LI Corp*, AIR 1965 Mad 440: (1965) 2 Mad LJ 185; to the same effect, *Shailesh N Shah v Regional Commr., Employees' Provident Fund*, (1993) 1 Mad LJ 328, **followed** in *Nagalakshmi v Thirugnansumbhandan*, AIR 1995 Mad 120, burden of proof in a suit for partition.

211. *Rango v Mudiyeppa*, (1898) 23 Bom 296, 306; *Narayan v Shriniwas*, (1905) 8 Bom LR 226; *Jayawant Jivanrao v Ramachandra Narayan*, (1915) 40 Bom 239 : 18 Bom LR 14; *Gopal Bhimji v Manaji Ganuji*, (1922) 47 Bom 451 : 25 Bom LR 134; *Lalchand Marwari v Mahanth Ramrup Gir*, (1925) 5 Pat 312 : 28 Bom LR 855 : 53 IA 24; *Ganesh Das Aurora, Re*, (1926) 54 Cal 186; *Dharup Nath v Govind Saran*, (1886) 8 All 614; *Fani Bhushan Banerji v Surjya Kanta Roy Chowdhry*, (1907) 35 Cal 25; *Narki v Lal Sahu*, (1909) 37 Cal 103; *Basharat v Najib Khan*, (1917) PR No. 38 of 1918 (Civil); *Tirathpathi v Ranjit Singh*, (1930) 6 Luck 407; *Punjab v Natha*, (1931) 12 Lah 718 (FB) overruling *Tani v Rikhi Ram*, (1920) 1 Lah 554; *Rowther Abdul Rahiman v Narayana Pillai*, (1957) Ker 53; *Re V Seshi Ammal*, AIR 1958 Mad 463; *Mukunda Behera v Subarna Bewa*, AIR 1962 Ori 3; *Parikhit Muduli v Champa Dei*, AIR 1967 Ori 70.

212. *Ganesh Bux Singh Thakur v Mohammad*, (1944) 19 Luck 581; *Venkata Subba Rao v G Subba Rao*, AIR 1964 AP 326; *Narayan Pillai v Velayuthan*, AIR 1963 Mad 385; *AV Narayana Vadhyar v Venkateswara*, AIR 1971 Ker 85 (FB). See also *N Jayalakshmi Ammal v R. Gopala Pathar*, AIR 1995 SC 995 : 1995 Supp (1) SCC 27.

213. *Hemant Kishore v Brij Raj Kishore*, AIR 1998 All 328. In this case even presumption of death could not be raised because while the legal heirs testified to no whereabouts for seven years, the father testified about his whereabouts *Barn v Tej Pal*, AIR 1998 All 230 here also no presumption could be raised because the requirement of 7 year unheard absence was not proved. Adoption deed, which was sought to be challenged for that reason, was not set aside.

214. *Sahdeo v State of UP*, (2010) 3 SCC 705.

The earliest date to which the death can be presumed can only be the date when the suit to claim that right is filed. It cannot have a further retrospective effect.[215] Where a suit was filed exactly after the expiry of seven years, the court said that without proof of the fact that death occurred before the enforcement of the 1937 Act, rights under the Act could not be acquired.[216] The Supreme Court observed in a case before it[217] that the presumption about the death of Sardul Singh, even if raised, would be restricted to the date of the filing of the petition. The court cited the Privy Council decision to the effect that "there is only one presumption, and that is that when these suits were instituted in 1916 Bhagwan Gir was no longer alive. There is no presumption at all as to the time he died. That, like any other fact, is a matter of proof."[218] Where the plaintiff respondent was kidnapped during the pendency of appeal and could not be traced, the High Court exercising its inherent powers allowed his wife and children to file the second appeal even before the lapse of seven years to meet the ends of justice.[219] The court can presume the date of death of an unheard person on the basis of attending circumstances and the reliable material on record of a case.[220]

The presumption of Muhammadan Law that, when a person has disappeared and has not been heard of for a certain number of years, he is dead, and further that, as regards property coming to him by inheritance, he must be deemed to have died at the date of his disappearance, is a rule of evidence only and is superseded by this section.[221] The rule of Muhammadan Law that a missing person is to be regarded as alive till the expiry of 90 years from the date of his birth is overruled by this section.[222] So is the rule of Hindu Law that 12 years must elapse before an absent person, of whom nothing has been heard during this period, can be presumed to be dead.

Where a woman obtained certificate of widowhood on the completion of seven years of the absence of her husband and obtained admission to MBBS course on that

---

215. *Jeshankar v Bai Divali,* (1919) 22 Bom LR 771.

216. *R. Gopala Pathar v N Jayalakshmi Ammal,* AIR 1984 Mad 340. An appeal before the Supreme Court, *Jayalakshmi Ammal N v Gopala Pathar,* AIR 1995 SC 995 : 1995 AIR SCW 983.

217. *Surjit Kaur v Jhujhar Singh,* AIR 1980 SC 274.

218. *Lal Chand v Ramrup Gir,* AIR 1926 PC 6. See also *Mathru v Rami,* AIR 1986 HP 6, presumption of death for succession. **Followed** in *Eliamma Simon v Seven Seas Transportation Ltd,* AIR 2002 Ker 219, date of death has to be proved in the same manner as any other fact is proved. The section does not automatically give rise to the presumption as to the exact date of death of the missing person. The Court cannot presume the date of death as the date that immediately followed the lapse of seven years from the date of his disappearance. Other cases on the same point, *Bhargavi Ammal v Bhaskara Pillai,* (1988) 2 Ker LT 537; *Appula Vadhyar v Venkateswara Vadhyar,* AIR 1971 Ker 85 : 1970 Ker LT 976 (FB); *Darshan Singh v Gujjar Singh,* AIR 2002 SC 606, there is no presumption of exact time of death. The plaintiff obtained succession to the estate of one J, the Court said that burden was upon him to show the date of death. The person in question who was not heard of for more than 7 years, he could not be presumed to be dead only on the date on which the suit was filed. The provisions of sections 107 and 108 were also. considered by the Supreme Court in *Sri Vidya Mandir Education Society v Malleswaram Sangeetha Sabha,* AIR 1994 SC 775 : 1994 AIR SCW 82 : 1995 Supp. 1 SCC 27.

219. *Chanda Devi v Shrinath Sharma,* AIR 1993 Pat 105.

220. *Subhash Ramchandra Wadekar v UOI,* AIR 1993 Bom 64, **dissenting** from *Ram Kali v Narain Singh,* AIR 1934 Oudh 298. The Court referred to *Ram Singh v Board of Revenue, UP, Allahabad,* AIR 1964 All 310 : 1993 All JJ 851.

221. *Mairaj Fatma v Abdul Wahid,* (1921) 43 All 673; *Azizul Hasan v Mohammad Faruq,* (1933) 9 Luck 401.

222. *Mazhar Ali v Budh Singh,* (1884) 7 All 297 (FB).

basis, it was held that the certificate was liable to be cancelled on her husband turning out to be alive.[223]

Where the certificate of death was taken on proving the completion of the statutory period and the Life Insurance claim lodged, it was held that if the insurer contended that the insured was still alive he would have to prove that fact. The fact that premiums were kept up for some years after disappearance was considered to be not material.[224]

[s 108.3] Simultaneous death.—When two individuals perish in a common calamity (*e.g.* shipwreck, train collision, air crash, earthquake etc.) and the question arises who died first, in the absence of evidence on the point, there is no presumption in law that the younger survived the elder. Such a question is always from first to last a pure question of fact, the *onus probandi* lying on the party who asserts the affirmative.[225] See also section 21 of the Hindu Succession Act, 1956, in the case of simultaneous death.

[s 108.4] CASES.—Division of estate among heirs.— A person was not heard of more than 18–20 years. Though the defendant claimed that he was writing letters to him, he could not produce any of such letters. The court said that presumption of his death could be drawn. The distribution of his property among his brothers and sisters was held to be permissible.[226] Whereabouts of an account holder in a bank were not known for years. His wife and children filed a writ petition for an order permitting to withdraw the money from the account and also to collect the contents of the locker, they being not able to file a case for succession certificate. The court said that they could not be denied such relief. They were allowed to collect their inheritance as being heirs of the first degree.[227]

[s 108.4.1] Joining as party to proceeding.—In a tenancy proceeding, an application was made by the mother of the tenant for her addition as a party on the ground that her son was not heard of for more than 13 years and should be presumed to be dead. The court said that section 108 does not provide any procedure to be followed, hence a separate suit for getting the declaration that the original tenant was dead was not necessary.[228]

[s 109] Burden of proof as to relationship in the cases of partners, landlord and tenant, principal and agent.—When the question is whether persons are partners,[s 109.2] landlord and tenant,[s 109.3] or principal and agent,[s 109.4] and it has been shown that they have been acting as such, the burden of proving that they do not stand, or have ceased to stand, to each other in those relationships respectively, is on the person who affirms it.

---

223. *N Prem Ananthi v Tahsildar, Coimbatore,* AIR 1989 Mad 248.
224. *Bhanumati Dayaram Mhatri v LIC,* AIR 2008 Bom 196.
225. *Agha Mir Ahmad v Mudassir Shah,* (1944) 71 IA 171.
226. *Kalyan Kumar Bhattacharjee v Pratibha Chakraborty,* AIR 2010 NOC 646 (Gau).
227. *Pooja V Raichandani v State Bank of India,* AIR 2009 NOC 685 (Guj).
228. *Panchanan Chandra v Kamala Biswas,* AIR 2000 NOC 19 (Cal) : 2000 AIHC 566. *Chami Narayanan v VR Krishna Iyer,* AIR 1998 Ker 365, impleading of legal heirs after seven years' of absence, civil death taken place on the expiry of the period and not on the last breath.

SYNOPSIS

COMMENT

[s 109.1] Principle.—When the existence of a personal relationship, or a state of things, is once established by proof, the law presumes that the relationship or state of things continues to exist as before, till the contrary is shown, or till a different presumption is raised, from the nature of the subject in question. A partnership, tenancy, or agency, once shown to exist, is presumed to continue, till it is proved to have been dissolved.

[s 109.2] "Partners".—Partnership once shown to exist is presumed to continue until the contrary is proved.[229]

After a firm is dissolved, the partners continue to be liable to third parties for any act done which would have been an act of the firm if done before the dissolution, until public notice of dissolution is given (section 45, Indian Partnership Act, 1932).

[s 109.3] "Landlord and tenant".—Where the relationship of landlord and tenant is admitted or proved to exist it will be presumed to continue until it is shown by affirmative proof that it has ceased to exist. Mere non-payment of rent, though for many years, is not sufficient to show that such relationship has ceased.[230] The mere entry in the record of tenancy rights Register does not by itself confer any right on a person as a cultivating tenant.[231]

[s 190.4] "Principal and agent".—Where an authority to do an act is once shown to exist, it is presumed to continue until the contrary is proved. Sections 182–238 of the Indian Contract Act, 1872, deal with the relationship of principal and agent. Section 206 provides that a reasonable notice must be given of revocation or renunciation of agency. Section 208 provides when the authority of an agent is terminated.

[s 110] Burden of proof as to ownership.—When the question is whether any person is owner of anything of which he is shown to be in possession, the burden of proving that he is not the owner is on the person who affirms that he is not the owner.

COMMENT

This section gives effect to the principle that possession is *prima facie* evidence of complete title; anyone who intends to oust the possessor must establish a right to do

---

229. *Liladhar Ratanlal v Holkarmal*, (1958) 60 Bom LR 203.

230. *Rungo Lall Mundul v Abdool Guffoor*, (1878) 4 Cal 314; *The British India Steam Navigation Co v Hajee Mahomed Esack and Co*, (1881) 3 Mad 107; *Attar Singh v Ramditta*, (1881) PR No. 110 of 1881 (Civil); *Harish Chandra v Ghisa Ram*, AIR 1981 SC 695 : (1981) 1 SCC 431, recorded in Jamabandi as a tenant, presumption. *Raees Ahmed v Shrigopal Prakash*, AIR 2002 NOC 178 (Raj) : 2002 AIHC 2152, denial of landlordship, burden on the tenant. The right of the landlord was otherwise also sufficiently proved.

231. *JM Jeyachandran Samuel v GSS Masilamani*, AIR 2007 NOC 1853 (Mad).

so.[232] This is to be presumed from lawful possession until the want of title or a better title is proved.[233]

Longer the possession, stronger is the presumption. This observation occurs in a judgment of the Supreme Court: A presumption of an origin in lawful title can be drawn... in order to support possessory rights, long and quietly enjoyed, where no actual proof of title is forthcoming. It is not a mere branch of the law of evidence. It is resorted to because of the failure of actual evidence. The matter is one of presumption based upon the policy of law. A presumption should be allowed to fill in gaps disclosed in the evidence. The presumption, not to supplement but to contradict the evidence would be out of place. It is not a presumption to be capriciously made nor is it one which a certain class of possessor is entitled to, *de jure*." In a case such as the one in question where it was necessary to indicate what particular kind of lawful title was being presumed, the court must be satisfied that such a title was in its nature practicable and reasonably capable of being presumed without doing violence to the probabilities of the case. It is the completion of a right to which circumstances clearly point where time had obliterated any record of the original commencement. The longer the period within which and the remoter the time when first a grant might be reasonably supposed to have occurred the less force there is in an objection that the grant could not have been lawful.[234]

The principle of the section does not apply where the possession has been obtained by fraud or force. The term "possession" in this section is to be understood as opposed to juridical possession and to denote actual present possession.

A person in possession of land without title has an interest in the property which is heritable and good against all the world except the true owner, an interest which unless and until the true owner interferes, is capable of being disposed of by deed or will, or by execution sale, just in the same way as it could be dealt with if the title were unimpeachable.[235]

Possession is *prima facie* proof of ownership; it is so, because it is the sum of acts of ownership. This applies both to prior and to present possession. Possession has a two-fold value; it is evidence of ownership, and is itself the foundation of a right to possession. To recover possession a plaintiff must show a better right in himself to possession than is in the defendant. He may, within the period prescribed by the

---

232. *Churharmal v CIT,* AIR 1988 SC 1384 : 1988 Tax LR 1205 : (1988) 172 ITR 250 : (1988) 3 SCC 588; *Ramchandra Apaji v Balaji Bhaurav,* (1884) 9 Bom 137; *Hassan v Fazal Wahid,* (1882) PR No. 121 of 1882 (Civil); *Pir Baksh v Jhanda Mal,* (1882) PR No. 157 of 1882 (Civil); *Nihal Chand v Teju,* (1883) PR No. 74 of 1883 (Civil); *Nihal Singh v Jiwanda,* (1888) PR No. 116 of 1888 (Civil); *Ram Chand v Bhana Mal,* (1900) PR No. 71 of 1900 (Civil); *U Nyo v Ma Shwe Meik,* (1899) PJLB 514; *Ma Ba v Maung Kun,* (1889) SJLB 474; *Maung Ya Baing v Ma Kyin Ya,* (1895) 2 UBR (1892-96) 234; *Ma Hla Gywe v Ma Thaik,* (1896) 2 UBR (1892-96) 377; *Maung Thit v Maung Kin,* (1898) 2 UBR (1897-1901) 412; *Maung Nwe v Maung Po Gyi,* (1897) 2 UBR (1897-1901) 416; *Maung Lu Pe v Maung Lu Gale,* (1899) 2 UBR (1897-1901) 418; *Ma Ngwe Zan v Mi Shwe Taik,* (1910) 1 UBR (1910-1913) 61.

233. *Jadh Singh v Sundar Singh,* (1882) PR No. 122 of 1882 (Civil).

234. *Vatticherukuru Village Panchayat v Nori Venkatarama Deekshithulu,* 1991 Supp (2) SCC 228.

235. *Gobind Prasad v Mohan Lal,* (1901) 24 All 157.

Limitation Act, 1963, succeed in a case where he is dispossessed, either by establishing title or by showing a prior legal possession entitling him to be restored to the same.[236]

There is a conflict of opinion between the High Courts as to whether a plaintiff in a suit for possession of immovable property, other than a suit under section 9 of the Specific Relief Act (I of 1877), is entitled to succeed merely upon proof of previous possession and dispossession by the defendant within 12 years prior to the suit, or whether he is bound to prove title.

A Full Bench of the Bombay High Court has held that possession is a good title against all persons except the rightful owner, and entitles the possessor to maintain ejectment against any person other than such owner who dispossesses him.[237] A person, although suing more than six months after the date of dispossession and without resorting to a possessory suit,[238] is entitled to rely on the possession previous to his dispossession as against a person who has no title.[239] The view of the Bombay High Court is in accordance with the English law. The effect of the Bombay cases is that when there is wrongful ouster of the person in possession, the person who comes into Court to oust such tort-feasor need not prove more than his possession of the land in dispute, and that he had been ousted by the defendant, and that the plaintiff's prior possession was *prima facie* evidence of his title. According to this view, it is not necessary to show title in the absence of any title shown by the defendant. The word "possession" denotes actual present possession. In *Hanmantrav v The Secretary of State for India*[240] Jenkins CJ, said:

> To say that a possession is not within the meaning of section 110, unless it is a possession according to title, would be to render that section meaningless, and to introduce a doctrine subversive of the established principles of property law.

But Ranade J, struck a different note: Under section 110, possession, when long and continued up to a recent date, leads to a presumption of title. Where the conflict is between mere previous possession and recent actual possession, the fact of previous possession will not entitle plaintiff to a decree except in suits under section 9, Act I of 1877, brought within six months from dispossession. Where this period is exceeded before a suit is brought, and is less than the limitation law requires, he must make out a *prima facie* title... And section 110 [Evidence Act] refers to the presumption to be made of ownership based on the circumstance of such possession, and allows the plaintiff with such *prima facie* title to claim a decree where no superior title is proved on the other side. It is in reference to such cases that it has been held that possession is evidence of

---

236. *Hari v Dhondi,* (1905) 8 Bom LR 96; *Phool Chand v Amrit Lal,* AIR 1980 P&H 122, party claiming under a will, unable to prove it. *State of Gujarat v Allauddin Babumiya Shaikh,* AIR 1990 SC 2220, the plaintiff in possession of the land over 60 years period to the institution of the proceedings.

237. *Pemraj Bhavaniram v Narayan Shivaram Khisti,* (1882) 6 Bom 215 (FB); *Ramchandra Narayan v Narayan Mahadev,* (1886) 11 Bom 216; *Krishnacharya v Lingawa,* (1895) 20 Bom 270; *Ambalal v The Secretary of State,* (1899) 1 Bom LR 45; *Basapa v Basapa,* (1900) 2 Bom LR 410; *Fatan v Emad,* (1901) 3 Bom LR 246.

238. Specific Relief Act, section 9.

239. *Krishnarav Yashwant v Vasudev Apaji Ghotikar,* (1884) 8 Bom 371; *Pemraj Bhavaniram v Narayan Shivaram Khisti,* (1882) 6 Bom 215 (FB) followed, and *Dadabhai Narsidas v The Sub-Collector of Broach,* (1870) 7 BHC (ACJ) 82, dissented from; *Wa Tha v Pe Hlaw,* (1905) 3 LBR 27.

240. *Hanmantrav v The Secretary of State for India,* (1900) 25 Bom 287, 290 : 2 Bom LR 1111, 1114; *Ali v Pachubibi* (1903) 5 Bom LR 264; *Rajaram v Nanchand,* (1903) 5 Bom LR 225, 227.

title, and the plaintiff who proves such possession and subsequent disturbance, shifts the burden of proof on the defendant when the *prima facie* title is made out...Where no such title is made out, and plaintiff comes to the court and asks for a declaratory decree, he cannot obtain that decree on the mere ground that he was in possession and the defendant had no title. Mere wrongful possession is insufficient to shift the burden of proof.[241] This means that possession must be of such a character as leads to a presumption of title.[242]

A suit on a possessory title must be distinguished from a suit filed under section 6 of the Specific Relief Act, 1963, within six months of dispossession. The latter type of suit cannot be resisted on the ground of title, so that the suit can be maintained even against a true owner if he has dispossessed the plaintiff otherwise than in due course of law. A suit on possession title, on the other hand, can be filed within 12 years of dispossession (Article 64 of the Limitation Act, 1963) and the plaintiff can maintain it against any person who does not have a better title.[243]

The Calcutta High Court held that mere previous possession will not entitle a plaintiff to a decree for the recovery of possession except in a suit under section 9 of the old Specific Relief Act.[244] In a suit to recover possession brought more than six months after the date of dispossession, the plaintiff must prove title, and mere previous possession for any period short of the statutory period of 12 years cannot be sufficient for the purpose.[245] Thus, in cases other than possessory suits under the Specific Relief Act the plaintiff must show title or such adverse possession as confers a title under the Limitation Act.

To succeed on the plea of adverse possession, the plaintiff should disclose and prove as to when the adverse possession started and when it was perfected.[246]

The Madras High Court held that, as against a wrong-doer, prior possession of the plaintiff in an action of ejectment was a sufficient title, even if the suit be brought more than six months after the act of dispossession complained of, and the wrong-doer could

---

241. *Hanmantrav v The Secretary of State for India,* (1900) 25 Bom 287, 303 : 2 Bom LR 1111, 1126; *Achut v Shivajirao,* (1936) 39 Bom LR 224. In an ejectment suit the defendant, though a trespasser, is entitled to require the plaintiff who seeks to eject him to prove that he has a superior title: *Kalu v Barsu,* (1894) 19 Bom 803. Plaintiff in an action of ejectment must recover by the strength of his own title, not the weakness of his adversary's: *Jowala Buksh v Dharum Singh,* (1866) 10 Moo Ind App 511; *Thakur Basant Singh v Mahabir Pershad,* (1913) 15 Bom LR 525, 530 : 40 IA 86 : 35 All 273; *Dharani Kanta v Gabar Ali,* (1912) 15 Bom LR 445 (PC); *Ramchandra v Vinayak,* (1914) 16 Bom LR 863, 900 : 41 IA 290: 42 Cal 384; *Bapuji v Bhagvant,* (1918) 20 Bom LR 346 : 42 Bom 357. The plaintiff must establish such title as carries a present right to possession: *Sitaram v Sadhu,* (1913) 16 Bom LR 132 : 38 Bom 240.

242. *Vasta v Secretary of State for India,* (1920) 45 Bom 789 : 23 Bom LR 238.

243. *Mariumbi Aslamkhan v Vithoba,* (1969) 72 Bom LR 142.

244. *Ertaza Hossein v Bany Mistry,* (1882) 9 Cal 130; *Debi Churn Boido v Issur Chunder Manjee,* (1882) 9 Cal 39; *Purmeshur Chowdhry v Brijo Lall Chowdhry,* (1889) 17 Cal 256.

245. *Nisa Chand Gaita v Kanchiram Bagani,* (1899) 26 Cal 579, 584; *Shama Churn Ray v Abdul Kabeer,* (1898) 3 Cal WN 158. Doubted in *Shyama Charan Ray v Surya Kanta Acharya,* (1910) 15 Cal WN 163; *Manik Borai v Bani Charan Mandal,* (1910) 13 Cal LJ 649; and *Adhar Chandra Pal v Dibakar Bhuyan,* (1913) 41 Cal 394. Approved in *Naba Kishore Tilakdas v Paro Bewa,* (1922) 50 Cal 23.

246. *State of MP v Nomi Singh,* (2015) 14 SCC 450, para 13.

not successfully resist the suit by showing that the title and right to possession were in a third person. It was immaterial however short or recent the plaintiff's possession was.[247]

The Allahabad High Court held that section 9 of the old Specific Relief Act did not debar a person who had been ousted by a trespasser from the possession of immovable property to which he had merely a possessory title, from bringing a suit in ejectment on his possessory title after the lapse of six months from the date of his dispossession.[248]

The Patna High Court held that a plaintiff who had omitted to sue under section 9 of the old Specific Relief Act, when first dispossessed, was not debarred from relying, in a suit for ejectment, on this section. As soon as he proved that the defendant had dispossessed him the onus was thrown upon the latter to prove his title.[249]

The Privy Council laid down in a case in which the plaintiff was a purchaser in possession and the defendant had no title at all, that lawful possession of land is sufficient evidence of right as owner, as against a person who has no title whatever, and who is a mere trespasser. The former can obtain a declaratory decree and an injunction restraining the wrong-doer.[250] In this case the plaintiff was in possession when he brought his suit and he asked for a decree declaring his right, and an injunction restraining the defendant from disturbing his possession.

Proof of the fact of possession varies with the nature of the property which is under the scrutiny of the court. It can be proved by credible oral evidence as well.[251]

[s 110.1] Chose-in-action.—In the context of the word "anything", it has been held that a chose-in-action or actionable claim (bends in this case) is not a thing which is capable of being possessed. The reversal of burden of proof does not apply to the case of a chose-in-action.[252]

[s 111] Proof of good faith in transactions where one party is in relation of active confidence.—Where there is a question as to the good faith of a transaction between parties, one of whom stands to the other in a position of active confidence,[s 111.2] the burden of proving the good faith of the transaction is on the party who is in a position of active confidence.

ILLUSTRATIONS

(a) The good faith of a sale by a client to an attorney is in question in a suit brought by the client. The burden of proving the good faith of the transaction is on the attorney.

(b) The good faith of a sale by a son just come of age to a father is in question in a suit brought by the son. The burden of proving the good faith of the transaction is on the father.

---

247. *Narayana Row v Dharmachar,* (1902) 26 Mad 514. See *Krishna Aiyar v The Secretary of State for India,* (1909) 33 Mad 173.

248. *Wali Ahmad Khan v Ajudhia Kandu,* (1891) 13 All 537. See *Lachho v Har Sahai,* (1887) 12 All 46; *Gobind Prasad v Mohan Lal,* (1901) 24 All 157.

249. *Haradhan Mondal Modak v Iswar Das Marwari,* (1916) 2 PLJ 61; *Bodha Ganderi v Ashloke Singh,* (1926) 5 Pat 765.

250. *Ismail Ariff v Mahomed Ghouse,* (1893) 20 IA 99: 20 Cal 834; *Sundar v Parbati,* (1889) 12 All 51: 16 IA 186.

251. *Kantilal v Shanti Devi,* AIR 1997 Raj 230.

252. *Standard Chartered Bank v Andhra Bank Financial Services Ltd,* (2006) 6 SCC 94 : AIR 2006 SC 3626.

SYNOPSIS

COMMENT

[s 111.1] Principle.—The principle of the rule embodied in this section which was called "the great rule of the Court" is "he who bargains in a matter of advantage with a person placing confidence in him is bound to show, that a reasonable use has been made of that confidence; a rule applying to trustees, attorneys, or anyone else."[253] Where a fiduciary or quasi-fiduciary relationship exists, the burden of sustaining a transaction between the parties rests with the party who stands in such relation and is benefitted by it. The plaintiff having been entirely in the hands of the defendant, would be destitute of the means—of proving affirmatively the *mala fides* of the transaction; whilst the defendant in such a transaction may fairly be subjected to the duty not only of dealing honestly but of preserving clear evidence that he has done so.[254] In such cases it is seldom, if ever, possible to prove specific acts of deception, or of exercise of authority amounting to moral coercion. Yet the risk of abuse is obviously great. The law therefore reverses its usual rule of evidence in dealings between man and man. Commonly we do not presume, without specific indications, that there is anything contrary to good faith in transactions which on the face of them are regular...But this is the rule as between equals, persons who are capable of dealing with one another, as the accustomed forensic phrase goes, "at arm's length." When one party habitually looks up to the other and is guided by him, he can no longer be supposed capable, without special precautions, of exercising that independent judgment which is requisite for his consent to be free.[255] A person who claims to have acted under a *bona fide* belief must himself appear as a witness to establish his claim. The version of other persons in that respect may not be sufficient.[256]

[s 111.2] "Active confidence".—These words indicate that the relationship between the parties must be such that one is bound to protect the interests of the other. This had been held to apply to a trustee, an executor, an administrator, a guardian, an agent, a minister of religion, a medical attendant, an auctioneer, and attorney. Persons standing in a confidential relation towards others cannot entitle themselves to hold benefits which those others may have conferred upon them unless they can show to the satisfaction of the court that the person by whom the benefits have been conferred had competent and independent advice in conferring them.[257]

---

253. *Gibson v Jeyes*, (1801) 6 Ves Jun 266, followed in *Nisar Ahmad Khan v Mohan Manucha : Mohan Monucha v Nisar Ahmad Khan*, (1940) 43 Bom LR 465, 469 (PC).

254. Markby.

255. *Pollock's Law of Fraud In British India*, pp 63-64.

256. *Jawahar Lal Wali v State of J&K*, (1993) 2 SCC 381.

257. *Raghunathji v Varjiwandas*, (1906) 8 Bom LR 525 : 30 Bom 578; *Hoti Lal v Mussammat Ram Piari*, (1903) PR No. 77 of 1903 (Civil). *Anil Rishi v Gurbaksh Singh*, AIR 2006 SC 1971 : (2006) 5 SCC 558, the relationship of active confidence has to be proved in the first place before anyone can be put under the burden of proving his good faith. *Krishna Mohan Kul v Pratima Maity*, AIR 2003 SC 4351 : (2004) 9 SCC 468, burden on the dominant party enjoying the position of active confidence to show that the gift deed was fair and made of free will.

[s 111.3] *Pardanashin* ladies.—In the case of deeds and powers executed by *pardanashin* ladies, it is requisite, that those who rely upon them should satisfy the court that they had been explained to, and understood by those who executed them.[258]

In the case of a *pardanashin* lady the law throws around her a special cloak of protection. It demands that the burden of proof shall in such a case rest not with those who attack, but with those who found upon a deed executed by her, and the proof must go so far as to show affirmatively and conclusively that the deed was not only executed, but was explained to and was really understood by her.[259] Even in cases where a *pardanashin* lady had independent advice the court will scrutinize the transaction very closely to see that it is a fair one.[260] Her free and intelligent consent to a transaction is necessary.[261] The rule of special protection of a *pardanashin,* old and illiterate woman should not be applied in each and every case but should be applied in the light of the facts of each case.[262] The expression *"pardanashin"* is not to be confused with a lady observing *pardah.* The word has special legal significance and means one who is unable to understand the transaction by virtue of the manner in which she has been brought up.[263]

A *pardanashin* lady accused will not be exempted from personal attendance at Court as a matter of right. But at the same time the court must reasonably use the discretion of granting such exemption under section 205 of the Code of Criminal Procedure, 1973, after due consideration of all the attending circumstances including the social status, custom and practice of the accused as well as the necessity of her personal presence having regard to the nature of the offence and the stage of the trial. No strict test as to the *pardanashin* status can be laid down, and non-observance of rigidity with regard to *pardah,* e.g. attending social and religious functions or going to bathe in the river, etc. with veils on would not take the accused out of that category. The court is to be guided by the prevailing habits and customs.[264] An illiterate and rustic village woman is entitled to the same benefits as are available to

---

258. *Sudisht Lal v Musummat Sheobarat Koer,* (1881) 8 IA 39 : 7 Cal 245; *Annoda v Bhuban,* (1901) 3 Bom LR 386 : 28 IA 71 : 28 Cal 546; *Shambati v Jago Bibi,* (1902) 4 Bom LR 444: 29 IA 127: 29 Cal 749; *Mirza Sajjad Ali v Nawab Wazir Ali,* (1912) 14 Bom LR 1055 : 39 IA 156: 34 All 455; *Kali Bakhsh v Ram Gopal,* (1913) 16 Bom LR 147 : 41 IA 23 : 36 All 81; *Sunitabala Debi v Dharasundari Debi,* (1919) 22 Bom LR 1 : 46 IA 272: 47 Cal 175; *Kamawati v Digbijai Singh,* (1921) 24 Bom LR 626 : 48 IA 381 : 43 All 525; *Farid-un-nisa v Mukhtar Ahmed,* (1925) 28 Bom LR 193 : 52 IA 342 : 47 All 703; *Ramanamma v Viranna,* (1931) 33 Bom LR 960 PC; *Tara Kumari v Chandra Mauleshwar Prasad,* (1931) 34 Bom LR 222 : 11 Pat 227 : 58 IA 450; *Sheoparsan Singh v Narsingh Sahai,* (1932) 34 Bom LR 890 (PC); *Kundan Lal v Musharrafi Begum,* (1936) 38 Bom LR 783 : 63 IA 326 : 11 Luck 346; *AV Palanivelu v Neelavathi,* (1937) 39 Bom LR 720 (PC); *Kharbuja Kuer v Jangabahadur,* AIR 1963 SC 1203.

259. *Bank of Khulna, Ltd v Jyoti Prokash Mitra,* (1940) 42 Bom LR 1139 : 67 IA 377; *Tulshiram v Chunilal,* (1940) Nag 149; *Jaibunisa v Abdul Gafoor,* AIR 1984 Pat 257, a *pardanashin* lady pleaded that her signature was obtained by fraud, held, heavy burden of proof lay upon the other party.

260. *Nathusa v Mohammad Siddique,* (1941) Nag 418.

261. *Hem Chandra Roy Choudhuri v Suradhani Debya Choudharani,* (1940) 42 Bom LR 993 : 67 IA 309; *Vinayak v Sk. Md. Hanif,* (1953) Nag 281; *Pathumma v Vadhyar Namboori,* (1951) TC 320.

262. *Kulsumun-nisa v Ahmadi Begum,* AIR 1972 All 219.

263. *Andhi Kuer v Rajeshwar Singh,* AIR 1972 Pat 325; *Ghulam Zubra v Habla Begum,* AIR 1985 J&K 22, a lady leading public life and appearing in courts is not *pardanashin.*

264. *Rajlakshmi Devi v The State,* (1953) 1 Cal 78.

a *pardanashin*. An old woman suffering from infirmity, ignorance, illiteracy, mental deficiency, inexperience and dependence upon others, intended to create a *wakf* and not a sale, heavy burden of proof lay upon those who alleged it to be sale.[265] Similar burden lay upon those who dealt with a person suffering from apparent mental or physical incapacity.[266]

[s 111.4] Blind.—Mere signature of a blind person on the sale-deed cannot have any force. Where an illiterate and blind woman is alleged to have executed a sale-deed, the execution of which is denied by her, a heavy burden is laid on the purchaser to prove that she not only agreed to sell but she knew what was being written and the document was in accordance with the terms of the agreement.[267]

The presumption under the section cannot go beyond the relations stated therein. Any other presumption has to be brought under section 114.[268]

[269]**[[s 111A] Presumption as to certain offences.—(1) Where a person is accused of having committed any offence specified in sub-section (2), in—**

(a) any area declared to be a disturbed area under any enactment, for the time being in force, making provision for the suppression of disorder and restoration and maintenance of public order; or

(b) any area in which there has been, over a period of more than one month, extensive disturbance of the public peace,

and it is shown that such person had been at a place in such area at a time when firearms or explosives were used at or from that place to attack or resist the members of any armed forces or the forces charged with the maintenance of public order acting in the discharge of their duties, it shall be presumed, unless the contrary is shown, that such person had committed such offence.

(2) The offences referred to in sub-section (1) are the following, namely:—

(a) an offence under section 121, section 121A, section 122 or section 123 of the Indian Penal Code;

(b) criminal conspiracy or attempt to commit, or abetment of, an offence under section 122 or section 123 of the Indian Penal Code.]

[s 112] Birth during marriage conclusive proof of legitimacy.—The fact that any person was born during the continuance of a valid marriage between his mother and any man,[s 112.2] or within two hundred and eighty days after its dissolution, the mother remaining unmarried,[s 112.3] shall be conclusive proof that he is the legitimate son of that man, unless it can be shown that the parties to the marriage had no access to each other[s 112.4] at any time when he could have been begotten.

---

265. *Ashok Kumar v Gaon Sabha,* AIR 1981 All 222; *Narayan Mishra v Champa Dibya,* AIR 1986 Ori 53.
266. *Daya Shanker v Bachi,* AIR 1982 All 376. The Court explained the meaning and scope of "fiduciary relations".
267. *Sivamma v Abdur Rahman,* (1952) Hyd 668.
268. *Surendra Pal v Saraswati,* AIR 1974 SC 1999 : (1974) 2 SCC 600.
269. Section 111-A, inserted by the Terrorist Affected Areas (Special Courts) Act, 1984, (w.e.f. 14-7-1984).

SYNOPSIS

COMMENT

[s 112.1] Principle.—The section is based on the principle that when a particular relationship, such as marriage, is shown to exist, then its continuance must *prima facie* be presumed.[270] Under the section the fact that any person was born—

(a) during the continuance of a valid marriage between his mother and any man, or

(b) within 280 days after its dissolution, the mother remaining unmarried,

shall be conclusive proof that he is the legitimate son of that man unless the parties had no access to each other at any time when he could have been begotten.

Evidence that a child is born during wedlock is sufficient to establish its legitimacy, and shifts the burden of proof to the party, seeking to establish the contrary.

According to the legislative intention and spirit behind section 112, once the validity of marriage is proved then there is strong presumption about the legitimacy of children born from that wedlock. The presumption can only be rebutted by strong, clear, satisfying and conclusive evidence. The presumption cannot be displaced by mere balance of probabilities or any circumstance creating doubt. It is well-settled principle of law that *odiosa et inhonesta non sunt in lege praesumenda* (nothing odious or dishonourable will be presumed by the law). The law presumes against vice and immorality. In a civilised society it is imperative to presume the legitimacy of a child born during continuation of a valid marriage and whose parents had "access" to each other. It is undesirable to enquire into the paternity of a child whose parents "have access" to each other. section 112 is based on presumption of public morality and public policy.[271]

The presumption under this section is a conclusive presumption of law which can be displaced only by proof of non-access between the parties to the marriage at a time when according to the ordinary course of nature the husband could have been the father of the child. Access and non-access connote the existence and non-existence of opportunities for marital intercourse. Non-access can be proved by evidence direct or

---

270. *Bhima v Dhulappa,* (1904) 7 Bom LR 95.

271. *Sham Lal v Sanjeev Kumar,* (2009) 12 SCC 454.

circumstantial though the proof of non-access must be clear and satisfactory as the presumption of legitimacy is highly favoured by law.[272]

Sections 41, 112 and 113 are the only sections which deal with matters which are to be regarded as "conclusive proof". No rule of the kind can be based on considerations of evidence, because enquiry is altogether excluded. The basis of the rule in the first case (section 112) seems to be a notice that it is undesirable to enquire into the paternity of a child whose parents "have access" to each other. This section refers to the point of time of the birth of the child as the deciding factor and not to the time of conception of that child; the latter point of time has to be considered only to see whether the husband has no access to the mother.[273]

[s 112.2] "During the continuance of a valid marriage between his mother and any man".—The presumption as to paternity in this section only arises in connection with the offspring of a married couple. The section applies to the legitimacy of the children of a married person only.[274] On the birth of a child during marriage the presumption of legitimacy is conclusive, no matter how soon the birth occurs after the marriage.[275] There is presumption of valid marriage from the fact of living together as husband and wife for continuous and long period and sons born to them from such marriage are legal heirs over the property of the husband.[276]

Even children born with only a gestation period of six months have been known to survive and live. Where a child was born eight months after date of marriage there could be no doubt that she could very well be the child of the father.[277]

A person claiming as an illegitimate son must establish his alleged paternity in the same manner as any other disputed question of relationship is established.[278] The presumption that children born of a married woman, during the lifetime of her husband are the legitimate offspring of that woman and her husband, is not conclusive proof of their legitimacy and must be regarded as fully rebutted where the woman admittedly lived for years with another person and they both asserted such children to be the offspring of their union.[279] It is upon the person who claims to be the legitimate issue of his parents to bring forward satisfactory evidence in support of their marriage.[280] Where documentary evidence adduced was sufficient to draw the presumption of marriage

---

272. *Chilukuri Venkateswarlu v Chilukuri Venkatanarayana,* (1954) SCR 424 : AIR 1954 SC 176.

273. *Palani v Sethu,* (1924) 47 Mad 706; *Pal Singh v Jagir,* (1926) 7 Lah 368. *Laxmi Kom Venkanna Nayak v Govt of India,* AIR 2002 Kant 54, the Court noted human experience which shows that it is very rarely that a woman with children would claim that she was the wife of a person who was not her husband. The case was about the right of a woman to family pension.

274. *XXX v Ma Son,* (1896) 1 UBR (1892-1896) 74. A marriage presumed from a long cohabitation is also a marriage within the meaning of the section for giving rise to this presumption. *SPS Balasubramanayam v Surattayan,* AIR 1952 SC 756 : 1992 Supp (2) SCC 304.

275. *Umra v Muhammad Hayat,* (1907) PR No. 79 of 1907 (Civil).

276. *Ranganath Parmeshwar P Mali v EG Kulkarni,* AIR 1996 SC 1290 : (1996) 7 SCC 681, finding of High Court that such presumption would arise only if factum of marriage is proved, held improper, decision reversed.

277. *Ponnammal v Andi Aiyyan,* (1953) TC 726.

278. *Gopalasami Chetti v Arunachelam Chetti,* (1903) 27 Mad 32, 33.

279. *Bahadur Singh v Viru,* (1905) PR No. 28 of 1906 (Civil).

280. *Thakur Amjal v Nawab Ali Khan,* (1906) 9 Bom LR 264 (PC).

between the plaintiffs' mother and their alleged father, the mere fact of non-examination of independent witnesses would not be fatal to the presumption.[281]

Reading section 120 with this section it is clear that there is no prohibition to the parents of a child from deposing whether or not they had at any time, when the child would have been begotten, access to one another.[282] In a case for maintenance, the father denied paternity to his second daughter. Evidence showed that his wife was pregnant when she left the house of her husband and there was no evidence of her illicit relations with anyone. He had admitted paternity in earlier petition. It was held that the daughter was entitled to maintenance.[283]

[s 112.2.1] Paternity of child—Blood test.—Section 112 requires the party disputing the paternity to prove non-access in order to dispel the presumption. "Access" and "non-access" mean the existence or non-existence of opportunities for sexual contact; it does not mean actual cohabitation. It is a rebuttable presumption of law under section 112 that a child born during the lawful wedlock is legitimate, and the access occurred between the parents. This presumption can only be displaced by a strong preponderance of evidence, and not by a mere balance of probabilities. Thus following is the position as to permissibility of blood test to prove paternity: (1) That Courts in India cannot order blood test as a matter of course. (2) Wherever applications are made for such prayers in order to have roving inquiry, the prayer for blood test cannot be entertained. (3) There must be a strong *prima facie* case in that the husband must establish non-access in order to dispel the presumption arising under section 112. (4) The court must carefully examine as to what would be the consequence of ordering the blood test, whether it will have the effect of branding a child as a bastard and the mother as an unchaste woman. (5) No one can be compelled to give sample of blood for analysis.[284] The use of DNA test is an extremely delicate and sensitive aspect. There is an apparent conflict between the right to privacy of a person not to submit himself forcibly to medical examination and the duty of court to reach the truth. The court must exercise its discretion only after balancing the interest of the parties. DNA test should be allowed only when it is eminently needed. It should not be directed as a matter of course or in a routine manner. Diverse aspects have to be considered including presumption under section 112 and whether it is not possible for the court to reach the truth without resorting to DNA test.[285]

Even the result of a genuine DNA test may not be enough to escape from the conclusiveness of section 112 of the Evidence Act like a case where a husband and wife were living together during the time of conception. Therefore, when there is apparent conflict between the right to privacy of a person not to submit himself forcibly to

---

281. *Sarangapani v Varadhan,* AIR 1995 Mad 188.

282. *Shantabai v Dalchand,* (1954) Nag 204.

283. *Alpana v Mohanlal,* 1993 Cr LJ 1008 (HP).

284. *Goutam Kundu v State of WB,* AIR 1993 SC 2295 : 1993 Cr LJ 3233 : (1993) 3 SCC 418. See also *Gomathi v Vijayaraghavan,* 1995 Cr LJ 81 (Mad) and *Tushar Roy v Sukla Roy,* 1993 Cr LJ 1659 (Cal) where the English Law on the subject is discussed.

285. *Bhabani Prasad Jena v Convenor Secretary, Orissa State Commission for Women,* AIR 2010 SC 2851 : (2010) 8 SCC 633. *Sunil Kumar Jangde v Manju Jangde,* AIR 2010 NOC 696 (Chh), DNA not allowed because they delivered a child 4 months after she was expelled from the home, they were together before pregnancy and also for major period after it, access not disproved, presumption prevailed.

medical examination and duty of the court to reach the truth, the court must exercise its discretion only after balancing the interests of the parties and on due consideration whether for a just decision in the matter, DNA test is eminently needed. DNA test in a matter relating to paternity of a child should not be directed by the court as a matter of course or in a routine manner, whenever such a request is made. The court has to consider diverse aspects including presumption under section 112 of the Evidence Act; pros and cons of such order and the test of "eminent need" whether it is not possible for the court to reach the truth without use of such test.[286]

Therefore, the direction for a DNA test cannot be granted mechanically. In a case for maintenance, a prayer for DNA test was made eight years after the birth of the child. No explanation for the delay was submitted. The court refused to grant the prayer.[287]

Where the wife was not able to reach for the test because of her pecuniary inability, the court said that no adverse presumption could be drawn against her. Even otherwise the access between the parties was an admitted fact and the delivery was that of a normal child. The presumption under section 112 was not rebutted in the circumstances.[288]

The general view in the courts is that no one can be compelled to undergo blood test. Blood test should be conducted only with the consent of the person concerned.[289] The courts are also of the view that the alleged father could not be compelled to submit himself to DNA test.[290]

The Karnataka High Court held that the court cannot exercise its inherent power to nullify the effect of the presumption. The provisions of the Act completely debar leading of evidence with respect to the fact which the law says is conclusive proof of the legitimacy and paternity of a child.

To compel a non-consenting person to submit himself for medical test or for blood group test under the exercise of inherent powers for determining paternity would run counter to the mandate of Article 21, i.e., interference with the fundamental right of life and liberty. An order of this kind would create a doubt about the chastity of the woman, and also about the paternity.[291] The Madras High Court has spoken with a different voice. It observed that passing an order directing the wife to undergo a DNA test is not an intervention in her personal liberty, without such test, it is difficult to

---

286. *Bhabani Prasad Jena v Orissa State Commission for Women,* (2010) 8 SCC 633.

287. *Kuldeep Singh v Joginder Kaur,* AIR 2007 NOC 185 (P&H) : (2007-1) 145 Pun LR 91; *Banarsi Dass v Teeku Dutta,* (2005) 4 SCC 449 : (2005) 3 SCR 923, the court did not direct DNA test of a claimant to property only because one of her brother was saying that she was the daughter of their father's brother. *Kamalamonta v State of TN,* AIR 2005 SC 2132 : (2005) 5 SCC 194, DNA test of dead foetus ordered to establish paternity in rape case. The expert affirmed paternity by the test, concurrent finding of DNA experts was upheld.

288. *Devesh Pratap Singh v Sumita Singh,* AIR 1999 MP 174.

289. *Sajeera v PK Salim,* 2000 Cr LJ 1208 (Ker).

290. *Syed Mohd Ghouse v Noorunnisa Begum,* 2001 Cr LJ 2028 (AP). *Master "X" v "Y",* AIR 2003 Delhi 195, suit by son against father for interim maintenance and praying that father be subjected to DNA test. There were documents and conversations showing that the plaintiff's mother was married to some other person. This raised doubt. DNA test and interim maintenance not ordered.

291. *Ningamma v Chikkaiah,* AIR 2000 Kant 50 **following** *Revamma v Sri Shanthappa,* AIR 1972 Mys. 157.

come to the conclusion about the divorce application based on the ground of adultery as a result of which she gave birth to a child.[292]

In case of proof of non-access, the court can direct the respondent wife to give blood sample to determine the paternity of the child born to her and in case of her refusal from doing so, the court can draw adverse inference against her.[293]

Where the husband with the order of the court obtained DNA report, refusal by the court to let him submit his report was held to be improper. He had a right to tender the document in evidence.[294]

Where the alleged father denied paternity of the child depriving her of the maintenance, it was held that the presumption under section 112 of the Evidence Act, 1872 does not bar the DNA test to prove the fatherhood of a child.[295] Where the husband claimed divorce on the ground of unfaithfulness of his wife on the ground that the child born to her was illegitimate but the wife volunteered to furnish DNA sample of herself and the child, it was held that the court should have forced the husband to furnish his blood sample for DNA matching before granting divorce.[296]

Section 112 of the Indian Evidence Act, 1872 was enacted at a time when the modern scientific advancements and DNA test were not even in the contemplation of the legislature. The result of DNA test is said to be scientifically accurate. Although s. 112 raises a presumption of conclusive proof on satisfaction of the conditions enumerated therein but the same is rebuttable. The presumption may afford a legitimate means of arriving at an affirmative legal conclusion. While the truth or fact is known, there is no need or room for any presumption. Where there is evidence to the contrary, the presumption is rebuttable and must yield to the proof. The interest of justice is best served by ascertaining the truth and the court should be furnished with the best available science and may not be left to bank upon presumptions, unless science has no answer to the facts in issue. When there is a conflict between a conclusive proof envisaged under law and a proof based on scientific advancement accepted by the world community to be correct, the latter must prevail over the former.[297] It is in the process of substantiating his allegation of infidelity of the his wife that the husband made an application before the Family Court for conducting a DNA test which would establish whether or not he had fathered the male child born to his wife. He feels that it is the only way to substantiate his allegations. The Supreme Court observed that DNA testing is the most legitimate and scientifically perfect means, which the husband could use to establish his assertion of infidelity. This simultaneously be taken as the most authentic, rightful and means also with the wife, for her to rebut the assertions made by her husband and to establish that she had not been unfaithful, adulterous or disloyal. It observed that the High Court had rightly directed for the same.[298]

---

292. *VK Bhurvaneswari v N Venugopal,* AIR 2007 NOC 158 (Mad) : (2007) 1 LW 318.

293. *Sadashiv M Kheradkar v Nandini S. Kheradkar,* 1995 Cr LJ 4090 (Bom). *Sadshiv S Kheradkar v NM Kheradkar,* 1995 Cr LJ 4090, suitable amendment recommended to cover cases of refusal to submit to blood test.

294. *Radhey Shyam v Pappi,* AIR 2007 Raj 42.

295. *Babu Remyalayam Veettil v Vidya,* 2015 Cr LJ 1049 (para 20) (Ker-DB).

296. *Rekha Devi v Sanjeev Kumar Jha,* AIR 2015 Pat 177, para 4 (DB). See also *Ranatish Saha v Soma Saha,* AIR 2016 NOC 268 (Cal).

297. *Nandlal Wasudeo Badwaik v Lata Nandlal Badwaik,* (2014) 2 SCC 576 (para 17).

298. *Dipanwita Roy v Ronobroto Roy,* (2015) 1 SCC 365 (para 17).

[s 112.3] "Within two hundred and eighty days after its dissolution, the mother remaining unmarried".—The section does not lay down a maximum period of gestation, and therefore does not bar the proof of the legitimacy of a child born more than 280 days after dissolution of marriage, the effect of the section being merely that no presumption in favour of legitimacy is raised, and the question must be decided simply upon the evidence for and against legitimacy.[299] A person born within 280 days after the death of his father is presumably his legitimate son.[300] When a person claims, under this section, to be the son of deceased person, he must prove that he was born within 280 days after the death of his father.[301]

[s 112.4] "Unless it can be shown that the parties to the marriage had no access to each other".—Meaning of access.—The Supreme Court considered the meaning of the word "access" in *Kamti Devi v Poshi Ram.*[302] Thomas J said: Earlier there was a controversy as to what is the true import of the word "access". Some High Courts held that access means actual sexual intercourse between the spouses. However, the controversy came to a rest when the Privy Council held in *Karapaya Servai v. Mayandi,*[303] that the word 'access' connotes only existence of opportunity for marital intercourse. The said legal principle gained the approval of this Court when a three Judge Bench held in *Chilukuri Venkataswarlu v Chilukuri Venkatanarayana,*[304] that the law has been correctly laid down therein.

Section 112 of the Evidence Act provides for a presumption of a child being legitimate and such a presumption can only be displaced by a strong preponderance of evidence and not merely by a balance of probabilities as the law has to live in favour of an innocent child from being bastardised. In the given case, as the proof of non-access between spouses had never been even pleaded, the matter was not examined by the High Court in correct perspective. It was held by Supreme Court that as per the settled legal proposition, proof of non-access between the parties to marriage during the relevant period is the only way to rebut that presumption.[305]

The principle of this section does not apply to the case of a paramour and the presumption can be rebutted when the mother of the child is not a wife but a mistress

---

299. *Rahmat Ali v Musst Allahdi,* (1883) PR No. 1 of 1884 (Civil); *Uttamrao Rajaram v Sitaram,* (1962) 64 Bom LR 752.

300. *Ghulam Mohy-ud-din Khan v Khizar Hussain,* (1928) 10 Lah 470; *Misir Bhairon Prasad v Gopi Kunwar,* (1930) 32 Bom LR 871 (PC).

301. *Narendra v Ram Govind,* (1901) 4 Bom LR 243 : 29 Cal 11 : 29 IA 17; *Karapaya Servai v Mayandi,* (1933) 12 Ran 243 : 36 Bom LR 394 (PC); *Zahoor Ahmad v Nadia,* 2003 Cr LJ 1393 (J&K), in a claim for maintenance for child, the alleged father disputed the paternity. The child was born within six months of the dissolution of the marriage and there was nothing to controvert this fact. It was not made out that the birth was premature. No proof of access of any stranger to the mother. The paternity of the child was not allowed to be disputed. The order granting maintenance was proper.

302. *Kamti Devi v Poshi Ram,* AIR 2001 SC 2226.

303. *Karapaya Servai v Mayandi,* AIR 1934 PC 49. *Asiya v Hameed,* AIR 2009 Ker 163, rebuttal of presumption of legitimacy can be solely on the ground of non-access and not in any other manner. Access connotes opportunity for coitus. It can be established by direct evidence of positive nature or by circumstantial evidence of cogent and conclusive nature.

304. *Chilukuri Venkataswarlu v Chilukuri Venkatanarayana,* AIR 1954 SC 176. 1954 SCR 424. *Usman v Badarunisa,* AIR 2007 NOC 371 (Ker), no evidence produced by the man to shown non-access, refusing to submit to DNA test, presumption of paternity prevailed.

305. *Bharatha Matha v R Vijaya Renganathan,* (2010) 11 SCC 483.

and it may be open for the mistress to prove that the real father of the child born during the period of her concubinage is different from her paramour.[306] A married woman was not allowed to claim maintenance for her child from a person other than her husband when there was neither divorce nor proof of lack of access to the husband.[307]

[s 112.4.1] ***Birth within Shorter Period after Marriage.***—The mother of the daughter (plaintiff) stated that before marriage she had relations with a person and became pregnant of him and gave birth to the daughter after three months of marriage. The court said that the mother was the best person to prove paternity of the daughter. The fact that her husband married her knowing that she was pregnant and took the responsibility of bringing up the daughter could not give the plaintiff the legal status of being his daughter. She had no right to challenge the "will" of the husband which did not carry her name.[308]

[s 112.5] Standard of proof.—The Supreme Court observed:[309] The standard of proof in such cases must at least be of a degree in between the two as to ensure that there was no possibility of the child being conceived through the plaintiff's husband. In *Gautam Kundu v State of West Bengal*[310] this Court after considering an earlier three-Judge Bench decision in *Dukhtar Jahan v Mohammed Farooq*,[311] held that this presumption can only be displaced by a strong preponderance of evidence and not by a mere balance of probabilities.

A dissolution of marriage was sought by the husband on the ground that his wife left him after eight days of marriage. He also alleged that she had illicit relationship with another person and also bore him a child. The court said that he failed to prove that after marriage the wife stayed with him only for eight days and that the marriage was not consummated. The presumption of marriage could be dispelled by proof of non-access, which the husband could not do. Dismissal of the dissolution petition was proper.[312] Where non-access was not pleaded and proved, it was held that even a negative DNA test report could not help to rebut the presumption. The unwillingness of wife to undergo DNA test could not tilt the scales against her.[313]

The court said that the criminal law standard of proof beyond reasonable doubt could not be applied because it would create the risk of many a children being rendered homeless.

[s 112.6] Mohammedan law.—According to Mohammedan law a child born six months after marriage or within two years after divorce or the death of the husband is presumed to be his legitimate offspring. If the question for decision be one of evidence

---

306. *Maina v Deorao*, (1942) Nag 383.

307. *Jit Ram v Cheli*, 1989 Cr LJ 1852 (HP), The Court referred to *Padmanabhan Kesavan v Bhargavi Krishnamma*, 1981 Cr LJ 156 and *Raghavan Pillai v Gourikutty Amma*, AIR 1960 Ker 119 : 1960 Cr LJ 476, on rebuttal of the presumption under the section.

308. *Bessi Devi v Chatru Devi*, AIR 2010 HP 26.

309. *Kanti Devi v Poshi Ram*, AIR 2001 SC 2226.

310. *Gautam Kundu v State of West Bengal*, AIR 1993 SC 2295 : 1993 Cr LJ 3233 : (1993) 3 SCC 418.

311. *Dukhtar Jahan v Mohammed Farooq*, AIR 1987 SC 1049 : 1987 Cr LJ 849. *Banarsi Dass v Teeku Dutta*, (2005) 4 SCC 449 : (2005) 2 KLT 729 : (2005) 4 SCC 449, the presumption can be overthrown not by a mere balance of probability, but strong preponderance of evidence.

312. *Ramroop Rathore v Rajkumari*, AIR 2009 MP 82.

313. *Laila v Muhammedali*, AIR 2009 Ker 173.

only it will be governed by this section[314] and the child will be considered legitimate if born within six months after marriage of its parents.[315] A child born more than 280 days after the dissolution of his mother's marriage with her first husband but less than six months after her marriage with her second husband was held entitled to inherit as the legitimate son of the second husband.[316]

It was established by evidence that the Muslim male and Hindu women were living together under one roof as husband and wife. The court said that marriage could be presumed from prolonged and continuous cohabitation as husband and wife. A child was born to them. The Birth Register extract showed the Muslim male as the father and the Hindu woman as the mother. This was a relevant proof of paternity.[317]

[s 112.6.1] ***Birth certificate.***—Birth certificate proceedings were taken on the basis of Baptism certificate. The proceedings contained the fact that the Baptismal record was read and checked before the God parents and signed by parents along with God parents. Thus, the Baptism certificate was a valid document. The birth certificate proceedings legally recognised legitimacy.[318] Extracts from birth register were produced to prove paternity of the child. The information recorded in the birth register was supplied by the mother who was interested in making maintenance for the child. The court said that the contents of the birth register cannot be presumed as absolute proof of paternity. But in view of the other documents like High School certificate and other documents produced by the mother in which also the defendant was described as the father of the child, the birth register could be relied on.[319]

[s 112.6.2] ***Circumstantial Evidence.***—Maintenance was granted on the basis of circumstantial evidence. The mother alleged sex with the father of the child (boy) on several occasions and the birth was consequence of that relationship. She produced birth certificate and baptism certificate. There was evidence of her mother and other relatives. She had approached the local *Pariah* for help. The man took the plea that she was of loose character but did not substantiate it. She had no motive against him. The court ordered paternity and maintenance on the basis of such circumstances.[320]

[s 113] Proof of cession of territory.—A notification in the Official Gazette that any portion of British territory has [321][before the commencement of Part III of the Government of India Act, 1935 (26 Geo. 5, ch. 2)], been ceded to any Native State, Prince or Ruler, shall be conclusive proof that a valid cession of such territory took place at the date mentioned in such notification.

---

314. *Mazhar Ali v Budh Singh,* (1884) 7 All 297 (FB); *Musammat Kaniza v Hasan Ahmad Khan,* (1925) 1 Luck 71.

315. *Sibt Muhammad v Muhammad Hameed,* (1926) 48 All 625; *Muhammad Allahabad Khan v Muhammad Ismail Khan,* (1888) 10 All 289.

316. *Nur-ul-Hasan v Muhammad Hasan,* (1910) PR No. 78 of 1910 (Civil); *P v R,* (1911) PR No. 77 of 1911 (Civil). Where a child was born after 7 months of marriage, this presumption applied and no weight was given to the mother's opinion that the child was mature. *Dukhtar Jahan v Mohd Farooq,* AIR 1987 SC 1049 : 1987 Cr LJ 849 : (1987) 1 Hindu LR 362 : (1987) 1 SCC 624.

317. *Shamsudeen M Illias v Mohammed Salim M Idris,* AIR 2008 Ker 59.

318. *Luis Caetano Viegas v Estreline Mariana RMA Da' Costa,* AIR 2003 SC 630.

319. *Dibakar Behera v Padmabati Behera,* AIR 2008 Ori 92.

320. *Master Leonard Mark v Seby Hillario,* AIR 2007 NOC 2348 (Bom).

321. Ins. by the A.O. 1937, (Pt. III of the Government of India Act, 1935 came into force on the 1st April, 1937).

COMMENT

[s 113.1] Object.—This section was enacted to exclude inquiry by Court of Justice into the validity of the acts of the Government so far as cession of territory to any Indian State was concerned. But the section is a dead-letter because it is declared to be *ultra vires* by the Privy Council in a case in which it is decided that the Governor-General-in-Council being precluded by 24 & 25 Vic. clause 67, section 22, from legislating directly as to sovereignty or dominion of the Crown over any part of its territories in India, or as to the allegiance of British subject, could not, by any legislative Act, purporting to make a notification in the Government Gazette conclusive evidence of a cession of territory, exclude inquiry as to the nature and lawfulness of that cession.[322] The section now is obsolete.[323]

[324]**[[s 113-A] Presumption as to abetment of suicide by a married woman.—When the question is whether the commission of suicide by a woman had been abetted by her husband or any relative of her husband and it is shown that she had committed suicide within a period of seven years from the date of her marriage and that her husband or such relative of her husband had subjected her to cruelty, the Court may presume, having regard to all the other circumstances of the case, that such suicide had been abetted by her husband or by such relative of her husband.**

Explanation.—For the purposes of this section, 'cruelty' shall have the same meaning as in Sec. 498A of the Indian Penal Code (45 of 1860).]

SYNOPSIS

COMMENT

The words "having regard to all the other circumstances of the case" in this section give wide powers to the court to appraise evidence and come to conclusion whether there was some extraneous cause for a woman to commit suicide.[325]

The words "all other circumstances of the case" require that a cause and effect relationship between the cruelty and suicide has to be established before drawing the presumption. Therefore, the presumption is not of mandatory nature.[326] The mere fact that if a married woman commits suicide within a period of seven years of her marriage, the presumption under this section would not automatically apply. The term

---

322. *Damodhar Gordhan v Deoram Kanji,* (1875-1876) 31 A 102 : 1 Bom 367.

323. *Maganbhai v UOI,* AIR 1969 SC 783, 794 : (1970) 3 SCC 400. One of the effects of cession is that the inhabitants of the territory can enforce only such rights as the new sovereign recognised. *Govindrao v State of UP,* AIR 1982 SC 1201 : (1982) 2 SCC 414.

324. Ins. by Act 46 of 1983, section 7 (w.e.f. 25-12-1983).

325. *Krishan Lal v UOI* (FB), 1994 Cr LJ 3472 (P&H).

326. *Ramesh Kumar v State of Chhatisgarh,* 2001 Cr LJ 4724 (SC), the cause of cruelty and beating as indicated in the deceased woman's letters and the statements of witnesses was forgetful nature and not dowry, presumption not applicable.

"the Court may presume, having regard to all the other circumstances of the case, that such suicide has been abetted by her husband" would indicate that the presumption is discretionary.[327]

In a dowry death case, the presumption that suicide was abetted by the accused-husband of the deceased could be drawn only when prosecution has discharged the initial onus of proving cruelty.[328] In *State of WB v Orilal Jaiswal*,[329] it was held that the requirement of proof beyond reasonable doubt in dowry death cases does not stand altered even after the introduction of section 498A of the IPC and section 113A of the Evidence Act. "Although, the Court's conscience must be satisfied that the accused is not held guilty when there are reasonable doubts about the complicity of the accused in respect of the offences alleged, it should be borne in mind that there is no absolute standard for proof in a criminal trial and the question whether the charges made against the accused have been proved beyond all reasonable doubts must depend upon the facts and circumstances of the case and the quality of the evidences adduced in the case and the materials placed on record. The doubt must be of a reasonable man and the standard adopted must be a standard adopted by a reasonable and just man for coming to a conclusion considering the particular subject-matter."[330] The scope of the pronouncement of the Apex Court that the offence of attempt to commit suicide is *ultra vires* the Constitution does not make the offence of abetment to commit suicide *ultra vires* the Constitution because the former is volitional and well-planned act of the person concerned whereas the latter is on the different footing as a third person forces the other person to take his life by committing suicide.[331]

[s 113A.1] Retrospective application.—The section embodies a rule of evidence. It would, therefore, also apply to incidents prior to its enforcement date, i.e., 25 December

---

327. *Mangat Ram v State of Haryana*, (2014) 12 SCC 595 (para 30).

328. *Basappa Dattu Hegade v State of Karnataka*, 1994 Cr LJ 1602 (Kant); *Pawan Kumar v State of Haryana*, AIR 2001 SC 1524 : 2000 Cr LJ 1679, the requirement of cruelty was proved by preponderance of evidence of unmet dowry demands, death had taken place by burning, theory of accident because of mis-handling of kerosene stove was found to be false. *Nandlal v State of MP*, 2000 Cr LJ 794 (MP), cruelty not proved, the allegation was that the husband has recalled his first wife and beat up the second (deceased), but this was not proved. Hence, the presumption did not arise. *Sarwan Kumar v State of HP*, 2000 Cr LJ 4002 (HP), onus is on the prosecution to prove that the accused had abetted suicide, the deceased-wife had not complained to her mother of harassment or cruelty. The explanation put forth by the accused-husband was that she was short tempered and was unhappy because of poor financial condition. The Court described the explanation as plausible and, though not proved it could be accepted. *State of Rajasthan v Kesa*, 2002 Cr LJ 432 (Raj) the initial burden of proving cruelty not discharged, presumption could not be raised. *Chandra Devi v State of Rajasthan*, 2002 Cr LJ 1075 (Raj), unnatural death of wife by burning within 7 years, she was unconscious and not in mental or physical condition to give statement as for medical opinion, statement recorded by police did not inspire confidence, not a genuine document, no evidence of cruelty or harassment for dowry, no presumption. *Dwarika Prasad Soni v State of MP*, 2002 Cr LJ 1080 (MP) no proof of cruelty during the preceding three years after the settlement, earlier cruelty not relevant, no presumption.

329. *State of WB v Orilal Jaiswal*, AIR 1994 SC 1418 : 1994 Cr LJ 2104 : (1994) 1 SCC 73 : 1994 SCC (Cri) 107.

330. See also *Dhobilal v State*, 1998 Cr LJ 4108 (MP), the wife committed suicide within 5 years from the date of marriage. She lived with her parents for 2-3 years. She returned to her matrimonial home and within a month thereafter she jumped into a well. Harassment by the husband and in-laws during this month was not proved. Hence, no presumption under the section.

331. *Krishan Lal v UOI (FB)*, 1994 Cr LJ 3472 (P&H).

1983.[332] The section is procedural in nature. It would, therefore, have retrospective operation.[333]

The provisions of the section are applicable to the pre-amendment cases also. In the words of the Supreme Court:[334] "These provisions do not create any new offence, (or any substantive right), but merely a matter of procedure and as such are retrospective and applicable to the present case. The presumption against retrospection does not apply to legislation concerned merely with matters of procedure or of evidence; on the contrary, the provisions of that nature are to be construed as retrospective unless there is a clear indication that such was not the intention of Parliament."[335]

[s 113A.1.1] ***Legislative intent.***—The legislative intent is clear, i.e., to curb the menace of dowry deaths, *etc.*, with a firm hand. One must keep in mind this legislative intent. It must be remembered that since such crimes, *e.g.*, dowry death, cruelty, etc., are generally committed in the privacy of residential homes and in secrecy, independent and direct evidence is not easy to get. That is why the legislature has by introducing sections 113-A and 113-B in the Evidence Act tried to strengthen the hands of the prosecution by permitting a presumption to be raised if certain foundational facts are established and the unfortunate event has taken place within seven years of marriage. This period of seven years is considered to be the turbulent one after which the legislature assumes that the couple had time enough to settle down in life.[336]

[s 113A.2] No presumption where charge under section 302, IPC.—Where the accused was charged under section 302, IPC, the presumption under section 113-A, Evidence Act, is not available. In such a case conviction and sentence has to be based on cogent and reliable evidence.[337]

[338]**[[s 113-B] Presumption as to dowry death.—When the question is whether a person has committed the dowry death of a woman and it is shown that soon before her death such woman had been subjected by such person to cruelty or harassment for, or in connection with, any demand for dowry, the Court shall presume that such person had caused the dowry death.**

***Explanation.*—For the purposes of this section, "dowry death" shall have the same meaning as in s. 304B of the Indian Penal Code (45 of 1860).]**

---

332. *State of Punjab v Iqbal Singh,* 1991 Cr LJ 1897 : AIR 1991 SC 1532.

333. *Arvind Kumar v State of MP,* 2001 Cr LJ 2317 (MP).

334. *Gurbachan Singh v Satpal Singh,* AIR 1990 SC 209 at p 218 : 1990 Cr LJ 562. **Followed** in *Bhoora Singh v State of UP,* 1992 Cr LJ 2294; *Vranta Tulshiram v State of Maharashtra,* 1987 Cr LJ 901, see also *Shanti v State of Haryana,* AIR 1991 SC 1226 : 1991 Cr LJ 1713 : (1991) 1 SCC 371; *State of Punjab v Kirpal Singh,* 1992 Cr LJ 2472 (P&H).

335. The court cited *Halsbury's Laws of England,*Vol 44 para 570.

336. *State of Punjab v Iqbal Singh,* (1991) 3 SCC 1, 9 : 1991 SCC (Cri) 513 : AIR 1991 SC 1532 : 1991 Cr LJ 1897.

337. *P Mani v State of TN,* AIR 2006 SC 1319 : (2006) 3 SCC 161 : 2006 Cr LJ 1629.

338. Ins. by Act No. 43 of 1986, section 12 (w.e.f. 19-11-1986).

SYNOPSIS

COMMENT

When the question at issue is whether a person is guilty of dowry death of a woman and the evidence discloses that immediately before her death she was subjected by such person to cruelty and/or harassment for, or in connection with, any demand for dowry, section 113-B, provides that the court shall presume that such person had caused dowry death. Of course if there is proof of the person having intentionally caused her death that would attract section 302, IPC.[339]

Presumption of dowry death under this section has a purpose. It is a beneficial provision aimed at giving relief to a woman subjected to cruelty routinely in an Indian household. The meaning to be applied to each word of this provision has to be in accord with the legislative intent. Even while construing this provision strictly, care will have to be taken to see that its object is not frustrated.[340]

The presumption under this section is attracted only in case of suicidal or homicidal death and not in case of an accidental death.[341]

Presumption under this section is a presumption of law. On proof of the essentials mentioned therein, it becomes obligatory on the court to raise a presumption that the accused caused the dowry death.[342] While the words "shall presume" in section 113-B mandate that the court is duty bound to proceed on the basis that the person has caused the dowry death, the presumption is rebuttable and it is open to prove that the ingredients of section 304-B IPC are not satisfied.[343]

Section 113B of the Evidence Act being procedural, it has been held that it is retrospective in operation.[344]

[s 113B.1] Presumption—When may be raised.—The presumption under section 113B shall be raised only on the proof of the following essentials:—

(1) The question before the court must be whether the accused has committed the dowry death of a woman. This means that the presumption can be raised only if the accused is being tried for the offence under section 304B, IPC.

(2) The woman was subjected to cruelty or harassment by her husband or his relatives.

---

339. *State of Punjab v Iqbal Singh*, (1991) 3 SCC 1 : AIR 1991 SC 1532 : 1991 Cr LJ 1897; *Lakhjit Singh v State of Punjab*, (1984) Supp. 1 SCC 173, the offence in this case was committed prior to the enforcement date of section 113-B. Evidence showed that the death in question could be suicidal. Section 113-B was held to be not applicable.

340. *Surinder Singh v State of Haryana*, (2014) 4 SCC 129 (para 26).

341. *Sultan Singh v State of Haryana*, (2014) 14 SCC 664 (para 8).

342. *Rajinder Kumar v State of Haryana*, (2015) 4 SCC 215 (para 15).

343. *Jagjit Singh v State of Punjab*, AIR 2018 SC 5719 : 2018 (105) ACC 613.

344. *Bhoora Singh v State of UP*, 1992 Cr LJ 2294 (All).

(3) Such cruelty or harassment was for or in connection with any demand for dowry.

(4) Such cruelty or harassment was taking place soon before her death.[345]

The requirements of this presumption in offence under section 304-B of IPC for the purposes of its applicability, have been thus re-phrased by Supreme Court –

(i) death should be of burns or bodily injury or has occurred otherwise than under normal circumstances;

(ii) within seven years of the marriage; and

(iii) that soon before her death she had been subjected to cruelty or harassment by her husband or his relatives.

Even if one of the ingredients is not made out, the presumption under section 113-B of the Evidence Act would not be available to the prosecution and the onus would not shift to the defence.[346]

The provisions of this section, although mandatory in nature, simply enjoin upon the court to draw such presumption of dowry death on proof of circumstances mentioned therein which amount to shifting the onus on the accused to show that the married woman was not treated with cruelty by her husband soon before her death.[347] In a dowry death case, it is a condition precedent to the raising of the presumption that the deceased married woman was subjected to cruelty or harassment for and in connection with the demand for dowry soon before her death.[348]

[s 113B.1.1] No presumption against wife where husband commits suicide.—A husband committed suicide. The alleged cause was cruelty by wife. The court said that a presumption under the section could not be raised against the wife.[349]

---

345. *Keshab Chandra Panda v State of Orissa,* 1995 Cr LJ 174 (Ori); *Rajinder v State of Haryana,* 2000 Cr LJ 2492 (P&H), the accused demanded money after 6 months of marriage which was paid. After 2 years he raised another demand. Death took place 2 years after the second demand. The Court refused to raise presumption under the section. The requirement of "soon before" was not satisfied. *Amar Singh v State of Rajasthan,* AIR 2010 SC 3391 : (2010) 9 SCC 64, harassment one month before death, held to be covered by the words "soon before." *Prem Kanwar v State of Rajasthan,* AIR 2009 SC 1242 : 2009 Cr LJ 1123 : (2009) 3 SCC 726, the expression "soon before her death" requires that there must be a live-link between the effect of cruelty based on dowry demand and concerned death. *Tarsem Singh v State of Punjab,* AIR 2009 SC 1454 : (2008) 16 SCC 155, presumption available only when the trial is for dowry death. *M Sirinvaslu v State of AP,* AIR 2007 SC 3146 : (2007) 12 SCC 443, the expression "soon before" is very much relevant when section 304-B, IPC and section 113-B, Evidence Act are pressed into service. It embodies the concept of proximity. There must be proximate and live link between the effect of cruelty based on dowry demand and concerned death. *Kailash v State of MP,* AIR 2007 SC 107 : (2006) 12 SCC 667, the words "soon before" cannot be limited to fixed time-limit. *Thakkan Jha v State of Bihar,* (2004) 13 SCC 348, deceased tortured and harassed for non-supply of articles, death not in normal circumstances, within 7 years of marriage, presumption attracted, the court also explained in detail the scope of the expression soon before, one circumstance was that there was settlement after the demand and before death.

346. *Gurdeep Singh v State of Punjab,* (2011) 12 SCC 408.

347. *Krishan Lal v UOI (FB),* 1994 Cr LJ 3472 (P&H).

348. *Bhoora Singh v State of UP,* 1993 Cr LJ 2636 (All). See also *Keshab Chandra Panda v State of Orissa,* 1995 Cr LJ 174 (Ori); *Chando Devi v State of Bihar,* 2002 Cr LJ 2783 (Pat), death by hanging, no proof of dowry demand or torture for it. There was demand for money for starting business but there was no torture for it. Presumption not applicable.

349. *Alka Grewal v State of MP,* 2000 Cr LJ 672 (MP).

[s 113B.1.2] Soon before her death.—The term "soon before her death" has been employed by Parliament to refer to cruelty or harassment which was meted out in proximity to the death and has to be considered as the cause of death. The provision does not employ the term "at any time before" nor "immediately before" and must be construed in its true import.[350]

The term "soon before" is a relative term. In matters of emotions, there cannot be a fixed formula. The time lag may differ from case-to-case. There must be a nexus between the demand of dowry, cruelty and harassment, based upon such demand and the date of death. The test of proximity will have to be applied. But, it is not a rigid test. It depends on the facts and circumstances of each case and calls for a pragmatic and sensitive approach of the court, within the confines of law.[351]

The expression "soon before" would normally imply that the interval should not be much between the cruelty and harassment concerned and the death in question. There must be existence of a proximate and live link between the effect of cruelty based on dowry demand and the death concerned. If the alleged incident of cruelty is remote in time and has become stale enough not to disturb the mental equilibrium of the woman concerned, it would be of no consequence.[352]

[s 113B.1.3] Cruelty or harassment.—Cruelty or harassment differs from case-to-case. It relates to the mindset of the people, which varies from person to person. Cruelty can be mental or it can be physical. Mental cruelty is of different shades. It can be verbal or emotional like insulting or ridiculing or humiliating a woman. It can be giving threats of injury to her or her near and dear ones. It can be depriving her of economic resources or essential amenities of life. It can be putting restraints on her movements. It can be, not allowing her to talk to the outside world. The list is illustrative and not exhaustive. Physical cruelty could be actual beating or causing pain and harm to the person of a woman. Every such instance of cruelty and related harassment has a different impact on the mind of a woman. Some instances may be so grave so as to have a lasting impact on a woman. Some instances which degrade her dignity may remain etched in her memory for a long time.[353]

[s 113B.2] Introduction of sections 113A and 113B.—In a case where demand of dowry is alleged, such demands are confined within four walls of the house and known only to members of both sides of family. In such cases independent and direct evidence with regard to the occurrences is ordinarily not available. That is why the legislature has introduced sections 113A and 113B in the Evidence Act by permitting presumption to be raised in certain circumstances.[354]

[s 114] Court may presume existence of certain facts.—The Court may presume the existence of any fact which it thinks likely to have happened, regard being had

---

350. *Tummala Venkateswar Rao v State of AP*, (2014) 2 SCC 240 (para 10). .
351. *Surinder Singh v State of Haryana*, (2014) 4 SCC 129 (paras 17 and 18).
352. *Hira Lal v State (Govt of NCT of Delhi)*, (2003) 8 SCC 80, para 9 : AIR 2003 SC 2865. See also *Major Singh v State of Punjab*, (2015) 5 SCC 201, para 16; *VK Mishra v State of Uttarakhand*, (2015) 9 SCC 588, para 7.
353. *Surinder Singh v State of Haryana*, (2014) 4 SCC 129 (para 17).
354. *VK Mishra v State of Uttarakhand*, (2015) 9 SCC 588, para 28.

to the common course of natural events,[s 114.4] **human conduct,**[s 114.5] **and public and private business,**[s 114.6] **in their relation to the facts of the particular case.**

ILLUSTRATIONS

The Court may presume—

(a) that a man who is in possession of stolen goods soon after the theft is either the thief or has received the goods knowing them to be stolen, unless he can account for his possession;[355]

(b) that an accomplice is unworthy of credit, unless he is corroborated in material particulars;[356]

(c) that a bill of exchange, accepted or endorsed, was accepted or endorsed for good consideration;

(d) that a thing or state of things which has been shown to be in existence within a period shorter than that within which such things or states of things usually cease to exist, is still in existence;

(e) that judicial and official acts have been regularly performed;

(f) that the common course of business has been followed in particular cases;

(g) that evidence which could be and is not produced would, if produced, be unfavourable to the person who withholds it;[357]

(h) that if a man refuses to answer a question: which he is not compelled to answer by law, the answer, if given, would be unfavourable to him;

(i) that when a document creating an obligation is in the hands of the obligor, the obligation has been discharged.

But the Court shall also have regard to such facts as the following, in considering whether such maxims do or do not apply to the particular case before it:—

as to *illustration* (a)—a shop-keeper has in his till a marked rupee soon after it was stolen, and cannot account for its possession specifically, but is continually receiving rupees in the course of his business:

as to *illustration* (b)—A, a person of the highest character, is tried for causing a man's death by an act of negligence in arranging certain machinery. B, a person of equally good character, who also took part in the arrangement, describes precisely what was done, and admits and explains the common carelessness of A and himself:

as to *illustration* (b)—a crime is committed by several persons. *A*, *B* and *C*, three of the criminals, are captured on the spot and kept apart from each other. Each gives an account of

---

355. *Deivendran A v State of TN*, 1998 Cr LJ 814 : AIR 1998 SC 2821, an explanation of the circumstances in which presumption of this kind can be drawn.

356. *Francis Stanly v Intelligence Officer, Narcotic Control Bureau*, AIR 2007 SC 794 : 2007 Cr LJ 1157, evidence of an accomplice should ordinarily be corroborated. *K Hashim v State of TN*, AIR 2005 SC 128 : (2005) 1 SCC 237 : 2005 Cr LJ 143, corroboration means that there should be some additional independent evidence rendering it probable that the story told by the accomplice is true and it is reasonably safe to act upon it. The statement should identify the accused as the one or one of those who committed the offence. It may not be direct evidence, it would be enough to show circumstantial connection. Testimony of one accomplice cannot be used as corroboration. In this case there was sufficient corroborative evidence.

357. *Prabha Shanker Shukla v Shrikant Tiwari*, AIR 2006 NOC 1115 (All), the driver put forth by the claimant had no valid driving licence, hence no liability of insurer for the accident, Motor Vehicles Act, 1988, section 149.

the crime implicating *D*, and the accounts corroborate each other in such a manner as to render previous concert highly improbable;

as to *illustration* (c)—*A*, the drawer of a bill of exchange, was a man of business. *B*, the acceptor, was young and ignorant person, completely under *A*'s influence;

as to *illustration* (d)—it is proved that a river ran in a certain course five years ago, but it is known that there have been floods since that time which might change its course;

as to *illustration* (e)—a judicial act, the regularity of which is in question, was performed under exceptional circumstances;

as to *illustration* (f)—the question is, whether a letter was received. It is shown to have been posted, but the usual course of the post was interrupted by disturbance;

as to *illustration* (g)—a man refuses to produce a document which would bear on a contract of small importance on which he is sued, but which might also injure the feelings and reputation of his family;

as to *illustration* (h)—a man refuses to answer a question which he is not compelled by law to answer, but the answer to it might cause loss to him in matters unconnected with the matter in relation to which it is asked;

as to *illustration* (i)—a bond is in possession of the obligor, but the circumstances of the case are such that he may have stolen it.

SYNOPSIS

COMMENT

[s 114.1] Presumption and burden of proof.—Sections 104–113 direct on whom burden of proof will lie. The court is bound in every instance to presume against that party on whom the burden of proof is directed to lie. No option is given to the court as to whether it will presume the fact or not. But there are various presumptions where room is left for the court to exercise its powers of inference; the court can throw the burden of proof on whichever side it chooses. This section deals with cases of the description. It declares that the court may, in all cases whatever, draw from the facts before it, whatever inferences it thinks just. The terms of the section are such as to reduce to their proper position of mere maxims, which are to be applied to facts by the courts in their discretion, a large number of presumptions to which English law gives, to a greater or less extent, an artificial value. Nine of the most important of them are given by way of illustrations.[358]

The effect of this provision is to make it perfectly clear that Courts of Justice are to use their own common sense and experience in judging of the effect of particular facts, and that they are to be subject to no particular rules whatever on the subject. The illustrations given are, for the most part, cases of what in English law are called presumptions of law: artificial rules as to the effect of evidence by which the court is

358. *Stephen's Introduction to Evidence Act.*

bound to guide its decision, subject, however, to certain limitations which it is difficult either to understand or to apply, but which will be swept away by the section 114 in question.[359] A presumption is not evidence or proof. It only shows on whom the burden of proof lies.[360]

Venkatramiah J of the Supreme Court observed:

> A presumption is not in itself evidence but only makes a *prima facie* case for party in whose favour it exists. It indicates the person on whom the burden of proof lies. When presumption is conclusive, it obviates the production of any other evidence. But when it is rebuttable it only points out the party on whom lies the duty of going forward with evidence on the fact presumed, and when that party has produced evidence fairly and reasonably tending to show that the real fact is not as presumed the purpose of presumption is over.

Pelting of stones on passengers in a train whether by a mob or otherwise creates an adverse presumption against railways. Responsibility for an untoward incident arises unless it is explained otherwise.[361]

[s 114.2] Scope.—This section authorises the court to make certain presumptions of fact. They are all presumptions which may naturally arise, but the Legislature, by the use of the word "may" instead of "shall" both in the body of the section and in the illustrations, shows that the court is not compelled to raise them but is to consider whether in all the circumstances of the particular case they should be raised.[362] The section does not lay down any hard and fast rule with regard to the circumstances in which any fact or facts may be presumed to exist nor does it contain an exhaustive list of such facts, though it gives a few illustrations from various walks of life.[363] In order to draw an inference that a fact in dispute has been established, there must exist, on record, some direct material facts or circumstances from which such an inference could be drawn.[364] Genuineness of a document cannot be presumed merely because of it having been exhibited.[365]

In a case under the Prevention of Corruption Act, 1988, it was proved that a sum of money was paid to the accused. The court said that it could be presumed that payment was made for the performance of an official act. This presumption could be based upon a proved fact, but there could not be further presumption on the basis of this presumption.[366] The court relied upon its own decision in which it was observed:

---

359. Gazette of India, March 30, 1872 Supplement pp 234-235.

360. *Sodhi Transport Co v UP,* AIR 1986 SC 1099 : (1986) 2 SCC 486 : (1986) 2 SCC 486 : 1986 SCC (Tax) 410.

361. *Lakhi Barua v UOI,* AIR 2008 Cal 59.

362. *Muthukumaraswami Pillai v King-Emperor,* (1912) 35 Mad 397 (FB); *Sadashib Das v State,* (1957) Cut 680.

363. *Mahabir Singh v Anant Ram,* AIR 1966 All 214.

364. *R Puthunainar Alhithan v PH Pandian,* AIR 1996 SC 1599 : (1996) 3 SCC 624.

365. *Hari Kumar v Sat Narain Mehra,* 1996 AIHC 2700 (Del), explaining and distinguishing *Ali Hasan v Matiullah,* AIR 1988 All 57.

366. *M Narsinga Rao v State of AP,* AIR 2001 SC 318 at p 322; *Suresh Bhudarmal Kalani v State of Maharashtra,* 1998 Cr LJ 4592 : AIR 1998 SC 3258, presumption can be drawn only from facts and not from other presumptions by a process of probable and logical reasoning.

"A presumption can be drawn only from facts—and not from other presumptions—by a process of probable and logical reasoning."[367]

"When a rule prescribed only a formula of presumptions based on facts, the prescription is only of a directory nature and not of a mandatory nature." Thus spoke the Supreme Court in *Ammal Chandra Dutt v IInd ADJ*,[368] The following passage wad cited by the court from Phipson on Evidence:[369]

> Presumptions are either of law or fact. Presumptions of law are arbitrary consequences expressly annexed by law to particular facts; and may be either conclusive, as that a child under a certain age is incapable of committing any crime; or rebuttable, as that a person not heard of for seven years is dead, or that a bill of exchange has been given for value.
>
> Presumptions of fact are inferences which the mind naturally and logically draws from given facts, irrespective of their legal effect. Not only are they always rebuttable, but either the trier of fact may refuse to make the usual or natural inference notwithstanding that there is no rebutting evidence.

A presumption can be raised to fill the gaps in evidence, but it cannot be used to contradict evidence.[370]

The power conferred by section 114 is in respect of inferences which may be drawn by the court. The section does not authorise the courts to legislate as to the manner in which human beings should conduct themselves.[371]

[s 114.3] Presumptions.—Presumptions may be either of law or fact, and when of law may be either *conclusive* (*proesumptiones juris et de jure*), or *rebuttable* (*proesumptiones juris*), but when of fact (*proesumptiones hominis*) are always rebuttable. Mixed presumptions are those which are partly of law and partly of fact.[372]

Presumptions of law differ from presumptions of fact in the following respects:

(1) Presumptions of law derive their force from law; while presumptions of fact derive their force from logic. And though many of the former have intrinsic logical weight, being indeed derived from the latter, yet there are others which have none.

(2) A presumption of law applies to a class, the conditions of which are fixed and uniform; a presumption of fact applies to individual cases, the conditions of which are inconstant and fluctuating.

(3) Presumptions of law are drawn by the court, and in the absence of opposing evidence are conclusive for the party in whose favour they operate; presumptions of fact are drawn by the jury, who may disregard them however cogent.[373]

---

367. *Suresh Budharmal kalani v State of Maharashtra*, AIR 1998 SC 3258 : 1998 AIR SCW 3182 : (1998) 7 SCC 337.

368. *Ammal Chandra Dutt v IInd ADJ*, AIR 1989 SC 255 : (1989) 1 SCC 1.

369. *Phipson on Evidence*, 13th Edn, p 4.

370. *Vattacherukuru Village Panchayat v Nori Venkatarama Deckshuthulu*, 1991 Supp. 2 SCC 228.

371. *State v Bhera*, 1997 Cr LJ 1237 (Raj) see generally, *State of AP v Gangula Satya Murthy*, AIR 1997 SC 1588 : 1997 Cr LJ 774.

372. *Phipson*, 10th Edn, p 2012.

373. *Ibid*, *p* 2016.

Venkatramaiha J of the Supreme Court said:

> In the Indian Evidence Act, 1872, there are three cases where conclusive presumption may be drawn. They are sections 41, (judgments in *rem*) 112 and 113. These are cases where law regards that any amount of other evidence will not alter the conclusion to be reached when the basic facts are admitted or proved.[374]

As to statutory presumptions, see sections 118, 119–122, 137 of the Negotiable Instruments Act, 1881; sections 53 and 101 of the Transfer of Property Act, 1882; section 6 of the Land Acquisition Act (I of 1894). There are various other statutory presumptions.

The chief function of rebuttable presumptions of law is to determine on whom the burden of proof rests.[375]

[s 114.4] "Common course of natural events".—A presumption of facts is an assumption resulting from one's experience of the course of natural events of human conduct and human character. Such experience can be made use of in the ordinary course of life as well as in the business of courts.[376]

It is settled law that presumption of fact is a rule in law of evidence that a fact otherwise doubtful may be inferred from certain other proved facts. When inferring the existence of a fact from other set of proved facts, the court exercises a process of reasoning and reaches a logical conclusion as the most probable position. The above position is strengthened in view of section 114 of the Evidence Act, 1872. It empowers the court to presume the existence of any fact which it thinks likely to have happened. In that process, the courts shall have regard to the common course of natural events, human conduct, etc. in addition to the facts of the case. In these circumstances, the principles embodied in section 106 of the Evidence Act can also be utilised. This section is not intended to relieve the prosecution of its burden to prove the guilt of the accused beyond reasonable doubt, but it would apply to cases where the prosecution has succeeded in proving facts from which a reasonable inference can be drawn regarding the existence of certain other facts, unless the accused by virtue of his special knowledge regarding such facts, failed to offer any explanation which might drive the court to draw a different inference.[377]

This expression is appropriate in regard to such matters as the period of gestation or the continuance of life. The legitimacy of a child may have to be decided by reference to the term during which in the ordinary course of nature gestation may continue.

A case of adultery must be judged having due regard to the social conditions and the manner in which the parties are accustomed to live. If there is evidence enough to show that they had reasonable opportunities of having sexual intercourse in the

---

374. *Sodhi Transport Co v State of UP,* AIR 1986 SC 1099 : (1986) 2 SCC 486.

375. *Syad Akbar v Kant,* AIR 1979 SC 1848 : 1979 Cr LJ 1374 explaining the difference between the operation of a presumption of fact and that of law. *Krishna Murari Prasad v Mitar Singh,* AIR 1994 SC 489 : 1993 Supp (1) SCC 439, a fallacious statutory presumption.

376. *State of Karnataka v David Rozario,* 2002 Cr LJ 4127 (SC).

377. *Tulshiram Sahadu Suryawanshi v State of Maharashtra,* (2012) 10 SCC 373.

conditions of life in which they live for days together then the court may be justified in raising an inference of adultery.[378]

[s 114.5] "Human conduct".—As an example of an inference to be drawn from the conduct of a person the following is apposite. It is settled law that where property is entrusted to a servant, it is the duty of the servant to give a true account of what he does with the property so entrusted to him. If such servant fails to return the property or to account or gives an account which is shown to be false and incredible, it is ordinarily a reasonable inference that he has criminally misappropriated the property so entrusted to him and dishonestly converted it to his own use. In such cases the court is entitled to draw hostile inferences and presumptions from the action and statements of the servant.[379] Where one member of the family claimed that the property in question was his self-acquired property and, therefore, was not liable to partition, and the other members showed that he had no source of income and in fact, payment was out of joint family fund, the court said that a presumption arose that the property was for the benefit of the whole family and was liable to partition. No evidence to counteract this presumption was given.[380] In the matters of partnership, the managing partner having a fiduciary character is bound to protect the interest of other partners and to make full and correct disclosure of accounts to them and presumption of genuineness of books of account is not be available to him.[381] Where a Hindu male performed second marriage during the life time of the first wife before coming into force of the Hindu Marriage Act, 1955 and a child was born out of that wedlock, presumption of the second marriage being legal could be drawn.[382]

In a husband's suit against his wife for divorce on the ground of mental cruelty being caused by repeated accusations of adultery with his brother's wife, his father and a social friend testified to the accusations, the court, having regard to human conduct, said that the father, an old and respectable person, would not testify to a fact which would disgrace his family, unless it was true.[383]

Where one joint owner was permitted to be in possession for a long period of over 50 years and that too without any protest or objection, a presumption arose that he was the exclusive owner.[384] A statement in a judgment as to things happening before the judge is not ordinarily permitted to be questioned.[385] Where an examinee's answer showed correct answer to a mathematical problem without showing the detailed calculation work in solving the problem and he was charge sheeted on the ground that he could

---

378. *Devyani v Kantilal Gamanlal,* (1962) 65 Bom LR 24.

379. *Sona Meah v King Emperor,* (1924) 2 Ran 476, 477. See *Emperor v Abdul Gani,* (1925) 27 Bom LR 1373. See further *Bank of India v Y Maredi,* 1987 Cr LJ 722 : AIR 1987 SC 821, withdrawing money from another's account, presumption of intention.

380. *Packsyam Ammal v Pattu Ammal,* AIR 1999 Mad 383.

381. *Y Venkanna Chowdry v G Lakshmidevamma,* AIR 1994 Mad 140.

382. *Nera Bai v Pusia Bai,* 1996 AIHC 122 (MP).

383. *Kiran Mandal v Mohini Mandal,* AIR 1989 P&H 310. See also *State of UP v Chetram,* AIR 1989 SC 1543 : (1989) 2 SCC 425 : 1989 Cr LJ 1785, a lantern recovered from the room of murder was deposed by the witnesses to be carrying a wick and chimney, presumption that those things must have disappeared while in the property room. *Virendra Kumar Tripathy v Nirmala Devi,* AIR 2006 SC 1724 : (2006) 3 SCC 615, presumption as to reality of relationship drawn from expression employed in the ordinary course of social life.

384. *Khan Ali Md. Khan v Abdul Rahim,* AIR 1981 J&K 57.

385. *State v Orissa Oil Industries,* AIR 1982 Ori 245.

not have done so without using unfair means, it was held that such a presumption was not justified. The court said that having regard to human possibilities, one can as well imagine that the examinee in question might have learned his lessons by heart.[386] Where the accident was not caused due to collusion and the plea of failure of lights and foggy weather being the cause was not established, negligence on the part of the driver could be presumed.[387] Where in a suit for eviction on the ground of sub-letting, the tenant's plea that the other person was running a joint business with him was not substantiated, adverse inference could be drawn against the tenant and he could be evicted.[388] The conduct of the eyewitness, the daughter of the deceased in apprising her maternal uncles about the murder of her father and brother first and then going along with the *Sarpanch* to inform the police was held to be normal and natural and this was no ground for drawing adverse conclusions against her conduct.[389]

The petitioner claimed that his mother was in the train which met with an accident and died. The body was so badly charred that even DNA test was not possible. No concrete evidence was produced against this contention. So the court presumed that the woman must have been the mother of the petitioner. The court issued direction for issue of death certificate.[390]

[s 114.5.1] Void or illegal marriage.—Where by reason of the provisions in the Hindu Marriage Act, 1955 the second marriage, during the subsistence of the first, is void *ab initio*, there would be no presumption of validity even if the couple is living together as husband and wife and the society recognised them as such. Such marriage does not create any right of succession.[391]

[s 114.5.2] Presumption of divorce—Child Marriage.—When the child was eight years old, there was marriage. The marriage was never consummated. The wife left him immediately after and never came to live with him. Divorce was permissible in the community. The husband himself cohabited subsequently with another woman for a long period. The court said that in the light of such facts the marriage could be presumed to have been terminated.[392]

---

386. *Naresh Pal v High School and Intermediate Education Board*, AIR 1995 All 81.

387. *Krishna Kapoor v Himachal Road Transport Corp*, AIR 1994 NOC 308 (HP).

388. *Bansilal v Mohan Lal*, AIR 1995 Raj 167.

389. *State of Punjab v Surja Ram*, AIR 1995 SC 2413 : 1995 Cr LJ 4161. *Crystal Developers v Asha Lata Ghose*, AIR 2004 SC 4980 : (2005) 9 SCC 375, inferences must be drawn from a given set of facts and circumstances as they operate upon realistic diversity. *T Shankar Prasad v State of AP*, AIR 2004 SC 1242 : 2004 Cr LJ 884 : (2004) 3 SCC 753, factual or discretionary presumptions should not be used to draw yet another discretionary presumption unless there is a statutory compulsion. *State of MP v Sanjay Rai*, (2004) 10 SCC 570 : AIR 2004 SC 2174, opinion in standard test books may be used for help and guidance, though the court has to form its own opinion. The court's conclusion that the accused strangulated the victim arrived at only on the basis of text books on medical jurisprudence without getting the passages examined by experts was held to be not sustainable.

390. *N Suryanarayana Raju v South Central Railways*, AIR 2010 NOC 625 (AP).

391. *Swaminathan v Palaniammal*, AIR 2009 NOC 221 (Mad). To the same effect is the decision in *Parmanand v Jagrani*, AIR 2007 MP 242, no presumption of marriage when the wife started living with another during the life time of her husband. No custom to that effect in the community was shown. She could not be regarded on the wedded wife of the other person.

392. *Sobha Hymavathi Devi v Setti Gangadhara Swamy*, (2005) 2 SCC 244 : AIR 2005 SC 800.

[s 114.5.3] Blank signature.—A person who said that he put his signature on a blank paper was not taken to mean that he had executed a document. There could be no presumption or inference of that kind.[393]

[s 114.5.4] Condonation of adultery presumed.—Where the husband had alleged adultery against his wife and sought divorce but he had given his wife an opportunity to mend her ways and they both lived together thereafter, condonation of the offence of adultery by the husband could be presumed.[394]

[s 114.5.5] Presumption of mens rea.—There is a presumption that *mens rea* or guilty intent is an essential ingredient of offences created by the law maker. But the legislature may create an offence with absolute liability requiring neither *mens rea* nor any other state of mind.[395]

The number of injuries caused to the victim was not considered by the court to raise the presumption of intention to kill. But the Supreme Court said that taking into consideration the number of injuries and medical evidence corroborating ocular evidence, there could no doubt that the accused entertained the intention to kill.[396]

[s 114.6] "Public and private business".—A catalogue which embodies a statement of the firm regarding the price at which it is prepared to sell its articles is not hearsay and is admissible in evidence in proof of the price.[397] There is a presumption that every person in his private character does his duty and unless the contrary is proved, it is presumed that all things are rightly and regularly done.[398] The plaintiff could not prove that he had kept jewellery in his bank locker. The court said that hiring a locker is not entering into a contract of bailment, and that, even if it were a contract of bailment, it could not be said that the bank had not exercised proper care. The court was not to presume, in the absence of evidence that the lockers installed were not built according to specifications.[399]

An adoption deed which was also registered mentioned all the ceremonies which were performed for carrying out the adoption. It was not allowed to be challenged simply because the presiding pandit was not examined. Presumption as to the regularity of social acts and ceremonies prevailed.[400]

"There must be an assumption that whatever is published in the Government owned paper correctly represents the actual state of affairs relating to governmental business

---

393. *Kiutadan Velyaudhan Re,* AIR 2001 Ker 123.

394. *Arun Kumar Bhardwaj v Anila Bhardwaj,* AIR 1993 P&H 33.

395. *State v Jagdish Chandra Jena,* 1998 Cr LJ 4771 (Ori).

396. *Benjamin v State,* AIR 2008 SC 1383 : 2008 Cr LJ 1806 : (2008) 3 SCC 745.

397. *Hansanali v Darashah,* (1948) Nag 922.

398. *Zeenat v Prince of Wales Medical College,* AIR 1971 Pat 43; *Taneja Skins Co Pvt Ltd v Bharath Skins Corp,* AIR 2002 Delhi 179, goods delivered and taken delivery of at Delhi, the person selecting and taking delivery was an employee of the buyer. Since he was so acting openly, the presumption prevailed that he was an employee of the buyer at Delhi. The High Court of Delhi accordingly had jurisdiction.

399. *Atul Mehra v Bank of Maharashtra,* AIR 2003 P&H 11, the bank was the victim of robbery.

400. *Baru v Tejpal,* AIR 1998 All 230, *PS. Manoharan v State of TN,* AIR 1999 Mad 208, merely because a file in a Government office is destroyed, the genuineness and correctness of a certificate (certificate of permanent residence in the state) was not to be doubted unless there are other circumstances to rebut the presumption as to official acts.

until the same is successfully challenged and the real state of affairs is shown to be different from what is stated in the Government publication."[401]

[s 114.7] Illustrations not exhaustive.—The illustrations given under this section are not exhaustive. They are merely a few examples of this class of "natural" presumptions, and they do not exclude the other numerous cases in which such presumptions are constantly drawn. The court need not draw the presumption in any particular case. The word used is "may"; and wherever the informative facts proved over-balance the probability that the inference would be a sound and just one, the court will exercise its sound discretion in electing not to rest upon the presumption.[402] The illustrations are merely examples of circumstances in which certain presumptions may be good and other presumptions, of a similar kind in similar circumstances, may be made under the provisions of the section itself. Every one of the illustrations is followed by an exception.[403] There are several presumptions recognised in Hindu law, Mahammadan law, criminal law, etc., e.g., the original status of a Hindu family must be presumed to be joint and undivided; in a joint Hindu family the whole property of the family is joint estate; in the absence of express contract a Mahammadan dower is presumed to be prompt; every person is presumed to be acquainted with the law of the land; the accused is presumed to be innocent.

[s 114.8] Stolen property—*[Illustration (a)]*.—This illustration raises two presumptions, viz., that the person in possession of stolen goods soon after the theft is either (1) the thief, or (2) has received the goods knowing them to be stolen. The question as to which of the two presumptions is to be drawn will depend upon the facts of each particular case. This is a presumption which the court is not bound to draw but it is in the option of the court to draw it. But it does not, in any way, shift the burden of proof to the accused. The words "can account for its possession" do not mean that the accused must prove it positively that he received the property in the manner indicated by him. If the explanation given is not inherently improbable or palpably false and the court or the jury trying the case find it to be reasonably true, the adverse presumption shall be deemed to have been rebutted. The meaning of the words "reasonably true" appears to be that the explanation must be sufficient to cast a doubt on the guilt of the accused and in that case unless the prosecution proves beyond reasonable doubt that the accused received the property knowing it to be stolen, the benefit of the doubt shall go to him.[404]

---

401. *RS Nayak v AR Antulay,* (1986) 2 SCC 716 : AIR 1986 SC 2045 : 1986 Cr LJ 1922 per Ranganath Misra J. There is a presumption in favour of the contents of a Government publication *Pushpa Devi M Jatia v ML Wadhawan,* (1987) 3 SCC 367 : AIR 1987 SC 1748 : 1987 Cr LJ 1888, official acts of the holder of an existing office are recognised as valid.

402. Norton, 299; *Sabitri Sharma v State of Orissa,* 1987 Cr LJ 950 (Ori), proof of mere possession, no presumption. *Jogendra Singh v State of Orissa,* 1991 Cr LJ 2331 (Ori), driver of a truck not to be convicted on mere proof that he was carrying the goods. *Abdul Rashid v State of UP,* 1991 Cr LJ 3065 (All), property found on land adjoining that of the accused, no presumption.

403. *Emperor v Chhidda,* (1944) All 694.

404. *Emperor v Jagannath,* (1945) All 11; *Amar Singh v MP,* AIR 1982 SC 129 : 1982 Cr LJ 610 : (1982) 3 SCC 214 recovery of property shortly after dacoity; *Virumal v Gujarat,* AIR 1974 SC 334 : 1974 Cr LJ 277 : (1974) 3 SCC 565, stolen goods found possession within 2 days; *Thulia Kali v TN,* AIR 1973 SC 501 : 1972 Cr LJ 1296, a person from whose custody things are recovered must be examined. See generally, *Rameshkumar Soni v State,* 1997 Cr LJ 3418 (MP).

The presumption under this illustration arises only when the prosecution has established, (1) the ownership of the article in question, (2) theft of the article, and (3) its recent possession by the accused. Before a presumption can arise it must necessarily be proved that the goods found in possession of the accused had been stolen.[405] The words "receives" and "retains" are generally used together and though Illustration (a) expressly refers to dishonest receipt of stolen property, a presumption about dishonest retention of the stolen property may equally be made by virtue of that illustration even though in the charge it is stated that the accused dishonestly received (not retained) the stolen property.[406]

The Supreme Court has held that the presumption permitted to be drawn under this illustration has to be read along with the important time factor.[407] If the gap of time is too large, the presumption that the accused was concerned with the crime itself gets weakened. The presumption is stronger when the discovery of the fruits of crime is made immediately after the crime is committed.[408] The question what period is covered by the expression "soon after" depends upon the circumstances of each case. Where the articles stolen in dacoity were found in the possession of the accused "soon after" the commission of the offence, it was presumed under section 114 that the accused were dacoits and offence of dacoity was thereby proved.[409]

---

405. *Sohan Singh v State,* (1955) Patiala 601. See, *Shankar v State,* 1989 Cr LJ 1066 (Del), where this presumption was resorted to though only some of the robbed articles were recovered. *Guman v State of MP,* 1989 Cr LJ 1425 (MP), where the property recovered from the accused was that of a deceased person and there was no proof whether the same was removed before or after death, hence no proof of theft and no presumption. *Limbaji v State of Maharashtra,* AIR 2002 SC 491 : 2002 Cr LJ 590, test of recent possession, the accused came into possession of ornaments soon after the commission of robbery and murder, one article sold very next day to a shop keeper, other articles were discovered from places of concealment within a short time as disclosed by the accused. This created the presumption that the accused were themselves involved in the commission of robbery and murder. *Deivendran A v State of TN,* 1998 Cr LJ 814 : AIR 1998 SC 2821 in a case of murder and robbery, the main accused was convicted of murder, the other accused persons from whom only articles were recovered were not convicted for murder. In contrast to this is the decision in *Ronny v State of Maharashtra,* 1998 Cr LJ 1638 : AIR 1998 SC 1251, articles belonging to the family of the deceased were recovered from the possession of the accused soon after the incident of robbery and murder. The accused person could not explain his possession. Murder and robbery were found to be a part of the same transaction. The Supreme Court concluded that the accused and none else committed murder and robbery. *Ezhil v State of TN,* 2002 Cr LJ 2799 : AIR 2002 SC 2017, dead body was recovered from near a bridge in the village, articles belonging to him were recovered from the two accused persons who were moving in a car, very proximately to the time of death, blood stained articles recovered from the dicky of the car, no plausible explanation by them, presumption of robbery and murder against them. *State of Orissa v Dayanidhi Bisoi,* 2003 Cr LJ 123 (Ori), recovery of incriminating materials, presumption that the accused persons were responsible for murder and robbery.

406. *Bama v State,* (1958) Cut 131. *Praveen Kumar v State of Karnataka,* (2003) 12 SCC 199 : 2003 (4) Crimes 358 (SC), accused was in constructive possession of ornaments belonging to the deceased immediately after the murder, he offered no explanation, inference that the accused robbed the victim and committed murder in that process. *Gilbert Pereira v State of Karnataka,* (2004) 12 SCC 281 : AIR 2004 SC 4454, robbery and murder, gold chain worn by the deceased missing, presumption.

407. *Tulsiram v State,* AIR 1954 SC 1 : 1954 Cr LJ 236.

408. *Shivappa v State of Mysore,* AIR 1971 SC 196 : 1971 Cr LJ 260. *Thavaraj Pandian v State,* 2003 Cr LJ 2642 (Mad), recovery of stolen jewels from the accused one month after the incident. Presumption against the accused drawn. Mere length of time did not matter. The accused was not able to explain how the articles came into his possession.

409. *State of Karnataka v Rajan,* 1994 Cr LJ 1042 (Kant).

The various factors that have a bearing on this presumption have been restated by the Supreme Court thus: the presumption depends on the nature of the article, the manner of acquisition by the accused, the nature of evidence about its identification, the manner in which the accused dealt with it, the place and circumstances of recovery, the length of intervening period, the ability or otherwise of the accused to explain his possession.[410] Recovery in pursuance of information is an important piece of evidence.[411]

[s 114.8.1] Application of this presumption to other matters.—The presumption in this illustration is not confined to charges of theft, but extends to all charges, however, penal, not excluding even murder. Therefore where a person charged with dacoity is shown to have been in possession of part of the stolen property soon after the dacoity, it may be presumed that he was one of the dacoits or that he received the property knowing it to have been stolen at the dacoity. The principle of Illustration (a) applies not only to cases of ordinary theft but also to cognate offences such as dacoity and robbery. The presumption arising under this illustration extends to all charges, however penal, including murder.[412] Where a watch belonging to the deceased was recovered from the possession of the accused, it was held that, that by itself could not connect the accused with the offence of murder by invoking section 114.[413] Merely because death of the person occurred in police custody, an immediate inference of murder cannot be drawn against the police.[414]

The Supreme Court held in *Navalshankar Ishwarlal Dave v State of Gujarat,* that mutation of name in revenue record is not evidence of title.[415] The statements of police witnesses are entitled to the same weight and the same consideration which are attached to the statements of a member of the public. However, the impugned statement must inspire confidence to be relied upon.[416]

Where an officer was found in possession of money, the court applied the presumption that he must have accepted bribe.[417]

[s 114.8.2] Long stay in India and citizenship.—In a case before the Supreme Court[418] the facts were that the appellant had gone to Pakistan and acquired a Pakistani passport voluntarily. He obtained a visa to visit India. On the expiry of the visa, he neither went back nor sought extension of visa, but, instead went underground. There was no evidence to show that the Pakistani passport was obtained under compelling circumstances. It was held that a conclusive presumption could be raised that Pakistani citizenship was taken voluntarily. The claim for Indian citizenship was rejected. The court said that a long stay in a country and enrolment in voters' list does not confer any right on an alien to continue to stay in the country.

---

410. *Baiju v MP,* AIR 1978 SC 522 : 1978 Cr LJ 646 : 1978 Mad LJ (Cr) 300.
411. *Mohan Lal v Ajit Singh,* AIR 1978 SC 1183 : 1978 Cr LJ 1107.
412. *Ramasarup Singh v King-Emperor,* (1929) 9 Pat 606; *Queen-Empress v Sami,* (1890) 13 Mad 426; *Bandhan Sao,* (1960) Pat 361; *Dhyanigope v King-Emperor,* (1946) 25 Pat 262; *Pritam Singh v The State,* (1954) Pun 907.
413. *Surjit Singh v State of Punjab,* AIR 1993 SC 110 : 1993 Cr LJ 3901 : 1993 Supp (1) SCC 208.
414. *State v Balakrishnan,* 1992 Cr LJ 1872 (Mad).
415. AIR 1994 SC 1496 : 1994 Cr LJ 2170.
416. *Gurucharan Singh v State,* 1993 Cr LJ 1622 (Del).
417. *State of AP v Vasudeva Rao,* AIR 2004 SC 960 : (2004) 9 SCC 319 : 2004 Cr LJ 620.
418. *Bhanwaroo Khan v UOI,* AIR 2002 SC 1614.

[s 114.8.3] Possession.—Person driving a vehicle and others who were travelling in the vehicle from which two bags of poppy husk were seized, it could not be said about them that they were in possession of the contraband, though two of them were sitting on the two bags and both of them ran away on the vehicle being stopped for checking.[419]

[s 114.8.4] Purchaser of property already sold to another.—Where there was an oral agreement of sale and the fact of the agreement and payment of earnest money made under it were proved. The suit for specific performance was resisted on the ground of subsequent sale. It was held that the burden of proving that the subsequent buyer was a *bona fide* buyer without notice was illegally put on the plaintiff (the first buyer). The court said that an adverse inference had to be drawn against the subsequent buyer. The court accordingly granted the decree of specific performance.

[s 114.9] Accomplice—*[Illustration (b)]*.—An accomplice is one who is a guilty associate in crime. Where the witness sustains such a relation to the criminal act that he could be jointly indicted with the accused, he is an accomplice.[420] It is a rule of prudence and practice which practically amounts to a rule of law that the evidence of an accomplice ought not to be acted upon unless it is corroborated as against the particular accused in material respects.[421] Corroborative evidence is evidence which shows or tends to show that the story of the accomplice that the accused committed the crime is true, not merely that the crime has been committed, but that it was committed by the accused.[422] The confession of a co-accused cannot be used to corroborate the evidence of an accomplice.[423] The corroboration in the case of an accomplice must point to the identification of the person charged with the particular act with which the direct evidence connects him.[424] The corroboration in material particulars must be such as to connect or identify each of the accused with the offence.[425] The evidence of an accomplice ought to be regarded with suspicion. The degree of suspicion which will attach to it must vary according to the extent and nature of the complicity.[426]

Where the accomplice is not really a criminal but a spy or informer his evidence does not require any corroboration.[427]

The rule in this illustration is to be read along with section 133, and neither rule is to be ignored in the exercise of judicial discretion. In point of law an accomplice is a competent witness against an accused person (*vide* section 133). But great caution in weighing his testimony is dictated by prudence and reason. Unless the case is a very exceptional one, an accomplice's evidence should not be accepted as being sufficient.[428]

---

419. *Avtar Singh v State of Punjab,* AIR 2002 SC 3343 : 2002 Cr LJ 4330.

420. *Ramaswami Gounden v Emperor,* (1903) 27 Mad 271, 277.

421. *Emperor v Mataprasad Shivharak,* (1942) 45 Bom LR 64; *State v Ram Singh,* (1954) Cut 309.

422. *Noor Ahmad v Emperor,* (1933) 62 Cal 527.

423. *Provincial Government, Central Provinces and Berar v Raghuram,* (1942) Nag 749.

424. *Emperor v Kalwa,* (1926) 48 All 409.

425. *Rebati Mohan Chakravarty v Emperor,* (1928) 56 Cal 150. See also *Rampal Pithwa Rahidass v State of Maharashtra,* 1994 Cr LJ 2320 : 1994 Supp (2) SCC 73 (SC) and *S.C. Bahri v State of Bihar,* AIR 1994 SC 2020 : 1994 Cr LJ 3271.

426. *Srinivas Mall Bairoliya v Emperor,* (1947) 49 Bom LR 688 (PC).

427. *Queen-Empress v Bastin,* (1897) PJLB 365, *contra, Mi The U v Queen-Empress,* (1881) SJLB 146.

428. *Rajagopal,* (1944) Mad 308 (FB).

In England it is regarded as the settled course of practice not to convict a prisoner, excepting, under very special circumstances, upon the un-corroborated testimony of an accomplice.[429] The corroboration which the common law requires is corroboration in some material particular tending to show that the accused committed the crime charged. It is not enough that the corroboration shows the witness to have told the truth in matters unconnected with the guilt of the accused.[430] See comment on section 133, *infra.*

One accomplice cannot corroborate another. However, if several accomplices simultaneously and without previous concert give a consistent account of the crime implicating the accused, the court may accept the several statements as corroborating each other, but it must be established that the several statements of accomplices were given independently and without any previous concert.[431]

It is now well settled that the minimum amount of corroboration required to make it safe to act on the testimony of an approver is that the evidence must be corroborated not only as to the *corpus delicti* but also as to the identity of the accused persons. The corroborative evidence must show or tend to show that the story of the approver that the accused committed the crime is true; in other words, the corroborative evidence must be such which confirms not only the evidence that the crime has been committed but also the evidence that the accused committed that crime.[432]

In a case where there are a large number of accused it is essential that the evidence of an accomplice be corroborated by evidence which implicates each of the accused individually. Independent evidence which corroborates the evidence of an accomplice so far as one of several co-accused is concerned is not necessarily evidence which corroborates the statement of the accomplice so far as the other accused are concerned.[433]

The Bombay High Court has laid down the following four principles with regard to the nature and extent of corroboration:

(1) that it is not necessary that there should be independent confirmation of every material particular,

(2) that independent evidence must not only make it safe to believe that the crime was committed, but in some way reasonably connect or tend to connect the accused with it by confirming in some material particular the testimony of the accomplice or complainant that the accused committed the crime,

(3) that the corroboration must come from independent sources, and

(4) that the corroboration need not be direct evidence that the accused committed the crime—it is sufficient if it is merely circumstantial evidence of his connection with crime.[434]

---

429. *Reg v Gallagher,* (1875) 13 Cox 61.
430. *Rex v Baskerville,* (1916) 2 KB 658.
431. *Hussain Umar v Dalipsinghji,* AIR 1970 SC 45 : 1970 Cr LJ 9.
432. *Ram Singh v The Crown,* (1950) Pun 209; *Bhima Swa v State,* (1956) Cut 195.
433. *Kedar v Rex,* (1949) All 152.
434. *Raju v State of Mysore,* (1953) 55 Bom LR 191.

In a case of corruption the accused offered the Minister of State an amount of Rs 3 lakhs for certain favours and the Minister gave them the impression that he was willing to consider their offer but he informed the Anti-Corruption Bureau (ACB) and filed a complaint whereupon a trap was laid by ACB. It was held that unlike other normal corruption cases, where the complainants are members of public and the complaints are against the public servants, the complainant could not be equated with the position of an accomplice and in such unusual cases the accused could be convicted even on uncorroborated testimony of the complainant.[435]

[s 114.9.1] Rape cases.—The Supreme Court of India has held that though a woman who has been raped is not an accomplice, her evidence has been treated by the courts on somewhat similar lines, and the rule which requires corroboration of such evidence save in exceptional circumstances has now hardened into law. The view that though corroboration should ordinarily be required in the case of a grown-up woman, it is unnecessary in the case of a child of tender years is not correct. The true position is that in every case of this type the rule about the advisability of corroboration should be present to the mind of the judge; whether corroboration is unnecessary is a question of fact in every case.[436] As a rule of prudence the court normally looks for some corroboration of her testimony so as to satisfy its conscience that she is telling the truth and that the person accused of rape on her has not been falsely implicated.[437] Where in a prosecution for rape there was variance on material points between FIR and statements made during trial and the eyewitnesses denied any such occurrence so that the only evidence on record was the uncorroborated testimony of the prosecutrix, the conviction was held to be not proper.[438]

The Supreme Court has spoken thus on the matter:[439] A prosecutrix of a sex offence cannot be put on par with an accomplice. She is in fact a victim of the crime. The Evidence Act nowhere says that her evidence cannot be accepted unless it is corroborated in material particulars. She is undoubtedly a competent witness under section 118 and her evidence must receive the same weight as is attached to an injured person in cases of physical violence. The same degree of care and caution must be taken in the evaluation of her evidence as in the case of an injured complainant or witness and no more. What is necessary is that the court must be alive to and conscious of the fact that it is dealing with the evidence of a person who is interested in the outcome of the charge levelled by her. If the court keeps this in mind and feels satisfied that it can act on the evidence of the prosecutrix, there is no rule of law or practice incorporated in the Evidence Act similar to Illustration (b) to section 114 which requires the court to look for corroboration. If for some reason the court is hesitant to place implicit reliance on the testimony of the prosecutrix, it may look for evidence which may lend assurance to her testimony short of corroboration required in the case of an accomplice.

---

435. *CR Mehta v State of Maharashtra,* 1993 Cr LJ 2863 (Bom).

436. *Rameshwar v State of Rajasthan,* (1952) SCR 377 : AIR 1952 SC 54; *Bhownri v The State,* (1952) Raj 817.

437. *Gurcharan Singh v State of Haryana,* AIR 1972 SC 2661 : 1973 Cr LJ 179. But corroboration can be waived in the light of apparent circumstances, *Krishan Lal v Haryana,* AIR 1980 SC 1252 : 1980 Cr LJ 926; *State of Maharashtra v CK Jain,* 1990 Cr LJ 889 : AIR 1990 SC 658, rape by police officer, no corroboration was considered necessary.

438. *Ashok Kumar v State of UP,* 1991 Cr LJ 2859 (All).

439. *State of Maharashtra v Chandraprakash Kewalchand Jain,* (1990) 1 SCC 550 : AIR 1990 SC 658 : 1990 Cr LJ 889.

The nature of evidence required to lend assurance to the testimony of the prosecutrix must necessarily depend on the facts and circumstances of each case.

The same approach was adopted in *Sheikh Zakir v State of Bihar.*[440] The court said:

> If a conviction is based on the evidence of a prosecutrix without any corroboration, it will not be illegal on that sole ground. But in the case of a grown-up or married woman, it is always safe to insist on corroboration, which can be sought from either direct or circumstantial evidence or both.

[s 114.9.2] Rape in Custody.—This line of development has been applied to rape in custody. A teenage girl was raped by a police officer, Ahmadi J observed:[441]

> A prosecutrix of a sex offence cannot be put on par with an accomplice. She is in fact a victim of the crime. The same degree of care and caution must attach in the evaluation of her evidence as in the case of an injured complainant. What is necessary is that the court must be alive to and conscious of the fact that it is dealing with the evidence of a person who is interested in the outcome of the charge levelled by her. If the court keeps this in mind and feels satisfied that it can act on the evidence of the prosecutrix, there is no rule of law or practice incorporated in the Evidence Act similar to the illustration (6) to s. 114 which requires (the court) to look for corroboration. If for some reason the court is hesitant to place implicit reliance on the testimony of the prosecutrix it may look for evidence which may lend assurance to her testimony short of corroboration required in the case of an accomplice.

[s 114.9.3] Bigamy.—A mere presumption or admission by the accused is not sufficient to prove bigamy. Requisite form and performance of necessary ceremonies should affirmatively be proved.[442] A man married second wife while the first was living. The second marriage took place in 1950 when polygamy was permissible. She was driven out from the house 35 years after their marriage. The witnesses to marriage and other documents pertaining to marriage could not be produced and the husband denied marriage. It was held that on the basis of long cohabitation and numerous other documents, presumption regarding the second marriage could be drawn.[443]

[s 114.10] Presumption as to consideration—*[Illustration (c)]*.—The presumption on which this illustration is founded is in accordance with the maxim *omnia praesumuntur rite, esse acta,* i.e., all things are presumed to be done in due form. The principle of the maxim "has, in many instances, been recognised in support of the solemn acts of even *private* person...Thus, if an act can only be lawful after the performance of some prior act, due performance of that prior act will be presumed. Again, although in the case of contracts not under seal, a consideration must in general be averred and proved, yet bills of exchange and promissory notes enjoy the privilege of being presumed, *prima facie,* to be founded on a valuable consideration. The law raises this presumption in favour of these instruments, partly because it is important to preserve their negotiability intact, and partly because the existence of a valid consideration may reasonably be inferred from the solemnity of the instruments themselves, and the deliberate mode in which they

---

440. *Sheikh Zakir v State of Bihar,* AIR 1983 SC 911 : 1983 Cr LJ 1285.
441. *State of Maharashtra v CK Jain,* AIR 1990 SC 658 at 664-665 : 1990 Cr LJ 889.
442. *Subir Kumar Kundu v State of West Bengal,* 1992 Cr LJ 1502 (Cal).
443. *A Bal Reddy v Saraswathi,* 1994 Cr LJ 1124 (AP), the case was for maintenance.

are executed.[444] An effect of the presumption is that the plaintiff has not to produce account books to substantiate consideration. The burden is upon the other party.[445]

The explanation to this illustration speaks of "a man of business," which in its well-known popular sense must mean a man habitually engaged in mercantile transactions or trade.[446]

[s 114.10.1] Presumption under this section and under Negotiable Instruments Act.— Sections 118 and 119 of the Negotiable Instruments Act, 1881 lay down certain other presumptions. The Lahore High Court has held that section 118 of the Negotiable Instruments Act, 1881 replaces the explanation attached to this illustration and therefore the rule laid down in this illustration is modified by section 118. What was permissible in the Evidence Act was converted into a statutory obligation in the Negotiable Instruments Act, 1881. While illustration

(c) is confined to the acceptance or endorsement of a bill of exchange, section 118 of the Negotiable Instruments Act, 1881 applies to the making or drawing of it also.[447] The Madras High Court has held that the difference between this section and section 118 of the Negotiable Instruments Act, 1881, consists only in this, that under the first, the court has a discretion to make the presumption or not, whereas, under the second, the court is bound to start with the presumption; but once the presumption is made there is no difference between the two cases, in the manner of displacing the presumption or disproving the "presumed" fact. Any presumption as to *quantum* of consideration as distinguished from the mere existence of consideration, has accordingly to be drawn, not by virtue of section 118 of the Negotiable Instruments Act, 1881 or even under this section, but only from the recitals, if any that the instrument may contain. As to such recitals, it has long been established that being *prima facie* evidence against the parties to the instruments, they may operate to shift on to the party pleading the contrary the burden of rebutting the inference raised by them. But the *weight* due to recitals may vary according to circumstances and, in particular circumstances, the burden of rebutting them may become very light, especially when the court is not satisfied that the transaction was honest and *bona fide*.[448] Section 118 of the Negotiable Instruments Act, 1881 enacts a special rule of evidence which operates between parties to the instrument or persons claiming under them in a suit or proceeding relating to the bill of exchange and does not affect the rule contained in this section in cases not falling within section 118 of the Negotiable Instruments Act, 1881.[449]

A bill of exchange given to a bank was dishonoured. The bank did not give to the drawer (defendant) notice of dishonour within reasonable time. The bank was withholding evidence as to the date of dishonour. The notice being not within reasonable time, the bank was not entitled to compensation.[450]

---

444. *Taylor*, 12th Edn, section 148, p 139.

445. *Gulab Chand v Satya Vrat*, AIR 1983 SC 54. *State of Haryana v Manoj Kumar*, AIR 2010 SC 1779 : (2010) 4 SCC 350, the fact that the sale deed was executed under the decree of a court was held to be not a ground to presume the genuineness of the sale price mentioned in the deed.

446. *Ningawa v Bharmappa*, (1897) 23 Bom 63, 66.

447. *Bannu Mal v Munshi Ram*, (1935) 17 Lah 107, 113.

448. *Narasamma v Veeraju*, (1934) 58 Mad 841, 850.

449. *Official Receiver v Abdul Shakoor*, AIR 1965 SC 920 : (1965) 1 SCR 254.

450. *Indian Bank v Booruga Nagaiah Rajanna*, AIR 2000 AP 289.

[s 114.10.1.1] ***Presumption under sections 138 and 139, NI Act.***—In the context of the dishonour of a cheque a presumption has to be drawn under section 139 of the Negotiable Instruments Act, 1881 that the cheque was issued for discharge of debt or liability of the drawer to the payee. This is a legal presumption and, therefore, it has to be drawn in every case. The presumption is rebuttable. The evidence which has to be adduced in rebuttal must not be merely a plausible explanation. Some evidence in proof of the explanation would be necessary.[451]

Dealing with the use of phrases *"until the contrary is proved"* in section 118 and *"unless the contrary is proved"* in section 139 of Negotiable Instruments Act, 1881 read with definitions of *"may presume"* and *"shall presume"* as given in section 4 of Evidence Act, it has been explained by Supreme Court that presumptions to be raised under both the provisions are rebuttable. When a presumption is rebuttable, it only points out that when the party against whom the presumption is drawn produces evidence fairly and reasonably tending to show that real fact is not as presumed, the purpose of the presumption is over.[452]

[s 114.10.1.2] ***Notice of demand.***—It is not necessary that the notice of dishonour and demand should be sent by registered post only. It can also be sent under certificate of posting. It has been held that once notice is sent by registered post by correctly addressing to the drawer of the cheque, the service of notice is deemed to have been effected. But, the drawer is at liberty to rebut this presumption.[453] The notice sent by speed post is presumed to have been served even if it was not sent by registered post.[454]

[s 114.11] Continuity of things—*[Illustration (d)]*.—This illustration is founded on the presumption which exists in favour of continuance or immutability.

If a thing or a state of things is shown to exist, an inference of its continuity within a reasonably proximate time both forwards and backwards may sometimes be drawn. The rule that the presumption of continuance may operate retrospectively also has been recognised in India. How far the presumption may be drawn backwards and forwards depends upon the nature of the thing and surrounding circumstances.[455]

The ordinary legal presumption is that things remain in their original state.[456] If a person is shown at one time to be a member of a joint Hindu family, it will be held under this illustration that he never separated at all unless the contrary is proved. Property which was shown to be ancestral would continue to be so until the contrary is shown.[457] But where the property was shown to be in the name of a co-sharer, there was no presumption that it was ancestral property.[458] The name of the husband

---

451. *Hiten P Dalal v Bratindranath Banerjee,* 2001 Cr LJ 4647 (SC) at p 4653; *Malanbai Ratnaparkhi v Govind R Motade,* 2002 Cr LJ 1188 (Bom) presumption of service of notice, sent by post at correct address. *Suresh Kanhaiyalal Prajapat v Manoj Balkrishna Bansal,* 2003 Cr LJ (NOC) 94 (MP), no such presumption was raised where the address was not correct. The court also said that an inference of delivery was not to be made from the remark that the "addressee was not found".

452. *Kumar Exports v Sharma Carpets,* (2009) 2 SCC 513.

453. *N Parameswaran Unni v G Kannan,* AIR 2017 SC 1681 : (2017) 5 SCC 737.

454. *Jaswant Kaur v Additional District Judge Court, Faizabad,* 2017 (5) ADJ 72 : 2017 (123) ALR 104.

455. *Ambika Prasad v Ram Ekbal Rai,* AIR 1966 SC 605 : (1966) 1 SCR 758.

456. *Mussammat Jariutool-Butool v Mussumat Hoseinee Begum,* (1867) 11 Moo Ind App 194, 209.

457. *Chito Mahto v Lila Mahto,* AIR 1991 Pat 186.

458. *Raghunath Tiwari v Ramakant Tiwari,* AIR 1991 Pat 145.

was recorded as a tenant in revenue records and after his death his wife's name and thereafter she was recorded as a mortgagee. Change of revenue entries will not raise a presumption of cessation of the wife's tenancy and it will revert to her on redemption of mortgage.[459]

Sections 107–109 deal with particular applications of the principle of which this illustration is the general expression.

[s 114.12] Judicial and official acts—*[Illustration (e)]*.—The rule embodied in the illustration flows from the maxim *omnia praesumuntur rite et solemniter esse acta,* i.e., all acts are presumed to have been rightly and regularly done. "The true principle intended to be conveyed by the rule, *"omnia praesumuntur rite et solemniter esse acta,"*...seems to be, that there is a general disposition in court of justice to uphold official, judicial, and other acts, rather than to render them inoperative, and with this view, where there is general evidence of acts having been legally and regularly done, to dispense with proof of circumstances, strictly speaking essential to the validity of those acts, and by which they were probably accompanied in most instances, although in other the assumption rests solely on grounds of public policy".[460] The presumption is in favour of the constitutional validity of an Act passed by the parliament.[461]

The court cited the following passage from Herbert Broom's *A Selection of Legal Maxims*:[462]

> In these cases the ordinary rule is that everything is presumed to be duly and rightly performed until the contrary is shown. The following may be mentioned as general presumptions of law illustrating this maxim: that a man, in fact acting in a public capacity, was properly appointed and is duly authorised so to act; that in the absence of proof to the contrary, credit should be given to public officers who have acted *prima facie* within the limits of their authority, for having done so with honesty and discretion.

Where a statement appears in the judgment of a court that a particular thing happened or did not happen before it, it ought not ordinarily to be permitted to be challenged by a party unless both the parties to the litigation agree that the statement is wrong, or the court itself admits that the statement is erroneous.[463] Whether a presumption should or should not be made must depend upon the particular circumstances of each

---

459. *Ram Rakhi v Atti,* AIR 1993 HP 137. *T Siddoshi v Deputy Commissioner,* AIR 2001 Kant 297, change in mutation of records in favour of a partnership firm by a sale deed does not affect the legality of the possession of the person who was already in possession. *S. Venkatappa v Narayanappa,* AIR 2001 SC 2148, occupancy rights of the person proved to be in possession not allowed to be affected by the declaration in the sale deed that vacant possession was being given to the buyer.

460. BEST, 12th Edn, section 353, p 312; *Narendra Lal Khan v Jogi Hari,* (1905) 32 Cal 1107, 1121; *Emperor v Leslie Gwill,* (1944) 47 Bom LR 431 : (1945) Bom 681. *Narayan v Maharashtra,* AIR 1977 SC 183 : (1977) 1 SCC 133, presumption as to public purpose in acquisition. *Kashmiri Lal v Punjab,* AIR 1984 P&H, 87, notification is different from order. The latter does not amount to public knowledge. *Achchey Lal v VC Gpr. University,* AIR 1985 All 1, admissions beyond prescribed limit can be questioned. *Twarku v Surti,* AIR 1997 HP 76, entries in a family Register maintained in accordance with Rules created the presumption of correctness as they were made and maintained by public officers in due discharge of their duties.

461. *Harpal Singh v Union Territory, Chandigarh,* AIR 1978 P & H 68 at 71.

462. Page 642 (1939 Edn).

463. *Bank of Bihar v Mahabir Lal,* AIR 1964 SC 377 : (1964) 2 SCJ 611; *State v Orissa Oil Industries,* AIR 1982 Ori 245.

case.[464] This illustration only means that, if an official act is proved to have been done, it will be presumed to have been regularly done,[465] but it does not raise any presumption that an act was done for which there is no evidence and proof. When the Government accords sanction, section 114 Illustration (e) of the Evidence Act raises a presumption that the official acts were regularly performed. The burden is heavier on the accused to rebut that statutory presumption.[466] Neither motives can be presumed nor bad faith or abuse of power.[467] The appointment of teachers being governed by statutory regulations is an official act and a presumption of regularity attaches to it.[468]

An order was passed by a magistrate in the course of performing his official duty by which a prosecution was sanctioned under the Prevention of Corruption Act, 1988. Presumption of validity attached to the order. Examination of the magistrate was not necessary.[469]

Where under an Act certain things are required to be done before any liability attaches to any person in respect of any right or obligation, it is for the person who alleges that that liability has been incurred to prove that the things prescribed

---

464. *Harkishan Das v The Crown,* (1943) 25 Lah 245 (FB). Things forming part of judicial records, such as a person's signature upon a plaint filed in a court, are presumed to be true, *Shahnaz v Dr Vijay,* AIR 1995 Bom 30, after a divorce decree, the allegation by wife that her signature on petition was obtained by force was not entertained.

465. *Pratap Singh v Manmohan Dey,* AIR 1966 SC 1931 : (1966) 3 SCR 663; *MB State v Beharamji D & Co,* AIR 1958 MP 71; *Krishna Murthy v Abdul Shubhan,* AIR 1965 (Mys) 128; *State of Rajasthan v Shamsher Singh,* AIR 1985 SC 1082 : 1985 Cr LJ 1348, opinion expressed by a Board under MISA; *Sone Lal v UP,* AIR 1978 SC 1142 : 1978 Cr LJ 1122, regular entries in public documents, allegation of fabrication and delay in lodging FIR; *Shankaranlingappa v Nanji Gowda,* AIR 1981 Kant 78, entry in record of rights. *Laxmibai v Thoreppa,* AIR 1982 Kant 248, entries in death register. *Ashim Kumar Dutta v State of WB,* 1989 Cr LJ 1797, presumption that a sanction under the Prevention of Food Adulteration Act, 1954 for prosecution must have been granted after due consideration. *Mathukutty v State of Kerala,* 1988 Cr LJ 898 : AIR 1988 Ker 60, presumption that sampling was properly done. *Nirmal Kumar v State,* 1987 Cr LJ 46 (MP), in spite of the presumption of proper sample, the court has to form opinion whether it was really so. *Revta v State,* 1987 Cr LJ 1967 (MP), proceedings proper, presumption. *Madhu Khanna v Administrator, Delhi,* 1987 Cr LJ 318 : AIR 1987 SC 48, presumption that the confirming authority considered all relevant material. *Food Inspector v V Velayudhan,* 1987 Cr LJ 1137 (Ker), Municipal Commissioner authorised by notification under the Act to act as a Local Authority, presumption of authority. *Kartar Singh v DDA,* AIR 2000 Delhi 184, demarcation of plot of land, Revenue Officials are supposed to be conversant with relevant rules, demarcation was done in the performance of official acts, presumed correct, objections would have to be substantiated with evidence. *Kamal Singh v State of UP,* AIR 1998 All 220, cancellation of mining lease on the ground that the area fell within the forest area. There was expert report to that effect. Presumption prevailed. No evidence to the contrary produced.

466. *MS Reddy v State Inspector of Police, AC.B, Nellore,* 1993 Cr LJ 558 (AP). *Ranganathan v State,* 1996 Cr LJ 2041 (Mad). *Devender Pal Singh v State NCT of Delhi,* 2002 Cr LJ 2034 (SC), TADA, 1987, confessional statement, the mere statement that the requisite procedures and safeguards were not observed or that the statement was taken under duress or coercion, was held to be of no consequence. There is the presumption that a person acts honestly which applies as much in favour of police officers as to others. The contrary must be proved. *Kshudiram Pal v West Bengal Financial Corpn.,* AIR 1998 Cal 52, notice issued by an officer valid delegation of power, presumption as to official acts applied.

467. *SR Bommai v UOI,* AIR 1994 SC 1918 : (1994) 3 SCC 1.

468. *Naseem Bano v State of UP,* AIR 1993 SC 2592 : 1993 Supp (4) SCC 46 : (1993) 4 Serv LR 803, the appointees were not qualified for promotion and therefore, the presumption was that the appointment was not on promotion.

469. *State of MP v Jiyalal,* AIR 2010 SC 1451 : (2009) 15 SCC 72.

in the Act have been actually done. No presumption can be made in favour of the things prescribed by the Act having been done. If, for example, publication of a notice was essential under an Act in order to bind a person, such publication must be distinctly proved.[470] But the Privy Council held that in the absence of evidence to the contrary it has to be presumed that the procedure laid down in a statute was duly followed and that proper statutory notice was given.[471] Where a warrant contains a preamble that the requirement of a section of an Act has been fulfilled, a presumption arises under this illustration that the officer issuing the warrant has performed his duty correctly.[472] The Calcutta High Court has held that the Privy Council has virtually overruled the decisions which laid down that it is not sufficient for the purpose of proving service of notice to rely on the presumption arising out of this section.[473]

A registered sale deed carries the presumption of genuineness. The burden of proving that it is not so, lies on the person who denies its genuineness.[474]

The mere fact that the impugned order of suspension did not contain a recital that the Governor was satisfied that it was either necessary or desirable to place the delinquent under suspension did not render the said order invalid.[475]

Entries in *Record of Rights* are presumed to be correct. Such record stands on a different footing than village papers or mutation papers. The law does not attach so much sanctity to such papers as it does to Record of Rights. It has to be presumed to be correct. Where any party alleges that an entry in the Record of Rights was not correct, the burden would lie on him to prove it.[476]

A presumption arises under this section as to legality and correctness of a court's proceedings.[477] Factual recitals or observations made in a judgment or order are taken

---

470. *Ashanullah Khan Bahadur v Trilochan Bagchi,* (1886) 13 Cal 197; *Walvekar v Emperor,* (1926) 53 Cal 718.

471. *Jitendra Nath Ghose v Monmohan Ghose,* (1930) 57 IA 214 : 58 Cal 301. See *Balakrishna Pillai v State of Kerala,* AIR 1992 Ker 136, an endorsement by village officer that the substance of the notification of acquisition of land was announced in the locality was presumed to be true until rebutted.

472. *Emperor v Savlaram Kashinath,* (1947) 49 Bom LR 798.

473. *Sasi Sekhar Sen Biswas v Maharaja Bir Bikram Kishore Manikya,* (1931) 35 Cal WN 1239. *Lumbini Baruah v Cotton College,* AIR 1997 Gau 87, the application of the candidate was duly processed and scrutinised through sub-committee, which recommended her name for admission on being fully satisfied about eligibility, presumption applicable to performance of official acts arose. The candidate pursued her course for a whole year. Withholding of her result for verification of eligibility was held to be not proper. The candidate had done nothing wrong and was not trying for any undue advantage.

474. *Govind Anant Goltekar v Dasharath Deoba Goltekar,* AIR 2006 Bom 174.

475. *State of Haryana v Hari Ram Yadaw,* AIR 1994 SC 1262 : (1994) 2 SCC 277.

476. *Janadan Rai v Mandeo Rai,* AIR 1997 Pat 124.

477. *Munshi Raghubir Singh v Rani Rajeshwari Devi,* (1933) 9 Luck 90; *Sheikh Ala Baksh v Thakur Durga Baksh Singh,* (1933) 9 Luck 162; *Laikunnissah v Hari Pd,* AIR 1980 All 63, Court auction sale, presumption of validity. *Rama Krishna v Lakshminaryayana,* AIR 1984 Kant 45, presumption that all official acts are in accordance with proper order. *Rudnap Export-Import v Estern Associates Ltd,* AIR 1984 Del 20, presumption of validity of documents authenticated by a foreign judge. *Vijaya College Trust v Kumta Co-op Arecanut Sales Society Ltd,* AIR 1995 Kant 35, an order of attachment before judgment does not create a presumption that the attachment must in fact have been carried out.

to be correct unless rebutted.[478] Where the special appeals were filed under section 18 of the Rajasthan High Court Ordinance and Rule 134 of the Rules for the High Court of Judicature for Rajasthan by the Additional Advocate General, it may be presumed that he was duly authorised to file the said special appeals.[479]

"A presumption has to be drawn under section 114(e) that the competent authority must have before it the necessary materials which *prima facie* establish the commission of the offence charged and that the competent authority had applied its mind before tendering the consent. All the reasons for the consent order need not be set out."[480]

Presumption of regularity of acts extends to testamentary documents.[481] It also extends to appointments and removals. They are also presumed to have been effected in due observance of applicable Rules and Regulations.[482] But the Government has, in the first instance, to justify its action either by proper pleadings or by producing records. A termination was declared to be invalid because the Government's failure to do so.[483]

Entries in Collector's books are presumed to be correct having regard to Illustrations (e) and (f).[484] A report signed by a Public Analyst under the Prevention of Food Adulteration Act, 1954 is, without any other proof, admissible in evidence under this clause.[485] The confidential reports submitted by the medical examiners of the Life Insurance Corporation will have to be accepted as true.[486] First Information Report is a public document.[487] The certificate by Board of Censor is relevant but does not create a presumption that sections 292 and 293 of IPC are not violated.[488] Where the entries in the record of rights maintained under the Punjab Land Revenue Act, 1887 did not

---

478. *State of Maharashtra v Admane Anita Moti,* AIR 1995 SC 350 : (1994) 6 SCC 109; *Krishna Rani Kwatra v DDA,* AIR 1999 Del 194, auction of shops, plaintiff's bid accepted for a shop, cancellation afterwards on the ground that the vice-chairman had not accepted the bid. Cancellation not allowed. Presumption that official acts must have been performed properly.

479. *Regional Transport Authority, Jodhpur v Sita Ram,* AIR 1993 Raj 76. Proof of notification and its publication in the locality under the Land Acquisition Act, 1894, evidence of peon that he affixed the copy at a conspicuous place in the locality, enough, *Ajai Krishan v UOI,* AIR 1996 SC 2677 : (1996) 10 SCC 721.

480. *State of Bihar v PP Sharma,* AIR 1961 SC 1260 : 1991 Cr LJ 1438. *Zorawar Singh v Sarwan Singh,* AIR 2002 SC 1711 : (2002) 4 SCC 460, a document was filed with an authority, it returned the document without making any entry in any official record. The plea as to filing was belatedly raised. Authority not examined. Presumption as to correctness of official acts could not be applied to such a document.

481. *Satipada Chatterjee v Annakali Debya,* (1955) 1 Cal 94.

482. *Naseem Bano v State of UP,* AIR 1993 SC 2592 : 1993 Supp (4) SCC 46.

483. *Vijay Narain Singh v Supdt. of Police,* 1994 SCC (L & S) 796 : (1994) 27 ATC 405.

484. *Mahomed Solaiman v Birendra Chandra Singh,* (1922) 50 Cal 243: 50 IA 247; *Emperor v Shib Charan,* (1938) All 386; *Karewwa v Hessensab Khansaheb,* AIR 2002 SC 504, presumption as to correctness of entries in revenue record, this presumption can be rebutted by leading evidence. Such entries do not stand rebutted by a mere denial statement made in the written statement.

485. *State v Chhotekhan,* AIR 1970 MP 29 (FB); *Lacho Devi v State,* 1991 Cr LJ 2793 (Del); the fact that the secret information was not recorded before the raid is not material, but the authorities have to show observance of proper procedure for sampling and no tampering till laboratory test. On the report of Public Analyst and Food Inspector, Competent Authority issued order for prosecution, Court could draw presumption that the said authority applied its mind before tendering "consent", Senior Food Inspector, *Ananthapur v Ravuru Subbaiah,* 1992 Cr LJ 2289 (AP), **following** *Bihar v PP Sharma,* AIR 1991 SC 1260 : 1991 Cr LJ 1438.

486. *LI Corp v B Chandravathamma,* AIR 1971 AP 41.

487. *Krishan Ram v Chuni Lal,* AIR 1981 P&H 120.

488. *Raj Kapoor v State (Delhi Admn.),* AIR 1980 SC 258 : 1980 Cr LJ 202.

show that a particular chunk of Brick-earth vested in the State, it was held that it created an irrebuttable presumption that it vested in the owner of the land.[489] Showing mutation as a sale in a land record does not create a presumption that the entry was correct. No proof of sale being the entry was rejected as being of any value.[490] Where the Magistrate has not recorded in the order-sheet the ascertainment of intactness of seal and mark and non-tampering of signature of the accused on the sample received from the Local Health Authority before sending it to the Director of Central Food Laboratory which was not challenged before the Magistrate, presumption of regular performance of judicial act could be drawn.[491] National Savings Certificates are the property of the Post Office and when the Post Master pledged them, the presumption would be that the same had been done properly.[492]

[s 114.12.1] Legislature.—Courts always presume that the legislature inserted every part of the statute for a purpose and legislative intention is that every part of it should have effect. This presumption is equally applicable to rule making authorities.[493]

The general presumption available for a statute cannot be invoked for an executive action.[494]

[s 114.12.2] Notified order of Government.—The natural presumption is that this official act of the Government has been done after due application of mind.[495]

[s 114.12.2.1] ***Rules and Regulations made under Statute.***—Rules or regulations made under a statute become a part of the statute. They have the same statutory force and effect as the statute itself. A presumption arises that the rules or regulations have been made for a particular purpose and that purpose should be given effect to.[496]

[s 114.12.2.2] ***Constitutionality.***—There is a presumption of validity of statutes. The courts presume that the legislature understands and correctly appreciates situations and, therefore, there is always a presumption in favour of constitutionality. The person who alleges that there is a transgression of constitutional provisions, has to prove that fact.[497]

[s 114.12.3] Acceptance of illegal gratification.—There is a presumption under section 20(1) of the Prevention of Corruption Act, 1988, which is of mandatory nature,

---

489. *State of Punjab v Subash Chander,* AIR 1991 P&H 134.

490. *Ram Sarup v State of Punjab,* 1987 Cr LJ 928 (P&H). *Sukumar Roy v Rabindra Chandra Roy,* AIR 1994 Gau 67, certified copy issued by the sub-Registrar, the scribe of the original document was also examined correctness presumed.

491. *Kailash Chand Gaggar v State of Assam,* 1993 Cr LJ 2632 (Gau). The preparation of crop record by Tehsildar is an official act, presumption of regular performance arises, *Pabbathi Reddy v PRS,* AIR 1996 AP 300.

492. *Gorakhnath Upadhyaya v State of UP,* AIR 1994 All 283; *DSE Brokers Forum, Bombay v SEBI,* AIR 2001 SC 1010, fee levied by SEBI on stock brokers and sub-brokers is both registration and regulatory fee. The Board had competence to levy it.

493. *Balkishan v Shrilal,* AIR 1994 MP 14.

494. *Baby P v Hindustan Petroleum Corp Ltd, Mumbai,* AIR 2016 Ker 184, para 7.vii.

495. *Marie Emmanuelle Verhoeven v UOI,* (2016) 6 SCC 456, para 123.

496. *Peerless General Finance and Investment Co Ltd v RBI,* (1992) 2 SCC 343 : AIR 1992 SC 1033 : (1992) 75 Comp Cas 12.

497. *Rakesh Bansal v State of Rajasthan,* AIR 2003 NOC 68 (Raj) : (2002) 2 Raj LR, 153, the provision in a taxing statute that for every evasion, 4 times more would have to be paid. This was held to be valid.

that gratification was accepted for performance of some official act. The prosecution proved in this case that the accused received gratification from the complainant. The court could draw the legal presumption that the gratification was accepted as a reward for doing public duty.[498]

See sections 79–86 as to the presumptions of this kind in respect of documents.

[s 114.12.4] Proceedings of meetings.—It is not obligatory that the minutes of proceedings of a meeting (corporators, in this case) should be confirmed at the subsequent meeting. The only requirement is that the presiding officer of the next ensuing meeting should sign the minutes. Presumptive value can be given to minutes, but this presumption is rebuttable. The corporators are not estopped from disputing the correctness of the minutes by adducing evidence.[499]

[s 114.13] Common Course of business—Delivery of letters.—*[Illustration (f)]*.—This illustration leaves it to the discretion of the court to presume that a common course of business has been followed: but the court is not bound to presume it.[500] In commercial transactions the presumption is that the usual course of business was followed by the parties thereto.

"Many presumptions are drawn from the usual course of business in public offices. With regard to the course of the post...if a letter is put into a post office, that is *prima facie* proof, until the contrary appears, that the party to whom it is addressed received it in due course."[501] "Postmarks on letters are *prima facie* evidence that the letters were in the post at the time and place therein specified if a letter properly directed, is proved to have been either put into the post-office or delivered to the postman, it is presumed, from the known course of business in that department of public service, that it reached its destination at the regular time, and was received by the person to whom it was addressed".[502]

The presumption is stronger when the letter is sent by registered post and the acknowledgement is signed by someone at the other end.[503] In the case of a public analyst's report, the requirement of law is to send the report to concerned persons by Regd. Post and not with acknowledgement due also. The report was sent with acknowledgement due which fact was not proved. It was held that if any excess has been done beyond the requirement of law that will not affect the legal position as stands under the law. Hence, non-proving of acknowledgement due does not affect the

---

498. *M Narsinga Rao v State of AP*, 2001 Cr LJ 515 (SC).

499. *Tarvindersingh Mahendra Singh Dhillon v State of Maharashtra*, AIR 2000 Bom 223.

500. *Ram Das Chakarbati v The Official Liquidator, Cotton Ginning Co Ltd, Caunpore*, (1887) 9 All 366, 376.

501. *Best*, 12th Edn, section 403, p 344.

502. *Taylor*, 12th Edn, section 179, p 163; *Harihar Banerjee v Ramshashi Roy*, AIR 1918 PC 102. Where the invitation cards bore postal stamps of the place of posting and also the place of destination, inference could be drawn that in the normal course of things they were posted and received by the addressee. *Vandavasi Karthikeya v S Kamalamma*, AIR 1994 AP 102. Refusal by tenant to receive notice, presumption of service, *R.A Qureshi v Xth Addl DJ, Meerut*, AIR 1995 All 345. *P Purushotham Reddy v Pratap Steels Ltd*, AIR 2003 AP 141, despatch of registered letter proved, presumption of delivery was not rebutted by the addressee by showing that the address put on the cover was incorrect, or that the postal authorities never tendered that letter or that there was endorsement by the postal authority that the letter could not be delivered. Mere denial of receipt was not sufficient.

503. *Hazaribagh Municipality v Fulchand*, AIR 1966 Pat 434.

presumption of the service of the report.[504] In *VP Shivanna v Bhadramma*[505] it was held that, in a case of recovery of maintenance, notice sent to the husband by Registered AD and not as contemplated under section 125(3), CrPC was illegal and question of any inference about its receipt to be drawn under section 114 does not arise. Where a notice was sent by registered post AD and it was duly received and acknowledgement signed, presumption of service arises and it was not necessary to examine the postman simply because the receipt of notice was denied.[506]

In view of the provisions of section 114 Illustration (*f*) of the Evidence Act and section 27 of the General Clauses Act, 1897, there is a presumption that the addressee has received the letter sent by registered post. However, the presumption is rebuttable on a consideration of evidence of impeccable character.[507]

It will all depend on the facts of each case whether the presumption of service of a notice sent under postal certificate should be drawn. It is true that the presumption would apply with greater force to letters which are sent by registered post, yet, when facts so justify, such a presumption is expected to be drawn even in the case of a letter sent under postal certificate.[508]

[s 114.13.1] Open post card.—Where a post card was delivered through the post office, the court said that there was no presumption that it was written by the sender. The only presumption was that it reached the addressee in the ordinary course of post.[509]

See sections 16 and 32(2). Entries in the regularly maintained register of a nationalised company have been held to be perfectly reliable.[510] A cheque of a customer was honoured beyond his balance without any agreement as to overdraft. It was presumed to be a loan.[511] Where two sets of account were seized, the court refused to draw the presumption that accounts showing less turnover were correct.[512]

---

504. *State of MP v Ramdeo Agrawal,* 1995 Cr LJ 1512 (MP). A letter sent by registered post, if not returned to the sender within 30 days, creates a presumption of delivery, *Piara Singh v A S. Lyalpuri,* AIR 1994 NOC 335 (Del). Notice sent in accordance with law, presumption of due services arises, *Vinod Khanna v Bakshi Sachdev,* AIR 1996 Delhi 32. *GS. Shrikanth v Sri Lakshmi Financers,* 1999 Cr LJ 329 (AP), demand notice under section 138, Negotiable Instruments Act, 1881, sent by Regd. AD Post, neither the letter came back, nor AD slip, delivery presumed.

Aparna Agencies v P Sudhakar Rao, 2000 Cr LJ 1005 (MP), notice for dishonour of cheque, Regd. post came back with the endorsement that the addressee was out of station. The notice was deemed to have been duly served. *Jameel v State of UP,* 2000 Cr LJ 3049 (All), report of Public Analyst, copy sent by Regd. Post, remark of the post man did not make it clear whether the addressee was avoiding delivery. The court said that presumption of delivery could not be made from the fact that the addressee was absent from home. No alternative or second attempt was made for service. The addressee was deprived of his rights under the Prevention of Food Adulteration Act, 1954. His conviction was held to have been vitiated.

505. *VP Shivanna v Bhadramma,* 1993 Cr LJ 418 (Kant).

506. *Shashikant Sadashiv Bagwe v State of Maharashtra,* AIR 1995 Bom 172.

507. *Parimal v Veena,* (2011) 3 SCC 545. Also see, *RS Sujatha v State of Karnataka,* (2011) 5 SCC 689.

508. *Samittri Devi v Sampuran Singh,* (2011) 3 SCC 556.

509. *Ashok Kumar Uttamchand Shah v.Patel Mohmad Asmal Chanchd,* AIR 1999 Guj 108.

510. *SKARSM Ramanathan v NTC Ltd,* AIR 1985 Ker 262.

511. *Bank of Maharashtra v United Construction Co,* AIR 1985 Bom 432. False explanation does not create any presumption. *Abdul Karim v Mys.,* 1979 Cr LJ 1123 : AIR 1979 SC 1506.

512. *State of Ker. v MM Mathew,* AIR 1978 SC 1571 : 1978 Cr LJ 1690; *KM Patel v Mohd. Rahimbux,* AIR 1981 SC 977 : 1980 Supp SCC 1, accounts not produced.

From the publication of statements in the shape of advertisements identical to those issued by an elected candidate, no inference could be drawn that they too were issued by the same candidate.[513]

[s 114.14] Withholding of evidence—*[Illustration (g)]*.—The presumption under section 114, illustration (g) is only a permissible inference and not a necessary inference. The court has the option, it may or may not raise presumption on the proof of certain facts. It depends upon the nature of the fact required to be proved and its importance in the controversy, the usual mode of proving it, the nature, quality and cogency of evidence, which has not been produced and its accessibility to the party concerned, all of which have to be taken into account. It is only when all these matters are duly considered that an adverse inference can be drawn against the party.[514] This illustration deals with the presumption arising from withholding evidence. The aspect of adverse inference under section 114, illustration (g) could arise in a case where there is no evidence insofar as the evidence that was available was suppressed or not produced. But in a situation where the material produced by the prosecution is itself sufficient, section 114, Illustration (g) cannot come to the assistance of the accused.[515] The conduct of the person withholding the evidence may be attributed to a supposed consciousness that the evidence, if produced, would operate against him. In a criminal. case failure to give evidence of relevant facts leads to the presumption, that evidence which could be produced and is not produced would, if produced, be unfavourable to the person who withholds it.[516] Though the prosecution is not bound to call all available witnesses irrespective of considerations of number[517] or reliability, witnesses essential to the unfolding of the narrative on which the prosecution is based must be called by the prosecution, whether in the result the effect of their testimony is for or against the case for the prosecution. It, therefore, becomes necessary to prove that the witnesses in question had seen the occurrence and, therefore, their evidence was material and the same has been deliberately withheld.[518] Explaining the role of the court in this connection the Supreme Court observed:[519]

---

513. *Gajanan Krishnaji Bapat v Dattaji Raghobaji Meghe*, AIR 1995 SC 2284 : (1995) 5 SCC 347. *Emess Advertising Service v Hindustan Times Ltd*, AIR 1998 Del 14, service of summons through newspaper publication was not rebutted.

514. *Tomaso Bruno v State of UP*, (2015) 7 SCC 178, para 27.

515. *State of Maharashtra v Jethmal Himatmal Jain*, 1994 Cr LJ 2613 (Bom). Where no neighbours witnessed the incident, non-production of neighbours, no adverse inference, *Sat Pal v State of Punjab*, AIR 1996 SC 201 : 1996 Cr LJ 406 : 1995 SCC (Cri) 1039. Non-production of FIR, adverse presumption, *Ranganathan v State*, 1996 Cr LJ 2041 (Mad).

516. *Mahendrapal v State*, (1955) 2 All 325. See *Harbhajan v State of MP*, 1989 Cr LJ 2205 (MP), prosecution not explaining serious injury on the person of the accused which was not self-caused, adverse presumption; *State of Rajasthan v Madho*, 1991 Cr LJ 1343: AIR 1991 SC 1065. But no such presumption where unexplained injuries were of minor nature. *Man Singh v State of UP*, 1987 Cr LJ 693 (MP).

517. *Khazan Singh v State of Punjab*, 1989 Cr LJ 1555 (P&H) : AIR 1989 SC 374, where a third witness, not produced, would have only added to multiplicity, no presumption. To the same effect, *Radhakishan Prashar v State*, 1988 Cr LJ 17 (Bom); *Waisuddin v State (Delhi Admn.)*, 1991 Cr LJ 134 (Del).

518. *Pattad Amarappa v State of Karnataka*, AIR 1989 SC 2004 at 2012. Dropping of some witnesses may attract this presumption, but will be of no consequence where the case proved. *Gurmej Singh v State of Punjab*, AIR 1992 SC 214 : 1992 Cr LJ 293. Prosecution was not allowed to be thrown out only on the ground that independent witnesses were not produced. *Appabhai v State of Gujarat*, 1988 Cr LJ 848 : AIR 1988 SC 696. A complaint cannot be thrown out by reason of the fact that the State has not filed written statement particularly when the stage is still not mature for the same. *State of Haryana v Bhajan Lal*, AIR 1992 SC 604 : 1992 Cr LJ 527.

519. *Mohanlal Shamji Soni v UOI*, AIR 1991 SC 1346 : (1991) 2 Guj LH 11 : 1991 Cr LJ 1521.

> It is a cardinal rule in the law of evidence that the best available evidence should be brought before the court to prove a fact or the points in issue. But it is left either for the prosecution or for the defence to establish its respective case by adducing the best available evidence and the court is not empowered under the provisions of the Code of Criminal Procedure to compel either the prosecution or the defence to examine any particular witness or witnesses on their sides. Nonetheless if either of the parties withholds any evidence which could be produced and which, if produced, be unfavourable to the party withholding such evidence, the court can draw a presumption under Illustration (*g*) to section 114 of the Evidence Act. In such a situation a question that arises for consideration is whether the presiding officer of a court should simply sit as a mere umpire at a contest between two parties and declare at the end of the combat who has won and who has lost or is there not any legal duty of his own, independent of the parties, to play an active role in the proceedings in finding out the truth and administering justice? It is a well accepted and settled principle that a court must discharge its statutory function, whether they be discretionary or obligatory it is the duty of a court not only to do justice but also to ensure that justice is being done.

Before drawing an adverse inference against a party for non-production of a document, it must be ascertained whether the document actually existed and whether it was in the possession of the party.[520] A party cannot be called upon to produce evidence with regard to an issue which is not part of its case. There can be no adverse presumption in such a case.[521]

Where in an accident claim, the insurer pleaded limited liability and produced only the attested copy of the policy on a different form, adverse inference could be drawn against the insurer for non-production of the original or office copy of the policy.[522] An adverse presumption was drawn against the driver of a truck which was involved in a head on collision because he refused to appear in the witness box to avoid cross-examination. His helper was testifying about matters.[523] The complainant alleged that a cheque was given to him under a share transaction; but he did not produce his statutory books of account relating to the transaction. An adverse inference was drawn against him.[524]

The presumption laid down in this illustration was held to apply to the case of counsel, engaged in a suit, who should not have been, under the circumstances counsel but should have been called as a witness.[525] An adverse presumption arose where a notification declared certain premises as shops without giving any opportunity to the owner. The relevant material justifying the notification was also not produced in the court.[526] Where the defendant Government failed to produce the original document for

---

520. *Bhoolchand v Kay Pee Cee Investments,* AIR 1991 SC 2053 : (1991) 1 SCC 343.

521. *Standard Chartered Bank v Andhra Bank Financial Services,* (2006) 6 SCC 94 : AIR 2006 SC 3626.

522. *Krishan Lal v Mohd. Din,* AIR 1994 Del 10.

523. *Krishna Dey v National Insurance Co Ltd,* AIR 2008 NOC 2190 (Cal—DB). See also *Abdul Mannan v Pawdhari Chouhan,* 2016 AIR CC 2749, para 10 (Gau).

524. *MS. Narayana Menon v State of Kerala,* (2006) 6 SCC 39 : AIR 2006 SC 3366.

525. *Weston v Peary Mohan Dass,* (1912) 40 Cal 898.

526. *Lipton India Ltd v West Bengal,* AIR 1984 Cal 109.

a long time of five years, an adverse inference was drawn.[527] A written report was made by the deceased's father to the police and that was the first contemporaneous document putting on record the true facts pertaining to the incident. It was not produced by the prosecution despite directions by the Sessions Judge. The court said that this raised a doubt against the prosecution case.[528] A worker claimed to have become permanent on account of continuous service. The Reserve Bank failed to produce any records. The worker's case was presumed to be true.[529] Where the plaintiff brought a suit for the recovery of loan amount on the basis of pro-note from the defendant who pleaded repayment and the plaintiff, though he maintained an account, did not produce it in the court, an adverse inference was drawn against him.[530] A supplier on instalments wanted to impose a penalty on the failure of the buyer to pay an instalment. But he did not produce the agreement which enabled him to do so. An adverse presumption was drawn against him.[531]

Where a suit was filed for specific enforcement of an agreement as to an immovable property, the vendor did not step into the witness box to depose in support of her case, the court drew the adverse inference that the case set up by her was not true.[532] The court said:[533] The party has not stepped into the witness box to depose in support of her case and to subject herself to cross-examination. It has been held by the Hon'ble Supreme Court in *Ishwar Bhai C. Patel v. Harihar Behara,*[534] that if a defendant does not enter the witness box to make a statement on oath in support of the pleadings set out in the written statement, an adverse inference would arise that what he had stated in the written statement was not correct. In the present case as well on the failure of defendant No. 3 to step into the witness box, an adverse inference will have to be drawn against her that the case set up by her is not true.

Where a party refuses to submit to a medical examination in a case where the whole case depends on the state of his or her mind or body, it will be open to the court to draw an adverse inference or presumption against the recalcitrant party.[535]

Where the plaintiff refused to give his specimen signature for the purpose of comparison with disputed signature, the court refused to draw any adverse presumption against him, because admitted signature of the plaintiff was already there on record and no effort was made to use the same for comparison purposes.[536] However, where

---

527. *State v Rikhab Das Jain,* AIR 1994 Raj 114.

528. *SK Meheboob v State of Maharashtra,* AIR 2005 SC 1805 : (2005) 10 SCC 387 : 2005 Cr LJ 2136.

529. *HD Singh v RBI,* AIR 1986 SC 132 : (1985) 4 SCC 201.

530. *HN Nanjundappa v CV Shashidhara Murthy,* 1996 AIHC 1916 (Kant). *Collector, Land Acquisition, UEED v Zamindarani Nambal,* AIR 1999 J&K 93, the Revenue Minister slashed down the temporary assessment of compensation made by the collector. No speaking order was passed, the record of the case not produced by the collector before the court despite sufficient opportunities. The court said that an adverse inference could be drawn that the record was intentionally withheld.

531. *Ganga Maruthi v Nagaraj,* AIR 1998 Kant. 407.

532. *Ranjana Nagpal v Devi Ram,* AIR 2002 HP 166.

533. *Ibid,* p 175.

534. *Ishwar Bhai C. Patel v Harihar Behara,* AIR 1999 SC 1341 : (1999) 3 SCC 457.

535. *Sulabai v Jagannath,* (1971) 74 Bom LR 295; *Swati Lodha v State of Rajasthan,* 1991 Cr LJ 939 (Raj), refusal to give blood sample to determine paternity, presumption. Where divorce was sought on the ground of impotency and the husband refused to undergo medical examination, adverse inference could be drawn against him, *George Philip v Saly Elias T,* AIR 1995 Ker 289.

536. *Kalyan Singh v Ranjot Singh,* AIR 2002 HP 180.

a witness filed "evidence affidavit" and refused to undergo a cross-examination or was withheld and not offered for cross-examination, an adverse inference could be drawn against such witness or the party. "Evidence affidavit" was to be ignored.[537]

In a trial for the offence of rape, it was alleged that the woman was raped when her husband was sleeping in the same room. It was held that the failure to examine the husband was fatal to the prosecution and an adverse inference could be drawn under section 114, Illustration (g).[538]

No presumption is created against the prosecution by reason of any conflict between medical version of the incident and that of the eyewitnesses.[539]

The object of O XII, rule 8 of the Civil Procedure Code, 1908 is to facilitate the plaintiff or any other party to get a document on record, which is not in their possession or in the possession of the other party. If a document has been produced then it is the duty of the party who has asked for such production to get it placed on record. If, however, the said document is not placed on record, then adverse inference against the party who has produced the same cannot be drawn, more so, when the party who has produced the said document before the court has been cross-examined *vis-à-vis* that document.[540]

[s 114.14.1] Government claim of privilege.—The High Court directed the Central Government to produce a copy of the note put up before the cabinet and its decision on the point. The Central Government refused to comply with the direction claiming privilege in regard to the document. The court said that in the facts of the case, such act of the Government indicated *mala fides*.[541]

[s 114.14.2] Failure to produce leave register.—A public servant who was facing the charge of bribery failed to produce the casual leave register of his Department for the purpose of showing that he was on leave on the alleged date of acceptance of bribe at office. An adverse inference on this ground in the circumstances of the case was held to be not proper. He was able to show his application for caused leave for that particular day and his absence from the office was proved by the evidence of an officer. Such evidence could not have been discarded.[542] The presumption under the section being non-obligatory, the background facts play an important role. No adverse inference can be drawn for non-production of evidence which had not even been called for.[543] Documents called for in the absence of any pleadings are not relevant.[544]

[s 114.14.3] Failure to produce document in proof of age.—In a charge under the Prevention of Food Adulteration Act, 1954 the accused wanted the benefit of probation on the ground that he was below 18 years of age. But he did not produce his school

---

537. *Banganga Co-op Housing Society Ltd, Mumbai v Vasanti Gajanan Nerurkar*, AIR 2015 NOC 1132 (Bom).
538. *Vijayan v State*, 1993 Cr LJ 2364 (Mad).
539. *Raja Ram v State of UP*, 1991 Cr LJ 3227 (All).
540. *Rohini Traders v JK Lakshmi Cement Ltd*, (2015) 12 SCC 46, para 14.
541. *UOI v Raja Mohd. Amir Mohd. Khan*, (2005) 8 SCC 696 : AIR 2005 SC 4383.
542. *Ganga Kumar Srivastva v State of Bihar*, AIR 2005 SC 3123 : (2005) 6 SCC 211 : 2005 Cr LJ 3454.
543. *Manager, RBI v S Mani*, AIR 2005 SC 2179 : (2005) 5 SCC 100 : (2005) 3 Serv LR 333.
544. *Mahendra L Jain v Indore Development Authority*, AIR 2005 SC 1252 : (2005) 1 SCC 639 : (2005) 1 Serv LR 39.

leaving certificate in proof of his age in spite of opportunity. Municipal birth certificate was also not produced. The court said that a presumption under section 114(g) of the Evidence Act could be raised against the accused that if the evidence in question had been produced it would have gone against him.[545]

[s 114.14.4] Public functionary's failure to produce document.—A document was in possession of a public functionary and he was under a statutory duty to produce the same before the court. The court said that on his failure to do so an adverse presumption could be drawn against him.[546]

[s 114.14.5] Statement to police before becoming approver.—Copies of statements made by an approver witness before police must be supplied to the defence on demand, otherwise an adverse inference could be drawn against his testimony. The defence could not be deprived of or denied the right to avail of the statements made before the police so as to enable them to test the evidence of the concerned witness or confront him with his earlier version and to find out whether the evidence in court was inconsistent with the earlier statements made before the police. In the present case, copies of those statements were not made available to the defence. The evidence of the approver had to be assessed in the light of this infirmity, which gave rise to an adverse inference to the effect that if the statements had been made available in response to the demand made by the defence, the same would have impaired the value of his testimony.[547]

[s 114.14.6] Compromise agreement.—A wife filed maintenance case and also criminal proceedings against the husband for cruelty. They entered into a compromise agreement. The proceedings were withdrawn and the wife came back to live with her husband. After about one and a half years the husband filed a case for divorce on the ground of cruelty by filing criminal proceedings. It was held that there was no cruelty by the wife. Her complaint was genuine, that is why the husband entered into the compromise. The failure on the part of the husband to produce a copy of the compromise agreement was a withholding of evidence creating a presumption against him.[548]

[s 114.14.7] Refusal to submit to medical examination.—The plaintiff brought an action for damages for personal injuries, but refused to submit for medical examination by the defendant's neurosurgeon. The court postponed the trial because with such report it was not possible to hold a fair trial. The court said: The plaintiff had blocked a potential solution to the problem by refusing to be examined by the neurosurgeon. It was not then open to her to insist the trial proceed without the defendant being able to produce evidence, whether orthopaedic or neurological, to counter that of the plaintiff's neurosurgeon. The judge had attempted to give the defendant a proper opportunity to respond to all the medical evidence which his expert had not had the chance to consider and the plaintiff should have attended the appointment despite the defendant choosing to go to a neurosurgeon.[549]

---

545. *Rakesh Kumar v State,* 2001 Cr LJ 2978 (Del).

546. *State Inspector of Police v Surya Sankaran Karri,* (2006) 7 SCC 172 : (2006) 3 SCC (Cri) 225 : 2006 Cr LJ 4598.

547. *Lal Chand v State of Haryana,* (1984) 1 SCC 686, 690 : 1984 SCC (Cri) 355 : AIR 1984 SC 226 : 1984 Cr LJ 164.

548. *Tapan Kumar Chakraborti v Joytsna,* AIR 1997 Cal 134.

549. *Wilson v Fylde Borough Transport,* June 22, 1998 (CA) : 1998 CLY 101 (351).

[s 114.14.8] Refusal to participate in DNA test.—It was alleged that the accused had sexual intercourse with the victim girl as a result of which she was blessed with the child and in case the accused chose to decline the direction of the court to undergo the DNA test to decide the paternity of the child, an adverse inference could be drawn against him.[550]

[s 114.14.9] Refusal to attend occupational therapy report.—The plaintiff suffered a crushing injury to his left dominant hand and traumatic amputation of all four fingers at the proximal interphalangeal joints in an industrial accident. Both parties instructed surgeons to examine the plaintiff and prepare reports on his injuries and future prognosis. The plaintiff's solicitors also obtained a report from an occupational therapist which assessed his disability and made suggestions to assist him in coping with his disability. He brought an action claiming damages for personal injuries. The defendant's solicitors requested facilities for an occupational therapist specialist to interview him with a view to preparing a report. His solicitors refused interview facilities with him but allowed the defendant's expert limited access to his flat to consider possible adaptations. The defendant's sought a stay of proceedings on the basis that the plaintiff unreasonably refused to be interviewed by his specialist. *A* argued that a comparison should be drawn between occupational therapists and employment consultants. It was held granting a stay of proceedings, that this was a claim where occupational therapist evidence was of importance for the just determination of the case. There was no similarity between occupational therapist specialists and employment consultants. It was necessary for the defendant's occupational therapist expert to interview the plaintiff as opposed to preparing a report from the medical evidence alone.[551]

[s 114.15] Refusal to answer questions—*[Illustration (h)]*.—Refusal to answer a question is a legitimate ground of unfavourable inference against the person who has to answer the question. See section 148(4), *infra*. But this illustration does not contemplate the case of witnesses who are not compelled to answer on grounds of privilege (*vide* sections 121–129).

[s 114.15.1] No presumption in criminal matters.—The Supreme Court has laid down that in criminal matters no presumption should be raised which does not have any origin in any statute as it may cause great prejudice to the accused.[552]

[s 114.15.2] Failure to traverse allegations.—An adverse inference can ordinarily be drawn in respect of allegations which are not traversed. But there is no rule that an adverse inference must always be drawn whatever the facts and circumstances may be.[553] There is also the rule that everybody has to prove his own case and no one can take advantage of the weakness in evidence of the other side.

[s 114.15.3] Compliance with or disregard order of High Court—In a case involving illegitimacy of a child, the High Court had ordered the wife to undergo a DNA test. The Supreme Court gave liberty to her to comply with or disregard the order passed by the High Court and if she declined to comply with the direction issued

---

550. *Bappaditya Ghosh v State of WB*, 2016 Cr LJ 5011, para 22 (Cal).
551. *Barresi v Acton & Borman Ltd*, May 15, 1998 : 1998 CLY 102 (353).
552. *Kailash Gour v State of Assam*, AIR 2008 SC 2467 : (2008) 9 SCC 204.
553. *Jagjit Singh v State of Haryana*, AIR 2007 SC 590 : (2006) 11 SCC 1.

by the High Court, an adverse inference could be drawn against her, in terms of the provisions of this section.[554]

See section 313, Code of Criminal Procedure (Act V of 1973).

[s 114.16] Document in the hands of the obligor—*[Illustration (i)]*.—This presumption is founded on the natural supposition that a man will protect his own interests by securing his bond before or at the time of discharging it. Where the instrument of a debt and the security for that debt are found in the hands of the debtor, the *prima facie* presumption is that the debt has been discharged.[555] If a pro-note is in the hands of the maker, there is a presumption that it has been paid off. If the drawee alleges that the maker came into possession of the note unlawfully, the onus is on him to prove it. This illustration only refers to presumption that may be raised. It does not follow that such presumption would shift the onus of proof.

In a suit on a bond for money, plaintiff alleged that his non-production of the document was due to the fact that the defendant had stolen it. The defendant admitted the execution of the bond, but alleged that he had paid it; it was held that the burden of proof was on the defendant to prove payment, either by the production of the bond, or other evidence or by both.[556]

Where plaintiff sued for money due upon *hundis* (bills of exchange), but alleged their loss, whilst defendant admitted execution, but pleaded payment and subsequent destruction of the documents, it was held that failing production of the *hundis* by the defendant there was no presumption that the *hundis* had been discharged and the onus was upon the defendant to prove payments.[557]

In a suit for money due on a mortgage bond, the plaintiff produced only a copy of the document, alleging in his plaint that it had been lost. The defendant admitted its execution, but alleged that the debt had been discharged, and in support of his allegation he produced the original document containing the endorsement of the mortgagee through her agent of payment of the debt. It was held that the production by the defendant of the bond with the endorsement of payment cast on the plaintiff the burden of proving that the debt was still outstanding.[558]

[559]**[[s 114A] Presumption as to absence of consent in certain proscecution for rape.—In a prosecution for rape under clause (a), clause (b), clause (c), clause (d),**

554. *Dipanwita Roy v Ronobroto Roy*, AIR 2015 SC 418 (para 12), **followed in** *Govindula Sathaiah v Govindula Manjula*, AIR 2016 AP 160, paras 7 and 8.

555. *Bhoy Hong Kong v Ramanathan Chetty*, (1902) 29 IA 43: 29 Cal 334: 4 Bom LR 378. *Citi Bank NA v Standard Chartered Bank*, (2004) 1 SCC 12 : AIR 2003 SC 4630, bank receipts in possession of the bank, presumption, payment had been made.

556. *Chuni Kuar v Udai Ram*, (1883) 6 All 73; *Aung Myat v Hla May*, (1918) 10 LBR 26.

557. *Dhian Singh v Gurdit Singh*, (1925) 6 Lah 297.

558. *Mohamad Mehdi Hasan Khan v Mandir Das*, (1912) 39 IA 184: 34 All 511: 14 Bom LR 1073.

559. Subs. by Act 13 of 2013, section 26, for section 114A (w.r.e.f. 3-2-2013). Earlier section 114A was inserted by Act 43 of 1963, section 6 (w.e.f. 25-12-1989). Section 114A, before substitition by Act 13 of 2013, stood as under:

> "*114A. Presumption as to absence of consent in certain prosecutions for rape.*—In a prosecution for rape under clause (a) or clause (b) or clause (c) or clause (d) or clause (e) or clause (g) of sub-section (2) of section 376 of the Indian Penal Code (45 of 1860), where sexual intercourse by the accused is proved and the question is whether it was without the consent of the woman alleged to have been raped and she states in her evidence before the Court that she did not consent, the Court shall presume that she did not consent.".

clause (e), clause (f), clause (g), clause (h), clause (i), clause (j), clause (k), clause (l), clause (m) or clause (n) of sub-section (2) of section 376 of the Indian Penal Code (45 of 1860), where sexual intercourse by the accused is proved and the question is whether it was without the consent of the woman alleged to have been raped and she states in her evidence before the Court that she did not consent, the Court shall presume that she did not consent.

***Explanation.*—In this section, "sexual intercourse" shall mean any of the acts mentioned in clauses (a) to (d) of section 375 of the Indian Penal Code (45 of 1860).]**

SYNOPSIS

COMMENT

[s 114A.1] Principle.—Evidence of bad character of an accused person (of whose good character evidence has not been given) is not relevant under this section for the purpose of raising a general inference that the accused is likely to have committed the offence charged. Such evidence is irrelevant and cannot be legally admitted in evidence whether elicited by the prosecution or by the defence.[560] This description of the accused as a law-breaker amounted to evidence of character. The Supreme Court excluded it.[561] A man's guilt is to be established by proof of the facts alleged and not by proof of his character; such evidence might create prejudice but not lead a step towards substantiation of guilt.[562] The prohibition does not in any way affect evidence which is required to prove a motive for the crime or which is otherwise relevant.[563] But in assessing punishment the court may take into consideration the accused's character and antecedents or the state of crime in the country or locality.[564]

Section 114-A no doubt addresses the consent part of the woman only, when the offence of rape is proved but it also impliedly would be applicable in a matter where the victim girl had gone to the extent of committing suicide due to the trauma of rape, and yet was sought to be disbelieved at the instance of the defence that she had woven a concocted story, even though she suffered the risk of death after consuming poison. If this were to be accepted, then what was the need of incorporating an amendment by incorporating section 114-A, which clearly has been added to add weight and credence to the statement of the victim woman, who suffers the offence of rape and a claustrophobic interpretation of this amended provision cannot be made to infer that the version of the victim should be believed relating merely to consent in a case where the offence of rape is proved by other evidence on record. If this view of the matter is taken into account relying upon the amended section 114-A as was done by the Apex Court, then even if there had been a doubt about the medical evidence regarding non-rupture of hymen, the same would of no consequence as it is well settled that the offence of rape would be held to have been proved even if there is an "attempt of rape on the woman and not the actual commission of rape". Thus, if the version

---

560. *Mi Myin v King-Emperor,* (1908) 5 LBR 4; *Emperor v Gangaram,* (1920) 22 Bom LR 1274.
561. *Ram Lakhan v State of UP,* AIR 1977 SC 1936 : 1977 Cr LJ 1566.
562. *Amrita Lal Hazra v Emperor,* (1915) 42 Cal 957.
563. *Jagwa Dhanuk v King-Emperor,* (1925) 5 Pat 63.
564. *King-Emperor v Nga Ba Shein,* (1928) 6 Ran 391 FB

of the victim girl is fit to be believed due to the attending circumstances that she was subjected to sexual assault of rape and the trauma of this offence on her mind was so acute that led her to the extent of committing suicide, which she miraculously escaped, it would be a travesty of justice if the court disbelieves her version which would render the amendment and incorporation of section 114-A as a futile exercise on the part of the legislature which in its wisdom has incorporated the amendment clearly implying and expecting the court to give utmost weightage to the version of the victim of the offence of rape which definition includes also the attempt to rape.[565]

[s 114A.2] 2013 Amendment.—This section was amended vide the Criminal Law (Amendment) Act, 2013[566] on the basis of recommendations given by the Justice JS Verma Committee, constituted in the aftermath of December 2012 Nirbhaya rape incident, whereby changes were made in section 376(2) of Indian Penal Code. By making necessary amendment in this section, the newly classified offence under up to clause (n) of section 376(2) has also been brought within the bracket of statutory presumption of non-consensual intercourse prescribed in this section.

The convicts who commit the offence of rape, and fall within any of the clauses (a) to (n) of sub-section (2), because of their special position by virtue of which they can exert influence upon the victim, have been classified differently. The statutory presumption of non-consensual intercourse is based on the proposition that because of their special position, the convict was in a position to exert influence upon the victim.

Further, an Explanation has been also inserted in this section so as to clarify that the meaning of "Sexual Intercourse" shall be the same that has been attributed to any of the acts mentioned in clauses (a) to (d) of section 375 of the Indian Penal Code.

---

565. *Puran Chand v State of HP*, (2014) 5 SCC 689 (para 16).
566. Act 13 of 2013, vide section 26, (w.e.f. 03.02.2013).

CHAPTER VIII

ESTOPPEL

[s 115] Estoppel.—When one person has, by his declaration, act or omission,[s 115.17] intentionally caused or permitted another person to believe a thing to be true and to act upon such belief,[s 115.18] neither he nor his representative shall be allowed, in any suit or proceeding between himself and such person or his representative, to deny the truth of that thing.

ILLUSTRATION

A intentionally and falsely leads *B* to believe that certain land belongs to *A*, and thereby induces *B* to buy and pay for it.

The land afterwards becomes the property of *A*, and *A* seeks to set aside the sale on the ground that, at the time of the sale, he had no title. He must not be allowed to prove his want of title.

SYNOPSIS

COMMENT

[s 115.1] Principle.—Estoppel is based on the principle that it would be most inequitable and unjust that if one person, by a representation made, or by conduct amounting to a representation, had induced another to act as he would not otherwise have done, the person who made the representation should not be allowed to deny or repudiate the effect of his former statement, to the loss and injury of the person who acted on it.[1]

The section says that when one person has by his,

(a) declaration, (b) act or (c) omission,

intentionally caused or permitted another person,

(i) to believe a thing to be true and (ii) to act upon such belief, then neither he nor his representative shall be allowed to deny the truth of that thing in any suit or proceeding between himself and such person or his representative. To invoke the doctrine of estoppel three conditions must be satisfied; (1) representation by a person to another, (2) the other shall have acted upon the said representation and (3) such action shall have been detrimental to the interests of the person to whom the representation has been made. Even where the first two conditions are satisfied but the third is not, there is no scope to invoke the doctrine of estoppel.[2] As a doctrine based on equity, the principle of estoppel is only applicable in cases where the other party has changed his position relying upon the representation thereby made.[3] The doctrine is premised

1. *Sarat Chunder Dey v Gopal Chunder Laha,* (1892) 19 IA 203, 215, 216 : 20 Cal 296; *Pickard v Sears,* (1837) 6 Ad & El 469. For a parallel example see *Gulam Abbas v Haji Kayyam Ali,* AIR 1973 SC 554 : (1973) 1 SCC 1, relinquishment of the future possible right of inheritance by a Muslim heir for a consideration may debar him from setting up his right when it actually comes into being. *RN Gosain v Yashpal Dhir,* (1992) 4 SCC 683 : AIR 1993 SC 352, a party who chooses to accept a transaction and to take an advantage under it, cannot afterwards be permitted to challenge the validity of the transaction. See generally, *Advocate-General of Andhra Pradesh v Chennamsetty Chakrapani CI of Police CCS Guntur,* 1997 Cr LJ 3333; *Karunakaran APKMP v State,* 1997 Cr LJ 3618 (Ker).
2. *Gyarsi Bai v Dhansukh Lal,* AIR 1965 SC 1055 : (1965) 2 SCR 154.
3. *HB Basavaraj v Canara Bank,* (2010) 12 SCC 458 : [2010] 1 Mad LJ 383 : LNIND 2009 SC 1936.

on the conduct of party making a representation to the other so as to enable him to arrange its affairs in such a manner as if the said representation would be acted upon.[4]

The doctrine of Estoppel is steeped in the principles of equity and good conscience. Equity will not allow a person to say one thing at one time and the opposite of it at another time. It would "estop" him from denying his previous assertion, act, conduct or representation, to say something contrary to what was implied in the transaction under which he obtained the benefit of being let in possession of the property to be enjoyed by him as a tenant.[5]

Estoppel is a principle of equity which deals with the effect of contract and not with its cause.[6] The burden of proving the ingredients of this section lies on the party claiming estoppel. The representation which is the basis for the rule must be clear and unambiguous and not indefinite, upon which the party relying on it is said to have, in good faith and in belief of it, acted.[7]

This section is founded upon the doctrine laid down in *Pickard v Sears*,[8] namely, that where a person "by his words or conduct wilfully causes another to believe the existence of a certain state of things, and induces him to act on that belief, so as to alter his own previous position, the former is concluded from averring against the latter a different state of things as existing at the same time." The doctrine embodied in this section is not a rule of equity, but is a rule of evidence formulated and applied in courts of law.[9] It precludes a person from denying the truth of some statement previously made by himself. No cause of action arises upon estoppel itself.[10]

Estoppel is based on the maxim, *allegans contraria non est audiendus* (a person alleging contradictory facts should not be heard), and is that species of *presumptio juris et de jure,* where the fact presumed is taken to be true, not as against all the world, but as against a particular party, and that only by reason of some act done; it is in truth a kind of *argumentum and hominem.* Hence it appears that "estoppel" must not be understood as synonymous with "conclusive evidence"—the former being conclusions drawn by law against parties from particular facts, while by the latter is meant some piece or mass of evidence, sufficiently strong to generate conviction in the mind of a tribunal, or rendered conclusive on a party, by either common or statute law.[11]

---

4. *LML Ltd v State of Uttar Pradesh,* (2008) 3 SCC 128; also see *UP Power Corp Ltd v Sant Steels & Alloys Pvt Ltd,* (2008) 2 SCC 777 : AIR 2008 SC 693, wherein it was held that once a representation is been made by one party and the other party acts on that representation and makes investment and thereafter the first party resiles, such act cannot be stated to be fair and reasonable.

5. *Kamaljit Singh v Sarabjit Singh,* (2014) 16 SCC 472 : LNIND 2014 SC 768, para 11.

6. *Ariane Orgachem Pvt Ltd v Wyeth Employees Union,* (2015) 7 SCC 561, para 33.

7. *B Coleman & Co v PP Das Gupta,* AIR 1970 SC 426 : (1961) 2 SCC 1.

8. *Pickard v Sears,* (1837) 6 Ad & El 469, 474.

9. *Municipal Corp of Bombay v Secretary of State,* (1904) 29 Bom 580 : 7 Bom LR 27.

10. *Banwari Lal v Sukhdarshan,* AIR 1973 SC 814 : (1973) 1 SCC 294, estoppel does not create interest in property. *Sukumabai v Chandgonda Kalgonda Patil,* AIR 2003 Bom 131, it was a suit for possession of land, the defendant pleaded that he was a tenant, he also pleaded in the alternative that he was a trespasser. His plea failed. He could not approbate and reprobate at the same time. *Dhaniya Bai v Jiwan,* AIR 2003 MP 71, construction by a sister adjacent to the house of his brother, the latter actively participated in the construction and allowed her to take the support of his wall. The brother not allowed subsequently to such removal of construction, but the sister not allowed further construction not even under easement.

11. *BEST ON EVIDENCE,* 12th Edn, section 533, p 463.

Estoppel is a complex legal notion, involving a combination of several essential elements, namely, statement to be acted upon, acting on the faith of it, resulting detriment to the actor. Estoppel is often described as a rule of evidence, as indeed it may be so described. But the whole concept is more correctly viewed as a substantive rule of law. Estoppel is different from contract in its both nature and consequences. But the relationship between the parties must also be such that the imputed truth of the statement is a necessary step in the constitution of the cause of action. But the whole case of estoppel fails if the statement is not sufficiently clear and unqualified.[12]

Estoppel depends on the existence of some duty; and that is peculiarly so in the case of an omission. In order to succeed on a plea of estoppel it must be shown that there was a neglect of some duty owing to the person led into a particular belief, or to the general public of whom that person is one, and not merely neglect of what would be prudent in respect to the party prejudiced, or even of some duty owing to third persons, with whom those seeking to set up estoppel are not privy. There is a breach of the duty if the party estopped has not used due precautions to avert the risk.[13]

It is only an unambiguous and definite promise, which is otherwise enforceable in law upon which, the other party has acted, that comes within the ambit and scope of enforcement, based on the principle of legitimate expectation, and binding on the parties for their promise and representation.[14]

Estoppel applies not only in favour of the person induced to change his position but of a transferee from such person, and it binds not only the persons whose representations or actions have created it, but all persons claiming under or through him by gratuitous title.[15] A person transferred his import licence. The transferee imported the goods. The original licencee had committed irregularities in obtaining the licence; it was held that the transferee could not be made to suffer on that basis.[16] The Supreme Court observed that the doctrine of estoppel could be described as a rule capable of creating or defeating rights.[17]

Estoppel is essentially a rule of civil action. It has limited application to criminal proceedings, though in such proceedings it would be prejudicial to set up a different story.[18] In a criminal trial, where an issue of fact has been tried by a competent Court on an earlier occasion and a finding has been recorded in favour of the accused, such a finding would constitute an estoppel or *res judicata* against the prosecution, not as

12. *HR Basavaraj v Canara Bank,* (2010) 12 SCC 458.
13. *Mercantile Bank of India Ltd v Central Bank of India Ltd,* (1937) 40 Bom LR 713 : 65 IA 75: (1938) Mad 360; *Canara Bank v Canara Sales Corp,* AIR 1987 SC 1603 : (1987) 62 Comp Cas 280 : (1987) 2 SCC 666.
14. *AP TRANSCO v Sai Renewable Power Pv tLtd,* (2011) 11 SCC 34.
15. *Raj Kumar Jagannath Prashad v Syed Abdullah,* (1918) 20 Bom LR 851, 45 IA 97, 45 Cal 909; *Sebina v State of Kerala,* 1994 Cr LJ 1291 (Ker).
16. *Chemi Colour Agency v Chief Controller of Imports,* AIR 1985 Cal 358. See also *Chhaganlal v Narandas,* AIR 1982 SC 121 : (1982) 1 SCC 223. Where the claim of estoppel was not allowed to the assignee of the person to whom the representation was made.
17. *BL Shreedhar v KM Munireddy,* AIR 2003 SC 578 : 2002 (9) Scale 183 : LNIND 2002 SC 779, grant of land made under an Act to a family member. The benefit of it ensured to the whole family.
18. A limited application can take place in criminal matters also. See, for example, *Sukhdev Singh v UOI,* 1989 Cr LJ 1340 (Del), copies of the documents mentioned in the statement of grounds of detention not supplied to the prisoner, and, therefore, he could not make effective reply, the Government was not heard to say that the documents were only casually mentioned.

a bar to the trial and conviction of the accused for a different or distinct offence, but as precluding the acceptance/reception of evidence to disturb the finding of fact when the accused is tried subsequently for a different offence. This rule is distinct from the doctrine of double jeopardy as it does not prevent the trial of any offence but only precludes the evidence being led to prove a fact in issue as regards which evidence has already been led and a specific finding has been recorded at an earlier criminal trial. Thus, the rule relates only to the admissibility of evidence which is designed to upset a finding of fact recorded by a competent Court in a previous trial on a factual issue.[19] However, since the principles of estoppel, waiver and *res judicata* are procedural in nature, the same will have no application in a case where judgment has been rendered wholly without jurisdiction or issues involve only pure questions of law.[20]

Although the principle of estoppel or *res judicata* does not strictly apply to the Income Tax Authorities, it is not open to a Tribunal to come to a different conclusion to the one arrived at by that very Tribunal earlier without any limitation whatsoever. An earlier decision on the same question cannot be reopened if that decision is not arbitrary or perverse, if it has been arrived at after due inquiry, if no fresh facts are placed before the Tribunal giving the later decision, and if the Tribunal giving the earlier decision has taken into consideration all material evidence.[21]

It needs to be understood that the rule of estoppel is a doctrine based on fairness. It postulates the exclusion of the truth of the matter. All, for the sake of fairness.[22]

[s 115.2] Estoppel and presumption.—Estoppel differs from presumption. An estoppel is a personal disqualification laid upon a person peculiarly circumstanced from proving peculiar facts; whereas a presumption is a rule that particular inferences shall be drawn from particular facts, whoever proves them.[23]

[s 115.3] Estoppel and *res judicata*.—Estoppel differs from *res judicata*: (1) Estoppel is part of the law of evidence and proceeds upon the equitable principle of altered situation; the doctrine of *res judicata* belongs to procedure and is based on the principle that there must be end to litigation.

(2) Estoppel prohibits a party from proving anything which contradicts his previous declarations or acts, to the prejudice of party, who, relying upon them, altered his position; *res judicata prohibits the Court from enquiring into a matter already adjudicated.*

(3) Estoppel shuts the mouth of a party; *res judicata* ousts the jurisdiction of the court.[24]

---

19. *Sangeetaben Mahendrabhai Patel v State of Gujarat,* (2012) 7 SCC 621 : LNIND 2012 SC 1473.

20. *Dadu Dayalu Mahasabha, Jaipur (Trust) v Mahant Ram Niwas,* (2008) 11 SCC 753—referred to *Bhanu Kumar Jain v Archana Kumar* (supra)

21. *HA Shah & Co v CIT, Bombay,* AIR 1956 Bom 375 : (1956) 58 Bom LR 45 : ILR 1956 Bom 79.

22. *Pratima Chowdhury v Kalpana Mukherjee,* AIR 2014 SC 1304 : (2014) 4 SCC 196 : LNIND 2014 SC 80, (para 35).

23. Stephen, 175.

24. *Woodroffe and Ameer Ali,* 9th Edn, p 850.

Put in the most simple and colloquial way, *res judicata* precludes a man averring the same thing twice over in successive litigations, while estoppel prevents him saying one thing at one time and the opposite at another.[25]

An erroneous determination of a pure question of law in a previous judgment will not operate as *res judicata,* in a subsequent proceeding for a different property, though between the same parties.[26]

[s 115.4] Estoppel and waiver.—Estoppel and waiver are different. Estoppel is not a cause of action. It may, if established, assist a plaintiff in enforcing a cause of action by preventing a defendant from denying the existence of some fact essential to establish the cause of action; or, in other words, by preventing a defendant from asserting the existence of some fact the existence of which would destroy the cause of action. Waiver, on the other hand, is contractual, and may constitute a cause of action; it is an agreement to release or not to assert a right.[27] If an agent, with authority to make such an agreement on behalf of his principal, agrees to waive his principal's rights, then, subject to any other question such as consideration, the principal will be bound, but he will be bound by contract, not by estoppel. There is no such thing as estoppel by waiver.[28]

The generally accepted connotation of waiver is that to constitute waiver there must be an intentional relinquishment or abandonment of a known existing legal right, or conduct such as warrants an inference of the relinquishment of a known right or privilege.[29] The plaintiff wrote to her bank manager that she had joined nunnery and,

---

25. *Casamally v Sir Currimbhai Ebrahim,* (1911) 13 Bom LR 717, 760 : 36 Bom 214. *Amita Shekhawat v State of Rajasthan,* AIR 2003 SC 230, directions were given by the High Court for redetermination of dead rent, this order was challenged by a writ petition. Not allowed to do so, because once the party had agreed to pay the rent in a particular manner, the matter could not be relitigated. *Yamunabai Purushottam Deogirikar v Mathurabia Nilkanth Choudhary,* AIR 2010 NOC 109 (Bom), points of difference restated.
26. *Satyendra Kumar v Raj Nath Dubey,* AIR 2016 SC 2231, para 13.
27. *LIC of India v OP Bhallah,* AIR 1989 Pat 269. *Vijya Kumari Gujral v UOI,* 1988 Cr LJ 1198 (Del), waiver from not asking for examination of a witness; *RF Charitable Trust v Spl. Dy. Collector (General) Land Acquisition,* AIR 1992 AP 130, the land of the Trust was acquired on agreed compensation, the trust waiving the right to ask for any addition amount, held bound by the waiver.
28. *Dawsons Bank Ltd v Nippon Menkwa Kabushiki Kaisha,* (1935) 37 Bom LR 544 : 62 IA 100; *Uniply Industries Ltd v Unicorn Plywood Pvt Ltd,* AIR 2001 NOC 49 (Mad) : 2001 CLC 411, no waiver or estoppel where the owner of a trade mark, having come to know of the infringement, could not do anything for a certain period because of the inability to know the particulars of the industry committing the infringement. *Rhodia Ltd v Neon Laboratories Ltd,* AIR 2002 Bom 502, the defendant filed an application under section 9-A, Maharashtra (Amendment) of CPC questioning jurisdiction of the court. He also filed reply to the plaintiff's application for temporary injunction without prejudice to his application under section 9-A Plea of waiver raised for the first time in Civil Revision was rejected. *Shiv Kumar Sharma v Wazir Ajay Vir Chand,* AIR 1998 J&K 100, plea of waiver not established. *Babu Ram v Indra Pal Singh,* AIR 1998 SC 3021 : (1998) 6 SCC 358, there was an agreement preceding a sale deed which contained a clause for reconveyance. The sale-deed was executed subsequently. It did not make any reference to the agreement of reconveyance. The Court said that the failure to mention the right of reconveyance in the sale deed could not lead to the inference that the right was given up by the plaintiff.
29. *Basheshar Nath v IT Commissioner,* AIR 1959 SC 149 : 1959 Supp (1) SCR 528; *Provash Chandra Dalui v Biswanath Banerjee,* AIR 1989 SC 1834 : 1989 Supp (1) SCC 487. See also *Malina Mondal v Pushpa Rani,* AIR 1991 Cal 291, where a quit notice was followed by another quit notice, the effect was that the first stood waived and the second was valid for proceedings; *Municipal Corporation of Greater Bombay v Dr Hakim Waddi Tenants' Assn.,* AIR 1988 SC 233 : 1988 Mah LJ 1 : 1988 Supp SCC 55.

therefore, had no claim or interest in paternal property. This did not estop the plaintiff from claiming her share. The letter did not amount to surrender or waiver.[30] There is no question of waiver where the party is not even aware of his right.[31] Waiver of a right cannot be lightly inferred and something more than inaction of the right holder in exercising the right is necessary.[32] Therefore, where a party to a litigation not only fails to invoke the doctrine of estoppel before the judge but joins issue with the opposite party upon the question and accordingly an issue is raised and evidence adduced on this question, such a party is precluded from relying on the doctrine of estoppel to prevent the other party from proving that question.[33]

For attracting the principle of waiver, there are two essential elements to be satisfied. Firstly, waiver should be voluntary and intentional and secondly, there should be two parties—one waiving and the other getting benefit from such waiver.[34]

These requirements were not satisfied in a case before the Delhi High Court.[35] The plaintiff's predecessor inducted the defendant as a tenant in respect of the suit property. The lease required renewal after the initial 11 months, but it was never renewed. The tenant stopped paying rent after death of the plaintiff's predecessor. There was no evidence to show that the predecessor consented to the tenant continuing in the premises in perpetuity. The court refused to accept the contention that the plaintiff was bound by waiver in favour of the tenant.

After the accession of the state of J&K to India, articles of great value were left in the treasury of J&K. The former Maharaja or his sons did not claim the articles as

---

30. *GK Kempegowda v Lucinda,* AIR 1985 Kant 231.

31. *Rameshwar Pd v Bihar,* AIR 1984 Pat 61. See further *Sen & Co v Mani Mala Sadhu,* AIR 1980 SC 155, where the Supreme Court explains the difference between waiver and estoppel; *Chief Wild Life Warden v NK Joshi,* 1987 Cr LJ 1506 (Cal), a concession without knowledge of the subject, held to be revocable.

32. *Ram Raksh Pal v Brij Nandan,* AIR 1967 All 325.

33. *Rajendra Ram v Devendra Doss,* AIR 1973 SC 268 : (1973) 1 SCC 14. Where no public interest is involved and an assessee of property tax chooses to file a complaint against the proposal to fix or increase the rateable value, even without the issuance of a valid special notice, the principle of waiver would apply, *Municipal Corp, Ahmedabad v Oriental F&G Insurance Co Ltd,* AIR 1994 Guj 167. Acceptance of compensation for acquisition of land under oral protest did not amount to waiver of the right to claim proper compensation, *Basant Kumar Jena v State,* AIR 1995 Ori 288.

34. *Chetan Das v Annusuiya,* 1996 AIHC 1706 (Raj), landlord withdrawing default rent from the Court. *Radha Kishan v Election Tribunal-cum-sub-Judge,* AIR 2001 SC 68, consent given to a petition for recounting in an election prevented such party from questioning the validity of the order of recounting. *St Anne's School Society v Urban Improvement Trust,* AIR 2000 Raj 70, a party accepted half of the plot which was allotted to him and remained satisfied, he claimed the other half after a gap of about a year, but it was allotted to a school which had done some construction work on it. The doctrine of waiver of rights came into play. *Anto Nitto v South Indian Bank Ltd,* AIR 1998 Ker 219, the Court adopted the price which was offered by the decree-holder, it was less than the amount due under the decree. The judgment-debtor made no objection. Fixation of reserve price was mandatory as per rules, which was not done in this case. No objection by the judgment debtor did not have the effect of waiver because there could be no waiver of mandatory rules. *Auto Trade and Transport v National Insurance Co,* AIR 1998 MP 147, suit against carrier for recovery of loss, the requirement of notice before filing a suit was not complied with. The carrier raised objections only belatedly. This was taken to be a waiver of the requirement of notice.

35. *Prithvi Raj Bhalla v Industrial Cables (India) Ltd,* AIR 2002 Del 539. *Ferro Alloys Corp Ltd v UOI,* AIR 1999 SC 1236 : (1999) 4 SCC 149, an area of mining lease distributed among two claimants in terms of a committee report which was not challenged. This amounted to waiver.

their private property for over 30 years. The court held that it could be said that either there was relinquishment of the right or waiver of it voluntarily.[36]

A mandatory provision of a statute can be waived if it deals with individual rights. The requirement of notice under section 28 of the Customs Act could be waived by the individual who is entitled to such notice.[37] In the matter of execution of an order of a tribunal, no objection was raised on the ground that the tribunal had no jurisdiction where the order was being executed. It was held that the failure to object at the initial stage did not operate as waiver. No jurisdiction was conferred at the tribunal at that place by such failure.[38]

A person who is entitled to the benefit of a stipulation in a contract or of a statutory provision may waive it and allow the contract or transaction to proceed as though the stipulation or provision did not exist. Waiver of this kind depends upon consent and the fact that the other party has acted upon it is sufficient consideration.[39]

A suit was filed by an advocate for recovery of his professional fee. In the letter of appointment it was mentioned that the fee would be payable at the maximum rate. He accepted the appointment at the minimum rate provided payments were made without delay. Even so payments were delayed for months together. The advocate withdrew his offer of working at minimum rates. The court said that the plaintiff's claim was not lost by reason of waiver.[40]

[s 115.4.1] ***Pre-emption and Waiver.***—The co-sharer (plaintiff) kept his right of pre-emption hanging in balance. When the transaction with the purchaser (defendant) was finalised, the plaintiff acquiesced in the matter and actively participated in the sale transaction. He was also present at the time of registration. The court said that waiver of his right could be inferred.[41]

[s 115.5] Kinds of estoppel.—There are different kinds of estoppels: (1) estoppels by matter of record; (2) estoppels by deed; and (3) estoppels *in pais*.

(1) Estoppel by matter of record.—A matter of record is something part of the records of a Court. It is at once the narrative and the proof of its proceedings. Estoppel by records results from the judgment of a competent Court. The law allows a party ample opportunity, by way of appeal and otherwise, of upsetting a wrong decision.

---

36. *State of J&K v Karan Singh,* AIR 1997 J&K 132. *Amar Nath Misra v District Inspector of School, Ballia,* AIR 1997 All 358, High Court order found elections to be valid but allowed representations to be filed before the District Inspector of Schools over some issues, representations were accordingly made, parties who made the representations were not debarred from jointing appeal. *Mohinder Singh v District Election Officer,* AIR 1997 P&H 272, employees who had earlier performed election duties, not barred from contending that they should not be put under such duty. *Subhash Chand Agarwal v Murli Manohar Lal,* AIR 2000 Del 357 (Del), estoppel cannot be used to defeat a right conferred by law but there can be waiver of such a right. It was an order of eviction which affected the sub-tenant also. *Jagdishbhai Mafatlal Patel v State of Gujarat,* AIR 2002 Guj 329, the plea that certain bye-laws *ultra vires* was not taken at the appropriate time and, therefore, the principle of acquiescence applied.
37. *Commissioner of Customs, Mumbai v Virgo Steels, Bombay,* AIR 2002 SC 1745.
38. *Correspondent and Chairman, Standing Committee MES v M Syed Mohd,* AIR 2007 NOC 882 (Ker).
39. *Seth Satnarain v Dominion of India,* (1968) 2 SC WR 335.
40. *Pushpa Verma v UOI,* AIR 2008 Jhar 54.
41. *Rukmani Devi v Prabhu Narayan,* AIR 2007 NOC 1748 (Raj).

And if he takes the opportunity and fails, or does not choose to avail himself of it, he cannot subsequently re-open or dispute that decision.

And not only the parties themselves, but also the heir, executor, administrator and assign of each of them are bound by the decision, for they are "privy to the estoppel".

Estoppel by matter of record is chiefly concerned with the effect of judgments and their admissibility in evidence, and this kind of estoppel is dealt with by sections 11–14, Code of Civil Procedure, and sections 40–44 of the Evidence Act. It is the final decision and not any and every expression of opinion in a judgment which gives rise to an estoppel by record, and the actual decision cannot be carried further than the circumstances warrant.[42] The general principle which runs through the doctrine of estoppel by record is that a decree is an order of the court and the judgment debtor must, when it has once been completed, obey it unless and until he can get it set aside in proceedings duly constituted for the purpose.[43]

The force and effect of a judgment depend first upon the nature of the proceedings in which it was rendered, i.e. upon the question whether it was an action *in rem* or *in personam*; and second upon the *forum* in which it was pronounced, i.e., upon the question whether it was a judgment of a domestic or foreign Court. The record of a judgment *in rem* is generally conclusive upon all persons. In other cases, so far as the record purports to declare rights and duties, its material recitals import absolute verity between the parties to it and those who claim under them. The estoppel arising from or fixed by the fact enrolled constitutes the estoppel of a judgment. And to the question whether the judgment necessarily creates an estoppel, the general answer is, yes, if it results in *res judicata*: no, if it does not.[44] A party accepting payment under an arbitrator's award cannot afterwards challenge it.[45] Similarly, a party accepting costs under a judgment, even if under protest, was held to have amounted to accepting the order of the court as the correct order.[46] The principle is applicable to execution proceedings as well. [47]

---

42. *Ghasiram v Kundanbai,* (1941) Nag 513.

43. *Ramrao v Dattadayal,* (1947) Nag 889.

44. *Bigelow,* 6th Edn, pp 406, 410, *Woodroffe and Ameer Ali,* 9th Edn, p 850.

45. *Govindiji Javat & Co v Shree Saraswat Mills,* AIR 1982 Bom 76. A Party accepting the award of a reference court was not allowed afterwards to challenge it. See *Krishi Upaj Mandi Samiti v Ashok Singhal,* AIR 1991 SC 1320 : 1991 Supp (2) SCC 419.

46. *Amar Singh v Prahlad,* AIR 1989 P&H 229. But a party accepting compensatory costs for the restoration of a case dismissed in default has been held not to lose his right to question the validity of the restoration order. *KR Singh v AG Thakare,* AIR 1991 Bom 296.

47. *Radheshyam Modi v Jadunath Mohapatra,* AIR 1991 Ori 88. Tax assessing officers are not bound by the method adopted in earlier assessments. *CIT v British Paints,* AIR 1991 SC 1338 : 1992 Supp (1) SCC 55. *Chandrika Singh v Additional Member, Board of Revenue,* AIR 1998 Pat 118, parties who participated in the proceedings before the court after restoration of revision were not allowed to challenge the validity of the proceedings. *Food Corp of India v Dilip Kumar Dutta,* AIR 1999 Cal 75, under the Arbitration Act, 1940, a party volunteered before the arbitrator for extension of time, the same party questioned before the court the validity of extension of time. The court said that a party would not be allowed to approbate and reprobate at the same time. Irregularity in extension of time could be regularised. *United Bank of India v Abhijit Tea Co Pvt Ltd,* AIR 1999 Cal 81, accepting part payment in terms of compromise, not debarred from appealing against it. *State of TN v K Sabanayagam,* AIR 1998 SC 344 : (1998) 1 SCC 318, exemption under the Payment of Bonus Act, 1965, became waived because of the consistent stand taken by the Housing Board.

In a suit for partition, the court found that there were earlier two suits which recorded a finding of oral partition. The plaintiff was a minor at that time but he was a party to those suits and was represented by his guardian. There was no plea that the two earlier proceedings were null and void, nor any prayer for setting aside decrees passed in those suits. There was also no evidence to show that the minor was adversely affected. He obtained fruits of those two decrees. He was not allowed to turn around and say that those decrees should be ignored as they had affected his interest.[48]

Where there were cross suits between the same parties relating to the same property involving the same issues and they were disposed of by a common judgment involving the passing of two decrees, it was held that an appeal against only one decree was not maintainable.[49]

The licencee of a corporation filed a compromise in an earlier proceeding, but the corporation did not accept the compromise. The licencee abandoned the compromise and withdrew his petition. It was held that he was not bound in his subsequent petition by the statements made by him in his earlier petition.[50]

(2) Estoppel by deed.—Where a party has entered into a solemn engagement by deed as to certain facts, neither he nor any claiming through or under him is permitted to deny such facts. This rule, however, is subject to certain, qualifications:

(1) The rule applies only between parties and privies, and only in actions on the deed. (2) No estoppel arises upon recitals or descriptions which are either immaterial or not intended to bind. (3) No estoppel arises where the deed is tainted by fraud or illegality. (4) A deed which can take effect by interest shall not be construed to take effect by estoppel. Thus if a party leases premises to another for a longer term than he himself possesses, it only enures to the extent of his own interest and no further.[51]

Where the petitioner claimed his possession on the land of a tribal by virtue of a registered sale deed obtained with due permission, the plea raised by the petitioner must be considered before drawing the conclusion that the possession was without lawful authority.[52]

The doctrine of English law as to estoppel by deed does not apply to written instruments in India. Deeds and contracts in this country are to be liberally construed. The form of expression, the literal sense, is not to be so much regarded as the real meaning of the parties which the transaction discloses.[53] The art of conveyancing in this country is of so simple and informal a character, that estoppel by deed has been expressly discountenanced by courts. "Justice and equity" require no more than that

---

48. *Muthakke v Devanna Rai,* AIR 2002 Ker 301.

49. *Darayas Bamanshah Medhora v Nariman Bamanshah Medhora,* AIR 2002 Guj 166.

50. *MS Baliga v Mangalore City Corporation,* AIR 1998 Kant 76 : LNIND 1997 Kant 428.

51. *Phipson,* 10th Edn, p 848. *PG Hariharan v Padaril,* AIR 1994 Ker 36, the party himself going against the terms of family arrangement cannot be allowed to raise the plea of estoppel against the other party.

52. *Atmaram v State,* AIR 1995 MP 225. *Chetak Constructions Ltd v Om Prakash,* AIR 2003 MP 145, the agreement for transfer of property stated that the vendors, who had received their price, transferred possession also at the time of the agreement. They were not permitted to deny the fact of handing over of possession also.

53. *Ram Lal Sett v Kanai Lal Sett,* (1886) 12 Cal 663; *Hunoomanpersaud Panday v Mussumat Babooee Munraj Koonweree,* (1856) 6 Moo Ind App 393, 411; *Johnston v Gopal Singh,* (1931) 12 Lah 546.

a party to an instrument should be precluded from contradicting it to the prejudice of another person, when that other person or person through whom the other person claims has been induced to alter his position by virtue of the instrument; but when the question arises between the parties or the representatives of parties who at the time of the execution of the instrument were aware of its intention and object and who have not been induced to alter their position by its execution, justice in India will be more surely obtained by allowing any party, whether he be plaintiff or defendant, to show the truth.[54]

(3) Estoppel *in pais* by conduct.—Estoppel *in pais* (i.e. "in the country", or "before the public"), or more fully "estoppel *in pais* dehors the instrument" (i.e. with regard to matters outside a record or deed) as known to the common law was of an entirely different character to the estoppel *in pais* of the present days. "Indeed the estoppel *in pais* of the present day has grown up entirely since the time of Coke, and embraces cases never contemplated in that character by him or by the lawyers of even much later times though the old lines are often visible in the newer pathways."

Estoppel *in pais* arises (1) from agreement or contract and (2) from act or conduct of misrepresentation which has induced a change of position in accordance with the intention of the party against whom the estoppel is alleged. To raise an estoppel by conduct, a person must by word or conduct induce another to believe that a certain state of things exists, and to cause that other to act on that belief in a way he would not have done had he known the facts, so that, if in an action between them the person making a representation were allowed to prove the true facts—to tell the truth—the other person would be prejudiced. If these two conditions are fulfilled, then the person making the representation will not be allowed to deny its truth in any action between him and the person to whom he made it or the persons who claim in the same right. But in any other action he can deny its truth. The ways in which a person may make such a representation are infinite. He may speak or write, act or omit to act, or act negligently.

The following are the recognised propositions of an estoppel *in pais*: (1) If a man by his words or conduct wilfully endeavours to cause another to believe in a certain state of things which the first knows to be false, and if the second believes in such state of things, and acts upon his belief, he who knowingly made the false statement is estopped from averring afterwards that such a state of things did not in fact exist.

(2) If a man, either in express terms or by conduct, makes a representation to another of the existence of a certain state of facts which he intends to be acted upon in a certain way, and it be acted upon in that way, in the belief of the existence of such a state of facts, to the damage of him who so believes and acts, the first is estopped from denying the existence of such a state of facts.

(3) If a man, whatever his real meaning may be, so conducts himself that a reasonable man would take his conduct to mean a certain representation of facts, and that it was a true representation, and that the latter was intended to act upon it in a particular way, and he with such belief does act in that way to his damage, the first is estopped from denying that the facts were as represented.

54. *Param Singh v Laji Mal,* (1877) 1 All 403; *Johnston v Gopal Singh,* (1931) 12 Lah 546; *Deena Bandhu Gan v Makim Sardar,* (1935) 63 Cal 763.

(4) If, in the transaction itself which is in dispute, one has led another into the belief of a certain state of facts by conduct of culpable negligence calculated to have that result, and such culpable negligence has been the proximate cause of leading and has led the other to act by mistake upon such belief, to his prejudice, the second cannot be heard afterwards, as against the first, to show that the state of facts referred to did not exist.[55]

The conduct of appearing before a selection committee without any objection as to the constitution of the committee would create an estoppel preventing the candidate from challenging the constitution of the committee even if the decision was against him.[56] Where in the selection of District judges, minimum qualifying marks to be obtained in interview were prescribed without any authority under the selection rules, no estoppel was created against a candidate appearing at the interview. He was allowed to challenge the validity of the procedure.[57] Allocation of 50% marks was held to be not arbitrary when promotion was to be to higher managerial posts. The appellant participated in the selection. He could not turn around subsequently to say that the process of interview was unfair.[58] Arbitrators failed to make an award within time. The court passed a consent order entitling the umpire to proceed. The party who submitted to his jurisdiction and participated in the proceeding was held precluded from challenging it.[59] A candidate appeared at a competitive examination on the basis of a prospectus. He failed. He was not allowed to challenge the validity of the prospectus as to the selection already made.[60] A candidate having participated in the selection process along with others without any demur or protest cannot be allowed to turn round and question the very same process after having failed to qualify for the promotion.[61] A candidate who applies for revaluation is bound by the new result

---

55. Per Brett, J, in *Carr v London and North Western Railway Co,* (1875) LR 10 CP 307, 316, 317, 318. No estoppel arises from a mere participation in the selection of a lessee. *Pukh Raj v Rajasthan,* AIR 1980 Raj 83. *Dhirubhai D & Co v Nizam Sugar Factory Ltd,* AIR 2010 NOC 660 (AP), till the time of preparation of final bill, the contractor's claim for higher rates was under consideration and not rejected. After about 2 years a small amount was paid. Its acceptance by the contractor did not estop him from claiming higher rates.

56. *G Sarana v Lucknow University,* AIR 1976 SC 2428 : (1976) 3 SCC 585.

57. *Ramesh Kumar v High Court of Delhi,* AIR 2010 SC 3714 : (2010) 3 SCC 104.

58. *KA Nagamani v Indian Airlines,* AIR 2009 SC 3240 : (2009) 5 SCC 515.

59. *N Chellappan v Kerala SE Board,* AIR 1975 SC 230 : (1974) 2 SCC 660. Submitting to the award of a Tribunal as to surplus land, cannot question afterwards. *State of Maharashtra v Harischandra,* AIR 1986 SC 1192 : (1986) 3 SCC 349. A simple participation in the proceedings after the expiry of 4 months does not debar. *State of Punjab v Hardayal,* AIR 1985 SC 920 : (1985) 2 SCC 629.

60. *S Muthumanicakam v State,* AIR 1986 Mad 179; *R Murali (Dr) v Dr R Kamalakhanan,* AIR 2000 Mad 174, the petitioner appeared for admission to PG Medical courses on the basis of a prospectus which contained fixation of quota for in service candidates by Government. He was not allowed to challenge the prospectus. *Kundan Mal v District College, Pali,* AIR 2000 Raj 152, the petitioner ordered to pay charges for conversion of land to commercial purposes and he complied with the orders, not allowed subsequently to challenge the order by writ petition.

61. *KA Nagamani v Indian Airlines,* AIR 2009 SC 3240 : (2009) 5 SCC 515; *Manish Kumar Shahi v State of Bihar,* (2010) 12 SCC 576. Also see—*Amlan Jyoti Borooah v State of Assam,* (2009) 3 SCC 227 (wherein it was held that the appellant, having accepted the change in the selection procedure *sub silentio,* cannot be permitted to turn round and contend that the procedure adopted was illegal); *UOI v Dalbir Singh,* (2009) 7 SCC 251 (wherein the candidate having applied only for the OBC vacancy, when his OBC certificate was found to be defective, he was held to be estopped from seeking his inclusion in the general list on the ground that the last candidate in the general list had scored less marks than him).

even if his score is reduced.[62] Where in an accident claim petition the owner of the vehicle did not file the original policy and made no objection to the genuineness of the printed copy filed by the insurance company, the owner cannot later on make objection to its genuineness.[63]

Similarly, bidders who participated in the tender process offering petrol vehicles, where the authorities had to decide what kind of vehicle they would hire for use as ambulance, were held to be estopped from questioning or objecting to the conditions of tender that it were meant to favouring only the owners of diesel vehicles, after they participated in the process.[64]

Estoppel *in pais* is dealt with in sections 115–117. sections 116 and 117 are instances of estoppel by contract, *viz.*, that of the tenant, the licensee, the bailee and the acceptor of a bill of exchange. But the distinction between estoppel by contract and estoppel by conduct is not preserved in the Evidence Act. The sections relating to estoppel in the Evidence Act are not exhaustive. Cases of estoppel may arise which are not within the purview of these sections.[65] As to other instances of estoppel, see section 234 of the Indian Contract Act, 1872; section 18 of the Specific Relief Act, 1877; sections 41 and 43 of the Transfer of Property Act, 1882; sections 27 and 53 of the Indian Sale of Goods Act, 1930; and section 28 of the Indian Partnership Act, 1932.[66]

The members of a joint family arrived at an informal family arrangement under which possession and enjoyment of the share in property of each member was handed over to him. All the members had signed the agreement. They considered the partition so made as final as between all of them and nobody made any objection for a number of years. The court said that in such circumstances even if it were to be assumed that the document required registration, the conduct of members operated as an estoppel which prevented them from resiling from the arrangement. No member could seek an injunction or a restraint order in respect of property partitioned and mutated in favour of another member.[67] The court said[68] that this principle has become established through several decisions of the court as also of the Privy Council. "In *Kanhailal v Brijlal*[69] the privy council applied the principle of estoppel to the facts of the case and observed: "Kanhailal was a party to that compromise. He was one of those whose claims to the family property or to share in it, induced Ram Dei against her daughter, Kripa, and

---

62. *Lalit Taori v Nagpur University*, AIR 1986 Bom 255.

63. *Amrit Kaur v Chaman Lal*, AIR 1994 HP 21. *Balkrishna Menon v Padmavathy Amma*, AIR 1993 Ker 218, first fact-finding commissioner's report not accepted by the party, got his replacement and on receiving the second report, not allowed to rely on the first report. *Pine Chemical Suppliers v Collector of Customs (Bombay)*, AIR 1993 SC 1185 : 1993 Supp(2) SCC 124, an importer accepted test reports indicating misdeclaration of goods, valuation on the basis of the test reports could not be challenged.

64. *Dr Hafzur Rahaman Quadri v State of West Bengal* , AIR 2012 NOC 235 (Cal.).

65. *Rup Chand Ghosh v Sarveswar Chandra*, (1906) 33 Cal 915. There are decisions which lay down that these sections are exhaustive: see *Asmatunnessa Khatun v Harendra Lal Biswas*, (1908) 35 Cal 904.

66. *Ganesh Shet v Dr CSGK Setty*, AIR 1998 SC 2216 : (1998) 5 SCC 381, specific relief not allowed on the evidence of incomplete contract and the plaintiff not competing even after opportunity.

67. *PN Wankundre v CS Wankundre*, AIR 2002 Bom 129 : 2002 1 Bom LR 613.

68. At p 133.

69. 45 Indian Appeals 118 at 124 : AIR 1918 PC 70, at P 74.

greatly to her own detriment to alter her position by agreeing to the compromise, and under that compromise he obtained a substantial benefit which he has hitherto enjoyed. In their Lordship's opinion he is bound by it and cannot now claim as a reversioner". For the issue of a stage carriage permit one of the conditions was that there would be levy of stand fee on per trip basis. This was held to be not violative of Article 19(1)(g). The permit holder had accepted the condition and, therefore, he was estopped from challenging the validity of the levy.[70] Where the grantee of stage coach permit challenged the proceedings on the ground that the State Transport Authority had imposed improper conditions but no such grounds were raised before the Tribunal, it was held that the applicant was debarred from her conduct from raising the point in a writ petition.

Where the consignee accepted the delivery of bulk goods from the ship after inspecting them and finding damage, he was not allowed afterwards to raise any claim for short delivery.[71] Where the licencee accepted the licence under the UP Cinemas (Regulation) Act, 1956 with a clause in the agreement that he would not claim grants-in-aid, it was held that he having enjoyed the other benefits under the agreement was not entitled to wriggle out of the agreement and claim the benefit of grant-in-aid.[72] Where all along the LIC had been accepting premiums and granting receipts without demur and there was not a single document on record or any pleading on its behalf that at any time it had informed the insured that, in fact, what it was depositing was the premium of the previous month, the LIC by so accepting the premium as valid payments for long years was estopped from taking the plea that the premium paid was not valid.[73]

---

70. *Haryana Cooperative Transport Societies Welfare Assn. v State of Haryana,* AIR 2000 P&H 230. *Navayuga Exports Ltd v AP Mineral Development Corp,* AIR 1998 AP 391, acceptance of mining rights for 6 months period, not allowed to say afterwards that under the relevant Act, lease should have been for 20 years.

71. *Scindia Steam Navigation Co Ltd v UOI,* AIR 1998 Ker 250. *Bapulal Walchand Jain v Pandurang Vithal Pingle,* AIR 2003 Bom 5, payment of decree, the judgment debtor pleaded that only a small amount remained to be paid, the decree-holder's income-tax return also showed the same fact, he was estopped from saying that no payment had been made. *Syed Ali Mossa Raza v Razia Begam,* AIR 2003 AP 2, construction over the plaintiff's property under *bona fide* belief, but not able to show any conduct on the part of the plaintiff to create an estoppel against him. The plaintiff could assert his normal property rights. *State of Karnataka v Stellar Construction Co,* AIR 2003 Kant 6, the contractor had nothing more than the agreed work, no claim for extra-expenditure could be built on the basis of a letter, a part of internal correspondence, from a lower officer to a higher officer. *Parvatewava v Bhagawwa,* AIR 2003 NOC 116 (Kant) : 2002 AIHC 3395, an *ex parte* order was set aside subject to payment of costs, the defendant paid belatedly but even so the plaintiff withdrew it. He was not allowed to challenge the restoration. *Heirs Kantilal Purshottamdas patel v Dahlben Jagdish Rathod,* AIR 2003 Guj 82, questioning validity of *sale deed* by legal heir after 4 years, after the death of her husband she operated the account in which the sale consideration was deposited, sale deed contained clear recitals about legal necessity. Sale deed not liable to be set aside. *MTW Tenzing Namgyal v Motilal Lakhotia,* AIR 2003 SC 1448, plaintiff's suit for possession of immovable property on the basis of ownership, the plaintiff failed to prove ownership on the basis of documents on record, the *Khasra* entry was found to be of no evidentiary value. The land in question was acquired and the plaintiff's predecessor in title received compensation without any objections. The plaintiffs became estopped from claiming title.

72. *Shitla pd. Dubey v State of UP,* AIR 1999 All 260.

73. *Life Insurance Corp of India, Patna v Lalita Devi,* AIR 2016 Pat 6, para 11.

[s 115.6] Equitable estoppel.—A man may be estopped, not only from giving particular evidence, but from doing acts, or relying upon any particular argument or contention which the rules of equity and good conscience prevent his using as against his opponent.[74] The law of estoppel by representation is confined to the provisions of this section and apart from the provisions of this section there is nothing like what is called "equitable estoppel" evolved by the English judges. The provisions of this section are in a sense a rule of evidence.[75] Where the Government caused delay in communicating adverse remarks to an employee, the Government was not permitted to reject the representation of the employee as belated. The Government was held to be bound by an equitable estoppel to consider the representation on merits.[76] Estoppel being a product of equity the court has to go by equities on both sides so as to hold them in a balance. A scheme for allotment of plots to non-resident Indian generated a poor response. Time was extended. It resulted in a long gap of time from the original date. In between the cost of development increased substantially. The Central Government was held to be justified in dropping the scheme.[77]

[s 115.7] Proprietary Estoppel.—The claimant lived for more than 30 years on an agricultural land of which the landlord lady was the half owner. She had given a promise to the claimant that she would leave her share in the land to him on her death if he cared for the land until her death and cultivated it. The claimant paid no rent, but he continued to fulfil the conditions in the owner's promise. He sold the surplus agricultural produce and retained the proceeds for himself. But the owner sold the land to a purchaser for value, who notified the claimant to quit the land. The claimant brought an action against the purchaser on the basis of promissory estoppel. The court ruled that he was entitled to half the share of the land. The court said that the question depended on what assurances were given to him and what was the degree of his reliance on those assurances and the detriment which was likely to be caused to him.

[s 115.8] Promissory estoppel.—When one party has, by his words or conduct, made to the other a promise or assurance which was intended to affect the legal relations between them and to be acted on accordingly, then, once the other party has taken him at his word and acted on it, the one who gave the promise or assurance cannot afterwards be allowed to revert to their previous legal relations as if no such promise or assurance had been made by him, but he must accept their legal relations subject to the qualification which he himself has so introduced. This doctrine, which is derived from a principle of equity enunciated in 1877, has been the subject of considerable recent development. This

---

74. *Ganges Manufacturing Co v Sourujmull,* (1880) 5 Cal 669, 678; *S. Butail v HP Forest Corp,* AIR 2002 HP 1, the fact that the plaintiff (chartered accountant) repeatedly asked for payment of the balance fee after he received the initial payment, showed that the payment was not received by him in full and final settlement and, therefore, his subsequent claim for full payment could not be prevented by invoking the doctrine of estoppel. It would be inequitable to do so.
75. *Maddanappa v Chandramma,* AIR 1965 SC 1812 : (1965) 3 SCR 283.
76. *Baidyanath Mahapatra v State of Orissa,* AIR 1989 SC 2218 : (1989) 4 SCC 664.
77. *RK Deka v UOI,* AIR 1992 Del 53.

is a doctrine evolved by equity in order to prevent injustice.[78] It differs from estoppel properly so called because the representation relied upon need not be one of present fact.[79]

The doctrine of promissory estoppel is premised on conduct of party making a representation to the other so as to enable him to arrange its affairs in such a manner as if the said representation would be acted upon. It provides for a cause of action. It need not necessarily be a defence.[80]

In granting relief on the basis of the doctrine of promissory estoppel, it is the duty of courts to analyse the facts to ensure that the principles of estoppel could appropriately be invoked to help the respondents. Where the respondents were not put to disadvantage acting upon any unequivocal promise made by the appellants, it was held that no relief can be granted by resorting to the doctrine of promissory estoppel.[81]

The Supreme Court observed in a case that in order to invoke the doctrine of promissory estoppel, a clear, sound and positive foundation must be laid by the party in the petition itself.[82] A plea of estoppel cannot be availed of if there is duty owed by the person sought to be estopped, nor any representation made by such person. Before anyone can be estopped by a representation inferred from negligent conduct there must be a duty to use due care towards the person misled, or towards the general public of which that person is one.[83]

---

78. *Motilal Padampat Sugar Mills Co Ltd v State of Uttar Pradesh,* (1979) 2 SCR 641, AIR 1979 SC 621—**referred** to and **followed** in *D Boopalan v Madras Metropolitan Water Supply and Sewerage Board,* (2007) 12 SCC 569.

79. Halsbury's Laws of England (3rd Edn), Vol 15, p 175, para 344, **applied** by VIMADALAL J, in *Air Corp. Emp. Union v GB Bhirade,* (1969) 71 Bom LR 707. Doctrine of promissory estoppel is evolved by equity in order to prevent injustice, *Intrans Systems Pvt Ltd v State of Kerala,* AIR 1996 Ker 161. The doctrine cannot be invoked against public interest, *National Oxygen Ltd v TN Electricity Board,* AIR 1996 Mad 229. Promissory estoppel proceeds on the footing that when on the representation of a promisor, a promisee alters his position, then the former should keep his words and should not be allowed to recede from them, *Kimti Lal Rahi v UOI,* AIR 1993 Del 211. The rule of promissory estoppel being an equitable doctrine is not a rule of thumb or a hard and fast rule but elastic one in the hands of courts to do complete justice between the parties, *State of HP v Ganesh Wood Products,* AIR 1996 SC 149 : (1995) 6 SCC 363. No clear cut promise or representation, doctrine of promissory estoppel not attracted, *Ude Ram v State of Haryana,* AIR 1994 P&H 175. No assurance or promise, no estoppel, *Paschimanchal Vidyut Vitran Nigam Ltd v Adarsh Textiles,* AIR 2015 SC 511 (paras 29 and 30); no fraudulent misrepresentation or false statement to other party, no estoppel, *Bhagwati Vanaspati Traders v Senior Superintendent of Post Offices, Meerut,* AIR 2015 SC 901 (para 7). A promise of full efforts to secure employment to trainees does not create any estoppel, *UPSRTC v UP Parivahan Sangh,* AIR 1995 SC 1115 : (1995) 2 SCC 1. Recognition as freedom fighter, type of evidence in one case (certificate from another freedom fighter) does not estop the Government from rejecting similar evidence in other cases, *Chaitnya Charan Das v State of WB,* AIR 1995 Cal 336. Doctrine of promissory estoppel cannot be invoked outside the terms of contract, *Nagappa v State,* AIR 1994 Kant 77. The principle of promissory estoppel is akin to the principle of legitimate expectation. Unless there is overriding reason of public policy or other compelling or overriding consideration of public interest or other extenuating circumstances the State is bound to fulfil its promise, *Shakti Tubes Ltd v State of Bihar (FB),* AIR 1994 Patna 162.

80. *LML Ltd v State of Uttar Pradesh,* (2008) 3 SCC 128.

81. *Managing Director, Tamil Nadu Magnesite Ltd v S Manickam,* (2010) 4 SCC 421.

82. *State of Arunachal Pradesh v Nezone Law House, Assam,* AIR 2008 SC 2045 : (2008) 5 SCC 609, which was not the case here. *Ansal Properties and Infrastructure Ltd v State of Haryana,* AIR 2008 NOC 2045 (P&H-DB), acquisition of land, departmental correspondence for allotment, not communicated to any hopeful builder, no estoppel.

83. *Standard Chartered Bank v Andhra Bank Financial Services Ltd,* (2006) 6 SCC 94 : AIR 2006 SC 3626.

No promissory estoppel arose where the Government granted a cement permit and afterwards cancelled it on account of a change in policy.[84] The doctrine of promissory estoppel cannot be invoked when the representation or promise made by Government officials or public authority is beyond its power or is prohibited by law.[85] The mere fact that the tenderer had agreed to the proposal to pay the entire bid amount, was held to be not an automatic acceptance of the tender on the principle of promissory estoppel.[86] Promissory estoppel is neither available against the abolition of a Government post[87] nor against the levy of a tax on sale of country liquor which was exempted by an earlier Government.[88] A long course of dealing (oil distribution agency in this case) does not create an estoppel that the agency will not be terminated or its terms will not be reviewed.[89] Deemed promotion from a past date cannot be granted but the Government can be held bound to adhere to the time bound promotion scheme promised to employees.[90] Where employees were shifted from one Department into another on assurance that no change would be made in their service conditions, they were allowed to claim estoppel against proposed changes.[91] Where certain mortgaged lands had reverted to the State and orders were passed to transfer the lands to the persons to whom they were allotted after receiving from them the mortgage money, the Government was not allowed to resile from its orders after accepting payments.[92] Sale of pledged goods by a bank under an assurance to the borrower by the bank manager that he would be discharged from liability created an estoppel preventing the bank from proceeding against the borrower for any deficiency.[93]

A person to whom the right to collect Zila Prishad fee on vehicles entering its territories was allotted was not permitted afterwards to refuse to hand over the collection by saying that the contract was not lawful.[94]

Where the petitioner accepted the proposal to produce a serial for Doordarshan in 13 episodes but subsequently he sought permission to produce the said serial in 26 episodes, he was barred by estoppel.[95] Where the railway authorities promised the petitioner that freight for goods would be charged by the shortest route, they were

---

84. *Jacob Philip v UOI,* AIR 1985 Ker 255; *R.B Jodhanand v State,* AIR 1984 J&K 10. *Ashok Kumar v Union Territory, Chandigarh,* AIR 1995 SC 461 : (1995) 1 SCC 631, change of policy in licencing rules. *Haryana State Industrial Devp. Corp v Inderjeet,* AIR 1996 SC 2244 : (1996) 9 SCC 49, offered plot size reduced, accepted by the applicant, not allowed to go back on his acceptance. *Bharat Wools v State of Punjab,* AIR 1996 P&H 215, invitation for applications, does not bind the Government.

85. *Bajrang Industries v General Manager, DIC., Vizianagaram,* AIR 1994 AP 10, relying upon *UOI v Godfrey Philips India Ltd,* AIR 1986 SC 806 : (1985) 4 SCC 369, *Jit Ram Shiv Kumar v State of Haryana,* AIR 1980 SC 1285 : (1981) 1 SCC 11 and *Motilal Patampat Sugar Mills Co Ltd v State of UP,* AIR 1979 SC 621 : 1979 All LJ 368 : (1979) 2 SCC 409 and **distinguishing** *Pournami Oil Mills v State of Kerala,* AIR 1987 SC 590 : 1986 Supp SCC 728.

86. *C Jayasree v Commissioner, MC.H,* AIR 1994 AP 312.

87. *Dasarathi v AP,* AIR 1985 AP 136; *Pramodhbhai v Officer on Spl. Duty No. 2,* AIR 1989 Guj 187, notification can be withdrawn before acted upon.

88. *Excise Commr. UP v Ram Kumar,* AIR 1976 SC 2237 : (1976) 3 SCC 540.

89. *Mahabir Auto Stores v IOC Ltd,* AIR 1989 Del 315. See also *Ramlal Khurana v State of Punjab,* AIR 1989 SC 1985 : (1989) 4 SCC 99, no estoppel against compulsory retirement.

90. *TR Kapoor v State of Haryana,* AIR 1989 SC 2082 : (1989) 4 SCC 71.

91. *Bhim Singh v Haryana,* AIR 1980 SC 768 : (1981) 2 SCC 673.

92. *Tara Singh v Kehar Singh,* AIR 1989 SC 1426 : 1989 Supp (1) SCC 316.

93. *Syndicate Bank v Sudhir Surgicals & Allied Industries,* AIR 1992 Ker 146.

94. *Surendra Kumar Rai v Zila Parishad, Jhansi,* AIR 1997 All 387.

95. *Gopi Chand Television v Director, Doordarshan Kendra, Hyderabad,* AIR 1995 AP 199.

estopped from rationalising the longest route subsequently.[96] Where the petitioner failed to construct the cinema hall within the specified period, he could not claim exemption from entertainment tax as promised by the Government by invoking the doctrine of promissory estoppel.[97] Where a certain small scale industrial unit, sick due to its own mismanagement, was unwilling to fulfil the suggested conditions, the bank could not be directed to fulfil the promise of its rehabilitation.[98] The Government held out a promise to a company to supply specified quantity of wood at a specified rate and the company on that assurance set up a factory by investing a huge amount, subsequent unilateral decision of the Government to enhance the rate of royalty would be hit by the principle of promissory estoppel.[99]

Where two people with the same source of information assert the same truth or agree to assert the same falsehood at the same time, neither can be estoppel against the other.[100]

[s 115.8.1] Promissory estoppel against Government and its Agencies.—Government and its agencies are no longer immune from the operation of the doctrine of promissory estoppel. Government agencies have to work within the framework of the legal system.[101] A contractor was promised renewal of a forest lease. He paid the requisites and incurred expenditure on improvement of the site. There was some delay in granting formal renewal.

---

96. *Gujarat Ambuja Cements Ltd v UOI,* AIR 1994 Guj 104. *Davinder Singh v State,* AIR 1995 J&K 77, transport authorities asked the bus owner to complete all the formalities and he complied with the order by depositing fee etc., the authority was not permitted to go back, relying on AIR 1979 SC 1628 : (1979) 3 SCC 489.

97. *Tilak Chitra Mandir v State,* AIR 1993 All 30. *Akhara Brahm Buta v State of Punjab,* AIR 1993 SC 366 : (1992) 4 SCC 243, acquisition of land against promise, houses built, market- value allowed as compensation. *Tulsi v State of Rajasthan,* 1996 AIHC 1824 (Raj) promise of land at certain rate to land oustees, not allowed to be altered to commercial value. Promise of loan for rebuilding cinema hall damaged in cyclone, the successor party to power not allowed to resile, *B Sanjeeva Reddy v Govt of AP,* 1996 AIHC 2426 (AP). Belated compliance with terms and conditions did not create estoppel, *Chemech Engineers P Ltd v Director of Industries and Commerce,* AIR 1994 Mad 14. Failure to observe packing rules, no estoppel against licencing authority, *GTN Textiles Ltd v R.OT Commr.,* AIR 1993 SC 1596 : (1993) 3 SCC 438. Withdrawal of proposed rebate on electricity charges before compliance by anybody with the scheme, held effective, *APSEB v Sarada Ferro Alloys,* AIR 1993 SC 1521 : (1993) 2 SCC 425; *Hindustan Ferro Alloys Ltd v UPSEB,* AIR 1995 All 209.

98. *Sanjiv Textiles Pvt Ltd v State Bank of India,* AIR 1993 Guj 132. For promissory estoppel to arise it is necessary that the contract between the parties is made in the prescribed form and manner, *BC Raju v Karnataka Housing Board,* AIR 1995 Kant 356. Non-compliance with requirements, no estoppel, *Kimti Lal Rahi v UOI,* AIR 1993 Del 211.

99. *Mangalam Timber Products Ltd v State,* AIR 1996 Ori 13; *Suvarna Cements Ltd v UOI,* AIR 2002 AP 244, accepting base on certain terms including the term as to interest on late payments, not allowed to say that those terms are not to be of binding effect.

100. *Bhagwati Vanaspati Traders v Senior Superintendent of Post Offices, Meerut,* (2015) 1 SCC 617 (para 8), **approving** *Moorgate Mercantile Co Ltd v Twitchings,* 1977 AC 890 : (1976) 3 WLR 66 : (1976) 2 All ER 641 (HL).

101. The Government has to place before the Court all the necessary material to enable the court to decide whether estoppel would arise or not. The mere *ipse dixit* of being a Government is not enough for this purpose. *American Dry Fruit Stores v UOI,* AIR 1990 Bom 376. Promissory estoppel cannot be used to compel the Government or a public authority to carry out a representation or a promise which is contrary to law or which was outside the authority or power of the officer of the Government or of the public authority to make, *Ram Nath Sahu v UOI,* AIR 1996 All 19. Where sanction or promise is *ultra vires* of the authority, no estoppel arises, *PV Balakrishnan Nair v State of Kerala,* AIR 1994 Ker 6, holding *Robertson, Robertson v Minister of Pensions,* (1949) 1 KB 227 not a good law.

Ultimately the contractor was refused because of a shift in policy. The Madras High Court did not permit the Government to go back upon its promise.[102] Where the right of collection of terminal tax was allotted at an auction to a bidder who had also deposited the bid amount and, before the final contract was executed, the Government adopted the policy of not granting such rights, the Government was held to be precluded from cancelling the auction.[103] The Government announced a scheme of exemptions under the Industries Act. The applicant submitted his documents within the time delimited and commenced working. The Government took four years to dispose of his application telling him that the scheme was withdrawn. The High Court of Delhi ordered the Government to grant the intended benefits to the applicant.[104] The moral of these cases is that there can be no whimsical withdrawal from a declared programme which has already generated action.[105] Where an industrialist went to the extent of erecting a factory in response to declarations of vital exemptions, Supreme Court held the Government bound by the scheme in reference to the petitioner. It was immaterial that his factory was running at a profit. The doctrine of estoppel is not based upon loss or detriment or fraud but upon alteration of position in response to a representation.[106]

It reviewed all the English cases on the subject, particularly relating to the position that promissory estoppel cannot be used as a cause of action and it only affords a

---

102. *AK Thangudrai v DFO, Madurai,* AIR 1985 Mad 104. Similarly, the extension of lease of fishery was not allowed to be withdrawn after the grantee had acted upon it. *Ikop Laidakol Fishing Corp v State of Manipur,* AIR 1982 Gau 14.

103. *Nandkishore v Nagar Palika Shajapur,* AIR 1991 MP 99.

104. *Dhampur Sugar Mills v UOI,* AIR 1985 Del 344.

105. See *UOI v Indo-Afghan Agencies,* AIR 1968 SC 718 : (1968) 2 SCR 366.

106. *Motilal Padmapat Sugar Mills v UP,* (1979) 2 SCR 641: AIR 1979 SC 621 : (1979) 2 SCC 409. Followed in *Indo-American Hybrid Seeds v Chandigarh I & TD Corporation,* AIR 1995 P&H 134. The same result followed where there was incentive scheme for industry in backward areas. *Tapti Oil Industries v Maharashtra,* AIR 1984 Bom 161. Followed by the Calcutta High Court in *Steel Crakers Ltd v MSTC,* AIR 1992 Cal 86 emphasising the duty of the Court as laid down by the Supreme Court in successive cases like *Mahabir Auto Stores v IOC,* AIR 1990 SC 1031 : (1990) 3 SCC 752, and *Kumari Shrilekha Vidyatri v State of UP,* 1990 (4) JT SC 211 to set right arbitrary Government action. *Modi Alkalies & Chemicals Ltd v State of Rajasthan,* AIR 1992 Raj 51, remission of electricity duty announced to promote industry, the Government held bound. *Vinay Cement Ltd v State of Assam,* AIR 1997 Gau 34, the promoter of a company acted on a scheme sponsored by the Government and established an industry in the notified backward area. He obtained letters of intent and necessary licences and all clearance certificates and also booked machinery supplied at a cost of crores of rupees. The State Government was not allowed to go back on its assurances. *Arya Durga Industries v GM, District Industries Centre,* acting on Government scheme for setting up industry. Government not allowed to revoke the scheme retrospectively. *Kalu Chand v State of Rajasthan,* AIR 1998 Raj 33, allotment of plot of land by Municipal Board. The allottee made heavy payments to the Board and also for securing water and electricity connection, construction was also done after securing sanction of the Board. Refusal by the Board at this stage to execute lease deed was held to be improper. Equitable considerations and legitimate expectation demanded that the Board be directed to execute lease in favour of the allottee. *National Engineering Industries Ltd v State of Rajasthan,* AIR 1998 Raj 229, an area of agricultural land officially converted into industrial for the use of the allottee which spent money on its use, the Government not allowed to go back on the promise. *UNI-ADS Pvt Ltd v Commissioner of MCH, Hyderabad,* AIR 1999 AP 278, the corporation invited tenders for leasing out electricity poles for advertising in the city. The petitioner company was the highest bidder. The petitioner acted in a *bona fide* manner on the representations made by the corporation and deposited the requisite amounts as well as made certain other expenses. The action of the corporation in not entering into the agreement was held to be not proper. The Court directed it to honour its promised commitments.

defence. The learned judge said:[107] "It is, however, necessary to make it clear that though the doctrine has been called in various judgments and text-books as promissory estoppel, and it has been variously described as "equitable estoppel", "quasi estoppel" and "new estoppel", it is not really based upon the principle of estoppel, but it is a doctrine evolved by equity in order to prevent injustice where a promise made by a person knowing that it would be acted on by the person to whom it is made and in fact it is so acted on and it is inequitable to allow the party making the promise to go back upon it."[108] The doctrine of promissory estoppel need not, therefore, be confined to the limitations of estoppel in the strict sense of the word. Even Lord Denning recognised in *Crabb v Arun District Council,*[109] that, "there are estoppels and estoppels. Some do give rise to a cause of action. Some do not." He added that promissory estoppel often gives rise to a cause of action. Stating the effect of estoppel on the position of the true owner, his Lordship observed that the owner's title to the property, be it land or goods, has been held to be limited or extinguished, and new rights and interests have been created therein. And this operates by reason of his conduct—what he has led the other to believe—even though he never intended it. "New rights and interests, so created by estoppel, in or over land, will be protected by the courts and in this way give rise to a cause of action." A declaration of the right of way against the District Council was granted in this case. It referred to the treatise by Spencer Bower and Turner on the Law Relating to Estoppel by Representation who have explained this decision on the basis that it is an instance of the application of the doctrine of estoppel by encouragement or acquiescence or what has now come to be known as proprietary estoppel which forms an exception to the rule that estoppel cannot found a cause of action.

The Supreme Court cited[110] the 13th Report of the Law Commission of India where it is recommended that, by way of an exception to section 25 of the Contract Act, 1872, a promise, express or implied, which the promisor knows or reasonably should know, will be relied upon by the promisee, should be enforceable, if the promisee has altered his position to his detriment in reliance on the promise. The learned judge added:

> We do not see any valid reason why promissory estoppel should not be allowed to found a cause of action where, in order to satisfy the equity, it is necessary to do so.[111]

---

107. AIR 1979 SC 61 : (1979) 2 SCC 409, at 426.

108. **Relying** upon similar statements in *Municipal Corporation of Bombay v Secretary of State,* ILR (1905) 29 Bom 580 at p 607 : 7 Bom LR 27. Commercial contracts already concluded, remedies have to be provided have to be for their breaches under the law of contract and not that of estoppel, *Trident Tubes Ltd v Govt of Bihar,* AIR 1995 Pat. 50.

109. *Crabb v Arun District Council,* (1975) 3 All ER 165 : (1975) 3 WLR 847.

110. (1979) 2 SCC 409, at p 430 : AIR 1979 SC 61.

111. The court also cited *Robertson v Minister of Pensions* and *Evenden v Guildfold City Assn Football Club Ltd,* (1949) 1 KB 227 : (1948) 2 All ER 767 and (1975) 3 All ER 269, where it is observed that promissory estoppel is no longer the same passive equity. *Vinjay Cements Ltd v Assam,* AIR 1997 Gau 34, the Government restrained from resiling from an announced scheme. The Government was required to give eligibility certificate to an entrepreneur who acting on the basis of the scheme prepared to establish an industry in the most backward area and obtained final licences, and clearance from Pollution Board and placed firm orders upon suppliers. Arguments were built upon the following authorities: *MP Sugar Mills v UP,* AIR 1979 SC 621 : (1979) 2 SCC 409; *UOI v Godfrey Philips (India) Ltd,* AIR 1986 SC 806 : (1985) 4 SCC 369; *Bakul Oil Industries v Gujarat,* (1987) 1 SCC 31 : AIR 1987 SC 142; *Pine Chemicals Ltd v Assessing Authority,* (1992) 2 SCC 683 : 1992 AIR SCW 702.

> The doctrine of promissory estoppel can be invoked even where a case does not satisfy the requirements of estoppel as enshrined in s. 115. It would be open to a party who has acted on a representation made by the Government to claim that the Government should be bound to carry out the promise made by it even though the promise was not recorded in the form of a formal contract.[112]

Where the mining lease granted was stopped on the ground that the detailed study on the environment will be undertaken before taking further action in the matter, the rule of promissory estoppel can be invoked only if on the basis of the representation made by the Government, the party has substantially altered its position. However, it was held that within a short time of ten days the party could not have altered its position so as to invoke the doctrine of promissory estoppel.[113] Where the sale deed of area comprising in "reserve forest", initially the registering authority refusing to register the same, was got registered under the directions issued by the High Court, that does not mean that the High Court had pronounced about the validity or otherwise of the document, the State was not estopped from raising its objection under section 22 of the Kerala Forest Act, 1962 for its violation.[114]

The court will not pass any order binding the government by its promises unless it is so necessary to prevent manifest injustice or fraud, particularly, when the Government acts in its governmental, public or sovereign capacity. Estoppel does not operate against the Government or its assignee while acting in such capacity.[115]

Before laying down any policy which would give benefit to its subjects, the State must think about the pros and cons of such policy and its capacity to give the benefits. Without proper appreciation of all the relevant factors, the State should not give any assurance, not only because that would be in violation of the principles of promissory estoppel but it would be unfair and immoral on the part of the State not to act as per its promise.[116]

[s 115.8.2] Relief against Government under Promissory Estoppel.—The extent of relief available against the Government on the plea of promissory estoppel was summarised by the Patna High Court,[117] citing Kailasam J.[118]

The scope of the plea of doctrine of promissory estoppel against the Government may be summed up as follows:

1. The plea of promissory estoppel is not available against the exercise of the legislative functions of the State. Thus where the Government changed its export policy by an order which had the force of legislation, exporters who

---

112. *Ashok Kumar Maheshwari v State of UP,* (1998) 2 SCC 502 : AIR 1998 SC 966.
113. *State of Kerala v Kerala Rare Earth and Minerals Ltd,* AIR 2016 SC 1817, para 58.
114. *State of Kerala v New World Investment Pvt Ltd,* AIR 2016 NOC 369 (Ker) : 2016 AIR CC 426 (Ker).
115. *AP Dairy Development Corp Federation v B Narasimha Reddy,* (2011) 9 SCC 286.
116. *SVA Steel Re-rolling Mills Ltd v State of Kerala,* (2014) 4 SCC 186 (para 30).
117. *Sah Mahadeo Lal Mohan Lal v State of Bihar,* AIR 1982 Pat. 158.
118. This also emerges from the decision of the Supreme Court in *Jit Ram Shiv Kumar v State of Haryana,* AIR 1980 SC 1285 : (1981) 1 SCC 11.

had contracted on the basis of earlier policy were not permitted to claim any estoppel against the State.[119]

2. The doctrine cannot be invoked for preventing the Government from discharging its functions under the law or to act contrary to law.
3. When an officer of the Government acts outside the scope of his authority, the plea of promissory estoppel is not available. The doctrine of *ultra vires* will come into operation and the Government cannot be held bound by the unauthorised acts of its officers.
4. When the officer acts within the scope of his authority under a scheme and enters into an agreement and makes a representation and a person acting on that representation puts himself in a disadvantageous position, the court is entitled to require the officer to act according to the scheme and the agreement or representation. The officer cannot arbitrarily act on his mere whim and ignore his promise on some undefined and undisclosed grounds of necessity or change the conditions to the prejudice of the person who had acted upon such representation and put himself in a disadvantageous position.
5. The officer would be justified in changing the terms of the agreement to the prejudice of the other party on special circumstances, such as difficult foreign exchange position or other matters which have a bearing on general interests of the State.

The decision in *Motilal Padmapat* case should be contrasted with the decision of the Madras High Court in *Shanmugraja v Superintending Engineer.*[120] In this case, concession was given in the tariff of power supply to new industries for a period of five years. The same was withdrawn in respect of an industry which started earning profit within the concession period of five years. The court said that such withdrawal was reasonable and also necessary in public interest. The doctrine of promissory estoppel would not apply.

Where the Government makes a promise knowing or intending that it would be acted on by the promisee and, in fact, the promisee, acting in reliance on it, alters his position, the Government would be held bound by the promise and the promise would be enforceable against the Government at the instance of the promisee notwithstanding that there is no consideration for the promise and the promise is not recorded in the form of a formal contract as required by Article 229 of the Constitution. The rule of promissory estoppel being an equitable doctrine has to be moulded to suit the particular situation. It is not a hard-and-fast rule but an elastic one, the objective of which is to do justice between the parties and to extend an equitable treatment to them. This doctrine is a principle evolved by equity, to avoid injustice and though

---

119. *State of Karnataka v KK Mohandas*, AIR 2007 SC 2917 : (2007) 6 SCC 484, no estoppel on the basis of a speech of a minister as to ban on sale of toddy. The Government had revised policy in the meantime.

120. *Shanmugraja v Superintending Engineer*, AIR 2002 Mad 159. The court also held that the plea of estoppel would have to be taken in the petition itself. It cannot be raised for the first time at the hearing.

commonly named promissory estoppel, it is neither in the realm of contract nor in the realm of estoppel. For application of the doctrine of promissory estoppel the promisee must establish that he suffered in detriment or altered his position by reliance on the promise.[121]

Normally, the doctrine of promissory estoppel being applied against the Government and defence based on executive necessity would not be accepted by the court. However, if it can be shown by the Government that having regard to the facts as they have subsequently transpired, it would be inequitable to hold the Government to the promise made by it, the court would not raise an equity in favour of the promisee and enforce the promise against the Government. Where public interest warrants, the principles of promissory estoppel cannot be invoked. The Government can change the policy in public interest. However, it is well settled that taking cue from this doctrine, the authority cannot be compelled to do something which is not allowed by law or prohibited by law. There is no promissory estoppel against the settled proposition of law. Doctrine of promissory estoppel cannot be invoked for enforcement of a promise made contrary to law, because none can be compelled to act against the statute. Thus, the Government or public authority cannot be compelled to make a provision which is contrary to law.[122]

Estoppel can be invoked to hold the Government bound to its promises and agreements whether they are of executive or administrative character.[123] The courts have to strike a balance between individual rights and larger public interest.[124] A Town Development Authority was not permitted to raise prices arbitrarily.[125] Cigarette manufacturers did not collect excise on corrugated fibre board containers in which cigarettes were delivered at the factory gates on the basis of a Departmental letter. It was

---

121. *Shree Sidhbali Steels Ltd v State of Uttar Pradesh,* AIR 2011 SC 1175 : (2011) 3 SCC 193.

122. *Shree Sidhbali Steels Ltd v State of Uttar Pradesh,* AIR 2011 SC 1175 : (2011) 3 SCC 193.

123. See cases cited under "promissory estoppel". *KML Narasimhan, Larsen & Toubro Ltd v UOI,* AIR 1994 Mad 82 **following** *Motilal Sugar Mills v UP,* (1979) 2 SCR 641: AIR 1979 SC 621 : (1979) 2 SCC 409 and dissenting from *Jeet Ram v State of Haryana,* (1980) 3 SCR 689 : AIR 1980 SC 1285 : (1981) 1 SCC 11 to the extent it is in conflict with *Motilal's* case. Where the Government resolution assured the petitioners to supply them timber for twenty years at the prevailing market rate to be revised after every three years, the show cause notice to reduce the price revision period from three years to one year would not amount to breach of any material promise on the part of the Government, *Vidarbha Veneer Industries Ltd v State of Maharashtra,* AIR 1994 Bom 155. Subsequential change of export policy by the Government, doctrine of promissory estoppel applies, *UOI v Rizwan International,* AIR 1993 Mad 336. Withdrawal of customs duty exemption notification in public interest would not attract promissory estoppel, *Kasinka Trading v UOI,* AIR 1995 SC 874 : (1995) 1 SCC 274; *Darshan Oils P Ltd v UOI,* AIR 1995 SC 370 : (1995) 1 SCC 345. Where the Government granted facility to operate pay phone on commission basis with a right to vary the conditions of agreement, the Government was not estopped from changing the commission of operators as a public policy to augment public revenue, *UOI v Binani Consultants Pvt Ltd,* AIR 1995 Cal 234. Where the Government granted licences to open bars only to those who had licences for retail selling shops without any representation by Government that the bars would be for a certain period, the Government was not estopped from rescinding the Rules of granting licences in public interest, *AJ Joy v Govt of Tamil Nadu,* AIR 1993 Mad 282.

124. *MP Mathur v DTC,* AIR 2007 SC 414 : (2006) 13 SCC 706.

125. *Sadhna Agarwal v Indore Devp. Auth.,* AIR 1986 MP 88. *Tandon Brothers v State of WB,* AIR 2001 SC 1866, a notification under the West Bengal Estate Acquisition Act, 1954 was not allowed to be superseded for changing its conditions by a subsequent notification.

held that promissory estoppel was attracted.[126] A land which had been already subjected to one-time tax was not allowed to be subjected to another dose of one-time tax assessment on its sale by the original assesse.[127] An invitation by the State Government to companies to set up industries by assuring them of the supply of raw material was not allowed to be changed in reference to companies which had already established factories and were in a position to use the promised raw material.[128] A letter of intent on the basis of which the grantee had been going round fulfilling formalities was not allowed to be cancelled without show cause notice to him.[129] An announced scheme of export promotion by providing cash assistance to persons qualifying under the scheme not allowed to be withdrawn retrospectively.[130] Where additional import licence was granted to the petitioner against admissible exports as an incentive, the Government was estopped from withdrawing such incentive in view of new policy unless it was done in public interest.[131] There was grant of quarry lease for quarrying granite on priority basis. Approval was granted by the Forest Department. Lessees incurred expenditure for preparatory work. The lease was subsequently cancelled without giving notice to the lessees and without any opportunity of hearing. This was held to be violative of the rules of natural justice. It was also hit by the principle of promissory estoppel, and the doctrine of legitimate expectations.[132] Where relying on the cash compensatory scheme of the Government to exporters of readymade garments, the petitioner priced

---

126. *UOI v Godfrey Philips India Ltd,* AIR 1986 SC 806 : (1985) 4 SCC 369. Where the Government promised to give interest free sales tax loan to industrial units and it did not go back from its promise but pleaded its inability due to paucity of funds, promissory estoppel was not applicable, *Shakti Tubes Ltd v State of Bihar (FB),* AIR 1994 Pat 162. Taxes already realised (sales-tax year) cannot be promised to be refunded. That would be against public interest, *Intrans Systems P Ltd v State of Kerala,* AIR 1996 Ker 161. The terms, restrictions and conditions of the import policy of the Government announced for a financial year could be changed only prospectively, *Nath Bros. Exim International Ltd v UOI,* AIR 1995 Del 280.

127. *East India Hotels Ltd v State of Rajasthan*, AIR 2001 Raj 286.

128. *Vij Resins P Ltd v State of J&K,* AIR 1989 SC 1629 : (1989) 3 SCC 115; *Uma Paliwal v UOI,* AIR 2002 Raj 348, grant of forest lease on acceptance of deposit on the expectation the contractor had employed a large number of workers, not allowed to be cancelled. There was no illegality in the initial renewal of the lease.

129. *Vinod Kumar Mittal v UOI,* AIR 1991 All 1. Promise of allotment of land to schools on no profit no loss basis not permitted to be shifted to market value basis. *Delhi Development Authority v Lala Amar Nath Educational Human Society,* AIR 1991 Del 96. *Hitech Electro Thermics & Hydropower Ltd v State of Kerala,* AIR 2003 SC 2091, the owner of the unit was allowed to claim benefits of the announced scheme under which he acted though he could not commission it within the time period, the delay in commissioning being due to delay in providing electric energy. *Ras Resorts & Apart Hotels Ltd v UOI,* AIR 2010 SC 2599 : (2010) 11 SCC 601, plot allotted for construction of hotel, proposal in the draft five year plan, and annual plan of UT to grant interest subsidy on loan taken to construct hotel, created no promissory estoppel because it was not a firm offer or representation.

130. *Garments International Pvt Ltd v UOI,* AIR 1991 Kant 52. *Sree Rayalaseema Alkalies & Allied Chemicals Ltd v Govt of AP (FB),* AIR 1993 AP 278, where the petitioner never applied for registration under the new incentive scheme of the Government, he was not entitled to invoke the doctrine of promissory estoppel. *Arivind Industries v State of Gujarat,* AIR 1995 SC 2477 : (1995) 6 SCC 53, the notification by the Government to give certain benefits to new industries did not contain any promise that the benefits given would not be altered from time to time, the Government was not estopped from modifying the same.

131. *Sanjaya Sales Corp v National Mineral Development Corporation Ltd,* AIR 1993 AP 62. Where the policy of the Government was provisional and was liable to change, doctrine of estoppel would not be attracted, *Kimti Lal Rahi v UOI,* AIR 1993 Del 211.

132. *Exotic Granite Exports v Govt of AP*, AIR 2008 NOC 2109 (AP).

its goods for export, the Government subsequently could not discontinue the scheme with retrospective effect.[133] Where under the export policy an exporter had incurred heavy loans and started production, the Government could subsequently not ban the export of goods ready for export.[134] An agreement as to the amount of property tax in lieu of the exemption to which the Government company in question was entitled was held to be binding on the taxing authority.[135]

In a case under the Drugs and Cosmetics Act, an understanding was arrived at between the Government and the accused that, if the accused surrendered his licence, the Government would not proceed further with the case. The licence was surrendered by the accused but, later on, the Government reversed its decision. It was held that the doctrine of promissory estoppel does not apply to criminal cases.[136] The principle of promissory estoppel has no application in a case of concluded commercial contract between the private party and the State.[137] Where assurance of rebate in electricity tariff was held out but the same was not incorporated in the written agreement, no rebate could be claimed.[138] The Government can be bound by the principle of promissory estoppel when it tries to wriggle out of the promises made by it through the announcement of schemes for providing incentives to the entrepreneurs to open industries in backward areas.[139] Where the recognised travel agents invested considerable amounts for the purpose of fulfilling conditions imposed for obtaining recognition under the new circular, subsequent withdrawal of recognition by the Government was covered by the principle of promissory estoppel.[140]

---

133. *Old Village Industries Ltd v UOI,* AIR 1993 Del 321.

134. *Rizwan International v UOI,* AIR 1994 Mad 112.

135. *Bhilai Steel Plant v Special Area Devp. Authority,* AIR 1991 MP 332. Promise to allot land for HAL colony has been held to be similarly binding. *Aeronautic Employees v AP Govt,* AIR 1990 AP 331. MN Rao J said [at p 335] : "Had the Government told the management of the HAL in the beginning itself in 1981 when vast tracts of land were readily available for construction purposes, the management would have explored alternative arrangements to provide housing accommodation to their employees. Because of the promise made by the State Government, the management, thinking that the promise would be [fulfilled], did not explore other possibilities. It is the promise of the Government that altered the position of the petitioner society."

136. *State of Maharashtra v Jethmal Himatmal Jain,* 1994 Cr LJ 2613 (Bom); *Laxmi Udyog Rock Cement Pvt Ltd,* AIR 2001 Ori 51, exemptions granted for a certain period can be withdrawn before the expiry of the period in public interest. The principle of promissory estoppel would not be applicable.

137. *Trident Tubes Ltd v Govt of Bihar,* AIR 1995 Pat 50.

138. *Bhoruka Power Corp Ltd v State of Karnataka,* AIR 1994 NOC 314 (Kant); *UP Power Corp Ltd v Sant Steels & Alloys P Ltd,* AIR 2008 SC 693 : (2008) 2 SCC 777, promised concession to new connections in hire areas could not be withdrawn because of theft of energy. Concessions ceased after statutory changes. *Saini Alloys P Ltd v UP Power Corp,* AIR 2007 NOC 978 (All-DB) : (2007) 2 All LJ 5, exemptions or concessions can be granted only by the authorised person or body under statutory provisions, otherwise there would be no estoppel. *Saharanpur Electric Supply Co Ltd v State of UP,* AIR 2007 NOC 145 (All-DB) : (2006) 6 All LJ 588, change in market value on basis of subsequent Amendment Act, not hit by promissory estoppel, it does not apply against statute. *AP Steel Rerolling Mill Ltd v State of Kerala,* AIR 2007 SC 797 : (2007) 2 SCC 725, no concession could be claimed by a party who failed to comply with terms and conditions of the scheme within reasonable time.

139. *Shri Bajrang Extraction Pvt Ltd v Secretary, Govt of MP,* AIR 1993 MP 202.

140. *Selvi Travels v UOI,* AIR 1993 Mad 216.

The other parties are also bound to use Government aids only for sanctioned objects. Money sanctioned for payment of rent of school building was not allowed to be diverted to other heads.[141]

Estoppel cannot be stretched to the extent of restraining the State from exercising its sovereign and legislative powers.[142] The Government can, for example, change export policy and thereby upset many a contractual commitments.[143] Speech made in Parliament by a Minister cannot be treated as a promise or representation made to a person attracting the principles of promissory estoppel.[144] The Government is also not bound by the acts of its Departments or officers which are beyond their powers, *ultra vires*.[145] Estoppel cannot be claimed on the basis of a contract which does not satisfy the requirements of Article 299 of the Constitution.[146] No estoppel can arise from simple or casual statements as to future programmes.[147] No estoppel was created by a Minister's statement in the House and reported in newspapers that no import tax would be levied on rice brought into the State.[148] Statements on behalf of Government in affidavits in previous proceedings and in Parliament about the promotion of a candidate did not constitute estoppel.[149] A housing society which accepted land from the Government on agreed rent was held to be free to apply to the Government for rent reduction and the

---

141. *TK Ghosh's Academy v TC Palit*, AIR 1975 SC 1496 : 1975 Cr LJ 1233.

142. Even in the case of legislative functions an overriding public necessity would be necessary to change a policy. *UOI v JK Industries Ltd*, AIR 1991 Raj 45, a matter of Central Excise Rules; *Nilagiri Tea Emporium v Govt of India*, 1990 Cr LJ 155 (AP), change in Tea Standard Rules, a matter of delegated legislation, no estoppel. *Pioneer Agro Extracts Ltd v State of Punjab*, AIR 2002 P&H 135, the fact that under a package of incentives, exemption from payment of sales tax was granted by the State Government for growth of industry in the State, did not estop the Government from imposing social security cess under an Act. *MP Cement Mfr's Assn. v State of MP*, AIR 2002 MP 62, the state permitted the petitioners to set up captive power plants for production of electrical energy in their industries, the State Government was held to be not prevented by promissory estoppel from imposing cess on energy produced by the petitioners. *Dayalbagh Educational Institute v State of UP*, AIR 2001 All 290, no estoppel by constructing building on land allocated under the Master Plan for educational purposes *Shiv Kr. Pandit v State of Assam*, AIR 1999 Gau 68, no estoppel in matters of tax.

143. *Bansal Exports v UOI*, AIR 1983 Del 443.

144. *State of Karnataka v KK Mohandas & Etc.*, 2008 (4) CCC 492 (SC).

145. *CV Enterprises v Brathwait & Co*, AIR 1984 Cal 306, a Govt. Co. not bound by contracts entered into under mistake of its rights; *Chatlal Sao v State*, AIR 1986 Pat 267, acts done in violation of directions or adminsitrative instructions; *Chandrakant Bhailal Patel v TV Krishnamurthy*, AIR 1991 Cal 63, grant of extension of lease on a well without observing the prescribed procedure, being *ultra vires* was open to challenge.

146. *Bihar EGP Co-op Soc v Sipahi Singh*, AIR 1977 SC 2149 : (1977) 4 SCC 145. Similarly there can be no estoppel where the requirements of exemption are not satisfied. *DR Kohli v Atul Products Ltd*, AIR 1985 SC 537 : (1985) 2 SCC 77.

147. *Turner Morrison & Co v Hungerford Investment*, (1972) 1 SCR 711: AIR 1972 SC 1311 : (1972) 1 SCC 857; *Jasjeet Films v DDA*, AIR 1980 Del 83, programme for the development of area adjoining a cinema site; *Assistant Custodian of EP v Brij Kishore*, (1975) 2 SCR 359 : AIR 1974 SC 2325 : (1975) 1 SCC 21, declaration about evacuee property; *Paradise Printers v UT of Chandigarh*, (1988) 1 SCC 440 : AIR 1988 SC 354, promise of allotment of land for industrial purposes; *Chandigarh Food And Services Ltd v UOI*, AIR 1990 P&H 206, promise to allot a contract by negotiations and not by tender, no estoppel.

148. *Sah Mahadeo Lal v State*, AIR 1982 Pat 158.

149. *PC Sethi v UOI*, AIR 1975 SC 2164 : (1975) 4 SCC 67.

Government was also free to consider the application. The Supreme Court said that no principle of promissory estoppel could be applied to the circumstances of the case.[150]

The Land Acquisition Officer (Collector) assured the landowner that a reference would be made to the civil court over the matter of valuation. It was held that the collector was a statutory authority. He became bound to fulfil the promise under the doctrine of promissory estoppel. The reference was made under a writ petition. The parties participated. The proceedings attained finality. The participating parties could not question the validity of the reference.[151]

No estoppel arose against land acquisition authorities where the amount of compensation was agreed through amicable settlement. No further compensation could be allowed because of the agreement.[152]

An exemption from levy on rice granted to rice millers on the stock held by them was subsequently withdrawn. It was held that withdrawal of any such exemption in public interest was a matter of Government policy. It could not be assailed under

---

150. *Foreshore Co-op Housing Society v N H S Samiti,* (1991) 2 SCC 75. Doctrine of promissory estoppel cannot be invoked for preventing Government from discharging its duty under the law. *Intrans Systems Pvt Ltd v State of Kerala,* AIR 1996 Ker 161. *State of HP v Padam Devi,* AIR 2002 SC 2477, two schemes formulated by the State Government for providing training to unemployed educated youth, they were found to be valid because of intelligible differentia. Refusal to give additional training under one scheme to those who joined the other schemes was held to be neither arbitrary nor discriminatory. No estoppel in spite of litigation. *Summer Chand Chhajed v Administrator,* AIR 2002 Raj 76, State Government appointed administrator for a society, subsequently notification issued for holding election to constitute the managing committee. The administrator was not allowed to claim any injunction against the notification for election. *Riaz Construction Co v UOI,* AIR 2001 J&K 7, a tender admitted by subsequently rejected because both the requirements of technical and financial capability were found to be not satisfied. No unfairness and no estoppel. *Prashant K Patel v UOI,* AIR 2001 Guj 58, National Savings Certificates taken by a person by virtue of power of attorney holder of another person, the account operating for 10 years, the Government was not allowed to deny interest on the ground that such accounts were not allowed. *NK Mettala High School v State of Gujarat,* AIR 2001 63, issuance of general policy resolution inviting applications for opening schools does not create an estoppel compelling the Government to do so, the same being a matter of policy and financial considerations. *Lotus Constructions v Govt of AP,* AIR 1997 AP 200, the Government sponsored a scheme for development of tourism and other related activities in certain areas. The petitioner's proposal was approved and negotiations were going on when the government, acting in public interest withdrew the scheme. The decision was not of *malafide* nature. No estoppel against Government. *KAS Semthinathan v UOI,* AIR 1997 Mad 208, revision of PCO commission rates from time to time, being a policy matter, no PCO owner can present a challenge against it. *Ajantha Travels v Govt of India,* AIR 2001 Ker 112, the system of recognising travel agents and renewal of agencies was changed in view of larger public interest and national security was held to be not arbitrary. There was no estoppel against the Government. *Y Konda Reddy v State of AP,* AIR 1997 AP 121, a letter of provisional acceptance was issued to a tenderer. He was fully aware that the matter was under consideration. The Government cancelled the tender. The tenderer was held to be not entitled to invoke the doctrine of promissory estoppel and legitimate expectation on the basis of the letter of provisional acceptance. *AND Adasingarahar v Collector of Dharmapuri,* AIR 2000 Mad 71, there is no question of promissory estoppel or isolation of natural purposes in the Government carrying out anti-encroachment operations. *Cosmopolitan Club v Govt of Tamil Nadu,* AIR 2000 Mad 120 : 2000 1 , non-renewal of the lease of the Golf Club in the interest of bringing it up to the international standard, the decision being in public interest, it could not be said to be unfair or unjustified, no violation of legitimate expectations.

151. *Steel Authority of India Ltd v SUTNI Sangam,* AIR 2010 SC 112 : (2009) 16 SCC 1.

152. *ML Dhar v Collector Land,* AIR 2007 J&K 15.

the doctrine of promissory estoppel.[153] The withdrawal of a tax exemption contrary to industrial policy announced for a particular period was not estopped since the Government could, in public interest revise its policies. The exemption in this case was not a part of any industrial policy. It was granted by a Notification under the Sales Tax Act and the same could be amended at any time.[154] Where a notification superseded exemption granted earlier for a specified period, it was held that the principle of promissory estoppel was not attracted.[155] An incentive granted under a scheme could be withdrawn or the scheme amended even during the currency of the scheme if public interest so demanded.[156]

The doctrine of promissory estoppel cannot be built upon promises which are contrary to law. An assurance was given by the State Government to the demonstrators in the Pharmacy Department that they would be promoted to the post of lecturers. There was no room for such promotion under applicable Rules and Regulations. The promotion would have been contrary to the law because under the legal provisions, the posts of lecturers had to be filled by selection.[157]

[s 115.8.2.1] ***Delay in invoking promissory estoppel.***—The delay in invoking the promissory estoppel has to be explained by cogent, convincing and persuasive explanation to justify condonation thereof. In the instant case the deliberate delay of more than two years was not so explained.[158]

[s 115.8.2.2] ***Continuation of temporary appointment against Rules.***—A doctor was appointed temporarily. His appointment was to come to an end automatically on the selection of a candidate by the service commission. Even otherwise the appointment was not to be continued beyond one year without the concurrence of the Commission. Such concurrence was not obtained even when the appointment was continued for a long period. It was held that concurrence could not be presumed from the fact of continuation. There could be no waiver of the requirement of compliance of the applicable Rules. The petitioner could not claim regularisation. The challenge to his order of dismissal was not tenable.[159]

Instead of the candidate recommended through the Employment Exchange, another candidate was taken because of better merit. The Supreme Court said that he could not be denied appointment. There was no estoppel because of the Employment Exchange recommendation.[160]

[s 115.9] Housing.—Where the Development Authority invited applications from the retired and retiring Government servants for out of turn allotment of flats on hire purchase basis, the doctrine of promissory estoppel would be attracted if it subsequently

---

153. *Himalaya Rice Mills v State of UP,* AIR 1997 All 155; *Punjab Travel Co v UOI,* AIR 2000 Raj 294, the doctrine cannot be used to prevent the Government from exercising its taxing power.

154. *Sales Tax Officer v Shree Durga Oil Mills,* AIR 1998 SC 591 : (1998) 1 SCC 572.

155. *UOI v Godhawani Bros.,* AIR 1999 SC 1604 : (1997) 11 SCC 173.

156. *State of Rajasthan v Mahavir Oil Industries,* AIR 1999 SC 2302 : (1999) 4 SCC 357.

157. *Ashok Kumar Maheshwari (Dr) v State of UP,* AIR 1998 SC 966 : (1998) 2 SCC 502.

158. *UOI v Shri Hanuman Industries,* (2015) 6 SCC 600, para 20.

159. *Chanchal Goyal v State of Rajasthan,* AIR 2003 SC 1713.

160. *UOI v Pritilata Nanda,* AIR 2010 SC 2821 : (2010) 11 SCC 674.

demanded cash down payment from the applicants.[161] Where the Housing Board had earmarked a certain area for providing community facilities, it could not subsequently convert the area for residential and commercial complex.[162] Where the petitioner sent some amount along with an application for allotment of a plot by the Government and the authorities requested him to pay the balance price so that letter of allotment could be issued which he did, allotment could not be refused on the plea of subsequent change of policy.[163] The Delhi Development Authority allotted flats on the basis of brochures inviting applications indicating estimated provisional costs. The allottee was fully aware of the fact that the cost was subject to change as per prevailing rates at the relevant time. The plea that the costs indicated in the brochures was final and binding was held to be untenable. There was no estoppel against escalation based revision of costs to the consumers.[164]

The Housing Board had promised the petitioner (allottee) to provide the flat to him on hire purchase basis. The petitioner had acted on the promise and changed his legal position by depositing two instalments. The Board was not allowed to go back upon its promise.[165]

[s 115.9.1] ***Exemption from building tax.***—At the time when construction of the building for promotion of tourism commenced, there was no provision in the relevant Act for exemption from building tax. A provision came into being subsequently and before the petitioner could make any claim, the provision was dropped. No claim under promissory estoppel was allowed.[166]

[s 115.9.2] ***Auction of shops in Malls and Multiplexes.***—The advertisement for auction of shops in Malls and Multiplexes clearly stated the floor area. The subsequent attempt to reduce the floor area without any genuine ground was prevented under the doctrine of promissory estoppel.[167]

[s 115.10] Financing.—Where the State Financial Corporation by issuing a notice abruptly refused to give the promised facilities to a company, the notice was quashed.[168]

---

161. *Sheelawanti v DDA (FB),* AIR 1995 Del 212; *Mangalore Municipal Market Welfare Socy. v Corp of Mangalore,* AIR 1993 Kant 220, no proof of promise to provide alternative accommodation. *Samsuddin v State of WB,* 1996 AIHC 930 (Cal), ferry operator handing over ferry to Zila Parishad for auction, bound, **distinguishing** *Narendra Prosad Singh v The State of West Bengal,* (1959) 63 Cal WN 158.

162. *Bhagat Singh Negi v HP Housing Board,* AIR 1994 HP 60. Acceptance of the scheme of plot allotment on the basis of the brochures and also payments thereunder, no change could be demanded, *Ghaziabad Devp. Authority v Sanchar Vihar Sahkari Avas Samiti Ltd,* AIR 1996 SC 2021 : (1996) 9 SCC 314.

163. *Anokh Singh v State of Punjab,* AIR 1994 P&H 157. Those who apply for after change or modification of the scheme are not entitled to claim under the original scheme, *Jai Prasad Singh v State of UP,* 1996 AIHC 3639 (All). *Rajiv Moudgil v HP Housing Board,* AIR 2000 HP 77, escalation costs in accordance with the rules of the scheme allowed to be recovered. No estoppel against it.

164. *DDA Self Finance Flats Owners Society v UOI,* AIR 2001 Delhi 39. *Sukhpal Singh Kang v Chandigarh Admn,* AIR 1999 P&H 156, terms and conditions of auction of leasehold sites not challenged at that time, not allowed to be challenged subsequently.

165. *Raja Ram Gaur v Rajasthan Housing Board,* AIR 2010 NOC 525 (Raj).

166. *Mayflower Hotels P Ltd v State of Kerala,* AIR 2007 NOC 827 (Ker-DB).

167. *Ganpati Shopping Mall P Ltd v State of Haryana,* AIR 2007 NOC 793 (P&H-DB).

168. *Bharat Explosives Ltd v Pradeshiya Industrial Corp of UP Ltd,* AIR 1994 All 123.

An entrepreneur under took the construction of a hotel complex on the basis of grant of loans by certain financial institutions. He received huge sums under sanctioned loans and also from certain private sources. He invested all such sums in the project. The superstructure was completely constructed and was then waiting for finishing touches when some of the promisors and institutions failed to release the balance of sanctioned loans. The court said that the entrepreneur had altered his position to his disadvantage on the basis of the promised loans and therefore, the lending institutions could not be allowed to go back upon their promises. Directions were issued to the institutions to release the balance of the promised loans.[169]

[s 115.10.1] ***Scheme of Cash Subsidy.***—A cash subsidy scheme was adopted for new industrial units to be set up in developing areas. The petitioner's two units fulfilled the requirements of the scheme. He was given positive opinion on his application to the competent authority. Cash subsidy was granted to him for five years. Later the scheme was cancelled by a State Level Committee. The court held the order of cancellation to be improper.[170]

[s 115.10.2] ***Power Supply.***—A representation was made to the consumer of electrical energy in furtherance of which he had altered his position. It was held that the doctrine of promissory estoppel applied.[171]

Promissory estoppel has the effect of preserving a right. Exemption was granted from payment of electricity tax. It was held to be an accrued right and not a mere concession. Grant was in favour of those setting up power generating plants. The right remained safe even though the scheme of the new Act on the subject was different.[172]

The principles of promissory estoppel cannot be pressed into service to prevent the State Electricity Board from realising the expenses, which it is statutorily empowered to realise.[173]

[s 115.10.3] ***Investment.***—Kisan Vikas Patras were issued to a company at a time when issue to companies was banned by change of Rules. On maturity the Authorities refused to pay interest. The investing company was not aware of any such ban. The Authority was held bound by promissory estoppel to repay on maturity the principal amount with interest.[174]

[s 115.10.4] ***Scheme of Loan for Rural Housing.***—A credit-cum-subsidy scheme was adopted for rural housing. The loan was sanctioned to the petitioner and on the faith of it he mortgaged his land for a loan. The benefit of the scheme was denied to him on the ground that he was already in possession of excess land. He disproved all the allegations by producing sufficient evidence. The court said that the principle of promissory estoppel applied. Refusal of the grant was not proper.[175]

---

169. *Kranti Hotels P Ltd v State of J&K,* AIR 1997 J&K 91.

170. *Atul Products Ltd v State of Gujarat,* AIR 2007 NOC 662 (Guj).

171. *Badri Kedar Paper P Ltd v UP Electricity Regulatory Commission,* AIR 2009 SC 1783 : (2009) 3 SCC 754.

172. *Southern Petrochemical Industries Ltd v Electricity Inspector,* AIR 2007 SC 1984 : (2007) 5 SCC 447.

173. *Kerala State Electricity Board v Hamsaveni Carbides,* AIR 2014 Ker 57 (para 27).

174. *UOI v Kashmir Finance Ltd,* AIR 2007 J&K 4.

175. *Dalbir Singh Sihag v Minister of Rural Development,* AIR 2006 P&H 191.

[s 115.11] Estoppel against Universities and other educational Institutions.—Estoppel was pushed to service in the favour of a person who was appointed the Vice Chancellor of a University for one term on the assurance that his appointment would be extended for one more term and he had on that basis given up his political career and his seat in the Assembly.[176]

Estoppel presupposes equity in the conduct of the claimant. A student who is a party to the issue of a false marks sheet cannot rely on it.[177] Where a marks sheet showed failing marks but the remarks column showed "passed", the mistake being patent, the Board was not estopped from cancelling the result.[178] Where a candidate was declared successful at BA I exam and had pursued her studies right up to BA final when the error in the result was detected and the court held that the error may be rectified and the candidate may be asked to clear her BA I papers without cancelling her subsequent papers.[179] The admission of a candidate to the engineering course in a private college was not allowed to be questioned on the ground that he had not secured qualifying marks, the University prescribing no standard.[180] A published merit list for house jobs was not challenged by the candidate but when the same list was published again for finalising admission course, the candidate challenged it. The acceptance of the list for one purpose was held to be an acceptance for all other allied purposes and thus the candidate was precluded from challenging it.[181] A revision of marks on the basis of revaluation done before the publication of the result was held to be within the discretion of the examining authority, there being no estoppel against it before the publication of the result.[182] A marks sheet obtained by fraud can be rectified.[183]

The Andhra Pradesh High Court allowed an institution to cancel an admission obtained on the basis of a false certificate even though the falsity was discovered after

---

176. *Hardwari Lal v GD Tapase*, AIR 1982 P&H 439.

177. *Satish Kumar v Gorakhpur University*, AIR 1981 All 377.

178. *Kedar Lal v Secy., HS. Board*, AIR 1980 All 32. For another case of patent error on the marksheet and, therefore, cancellation of the result, see *Prabhat Kishor Sahu v Sambal University*, AIR 1992 Ori 83.

179. *Bharti Shrivastva v Jiwaji University*, AIR 1989 MP 197. But see *Basanta Kumar Mohanty v Utkal University*, AIR 1990 Ori 10, a marksheet not allowed to be rectified after 5 years. *Maxey Charan v Rohilkhand University*, AIR 1992 All 122, University not allowed to cancel marksheet which showed the candidate successful, she taking further admission and there was no fraud in her. *Reeta v Berhampur University*, AIR 1993 Ori 27 (FB), the petitioner suppressed the knowledge of cancellation of his result of BA. Final and sought admission to higher studies, he was not entitled to any relief by invoking promissory estoppel, overruling *Rajkishore Senapati v Utkal University*, AIR 1982 Ori 189.

180. *Ambika Pd Mohanty v Orissa Engg. College*, AIR 1989 Ori 173; *M Hussain v Bharathiyar University*, AIR 1991 Bom 45, MBBS admissions not allowed to be cancelled after semester on the ground of ineligibility. *NE Krishna Murthy v University of Mysore*, AIR 1991 Kant 35, a provisional result permitted to be revised when that was being done within two and a half months. *Shri Prashant Kanabar v Gujarat University*, AIR 1991 Guj 23, subsequent changes in criteria under statutory rules, not precluded, *Rafia Durani v University of Kashmir*, AIR 2002 J&K 126, the candidate was admitted on the basis of declared result, she was allowed to attend and complete the course and to appear at the final examination as a regular candidate, the University Authorities, were not allowed to withhold her result by questioning the validity of the original admission.

181. *Nilofar Insaf v State of MP*, AIR 1991 SC 1872 : (1991) 4 SCC 279.

182. *Reetanjali Pati v Board of Secondary Education*, AIR 1990 Ori 90.

183. *Karupa Sindhu v Orissa Board of Sec. Edu.*, AIR 1981 Ori 91.

four years of study.[184] The Supreme Court allowed discontinuation of an admission which was obtained on the basis of a false certificate of belonging to a tribe.[185] Where a candidate, though not eligible, secured admission to a teachers' training school on payment of capitation fee and completed two years of the course, it was held that the withholding of his result on the basis of ineligibility was not improper. The plea of estoppel raised by the candidate was not tenable.[186] But the Patna High Court did not allow this to be done when the candidate was in the fifth year.[187] An admission on the basis of a false certificate of caste can be cancelled.[188] The Rajasthan High Court did not permit it to be cancelled after three to four years.[189] Where the petitioners had passed their examinations from Hindi Vishwavidyalaya, Allahabad and their testimonials were duly checked at the time of their admission to Nursing and Midwifery course and they were able to follow the instructions in English, the Government was estopped from cancelling their admission on the ground of not possessing the minimum qualification when they had almost completed their courses of studies.[190]

Where the parent University conferred degrees on students of the affiliated colleges, it was not allowed to cancel their degrees by pleading that the colleges had not complied with the statutes. Such action of the University defeated the legitimate expectation of the students.[191] The Allahabad University Statutes limited the admission of autonomous college students to post-graduate courses of the University. This was held to be discriminatory and also violative of UGC guidelines.[192]

---

184. *NB Rao v Principal, Osmania Medical College*, AIR 1986 AP 196. *State of TN v A Gurusamy*, AIR 1997 SC 1199 : (1997) 3 SCC 542, an admission obtained on the basis of a false caste certificate allowed to be cancelled. *PN Bhadra v Registrar, University of Agricultural Sciences*, AIR 1997 Kant 100, admission obtained by submitting false marks card, allowed to be cancelled. *K Shashidhara Rao v Ambedkar Institute of Technology*, AIR 1998 Kant 294, an admission made in violation of rules was held to be cancellable. *Sitam Seshanka v Principal, College Pharmaceutical Societies*, AIR 1997 Ori 62, admission cancelled, it was made on the recommendation of a colledge which had not scrutinised papers carefully. *Charan Singh v Punjab University*, AIR 1997 P&H 278, mistaken admission allowed to be cancelled. *SD Kapoor v Chancellor, Jai Narain Vyas University*, AIR 1997 Raj 217, nomination to membership at syndicate for a period of three years was superseded by the Chancellor in public interest and in the interest of the University, no estoppel. *Abila v MDS University*, AIR 1998 Raj 328, admission granted on the basis of qualifying marks obtained at the post-graduate examination was not allowed to be cancelled by saying that qualifying marks were not there at the graduate level examination.

185. *Madhuri Patil v Addl. Commr., Tribal Development*, AIR 1995 SC 94 : (1994) 6 SCC 241. Where an error in the admission merit list was detected in just three days, the admission was allowed to be cancelled because the candidate had not yet lost anything in terms of other opportunities, *Brajendra Singh Chouhan v State of MP*, AIR 1995 MP 23.

186. *MK Sankaran v Govt of TN*, AIR 1998 Mad 332.

187. *Amresh Kumar v Principal, Bhagalpur Medical College*, AIR 1982 Pat 122.

188. *Israr Ad. Mansuri v MP*, AIR 1982 MP 205.

189. *Harpal Singh v Rajasthan*, AIR 1981 Raj 8. See also *Jaisree Pal v State of WB*, AIR 1990 Cal 253, admission not allowed to be cancelled after the completion of one year. *Amarjeet Jena v Council of Higher Secondary Education*, AIR 1999 Ori 129, help to a student in matters where his father was transferred to a place where there was a different Board of Examination and Education.

190. *Neelam Kumar v State of Bihar*, AIR 1994 Pat 15; *Rajkumar Gadpayle v State of MP*, AIR 1997 MP 85, new conditions on admission to medical and technical education which were not announced before were not allowed to be enforced.

191. *Shruti Chaturvedi v Allahabad University*, AIR 1998 All 291.

192. *Ibid. Biju Patnaik University of Technology v Sairam College*, AIR 2010 NOC 691 (Ori), private University permitted to conduct special examination and result declared, not permitted to cancel affiliation. *Vedica College of Education, Bhopal v Barkatullah University*, AIR 2008 MP 219, DB, institution recognised for B.Ed. course. Results of candidates not allowed to be withheld for the reason that the recognition was not published in the Official Gazette.

Where an institution makes an error in an admission it may cancel the same if the mistake is on a point of law.[193] An admission which slipped through in spite of inadequate percentage of marks was not allowed to be cancelled right on the verge of examinations.[194] An admission to LLB class was made on provisional basis and the candidate was treated all along as provisionally admitted until the University sought to cancel the admission. It was held that the University had become bound to honour the admission notwithstanding the fact that the admission committee had no power to make a provisional admission of a candidate who had apparently less than qualifying marks.[195] Where the admission rules were abruptly changed, a candidate was not debarred from challenging them by the mere fact that he participated in the changed procedure.[196]

Where reservation for admission was claimed on the basis of being wards of police officers holding gallantry awards, but the University admission carried no such reserved category, the candidates were not allowed to claim such reservation. They were only able to cite an instruction by the Chief Minister for creating such reserved category. The court said that such reservation could only be prospective.[197]

Where a candidate securing lesser marks in MSc Part I, appeared in the improvement test and was allowed to appear at MSc Part II examination in the same academic year, her result could not be withheld on the basis of a resolution prohibiting students from taking two examinations in a year when such resolution was never communicated to her.[198]

---

193. *Dalip Singh v Pracharya & Adhikshak,* AIR 1986 All 158; *Baldev Singh Rana v State of HP,* AIR 2002 HP 41, the appointment of the petitioner to the post of demonstrator which was made due to some mistake and inadvertence, did not attract the doctrine of promissory estoppel. The mistake could not be allowed to be perpetuated by applying the doctrine of estoppel.

194. *Sangeeta Srivastva v UN Singh,* AIR 1980 Del 27. For other admission cases see *Manoj Kumar v Co-ordinator, MNR,* AIR 1985 All 257; *Gladson Menino Vaz v Goa Medical College,* AIR 1981 Goa 21.

195. *Kaniska Agarwal v University of Delhi,* AIR 1992 Del 105. A student got admission in a particular course by the mistake of the academic body and she pursued the course for a reasonable period, her admission could not be cancelled subsequently. However, the admission sought fraudulently by the student will not attract estoppel, *Smita Shukla v University of Allahabad,* AIR 1994 NOC 109 (All). Fake and bogus certificates, admission cancelled, *Dinesh v State,* AIR 1993 Raj 187.

196. *Anjum Afshan v State of J&K,* AIR 1994 NOC 313 (J&K); *State of TN v G Samathi,* AIR 1999 Mad 327, a candidate who acquiesces in the terms of a prospectus may not afterwards question them. *N Vanajakshi v Principal, University College for Women,* AIR 1999 AP 323, the examinee who had, in fact, failed, was declared successful due to typographical error, she was not allowed to claim the benefit of promissory estoppel.

197. *Harpreet Singh Randhawa v State of Punjab,* AIR 2001 P&H 107.

198. *Ruchira Chauhan v Rohilkhand University, Bareilly,* AIR 1996 All 12, the two examinations were the improvement test and the M Sc. Part II examination. *Surendra Kumar v Board of Secondary Education,* AIR 1995 Raj 115, a private school admitting a failed High School candidate into XI, did not prevent the Board from refusing to permit him intermediate examination. *Mukund Prasad Khare v State,* AIR 1996 MP 130, admission not allowed to be cancelled after three and a half years without giving opportunity, the allegation was that his certificate of being an agriculturist's son was false. *Naresh Singh v State,* AIR 1994 J&K 42, caste certificate not filed at right time, refusal to provide caste benefit not allowed to be challenged. *B Seenaiah v Health Ministry, Vijayawada,* AIR 1995 AP 181, caste status not proved up to II-yr in MBBS, admission liable to be cancelled. *Prabhjot Wahi v Guru Nanak Dev University,* AIR 1995 P&H 269, admission under pressure and connivance, cancelled. *Vinod Kumar Razdan v State,* AIR 1995 J&K 68, ineligibility detected after permission for entrance, cancellation of candidature allowed, **distinguishing** AIR 1976 SC 376 : (1976) 1 SCC 311.

Undertaking by students at the time of admission not to approach any Court against the school did not have the effect of debarring them from filing a writ petition.[199]

Where admission of a candidate to Medical College was done due to the mistake of the selection committee, her admission was not allowed to be cancelled four months after her joining the Medical College, more so when she had given up her studies in an agricultural college.[200] Where the petitioner was admitted to the course of Physical Training Instructor and was allowed to undergo full training for about a year, cancellation of his admission on the ground that sports certificate given by him was not properly authenticated, was held to be not proper.[201] An institution cannot change examination rules after the tests have already been conducted.[202] In a test for admission to post graduate degree and diploma in medical course, there was a provision in the prospectus for preference to in-service candidates and this was also made known to the candidates at the interview. The court allowed the provision to be challenged by open merit candidate. The participation in the test did not debar from challenging some of the provisions of the prospectus.[203]

One of the rules for the conduct of entrance tests to professional courses was that there would be no revaluation or rechecking of answer books. A candidate who took the test subject to the rules was not afterwards allowed to claim revaluation or rechecking. His request for disclosure of key answers was also not allowed. The court, however, directed the authorities to disclose key answers immediately after the declaration of result.[204]

Conditions of affiliation and of granting recognition to colleges and their degrees and diplomas can be altered for the future. The okay report of inspectors for affiliation does not bind the University so as to create an estoppel against it.[205]

One of the conditions in the brochure issued for admission to homeopathic diploma course was that the Central Council approved that the diploma holders would be treated eligible for registration to degree course. It was found that there was no such authorisation in favour of the college. The students who passed the diploma course could not get any relief in terms of this condition. But having regard to their reasonable expectation, the authorities were directed that students should be given permission to

---

199. *Abu Zaid v Principal, Madrasa,* AIR 1999 All 64.

200. *B Jayalakshmi v SC University of HS Vijayawada,* AIR 1994 AP 297. Calling a candidate for interview does not create a promise of admission, AIR 1994 Sikkim 1.

201. *Randhir Singh v State,* AIR 1995 Raj 44, **relied on** *Sanatan Gauda v Berhampur University,* AIR 1990 SC 1075 : (1990) 3 SCC 23.

202. Competitive test held without reservation, subsequent reservations not allowed. *Anand Kumar v State,* AIR 1981 Pat 104; *Deepak v State,* AIR 1981 Pat 104. See also *Tripureswar Malik v Council of Higher Secondary Education,* AIR 1990 Ori 228, exemption from papers in which the candidate passed, not allowed to be withdrawn.

203. *AV Gopalakrishnan v Byju N,* AIR 1999 Ker 10.

204. *Nishant Singh Sipehia v Regional Engineering College,* AIR 2000 HP 99; *V Ramalakshmi (Dr.) v Director of Medical Education,* AIR 1998 Mad 55, candidate not allowed to challenge admission rules contained in the prospectus.

205. *Meenakshi College for Women v University of Madras,* AIR 1991 Mad 32. Procedural matters as distinguished from substantive rights do not create an estoppel. *Anant Kumar v VC, Magadh University,* AIR 1990 Pat 205; *Ashwin Prafulla Pimpalwar v State,* AIR 1992 Bom 233, an educational institution (medical college here), whether private or public, can change rules for the future including curtailment of privileges after completion even if they deprive the candidates of their expectations.

join second year degree course after completion of 1750 hours of study and on passing examination thereafter.[206]

The candidates who had applied for a post and appeared at the interview without protesting against the change of eligibility criteria were not subsequently allowed to plead that the eligibility criteria were wrongly framed.[207] The appellant was working as a lecturer in a college. The District Inspector of Colleges approved his appointment on yearly basis. Such approval was not granted after 1973. Another person (respondent in this case) was selected as lecturer and appointed by the Education Department. Appellant filed his suit only against the college. Declaration by the Civil Court that the appellant was permanent on his post was held not to bind the Education Department or the respondent because they were not parties to the suit. There was no estoppel against the Education Department.[208]

A party claimed title to the property in question under a will and also set up the plea of adverse possession. The court said that such alternative pleas are possible. It was held that the trial Court holding that the appellant was not entitled to set up the right of adverse possession and rejected it at threshold without scrutiny of evidence. This was held to be improper.[209]

Where the candidate had failed both in the aggregate as well as in an individual paper, a pass mark sheet, having been issued to him by mistake, was allowed to be cancelled.[210]

[s 115.11.1] CASES.—An admission Regulation required candidates to secure minimum 50% marks in the Joint Entrance Test. The University in question did not mention it in its information brochure. The petitioner was offered admission without securing the requisite percentage. The University was not allowed to cancel the admission when he had already pursued the medical course for more than a year, being against the equitable doctrine.[211]

[s 115.12] Revision of admission rules.—Where students were allowed admission to higher semester pending the result of revaluation, the facility being offered only as a concession, it was held that the withdrawal of the facility after some years due to chaotic conditions caused by the scheme could not be condemned as something arbitrary. The doctrines of legitimate expectations and promissory estoppel were not applicable. Public interest can override legitimate expectations. The decision lies with the Government. The court can only see that the new policy is not irrational or perverse.[212] An exemption from fee was granted to such medical and engineering

---

206. *Varinder Singh v State of Punjab,* AIR 1998 P&H 42.

207. *GN Nayak v Goa University,* AIR 2002 SC 790. The court cited the following authorities *Madan Lal v State of J&K,* AIR 1995 SC 1088 : (1995) 3 SCC 486; *Om Prakash Shukla v Akhilesh Kumar,* AIR 1986 SC 1043 : 1986 Supp SCC 285.

208. *Shiv Kumar Tiwari v Jagat Narain Rai,* AIR 2002 SC 211.

209. *A Krishnappa v Thinunarajappa,* AIR 2001 Kant 470.

210. *Vice Chancellor, University of Allahabad v Som Prakash,* AIR 2001 All 319.

211. *Principal, Kalinga Institute of Medical Sciences v State of Orissa,* AIR 2010 Ori 124.

212. *G Sreenivasan v Principal, Regional Engg. College,* AIR 2000 Ori 56. *Jesja PK v Director, School of Distance Education,* AIR 2000 Ker 281, choices already made by candidates on the basis of existing cannot be upset by changing admission rules. *Anop Singh Ratnu v Maharishi Dayanand Sarswati University,* AIR 1998 Raj 54, eligibility percentage revised, in accordance with the law from 40% to 45% no estoppel against it.

candidates who had undergone sterilisation operation. The Notification to that effect was subsequently modified by providing that the scheme was not to apply to private educational institutions. The candidates of such institutions were not allowed to claim estoppel against the Government.[213]

A university was running non-formal distant education system and had followed it for a decade. All such Universities had to modify the system as per UGC guidelines. It could not be said that they had acted against the law. The writ of mandamus could not be issued.[214]

[s 115.13] Revaluation.—A student sought revaluation of some of his answer books. The University, carried out revaluation of papers applied for and also revalued another paper which was not applied for. This was done because some other wrongs were also detected. The court said that there was nothing illegal in that respect. The principle of promissory estoppel was not applicable.[215]

[s 115.13.1] ***Admission Fee.***—Where a University was charging different fee from different batches and the batch of the petitioners was subjected to higher fee and the structure of the fee was clearly disclosed in the prospectus, it was held that the fact that the petitioners accepted the fees structure while taking admission could not be a ground for estopping them from challenging the validity of the discriminatory fees structure. They could not be said to have given up their right to a parity of treatment with others with whom they were similarly situated.[216]

[s 115.13.2] ***Cancellation of result.—Mass copying.***—Where the petitioner was declared to have passed BA Final examination and he applied for job and received call letter, he could not be said to have "changed or altered" his position and the university could not be precluded from cancelling his result on the ground of mass copying by invoking doctrine of estoppel.[217] Where the students using unfair means were allowed to join the next year courses under an interim order of the High Court, the University was not estopped from altering their results subsequently on the basis of the syndicate finding them to be guilty of using unfair means.[218]

[s 115.14] Permission for establishing college.—A permission to establish and run a private college was granted in accordance with applicable Rules and subject to the conditions mentioned in the Government Order. Acting on the basis of the permission, the founders spent huge sums of money in establishing the institution. Subsequently to all this, the government issued an executive order declaring 50% seats as Government seats, and also assuming the right to admit students to that extent. The court ordered otherwise. The doctrine of promissory estoppel prevailed over the executive order.[219]

[s 115.14.1] ***Minority status.***—The right to establish and administer educational institutions by minorities cannot be whittled down by doctrines of estoppel and waiver.

---

213. *Principal, Madhav Institute of Technology and Science v Rajendra Singh,* AIR 2000 SC 2487 : (2000) 6 SCC 608.
214. *Osmania University v R. Madhavi,* AIR 1998 AP 130.
215. *Birendra Nath Mondal v Vidyasagar University,* AIR 1999 Cal 283.
216. *Thomas P John v Cochin University of Science and Technology,* AIR 2003 Ker 238.
217. *Reeta v Behrampur University,* AIR 1993 Ori 27 (FB).
218. *Desai Devang V v Registrar, South Gujarat University,* AIR 1996 Guj 96.
219. *Association of Management of Pvt Colleges v State of TN,* AIR 1998 Mad 34.

The educational agency in this case took inconsistent stands in claiming minority status. The court said that the claim could not be rejected on that ground. A detailed and deeper probe would be required.[220]

[s 115.14.2] ***Religious institutions or places.***—A temple was being administered by the plaintiff community. On representation of the plaintiff along with the general public, the defendant was allowed to administer the temple. It was taken over by the defendant administering it for more than 35 years. The temple lost its character by efflux of time and also because of the conduct of the plaintiff community as being a denomination temple. The defendant appointed persons of other communities as trustees. The plaintiff community became estopped from challenging the administration by the defendant saying that it was violation of Article 26 of the Constitution, being against interests of the plaintiff community.[221]

[s 115.15] Issue estoppel.—The basic principle underlying the rule of issue estoppel is that the same issue of fact and law must have been determined in the previous litigation.[222] The doctrine of issue estoppel in a criminal proceeding would come into play only if the earlier and subsequent proceedings were criminal prosecutions.[223] Where the issue of facts in petty cases in relation to the accused was already tried and findings were reached thereon, it was held that the reception of evidence as to the same issue of facts in respect of the same accused in a murder trial was barred. Findings in petty cases would constitute an estoppel against the prosecution in a murder case.[224] The Court has inherent jurisdiction as a matter of discretion in the interests of finality not to allow a particular issue which has already been litigated to be reopened,[225] nor to permit a party to change his pleadings.[226] Commons Commissioner decided a dispute between a County Council and Crown Estate Commissioners by declaring that the grass verges (which were in dispute) were a part of the highway and not registrable as common land. Subsequently the Crown Estate Commissioners brought an action against

---

220. *Ummul Qura Educational Society Govt of AP,* AIR 2002 NOC 121 : (2001) 5 Andh LT 422 (AP).

221. *Kuzhithurai Peruntheru Vellalar Samudayam Sreerooba Narayanapillayar Devasthanam, v The Commissioner,* AIR 2007 NOC 585 (Mad).

222. *GP Sinha v State of Bihar,* AIR 1971 SC 458 : 1971 Cr LJ 420 : (1970) 2 SCC 905; *Nilofar Insaf (Dr. Kumari) v State of MP,* AIR 1991 SC 1872 : (1991) 4 SCC 279, a settled issue cannot be sought to be unsettled belatedly particularly when it is sought to be done in a collateral attack and on a ground which does not go to the root of the matter.

223. *GN Deshpande v Ishwaribai U Ahuja,* 1992 Cr LJ 2665 (Bom).

224. *Ramesh Chandra Biswas v State,* 1994 Cr LJ 1134 (Cal). See also *Sangeetaben Mahendrabhai Patel v State of Gujarat,* (2012) 7 SCC 621, para 23.

225. *R v Secy of State,* (1984) 1 All ER 956 at 964 and *Ali v Secy. of State,* (1984) 1 All ER 1009, noted All ER Annual Rev 1984 at 160-161.

226. *Thayammal v K Subramaniam,* AIR 1989 Mad 317. Issue estoppel would not have the effect of compelling the Government which filed two identical cases and withdrew one, to withdraw the other also. *PR. Rao v G Soma Reddy,* 1987 Cr LJ 1629 (AP). *Roop Kumar v Mohan Thedani,* AIR 2003 SC 2418, the parties agreed that instead of remanding the matter, the appellate court should consider the material on record and render a verdict. The Supreme Court said that it was not open to any party to take the plea that no concession was given. *Muthake v Devanna,* AIR 2002 Ker 301, in a suit for partition, there were findings of courts in earlier two suits that there had been oral partition, the plaintiff, a minor at the time was represented through guardian, there was no plea that the earlier proceedings were null and void, or that the decrees passed in those suits should be set aside, no evidence to show that the minor was adversely affected, rather he had the fruits of the decrees, not allowed to sue.

the County Council for trespass on verges and the Council claimed estoppel against them because the issue had already been decided. The court said:[227]

> There was no reason why the decision of an inferior tribunal with a limited jurisdiction and a strictly limited function to perform should not be capable of creating an issue estoppel, subject always to the constitutional principles that a tribunal of limited jurisdiction could not be permitted conclusively to determine the limits of its own jurisdiction and that a public official could not be barred by issue estoppel from performing his statutory duty. Since the Commissioner had a statutory jurisdiction to decide whether the road verges should be registered as common land and for that purpose had to determine whether they formed part of a highway, he had jurisdiction to determine that question also. Furthermore, that was not a jurisdictional question, since the Commissioner's jurisdiction to decide it did not depend on the correctness of the answer he gave. All the requirements of issue estoppel were therefore satisfied.

Where the purchaser of the assets of a company submitted before the High Court that as per terms of the settlement, he would abide by the terms as modified by the High Court, it was held that the Supreme Court could again modify the terms and no estoppel would be attracted.[228]

The principle of cause of action or issue estoppel applies to an industrial tribunal application which has been formally dismissed following its withdrawal by the applicant. The fact that the tribunal heard no evidence or argument on the issues of fact or law would not prevent the decision from operating as *res judicata*. It was a judicial decision by a tribunal in the exercise of its statutory powers and not a mere administrative act. In the absence of any exceptional circumstances, the employee was disentitled from bringing a further claim for a redundancy payment.[229]

Under the principle of issue estoppel a party was not allowed to raise the matter of copyright where it was not raised in the course of the parties' without prejudice correspondence.[230]

[s 115.16] Scope.—In order to hold that a case comes within the scope of this section a Court must find.

(1) That party A believed a thing to be true,

(2) That, in consequence of that belief, he acted in a particular manner,

---

227. *Crown Estate Commissioners v Dorset County Council,* (1990) 1 All ER 19 (Chapter D).

228. *Industrial Finance Corp v Official Liquidator,* AIR 1993 SC 1524 : (1993) 3 SCC 40; *Shree Anupar Chemical (India) Pvt Ltd v Dipak G Mehta,* AIR 1999 Bom 349, averment in the petition of 20% shareholding, objection to the petition that on account of subsequent increase of capital, the petitioner's shareholding was reduced to less than 10% and therefore, he was not qualified for the petition. The objection was held to be not maintainable. The objector had agreed in an earlier proceeding not to raise any such objection.

229. *Barber v Staffordshire County Council,* (1996) 2 All ER 748 (CA); *Udit Gopal Beri v State of Rajasthan,* AIR 2001 Raj 147, petition for conversion of agricultural land, the same plea was taken by the predecessor of the petitioner and was negatived by a reasoned order which was confirmed by a Division Bench. Thus the plea was directly and substantially in issue in the earlier proceeding, not allowed to be reopened in a subsequent writ petition.

230. *Hodgkinson and Corby Ltd v Wards Mobility Services Ltd,* 1997 FSR 178 (ChD).

(3) That that belief, and A's so acting, were brought about by some representation by party B, either by declaration, act or omission, which representation was made intentionally to produce that result.

If these be established, then B is prohibited by law from denying, in a proceeding against A or A's representative, the truth of his representation.

It is not necessary to prove an intention by B to deceive, or any fraudulent intention. He will nonetheless be estopped if he himself was acting under a mistake or misapprehension. It is also not necessary that the party claiming estoppel should have suffered any loss or detriment.[231] The court said: "Gradually the doctrine of promissory estoppel has developed to an extent that it is no longer necessary that the party seeking to enforce the principle must have suffered a detriment."

The Supreme Court has stated the requirements in terms of a larger number of points:[232]

"To bring the case within the scope of estoppel as defined in section 115 of the Evidence Act;

(1) there must be a representation by a person or his authorised agent to another in any form—a declaration, act or omission;

(2) the representation must have been of the existence of a fact and not of promises *de futuro* or intention which might not be enforceable in contract;

(3) the representation must have been meant to be relied upon;

(4) there must have been belief on the part of the other party in its truth;

(5) there must have been action on the faith of that declaration, act or omission, that is to say, the declaration, act or omission must have actually caused another to act on the faith of it, and to alter his former position to his prejudice or detriment;

(6) the misrepresentation or conduct or omission must have been the proximate cause of leading the other party to act to his prejudice;

(7) the person claiming the benefit of an estoppel must show that he was not aware of the true state of things—if he was aware of the real state of affairs or had means of knowledge, there can be no estoppel;

(8) only the person to whom representation was made or for whom it was designed can avail himself of it. A person is entitled to plead estoppel in his own individual character and not as a representative of his assignee."

The law of estoppel cares nothing for the motive or state of knowledge of the party upon whose representation the action took place. What it does care about is the position of the party who was induced to act. That party can only use as an estoppel a statement by which he was actually misled.

---

231. *RK Kawatra v DSIDC,* AIR 1992 Del 28.

232. *Chhaganlal Keshavlal Mehta v Patel Narendas Haribhai,* AIR 1982 SC 121 : (1982) 1 SCC 223 : (1982) 1 Guj LR 325. No estoppel arose on the facts of the case because there was no representation by the legal heirs of the mortgagors to the mortgagee.

The Government is not exempt from the equity arising out of the acts done by citizens to their prejudice, relying upon the representations as to its future conduct made by the Government.[233] Public bodies are as much bound as private individuals to carry out representations of facts and promises made by them, relying on which other persons have altered their position to their prejudice.[234]

If a document is void *ab initio* there would be no question of estoppel.[235]

The general notion about doctrine of estoppel has all along been that it can be used as a defence and not as a cause of action. But now under the impact of its application and extension to promissory estoppels, it is capable of affording a cause of action also. Noting this development, the High Court of Delhi observed:

> The modern doctrine of promissory estoppel is of comparatively recent origin in the field of public law. The provisions regarding estoppel contained in ss. 115–117 are a mere shadow of what the modern principles of promissory estoppel have come to be. The present development in this area is that an independent action can now be founded on a promissory estoppel and it is no longer a principle available only as a shield. It can be used as a weapon of offence.[236]

[s 115.17] "When one person has by his declaration, act or omission?"—The term "person" applies only to a person of full age and competent to enter into contracts. If an infant represents fraudulently or otherwise that he is of age and thereby induces another to enter into a contract with him, the infant is not estopped from setting up infancy in an action founded on the contract.[237] But the court has discretion in equity to direct the minor to return the benefit he has received by false representation to the person he has deceived.[238] The Allahabad High Court has held that upon equitable grounds he may be made liable for any loss which the plaintiff has suffered.[239] The Privy Council has not decided the point though the Calcutta High Court in its decision had expressly decided it.[240]

A declaration of age, other than in the case of a minor, creates an estoppel.[241]

There is a clear distinction between a representation of an existing fact and a representation that something will be done in future. The former may, if it amounts to a representation as to some fact alleged at the time to be actually in existence, raise

---

233. *UOI v Indo-Afghan Agencies Ltd*, (1968) 2 SCR 366 : AIR 1968 SC 718.

234. *Century Spg & Mfg Co v Ulhasnagar Municipality*, AIR 1971 SC 1021 : (1970) 1 SCC 582.

235. *Niranjan Panda v Narayan Panda*, (1953) Cut 508.

236. *RK Kawatra v DSIDC*, AIR 1992 Del 28.

237. *Gadigeppa v Balangowda*, (1931) 33 Bom LR 1313 : 55 Bom 741 (FB); *Brohmo Dutt v Dharmo Das Ghose*, (1898) 26 Cal 381; *Manmatha Kumar Shaha v Exchange Loan Co Ltd*, (1937) 1 Cal 283; *Nakul Chandra v Sasadhar*, (1941) 45 Cal WN 907; *Vaikuntarama Pillai v Authimoolam Chettiar*, (1914) 38 Mad 1071; *Radhe Shiam v Behari Lal*, (1918) 40 All 558; *Radha Kishan v Bhore Lal*, (1928) 50 All 862; *Kumar Ganganand Singh v Maharaja Sir Rameshwar Singh Bahadur*, (1927) 6 Pat 388; *Khan Gul v Lakha Singh*, (1928) 9 Lah 701 (FB). The former Judicial Commissioner's Court at Nagpur had held likewise; *Gulabchand v Chunnilal*, (1929) 25 NLR 85.

238. *Khan Gul v Lakha Singh*, (1928) 9 Lah 701 (FB); *Vaikuntarama Pillai v Authimoolam Chettiar*, (1914) 38 Mad 1071; *Kumar Ganganand Singh v Maharaja Sir Rameshwar Singh Bahadur*, (1927) 6 Pat 388.

239. *Jagar Nath Singh v Lalta Prasad*, (1908) 31 All 21; *Radha Kishan v Bhore Lal*, (1928) 50 All 862.

240. *Mohori Bibee v Dharmodas Ghose*, (1903) 30 IA 114, 122 : 30 Cal 539, 545 : 5 Bom LR 421, 424.

241. *Devi Dayal v Secy. to Govt, Haryana*, AIR 1985 P&H (NOC) 223.

an estoppel, if another person alters his position relying upon that representation. A representation that something will be done in the future may result in a contract if another person to whom it is addressed acts upon it.[242]

Under the English law a minor is not estopped from pleading his minority. An infant by fraudulently representing that he was of full age induced the plaintiffs to lend him a sum of money. In an action by the plaintiffs to recover the money it was held that the cause of action was in substance *ex contractu*, that the plea of infancy was a good answer to the action, and that the defendant was under no equitable liability to the plaintiffs.[243] "When an infant obtained an advantage by falsely stating himself to be of full age, equity required him to restore him ill-gotten gains, or to release the party deceived from obligations or acts in law induced by the fraud, but scrupulously stopped short of enforcing against him a contractual obligation, entered into while he was an infant, even by means of fraud."[244] This case has been approved of by the Privy Council.[245]

Where the construction of a building has been sanctioned by the Development Authority of the Town under ministerial orders, the validity of the sanction cannot be questioned by the Government after the commencement or completion of construction.[246] Similarly, a Town Planning Authority cannot change the scheme of the area of a residential colony.[247] A person tolerated an encroachment wall obstructing passage for nine years. He commenced proceedings but claimed removal only after four years of the proceedings. The court would not allow him to do so but ordered the defendant not to obstruct the passage further still by dumping material.[248] Where requisite fee has been paid on the basis of valuation made by the Government, the latter cannot afterwards challenge the valuation.[249] Where all the members of a family accepted an assessment to estate duty permitting one of them to act as the accountable person, none of them was subsequently allowed to challenge the assessment on the ground that the person so assumed to be accountable was not really so.[250] Full professional charges were paid to a claimant by the Government as a special case by waiving normal procedures. The person who accepted the payment was not allowed afterwards to claim interest on delayed payment.[251]

Where the Advocate General made a statement that a Government order stood superseded by subsequent rules, the Government could not contend that the said GO was still alive.[252] Where royalty imposed on timber mills was found to be illegal, the

---

242. *Centrury Spg & Mfg Co v Ulhasnagar Muncply.*, AIR 1971 SC 1021 : (1970) 1 SCC 582. *Abdul Dadamiya Shaikh v Murlidhar Rathi,* AIR 2002 Bom 413, the vendor made no representation about his ownership of land about which the purchaser could say that he acted on it, the vendor became the owner by some alteration in the mutation records. He was not bound by any estoppel.

243. *R Leslie, Ltd v Sheill,* (1914) 3 KB 607.

244. *Ibid.* p 618.

245. *Mahomed Syedol Ariffin v Yeoh Ooi Gark,* (1916) 43 IA 256: 19 Bom LR 157: (1916) 2 AC 575, followed in *Mt. Muliabai v Garud,* (1919) 15 NLR 149.

246. *Express Newspapers Ltd v UOI,* AIR 1986 SC 872 : (1986) 1 SCC 133.

247. *Kantilal v Chairman, Improvement Trust, Ratlam,* AIR 1986 MP 134.

248. *K Satyanarayanan v K Ramaiah,* AIR 1983 SC 452 : (1984) 2 SCC 439.

249. *Abdul Wahid v UOI,* AIR 1982 Del 291.

250. *Kalyani Sundaram v ASST Controller of Estate Duty,* AIR 1989 SC 1654 : 1989 Supp (1) SCC 635.

251. *P Ram Reddy v State of AP,* AIR 1990 AP 76.

252. *Amali English Medium H School v Govt of AP,* AIR 1993 AP 338 (FB). Appointment of Commission of Inquiry after court order, the Govt not allowed to go against the Report, *State v Janmohan Das,* AIR 1993 Ori 180.

petitioner mill owner could not be refused relief by applying principle of estoppel, merely because of some discussion between the Government and mill owners before order of realisation of royalty was passed.[253]

[s 115.18] "Intentionally caused or permitted another person to believe a thing to be true and to act upon such belief".—A person who, by his declaration, act or omission, had caused another to believe a thing to be true and to act upon that belief, must be held to have done so "intentionally" if a reasonable man would take the representation to be true, and believe it was meant that he should act upon it.[254] The words "caused person to believe a thing to be true" refer to the belief in a fact and not in proposition of law.[255] "Believe a thing to be true", i.e., believe a fact to be true. The word "thing" means fact.[256] It must be found that the defendant by his act or omission intentionally caused or permitted another person to believe a thing to be true and to act upon such belief. It is not sufficient to say that it may well be doubted whether the plaintiff would have acted in the way he did but for the way in which the defendant had acted. It must be found that the plaintiff would not have acted as he did.[257] If a man, either by words or by conduct has intimated that he consents to an act which has been done, and that he will offer no opposition to it, although it could not have been lawfully done without his consent and he thereby induces others to do that from which they otherwise might have abstained, he cannot question the legality of the act he had so sanctioned, to the prejudice of those who have so given faith to his words, or to the fair inference to be drawn from his conduct.[258] A teacher of a recognised school who was facing inquiry for misconduct demanded that the enquiry should be held by educationists other than the members of the school committee. An inquiry committee was so constituted and the teacher participated in its proceedings without any objection as to its jurisdiction etc. No such objections were allowed to be raised afterwards.[259] The petitioner represented that he wanted to hold ice shows for a limited duration. The first round of shows in the various cities of India was over. The Reserve Bank was not estopped from refusing further permission. There was no representation that they would be permitted till their foreign exchange was exhausted.[260]

A party relying upon this section has to establish not only that the opposite party had made a certain declaration, but that the said declaration had been believed and had

---

253. *S. Veneer and Saw Mills, Dimapur v State of Nagaland*, AIR 1995 Gau 37, **following** *Amalgamated Coalfields Ltd v Janapada Sabha, Chhindwara*, AIR 1961 SC 964 : (1962) 1 SCR 1 and *Indira Bai v Nand Kishore*, (1990) 4 SCC 668 : AIR 1991 SC 1055.

254. *Sarat Chunder Dey v Gopal Chunder Laha*, (1892) 19 IA 203, 219 : 20 Cal 296, 314, quoted in *Niharbala Debi v Shasdhar Ray Chaudhuri*, (1930) 58 Cal 358, 364.

255. *Rajnarain Bose v Universal Life Assurance Co*, (1881) 7 Cal 594. The principle of estoppel will come into play only in case the plaintiff had accepted an agreement and had acted in accordance with that in detriment to his own interest, *State of Haryana v Bharat Steel Tubes Ltd*, AIR 1996 Del 198.

256. *Vishnu v Krishnan*, (1883) 7 Mad 3 (FB); *Sarat Chunder Dey v Gopal Chunder Laha*, (1892) 19 IA 203 : 20 Cal 296; *Tek Chand v Mussammat Gopal Devi*, (1912) PR No. 46 of 1212 (Civil).

257. *Narsingdas v Rahimanbai*, (1904) 28 Bom 440 : 6 Bom LR 440; *Jhinguri Tewari v Durga*, (1885) 7 All 878 (FB); *Hem Nolini v Isolyne Sarojbashini*, AIR 1962 SC 1471 : 1962 Supp (3) SCR 294.

258. *UOI v KP Mandal*, AIR 1958 Cal 415.

259. *National High School, Madras v Education Tribunal*, AIR 1992 SC 717 : 1992 Supp (3) SCC 106. See also *Rajendra Kumar Arya v New India Assurance Co Ltd*, AIR 1992 Cal 110, prolonged negotiations about an insurance claim with no indication that the claim would be refuted, disclaimer of the claim not allowed.

260. *Arun Kumar v RBI*, AIR 1981 Del 314.

been acted upon and that it was not reasonably possible for the said party to know the true state of affairs by pursuing inquiries reasonably and with diligence. Where truth is accessible to a party, the plea of estoppel upon representation fails.[261] A person cannot invoke the doctrine of estoppel unless he proves that he has been induced to change his position to his detriment by relying upon any declaration, act or omission of the person against whom the doctrine is invoked.[262]

Where the Government declared a scheme of giving incentive to Rice Mill Industries and a party made heavy investments for modernisation of the mill but prior to introduction of the scheme and did not obtain approval as required under the scheme, he was entitled to no benefit by applying the doctrine of promissory estoppel on Government subsequently withdrawing the scheme.[263]

[s 115.19] Permission for employment abroad, with right of lien on existing job.—An employee was allowed to join an employment abroad with two years lien on the existing job. The sanction order clearly stipulated that if the employee failed to resume his duty within two years his lien would end. The employee did not return within the stipulated period and, therefore, his employment was terminated. He was not allowed to challenge the validity of two years restriction on the right of lien.[264]

[s 115.20] Future promise does not create estoppel.—To create an estoppel there must be a representation by means of a declaration, act or omission that a thing is true, i.e., that the representation is as to some state of facts alleged to be at the time actually in existence. If the representation relates to a promise *de futuro*, it can be binding not as an estoppel but as a contract.[265] A mere promise to do something in future will not create an estoppel.[266]

[s 115.20.1] ***Agreement in Praesenti.***—A question arose about the extension of time for the telecast of a TV Serial. There was a letter from the Prasar Bharti stating that an extension of time would not be granted after 52 episodes. Both parties kept on acting on this letter. The court said that the letter served as an agreement between the parties. Both parties thus became bound. The applicant could not compel the authorities to grant extension on the basis of the revised policy. Neither the principle of promissory estoppel nor that of legitimate expectation could be invoked.[267]

[s 115.21] True facts known to both the parties.—The section does not apply to a case where the statement relied upon is made to a person who knows the real facts

---

261. *Muhammad Shafi v Muhammad Said*, (1929) 52 All 248; *Sarat Chunder Dey v Gopal Chunder Laha*, (1892) 19 IA 203 : 20 Cal 296.

262. *Kazi Syed Karimuddin v Meherunisa Begum*, (1947) Nag 341; *Muddanappa v Chandramma*, AIR 1965 SC 1812 : (1965) 3 SCR 283; *Abdul Dadamiya v Jagannath Murlidhar*, AIR 2002 Bom 413, a buyer of property did not part with his money and thus, having not acted on the basis of the representations made to him, he was not allowed to say that the seller was bound by his representations.

263. *Mahalaxmi Rice Mills v State of WB*, AIR 1996 Cal 162.

264. *Anil Bajaj (Dr) v PG Institute of Medical Education and Research*, AIR 2002 SC 2414.

265. *Jethabhai v Nathabhai*, (1904) 28 Bom 399, 407 : 6 Bom LR 428; *Rivett Carnac v New Mofussil Co*, (1901) 26 Bom 54 : 3 Bom LR 846; *Parshottam v Secretary of State*, (1937) 39 Bom LR 1257.

266. *Ma Pyu v Maung Po Chet*, (1916) 2 UBR (1914-1916) 148.

267. *AAA Film Motion Picture Producers v UOI*, AIR 1999 Delhi 178.

and is not misled by the untrue statement. There can be no estoppel where the truth of the matter is known to the both parties.[268]

The husband who contracted second marriage was fully conscious of the fact that the second wife was earlier married and divorced. The fact was duly included in the matrimonial advertisement. The Church Marriage Register Book was also signed by both the parties. The husband was not allowed to plead that his marriage was invalid because the divorce to the wife from the first marriage was granted by a Court of incompetent jurisdiction. The plea was barred by estoppel and also contrary to public policy.[269]

Where the defendant knew that the buildings in dispute did not belong to him, but had been sold to the plaintiff, and, in spite of that fact, he chose of his own accord to incur expenditure by repairing these buildings, it was held that he could not raise any plea of estoppel.[270] The fact that a workman continued in service for a number of years on the basis of bogus and forged casual labourer service cards, cannot create an estoppel against the employer Government to remove him after holding departmental proceedings.[271]

[s 115.22] Estoppel does not require fraudulent intention.—It is not essential that the person making the representation which induces another to act must be influenced by a fraudulent intention. A fraudulent intention is not necessary to create an estoppel. The determining element is not the motive with which the representation has been made, nor the state of knowledge of the party making it, but the effect of the representation as having caused another to act on the faith of it.[272] The Allahabad High Court has held that the word intentionally does not mean that the conduct of the person making the representation should have been fraudulent or that it should not have been made under a mistake or misapprehension. The motive or state of knowledge of the representor is immaterial. The law only considers the position of the person to whom the representation was made.[273] The section "does not make it a condition of estoppel resulting that the person who by his declaration or act had induced the belief on which another has acted was either committing or seeking to commit a fraud, or that he was acting with a full knowledge of the circumstances, and under no mistake or misapprehension...What the law and the Indian statute mainly regard is the position of the person who was induced to act; and the principle on which the law and the statute rest is, that it would be most inequitable and unjust to him that if another, by a representation made, or by conduct amounting to a representation, has induced him to act as he would not otherwise have done, the person who made the representation should be allowed to deny or repudiate the effect of his former statement, to the loss and injury of the person who acted on it." If the person who made the statement did so without full knowledge, or under error, *sibi imputet*, it may, in the result, be unfortunate for him, but it would be unjust, even though he acted under error, to

---

268. *Honapa v Narsapa*, (1898) 23 Bom 406; *Mohori Bibee v Dharmodas Ghose*, (1903) 30 IA 114: 5 Bom LR 421: 30 Cal 539; *Ranchhodlal v Secretary of State*, (1910) 13 Bom LR 92 : 35 Bom 182; *Jacks & Co v Joosab Mohomed*, (1923) 48 Bom 38 : 25 Bom LR 1170.

269. *Deva Prasad Reddy v Kamini Reddy*, AIR 2000 Kant 356.

270. *Nawab Zakia Begam v The Lucknow Improvement Trust*, (1937) 13 Luck 192; *Rai Sunil Kumar v Thakur Singh*, AIR 1984 Pat 80, where the truth of the matter was known to both parties.

271. *UOI v M Bhaskaran*, AIR 1996 SC 686 : 1995 Supp (4) SCC 100.

272. *Cairncross v Lorimer*, (1860) 3 Macq. HLC 827.

273. *Harbans Lal v Divl Supdt, Central Rly*, AIR 1960 All 164.

throw the consequences on the person who believed his statement and acted on it as it was intended he should do.[274]

"An estoppel does not in itself give a cause of action; it prevents a person from denying a certain state of facts. One ground of estoppel is where a man makes a fraudulent misrepresentation and another man acts upon it to his detriment. Another may be where a man makes a false statement negligently, though without fraud, and another person acts upon it. And there may be circumstances under which, where a misrepresentation is made without fraud and without negligence, there may be an estoppel."[275] There may be statements made, which have induced another party to do that from which otherwise he would have abstained, which cannot properly be characterised as misrepresentation, but which amount to estoppel.[276]

[s 115.23] Estoppel must be unambiguous.—To create an estoppel against a party, his declaration, act or omission must be of an unequivocal and unambiguous character.[277] An estoppel to have any judicial value, must be clear and non-ambiguous; it must also be free, voluntary and without any artifice.[278]

[s 115.24] Estoppel on point of law.—There is no estoppel on a point of law.[279] In *CIT v BN Bhattacharjee, CIT v BN Bhattacharjee,*[280] the court said: "The soul of estoppel is equity, not facility for inequity nor is estoppel against statute permissible because public policy animating a statutory provision may then become the casualty." Halsbury has noted this sensible nicety.[281] "Where a statute, enacted for the benefit of a section of the public, imposes a duty of a positive kind, the person charged with the performance of the duty cannot by estoppel be prevented from exercising his statutory powers."[282]

Estoppel refers to a belief in a fact and not in a proposition of law. A person cannot be estopped for a misrepresentation on a point of law. An admission on a point of law is not an admission of a "thing" so as to make the admission matter of estoppel.[283] An

---

274. *Sarat Chunder Dey v Gopal Chunder Laha*, (1892) 19 IA 203, 215 : 20 Cal 296, 311, overruling *Ganga Sahai v Hira Singh*, (1880) 2 All 809 (FB); *Vishnu v Krishnan*, (1883) 7 Mad 3 (FB); *Assudibai v Haribai*, (1943) Kar 227.

275. *Per* Lord Esher, MR, in *Seton v Lafone*, (1887) 19 QBD 68, 70.

276. *Sarat Chunder Dey v Gopal Chunder Laha*, (1892) 19 IA 203 : 20 Cal 296.

277. *Gajanan v Nilo*, (1904) 6 Bom LR 864; *Gaura Dei Musammat v Raja Mohammad Yasin Ali Khan*, (1934) 10 Luck 361.

278. *Mowji v National Bank of India*, (1900) 2 Bom LR 1041: 25 Bom 499; *Rani Mewa Kuwar v Rani Hulas Kuwar*, (1874) 1 IA 157.

279. *Raghava Rajagopala Chari v State of Assam*, AIR 1965 Assam, 109. Operation of law cannot be prevented by estoppel. *CIT v BN Bhattacharjee*, 118 ITR 461 : 1979 Tax LR 1180; *Elson Machines Pvt Ltd v Collector of Central Excise*, AIR 1989 SC 617; (1989) 9 ECC 80 : 1989 Supp (1) SCC 671. There cannot be any estoppel against settled principles of law, nor against any person who is not the maker of the statement, *C Doctor & Co Ltd v Belwal Spinning Mills Ltd*, AIR 1995 All 19. The constitutional validity of admission rules was allowed to be challenged though they had been there for 29 years, *Ekta Arvind Kumar Shah v HS. Shah*, AIR 1993 Guj 90. See also *Dugar Tea Industries Pvt Ltd v State of Assam*, AIR 2016 SC 4696, para 21.

280. *CIT v BN Bhattacharjee*, AIR 1979 SC 1725 at 1738 : (1979) 4 SCC 121.

281. *Halsbury's Law of England*, para 1515 (Vol 4).

282. *Maritime Electric Co Ltd v General Dairies Ltd*, 1937 AC 610; *Hudson v Hudson*, (1948) 1 All ER 748 (PC).

283. *Jagwant Singh v Silan Singh*, (1899) 21 All 285; *UOI v KS Subramaniam*, AIR 1989 SC 662 : 1989 Supp (1) SCC 331 : 1989 SCC (L&S) 404, party not estopped from pleading against earlier admissions made in court on a wrong apprehension of law.

agreement contrary to public policy does not create an estoppel. It would not prevent the party from pleading the illegality.[284] Where certain claims have been allowed in a tax matter, there is no estoppel as against similar claims in future.[285] Any act done under misapprehension of legal right does not create estoppel, nor does a question of estoppel arise when the parties know the correct position.[286] Where persons merely represent their conclusions of law as to the validity of an assumed or admitted adoption, there is no representation of a fact to constitute an estoppel.[287]

Where an appointment was made clearly against the regulations, it was liable to be set aside. There arises no question of estoppel though the appointee was even promoted.[288]

A student in a Polytechnic failed to put in a minimum prescribed percentage of attendance. But the principal permitted him to take his examination. The principal spoke of superior orders but the persons making such orders had no jurisdiction in the matter. The permission was against Rules and, therefore, it was cancellable leaving no scope for invocation of the doctrine of promissory estoppel.[289]

A party is not bound by his pleader's admission on a point of law.[290]

The doctrine of estoppel is not applicable to a decision on a pure question of law such as the question of jurisdiction of courts.[291] Where a cooperative bank alleged before the MRTP Commission that it was a full-fledged banking company within the meaning of the Banking Regulation Act, 1949, the same being against the law, it was held that the party making the averment was not estopped from averring that it was not a banking company.[292]

The right of pre-emption, though a legal right, is in its nature a very weak right, and, therefore, can be defeated by estoppel.[293] A suit for pre-emption on the basis of an alleged sale of land did not prevent the party from subsequently challenging the validity of the sale.[294] In a contract under which timber was to be supplied and price could not be fixed, because the timber had still to be ascertained the court said that sections 18, 19 and 20 of the Sale of Goods Act, 1930 would govern the right and duties of the parties, and not the principle of promissory estoppel.[295]

---

284. *Union Carbide Corp v UOI*, AIR 1992 SC 248 : (1991) 4 SCC 584.

285. *Dunlop India Ltd v UOI*, AIR 1977 SC 597 : (1976) 2 SCC 241; *Hamir Ram v Varisng Ramal*, AIR 1998 Guj 165, application in administrative law explained.

286. *Shanker Lal v Narendra*, AIR 1967 All 405.

287. *Dhanraj v Soni Bai*, (1925) 27 Bom LR 837: 52 IA 231: 52 Cal 482.

288. *Ravinder Sharma v State of Punjab*, AIR 1995 SC 277 : (1995) 1 SCC 138;. *Jagdish Chandra Mitra v District Municipal Election Officer*, 1996 AIHC 101 (Cal), however, the case involved pure question of law and there can be no estoppel against statute. Service of notice and its receipt do not amount to submission to jurisdiction.

289. *MR Jayaswal v Secretary, State Board of Technical Education and Training*, AIR 1998 AP 263.

290. *Narayan v Venkatacharya*, (1904) 28 Bom 408 : 6 Bom LR 434; *Krishnaji v Rajmal*, (1899) 24 Bom 360 : 2 Bom LR 25; *Shanti Prasad v Kalinga Tubes Ltd*, AIR 1962 Ori 202. *Jagannatha Swamy Varu v Vana Venugopalanaidu*, 1996 AIHC 1397 (AP), relying on *Veeramma v Appayya*, AIR 1957 AP 965.

291. *Isabella Johnson v MA Sasai*, AIR 1991 SC 993 : (1991) 1 SCC 494.

292. *Phoneix Impex v State of Rajasthan*, AIR 1998 Raj 100.

293. *Indira Bai v Nand Kishore*, AIR 1991 SC 1055 : (1990) 4 SCC 668.

294. *Munshi Singh v Sohan Bai*, AIR 1989 SC 1179 : (1989) 2 SCC 265.

295. *Ghulam Md. v State of J&K*, AIR 1999 J&K 74. *Lords Food Products (India) Pvt Ltd v Orissa State Provincial Corp*, AIR 2002 Ori 156, the borrower unit participated in auction proceedings without any objection to the rejection of the proposal at Branch level.

A life convict accepted certain conditions for his release as to his surety. One of the conditions was that surety should be for an indeterminate period commensurate with the life of the released prisoner. After his release he questioned the condition on the ground that it was neither reasonable nor fair. It was contended by the other side that he should not be allowed to do so because he had accepted it as a part of his package of release. The court did not accept this condition and allowed questioning. The court said that the principles of estoppel did not apply in this area.[296]

[s 115.24.1] ***Allotment of flat.***—After allotment, the Housing Board demanded additional price. The allottee paid it and took possession. He was not allowed afterwards to challenge the validity of the additional price demand.[297] The allotment letters stipulated norms for fixing price, payment schedule of installments and interest chargeable for default. An office order was issued subsequently for levying 20% surcharge for restoration. In spite of this office order, the Authority condoned the default of the allottee as per terms of the allotment letter and restored the allotment. The Authority was not allowed to enforce the office order of surcharge.[298]

[s 115.25] Allotment of plot of land in legal violation.—The allottee (petitioner) himself cancelled the allotment saying that it was illegal. He also claimed refund of earnest money. His claim for refund was not granted and probably for that reason he changed his stand saying that the allotment was valid and deposited the bid money. The deposit was accepted by the Authority under protest. It was held that such conduct could not estop the authorities from cancelling something which was against law.[299]

[s 115.25.1] ***Allotment of Land for Petrol Pump.***—A site was allotted and a no objection certificate for installing a petrol pump was issued. Subsequent to this, the Indian Road Congress issued a Circular for maintaining prescribed distance between two petrol pumps. For this reason the NOC was cancelled. In the meantime, the petitioner had by acting on instructions and guidelines then prevalent, altered his position by making a huge investment. It was held that the authorities were estopped from withdrawing the NOC on the basis of a subsequent Circular.[300]

[s 115.26] No estoppel against statute.—The principle of estoppel cannot be invoked to defeat the plain provisions of a statute.[301] There is no estoppel against an

---

296. *Hari Singh v State*, 2000 Cr LJ 1964 (Delhi).

297. *Tamil Nadu Housing Board. v Sea Shore Apartments Owners Welfare Assn.*, AIR 2008 SC 1151 : (2008) 3 SCC 21.

298. *Delhi Development Authority v Joint Action Committee of SFS Flats*, AIR 2008 SC 1343 : (2008) 2 SCC 672.

299. *G Ram v Delhi Development Authority*, AIR 2003 Delhi 120.

300. *Kailash Chand Poddar v State of Rajasthan*, AIR 2008 NOC 1497 (Raj).

301. *Jagabandhu Saha v Radha Krishna Pal*, (1909) 36 Cal 920; *Abdul Aziz v Kanthu Mallik*, (1910 39 Cal 512; *Dhanu Pathak v Sona Koeri*, (1936) 15 Pat 589 (SB); *Ma Mo E v Ma Kun Hlaing*, (1941) Ran 309; *Workmen v Hindustan Lever Ltd*, AIR 1984 SC 516 : (1984) 1 SCC 728; *Yamunabai Anantrao Adhav v AS Adhav*, AIR 1988 SC 644 : 1988 Cr LJ 703 : 1988 Mah LJ 335 : (1988) 1 Ker LT 416; *Aliakutty Paul v State*, AIR 1995 Ker 291; *Bengal Iron Corp v CTO*, AIR 1993 SC 2414 : (1994) Supp (3) SCC 310; *National Textile Corp v Bank of Madura Ltd*, AIR 1998 Mad 113, the remand of a case in violation of the Sick Textile Undertakings (Nationalisational) Act, 1974 was held to be not binding. It created no estoppel.

Act of Legislature.[302] There can be no estoppel against the law. The doctrine of estoppel cannot be invoked to render valid a transaction which the legislature has, on the grounds of general public policy, enacted to be invalid, or to give the court a jurisdiction which is denied to it by statute, or to oust the court's statutory jurisdiction under an enactment which precludes the parties contracting out of its provisions.[303] Estoppel only applies to a contract *inter partes* and it is not competent to parties to a contract to estop themselves or anybody else in the face of an Act.[304] Statutory protection granted to persons below age and to persons of unsound mind cannot be defeated by resorting to the doctrine of estoppel.[305] Where a statute imposes a duty by a positive action, estoppel cannot prevent it. Estoppel is only a rule of evidence which can be invoked under special circumstances but is not available to release a party from the obligation to obey a statute.[306] Nor it can be used to prevent legislative and executive organs of the State from performing their functions. Estoppel is not available for preventing a Municipal Committee from acting according to law. A Municipality granted exemption from Octroi for developing a Mandi, but subsequently revoked it. It again granted exemption in keeping with the terms of the original sale of plots, but again levied the tax. Even so a claim of estoppel against its legislative power was not allowed.[307] A Municipality (Mahapalika) handed over the contract of building a shopping complex in a public park to a private builder. It found subsequently that its action was contrary to the statute under which it was constituted. It was held that the Mahapalika could reverse its action and would not be bound in that respect by the doctrine of promissory estoppel. Its promise was against the law.[308] Where plots could be allotted under the applicable rules only to persons who qualified as locally displaced persons, but they happened to be allotted to persons who were similarly situated. Because of this allotment, others also claimed equal treatment. It was held that a wrongful allotment would not give anybody the right to seek a further wrongful allotment. Wrongly allotted plots were liable to be cancelled. The acceptance of consideration in respect of those plots would not protect the allotment. There could not be estoppel against law.[309] Where a person had acted on the terms and conditions

---

302. *Shridhar v Babaji*, (1914) 16 Bom LR 586: 38 Bom 709; *Ahmed Bhauddin v Babu*, (1929) 31 Bom LR 778 : 53 Bom 676; *Mathra Parshad v State of Punjab*, AIR 1962 SC 745 : 1962 Supp (1) SCR 913; *BN Ellias & Co v Fifth Industrial Tribunal*, AIR 1965 Cal 166; *Gopi Krishna v Anil Bose*, AIR 1965 Cal 59. The course of legislation cannot be prevented by estoppel. *Amrit Bhikaji Kale v Kashinath Janardan*, AIR 1983 SC 643 : (1983) 3 SCC 437 : 1983 Mah LJ 711. Estoppel not available against statute, *Vishnu Kumar Khatar v State*, AIR 1995 Pat 168 (FB). Change of sales- tax law with retrospective effect, refund due under changed law, recoverable, no question of estoppel or *res judicata*, *Comorin Match Industries Pvt Ltd v State of TN*, AIR 1996 SC 1916 : (1996) 4 SCC 281.

303. *Hackbridge Hewitic & Easun Ltd v Provident Fund Inspector, Madras*, 1992 Cr LJ 303 (Mad). See also *Ramesh Narang v Rama Narang*, 1995 Cr LJ 1685 (Bom). *National Oxygen Ltd v TN Electricity Board*, AIR 1996 Mad 229, not compelled to act against the provisions of a statute.

304. *Barrow's Case*, (1880) 14 Chapter D 432, 441; *Madras Hindu Mutual Benefit Permanent Fund v Ragava Chetti*, (1895) 19 Mad 200.

305. *Johri v Mahila Drupati*, AIR 1991 MP 340.

306. *Harda Municipality v H Electric Supply Co*, AIR 1964 MP 101; *Municipal Board v Mahendra Singh Chawla*, AIR 1982 SC 1493 : (1982) 3 SCC 331 : 1983 SCC (L&S) 19 : 1982 Lab IC 1783.

307. *Jit Ram Shiv Kumar v Haryana*, AIR 1980 SC 1285 : (1981) 1 SCC 11. Relying upon, *Excise Commr., UP v Ram Kumar*, AIR 1976 SC 2237 : 1976 Supp SCR 532; *N Ramanatha Pillai v Kerala*, (1974) 1 SCR 515 : AIR 1973 SC 2641 and *State of Kerala v Gwalior Rayon*, (1974) 1 SCR 671: AIR 1973 SC 2734.

308. *MI Builders v Radhey Shyam Sahu*, AIR 1999 SC 2468 : (1999) 6 SCC 464.

309. *Jallandhar Improvement Trust v Sampuran Singh*, AIR 1999 SC 1347 : (1999) 3 SCC 494 : 1999 (2) SC 598.

of a code for several years even he was not estopped from challenging its validity.[310] Where an exemption from tax is granted to save an industry, the doctrine of estoppel is not attracted.[311] If an item has been listed in a wrong category for excise purposes, the Department cannot be prevented from revising the classification.[312]

A Government authority was allowed to withdraw the promise of exemption from Mandi tax when it was found that there was no provision in the underlying Act enabling or justifying such exemption. Even the opinion of the Advocate General could not justify the exemption.[313]

It has been held that coffee is a plantation crop and not a first produce. The Forest Department collected tax from dealers in coffee seeds and coffee powder. This was held to be not permissible. The fact that the respondent voluntarily remitted the tax amount pursuant to a clause in the terms and conditions of the auction, did not have the effect of precluding him from claiming refund.[314]

No person can be precluded from pleading that certain orders are illegal or invalid, because the question as to whether orders are illegal or invalid is a pure question of law and there can be no estoppel against law.[315] An undertaking was given before the High Court in a writ proceeding on behalf of the hut and pavement dwellers that they would not claim any fundamental right to put up huts on pavements or public roads and that they would not obstruct the demolition of the huts after a certain date. They were not estopped from contending before the Supreme Court that their huts could not be demolished because of their right to livelihood comprehended in Article 21.[316] No

310. *Monte De Guirim Edul Soc. v UOI,* AIR 1980 Goa 1, Minority institutions; *Preethi Srinath v Saleedion Com Govt and Pvt Med College,* AIR 1981 Kant 58, no reservation made for sportsmen. *KR. Shenoy v Udipi Municipality,* AIR 1974 SC 2177 : (1994) 2 SCC 506, exercise of statutory power. The right of a Road Transport Corpn. to allot routes to a fresh lot of unemployed graduates cannot be questioned because the earlier allottees had been allowed good time. *Krishan Gopal Dixit v SRTC,* AIR 1986 MP 103.

311. *Filter Co v Sales Tax Commissioner* AIR 1986 SC 626 : (1986) 2 SCC 103.

312. *Plasmac Machine Mfg. Co P Ltd v Collector of Central Excise,* AIR 1991 SC 999 : 1991 Supp (1) SCC 57. The authority sealing the cinema tickets is not bound by the tax mentioned on the tickets and is not estopped from raising any demand of tax more than what is specified thereon, Theatre, *Sangamesh v Entertainment Tax Dy. Commr., Kurnool,* AIR 1993 AP 137 (FB).

313. *Krishi Upaj Mandi Samiti v Shree Gopal Products,* AIR 2009 Raj 121 (DB).

314. *Divisional Forest Officer v CC Aravindan,* AIR 2000 Ker 121.

315. *Dinbai Petit v Dominion of India,* (1950) 53 Bom LR 229; *S.B Noronah v Prem Kumari,* AIR 1980 SC 193 : (1980) 1 SCC 52; *Subhash Kumar v R.C. Chibba,* (1988) 4 SCC 709 : AIR 1989 SC 458 where the tenants were not estopped from challenging the validity of a lease under Delhi Rent Control Act, 1958; *Indra Bahadur Singh v Bar Council of UP,* AIR 1986 All 56, no estoppel against statute. *Kakubhai & Co v Nathmal,* AIR 1980 Bom 25, proceeding about validity of lease withdrawn, no estoppel against proceeding again. *3 ACES, Hyderabad v MC. of Hyderabad,* AIR 1995 AP 17, approval of a building map plan does not create an estoppel against the authority. The building can be pulled if the construction was against regulations provided that the deviation from prescribed regulations endangered public safety but not if it is of minor nature. *Karnataka State Road Transport Corp v Karnataka State Transport Appellate Tribunal,* AIR 1995 Kant 103, renewal of a road permit in violation of statute, no estoppel against renewing authority. *Adhartal Shiksha Samiti v State of MP,* AIR 2001 MP 3, allotment of land for school building on concessional rate, without taking approval of the State Government, as required under the statute, was held to be not capable of creating any estoppel against cancellation of the allotment.

316. *Olga Tellis v Bom MC,* AIR 1986 SC 180. Followed in *Ammini EJ v UOI,* AIR 1995 Ker 252 (SB).

estoppel arises where a promise given by an executive authority is beyond its powers, *ultra vires*,[317] or when a statement is made under a misapprehension of legal rights.[318]

The plaintiff and the defendant exchanged adjacent plots of land each worth more than Rs 100 by means of an unregistered deed, both believing that they had effected a valid transfer. Possession was taken by each party and defendant began to erect a very costly building placing a wall thereof in the land he had acquired in exchange. While the building was in progress, the plaintiff demanded and obtained Rs 525 from the defendant on the ground that the plot he parted with was found to be more in extent than the defendant's. After the completion of the building the plaintiff sued the defendant for recovery of his plot after removal of the defendant's building on it. The defendant pleaded that the plaintiff was estopped by his conduct from recovering the plot. It was held that the plaintiff was not estopped and that he was entitled to recover his plot owing to the absence of a registered deed of exchange as required by sections 54 and 118 of the Transfer of Property Act, 1882.[319]

Where the percentage prescribed for admission to a particular course had the force of statutory operation, it was held that the admission granted by a college of the University to a candidate with 39.1% marks (prescribed percentage being 40) was liable to be examined and the University's cancellation on the eve of the examination was well within time because the University came to know of the irregular admission only on receiving the examination form.[320] The statutory rights of a landlord under a tenancy are not defeasible by means of an estoppel.[321] No one can be estopped from asserting his statutory rights even if he had been declaring that he would not insist upon them.[322] Whether an estoppel will operate against a statute depends on the nature of the statute and objects sought to be achieved by it.[323] But abandonment of rights may change the position between the parties. A party suffering a wrong remand for five years was precluded from challenging its validity.[324] Similarly in a case, the landlord claimed rent at an excess rate, which was tendered by the tenant under protest, whereafter two eviction petitions were withdrawn by the landlord without protest by tenant to proceed further to determine the rate of rent. Even a petition for refund of excess rent paid by

---

317. *Vasantkumar Radhakisan Vora v Board of Trustee of the Port of Bombay*, AIR 1991 SC 14 · (1991) 1 SCC 761, an *ultra vires* promise in this case by the estate manager to allot premises.

318. *Sukumar Chakraborty v Asst. Assessor-Collector*, AIR 1991 Cal 181.

319. *Ramanathan v Ranganathan*, (1917) 40 Mad 1134. No conduct or agreement can amount to waiver of the right to insist upon the law of limitation. *Ajab Enterprises v Jayant Vegoiles and Chemicals Ltd*, AIR 1991 Bom 35. Where ceiling was retrospectively imposed by the statute upon the incentive granted to industries, promissory estoppel could not be invoked, *Sree Rayalaseema Alkalies & Allied Chemical Ltd v Govt of AP*, AIR 1993 AP 278 (FB). *Bankey Bihari v Surya Narain*, AIR 1999 All 167, a document under the title of family arrangement in fact involved partition of family property and, therefore, required a registered deed. The arrangement was acted upon by all members drawing their respective benefits. When it was ultimately questioned, it was held that estoppel was not applicable because it would defeat the purposes of the Registration Act and the Stamp Act.

320. *Mahesh Kumar Tewari v RD Vishwavidaya*, AIR 1989 MP 292.

321. *Pundalik Vishram Patil v Bandu Chintaman Sonar*, AIR 1991 SC 486 : 1991 Supp (2) SCC 590.

322. *Sidi Nitinkumar v Gujarat University*, AIR 1991 Guj 43, right of a candidate belonging to reservation category to seek admission in general category.

323. *Tamil Nadu Electricity Board v Status Spinning Mills Ltd*, AIR 2008 SC 2838 : (2008) 7 SCC 353, industries which had started production before the cut-off date and had applied for connection, were held entitled to the benefit of concession.

324. *Sigma Agencies Pvt Ltd v PV Thomas*, AIR 1991 Ker 102.

him was also not filed by the tenant. In the third petition, it was held that the tenant was estopped from disputing his liability to pay rent at a higher rate as claimed in the earlier eviction petition.[325]

Where a person (full-time law teacher) not entitled to be enrolled as an Advocate, was granted enrolment by a State Bar Council by misinterpreting the relevant rules, it was held that the cancellation of the enrolment by the Bar Council of India was proper. The teachers concerned could not raise the plea of estoppel because they suffered the bar at the threshold and were given enrolment in violation of and contrary to Rules.[326]

A right of appeal cannot be created by consent or agreement. Parties cannot confer jurisdiction on Court and then claim estoppel.[327]

[s 115.27] No estoppel against a Constitutional right.—Principle of estoppel cannot be invoked against a Constitutional right guaranteed to the citizens of India.[328]

[s 115.27.1] ***Transfer of Right of Succession.***—Both under the Transfer of Property Act and Mohammedan Law, a bare chance of succession is not transferable. Hence, no estoppel would arise by reason of any such transfer. But she (the legal heir) had accepted money to give up her right during father's life time. Her father died intestate. She became under estoppel from claiming her share. The court said that estoppel as a rule of evidence could be applied to estop her on account of her conduct from succeeding to the estate.[329]

[s 115.28] Criminal proceedings.—The doctrine of estoppel would not apply where parties agreed to compound an offence which is otherwise not compoundable. A petition was filed for quashing proceedings under sections 498A, 304, IPC and under the Dowry Prohibition Act because of the agreement between the parties. The petition

---

325. *Darshan Singh v Kartar Singh,* 2007 (4) CCC 344 (P&H).

326. *Anees Ahmed v University of Delhi,* AIR 2002 Delhi 440. *Association of Independent Schools, Bihar v State of Bihar,* AIR 2002 Pat 9, requisitioning of accommodation of private schools or state managed schools for holding a convention of newly elected members of *Panchayat Samitis* was held to be violative of Articles 300-A, 19(1)(d), 21, 25 of the Constitution, the fact that school managements had not protested against it did not create an estoppel against them by acquiescence. *Kanchan Bhai Kanbhai v MC of Vadodra,* AIR 2002 Guj 31, written petition to question the validy of acquisition of property in public interest (for establishing the press of a daily newspaper was allowed because the facts showed that such installation of press was done at the site. *Kamala Solvent v Manipal Finance Corp Ltd,* AIR 2001 Mad. 440, under the Arbitration and Conciliation Act, 1996, the High Court is vested with jurisdiction to pass interim orders to safeguard and protect the interests of the parties but not to challenge the appointment of an arbitrator and the venue. *Pritam Kaur v Harpal Singh,* AIR 2001 P&H 300, right to question the validity of a will is a statutory right. An agreement not to exercise that right by raising objections to validity or otherwise did not create any estoppel. The right to question validity remained available. *Star Diamond Co v UOI,* AIR 1987 SC 179 : (1986) 4 SCC 246, an earlier letter issued by the Government did not have the effect of creating any estoppel against the subsequent letter issued by the Government for the purpose of clarifying the correct position. *Kennedy Sigamani v Kiruba Gnanaseeli Prema,* AIR 2000 Mad 357, concurrent finding by courts below on the basis of oaths taken by both parties that they were married was not disturbed, though it was a question of law but it did not mean that there could be an estoppel against a statute.

327. *Suresh Saggar v Vijay Saggar,* AIR 2010 P&H 104.

328. *Madala Venkata Akshay v Comedk Uget,* AIR 2016 NOC 219 (Kar).

329. *Hameed v Jameela,* AIR 2010 Ker 44.

was dismissed. The party to the agreement was not bound by the unlawful compromise and, therefore, there was no question of estoppel either.[330]

[s 115.28.1] ***Statement Before Court.***—A statement was made by the party's counsel before the court. The matter had come before the court in connection with illegal construction of an approach road. The party wanted to withdraw the statement saying that the counsel had misconception about facts and failed to take instructions. The court did not permit. Withdrawal was sought not immediately after the statement but after several adjournments. It was a high profile case and was being conducted by an experienced counsel.[331]

[s 115.29] Estoppel by silence and acquiescence.—Whenever there is a duty owing by one person towards another to speak or act which he has failed to perform and the other party has been led by such silence to change his position, such silence would operate as estoppel against the former. But where there is no duty to speak, no estoppel can arise.[332] When silence is of such a character and under such circumstances that it would be fraud upon the other party, for the party which has kept silence to deny what his silence has induced, it will operate as an estoppel.[333] A man is bound to speak out in certain cases, and his very silence becomes as expressive as if he has openly consented to what is said or done and had become a party to the transaction. The ostensible owner sold certain land and his son, the real owner, remained silent. The acquiescence resulted in an estoppel.[334] Where a forest coupe was knocked down in favour of a person at an auction was put to re-auction after cancelling the earlier and he participated in the second auction, he was not allowed subsequently to question the validity of the cancellation. His silence amounted to an acceptance of the cancellation.[335] A landlord, who had let out the house for residential purposes tolerated non-residential use for as many as seven years, was estopped from seeking eviction on that ground.[336] Where the plaintiffs came to know about the sale of property to the defendants beforehand and made no objection to the transaction, they lost their right of pre-emption by acquiescence.[337] Wherein a suit for declaration of rights in the management of a temple, the matter was settled between the main parties before the High Court, the other signatory defendants, by their silence, were estopped from contending that the order was not binding on them.[338] Where the owners of certain industries acquiesced in their treatment as a separate class, subsequently while fixing electricity tariff, they could not say that the classification was discriminatory.[339] Where the applicant-manufacturer

---

330. *Madhumuri Surya Narayana Raja v State*, 2003 Cr LJ (NOC) 75 (Kant).

331. *Vilas Shankar Donode v State of Maharashtra*, AIR 2008 Bom 10 (DB).

332. *Jones Brothers (Holloway) Ld. v Woodhouse*, (1923) 2 KB 117; *Delhi University v Ashok Kumar*, AIR 1968 Del 131.

333. *Jokhomull Mehera v Saroda Prosad Dey*, (1908) 7 Cal LJ 604; *Dhanpat Rai v Gurunditta Mal*, (1921) 2 Lah 258.

334. *Syed Abdul Khader v Rami Reddy*, AIR 1979 SC 553 : (1979) 2 SCC 495; *Sailala v Ngurtaiveli*, AIR 1980 Gau 70.

335. *Rahaman Bhai v State of Orissa*, AIR 1989 Ori 233.

336. *DC Oswal v VK Subbiah*, AIR 1992 SC 184 : (1992) 1 SCC 370.

337. *Roopi Bai v Mahaveer*, AIR 1994 Raj 133.

338. *Shanimahatma Swamy v C Gangaiah*, AIR 1994 Kant 303.

339. *Ferro Alloys Corp Ltd v APS.E Board*, AIR 1993 AP 183.

allowed a sister concern to use his registered trade mark for a long period, doctrine of acquiescence and honest and concurrent user was attracted.[340]

Where in an order of eviction the second revision did not lie before the High School but this plea was not raised when the matter was remitted to trial Court in the second revision, acquiescence extinguished the plea from being raised by taking the matter in appeal.[341] Where the Central Government did not question the calculation of payment of solatium and interest before the tribunal, it was not allowed to say that the same were not payable under the Coal-Bearing Areas (Acquisition and Development) Act, 1957.[342] Acquisition of title is inference of law arising out of certain set of facts. A person who has not acquired any title in law, the title cannot be vested in him by reason only of acquiescence or estoppel on the part of the other. A presumption by itself does not discharge the burden of proof which lies on the claimant and would not create title.[343]

Where a party without raising any objection regarding the terms and conditions of a tender, participated in a tender process, it would be estopped from raising any objection at the subsequent stage.[344] Where the successful bidder paid only a small amount as earnest money and took no further steps to implement the project tendered for, it was decided by the Port Trust to cancel the tender process. It was held that the Port Trust Authorities were not bound by their promise.[345]

A party by committing a fraud during consolidation proceedings got her name recorded in revenue records in relation to the other person's half-share in the ancestral property concerned. The other party raised objection before the Consolidation Officer, but later on withdrew the same. It was held that the other party's right over the said property did not stand extinguished by the withdrawal of the said objection.[346]

[s 115.29.1] ***Acquiescence and waiver.***—The students of certain medical and technical institutions were to be exempted from payment of tuition fee. Grant was to be given to green card holders, namely parents who had undergone family planning operation. The institutions were not allowed to withhold accrued benefits. The institutions were already receiving grants-in-aid. Their claim of refund by Government was something different from benefit to students.[347]

Levy was imposed for extra tariff for peak hour consumption by wind mill owners. For more than five years they did not challenge the levy. How much more energy was

---

340. *Power Control and Appliances Co v Sumeet Machines Pvt Ltd*, AIR 1993 Mad 120.

341. *Rukmini Amma Saradamma v Kallayani Sulochana*, AIR 1993 SC 1616 : (1993) 1 SCC 499; *Ganpat Lal v State*, AIR 1999 Raj 225, land donated by owner to Government for establishing school, a further area of adjoining land taken from him for expansion of school and another area of land was allotted to him in lieu thereof. This allotment was cancelled by the Government after 13 years and without any notice to the allottee. The cancellation was held to be illegal. *Hindustan Copper Ltd v Rana Builders Ltd*, AIR 1999 Cal 229, enforcement of bank guarantee, bank honoured it. The amount had to be returned subsequently on appeal being filed. The plaintiff was held not debarred from filing an appeal because of acquiescence or waiver.

342. *UOI v Kashinath Mahto*, AIR 1998 Pat. 100.

343. *Kamakshi Builders v Ambedkar Educational Society*, AIR 2007 SC 2191 : (2007) 12 SCC 27.

344. *B Himmatlal Agarwal v Maharashtra State Power Generation Co Ltd, Nagpur*, AIR 2014 Bom 108 (para 34) (DB). See also *Ashok Thakur v State of HP*, AIR 2014 HP 30 (para 23) (DB).

345. *Rishi Kiran Logistics Pvt Ltd v Board of Trustees of Kandla Port Trust*, AIR 2014 SC 3358 (para 25).

346. *Amar Nath v Kewla Devi*, (2014) 11 SCC 273 (para 16).

347. *Ku Tarang Kapil v State of MP*, AIR 2008 NOC 184 (MP).

generated than the power consumed by the wind mills was not worked out. They were held to be estopped by waiver and acquiescence from challenging the levy.[348]

For a waiver of a legally enforceable right earned by an employee, it is necessary that the same is clear and unequivocal, conscious and with full knowledge of the consequences.[349] An agreement or a contract, which seeks to waive an advantage of law, is void *ab initio* on the ground of public policy.[350]

Where there was no pleading and no issue was framed in regard to the validity of the gift in question in the courts below, it was held to be too late in the day for the parties concerned to question the validity of the said gift for the first time before the Supreme Court.[351] A dispute alleging termination and demanding reinstatement was raised by the workman after the lapse of 14 years, it was held that it could be said that the dispute no longer existed and there was no "live dispute" due to acquiescence of the workman.[352]

[s 115.29.2] ***Acceptance of final bill.***—In a works contract, the contractor accepted the final bill, without raising any objection about any item. It was held that the bill became binding on the contractor by virtue of the agreement. A claim for additional payment and damages raised by the contractor two years after acceptance of the bill was barred by estoppel.[353]

In a suit for an injunction to restrain the publication of an autobiography which was alleged to contain derogatory and defamatory matter, it was shown that the passages complained of had already been published in magazines and books and that the nature of the controversy was also the same as was commented upon in the proposed book. It was held that the plaintiff could not make any grievance of the same matter being published again so as to seek prevention of the publication itself. The plaintiff's silence and not making any grievance against the prior publication amounted to acquiescence.[354]

In an election to the post of the president of a cooperative society, the defeated candidate signed the proceedings and the certificate that he was 100% satisfied with the polling. It was held that he was estopped by acquiescence from challenging the validity of the election process.[355] Where the licence fee for draftsmen was enhanced and all draftsmen, including the present protestor agreed to the enhancement and also started paying, there was acquiescence and, therefore, no challenge could be presented to the process of enhancement.[356]

---

348. *BMF Beltings Ltd v Chairman TNEC*, AIR 2007 NOC 529 (Mad-DB).

349. *Shashikala Devi v Central Bank of India*, AIR 2015 SC 2434 (para 14).

350. *RCC (Sales) Pvt Ltd v ES.I Corp*, AIR 2015 AP 134 (para 26) (FB).

351. *Phool Patti v Ram Singh*, (2015) 3 SCC 164 (para 28). See also *Rajesh Vig v Shiv Prakash Mundra*, AIR 2015 Ori 161, para 11.

352. *Prabhakar v Joint Director Sericulture Department*, AIR 2016 SC 2984, para 34. See also *PEPSU Road Transport Corp v S.K Sharma*, AIR 2016 SC 3662, para 17.

353. *Government of Gujarat v RL Kalathia*, AIR 2003 Guj 185.

354. *Khushwant Singh v Maneka Gandhi*, AIR 2002 Del. 58.

355. *Nand Prakash Vohra v State of HP*, AIR 2000 HP 65.

356. *Municipal Council, Pali v State*, AIR 2000 Raj 157; *Badam Singh v UOI*, AIR 1998 Del. 162, land acquisition, challenge after 20 years, compensation was also accepted, not allowed. *Girdharilal M Pittie v AAIFR*, AIR 1998 Del 400, negligence in obtaining copy, delay in filing appeal, no condonation.

A grant of temporary affiliation to a college by the State Government which was not illegal and the benefit of it was also accepted by the college, was not allowed to be challenged afterwards for its validity.[357]

[s 115.29.3] ***Acknowledgement of liability.***—The defendants acknowledged their liability in a suit by the bank for recovery of loan. They were not subsequently permitted to deny their liability saying that a higher rate of interest could not have been charged. The court said that acknowledgement of liability by a party not only saves limitation, it also gives a cause of action to the plaintiff to base its (bank's) claim.[358]

[s 115.29.4] ***Acceptance of Tender.***—The State invited tenders for installation and maintenance of double hoarding. In response to this tender, the petitioners were permitted to go ahead with the work. they incurred huge expenditure in erecting the hoarding. The attempt on the part of the State to allot the work to someone else was held to be arbitrary and not allowed. Writ petition was maintainable for enforcement of the contract even if the contract was non-statutory.[359]

[s 115.30] Estoppel by standing by.—When A stands by while his right is being infringed by B, the rule of estoppel by acquiescence applies under the following conditions: (1) B must be mistaken as to his legal rights; (2) B must expend money or do some act on the faith of his mistaken belief; (3) A must know his own rights; (4) A must know of B's mistaken belief; and (5) A must encourage B in his expenditure of money or other act directly or by abstaining from asserting his legal rights.[360] On the expiry of a lease term, the Government put up the property on auction for further lease and the erstwhile lessee participated in all the auctions. He did not insist upon his rights under the relevant rules at the proper moment. He was not allowed to protest against the auctions at a later stage.[361]

[s 115.31] Estoppel by negligence.—In support of a plea of estoppel on the ground of negligence it must be shown that the party against whom the plea is raised owed a duty to the party who raises the plea, or towards the general public of which he is one and that the negligence on which it is based should not be indirectly or remotely connected with the misleading effect assigned to it but must be proximate or real cause of that result i.e. the negligence which can sustain a plea of estoppel must be in the transaction itself and it should be so connected with the result to which it led that it is impossible to treat the two separately.[362]

[s 115.32] Estoppel by recital in deed.—A recital in a deed or other instrument is in some cases conclusive, and in all cases evidence as against the parties who make it, and it is of more or less weight or more or less conclusive against them according to circumstances. It is a statement deliberately made by those parties, which, like any other statement, is always evidence against the persons who make it. But it is no more evidence as against third persons than any other statement would be.[363]

---

357. *Managing Director, Rajkot Homeopathic Medical College,* AIR 1998 Guj 161.

358. *Syndicate Bank v R Veeranna,* AIR 2003 SC 2122.

359. *Enkon P Ltd v Bijoli Studio Pvt Ltd,* AIR 2008 NOC 179 (Cal-DB).

360. *Sidde Gowda v Sidda Naika,* (1952) Mys 384.

361. *Murali Krishnan v A Nagarajan,* AIR 1991 Mad 108.

362. *New Marine Coal Co v UOI,* AIR 1964 SC 152 : (1964) 2 SCR 859.

363. *Brajeshware Peshakar v Budhanuddi,* (1880) 6 Cal 268; *Tehilram Girdharidas v Kashibai,* (1908) 10 Bom LR 403 : 33 Bom 53.

Where the lease deed contained that a certain HUF was the owner of the premises which was let out, the tenant could not challenge that the HUF was not the owner.[364]

[s 115.33] Estoppel by election.—Where a man has an option to choose one or other of two inconsistent things, when once he has made his election, it cannot be retracted; it is final and cannot be altered.[365] Where a person having two inconsistent alternative remedies chooses to enforce one and thereby induces another to alter his position, an estoppel may arise on the principle that no man can approbate and reprobate at the same time. If a person chooses to accept a legacy under a will, he will be estopped from setting up a title contrary to its provisions.[366] Where the Collector, having exercised his alternative power either to exclude the lands or to proceed to acquire the lands for a wildlife sanctuary, proceeded to acquire the lands, it is no longer open to the Collector to exclude the lands by a subsequent order.[367]

The doctrine of election is based on the rule of estoppel—the principle that one cannot approbate and reprobate inheres in it. The doctrine of estoppel by election is one of the species of estoppels in pais (or equitable estoppel), which is a rule in equity. By that law, a person may be precluded by his actions or conduct or silence when it is his duty to speak, from asserting a right which he otherwise would have had.[368]

A party cannot say at one time, that the transaction is valid and thereby obtain some advantage to which he could only be entitled on the footing that it is valid, and at another say it is void for the purpose of securing some further advantage.[369] Estoppel by election is applicable to all kinds of proceedings including civil and criminal.[370]

[s 115.34] Estoppel by taking up a particular position.—If the parties have taken up a particular position before the court at one stage of the litigation it is not open to them to approbate and reprobate and to resile from that position.[371] This principle is based on the maxim "*allegans contraria non est audiendus*". It means he shall not be

---

364. *Kelvinator of India Ltd v AF Bagai*, AIR 1994 NOC 297 (Del); *Noor Md. v SH Amin*, 1996 AIHC 2550 (Ker), position taken under a settlement deed.

365. *Scarf v Jardine*, (1882) 7 App Cas 345, 360.

366. *Probodh Lal Kundu v Harish Chandra Dey*, (1904) 9 Cal WN 309; *MP Rajan v Kerala State Election Commission*, AIR 1999 Ker 399, members of the *Panchayat* who approached the Election Commission to determine whether they were in fact disqualified. They were held bound by their choice of the remedy. *Purshottam v Bhagwat Sharan*, AIR 2003 MP 128, the plaintiff claimed property as coparcenary in a suit for partition. He had also claimed a part of the property under a will in a suit against the tenant. The doctrine of election was held to be not attracted.

367. *NSV Ramanuj Jeer Swamigal v State of TN*, 1996 AIHC 204 (Mad).

368. *Cauvery Coffee Traders v Hornor Resources (International) Co Ltd*, (2011) 10 SCC 420. See also *State of Punjab v Dhanjit Singh Sandhu*, (2014) 15 SCC 144, para 26.

369. *Ambu Nair v Kelu Nair*, (1933) 35 Bom LR 807 : 60 IA 266 : 56 Mad 737.

370. *PJ Kurien v Renjitha*, 2000 Cr LJ 1731 (Ker).

371. *Udraj Raj Singh v Ram Bahal Singh*, (1946) All 549; see also *State of Bihar v BL Agarwalla*, AIR 1966 Pat 410; *IT Commr., Mysore v Canara Bank*, AIR 1967 SC 417 : (1967) 1 SCR 859. For estoppel by pleadings see *Jai Kishan v Mumtaz Beg*, AIR 1984 SC 1890 : (1984) SCC 623; *M Printer v Mareel Martins*, AIR 2002 Kant 191, a person in whose name the purchase of a property was effected contended that he alone paid for but some others contended that he was a part *benami* and that the latter also contributed towards the purchase price, the Court said that the purchaser having taken up the position that he was the sole buyer was estopped from going against his stand. The Benami Transactions (Prohibition) Act, 1988 was not applicable. *Raghu Forwarding Agency v UOI*, AIR 2000 Gau 27, railway asking for reweighment of the consignment was held to be not bound by the result of reweighment.

heard to say things contrary to each other.[372] Where payment of costs is a condition precedent to the amendment in petition being allowed and the other party accepts the costs, he cannot subsequently challenge the order on merits.[373] Relationship between pay phone operators and the Government is that of an agent and the principal, and change in the rate of commission and billing period is within the domain of the principal and doctrine of estoppel is not attracted.[374] Once having questioned the jurisdiction of the Co-operative Court, it is not open for the petitioner to say that the dispute before the Co-operative Court was maintainable. It is not possible for him to approbate and reprobate at the same time.[375] Acceptance of premature retirement and of benefits due thereon as ordered by the Service Tribunal could not be set at naught by writing a letter to the Government that he should be allowed to continue till superannuation, though the letter remained unreplied.[376]

Where the insurance claim of the petitioner was processed by surveyors appointed by the insurance company, the latter was not allowed to repudiate the claim as processed by the surveyor.[377]

[s 115.35] Estoppel by attestation.—The Privy Council has held that attestation of a deed does not by itself estop the person attesting from denying that he knew of its contents or that he consented to the transaction which it effects, and that knowledge of the contents of a deed is not to be inferred from the mere fact of attestation.[378] If A, with the knowledge that the recital in a sale deed that the land, thereby conveyed, belongs to B, and is in his (B's) enjoyment as owner, attests the sale deed executed by B in favour of the plaintiff he is estopped from setting up thereafter his title to the land, even though he (A) might be the certified purchaser of the same in a previous Court auction.[379] A person, who to his knowledge is entitled to one-half share in a shop and who allows his co-sharer to mortgage the whole shop, signing the mortgage deed as a witness and identifying the mortgagor and mortgagee at the time of registration, is estopped from bringing a subsequent suit against the mortgagee claiming a declaration of his right to one-half share in the mortgaged property.[380] Where a person attested a settlement deed which was in favour of the defendant, and there was nothing to show that the attesting witness (plaintiff) had acquainted himself with the contents of the deed or he was made aware of those contents, he was prevented from challenging the deed. No estoppel arose against him by attestation in ignorance.[381] In a sale of land by

---

372. *BS Lail v Sardar Mal*, AIR 1964 MP 124; *Bhopal Singh v Chatter Singh*, AIR 2000 P&H 34, withdrawal of a suit and its settlement were the necessary consequences of the opposite party's statement, the latter was held estopped from resiling from his statement.

373. *Bijendra Nath Srivastawa v Mayank Srivastawa*, AIR 1994 SC 2562 : (1994) 6 SCC 117. *Radheshyam Palod v Shantidevi*, AIR 1994 NOC 191 (MP), estopped from challenging amendment after accepting costs for the same.

374. *UOI v Binani Consultants Pvt Ltd*, AIR 1995 Cal 234.

375. *Mario Shaw v Martin Fernandez*, AIR 1996 Bom 116.

376. *GM Telephones v VG Desai*, AIR 1996 SC 2062 : (1996) 7 SCC 444; *Jagdishbhai Mafatlal Patel v State of Gujarat*, AIR 2002 Guj 320, estoppel by acquiescence arose when the validity of bye- laws was challenged at a belated stage and not when they were first put in question.

377. *Nand Construction Co v Regional Manager, Oriental Ins Co*, AIR 2002 Raj 272.

378. *Pandurang Krishnaji v Markandeya Tukaram*, (1921) 49 Cal 334 : 24 Bom LR 557 : 49 IA 16.

379. *Kandasami v Nagalinga*, (1912) 36 Mad 564.

380. *Shori Lal v Damodar Das*, (1937) 18 Lah 783.

381. *Annadurai v Mayazaghu*, AIR 2001 NOC 44 (Mad) : 2001 AIHC 1677.

a Muslim father, the son attested the sale deed and raised no objection though the sale was against his interest, the son was estopped from challenging the sale subsequently.[382]

[s 115.36] Constructive estoppel.—There is no such thing known to the law as constructive estoppel.[383]

[s 115.37] Plea estoppel.—Alternative plea.—The plaintiff pleaded that the agreement entered into by him for development of a plot and construction thereon was void because he was deceived into the transaction for lesser consideration. He also pleaded in the alternative for an order of specific performance. The alternative was allowed to be raised. There was no estoppel against it because of the first plea. The defendant himself had pleaded for specific performance.[384]

[s 115.38] Estoppel by crediting cheque.—Credit given in a passbook binds the banker, if on the faith of such credit the customer has altered his position, as by drawing on the credit, etc., for by entering the sums to the customer's credit, they lead him to suppose that they have received them on his account. When, however, there has been no such alteration, the banker is allowed to show that the entries were made by mistake; for the passbook is only *prima facie* evidence against him.[385]

[s 115.39] Estoppel by consent.—Consent given in a Court that a controversy is covered by a judgment which has no applicability whatsoever and pertains to a different field, cannot estop the party from raising the point that the same was erroneously cited.[386]

In case of consent award of compensation, the question of seeking any amount over and above the amount settled in the consent award does not arise.[387]

[s 115.40] Estoppel by consent/compromise decree.—A compromise decree is the acceptance by the court of something to which the parties had agreed. Such a decree might create an estoppel by conduct between the parties but such an estoppel must be specially pleaded.[388] An estoppel by consent decree can arise only when the question raised in the subsequent suit was present to the minds of the parties and was actually dealt with by the consent decree. In order to effect an estoppel it is also necessary that it should appear on record that the question had been put in issue.[389] The consent decree, resulting from the settlement entered by the Government pleader, operates as an estoppel and is binding on the parties from which the Government cannot wriggle out by taking an afterthought plea that its lawyer was not authorised to enter into such a settlement.[390]

---

382. *Mahboob Sahab v Syed Ismail*, AIR 1995 SC 1205 : (1995) 3 SCC 693.

383. *Parsomtad Gir v Narbada Gir*, (1899) 26 IA 175 : 1 Bom LR 700 : 21 All 505.

384. *Krishnabai C Kadam v Wellworth Developers*, AIR 2001 Bom. 9.

385. *Mowji v National Bank of India*, (1900) 2 Bom LR 1041 : 25 Bom 499.

386. *State of Rajasthan v Surendra Mohnot*, (2014) 14 SCC 77 (para 17).

387. *Sidramappa v State of Karnataka*, AIR 2014 Kar 100 (para 10) (FB).

388. *Subba Rao v Jagannadha Rao*, AIR 1967 SC 591.

389. *Gokul Prasad v Saran Das Mahant*, (1946) 22 Luck 270; *AP Sarpanchs Assn v Govt of AP*, AIR 2001 AP 474, directions were issued by the Court on consensus of parties as to identification of backward classes on the basis of voters' lists. The Court did not sustain the objection that the process would result absurdity because no door to door survey was conducted.

390. *Y Sleebachen v State of Tamil Nadu*, (2015) 5 SCC 747, para 23.

Where in a suit to set aside alienation of property filed by remote reversioners of the alienor, a compromise decree in the shape of decree of declaration was passed which was to take effect after the death of the alienor, declaring shares of the parties, and the decree had become final, the alienee could not take objection in a subsequent suit filed by the said remote reversioners for their share in terms of compromise that the next reversioner of the alienor being alive, the suit was not maintainable.[391] Where the property subjected to mortgage in four suits for claim was one and the same and the appellant failed to contend before the trial Court that all the claims should have been consolidated in one suit as required under section 67A of the Transfer of Property Act, 1882 and consented to decrees being passed separately, he was estopped from raising that plea in appeal.[392]

[s 115.41] Estoppel by participating in arbitration or other proceedings.—A person who participates in arbitration proceedings as a party may become estopped afterwards from dragging the same matter to civil courts, but he can nevertheless still question the validity of the underlying arbitration agreement.[393] Participation without filing counter statements does not create an estoppel, particularly where immediately after inspecting the papers, the party challenged the existence of the arbitration agreement.[394] Where a Government servant was acting *ex officio* as an arbitrator and continued, to the acceptance of the parties, even after his retirement, the parties were not permitted to challenge his competence.[395] Where a party first moved the court in a pending suit for stay under section 34 of the Arbitration Act and then resiled from the stay application and thus permitting the suit to go on and abandoning the rights under the arbitration agreement, a subsequent application for reference was not allowed.[396] Where one party concurred to the appointment of an officer of the other party as an arbitrator and he participated in the proceedings, subsequently objection of bias could not be raised by him against the arbitrator.[397]

Where the objections as to the arbitration award were rejected by the court as time-barred and no review petition was filed against the judgment, it was held that the party was estopped from raising those objections on appeal to the High Court.[398]

An Indian company and a foreign company agreed that their agreement including the arbitration under it would be governed by laws of India. The court held that the

391. *Bakshi Ram v Brij Lal*, AIR 1995 SC 395 : 1994 Supp (3) SCC 198.

392. *Annapurna Industries v Syndicate Bank*, AIR 1993 Kant 279.

393. *Waverly Jute Mills v Raymon & Co*, AIR 1963 SC 90 : (1963) 3 SCR 209.

394. *Hindustan Cables Ltd v Bombay Metal Co*, AIR 1981 Cal 350. *Bharat Sanchar Nigam Ltd v Motorola India P Ltd*, AIR 2009 SC 357 : (2009) 2 SCC 337, the High Court appointed an arbitrator on the application of the respondent. The appellant did not raise any objection prior to the first hearing. The appellant was deemed to have waived the right of objection.

395. *Mohinder Pal Mohindra v Delhi Admn*, AIR 1989 Del 270.

396. *Kishandas Parasram Ahuja v Bhagchand Dwarkadas Nagdev*, AIR 1991 MP 309.

397. *Noble Engineering Works v HP State Electricity Board*, AIR 1994 HP 153. Where a party participated in the proceedings of division of assets and liabilities of a firm, he could not be allowed to make an objection that the assets and liabilities were not the part of reference and division was beyond the scope of arbitration. *RC Bhalla v NC Bhalla*, AIR 1996 Del 24. *Mokha Light House v Indian Tourism Development Corp*, AIR 2003 NOC 9 (Del), a clause in the agreement gave power to the chief engineer or managing director to appoint arbitrator. No objections raised to the appointment. No objection was allowed to be raised after the death of the arbitrator.

398. *Shiv Lal v Food Corp of India*, AIR 1997 Raj 93.

arbitral award made under the agreement could be regarded as made under Part I of the Arbitration and Conciliation Act, 1996. It was a domestic award though made on a foreign soil according to the ICC Rules and procedure. Recourse to section 34 of the Act could not be said to have been waived by subscribing to the ICC Rules.[399]

The competency of the arbitrator was challenged after long participation in proceedings without protest. It was held that this precluded the party from saying that the proceedings were without jurisdiction. The move seemed to have been promoted by the fact that the party saw that the award was likely to go against him.[400]

[s 115.42] Estoppel by participating in election and Assembly.—Where a member challenged by a writ petition the election of a person as the Speaker of the assembly (State Legislative Assembly) by elected representatives filing his petition after six months and himself taking part in the proceedings of the Assembly for all the six months, it was held that his writ petition was barred by delay and estoppel.[401]

Where a party acquiesced in the invalidity in the conduct of arbitration proceedings and took chances, it was held that he could not thereafter object to the award which went against him. He could not say that the arbitrator had no jurisdiction to pass the award. The right of the party to raise the objection was deemed to have been waived.[402]

Where the parties agreed to refer all their disputes to arbitration and identical disputes were referred by the Municipal Corporation, the court said that the latter was estopped by its conduct from raising the plea that the claims raised by the claimants were outside the scope of the arbitration agreement particularly when the award was against it.[403]

Where an industrial unit participated in an auction proceeding without objecting to the rejection of the proposal at the branch level, it was held that the rejection of the proposal could not be challenged on the ground that it should have been considered by the Board of directors of the State Financial Corporation.[404] Where the party participated in the arbitration proceedings without protest and allowed the award to be passed, it was held that he was estopped from challenging the award on the ground that the arbitrator had no jurisdiction.[405]

[s 115.43] Estoppel against estoppel.—The maxim is "estoppel against an estoppel setteth the matter at large." In a case of one estoppel against another, the parties are set free and the court has to see what their original rights really are.

[s 115.44] Estoppel by participation in selection.—The Kerala State and Subordinate Services Rules, 1958 provided for reservation of posts, for SC/ST candidates. They were adopted by the University. Certain posts were advertised for selection of SC/ST candidates. The candidate who participated in the selection but was not taken was not allowed to challenge the process. Omission in the advertisement to state that it was a

---

399. *Nirma Ltd v Lurgi Energic Und Entsorgung GmbH,* AIR 2003 Guj 145.
400. *Soyabean Processors Assn. of India v Assardas Wadhwani (Constructions) Pvt Ltd,* AIR 2010 MP 179.
401. *AElumalai v Administrator-cum-Lt. Governor of Pondicherry,* AIR 2001 Mad 265.
402. *Inder Sain Mittal v Housing Board, Haryana,* AIR 2002 SC 1157.
403. *International Security to Intelligence Agencies Ltd v MCD,* AIR 2001 Del. 283.
404. *Lords Food Products (India) Pvt Ltd v Orissa State Financial Corp,* AIR 2002 Ori. 156.
405. *Vaish Bros & Co v UOI,* AIR 1999 Del. 105.

special selection was held to be not material.[406] The challenge to eligibility criteria as being contrary to service Rules was not allowed to be raised by candidates who had participated in the selection process.[407]

[s 115.45] No estoppel as to jurisdiction.—An estoppel against a party cannot give the court jurisdiction where it has none.[408] There can be no estoppel against a statute and that consent cannot confer jurisdiction.[409] Admissions were made by parties that the subject-matter of the suit was cognizable by the Wakf Tribunal. The disposal of the case on the basis of such admissions was held to be not proper. The admission about the jurisdictional aspects was challenged on the first occasion itself. The court said that it was a question of law. Parties could not be bound by their statements about law. The question had to be considered on merits.[410]

[s 115.46] Family arrangement.—A family arrangement is an agreement between members of the same family intended to be generally and reasonably for the benefit of the family either by compromising doubtful or disputed rights or by preserving the family property or the peace and security of the family by avoiding litigation or by saving its honour.[411] Parties agreeing to the arrangement and acting upon it are estopped from questioning its validity or legality. Where the head of a family converted his self-acquired property into HUF property, leaving out his son and daughter from the first wife, subsequent suit for partition by the son was not maintainable, particularly when he had accepted his left out position in other proceedings.[412] The provision by the father-in-law in his property his daughter-in-law made at the marriage was protected by the Supreme Court by awarding her an amount out of the sale proceeds of the property.[413] Where *ex parte* divorce decree was passed in favour of husband by a foreign Court which was a nullity under the Indian Act, the husband having married a second wife there the wife was not estopped from bringing a subsequent petition for divorce in India on the ground of adultery, cruelty and desertion simply because she had accepted maintenance under the foreign judgment.[414]

[s 115.47] Maintenance allowance.—The right of maintenance is a substantive and a continuing right and the quantum of maintenance is variable from time-to-time. Neither the doctrine of *res judicata* nor that of estoppel can be used to defeat the right of the claimant to seek revision of the amount of maintenance according to the cost

---

406. *University of Cochin v NS. Kanjoojamma*, AIR 1997 SC 2083 : (1997) 5 JT 379.

407. *Dhananjay Malik v State of Uttaranchal*, AIR 2008 SC 1913 : (2008) 4 SCC 171.

408. *Saiyid Mohd. Mohsin v Saiyid Ainul Husain*, (1946) 22 Luck 283.

409. *Uda v Jagdish Narayan*, (1963) Raj 652; *Hari Nath v Raghu Nath*, AIR 1998 HP 28, earlier judgment of the High Court holding that the jurisdiction of the civil court to decide the disputed question of title to the suit land was not barred by the HP Land Revenue Act. The same jurisdiction could not be challenged again in a civil proceeding. *State of Gujarat v Vishnu Automobiles*, AIR 1999 Guj 92, an order against a statute, an appeal against such order not barred, it being without jurisdiction. *IFB Automotive Seating and System Ltd v UOI*, AIR 2003 Cal 80, question of jurisdiction, no estoppel by reason of filing of papers.

410. *Abdul Rahiman Musaliar v TR Muhammed Sahib*, AIR 2003 Ker 84.

411. Halsbury's Laws of England, 3rd EdnVol 17, pp 215-216; *Dhiyan Singh v Jugal Kishore*, (1953) 1 All 25.

412. *Partha Talukdar v Mina Hardinge*, AIR 1993 Cal 118; *Papanna v Madappa*, AIR 1993 Kant 24, no evidence of exclusion from family, no estoppel against claiming family rights.

413. *NA Md Kasim v Sulochana*, AIR 1995 SC 1624 : (1995) Supp 3 SCC 128.

414. *Ram Shanker Rastogi v Vinay Rastogi*, AIR 1991 All 255.

of living structure.[415] Where a compromise was reached by the parties in a case for enhancement of maintenance to the wife and daughter, on the subsequent application by the wife for enhancement of maintenance, it was held that the doctrine of estoppel or waiver did not apply in the changed circumstances.[416] Where in a maintenance proceedings, the parties were Muslims and the order of maintenance was passed without obtaining the necessary consent of the husband in writing with regard to his preference to be governed by section 125, CrPC, the order was not binding upon the husband even if he had paid some amount in the first execution petition and he was not estopped from contending that the order was not binding upon him.[417]

Where the right to maintenance was granted to the wife under a compromise decree against the husband, it was held that a subsequent cohabitation between them had no effect on the decree. The decree was final and could be modified only by a competent Court.[418]

Where the wife was granted relief of maintenance by a civil court in the presence of the husband who did not object, and it was clarified that the amount of maintenance was in addition to the maintenance granted by a magistrate under section 125 CrPC, the husband is estopped from challenging the same.[419]

[s 115.48] Feeding the estoppel.—The equitable principle of feeding the estoppel has been recognised to some extent in section 43 of the Transfer of Property Act, 1882, which says that where a person fraudulently or erroneously represents that he is authorised to transfer certain immovable property and professes to transfer such property for consideration, such transfer shall, at the option of the transferee, operate on any interest which the transferor may acquire in such property at any time during which the contract of transfer subsists. But the right of transferees in good faith for consideration without notice of the existence of the said option shall not be impaired. In such cases the subsequent interest enuring to the benefit of the transferor is said to feed the estoppel which is subsisting in the transferee so as to preclude the transferor from contending that the transferee has no right to his subsequently acquired property.[420] This principle applies in the case of sale, mortgage, lease, or any such grant.[421]

---

415. *Veena Kalia v Jatinder Nath Kalia*, AIR 1996 Del 54; *Jawan v Mewa Singh*, AIR 2001 P&H 344, matters of partition of agricultural land between family members not allowed to be raised in an application by tenants for grant of proprietary rights.

416. *Joydel Kumar Biswas v Maduri Biswas*, 1994 Cr LJ 3342 (Cal).

417. *Nazimunnisa Begum v Abdul Majeeth*, 1995 Cr LJ 3156 (Mad); *Bansidhar Mohanty v J Mohanty*, AIR 2002 Ori 182, grant of maintenance to wife under the Hindu Adoption and Maintenance Act, 1956, she was estopped from claiming maintenance under section 125, CrPC. *Surendra Bhatia v Punam Bhatia*, AIR 2001 Raj 338, admission by the defendant in his written statement that the deceased testator and the plaintiff were husband and wife. He also led evidence to that effect. He was not allowed to retract the admission and raise the plea that there was no marriage at all.

418. *Kudupudi Lakshmi v Kudupudi Srikrishna*, AIR 1999 AP 226.

419. *Anant Tukaram Nalawade v Sou. Latika Anant Nalwade*, 2008 Cr LJ (NOC) 1291 (Bom.).

420. *Krishna Chandra Ghosh v Rasik Lal Khan*, (1916) 21 Cal WN 218.

421. *Deolie Chand v Nirban Singh*, (1879) 5 Cal 253; *Vithabai v Malhar*, (1937) 40 Bom LR 147. *Renu Devi v Mahendra Singh*, AIR 2003 SC 1608, property coming to the share of certain family members under a priliminary decree passed in a suit for partition. They donated it to their sons and daughters. The donation being valid, they became estopped from denying its validity. When the preliminary was confirmed by the final decree, it operated as feeding the grant by estopped.

[s 115.49] Banker's general lien.—The bank cannot be estopped from retaining pledged goods under the exercise of its general lien if the debtor had not cleared his amount in connection with another loan.[422]

[s 115.50] CASES

[s 115.50.1] Mortgagee concealing his lien.—A mortgagee who caused the mortgaged property to be sold in execution of a decree other than a decree obtained upon his mortgage, without notifying to intending purchasers the existence of his mortgage lien, was held to be estopped for ever from setting up that lien against the title of a *bona fide* purchaser.[423]

[s 115.50.2] Representation that lease is permanent.—Where a lessor, being either ignorant of his rights or uncertain of their extent, by his own act or representation created or induced in the mind of his tenant a mistaken belief that he had a permanent interest in the land and might build thereon, and the tenant, relying upon the act or representation so made, treated his interest as permanent and incurred expense in building which he would not otherwise have done, it was held that the lessor was estopped from denying the truth of that which it represented.[424] In 1894 the appellant agreed in writing to give the respondent a lease of a plot of land "for the purpose of erecting buildings...from year to year at an annual rental of Rs.180," and the respondent took possession. In 1903 the respondent wished to build a pucca house upon the land, and in answer to inquiries the appellant wrote a letter stating that the lease was a permanent lease though the rent was liable to enhancement. Acting upon that letter the respondent built a house; the appellant knew of the building and received a bonus in respect of it. In 1916, the appellant sued to eject the respondent from the land. It was held that, whether or not the letting was a permanent one upon the construction of the agreement, the statement in the letter that it was so was a representation of fact, not an expression of opinion and that the appellant was estopped from denying that the letting was of that character though subject to enhancement of rent.[425]

In a lease by the Government of a sea shore plot for carrying on the business of manufacturing salt, the lessee was permitted to induct a financial partner on certain conditions to render financial assistance only. The lessee retired from the firm leaving the lease to the exclusive care of the financial partner. The leasehold right did not become a part of the partnership properties. The fact that the Government accepted royalty from the financial partner did not attract promissory estoppel.[426]

[s 115.50.3] Trustee mortgaging trust property as his own cannot dispute sale by mortgagee.— A trustee, alleging that the trust property, consisting of land was

---

422. *State Bank of India, Kanpur v Deepak Malviya,* AIR 1996 All 165, **distinguishing** *Syndicate Bank v Devendra Karkera,* AIR 1994 Kant 1; *State Bank of India v Javed Akhtar Hassan,* (1992) 2 Bank CLR 339 : AIR 1993 Bom 87 and *RK Agency v Central Bank of India,* 1992 (2) Bank CLR 453 : AIR 1992 Cal 193.

423. *Muhammad Hamid-ud-din v Shib Sahai,* (1899) 21 All 309; *Agarchand Gumanchand v Rakhma Hanmant,* (1888) 12 Bom 678; *RMPAL Chettiar Firm v Ko Maung Gale,* (1935) 13 Ran 346.

424. *Forbes v Ralli,* (1925) 27 Bom LR 860: 52 IA 178: 4 Pat 707; *Bansi Singh v Chakradhar Prashad,* (1938) 17 Pat 358.

425. *Fobres v Ralli, ibid; Bahir Das Chakravarti v Nobin Chunder Pal,* (1901) 29 Cal 306. For an example of estoppel by acceptance of rent see *Narendra Bahadur Tandon v Shanker Lal,* AIR 1980 SC 575 at 579 : (1980) 2 SCC 253.

426. *Ganpat Salt Works v State of Gujarat,* AIR 1995 Guj 61, applying the ratio laid down in *Ved Gupta v Apsara Theatres, Jammu,* (1983) 4 SCC 323 : AIR 1983 SC 978.

his own property, mortgaged it. The mortgagee took the mortgage in good faith, for valuable consideration, and without notice of the trust. The mortgagee obtained a decree against the trustee for the sale of the land, and the land was sold in execution of that decree. The trustee subsequently brought a suit to recover the land from the purchaser on the ground that it was trust property and that he had no power to transfer it. To this none of the beneficiaries under the trust were parties. It was held that the plaintiff was estopped by his conduct from recovering possession of the land.[427] A valid trust was created by the donor in respect of the suit property. The donor was one of the trustees. The property was sold for recovering income tax dues of the donor. It was held that the trustees were not estopped from challenging the auction sale of the trust property on the ground that they were aware of the Notification of sale.[428]

[s 115.50.4] School tenancy in name of Head Master.—The landlord was not allowed to contend that the tenancy of his premises which to his knowledge was all along being used by the school was not that of the school because it was held in the name of the headmaster. The school had been paying the rent out of its funds.[429]

[s 115.50.5] Profession of Muhammadanism.—In a suit for divorce from a Muhammadan husband, brought by a Burmese woman professing the Buddhist faith, but at the time of her marriage, simulating conversion to Islam, and married with Muhammadan ceremonies, it was held that the Muhammadan law should form the rule of decision.[430]

[s 115.51] Adoption.—In a suit to set aside an adoption brought by the adoptive mother against her adopted son it was found that the plaintiff had represented that she had authority to adopt, and this representation was acted on by the defendant; that the ceremony of adoption was carried out on the faith of this representation; that the marriage of the defendant was likewise on the strength of it celebrated, and the defendant performed the *shradha* ceremony of his adoptive father. It was further found that the defendant had been obliged to defend a suit brought against him by an alleged reversioner to the estate of his adoptive father, and that for this purpose he had incurred heavy liabilities. It was held that the plaintiff was estopped from maintaining a suit for a declaration that the adoption was without authority and void.[431] A childless Hindu widow agreed with the plaintiff's father to adopt the plaintiff, stating that her husband had given her authority to adopt. Subsequently she adopted the plaintiff and had his thread ceremony performed in the adoptive family next day, and administered her husband's property as the minor's guardian for about 18 months, when she repudiated the adoption and refused to maintain the plaintiff. It was held that the adoption being invalid on the ground that the widow had not as a fact, acted under authority from her husband, she was not estopped from denying the adoption by the fact of her having treated it as effective for the period of 18 months. In order that an estoppel by conduct may raise the invalid adoption to the level of a valid adoption, there must have been a course of conduct long continued on the part of the adopting family, and

427. *Gulzar Ali v Fida Ali*, (1883) 6 All 24.

428. *Institute of Education Saraswathipuram v Sri Sowcar A Siddanna Endowment*, AIR 2003 Kant 226.

429. *Anadi Mohan Rashit v Nalin Sarkar Street UP School*, AIR 2002 Cal 22.

430. *Kumal Sheriff v Mi Shwe Ywet*, (1875) SJLB 49.

431. *Dharam Kunwar v Balwant Singh*, (1908) 30 All 549. See *Muhammad Niaz-ud-din Khan v Muhammad Umar Khan*, (1906) PR No. 1 of 1907 (Civil).

the situation of the adoptee in his original family must have become so altered that it would be impossible to restore him to it.[432]

[s 115.52] Acquisition of Land.—The petitioner company had purchased the land in question after an earlier notification for acquisition had lapsed. The company spent huge amounts on external development charges and obtained permission. The court said that the issue of a subsequent notification for acquisition was hit by the principle of promissory estoppel[433] and legitimate expectations.

The State had granted permission to the land owners for change of land use and developing the area as an industry. It turned around after 26 years to acquire the said land to develop it for residential purpose. It was held that permission for change of land use as an industry has no relevance while considering the validity of acquisition, otherwise a particular area could not be acquired for all times to come. Public interest overrides the individual interest. Therefore, the State could not be estopped from acquiring back the said land, of course, after appropriate compensation.[434]

[s 115.53] Valuation of land.—Where the Sarpanch himself participated in the meeting and passed a resolution allowing exchange of land in his own favour and the land given to him was found to be more valuable as compared to land given by him in exchange, it was held that the order according approval to the exchange granted by the Collector was rightly set aside as the question of promissory estoppel did not arise.[435]

[s 115.53.1] ***Valuation of land in acquisition.***—A question before the J&K High Court was whether a claim for enhancement of compensation was maintainable and a restricted claim was raised before the Collector, it was held that the claimant was not estopped from claiming enhanced compensation before the arbitrator. This was more particularly so because the land adjacent to the land of the claimant which had similar soil and status and in the same village was notified for compensation at enhanced rates.[436]

[s 115.53.2] ***Rehabilitation on Acquisition of Lands.***—Agricultural land was to be offered to displaced families under a Policy of Rehabilitation and settlement. The court said that it was the fundamental right of the oustees and also the right of livelihood as a human right. It could not be defeated by the Government under the plea that the oustees had accepted full compensation for acquisition. The plea of waiver or estoppel could not defeat that right.[437]

[s 115.54] Employment.—Where an appointment was anti-dated by 10 years on the ground that the appointment was denied to him for all that period under a finding that he was not qualified and the grant of the seniority were held to be not permissible.[438] Where certain applicants were included in the panel made on merit basis but could

---

432. *Parvatibayamma v Ramakrishna Rau*, (1894) 18 Mad 145.

433. *Eros City Developers Pvt Ltd v State of Haryana*, AIR 2008 NOC 1565 (P&H-DB).

434. *State of Haryana v Vinod Oil and General Mills*, (2014) 15 SCC 410, paras 8 and 9. See also *Maheshwari Vani Prakashan Pvt Ltd v State of Rajasthan*, AIR 2016 NOC 237 (Raj).

435. *M Pyarali v M Sarifbhai*, 1996 AIHC 716 (Guj), **distinguishing** *BK Srinivasan v State of Karnataka*, AIR 1987 SC 1057 : (1987) 1 SCC 471.

436. *UOI v Kamal Kant Gupta*, AIR 2002 J & K 115.

437. *Narmada Bachan Andolan v State of MP*, AIR 2008 MP 142.

438. *Ramvir Singh v UOI*, (1993) Supp 2 SCC 262 : (1993) 24 ATC 255.

not be appointed because their number happened to go beyond the available posts, and they accepted the option of being absorbed on lower posts on an undertaking that they would not lay claim to the posts on which they were initially selected, it was held that the undertaking given by them did not have the effect of preventing them from claiming absorption on senior posts in accordance with the applicable Rules whenever any such posts fell vacant.[439] Where a candidate got selected to a post by showing that he had the basic qualifications but that was in fact a misrepresentation, it was held that the authorities were not estopped from cancelling his selection.[440]

In a dispute over termination of service, it was contended that the employees having accepted benefits of VRS cannot raise dispute about termination, the same was held to be not tenable as estoppel does not bar Courts from adjudicating upon validity of a contract.[441]

[s 115.54.1] ***Terms of appointment.***—A person was appointed as advisor to a company on retainership basis. A letter of appointment containing terms and conditions was issued to him. He admitted in his correspondence with the company that the understanding arrived at as to terms was final. He was also accepting periodical payments on those terms. He was not allowed to say that the letter was issued by an unauthorised person and, therefore, he was not bound to comply with the terms.[442]

[s 115.54.2] ***Re-employment.***—The employer company was fully owned by the Government. Certain employees were permanently transferred to a joint venture company (JVC). After acceptance of the option they were not put on deputation. Fresh appointment letters were issued to them. Their original employment was terminated. Their lien on the job ended. No assurance was given to them that they would be retained by the JVC till superannuation. They were held to be not entitled to be reabsorbed. There was no estoppel in their favour.[443]

[s 115.54.3] ***Resignation.***—The president of a Municipal Council resigned his office. The fact of resignation was admitted by him in a subsequent meeting of the council. He also made a demand for fresh election to the post. It was held that such conduct disentitled him from subsequently claiming that as his letter of resignation was not properly addressed, he had not effectively resigned.[444]

[s 115.55] Promise of deposit on application for bail.—A condition for making a deposit was imposed for grant of bail. The court said that such condition should not be unreasonable and unjust. In the context of the offence of criminal breach of trust, the court cannot proceed to recover the amount which is the subject-matter of the complaint as a condition for grant of bail. But if the accused has himself given the undertaking that he would deposit the amount by way of FDRs every month for earning indulgence of the court, then he could not be permitted to resile from such terms and conditions by reason of the doctrine of estoppel.[445]

---

439. *Rakesh Ranjan Verma v State of Bihar*, AIR 1992 SC 1348 : 1992 Supp (2) SCC 343.
440. *Central Airmen Selection Board v Surinder Kumar Das*, AIR 2002 SC 240.
441. *Ariane Orgachem Pvt Ltd v Wyeth Employees Union*, AIR 2016 1761, para 26.
442. *Sociedale de Fomento Industries Ltd v Ravindranath Subraya Kamal*, AIR 1999 Bom. 158.
443. *MD, TN Magnestite Ltd v S Manickam*, AIR 2010 SC 3125 : (2010) 4 SCC 421.
444. *Prabharani Vishwakarma v State of MP*, AIR 1999 MP 223.
445. *MR Narayanan v State*, 2003 Cr LJ 1472 (Del).

[s 115.56] Estoppels under Negotiable Instruments Act.—The Negotiable Instruments Act binds the parties liable upon an instrument by certain estoppel. The estoppels are as follows:

(1) *Against Denial of Validity* [section 120].—The maker of a promissory note, the drawer of a bill or cheque and the acceptor of a bill for the honour of drawer are not permitted, as against a holder in due course, to deny the validity of the instrument as originally made or drawn.

(2) *Against Denial of Payee's Capacity* [section 121].—The maker of a promissory note and the acceptor of a bill payable to order are not permitted, as against a holder in due course, to deny the payee's capacity at the time to indorse the instrument.

(3) *Against Endorser* [section 122].—The endorser of a negotiable instrument is not permitted, as against a subsequent endorser, to deny the signature or capacity of any prior party to the instrument. The benefit of these estoppels is available only when due execution of the instrument has been proved. There should be proof that the cheque was signed by the party against whom the estoppel is claimed.[446]

[s 115.57] Age.—A person who declares his age at the time of appointment is bound by it. Under the Rules contained in the All India Services (Death and Retirement) Benefits Rules, 1958, Rule 16-A as amended in 1978, he is entitled to seek a change only in case of a *bona fide* mistake in recording the date of birth at the time of employment. The principle of estoppel applies otherwise.[447]

[s 115.58] Extension of service.—Before the superannuation of an employee, an order was issued for extension of his service. The order was subsequently cancelled before the extension had become operative. No hearing was given to him before cancelling his extension. The court did not allow any challenge to the cancellation either on the ground of violation of natural justice or on the basis of the doctrine of estoppel.[448]

[s 115.59] Execution of decree.—Where the objections to the execution of a decree were allowed to be dismissed for non-prosecution, fresh objections were allowed to be made. The principles of promissory estoppel and *res judicata* were not applicable.[449]

[s 115.60] Recounting in election.—Where a party consented to recounting and an order was accordingly issued, it was held that such party would be estopped from challenging the correctness of the order on the ground that the consent order was not permissible under the Haryana Panchayati Raj Act, 1994.[450]

The Orissa High Court held that the declaration of results on the basis of draw of lot on the consent of the parties did not create any estoppel against the candidate who lost on the lot. The election was held under the Orissa Gram Panchayat Election Rules, 1965. There was a dispute about acceptance and rejection of invalid and valid votes. The court said that the dispute could not be adjudicated effectively without recounting

---

446. *CT Joseph v IV Philip,* AIR 2001Ker 300.
447. *UOI v C Ramaswamy,* AIR 1997 SC 2055 : (1997) 4 SCC 647.
448. *State of UP v Girish Bihari,* AIR 1997 SC 1354 : (1997) 4 SCC 362.
449. *Kamta Prasad v 2nd Addl. DJ,* AIR 1997 All 201.
450. *Radha Kishan v Election Tribunal-cum-Sub-judge,* AIR 2000 P&H 1.

of votes. The order of the trial judge declaring the opposite party elected on recounting of and scrutiny of votes was held to be proper.[451]

[s 115.61] Tenancy.—Where the tenant in Form No. C, under Maharashtra Housing and Area Development Act, 1977, indicated at the time of allotment that his brother with his wife would be occupying the premises and the Form was accepted by the Board, it was held that the subsequent termination of the tenancy on the grounding that there was a sub-letting to the brother and its regularisation was illegal.[452]

Under the terms of a compromise, a declaration was made by the person concerned that he was not a tenant of the land in question. His name was accordingly deleted. The order of the court in the terms of the compromise had become final. It was held that a subsequent order of the Tehsildar under section 49-B of the Bombay Tenancy and Agricultural Lands (Vidharbh Region) Act, 1958 declaring that person to be still a tenant, was without jurisdiction.[453]

A tenant gave an undertaking to the court that he would vacate the premises. But he filed an appeal against the order of eviction. The appeal was held to be maintainable.[454]

Where the entire undertaking of a company including let-out premises were taken over by another company, it was held that the tenants could not refuse to deal with the successor company as their new landlord. Ownership is not necessary for being a landlord.[455]

[s 115.62] Long enjoyment of caste benefits.—Where a person enjoyed caste benefits on false basis for a pretty long time, it was held that his caste certificate was liable to be cancelled and his benefits terminated. Long-period misuse of a privilege does not create an estoppel.[456]

[s 115.63] Certificate of final settlement.—In the context of a dispute as to the contractor's claim under a works contract, it was held that once the claimant issued a certificate of final settlement of his claim, he was estopped from raising further claims under the contract and demand reference to arbitration.[457] Where, in a consumer complaint, the insured had executed a discharge voucher in full satisfaction of his claim, the court said that his challenge to the discharge voucher would have been tenable only by showing that he executed it under fraud or coercion, etc. Appropriate relief could be granted by the Consumer Commission on such proof.[458]

[s 115.64] Application for amendment of plaint.—An application for amendment of plaint was allowed subject to payment of costs of Rs 50. A certified copy of the memo was filed showing receipt of the money by the defendant without any objection. It was held that the defendant was estopped from challenging the order allowing the amendment of the plaint.[459]

---

451. *Basanti Das v Kamala Nayak,* AIR 1999 Ori. 187.

452. *Dattaram S Vichare v Thukaram S Vichare,* AIR 2000 SC 103 : (1999) 6 SCC 764; *Kusum Anand v Mohinder Kaur,* AIR 1999 Del. 221, tenancy through power of attorney holder, the owner could not prove lack of authority.

453. *Vijyabai v Shriram Tukaram,* AIR 1999 SC 431 : (1999) 1 SCC 693. *PK Vasudeva v Zenobia Bhanot,* AIR 1999 SC 3322 : (1999) 7 SCC 377, estoppel arising out of review petition against eviction order.

454. *AVGP Chettiar & Sons v JPalanisamy,* AIR 2002 SC 2171.

455. *Kamla Rani v Texmaco Ltd,* AIR 2007 Del 147.

456. *KS. Vijayalakshmi v Tahasildar,* AIR 2000 Ker 262.

457. *UOI v Raj Brothers,* AIR 2000 Gau 132.

458. *United India Insurance v Ajmer Singh,* AIR 1999 SC 3027 : (1999) 6 SCC 400.

459. *Sk. Zahural Islam v Tanweer Jahan Begum,* AIR 2000 Ori 140.

[s 115.65] Lease agreement.—There was an agreement of lease between the parties in writing under which the owner of the property was to bring the construction up to plinths and thereafter the lessee was to take over the property under the lease for a period of 3 years. The owner invested a huge sum of money in providing plinth level construction, but the lessee backed out. The court held that he could not do so and that too just only under the technical plea that the agreement was not a registered tenancy and, therefore, it being only a month–to–month tenancy, it could be terminated under section 106 of the Transfer of Property Act, 1882.[460]

[s 115.66] Void order.—A void order can create neither legal rights nor obligations. Therefore, the appellant cannot be denied his right to recover possession of the property in dispute on the ground that he did not choose to challenge such a void order.[461]

[s 115.67] Levy of composite fee on tourists transport vehicles.—A scheme for tourism promotion was adopted under the Motor Vehicles (All India Permit for Tourist Transport Operators) Rules, 1993 and they contemplated levy of composite fee only. The operators spent substantial sums of money on expensive vehicles and undertook the work of carrying tourists. It was held that the authorities were estopped from levying anything beyond composite fee.[462]

[s 116] Estoppel of tenant; and of licensee of person in possession.—No tenant of immoveable property,[s 116.3] or person claiming through such tenant, shall, during the continuance of the tenancy,[s 116.4] be permitted to deny that the landlord of such tenant had, at the beginning of the tenancy,[s 116.5] a title to such immoveable property; and no person who came upon any immoveable property by the license of the person in possession[s 116.6] thereof shall be permitted to deny that such person had a title to such possession at the time when such license was given.

SYNOPSIS

COMMENT

This section enumerates the principle of estoppel which is merely an extension of the principle that no person is allowed to approbate and reprobate at the same time.[463] The

460. *Food Corp of India v Babulal Agarwal*, AIR 1998 MP 23.
461. *Shivshankar Gurgar v Dilip*, (2014) 2 SCC 465 (para 14).
462. *Indo Canadian Transport Co v UOI*, AIR 1999 P&H 130.
463. *Kusum Lata Bansal v Avadhesh Kumar Gupta*, 2017 (9) ADJ 638 : 2017 (124) ALR 371.

section deals with estoppel of (1) a tenant, and (2) a licensee of the person in possession. It is not exhaustive as containing all kinds of estoppel which may arise between landlord and tenant. It postulates that there is a tenancy still continuing[464] and that it had its beginning at a given date from a given landlord, and provides that neither a tenant nor any one claiming through a tenant shall be heard to deny that the particular landlord had at that date a title to the property, and there is no exception even for the case where the lease itself discloses the defect of title. In the ordinary case of a lease intended as a present demise the section applies against the lessee, any assignee of the term and a sub-lessee or licensee.[465] Even before the Act came into force, the Bombay High Court recognised an estoppel of this kind.[466] After the Act came into force, the Privy Council in *Kumar Raj Krishna Prosad Lal v Baraboni Coal Concern Ltd*,[467] declared that the section does not deal with all kinds of estoppel which might arise between the landlord and tenant. The estoppel under this section is wide enough to cover the case of a grantee who occupies and enjoys under a grant disputing the grantor's title. Even a mere attornment creates an estoppel against the tenant but that estoppel is not the same as is given statutory effect by this section. There are other kinds of estoppel between tenant and landlord which fall outside the scope of the section. Such an estoppel does not prevent the tenant from showing that he attorned in ignorance of the fact that the landlord had no title. The test for the purposes of this section is whether the attornment creates a new tenancy.[468] This happened in *Adyanath Ghatak v Krishna Pd Singh*,[469] where the attornment was under the threat of eviction by the title paramount and a new jural relationship of landlord and tenant was created. The estoppel thereafter arises against the attorned landlord.[470] The rule of estoppel embodied in this section is not applicable to the case of a tenant who purchases subsequently the share of a co-sharer in the leased property and files a suit

---

464. *Sheikh Rashid v Hussain Baksh*, (1943) Nag 340; *Dangam Venkat Rajam v Peddi Gundla Rajia*, (1953) Hyd 288. *Bansraj Lalta Prasad Mishra v Stanley Parker Jones*, (2006) 3 SCC 91 : AIR 2006 SC 3569, the Supreme Court discussed in detail the object and scope and underlying policy of the provision enshrined in the section.

465. *Krishna Prosad Lal Singha Deo v Baraboni Coal Concern*, (1937) 64 IA 311: 39 Bom LR 1034: (1938) 1 Cal 1; *Ata Muhammad v Shankar Das*, (1925) 6 Lah 319; *Yusuf v Jyotishchandra Banerji*, (1931) 59 Cal 739; *M Manphul Bai v Ladhuram*, (1952) Raj 58; *UG Sakhare v C.G Gawande*, AIR 1960 Bom 238; 60 Bom LR 1150.

466. *Vasudev Daji v Babaji Ranu*, (1871) 8 Bom HCR 175. The section is a recognition and adoption of the same demand of equity. *Pal Singh v Sunder Singh*, AIR 1989 SC 758: (1989) 1 SCR 67 : (1989) 1 SCC 444.

467. (1937) 64 IA 33: AIR 1937 PC 251. See also *Harbans Singh v Tekamani Devi*, AIR 1990 Pat 26, a tenant not allowed to challenge the title of the person with whom he entered into the *kirayanama*.

468. *Nadjarian v Trist*, (1944) 47 Bom LR 209: (1945) Bom 343; *Amar Devi v Nathu Ram*, (1994) 4 SCC 250, the buyer of the premises became a new landlord who sued for eviction on a permitted ground. The tenant not allowed to challenge his title.

469. *Adyanath Ghatak v Krishna Pd. Singh*, AIR 1949 PC 124. Followed by the Supreme Court in *D Satyanarayana v P Jagadish*, AIR 1987 SC 2192 : (1987) 4 SCC 424.

470. *Tej Bhan Madan v II Addl DJ*, AIR 1988 SC 1413 : 1988 1 KLJ 686 : (1988) 3 SCC 137; *JJ Lal Pvt Ltd v MR Murali*, AIR 2002 SC 1061, eviction suit against tenant on ground of default in payment of rent, plea by the tenant that he was willing to pay the overdue amount, could not be construed as *bona fide* denial of title. *Badrinath v Gaushala Trust Society*, AIR 2010 NOC 890 (P&H), in his written statement, the tenant admitted the relationship of landlord and tenant, estopped from challenging the title of the landlord; *Nirmala Devi v Jai Dutt*, 240 (2017) DLT 424 : 2017 SCC Online Del 7353 : LNIND 2017 Del 807, once the tenant admitted the relationship of the landlord and tenant, he is estopped from denying the title of the legal heir during the continuance of the benefit that he had drawn under this relationship.

for partition on the basis of such purchase. The Supreme Court also pointed out in this case that the rule of estoppel stated in this case is not exhaustive of the law of estoppel.

The underlying policy of section 116 is that where a person has been brought into possession as a tenant by the landlord and if that tenant is permitted to question the title of the landlord at the time of the settlement, then that will give rise to extreme confusion in the matter of relationship of the landlord and tenant and so the equitable principle of estoppel has been incorporated by the legislature in the said section.[471]

The doctrine of estoppel which operates between landlord and tenant has no application to the same parties even while the tenancy exists, where the question of title arises between them, not in the relation of landlord and tenant, but of vendor and purchaser.[472] Where the tenant was eager to pay the rent due to the transferee but demanded certain documents from him proving his title, it was not a denial of the title of the landlord.[473] Where the executant of a lease deed and to whom the rent was paid brought a suit for eviction, the tenant was estopped from challenging the title of the landlord.[474]

This section estops a defendant from challenging the title of the predecessors in interest of the plaintiff from whom he takes the land. Apart from the section the doctrine of estoppel applies even to a case where the tenant attorns to the landlord. The estoppel to deny the title of the lessor continues to apply to the lessee until he has given possession to the lessor on determination of the tenancy. If there has been eviction by title paramount the lessee is not estopped from denying the title of the lessor.[475]

The estoppel of a tenant is founded upon contract between the tenant and his landlord. It is one of the most noticeable instances of estoppel by contract. The estoppel disappears if the landlord's title is extinguished subsequent to the inception of the tenancy,[476] or if there is eviction by title paramount.[477]

---

471. *Bansraj Laltaprasad Mishra v Stanley Parker Jones,* (2006) 3 SCC 91.

472. *Muhammad Hussain v Abdul Gaffoor,* (1946) Mad 44.

473. *Gandabhai Ranchhodji Gandhi v Noshir Ka Vasji Sabowala,* AIR 1994 Guj 18. *Rajendra Kumar v DJ, Jaunpur,* AIR 1996 All 178, paying rent to the plaintiff, not allowed to question his title as a landlord.

474. *PS Bedi v Project & Equipment Corporation of India Ltd,* AIR 1994 Del 255.

475. *Gajadhar Lodha v Khas Mahatadih Colliery Co,* (1959) Pat 806; A person admitted in the cross-objections and also admitted before the Municipal Authorities under a document, to be a tenant, held, estopped from claiming to be owner of the property against the lessor which was a trust, even if he had a registered sale deed, executed by the Managing Trustee in his favour. In view of such admissions, his contention that subsequent to entering the property as a tenant he had acquired ownership thereof, refused to be examined in SLP.See also *Orissa Olympic Association v State of Orissa,* (2015) 13 SCC 417, para 3 : 2017 (4) Scale 217; *Om Prakash v Mishri Lal,* AIR 2017 SC 1597 : 2017(122) ALR 123 : (2017) 5 SCC 451, a tenant during the continuance of the tenancy is debarred from denying the title of his landlord through whom he claims tenancy.

476. *Mangat Ram v Sardar Meharban Singh,* AIR 1987 SC 1656 : (1987) 4 SCC 319.

477. *Krishna Prasad Singh v Adyanath Ghatak,* (1943) 22 Pat 513. The section does not create a ground for eviction. *Lena Pereira v Mary Boracho,* AIR 1992 Bom 93; *Nirvikar Gupta v Ram Kumar,* AIR 1992 MP 115, the denial of the landlord's title is not a ground for eviction. *Rita Lal v Raj Kumar Singh,* AIR 2002 SC 3341, rent note proved to have been signed by the tenant, he also admitted the title of the landlord in his deposition in an earlier judicial proceeding. Denial by him of his landlord's title did not raise any triable issue, because he was already under an estoppel. *C. Chandramohan v Sengottaiyan,* AIR 2000 SC 568 : (2000) 1 SCC 451, the mere assertion by the tenant that his landlord was co-owner and that too because he was not aware of the release of the other co-owner's share to the landlord, was held to be not denial of the position of the landlord so as to enable the latter to evict him. *Dunlop India Ltd v TK Mukhopadhayay,* AIR 1998 Cal 59, a tenant can show that he has acquired title to the property.

Where a man having no title obtains possession of land under a demise by a man in possession, who assumes to give him a title as tenant, he cannot deny his landlord's title; as, for instance, if he takes for 21 years and he finds the landlord has only five years' title, he cannot after the five years set up against the landlord the *jus tertii*, though, of course, the real owner can always recover against him. That is a perfectly intelligible doctrine. He took possession under a contract to pay the rent as long as he held possession under the landlord, and to give it up at the end of the term to the landlord, and having taken it in that way he is not allowed to say that the man whose title he admits, and under whose title he took possession, has not a title.[478] This is estoppel by contract. The estoppel arises, not by reason of some fact agreed or assumed to be true, but as the legal effect of carrying the contract into execution, of the tenant taking possession of the property from the hand of the lessor.[479] Where occupants were occupying the land in question of the Gram Panchayat from time-to-time on payment of specified rate of rent, they were held to be lessees under the Gram Panchayat and they could not dispute the title of their landlord.[480] An unauthorised occupant of a property, subsequently converting his possession into that of a tenant by executing a rent note, would be estopped from challenging the title of the landlord and his right to recover rent or arrears of rent.[481]

[s 116.1] Title paramount.—Exceptional situation.—An exceptional situation is to be found in the following statement of the Supreme Court in *D Satyanarayana v P Jagdish*:[482] "During the continuance of the tenancy, the tenant cannot acquire by prescription a permanent right of occupancy in derogation of the landlord's title by mere assertion of such a right to the knowledge of the landlord. The general rule is, however, subject to certain exceptions. Thus, a tenant is not precluded from denying the derivative title of the persons claiming through the landlord. Similarly, the estoppel under section 116 of the Evidence Act is restricted to the denial of the title at the commencement of the tenancy. From this, the exception follows, that it is open to the tenant even without surrendering possession to show that since the date of the tenancy, the title of the landlord came to an end or that he was evicted by a paramount title holder or that even though there was no actual eviction or dispossession from the property, under a threat of eviction, he had attorned to the paramount title-holder. In order to constitute eviction by title paramount, it has been established by decisions in England and in India that it is not necessary that the tenant should be dispossessed or even that there should be a suit for ejectment against him. It will be sufficient if there was threat of eviction and if the tenant as a result of such threat attorns to the real owner, he sets up such eviction by way of defence either to an action for rent or to a suit in ejectment. If the tenant gives up possession voluntarily to the title-holder, he cannot claim the benefit of this rule. When the tenancy has been determined by eviction by title paramount, no question of estoppel arises under section 116 of the Evidence Act. The principle must equally apply when the tenant has attorned under a threat of eviction by the title paramount and there comes into existence a new jural

478. *Per* JesseL, MR, in *Re Stringer's Estate, Shaw v Jones-Ford*, (1877) 6 Ch D 1, 9; *Vertannes v Robinson*, (1927) 29 Bom LR 1017: 54 IA 276: 5 Ran 427; *Musammat Bilas Kunwar v Desraj Ranjit Singh*, (1915) 17 Bom LR 1006: 42 IA 202: 37 All 557.

479. *Bamandas Bhattacharjee v Nilmadhab Sahu*, (1916) 44 Cal 771, 777.

480. *Kartar Singh v Collector, Patiala*, 1996 AIHC 1538 (P&H).

481. *Ziauddin v Bansi Lal*, 1996 AIHC 1425 (Del). *Jagmohan Singh Wadhera v K M Bhatnagar*, 1996 AIHC 415 Del, failure to examine ex-landlord, no adverse presumption.

482. *D Satyanarayana v P Jagdish*, AIR 1987 SC 2192 : (1987) 4 SCC 424, 427, 428.

relationship of landlord and tenant as between them. The law is thus stated in *Halsbury's Laws of England*:[483]

238. *Eviction under title paramount*, In order to constitute an eviction by a person claiming under the title paramount, it is not necessary that the tenant should be put out of possession, or that proceedings should be brought. A threat of eviction is sufficient, and if the tenant, in consequence of the threat, attorns to the claimant, he may set this up as an eviction by way of defence to an action for rent, subject to his proving the evictor's title. There is no eviction, however, if the tenant gives up possession voluntarily.

The ruling in the *Satyanarayana*[484] case could not be applied to a case in which there was no finding that the title of the landlord had come to an end. The corporation (which was the other claimant of title over the suit property) had not established its title in any proceedings in accordance with the law. In these circumstances, the exception to the rule of estoppel embodied in section 116 could not be pleaded by the licencee.[485]

However, in a case,[486] the respondents had filed a suit against appellants 1 to 4 for ejectment and resumption of possession of the suit land. The case of the respondents in the plaint was that the appellants had taken lease of the suit land from their common ancestor, late Shri Dwaraka Pershad who had purchased the suit land from Nawab Rayees Yar Bahadur. The further case of the respondents was that as the appellants failed to pay any rent from 1986 and renewed the lease after 1986, the respondents gave a notice to the appellants to vacate the suit land. Referring to the law laid down in D Satyanarayana's case,487 that the tenant who has been let into possession by the landlord cannot deny the landlord's title, however defective it may be, so long as he has not openly surrendered possession by surrender to his landlord, it was held by Supreme Court that although, there are some exceptions to this general rule, none of the exceptions have been established by appellants in the instant case. Accordingly, the appellants who were the tenants of respondents were required to surrender possession to the respondents before they can challenge the title of the respondents.[488]

[s 116.2] Whether tenant should be in possession of property to estop him from denying his landlord's title.—The Privy Council has laid down that a tenant is estopped from denying his landlord's title whether he was or was not already in possession of the property at the time when he took his lease.[489] The Bombay,[490] the Madras,[491] and the Allahabad[492] High Courts have held similarly. The decisions of

483. Vol 27, 4th Edn, para 238. Another decision of the Supreme Court on the point is in *S. Thangappan v P Padmavathy*, AIR 1999 SC 3584 : (1999) 7 SCC 474, the tenant was not allowed to say that the property did not belong to his landlord but to a Devasthanam. The latter had never made any such claim on the tenant.

484. *D Satyanarayana v P Jagdish*, AIR 1987 SC 2192 : (1987) 4 SCC 424.

485. *E Parshuraman v V Doraiswamy*, (2006) 1 SCC 658 : AIR 2006 SC 376.

486. *State of AP v D Raghukul Pershad*, (2012) 8 SCC 584.

487. *D Satyanarayana v P Jagadish*, AIR 1987 SC 2192 : (1987) 4 SCC 424.

488. *State of AP v D Raghukul Pershad*, (supra).

489. *Krishan Prosad Lal Singha Deo v Baraboni Coal Concern*, (1937) 64 IA 311: 39 Bom LR 1034 : (1938) 1 Cal 1; *Musammat Bilas Kunwar v Desraj Ranjit Singh*, (1915) 17 Bom LR 1006: 42 IA 202: 37 All 557, 567; *Vertannes v Robinson*, (1927) 29 Bom LR 1017: 54 IA 276 : 5 Ran 427.

490. *Vasudev Daji v Babaji Ranu*, (1871) 8 BHCR (ACJ) 175; *Shankar v Jagannath*, (1928) 33 Bom LR 741.

491. *Venkata Chetty v Aiyanna Goundan*, (1916) 40 Mad 561 (FB).

492. *Ganpat Rai v Multan*, (1916) 38 All 226, 228.

the Calcutta High Court are not unanimous on the point.[493] A tenant who wishes to dispute his landlord's title must not only see that the tenancy has come to an end, but that the possession which was in him as a tenant has been surrendered. A tenant who holds over and remains in possession cannot be allowed to use that possession as a lever to support a case in which he denies the landlord's title.[494] The estoppel operates in the case of a tenant who remains in possession even after the termination of the tenancy by notice to quit.[495] A tenant who has been let into possession cannot deny his landlord's title, however defective it may be, so long as he has not openly restored possession by surrender. Without openly and actually going out of the occupation, the tenant cannot deny the landlord's title.[496] Where a tenant denied the title of his landlady claiming himself to be absolute owner of the premises in his occupation but could produce no evidence for his claim, it was held that the denial was *mala fide* and the tenant was liable to be evicted on that ground.[497]

[s 116.3] "Immoveable property".—A several fishery is considered immoveable property for the purposes of this section.[498]

[s 116.4] "During the continuance of the tenancy".—A tenant is only precluded, during the continuance of the tenancy, from denying that the landlord had "at the beginning of the tenancy" a title to the property, the subject of the tenancy. The section is no bar to a tenant showing that his landlord had no title at a date previous to the commencement of the tenancy. The words of the section leave it open to the tenant to show that his landlord's title has subsequently expired.[499] If the term of lease has expired when a suit is brought, the tenant can dispute the title of the landlord. Though the tenancy may be continuing, it is quite open to the tenant to plead and show that his liability to pay the rent has wholly or partially or for a time ceased: such a plea is really one of confession and avoidance (not denial), and has been held available to the tenant.[500] A tenant is estopped from challenging the title of the co-owner landlord.[501]

---

493. *Lal Mohomed v Kallanus*, (1885) 11 Cal 519, dissented from in *Nagindas Sankalchand v Bapalal Purshottam*, (1930) 54 Bom 487 : 32 Bom LR 692; *Ketu Das v Surendra Niath Sinha*, (1903) 7 Cal WN 596.

494. *Ekoba v Dayaram*, (1919) 22 Bom LR 82; *Patel Kilabhai Lallubhai v Hargovan Mansukh*, (1894) 19 Bom 133; *Nadri Begum v Nasrat Bibi*, AIR 1980 All 210, the defendant continued in possession after expiry of licence in the right of his father, estopped from denying the plaintiffs title.

495. *Mujibar Rahman v Isub Surati*, (1928) 56 Cal 15; *Re Ganesh Trading Co Pvt Ltd*, AIR 1985 Cal 37, lessee remained bound by estoppel as long as he was in actual possession; *Mahabir Pd v KC Thapar & Bros Ltd*, AIR 1985 Cal 209; *Sri Ram Pasricha v Jagannath*, AIR 1976 SC 2335 : (1976) 4 SCC 184.

496. A clear decision of the Supreme Court to this effect is to be seen in *D Satyanarayana v P Jagadish*, 1987 4 SCC 424 : AIR 1987 SC 2192. *Jamila Khatoon v Ajodhya Pathak*, 1996 AIHC 2928 (Gau). In the instant case the tenant purchased the house in his occupation from a third person under belief that he was the owner and not the person who let him the house. He must prove the ownership of that third person or face the consequences of denial of title of the person who let him the premises.

497. *M Narayanaswami v Roya Poulle Amala*, 1994 AIHC 2591 (Mad).

498. *Lakshman v Ramji*, (1920) 23 Bom LR 939.

499. *Bala v Abai*, (1909) 11 Bom LR 1093; *Devidas v Shamal*, (1919) 22 Bom LR 149; *Ata Muhammad v Shankar Das*, (1925) 6 Lah 319; *Deena Bandhu Gan v Makim Sardar*, (1935) 63 Cal 763; *Krishna Prosad Lal Singha Deo v Baraboni Coal Concern*, (1937) 64 IA 311: 39 Bom LR 1034: (1938) 1 Cal 1.

500. *Jogendra Lal Sarkar v Mohesh Chandra Sadhu*, (1928) 55 Cal 1013; *Shantabhai v Narayan Rao*, (1948) Nag 290.

501. *Kishan Gopal Agarwalla v Ramdulari Sah*, AIR 1996 Gau 39.

A tenanted trust property was sold by public auction for recovery of tax dues. It was purchased by the tenant himself. The sale was subsequently set aside. The property came back to the trustees. They sued the tenant for recovery of possession. It was held that the tenancy had ended when the tenant purchased the property. He was not entitled to be restored to his tenancy after the sale to him had been set aside.[502] In a case, the suit filed by a Club questioning the title of the Trust as its lessor, was dismissed and nothing was given to show that it was restored. It was held that the Club was not facing the threat of eviction from anybody except the Trust and there was no question of a superior landlord. Therefore, section 116 was held to be *prima facie* applicable and the Club was estopped from challenging the title of the Trust.[503]

Possession and permission being established, estoppel would bind the tenant "during the continuance of the tenancy" and until he surrenders his possession. The words "during the continuance of the tenancy" have been interpreted to mean during the continuance of the possession that was received under the tenancy in question, and the courts have repeatedly laid down the estoppel operates even after the termination of the tenancy so that a tenant who had been let into possession, however defective it may be, so long as he has not openly surrendered possession, cannot dispute the title of the landlord at the commencement of the tenancy. The rule of estoppel is thus restricted not only in extent but also in time *i.e.* restricted to the title of the landlord and during the continuance of the tenancy; and by necessary implication, it follows that a tenant not estopped, when he is under threat of eviction by the title paramount, from contending that the landlord had no title before the tenancy commenced or that the title of the landlord has since come to an end. The rule of estoppel embodied under section 116 of the Evidence Act is that, a tenant who has been let into possession cannot deny his landlord's title, however defective it may be, so long as he has not openly restored.[504]

Where the tenant has been evicted or has surrendered possession, the rule of estoppel ceases to operate.[505]

[s 116.5] "At the beginning of the tenancy".—This section only provides that a tenant cannot be permitted to deny that the landlord at the beginning of the tenancy had a title to the property. The section does not disentitle a tenant to dispute the derivative title of one who claims, since the beginning of the tenancy, to have become entitled to the reversion. In that sense the principle only applies to the title of the landlord who "let the tenant in" as distinct from any other person claiming to be reversioner.[506] The tenancy under this section does not begin afresh every time the interest of the tenant or of the landlord devolves upon a new individual by succession or assignment.[507]

---

502. *Institute of Education, Saraswathipuram v Sri Sowcar A Siddanna Endowment,* AIR 2003 Kant 226.

503. *Karam Kapahi v Lal Chand Public Charitable Trust,* (2010) 4 SCC 753.

504. *D Satyanarayana v P Jagadish,* AIR 1987 SC 2192: (1987) 4 SCC 424.

505. *Brij Lal Sharma v Kanhiya Lal,* AIR 2009 NOC 175 (Del).

506. *Krishna Prosad Lal Singha Deo v Baraboni Coal Concern,. supra. Pushpa Sharma v Gopal Lal,* AIR 1986 Raj 187, the tenant led evidence and proved the title of a third person. See also *Aras Khan v Ali Mian,* AIR1985 Pat 126, where in a suit for ejectment the plaintiff was not able to establish relationship of landlord and tenant, but did establish his ownership. There was no reason to deny him the equitable relief of recovery of possession.

507. *Krishna Prosad Lal Singha Deo v Baraboni Coal Concern, supra.*

[s 116.6] "No person who came upon any immoveable property by the license of the person in possession".—Where it is proved that the occupation by a person of immoveable property is by permission of another, the occupier is estopped from denying that other's title.[508] "There is no distinction between the case of a tenant and that of a common licensee. The licensee, by asking permission, admits that there is a title in the licensor. The law would imply a tenancy under such circumstances".[509] Where defendant No. 1 came into possession of certain coal mining lands as a licensee of the plaintiff, and subsequently defendant No. 2, as the assignee of, and claiming through, defendant No. 1, entered into possession thereof, it was held that the possession of the lands by both the defendants must be attributed to the possession given to defendant No. 1 by the plaintiff and they were both barred by this section from questioning the plaintiff's title to those lands until they had surrendered possession thereof again to him.[510] A tenant surrendered his tenancy right in favour of a registered society without the consent of the landlord. The tenant paid the rent in the name of the registered society. The acceptance of such rent was held as not constituting tenancy in favour of the society.[511]

[s 116.7] Suit by a co-owner.—A suit for eviction could not be dismissed on the ground that all the co-owners were not impleaded. The court said that a suit for eviction at the behest of one of the co-owners of the property in question is maintainable. The premise were handed over under tenancy by the plaintiff co-owner and, therefore, the tenant was estopped from challenging the right of the plaintiff co-owner.[512] However, in a case it was urged by the appellant that in the suit filed by respondents they had not asserted that they were filing it as co-owners but they claimed that they were filing it as executors/executrix. Rejecting this contention, it was held by Supreme Court that if the status of the respondents as co-owners of the property transpires clearly from the admitted facts of the case, they cannot be denuded of the said status at the instance of some objections by the tenants. Normally, a tenant's right to question the title of a landlord is very limited in view of the rule of law which is codified in section 116 of the Evidence Act. A co-owner of a property is an owner of the property, till the property is partitioned.[513]

---

508. See *Mah Hli v Maung San Dun*, (1892) PJLB 4. Also *Ramuthi Madalaichamy v Thangarathina Nadar*, AIR 1991 Mad 229, involving denial of title and eviction proceeding on that ground. *SK Sarma v Mahesh Kumar Verma*, 2002 Cr LJ 4318 (SC), a premises allotted to an employee by the railway. He was not allowed to raise the question that the railway had no rights over the property. He came into possession taking it from railway. section 116 squarely applied. *Karam Kapahi v Lal Chand Public Charitable Trust*, AIR 2010 SC 2077 : (2010) 4 SCC 753, estoppel of lessee against challenging the title or right of the lessor.

509. *Per* Coleridge J, in *Doe dem Johnson v Baytup*, (1835) 3 Ad & El 188, 192.

510. *Currimbhoy & Co v Creet*, (1932) 35 Bom LR 223 : 60 IA 297 : 60 Cal 980. *Bansraj Lalta Prasad Mishra v Stanley Parker Jones*, (2006) 3 SCC 91 : AIR 2006 SC 3569, emphasising the irrelevance of the title of the licensor in respect of the immovable property in question to the position of the licencee, the concept of construction possession applicable under the section. The person from whom possession was taken would have right to take back possession irrespective of questions of title.

511. *Ram Saran v Pyare Lal*, AIR 1996 SC 2361 : (1996) 11 SCC 728.

512. *Dhanraj Bhuddsingh Gupta v Dinesh Purshottam*, AIR 2002 Bom 456. The suit was filed by the plaintiff under his ownership created by a registered deed of partition and, therefore, he could not be non-suited by saying that there was a will also which was not probated.

513. *FGP Ltd v Saleh Hooseini Doctor*, (2009) 10 SCC 223, 2010 (1) CCC 14 (SC).

[s 116.8] Sub-lease or Sub-tenancy.—In a case before the Calcutta High Court[514] a sub-tenant questioned the right of the tenant to ask for eviction. His ground was that the tenant had himself lost his right to possession. The court said:[515]

> The point is well-settled by the authorities and is a hardened principle of law. A tenant, in so far as he claims as a tenant, is not permitted to dispute the title of the landlord from whom his tenancy and possession have been derived. On that basis, even a trespasser landlord can maintain a suit for eviction as against his tenant and it would not be open to the tenant to challenge the title of the landlord in any manner whatsoever. The reason for this long standing rule is simple to understand. The tenant comes into possession from and by reason of the landlord. As such, he shall hand over possession to that person from whom he originally came to acquire it and shall not raise pleas or obstacles in that regard.

> The expiry of the lease of the tenant was not a matter about which the sub-tenant could enquire. There is a decision on another cause between the same parties. In this case a head-lessee filed a suit against his sub-lessee for eviction. The lease in favour of the head-lessee expired while the suit was still pending. The lessor also filed a suit against his lessee as a result of which the sub-lease would also come to an end and the sub-lessee would be evicted. The court said that the sub-lessee was entitled to deny the title of the head-lessee in view of the subsequent developments, namely the termination of the lease. The actual eviction of the head-lessee was not necessary to enable him to do so.[516] Railways allotted premises to one of its officers. He refused to vacate on retirement. The Railway's suit to eject him was allowed. He was not entitled to deny the person from whom the premises were taken.[517]

[s 116.9] Transfer of premises by will.—Where the landlord transferred his premises, which was under tenancy, to a legatee by his will, the questioning of the title of the new owner by the tenant was held to be wrongful. The tenant remained by the estoppel even when the premises came into the hands of the new owner. The court said that the tenant had incurred a ground for his eviction.[518]

[s 116.10] Mortgagor and mortgagee.—As between a mortgagor and his mortgagee neither can deny the title of the other for the purposes of the mortgage. A mortgagor cannot derogate from his grant so as to defeat his mortgagee's title, nor can the mortgagee deny the title of his mortgagor to mortgage the property.[519] The rule of estoppel between the mortgagor and the mortgagee cannot be invoked in a case where the suit is not based on the mortgage, but is one in repudiation of the mortgage.[520] Where the object of a mortgage is to defraud a third person and the mortgagee is cognisant of and indeed a party to that intended fraud, the mortgagor is not estopped from pleading and proving against his mortgagee seeking to enforce the mortgage that it was a sham transaction a device to defeat a possible attachment of the properties by a creditor.[521] A mortgagor of immoveable property is not estopped from pleading, or taking advantage of, the invalidity of his mortgage deed on the ground that, by the inclusion of a fictitious property in the document and getting it registered in an office

---

514. *Vithalbhai Pvt Ltd v Union Bank of India*, AIR 1992 Cal 283.
515. *Ibid*, at p 284.
516. *UOI v Vithalbhai Pvt Ltd*, AIR 2002 Cal 144.
517. *SK Sarma v Mahesh Kumar Verma*, AIR 2002 SC 3294.
518. *Jalal & Sons v Sita Bai*, AIR 2001 NOC 41 (AP) : 2001 ALHC 1860.
519. *Hillaya v Narayanappa*, (1911) 13 Bom LR 1200 : 36 Bom 185.
520. *Musammat Rajna v Musaheb Ali*, (1937) 13 Luck 178.
521. *Arunachalam v Rengaswami*, (1935) 59 Mad 289.

where otherwise it could not have been registered, a fraud on the registration law was committed in which he participated.[522]

[s 116.11] *Benami* title.—The Madras High Court has held that where a lease is executed by a tenant in favour of a *benamidar*, the real owner and not the *benamidar* is regarded as the landlord whose title the tenant is estopped from denying under this section. In a suit by such *benamidar* for rent, the tenant can deny his right to sue on the ground that he is not the person entitled. A *benamidar* has no right to sue unless he can show a legal right to sue under the general law.[523] The Calcutta High Court is of the opinion that a tenant is estopped from raising the question that his lessor is a *benamidar* of someone to whom he has paid rent.[524]

The defendants entered into possession of plaintiff's property by executing a registered agreement, but no lease was executed. In a suit by the plaintiff to recover rent, the defendants pleaded that without a lease there was no contract of tenancy and that the plaintiff was not entitled to recover the rent. It was held that in view of the fact that the defendants entered into and continued in occupation of the land with the plaintiff's consent, they could not be heard to say that they were not liable for rent for use and occupation.[525]

[s 116.12] Sale of tenanted premises.—A tenant was not allowed to claim that the sale of the tenanted premises to the new owner was null and void because he had not raised that plea in the earlier suit by the erstwhile landlord. An acknowledgement of the title of the owner was held to have taken place by reason of payment of rent and tax in the name of the real owner. Such payment amounted to acknowledgement unless it could be shown that it was made under compelling circumstances.[526]

[s 117] Estoppel of acceptor of bill of exchange, bailee or licensee.—No acceptor of a bill of exchange shall be permitted to deny that the drawer had authority to draw such bill or to endorse it; nor shall any bailee or licensee be permitted to deny that his bailor or licensor had, at the time when the bailment or license commenced, authority to make such bailment or grant such license.

***Explanation (1).*—The acceptor of a bill of exchange may deny that the bill was really drawn by the person by whom it purports to have been drawn.**

***Explanation (2).*—If a bailee delivers the goods bailed to a person other than the bailor, he may prove that such person had a right to them as against the bailor.**

SYNOPSIS

---

522. *Ramnandan Prasad Narayan Singh v Chandradip Narain Singh*, (1940) 19 Pat 578.
523. *Kuppu Konan v Thirugnana Sammandan Pillai*, (1908) 31 Mad 461; *Bogar v Karan Singh*, (1906) PR No. 141 of 1906 (Civil).
524. *Deena Bandhu Gan. v Makim Sardar*, (1935) 63 Cal 763.
525. *Sheo Karan Singh v Maharaja Parbhu Narain Singh*, (1909) 31 All 276 (FB).
526. *Bhagwan Agarwalla v Puranmal Bhut*, AIR 2003 Ori 75.

COMMENT

This section deals with further instances of estoppel by agreement. Sections 116 and 117 are however not exhaustive of the doctrine of estoppel by agreement.[527] Agents, for instance, are not ordinarily permitted to set up the adverse title of a third person defeat the rights of their principals.

Under this section an acceptor of a bill of exchange cannot deny that the drawer had authority to draw such bill or to endorse it. But he may deny that the bill was really drawn by the person by whom it purports to have been drawn (Explanation 1). A bailee or licensee cannot deny that his bailor or licensor had, at the commencement of the bailment or license, authority to make the bailment or grant the license. But a bailee, if he delivers the goods bailed to a third person, may prove that such person had a right to them as against the bailor (Explanation 2).

[s 117.1] Bill of exchange.—Estoppels in the case of negotiable instruments are instances of estoppel by agreement or contract. See sections 41 and 42 of the Negotiable Instruments Act.

[s 117.2] Forged endorsement.—No person can claim a title to a negotiable instrument through a forged endorsement. Such endorsement is a nullity and must be taken as if no such endorsement was on the instrument.[528]

[s 117.3] Bailee.—The bailee and the licensee are placed in the same position as the tenant in the preceding section. The bailee is protected by the bailor's title so long as any better title is not advanced. A bailee entrusted with the care of goods is estopped from claiming that the bailor had no title at the time of bailment. He cannot set up the title of a third person. But the bailee has no better title than the bailor, and consequently if a person entitled as against the bailor claims the goods, the bailee has no defence against him.

[s 117.4] Licensee.—As between landlord and tenant so between licensor and licensee the former's right cannot be questioned by the latter. A licensee cannot be permitted to deny that his licensor had at the time when the license commenced authority to grant such license. The licensee of a trademark cannot put an end to the relation of licensor and licensee by repudiating the contract, inasmuch as the concurrence of the other party is essential. In a suit for royalty, brought by the licensors of certain jute trademarks against the licensees, the defence taken was that the plaintiffs had no title to the marks in question, and that the license was void. It was held that by virtue of this section the licensees were estopped from questioning their licensors' title, or the validity of the license.[529]

---

527. *Rup Chand Ghosh v Surveswar Chandra*, (1906) 33 Cal 915.
528. *Banku Behari Sikdar v Secretary of State for India*, (1908) 36 Cal 239.
529. *Hannah v Juggernath & Co*, (1914) 42 Cal 262.

CHAPTER IX

OF WITNESSES

[s 118] Who may testify.—All persons shall be competent to testify[s 118.3] unless the Court considers that they are prevented from understanding the questions put to them, or from giving rational answers to those questions, by tender years, extreme old age, disease, whether of body or mind, or any other cause of the same kind.

***Explanation*.—A lunatic is not incompetent to testify, unless he is prevented by his lunacy from understanding the questions put to him and giving rational answers to them.**

SYNOPSIS

COMMENT

Under this section all persons are competent to testify, unless they are, in the opinion of the court (a) unable to understand the questions put to them, or (b) to give rational answers to those questions, owing to (i) tender years, (ii) extreme old age, (iii) disease of mind or body or (iv) any other such cause. Even a lunatic, if he is capable of understanding the questions put to him and giving rational answers, is a competent witness.

The position as to who should give evidence in regard to matters involving personal knowledge, has been summarized by Supreme Court[1] in the following words:

(a) An attorney-holder who has signed the plaint and instituted the suit, but has no personal knowledge of the transaction can only give formal evidence about the validity of the power of attorney and the filing of the suit.

(b) If the attorney-holder has done any act or handled any transactions, in pursuance of the power of attorney granted by the principal, he may be examined as a witness to prove those acts or transactions. If the attorney-holder alone has personal knowledge of such acts and transactions and not the principal, the attorney-holder *shall* be examined, if those acts and transactions have to be proved.

(c) The attorney-holder cannot depose or give evidence in place of his principal for the acts done by the principal or transactions or dealings of the principal, of which principal alone has personal knowledge.

---

1. *Man Kaur v Hartar Singh Sangha*, (2010) 10 SCC 512.

(d) Where the principal at no point of time had personally handled or dealt with or participated in the transaction and has no personal knowledge of the transaction, and where the entire transaction has been handled by an attorney-holder, necessarily the attorney-holder alone can give evidence in regard to the transaction. This frequently happens in case of principals carrying on business through authorised managers/attorney-holders or persons residing abroad managing their affairs through their attorney-holders.

(e) Where the entire transaction has been conducted through a particular attorney-holder, the principal has to examine that attorney-holder to prove the transaction, and not a different or subsequent attorney-holder.

(f) Where different attorney-holders had dealt with the matter at different stages of the transaction, if evidence has to be led as to what transpired at those different stages, all the attorney-holders will have to be examined.

(g) Where the law requires or contemplated the plaintiff or other party to a proceeding, to establish or prove something with reference to his "state of mind" or "conduct", normally the person concerned alone has to give evidence and not an attorney-holder. A landlord who seeks eviction of his tenant, on the ground of his "bona fide" need and a purchaser seeking specific performance who has to show his "readiness and willingness" fall under this category. There is however a recognised exception to this requirement. Where all the affairs of a party are completely managed, transacted and looked after by an attorney (who may happen to be a close family member), it may be possible to accept the evidence of such attorney even with reference to bona fides or "readiness and willingness". Examples of such attorney-holders are a husband/wife exclusively managing the affairs of his/her spouse, a son/daughter exclusively managing the affairs of an old and infirm parent, a father/mother exclusively managing the affairs of a son/daughter living abroad.

[s 118.1] Scope.—This section does no more than enunciate the English rule with regard to the competency of parties as witnesses without in any way making admissible all the evidence, which might be given by them. In this connection the provisions of section 112 must not be overlooked.[2]

[s 118.2] *Oath.*—It has been held that an omission to administer oath under the Oaths Act, 1969 does not affect the admissibility of evidence unless the judge considers the witness to be otherwise incompetent.[3] In a murder trial, the child witness who was below 12 years in age, clearly deposed in terms of the prosecution case. His evidence was found reliable and corroborated with the evidence of other witness. The Session Court was satisfied that he was giving the truthful evidence. Mere absence of oath alone will not make his evidence disbelievable.[4]

---

2. *Sweenney v Sweenney*, (1935) 62 Cal 1080; *Musunuri Anjaneyulu v Koona Lakshmi*, AIR 1998 AP 204, endorsement on a pronote, it is not a document which is required by law to be attested or scribed. It was not necessary that the scribe should have been examined.
3. *Bhagwania v State of Rajasthan*, 2001 Cr LJ 3719 (Raj).
4. *Mamachan v State of Kerala*, 2008 CrLJ (NOC) 257 (Ker.) (DB).

Once the child-witness is found competent, his inability to take or understand oath or omission in administering it, neither invalidates the proceedings nor renders his evidence inadmissible.[5] The testimony of a child witness must find adequate corroboration before it is relied on. However, it is more a rule of practical wisdom than of law. It cannot be held that the evidence of a child witness would always stand irretrievably stigmatised. It is not the law that if a witness is a child, his evidence shall be rejected, even if it is found reliable. The law is that evidence of a child witness must be evaluated more carefully and with greater circumspection because a child is susceptible to be swayed by what others tell him and thus a child witness is an easy prey to tutoring.[6]

[s 118.3] "Competent to testify".—The competency of a person to testify as a witness is a condition precedent to the administration to him of an oath or affirmation, and is a question distinct from that of his credibility when he has been sworn or has been affirmed. In determining the question of competency the court, under this section, has not to enter into inquiries as to the witness's religious belief or as to his knowledge of the consequences of falsehood in this world or the next.[7] It has to ascertain, in the best way it can, whether, from the extent of his intellectual capacity and understanding, he is able to give a rational and intelligent account of what he has seen or heard or done on a particular occasion. If a person of tender years or of very advanced age[8] can satisfy these requirements, his competency as a witness is established.[9] If a boy in spite of his young age can both understand questions and give rational answers to them he should be examined.[10]

[s 118.4] Role of Magistrates/Judges.—The child has to be handled in a manner where he/she finds a friend in the judge. Consultation with the child should be done in the language which the child understands. The child should never be called to the court room but only to chamber. The judge must make an effort to build up relationship with the child to find out truth from the child.[11]

[s 118.5] Explanation.—Lunatic.—The explanation applies to the case of a monomaniac or person afflicted with partial insanity. Such a person will be an admissible witness if the judge finds him upon investigation capable of understanding the subject in respect of which he is required to testify.[12] An insane or an idiot is not a competent witness if he is incapacitated to such an extent that he is unable to understand the subject

5. *Ghewar Ram v State of Rajasthan*, 2001 Cr LJ 4460 (Raj).
6. *Panchhi v State of UP*, (1998) 7 SCC 177 (SCC p 181, para 11).
7. *State of Kerala v Naduveetil Viswanathan*, 1991 Cr LJ 1501 (Ker), the court was not concerned with the profession of the witness as an illegal arrack dealer.
8. *Prafulla Bora v State of Assam*, 1988 Cr LJ 428 (Gau), an aged lady of 80 years with weak vision and hard hearing was not trusted as an eye-witness of a crime taking place in dark.
9. *Queen-Empress v Lal Sahai*, (1888) 11 All 183; *Quasim Ali v State*, (1952) Raj 435; *Purna Chandra v State*, AIR 1959 Cal 306.
10. *Queen-Empress v Ram Sewak*, (1900) 23 All 90.
11. *Sreeparna Banik (Saha) v Ankur Saha*, AIR 2016 NOC 541 (Tri).
12. *Hill's case*, (1851) 2 Den CC 254; *Spittle v Walton*, (1871) LR 11 Eq 420. See also *R v Spencer and R v Smails*, (1986) 2 All ER 928 (HL), where the House of Lords found that the judge had told the jury in the clearest possible terms that they must approach the evidence of the patients (mental condition and criminal connections) with great caution and since having given the warning, he identified the very dangers which justified the exercise of great caution, it was held that the judge's direction were fair and adequate. Approving, *R v Beck*, (1982) 1 All ER 807 and **overruling** *R v Bagshaw*, (1984) 1 All ER 971.

in reference to which he is called as a witness. Where the witness was suffering from mental defect, her evidence was recorded without any finding that she was competent to depose, the whole trial was held to be vitiated. Re-trial was ordered.[13]

[s 118.5.1] ***Disease of body.***—The word "disease" as used in section 118 refers to such a disease which affects the sufferer mentally so as to prevent him from understanding the questions put to him and giving rational answers. Mere restrictions on the movement of the plaintiff due to diseases like "heart ailment" would be of no consequence because the plaintiff could apply for her examination on commission.[14]

[s 118.6] When accused competent witness.—An accused person is competent to testify within this section, but before the amendment of the Code of Criminal Procedure in 1956 he was incompetent to be a witness, for an oath could not be administered to him, and without it no witness can be lawfully examined, or give evidence, by or before a Court.[15] Where there are two accused a magistrate cannot convert one of them into a witness against the other except when a pardon has been lawfully granted.[16]

[s 118.7] Power of attorney holder.—A power of attorney holder can testify as a witness. He is a competent witness. His deposition would become part of the evidence on record.[17] An earlier decision of the same High Court was to the effect that a power of attorney holder was not entitled to appear as witness for the party appointing him.[18] An attorney has been held to be competent to depose in respect of all matters except matters which are required to be done personally by the principal. His statement can be taken as that of the party to the list. It was a suit for eviction by an NRI landlord. The attorney holder testified to the *bona fide* personal need of the landlord. The order of eviction passed on that basis was held to be not illegal.[19]

The evidence of power of attorney was not allowed to be ignored only on the ground that the parties to the suit did not appear in the witness box.[20]

[See also Notes under section 3 under the heading "Appreciation of Evidence"]

[21][[s 119] Witness unable to communicate verbally.—A witness who is unable to speak may give his evidence in any other manner in which he can make it intelligible, as by writing or by signs; but such writing must be written and the signs made in open Court, evidence so given shall be deemed to be oral evidence:

Provided that if the witness is unable to communicate verbally, the Court shall take the assistance of an interpreter or a special educator in recording the statement, and such statement shall be video graphed.]

---

13. *State of Karnataka v Shabuddin*, 1995 Cr LJ 3237 (Kant).

14. *Rajni Shukla v Special Judge*, AIR 2008 NOC 474 (All).

15. *King-Emperor v Nga Po Min*, (1932) 10 Ran 511 (FB).

16. *Reg v Hanmanta*, (1877) 1 Bom 610. See *Nabi Bakhsh v The Emperor of India*, (1902) PR No. 12 of 1902 (Cr); *Alladad v The King-Emperor of India*, (1906) PR No. 9 of 1906 (Cr).

17. *Raees Ad v Shrigopal Prakash*, AIR 2002 NOC 178 (Raj) : 2002 AIHC 2152.

18. *Ram Prasad v Hari Narain*, AIR 1998 Raj 185.

19. *Satnam Channan v Darshan Singh*, AIR 2007 NOC 216 (P&H).

20. *Bhimappa v Allisab*, AIR 2006 Kant 231 : (2007() 6 Kar LJ 286.

21. Subs. by Act 13 of 2013, section 27 for section 119 (w.r.e.f. 3-2-2013). Section 119, before subsitution, stood as under:

"*119. Dumb witnesses.*—A witness who is unable to speak may give his evidence in any other manner in which he can make it intelligible, as by writing or by signs; but such writing must be written and the signs made in open Court. Evidence so given shall be deemed to be oral evidence.".

COMMENT

When a deaf-mute is a witness the court will ascertain before he is examined that he possesses the requisite amount of intelligence, and that he understands the nature of an oath. A deaf-mute's evidence may be taken (a) by written questions to which he may reply in writing or (b) by means of signs.

The object of enacting the provisions of section 119 of the Evidence Act reveals that deaf and dumb persons were earlier contemplated in law as idiots. However, such a view has subsequently been changed for the reason that modern science revealed that persons affected with such calamities are generally found more intelligent, and to be susceptible to far higher culture than one was once supposed. When a deaf and dumb person is examined in the court, the court has to exercise due caution and take care to ascertain before he is examined that he possesses the requisite amount of intelligence and that he understands the nature of an oath. On being satisfied on this, the witness may be administered oath by appropriate means and that also with the assistance of an interpreter. However, in case a person can read and write, it is most desirable to adopt that method being more satisfactory than any sign language. The law requires that there must be a record of signs and not the interpretation of signs.

A dumb person need not be prevented from being a credible and reliable witness merely due to his/her physical disability. Such a person though unable to speak may convey himself through writing, if literate or through signs and gestures, if he is unable to read and write. A case in point is the silent movies which were understood widely because they were able to communicate ideas to people through novel signs and gestures. Emphasised body language and facial expression enabled the audience to comprehend the intended message. Therefore, a deaf and dumb person is a competent witness. If in the opinion of the court, oath can be administered to him/her, it should be so done. Such a witness, if able to read and write, it is desirable to record his statement giving him questions in writing and seeking answers in writing. In case the witness is not able to read and write, his statement can be recorded in sign language with the aid of interpreter, if found necessary. In case the interpreter is provided, he should be a person of the same surrounding but should not have any interest in the case and he should be administered oath.[22]

Where the witness had taken a religious vow of silence, and the magistrate took his evidence in writing in open Court when he could not get it in any other way without forcing the witness to break his religious vow, it was held that the witness should be deemed unable to speak within the meaning of this section and the course adopted by the magistrate was correct.[23] Where a witness having become dumb was physically incapable to give his statement, it was held that no adverse inference could be drawn against the prosecution in not examining him.[24]

[s 119.1] 2013 Amendment—This section was amended *vide* the Criminal Law (Amendment) Act, 2013 on the basis of recommendations given by the Justice JS Verma Committee, constituted in the aftermath of December 2012 Nirbhaya rape incident. The title of this section has been changed by this amendment, so as to enable the

---

22. *State of Rajasthan v Darshan Singh*, (2012) 5 SCC 789.
23. *Lakhan Singh v King-Emperor*, (1941) 20 Pat 898.
24. *Kishan Singh v State*, 1995 Cr LJ 2027 (Raj).

courts to take resort to the modalities during the course of recording of evidence, as prescribed in this section, to not merely the dumb witnesses, but to all those witnesses who are unable to communicate verbally.

The effect of this section is that all such victims of sexual offences or any other offence, who are having problems in communicating verbally, can be a witness and the court can record their statements during trial. A proviso has also been added to this section whereby the court has been obligated to take the assistance of an interpreter or a special educator in recording the statement, and get the recording of such statement videographed, if the witness is unable to communicate verbally.

[s 120] Parties to civil suit, and their wives or husbands. Husband or wife of person under criminal trial.—In all civil proceedings the parties to the suit, and the husband or wife of any party to the suit, shall be competent witnesses. In criminal proceedings against any person, the husband or wife of such person, respectively, shall be a competent witness.

SYNOPSIS

COMMENT

[s 120.1] Principle.—In civil proceedings parties to the suit are competent witnesses. Husbands and wives are competent witnesses for or against each other in civil as well as criminal proceedings.

Parties in civil proceedings are competent witnesses and therefore their testimony is to be scrutinised in the same manner as that of any other witness. There is no inflexible rule that if a party gives his testimony he must be disbelieved because he is a party to the suit.[25] In *Aidan v State of Rajasthan,*[26] it was held that truthfulness of the statement of wife could not be disbelieved merely because her emotional reaction was different from what it should have been, in the opinion of the court.

The husband was his wife's power of attorney. In that capacity he had made a statement on behalf of wife. The wife wanted to examine him as a witness. The court said that in spite of the suit between them, they continued to be man and wife. Whether the evidence of the husband was useful or not in deciding the matter between them would be decided at the stage of judgment and not at the stage of recording evidence.[27]

[s 120.2] Privilege as to statements.—The plaintiff brought proceedings against B in Watford country Court and against D in Brentford country Court, alleging unlawful eviction in both cases. B, in support of his application to strike out the proceedings, swore an affidavit raising serious allegations against the plaintiff concerning the proceedings. The affidavit was made available to D to assist her in her own application to strike out the plaintiffs claim against her. The plaintiff subsequently sued B for damages for libel and slander, contending that defamatory statements contained in the affidavit, when

---

25. *Bhanwar Lal Vaid v Bhanwar Lal Agarwal,* (1951) Raj 1.
26. *Aidan v State of Rajasthan,* 1993 Cr LJ 2413 (Raj).
27. *Shaik Rafath Begum v TVR. Anjaneyulu,* AIR 2007 AP 23 : (2006) 6 Andh LD 769.

used by D, were not protected by privilege. The court said that the test for deciding if absolute privilege attracted to defamatory remarks made in witness statements used in court proceedings is whether the statements are made with reference to the subject matter of those proceedings. There is no dispute that test was satisfied in respect of the use of the defamatory statements in the Watford proceedings, for which B's affidavit was originally prepared. Equally, as the affidavit included allegations referring to other cases involving the plaintiff including his claim against D, the statements had direct reference to the Brentford proceedings and thus absolute privilege applied, particularly as it was clear that the material was published to D to assist in the ongoing proceedings against her.[28]

[s 120.2.1] ***Refusal to enter witness box.***—The failure as the part of the defendant to step into the witness box to make statements on oath in support of pleadings set out in the written statement led to an adverse inference. But the court refused to decree the suit of the plaintiff on the basis of pleadings only. There was no independent evidence.[29]

[s 121] Judges and Magistrates.—No Judge or Magistrate shall, except upon the special order of some Court to which he is subordinate, be compelled to answer any questions as to his own conduct in Court as such Judge or Magistrate, or as to anything which came to his knowledge in Court as such Judge or Magistrate; but he may be examined as to other matters which occurred in his presence whilst he was so acting.

ILLUSTRATIONS

(a) *A*, on his trial before the Court of Session, says that a deposition was improperly taken by *B*, the Magistrate. *B* cannot be compelled to answer questions as to this, except upon the special order of a superior Court.

(b) *A* is accused before the Court of Session of having given false evidence before *B*, a Magistrate. *B* cannot be asked what *A* said, except upon the special order of the superior Court.

(c) *A* is accused before the Court of Session of attempting to murder a police-officer whilst on his trial before *B*, a Sessions Judge. *B* may be examined as to what occurred.

SYNOPSIS

COMMENT

[s 121.1] Principle.—Under this section a judge or magistrate shall not be compelled to answer questions as to (a) his conduct in court as such judge or magistrate, or (b) anything which came to his knowledge in court as such judge or magistrate, except upon the order of a Court to which he is subordinate. He may be examined as to other matters which occurred in his presence while he was so acting.

---

28. *Smeaton v Butcher (No. 1)*, (2000) EMLR 985, CA. The court applied the principles laid down in *Seaman v Netherclift*, (1876) LR 2 CPD 53 and *Samuels v Coole & Haddock*, (Unreported, May 22, 1997) : (1997) CLY 4860. The judge was therefore right to strike out S's libel claim.

29. *Onkar Chand v Jagtamba Devi*, AIR 2003 NOC 124 (HP) : 2002 AIHC 3501.

Sections 121–132 declare exceptions to the general rules that a witness is bound to tell the whole truth, and to produce any document in his possession or power relevant to the matter in issue.[30] They deal with the privilege of certain classes of witnesses.

The privilege given by this section is the privilege of the witness, that is, of the judge or magistrate of whom the question is asked. If he waives such privilege, or does not object to answer such question, it does not lie in the mouth of any other person to assert the privilege.[31] The privilege of the judge or the magistrate, extends only "to his own conduct in court as such Judge or Magistrate, or as to anything which came to his knowledge in court as such Judge or Magistrate".

A distinction should be drawn between questions which a witness cannot be compelled to answer (sections 121, 124 and 125) and those which he cannot be permitted to answer (sections 123 and 126). The latter class of questions might properly be forbidden but questions of the former class are in no way barred; a witness has merely the right of refusing to answer such questions, without any hostile inference being drawn from his refusal. The most that a Court can do, in the case of a witness who is ignorant of his privilege, is to warn him that he need not answer. But if the witness elects to waive his privilege of refusing to answer, his answer is admissible in evidence.[32]

[s 121.2] Judge or Magistrate as witness.—"A Judge, before whom the cause is tried, must conceal any fact within his own knowledge, unless he be first sworn, and, consequently, if he be the sole Judge, it seems that he cannot depose as a witness, though if he be sitting with others, he may then be sworn and give evidence. In this last case, the proper course appears to be that the Judge, who has thus become a witness, should leave the bench, and take no further judicial part in the trial, because he can hardly be deemed capable of impartially deciding on the admissibility of his own testimony, or of weighing it against that of another."[33]

A person having to exercise judicial functions may give evidence in a case pending before him when such evidence can and must be submitted to the independent judgment of other persons exercising similar judicial functions sitting with him at the same time.[34]

Where a judge is the sole judge of law and fact, he cannot give evidence before himself or import matters into his judgment not stated on oath before the court in the presence of the accused.[35] The accused is entitled to have nothing stated against him in the judgment which was not stated on oath in his presence, and which he had no opportunity of testing by cross-examination and rebutting.[36] If the judge knew any facts concerning the case, he is bound to state to the accused, so far as he could, what were the facts he himself observed, and to which he himself could bear testimony; and the accused in such situation has a right, if he thought it desirable, to cross-examine the

30. *The Queen v Gopal Doss*, (1881) 3 Mad 271, 277 (FB).

31. *Empress of India v Chidda Khan*, (1881) 3 All 573 (FB). See also *Supreme Court Advocates-on- Record Association v UOI*, (2016) 5 SCC 1.

32. *Mahomed Ally v Emperor*, (1909) 12 Cr LJ 277.

33. *TAYLOR*, 12th Edn section 1379, p 870.

34. *The Queen v Mookta Singh*, (1870) 13 WR (Cr) 60.

35. *Queen-Empress v Manikam*, (1896) 19 Mad 263; *Empress v Donnelly*, (1877) 2 Cal 405.

36. *Girish Chunder Ghose v The Queen-Empress*, (1893) 20 Cal 857, 866; *Hari Kishore Mitra v Abdul Baki Miah*, (1894) 21 Cal 920.

judge, whose evidence should be recorded, and form part of the record in the case.[37] The privilege extends to arbitrators also. In no case an arbitrator can be summoned to explain how he came at his award.[38]

[s 122] Communications during marriage.—No person who is or has been married shall be compelled to disclose any communication[s 122.2] made to him during marriage[s 122.3] by any person to whom he is or has been married; nor shall he be permitted to disclose any such communication,[s 122.4] unless the person who made it, or his representative in interest,[s 122.5] consents, except in suits between married persons, or proceedings in which one married person is prosecuted for any crime committed against the other.

SYNOPSIS

COMMENT

[s 122.1] Principle.—This section "rests on the obvious ground that the admission of such testimony would have a powerful tendency to disturb the peace of families to promote domestic broils, and to weaken, if not to destroy, that feeling of mutual confidence which is the most endearing solace of married life. The protection is not confined to cases where the communication sought to be given in evidence is of a strictly confidential character, but the seal of the law is placed upon all communications of whatever nature which pass between husband and wife. It extends also to cases in which the interests of strangers are solely involved, as well as to those in which the husband or wife is party on the record. It is, however, limited to such matters as have been communicated 'during the marriage'."[39] This section limits the rule enunciated in section 120.

Under this section a married person shall not be—

(1) compelled to disclose any communication made to him during marriage by any person to whom he is married; and

(2) permitted to disclose any such communication, except—

   (a) when the person who made it or his representative in interest consents, or

   (b) in suits between married persons, or

   (c) in proceedings in which one married person is prosecuted for any crime committed against the other.

[s 122.2] "Compelled to disclose any communication".—This expression implies that the party concerned is made or allowed to say or do something by way of disclosing a communication made during marriage.[40] Thus a wife was not allowed to tell what

37. *Re Hurro Chunder Paul*, (1873) 20 WR (Cr) 76.

38. *UOI v Orient Engg. and Commrl Co*, AIR 1977 SC 2445 : (1978) 1 Serv LR 632 : (1978) 2 SCJ 83.

39. *Taylor*, 12th Edn, section 909-A, p 572; *Emperor v Ramchandra*, (1932) 35 Bom LR 174.

40. *Queen-Empress v Donaghue*, (1898) Mad 1, 4.

her husband told her about a murder with which he was charged.[41] A document, even though it contains a communication from a husband to a wife or *vice versa*, in the hands of third persons, is admissible in evidence; for, in producing it, there is no compulsion on or permission to the wife or husband to disclose any communication. The section protects the individuals, and not the communications if it can be proved without putting into the box for that purpose the husband or the wife to whom the communication was made.[42] Marital communications can be proved by evidence of the over-hearers.[43] Confession to wife in the presence of others was allowed to be proved by others.[44] Letters written by husband to wife were held to be provable otherwise than through wife.[45]

[s 122.3] "During marriage".—The protection conferred by the section is limited to such matters as have been communicated during marriage. A communication made to a woman before marriage would not be protected. But the privilege continues even after the marriage has been dissolved by death or divorce. The bar to the admissibility in evidence of communications made during marriage attaches at the time when the communication is made, and its admissibility will be adjudged in the light of the status at that date and not the status at the date when evidence is sought to be given in court.[46] So, where the accused had made extra-judicial confession to his wife, it was held that the said extra-judicial confession cannot be taken into consideration as evidence.[47]

[s 122.4] "Permitted to disclose any such communication."—Even if one of the spouses is willing to disclose a communication, he or she will not be permitted to disclose it unless the person who made it or his representative in interest consents, except in suits or prosecutions between married persons. The consent cannot be implied. It is incumbent upon the court to ask the party against whom the evidence is to be given.

On a trial for the offence of breach of trust by a public servant, a letter was tendered in evidence for the prosecution which has been sent by the accused to his wife at Pondicherry and had been found on a search of her house made there by the police; it was held that the letter was admissible in evidence against the accused.[48]

The ban of the section is confined to communications only. A wife can testify to the deeds of her husband of which she was the eyewitness.[49] This is so because section 120 declares her to be a competent witness against her husband. This approach obviates the difficulties experienced by English law in this respect. One example is *R v Pitt*.[50] The accused was charged with two counts of assault occasioning actual bodily harm on his eight-month-old daughter. On both the occasions the baby suffered multiple injuries to her face and head. The wife implicated her husband. It was not disputed

---

41. *Ram Chandra Shanker Shet v Emperor*, AIR 1933 Bom 153.
42. *Queen-Empress v Donaghue, Ibid.*
43. *Appu v State*, AIR 1971 Mad 194.
44. *Ibid*
45. *A Manibhushana Rao v A Surya Kantam*, AIR 1981 AP 58.
46. *MC Verghese v TJ Ponnan*, AIR 1970 SC 1876 : 1970 Cr LJ 1651.
47. *Vilas Raghunath Kurhade v The State of Maharashtra*, 2011 Cr LJ 3300 (Bom).
48. *Queen-Empress v Donaghue*, (1898) 22 Mad 1, 4.
49. *Ram Bharosey v UP*, AIR 1954 SC 704 : 1954 Cr LJ 1755.
50. *R v Pitt*, (1982) 3 All ER 63, noted all ER Annual Rev. 1982 at 138 a direct consequence of the rulings in *Leach v R*, (1912) AC 304 and *R. v Hoskyn*, 1978 2 All ER 136 to the effect that even when she is competent she is not compellable.

that the accused was left at home with the baby and that the baby suffered injuries. The accused tried to lay the blame upon the 2½ year old brother of the baby but that was found to be factually false. Even so the court held that the wife was not a compellable witness. She could choose to save her marriage by refusing to testify. Where there was no evidence that the accused consented to disclosure of communications allegedly made by him to his wife, it was held that evidence of the wife of only such portions as were communications from her husband in connection with the murder, were inadmissible under section 122.[51]

[s 122.5] "Representative in interest".—Where there is no "representative in interest" who can consent, under this section, to the disclosure of communications made by a deceased husband to his wife during marriage, the wife should not be permitted, even if willing, to disclose such communications. The widow of a deceased husband is not his "representative in interest," for the purpose of giving such consent.[52]

[s 122.6] Evidence of mistress cohabitee.—Where the accused confessed his offence to his mistress, it was held that section 122 did not in any manner come in the way of the evidence of a mistress and such evidence could be relied upon.[53] The same principle has been applied by the [English] Court of Appeal to a cohabitee. In this case the accused appealed against his conviction for murder. At his trial, his longstanding cohabitee had given evidence. Had she been married to him she would have been, non-compellable witness. The accused contended *inter alia*, that her evidence should have been treated in the same way as that of a spouse. He maintained that the rationale for the rule in relation to spouses was to protect family relationships and that the courts should assess the substance of such relationships as well as the form in order to prevent a breach of the right to family life under the Human Rights Act 1998 Sch I, Pt I, Article 8. It was held that it was not possible to expand the provision so as to include partners. If the existing concession were to be widened it would be difficult to find a logical end point and potentially cause grave difficulties in the enforcement of the criminal law.[54]

[s 123] Evidence as to affairs of State.—No one shall be permitted to give any evidence derived from unpublished official records relating to any affairs of State,[s 123.2] except with the permission of the officer at the head of the department concerned, who shall give or withhold such permission as he thinks fit.[s 123.3]

SYNOPSIS

COMMENT

[s 123.1] Principle.—This section involves two things: (1) That the document is an unpublished official record relating to any affairs of State and (2) that the officer at

51. *Fateh Singh v State*, 1995 Cr LJ 88 (All).
52. *Nawab Howladar v Emperor*, (1913) 40 Cal 891.
53. *Shankar v State of TN*, 1994 Cr LJ 3071 : (1994) 4 SCC 478 : (1994) 2 Andh LT (Cri) 429 : 1994 Cr LJ 3071.
54. *R v Pearce*, (2001) EWCA Crimes 2834.

the head of the department concerned may give or withhold the permission for giving the evidence derived therefrom. On grounds of public policy, evidence derived from unpublished official records of State cannot be given, except with the permission of the head of the department concerned. The court is bound to accept without question the decision of the public officer.

Section 122 prevents communications between a man and his wife from being disclosed. Marriage inspires confidence and confidence inspires openness of heart and feeling. This enables a married person to make a clean breast of everything to his or her spouse. Naturally, therefore, such matters should be free from the risk of being disclosed.[55] The policy of protection is thus stated by an American judge: Communications and transactions between husband and wife were early recognised as privileged and neither could be compelled to disclose what took place between them and neither was a competent witness to testify to such transactions or communications of a confidential nature or induced by marital relations. From experience it was found that far less evil would result from the exclusion of such testimony than from its admission. It may in individual cases work hardship, but the destruction of confidence between a husband and wife would cause much misery and affect the marriage relation. This rule is founded upon sound public policy. Those living in the marriage relation should not be compelled or allowed to betray the mutual trust and confidence which such relation implies.[56]

The only ground sufficient to justify non-production of an official document marked confidential is that production would not be in the public interest, for example where disclosures would be injurious to national defence or to good diplomatic relations or where the practice of keeping a class of documents secret is necessary for the proper functioning of the public service.[57] Care has, however, to be taken to see that interests other than the interest of the public do not masquerade in the garb of public interest and take undue advantage of the provisions of this section. Subject to this reservation the maxim *salus populi est suprema lex*, which means that regard for public welfare is the highest law, is the basis of the provisions contained in this section.[58] Referring to the facts of case, the Supreme Court said:[59] The court would not have rejected the State's claim of privilege in regard to departmental nothings contained in official files, except for the fact that the affidavit filed on behalf of the Government did not adequately bring out the involvement of public interest consequent upon the disclosure of the nothings.

The term "evidence" refers to both oral and documentary evidence.[60]

[s 123.2] "Unpublished official records relating to any affairs of State".—It is for the court to decide whether a document falls within the category "unpublished official records relating to any affairs of State." In doing so the court can have regard to all the circumstances, barring the inspection of the document itself. Apart from this, there is no fetter to the jurisdiction of the court looking at whatever materials

55. See Dr Avtar Singh, *Principles of the Law of Evidence*, p 425 (13th Edn 2002).

56. *Stillman v Stillman*, 115 Mis C 106 : 187 NYS 383 See RICHARDSON ON EVIDENCE, p 453.

57. *Tukaram v King-Emperor*, (1946) Nag 385.

58. *State of Punjab v Sodhi Sukhdev Singh*, AIR 1961 SC 493 : (1961) 2 SCR 371; **Overruled** by the Supreme Court on another point in *SP Gupta v UOI*, AIR 1982 SC 149 : 1981 Supp SCC 87.

59. *State of Orissa v Jagannath*, AIR 1977 SC 2201 : (1977) 2 SCC 165.

60. STOKES,Vol II, p 919, fn 2.

are available for the purpose of ascertaining whether the document is an unpublished official record relating to affairs of State. "Affairs of State" is a very wide expression. Every communication which proceeds from one officer of State to another officer of the State is not necessarily relating to the affairs of State. What are the "affairs of State" has got to be determined by a reference to the grounds on which privilege can be claimed in respect of a particular document. It is only such documents which relate to the affairs of the State the disclosure of which would be detrimental to the public interest that come within the category of unpublished official records relating to affairs of State entitled to protection under this section.[61]

"Affairs of State" will include any matter of a public nature with which the Government is concerned, i.e., all secrets of State, such as State papers and all communications between Government and its officers—the privilege in such cases not being that of the person who is in possession of the secret, but that of the public, as a trustee for whom the secret has been entrusted to him.[62] Under this section and section 162, the court cannot hold an enquiry into the possible injury to public interest which may result from the disclosure of the document in respect of which privilege is claimed under this section. That is a matter for the authority concerned to decide; but the court is competent, and indeed is bound to hold a preliminary enquiry and determine the validity of the objections to its production, and that necessarily involves an enquiry into the question as to whether the evidence relates to an affair of the State under this section or not. In this enquiry the court has to determine the character or class of the document. Although in such an enquiry the court cannot permit any evidence about the contents of the document, other collateral evidence can be produced which may assist the court in determining the validity of the objection under this section. The question as to whether any particular document answers the description of a document relating to affairs of State must be determined in each case on the relevant fact and circumstances adduced before the court.[63]

Before any document is excluded in such a case on the ground that it relates to affairs of State, the court must be satisfied that the mind of a responsible officer of Government has been brought to bear upon the question whether it is expedient in the public interest to give or withhold the information asked for, and that he has made his decision solemnly and with a due sense of responsibility.[64]

The orders made by the Chief Minister of which the result alone is communicated by his Secretary to a public servant interested in knowing it, are still unpublished records contemplated by this section. Every communication that passes between different departments of the Government or between members of the same department *inter se*

---

61. *Chamarbaghwalla v Parpia*, (1948) 52 Bom LR 231. The Union Government can claim no privilege or protection against the disclosure of any such information in its possession which was made the basis of proclamation of the President's rule. *Sunderlal Patwa v UOI (FB)*, AIR 1993 MP 214. *Sathyanarayana Bros. Pvt Ltd v TN Water Supply & Drainage Board*, (2004) 5 SCC 314 : AIR 2004 SC 651, a "handing over note" prepared by the chief engineer, held, the arbitrator could not refuse to consider such a document on the ground of confidentiality at a time when there is a greater stress of transparency in state affairs. *People's Union for Civil Liberties v UOI*, AIR 2004 SC 1442 : (2004) 2 SCC 476, withholding of information by the State, claim of privilege to be considered by the court in exercise of discretionary jurisdiction under Article 136 of the Constitution.

62. *Best*, 12th Edn, section 578, p 495.

63. *State of Punjab v SS Singh*, AIR 1961 SC 493 : (1961) 2 SCR 371.

64. *Bhaiya Saheb v Pt Ramnath Rampratap Bhadupote*, (1940) Nag 280.

and every order made by a Minister, departmental head or a responsible officer cannot be deemed to relate to an affair of State unless it refers to a matter of vital importance the disclosure of which is likely to prejudice the interest of the State.[65] A Government supplier of chrome ore wanted to recover the price fixed by the Department in their files. The court held that the document concerning fixation related to a commercial transaction in respect of which no privilege could be claimed.[66] As against it, in *Durga Pd v Parveen,*[67] it was held that the State was justified in claiming a privilege against production of the relevant file concerning the grant of mining lease as it contained letters written by the Head of the Department to the subordinate officers of the Department and vice versa and between that Department and other Departments which were unpublished and contained State secrets.

The approach to this question has now acquired new dimensions particularly since the decision of a Bench of seven Supreme Court judges in *SP Gupta v UOI.*[68] The case arose out of the matter of the transfer of a High Court judge and the non-renewal of the term of an additional judge. The correspondence between the Law Minister and the Chief Justice of India and that between the Chief Justice of the High Court and the State Government was required to be produced. It was held that though the "advice" was protected from judicial scrutiny by virtue of Article 74 of the Constitution, the material on the basis of which the advice was formulated was not protected.[69]

The court also added that the common law protection known as the "Crown privilege" or "public interest immunity" does not apply in India and observed as follows: "Meaning and scope of section 123 cannot remain static. It must be interpreted keeping in view our new democratic society wedded to the basic values enshrined in the Constitution."

"The concept of an open government is the direct emanation from the right to know which seems to be implicit in the right of free speech and expression guaranteed under Article 19(1)(*a*). Therefore, disclosure of information in regard to the functioning of Government must be the rule and secrecy an exception justified only where the strictest requirements of public interest so demands. The approach of the Court must be to attenuate the area of secrecy as much as possible consistently with the requirement of

---

65. *Gursewak Singh v The State,* (1953) Pat 626.

66. *Ferroy Alloys Corp Ltd v Industrial Devp. Corporation of Orissa,* AIR 1986 Ori 199. The Court relied upon *State of Punjab v Sodhi Sukhdev Singh,* AIR 1961 SC 493 : (1961) 2 SCR 371 (partly overruled by the SC in *SP Gupta v UP,* AIR 1982 SC 149 : 1981 Supp SCC 87 and section 162 which requires documents to be produced. Followed in principle in *Subhasini Jena v Commandant,* 1988 Cr LJ 1570 (Ori), documents connected with mobilisation etc. of armed forces allowed to remain; even if disclosed they would have served no purpose in connection with misconduct of army personnel.

67. *Durga Pd v Parveen,* AIR 1975 MP 196.

68. *SP Gupta v UOI,* AIR 1982 SC 149 : 1981 Supp SCC 87. **Followed** in *Sundaresan v Ramchandran,* 1987 Cr LJ 108 (Ker) where in a complaint against illegal immigration allowed by officers, certain documents were demanded and the court held that greater harm would be done to public interest by disclosure than by keeping them secret. *State of Bihar v Kripalu Shankar,* 1987 Cr LJ 1860 : AIR 1987 SC 1554 : (1987) 3 SCC 34 : 1987 SCC (Cri) 442, notings in files cannot be used for supporting a contempt petition.

69. Overruling its own earlier decision in *State of Punjab v Sodhi Sukhdev Singh,* AIR 1961 SC 493 : (1961) 2 SCR 371, to the effect that the underlying report on the basis of which the advice was prepared was equally protected. For developments in this respect in English law see *Hasselblad (GB) Ltd v Orbinson,* (1985) 1 All ER 173 and All ER Annual Rev. 1985 p 167.

public interest, bearing in mind all the time that disclosure also serves an important aspect of public interest."

"Though public interest lies at the foundation of the claim for protection against disclosure enacted in section 123, Evidence Act, 1872, the claim which comes into conflict with it is not private interest of the litigant in disclosure but the public interest in fair administration of justice. Court has to balance these two public interests and decide which aspect predominates in each particular case before it."[70]

The mere fact that a document is marked confidential will not afford sufficient justification for objecting to its production under this section, nor will it be a good ground that the production may involve a department of the Government in a discussion in the Legislative Assembly or in public criticism. Neither will it be a good ground that production may tend to expose want of efficiency in administration or to lay the department open to claim for compensation,[71] or it is apprehended that the document if produced would defeat the defence raised by the State. The impact of the document on the head of the department or the Minister in charge of the department or even the Government in power, has no relevance in making a claim for privilege under this section.[72] Where the contents of the Report of the Committee inquiring into the allegations of sexual harassment by the officials were not related to the affairs of the State, neither was there anything concerning the national security, nor were the accompanying documents detrimental to the interest of the country, the Union of India could not claim the privilege in respect of the said report.[73]

The High Court in exercise of its powers under Article 226 of the Constitution of India can call for scrutiny and perusal by it unpublished official records. In so doing the court is not permitting anybody to give any evidence from these records relating to any affairs of State within the meaning of this section.[74]

Where the original records were produced by the Government for the court's perusal and they contained secret documents, it was held by the Supreme Court that the High Court had no jurisdiction under Articles 226 to wade through them for the purpose of deciding controversial issues.[75]

The Government claimed privilege in respect of records relating to action by the Government for the formation of the State Human Rights Commission. The court rejected the claim. All the documents could be looked into barring the advice tendered by the cabinet to the Government.[76]

[s 123.3] "Who shall give or withhold permission as he thinks fit".—These words clearly indicate that the Head of the Department, who is in possession of the document is the exclusive judge of the fact whether the unpublished records are protected from production on the ground of their being related to affairs of State, and, therefore, the

---

70. *Per* Bhagwati J.

71. *Tukaram v King-Emperor*, (1946) Nag 385; *Jaggannath Dwarkanath v State*, (1971) 74 Bom LR 320.

72. *State of Punjab v S..Singh*, AIR 1961 SC 493 : (1961) 2 SCR 371; *Amar Chand Butail v UOI*, AIR 1964 SC 1658 : (1965) ISCJ 243.

73. *Nisha Priya Bhatia v Ajit Seth*, AIR 2016 SC 2319, paras 12 and 13.

74. *R. Ramanna v State*, AIR 1971 AP 196.

75. *UOI v WN Chadha*, AIR 1993 SC 1082 : 1993 Cr LJ 859 : (1993) 1 SCC 154.

76. *People's Union for Civil Liberties v State of UP*, AIR 2000 All 103.

privilege claimed under the section by the Head of the Department that the document relates to the affairs of State has got to be allowed although the decision would be that of the court. The court simply gives effect to the decision of the Head of the Department by adding its own command to it but the court has no power to examine the document in order to verify the correctness of the allegations or the grounds on which the privilege was claimed.[77] The privilege should be claimed generally by the Minister in charge who is the political head of the department concerned, if not, the Secretary of the department who is the departmental head should make the claim; and the claim should always be made in the form of an affidavit. When the affidavit is made by the Secretary, the court may, in a proper case, require an affidavit of the Minister himself. The affidavit should show that each document in question has been carefully read and considered, and the person making the affidavit is satisfied that its disclosure would lead to public injury. The affidavit should also indicate briefly within permissible limits the reason why it is apprehended that their disclosure would lead to injury to public interest. In a proper case the person making the affidavit whether he is a Minister or the Secretary should be summoned to face cross-examination on the relevant points.[78]

Reports by police officers to the Government about the investigation of allegations of the commission of an offence are privileged under this section and section 124 as they are unpublished records and are submitted in official confidence. The privilege which the Government can claim in respect of documents relating to matters of State is a narrow one and must be sparingly used.[79] Privilege under section 123 can be claimed in respect of ministerial advice tendered to the President of India.[80]

Where the document was not a confidential correspondence, nor relating to the transaction of business by the Council of Ministers in respect of affairs of State or communication of policy decision taken at ministerial or secretariat level, immunity from disclosure could not be claimed.[81]

In claiming privilege under the section the head of the department should not confine himself to saying that the disclosure of the document would be against public interest but should indicate the nature of the suggested injury to the interests of the public.[82]

[s 123.4] Production without claim of privilege.—It has been held that notwithstanding the bar contained in Article 163(3) of the Constitution it shall be the sole discretion of the Governor concerned to produce the proceedings of the Council of Ministers without any objection and without any claim of privilege before any Court of law and then there is nothing to debar the court from looking into the same. This proposition of law was affirmed by the Apex Court in *Chaudhary v Governor of Bihar,*[83] *overruling the judgment of Patna High Court in Ram Nagina v Sohni.*[84]

---

77. *Khawaja Nazir Ahmad v The Crown,* (1944) 26 Lah 219.

78. *State of Punjab v SS Singh,* AIR 1961 SC 493 : (1961) 2 SCR 371.

79. *Rajul Raojee v Provincial Government, Central Provinces,* (1950) Nag 690.

80. *SR Bommai v UOI,* AIR 1994 SC 1918 : (1994) 1 SCC 754, dissenting from *State of Rajasthan v UOI,* (1978) 1 SCR 1 : AIR 1977 SC 1361 : (1977) 3 SCC 592.

81. *Baburao Vishwanath Mathpati v State,* AIR 1996 Bom 227.

82. *Chamarbaghwalla v Parpia,* (1948) 52 Bom LR 231.

83. *Chaudhary v Governor of Bihar,* AIR 1980 SC 383 : 1980 Supp SCC 374, **followed** in *Shree Swami v State of Rajasthan,* AIR 1995 Raj 69.

84. *Ram Nagina v Sohni,* AIR 1976 Pat 36.

The oath of secrecy does not absolve the Minister from filing affidavit stating grounds or reasons in support of his claim for public interest immunity.[85] The court said in this case that immunity could not be claimed by way of mere administrative routine. It must be shown that the documents relate to the affairs of the State and disclosure thereof would be against interest of the State or public service and public interest must be so strong as to outweigh the private or any other interest. Affidavit should generally be filed by the Minister concerned precisely stating reasons or grounds for claim of immunity. The court should normally be slow to question the opinion of the Minister given in the affidavit. However, the court may seek additional affidavit or summon the Minister concerned for cross-examination. The court may also examine the documents in camera. Court should weigh the competing claims of public interest immunity from disclosure of the documents and public interest of doing justice to the litigating parties in the light of those documents and decide accordingly. The Government can claim privilege from disclosure in respect of the relevant files on which the appointment of the President of Customs, Excise and Gold Control Appellate Tribunal was made.[86] Where an affidavit was filed claiming the case diaries to be unpublished official records and that the disclosure of their contents would be against public interest, the claim of privilege from disclosure could be allowed.[87] Merit alone should be the criterion of admission of foreign students to professional (medical) colleges in India, the Government should not claim privilege under sections 123 and 124 in such matters.[88] The Commission appointed to inquire into a caste war resulting in many deaths cannot direct the Government and CBI to produce the documents for public inspection over which privilege has been claimed.[89] The records of an abortion clinic are subject to public interest immunity. They were not ordered to be disclosed to a person who wanted to prove as a part of his defence that illegal abortions were taking place at the clinic.[90]

[s 124] Official communications.—No public officer shall be compelled to disclose[s 124.3] communications ma barrister, attorney, pleader de to him in official confidence,[s 124.4] when he considers that the public interests would suffer by the disclosure.[s 124.5]

SYNOPSIS

85. *RK Jain v UOI*, AIR 1993 SC 1769 : (1993) 4 SCC 119. On the facts of the case, the court held that it was not necessary to disclose the contents of the records to the petitioner or his counsel.
86. *Ibid*
87. *CBI v Kumher Inquiry Commission*, 1995 Cr LJ 3917 (Raj).
88. *Sajitha G v Secy to Govt of India, Ministry of External Affairs*, AIR 1994 Mad 204.
89. *CBI v Kher Inquiry Commission*, 1996 AIHC 1971 (Raj).
90. *DPP v Morrow, The Guardian*, 5 April 1993 (DC).

COMMENT

[s 124.1] Object.—This section is designed to prevent the knowledge of official papers, that is to say papers in official custody, beyond that circle which would obtain knowledge of them in confidence whether the confidence was express or implied. It would normally include all officers including clerks of superior officers and might also apply to non-officials to whom such papers were disclosed on the understanding express or implied that the knowledge should go no further.[91] Public interests are paramount as compared with the individual interests of a party in a Court of Justice. It is absolutely essential to the welfare of the State that the names of parties who interpose in situations of this kind should not be divulged, for otherwise—be it from fear or shame, or the dislike of being publicly mixed up in inquiries of this nature—few men would choose to assume the disagreeable part of giving or receiving information respecting offences, and the consequence would be that many great crimes would pass unpunished.[92]

There is a privilege which attaches, under certain circumstances, to communications made to public officers. State secrets, or matters which govern the administration of Government should not be disclosed, since to reveal them might be highly prejudicial to public interest. Therefore, communications relating to affairs of State are generally held to be privileged, and the officers may refuse to disclose them.[93]

[s 124.2] Principle.—A public officer cannot be compelled to disclose communications made to him in confidence if he considers that public interests would suffer by this disclosure.

This section is confined to public officers; section 123 embraces everyone. Section 123 deals with unpublished records; this section deals with communications made in official confidence.

[s 124.3] "No public officer shall be compelled to disclose".—The term "public officer" means an officer with public, as opposed to private, duties who receives communications made to him in official confidence of such a nature that disclosure in certain cases would injure the public interests. The word "disclose" means the first disclosure of communications made in official confidence and does not apply to a disclosure in a Court of law of what has already been disclosed outside it. The object of the section is to prevent the disclosure of things not known outside that circle which is in confidence and the section has no application when once there has been disclosure to a member of the public to whom the contents of such papers have not been made known in confidence.[94]

The Vice-Chancellor of Punjab University is a "public officer" within the meaning of this section.[95] The privilege can only be claimed by the head of the department or by the Secretary of that department on an affidavit. Filing of a certificate only is not enough.[96] Where it is an unpublished official record relating to an affair of the State, the question whether the disclosure of its contents would be against public interest

---

91. *Pandit Chandra Dhar Tewari v The Deputy Commissioner, Lucknow*, (1938) 14 Luck 351.
92. Taylor, 12th Edn, section 941, p 597.
93. *Richards on the Law of Evidence*, 461 (7th Edn, 1948).
94. *Pandit Chandra Dhar Tewari v Deputy Commissioner, Lucknow*, (1938) 14 Luck 351.
95. *The University of the Punjab, Lahore v Jaswant Rai*, (1945) 27 Lah 561.
96. *S Ajit Singh v Shri Ashwani Kumar*, (1954) Pun 359.

and whether privilege could be claimed rested with the head of the department and if the head of the department refused to disclose it, the court would not compel him to produce the document or disclose its contents.[97]

[s 124.4] "Communications made to him in official confidence".—The question that arises under this section is whether the communication in question was made to the public officer in official confidence. This is a condition precedent to the claim, and the question is to be primarily decided by the court before whom the privilege is claimed. There is no clear-cut rule of procedure as to when and how the privilege should be claimed. It should be claimed at the earliest opportunity by the public officer concerned when in reply to the summons he produces the document in his control or charge.[98] Communications in official confidence import no special degree of secrecy and any pledge or direction for its maintenance, but include generally all matters communicated by one officer to another in the performance of their duties. The question whether such communication was made in the course of such performance is for the court to decide.[99] A demi-official letter addressed by one officer by name to another officer by name in view of the reasons for which demi-official letters are usually written is written in official confidence within the meaning of this section.[100] If communications are not made in official confidence, they cannot be regarded as privileged, e.g., statements made to a station-master of a railway in the course of an inquiry of a theft by some railway employees.[101]

A Government Resolution, containing opinions of Government officers, including a legal adviser, is a privileged document within the meaning of this section.[102] A statement made to the Collector by a person applying to have his estate taken under the court of Wards setting forth his financial position, that is to say, the details of his property and liabilities, is a communication made to a public officer in official confidence within the meaning of this section and cannot be used as acknowledgment of any liability mentioned therein.[103]

[s 124.5] "When he considers that the public interests would suffer by the disclosure".— The sole judge as to whether disclosure will harm the public interest is the public officer concerned and it is not for the court to decide whether public interests would or would not suffer.[104] The public officer claiming privilege has to exercise his own discretion in giving or refusing disclosure.[105] His decision must not be arbitrary or capricious. He should not claim privilege merely because such disclosure would either advance the case of the adversary or damage his case. This section must in no event be resorted to as a cloak to shield the truth from the court.[106] Where the secretary, Ministry of Home Affairs, Government of India, claimed that production of

97. *Mutsadilal v UOI*, (1955) Hyd 256; *Public Prosecutor v Narasayya*, (1957) AP 174.
98. *Bhalchandra v Chanbasappa*, (1938) 41 Bom LR 391.
99. *Nagaraj Pillai v The Secretary of State*, (1914) 39 Mad 304, 311.
100. *Pandit Chandra Dhar Tewari v The Deputy Commissioner, Lucknow*, (1938) 14 Luck 351.
101. *King-Emperor v Bhagwati Prasad*, (1929) 5 Luck 297.
102. *Sursingji Dajiraj v Secretary of State*, (1926) 28 Bom LR 1213.
103. *Collector of Jaunpur v Jaman Prasad*, (1922) 44 All 360.
104. *Nagaraja Pillai v The Secretary of State*, (1914) 39 Mad 304; *Pandit Chandra Dhar Tewari v The Deputy Commissioner, Lucknow*, (1938) 14 Luck 351.
105. *Jehangir v Secretary of State*, (1903) 6 Bom LR 131; *King-Emperor v Bhagwati Prasad*, (1929) 5 Luck 297.
106. *Excelsior Film v UOI*, (1966) 69 Bom LR 878.

documents and video cassettes collected by CBI regarding newspaper report involving IGP in ISRO espionage case was privileged from disclosure, it was held that the said documents had no bearing to the security of the nation as well as friendly relations with various countries, hence the privilege could not be claimed in respect of such documents.[107]

In a case before the Bombay High Court,[108] the society in question was put under prohibition in public interest from accepting foreign contributions because of alleged violations of Foreign Contribution (Regulation) Act. The Authority under the Act claimed privilege in respect of basic document on the basis of which the prohibition order was issued. An affidavit to that effect was filed by a joint secretary in the Home Ministry. The court examined the document and found that there was sufficient indication of a possible injury to public in disclosure of the document. The court held that the claim as to privilege was well-founded.

[s 124.6] Income tax return.—A party in a civil suit sought production of the income-tax return of the opposite party. The court refused to summon the document asked for considering it to be a privileged document. This was held to be not justified. It was up to the Commissioner of Income-tax to claim privilege when a document has been summoned. It is then for the court to decide whether the privilege is to be granted or not.[109]

[s 124.7] Document disclosed for taxation of costs.—It has been held that documents disclosed for taxation of costs remained privileged for any collateral purposes notwithstanding the US Law. The court said:[110] Where privilege in respect of confidential documents was waived for specific purposes, for example taxation of costs, there was no waiver for collateral purposes. Had the documents been disclosed by order of the taxing master they would have retained privilege pursuant to the Rules of the Supreme Court O LXII, rule 20(d) and the lack of an order should make no difference to their status. The expert witness had denied that the documents had affected his evidence and privilege could not be lost in that manner.[111] It was inappropriate to consider US law and practice in relation to such matters in this jurisdiction. The implied undertaking was imposed on public interest grounds and any relief from its obligations should be rare in case it deterred parties from giving full discovery.

[s 124.8] Information in investigation by Foreign Authorities.—The court was considering Mutual Legal Assistance in Criminal Matters Act 1985 (Canada) section 18, section 20. Authorities in the Russian Federation were investigating allegations of theft and corruption involving Russian citizens and government officials. The investigation led to Canada and the assistance of the Canadian Authorities was sought. Documents were seized from the X's business premises and three banks and detained by the Canadian

---

107. *Niyamavedi v Raman Srivastawa*, 1995 Cr LJ 1976 (Ker).

108. *Watch Tower Bible & Tract Society of India v UOI*, AIR 2002 Bom 83. The Court **followed** authorities like *SP Gupta v President of India*, AIR 1982 SC 149 : 1981 Supp SCC 87; *Chamanlal v State of Punjab*, AIR 1970 SC 1372 : 1970 Cr LJ 1266 : (1970) 1 SCC 590.

109. *Debasis Sahu v Nabeen Chandra Sahu*, AIR 2002 Ori 211. The Court **followed** the Supreme Court decision in *Lagiram Pindilal v Trilok Chand Jain*, AIR 1992 SC 990 : (1992) 2 SCC 13 : 1992 AIR SCW 913 : 1992 Tax LR 856 and also *SP Gupta v UOI*, AIR 1982 SC 149 : 1981 Supp SCC 87.

110. *Bourns Inc. v Raycham Corp., (No. 3)*, (1999) 3 All ER 154 (CA).

111. The court **followed** *Marubeni Corp. v Alalouzos*, 1988 CLY 2841.

Authorities under search warrants issued in connection with the investigation. There was an appeal against the direction that copies of the documents be turned over to a specified official and an order under section 20 for the documents be sent to the Russian Federation. The appeal was dismissed. The court said that the Act did not require that a foreign state's request for assistance should comply with section 18(1); the issue of "relevance" had to be given a wide judicial interpretation at the investigative stage of criminal proceedings, especially where commercial matters were concerned, as in the instant case. The judge making an order under section 20 was not concerned, with the ultimate admissibility of any of the documents in a Russian Court, and "relevance" therefore meant information that would assist the foreign authorities in discovering and proving the events underlying the allegations that formed the subject matter of the Russian investigation.[112]

[s 124.9] **Information generated by investigation.**—The flat occupied by the accused became the victim of burglary. A burglary search discovered a unique mix of heroin and methaqualone. A similar mix was recovered from the house of the burglar. The court okayed the use of this report in the heroin case also.[113]

[s 124.10] **Confidential Information between bank and customer.**—A conflict arose between the bank's duty of maintaining secrecy of the customer's account and the duty to disclose the same because of court orders. The customer had obtained an injunction under the English jurisdiction restraining disclosure of documents and a subpoena was issued under the US jurisdiction for discovery of documents. The court held as follows: The public interest in upholding the duty of confidentiality existing between banker and customer is subject to being overridden by the greater public interest in making confidential documents relating to the alleged fraud of an international bank available to the parties to private foreign proceedings for the purpose of uncovering that fraud. But such disclosure should be limited to what is reasonably necessary to achieve the purpose of the public interest in disclosure. In the instant case, the public interest in making the documents requested available in the US proceedings, which, if successful, would result in significant further recoveries for the benefit of the BCCI depositors, outweighed the public interest in preserving confidentiality as to those documents, notwithstanding that such disclosure could result in breaches of confidentiality and the terms of the injunction obtained by the customer, as well as the risk that the documents would become available to the world at large. Accordingly, liberty to disclose the documents would be granted, subject to the proviso that disclosure should not be made without taking all reasonably practicable steps to ensure that the documents were suitably redacted.[114]

---

112. *Re Mutual Legal Assistance in Criminal Matters*, (2001) IL Pr 11, CA (Ont). *Atlan v UK*, (2002) 34 EHRR 33 (ECHR) the court considered the impact of the claim of public interest immunity on the right to fair trial.

113. *R v Jamil (Mohd. Ali)*, (2001) EWCA Crimes 1687.

114. *Pharaon v Bank of Credit and Commerce International SA (in liquidation) (Price Waterhouse (a firm) intervening) Price Waterhouse (a firm) v Bank of Credit and Commerce International SA (in liquidation)*, (1998) 4 All ER 455 : (1998) 142 SZLR 251. The court applied the dictum of Sir Richard Scott VC, in *First American Croporation v Sheikh Zayed Al-Nahyan, Clifford v First American Corporation*, (1998) 4 All ER 439 at 448-449.

[115]**[s 125] Information as to commission of offences.—No Magistrate or Police-officer shall be compelled to say whence he got any information as to the commission of any offence, and no Revenue-officer shall be compelled to say whence he got any information as to the commission of any offence against the public revenue.**

***Explanation.*—"Revenue-officer" in this section means any officer employed in or about the business of any branch of the public revenue.**

SYNOPSIS

COMMENT

[s 125.1] Principle.—On grounds of public policy, a magistrate or a police-officer[116] cannot be compelled to give the source of information received by him as to the commission of an offence.[117] Similarly, a revenue-officer cannot be compelled to say whence he got information as to any offence against the public revenue. Such officer may, if he likes, disclose the name of the informant. It is of importance to the public for the detection of crimes that those persons who are the channel by means of which the detection is made should not be unnecessarily disclosed.

The accused is not entitled to elicit from individual prosecution witnesses whether he was a spy or an informer, or discover from police officials the names of persons from whom they had received information; but a detective cannot refuse, on grounds of public policy, to answer a question as to where he was secreted.[118]

Although this section does not in express terms prohibit a witness, if he be willing, from saying whence he got his information, the protection afforded by this section does not depend upon a claim of privilege being made, but it is the duty of the court, apart from objection taken, to exclude such evidence. If objection is taken, it cannot, since the law allows it, be made the ground of adverse inferences against the witness.[119]

In the application of this privilege, the criminal procedure has to accommodate two goals which are at times at odds with each other. On the one hand, it has to afford accused persons an adequate opportunity to establish their innocence. An accused must have an uninhibited right to challenge the evidence against him and establish his innocence. On the other hand, the criminal procedure has to promote the detection of crime. This accommodating process was in evidence in *R v Johnson*.[120] The charge against the accused was supplying controlled drugs. The evidence against him consisted of the testimony of police officers who secretly observed the accused from premises belonging to private residents, who agreed to provide the police with observation posts. The prosecution was granted permission to withhold any information which could lead

---

115. Subs. By Act 3 of 1887, sec 1, for section 125.

116. *Emperor v Bilal Mahomed*, (1940) 42 Bom LR 787 : (1940) Bom 768.

117. *Assistant Collector of Central Excise v TK Prasad*, 1989 Cr LJ (NOC) 28 Mad, recorded information of prizes granted to informants, held privileged. See also *Munna Singh v State of MP*, 1989 Cr LJ 580 (MP), FIR is not a privileged document.

118. *Amrita Lal Hazra v Emperor*, (1915) 42 Cal 957.

119. *Weston v Peart v Mohan Dass*, (1912) 40 Cal 898, 920.

120. *R v Johnson*, (1989) 1 All ER 121.

to the identification of these premises. As a result, the counsel for the accused was not allowed to cross-examine the officers about the location of their observation posts and of the nature of any obstructions to their view. The prosecution relied on public interest immunity as justifying the withholding of information about the observation posts. It is well established that the police may suppress the identity of informants in the interests of combating crime. It was, therefore, held that within the scope of this principle the secrecy of observation posts could be maintained.[121] It was as important to secure public co-operation in providing suitable observation posts as it is to encourage the public to come forward with information. However, it is necessary for the claim for immunity to be entertained that the owners of the premises should object to being identified.[122]

[s 125.2] Informer's identity not allowed to be revealed even *in camera*.—The court of Appeal in England held as follows: Where it was accepted by the judge in an action for wrongful imprisonment and malicious prosecution that to admit evidence as to the identity of an informer would hinder future police investigations and endanger the informer, then it was not open to the court to devise a means for circumventing that, such as requiring the evidence to be given in camera. The court is required to balance the interests of someone seeking damages, with those of the public interest in maintaining the anonymity of informers. Once it is accepted that the public interest in concealing the identity of the informer is greater, and any benefit to the claimant minimal, then there is no residual discretion to order evidence to be given in camera.[123]

[s 126] Professional communications.—No barrister, attorney, pleader or vakil shall at any time[s 126.3] be permitted, unless with his client's express consent, to disclose any communication made to him in the course and for the purpose of his employment as such barrister, pleader, attorney or vakil,[s 126.4] by or on behalf of his client, or to state the contents or condition of any document with which he has become acquainted in the course and for the purpose of his professional employment,[s 126.5] or to disclose any advice given by him to his client in the course and for the purpose of such employment:

Provided that nothing in this section shall protect from disclosure—

(1) any such communication made in furtherance of any [124][illegal] purpose;

(2) any fact observed by any barrister, pleader, attorney or vakil, in the course of his employment as such, showing that any crime or fraud has been committed since the commencement of his employment.

It is immaterial whether the attention of such barrister, [125][pleader], attorney or vakil was or was not directed to such fact by or on behalf of his client.

***Explanation*.—The obligation stated in this section continues after the employment has ceased.**

---

121. See also *R v Rankine*, (1986) 2 All ER 566.
122. For criticism see, 1989 All ER Annual Review, p 154. *Sunil Kumar v State*, 1990 Cr LJ 414 (Del), secret information received under Narcotic Drugs etc. Act, 1985 not recorded before search, not fatal.
123. *Powell v Chief Constable of North Wales, The Times*, February 11, 2000 (CA). The court followed *Marks v Beyfus*, (1890) LR 25 QBD 494.
124. Subs. By Act 18 of 1872, sec. 10, for "criminal".
125. Ins. By Act 18 of 1872, sec. 10.

ILLUSTRATIONS

(a) *A*, a client, says to *B*, an attorney—"I have committed forgery and I wish you to defend me."

As the defence of a man known to be guilty is not a criminal purpose, this communication is protected from disclosure.

(b) *A*, a client, says to *B*, an attorney—"I wish to obtain possession of property by the use of a forged deed on which I request you to sue."

This communication, being made in furtherance of a criminal purpose, is not protected from disclosure.

(c) *A*, being charged with embezzlement, retains *B*, an attorney, to defend him. In the course of the proceedings, *B* observes that an entry has been made in *A*'s account book, charging *A* with the sum said to have been embezzled, which entry was not in the book at the commencement of his employment.

This being a fact observed by *B* in the course of his employment, showing that a fraud has been committed since the commencement of the proceedings, it is not protected from disclosure.

SYNOPSIS

COMMENT

[s 126.1] Principle.—This section is based upon the principle that if communications to a legal adviser were not privileged, a man would be deterred from fully disclosing his case, so as to obtain proper professional aid in a matter in which he is likely to be thrown into litigation.

Under this section no barrister, attorney, pleader or vakil shall at any time be permitted to—

(1) disclose (i) any communication made to him by or on behalf of his client or (ii) any advice given by him to his client in the course and for the purpose of his employment;

(2) to state the contents or conditions of any document with which he has become acquainted in the course and for the purpose of his employment.

The privilege also extends to documents prepared in connection with the client's claim for the dominant purpose of preparing for litigation.[126]

---

126. *Silver Hill Duckling v Minister of Agriculture, Ireland,* 1987 Irish Reports, 289; 1988 CLY 1593. Communication with a lawyer is thus not a publication for the purposes of the law of defamation. *PR. Ramakrishnan v Subramania,* 1988 Cr LJ 124 : AIR 1988 Ker 18; *Rev Fr Bernad Thattil v Ramchandran Pillai,* 1987 Cr LJ 739 (Ker).

The section does not protect from disclosure—

(1) any communication made in furtherance of any illegal purpose;

(2) any fact observed in the course of employment showing that any crime or fraud has been committed since the commencement of the employment. Under section 127 the above provisions apply to interpreters and the clerks or servants of barristers, pleaders, attorneys and vakils.

The section not only protects the legal adviser from disclosing communications made to him by his client when interrogated as a witness, but he is not permitted to do so even if he is willing to give evidence unless with the express consent of his client.[127]

The privilege under this section is not absolute. When defamatory questions are put by a lawyer to a witness in cross-examination on client's instructions without any reasonable basis for putting them, such a communication is not professional and its disclosure is not protected under this section.[128]

[s 126.2] Scope.—Sections 126 to 129 deal with the privilege that is attached to professional communications between the legal adviser and the client. Sections 126 and 128 mention the circumstances under which the legal adviser can give evidence of such professional communications. Section 127 provides that interpreters, clerks or servants of legal advisers are restrained similarly. Section 129 says when a legal adviser can be compelled to disclose the confidential communication which has taken place between him and his client. Law officers have been held to be within the scope of the section.[129] Communications between an insurer and his counsel are also privileged.[130] Notes made by lawyers of statements of witnesses are within the range of protection.[131]

The protection afforded under this section cannot be availed of against an order to produce documents under section 91 of the Code of Criminal Procedure. The documents must be produced, and then, under section 162 of this Act, it will be for the court, after inspection of the documents, if it deems fit, to consider and decide any objections regarding their production or admissibility.[132] Under this section an advocate is not permitted to state the contents or condition of any document with which he has become acquainted in the course and for the purpose of his professional employment. The protection against production or disclosure does not extend to any original document which might have come into the possession of the advocate from his client e.g. a letter addressed to the client which was alleged to be in the brief of the counsel.[133]

---

127. *Mandesan v State of Kerala*, 1995 Cr LJ 61 (Ker).

128. *Deepchand v Sampathraj*, AIR 1970 Mys 34.

129. *MC of Greater Bombay v Vijay Metal Works*, AIR 1982 Bom 6.

130. *R. Ramalingam v PR Thakar*, AIR 1982 Del 486.

131. *Superintendent & LR. v S. Bhowmick*, AIR 1981 SC 917 : 1981 Cr LJ 341 : (1981) 2 SCC 109, a case under the Official Secrets Act, 1923.

132. *Ganga Ram v Habib Ullah*, (1935) 58 All 364.

133. *Chandubhai v State*, AIR 1962 Guj 290.

No privilege can be claimed in respect of a document which came into the possession of the opposite party and has been filed in the court, though it might contain legal advice.[134]

[s 126.3] "At any time".—These words indicate that the legal adviser is not to disclose the communication even when the relation is ended or even after the client's death. The rule is "once privileged always privileged." The explanation to the section clearly shows this.

[s 126.4] "To disclose any communication made to him in the course and for the purpose of his employment as such barrister, pleader, etc.".—Communications protected by the section must be confidential. The word "disclose" shows that the privileged communication must be of a confidential or private nature.[135] It is not every communication made by a person to his legal adviser that is privileged from disclosure. The privilege extends only to communications made to him confidentially, and with a view to obtaining professional advice.[136] Illustration (a) exemplifies this. The section applies as much to what a witness has learned by observation, e.g., by watching a manufacturing process being carried on, as to what is communicated to him by word of mouth or writing.[137] The privilege in respect of professional communication is intended only to protect the interests of a client in respect of any action or prosecution for any prior act or offence. The privilege is not intended for committing any offence.[138]

The section protects from publicity not merely the details of the business, but also its general purport, unless it be known *aliunde* that such business falls within proviso 1 or 2. A solicitor is not at liberty to disclose the nature of his professional employment.[139] If an attorney discloses the facts which came to his knowledge while he was engaged as an attorney, he will be guilty of professional misconduct.[140]

There is no privilege to communications made before the creation of relationship of pleader and client. Where two persons have a dispute about a claim made by one of them upon the other, and both seek the help of a pleader, and one of them makes a statement to the pleader, the statement so made to the pleader by one of the parties is admissible in evidence. If the communication or admission be made by the plaintiff to the witness in the character of his own exclusive pleader or legal adviser, the bond of secrecy is upon the witness; if not, the communication is not privileged.[141]

---

134. *Daya Shanker Dubey v Subhas Kumar*, 1992 Cr LJ 319 (All); *PG Anantasayanam v Miriyala Sathiraju*, AIR 1998 AP 335, an advocate was sought to be summoned to prove sending of notice to the defendant. The contents of the notice were in no way confidential being already communicated. Claim of privilege under the section was not allowed.

135. *Framji Bhicaji v Mohansingh Dhansing*, (1893) 18 Bom 263, 272; *Memon Hajee Haroon Mahomed v Molvi Abdul Karim and Moola Ahmed Moola Abdulla*, (1878) 3 Bom 91; *Emperor v Rodrigues*, (1903) 5 Bom LR 122; *Kalikumar Pal v Rajkumar Pal*, (1931) 58 Cal 1379.

136. *Framji Bhicaji v Mohansingh Dhansing*, (1893) 18 Bom 263; *Emperor v Bala*, (1902) 4 Bom LR 460.

137. *Gopi Lal v Lakhpat Rai*, (1918) 41 All 125.

138. *Antony v GS Naidu*, AIR 1967 Mad 395.

139. *Framji Bhicaji v Mohansingh Dhansing*, (1893) 18 Bom 263.

140. *Re an Attorney*, (1924) 26 Bom LR 887 (FB).

141. *Kalikumar Pal v Rajkumar Pal*, (1931) 58 Cal 1379; *Ditta v Duport Harper Foundries Ltd*, 1998 CLY 96 (336), documentation and audiogram on worker's industrial deafness did not attract legal professional as the dominant purpose of the report prepared by the Bangladeshi Workers' Assn. was not for enabling the worker's solicitor to advice or act with regard to litigation.

[s 126.5] "State the contents...of any document with which he has become acquainted in the course...of his professional employment".—A legal adviser is not bound to produce or to answer any questions concerning the nature or contents of a document entrusted to him professionally by his client. The court has no power to order production of such a document.[142] A pleader is not bound to disclose, at the instance of a third party, the contents of a will that came to his hands in the course of his professional employment even if it is subsequently lost.[143]

[s 126.6] Illegal Purpose *[Proviso 1]*.—This proviso differs from the English law. Under it any communication made in furtherance of an "illegal purpose" is not privileged. Under the English law the purpose must be "criminal" and not merely "illegal."

Disclosure was allowed where the client desired to obtain decree for money on the basis of forged promissory notes.[144]

Communications between solicitors and their clients are protected even if they contain information from third parties.[145] Communications between the solicitors and third parties were disclosable unless they came into existence for the purpose of existing or contemplated litigation.[146]

Legal professional privilege would be overridden where the documents existed to further a fraudulent or criminal purpose. There is no precise definition of the purpose which invokes the exception, although a deliberate misrepresentation by a borrower to a lender to secure a mortgage was within its scope. Privilege would be waived provided that impropriety or bad faith was pleaded, the advice given by the solicitor was used to further the wrongdoing and there was a sufficient factual basis to support the allegation of impropriety.[147]

The privilege of professional communication to the Advocate is not given relating to the signed pleadings filed in the court. A party can be permitted to examine an Advocate of the other party as a witness for the purpose of proving pleadings filed in the court.[148]

[s 126.6.1] *Privilege not abrogated by Right to Information Act, 2005*.—This privilege has not been done away with by the RTI Act. It has to be given effect to notwithstanding the RTI Act. Communications between a client and his lawyer remain protected.[149]

[s 127] Section 126 to apply to interpreters, etc.—The provisions of section 126 shall apply to interpreters, and the clerks or servants of barristers, pleaders, attorneys and vakils.

---

142. *Vishnu v New York Ins. Co*, (1905) 7 Bom LR 709.

143. *Bai Kanta v Bhailal*, (1929) 31 Bom LR 1046.

144. *Gurunanak Provisions Stores v Dalhonumal Savanmal*, AIR 1994 Guj 31.

145. *Balabel v Air India*, (1988) Ch 317 : 1988 CLY 1594.

146. *Birmingham Midshires Mortgage Services Ltd v Ansell*, [1998] PNLR 237 (Ch. D). The court **followed** *Wheeler v Le Marchant*, (1881) 17 Ch D. 675.

147. *Nationwide Building Society v Various Solicitors*, [1999] PNLR 52, (Ch. D). The court considered the decision in *Barclays Bank plc v Eustice*, (1995) 1 WLR 1238 : 1999 CLY 3510.

148. *Chaman Lal v Sunder Lal*, AIR 2016 HP 83, paras 11 and 13.

149. *Karamjit Singh v Govindan Chettiyar*, AIR 2010 NOC 699 (P&H).

COMMENT

This section extends the privilege given by section 126 to interpreters, clerks, or servants of lawyers. It extends to a communication made to a pleader's clerk the same confidential character that attaches to a communication to the pleader direct under section 126.[150]

[s 128] Privilege not waived by volunteering evidence.—If any party to a suit gives evidence therein at his own instance or otherwise, he shall not be deemed to have consented thereby to such disclosure as is mentioned in section 126; and, if any party to a suit or proceeding calls any such barrister, [151][pleader] , attorney or vakil as a witness, he shall be deemed to have consented to such disclosure only if he questions such barrister, attorney or vakil on matters which, but for such question, he would not be at liberty to disclose.

COMMENT

[s 128.1] Waiver of privilege.—The privilege belongs to the client and therefore he alone can waive it. The privilege is not lost by calling the legal adviser as a witness, unless the party having the privilege questions him relating to confidential matters.

[s 129] Confidential communications with legal advisers.—No one shall be compelled to disclose to the Court any confidential communication which has taken place between him and his legal professional adviser, unless he offers himself as a witness, in which case he may be compelled[s 129.3] to disclose any such communications as may appear to the Court necessary to be known in order to explain any evidence which he has given, but no others.

SYNOPSIS

COMMENT

[s 129.1] Scope.—Sections 126, 127 and 128 prevent a legal adviser or his clerk, servant, etc. from disclosing professional communications. This section applies where the client is interrogated, whether he is a party to the suit or not. Documents prepared for litigation or for the purpose of legal advice are privileged even if they are copies of documents which may not be privileged. In the plaintiff's claim against the defendant in respect of an accident, his solicitors obtained copies of hospital records concerned with the plaintiff's treatment. The court of Appeal held that these copies were privileged notwithstanding that the originals could be obtained by the defendant from the hospital by means of a Court order. This is a part of the privilege that the advice given by a

150. *Kameshwar Pershad v Amanutulla*, (1898) 26 Cal 53.
151. Ins. by Act 18 of 1872, sec. 10.

lawyer to his client is not disclosable, the reason being that by revealing the lawyer's copies, the lawyer's advice or strategy would emerge. Copies made by a lawyer are the fruits of his expertise; "in so far as skill is involved it was part of his professional skill in assisting his client to go to the hospital" and get copies.[152]

"Legal professional privilege entitles lawyers and their clients to keep their communication to themselves. They are immune from compulsory process. This immunity may extend to third parties, such as consultants who are recruited to help with the preparation of a case for trial. However, once the material has got out, it should not be kept out of court on account of its confidential nature any more than would any other confidential material. The exercise of the discretion in deciding whether to restrain the use of confidential material involves the striking of a balance between the interests of the plaintiff who seeks to suppress confidential information and the interest of the defendant who seeks to use it."[153]

[s 129.2] Documents pre-read and referred to in judgment.—Where a document relating to a patent revocation was submitted in a Court from where it happened to be read by a judge deciding another case and he referred to it in his judgment, it was held that such a document was in public domain. The court said that it was the effect of rules of the Supreme Court, O XXIV, rule 14A.[154]

If a party becomes a witness of his own accord he shall, if the court requires it, be made to disclose everything necessary to the true comprehension of his testimony.[155]

[s 129.3] "Compelled".—This word does not mean subpoenaed. The section uses the words "compelled to disclose" with reference to the case when a man has offered himself as a witness, and must refer to some force put upon the witness after he is in the witness-box.[156] Once a client reveals in court part of the communication between himself and his legal adviser regarding a transaction in issue, the client thereby waives his privilege with respect to all communications connected with the same transaction. Where a solicitor is employed by two clients in a conveyancing transaction, the communications concerning the transaction between either of them and the solicitor are disclosable in favour of the other.[157] The legal privilege is overridden by the consideration that the client acted in furtherance of crime.[158]

[s 129.4] Chartered Accountant.—A chartered accountant disclosed information which had come to him during the statutory audit of a banking company. Communications were made to several persons including the Prime Minister about the alleged irregularities by the bank. This was held to be a grave professional misconduct.[159]

---

152. *Watson v Cammell Laird & Co (Shipbuilders and Engineers) Ltd,* (1959) 2 All ER 757; *R v Board of Inland Revenue, ex p Goldberg,* (1988) 3 All ER 248, photocopy of a document made for purpose of legal advice, held, privileged, though the original was not.

153. 1989 All ER Annual Review, 152.

154. *Smithkline Beecham Biologicals SA v Connaught Laboratories INC (Disclosure of Documents),* (1999) 4 All ER 498 (CA). The court applied the ruling in *Derby & Co Ltd v Weldon (Documents : Disclosure) The Times,* October 20, 1988.

155. See *Munchershav Bezanji v The New Dhurumsey S & W Co,* (1880) 4 Bom 576, 581.

156. *Moher Sheikh v Queen-Empress,* (1893) 21 Cal 392, 400.

157. *Re Konigsberg (a bankrupt) ex parte the trustees v Konigsberg,* (1989) 3 All ER 289.

158. *R v Governor of Pentonville, ex p Osman,* (1989) 3 All ER 701.

159. *Council of the Institute of Chartered Accountants v Mani S. Abraham,* AIR 2000 Ker 212.

[s 129.5] Medical report, psychiatrist's opinion obtained at request of defendant's solicitors.—It was held that the judge had erred in ordering disclosure of the report. Where, in criminal proceedings, the opinion of an expert had been obtained at the request of the solicitors to a party to the proceedings in circumstances where section 10(1)(b) of the Act[160] applied and that opinion was derived from privileged information from which it could not be separated, it was itself privileged. In the instant case, the predominant purpose of the psychiatrist's examination of the accused had been to report on his mental state to his solicitors. The judge had been wrong, therefore, to conclude that the psychiatrist's opinion resulted from a doctor/patient relationship. A verdict of manslaughter by reason of diminished responsibility was substituted.[161]

[s 129.5.1] ***Communications between DPP and Police.***—Communications between the Director of Public Prosecutions and the police are not subject to the legal professional privilege. The public interest has to be balanced against the need to do justice.[162] The court said that it would examine the documents itself. Legal professional privilege extends to communications with salaried legal advisers, including internal legal departments.[163] The statutory provisions governing the relationship between the police and the DPP are such that where the police sought the DPPs advice on certain matters both the request for advice and the advice given would be protected by legal professional privilege. In the instant case, there was no suggestion that C or W were seeking legal advice from the DPP. The reports were information provided in connection with the investigation of M's murder, in accordance with the statutory framework. Accordingly, they did not attract legal professional privilege. In order to show that the inspection by a party of a particular document was necessary for the fair disposal of a case that party had to show that he would suffer litigious disadvantage if he failed to see the document.[164] If that threshold test is satisfied, an order for inspection would normally only be refused after the court had itself examined the document in the context of material already held by the party.[165] In the instant case, given that the main issues concerned W's state of mind as regards, *inter alia,* his belief in G's guilt, it was likely that the documents would further illuminate the main questions in the case. Where, as in the instant case, the documents as a class were subject to public interest immunity, the court should balance the need for proper protection of the public interest with the need to do justice for the plaintiff in order to determine whether discovery should be ordered. Since G had passed the threshold test, the court would examine the documents and undertake the balancing exercise in order to determine whether they should be disclosed.

[s 130] Production of title-deeds of witness, not a party.—No witness who is not a party to a suit shall be compelled to produce his title-deeds to any property or any document in virtue of which he holds any property as pledgee or mortgagee or any document the production of which might tend to criminate him,[s 130.2] **unless he**

---

160. *Police and Criminal Evidence Act, 1984 [English].*

161. *R v Davies,* [2002] EWCA Crimes 85, *The Times,* March 4, 2002, LJ, CA (Crim Div).

162. *Goodridge v Chief Constable of Hampshire,* (1999) 1 WR 1558 (QBD).

163. *Alfred Crompton Amusement Machines Ltd v Customs and Excise Commissioners (No. 2)* (1974) ACT 405, the court **considered** this case.

164. *Taylor v Anderton,* (1995) 1 WLR 447 **followed.**

165. *Wallace Smith Trust Co Ltd v Deloitte Haskins & Sells,* (1997) 1 WLR 257, the principle of this case was applied.

has agreed in writing to produce them with the person seeking the production of such deeds or some person through whom he claims.

SYNOPSIS

COMMENT

[s 130.1] Principle.—This section is based on the principle that great inconvenience and mischief would result to witnesses if they are compelled to disclose their titles by the production of their title-deeds. The object of the privilege is that the title may not be disclosed and examined.

The section protects a witness, who is not a party to the suit in which he is called, from producing—

(1) title-deeds to any property,

(2) any document in virtue of which he holds any property as pledgee or mortgagee, or

(3) any document the production of which might tend to criminate him, unless he has agreed in writing to produce such document.

It would be entirely optional for the witness to produce his title-deeds, and to raise any objection whatever.

[s 130.2] "Any document the production of which might tend to criminate him".—A book of accounts cannot be withheld on the ground that it tends to incriminate a witness. The mere circumstance that the production of a document may render the witness liable to a civil action does not come within this section.

[166]**[[s 131] Production of documents or electronic records which another person, having possession, could refuse to produce.—No one shall be compelled**[s 131.1] **to produce documents in his possession or electronic records under his control, which any other person would be entitled to refuse to produce if they were in his possession or control, unless such last-mentioned person consents to their production.]**

SYNOPSIS

COMMENT

Persons in possession of documents on behalf of others are generally agents, attorneys, mortgagees, trustees, etc. This section extends to these persons the same protection which the preceding section provides for a witness who is not a party to a suit.

---

166. Subs. by Act 21 of 2000, section 92 and Sch. II–16, for section 131 (w.e.f. 17-10-2000).

It is not open to a litigant to refrain from producing a document which he considers to be irrelevant and if the opposing litigant is dissatisfied he may apply for its production and inspection. If he fails to do so, neither he nor the court at his suggestion is entitled to draw any inference as to its contents.[167]

[s 131.1] "Compelled".—The use of this word indicates that the person in possession of the document will be "*allowed* to produce documents which other persons would be entitled to refuse to produce if such were in their possession. This is in accordance with English law. It would seem to follow that, although a barrister, pleader, attorney, or vakil is forbidden (by section 126) to state the contents of any documents with which he has become acquainted in the course and for the purpose of his professional employment, he will be permitted to produce the document itself if it happen to be in his possession and he choose to do so."[168]

[s 131.2] Information Technology Act, 2000.—***Production of documents [section 131].***— Section 131 has been substituted for the purpose of accommodating electronic records along with documents. The new section says that no one shall be compelled to produce documents in his possession or electronic records under his control which any other person would be entitled to refuse to produce if they were in his possession or control unless he consents to their production.

[s 132] Witness not excused from answering on ground that answer will criminate.—A witness shall not be excused from answering any question as to any matter relevant to the matter in issue[s 132.2] in any suit or in any civil or criminal proceeding, upon the ground that the answer to such question will criminate, or may tend directly or indirectly to criminate, such witness, or that it will expose, or tend directly or indirectly to expose, such witn and, in the absence of any ess to a penalty or forfeiture of any kind:

Proviso.—Provided that no such answer, which a witness shall be compelled to give, shall subject him to any arrest or prosecution, or be proved against him in any criminal proceeding, except a prosecution for giving false evidence by such answer.

SYNOPSIS

COMMENT

[s 132.1] Principle.—Under this section a witness is not excused from answering any question relevant to the matter in issue on the ground that answer to such question may criminate him or expose him to a penalty or forfeiture.

---

167. *Chandra Narayan Deo v Ramchandra*, (1945) 24 Pat 541.

168. See *Field*, 8th Edn, p 803.

[s 132.2] "Any question as to any matter relevant to the matter in issue".—The section does not in terms deal with all criminatory questions which may be addressed to a witness, but only with questions as to matters relevant to the matter in issue. Irrelevant questions should not be allowed, and it may be implied from the limitation in this section that a witness should be excused from answering questions tending to criminate as to matters which are irrelevant.[169] A witness who answers a questions or question put to him by counsel without seeking the protection of this section is not entitled to that protection.[170]

[s 132.3] Protection against prosecution *[Proviso]*.—The section makes a distinction between those cases in which a witness voluntarily answers a question and those in which he is compelled to answer, and gives him a protection in the latter of these cases only. Protection is afforded only to answers which a witness has objected to give or which he has asked to be excused from giving, and which then he has been compelled by the court to give.[171] The mere subpoenaing of a witness or ordering him to go into the witness-box does not compel him to give any particular answer or to answer any particular question. The words "shall be compelled to give" in the proviso apply to pressure put upon a witness after he is in the box, and when he asks to be excused from answering a question.[172] Section 132 existed on the statute book from 1872, i.e., for 78 years prior to the advent of the guarantee under Article 20 of the Constitution of India. The policy under this section appears to be to secure the evidence from whatever sources it is available for doing justice in a case brought before the court. In the process of securing such an evidence, if a witness who is under obligation to state the truth because of the oath taken by him makes any statement which criminate or tend to expose such a witness to a "penalty or forfeiture of any kind etc.," the proviso grants immunity to such a witness by declaring that "no such answer given by the witness shall subject him to any arrest or prosecution or be proved against him in any criminal proceeding."[173]

The proviso to section 132 is a facet of the rule against self-incrimination and the same is statutory immunity against self-incrimination, which deserves the most liberal construction. Therefore, no prosecution can be launched against the maker of a statement falling within the sweep of section 132 on the basis of the "answer" given by a person while deposing as a "witness" before a Court.[174] Refusal to answer any question put to the accused by the court in relation to any evidence that may have been presented against him by the prosecution or the accused giving an evasive or unsatisfactory answer, would not justify the court to return a finding of guilt on this score.[175]

---

169. *Queen v Gopal Doss*, (1881) 3 Mad 271, 277, 278 (FB).

170. *Peddabba Reddi v Varada Reddi*, (1928) 52 Mad 432.

171. *Queen-Empress v Ganu Sonba*, (1888) 12 Bom 440; *Queen v Gopal Doss*, (1881) 3 Mad 271 (FB); *Queen-Empress v Moss*, (1893) 16 All 88; *Kallu v Sital*, (1918) 40 All 271; *Emperor v Pramatha Nath Bose*, (1910) 37 Cal 878; *Jagannath v King-Emperor*, (1934) 10 Luck 169; *Rasool Bhai v Lall Khan*, (1939) Ran 479.

172. *Moher Sheikh v Queen-Empress*, (1893) 21 Cal 392.

173. *R Dineshkumar v State*, AIR 2015 SC 1816 (para 46).

174. *R Dineshkumar v State*, AIR 2015 SC 1816 (para 47). See also *R. Dineshkumar v State Rep. by Inspector of Police*, 2015 Cr LJ 2362 (para 47) (SC).

175. *Nagaraj v State*, (2015) 4 SCC 739 (para 15).

The Allahabad High Court has held that this is too narrow an interpretation. A common sense meaning should be given to the word "compelled". It is impossible to deny that in the case of ordinary laymen unacquainted with the technical terms of this section, they are compelled to answer on oath questions put either by the court or by the counsel, especially when the question is relevant to the case. An answer given by a witness under such circumstance is protected by this section. Whether or not a witness is "compelled" within the meaning of this section to answer any particular question put to him while in the witness-box is in each case a question of fact.[176] The Kerala High Court has similarly held that a witness who is summoned by the court feels the compulsion not only in appearing but also that he is bound to answer questions put to him and is, therefore, entitled to the protection of the proviso.[177]

The Calcutta High Court has held that a witness who makes a voluntary and irrelevant statement not elicited by any question put to him while under examination is not protected by this section. It has, therefore, held that a witness making a voluntary and irrelevant statement to injure the reputation of another is guilty of defamation.[178]

According to an earlier decision of the Madras High Court a witness is not guilty of defamation for any statements made in the witness-box.[179] But subsequently it has held that a witness who answers a question put to him by counsel without seeking the protection of this section is not entitled to any protection as the statements made by him are entitled not to an absolute but only to a qualified privilege.[180]

The Bombay High Court has in a Full Bench case laid down that relevant statements made by a witness on oath or solemn affirmation in a judicial proceeding are not protected by this proviso where the witness has not objected to answering the questions put to him.[181] A witness who makes defamatory statements in a witness-box comes within the purview of section 499, Indian Penal Code.[182]

The former Nagpur High Court has held that there is no essential difference between this section and section 161(2), Code of Criminal Procedure, 1973. Section 161(2) does not go further than this section.[183]

Protection under the proviso to this section cannot be granted to an officer of a company with regard to answers given by him in his public examination which might tend to incriminate him and can be used in criminal as well as civil proceeding that might ensue, even though he may be compelled to give the same by reason of the

---

176. *Emperor v Banarsi*, (1923) 46 All 254; *Emperor v Chatur Singh*, (1920) 43 All 92; *Emperor v Ganga Sahai*, (1920) 42 All 257.

177. *MP Gangadharan v State SI of Police*, 1989 Cr LJ 2455 (Ker), following *Kunhappan v State of Kerala*, (1987) 2 Ker LT 222. The court would not refuse summoning a witness only because he would have to testify against himself. There is enough protection in the proviso. *Usha Devi v Jagdish Prasad*, 1988 Cr LJ 1239 (All). *Janardan Subrao Pal v Chandra Kamalaksha Pal*, 2003 Cr LJ 2909 (Bom), the accused deposed as a prosecution witness in another criminal case under court's summons, it could not be regarded as a voluntary statement, not allowed to be used against him in a pending prosecution, except if he were charged with giving false evidence.

178. *Haidar Ali v Abru Mia*, (1905) 32 Cal 756.

179. *Manjaya v Sesha Shetti*, (1888) 11 Mad 477.

180. *Peddabba Reddi v Varada Reddi*, (1928) 52 Mad 432.

181. *Bai Shanta v Umrao Amir*, (1925) 28 Bom LR 1 : 50 Bom 162 (FB).

182. *Ibid.*

183. *Hittu v Sheolal*, (1947) Nag 899.

provisions of section 478(5) of the Companies Act, 1956.[184] Similarly section 171A of the Sea Customs Act, 1878, does not limit the right of interrogation to questions the answers whereto may not incriminate the person interrogated.[185]

It has been held that the privilege against self-incrimination could rightly be claimed by a defendant who had been ordered to be cross examined in contemplation of possible contempt proceedings in the same action. The argument that privilege was unavailable where the contempt arose out of statements made in the instant case was not borne out by the authorities.[186]

In a case, the Public Prosecutor realised that the approver who was appearing as witness was not desirous of telling the court about the conspiracy. The Special Public Prosecutor put a specific question to the approver as to whether he wanted to tell the court about the conspiracy to which his answer was in the negative. Immediately, the Special Public Prosecutor issued a certificate under section 308, CrPC that the approver had not complied with the condition on which pardon was tendered to him and, therefore, he may be tried separately. Upon this, when the defence requested to cross-examine the approver, the request was opposed by the Special Public Prosecutor on the ground that once the Public Prosecutor forfeits the pardon, the witness is relegated back to the status of accused to be tried separately for the same offence and as such, the approver loses his status as witness of the prosecution, and therefore, his entire evidence though will be on record but cannot be used for any purpose and as such the question of cross-examining such hostile witness by other accused does not arise. Referring to section 132 of the Evidence Act, it was held by Supreme Court that once the pardon forfeits, the approver becomes an accused and he cannot be compelled to be a witness in view of the protection of Article 20(3) of the Constitution of India. Accordingly, it was held that there is no question of such person being further examined for the prosecution and, therefore, no occasion arises for the defence to cross-examine him.[187]

---

184. *Gill & Co v Madhav Mills*, (1969) 72 Bom LR 679; *Odyssey Re (London) Ltd v OIC Run off Ltd*, The Times Mar 17, 2000 CA : 2000 CLY 106, a company is bound by the perjured evidence of a director. In a previous proceeding the evidence given by the director and general manager of the company was held to be credible and as a result judgment was given in favour of the company. It emerged in a subsequent proceeding before a different judge that the evidence given in the earlier case was perjured, the judgment was set aside. The court said that it was a common ground that where fraud was that of a party to the action, or, where a corporation was a party and the fraudulent evidence could be treated as that of the corporation, then the judgment could be set aside, but it was necessary to determine whether S had possessed sufficient status to make his fraudulent evidence that of OIC. Although the perjured evidence was that of a director and managing director of a party and not that of a party to the action, nevertheless it would be unjust not to treat it as being that of the company. The court **followed** *Hunter v Chief Constable of the West Midlands*, (1980) QB 283 : (1980) CLY 2609 and *R v Andrews-Weatherfoil Ltd*, (1972) 1 WLR 118 : (1972) CLY 594.

185. *Hira H Advani v The State*, (1969) 73 Bom LR 112 (SC). The section is not violative of Article 20(3) of the Constitution which provides a protection to an accused person from being compelled to be a witness against himself. See *S Raghbir Singh Gill v Gurcharan Singh Tohra*, (1980) 2 SCJ 454 : AIR 1980 SC 1362 : 1980 Supp SCC 53.

186. *Memory Corp Plc v Sidhu (No. 2)*, (2000) Ch 645, Ch D. The court **followed** *Comer Products (UK) Ltd v Hawtez Plastics Ltd*, (1971) 2 QB 67 and distinguished *Rice v Gonden*, (1843) 13 Sim 580.

187. *State of Maharashtra v Abu Salem Abdul Kayyum Ansari*, (2010) 10 SCC 179.

A witness is entitled to claim privilege in relation to any piece of information of evidence on which the prosecution might wish to rely not only in establishing guilt but also in making their decision whether to prosecute or not.[188]

[s 132.3.1] ***Claim of privilege through solicitor.***—The privilege against self-incrimination cannot be claimed on an affidavit by a solicitor on behalf of his client. The authorities showed that the privilege had to be claimed on oath by the witness who sought to rely on it, whether as a reason for refusing to answer a question in the witness box, not disclosing a document on discovery or not answering an interrogatory. It was not necessary that the witness seeking to rely on the privilege describe in detail how he might be incriminated, as to do so could render him vulnerable to the danger from which the privilege is designed to protect him. But that does not remove the obligation on the witness to swear an oath in person, even where support for the claim and its substantiation came from another source.[189]

[s 132.3.2] ***Right of accused to maintain silence.***—There is no cavil over the proposition that an accused has the right to maintain silence and not to disclose his defence before trial.[190]

[s 133] Accomplice.—An accomplice shall be a competent witness against an accused person; and a conviction is not illegal merely because it proceeds upon the uncorroborated testimony of an accomplice.

SYNOPSIS

COMMENT

[s 133.1] Principle.—The evidence of an accomplice, though it is uncorroborated, may form the basis for a conviction.

This section is the only absolute rule of law as regards the evidence of an accomplice. But illustration (b) to section 114 is a rule of guidance to which also the court should have regard. It is, however, not a hard-and-fast presumption, incapable of rebuttal, a *presumptio juris et de jure*.[191] The combined effect of this section and section 114, Illustration (b), is that though the conviction of an accused on the testimony of an accomplice cannot be said to be illegal, yet the courts will, as a

---

188. *Den Norske Bank A/A v Antonatos*, [1998] 3 WLR 711 (CA). The court applied *Sociedade Nacional de Combustiveis de Angola UEE v Lundqvist*, [1990] 3 All ER 283.

189. *Downie v COE, The Times*, November 28, 1997 (CA).

190. *Yogendra Kumar Jaiswal v State of Bihar*, (2016) 3 SCC 183, para 161.

191. *Emperor v Shrinivas*, (1905) 7 Bom LR 969.

matter of practice, not accept the evidence of such a witness without corroboration in material particulars.[192]

A statement to this effect to be found in the judgment of Supreme Court in *Dagdu v State of Maharashtra*:[193]

> There is no antithesis between S. 133 and illustration (b) to S. 114, because the illustration only says that the court 'may' presume a certain state of affairs. It does not seek to raise a conclusive and irrebuttable presumption. Reading the two together the position which emerges is that though an accomplice is a competent witness and though a conviction may lawfully rest on his uncorroborated testimony yet the court is entitled to presume and may indeed be justified in presuming that no reliance can be placed on the evidence of an accomplice unless that evidence is corroborated in material particulars, by which it meant that there has to be some independent evidence tending to incriminate the particular accused in the commission of the crime. It is hazardous, as a matter of prudence, to proceed upon the evidence of a self-confessed criminal, who, in so far as an approver is concerned has to testify in terms of the pardon tendered to him.

Reading section 133 and Illustration (b) to section 114 of the Evidence Act, 1872 together, the courts in India have held that while it is not illegal to act upon the uncorroborated testimony of the accomplice, the rule of prudence so universally followed has to amount to the rule of law, that it is unsafe to act on the evidence of an accomplice unless it is corroborated in material aspects, so as to implicate the accused. The reasons for requiring corroboration of the testimony of an accomplice are that an accomplice is likely to swear falsely in order to shift the guilt from himself and that he is an immoral person being a participator in crime who may not have any regard to any sanction of the oath and in the case of an approver, on his own admission, he is a criminal who gives evidence under a promise of pardon and supports the prosecution with the hope of getting his freedom.[194]

The testimony of an accomplice cannot be used against another accused.[195]

The court may consider, though it is not bound to consider, an accomplice unworthy of credit unless he is corroborated in material particulars. The evidence of an accomplice requires to be accepted with a great deal of caution and scrutiny because—

(a) he has a motive to shift guilt from himself;

(b) he is an immoral person likely to commit perjury on occasion;

---

192. *Bhiva Doulu Patil*, (1962) 65 Bom LR 347; *Khokan Giri v State of West Bengal*, AIR 2017 SC 668 : LNIND 2016 SC 639, such corroboration must connect the accused with crime and also the corroboration must be from an independent source, meaning thereby, one accomplice cannot corroborate another; *State of Kerala v Thomas*, (1986) 2 SCC 411, 413 : 1986 SCC (Cri) 176, the testimony of *particpas criminis* requires some independent corroboration for acceptance. *Shankar v State of MP*, 1997 Cr LJ 3876 (MP), the accomplice did not disclose the ghastly incident for 7 days without any reason, nor there was any corroboration. The testimony was held to be not reliable.

193. *Dagdu v State of Maharashtra*, (1977) 3 SCC 68 at pp 74-75 : AIR 1977 SC 1579 : 1977 Cr LJ 1206.

194. *D Velayutham v State*, AIR 2015 SC 2506 (para 6).

195. *Krishnan v State of TN*, AIR 2014 SC 2548 (para 20).

(c) he hopes for pardon or has secured it, and so favours the prosecution.[196]

However, if the statement of the accomplice/approver implicating the accused is otherwise admissible and reliable, it can sustain conviction.[197]

[s 133.2] Who is an accomplice.—The word "accomplice" has not been defined under the Evidence Act and therefore presumed to have been used in the ordinary sense. A person concerned in the commission of crime, a partner in crime and associate in guilt is an accomplice. He takes part in the crime and is privy to the criminal intent. However, a witness forced to pay on promise of doing or forbearing to do any official act by a public servant, is not a partner in crime and associate in guilt and therefore cannot be said to be an accomplice. It has long been a rule of practice, which has become equivalent to the rule of law, that the evidence of an accomplice is admissible but to be acted upon, ordinarily requires corroboration. The contractor who gave bribe, therefore, cannot be said to be an accomplice as the same was extorted from him.[198] An accomplice by becoming an approver becomes a prosecution witness. An approver's evidence has to satisfy a double test: (1) his evidence must be reliable and (2) his evidence should be sufficiently corroborated.[199]

An accomplice cannot corroborate himself; tainted evidence does not lose its taint by repetition. "The danger of acting on accomplice evidence is not merely that the accomplice is on his own admission a man of bad character who took part in the offence and afterwards to save himself betrayed his former associates, and who has placed himself in a position in which he can hardly fail to have a strong *bias* in favour of the prosecution; the real danger is that he is telling a story which in its general outline is true, and it is easy for him to work into the story matter which is untrue. He may implicate ten people in an offence, and the story may be true in all its details as to eight of them, but untrue as to the other two, whose names have been introduced because they are enemies of the approver. This tendency to include the innocent with the guilty is peculiarly prevalent in India, and it is very difficult for the courts to guard against the danger. The only real safeguard against the risk of condemning the innocent with the guilty lies in insisting on independent evidence which in same measure implicates each accused."[200]

---

196. *Barkat Ali v The Crown,* (1916) PR No. 2 of 1917 Cr. The evidence of an approver has more sanctity than a mere confession under section 164 CrPC because an approver deposes in open court and is subject to cross-examination by the other accused, *Re Deivendran,* 1994 Cr LJ 2209 (Mad); *Lal Chand v State of Haryana,* AIR 1984 SC 226 : 1984 Cr LJ 164 : (1984) 1 SCC 686, where the Supreme Court said : The evidence of a witness, who on his own admission, was a person who had no compunction in betraying an illiterate woman who had engaged him to look after her affairs and had placed implicit trust in him, deserved to be scrutinised closely and carefully and in the absence of corroboration in regard to material aspects of the case, the court would be reluctant to accept his testimony apart from the fact that he being an approver his evidence calls for corroboration even otherwise.

197. *Air Customs Officer v Pramod Kumar Dhamija,* (2016) 4 SCC 153, para 13.3.

198. *CM Sharma v State of AP,* (2010) 15 SCC 1.

199. *Shankar v State of TN,* 1994 Cr LJ 3071. *MO Shamshudin v State of Kerala,* (1995) 3 SCC 351 : (1995) 2 Andh LT 114 (Cri), the word "accomplice" is not defined in the Act. The word has been used in its ordinary sense which means guilty partner or associate in a crime.

200. *Bhuboni Sahu v The King,* AIR 1949 PC 257 at para 4 : (1949) 51 Bom LR 955. There are somewhat similar observations of the Supreme Court. See, for example, *State of TN v Suresh,* AIR 1998 SC 1044 : (1998) 2 SCC 372, the evidence of an accomplice is not totally bereft of value, can be relied upon for recording conviction.

An accomplice is a person who participates in the commission of the actual crime charged against an accused. He is to be a *participes criminis*. There are two cases, however, in which a person has been held to be an accomplice even if he is not a *participes criminis*. Receivers of stolen property are taken to be accomplices of the thieves from whom they receive goods, on a trial for theft. Accomplices in previous similar offences committed by the accused on trial are deemed to be accomplices in the offence for which the accused is on trial when evidence of the accused having committed crime of identical type on other occasions be admissible to prove the system and intent of the accused in committing the offence charged.[201] A witness, who assisted the criminals to the extent of keeping a look out to see whether the police were approaching, is in the position of an accomplice.[202] A witness who is not a guilty associate in crime or who does not sustain such a relation to the criminal act that he could be jointly indicted with the principal is not an accomplice as the element of *mens rea* is entirely absent. A witness who only happens to be conversant with a crime or who makes no attempt to prevent it or who does not disclose it, is not an accomplice and the rule of practice as to corroboration does not apply to his evidence.[203]

There is no warrant for the proposition that if a man sees the perpetration of a crime and does not give information of it to anyone else, he might well be regarded as an accomplice.[204] A rustic villager acting according to the advice of his master and not disclosing under the threat of death the commission of an offence by his master for some time and thereafter disclosing the same to a police informant and before a magistrate, such person could be called as an active participant in the crime. He could be termed to be an accomplice.[205] A pretended confederate such as a detective, spy or decoy is not an accomplice. "If such a person has made himself an agent for the prosecution before associating with the wrongdoers or before the actual perpetration of the offence he is not an accomplice; but he may be an accomplice if he extends no aid to the prosecution until after the offence has been committed."[206]

The Supreme Court of India held that the rule laid down in *Rex v Baskerville*[207] with regard to the admissibility of the uncorroborated evidence of an accomplice is the law in India also so far as accomplices are concerned and it is not any higher in the case of sexual offences. The only clarification of the rule that is necessary for the purposes of India is where this class of offence is tried by a judge without the aid of jury. In such cases it is necessary that the judge should give some indication in his judgment that he has had the rule of caution in his mind and should proceed to give reasons for considering it unnecessary to require corroboration on the facts of the particular case before him and show why he considers it safe to convict without corroboration in that particular case. There is, however, no rule of law or practice that there must in every

201. *RK Dalmia v Delhi Administration*, AIR 1962 SC 1821 : (1962) 2 Cr LJ 805.
202. *Dhanapati De v Emperor*, (1944) 2 Cal 312.
203. *Ghudo v King-Emperor*, (1945) Nag 315.
204. *Vemi Reddy Sathyanarayan Reddy v The State of Hyderabad*, (1956) Hyd 386.
205. *Subash Chandra Pandia v State of Orissa*, 2001 Cr LJ 4108 (Ori).
206. *Basheeruddin Ahamed v State of Mysore*, (1951) Mys 464.
207. *Rex v Baskerville*, (1916) 2 KB 658. After some difference of opinion with this decision in *Director of Public Prosecutions v Kilbourn*, (1973) AC 729; (1973) 1 All ER 440, the supremacy of the rule in *Baskerville* was again restored in *R v Beck*, (1982) 1 All ER 807 (CA), that the corroborative evidence should not only show that part of the accomplice testimony is true; but should go further and also implicate the other accused. To the same effect, *R v Donat*, (1986) 2 Cr App R 1973.

case be corroboration before a conviction can be allowed to stand.[208] The Supreme Court has also held that a conviction can be based on the uncorroborated testimony of an accomplice provided the judge has the rule of caution in mind.[209] The evidence of an accomplice being that of an interested witness or tainted one, caution requires that there should be corroboration from an independent source in some material aspect of not only of the commission of crime but also his involvement in it, before its acceptance.[210]

An accomplice is a competent witness and conviction can lawfully rest upon his uncorroborated testimony, yet the court is entitled to presume and may indeed, be justified in presuming in the generality of cases that no reliance can be placed on the evidence of an accomplice unless the evidence is corroborated in material particulars, which means that there has to be some independent witness tending to incriminate the particular accused in the commission of the crime. Since he is an accomplice in a crime who has not been made an accused/put to trial, his evidence is required to be considered with care and caution. An accomplice who has not been put on trial is a competent witness as he deposes in the court after taking oath and there is no prohibition in any law not to act upon his deposition without corroboration.[211]

Therefore, a definite rule has become crystallised to the effect that though a conviction can be based on uncorroborated evidence of an accomplice, as a rule of prudence it is unsafe to place reliance on the uncorroborated testimony of an approver as required by Illustration (b) of section 114 of the Act.[212]

According to the Supreme Court the four principles with regard to the nature and extent of corroboration are: (1) that it is not necessary that there should be independent confirmation of every material circumstance in the sense that the independent evidence in the case, apart from the testimony of the complainant or the accomplice, should in itself be sufficient to sustain conviction; all that is required is that there must be some additional evidence rendering it probable that the story of the accomplice (or complainant) is true and that it is reasonably safe to act upon it, (2) that independent evidence must not only make it safe to believe that the crime was committed, but must in some way reasonably connect or tend to connect the accused, with it by confirming in some material particular the testimony of the accomplice or complainant that the

---

208. *Rameshwar v State of Rajasthan*, (1952) SCR 377 : AIR 1952 SC 54; *Jasbir Singh v Vippin Kumar Jaggi*, 2001 Cr LJ 3993 : AIR 2001 SC 2734, approver's evidence is looked upon with great suspicion. But if found trustworthy, it can be decisive in securing conviction. [at p 3998].

209. *Kashmira Singh v State of Madhya Pradesh*, (1952) SCR 526 : AIR 1952 SC 159 : 1952 Cr LJ 839; *Bhairon Lal v The State*, (1952) Raj 669; *Autar Singh* (1960) Pun 111.

210. *Vimit v State of Maharashtra*, 1994 Cr LJ 1791. *Vasudevan v State*, 1993 Cr LJ 3151, there must be additional evidence rendering it plausible.

211. *Prithipal Singh v State of Punjab*, (2012) 1 SCC 10.

212. *Suresh Chandra Bahri v State of Bihar*, AIR 1994 SC 2420 : 1994 Cr LJ 3271. *Sevaka Perumal v State of TN*, AIR 1991 SC 1463 : 1991 Cr LJ 1845 : (1991) 3 SCC 1463, approver's evidence is acceptable if corroborated by independent evidence, ocular or circumstantial in respect of general particulars. *MO Shamshudin v State of Kerala*, (1995) 3 SCC 351 : (1995) 2 Andh. LT 114 (Cri), whether in a particular case the evidence of accomplice should be accepted without corroboration would depend upon the facts and circumstances of each case. *UOI v JS Brar*, AIR 1993 SC 773 : (1993) 1 SCC 176 : 1993 All LJ 807, the accomplice completed his deposition on behalf of the prosecution, the defence was afforded opportunity to cross-examine him, his evidence became admissible. *Joseph v State of Kerala*, 1993 Supp 4 SCC 7 : 1993 Cr LJ 3538, the testimony of the approver was amply corroborated by eye-witnesses and recovery of weapons, etc., held, the prosecution established their case to that extent beyond a reasonable doubt.

accused committed the crime, (3) that the corroboration must come from independent sources and thus ordinarily the testimony of one accomplice would not be sufficient to corroborate that of another, (4) that the corroboration need not be direct evidence that the accused committed the crime—it is sufficient if it is merely circumstantial evidence of his connection with the crime.[213]

The Supreme Court also held that while approver's evidence has to be looked upon with great suspicion, it could be decisive in securing conviction if it is found to be trustworthy.[214]

[s 133.3] Disclosure of accomplice's criminal record.—It has been suggested that it ought to be a normal practice for the previous convictions of an accomplice giving evidence to be disclosed to the crown at the outset. The court said that if an accomplice witness with a heavy criminal record was protected against disclosure of such record, then, as against the crown witnesses, such witnesses be enjoying too much freedom.[215]

[s 133.4] Partisan witness.—In the case of evidence of an accomplice no conviction can be based on his evidence unless it is corroborated in material particulars, but as regards the incidence of a partisan witness it is open to a Court to convict an accused person solely on the basis of that evidence if it is satisfied that that evidence is reliable. But it may in appropriate cases look for corroboration.[216] In a murder trial the evidence on behalf of the prosecution of the son or daughter of the victim cannot be discarded on the mere ground of their close interest in the deceased.[217] Evidence of related witnesses has to be scrutinized with caution.[218] In cases of communal disturbances the evidence given by witnesses should not be discarded only on the ground that the persons who

213. *Rameshwar v State of Rajasthan*, (1952) SCR 377 : AIR 1952 SC 54 : (1952) Cr LJ 547. In *Ram Narayan v Rajasthan*, AIR 1973 SC 1188 : 1973 Cr LJ 914 : (1973) 3 SCC 805, the Supreme Court reversed a High Court decision based on uncorroborated testimony. *Abdul Sattar v UT Chandigarh*, AIR 1986 SC 1438 : (1985) Supp SCC 599 : 1985 SCC (Cri) 505. Where the participation of the alleged accomplice was itself a doubtful fact; *Mukhtiar Kaur v State of Punjab*, AIR 1980 SC 1871; *Kannan Singh v State of TN*, AIR 1989 SC 396 : 1989 Cr LJ 825 : 1989 Supp (1) SCC 81, where all the above tests were satisfied and, therefore, the testimony was found to be acceptable without corroboration. See also *State v Jagjit Singh*, 1989 Cr LJ 986 : AIR 1989 SC 598, approver resiling from his earlier statement, not material.

214. *Jasbir Singh v Vipin Kumar Jaggi*, AIR 2001 SC 2734 : 2001 Cr LJ 3993.

215. *R v Taylor; R v Goodman*, 1998 CLY 302 (864) [CA (Crim. Div.)].

216. *Bhanuprasad v State of Gujarat*, (1968) 71 Bom LR 43 (SC). *State of Bihar v Basawan Singh*, AIR 1958 SC 500. A testimony cannot be rejected only on the ground that the witness was interested and inimical. *Babu v UP*, AIR 1980 SC 443 : (1979) 4 SCC 465 : 1980 Cr LJ 392; See further *Ram Ashrit v Bihar*, AIR 1981 SC 942 : 1981 Cr LJ 484 : (1981) 2 SCC 60 which explains the situation where all witnesses are interested; *State of UP v Manohar Lal*, AIR 1981 SC 2073 : 1981 Supp SCC 35 : 1981 Cr LJ 1701. For difference between interested and related witness see *State of Rajasthan v Kalki*, AIR 1981 SC 1390 : 1981 Cr LJ 1012. An interested witness is not like approver, only more precaution is necessary. *State of UP v Ballabh Das*, AIR 1985 SC 1384 : (1985) Cr LJ 2009 : (1985) 3 SCC 703; A son of the deceased cannot be disbelieved. *Natthu v UP*, AIR 1977 SC 2096 : (1977) 4 SCC 293 : 1977 Cr LJ 1578; *Guli Chand v Raj*, AIR 1974 SC 775 : 1974 Cr LJ 510.

217. *Bhupender Singh v State of Punjab*, AIR 1968 SC 1438 : 1969 Cr LJ 6; *Nafiz Ad v State*, 1989 Cr LJ 1296 (Bom), where the accomplice turned approver was a drug peddlar along with the accused persons, testimony uncertain, no corroboration available, hence not relied upon.

218. *Birender Poddar v State of Bihar*, 2011 Cr LJ 3120 (SC).

gave such evidence belong to one particular community and as such are partisan or interested witnesses.[219]

[s 133.5] Trap witness.—It is not safe to rely upon the evidence of a trap witness without corroboration.[220] However, it is not necessary to have corroboration of all the circumstances of the case or every detail of the crime. It will be sufficient if there is corroboration as to the material circumstances of the crime and of the identity of the accused in relation to the crime.[221] The Supreme Court has, however, cautioned against a harsh approach which would make things impossible to prove.[222]

[s 133.6] Nature of corroboration required.—Generally speaking the corroboration is of two kinds. Firstly, the court has to satisfy itself that the statement of the approver is credible in itself and there is evidence other than the statement of the approver that the approver himself had taken part in the crime.[223] In order to determine the creditworthiness of the testimony of the approver and the nature and the extent of the corroboration the court must consider the question as to how the approver came to be arrested and how did he become a participant in the crime, the role played by him in the crime and the circumstances in which he decided to become an approver.[224] Secondly, the court seeks corroboration of the approver's evidence with respect to the part of other accused persons in the crime, and this evidence has to be of such a nature as to connect the other accused with the crime.[225] The corroboration need not

---

219. *Manilal v State*, AIR 1969 Ori 176; *Vinod Chaturvedi v State of MP*, (1984) 2 SCC 350 : AIR 1984 SC 911 : 1984 Cr LJ 814. Testimony of a co-occupant that letting was not on leave and licence basis and that he would vacate whenever asked to do so was held to be not unnatural and hence reliable even if he was an interested witness. *Vishnudeo Kumar v State of Bihar*, 1986 Supp SCC 656 : 1987 SCC (Cr) 180 Evidence regarding recovery of cash and gold from accused's house which was not the subject-matter of the charge the evidence not sufficient to connect accused with the crime. *Ramprasad v State of Maharashtra*, 1999 Cr LJ 2889 : AIR 1999 SC 1969 conviction on sole basis is permissible if the accomplice passes the test of reliability and corroboration in material particulars. His statement before the magistrate before pardon can be used as former statement of the witness. He did not disclose the name of one of the accomplices. This was held to be of no significance because in his confessional statement he mentioned the other accused persons also.

220. *Ramnarayan Patnaik v State*, 1989 Cr LJ 172 (Ori), where no independent corroboration was available.

221. *Major E G Barsay v State of Bombay*, AIR 1961 SC 1762 : (1962) 2 SCR 195. *Raghubir Singh v Haryana*, AIR 1974 SC 1516 : 1974 Cr LJ 1062 : (1974) 4 SCC 560. *State of UP v Hakim Singh*, AIR 1980 SC 2128 : 1980 Cr LJ 1478, mid-night murder, home people only naturally witnesses; *Maharaj Singh v Rajasthan*, AIR 1981 SC 936 : 1981 Cr LJ 477.

222. *State of Maharashtra v Narsingrao*, AIR 1984 SC 63 : 1984 Cr LJ 4 : (1984) 1 SCC 446 : 1984 SCC (Cri) 109 : 1984 Mad LJ (Cri) 207. Accused trapped with the use of phenolphathalein, *Darshan Kumar v State of Punjab*, 1988 Cr LJ 1446 (P&H). *Sadashiv Mahadeo v State of Maharashtra*, 1990 Cr LJ 600 : AIR 1990 SC 287, unsuccessful evidence of trap and the Supreme Court explains ingredients.

223. *Chandan v State of Rajasthan*, AIR 1988 SC 599 : 1988 Cr LJ 842 : (1988) 1 SCC 696 : 1988 SCC (Cri) 238, the testimony of the approver seemed motivated in self-interest, hence rejected; evidence of test identification witnesses who were not examined, not good for corroboration.

224. *Rampal Pithwa Rahidas v State of Maharashtra*, 1994 Cr LJ 2320 : (1994) 1 Crimes 1017.

225. *Saravanbhavan v State of Madras*, AIR 1966 Mad 1273; See also *Lacchi Ram v State of Punjab*, AIR 1967 SC 792 : 1967 Cr LJ 671. See also *Balwant Kaur v UT Chandigarh*, AIR 1988 SC 139 : (1988) 1 SCC 1 : 1988 Cr LJ 398, where the corroborative evidence to connect the accused with the crime was not there. The wife of the deceased, the appellant in this case, was alleged to have exhorted the two killers to eliminate her husband. One of the killers became approver. He testified that she was involved in sex affairs with both of them and promised to live as the wife of one of them after the elimination of her husband. No corroboration of these particulars was available. The Supreme Court extended the benefit of doubt to the accused young girl.

be direct evidence of the commission of the offence by the accused. If it is merely circumstantial evidence of his connection with the crime it will be sufficient.[226] The corroboration need not consist of evidence which, standing alone, would be sufficient to justify the conviction of the accused. If that were the law, it would be unnecessary to examine an approver. All that seems to be required is that the corroboration should be sufficient to afford some sort of independent evidence to show that the approver is speaking the truth with regard to the accused person whom he seeks to implicate.[227]

Some of these points have been restated by the Supreme Court in terms of the following propositions. In reference to the requirement of corroboration, the word used is "may" and not "must". No decision of a Court can make it "must". It ultimately depends upon the court's view as to the credibility of the evidence tendered by an accomplice. If it is found credible and cogent, the court may record a conviction on its basis even if not corroborated. Corroboration in material particulars means that there should be some additional or independent evidence (i) rendering it probable that the story revealed by the accomplice is true and that it is reasonably safe to act upon it; (ii) identifying the accused as one of those or among those, who committed the offence; (iii) showing the circumstantial evidence of his connection with the crime, though it may not be direct evidence, and (iv) ordinarily the testimony should not be sufficient to corroborate that of the other.

In the words of the Supreme Court as uttered in *State of TN v Suresh*:[228] "The law is not that the evidence of an accomplice deserves outright rejection if there is no corroboration. What is required is to adopt great circumspection and care when dealing with the evidence of an accomplice. Though there is no legal necessity to seek corroboration of accomplice's evidence, it is desirable that the court seeks reassuring circumstances to satisfy the judicial conscience that the evidence is true." Applying it to the facts of the case, the court said:

> Where in a murder trial the evidence of the accomplice was not totally bereft of reassuring circumstances, the accused could be convicted on the basis of such evidence.

The fact that the testimony of an accomplice was found to be not acceptable in respect of one of the accused persons for want of independent corroboration should not be taken to cast a doubt upon her reliability as a witness in respect of other accused persons.[229]

---

226. *KK Jadav v State of Gujarat*, AIR 1966 SC 821 : 1962 Supp (2) SCR 726; see also *Ramanlal v State of Bombay*, AIR 1960 SC 961 : 1960 Cr LJ 1380; *Major EG Barsay v State of Bombay*, AIR 1961 SC 1762.

227. *Bishnu Pada Chatterji v Emperor*, (1944) 2 Cal 327; *Ranjeet Singh v State of Rajasthan*, AIR 1988 SC 672 : 1988 Cr LJ 845 : (1988) 1 SCC 633 : 1988 SCC (Cri) 229, corroborating evidence must be independent and reliable. Here the approver was related both ways and, therefore, could not have been interested in one or the other and also gave a detailed account of his own participation, testimony accepted. *Narayan Chetanram Chaudhary v State of Maharashtra*, 2000 Cr LJ 4640 (SC), the statement of the accomplice was vivid in explanations and inspired confidence of the court. Corroborative evidence left no doubt as to the involvement of the accused in the crime. Conviction of accused was held not liable to be set aside.

228. *State of TN v Suresh*, AIR 1998 SC 1044 at 1048 : (1998) 2 SCC 372.

229. *Ramadhar Basu v State of WB*, AIR 2000 SC 908 : 2000 Cr LJ 1417 : (2000) 3 SCC 161, *Mohan v State of Rajasthan*, 1997 Cr LJ 1179 : AIR 1997 SC 1704, the approver stated that he was a party to the conspiracy to murder. His statement was corroborated by prosecution witnesses and medical evidence. Some discrepancies in his version of injuries caused by blunt weapon did not make it as liable to be rejected. *Perajmal Ballaji v State of TN*, 1998 Cr LJ 1416 (SC), the evidence of accomplice in this was not bereft of reassuring circumstances. It could be relied on for convicting the accused.

The testimony of an accomplice can be made the basis of conviction without corroboration. The requirement of corroboration is a matter of prudence. The word "may" in section 114(b) cannot be converted to mean "must".[230]

[s 133.7] Bribery.—The rule requiring corroboration of the evidence of an accomplice applies with very little force where the accused is charged with the offence of extorting a bribe, and the accomplice is not a willing participant in the offence but a victim of that offence.[231] Persons coming technically within the category of accomplices cannot be treated as on precisely the same footing.[232] In a case of bribery where the person who pays the bribe is not a willing participant in the offence but is really a victim of the offence, conviction of the accused may be based on the evidence of the person paying the bribe if there is a slight independent corroboration of his evidence.[233] It is a rule of prudence because on the whole a person giving bribe is technically in the category of an accomplice.[234] The person, who pays bribe so as to expose the conduct of public servant and as directed by the police, is not an accomplice.[235]

The Supreme Court in *MO Shamshudin v State of Kerala,*[236] explained the position of such a person as follows: The person offering bribe to a public officer is in the same position as that of an accomplice but the nature of corroboration required in such a case should not be subjected to the same rigorous tests which are generally applied to a case of an approver in other crimes. Though bribe-givers are generally treated to be in the nature of accomplices but among them there are various types and gradations. In cases under the Prevention of Corruption Act the complainant is the person who gives the bribe in a technical and legal sense because in every trap case wherever the complaint is filed there must be a person who has to give money to the accused which in fact is the bribe money which is demanded and without such a giving the trap cannot succeed. When there is such a demand by the public servant from a person who is unwilling, and therefore, intending to do public good, he approaches the authorities and lodges a complaint, then in order that the trap succeeds he has to offer the money. There could be another type of bribe-giver who is always willing to give money in order to get his work done and having got the work done he may send a complaint. Here he is particeps criminis in respect of the crime committed and thus is an accomplice and therefore a distinction could as well be drawn between cases where a person offers a bribe to achieve his own purpose and where one is forced to offer bribe under a threat of loss or harm, that is to say, under coercion. A person who falls in this category and

---

230. *Sitaram Sao v State of Jharkhand,* AIR 2008 SC 391 : (2007) 12 SCC 630, the court stated the extent and nature of corroboration required.

231. *Emperor v Papa Kamalkhan,* (1935) 37 Bom LR 336 : 59 Bom 486; *Deo Nandan Pershad v Emperor,* (1906) 33 Cal 649. *CM Sharma v State of AP,* AIR 2011 SC 608 : 2010 (4) Crimes 347 (SC), a contractor gave bribe to a public servant was not regarded as a accomplice as the money was extorted from him. It would lead to absurd results if were treated an accomplice requiring corroboration.

232. *King-Emp. v Malhar,* (1901) 3 Bom LR 694 : 26 Bom 193; *Kamala Prasad v Sital Prasad, sup; Banu Singh v Emperor,* (1906) 33 Cal 1353.

233. *Narayan Prashad v King-Emperor,* (1948) Nag 276. The Supreme Court held in *Raghubir v Haryana,* AIR 1974 SC 1516 : (1974) 4 SCC 560 : 1974 Cr LJ 1062 that the evidence of a bribe payer carries little conviction in the absence of reassuring support; *Gulam Mahmood v Gujarat,* AIR 1980 SC 1558 : 1980 Cr LJ 1096 : 1980 Supp SCC 684.

234. *Devan v State,* 1988 Cr LJ 1005 (Ker). See *Sheo Nandan Paswan v State of Bihar,* 1987 Cr LJ 793 : AIR 1987 SC 877, solitary accomplice witness found to be not reliable.

235. *Rajasingh v State,* 1995 Cr LJ 955 (Mad).

236. *MO Shamshudin v State of Kerala,* (1995) 3 SCC 351 : (1995) 2 Andh LT 114 (Cri).

who becomes a party for laying a trap stands on a different footing because he is only a victim of threat or coercion to which he was subjected to. Where such witnesses fall under the category of "accomplices" by reason of their being bribe-givers, in the first instance, the court has to consider the degree of complicity and then look for corroboration if necessary as a rule of prudence. The extent and nature of corroboration that may be needed in a case may vary having regard to the facts and circumstances.

The word "corroboration" means not mere evidence tending to confirm other evidence. In trap cases if any of the witnesses are accomplices who are *particeps criminis* in respect of the actual crime charged, their testimony must be treated as that of an accomplice; if they are not accomplices in that sense but are only partisan or interested witnesses who are concerned in the success of the trap, their evidence must be tested in the same way as that of any other interested witness, corroboration in such cases may be of general nature. Where the bribe has already been demanded from a man and if without giving the bribe he goes to the police or magistrate and brings them to witness the payment it will be a legitimate trap and in such cases at the most he can be treated as an interested witness. Whether corroboration is necessary or not will be within the discretion of the court and will depend upon the facts and circumstances of each case. However, as a rule of prudence, the court has to scrutinise the evidence of such interested witnesses carefully.

It is well-settled that the corroborating evidence can be even by way of circumstantial evidence. No general rule can be laid down with respect to quantum of evidence corroborating the testimony of a trap witness. The court should weigh the evidence and then see whether corroboration is necessary. Therefore, as a rule of law it cannot be laid down that the evidence of every complainant in a bribery case should be corroborated in all material particulars and otherwise it cannot be acted upon. Whether corroboration is necessary and if so to what extent and what should be its nature depends upon the facts and circumstances of each case. In a case of bribe, the person who pays the bribe and those who act as intermediaries are the only persons who can ordinarily be expected to give evidence about the bribe and it is not possible to get absolutely independent evidence about the payment of bribe. However, it is cautioned that the evidence of a bribe-giver has to be scrutinised very carefully and it is for the court to consider and appreciate the evidence in a proper manner and decide the question whether a conviction can be based upon it in those given circumstances.

[s 133.8] Rape cases.—The Supreme Court has laid down this principle that the testimony of a rape victim is not to be treated as that of an accomplice. It should be treated as that of an injured person.[237]

[s 133.9] Identity.—It is the invariable practice of the courts to require the corroboration by an independent witness of so much of the evidence of an accomplice as goes to identify the accused person as the offender.[238] Such corroboration ought to be that which is derived from unimpeachable or independent evidence.[239]

---

237. *State of Rajasthan v Narayan,* AIR 1992 SC 2004 : (1992) 3 SCC 615.

238. *Emperor v Kostalkhan,* (1902) 4 Bom LR 431; *Queen-Empress v Krishnabhat,* (1885) 10 Bom 319.

239. *Emperor v Baji Krishna,* (1904) 6 Bom LR 481.

[s 133.10] Retracted statement.—It would be risky to base conviction on the sole retracted statement of the co-accused but conviction is not barred.[240]

[s 133.11] Abrogation of warning rule in England.—Section 32(1) of the Criminal Justice and Public Order Act, 1994 has abrogated the rule requiring compulsory warning for corroboration of the evidence of accomplices and complainant's in sexual cases. The Law Commission's proposals marked the culmination of a growing dissatisfaction among judges, practitioners and academic commentators at the complex and inflexible nature of the warning and its tendency to confuse rather than assist the jury in its deliberations.[241]

[s 134] Number of witnesses.—No particular number of witnesses shall in any case be required for the proof of any fact.

COMMENT

Under the Act no particular number of witnesses is required in any case. of course it is open to a final Court of fact to believe or disbelieve a statement, but simply because the statement is of one witness that cannot by itself be a ground for not acting upon that testimony.[242] Neither the number of witnesses, nor the quantity of evidence is material. It is the quality that matters.[243] There is a general public reluctance in appearing as witnesses. Hence there should be no insistence that there should be more witnesses than one.[244]

---

240. *Haji Abdulla Haji Ibrahim Mandhra v Supdt. of Customs, Bhuj*, 1992 Cr LJ 2800 (Guj).

241. 1995 All ER Annual Review at pp 230- 231. The courts had to give new guidelines to judges in the area of suspect witnesses generally in the wake of the demise of the corroboration rules. This opportunity came in *R v Makanjuola and R v Easton*, (1995) 3 All ER 730 (CA), signalling an end to the flow of technical appeals regarding corroboration rules.

242. *Ramnath v Extra Assistant Commissioner, Jabalpur*, (1953) Nag 361.

243. *Maqsoodan v State of UP*, AIR 1983 SC 126 : 1983 Cr LJ 218. *Ramashish Rai v State of Bihar*, 1989 Cr LJ 336 (Pat), sole witness, value of evidence explained; *Rameshwar v State of UP*, 1987 Cr LJ 442 (All), a village woman, wife of deceased, mentioning only herself as an eye-witness, sole testimony, relied upon. See also *Barkau v State of UP*, 1993 Cr LJ 2954 (All), evidence has to be weighed and not counted. *Kedar Behera v State*, 1993 Cr LJ 378 (Ori), it is the acceptability of evidence which is material. *State of MP v Dharkole*, (2004) 13 SCC 308 : AIR 2005 SC 44 : 2005 Cr LJ 108, non-examination of any particular witness does not affect the prosecution case when the witness examined by the prosecution without the cross-examination pointing to the guilt of the accused.

244. *State of UP v Anil Singh*, AIR 1988 SC 1998 : 1988 Supp SCC 686 : 1989 Cr LJ 88 : 1989 SCC (Cri) 48. It is not necessary to multiply witnesses, *State of UP v Hakim Singh*, AIR 1980 SC 184 : 1980 All LJ 16 : 1980 Cr LJ 46 (SC). The fact that some witnesses are not produced does not cast a reflection upon the probative value of the testimony of those who are actually produced. *Allaudin Mian v State of Bihar*, AIR 1989 SC 1456; 1989 Cr LJ 1466; *Appukuttan v State*, 1989 Cr LJ 2362 (Ker); *Gaital v State*, 1988 Cr LJ 960 (All), sole witness. Another case depending on sole witness, *Banshidhar Swain v State of Orissa*, 1987 Cr LJ 1819 (Ori). Conviction can be based upon the truthful testimony of a solitary witness, *Kartik Malhar v State of Bihar*, 1996 Cr LJ 889 : (1996) 1 SCC 614. To the same effect, see *SG Gundegowda v State*, 1996 Cr LJ 852 (Kant). *Munshi Prasad v State of Bihar*, AIR 2001 SC 3031 at 3038, certain independent witnesses to the fact of murder from the nearby residential area were not examined, the court said that it was not something which could be regarded as material because the evidence on record was of satisfactory and trustworthy nature. Increasing the number of witnesses only for the sake of increase was not necessary. *Gopal Mahadeo Tambada v State of Maharashtra*, 1997 Cr LJ 2425 (Bom), sole eye- witness, wife of the deceased, testimony supported by medical evidence, ballistic experts and witnesses of recoveries, conviction sustained on the basis of the account.

The court said: "The public are generally reluctant to come forward to depose before the court. It is, therefore, not correct to reject the prosecution version only on the ground that all witnesses to the occurrence have not been examined. Nor is it proper to reject the case for want of corroboration by independent witnesses if the case made out is otherwise true and acceptable."

In the matter of appreciation of evidence of witnesses, it is not the number of witnesses but quality of their evidence which is important, as there is no requirement in law of evidence that any particular number of witnesses is to be examined to prove/disprove a fact. It is a time-honoured principle that evidence must be weighed and not counted. The test is whether the evidence has a ring of truth, is cogent, credible and trustworthy or otherwise. The legal system has laid emphasis on value provided by each witness, rather than the multiplicity or plurality of witnesses. It is quality and not quantity, which determines the adequacy of evidence as has been provided by section 134 of the Evidence Act. Where the law requires the examination of at least one attesting witness, it has been held that the number of witnesses produced do not carry any weight.[245]

The Supreme Court has been sustaining convictions on the basis of the testimony of a sole witness. In one of the cases,[246] it remarked: "There is no computerised rule. Nor are judges computers. It must always depend on the circumstances of each case and the quality of the evidence of the single witness. In this case we find there is abundant evidence direct and circumstantial to prove the guilt of the appellants. The trial court called the appellants 'dare-devils of the locality'. No one was willing to come forward to depose against them. In such circumstances, as always, the court has to separate the grain from the chaff."

The Supreme Court in *Marwadi Kishore Parmanand v State of Gujarat*[247] explained the reliability factor in the following words: Generally speaking oral testimony may be classified into three categories, namely, (1) wholly reliable, (2) wholly unreliable and (3) neither wholly reliable nor wholly unreliable. So far as the first category of proof is concerned, the courts have no difficulty in coming to its conclusion either way, that is to say, it may convict or may acquit an accused on the testimony of the single witness, if his testimony is found to be above approach or suspicion of interestedness, incompetence or subordination. In the case of *second category* of the witness, the court

245. *Laxmibai v Bhagwantbuva,* (2013) 4 SCC 97.

246. *Madan Lal v State,* (1978) Cr LJ 1832 at 1835 (SC). *Ramesh Bhagwan Manjrekar v State,* 1997 Cr LJ 796 (Bom), a conviction on the basis of a sole eye-witness can be sustained if he is reliable. In the present case, however, there were three witnesses. *State v Datta Maruti Salagar,* 1998 Cr LJ 3756 (Bom) sole reliable witness, but some contradiction, not a ground for rejecting his evidence. *Shyamrao Vishnu Patil v State,* 1998 Cr LJ 3446 (Bom), conviction was based in this case on the solitary statement of the victim. The court said that the conviction was not bad in law because evidence has to be weighed not counted, *Sheelam Ramesh v State of AP*, 2000 Cr LJ 51 (AP), the prosecution did not examine other nearby persons. The court said that the evidence of eye-witnesses could not be minimised by that reason. The courts are concerned with quality and not quantity of evidence. *State of Maharashtra v Raju Dadaba Borge,* 2001 Cr LJ 3638 (Bom), plurality of evidence is only a rule of caution and not an inflexible legal requirement. Evidence has to be weighed, not counted. A conviction can be based on the testimony of a solitary witness. *Kewla Ram v State of Rajasthan,* 2000 Cr LJ 3077 (Raj), the testimony of the sole eye-witness to murder did not suffer from any infirmity, hence accepted.

247. *Marwadi Kishore Parmanand v State of Gujarat.* (1994) 4 SCC 549 : 1994 SCC (Cr.) 1294.

has equally no difficulty in coming to the conclusion. But in the *third category* of cases, the court has to be circumspect and has to look for corroboration in material particulars by reliable testimony, direct or circumstantial. More often than not there are situations where only a single person is available to give evidence in respect of a disputed fact. Naturally in such a situation the court has to weigh carefully such a testimony and if it is satisfied that the evidence is reliable and free from all taints which tend to render oral testimony open to suspicion, it becomes its duty to act upon such testimony.

CHAPTER X

OF THE EXAMINATION OF WITNESSES

[s 135] Order of production and statement to this effect to be found examination of witnesses.—The order in which witnesses are produced and examined shall be regulated by the law and practice for the time being relating to civil and criminal procedure respectively, and, in the absence of any such law, by the discretion of the Court.[s 135.4]

SYNOPSIS

COMMENT

This section deals with the order in which witnesses are to be examined; and not with the quantity or quality of the proof.

In civil proceedings the order is to be regulated by the provisions of the Civil Procedure Code; and in criminal proceedings, by those of the Criminal Procedure Code. Failing these, the order is to be determined by the discretion of the court. In practice, however, it is left largely to the option of the party calling witnesses to examine them in any order he chooses.

Where there is delay in examination of a particular witness and a plausible explanation has been offered for delayed examination of that witness, there is no ground to doubt the veracity of prosecution case.[1]

Merely because some of material witnesses were not examined by prosecution, a criminal Court would not lean towards drawing the adverse inference that if they were examined they would have given contrary version.[2]

At the same time, non-examination of named witness and merely giving statement that a particular witness is not ready to come and depose in support of prosecution charges, without assigning any substantial reason, may not be sufficient and good reasons for not examining witness, more so, when witnesses examined, appear deeply interested with prosecution and inimical to accused persons.[3]

[s 135.1] Civil proceedings.—In civil suits, it is the plaintiff who generally has the right to begin (Civil Procedure Code, O XVIII, rule 1). The other party has then to state his case (O XXVIII, rule 2). If the defendant admits the facts alleged by plaintiff and relies on a defence, it is for him to establish that defence. The plaintiff

---

1. *Abuthagir v State Rep. by Inspector of Police, Madurai*, 2009 Cr LJ 3987 (SC).
2. *Joginder v State*, 2010 Cr LJ 1770 (Del).
3. *Mrityunjay Mani Mishra v State of Bihar*, 2011 Cr LJ 1966 (Pat).

may then prove his case in rebuttal, if any (O XVIII, rule 3). Where a party is taken by surprise by a point made against him at the hearing, the judge may, if he thinks right, at any stage of the trial, allow him to produce rebutting evidence.[4] Such evidence must be that which goes to cut down the defence, without being in confirmation of the original case.[5]

In civil appeals, the appellant is heard first in support of his appeal. If the court does not dismiss the appeal at once, the respondent is heard against the appeal; and in such case the appellant is entitled to reply (O XLI, rule 16).

The Bombay High Court has upheld the court's power to direct witness to go out of court when the evidence of other witness is being recorded. Courts can exercise this power in civil cases also depending upon facts of each case. But at the same time, if a witness is present in court at the time of examination of other witnesses, the court has no power under Evidence Act or even under CPC to decline permission to examine witness on ground that he was present in court while evidence of other witnesses was being recorded. The issue as to whether the evidentiary value of evidence of such witnesses would be affected by reason of that witness remaining present in court during recording of evidence of other witnesses, will depend on facts of case.[6]

[s 135.2] Criminal proceedings.—In criminal proceedings, the complainant or the prosecutor, as the case may be, has the right to begin; and, if necessary, the accused is asked to adduce his evidence in defence. The trial before a magistrate may be (a) in summons cases (Criminal Procedure Code, sections 251–258), or (b) in warrant cases instituted by the Police, section 238; otherwise than on Police report (sections 244–249) or (c) summary (section 260). Where a trial takes place before a Court of Session, or High Court, the procedure as laid down in section 226, *et seq.* of the Criminal Procedure Code is followed. In hearing appeals, the appellant begins and if necessary the other side is heard next (section 385).

In a trial under section 138 of the Negotiable Instruments Act for dishonour of cheque, it was held that the procedure of filling affidavit in lieu of examination-in-chief as provided under section 145 of the Negotiable Instruments Act does not violate the right of accused to fair trial and an opportunity to cross examine the witness.[7]

However, where the accused was facing trial for possession of narcotic drugs, a prayer was made by the accused for deferring the cross-examination of official witness till the recording of examination-in-chief of all the witnesses. This prayer was declined by court on the ground that the same will delay the disposal of matter. Sections 231(2) and 243(3) of CrPC may be invoked only to have speedy trial and not otherwise.[8]

[s 135.3] Commission.—In both civil and criminal proceedings witnesses may be examined on commission, where evidently the same rules will apply respectively (see

4. *Bigsby v Dickinson,* (1876) 4 Ch D 24.
5. *Rex v Hilditch,* (1832) 5 C&P 299.
6. *Indur Kartar Chhugani v Ms Priya Sunil Dutt,* 2011 Cr LJ 3571 (Bom).
7. *Abdul Aziz Lokhandwala and etc etc v Nasir Ali,* 2010 Cr LJ 1981 (Bom).
8. *Shamoon Ahmed Sayed v Intelligence Officer, Narcotic Central Bureau, South Zonal Unit, Chennai,* 2009 Cr L J 1215 (SC).

Civil Procedure Code, O XXVI, rules 1–8; Criminal Procedure Code, sections 284–288). Evidence taken on commission is later put on the record of the case.[9]

[s 135.4] "Discretion of the Court".—The court is very slow to interfere with the discretion of counsel as to the order in which witnesses should be examined.[10] While counsel has discretion, the court has also the power to direct the order in which witnesses cited by the party shall be examined.[11]

[s 136] Judge to decide as to admissibility of evidence.—When either party proposes to give evidence of any fact, the Judge may ask the party proposing to give the evidence in what manner the alleged fact, if proved, would be relevant; and the Judge shall admit the evidence if he thinks that the facts, if proved, would be relevant, and not otherwise.

If the fact proposed to be proved is one of which evidence is admissible only upon proof of some other fact, such last-mentioned fact must be proved before evidence is given of the fact first mentioned, unless the party undertakes to give proof of such fact, and, the Court is satisfied with such undertaking.

If the relevancy of one alleged fact depends upon another alleged fact being first proved, the Judge may, in his discretion, either permit evidence of the first fact to be given before the second fact is proved, or require evidence to be given of the second fact before evidence is given of the first fact.

ILLUSTRATIONS

(a) It is proposed to prove a statement about a relevant fact by a person alleged to be dead, which statement is relevant under section 32.

The fact that the person is dead must be proved by the person proposing to prove the statement, before evidence is given of the statement.

(b) It is proposed to prove, by a copy, the contents of a document said to be lost.

The fact that the original is lost must be proved by the person proposing to produce the copy, before the copy is produced.

(c) A is accused of receiving stolen property knowing it to have been stolen. It is proposed to prove that he denied the possession of the property.

The relevancy of the denial depends on the identity of the property. The Court may, in its discretion, either require the property to be identified before the denial of the possession is proved, or permit the denial of the possession, to be proved before the property is identified.

(d) It is proposed to prove a fact (*A*) which is said to have been the cause or effect of a fact in issue. There are several intermediate facts (*B*, *C* and *D*) which must be shown to exist before the fact (*A*) can be regarded as the cause or effect of the fact in issue. The Court may either permit *A* to be proved before *B*, *C* and *D* is proved, or may require proof of *B*, *C* and *D* before permitting proof of *A*.

---

9. *Kusum Kumari Roy v Satya Ranjan Das*, (1903) 30 Cal 999; *Man Gobinda Choudhuri v Shashindra Chandra Chowdhuri*, (1907) 35 Cal 28; *Dhanu Ram Mahto v Murli Mahto*, (1909) 36 Cal 566.
10. *Per* Stanley J, in *Kedar Nath Ghose v Bhupendra Nath Bose*, (1900) 5 Cal WN xv.
11. *In the goods of Gopessur Dutt*, (1911) 16 Cal WN 265. This discretion should be fairly exercised. *Ram Singh v State of MP*, 1989 Cr LJ (NOC) 206 (MP).

SYNOPSIS

COMMENT

This section embodies three cardinal rules as to the admissibility of evidence.

Though proper time for objecting to the admissibility of a document is when it is tendered, mere omission to so object does not constitute an inadmissible document evidence. Party seeking to put a document in evidence must show under which section it is admissible. Improper admission or rejection of evidence will not by itself form ground for a new trial or reversal of a decision if, in view of the other evidence in the case, the decision would be the same even if there had been no such improper admission or rejection.[12]

[s 136.1] Evidence relating to facts in issue and also relevant facts.—*[Clause 1]*.—In order to focus the attention of the litigants to the points in dispute between them, issues are raised on the pleadings. The parties are called upon to lead evidence on them. Such evidence must primarily relate to facts in issue; but it may also refer to relevant facts (section 5). In the latter case, the first paragraph of this section enables the presiding judge to ask the party to show the relevancy of the fact which is sought to be proved. Questions of admissibility of evidence are to be determined by the judge.

In dealing with the relevancy of facts as above, two sets of special circumstances may arise; first, where the *evidence of one fact is admissible* only upon proof of some other fact, such last-mentioned fact must be proved first, unless the court accepts the undertaking by the party that it will be proved later on (clause 2); and, second, where the *relevancy of one fact depends* upon the proof of another fact, the judge may in his discretion permit either of them to be proved first (clause 3).

It is the bounden duty of a party, personally knowing the whole circumstances of the case, to give evidence on his own behalf and to submit to cross-examination. His non-appearance as a witness would be the strongest possible circumstance going to discredit the truth of his case.[13]

[s 136.2] Other Facts on assurance may be proved later.—*[Clause 2]*.—This clause should be read with section 104. Its purpose is to facilitate a party in laying his case before the court. Where a witness in the box deposes to a story, some portions of which would become admissible only on proof of certain other facts, it is convenient as well as economical in time to permit him to complete his story, as soon as the party calling him gives an assurance that such other facts will be proved by him later on. Illustrations (a) and (b) demonstrate the application of the rule.

[s 136.3] Judge's discretion—Either fact proved first.—*[Clause 3]*.—This clause is expressed in wider terms than clause 2. When the relevancy of one fact depends upon

---

12. *Dwijesh Chandra Ray Chaudhuri v Naresh Chandra Gupta*, (1946) 1 Cal 149.
13. *Gurbaksh Singh v Gurdial Singh*, (1927) 29 Bom LR 1392 (PC).

the proof of another fact, the judge has full discretion to allow either fact to be proved first. The clause is illustrated by illustrations (c) and (d).

Questions as to the admissibility of evidence should be decided as they arise and should not be reserved until judgment in the case is given.[14] Where a judge is in doubt as to the admissibility of a particular piece of evidence he should declare in favour of admissibility rather than of non-admissibility.[15] The Supreme Court upheld the rejection of the evidence of a living person by means of an affidavit. The proper course was for the signatory of the affidavit to appear in person.[16]

[s 137] Examination-in-chief.—The examination of a witness by the party who calls him shall be called his examination-in-chief.

Cross-examination.—The examination of a witness by the adverse party shall be called his cross-examination.

Re-examination.—The examination of a witness, subsequent to the cross-examination by the party who called him, shall be called his re-examination.

SYNOPSIS

COMMENT

Evidence of witnesses examined in defence on behalf of one accused and cross-examined on behalf of another accused is admissible as against the latter. It may be otherwise where that other accused had no opportunity of cross-examining them or where he has not been given an opportunity by the magistrate or the judge to explain the circumstances appearing in such evidence.[17]

The third para, means "where a witness has been cross-examined, and is then examined by the party who called him, such subsequent examination shall be called his re-examination."[18]

The evidence produced through the successive examinations has to be taken as a whole and not that one portion can be taken in by ignoring the others.[19]

---

14. *Jadu Rai v Bhubotaran Nundy*, (1889) 17 Cal 173; *Ramjibun Serowgy v Oghore Nath Chatterjee*, (1897) 25 Cal 401.

15. PER STRAIGHT, J, in *The Collector of Gorakhpur v Palakdhari Singh*, (1889) 12 All 1, 26 (FB).

16. *Munir Ad v State of Rajasthan*, AIR 1989 SC 705: 1989 Cr LJ 845 : 1989 Supp 119 SCC 377 : 1989 SCC (Cri) 455.

17. *Nandgopal v State*, (1951) Nag 172. *Chandan v State of Rajasthan*, (1988) 1 SCC 696 : AIR 1988 SC 599 : 1988 Cr LJ 842, where the son of the deceased identified certain articles, but was not examined and, therefore, his evidence was rejected as hearsay.

18. *Stokes*,Vol II, p 925, f.n. 1.

19. *Badhna Kharia v State of Assam*, 1988 Cr LJ 1412 (Gau).

A party must be given a fair chance to cross-examine the witness.[20] Summary procedure cannot take away the right of a party to cross-examine the other side.[21] In *State of Karnataka v S Dhandapani Modaliar*,[22] it was held that some time should intervene between framing of the charge and statement of the accused about his desire of cross-examination because in a large number of cases they are ignorant of the law and must need advice before they can make up mind whether to further cross-examine the witnesses already examined by the prosecution.

[s 137.1] Cross-examination without examination-in-chief.—Where a witness was not examined in examination-in-chief, tendering him for cross-examination is not permissible.[23] Section 138 envisages that a witness would first be examined-in-chief and then subjected to cross-examination and for seeking any clarification, the witness may be re-examined by the prosecution. There is no purpose in *tendering* a witness for cross-examination only. Tendering of a witness for cross-examination without examination-in-chief amounts to giving up of the witness by the prosecution. However, the practice of tendering witnesses for cross-examination in a sessions trial had been frequently resorted to since the enactment of the Code of Criminal Procedure, 1898. The reason behind taking recourse to such a practice, which undoubtedly was inconsistent with section 138 of the Evidence Act, is not far to seek. Under the old Code, as it stood prior to its amendment by Act 26 of 1955, a full-fledged magisterial enquiry was to be held in a case which was triable exclusively by the court of session or the High Court in accordance with the procedure laid down in Chapter XVIII thereof and in that enquiry prosecution was required to examine all its witnesses. Under section 288 of that Code the evidence of the witnesses so recorded by the committing magistrate could be treated, at the discretion of the sessions judge, as substantive evidence at the trial. The prosecution taking advantage of the above provision, used to ask for and obtain leave of the sessions Court to treat the depositions of those witness whom they did not intend to examine afresh, recorded in the committal enquiry as its evidence in the trial and then tender them for cross-examination.

The *Jaggo* case[24] (decided under old Code) cannot be read to lay down, as a matter of legal proposition, that a witness can be "tendered" for cross-examination even without there being any examination-in-chief. If there is some earlier statement of the witness recorded by a competent Court or an affidavit filed in the trial Court and the witness testifies to the correctness of that earlier statement at the trial, it may (in certain cases of witnesses of a formal nature) be permissible to tender a witness for cross-examination after he has sworn to the correctness of the earlier statement, because in that event that earlier statement is treated as the examination-in-chief of the witness, but that is not the same thing as tendering a witness for cross-examination only, without there being any examination-in-chief on the record. After the coming into force of the Criminal

20. *Pyarelal Sakseria v Devishankar Parashar*, AIR 1994 MP 115; *Modula India v Ramakshya Singh Deo*, AIR 1989 SC 162 : (1988) 4 SCC 619, a tenant defendant has a limited right of cross- examining the landlord where his defence has been struck out.

21. *Kalpanaben M Shah v Navinchandra Jeevanlal Acharya*, AIR 1995 Guj 176.

22. 1992 Cr LJ 24 (Karn).

23. *Tej Prakash v State of Haryana*, 1996 Cr LJ 394 : (1996) 7 SCC 322, **relying on** *Sukhwant Singh v State of Punjab*, 1995 (2) Scale 482 : 1995 AIR SCW 2521 : (1995) 3 SCC 367 : AIR 1995 SC 1601.

24. *State of UP v Jaggo*, AIR 1971 SC 1586 : (1971) 2 SCC 42.

Procedure Code, 1973, which replaced the Code of 1898, recording of evidence in committal proceedings has been totally dispensed with and section 288 of the old Code has been omitted. Consequently, the recourse to practice of tendering a witness for cross-examination, who had been examined in the committal Court, is no more relevant or available.[25]

The Evidence Act gives the right of cross-examination only to the adverse party. So, a defendant can cross-examine a co-defendant only when the interest of co-defendant is adverse to the interest of defendant.[26] A defendant having no conflicting interest with plaintiff cannot be permitted to cross-examine the plaintiff. The right of cross-examination is available only to an adverse party.[27]

The Supreme Court observed in light of its previous decision[28] that the object of section 311 is to bring on record evidence not only from the point of view of the accused and the prosecution but also from the point of view of the orderly society. If a witness called by the court gives evidence against the complainant, he should be allowed an opportunity to cross-examine. The right to cross-examine a witness who is called by a Court arises not under the provisions of section 311, but under the Evidence Act which gives a party the right to cross-examine a witness who is not his own witness. Since a witness summoned by the court could not be termed a witness of any particular party, the court should give the right of cross-examination to the complainant.

Where an application was moved by prosecution to cross-examine its witness in midst of cross examination and the same was allowed by trail Court without giving a reasoned order, it was held that the prayer was of exceptional nature which was likely to have a crucial bearing upon trial against accused. Hence, the order being non-speaking, was quashed.[29]

[s 137.1.1] ***Cross-examination in case of Evidence on Affidavit.***—A witness deposed by an affidavit. On the application of the accused he was summoned for cross-examination. The court said that he could be subjected to cross-examination only as to facts stated in his affidavit. It was not open to the accused to insist that before cross-examination he must first depose in examination-in-chief.[30]

[s 137.2] Witness not presenting himself for cross-examination.—Where a witness was examined-in-chief but he did not make himself available for cross-examination, the court said that his evidence had lost all credibility.[31]

A defence witness who was being cross-examined could not appear the next day for continuation because of illness for which medical certificate was filed. Other defence witnesses were present and could have been cross-examined but for the court's refusal. Such refusal was held to be improper. The court said that it is the bounden duty of

---

25. *Sukhwant Singh v State of Punjab,* (1995) 3 SCC 367 : 1995 SCC (Cri) 524 : AIR 1995 SC 1601 : (1995) 2 Andh LT (Cri) 201.

26. *Smt. Annapurn Devi v Administrator General, UP*, 2010 (1) CCC 501 (All.) (DB).

27. *Vijaya v Saraswathi* 2008 (3) CCC 535 (Mad.).

28. *Jamatraj Kewalji Govani v State of Maharashtra,* AIR 1968 SC 178, (1967) 3 SCR 415, 1968 Cr LJ 231 (SC).

29. *Sudhakar Tukaram Dhatrak v State of Maharastra*, 2010 Cr LJ (NOC) 217 (Bom).

30. *Mandvi Co-op Bank Ltd v Nimesh B Thakore*, AIR 2010 SC 1402 : (2010) 3 SCC 83.

31. *Paritosh Ghosh v Ashim Kumar Gupta,* AIR 2003 NOC 141 (Cal) : 2003 AIHC 291.

the court to record statements of witnesses present for cross-examination.[32] The right of the land acquiring body to cross-examine its officers who made promises against its interest could not be refused merely on the ground of common defence.[33]

[s 137.3] Keeping identity of witness secret.—The court may in exceptional circumstances order that the identity, names and addresses of certain witnesses be kept secret. The Court said that this may not affect fair trial.[34]

[s 137.4] Questions by Court.—Where the witness became confused in the course of his cross-examination, it was held that the court could put questions to him to elicit the truth.[35]

[s 138] Order of examination.—Witnesses shall be first examined-in-chief, then (if the adverse party so desires) cross-examined, then (if the party calling him so desires) re-examined.

The examination and cross-examination must relate to relevant facts, but the cross-examination need not be confined to the fact to which the witness testified on his examination-in-chief.

Direction of re-examination.—The re-examination shall be directed to the explanation of matters referred to in cross-examination; and, if new matter is, by permission of the Court, introduced in re-examination, the adverse party may further cross-examine upon that matter.

SYNOPSIS

COMMENT

The examination of witnesses is *viva voce* (O XVIII, rule 4). It is always in the form of questions and answers. The deposition is usually taken down in the form of a narrative formed out of the answers (O XVIII, rule 5). Where a question is objected to and yet allowed by the court to be put, the question and its answer are taken down

32. *Kailash Chandra Sharma v Siraj Krishna Das*, AIR 2009 Gau 73.
33. *Vidharbha Irrigation Development Corp v 3rd Ad hoc Addl. Distt. Judge.*, AIR 2008 NOC 1326 (Bom).
34. *Kartar Singh v State of Punjab*, (1994) 3 SCC 569 : 1994 Cr LJ 3139.
35. *State of Rajasthan v Ani*, AIR 1997 SC 1023 : 1997 Cr LJ 1529.

verbatim (O XVIII, rule 10). At the end of the deposition, it is read out to the witness and signed by the presiding officer (O XVIII, rule 5).

The *viva voce* examination consists generally of three stages: first of all, the witness is examined by the party who calls him; this is called examination-in-chief (section 137). He is next examined by the adverse party; this is called cross-examination (section 137). Finally he is examined again by the party who called him; this is called re-examination (section 137).

Section 246 of the Criminal Procedure Code, 1973 giving the accused a right in a warrant case to cross-examine the witnesses for the prosecution after a charge has been framed, is an exception to the general rule. In the exercise of the inherent power of the court, the magistrate in an inquiry under Chapter XIX of the Code of Criminal Procedure may allow the accused to reserve cross-examination for a future occasion in the special circumstances of a case.[36]

[s 138.1] Examination-in-chief.—This will ordinarily be in the form of a connected narrative, brought out by questions put to the witness by the party calling him. It must relate to relevant facts [section 138(2)]. No leading questions can be asked (section 142).

"Unless evidence of reputation be admissible, witnesses, must, in general merely speak to facts within their own knowledge, and they will not be permitted...to express their own belief or opinion...Though a witness, in general, must depose to such facts only as are within his own knowledge, the law does not require him to speak with such expression of certainty as to exclude all doubt. For, whatever may be the nature of the subject, if the witness has any personal recollection of the fact under investigation, he may state what he remembers concerning it, and leave the jury to judge of the weight of his testimony. If the impression on his mind be so slight as to justify the belief that it may have been derived from others, or may be some unwarrantable deduction of his own dull understanding or lively imagination, it will be rejected."[37]

On some particular subjects, positive and direct testimony may often be unattainable, and, in such cases, a witness is allowed to testify to his belief or opinion, or even to draw inferences respecting the fact in question from other facts, provided these last facts be within his personal knowledge.[38] This mode of examination, however, chiefly prevails on questions of *science or trade*, where, from the difficulty, and occasional impossibility, of obtaining more direct and positive evidence, persons of skill, sometimes called *experts*, are allowed, not only to testify to facts, but to give their opinions in evidence.[39]

It is the duty of counsel to bring out clearly and in proper chronological order every relevant fact in support of his client's case to which the witness can depose. This task is more difficult than may at first sight appear. The timid witness must be encouraged; the talkative witness repressed; the witness who is too strong a partisan must be kept in check. And yet counsel must not suggest to the witness what he is to say. An honest witness, however, should be left to tell his tale in his own way with as little interruption from counsel as possible.[40]

---

36. *GV Raman v Emperor,* (1929) 57 Cal 44.
37. Taylor, 12th Edn, sections 1414-15, pp 898-99.
38. *Ibid,* section 1416, p 899.
39. *Ibid,* section 1417, p 900.
40. *Powell,* 10th Edn, p 458.

Once examination-in-chief is conducted, the statement becomes part of the record. It is evidence as per law and in the true sense, for at best, it may be rebuttable. An evidence being rebutted or controverted becomes a matter of consideration, relevance and belief, which is the stage of judgment by the court. Yet it is evidence and it is material on the basis whereof the court can come to a *prime facie* opinion as to complicity of some other person who may be connected with the offence. On the basis of examination-in-chief, the court or the magistrate can proceed against a person as long as the court is satisfied that the evidence appearing against such person is such that it *prima facie* necessitates bringing such person to face trial. In fact, an examination-in-chief untested by cross-examination, undoubtedly in itself, is an evidence.[41]

However, the statements made in examination-in-chief, lose much of their credibility and weight unless they are put into the crucible of cross-examination and emerge unscathed from the test.[42]

No witness can be cross-examined unless he has been first examined-in-chief. This section provides that cross-examination follows examination-in-chief but it cannot be so without examination-in-chief.[43]

[s 138.2] Cross-examination.—The testimony of a witness is not legal evidence unless it is subject to cross-examination; and where no opportunity has been given to the appellant's counsel to test the veracity of the principal prosecution witness or where owing to the refractory attitude of the witness the court is constrained to terminate all of a sudden and prematurely the cross-examination of the witness, the evidence of such a witness is not legal testimony and cannot be the basis of a judicial pronouncement.[44] No evidence affecting a party is admissible against that party unless the latter has had an opportunity of testing its truthfulness by cross-examination.[45] "The exercise of this right [cross-examination] is justly regarded as one of the most efficacious tests which the law has devised for the discovery of truth. By means of it, the situation of the witness with respect to the parties and to the subject of litigation, his interest, his motives, his inclination and prejudices, his character, his means of obtaining a correct and certain knowledge of the facts to which he bears testimony, the manner in which he has used those means, his powers of discernment, memory, and description, are all fully investigated, ascertained, and submitted to the consideration of the jury, who have an opportunity of observing his demeanour, and of determining the just value of his testimony. It is not easy for a witness, subjected to this test, to impose on a Court or jury, for however artful the fabrication of falsehood may be, it cannot embrace all the circumstances to which cross-examination may be extended."[46]

---

41. *Hardeep Singh v State of Punjab*, (2014) 3 SCC 92 (paras 89 and 90).

42. See *Gopal Saran v Satyanarayna*, AIR 1989 SC 1785 : 1989 Cr LJ 2070, where the testimony of a witness who did not submit himself to cross-examination was held to be not reliable. *Ganesh Jadav v State of Assam*, 1995 Cr LJ 3748 (Gau), examination and cross-examination must relate to relevant facts and on failure of the defence to challenge the relevant facts brought in examination- in-chief, the court has discretion to accept that part of evidence.

43. *Sharadamama v Kenchamma*, AIR 2007 Kar 17.

44. *Ram Kumar v King-Emperor*, (1936) 12 Luck 552; *Food Inspector v James NT*, 1998 Cr LJ 3494 (Ker) the value of the evidence of a witness who died before cross-examination.

45. *Maganlal v King-Emperor*, (1946) Nag 126; *R. v Gokal (Abbas)*, (1997) 2 Cr App R 266 (CA (Crim Div)], statements of witnesses who were not cross-examined abroad were held to be unsafe evidence.

46. *Taylor*, 12th Edn, section 1428, p 910.

In the instant case, the Supreme Court observed that it is not at all appreciable to call a witness for cross-examination after a long span of time (here after one year and eight months). It is imperative if the examination-in-chief is over, the cross-examination should be completed on the same day. If the examination-in-chief continues till late hours, the trial can be adjourned to the next day for cross-examination. It is inconceivable in law that the cross-examination should be deferred for such a long time. It is an anathema to the concept of proper and fair trial.[47] However, in the instant case cross-examination was conducted nearly eight months later but the defence was unable to make any serious dent in the kernel of the evidence of the witness. The court accepted his evidence.[48]

In the case of uncross-examined testimony of a witness, the provision of section 32 clause (7) is not applicable. Such an uncross-examined testimony of a witness is not to be read into evidence with the aid of section 32 of the Evidence Act. In this case, the witness remained uncross-examined and subsequently could not be cross-examined as he became incapable of giving evidence due to infirmities of old age.[49]

A question arose before the Calcutta High Court as to the admissibility of the evidence of a person where cross-examination could not be finished. The evidence of the defendant witness was being recorded on commission. His cross-examination could only be partly held because of his death. The court was of the view that his evidence would not be inadmissible. The court said that there is no provision in the Act saying that if the cross-examination could not be held in part or in full, his testimony would be rendered absolutely inadmissible. How much weight is to be attached to such testimony should be decided by considering surrounding facts and circumstances.[50] The court found a line of authorities in favour of its opinion. There is the decision of the Madras High Court in *Maharaja of Kolhapur v S Sunderam Ayyar*.[51] The court held that where a witness was examined-in-chief and there was hardly any cross-examination and before it could be concluded, the witness died and the unfinished testimony of the deceased witness was not rejected or held to be inadmissible. Another decision was that of the Allahabad High Court in *Ahmad Ali v Joti Pd*,[52] hinting to the absence of any provisions in the Act against the inadmissibility of such evidence only because of the fact that the other party could not cross-examine him. The court pointed out that the distinction between the admissibility of evidence and the fact that the court would not put any belief upon it is very fine but it is important because if the evidence is inadmissible, the court cannot take it on record, but, if it is admissible, it has to be taken and considered with the rest of the evidence. The Patna High Court in *Horli Kumar v Rajab Ali*,[53] also regarded such evidence to be admissible but to be examined carefully to see whether, if cross-examination, it would have stood or not. An earlier

---

47. *Vinod Kumar v State of Punjab*, (2015) 3 SCC 220 (para 57.4).
48. *K Ramajayam v Inspector of Police, Chennai*, 2016 Cr LJ 1542, para 16 (Mad-DB).
49. *Ghasitibai v Ram Gopal Singh*, 2009 (4) CCC 578 (MP).
50. *Dever Park Builders Pvt Ltd v Madhuri Jalan*, AIR 2002 Cal 281.
51. *Maharaja of Kolhapur v S Sunderam Ayyar*, AIR 1925 Mad 497 at 538. The court did not attach any probative value to the evidence in the circumstances.
52. *Ahmad Ali v Joti Pd*, AIR 1944 All 188.
53. *Horli Kumar v Rajab Ali*, AIR 1936 Pat 34.

decision of the Calcutta High Court[54] was to the same effect. The court also cited two Lahore decisions.[55]

The objects of cross-examination are to impeach the accuracy, credibility, and general value of the evidence given in chief; to sift the facts already stated by the witness, to detect and expose discrepancies, or to elicit suppressed facts which will support the case of the cross-examining party.[56]

"Where the facts are in dispute, such cases, generally speaking, are proved by human testimony. The value of that testimony depends on the honesty of the witness, his means of knowledge, his memory, his intelligence and his impartiality. Every question is relevant which goes to indicate the presence or absence of these qualities or any of them. The object of cross-examination may be described as three-fold. First, to elicit from an adverse witness something in your favour; second, to destroy or weaken the force of what the witness has said against you, and third, to show from the present attitude of the witness or from his past experience that he is unworthy of belief in whole or in part."[57]

When the examination-in-chief has resulted in clear, conclusive, or unimpeachable evidence, it may be prudent for the adverse party not to cross-examine; for, in such a case, he may by so doing, instead of weakening the evidence, merely strengthen and confirm it. So, too, he will generally not cross-examine a witness, whose evidence he admits, or which cannot possibly injure his case. Reckless cross-examination, moreover, often lets in evidence which before was not admissible.[58]

The trend of the cross-examination is in most cases determined by the line of narrative unfolded in the examination-in-chief. It is usual to take each important item so deposed to and to cross-examine the witness upon it. Its purpose is two-fold. First of all, the cross-examiner tries to discover if the story told by the witness in examination-in-chief is tainted by exaggerations or falsehoods. Second, the adverse party can in some cases, construct his line of defence from out of the mouth of the witness.

The essence of cross-examination is that it is the interrogation by the advocate of one party of a witness called by his adversary with the object either to obtain from such witness admissions favourable to his cause, or to discredit him. Cross-examination is the most effective of all means for extracting truth and exposing falsehood.[59]

In a criminal trial,[60] leading questions were permitted to be asked to a prosecution witness in examination-in-chief in the absence of defence counsel. It was held that

---

54. *W Stewart v Newzeland Ins. Co Ltd*, 16 Cal WN 991. The plaintiff did not use his opportunity to cross-examine the witness.

55. *Mangal Sen v Emperor*, AIR 1929 Lah. 840, weight to be attached to such testimony would depend upon circumstances. *Diwan Singh v Emperor*, AIR 1933 Lah 561, the evidence of the witness who left before his cross-examination could be complied was admissible.

56. *Powell*, 10th Edn, p 463. Cross-examination is not the only method of demolishing a witness. The court may discard a testimony if it is not believable even if the witness has not been cross-examined. *Juwar Singh v State of MP*, AIR 1981 SC 373 : 1980 Cr LJ 1418 : 1980 CLR 605.

57. *Juwar Singh v State of MP*, AIR 1981 SC 373 : 1980 Supp SCC 417 : 1980 Cr LJ 1418.

58. *Powell*, 10th Edn, p 463.

59. *Meer Sujad Ali Khan Nawab Zoolfukar Dowla Bahadoor v Lalla Kasheenath Doss*, (1866) 6 WR (Civil) 181, 182. See *P v P*, AIR 1982 Bom 498 which explains the range of cross-examination. The Court permitted questions as to the social conditions of family life and the degree to which mixing with other people would give rise to inference of adultery.

60. *Madan Lal v State of Rajasthan*,2012 Cr LJ 1430 (Raj.).

asking of leading questions is not only against the tenor of section 142 of the Evidence Act but also violates the right of an accused to a fair trial when such leading questions are permitted to be asked in the absence of defence counsel. Such conduct of trial gives accused persons, a reasonable cause for their apprehension that justice is not being done to them.

A skilful cross-examination is the highest attainment of an advocate's art. It is, difficult to frame any rules governing it; its technique can be acquired only by natural instinct or by long practice. The Act has, however, laid down some rules of guidance.

Like examination-in-chief, cross-examination must "relate to relevant facts": but unlike re-examination, it need not be confined to facts deposed to in the preceding examination (section 138). Further, it differs from both of them, inasmuch as leading questions can be asked (sections 142, 143).

No cross-examination can be allowed of a witness who is "summoned to produce a document," (section 139), but it is competent of a witness to character (section 140). Similarly, a witness may be cross-examined as to previous statements made by him in writing or reduced into writing, and relevant to matters in question without such writing being shown to him or being proved (section 145).

The range of cross-examination is unlimited, the only circumscribing limits being that it must "relate to relevant facts" (section 138).

By sections 146–150 the Legislature has tried to give very wide powers to the cross-examiner to help him in finding out the truth in oral depositions laid out before the court. But the Legislature protects the witness (i) from consequences which he might incur from speaking the truth and (ii) from needless questions, for the cross-examiner has to see that the imputations he makes against the witness are well-founded.

In the course of cross-examination, a witness may be asked questions—

(1) to test his veracity;

(2) to discover who he is and what is his position in life;

(3) to shake his credit by injuring his character, although his answer might criminate him or expose him to penalty or forfeiture (section 146).

The cross-examiner is treading on safe ground so far as (1) and (2) are concerned. As regards (3), complex set of considerations present themselves.

If the questions refer to a relevant matter the provisions of section 132 are applicable (section 147). If, however, the questions refer to an irrelevant matter, they are proper—

(1) if the truth or imputation conveyed by them would seriously affect the opinion of the court as to the credibility of the witness.

They are improper—

(1) if the imputation conveyed by them relates to matters so remote in time or of such a character that they would not affect the credibility of the witness;

(2) if there is a great disproportion between the importance of the imputation made against the witness's character and the importance of his evidence (section 148).

Before such questions are asked, the person putting them must have reasonable grounds for thinking that the imputation was well-founded (section 149). If any lawyer asks such questions without reasonable grounds, the court may report the case to the High Court or other authority to which he is subject (section 148).

All questions or inquiries which are indecent or scandalous, unless they relate to facts in issue, are to be avoided (section 151); so also all questions which are calculated to insult or annoy or couched in a needlessly offensive form (section 152).

Cross-examination is in almost all cases undertaken by the adverse party; but the court may permit a party to cross-examine his own witness if he proves to be a hostile witness (section 154).

In criminal cases (warrant cases) tried by magistrates, the accused person can, after the charge has been framed and he has given his plea, re-call and cross-examine any witness for the prosecution (Criminal Procedure Code, section 246).[61]

An accused is entitled in law to put further questions to a prosecution witness by way of cross-examination in respect of what he had stated in reply to questions put to him in cross-examination by the other co-accused.[62] An accused person may cross-examine a witness called by a co-accused for his defence when the case of the second accused is adverse to that of the first.[63]

Where the prosecution declines to call in the court of Session a witness for the Crown who has been examined in the magistrate's Court, and such witness is thereupon placed in the witness-box by counsel for the defence, the counsel for the defence is not entitled to commence his examination of the witness by questioning him as to what he had deposed in the magistrate's Court. Questions as to his previous deposition are, under the circumstances, only admissible by way of cross-examination, with the permission of the court, if the witness proves himself a hostile witness.[64]

Where the defences of a co-respondent or a co-defendant and the respondent or the defendant are identical, neither is entitled to cross-examine the other. It is only where the evidence of a co-defendant or a co-respondent is adverse to the defendant or the respondent that the defendant or respondent has the right to cross-examine.[65] Where one of the partners of a firm borrowed money on behalf of the firm in his capacity as managing partner allegedly without the consent of the other partner, it was held that the latter had the right to cross-examine the former and the order denying the same was illegal and was set aside.[66]

Cross-examination is the right of the adverse party. The party itself cannot call his witness for cross-examination.[67]

---

61. *GH Iyar v State,* 1998 Cr LJ 1821. In respect of examination of witnesses, the provisions of section 138 of the Evidence Act and those of section 311 of CrPC are complementary of each other and not conflicting.

62. *Muniappan v State of Madras,* AIR 1961 SC 175 : (1961) 1 Cr LJ 315.

63. *Ram Chand Chatterjee v Hanif Sheikh,* (1893) 21 Cal 401.

64. *Queen-Empress v Zawar Husen,* (1897) 20 All 155.

65. *Ghadiali v Ghadiali,* (1946) 48 Bom LR 36.

66. *BS Balaji v T Govindaraju,* 1996 AIHC 2484 (Kant).

67. *Sudam Sahoo v District Judge, Cuttack,* AIR 2016 Ori 38 (para 6).

It is a settled principle of law that a witness should be cross-examined on each and every point and failure to cross-examine him/her on a particular point would entail a presumption that the party, not cross-examining the witness, had accepted the evidence.[68] Any fact asserted by a witness, if not challenged in his cross-examination by the adverse party, will certainly amount to acceptance of that fact. If the relevant facts in the examination-in-chief are not challenged in the cross-examination, they shall be deemed to be admitted.[69] Where the accused had an opportunity to cross-examine the witnesses but failed to avail himself of this opportunity and adopted the cross-examination done by other accused on the witnesses. He subsequently cannot be permitted to find fault in the evidence of the witnesses and rely upon some contradictions which otherwise do not show any contradiction much less major one affecting their testimony.[70]

[s 138.3] "Relevant facts".—"Relevant facts" in cross-examination must necessarily have a wider meaning than the term when applied to examination-in-chief. For instance, the facts though otherwise irrelevant may involve questions affecting the credibility of the witness and such questions are permissible in cross-examination. Cross-examination is not limited to matters upon which the witness has already been examined in chief but extends to the whole case.[71]

[s 138.4] Proforma party.—It has been held that a proforma defendant has no right to examine or cross-examine witnesses. He does not have the right to bring in his own witnesses and cross-examine the adverse party's witnesses. This will be particularly so when he has not filed any written statement.[72] The court relied upon the decision of the Gujarat High Court in *Hussens Hasanali v Sabbhirbhai Hasanali Pulavwala*[73] "in order to cross-examination a witness it must be shown that the party seeking cross-examination is an "adverse party". Merely because a party is shown as a defendant in the cause title of the plaintiff, that party cannot be styled as an adverse party, unless it is further shown that the party is a contesting party in the sense that he disputes the case put up by the plaintiff in the plaint. If a party accepts the plaintiff's case, there is no contest between the plaintiff and that party and such a defendant cannot be styled as an "adverse party" and would therefore, not be entitled to cross examine the plaintiff."[74]

[s 138.5] Cross-examination through questions handed over in advance.—The court did not consider it proper that a counsel should have been allowed to furnish a copy of questions proposed to be asked to the defendant in his cross-examination, the intention being to conclude the cross-examination expeditiously.[75] The court said: "However statutory that objective may be, it appears to be legally unchartered and destructive of the very purpose of cross-examination. This purpose has been succinctly stated in *Meer Sujad Ali v Kashee Nath*[76] that "a skilful interrogation may produce by

68. *Gujua Manjhi v State of Jharkhand*, 2015 Cr LJ 4303, para 22 (Jhar) (DB).
69. *Mariamma Itty v KJ Abraham*, AIR 2017 CC 5, para 12 (Ker-DB).
70. *Bilal Hajar v State*, AIR 2018 SC 4780 : 2018 (4) Crimes 103 : JT 2018 (10) SC 251 : 2018 (14) Scale 11.
71. *Prashant Maheshbhai Pandya v State of Gujarat*, 2016 Cr LJ 303, para 15 (Guj).
72. *State of WB v Rama Devi*, AIR 2002 Cal 235.
73. *Hussens Hasanali v Sabbhirbhai Hasanali Pulavwala*, AIR 1981 Guj 190.
74. AP p 237, AIR 2002 Cal 235.
75. *Khairati Lal and Sons v Hari Singh*, AIR 2002 Delhi 335, at p 336.
76. 6 WR 181. The court found the decision in *Regina N Da Silva*, (1990) 1 WLR 31 since it dealt with the right of the witness to refresh memory.

Article that which usually happens accidentally." In Sarkar on Evidence[77] it is stated that: "Cross-examination is directed to (1) credibility of the witness; (2) the facts to which he had deposed in examination-in-chief including the cross-examiner's version thereof and (3) the facts to which the witness has not deposed but about which the cross-examiner thinks that he is able to depose. The object of cross-examination is two-fold: to weaken quality or destroy the case of the opponent and to establish the party's own case by means of his opponent's witnesses. The objects are to impeach the accuracy, credibility and general value of the evidence given in chief, to sift the facts already stated by the witness, to detect and expose discrepancies or to elicit suppressed facts which will support the case of the cross-examining party." If a questionnaire is to be prepared and forwarded to the witness in advance, its essential purpose would be lost since truth is usually extracted from the witness by dexterous surprise."

[s 138.5.1] ***Filing of Affidavit of Witness in Advance.***—The court deprecated the practice of getting the affidavits of witnesses in advance. The court said that it amounts to an attempt to dissuade witnesses from speaking the truth before the court. This type of interference in criminal justice should not be encouraged and is to be viewed seriously.[78]

[s 138.5.2] ***Cross-examination of co-defendant by another co-defendant.***—An order allowing such cross-examination to the extent of clash of interest between the co-defendants was held to be permissible.[79] The parties arrayed as co-defendants in the suit took contradictory stand or relevant and material issues. It was held that the defendant could cross-examine his co-defendant and his witnesses.[80]

The Evidence Act gives the right of cross-examination only to the adverse party. So, a defendant can cross-examine a co-defendant only when the interest of that co-defendant is adverse to the interest of defendant.[81] A defendant having no conflicting interest with plaintiff cannot be permitted to cross-examine the plaintiff. The right of cross-examination is available only to an adverse party.[82]

[s 138.5.3] ***Re-cross-examination.***—A witness can be recalled for his further cross-examination (re-cross-examination). The court can exercise this power on an application by the defendant. The power is not confined for its exercise to the self-motion of the court.[83] The power under the section is the exclusive power of the court. It is to be exercised in exceptional circumstances.[84] It has been held by the Supreme Court that once a witness has been examined-in-chief and cross-examined fully, such a witness should not have been recalled and re-examined to deny the evidence he had already given before the court even though he had given an inconsistent statement before any

---

77. 19th Edn 2016, Vol 2.

78. *Bachapalli Abbulu v State of AP,* 2002 Cr LJ 2527 : AIR 2003 SC 1805.

79. *Kartar Singh v Thakur Singh,* AIR 2003 NOC 130 (P&H) : 2002 AIHC 3683.

80. *Saroj Bala v Dhanpati Devi,* AIR 2007 Del 105.

81. *Smt. Annapurn Devi v Administrator General, UP.,* 2010 (1) CCC 501 (All.) (DB).

82. *Vijaya v Saraswathi.,* 2008 (3) CCC 535 (Mad.).

83. *SSS Durian pandian v SA Samuthra Pandian,* AIR 1998 Mad 323; *State of Rajasthan v Teja Ram,* AIR 1999 SC 1776 : (1999) 3 SCC 507 : 1999 Cr LJ 2588.

84. *V Shanmugam v S Umamaheswaran,* AIR 2008 NOC 646 (Mad), petitioner failed to elicit certain facts, applied for recall of witness, six months time had already been given, that was sufficient time, application not allowed.

other forum or Court subsequently. A witness can be confronted only with a previous statement made by him.[85]

However, merely with the change of counsel, a witness cannot be recalled for further cross-examination, when the prosecutrix is thoroughly cross-examined and otherwise, no case for recalling the witness is made out. Hence, the order of trial Court re-summoning the prosecutrix for further cross-examination at belated stage was held to be illegal.[86]

[s 138.5.4] ***Cross-examination of co-respondent (Recall for further cross-examination).***—The right of cross-examination can be exercised by co-respondents when their interests are in direct conflict with each other.[87]

The only ground on which the witness was sought to be recalled for further cross-examination was that the earlier counsel representing the petitioner did not cross-examine the witness effectively due to inadvertence on the point of adverse possession. There was nothing in the application to show that new facts had come to knowledge which required recalling. Effective cross-examination was a very vague term. A witness cannot be allowed to be recalled merely on the change of counsel and that too for filling up the lacuna left in the case.[88]

[s 138.6] Re-examination.—The object of re-examination is to afford the party calling a witness an opportunity of filling in the lacuna or explaining the inconsistencies which the cross-examination has discovered in the examination-in-chief of the witness. It is accordingly limited to the explanation of matters referred to in cross-examination (section 138). It partakes of the nature of examination-in-chief inasmuch as no leading questions can be asked (section 142).

The party who calls a witness has the right to re-examine him on all matters arising out of the cross-examination for the purpose of reconciling any discrepancies that may exist between the evidence on the examination-in-chief and that which has been given in cross-examination; or for the purpose of removing or diminishing any suspicion that the cross-examination may have cast on the evidence-in-chief; or to enable the witness to state the whole truth as to matters which have only been partially dealt with in cross-examination.[89]

In re-examination the party has a right to ask all questions which may be proper to draw forth an explanation of the meaning of the expressions used by the witness on cross-examination, if they be in themselves doubtful, and also of the motive, or provocation, which induced the witness to those expressions, but he has not right to go further, and to introduce matter new in itself and not suited to explain either the expressions or the motives of the witness.[90] If the counsel chooses to cross-examine the witness as to *facts which were not admissible in evidence*, the other party has a right to re-examine him as to the evidence so given.[91] If a question has been omitted in the examination-in-chief, and cannot, in strictness, be asked on re-examination as not arising out of the cross-examination, it is usual for counsel to request the judge

85. *Mishri Lal v State of MP*, (2005) 10 SCC 701 : 2005 (2) Crimes 216 (SC).
86. *Baldev Singh v State of Punjab*,., 2007 Cr LJ (NOC) 251 (P&H).
87. *Ennen Castings Pvt Ltd v MM Sundaresh*, AIR 2003 Kant 293.
88. *Akash v Gian Singh*, AIR 2010 HP 93 : LNIND 2010 HP 235.
89. *Powell*, 10 Edn, p 469.
90. *Taylor*, 12th Edn, section 1474, p 939.
91. *Ibid*, section 1475, p 940.

to make inquiry and such a request is generally granted.[92] If the cross-examination is ineffective, no re-examination is, as a rule, made.

Questions in re-examination cannot be confined to ambiguities alone which became exposed in cross-examination. Questions can be put to seek explanation of any matter referred to in cross-examination.[93]

However, totally new facts which have no concern with the cross-examination cannot be introduced in re-examination.[94]

The court proceeded to explain the position as follows:[95] "There is an erroneous impression that re-examination should be confined to clarification of ambiguities which have been brought down in cross-examination. No doubt, ambiguities can be resolved through re-examination. But that is not the only function of the re-examiner. If the party who called the witness feels the explanation is required for any matter referred to in cross-examination he has the liberty to put any question in re-examination to get the explanation. The Public Prosecutor should formulate his questions for that purpose. Explanation may be required either when ambiguity remains regarding any answer elicited during cross-examination or even otherwise. If the Public Prosecutor feels that certain answers require more elucidation from the witness he has the freedom and the right to put such questions as he deems necessary for that purpose, subject of course to the control of the court in accordance with the other provisions. But the court cannot direct him to confine his questions to ambiguities alone which arose in cross-examination. Even if the Public Prosecutor feels that new matters should be elicited from the witness he can do so, in which case the only requirement is that he must secure permission of the court. if the court thinks that such new matters are necessary for proving any material fact, Courts must be liberal in granting permission to put necessary question. A Public prosecutor who is attentive during cross-examination cannot but be sensitive to discern which answer in cross-examination requires explanation. An efficient Public Prosecutor would gather up such answers falling from the mouth of a witness during cross-examination and formulate necessary questions to be put in re-examination. There is no warrant that re-examination should be limited to one or two questions. If the exigency requires any number of questions can be asked in re-examination."

The examination-in-chief cannot be supplemented by way of re-examination. Totally new facts cannot be introduced which have no concern with cross-examination.[96] During the cross-examination of a prosecution witness, doubts arose about interpretation of certain parts of his evidence. The prosecution failed to clarify the same by calling the witness for re-examination. The court said that the benefit of doubt had to go to the defence.[97]

[s 138.7] Tendering witness for cross-examination.—The practice of tendering witnesses for cross-examination is inconsistent with this section. It ought never to be

92. *Ibid*, section 1477, p 942. Where no such request was made by the prosecution and the evidence on both sides was closed, the Supreme Court held that re-examination should not have been allowed, *Mir Mohd Omar v State of WB*, AIR 1989 SC 1785 : 1989 Cr LJ 2070 : (1989) 4 SCC 436 : 1989 SCC (Cri) 750; *Jugroo v State of MP*, 2002 Cr LJ 1050 (MP), order of examination found to be proper.

93. *Rammi v State of MP*, AIR 1999 SC 3544 : (1999) 8 SCC 649 : 1999 Cr LJ 4561.

94. *Pannayar v State of Tamil Nadu by Inspector of Police*, 2009 Cr LJ 4454 (SC).

95. *Ibid*, pp 3547-48.

96. *Pannayar v State of TN*, AIR 2010 SC 85 : (2009) 9 SCC 152.

97. *Ramsewak v State of MP*, (2004) 11 SCC 259 : 2004 Cr LJ 3043.

employed in the case of a witness whose evidence is not merely formal. The practice leads only to confusion and does not induce to the discovery of the truth.[98]

[s 138.8] Recall of a witness.—The object of the provision for recall of witness, is to reserve the power with the court to prevent any injustice in the conduct of trial at any stage. The power available with the court to prevent injustice has to be exercised only if the court, for valid reasons, feels that injustice is caused to a party. Such a finding with reasons must be specifically recorded by the court before this power is exercised. It is not possible to lay down precise situations when such power can be exercised. The legislature in its wisdom has left the power undefined. Thus, the scope of the power has to be considered from case to case.[99]

[s 138.9] Examination by Court.—It is not the province of the court to examine the witnesses, unless the pleaders on either side have omitted to put some material question or questions; and the court should, as a general rule, leave the witnesses to the pleaders to be dealt with as laid down in this section.[100] The judge's right to question is circumscribed by the adversary system. Where the judge rebuked a witness and threatened him with prosecution for perjury, the whole trial was held to be vitiated.[101]

[s 138.10] Enquiry into perjury.—Certain witnesses were examined for the purpose of an inquiry into a complaint of perjury. It was held that persons against whom there were allegations of perjury could take part in the enquiry and cross-examine the witness examined by the court.[102]

[s 139] Cross-examination of person called to produce a document.—A person summoned to produce a document does not become a witness by the mere fact that he produces it and cannot be cross-examined unless and until he is called as a witness.

COMMENT

[s 139.1] Principle.—A witness summoned merely to produce a document does not become a witness for purposes of cross-examination, since he may either attend the court personally or may depute any person to produce the document in court (Civil Procedure Code, O XVI, rule 6; Criminal Procedure Code, section 91). If he intentionally omits to produce the document, he commits the offence punishable under section 175 of the Indian Penal Code, or section 345 of the Criminal Procedure Code, 1973. This section must be read with section 162.

The wife of a partner was called upon to produce the deed of dissolution of the firm. She was not permitted to be examined as a witness.[103]

Where a witness denies, on oath, that he has the possession or means of producing a particular document, he can, if he has been guilty of falsehood, be prosecuted for

98. *Emperor v Kasamalli Mirzalli*, (1941) 44 Bom LR 27 : (1942) Bom 384 (FB); *Emperor v Sadeppa Gireppa Mutgi*, (1941) 43 Bom LR 946 : (1942) Bom 115; *Re Veera Koravan*, (1929) 53 Mad 69.
99. *State (NCT of Delhi) v Shiv Kumar*, (2016) 2 SCC 402, para 11.
100. Per Garth CJ, in *Noor Bux Kazi v The Empress*, (1880) 6 Cal 279, 283.
101. *Ram Chander v State of Haryana*, AIR 1981 SC 1036 : 1981 Cr LJ 609 : (1981) 3 SCR 12 : (1981) 3 SCC 191 : 1981 SCC (Cri) 683.
102. *Kishorilal v State of Rajasthan*, 1999 Cri lJ 840 (Raj).
103. *Parmeshwari Devi v State*, AIR 1977 SC 403 : 1977 Cr LJ 245 : (1977) 1 SCC 169.

giving false evidence in a judicial proceeding.[104] The summons to produce a document is in English law called a *subpoena duces tecum.*

[s 140] Witnesses to character.—Witnesses to character may be cross-examined and re-examined.

COMMENT

This section must be read with section 53. In most cases, witnesses to character not only may but must be cross-examined. The use of character evidence is to assist the court in estimating the value of the evidence brought against the accused. Holt CJ, observed in a case that "a man is not born a knave; there must be time to make him so; nor is he presently discovered after he becomes one. A man may be reputed an able man this year, and yet be a beggar the next; it is a misfortune that happens to many men, and his former reputation will signify nothing to him upon this occasion."[105]

[s 141] Leading questions.—Any question suggesting the answer which the person putting it wishes or expects to receive is called a leading question.

[s 142] When they must not be asked.—Leading questions must not, if objected to by the adverse party, be asked in an examination-in-chief, or in a re-examination, except with the permission of the Court.

The Court shall permit leading questions as to matters which are introductory or undisputed, or which have, in its opinion, been already sufficiently proved.

[s 143] When they may be asked.—Leading question may be asked in cross-examination.

COMMENT

A "leading question" is one which suggests to the witness the answer which it is desired he should give. But if it merely suggests a subject, without suggesting an answer or a specific thing, it is not leading. Leading questions cannot ordinarily be asked in examination-in-chief or re-examination. The witness is presumed to be biased in favour of the party examining him and might thus be prompted. The reason for excluding leading questions is quite obvious: it would enable a party to prepare his story and evolve it in his very words from the mouth of his witnesses in court. It would tend to diminish chances of detection of a concocted story. If a witness is allowed to give his narrative in his own words, he is likely, if the story is made up, to leave some loopholes, to which the cross-examiner will scarcely fail to direct his attack.

Leading questions can only be asked in examination-in-chief when they refer to matters which are (1) introductory; (2) undisputed or (3) sufficiently proved. For, if it were not allowed to approach the points at issue by such questions, the examination would be most inconveniently protracted. To abridge the proceedings, and bring the witness as soon as possible to the material points on which he is to speak, counsel

---

104. Per West J, in *Re Premchand Dowlatram*, (1887) 12 Bom 63, 65.
105. *Haagen Swendsen*, (1902) How St Tr 559, 596.

may lead him on to that length, and may recapitulate to him the acknowledged facts of the case which have been already established.[106]

The reason why leading questions are allowed to be put to an adverse witness in cross-examination is that the purpose of a cross-examination being to test the accuracy, credibility and general value of the evidence given, and to sift the facts already stated by the witness, it sometimes becomes necessary for a party to put leading questions in order to elicit facts in support of his case, even though the facts so elicited may be entirely unconnected with facts testified to in an examination-in-chief. Where a general order is made that no leading questions shall be allowed in cross-examination, the order is illegal and vitiates the trial.[107]

It is the court, and not counsel for the State, who can determine whether leading questions should be permitted, and the responsibility for that permission rests on the court.[108]

In a criminal trial,[109] leading questions were permitted to be asked to a prosecution witness in examination-in-chief in the absence of defence counsel. It was held that asking of leading questions is not only against the tenor of section 142 of the Evidence Act but also violates the right of an accused to a fair trial when such leading questions are permitted to be asked in the absence of defence counsel. Such conduct of trial gives a reasonable cause to the accused persons for their apprehension that justice is not being done to them.

Leading questions can be freely asked in cross-examination: "First, and principally, on the supposition that the witness has a bias in favour of the party bringing him forward, and hostile to his opponent. Secondly, that the party calling a witness has an advantage over his adversary, in knowing beforehand what the witness will prove, or at least is expected to prove; and that, consequently, if he were allowed to lead, he might interrogate in such a manner as to extract only so much of the knowledge of the witness as would be favourable to his side, or even put a false gloss upon the whole."[110]

With respect to the mode of conducting a cross-examination, it is admitted on all hands that leading questions may in general be asked, but this does not mean that the counsel may go to the length of putting the very words into the mouth of the witness which he is to echo back again. Neither does it sanction the putting of a question assuming that facts have been proved which have not been proved, nor that particular answers have been given contrary to the fact. The rule ought also to receive some further qualification where the witness is evidently hostile to the party calling him, for although it appears in one case to have been laid down that leading questions may always be put in cross-examination, whether a witness be unwilling or not, some restriction should surely be imposed where the witness betrays a vehement desire to serve the cross-examining party. It is no answer to say that the party, who originally called the witness, has brought the evil on his own head, for a fraudulent witness might purposely conceal his bias in favour

106. *Taylor*, 12th Edn, section 1404, pp 890, 891. *Abdul Aziz Lokhandwala v Nasir Ali*, AIR 2010 NOC 613 (Bom), leading questions in examination-in-chief with the permission of the court.

107. *Sri LP v Inspector General of Police*, (1954) All LJ 316.

108. *Per Jenkins* CJ, in *Barindra, Kumar Ghose v Emperor*, (1909) 37 Cal 467, 509.

109. *Madan Lal v State of Rajasthan*,2012 Cr LJ 1430 (Raj.).

110. *Best*, 12th Edn, section 641, p 561.

of one party, and thus induce the other to call him, or he might be an attesting witness, or other person whom it was necessary to examine to establish some technical part of the case. To allow such a witness to have the most favourable answers suggested to him through the medium of leading questions would be obviously unjust.[111]

The prosecution cannot put leading questions on the material part of the evidence which the witness intends to give against the accused. It would be a method of eliciting evidence from the witness which is desired by the prosecutor. Such leading questions offend the right of the accused to fair trial enshrined in Article 21 of the Constitution. It is not a curable irregularity.[112] The court explained the effect of the provisions as follows: The criminal trial was unfair to the appellant and the procedure adopted in the trial was obviously illegal and unconstitutional. The Sessions Court in fairness recorded the evidence in the form of questions put by the prosecutor and defence counsel and answers given by each witness. The material part of the prosecution case to connect the appellant with the crime was from certain witnesses. The Sessions Court permitted even without objection by the defence to put leading questions in the chief examination itself suggesting all the answers which the prosecutor intended to get from the witnesses to connect the appellant with the crime. The attention of the witness cannot be directed in chief examination to the subject of the enquiry/trial. The court may permit leading question to draw the attention of the witness which cannot otherwise be called to the matter under enquiry, trial or investigation. The discretion of the court must only be controlled towards that end but a question which suggests to the witness the answer the prosecutor expects must not be allowed unless the witness, with the permission of the court, is declared hostile and cross-examination is directed thereafter in that behalf. Therefore, as soon as the witness has been conducted to the material portion of his examination, it is generally the duty of the prosecutor to ask the witness to state the facts or to give his own account of the matter making him speak as to what he had seen. The prosecutor will not be allowed to frame his questions in such a manner that the witness by answering merely "yes" or "no" will give the evidence which the prosecutor wishes to elicit. The witness must account for what he himself had seen. Section 142 does not empower the prosecutor to put leading questions on the material part of the evidence which the witness intends to speak against the accused and the prosecutor shall not be allowed to frame questions in such a manner to which the witness answer merely "yes" or "no"; but he shall be directed to give evidence of the facts which he witnessed. The question shall not be put to enable the witness to give evidence which the prosecutor wishes to elicit from the witness nor shall the prosecutor put into witness's mouth the words which he hoped that the witness will utter nor in any other way suggest to him the answer which it is desired that the witness would give. The counsel must leave the witness to tell unvarnished tale of this own account. In the instant case, the prosecutor led the witnesses to what he intended that they should say on the material part of the prosecution case to prove against the appellant. This was illegal and obviously unfair to the appellant offending his right to fair trial enshrined under Article 21 of the Constitution. It is not a curable irregularity.

The impact of a leading question has to be assessed on the facts of each case. It simply cannot be that every single leading question would invalidate the trial.[113]

---

111. *Taylor*, 12th Edn, section 1431, pp 912-913.

112. *Varkey Joseph v State of Kerala*, AIR 1993 SC 1892 : 1993 Cr LJ 2010 : AIR 1994 SC 1892 : (1993) 3 Punj LR 643 : (1992) 2 Ker LJ 617.

113. *Sidharth Vashisht @ Manu Sharma v State (NCT of Delhi)*, AIR 2010 SC 2352 : (2010) 6 SCC 1.

[s 144] Evidence as to matters in writing.—Any witness may be asked, whilst under examination, whether any contract, grant or other disposition of property, as to which he is giving evidence, was not contained in a document, and if he says that it was, or if he is about to make any statement as to the contents of any document, which, in the opinion of the Court, ought to be produced, the adverse party may object to such evidence being given until such document is produced, or until facts have been proved which entitle the party who called the witness to give secondary evidence of it.

***Explanation.*—A witness may give oral evidence of statements made by other persons about the contents of documents if such statements are in themselves relevant facts.**

ILLUSTRATION

The question is, whether *A* assaulted *B*.

C deposes that he heard *A* say to *D*—"*B* wrote a letter accusing me of theft, and I will be revenged on him." This statement is relevant as showing *A*'s motive for the assault, and evidence may be given of it, though no other evidence is given about the letter.

COMMENT

This section is meant to enable parties to carry out the provisions of sections 91 and 92. It should be read along with those sections. It refers both to the examination-in-chief and cross-examination. A party can compel the opposite party to produce a document (or to make out a case for letting in its secondary evidence)—

(1) when a witness is about to give evidence as to any (a) contract, (b) grant, or (c) other disposition of property, which is contained in a document; or

(2) when he is about to make any statement as to the contents of any document.

This rule does not forbid a witness to give oral evidence of statements as to relevant facts, made by other persons, about the contents of documents.

[114][s 145] Cross-examination as to previous statements in writing.—A witness may be cross-examined as to previous statements made by him in writing or reduced into writing and relevant to matters in question, without such writing being shown to him, or being proved; but, if it is intended to contradict him by the writing, his attention must, before the writing can be proved, be called to those parts of it which are to be used for the purpose of contradicting him.

SYNOPSIS

114. As to the application of section 145 to police-diaries, see the Code of Criminal Procedure, 1973 (2 of 1974), section 172.

COMMENT

In a way this section is an exception to the general rule forbidding all use of the contents of a written document until the document itself be produced.

[s 145.1] Principle.—A witness may be cross-examined as to any statements as to relevant facts made by him on a former occasion, in writing or reduced into writing, without showing the writing to him or proving the same. But if it is intended to contradict him by the writing, his attention must be called to the writing. The object of this provision is either to test the memory of a witness or to contradict him by previous statements in writing. Such writing may be documents, letters, depositions, police diaries, etc. It must be noted that the previous record should be in writing.[115] The witness may also be contradicted by his previous verbal statements (section 153, Exception 2).

Statements which are not fully recorded or statements which are recorded in the form of memorandum are statements falling within the ambit of this section. The statement may be either written by the witness himself or which was reduced into writing by someone else.[116] Unsigned statements cannot be used as previous statements to contradict the witness.[117] The first information report (FIR) is not substantive evidence. It is information of a cognizable offence given under section 154, CrPC. Statements made in it can be used for contradicting and discrediting a witness under section 143.[118] Evidence recorded in criminal proceeding was transferred to the Sessions trial for the purpose of contradicting a witness. That becomes substantive evidence.[119] Admissions should be tested by cross-examination.[120]

A witness may be questioned as to his previous written statements for two purposes: it may be to test his memory; and the very object would be defeated if the writing were placed in his hand before the questions were asked, or it may be to contradict him; and here it would be obviously unfair not to give him every opportunity of seeing how the matter really stands.

If you intend to impeach a witness you are bound, whilst he is in the box, to give him an opportunity of making any explanation which is open to him, and that is not only a rule of professional practice in the conduct of a case, but is essential to fair play and fair dealing with witnesses.[121]

---

115. *Majid v State of Haryana*, AIR 2002 SC 382, the son of the deceased deposed that he saw his mother being killed by the accused. He was sought to be contradicted by his earlier statement that his father had killed his mother. This was not allowed because the earlier statement was not in writing; *Balakram v State of Uttarakhand*, AIR 2017 SC 2375 : 2017 (5) Scale 220 : (2017) 7 SCC 668, a witness may be cross-examined as to his previous statements if such previous statements are brought on record in accordance with law, and if the contingencies as contemplated under section 172(3) of CrPC are fulfilled.

116. *President, SVV Mandal v Yellaiah*, AIR 1969 AP 148.

117. *State of Haryana v Harpal Singh*, AIR 1978 SC 1530 : 1978 Cr LJ 1603.

118. *Nankhu Singh v Bihar*, AIR 1973 SC 491 : 1972 Cr LJ 1204 .

119. *Ashok Kumar v State (Delhi Admn.)*, AIR 1977 SC 1304 : 1977 Cr LJ 814 : (1977) 2 SCC 233. Where such statements have not been transferred to the Sessions Judge they cannot be used as substantive evidence. *Jit Singh v State of Punjab*, AIR 1976 SC 1421 : 1976 Cr LJ 1162 : (1976) 2 SCC 836.

120. *Sitaram v Ram Chandra*, AIR 1977 SC 1712 : (1977) 2 SCC 49; *Public Prosecutor, HC of AP v Vendala Semaiah*, 2000 Cr LJ (NOC) 29 (AP), witnesses not standing the test of cross- examination.

121. Per Lord Herschell,LC in *Browne v Dunn*; (1893) 6 R 57—HL *Md. Badaruddin Ad v State of Assam*, 1989 Cr LJ 1876 (Gau), the requirement of the section is of compulsory nature. *Ganakanta Das v State of Assam*, 1990 Cr LJ 219 (Gau), that part of the statement which is to be used must be pin-pointed by marking it. Also on the same point, *Ghanshyam v State of MP*, 1990 Cr LJ 1017 (MP).

The expression "previous statements made" used in section 145 cannot be extended to include statements made by a witness, after the filing of the charge sheet. The expression must, therefore, be confined to statements made by a witness before the police during investigation and not thereafter.[122]

[s 145.2] Contradiction of witness.—As regards the contradiction of a witness by a previous statement, section 162 of the Code of Criminal Procedure, 1973 sanctions a very extraordinary procedure. This section in its ordinary application is intended for the purpose of such contradiction by a written previous statement for which the witness is responsible. This cannot in terms apply to a statement recorded under section 161 of the Code of Criminal Procedure, for the record of which he cannot be held to be directly responsible and which he does not sign. The Legislature, however, intended that the principle of this section should apply and that attention of the witness should be called to those parts of diary entries by which it is intended to contradict him by proving that they represent the actual statement of the witness to the police. In many cases the investigating officer may be able to prove that the writing is an accurate record or at any rate, a correct summary of the statements made to him by the witness during the course of the investigation. In that event, the writing comes on the record as proof of the statement of the witness.[123] The section is attracted only when two contradictory statements are made by the same witness and not when the statement of one witness is contradicted by another witness.[124] The court would not be permitted to accept the version of the defence witnesses as correct merely because the defence witnesses have not been contradicted by reference to their previous statements.[125] A witness can be contradicted only when he denies his statement and not when he admits it.[126]

---

122. *State (NCT of Delhi) v Mukesh*, (2014) 15 SCC 661, para 10.

123. *Heramba Lal Ghosh v Emperor*, (1945) 1 Cal 326 : AIR (32) **1945** Cal; *Santosh v State of Chhatisgarh*, 2002 Cr LJ 1180 : **2001 (4) MPHT 63 CG** (Chha), documents needed for contradiction can be ordered to be produced.

124. *Mohanlal v State of Maharashtra*, AIR 1982 SC 839 : 1982 Cr LJ 630(2) : (1982) 1 SCC 700 : 1982 SCC (Cri) 334.

125. *Balakrishnan v State of Tamil Nadu*, AIR 2018 SC 1153.

126. *Dhanbal v State of TN*, AIR 1980 SC 628; *State of Rajasthan v Kartar Singh*, (1971) 1 SCR 56. Minor contradictions not to rule out the witness. *Dharamvir v State*, 1990 Cr LJ 839 : 1989 All LJ 454; *Shaik Subhani v State of AP*, 2000 Cr LJ 321 (AP), putting suggestions to a witness which he goes on denying was held as not amounting to contradicting the witness. *Rajendra Singh v State of Bihar*, 2000 Cr LJ 2199: AIR 2000 SC 1779 : (2000) 4 SCC 298, the former statement of the witness which was exhibited to him did not carry any signature or seal of office. Hence, it could not be said to be the proved statement of the witness, the witness was also not confronted with that part of the statement with which the defence wanted to contradict him. The provisions of section 145 were not attracted. *Tahir v State of UP*, 2000 Cr LJ 1342 (All), a witness was sought to be recalled after he had concluded his evidence. The basis of the application was that he subsequently filed an affidavit which contradicted his previous statements made in the court. The court said that this was not allowable under section 145. *Shyam Singh Hada v State*, 2002 Cr LJ 1437 (Raj), contradiction must be of material nature otherwise the prosecution case cannot be jettisoned. *Bishna v State of WB*, (2005) 12 SCC 657 : AIR 2006 SC 302, cross-examination as to previous contradictory statements in writing. In certain cases omissions are also considered as contradictions. *Karan Singh v State of MP*, (2003) 12 SCC 587 : 2003 (4) Crimes 180 (SC), the previous statement of the witness was put to him, nor he was given an opportunity to explain it the statement could not be used to contradict the present statement of the witness. *Chaudhary Ramjibhai Narsangbhai v State of Gujarat*, AIR 2004 SC 313 : (2004) 1 SCC 184, the section comes into play when a witness makes contradictory statements.

[s 145.3] Prosecutrix.—A statement made by the prosecutrix to the doctor who examined her which was put before her during her cross-examination was not allowed to be used to contradict her.[127]

[s 145.4] Documents.—A witness can be confronted with the statements made in writing in his account-books: but a clerk who writes the accounts at the mere dictation of his employer cannot be so confronted. In a case, A was employed by B, at intervals of a week or fortnight, to write up B's account-books, B furnishing him with the necessary information either orally or from loose memoranda. It was held that the entries so made could not be given in evidence to contradict A under this section, as previous statements made by him in writing. The statements were really made, not by A but B, under whose instructions A had written them.[128]

Documents were produced without any objection as to admissibility. Objections cannot be raised for the first time in appeal. The Counsel endorsed the document with remark: "formal proof dispensed with." The party relying upon the document was absolved from proving.[129]

[s 145.5] Depositions.—This section, which has to be read with section 162 of the Code of Criminal Procedure, quite clearly indicates that the attention of a witness is to be called to the previous statement before the writing can be proved. If the witness admits the previous statement, or explains any discrepancy or contradiction, it becomes unnecessary for the statement thereafter to be proved. On the other hand, if the statement still requires to be proved that can be done by calling the person before whom the statement was made.[130] A statement made by a witness to a police-officer in the course of an investigation can be used only to contradict him in the manner provided by this section and for no other purpose.[131]

In a trial before a Court of Sessions, counsel for the accused is not entitled to refer to the depositions given before the committing magistrate for the purpose of contradicting the witnesses before the Sessions Court, without drawing their attention to the alleged contradictions in their previous depositions and giving them an opportunity of explaining the same.[132]

A first information report is not ordinarily substantive evidence. It is merely a previous statement, which may be proved by the prosecution for the purpose of corroborating the first informant, and may be used by the defence for the purpose of contradicting him.[133] For the latter purpose it is essential that the attention of the witness should be drawn to

---

127. *Narayanamma v State of Karnataka*, (1994) 5 SCC 728 at p 732 : 1994 SCC (Cr) 1573.

128. *Munchershaw Bezonji v The New Dhurumsey S & W Co*, (1880) 4 Bom 576.

129. *Daya Shankar v Bachi*, AIR 1982 All 376.

130. *Muzaffar Khan v The Crown*, (1939) 20 Lah 509.

131. *Prakash Chandra v State (Delhi Admn.)* AIR 1979 SC 400 : 1979 Cr LJ 329; *Guggiliasanthosh Reddy v State of AP*, 2001 Cr LJ (NOC) 110 (AP) : (2001) 1 Andh LJ (Cri) 76, the statement of a witness under section 164, CrPC is only a previous statement. It cannot be taken as a substantive evidence. It can be used for contradicting the witness. Convicting the accused on the basis of such a statement is not proper. An inquest report is also not a substantive piece of evidence. It can be used for corroborating the evidence of other witnesses.

132. *Emperor v Zawar Rahman*, (1902) 31 Cal 142 (FB); *Queen-Empress v Dan Sahai*, (1885) 7 All 862; *Reg. v Arjun Megha*, (1874) 11 BHC 281; *Emperor v Lakshman*, (1915) 17 Bom LR 590; *Bal Gangadhar Tilak v Shri Shriniwas Pandit*, (1915) 17 Bom LR 527 : 42 IA 135 : 39 Bom 441.

133. *Nankhu Singh v State of Bihar*, AIR 1973 SC 491 : 1972 Cr LJ 1204.

those parts of the document, which it is intended to use for the purpose of contradicting him, in order that he may be given an opportunity to furnish a suitable explanation with regard to the alleged contradictions. Statements in the first information report cannot be used for the purpose of discrediting any witness, other than the first informant, for such use is in effect to treat the first information report as substantive evidence in the case.[134]

[s 145.6] Police diaries.—"It is the absolute duty of Judges and Magistrates to entirely disregard all statements and entries in special diaries as being in any sense legal evidence for any purpose, except for one solitary purpose of contradicting the Police-officer who made the special diary when they do afford such a contradiction; and even in that case they are not evidence of anything except that such Police-officer made the particular entry which is at variance with his subsequently given evidence; they are not evidence that what is stated in the entry was true or correctly represents what was said or done."[135]

"Where the Police-officer who made the special diary is allowed to refresh his memory and does look at an entry in the Diary for the purpose of refreshing his memory, the provisions of section 161 of the Indian Evidence Act...apply, and the accused or his agent is entitled to see such entry in the special diary and to cross-examine such Police-officer thereupon. There is no provision in section 172 of the Code of Criminal Procedure, 1973 enabling any person other than the Police-officer who made the special diary to refresh his memory by looking at the special diary and the necessary implication is that a special diary cannot be used to enable any witness other than the Police-officer who made the special diary to refresh his memory by looking at it.[136] This is in truth a general principle of law. The Criminal Court, but not an accused person or his agent unless the Police-officer has been allowed to look at the diary in order to refresh his memory, can use the special diary for the purpose of contradicting the Police-officer who made it, but before doing so the court must comply with the specific enactment of section 145 of the Indian Evidence Act...and call the attention of the Police-officer to such parts of the special diary as are to be used for the purpose of contradicting him, otherwise such a use of the special diary would be illegal. There is no provision in section 172 of the Code of Criminal Procedure enabling the court, the prosecution or the accused to use the special diary for the purpose of contradicting any witness other than the Police-officer who made it, and the necessary implication is that the special diary cannot be used to contradict any witness other than the Police-officer who made it. Section 145 of the Indian Evidence Act does not either extend or control the provisions of section 172 of the Code of Criminal Procedure. It is only if the court uses the special diary for the purpose of contradicting the Police-officer who made it that section 145 of the Indian Evidence Act. applies, and in such case it applies for that purpose only, and not for the purpose of enabling the court or a party to contradict any other witness in the case, or to show it or any part of its contents to any other witness. No reading of section 172 of the Code of Criminal Procedure consistent with the rules of construction and a knowledge of the English language is possible by which the special diary is to be used to contradict any person except the

134. *Emperor v Rahenuddin Mandal,* (1943) 2 Cal 381; *Nisar Ali,* (1957) 1 All 361 SC. Also see, *Kirender Sarkar v State of Assam,* (2009) 12 SCC 342 at para 11 and 12; *Asharam v State of MP,* (2007) 11 SCC 164 at para 18.

135. *Per* EDGE, C.J, in *Queen-Empress v Mannu,* (1897) 19 All 390, 412 (FB); *Dadan Gazi v Emperor,* (1906) 33 Cal 1023, 1026, 1027.

136. These provisions are not discriminatory *Subhash Chandra v UOI,* 1988 Cr LJ 1077 Raj.

Police-officer who made it. It is not enacted in section 172 of the Code of Criminal Procedure by reference to section 145 of the Indian Evidence Act, or otherwise that if the special diary is used by the court to contradict the Police-officer who made it, it may thereupon or thereafter be used to contradict any other witness in the case."[137]

A certified copy of the statements recorded under section 176 of the Code of Criminal Procedure, 1973 does not constitute an evidence in itself. It can be used as an evidence under this section to contract the present statements of the witness. This would require the witness to be produced, cross-examined and an opportunity given to him either to admit the statement or to deny it.[138]

A statement of witness made before the investigating officer was not allowed to be used for the purpose of cross-examining the witness to establish contradiction between one statement and another.[139]

The statement made by the accused to the police during investigation is admissible in evidence in a civil suit. The fact that the signature of the maker was not obtained thereon does not make it inadmissible. The court will, however, consider such statement keeping in mind the rule of caution.[140]

The Supreme Court stated the position in this regard as follows:[141] "Section 162 of the Code of Criminal Procedure imposes a bar on the use of any statement made by any person to a police officer in the course of investigation at any inquiry or trial, except for the purpose of contradicting the witness in the manner provided by section 145 of the Evidence Act. Where any part of such statement is so used any other part may also be used in the re-examination of the witness for the limited purpose of explaining any matter referred to in the cross-examination. The only other exception to this embargo relates to the statements falling within the provisions of sec. 32(1) or permitted to be proved under section 27. Section 145 provides that a witness may be cross-examined as to previous statements made by him in writing and relevant to maters in question, without such statement being shown to him or being proved, but that if it is intended to contradict him by the writing, the attention must, before the writing can be proved, be called to those parts of it which are to be used for the purpose of contradicting him. The courts below were clearly wrong in using as substantive evidence statements made by the witness in the course of investigation. The definition of the word "proved" in sec. 3 does not enable the court to take into consideration matters, including statements whose use is statutorily barred."

Statements of witnesses recorded during inquest cannot be used as evidence.[142] An FIR is not a substantive piece of evidence. It can be used only to contradict or corroborate the version in the court of the person who filed the report. Where the

---

137. *Per* Edge CJ, in *Queen-Empress v Mannu*, (1897) 19 All 390, 393, 394 (FB); *Balakram v State of Uttarakhand*, AIR 2017 SC 2375 : 2017(5) Scale 220 : (2017) 7 SCC 668, unless the investigating officer or the court uses the case diary either to refresh the memory or contradicting the investigating officer as previous statement that too after drawing his attention thereto as is enjoined under section 145, the entries cannot be used by the accused as evidence.

138. *Gauri Shanker Sharma v State of UP*, AIR 1990 SC 709 : 1990 Supp SCC 656 : (1990) 1 Crimes 196.

139. *Kemparaju v State*, 2000 Cr LJ 4734 (Kant).

140. *Khair Mohamed Reas Mohamed v State of Maharashtra*, 1995 Cr LJ 568 (Bom). The court **referred** to *Zahiruddin v Emperor*, AIR 1947 PC 75 : (1947) 48 Cr LJ 679.

141. *Hazarilal v State (Delhi Admn.)*, AIR 1986 SC 1883 : 1999 Cr LJ 18.

142. *Malkiat Singh v State of Punjab*, (1991) 4 SCC 341 : 1991 SCC (Cr) 976.

inconsistent statements in the FIR are not shown to the witness during his examination, they cannot be used as evidence.[143]

Entries in a case diary cannot be relied upon by the prosecution as a substantive evidence. It can only be used for contradicting the prosecution witnesses.[144] Statements of a witness in a case diary of some other case can also be used.[145]

[s 145.6.1] ***Person not examined-in-chief, cannot be cross-examined as to previous statements.***—A person who was not examined-in-chief was not allowed to be cross-examined as to previous statements in writing. The Court said: By its very nomenclature section 145 deals with the aspect of cross-examination. The question of cross examination would arise if only a particular witness was examined-in-chief. Admittedly third party purchaser, in this case, was not examined-in-chief. Therefore, invoking section 145 in the context of the application made by her does not arise.[146]

[s 145.7] Supply of copy to accused.—Where the statement of the prosecutrix was recorded by the investigating officer in the course of investigation, it was held that not furnishing a copy of it to the accused was illegal. It violated the statutory right of the accused to test the veracity of the evidence of the proecutrix.[147]

[s 146] Questions lawful in cross-examination.—When a witness is cross-examined, he may, in addition to the questions hereinbefore referred to,[s 146.2] be asked any questions which tend—

(1) to test his veracity,[s 146.3]

(2) to discover who he is and what is his position in life,[s 146.4] or

(3) to shake his credit by injuring his character,[s 146.5] although the answer to such questions might tend directly or indirectly to criminate him or might expose or tend directly or indirectly to expose him to a penalty or forfeiture:

[148][*Provided* that in a prosecution for an offence under section 376, [149][section 376A, section 376AB, section 376B, section 376C, section 376D, section 376DA, section 376DB] or section 376-E of the Indian Penal Code (45 of 1860) or for attempt to commit any such offence, where the question of consent is an issue, it shall not be permissible to adduce evidence or to put questions in the cross-examination

---

143. *State of UP v Babul Nath*, (1994) 6 SCC 29 : 1994 SCC (Cr) 1585; *Surjit Singh v State of Punjab*, AIR 1992 SC 1389, an acquittal based on discrepancies in the FIR was held to be improper *Ibrahimkhan Prikhan v State of Maharashtra*, 2003 Cr LJ 1802 (Bom), the eye-witness was not confronted with the FIR and with additional police statements. This omission was held to be not fatal to the prosecution case. The accused could not claim any benefit from it as the FIR has never been regarded as substantive evidence.

144. *Bandhu v State*, 1997 Cr Lj 3010 : 1997 All LJ 136.

145. *State of Kerala v Babu*, 1999 Cr LJ 3491 : AIR 1999 SC 2161.

146. *Grandhi Narayanachetty v Vissannagasi*, AIR 2003 NOC 131 : 2003 AIHC 25.

147. *Dharamarajan v State*, 2002 Cr LJ 2751 (Ker).

148. Subs. by Act 13 of 2013, section 28, for the Proviso (w.r.e.f. 3-2-2013). Earlier the proviso was inserted by Act 4 of 2003, section 2 (w.e.f. 31-12-2002). The proviso, before substitution by Act 13 of 2013, stood as under:

"Provided that in a prosecution for rape or attempt to commit rape, it shall not be permissible to put questions in the cross-examination of the prosecutrix as to her general immoral character.".

149. Subs. by Act 22 of 2018, sec. 9, for "section 376A, section 376B, section 376C, section 376D" (w.r.e.f. 21-4-2018).

of the victim as to the general immoral character, or previous sexual experience, of such victim with any person for proving such consent or the quality of consent.]

SYNOPSIS

COMMENT

Sections 146–152 deal with questions which can be put to a witness with a view to shake his credit by damaging his character. These sections along with section 132 embrace the entire range of questions which can possibly be put to a witness.

[s 146.1] Scope.—This section gives very wide powers to the cross-examiner in addition to those given by section 138; and is more extensive in scope. As long as the cross-examiner confines his questions to the points of testing the veracity of a witness or discovering his status in life, there seem to be no limits to his power of putting questions. But when he undertakes the difficult yet delicate task of impeaching the character of witness, the following sections (sections 147–150) give ample protection to a witness in speaking the truth and impose wholesome restraints upon groundless assertions levelled against him. "If any such question relates to a matter relevant to the suit or proceeding, the provisions of section 132 are by section 147 declared applicable to it. If the question is as to a matter relevant only so far as affects the credit of the witness by injuring his character, the court is by section 148 directed to decide whether or not the witness is to be compelled to answer, and may...warn the witness that he is not obliged to answer it When there is a question asked to which the answer may tend to criminate a witness, he may object that it is not as to a matter relevant to a matter in issue, or that, if relevant, it is relevant only as affecting his credit by injuring his character."[150]

This section extends the power of cross-examination far beyond the limits of s.138, paragraph 2, which confines the cross-examination to relevant facts, including of course the facts in issue.[151]

Cross-examination to credit is necessarily irrelevant to any issue in an action, its relevancy consists in being addressed to the credit or discredit of the witness in the box so as to show that his evidence for or against the relevant issue is untrustworthy; it is most relevant in a case where everything depends on the judge's belief or disbelief in the witness's story.[152]

Where the cross-examination of a witness before a committing magistrate was deferred to the next date as the court time was over at the conclusion of the examination-in-chief of the witness but the witness breathed his last before the date fixed in the case and could not be cross-examined, it was held that it could not be said that the accused was given the opportunity to cross-examine the witness and had failed to avail of the

150. *Per* Turner, CJ, in *The Queen v Gopal Doss*, (1881) 3 Mad 271, 278 (FB).

151. Markby, p 107.

152. *Bombay Cotton Co v Raja Bahadur Shivlal Motilal*, (1915) 17 Bom LR 455 : 42 IA 110 : 39 Bom 386.

opportunity, therefore the statement of such a witness could not be received in evidence at the trial.[153]

[s 146.2] "Hereinbefore referred to", that is, referred to in section 138, para 2.

[s 146.3] "To test his veracity".—A witness may be examined not only as to the relevant facts but also as to all facts which reasonably tend to affect the credibility of his testimony. This is generally spoken of as cross-examination to credit, inasmuch as a large part at any rate of the facts which are relied on for the purpose are facts which touch the credit and good name of the witness. But no such cross-examination can be legitimate unless it has some reasonable bearing on his credibility.

When a witness is contradicted by his previous statement in the manner laid down in section 145, then that part of the statement which has been put to the witness will be considered along with the evidence to assess the worth of the witness in determining his veracity. The whole of the previous statement however cannot be treated as substantive evidence.[154]

[s 146.4] "To discover who is he," etc.—As preliminary to the cross-examination of a witness as to facts in the case, it is common practice to make inquiry into his relations with the party on whose behalf he was called—business, social and family; also to enquire as to his feelings towards the party against whom his testimony has been given. This is permissible in order to place his testimony in a proper light with reference to bias in favour of the one party or prejudice against the other.[155]

[s 146.5] "Credit... character".—The word "credit" is of a wide and varied connotation and has to be distinguished from the word "character", though the latter may include the former. "Credit" would take in belief, estimate of reputation, however, good character, and "creditable" so construed would mean honourable or trustworthy. The term "character" envisages a moral or ethical qualities of a person as a social being.[156]

[s 146.6] "Proviso" prior to the amendment of 2013.—Prior to the amendment of 2013, the proviso which was inserted by the Indian Evidence (Amendment) Act, 2002 (Act 4 of 2003), section 2 (w.e.f. 31 December 2002) read as under:

"Provided that in a prosecution for rape or attempt to commit rape, it shall not be permissible to put questions in the cross-examination of the prosecutrix as to her general immoral character."

[s 146.7] 2013 Amendment.—This section was amended *vide* Criminal Law (Amendment) Act, 2013[157] on the basis of recommendations given by the Justice JS Verma Committee, constituted in the aftermath of the December 2012, Nirbhaya rape incident. By way of necessary amendment in this section, the earlier proviso has been substituted by a new proviso so as to complete the entire legal scheme under which the questioning of a woman's character by way of an accused's defence has been completely ousted in the cases of rape falling under various species of the offence.

---

153. *State v Hazura Singh*, (1952) Pat 48.
154. *Som Nath v UOI*, AIR 1971 SC 1910 : 1971 Cr LJ 1422 : (1971) 2 SCC 387.
155. MaKelvey, section 259.
156. *Prashant Maheshbhai Pandya v State of Gujarat*, 2016 Cr LJ 303, para 20 (Guj).
157. Act 13 of 2013, *vide* section 26, (w.e.f. 3- 2-2013).

The effect of this amendment is that in a trial for the offence under sub-section (1) or sub-section (2) of section 376, section 376-A, section 376-B, section 376-C, section 376-D or section 376-E of Indian Penal Code or for attempt to commit any such offence, it is no longer permissible for the accused to adduce evidence or to put questions in the cross-examination of the victim as to her general immoral character, or her previous sexual experience, with any person for proving either her consensual participation in the offence consent or the quality of her consent.

Now, this newly amended section read with section 53-A, totally bars the leading of evidence about the character of the victim or her previous sexual experience with any person on the issue of consent given by her or the quality of consent, by making it not relevant as also inadmissible during the course of recording of evidence in a trial for the prescribed offences. However, a difference between these two newly inserted provisions is that while section 53-A includes within its fold, the various offences defined under section 354, section 354-A, section 354-B, section 354-C and 354-D also, the present section is confined only to the offence of rape and its various species made punishable differently.

In order to make the justice delivery system "gender-neutral", the Supreme Court,[158] entertained and allowed an appeal by a lady witness against an order of High Court transferring trial from a Fast Track Court presided over by a lady judge to another Fast Track Court presided over by a male judge in a case relating to making pornographic photos and videos in various acts of sexual intercourse and thereafter selling them to foreign websites. The Supreme Court was of the view that the recording of evidence as to the subject-matter of such an offence could cause embarrassment not only to the Presiding Officer, both male and female, but also to the lady witnesses/accused as well as to any decent person.

[s 146.8] 2018 Amendment.—Section 146 of the Indian Evidence Act, 1872 has been further amended *vide* the Criminal Law (Amendment) Act, 2018. In section 146 of the Evidence Act, in the proviso, for the words, figures and letters "section 376A, section 376B, section 376C, section 376D", the words, figures and letters "section 376A, section 376AB, section 376B, section 376C, section 376D, section 376DA, section 376DB" have been substituted. The section required amendment to bring sections 376AB, 376DA and 376DB of the Indian Penal Code within its purview.

[s 147] When witness to be compelled to answer.—If any such question relates to a matter relevant to the suit or proceeding, the provisions of section 132 shall apply thereto.

COMMENT

This section only applies to question referred to in clause (3) of the preceding section. If refers to "matters relevant to the suit or proceeding." The following section (i.e., section 148) refers to "matters not relevant to the suit for proceeding."

[s 148] Court to decide when question shall be asked and when witness compelled to answer.—If any such question[s 148.2] relates to a matter not relevant to the suit or proceeding, except in so far as it affects the credit of the witness by injuring his character, the Court shall decide whether or not the witness shall be compelled to answer it, and

---

158. *Fatima Riswana v State,* (2005) 1 SCC 582.

may, if it thinks fit, warn the witness that he is not obliged to answer it. In exercising its discretion, the Court shall have regard to the following considerations:—

(1) such questions are proper if they are of such a nature that the truth of the imputation conveyed by them would seriously affect the opinion of the Court as to the credibility of the witness on the matter to which he testifies;

(2) such questions are improper if the imputation which they convey relates to matters so remote in time, or of such a character, that the truth of the imputation would not affect, or would affect in a slight degree, the opinion of the Court as to the credibility of the witness on the matter to which he testifies;

(3) such questions are improper if there is a great disproportion between the importance of the imputation made against the witness's character and the importance of his evidence;

(4) the Court may, if it sees fit, draw, from the witness's refusal to answer, the inference that the answer if given would be unfavourable.

SYNOPSIS

COMMENT

[s 148.1] Object.—Sections 148–152 are intended to protect a witness against improper cross-examination—a protection which is often very much required. But the protection offered by section 148 is neither very effectual because an innocent man will be eager to answer the question, and one who is guilty will by a claim for protection merely confess his guilt, nor does the threat contained in section 149 and this section carry the matter much further.[159]

The object of this section is to prevent the unnecessary raking up of the past history of a witness, when it throws no light whatsoever on the questions at issue in a case. It protects a witness from the evils of a reckless and unjustifiable cross-examination under the guise of impeaching his credit. In the course of cross-examination, the temptation is always too great to run down a witness's character; the Legislature has, therefore, wisely provided ample safeguards for the unfortunate witness and placed wholesome checks on the wily cross-examiner. It would seem that under this section a witness cannot be compelled to answer irrelevant questions; but if he chooses to answer them, he cannot be contradicted by other evidence (section 153).

[s 148.2] "Any such question".—When any such question, that is, the question referred to in section 146, is *not relevant* to the suit or proceeding, the court must decide whether or not the witness should be compelled to answer it and may warn the witness that he is not obliged to answer it.

159. Markby, 107.

Such questions are *proper*—

(1) if they are of such a nature that the truth of the imputation made touches the credibility of the witness.

They are *improper*—

(1) if the imputation refers to matters (a) so remote in time, or (b) of such a character, that its truth does not affect the credibility of the witness; or

(2) if there is a great disproportion between the importance of the imputation and the importance of the evidence.

If the witness refuses to answer any question it is open to the court to draw the inference that the answer if given would be unfavourable [cf. section 114, Illustration (b)].

[s 148.2.1] CASES

[s 148.2.1.1] Prior consideration whether such questions proper or improper.—*[Clauses (1), (2)]*.—On an indictment for rape, or attempt at rape, or for an indecent assault, the prosecutrix cannot be asked in cross-examination whether she had connection with another person not the accused; and if she denies it, evidence cannot be called to contradict her.[160] But she can be asked whether she had on previous occasions connection with the accused,[161] or whether she was a common prostitute.[162]

[s 148.3] Remote imputation *[Clause (2)]*.—The following statement of the Supreme Court in *State of Punjab v Gurmit Singh*,[163] highlights the duty of the court in this respect: "There has been lately a lot of criticism of the treatment of the victim of sexual assault in the court during their cross-examination some defence counsel adopt the strategy of continual questioning of the prosecutrix as to details of the incident. The court should not sit as a silent spectator. While every latitude should be given to the accused to test the veracity of the prosecutrix and credibility of her version through cross-examination, the court must also ensure that cross-examination is not made a means of harassment or causing humiliation to the victim. A victim of rape has already undergone a traumatic experience and if she is made to repeat again and again, in unfamiliar surroundings what she had been subjected to, she may be too ashamed and even nervous or confused to speak and her silence or a confused stray sentence may be wrongly interpreted as discrepancies and contradictions in her evidence."

The Supreme Court[164] entertained and allowed an appeal by a lady witness against an order of High Court transferring trial from a Fast Track Court presided over by lady judge to another Fast Track Court presided over by male judge in a case relating to making pornographic photos and videos in various acts of sexual intercourse and thereafter selling them to foreign websites. Supreme Court, in order to make the justice delivery system "gender-neutral", held that recording of evidence in a case of pornographic materials under section 67 of the Information Technology Act, 2000

---

160. Per Kelley CB, in *Queen v Holmes*, (1871) LR 1 CC R 334, 336; *Hodgson's Case*, (1812) R & R CC 211; *Rex v Clarke*, (1817) 2 Stark 41.

161. *Rex v Martin*, (1834) 6 C&P 562; *Reg v Cockcroft*, (1870) 11 Cox 410.

162. *Rex v Barker*, (1829) 3 C&P 589.

163. *State of Punjab v Gurmit Singh*, (1996) 2 SCC 384, at 403 : AIR 1996 SC 1393 : 1996 Cr LJ 1728.

164. *Fatima Riswana v State*, (2005) 1 SCC 582.

could cause embarrassment not only to the Presiding Officer, both male and female, but also to lady witnesses/accused as well as to any decent person.

[s 149] Question not to be asked without reasonable grounds.—No such question as is referred to in section 148 ought to be asked, unless the person asking it has reasonable grounds for thinking that the imputation which it conveys is well-founded.

ILLUSTRATIONS

(a) A barrister is instructed by an attorney or vakil that an important witness is a dakait. This is a reasonable ground for asking the witness whether he is a dakait.

(b) A pleader is informed by a person in Court that an important witness is a dakait. The informant, on being questioned by the pleader, gives satisfactory reasons for his statement. This is a reasonable ground for asking the witness whether he is a dakait.

(c) A witness, of whom nothing whatever is known, is asked at random whether he is a dakait. There are here no reasonable grounds for the question.

(d) A witness, of whom nothing whatever is known, being questioned as to his mode of life and means of living, gives unsatisfactory answers. This may be a reasonable ground for asking him if he is a dakait.

COMMENT

The cross-examiner must have reasonable grounds to believe that the imputation made against the witness is well-founded. As for what are reasonable grounds which justify such question, see the illustrations.

[s 150] Procedure of Court in case of question being asked without reasonable grounds.—If the Court is of opinion that any such question was asked without reasonable grounds, it may, if it was asked by any barrister, pleader, vakil or attorney, report the circumstances of the case to the High Court or other authority to which such barrister, pleader, vakil or attorney is subject in the exercise of his profession.

COMMENT

[s 150.1] Object.—"The object of these sections [sections 149, 150, 151, 152] is to lay down, in the most distinct manner, the duty of counsel of all grades in examining witnesses with a view to shaking their credit by damaging their character. I trust that this explicit statement of the principles, according to which such questions ought or ought not to be asked, will be found sufficient to prevent the growth, in this country, of that which in England has on many occasions been a grave scandal. I think that the sections, as far as their substance is concerned, speak for themselves, and that they will be admitted to be sound by all honourable advocates and by the public..."[165]

"In order to protect witnesses against needless questions of this kind, we enact that any advocate who asks such questions without written instructions (which the court may call upon him to produce, and may impound when produced) shall be guilty of contempt of court, and that the court may record any such question, if asked by a party to the proceedings. The records of the question in the written instructions are

---

165. Abstract of Proceedings of the Council of the Governor General of India, Vol XI (1872) p 133.

to be admissible as evidence of the publication of an imputation intended to harm the reputation of the person affected, and such imputations are not to be regarded as privileged communications, or as falling under any of the exceptions to section 499 of the Indian Penal Code, merely because they were made in the manner stated. Upon a trial for defamation, it would, of course, be open to the person accused to show, either that the imputation was true, and that it was for the public good that the imputation should be made (Exception 1, section 499, Indian Penal Code), or that it was made in good faith for the protection of the interest of the person making it or of any other person (Exception 9). This is the only method which occurs to us of providing at once for the interests of a *bona fide* questioner and an innocent witness."[166]

[s 151] Indecent and scandalous questions.—The Court may forbid any questions or inquiries which it regards as indecent or scandalous, although such questions or inquiries may have some bearing on the questions before the Court, unless they relate to facts in issue, or to matters necessary to be known in order to determine whether or not the facts in issue existed.

COMMENT

This section forbids the putting of any question which is indecent or scandalous, unless it relates to facts in issue or is necessarily connected with them.

[s 151.1]CASE.—In a proceeding to recover maintenance by a married woman for her illegitimate children, under section 125 of the Criminal Procedure Code, she "can be examined to prove non-access of her husband during their married life, without independent evidence being first offered to prove the illegitimacy of the children."[167]

[s 152] Questions intended to insult or annoy.—The Court shall forbid any question which appears to it to be intended to insult or annoy, or which, though proper in itself, appears to the Court needlessly offensive in form.

COMMENT

The court has the power to forbid any question which is intended to insult or annoy, or which is couched in a needlessly offensive form.

[s 153] Exclusion of evidence to contradict answers to questions testing veracity.—When a witness has been asked and has answered any question which is relevant to the inquiry only in so far as it tends to shake his credit by injuring his character, no evidence shall be given to contradict him; but, if he answers falsely, he may afterwards be charged with giving false evidence.[s 153.3]

***Exception 1.*—If a witness is asked whether he has been previously convicted of any crime and denies it, evidence may be given of his previous conviction.**

***Exception 2.*—If a witness is asked any question tending to impeach his impartiality and answers it by denying the facts suggested, he may be contradicted.**

166. Proceedings of the Supreme Legislative Council, *Gazette of India*, pp 237, 238, of the Supplement, dated March 30, 1872.
167. *Rozario v Ingles*, (1893) 18 Bom 468, 472.

ILLUSTRATIONS

(a) A claim against an underwriter is resisted on the ground of fraud.

The claimant is asked whether, in a former transaction, he had not made a fraudulent claim. He denies it.

Evidence is offered to show that he did make such a claim. The evidence is inadmissible.

(b) A witness is asked whether he was not dismissed from a situation for dishonesty. He denies it. Evidence is offered to show that he was dismissed for dishonesty.

The evidence is not admissible.

(c) *A* affirms that on a certain day he saw *B* at Lahore.

A is asked whether he himself was not on that day at Calcutta. He denies it. Evidence is offered to show that *A* was on that day at Calcutta.

The evidence is admissible, not as contradicting *A* on a fact which affects his credit, but as contradicting the alleged fact that *B* was seen on the day in question in Lahore.

In each of these cases the witness might, if his denial was false, be charged with giving false evidence.

(d) *A* is asked whether his family has not had a blood feud with the family of *B* against whom he gives evidence.

He denies it. He may be contradicted on the ground that the question tends to impeach his impartiality.

SYNOPSIS

COMMENT

[s 153.1] Object.—The object of the section is to prevent trials being spun out to an unreasonable length. If every answer given by a witness upon the additional facts mentioned in section 146 could be made the subject of fresh inquiry, a trial might never end. These matters are after all not of the first importance, beyond what is comprised in the exceptions.[168]

[s 153.2] Principle.—When a witness deposes to facts which are relevant, evidence may be given in contradiction of what he has stated. But when what he deposes to affects only his *credit*, no evidence to contradict him can be led for the sole purpose of shaking his credit by injuring his character. However, a witness answering falsely can be proceeded against for giving false evidence under section 193 of the Indian Penal Code. There are two exceptions to this: (1) previous conviction when denied can be proved (section 298, Criminal Procedure Code); and (2) any fact tending to impeach his impartiality when denied can be proved. This is a salutary rule and is meant to curtail every inquiry. If contradictory evidence be allowed on side issues for instance, as shaking the witness's credit by injuring his character, there can be no limit to an enquiry. The main issue in the case is almost always likely to be fogged by subsidiary inquiries which are profitless as well as perplexing. The two exceptions engrafted on the

168. Markby, 108.

section are capable of easy proof and are material in assessing the weight to be attached to the testimony of an individual witness. The section should be strictly construed and narrowly interpreted, otherwise Courts would have to investigate, on most imperfect materials, questions which have no bearing upon the matter really in contest.[169]

The rule limiting the right to call evidence to contradict witnesses on collateral questions excludes all evidence of facts which are incapable of affording any reasonable presumption or inference as to the principal matter in dispute; the test being whether the fact is one which the party proposing to contradict would have been allowed himself to prove in evidence.[170]

The principle that evidence cannot be adduced to contradict the denials of a witness in cross-examination on matters going to collateral issues affecting credit only, although a general rule, is an absolute rule and the categories of exceptions to it are not closed.[171]

There was the allegation as shown by the testimony of the eyewitness in a case that the husband of the eyewitness and the father of the accused had loan transactions on which they later fell out. No questions were put to her to contradict her on this point. She was not allowed to be contradicted through the mouth of other witnesses by putting questions to them about her testimony.[172]

[s 153.3] "If he answers falsely, he may afterwards be charged with giving false evidence".—These words were apparently inserted in forgetfulness of the fact that the Indian law as to false evidence differs from the English law as to perjury in not requiring that the matter charged as false should have been material to the issue.[173]

[s 154] Questions by party to his own witness.—[174][(1)] The Court may, in its discretion,[s 154.2] permit the person who calls a witness to put any questions to him which might be put in cross-examination by the adverse party.

[175][(2) Nothing in this section shall disentitle the person so permitted under sub-section (1), to rely on any part of the evidence of such witness].

SYNOPSIS

169. *Bhogilal v Royal Insurance Co Ltd*, (1927) 30 Bom LR 818 : 6 Ran 142 (PC).
170. *Kazi Gulam Alli Bin Kasi Ismail v HH Aga Khan*, (1869) 6 BHC (OCJ) 93. The antecedents of the witness can be brought to light only for the purpose of shaking his credit. *Bhaskaran Nair v State of Kerala*, 1991 Cr LJ 23 (Ker).
171. *Urban Transport Authority v Nweiser*, 1993 ALMD 1487 (CA).
172. *State of Karnataka v K Varappa Reddy*, 2000 Cr LJ 400 : AIR 2000 SC 185 : (1999) 8 SCC 715.
173. *Stokes*, Vol II, p 929, f.n. 2.
174. Section 154 renumbered as sub-section (1) thereof by Act 2 of 2006, section 9 (w.e.f. 16-4-2006).
175. Ins. by Act 2 of 2006, section 9 (w.e.f. 16-4-2006).

COMMENT

[s 154.1] Principle.—Where a party calling a witness and examining him discovers that he is either hostile or unwilling to answer questions put to him, he can obtain permission of the court to put questions to him which may be put to him by way of cross-examination. The section does not say that a person who calls a witness may cross-examine him in certain circumstances, but he might put questions to him which might be put in cross-examination by the adverse party. That is not the same as cross-examination.[176] This section vests discretion in the court to permit such person to put any such question. Such a request can be made in civil as well as in criminal cases. Permission for cross-examination in terms of the section cannot and should not be granted at the mere asking of the party calling the witness. The courts are under a legal obligation to exercise the discretion vesting in them in a judicious manner by proper application of mind and keeping in view the attending circumstances.[177]

A discretion is given to the court to allow or not to allow a person to cross-examine his own witness as hostile. The witness may be asked leading questions (section 143); or questions as to his previous statements in writing (section 145); or any questions under section 146; or his credit may be impeached (section 155).

Under this section, before a party calling a witness can cross-examine him, it is not necessary that the witness should first be declared to be hostile to the party calling him, and the court has unfettered discretion to allow a counsel to put questions of a cross-examination nature to his own witness even though he did not show himself hostile to the party calling him, but the court ought not to exercise its discretion unless during the examination-in-chief something happens which makes it necessary for the facts to be got from that witness by cross-examination; it is necessary before the procedure under this section can be adopted that leave of the court should be asked for and obtained or permission given by the court *suo motu* for the said purpose before such questions are put to a witness though the section may not make such a procedure imperative and the permission contemplated by the section should be signified, if not in words, by some other action of the court indicating its permission during the cross-examination of the witness by the party calling him.[178]

[s 154.2] "The Court may, in its discretion".—A party who calls an opponent as a witness has no right to cross-examine him, however hostile he may be, without the leave of the judge. Whether a witness is a litigant or not, it is a matter of discretion in the judge whether he shows himself so hostile as to justify his cross-examination

---

176. *Bikram Ali Pramanik v Emperor*, (1929) 57 Cal 801; *Luchiram Motilal Boid v Radha Charan Poddar*, (1921) 49 Cal 93; *Khijiruddin Sonar v Emperor*, (1925) 53 Cal 372; See also *State v Bhera*, 1997 Cr LJ 1237 (Raj), evidence of hostile witness deserves to be scrutinized carefully. The prosecution should bring out contradictions in his testimony by confronting him with his previous statements, should the prosecution fail to do so, it would became the duty of the court to put such questions to him as may be necessary to ascertain the truth. *Public Prosecutor v Thummala Janaradhana Rao*, 1998 Cr LJ 4450 (AP), no permission to cross-examine one's own witness was granted where the witness had not shown any element of hostility to the party. *Samir Das v State of Tripura*, 1999 Cr LJ 953 (Gau), no permission to cross-examine a witness where there was nothing to show that he had resiled from his earlier statements.

177. *Mattam Ravi v Mattam Raja Yellaiah*, AIR 2017 Hyd 155 : 2017 (4) ALT 547.

178. *Ammathayarammal v Official Assignee, Madras*, (1932) 56 Mad 7; *Mohan Banjari v The King- Emperor*, (1933) 30 NLR 55.

by the party calling him.[179] The permission under the section should not and cannot be granted at the mere asking of the party calling the witness.[180] The court said that the fact that the witness was not concurring with the suggestion in respect of a post event detail was not sufficient for public prosecutor to proclaim that the witness had become hostile to the prosecution.

The court has the discretion under this section, to permit the prosecution to test, by way of cross-examination, the veracity of their own witnesses with regard to the (unconnected) matters elicited by the defence in cross-examination.[181] The discretion conferred on the court is to be exercised judicially and in the interest of justice. The witness in this case was deposing in favour of the opposite party but not against the interest of his party. The veracity of his statement could not be doubted. The court refused to declare him as a hostile witness.[182]

[s 154.3] Stage for seeking permission.—Where a witness called by the prosecution started giving statements in favour of the defence even in his examination-in-chief, but the public prosecutor did not immediately seek permission for getting the witness declared as hostile and allowed his cross-examination by the defence and then applied for permission to cross-examine him, the Supreme Court refused to interfere in the order refusing permission.[183]

[s 154.4] CASES.—Hostile witness.—A "hostile witness" is one who from the manner in which he gives evidence shows that he is not desirous of telling the truth to the court.[184] In *Shatrughan v State of MP*, a hostile witness is not necessarily a false witness.[185] The court can permit a person, who calls a witness, to put questions to him which might be put in the cross-examination at any stage of the examination of the witness, provided it takes care to give an opportunity to the adverse party to cross-examine him on the answers elicited which do not find place in examination-in-chief.[186] Where a party is allowed to cross-examine his own witness, the effect of that cross-examination must be to discredit that witness altogether and not merely to get rid of part of his testimony, and hence that witness's evidence must be excluded altogether. In the case of a witness for the prosecution, this means so far as it supports the case for the prosecution, for obviously the defence is entitled to rely on so much of his evidence as supports their case: otherwise a party who found that his witness had given evidence

---

179. *Price v Manning*, (1889) 42 Chapter D 372.

180. *Gura Singh v State of Rajasthan*, 2001 Cr LJ 487 (SC).

181. *Amrita Lal Hazra v Emperor*, (1915) 42 Cal 957; *Dadabuddappa Gouli v Kalu Kanto Gouli*, AIR 2000 Kant 158, the court has the power to permit a party to put any questions to his own witness which might be put in cross-examination when the witness turns hostile.

182. *S Murugesan v S Pethaperumal*, AIR 1999 Mad 76.

183. *State of Bihar v Lalu Prasad* 2002 Cr LJ 3236 (SC).

184. *Panchanan Gogai v Emperor*, (1930) 57 Cal 1266.

185. *Shatrughan v State of MP*, 1993 Cr LJ 120 (MP).

186. *Dahyabhai v State of Gujarat*, AIR 1964 SC 1563 : (1964) 2 Cr LJ 472 : (1964) 7 SCR 361. The value of his testimony is not destroyed by such a permission. *Lodai v State*, 1991 Cr LJ 1878 (All). Evidence of such witness need not be wholly discarded. *KP Rajan v State of Kerala*, 1991 Cr LJ 1859 (Ker); *Suyambu Re*, 1991 Cr LJ 2506 (Mad). At appellate stage, the prosecution cannot say that a statement of its own witness is not binding on it. *Murugan v State*, 1991 Cr LJ 1680 (Mad), his evidence can be used to the extent to which it is natural and supports the party's case. *Laxman Sahu v State of Orissa*, 1990 Cr LJ 821 (Ori).

which supported his adversary's case could get rid of the evidence by declaring him hostile.[187] The expression "hostile witness" has been avoided because of the confusion caused by it in English Law. The section confers a simple discretion upon the court to allow a party to cross-examine his own witness.[188] In short, the rule prohibiting a party to put questions to his own witness in the manner of cross-examination or in a leading form is relaxed not because the witness has already forfeited all right to credit but because of his antipathetic attitude or otherwise the court feels that for doing justice, his evidence will be more fully given, the truth more effectively extracted and credit more adequately tested by questions put in a more pointed, penetrating and searching way. The expression "any questions that may be asked by the adverse party in cross-examination" shows that neither party is excluded from relying on his testimony.

In a departmental enquiry against the appellant, the enquiry officer made adverse comments about the correctness or otherwise of the statements made by the witnesses examined on behalf of the department without assigning any reasons therefor. They were examined by the department. It was held that if those witnesses deposed falsely, they should have been cross-examined. Only because their evidence was totally against the department, the same per se would not mean that they deposed falsely.[189]

The mere fact that a party has cross-examined its own witness does not make him an unreliable witness. There must be some material to show that the witness has resiled from his earlier statements.[190] The evidence of a hostile witness can be relied upon to the extent to which it supports the prosecution version.[191] The testimony of a hostile witness need not be rejected in its entirety.[192]

In *Gulshan Kumar v State*,[193] it was held that the court is not precluded from taking into account the statement of a hostile witness altogether and it is not necessary to discard the same *in toto*. Thus, the statement of the hostile witness can be relied upon partly. In *Balu Sonba Shinde v State of Maharashtra*,[194] while it is true declaration of a witness to be hostile does not *ipso facto* amount to rejection of his evidence—and it is now well-settled that the portion of evidence being advantageous to the parties may be taken advantage of—but the court before whom such a reliance is placed shall have to be extremely cautious and circumspect in such acceptance. Reference in this context

---

187. *Emperor v Mokbul Khan*, (1928) 56 Cal 145; *Sohrai Sao v King-Emperor*, (1929) 9 Pat 474. *Jagir Singh v State*, AIR 1975 SC 1400. Prosecution case cannot be judged on the basis of testimony of hostile witnesses. *Keshoram Bros. v Assam*, AIR 1978 SC 1096 : (1978) 2 SCR 788.

188. *Sat Paul v Delhi Admn.*, AIR 1976 SC 294 : 1976 (1) Cr LJ 295. The Court explains at this stage (p 306) the purpose of cross-examination and the validity of some of the Cal HC decisions to the effect that once a witness is declared hostile his testimony cannot be used at all. **Followed** in *Ashim Das v State of Assam*, 1987 Cr LJ 1533 (Gau), so as to hold that it was a lame excuse not to produce the son of the deceased as a witness on the ground that he was won over by the defence. **Relied upon** in *Lalu v State*, 1988 Cr LJ 1301 (Cal), in connection with the testimony of child witness.

189. *MV Bijlani v UOI*, (2006) 5 SCC 88.

190. *Dhanu v State of Tripura*, 1999 Cr LJ 1231 (Gau).

191. *Koli Lakhmanbhai Chanabhai v State of Gujarat*, 2000 Cr LJ 408 : AIR 2000 SC 210.

192. *G Parshwanath v State of Karnataka*, AIR 2010 SC 2914 : (2010) 8 SCC 593.

193. *Gulshan Kumar v State*, 1993 Cr LJ 1525. See also *Kunwar v State of UP*, 1993 Cr LJ 3421 (All). *Haneefa v State of Kerala*, 1993 Cr LJ 2125 (Ker), such portions of the evidence which inspire confidence can be relied upon.

194. *Balu Sonba Shinde v State of Maharashtra*, AIR 2002 SC 3137 at p 3141 : 2002 Cr LJ 4650.

may be made to the decision of this Court in *State of UP v Ramesh Prasad Misra*,[195] wherein this Court stated:

> It is equally settled law that the evidence of a hostile witness would not be totally rejected if spoken in favour of the prosecution or the accused, but it can be subjected to close scrutiny and that portion of the evidence which is consistent with the case of the prosecution or defence may be accepted.[196]

In *Gurpreet Singh v State of Haryana*,[197] the Supreme Court relied on the observations passed in an earlier case in both of which similar facts were involved as cited the following passage: "Incidentally, it is now well-settled that in the event of a portion of evidence not being consistent with the statements given under 161, CrPC, and the witness stands declared hostile that does not mean and imply total rejection of the evidence. The portion which stands in favour of the prosecution or the accused may be accepted but the same shall be subjected to close scrutiny. It is in this context the observations of this Court in *State of UP v Ramesh Prasad Misra*,[198] seem to be rather apposite."

In another Supreme Court decision it was held that the mere fact that the prosecution witness was not concurring with a suggestion made by the public prosecutor which was dealing with a post event detail, was not sufficient to seek that the witness be declared hostile. The court observed that a declaration of this kind cannot be granted at the mere asking of the party who called the witness and that the evidence of such a person cannot be regarded as unworthy of credit only because he has been declared hostile.[199] Where hostile witness did not speak anything about the occurrence, his evidence was of no use.[200] Where in a murder case all the prosecution witnesses resiled from their earlier statements to the police and were treated hostile in wholesale, their testimony was of no use.[201]

This section does not warrant an inference that only when any previous statement of the witness is available and if he is alleged to have departed from that that the court can declare that witness hostile.[202] Inconsistent and contradictory statements are not enough. The witness must appear to be not desirous of telling the truth and it is necessary to regard him hostile for eliciting the truth.[203] The Supreme Court further elaborated this aspect in *RK Dey v State of Orissa*.[204] The court has a discretion but no guiding principles. The witness should exhibit an element of hostility or resile from a material statement made before an earlier authority or not be speaking the truth. There must be some material to show that the witness is not speaking the truth. Merely because a witness in an unguarded moment speaks the truth which may not suit the prosecution or which may be favourable to the accused, the discretion to allow cross-examination of one's own witness cannot be exercised. In this case the witnesses in their statements

---

195. *State of UP v Ramesh Prasad Misra*, AIR 1996 SC 2766 : AIR SCW 3468 : 1996 All LJ 1619 : 1996 Cr LJ 4002.

196. Also see, *Khachar Dipu v State of Gujarat*, (2013) 4 SCC 322; *Rameshbhai Mohanbhai Koli v State of Gujarat*, (2011) 11 SCC 111.

197. *Gurpreet Singh v State of Haryana*, AIR 2002 SC 3217 : 2002 Cr LJ 4688.

198. *State of UP v Ramesh Prasad Misra*, (1996) 10 SCC 360 : AIR 1996 SC 2766 : 1996 AIR SCW 3468 : 1996 Cr LJ 4002 : 1996 All LJ 1619.

199. *Gura Singh v State of Rajasthan*, AIR 2001 SC 330 at pp 334-335.

200. *Kathi Odhabhai Bhimabhai v State of Gujarat*, AIR 1993 SC 1193 : 1993 Cr LJ 187.

201. *Subbiramani v State*, 1995 Cr LJ 3382 (Mad).

202. *Sahdeo v Bipti*, AIR 1969 Pat 415.

203. *Phanindra Nath v Bholanath Banerjee*, AIR 1982 Cal 397.

204. *RK Dey v State of Orissa*, AIR 1977 SC 170 : (1976) 4 SCC 233 : 1977 Cr LJ 173.

before the police attributed a clear intention to the accused to commit murder but before the court they stated that the accused was insane. The right to cross-examine them was upheld. But this does not make him an unreliable witness so as to exclude his evidence from consideration altogether.[205] The evidence remains admissible in the trial and there is no legal bar to base a conviction upon his testimony if corroborated otherwise.

In a suit to recover moneys alleged to have been expended by the plaintiff in the performance of a ceremony, the plaintiff's witnesses having failed to prove any damages, he called the defendant as a witness who gave evidence to the effect that the plaintiff had no claim. The court refused to allow the plaintiff to cross-examine the defendant. It was held that the refusal to cross-examine was not justifiable.[206]

[s 154.4.1] ***Cross-Examining one's own Witness without being Hostile.***—The trial was under an election petition. The court said that the right to cross-examine one's own witness is not necessarily confined only to the situation where the witness exhibits hostility or is resiles from his earlier statement. Such cross-examination may be permitted to retract truth if the court finds that the witness is withholding the truth. Permission can be granted at any stage of the trial since the power of the court under section 154 is not fettered by section 137 or section 138.[207]

[s 154.5] Stage at which permission should be sought.—A witness made statements favourable to the defence even during his examination-in-chief. The public prosecutor allowed his cross-examination to proceed without making an application for permission for cross-examining him. He applied for permission after the cross-examination by the defence. The court refused it. The Supreme Court refused to interfere in the refusal.

Declaration of a witness as hostile is to be done immediately at the time of examination of witness and cannot be permitted to be done long after witness has been examined.[208]

[s 154.6] Effect upon testimony.—The testimony of a witness who has turned hostile is not to be excluded entirely or rendered unworthy of consideration.[209] His testimony remains admissible. A conviction can be based on it if it finds some corroboration.[210]

Referring to its earlier decisions on hostile witness,[211] the Supreme Court relied upon the examination in-chief of hostile witnesses only to the extent to which they

205. *Bhagwan Singh v Haryana*, AIR 1976 SC 202, 203 : 1976 Cr LJ 203. Where some witnesses of rape turned hostile, the evidence of others was not to be rejected and was to be considered independently of that fact and on its own intrinsic merit, *State of Karnataka v Mehaboob*, 1987 Cr LJ 940 (Karn).

206. *Radha Jeebun Moostuffy v Taramonee, Dosssee*, (1869) 12 Moo Ind App 380.

207. *Atul Bora v Akan Bora*, AIR 2007 Gau 51.

208. *Jatinder Singh Bhatia v State,*, 153 (2008) DLT 633.

209. *Gura Singh v State of Rajasthan*, 2001 Cr LJ 487 (SC).

210. *Anil Rai v State of Bihar*, 2001 Cr LJ 3969 (SC), the wife was the eye-witness to the fact of the murder of her husband.

211. *Koli Lakhmanbhai Chanabhai v State of Gujarat*, (1999) 8 SCC 624; *Prithi v State of Haryana*, (2010) 8 SCC 536; *Manu Sharma v State (NCT of Delhi)*, (2010) 6 SCC 1, and *Ramkrushna v State of Maharashtra*, (2007) 13 SCC 525. Also see, *Sidhartha Vashisht v State (NCT of Delhi)*, (2010) 6 SCC 1; *Paramjeet Singh v State of Uttarakhand*, (2010) 10 SCC 439; *Ramesh Harijan v State of UP*, (2012) 5 SCC 777 – para 23, 24; *Himanshu v State (NCT of Delhi)*, (2011) 2 SCC 36 – relied upon the previous decisions of Supreme Court in *Bhagwan Singh v State of Haryana*, (1976) 1 SCC 389; *Rabindra Kumar Dey v State of Orissa*, (1976) 4 SCC 233; *Syad Akbar v State of Karnataka*, (1980) 1 SCC 30; *Khujji v State of MP*, (1991) 3 SCC 627; *Koli Lakhmanbhai Chanabhai v State of Gujarat*, (1999) 8 SCC 624; *Prithi v State of Haryana*, (2010) 8 SCC 536;

supported the case of the prosecution and were duly corroborated, not only by other witnesses but even by the dying declaration and the medical evidence.[212]

The evidence of a witness who has been declared hostile can be relied if there are some other materials on the basis of which the said witness can be corroborated. More so, that part of evidence of a witness as contained in the examination-in-chief, which remains unshaken even after cross-examination, is fully reliable even though the witness has been declared hostile.[213] Evidence of a hostile witness can be accepted, if the same is otherwise worthy of trust though he was declared hostile with regard to some aspects of evidence tendered by him.[214]

[s 154.7] 2005 Amendment.—This section was amended in 2005 *vide* which the earlier section 154 was re-numbered as sub-section (1) of this section, and a new sub-section (2) was inserted. What was earlier being laid down through judicial pronouncements, was brought into the statute book by way of this insertion of sub-section (2) so as to re-affirm that the courts shall be entitled to rely upon any part of the evidence of a witness declared "hostile" by court.

In view of this amendment in section 154, the evidence of a hostile witness remains admissible and there is no legal bar to base conviction upon the testimony of such hostile witnesses if corroborated by other reliable evidence.[215] In view of the amended section 154, prosecution can rely on part of the evidence of a hostile witness.[216] The evidence of a person does not become effaced from the record merely because he has turned hostile and his deposition must be examined more cautiously to find out as to what extent he has supported the case of the prosecution.[217] The deposition of a hostile witness can be relied upon at least up to the extent he supported the case of the prosecution.[218] It is also now a settled canon of criminal jurisprudence that the part which has been allowed to be cross-examined can also be relied upon by the prosecution.[219]

[s 155] Impeaching credit of witness.—The credit of a witness may be impeached in the following ways by the adverse party, or, with the consent of the Court, by the party who calls him:—

(1) by the evidence of persons who testify that they, from their knowledge of the witness, believe him to be unworthy of credit;

(2) by proof that the witness has been bribed, or has [220][accepted] the offer of a bribe, or has received any other corrupt inducement to give his evidence;

(3) by proof of former statements inconsistent with any part of his evidence which is liable to be contradicted;

---

212. *Bhajju v State of MP* (supra).

213. *Devraj v State of Chhattisgarh*, AIR 2016 SC 3498 , para 19.

214. *SC Goel v State*, 2017 Cr LJ 536, para 4 (SC).

215. *Parimal Gowala v State of Tripura*, 2007 Cr LJ 2394 (Gau.).

216. *Shushendra alias Sushai Deb v State of Tripura*, 2010 Cr LJ 4777 (Gau).

217. *Paramjeet Singh v State of Uttarakhand*, (2010) 10 SCC 439.

218. *Govindappa v State of Karnataka*, (2010) 6 SCC 533; Also see *Prithi v State of Haryana*, (2010) 8 SCC 536.

219. *Bhajju v State of MP*, (2012) 4 SCC 327; Also see, *Manu Sharma v State (NCT of Delhi)*, (2010) 6 SCC 1.

220. Subs. by Act 18 of 1872, sec. 11, for "had".

[221][(4) * * *]

***Explanation.*—A witness declaring another witness to be unworthy of credit may not, upon his examination-in-chief, give reasons for his belief, but he may be asked his reasons in cross-examination, and the answers which he gives cannot be contradicted, though, if they are false, he may afterwards be charged with giving false evidence.**

ILLUSTRATIONS

(a) *A* sues *B* for the price of goods sold and delivered to *B*. *C* says that *A* delivered the goods to *B*.

Evidence is offered to show that, on a previous occasion, he said that he had not delivered the goods to *B*. The evidence is admissible.

(b) *A* is indicted for the murder of *B*.

C says that *B*, when dying, declared that *A* had given *B* the wound of which he died.

Evidence is offered to show that, on a previous occasion, *C* said that the wound was not given by *A* or in his presence.

The evidence is admissible.

SYNOPSIS

COMMENT

[s 155.1] Principle.—This section enables the parties to give independent testimony as to the character of a witness in order to indicate that he is unworthy of belief by the court. Its provisions apply to both criminal and civil cases.

The section indicates four ways in which the credit of a witness may be impeached; (a) by the adverse party, or (b) with the consent of the court by the party who calls him.[222] They are:—

(1) evidence of persons that the witness is unworthy of credit;

(2) proof that the witness (i) has been bribed; (ii) has accepted the offer of a bribe; or (iii) has received any other corrupt inducement;

---

221. Clause (4) omitted by the Indian Evidence (Amendment) Act, 2002 (Act 4 of 2003) w.e.f. 31-12-2002. Clause (4) prior to omission read as:

"(4) when a man is prosecuted for rape or an attempt to ravish, it may be shown that the prosecutrix was of generally immoral character."

222. The court may reject the testimony of a witness of its own even if he has not been exposed by cross- examination. *Juwar Singh v State of MP*, AIR 1981 SC 373 : 1980 Cr LJ 1418.

(3) former statements inconsistent with the present evidence and

(4) general immoral character of the prosecutrix in cases of rape or attempt to ravish.

The above sub-clause (i) has an explanation, which is a re-echo of section 153. Witnesses deposing to character can be asked in cross-examination to give reasons for their opinion. They are not liable to be contradicted in those reasons; but, if they are false, they can be charged with giving false evidence.

The first three grounds are general. They indicate that the credit of a witness may be impeached, first of all, by the best of evidence, that is, his own former statements to the contrary; secondly, he can be shown to be unworthy of credit by the oral testimony of other persons; and, lastly, his credit can be completely overthrown by proving that he had accepted (a) a bribe, or (b) an offer of a bribe, or (c) any other corrupt inducement. The fourth ground is a special one. If the woman complaining of rape or attempt to ravish is proved to be a woman generally of immoral character, her story in the complaint will necessitate strong proof.

This section should be strictly construed and narrowly interpreted, otherwise Courts would have to investigate, on most imperfect materials, questions which have no bearing upon the matter really in contest.[223]

[s 155.2] Witness unworthy of credit *[Clause 1]*.—In order to impeach the character of a witness for veracity, witnesses may be called to prove that his general reputation is such that they would not believe him upon his oath. Such evidence can be given, and the practice is ancient and undoubted.[224]

The opinion of another Court in another case as to a witness cannot be put in to impeach his credit.

[s 155.3] Bribe or corrupt inducement *[Clause 2]*.—The credit of a witness may be impeached on the ground that his evidence was obtained by corrupt inducement, and it was open to the defendant to contend that the application of a third degree method by the persistent questioning in the investigation constituted a form of unfair evil, the avoidance of which was a corrupt inducement to witness to say what was required of him. It would be open to the defendant also to attempt to establish this by evidence, and it was clear that an important witness for this purpose would be the counsel. There was also the possibility of certain contingencies in which the counsel's association with the enquiry may be unseemly.[225]

[s 155.4] Former inconsistent statements *[Clause 3]*.—The words "which is liable to be contradicted" mean "which is relevant to the issue,"[226] but, according to the Supreme Court this proposition has been too broadly laid down.[227]

223. *Bhogilal v Royal Insurance Co Ltd*, (1927) 30 Bom LR 818 : 6 Ran 142 (PC).
224. *The Queen v Brown and Hedley*, (1867) LR 1 CCR 70.
225. *Hussain Khan of Mamdot v Iftikhar Hussain Khan of Mamdot*, (1949) 2 Lah 844.
226. *Khadijah Khanum v Abdool Kurreem Sheraji*, (1889) 17 Cal 344, 347.
227. *Rama Reddy v VV Giri*, AIR 1971 SC 1162 : (1970) 2 SCC 340.

This sub-clause does not do away with the necessity of drawing the attention of the witness to the previous statement because this section is controlled by section 145.[228]

A conversation recorded in a tape-recorder is admissible in evidence under this clause.[229]

[s 155.4.1] Section 154, Criminal Procedure Code.—The first information report recorded under section 154, Criminal Procedure Code, may be used to contradict the informer under this section.[230]

[s 155.4.2] Section 164, Criminal Procedure Code.—A previous statement of a witness recorded under section 164, Criminal Procedure Code, can be used as provided for by this section, but it cannot be used as substantive evidence of the facts deposed to therein.[231]

[s 155.5] Immoral character of prosecutrix *[Clause 4]*.—In a case of rape the general immoral character of the complainant is relevant. The non-consent of the complainant is a material element; and the character of the woman as to chastity is of considerable probative value in judging of the likelihood of that consent.[232] Thus where the prosecutrix was asked the question about her previous sexual experience with other men and the question was not allowed, it was held on appeal that the question should have been allowed, for, if she had denied the imputation, she could have been contracted by citing her prior inconsistent statements about the matter and that would have very seriously affected her credibility as witness.[233]

Where the disclosure of incident of rape by the eyewitness the next day was supported by sound reasons, it was held that delayed disclosure *per se* was not fatal.[234]

[s 155.5.1] *Deletion of clause (4).*—Clause 4 has been deleted. It has been deleted in England also by the Youth Justice and Criminal Evidence Act, 1999. Now it is not permissible to ask any questions about the complainant's sexual history or previous sexual behaviour, not even under the guise of seeking information about previous false complaints.[235]

---

228. *Gopi Chand v The Crown*, (1930) 11 Lah 460; *Majid v State of Haryana*, AIR 2002 SC 382 : 2002 Cr LJ 938, a son deposed that his mother was killed by the accused. He was sought to be contradicted by an earlier statement to the effect that his father had killed his mother. This was not allowed because the earlier statement was not in writing. He was also not questioned about his earlier statement in cross-examination.

229. *Rup Chand v Shri Mahabir Pershad*, (1956) Pun 1351.

230. *Manimohan Ghosh v Emperor*, (1931) 58 Cal 1312; *Ramprasad v State of Maharashtra*, 1999 Cr LJ 2889 : AIR 1999 SC 1969 : (1999) 5 SCC 30, a dying declaration can be used for corroborating or contradicting the maker of the statement if he survives and appears as a witness. *State of Rajasthan v Teja Ram*, AIR 1999 SC 1776 : 1999 Cr LJ 2588, former statement of the witness, mode of proving.

231. *Emperor v Bishun Datt*, (1927) 50 All 242.

232. Cunnigham, 360.

233. *R v Funderburk*, (1990) 2 All ER 482 (CA), **applying** *R v Sweet Escote*, (1971) 55 Cr App R 316. It was pointed out per curiam that the court will be astute to see that such cross-examination is not abused or unnecessarily extended.

234. *Mukhera Belakota Reddi v State of AP*, 1992 Cr LJ 2236 (AP).

235. *R v T (complainant's Sexual History)*; *R v H (Complainant's Sexual History)*, (2002) 1 WLR 632 (CA) : (2002) 1 All ER 683. Questions about previous false complaints would require ruling from the

(Footnote No. 235 contd.)

[s 155.5.2] CASES.—The defendant was accused of indecently assaulting the complainant in a restaurant. There were no witnesses. The defence cross-examined the complainant as to allegations of sexual impropriety which she had made against other men. She denied making the complaints. The judge refused to allow the defence to call evidence as to the making of those complaints. On appeal it was contended that the judge erred in so ruling.

Held, allowing the appeal and ordering a retrial, that the judge should have permitted N to adduce the evidence of the making of the other complaints which went not merely to credit but to the central issue as to whether or not there had been any indecent assault in the instant case. As to that matter, only the complainant and the defendant were able to give evidence. If the evidence as to the other complaints had been called, it might well have caused the jury to take a different view.[236]

[s 155.6] Reasons for characterising witness hostile *[Explanation]*.—In the examination-in-chief a witness cannot be asked the reasons for his belief that another witness is unworthy of credit. Such questions can only be asked in cross-examination. But it is very dangerous in cross-examination to ask a witness his reasons for believing a witness to be untrustworthy. He is, by such a question, enabled to state any unfavourable fact without fear of contradiction.[237]

[s 156] Questions tending to corroborate evidence of relevant fact admissible.—When a witness whom it is intended to corroborate gives evidence of any relevant fact, he may be questioned as to any other circumstances which he observed at or near to the time or place at which such relevant fact occurred, if the Court is of opinion that such circumstances, if proved, would corroborate the testimony of the witness as to the relevant fact which he testifies.

ILLUSTRATION

A, an accomplice, gives an account of a robbery in which he took part. He describes various incidents unconnected with the robbery which occurred on his way to and from the place where it was committed.

(Footnote No. 235 contd.)

Judge. *R v Mohrecovas*, (20010 EWCA Crimes 1644 : (2002) 1 Cr App R 20, the complainant not allowed to be questioned on the point whether prior to the alleged rape by the accused, she had consensual sexual intercourse with the accused's brother. *R v A*(2001) 3 All ER 1 : (2002) 1 AC 45 : (2001) 2 WLR 1456 : (2001) 2 Cri App R 21 : (2001) UR HL 25 (HL). Their Lordships said that:

Under section 41(3)(c) of the 1999 Act, construed where necessary by applying the interpretative obligation under section 3 of the 1998 Act, and always paying due regard to the importance of seeking to protect the complainant from indignity and humiliating questions, the test of admissibility was whether the evidence, and questioning relating to it, was nevertheless so relevant to the issue of consent that to exclude it would endanger the fairness of the trial under Article 6 of the Convention. If that test were satisfied, the evidence should not be excluded. In the instant case the permissibility of questioning the complainant about the alleged recent sexual relationship between her and the accused and the admissibility of evidence on that point, were matters for the trial judge to decide at the resumed trial.

236. *R v Nagrecha (Chandu)*, (1997) 2 Cr App R 401 [CA (Crim Div)].

237. Cunnigham, 360.

Independent evidence of these facts may be given in order to corroborate his evidence as to the robbery itself.

COMMENT

[s 156.1] Principle.—It is a well-settled law that even where the evidence of the complainant is quite credible, no conviction can be based on such evidence unless it is corroborated by independent material.[238] This section permits the court to allow a witness, who has testified to a relevant fact, to corroborate his testimony by deposing to any circumstances which he observed at or near the time or place at which such relevant fact occurred. The frame of the section indicates what questions are to be asked in examination-in-chief. In most cases, it paves the way for cross-examination, which, if successful, brings out contradiction; but which, if unsuccessful, must inevitably result in corroboration. Like contradiction, corroboration is meant to test the truthfulness of a witness.

The Legislature has indicated how and when a witness may be contradicted (sections 145, 153 and 158). We have now to see in what circumstances a witness may be corroborated. First of all, he may be asked questions tending to corroborate evidence of a relevant fact (section 156); secondly, former statements made by him may be proved to corroborate later testimony to the same fact (section 157); thirdly, when any statement relevant under section 32 or section 33 is proved, all matters may be proved either to contradict or corroborate it (section 158).

[s 157] Former statements of witness may be proved to corroborate later testimony as to same fact.—In order to corroborate the testimony of a witness, any former statement[s 157.2] made by such witness relating to the same fact at or about the time when the fact took place,[s 157.3] or before any authority legally competent to investigate[s 157.4] the fact, may be proved.

SYNOPSIS

COMMENT

[s 157.1] Principle.—A witness's former statement relating to the same fact made at or about the time when the fact took place may be proved in order to corroborate his present testimony. There are only two things which are essential for the section to apply. The first is that a witness should have given testimony with respect to some fact. The second is that he should have made a statement earlier with respect to the same fact at or about the time when the fact took place or before any authority legally competent to investigate the fact. But in order to make the former statement admissible it is not necessary that the witness to be corroborated must also say in court in his testimony

---

238. *MG Thatte v State of Maharashtra*, 1993 Cr LJ 2878 (Bom).

that he had made the former statement.[239] The word investigate used in section 157 is not to be understood in narrow sense in which it is used in CrPC. It must carry its ordinary dictionary meaning in the sense of ascertainment of facts, sifting of materials and search of relevant data etc.[240]

A first information report is not a substantive piece of evidence and can only be used to corroborate the statement of the maker under this section or to contradict it under section 145 of this Act. It cannot be used as evidence against the maker at the trial if he himself becomes an accused, nor to corroborate or contradict other witnesses.[241]

[s 157.2] "Any former statement".—Such statement may be written or verbal, on oath, or in ordinary conversation. A witness's account-books, duly kept in the ordinary course of business, may be used under this section.[242]

The word "statement" means only "something that is stated" and the element of communication to another person is not necessary before "something that it stated" becomes a statement under this section.[243]

Statement of victim of sexual offence made immediately after the occurrence is admissible as a previous statement in terms of section 157 or section 8 of the Act.[244]

[s 157.3] "At or about the time when the fact took place".—These words mean that the statement must be made at once or at least shortly after when a reasonable opportunity for making it presents itself. What is a reasonable time is a question of fact in each case. The object of the section is to admit statements made at a time when the mind of the witness is still so connected with the events as to make it probable that his description of them then would be accurate. But if time for reflection passes between the event and the subsequent statement, it not only can be of very little value but may be actually dangerous as such statements can be easily brought into being. Such delayed statements are inadmissible. The section says that the statement must be made "at or about the time" not "at any time after the event."[245] The Supreme Court has held that the main test as to whether a previous statement was made "at or about the time when the fact took place" is whether the statement was made as early as could reasonably be expected in the circumstances of the case and before there was an opportunity for tutoring or concoction.[246]

The expression "at or about time when fact took place" in section 157 should be understood in the context according to facts and circumstances of each case. Where the testimony of witnesses is that soon after the incident when they arrived at the spot, eyewitnesses told them that accused chopped deceased by axe, while appellant-accused

---

239. *Ramratan v State of Rajasthan*, AIR 1962 SC 424 : (1962) 1 Cr LJ 473.
240. *Satendra Singh v State of Jharkhand* , 2009 Cr LJ 2280 (Jhar.).
241. *Nisar Ali*, (1957) All 361 SC.
242. Stokes,Vol II, p 931 fn 1.
243. *Bhogilal Chunilal*, (1958) 61 Bom LR 746 SC : (1958) 22 SCJ 240.
244. *Thottakkara Chanthan v State*, 2009 Cr LJ (NOC) 594 (Ker.).
245. *Re Appaduras*, (1945) Mad 821.
246. *Rameshwar v State of Rajasthan*, (1952) SCR 377 : AIR 1952 SC 54 : 1952 Cr LJ 547. Following this the Kerala High Court observed in *Rajan v State of Kerala*, 1992 Cr LJ 575, 578 (Ker), that the words "at or about the time" must mean that the statement was made at once or at least shortly after the event. The statement loses its value if the interval between the event and the statement is such as to afford opportunity for reflection. The court accordingly admitted the evidence of the statement of a bystander to another person who came running on hearing the sound of an explosion.

dealt Thunsa blow of lathi, the testimony is admissible in evidence and is relevant piece of evidence in terms of section 157.[247]

In *Mahabir Singh v State of Haryana*,[248] the Supreme Court construed the words "at or about the time when the fact took place." There was the solitary eyewitness to the fact of a murder. Soon after the incident he narrated the details to his father. The father narrated the same details in the FIR lodged by him. The court said that the interval between the occurrence and the time of communicating its details by the eyewitness to his father had not crossed the boundaries envisaged by the words "at or about the time when the fact took place." The testimony of father could be used to corroborate the evidence of his son, the eyewitness. The court said:[249] "It is useful to refer to the decision of this Court in *State of Tamil Nadu v Suresh*.[250] Following passage in that decision will be apposite: "We think that the expression "at or about the time when the fact took place" in section 157 of the Evidence Act should be understood in the context according to the facts and circumstances of each case. The mere fact that there was an intervening period of a few days, in a given case, may not be sufficient to exclude the statement from the use envisaged in section 157 of the Act. The test to be adopted, therefore, is this: Did the witness have the opportunity to concoct or to have been tutored? In this context the observation of Vivian Bose J in *Rameshwar v State of Rajasthan*[251] is apposite:

> There can be no hard and fast rule about the 'at or about' condition in Section 157. The main test is whether the statement was made as early as can reasonably be expected in the circumstances of the case and before there was opportunity for tutoring or concoction.

[s 157.4] "Any authority legally competent to investigate".—An Inspector of the Criminal Investigation Department is "an authority legally competent to investigate" within the meaning of this section.[252]

The first information report recorded under section 154, Criminal Procedure Code, is not a substantive piece of evidence; it can be used merely by way of corroboration or contradiction and not any further. It is inadmissible for the purpose of proving that the facts stated in it are correct.[253] The statement of a prosecution witness during the course of enquiry under section 202, CrPC cannot be proved under section 157 to corroborate evidence of other witnesses examined during trial.[254] Statements of witnesses before an investigating officer are also not evidence. Such statements can be used only to contradict a witness in the witness box.[255] The statements in an FIR also do not constitute a substantive evidence. They can also be used either for corroboration or

---

247. *Balram alias Ballu v State of MP*, 2011 Cr LJ 836 (MP).

248. *Mahabir Singh v State of Haryana*, AIR 2001 SC 2503 : 2001 Cr LJ 3945.

249. *Ibid*, p 2509.

250. *State of Tamil Nadu v Suresh*, AIR 1998 SC 1044 : (1998) 2 SCC 372 : 1998 AIR SCW 819 : 1998 Cr LJ 1416.

251. *Rameshwar v State of Rajasthan*, AIR 1952 SC 54 : 1953 Cr LJ 5471

252. *Muthukumaraswami Pillai v King-Emperor*, (1912) 35 Mad 397 (FB).

253. *Gajadhar Lal v King-Emperor*, (1931) 7 Luck 552, 562; *Manimohan Ghosh v Emperor*, (1931) 58 Cal 1312.

254. *Sashi Jena v Khadal Swain*, (2004) 4 SCC 236 : AIR 2004 SC 1492.

255. *Hamidulla Bismillakhan v State of Gujarat*, 1988 Cr LJ 981 (Guj); *VA Abraham v S P Cochin*, 1988 Cr LJ 1144 (Ker).

contradiction of the testimony of the witness.[256] It should not be admitted in evidence or placed before the jury unless it is admissible under one of the provisions of the Evidence Act. If, however, it is admissible it should be placed before the jury with proper directions. An information lodged by a person who died subsequently, relating to the cause of his death, is admissible as a substantive piece of evidence under the provisions of section 32(1). At the same time, the jury should be reminded that the statement in question had not been made on oath nor had it been tested by cross-examination but that after bearing these points in mind it would be for the jury to attach to it such weight as they considered necessary.[257]

When the prosecution has neither produced in evidence the person who made the first report in the Thana nor produced the person who wrote it out at the Thana, the first report cannot be referred to in evidence.[258]

[s 157.5] Effect of section 162, Criminal Procedure Code.—The general rule laid down in section 157 is controlled by the special provisions of section 162, Criminal Procedure Code, so far as statements to the police taken under section 161, Criminal Procedure Code, are concerned. Section 162 prohibits the use of the record containing the statement of a witness to the police as evidence against the accused as well as proof of such statement by oral evidence.[259] Such statements cannot be used as corroboration under this section.[260] Cases which laid down that the record was inadmissible but oral evidence as to the nature of those statements could be given to corroborate the testimony of a witness are no longer of any authority in virtue of the amended section 162, Criminal Procedure Code.[261] A first information does not prove itself; it has to be tendered under some section of the Evidence Act. The usual course is for the prosecution to tender it under this section to corroborate the informant, and the defence can prove it to impeach his credit under section 155, or to contradict him under section 145, of the Act. It is admissible also in proper cases under sections 8 and 32(1) of the Act.[262]

[s 157.6] Dying declaration.—Where a person making a dying declaration chances to live, his statement cannot be admitted in evidence as a dying declaration under section 32, but it may be relied on, under this section, to corroborate the testimony of the complainant when examined in the case.[263]

---

256. *Shayam Nandan Singh v State of Bihar*, 1991 Cr LJ 3350 (Pat).

257. *Emperor v Mohammad Shaikh*, (1942) 2 Cal 144; *Emperor v Rehenuddin Mondal*, (1943) 2 Cal 381.

258. *The State v Gajraj*, (1952) Raj 910.

259. *Rakha v The Crown*, (1925) 6 Lah 171, **disapproving** *Mam Chand v The Crown*, (1924) 5 Lah 324.

260. *Jagwa Dhanuk v King-Emperor*, (1925) 5 Pat 63; *King-Emperor v Maung Tha Din*, (1926) 4 Ran 72 (FB); *Rakha v The Crown*, (1925) 6 Lah 171, **disapproving** *Mam Chand v The Crown*, (1924) 5 Lah 324; *King-Emperor v Nga Lun Thoung*, (1935) 13 Ran 570 (FB).

261. The following cases are no longer of any authority: *Emperor v Hanmaraddi*, (1914) 16 Bom LR 603 : 39 Bom 58; *Fanindra Nath Banerjee v Emperor*, (1908) 36 Cal 281; *Muthukumaraswami Pillai v King-Emperor*, (1912) 35 Mad 397 (FB).

262. *Azimuddy v Emperor*, (1926) 54 Cal 237. *Shanker v State of UP*, AIR 1975 SC 757 : 1975 Cr LJ 634, FIR can be used as evidence under sections 32(1), 8, 154, 155 and 157.

263. *Emperor v Rana Sattu*, (1902) 4 Bom LR 434; *Maqsoodan v State of UP*, AIR 1983 SC 126 : (1983) 1 SCC 218 : 1983 SCC (Cri) 176 : 1983 Cr LJ 218 : 1982 All LJ 1524 ; *Ramprasad v State of Maharashtra*, 1999 Cr LJ 2889 : AIR 1999 SC 1969 : (1999) 5 SCC 30, which is to the same effect.

Where the maker of statement is alive and has also been examined, her statement is not admissible under section 32 but admissible under section 157.[264] In a case,[265] the statement of one of the victim was recorded as dying declaration, but subsequently, the victim survived and became an injured witness. Relying on its previous decisions,[266] it was held by Supreme Court that the statement cannot be treated as a dying declaration, but only as a previous statement made by that witness, but the statement has to be treated as of superior quality/high degree than that of the statement recorded under section 161, CrPC. It can also be used for the purposes of section 157 of Act.

Where a person in anticipation of death makes his dying declaration in terms of section 32 of Evidence Act but thereafter survives, in such an eventuality the statement so recorded has to be treated as of a superior quality/high degree than that of a statement recorded under section 161, CrPC and can be used as provided under section 157 of the 1872 Act.[267]

Where plaintiffs sought to establish their pedigree by proving *inter alia* that A and B were brothers, it was held that a statement to that effect made by one of the plaintiffs in a deposition given long before the controversy in suit arose was admissible in evidence.[268]

[s 158] What matters may be proved in connection with proved statement relevant under section 32 or 33.—Whenever any statement, relevant under section 32 or 33, is proved, all matters may be proved either in order to contradict or to corroborate it, or in order to impeach or confirm the credit of the person by whom it was made, which might have been proved if that person had been called as a witness and had denied upon cross-examination the truth of the matter suggested.

COMMENT

Sections 32 and 33 of the Act permit the putting in of statements, oral or written, or statements made in a judicial proceeding, by a person who cannot be examined as a witness. The Legislature intends by this section to submit such statements to the tests of contradiction and corroboration, in the same way as if those statements were made by the witness in the box. No sanctity attaches to such statements simply because the person is dead or cannot be examined as a witness. His credibility may be impeached or confirmed in the same manner as in the case of a living witness.

[s 159] Refreshing memory.—A witness may, while under examination, refresh his memory by referring to any writing made by himself at the time of the transaction concerning which he is questioned, or so soon afterwards that the Court considers it likely that the transaction was at that time fresh in his memory.

---

264. *Gajula Surya Parakash Rao v State of Andhra Pradesh*, 2010 Cr LJ 2102 (SC); Also see—*Mona Hang Subba v State of Sikkim*, 2012 Cr LJ 122 (SK); *Sunder Singh v State of Uttaranchal*, (2010) 10 SCC 611.

265. *Ranjit Singh v State of Madhya Pradesh*, 2011 Cr LJ 283 (SC).

266. *Sunil Kumar v State of MP*,(1997) 10 SCC 570, *Maqsoodan v State of UP*, (1983) 1 SCC 218, *Ramprasad v State of Maharashtra*, (1999) 5 SCC 30, *Gentela Vijayavardhan Rao v State of AP*, (1996) 6 SCC 241, *and State of UP v Veer Singh*, (2004) 10 SCC 117.

267. *Ranjit Singh v State of MP*, (2011) 4 SCC 336.

268. *Jadu Nath Sarker v Mahendra Nath Rai Chowdhury*, (1907) 12 Cal WN 266.

The witness may also refer to any such writing made by any other person, and read by the witness within the time aforesaid, if when he read it he knew it to be correct.

When witness may use copy of document to refresh memory.—Whenever a witness may refresh his memory by reference to any document, he may, with the permission of the Court, refer to a copy of such document:[s 159.1]

Provided the Court be satisfied that there is sufficient reason for the non-production of the original.

An expert may refresh his memory by reference to professional treatises.

SYNOPSIS

COMMENT

This section says how a witness may refresh his memory. He may, during his examination, refresh his memory by referring to—

(1) any writing made by himself (i) at the time of the transaction concerning which he is questioned, or (ii) so soon afterwards that the court considers it likely that the transaction was fresh in his memory;

(2) any such writing made by any other person and read by the witness within the time aforesaid;[269]

(3) professional treatises, if the witness is an expert (section 159).

It is not necessary that the writing referred to should be one which is admissible in evidence. A document not produced in court within proper time and, in consequence, rejected, may be referred to, to refresh memory if it comes within the purview of this section.[270] Even if a *panchanama* containing a statement made by a witness as to the crime committed is not admissible in evidence, a *panch* witness can make use of it for the purpose of refreshing his memory, where the *panchanama* is made by the police but is immediately read over to the *panch* and admitted by him to be correct.[271] But a Court should not take cognizance of the terms of a document which is inadmissible in evidence and has been referred to by a witness merely in order to refresh his memory as to a date.[272] The mere handing over of a document to a witness for the purpose of refreshing his memory does not make the document a piece of evidence in the case.[273] It is immaterial what the document is, whether it be a book of account, letter, tradesman's bill, notes made by the witness, or any other document which is likely to assist the memory of the witness. Where the question was whether a candidate appealed to voters on the ground of religion, short and long-hand notes made by persons who heard the speeches were permitted to be used by them for refreshing memory.[274] Their

---

269. *Burrough v Martin*, (1809) 2 Camp 112; *Abdul Salim v Emperor*, (1921) 49 Cal 573.
270. *Jewan Lal Daga v Nilmani Chaudhuri*, (1927) 30 Bom LR 305 : 55 IA 107 : 7 Pat 305.
271. *Emperor v Mahadeo Dewoo*, (1945) 47 Bom LR 992.
272. *Bhogilal Bhikachand v Royal Insurance Co Ltd*, (1927) 6 Ran 142 : 30 Bom LR 818 (PC).
273. *Tribhuvan Ojha v Ramchandra Dube*, (1934) 14 Pat 233.
274. *ZB Bukhari v BR Mehra*, AIR 1975 SC 1788 : (1976) 2 SCC 17.

contents can also be brought on record by direct oral evidence in the manner prescribed by section 160.

It is not necessary that the witness should have specific recollection of the facts themselves (section 160). But he has to appear before the court in person. Where the question was whether a marriage was solemnised before attaining the age of 15 years, the court said that the horoscope can be used in evidence by examining the person who prepared it not under section 32 but under sections 159–160.[275]

Deposition of complainant by referring to documents after permission from Court for the purposes of refreshing his memory does not result in any illegality or irregularity.[276]

The adverse party has the right of seeing the writing so used and cross-examining the witness thereupon (section 161).

The grounds upon which the opposite party is permitted to inspect a writing used to refresh the memory of a witness are threefold; (i) to secure the full benefit of the witness's recollection as to the whole of the facts; (ii) to check the use of improper documents; and (iii) to compare his oral testimony with his written statement.[277]

The section says a witness may refresh his memory as stated. He is not bound to do so; and the accused cannot compel him to do it.[278] Nor the accused can prevent from doing so. A person was charged with unlawfully possessing a controlled drug. The witness for the prosecution did not give at the trial as detailed a statement as he gave to the police when he was initially interviewed in relation to the offence. He was invited to refresh his memory from the record of his interview. The accused objected. The court said that there is no reason why a witness should not be allowed to supplement his testimony with certain essential details which are eluding him in oral testimony from his own earlier recorded statements. This is allowed in all cases where his testimony otherwise lays a proper foundation for his testimony.[279]

Records of investigating officers are in the nature of contemporaneous entries made by him for the purpose of refreshing his memory. The court said that it is always advisable to that he should look into his records before any concerned question.[280]

[s 159.1] "Copy of such document".—The Act does not require that this copy shall have been made by the witness himself, or in his presence, or so as to enable him to swear to its accuracy.[281] A register which is not a secondary evidence of the contents of a bond may be referred to by a witness for the purpose of refreshing his memory.[282]

Recovery memos and Discovery memos are used for the purposes of section 159. Statements of attesting witness to such memos are only corroborating evidence and their support to the prosecution cannot be considered as mandatory.[283]

---

275. *Savitri Bai v Sitaram*, AIR 1986 MP 218.
276. *Mahendra Amratlal Kayastha v State of Gujarat*, 2012 Cr LJ 959 (Guj.).
277. Per Field J, *In the matter of the petition of Jhubboo Mahton*, (1882) 8 Cal 739, 744.
278. *In the matter of the Petition of Kali Churn Chunari*, (1881) 8 Cal 154.
279. *R v Sutton*, (1992) Cr App R 70 (CA).
280. *State of Karnataka v R. Varappa Reddy*, 2000 Cr LJ 400 : AIR 2000 SC 185.
281. *Stokes*, Vol II, p 932, fn 3.
282. *Taruck Nath Mullick v Jeamat Nosya*, (1879) 5 Cal 353.
283. *Liyakat Ali v State of Rajasthan*, 2010 Cr LJ 2450 (Raj).

[s 159.2] Post-mortem examination reports.—A medical man in giving evidence may refresh his memory by referring to a report which he has made of his *post-mortem* examination, but the report itself cannot be treated as evidence.[284]

[s 159.3] Dying declaration.—The dying statement of a deceased person may be proved in the ordinary way by a person who heard it; and the writing may be used for the purpose of refreshing the witness's memory.[285]

[s 159.4] Special diary.—The special diary may be used by the police-officer who made it, and by no witness other than such officer, for the purpose of refreshing his memory.[286]

[s 160] Testimony to facts stated in document mentioned in section 159.—A witness may also testify to facts mentioned in any such document as is mentioned in section 159, although he has no specific recollection of the facts themselves, if he is sure that the facts were correctly recorded in the document.

ILLUSTRATION

A book-keeper may testify to facts recorded by him in books regularly kept in the course of business, if he knows that the books were correctly kept, although he has forgotten the particular transactions entered.

COMMENT

The principle of the foregoing section is carried a step further here. A witness may refresh his memory by a document even though he has no specific recollection of the facts themselves; but he must be sure that the facts were correctly recorded in the document. If the witness had not correctly recorded the words used by the speaker but only his impression, then the notes made by him would be inadmissible to prove the words used.[287] The section applies when the witness states in so many words that he does not recollect, and when the circumstances establish beyond doubt that this is so. Having no specific recollection of the facts he can only testify regarding the contents of the document before him and explain that he recorded correctly what the deponent said at the time.[288] A witness testifying to large number of transactions contained in account books or in other documents can be permitted to testify by referring to them.[289]

That a document may be used as the refresher of memory, it is by no means necessary that the witness, after having seen it, should have an independent recollection of the facts mentioned therein or connected therewith. It will suffice if he remembers that he has seen the paper before, and that, when he saw it, he knew its contents to be correct, or even if, entirely forgetting the circumstances themselves, and the fact of his having seen the paper, he can still, in consequence of recognising his signature or

284. *Roghuni Singh v The Empress*, (1882) 9 Cal 455; *Loku Basappa Pujari*, (1959) 61 Bom LR 1271.

285. *In the matter of the Petition of Samiruddin*, (1881) 8 Cal 211.

286. *Queen-Empress v Mannu*, (1897) 19 All 390 (FB); *King-Emperor v Nga Lun Thoung*, (1953) 13 Ran 570 (FB).

287. *Per* Wallis J, in *Mylapore Krishnasami v Emperor*, (1909) 32 Mad 384, 395.

288. *Partap Singh v The Crown*, (1925) 7 Lah 91.

289. *State of Andh. Pra. v Ganeswara Rao*, AIR 1963 SC 1850 : (1963) 2 Cr LJ 671.

writing upon it, vouch for the accuracy of the memorandum, or swear to the particular fact in question.[290]

A witness may refresh his memory from a writing made by another person and inspected and signed by him, at the close of the day on which it was made, when it brings to his mind neither any recollection of the facts mentioned therein nor any recollection of the writing itself but when it nevertheless enables him to testify to a particular fact from the conviction of his mind on seeing the writing which he knows to be genuine.[291]

The notes of a speech taken at the time by a police-officer should be proved in the following way. The police-officer should describe his attendance at the place where the speech was made by the accused and the making of the relevant speech, and give a description of its nature so as to identify his presence there and his attention to what was going on. After that it is quite enough if he says: "I wrote down that speech and this is what I took down."[292]

Where a commissioner's report was cancelled and a party sought to examine him as an ordinary witness and not in the capacity of commissioner, it was held that he could be allowed to refer to his report for refreshing memory.[293]

[s 161] Right of adverse party as to writing used to refresh memory.—Any writing referred to under the provisions of the two last preceding sections must be produced and shown to the adverse party if he requires it; such party may, if he pleases, cross-examine the witness thereupon.

COMMENT

[s 161.1] Principle.—This section gives the opposite party a right of inspecting documents used in court for the purpose of refreshing the memory of a witness. He may look at the writing to see what kind of writing it is in order to check the use of improper documents.[294] He has a right to look at any particular writing before or at the moment when the witness uses it to refresh his memory in order to answer a particular question; but if he then neglects to exercise his right, he cannot continue to retain the right throughout the whole of the subsequent examination of the witness.[295]

In all cases where documents are used to refresh the memory of a witness, it is usual and reasonable—and if the witness has no independent recollection of the fact, it is necessary—that they should be produced at the trial, and that the opposite counsel should have an opportunity of inspecting them, that, on cross or re-examination, he may have the benefit of the witness's refreshing his memory by every part. Neither is the adverse party bound to put in the document as part of his evidence, merely because he has looked at it, or examined the witness respecting such entries as have

290. *Taylor*, 12th Edn, section 1412, pp 896- 897.
291. *Abdul Salim v Emperor*, (1921) 49 Cal 573.
292. *Public Prosecutor v Venktarama Naidu*, (1944) Mad 113.
293. *VP Padmnabhan v Grassim Industries*, AIR 1997 Ker 356.
294. Per Field J, In the matter of the Petition of Jhubboo Mahton, (1882) 8 Cal 739, 745.
295. In the Matter of the Petition of Jhubboo Mahton, (1882) 8 Cal 739, 745.

been previously referred to, but, if he goes further than this, and asks questions about other parts of the memorandum, it seems that he thereby makes it his own evidence.[296]

[s 162] Production of documents.—A witness summoned to produce a document shall, if it is in his possession or power, bring it to Court, notwithstanding any objection which there may be to its production or to its admissibility. The validity of any such objection shall be decided on by the Court.

The Court, if it sees fit, may inspect the document, unless it refers to matters of State,[s 162.2] or take other evidence to enable it to determine on its admissibility.

Translation of documents.—If for such purpose it is necessary to cause any document to be translated, the Court may, if it thinks fit, direct translator to keep the contents secret, unless the document is to be given in evidence: and, if the interpreter disobeys such direction, he shall be held to have committed an offence under section 166 of the Indian Penal Code (45 of 1860).

SYNOPSIS

COMMENT

This section refers to official as well as private documents. The second paragraph of the section provides that when a document, in respect of which an objection to production or admissibility is raised, refers to matters of State, the court has no power to inspect the document. With regard to other documents in respect of which privilege is claimed, the court, if it thinks fit, may inspect the documents.

[s 162.1] Principle.—Under this section the validity of an objection to the production of a document has to be determined by the court. The only limitation on the power of the court is that in cases of documents where privilege is claimed under section 123, the court may not look at those documents but must determine the validity of the claim on materials other than the document itself.[297]

When a witness is summoned to produce a document which is in his possession or power, he must bring it to Court, notwithstanding any objection that he may have with regard to its production or admissibility. Under the provisions of O XVI, rule 6, of the Civil Procedure Code, a person may be summoned to produce a document without being summoned to give evidence. He may either attend the court personally or depute another to produce it. In neither case is he liable to be cross-examined (section 139). If the document be in his possession or power, he is bound, under this section, to bring the document with him to Court notwithstanding any objection he may have to its production (e.g., sections 130–131 or sections 126–129) or admissibility. Having brought it to Court, he is entitled to raise his objection to its production or admissibility. The court has then to decide the validity of any such objection. For the purpose of deciding on the validity of the reason that may be offered for withholding

---

296. *Taylor*, 12th Edn, section 1413, p 897.
297. *Dinbai Petit v Dominion of India*, (1950) 53 Bom LR 229.

them, the court may receive evidence[298] and in so doing it is entitled to inspect the document, if it does not refer to matters of State (section 123). If the document in question happens to be in a language not known to the presiding officer, he may get it translated, and call upon the translator to keep its contents secret.

In criminal cases, the protection under section 126 afforded to communications by a client to lawyers cannot be availed of against an order to produce the document; the document must be produced, and then, under this section it will be for the court, after inspection of the document, if it deems fit, to consider and decide any objections regarding its production or admissibility.[299] Where the matter in a Government was found to be of privileged character, the matter was held to be not available to support a contempt or defamation case.[300]

The party claiming privilege may waive it, either absolutely or subject to reservations. Where a document was disclosed for the purposes of criminal proceedings, it was held that there was no waiver of the privilege in the matter of civil proceedings.[301]

[s 162.2] "Matters of State".—See section 123 as to "affairs of State." Where an officer is summoned to produce an official document, he is bound to produce it in court. He should raise the objection in court, and the question whether that objection is well-founded is one for the court to decide. For this purpose the court is not entitled to inspect the document if it refers to matters of State. It must decide the question without such inspection by examining the officer producing it or otherwise. It is for the court to decide whether a particular document is an unpublished record relating to affairs of State, i.e., whether it is a document in respect of which privilege can properly be claimed. But once the court has decided that the document is one in respect of which privilege may be claimed, i.e., it is an unpublished record relating to matters of State, the question whether the document should be produced or not is one entirely in the discretion of the head of the department concerned, and the court has no power to inspect the document to determine the question of its admissibility. The officer claiming privilege for a document that he is summoned to produce must appear and produce the document in court and must satisfy the court that his claim is well-founded. It is for the court to decide whether the claim should be allowed or not. But once the court holds that the document is one with regard to which privilege can be claimed, in other words, that it is a communication made to a public officer in official confidence or that it is an unpublished official record relating to affairs of State which it would not be in the public interest to disclose, the question whether privilege should be claimed for it or not is entirely within the discretion of the officer in charge of the document. The court for the purpose of deciding whether the claim to privilege is well-founded or not is not entitled to look at the document. It must decide the question of the validity of the objection without looking at the document.[302]

---

298. *Venkatachella Chettiar v Sampathu Chettiar*, (1908) 32 Mad 62, 64.

299. *Ganga Ram v Habib-Ullah*, (1935) 58 All 364.

300. *State of Bihar v Kripalu Shankar*, AIR 1987 SC 1554 : (1987) 3 SCC 34 : 1987 SCC (Cri) 442. The court considered *Bachitar Singh v State of Punjab*, AIR 1963 SC 395 : 1962 Supp (3) SCR 713; *Home Office v Harman Singh*, (1981) 2 WLR 310; *Harman v Secy of State for Home Deptt*, 1983 AC 280.

301. *British Coal Corpn v Rye (Dennis) (No. 2)* The Times, March 7, 1988 CA; 1988 CLY 1592.

302. *Re Mantubhai Mehta*, (1943) 46 Bom LR 802.

This aspect was closely scrutinised by the Supreme Court in its decision in *SP Gupta v UOI,*[303] The case arose out of the matter of the transfer of a High Court judge and non-renewal of the terms of an additional judge. The correspondence between the Law Minister and the Chief Justice of India and that between the Chief Justice of the High Court and the State Government was required to be produced. It was held that though the advice was protected from judicial scrutiny by virtue of Article 74 of the Constitution, the material on the basis of which the advice was formulated was not protected. The approach adopted appears from the following statement: "So where an objection is taken against the disclosure of any document the court would allow the objection if it finds that the document relates to the affairs of the State and its disclosure would be injurious to public interest, but, on the other hand if the court reaches the conclusion that the document does not relate to the affairs of the State or that the public interest in the administration of justice in the particular case overrides all other aspects of public interest, the court will overrule the objection and order disclosure of the document. The final decision in regard to the validity of an objection against disclosure raised under section 123 would always be with the court by reason of section 162.

"The Court is not bound by the assertions made by a Minister or a Head of the Department in an affidavit in support of plea against non-disclosure. The Court retains the power to balance the injury to the State or the public service against the risk of injustice, before reaching the decision. At the same time the immunity against disclosure allowed under section 123 is not a privilege which can be waived by the State.

In the weighting process which the court has to perform in order to decide which of the two aspects of public interest should be given predominance, the character of the proceeding, the issues arising in it and the likely effect of the documents on the determination of the issues must form vital consideration.

Of course, there are certain classes of documents which should not be disclosed, no matter what a particular document in those classes may contain. Law recognises their immunity from disclosure as a class. It does appear that cabinet papers, minutes of discussions of Heads of Departments and high level documents relating to the inner working of the Government machinery which are concerned with the framing of Government polices belong to this class which in public interest must be regarded as protected against disclosure.

In this regard it is necessary to bear in mind that the burden of establishing a claim for class immunity is very heavy on the person making the claim.

So even where a claim for immunity against disclosure of a document is made under

section 123, the court may in an appropriate case inspect the document in order to satisfy itself whether its disclosure would, in the particular case before it, be injurious to public interest and whether the claim for immunity must, therefore, be upheld. This power of inspection is a power which is to be sparingly exercised, that is, only if the court is in doubt, after considering the affidavit, if any, filed by the Minister or the Secretary, the issues in the case and the relevance of the document whose disclosure is sought."

303. *SP Gupta v UOI,* AIR 1982 SC 149 : 1981 Supp SCC 87. The court **overruled** its own decision in *State of Punjab v Sodhi Sukhdev Singh,* AIR 1981 SC 493.

"What is impermissible under section 123 is giving evidence derived from unpublished official records relating to affairs of the State. Section 123 must be construed on its own terms. Undoubtedly, a century old provision enacted to some extent keeping in view the needs of the Empire builders must change in the context of the Republican Government and the open society which we have set up. Undoubtedly there must be such affairs of the Sate involving security of the nation and foreign affairs where public interest requires that the disclosure should not be ordered. It is, however, equally well recognised that fair administration of justice is itself a matter of vital public interest. Therefore, if the two public interest conflict, the court will have to decide whether the public interest which formed the foundation for claiming privilege would be jeopardised if disclosure is ordered and on the other hand whether fair administration of justice would suffer by non-disclosure and decide which way the balance tilts."

"The rules now developed by Supreme Court relating to the disclosure of documents need to be carefully applied. The balance between the conflicting claims of public interest represented by officialdom and the public interest flowing from the administration of justice often calls for a delicate assessment, into which per force must enter consideration vital to the operations of Government on the one hand and the demands of adjudication on the other. The responsibility fixed on the court is a serious one, and there is need to warn that this power which now vests in the court can have grave consequences if the content of its potential is not truly appreciated and realised by those who wield it. Whenever a court breaks new ground, the development and recognition of new rights is often accompanied by the birth of problems surfacing also for the first time. New doctrines must be cautiously applied. Yet no court can shirk its duty if it finds that its power has been rightly invoked."

The Supreme Court laid emphasis upon public interest aspects of the provisions: A plain reading of sections 123 and 124 of the Evidence Act, section 162 of the CrPC and Article 74(2) of the Constitution would show that these provisions are expressed in a negative form which is the clearest possible proof of the fact that the legislature has incorporated a direct prohibition against the use of documents mentioned in the aforesaid provisions.

Thus, a disclosure can be allowed only in exceptional circumstances where there is no injury to public interest because public interest is always paramount to private interest. In fact, those provisions clearly contain four important attributes of the doctrine of disclosure—(a) public interest, (b) confidentiality, (c) candour and (d) expediency. The legislature seems to have laid the greatest possible emphasis on public interest and confidentiality aspects of these documents.

Any revolutionary decisions so as to expose high confidential matters to public gaze by following a policy of liberal disclosure of documents ignoring the provisions of sections 123 and 124 of the Act would not only be detrimental to our progress but may cause serious obstruction in the practical running of day-to-day affairs of the Government or for that matter the governance of the country itself.

The statutory provisions of sections 123 and 124 of the Evidence Act as also those of Article 74(2) of the Constitution have fully safeguarded high Government and official secrets and disclosure is prohibited in public interest unless the court is fully satisfied that disclosure will not harm the public interest."

In a subsequent case,[304] the Supreme Court thus commented on this case: "Though the ratio of the court's decision in *Bachhittar Singh*[305] case outlines the conservative view in the law relating to privilege, the doctrine of privilege received a shock treatment against the State at the hands of the Supreme Court in *SP Gupta v UOI*"[306] It may be said that the legal milestone in *Gupta* case also needs to retreat a bit.

Statements made and documents produced by assesses before the Income-tax Officer for the purpose of showing the income of such assesses do not refer to matters of State.[307]

In an employment dispute, the employee had filed a suit against his employer seeking a declaration that he is entitled to promotion to the post of Senior Branch Manager with effect from the date when his batch mates were so promoted. The employee pleaded that his performance was admittedly comparatively better than his batch mates. During trial, a witness was summoned to produce the Annual Confidential Report of the employee when an application was filed seeking privilege on the ground that the Annual Confidential Report cannot be allowed to be produced in public interest. It was held by the Punjab & Haryana High Court that claim of privilege is not available to "Annual Confidential Report". Information cannot be protected from disclosure merely because it has been supplied in confidence. Accordingly, the claim of privilege in regard to the class of document known as Annual Confidential Report was declined.[308]

[s 162.3] Privilege of newspapers.—The privilege of newspapers (known as the newspaper rule) protects their sources of information. In a matter in which a privilege of this kind was claimed by a newspaper (a libel action), the court said:[309] In determining whether the disclosure of sources is "necessary" in the interests of justice, the court has first to identify and define the issue for which disclosure was required and then to decide whether, having regard to the nature of the issue and the circumstances of the case, it is in fact "necessary" to order disclosure. Although disclosure of sources might be relevant and important in determining whether the defendants had acted disgracefully and whether that should be reflected in an award of aggravated or exemplary damages, that does not make disclosure "necessary" in the interests of justice.[310]

Where a news reporter collected information from some hospital sources identifying the victims of AIDS admitted there and the newspaper was permanently restrained from publishing the matter because freedom of the press was comparatively less important than the secrecy of AIDS victims so that they may not be deterred from going to hospitals, the reporter was not compelled to disclose the source of his information because the plaintiff had to fail to prove on a balance of probability that the disclosure was necessary in public interest or interests of justice, such as for example, prevention of crime.[311]

---

304. *State of Bihar v Kripalu Shankar,* (1987) 3 SCC 34 : AIR 1987 SC 1554.

305. *Bachhittar Singh v State,* AIR 1963 SC 395 : 1962 Supp 3 SCR 713.

306. *SP Gupta v UOI,* AIR 1982 SC 149 : 1981 Supp SCC 87.

307. *Venkatachella Chettiar v Sampathu Chettiar,* (1908) 32 Mad 62; *Jadobram Dey v Bulloram Dey,* (1899) 26 Cal 281.

308. *LIC of India, Sector-17B, Chandigarh v BB Singla,,* 2008 (4) CCC 406 (P&H).

309. *Maxwell v Pressdram Ltd,* (1987) 1 All ER 656 (CA).

310. Applying the dictum of Lord DIPLOCK in *Secretary of State for Defence v Guardian Newspapers Ltd,* (1984) 3 All ER 606-607.

311. *X v Y,* (1988) 2 All ER 649 (SBD).

[s 163] Giving, as evidence, of document called for and produced on notice.—When a party calls for a document[s 163.3] which he has given the other party notice to produce, and such document is produced and inspected by the party calling for its production, he is bound to give it as evidence if the party producing it requires him to do so.

SYNOPSIS

COMMENT

[s 163.1] Principle.—Where a party to a suit gives notice to the other party to produce a document, and when produced, he inspects the same he is bound to give it as evidence if the other party requires him to do so.[312] The reason for this rule is that it would give an unconscionable advantage to a party to enable him to pry into the affairs of his adversary, without at the same time subjecting him to the risk of making whatever he inspects as evidence for both parties.[313]

A party is bound to give the opponent's documents as evidence in the case if three conditions are fulfilled: (1) the document should be required by that party to be produced in evidence; (2) it should be inspected by the party calling for its production; (3) the party producing the document should require the party calling for it to put it in evidence.[314]

[s 163.2] Scope.—This section is applicable to criminal trials as well as to civil actions.[315] Records of statements made not on oath in the course of a departmental inquiry by Government are not public documents. But, when the defence had called for their production and they were, thereupon, produced and inspected and used for the cross-examination of the prosecution witnesses, it was held that the Crown could insist on the entire statements being put in under this section.[316]

[s 163.3] "When a party calls for a document".—The terms of the section make it clear that the section refers to documents asked for by a party during trial. It does not refer to documents produced under O XI, rule 14, of the Civil Procedure Code.

[s 163.4] Foreign document, production in home country illegal.—The documents in question were involved in assisting banking fraud connected with BCCI. The French Law prohibited the documentary evidence of a business of a financial nature for use in foreign proceedings. It was held[317] that the court had a jurisdiction to order disclosure in such circumstances and could exercise its discretion in deciding whether or not to so order. The court would not have jurisdiction to order inspection where to do so would involve an offence under English law. It was, however, different where the obligation

---

312. *Mahomed v Abdul,* (1903) 5 Bom LR 380.
313. *Taylor,* 12th Edn, section 1817, p 1126.
314. *Liladhar Ratanlal v Holkarmal,* (1958) 60 Bom LR 203.
315. *Emperor v Makhan Lal Datta,* (1939) 2 Cal 429.
316. *Govt of Bengal v Santiram Mandal,* (1930) 58 Cal 96.
317. *Morris v Banque Arable Et International Dinvestissment SA (No. 1),* 2000 CP Rep 65 (Ch D).

to disclose was under English law but the offence was under a foreign jurisdiction.[318] The existing authorities indicate that the court has a discretion whether or not to order disclosure.

[s 164] Using, as evidence of document production of which was refused on notice.—When a party refuses to produce a document which he had notice to produce, he cannot afterwards use the document as evidence without the consent of the other party or the order of the Court.

ILLUSTRATION

A sues *B* on an agreement and gives *B* notice to produce it. At the trial *A* calls for the document and *B* refuses to produce it. *A* gives secondary evidence of its contents. *B* seeks to produce the document itself to contradict the secondary evidence given by *A*, or in order to show that the agreement is not stamped. He cannot do so.

COMMENT

[s 164.1] Principle.—If a party having a document in his possession refuses to produce it when called upon at the hearing to do so, he is not at liberty afterwards to give the document in evidence for any purpose without (1) the consent of the other party, or (2) the order of the court. This is meant as a penalty for unfair tactics. The Civil Procedure Code, O XI, rule 15, makes a similar provision.

This section does not contemplate the production of a document for inspection. It contemplates that one party should call upon another in court to produce a document of which the first party has given the other notice to produce. It does not give him any right, at any stage of the case, to call upon his opponent to produce the document and, after inspecting it, use it or not as he sees fit. It is doubtful if this section applies to criminal proceedings.[319]

[s 165] Judge's power to put questions or order production.—The Judge may, in order to discover or to obtain proper proof of relevant facts,[s 165.2] ask any question he pleases, in any form, at any time, of any witness, or of the parties about any fact relevant or irrelevant; and may order the production of any document or thing; and neither the parties nor their agents shall be entitled to make any objection to any such question or order, nor, without the leave of the Court, to cross-examine any witness upon any answer given in reply to any such question:[s 165.3]

Provided that the judgment must be based upon facts declared by this Act to be relevant, and duly proved:

Provided also that this section shall not authorize any Judge to compel any witness to answer any question or to produce any document which such witness would be entitled to refuse to answer or produce under sections 121 to 131, both inclusive, if the question were asked or the document were called for by the adverse party; nor shall the Judge ask any question which it would be improper for any other person to ask under section 148 or 149; nor shall he dispense with primary evidence of any document, except in the cases hereinbefore excepted.

---

318. The court applied the principle *Brannigan v Davison,* (1997) AC 238.
319. *Shyamdas Kapur v Emperor*, (1932) 60 Cal 341.

SYNOPSIS

COMMENT

[s 165.1] Principle.—This section is intended to arm the judge with the most extensive power possible for the purpose of getting at the truth. The effect of this section is that in order to get to the bottom of the matter before it, the court will be able to look at and enquire into every fact whatever.[320] Each party in a case is interested in setting up his own case and demolishing the one set up by his adversary. There is danger in some cases that the whole truth may not come out before the court. The judge, in order to discover, or to obtain proper proof of relevant facts, may exercise very wide powers indeed; but they all pivot upon the ascertainment of relevant facts. He may approach the case from any point of view, and is not tied down to the ruts marked out by the parties. He can ask (1) any question he pleases, (2) in any form, (3) at any time, (4) of any witness, (5) or of the parties, (6) about any fact relevant or irrelevant. No party is entitled to object to any such question or order, or to cross-examine the witness without the leave of the court. But out of the evidence so brought out, the judge can only use that which is relevant and duly proved. There are three exceptions to the very wide powers given to the judge. The witness cannot be compelled to answer (1) any question or to produce any document contrary to sections 121–131; (2) any question contrary to section 148 or 149; and (3) the judge shall not dispense with primary evidence of any document except as provided before.

A trial judge is not expected to act like a mere tape recorder to record whatever has been stated by the witnesses. Section 311 of CrPC and section 165 of Evidence Act confers vast and wide powers on Court to elicit all necessary materials by playing an active role in the evidence collecting process.[321]

In civil as well as in criminal proceedings the Legislature has vested ample powers in the courts to exercise this power (Civil Procedure Code, O X, rules 2, 4, O XVI, rule 14; section 311, Criminal Procedure Code).

The effect of this section is that in order to get to the bottom of a matter before it, the court will be able to look at and enquire into every fact whatever and thus possibly acquire valuable indicative evidence which may lead to other evidence strictly relevant and admissible.[322]

---

320. Stephen, 162; *Ramachandra Reddy*, (1957) AP 742.

321. *Vikas Kumar Roorkewal v State of Uttarakhand*, (2011) 2 SCC 178. Also see *Vijay Kumar v State of UP*, (2011) 8 SCC 136 wherein it was held that powers of court under section 165 of the Evidence Act is complementary to its power under section 311 of CrPC. These two sections between them confer jurisdiction on the court to act in aid of justice.

322. *Sky Land International Pvt Ltd v Kavita Lalwani*, RFA 697 of 2010 decided by the Delhi High Court on 25-5-2012 (JR. MIDHA, J).

This power has been explained by the Supreme Court as an extraordinary power conferred upon the court to elicit the truth and to act in the interest of justice. A wide discretion has been conferred on the court to act as the exigencies of justice require. Thus, in order to discover or obtain proper proof of the relevant facts, the court can ask the question to the parties concerned at any time and in any form. "Every trial is voyage of discovery in which truth is the quest". Therefore, power is to be exercised with an object to subserve the cause of justice and public interest, and for getting the evidence in aid of a just decision and to uphold the truth.[323]

Even the scheme and special procedure prescribed under sections 143–146 of the Negotiable Instruments Act does not in any way affect the judge's powers under section 165 of the Evidence Act.[324]

"When the counsel for the prisoner has examined or declined to cross-examine a witness, and the Court afterwards, of its own motion, examine him, the witness cannot then, without the permission of the Court, be subjected to cross-examination. When, after the examination of a witness by the complainant and the defendant, the Court takes him in hand, he is put under special pressure as the Judge is empowered to ask any question he pleases, in any form about any fact relevant or irrelevant. and he is, therefore, at the same time placed under the special protection of the Court, which may, at its discretion, allow a party to cross-examine him, but this cannot be asked for as a matter of right. This principle applies equally whether it is intended to direct the examination to the witness's statements of fact, or to circumstances touching his credibility, for any question meant to impair his credit tends (or is so designed) to get rid of the effect of all his answers, and of each of them just as much as one that may bring out an inconsistency or contradiction. It is then a cross-examination upon answers—upon every answer given to the Court, and is subject to the Court's control."[325]

In a great number of cases—probably, the vast numerical majority—the Judge has to conduct the whole trial himself. In all cases he has to represent the interests of the public much more distinctly than he does in England. In many cases he has to get at the truth, or as near to it as he can, by the aid of collateral inquiries, which may incidentally tend to something relevant; and it is most unlikely that he should ever wish to push an inquiry needlessly, or to go into matters not really connected with it. We have accordingly thought it right to arm Judges with a general power to ask any questions, upon any facts, of any witnesses, at any stage of the proceedings, irrespective of the rules of evidence binding on the parties and their agents, and we have inserted in the bill a distinct declaration that it is the duty of the Judge, especially in criminal cases, not merely to listen to the evidence put before him, but to inquire to the utmost into the truth of the matter. We do not think that the English theories, that the public have no interest in arriving at the truth and that even criminal proceedings ought to be regarded mainly in the light of private questions between the prosecutor and the prisoner, are at all suited to India, if indeed they are the result of anything better than carelessness and apathy in England.

323. *Ritesh Tewari v State of UP,* (2010) 10 SCC 677 : AIR 2010 SC 3823.
324. *Mandvi Co-op Bank Ltd v Nimesh B Thakore,* (2010) 3 SCC 83.
325. *Reg v Sakharam Mukundji,* (1874) 11 BHC 166, 168.

"In India, in an enormous mass of cases, it is absolutely necessary that the Judge should not only hear what is put before him by others, but that he should ascertain by his own inquiries how the facts actually stand. In order to do this, it will frequently be necessary for him to go into matters which are not themselves relevant to the matter in issue, but may lead to something that is, and it is in order to arm Judges with express authority to do this that this section has been framed."[326]

It is not the province of the court to examine the witnesses, unless the pleaders on either side have omitted to put some material question or questions, and the court should, as a general rule, leave the witnesses to the pleaders to be dealt with as laid down in section 138.[327]

The power to identify the matters in controversy by examination of parties at the pre-trial stage under O X, rule 2, is completely different from the power exercised by the court under section 165 of the Evidence Act to put any question it pleases in any form, to a witness or a party in order to discover or to obtain proper proof of relevant facts, or the power under O XVIII, rule 17 of the Code to recall and examine any witness. The court's anxiety to do justice by speeding up the process of the suit should not itself lead to injustice.[328]

Facts which are not properly proved cannot be considered by the Judge and cannot form the basis of a judgment. It is only those facts which are declared to be relevant and duly proved, which can be the basis of a judgment as provided by this section.[329]

Judges should avoid interrupting a witness, particularly a defendant, when he is being examined-in-chief or being cross-examined.[330]

The evidence that comes on record pursuant to the questions put by the court in exercise of powers under section 165 of the Evidence Act is outside the scheme for recording evidence under sections 137 and 138 of the Evidence Act. However, the adverse party against whom the witness has given evidence pursuant to the court question is entitled to cross-examine on matters referred to in the answer given in reply to any such Court question.[331]

Where a witness was a bit confused during his cross-examination and the trial Court intervened putting questions to him to elicit the truth, the Supreme Court said that the trial Court ought not to have done so.[332] The Supreme Court said:[333]

> Section 165 of the Evidence Act confers vast and unrestricted powers on the trial court to put *any* question *it pleases in any* form, at *any* time, of *any* witness, or of the parties, about *any* fact *relevant or irrelevant* in order to discover any relevant facts. The section was framed by lavishly studding it with the word "any" which could only have been inspired by the legislative intent to confer unbridled power on the trial court to use the power

326. Proceedings of the Legislative Council. Reiterated and also restated by the Supreme Court in *Zahira Habibullah Sheikh v State of Gujarat,* AIR 2006 SC 1367 : (2006) 3 SCC 374 : (2006) 2 Ker LT 350 : 2006 Cr LJ 1694.

327. *Noor Bux Kazi v Empress,* (1880) 6 Cal 279, 283.

328. *Kapil Corepacks Pvt Ltd v Harbans Lal,* (2010) 8 SCC 452.

329. *Miyana Hasan Abdulla,* (1961) 3 GLR 107.

330. *R v Marsh,* The Times, July 6, 1993 (CA).

331. *Popathal Jethabhai Shah v State of Maharashtra,* 2007 Cr LJ (NOC) 605 (Bom.).

332. *State of Rajasthan v Ani,* AIR 1997 SC 1023 : 1997 Cr LJ 1529 : (1997) 6 SCC 162.

333. 35. Ibid, p 166, (1997) 6 SCC 162 : AIR 1997 SC 1023 : 1997 Cr LJ 1529.

> whenever it deems it necessary *to elicit the truth.* Even if any such question crosses into irrelevancy, it would not transgress the contours of the powers of the court. This is clear from the words "relevant or irrelevant". Neither of the parties have any right to raise any objection to any such question.

The judges are not computers. In assessing the value to be attached to oral evidence, they are bound to call into aid their experience of life.[334]

It is the bounden duty cast upon the judge not merely to ensure that an innocent person is not punished but equally not to become a mute spectator to the spectacle of convict circumventing his conviction. If the court is derelict in doing its duty, the social fabric will be rent asunder and anarchy will rule everywhere. The criminal justice delivery system is being held to ransom by convicts who have developed the devious and dishonest practice of escaping punishment and thereafter disappearing beyond the reach of the arms of the law.[335] The court cannot be a silent spectator or a mute observer when it presides over a trial. It is the duty of the court to see that neither the prosecution nor the accused play truancy with the criminal trial or corrode the sanctity of the proceeding. They cannot expropriate or highjack the community interest by conducting themselves in such a manner as a consequence of which the trial becomes a farcical one. The law does not countenance a "mock trial". The court is duty bound to see that neither the prosecution nor the defence takes unnecessary adjournments and take the trial under their control. The court is under the legal obligation to see that the witnesses who have been cited by the prosecution are produced by it or if summons are issued, they are actually served on the witnesses. If the court is of the opinion that the material witnesses have not been examined, it should not allow the prosecution to close the evidence. There can be no doubt that the prosecution may not examine all the material witnesses but that does not necessarily mean that the prosecution can choose not to examine any witness and convey to the court that it does not intend to cite the witnesses. The court is also not expected to accept the version of the prosecution, as if it is sacred. It has to apply its mind on every occasion. Non-application of mind by the trial Court has the potentiality to lead to the paralysis of the conception of fair trial.[336]

[s 165.2] "In order to discover or to obtain proper proof of relevant facts".—The power of the court to direct production of any document under this section is subject to the plain proviso at the beginning of that section that the direction must be "in order to discover or obtain proper proof of relevant facts." The commentaries show clearly that the object of allowing the Judge to ask irrelevant questions under this section is to obtain "indicative evidence" which may lead to the discovery of relevant evidence.[337]

Although a statement made by an accused person to a police-officer on which the defence wishes to rely is shut out by section 162, Criminal Procedure Code, a Court, having a case diary in its possession, at the request of the defending counsel, would be justified in putting a question to a police-officer to elicit what the accused told him, purely in the interest of the accused, within its wide powers under this section.[338]

---

334. *Chaturbhuj Pande v Collector, Raigarh*, AIR 1969 SC 255 : (1969) 1 SCR 412.
335. *Surya Baksh Singh v State of UP*, (2014) 14 SCC 222 (paras 25 and 17).
336. *Bablu Kumar v State of Bihar*, (2015) 8 SCC 787, para 22.
337. *Krishna Ayyar v Balakrishna Ayyar*, (1933) 57 Mad 635.
338. *Molagan*, (1953) Mad 284.

The trial Court could not have first put a specific finding based on its own opinion to the expert witness and then ask him questions. The court said that the trial Court exceeded its jurisdiction under section 165.[339]

[s 165.3] "Cross-examine any witness upon any answer, etc."—A party to a proceeding is not allowed to cross-examine a witness upon an answer given by him to a question put by the court without the permission of such Court.[340] If what the witness has said in answer to the questions put to him by the Judge is adverse to either of the parties, the Judge ought to allow the witness to be cross-examined upon his answers. A general fishing cross-examination ought not to be permitted.[341] The accused should be given an opportunity to cross-examine a witness on the answers to questions put by the court.[342]

A Judge can himself look into previous statements of witnesses recorded in the police diary, even though the defence neither requested him to do so nor applied for copies of such statements, and if the interests of justice demand, the Judge may himself, under this section, put questions to witnesses to bring out discrepancies of a vital nature between such statements and the evidence of those witnesses in court.[343]

Where a witness was confused while facing his cross-examination, it was held to be not improper for the trial Court to ask questions to him to find out the truth.[344] The purpose of examination of a witness by the Judge is to ascertain the matter in controversy in the suit. The purpose is not to record evidence or to secure an admission or to conduct cross-examination. It was held that an answer given by a party under O X, rule 2, as to veracity of signature on the document is neither given under oath nor while being examined as a witness. It does not amount to fabricating or giving of false evidence.[345]

The power of the court of questioning parties is of extraordinary nature. It is to be used for eliciting truth in the interest of justice. The party cannot tell the court that the question put to him is irrelevant.[346] The presiding judge must not be a spectator and a mere recording machine.[347]

[s 165.4] Judgment to be on facts relevant and duly proved *[Proviso 1]*.—This proviso says that the judgment must be based upon facts declared by this Act to be relevant (sections 5–55) and duly proved (sections 56–100). The Judge will not be

---

339. *Sidhartha Vashisht @ Manu Sharma v State (NCT of Delhi)*, AIR 2010 SC 2352 : (2010) 6 SCC 1.

340. *Gopal Lall Seal v Manick Lall Seal*, (1897) 24 Cal 288, 290.

341. *Coulson v Disborough*, (1894) 2 QB 316.

342. *In the matter of The Empress v Grish Chunder Talukdar*, (1879) 5 Cal 614; *Mohendro Nath Das Gupta v Emperor*, (1902) 29 Cal 387.

343. *Emperor v Lal Miya*, (1943) 1 Cal 543.

344. *State of Rajasthan v Ani*, AIR 1997 SC 1023 : 1997 Cr LJ 1529 : (1997) 6 SCC 162. *Shri Ouz Pedro Pancheco v State*, 1998 Cr LJ 4628 (Bom), the material statement of the witness was that he had seen the witness setting fire to the shed. This vital fact was missing from his statement to the police. This amounted to a contradiction. No opportunity was given to the witness to explain this contradiction. Other witnesses also did not speak of his being present at the site. His evidence was discarded.

345. *Kapil Corepacks Pvt Ltd v Harbans Lal*, AIR 2010 SC 2809 : (2010) 8 SCC 452. Power under Order 10, Rule 2, CPC, is completely different from power under section 165.

346. *Ritesh Tewari v State of UP*, AIR 2010 SC 3823 : (2010) 10 SCC 677.

347. *Himanshu Singh Sabharwal v State of MP*, AIR 2008 MP 1943.

permitted to found his judgment upon the class of statements to which he may resort as indicative evidence, for the reason that it would tempt Judges to be satisfied with second-hand reports, would open a wide door to fraud, and would waste an incalculable amount of time.[348] It would be intolerable that the court should decide right upon suspicions unsupported by testimony.[349]

[s 165.5] Recalling witness.—In a suit by the plaintiff for declaration of title, the defendant claimed that he was the owner of the property and that the plaintiff was his labourer working for him on the land in question. The defendant applied for an order that the plaintiff be recalled in order to enable him to prove the receipts issued by the plaintiff acknowledging receipt of money for working charges. Rejection of the application was held to be improper.[350]

[s 165.6] Privilege of witness to refuse remains same *[Proviso 2]*.—This proviso subjects the judge to the provisions contained in sections 121–131, sections 148 and 149. The Judge has the power of asking irrelevant questions to a witness, if he does so in order to obtain proof of relevant facts, but if he asks questions with a view to criminal proceedings being taken against the witness, the witness is not bound to answer them, and cannot be punished for not answering them under section 179, Indian Penal Code.[351] A witness should not be coerced to answer a question.[352] Where a Judge rebuked a witness and threatened him with prosecution for perjury if he changed his statement, the Supreme Court held that the proceeding was vitiated.[353]

Section 165 would have no application in a situation where the evidence is concluded, where the prosecution has closed its case, where the judgment has commenced and where it appears to the court at that point of time that prosecution has failed on a material aspect. This section cannot be pressed into service to reopen the evidence to cover up the obvious lacuna at this point of time.[354]

[s 166] Power of jury or assessors to put questions.—In cases tried by jury or with assessors, the jury or assessors may put any questions to the witnesses, through or by leave of the Judge, which the Judge himself might put and which he considers proper.

COMMENT

The jury or assessors may put any questions to the witness, through or by leave of the Judge, which the Judge himself might put and which the Judge considers proper.

---

348. Stephen, 162, 163.

349. *Sreemutty Mohun Bibi v Saral Chand Mitter*, (1897) 2 Cal WN 18, 27.

350. *Surinder Singh v Sukhdev*, AIR 1999 HP 72.

351. *Queen-Empress v Hari Lakshman*, (1885) 10 Bom 185.

352. *Queen-Empress v Ishri Singh*, (1886) 8 All 672, 675.

353. *Ram Chandra v State of Haryana*, AIR 1981 SC 1036 : 1981 Cr LJ 609 : (1981) 3 SCC 191 : 1981 SCC (Cri) 683.

354. *Omprakash Shankarlal Sharma v State of Maharashtra*, 1993 Cr LJ 3175 (Bom); *Lalu v State of MP*, 2003 Cr LJ 1992 (MP), wife sitting by his side when her husband received knife blows but she did not speak anything, she avoided and evaded all questions put to her in cross-examination, the court said that her testimony was liable to be discarded completely. Other witness also turned hostile.

CHAPTER XI

OF IMPROPER ADMISSION AND REJECTION OF EVIDENCE

[s 167] No new trial for improper admission or rejection of evidence.—The improper admission or rejection of evidence shall not be ground of itself for a new trial or reversal of any decision in any case,[s 167.5] if it shall appear to the Court before which such objection is raised[s 167.6] that, independently of the evidence objected to and admitted, there was sufficient evidence to justify the decision, or that, if the rejected evidence had been received, it ought not to have varied the decision.[s 167.7]

SYNOPSIS

COMMENT

[s 167.1] Object.—The object of the section is that the court of appeal or revision should not disturb a decision on the ground of improper admission or rejection of evidence, if in spite of such evidence, there are sufficient materials in the case to justify the decision.[1] In other words, technical objections will not be allowed to prevail, where substantial justice appears to have been done.

[s 167.2] Principle.—The improper (a) admission or (b) rejection of evidence is no ground for a new trial or reversal of any decision, if—

(i) in the case of improper admission—

there is sufficient evidence to justify the decision independently of the evidence objected to and admitted; or

(ii) in the case of improper rejection—

the decision could not be varied, if the rejected evidence had been received.

[s 167.3] Civil and criminal cases.—The provisions of this section are made applicable by the clearest possible words to all judicial proceedings in or before any

1. *Mohur Sing v Ghuriba*, (1870) 6 Beng LR 495, 499 PC : 15 WR (PC) 8; *Dwijesh Chandra Ray Choudhuri v Naresh Chandra Gupta*, (1946) 1 Cal 149.

Court.[2] The section applies to civil cases and to criminal cases whether or not the trial has been had before a jury.[3]

[s 167.3.1] Civil.—In the case of first appeal, the provisions of this section have to be read with section 99 of the Civil Procedure Code (Act V of 1908), which provides: "No decree shall be reversed or substantially varied nor shall any case be remanded, in appeal on account of...any error, defect or irregularity in any proceeding in the suit not affecting the merits of the case..." See also O XLI, rules 27 to 29.

In second appeals, one of the grounds, justifying the appeal is "a substantial error or defect in the procedure...which may possibly have produced error or defect in the decision of the case upon the merits" [section 100(1)(c) of the Code of Civil Procedure of 1908].

There is, however, a great difficulty in applying the provisions of this section to the generality of cases which come before the High Court on second appeal. On second appeal, the High Court has no power to deal with the sufficiency of evidence; it has only a right to entertain questions of law. Its duty being thus confined, when evidence has been wrongly admitted by the court below, the High Court has, generally speaking, no right, to decide, whether the remaining evidence in the case, other than that which has been improperly admitted, is sufficient to warrant the finding of the court below. The only cases, which it may with propriety dispose of under such circumstances without a remand, are those where independently of the evidence improperly admitted, the lower Court has apparently arrived at its conclusion upon other grounds.[4]

Where the first Court improperly admits evidence the High Court has power to interfere and remand the case for a new trial.[5]

The omission to receive an important document[6] or to examine a material witness[7] justifies a reversal of the decision. Where a document has been acted upon while pronouncing the judgment and passing the decree in consequence of that, the said document cannot be challenged in appeal in view of this section.[8]

[s 167.3.2] Criminal.—In criminal cases also the legislature has provided a similar safeguard. No finding, sentence or order, passed by a Court of competent jurisdiction shall be reversed or altered...on appeal or revision, on account of any misdirection in any charge to a jury

unless such error, omission, irregularity, or misdirection has in fact occasioned a failure of justice [section 465 CrPC].

---

2. *Reg v Navroji Dadabhai*, (1872) 9 BHC 358, 374.
3. *Imperatrix v Pitamber Jina*, (1877) 2 Bom 61, 65; *Queen v Hurribole Chunder Ghose*, (1876) 1 Cal 207, 216; *Emperor v Panchu Das*, (1920) 47 Cal 671 (FB).
4. *Womesh Chunder Chatterjee v Chundee Churn Roy Chowdhry*, (1881) 7 Cal 293, 296.
5. *Palakdhari Rai v Manners*, (1895) 23 Cal 179.
6. *Devidas Jagjivan v Pirjada Begam*, (1884) 8 Bom 377; *Talewar Singh v Bhagwan Das*, (1907) 12 Cal WN 312 : 8 Cal LJ 147.
7. *Moni Lal Bandopadhya v Khiroda Dasi*, (1893) 20 Cal 740.
8. *Babulal v Mohammed Sharif*, AIR 1996 MP 147.

Where the order according sanction for the prosecution of the accused for non-filing of Provident Fund Return was on record but was not marked as exhibit, it was held that order acquitting the accused on that ground was liable to be set aside.[9]

[s 167.4] Letters Patent, clause 26.—The provisions of this section apply to the High Court when acting under clause 26 of the Letters Patent.[10]

[s 167.5] "In any case".—These words are very wide and include criminal trials by jury.[11]

[s 167.6] "The Court before which such objection is raised".—The court which is to decide upon the sufficiency of the evidence to support the conviction is the court of review or the appellate court,[12] but not the court below.[13]

[s 167.7] "Decision".—The word "decision" is more generally used as applicable to civil proceedings, but it is by no means inappropriate to criminal cases; and, if it was the intention of the legislature to use an expression which would apply equally to civil and to criminal proceedings, there is probably no other word which would have answered their purpose better.[14]

[s 167.8] Appreciation of evidence—improper admission or rejection of evidence.—In Election Appeals, while as a Court of first appeal there are no limitations on the powers of Supreme Court in reversing a finding of fact or law which has been recorded on a misreading or wrong appreciation of the evidence or law, it would not ordinarily disregard the opinion formed by the trial judge who has recorded the evidence and who has had the benefit of watching the demeanour of the witnesses in forming first hand opinion regarding their credibility.[15]

The legal position about appreciation of evidence in trial Court has been succinctly summed up by Supreme Court[16] as follows:

> 15. The golden thread which runs through the administration of justice in criminal cases is that if two views are possible, one pointing to the guilt of the accused and the other to the innocence, the view which is favourable to the accused should be adopted. The paramount consideration of the court is to ensure that miscarriage of justice is prevented. A miscarriage of justice which may arise from acquittal of the guilty is no less than from a conviction of an innocent.
>
> 16. The principle to be followed by the appellate court considering an appeal against an order of acquittal is to interfere only when there are compelling and substantial reasons to do so. Thus, in such cases, this court would usually not interfere unless:

---

9. *HS Sadashiva v MS Muthappa*, 1992 Cr LJ 2424 (Kant).
10. *Queen v Hurribole Chunder Ghose*, (1876) 1 Cal 207; *Imperatrix v Pitamber Jina*, (1877) 2 Bom 61; *Emperor v Narayen*, (1907) 9 Bom LR 789 : 32 Bom 111 (FB). See *Emperor v Panchu Das*, (1920) 47 Cal 671 (FB).
11. *Queen-Empress v Ramchandra Govind Harshe*, (1895) 19 Bom 749, 762.
12. *Per* WESTROPP CJ, in *Imperatrix v Pitamber Jina*, (1877) 2 Bom 61, 65.
13. *Queen v Hurribole Chunder Ghose*, (1876) 1 Cal 207, 217.
14. *Ibid*
15. *Pradip Buragohain v Pranati Phukan*, (2010) 11 SCC 108 **approving** *Sarju Pershad case*, AIR 1951 SC 120; *Gajanan Krishnaji Bapat*, (1995) 5 SCC 347; and *PC. Thomas v PM Ismail*, (2009) 10 SCC 239.
16. *State of Rajasthan v Islam*, (2011) 6 SCC 343, at p 348.

(i) The finding is vitiated by some glaring infirmity in the appraisal of evidence.[17]

(ii) The finding is perverse.[18]

(iii) The order suffers from substantial errors of law and fact.[19]

(iv) The order is based on misconception of law or erroneous appreciation of evidence.[20]

(v) The High Court has adopted an erroneous approach resulting in miscarriage of justice.[21]

(vi) Acquittal is based on irrelevant grounds.[22]

(vii) The High Court has completely misdirected itself in reversing the order of conviction by the trial court.[23]

(viii) The judgment is tainted with serious legal infirmities.[24]

17. In reversing an acquittal, this Court keeps in mind that presumption of innocence in favour of the accused is fortified by an order of acquittal and if the view of the High Court is reasonable and founded on materials on record, this Court should not interfere. However, if this Court is of the opinion that the acquittal is not based on a reasonable view, then it may review the entire material and there will be no limitation on this Court's jurisdiction under Article 136 to come to a just decision quashing the acquittal.[25]

THE SCHEDULE

Enactment repealed.—[*Rep. by the Repealing Act, 1938 (1 of 1938), S. 2 and Sch.*]

---

17. *State of UP v Sahai*, (1981) 1 SCC 352 at paras 20-22; AIR 1981 SC 1442 at paras 19-21.

18. *State of MP v Bacchudas*, (2007) 9 SCC 135 at SCC para 10; *State of Punjab v Parveen Kumar*, (2005) 9 SCC 769 at SCC para 9.

19. *Rajesh Kumar v Dharamvir*, (1997) 4 SCC 496 at SCC para 5.

20. *State of UP v Abdul*, (1997) 10 SCC 135; *State of UP v Premi*, (2003) 9 SCC 12 at SCC para 15.

21. *State of TN v Suresh*, (1998) 2 SCC 372 at SCC paras 31 and 32; *State of MP v Paltan Mallah*, (2005) 3 SCC 169 at SCC para 8.

22. *Arunachalam v PS.R. Sadhananthanı*, (1979) 2 SCC 297 at SCC para 4.

23. *Gauri Shanker Sharma v State of UP*, (1990) Suppl. SCC 656.

24. *State of Maharashtra v Narsingrao Gangaram Pimple*, (1984) 1 SCC 446 at para 45 : AIR 1984 SC 63 at para 45.

25. *State (Delhi Admn.) v Laxman Kumar*, (1985) 4 SCC 476 at para 45 and *Dharma v Nirmal Singh*, (1996) 7 SCC 471 at para 4.

SUMMARY

The law of evidence is the most important branch of adjective law. It is to legal practice what logic is to all reasoning. Without it, trials might be infinitely prolonged to the great detriment of the public and the vexation and expense of suitors. It is by this that the Judge separates the wheat from the chaff among the mass of facts that are brought before him, decides upon their just and mutual bearing, learns to draw correct inferences from circumstances, and to weigh the value of direct testimony. It is by this guide that he is able to tread his way with comparative safety among the burning ploughshares of perjury, forgery and fraud that beset his footsteps, and to rest his judgment on a basis of probabilities at least comparatively satisfactory to his own mind.[1]

The Indian Evidence Act codifies the rules of English law of evidence with such modification as are rendered necessary by the peculiar circumstances of this country. But the Act is not exhaustive, and cases do arise for the solution of which principles of common law are resorted to. The Act, though chiefly drawn upon the lines of the English law of evidence, was not intended to be a servile copy of it.

The object of codification is that, on any point specifically dealt with by an Act, the law should be ascertained by interpreting its language, instead of, as before, roaming over a vast number of authorities to discover what the law is, and extracting it by a critical examination of the prior decisions.[2]

One great object of the Evidence Act was to prevent laxity in the admissibility of evidence, and to introduce a more correct and uniform rule of practice than was previously in vogue. The Evidence Act is not intended to do more than prescribe rules for the admissibility or otherwise of evidence on the issues as to which the courts have to record findings.

The main principles which underlie the law of evidence are—

(1) evidence must be confined to the matters in issue;

(2) hearsay evidence must not be admitted; and

(3) the best evidence must be given in all cases.

The following tabular scheme[3] sufficiently explains the general arrangement of the Indian Evidence Act—

1. *Norton on Evidence.*
2. *Bank of England v Vagliano Bros,* (1891) AC 107.
3. Stephen's Introduction, p 12.

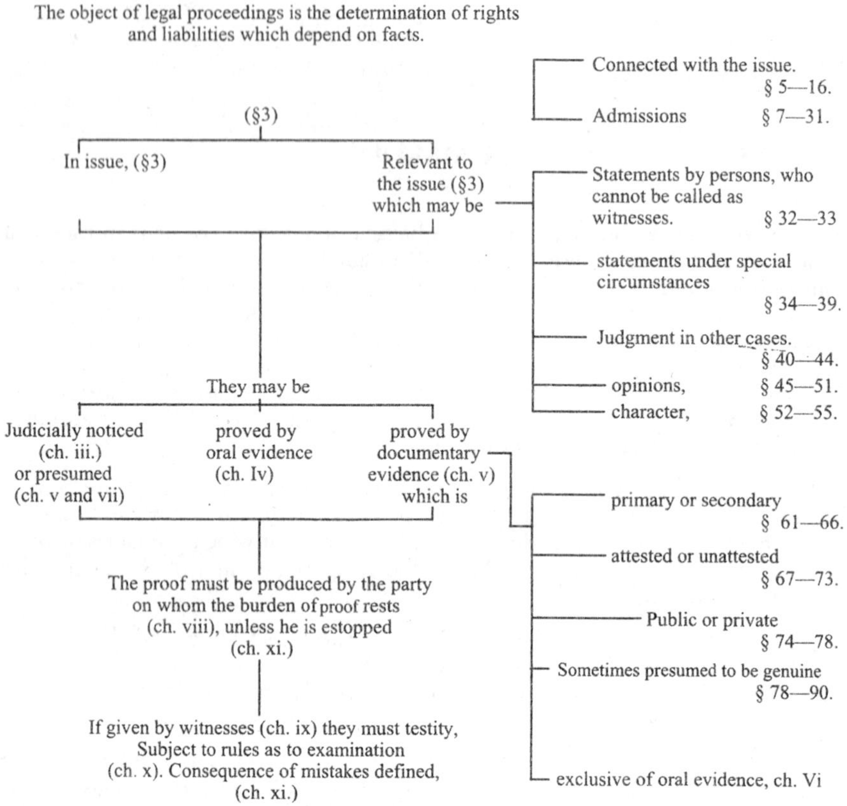

The Evidence Act is divided into three Parts comprising eleven Chapters—

Part I consists of two Chapters dealing with definitions and relevancy of facts.

Part II comprises Chapters III to V which provide for proof of facts by oral or documentary evidence.

Part III embodies Chapters VI to XI which contains rules for the production of evidence in court, the effect of presumptions and the duties of the court in dealing with the evidence produced before it.

PART I
RELEVANCY OF FACTS

The Evidence Act extends to the whole of India except the State of Jammu and Kashmir, and applies to all judicial proceedings and Courts-martial. Though not applicable to disciplinary proceedings and domestic inquiries, the provisions of the Act and judgments delivered under them are all helpful in the appreciation of evidence and standards of proof, etc. in those proceedings also.

Chapter I deals with definitions of various terms.

"Evidence" means and includes—

(1) Oral evidence, i.e., all statements which the court permits or requires to be made before it by witnesses, in relation to matters of fact under inquiry.

(2) Documentary evidence, i.e., all documents including electronic records produced for the inspection of the court.

Tape recordings can be legal evidence but the court must be satisfied beyond reasonable doubt that the record has not been tampered with. Similarly, if the court is satisfied that there is no trick photography and the photograph is above suspicion, it may allow the photograph to be received in evidence. Evidence of dog-tracking, even if admissible, is not of much weight. The definition of the term evidence is not complete. There are many other things, not included in this definition, on which judicial decisions may rest. In rare cases, evidence may include statements of a witness who has not been cross-examined. An FIR is not substantive evidence. But it can be used for contradicting or corroborating statements. *Bhimappa Janappa Naguna v State of Karnataka*, AIR 1993 SC 1469.

The mode of obtaining evidence, that is to say, whether by lawful or unlawful means has nothing to do with the intrinsic value of the evidence obtained. Wrongs committed by the investigating officer were not allowed to affect that part of the evidence which was trustworthy.

Evidence may be given in any suit or proceeding.

(1) of every fact in issue, and

(2) of relevant facts (**section** 3).

(1) **"Fact."**—It means and includes—

(i) any thing, state of things, or relation of things, capable of being perceived by the senses;

(ii) any mental condition of which any person is conscious (**section 3**).

The expression **"facts in issue"** means and includes any fact from which, either by itself or in connection with other facts, the existence, non-existence, nature or extent of any right, liability, or disability asserted or denied in any suit or proceeding, necessarily follows (**section 3**).

(2) **"Relevant fact."**—One fact is said to be relevant to another when the one is connected with the other in any of the ways relating to the relevancy of facts as provided in sections 6 to 55 of the Act. (**section 3**).

Presumptions.—The topic of "presumptions" has been referred to in section 4. A presumption means a rule of law that courts and Judges shall draw a particular inference from a particular fact, or from particular evidence, unless and until the truth of such inference is disproved. Presumptions are divided into presumptions of fact ("may presume" under the Evidence Act) and presumptions of law. Presumptions of law are again sub-divided into presumptions of law *absolute or conclusive* ("conclusive proof") and presumptions of law *disputable* or *rebuttable* ("shall presume").

Whenever it is provided by the Evidence Act that the court—

"may presume" a fact, it may either regard such fact as proved unless and until it is disproved, or may call for proof of it:

"shall presume" a fact, it must regard such fact as proved, unless and until it is disproved.

When one fact is declared by this Act to be "conclusive proof" of another, the court shall, on proof of the one fact, regard the other as proved, and shall not allow evidence to be given for the purpose of disproving it (**section 4**).

Chapter II.—Evidence may be given—

(1) of the existence or non-existence of every fact in issue, and

(2) of such other facts as are declared under the Act to be relevant, and of no others (**section 5**).

No evidence can be given of a fact which a person is disentitled from proving under the Civil Procedure Code (**section 5**). There is a difference between relevancy of evidence and admissibility of evidence.

What facts are relevant.—The following facts are relevant—

1. Facts so connected with a fact in issue as to form part of the same transaction (**section 6**). This section receives evidence of all acts and statements connected with a

happening in such-wise as to form an integral part of the happening. It is based upon the doctrine of *res gestae.*

2. Section 7 admits evidence of facts which provide the occasion, constitute the cause or show the effect, immediate or otherwise of either the relevant facts or of the facts in issue. It also admits evidence of facts showing the state of things or affording the opportunity for the happening of the facts in issue or the facts relevant to such facts. (**section** 7)

3. Facts showing motive or preparation for, or previous or subsequent conduct in relation to, any fact in issue or relevant fact (**section 8**). Motive plays an important part in the setting of circumstantial evidence, e.g., dowry-death cases which depend upon circumstantial evidence. *Kundula Bala Subramaniam v State of AP*, 1993 AIR SCW 1321 : (1993) 2 SCC 684 : 1993 Cr LJ 1635. The conduct declared relevant is that of the parties to the case, the accused person and the injured person. The conduct should have such connection with the facts in issue or relevant facts as influences them or is influenced by them. The word "conduct" for the purposes of section 8 does not include statements except when the statement in question accompanies or explains the relevant conduct or affects such conduct. If such connection is there, the conduct will be relevant whether it is previous or subsequent to the happening. (**section 8**)

4. Section 9 deals with facts (i) necessary to explain or introduce a fact in issue or relevant fact or (ii) which support or rebut an inference suggested by such a fact, or (iii) which establish the identity of anything or person whose identity is relevant, or (iv) which fix the time or place at which any fact in issue or relevant fact happened, or (v) which show the relation of parties by whom any such fact was transacted (**section 9**).

It is under this section that test identification parades are conducted and in the matter of their evidentiary value, they have generated much literature through Supreme Court decisions. All factors which can bring about identification are allowed, e.g., identification by voice, gait, foot-prints, finger-impressions, photographs, etc. Time factor is of crucial value in identification. Evidence of identification is of corroborative nature. It is not substantive evidence. Identification in court is substantive evidence. An adverse inference is drawn from refusal to appear in TI parade. Identification is also possible by voice, gait, footprints, etc.

5. Anything said, done, or written, by a conspirator in reference to the common intention of all the conspirators (**section 10**). The section comes into play only when there is a reasonable ground to believe that a conspiracy exists. For an act of one conspirator to be regarded as an act of all, it is necessary that the act was done at a time when the person in question was a party to the conspiracy and was related with the common intention of the parties. If this is so, it is not necessary to know that the conspirators knew or met each other or at what stages they joined.

6. Facts (i) that are inconsistent with any fact in issue or relevant fact, or (ii) which make the existence or non-existence of any fact in issue or relevant fact highly probable or improbable (**section 11**). It is under this section that the plea of *alibi*, that is to say, the presence of the accused elsewhere than at the place of the crime, is allowed and this plea has brought about a number of court decisions.

7. Facts which will enable the court to determine the amount of damages which ought to be awarded (**section 12**). Every fact that would help the court to quantify the amount of compensation that ought to be awarded in a particular case can be taken into account. Naturally, relevant facts are likely to be different from case to case. Even where the claimant fails to produce the best possible evidence, the court has to perform its duty to awarding and fixing the figure of damages.

8. Where the question is as to the existence of any right or custom (i) any transaction by which the right or custom in question was created, claimed, modified, recognised, asserted or denied, or which was inconsistent with its existence; (ii) particular instance in which the right or custom was (a) claimed, recognised or exercised, or (b) disputed, asserted, or

departed from (**section 13**). Judgments of courts of law and wills have been regarded by the courts as very important facts affecting rights.

9. Facts showing the existence of any state of (1) mind (e.g., intention, knowledge, good faith, negligence, rashness, ill-will, good-will) or (2) body or (3) bodily feeling, when such state of mind or body is relevant (**section 14**). It is necessary that the evidence produced must relate to the specific state of mind which is in question in the case and not to a general state of mind or tendency of the person in question. A previous conviction can be cited only if it will prove a specific state of mind.

10. When the question is whether an act was accidental or intentional—the fact that it formed part of a series of similar occurrences in which the same person was again and again involved (**section 15**). This section provides exceptions to the popular rule of excluding the evidence of similar facts.

11. Existence of any course of business according to which the act in question must have been done (**section 16**).

Relevancy : Admissibility.—The word "relevant" is not co-extensive with the word "admissible." A relevant fact is a fact that has a certain degree of probative force. Certain facts are relevant under sections 5-55, but all such facts are not admissible in evidence. There may arise restrictions as to their admissibility under sections 91-99 (exclusion of oral evidence by documentary evidence), 115-117 (parties estopped from proving certain facts) and 121-130 (communications and witnesses enjoying certain privileges). All admissible evidence is therefore relevant, but all relevant evidence is not necessarily admissible. Thus, admissibility includes relevancy, but not *vice versa*.

Sections 17-55 deal with statements which are relevant under certain circumstances. These include—

I. Admissions
II. Confessions
III. Statements by persons who cannot be called as witnesses
IV. Statements under special circumstances
V. Judgments of courts
VI. Opinions of third persons
VII. Character of parties

I. Admissions.—The Indian Evidence Act deals with admissions as follows:—

1. An admission is a statement, oral or documentary, or contained in electronic form which suggests any inference, as to any fact in issue or relevant fact, and which is made by—

(i) a party to the proceedings;
(ii) an agent authorised by such party;
(iii) a party suing or sued in a representative character making admissions while holding such character;
(iv) a person who has a proprietary or pecuniary interest in the subject-matter of the suit during the continuance of such interest;
(v) a person from whom the parties to the suit have derived their interest in the subject-matter of the suit during the continuance of such interest (**section 18**);
(vi) a person whose position it is necessary to prove in a suit, if such statements would be relevant in a suit brought by or against himself (**section 19**);
(vii) a person to whom a party to the suit has expressly referred for information in reference to a matter in dispute (**section 20**).

2. An admission is relevant and may be proved as against the person who makes it or his representative in interest. It cannot be proved by or on behalf of the person who makes it or by his representative, except in the following three cases—

(a) when it is of such a nature that, if the person making it were dead, it would be relevant as between third persons under section 32;

(b) when it consists of a statement as to the existence of any state of mind or body and made at or about the time when such state of mind or body existed and is accompanied by conduct rendering its falsehood improbable;

(c) if it is relevant otherwise than as an admission (**section 21**).

3. Oral admissions as to contents of a document are not relevant unless—

(a) the party proposing to prove them shows that he is entitled to give secondary evidence of the contents of such documents, or

(b) the genuineness of the document or an electronic record produced is in question (**section 22 and section 22A**).

4. An admission is not relevant in a *civil* case if it is made—

(a) upon an express condition that evidence of it is not to be given, this category cover cases of communications made "without prejudice", or

(b) under circumstances from which the court can infer that the parties agreed together that evidence of it should not be given (**section 23**).

A barrister, pleader, attorney, or vakil, is not exempted from giving evidence of any matter of which he may be compelled to give evidence under section 126 (**section 23, Explanation**).

5. An admission is not conclusive proof of the matter admitted, but it may operate as estoppel (**section 31**).

II. Confessions.—A "confession" is an admission made at any time by any person charged with a crime stating or suggesting an inference that he committed that crime. A brief view of the provisions dealing with confessions is as follows:

1. A confession is irrelevant.

(a) If it is obtained by any (a) inducement, (b) threat, or (c) promise;

(b) referring to the charge in question;

(c) proceeding from a person in authority; and

(d) sufficient to give the accused grounds for supposing that by making the confession he would gain an advantage or avoid an evil of a temporal nature in reference to the proceedings against him (**section 24**).

But a confession made after the removal of the impression caused by such inducement, threat, or promise, is relevant (**section 28**).

2. A confession made to a police officer is not admissible (**section 25**). A confession made to police in Departmental proceedings was held to be relevant because section 25 does not apply to such proceedings.

3. A confession made by a person in police custody is not admissible, unless it is made in the presence of a Magistrate (**section 26**).

But when any fact connected with the crime is discovered in consequence of information received from such person, so much of the information as relates to the facts discovered is admissible whether it amounts to confession or not (**section 27**).

4. A confession does not become irrelevant only because it is made—

(i) under a promise of secrecy; or

(ii) in consequence of a deception practised on the accused; or

(iii) when the accused was drunk; or

(iv) in answer to questions which the accused need not have answered; or

(v) when the accused was not warned that he was not bound to make it (**section 29**).

5. When more persons than one are tried jointly for an offence, and one of them makes a confession affecting himself and some other of such persons, the confession may be taken into consideration against such other person as well as against the person making it (**section 30**).

As to the difference between an "admission" and a "confession," see notes under section 24.

III. Statements by a witness who cannot be produced.—A statement of a relevant fact made by a person—

(i) who is dead;

(ii) who cannot be found;

(iii) who has become incapable of giving evidence; or

(iv) whose attendance cannot be procured without unreasonable delay or expense

is relevant under the following circumstances:—

(1) When it relates to the cause of his death (known as dying declaration).

(2) When it is made in the course of business; such as an entry in books, or acknowledgment of the receipt of any property, or date of a document.

(3) When it is against the pecuniary or proprietary interest of the person making it or when it would have exposed him to a criminal prosecution.

(4) When it gives opinion as to a public right or custom or matters of general interest and it was made before any controversy as to such right or custom had arisen.

(5) When it relates to the existence of any relationship between persons as to whose relationship the maker had special means of knowledge and was made before the question in dispute arose.

(6) When it relates to the existence of any relationship between persons deceased and is made in any will or deed or family pedigree, or upon any tombstone or family-portrait, and was made before the question in dispute arose.

(7) When it is contained in any deed, will or other document. This clause, however, does not allow introduction of parole evidence.

(8) When it is made by a number of persons and expresses feelings relevant to the matter in question (**section 32**).

Admissibility of depositions in former trials in subsequent trials.—Evidence given by a witness (i) in a judicial proceeding, or (ii) before any person authorised by law to take it, is relevant in a subsequent judicial proceeding or at a later stage of the same proceeding when—

(i) the witness is dead,

(ii) he cannot be found,

(iii) he is incapable of giving evidence,

(iv) he is kept out of the way by the adverse party, or

(v) his presence cannot be obtained without an amount of delay or expense which the court considers unreasonable.

Such evidence will only be admissible—

(1) if the proceeding was between the same parties, or their representatives in interest;

(2) if the adverse party in the first proceeding had the right and opportunity to cross-examine; and

(3) if the questions in issue were substantially the same in the first as in the second proceeding (**section 33**).

Evidence given on a different occasion is also admissible to contradict a witness (**section 155**) or to corroborate him (**section 157**).

IV. Statements made under special circumstances.—There are statements which are relevant under special circumstances. These are—

1. Entries in books of account including those maintained in electronic form regularly kept in the course of business. Such entries are not alone sufficient evidence to charge any person with liability (**section 34**).

2. Entries in public or official books or records or electronic records made by a public servant or by a person enjoined by law in the discharge of his duty (**section 35**).

3. Statements made in maps or charts offered for public sale or in maps or plans made under the authority of the Central Government or any State Government (**section 36**).

4. Statements of facts of public nature made in—

(1) an Act of Parliament;

(2) an Act of the Central Legislature or any other legislative authority in a State; and

(3) Notifications in the Official Gazette or the Government Gazette of any Dominion or Colony or Possession of Her Majesty or the London Gazette (**section 37**).

5. Statements of the law of any country contained in—

(1) a book published under the authority of the Government of that country, and

(2) published reports or rulings of the courts of such country (**section 38**). Opinions of persons skilled in foreign law may be invited by the court (**section 45**).

When the evidence to be given forms part of a statement, conversation, document, book, or in electronic record, or series of letters or papers, then so much of the statement, etc., as the court considers necessary to the full understanding of the nature and effect of the statement, shall only be given (**section 39**).

V. Judgments.—Judgments are relevant facts of great importance. Judgments in civil cases do not preclude any one but parties to the suit or their representatives from contesting the subject-matter upon which they are pronounced. There are four exceptions to this principle.

1. The existence of a judgment, decree or order is a relevant fact if by law it has the effect of preventing any court from taking cognizance of a suit, or holding a trial (the doctrine of *res judicata*) (**section 40**).

2. A final judgment of a court exercising (1) probate, (2) matrimonial, (3) admiralty, (4) insolvency jurisdiction which—

(i) confers upon or takes away from any person any legal character, or

(ii) declares any person to be entitled to (a) any such character, or (b) any specific thing absolutely,

is *relevant* when (a) the existence of any such legal character, or (b) the title of any such person to any thing, is relevant.

Such judgments are known as judgments *in rem*.

Such judgment is *conclusive proof*:

(1) that any legal character, which it confers, accrued at the time when such judgment came into operation;

(2) that any legal character to which it declares any person to be entitled accrued at the time mentioned in the judgment;

(3) that any legal character which it takes away from any person ceased at the time mentioned in the judgment;

(4) that any thing to which it declares a person to be entitled was that person's property at the time at which the judgment declares it to be his (**section 41**).

There are two other sections dealing with conclusive proof:

(1) birth during marriage is conclusive proof of legitimacy (**section 112**);

(2) notification in the Official Gazette that a portion of British territory is ceded to an Indian State before the commencement of Pt III of the Government of India Act, 1935, is conclusive proof of cession of that territory (**section 113**).

3. Judgment relating to matters of a public nature are relevant though such judgments are not conclusive proof of that which they state (**section 42**).

4. Judgments, the existence of which is a fact in issue or is relevant under some other provision of the Evidence Act (**section 43**).

Any party to a suit may show that a judgment which is relevant was delivered by a Court not competent to deliver it or was obtained by fraud or collusion (**section 44**).

VI. Opinions.—The court has often to form an opinion on technical matters. In such cases, extraneous assistance may become necessary. The Act allows such assistance in the following cases—

(1) Opinion of experts, i.e. persons specially skilled in (i) foreign law, (ii) matters of science, (iii) matters of art, (iv) handwriting, and (v) finger impressions (**section 45**)

(2) Opinion of Examiner of Electronic Evidence (as defined by section 79A of the Information Technology Act 2000) **(section 45A).**

2. Any fact which supports or is inconsistent with the opinion of experts (**section 46**).

3. Opinion of a person acquainted with the handwriting of the person by whom a document is written when the court has to form an opinion as to the person by whom it was written (**section 47**). When the court has to form an opinion as to the electronic signature of any person, the opinion of the Certifying Authority which has issued the electronic signature certificate is a relevant fact. **(section 47A)**

A person is said to be acquainted with the handwriting of another person when—

(i) he has seen that person write;

(ii) he has received documents purporting to be written by that person in answer to documents written by himself or under his authority and addressed to that person; or

(iii) in the ordinary course of business documents purporting to be written by that person have been habitually submitted to him (**section 47**).

4. Opinions as to the existence of a right or custom of a person who knows of its existence (**section 48**).

5. Opinions of persons having special means of knowledge regarding—

(i) usages and tenets of a body of men or family;

(ii) the constitution and government of any religious or charitable foundation;

(iii) the meaning of words or terms used in particular districts or by particular classes of people (**section 49**).

6. Opinion of a person, expressed by his conduct, who as a member of the family had special means of knowledge as to the relationship of one person to another, (**section 50**).

Whenever the opinion of a person is relevant, the grounds on which such opinion is based are also relevant (**section 51**).

VII. Character.— "Character" includes both reputation and disposition. Relevancy of character may arise both in (1) civil and (2) criminal cases.

(1) In civil cases the fact that the character of any person is such as to render probable or improbable any conduct imputed to him is irrelevant, except in so far as such character appears from facts otherwise relevant (**section 52**).

But the fact that the character of any person is such as to affect the amount of damages which he ought to receive is relevant (**section 55**).

(2) In criminal cases the fact that the accused is of *good character* is relevant (**section 53**). But the fact that he is of *bad character* is irrelevant unless—

(i) evidence has been given that he has a good character (**section 54**); or

(ii) the bad character is itself a fact in issue (**section 54, Explanation 1**).

A previous conviction is relevant as evidence of bad character (*ibid.*, **Explanation 2**)

(3) In a prosecution for an offence under section 354, section 354A, section 354B, section 354C, section 354D, sub-section (1) or sub-section (2) of section 376, section 376A, section 376AB, section 376B, section 376C, section 376D, section 376DA, section 376DB or section 376E of the Indian Penal Code or for attempt to commit any such offence, where the question of consent is in issue, evidence of the character of the victim or of such person's previous sexual experience with any person shall not be relevant on the issue of such consent or the quality of consent. **(section 53A)**

Part II—On Proof

Chapter III.—Facts which need not be proved.—These are:—

1. Facts of which the court will take judicial notice (**section 56**). Section 57 gives thirteen item list of facts of which the court is bound to take judicial notice.

2. Facts which the parties or their agents agree to admit at the hearing, or which, before the hearing, they agree to admit by any writing under their hands, or which, by any rule of pleading, they are deemed to have admitted by their pleadings (**section 58**).

3. Facts which are presumed to exist. Presumptions as to documents are drawn under sections 79-90; as to survivorship and death under sections 107-108; as to fiduciary relations under sections 109 and 111; as to ownership under section 110; as to certain offences under section 111-A; as to legitimacy under section 112; as to cessation of territory under section 113; as to abetment of suicide by married woman under section 113-A; as to dowry death under section 113-B; as to the existence of certain facts, under section 114 and as to absence of consent in certain rape cases, under section 114-A.

Chapter IV.—Oral evidence.—All facts, except the contents of documents, and of electronic records may be proved by oral evidence (**section 59**). Oral evidence must be direct, that is to say,

(1) if it refers to a fact which could be seen, it must be the evidence of a witness, who says he saw it;

(2) if it refers to a fact which could be heard, it must be the evidence of a witness, who says he heard it;

(3) if it refers to a fact which could be perceived by any other sense or in any other manner, it must be the evidence of a witness who says he perceived it by that sense or in that manner;

(4) if it refers to an opinion or to the grounds on which that opinion is held, it must be evidence of the person who holds that opinion on those grounds (**section 60**).

"Circumstantial evidence" is opposed to "direct evidence". It means a set of circumstances from which some other fact is inferred. "Direct evidence" means testimony given by a man as to what he has himself perceived by his own senses. It is the testimony of a witness (called eye-witness) to the existence or non-existence of the fact or fact in issue. As regards admissibility, direct and circumstantial evidence stand on the same footing.

Any other evidence would be *hearsay* evidence, that is, an evidence of a person who has not himself perceived the thing to which he testifies but has come to know of it from those who perceived it. Such evidence is excluded generally and is allowed only exceptionally. One of the exceptions is opinions on matters requiring special skill expressed in published books.

Opinion of an expert expressed in a book commonly offered for sale may be proved by the production of such book, if the author—

(1) is dead, or

(2) cannot be found, or

(3) has become incapable of giving evidence, or

(4) cannot be called as a witness without an amount of delay or expense, which the court regards as unreasonable (*ibid*).

Chapter V.—Documentary evidence.—The contents of documents may be proved either by (1) primary evidence, or (2) secondary evidence (**section 61**).

(1) **Primary evidence** means the document itself produced for the inspection of the court (**section 62**).

Where a document is executed in several parts, each part is primary evidence. Where a document is executed in counterpart, each counterpart is primary evidence as against the parties executing it (*ibid.*, **Explanation 1**).

Where a number of documents are made by uniform process, such as printing, lithography, or photography, each one is primary evidence of the contents of all the rest.

(2) **Secondary evidence** means and includes—

(i) certified copies given under provisions of this Act;

(ii) copies made from the original by mechanical processes, which in themselves ensure accuracy of the copy and, copies compared with such copies;

(iii) copies made from or compared with the original;

(iv) counterparts of documents, as against the parties who did not execute them;

(v) oral account of the contents of a document, given by some person who has himself seen it (**section 63**).

Documents must be proved by primary evidence (**section 64**).

Secondary evidence may be given of the existence, condition or contents of a document in the following cases:—

(1) When the document is in the possession of—

(i) the person against whom it is to be proved, or

(ii) any person out of the reach of, or not subject to, the process of the court, or

(iii) any person who is legally bound to produce it but does not produce it after notice to produce the same.

(2) When the existence or contents of the original have been proved to have been admitted in writing by the person against whom it is to be proved or his representative. In such a case the written admission is admissible.

(3) When the original has been destroyed or lost or when the party offering evidence of its contents cannot, for any other reason, not arising from his own neglect or default, produce it in reasonable time. In such a case any secondary evidence of its contents is admissible.

(4) When the original is of such a nature as not to be easily movable. In such a case any secondary evidence of its contents is admissible.

(5) When the original is a public document.

(6) When the original is a document of which a certified copy is permitted by this Act or any law in force in India, a certified copy is admissible.

(7) When the original consists of numerous accounts or other documents which cannot conveniently be examined in court, and the fact to be proved is the general result of the whole collection. Such result may be proved by the evidence of any person skilled in the examination of such documents (**section 65**).

Contents of electronic records [section 65A].—The contents of electronic record may be proved in accordance with the provisions of section 65-B Under this section a computer output is deemed to be a document subject to the conditions as to the maintenance and working of the computer machines from which the output has been taken.

When notice to produce a document is not required.—Notice under section 65 to produce a document is not required—

(1) when the document to be proved is itself a notice;

(2) when, from the nature of the case, the adverse party must know that he will be required to produce it;

(3) when the adverse party has obtained possession of the original by fraud or force;

(4) when the adverse party, or his agent, has the original in court;

(5) when the adverse party, or his agent, has admitted the loss of the document;

(6) when the person in possession of the document is out of reach of, or not subject to, the process of the court (**section 66**).

Signature and handwriting.—If a document is alleged to be signed or to have been written by any person, the signature or handwriting of so much of the document, as is alleged to be in that person's writing, must be proved to be in his handwriting (**section 67**).

Handwriting can be proved in the following ways:

(1) By the evidence of the writer himself.

(2) By the opinion of experts who can compare handwritings (**section 46**).

(3) By the evidence of a person who is acquainted with the handwriting of a person by whom the writing in question is supposed to have been written and signed (**section 47**).

(4) By the court comparing the writing or signature in question with any others proved to the satisfaction of the court to be genuine (**section 73**).

(5) The court may direct any person present to write any words or figures to enable the court to compare them with any words or figures alleged to have been written by him (*ibid*).

Where the electronic signature of any subscriber is alleged to have been affixed to an electronic record, the fact that such electronic signature is that of the subscriber has to be proved. This does not apply to the case of a secure electronic signature **(section 67A).**

Documents requiring attestation.—Documents required by law to be attested can be used in evidence as follows:—

1. One attesting witness at least must be called for proving its execution, if such witness is—

   (i) alive,

   (ii) subject to the process of the court, and

   (iii) capable of giving evidence (**section 68**).

But, if the document is a registered one and is not a will, then it is not necessary to call an attesting witness unless its execution is denied by the person who has executed it (*ibid*, proviso).

2. If such witness cannot be found, or if the document is executed in the UK, it must be proved—

   (i) that the attestation of a witness is in his handwriting, and

   (ii) that the signature of the person executing the document is in the handwriting of that person (**section 69**).

3. The admission of a party to an attested document of its execution by himself is sufficient proof of its execution as against him (**section 70**).

4. If the attesting witness denies or does not recollect the execution of the document, the execution may be proved by other evidence (**section 71**), i.e., it may be proved under sections 69 and 70.

An attested document, not required by law to be attested, may be proved as if it was unattested (**section 72**).

In order to ascertain whether a signature, writing or seal is that of the person by whom it purports to have been written or made, any signature, writing or seal, proved to have been written or made by that person, may be compared with the one which is to be proved (**section 73**).

For the verification of a digital signature, the court may direct the person concerned, or the Controller, or the Certifying Authority to provide the digital signature certificate. The court may direct any other person to apply the public key listed in the certificate and to verify the signature **(section 73-A).**

Public documents.—These are (1) documents forming the acts or records of the acts—

   (i) of the sovereign authority,

   (ii) of official bodies and tribunals, and

   (iii) of public officers, legislative, judicial and executive of any part of India or of the Commonwealth, or of a foreign country.

(2) Public records kept in any State of private documents (**section 74**).

All other documents are private (**section 75**).

Certified copies of public documents will be given by every public officer having the custody of them on payment of legal fees (**section 76**). Such copies may be produced in proof of the contents of the public documents of which they purport to be copies (**section 77**).

Certain public documents are proved in special ways, and not by certified copies. These are Acts or Notifications of the Central Government or of the Crown Representative, or of any State Government; proceedings of Legislatures; proclamations issued by Her Majesty or by the Privy Council; Acts or proceedings of the Legislature of a foreign country. As to how they are to be proved, see section 78.

Presumptions as to documents.—Sections 79-85 and section 89 provide for cases in which the court shall presume to be genuine certain facts about documents, that is, the court is bound to accept those facts as proved until they are disproved.

1. As to a certified copy or other document which is declared by law to be admissible as proof of any fact, and which purports to be certified by an officer of the Central Government or State Government or by an officer in the State of Jammu and Kashmir who is duly authorised by the Central Government, the court shall presume that it is genuine. It shall also presume that the officer who signed or certified it held at the time the official character which he claims in it (**section 79**).

2. As to (1) a record of evidence in a judicial proceeding, or

(2) a confession taken is accordance with law and purporting to be signed by a Judge or Magistrate or other officer authorized by law, the court shall presume—

(i) that the document is genuine;

(ii) that any statement as to the circumstances under which it was taken is true; and

(iii) such evidence or confession was duly taken (**section 80**).

3. As to the London Gazette, or any Official Gazette or the Government Gazette of any colony, dependency or possession of the British Crown, or a newspaper, or private Act of Parliament printed by the Queen's Printer, or a document coming from proper authority, the court shall presume that it is genuine (**section 81**).

The court has to presume the genuineness of every electronic record purporting to be the official *Gazette* or purporting to be the electronic record directed by any law to be kept by any person, if the electronic record has been kept substantially in the form required by law and has been produced from proper custody (**section 81A**).

4. As to a document which would be admissible in an English or Irish Court without proof of (a) its seal or stamp or signature, or

(b) the official character of the person signing it, the court shall presume (i) that the seal, etc., is genuine, and (ii) that the person signing it held that official position which he claims in it (**section 82**).

5. As to maps or plans purporting to be made by the authority of Central Government or State Government, the court shall presume that they were so made and are accurate (**section 83**). The section concludes by providing that maps, etc., made for any particular cause must be proved to be accurate.

6. As to (1) authorized law-books containing laws of any country, and

(2) books purporting to contain reports of decisions of courts of such country, the court shall presume that they are genuine (**section 84**).

7. As to powers-of-attorney executed before, and authenticated by, a notary public, or any Court, Judge, Magistrate, Indian Consul or representative of the Central Government, the court shall presume that they were so executed and authenticated (**section 85**). For creating the presumption about a foreign power of attorney, the document has to be authenticated by the Indian Counsel or relevant Indian Authority.

The court has to presume that every electronic record purporting to be an agreement containing the electronic signatures of the parties was concluded by affixing the electronic signatures of the parties (**section 85-A**).

In any proceedings involving a secure electronic record, the court has to presume that the record has not been altered since the specific point of time to which the secured status relates (**section 85B(1)**).

In a proceeding involving a secure electronic signature the court has to presume that (*a*) the secure electronic signature was affixed by the subscriber with the intention of signing or approving the electronic record; (*b*) apart from the secure electronic record or secure electronic signature, the section does not create any presumption relating to authenticity and integrity of the electronic record or electronic signature **(section 85-B(2))**.

The court has to presume that the information listed in an electronic signature certificate is correct, if the certificate was accepted by the subscriber. This does not apply to information specified as subscriber information and which has not been verified **(section 85-C)**.

8. As to a document called for and not produced after notice to produce, the court shall presume that it was duly attested, stamped and executed (**section 89**).

Sections 86-88 and 90 provide for cases in which the court may presume certain facts about documents, that is, the court is at liberty to accept those facts as proved until they are disproved, or to call for proof of them in the first instance.

1. As to a certified copy of any judicial record of a foreign country, certified by a representative of Her Majesty or of the Central Government, the court may presume that it is genuine and accurate (**section 86**).

2. As to (1) any book to which the court may refer on a matter of public or general interest, and

(2) any published chart or map produced for its inspection, the court may presume that it was written and published by the person, and at the time and place, by whom or at which it purports to have been written or published (**section 87**).

3. As to a message forwarded from a telegraph office, the court may presume that it corresponds with the message for transmission at the office from which it purports to be sent.

But it shall not make any presumption as to the person by whom such message was delivered for transmission (**section 88**).

The court may presume that an electronic message forwarded by the originator through an electronic mail server to the addressee to whom the message purports to be addressed corresponds with the message which was fed into his computer. But there is no presumption as to the person by whom the message was sent **(section 88-A)**.

4. As to a document proved to be **30 years old** and produced from proper custody, the court may presume—

(i) that the signature and every other part of such document, which purports to be in the handwriting of any particular person, is in that person's handwriting, and

(ii) that it was duly executed and attested by the person by whom it purports to be executed and attested (**section 90**).

Documents are said to be in proper custody if they are (i) in the place in which, and under the care of the person with whom, they would naturally be (*ibid*).

Where an electronic record which is *five years* old and is produced from a *proper custody*, the court may presume that the electronic signature appearing on the record was affixed by the person whose signature it purports to be or was affixed by the person authorised by him **(section 90-A)**.

Chapter VI.—Exclusion of oral by documentary evidence.—When—

(i) the terms of a contract, grant, or other disposition of property have been reduced to the form of a document, or

(ii) any matter is required by law to be in the form of a document—

(I) no evidence shall be given of the terms of (a) such contract, grant, or disposition of property, or (b) of such matter, except

(i) the document itself, or

(ii) secondary evidence of its contents in cases in which secondary evidence would be admissible (**section 91**);

(II) no evidence of any oral agreement or statement shall be admitted, as between the parties to any such instrument or their representatives in interest, for the purpose of (i) contradicting, (ii) varying, (iii) adding to, or (iv) subtracting from, its terms (**section 92**).

To this rule (I) there are two exceptions:—

(1) When a public officer is required by law to be appointed in writing, and when it is shown that any particular person has acted as such officer, the writing by which he is appointed need not be proved (**section 91, Exception 1**).

(2) Wills admitted to probate in India may be proved by the probate (**section 91, Exception 2**).

The statement, in any document, of a fact other than the terms of a contract, grant or disposition of property, or which is not required by law to be in writing, does not preclude proof of such fact by any other means (*ibid*, **Explanation 3**).

To the rule (II) there are six exceptions. Oral evidence is admissible in the following cases:—

(1) Any fact which would (i) invalidate any document, or (ii) entitle any person to any decree or order relating thereto, may be proved, i.e., fraud, intimidation, illegality, failure of consideration, mistake of fact or law.

(2) Any separate oral agreement as to any matter on which the document is silent, and which is not inconsistent with its terms, may be proved.

(3) Any separate oral agreement, constituting a condition precedent to the attaching of any obligation under the document, may be proved.

(4) A subsequent oral agreement to rescind or modify any such contract, grant or disposition of property, may be proved, except where such contract or grant is required to be in writing, or has been registered.

(5) Any usage or custom by which incidents not expressly mentioned in any contract are usually annexed to such contracts, may be proved if they are not inconsistent with its express terms.

(6) Any fact which shows in what manner the language of the document is related to existing facts may be proved.

Persons who are not parties to a document or their representatives in interest may give evidence of facts tending to show a contemporaneous agreement varying the terms of the document (**section 99**).

Construction of documents.—Latent and patent ambiguities.—Sections 93-100 embody the rules as to the admissibility of extraneous evidence to interpret documents. Such evidence is inadmissible in the following cases:—

1. When the language is, on its face ambiguous or defective, evidence cannot be given of facts which would show its meaning or supply its defects (**section 93**).

2. When the language is plain in itself, and when it applies accurately to existing facts, evidence cannot be given to show that it was not meant to apply to such facts (**section 94**).

Such evidence is admissible in the following cases:—

1. When the language is plain in itself, but is unmeaning in reference to existing facts, evidence may be given to show that it was used in a peculiar sense (**section 95**).

2. When the language is meant to apply to any one, but not to more than one, of several persons or things, evidence may be given to show to which of those persons or things it was intended to apply (**section 96**).

3. When the language applies partly to one set of facts and partly to another, but the whole of it does not apply correctly to either, evidence may be given to show to which of the two it was meant to apply (**section 97**).

4. Evidence may be given as to the meaning of illegible, foreign, obsolete, technical, local and provincial expressions, abbreviations and words used in a peculiar sense (**section 98**).

Part III—Production and Effect of Evidence

This Part deals with the production and effect of evidence. It comprises of—

(a) the question of burden of proof;

(b) the rules as to who is to give evidence and under what circumstances;

(c) the rules as to examination of witnesses; and

(d) the effect of improper reception or rejection of evidence.

Chapter VII.—Burden of proof.—Whoever desires any Court to give judgment as to any legal right or liability dependent on facts, which he asserts, must prove that those facts exist. The burden of proof lies on that person who is bound to prove any fact (**section 101**). The burden of proof in a suit or proceeding lies on that person who would fail if no evidence were given on either side (**section 102**). During the course of the trial the burden may shift from one side to the other.

Sections 103-113 lay down the rules as to burden of proof.—

1. The burden of proof as to any particular fact lies on that person who wishes the court to believe it unless the law has provided that its proof shall lie on any particular person (**section 103**).

2. The burden of proving any fact in order to enable any person to give evidence of any other fact is on the person who wishes to give such evidence (**section 104**).

3. When a person is accused of an offence, the burden of proving that his case falls within any exception in the Penal Code or any other law lies on him (**section 105**).

4. When a fact is especially within the knowledge of any person, the burden of proving it lies on him (**section 106**).

5. When it is shown that a man was alive within thirty years, the burden of proving that he is dead is on the person who affirms it (**section 107**).

6. When it is proved that a man has not been heard of for seven years by those who would naturally have heard of him if he had been alive, the burden of proving that he is alive lies on the person who affirms it (**section 108**). The presumption is as to the fact of death and not the time of death. The probability of the time of death may, however, be taken into account when it is necessary to meet the ends of justice.

7. When persons have acted as partners, or as landlord and tenant, or as principal and agent, the burden of proving that such relationship has ceased, lies on the person who affirms it (**section 109**).

8. When a person is in possession of any thing as owner, the burden of proving that he is not the owner is on the person who affirms that he is not the owner (**section 110**).

9. When a person stands towards another in a position of active confidence, the burden of proving the good faith of any transaction between them lies on the person in active confidence (**section 111**).

10. In reference to disturbed areas certain persons are presumed to have committed the offences stated in sections 121-123 of the Indian Penal Code, 1860 (**section 111-A**).

11. The fact that a person is born during a valid marriage between his mother and any man, or within 280 days after its dissolution, the mother remaining unmarried, then unless non-access is proved, it shall be conclusive proof of the legitimacy of the child (**section 112**).

12. A notification in the Official Gazette of a cession of British territory before the commencement of Pt III of the Government of India Act, 1935, to any Indian State is conclusive proof that a valid cession took place at the date mentioned in the notification (**section 113**).

Three sections deal with "conclusive proof" as defined in section 4, viz., sections 41, 112, 113.

Section 113-A deals with presumption as to abetment of suicide by a married woman.

Where the question is whether suicide by a married woman was abetted by her husband or in-laws, the fact that the suicide has taken place within seven years of marriage and she was subjected to cruelty would create the presumption that the suicide was the result of abetment. Thus the burden of proof would be shifted to in-laws to show that they had no role to play in the episode and it was the result of her own voluntary act. The word "cruelty" has the same meaning as in section 498-A of IPC.

Section 113-B creates a presumption as to dowry death. Where the question is whether a person has committed a "dowry death", the fact that such person "soon before her death" had subjected her to cruelty or harassment for dowry, he would be presumed to have caused the death. "Dowry death" here means the same as in section 113-B.

Section 114 lays down certain cases in which the court may presume the existence of any fact which it thinks likely to have happened, regard being had (i) to the common course of natural events, (ii) human conduct, and (iii) public and private business, in their relation to the fact of the particular case (**section 114**). See the illustrations to the section as to those cases. These illustrations deal with matters like receiving stolen property, testimony of an accomplice, bigamy, consideration, continuity of things, judicial and official acts, functioning of legislature and Government officer, common course of business, withholding of evidence, refusal to answer questions, etc.

Section 114-A deals with presumption as to absence of consent in prosecution for rape under clause (a), clause (b), clause (c), clause (d), clause (e), clause (f), clause (g), clause (h), clause (i), clause (j), clause (k), clause (l), clause (m) or clause (n) of sub-section (2) of section 376 of the Indian Penal Code. Where sexual intercourse by the accused is proved and the victim woman says in the court that she had not consented, the court would presume that there was no consent. This shifts the burden of proving consent on to the accused and, on his failure to do so, there would be a finding that he was guilty. In this section, "sexual intercourse" shall mean any of the acts mentioned in clauses (a) to

(d) of section 375 of the Indian Penal Code.

Chapter VIII.—Estoppel.—When one person has by his (a) declaration, (b) act, or (c) omission,

(1) intentionally caused or permitted another person to believe a thing to be true, and

(2) to act upon such belief, neither he nor his representative shall be allowed in any suit or proceeding between himself and such person or his representative, to deny the truth of that thing. The kinds of estoppel which have evolved through judicial process are equitable estoppel, promissory estoppel, including promissory estoppel against Government and its agencies, against universities and institutions, issue estoppel, etc.

The Evidence Act specially provides for the following estoppels:—

1. A tenant of immovable property or person claiming through such tenant cannot, during the continuance of the tenancy, deny that the landlord had, at the beginning of the tenancy, a title, to such property (**section 116**).

2. A person, who came upon immovable property by the license of the person in possession thereof, cannot deny that the person so in possession had a title at the time when such license was given (*ibid*).

3. An acceptor of a bill of exchange cannot deny that the drawer had authority to draw or endorse (**section 117**).

But the acceptor of a bill of exchange may deny that the bill was really drawn by the person by whom it purports to have been drawn (*ibid*, **Explanation 1**).

4. A bailee or a licensee cannot deny that his bailor or licensor had, when the bailment or license commenced, authority to make such bailment or grant such license (*ibid.*). But if a bailee delivers the goods bailed to a person other than the bailor, he may prove that such person had a right to them as against the bailor if he is sued by the bailor (*ibid*, **Explanation 2**).

Difference between estoppel and admission.—(1) Estoppel binds only parties and privies thereto. It cannot be taken advantage of by strangers. (2) Estoppel being a rule of evidence, an action cannot be founded on it. An action may be founded on an admission.

Difference between estoppel and presumption.—An estoppel is a personal disqualification laid upon a person peculiarly circumstanced from proving particular fact;

whereas a presumption is a rule that particular inferences shall be drawn from particular facts, whoever proves them. Estoppel is that species of presumption where the fact presumed is taken to be true, not as against all the world, but as against a particular party, and that only by reason of some act done.

Difference between estoppel and *res judicata*.—(1) Estoppel is part of the law of evidence and proceeds upon the equitable principle of altered situation; *res judicata* belongs to procedure and is based on the principle that there must be an end to litigation.

(2) Estoppel prohibits a party from proving anything which contradicts the previous declarations or acts, to the prejudice of a party who, relying upon them, altered his position; res judicata prohibits the court from enquiring into a matter already adjudicated.

(3) Estoppel shuts the mouth of a party; res judicata ousts the jurisdiction of the court.

Estoppel against Government and its agencies.—Government and its agencies are precluded by the doctrine of estoppel from going back upon their schemes of aid, subsidy, rebate, allowances, tax holidays etc. when once any such scheme has brought about some action in the desired direction on the part of a certain person. Such schemes may be reversed for the future.

Estoppel against educational institutions.—The doctrine of estoppel does not permit educational institutions to play hide and seek with the careers or prospects of students where there is no fraud in them, and admissions or results have been brought about by their own working errors.

Promissory estoppel.—Persons holding out promises intended to be acted upon and which have in fact been acted upon are not permitted to resile from their promises only because there was no consideration for the promise.

Difference between estoppel and waiver.—Estoppel being a rule of evidence may, if established, assist a plaintiff in enforcing a cause of action, but it is not a cause of action. Waiver on the other hand, is contractual, and may constitute a cause of action.

Chapter IX.—Witnesses.—All persons are competent to testify unless the court considers that they are prevented from understanding the questions put to them, or from giving rational answers to those questions (a) by tender years, (b) extreme old age, or (c) disease (**section 118**). No particular number of witnesses is required for the proof of any fact (**section 134**). The court has to apply its mind and restrict the number of witnesses to an extent which should cater to the requirements of the case and should not leave the number to the whims and fancies of the parties. In criminal cases in which the conviction rests solely on the testimony of one witness, it is necessary to make sure that he is wholly reliable. *Kathi Oudhubhai Bhimabhai v State of Gujarat*, AIR 1993 SC 1193 : 1993 Cr LJ 187.

The courts have to take special care of the testimony of a child witness, that of a person of unsound mind, partisan witnesses.

Dumb witnesses.—A witness who is unable to speak may give his evidence in any manner in which he can make it intelligible, e.g., by writing or signs. Such writing must be written and the signs made in open Court. Provided that if the witness is unable to communicate verbally, the court shall take the assistance of an interpreter or a special educator in recording the statement and such statement shall be videographed. (**section 119**).

Husband and wife.—Husband or wife (i) of any party to a civil suit, or (ii) of the accused in criminal proceedings, is a competent witness (**section 120**).

Privileged communications.—Certain witnesses cannot be compelled to disclose certain facts. The law excludes this evidence on the ground of public policy.

1. *Judge and Magistrate.*—A Judge or Magistrate cannot, except on the special order of some Court to which he is subordinate, be compelled to answer any question,

(i) as to his own conduct, or

(ii) as to anything which came to his knowledge, as such Judge or Magistrate.

He may be examined as to matters which occurred in his presence while he was so acting (**section 121**).

2. *Communications during marriage.*—A person cannot be compelled to disclose any communications made to him or her during marriage by any person to whom he or she is or has been married. He will not be permitted to disclose any such communication unless the person who made it or his representative in interest consents—except

(i) in suits between married persons, or

(ii) in proceedings in which one married person is prosecuted for a crime against the other (**section 122**).

3. *Affairs of State.*—No person can give evidence derived from unpublished official records relating to any affairs of State, except with the permission of the officer at the head of the department concerned (**section 123**). This should be read with S. 162 which requires a witness who has been called upon to produce a document to actually produce notwithstanding his objections and then the court will decide whether he ought to be given the privilege or not.

The privilege is a narrow one and must be sparingly used. Production of documents without any objection and without claim of privilege amounts to waiver and there would nothing to debar the court from examining the documents. *Chaudhary v Governor of Bihar*, AIR 1980 SC 383.

4. *Official communications.*—No public officer can be compelled to disclose communications made to him in official confidence, if public interest would suffer by the disclosure (**section 124**).

5. *Information as to crimes.*—A Magistrate or a police or revenue officer cannot be compelled to say whence he got any information as to the commission of an offence (**section 125**). A police officer may be compelled to disclose the source of his information when the police power is being abused. *R v Agar*, (1990) 2 All ER 442 (CA).

6. *Professional communications.*—A barrister, attorney, pleader, or vakil, cannot disclose, without the client's consent,

(i) any communication made to him in the course and for the purpose of his employment;

(ii) the contents or condition of any document with which he became acquainted in the course and for the purpose of his employment, or

(iii) any advice given by him to his client (**section 126**). Such protection from disclosure does not extend to—

  (i) any communication made in furtherance of any illegal purpose;

  (ii) any fact observed by a barrister, attorney, pleader, or vakil in the course of his employment, showing that a crime or fraud has been committed, since the commencement of his employment.

The principle of non-disclosure of professional communications applies also to the clerks or servants of barristers, attorneys, pleaders, or vakils (**section 127**).

If a party to a suit gives evidence *at his own instance* he is not to be deemed thereby to have consented to a disclosure of professional communications by his legal adviser; and if he calls any barrister, attorney, pleader, or vakil, as a witness he is only deemed to have consented to such disclosure if he questions him regarding it (**section 128**). A person cannot be compelled to disclose any confidential communication which has taken place between him and his legal adviser unless he offers himself as a witness, in which case he may be compelled to disclose any such communications as the court thinks necessary, in order to explain any evidence he has given (**section 129**).

Production of documents by witness.—A witness who is not a party to a suit cannot be compelled to produce—

(1) his title-deeds or any documents which might tend to criminate him unless he has agreed in writing to produce them (**section 130**);

(2) documents or electronic records in his possession which any other person would be entitled to refuse to produce if they were in his possession (**section 131**).

Criminating questions to a witness.—A witness cannot be excused from answering any relevant question upon the ground that the answer will tend (i) to criminate him, or (ii) to expose him to a penalty or forfeiture. But such answer cannot

(a) subject him to arrest or prosecution, or

(b) be proved against him in any criminal proceedings except a prosecution for giving false evidence (**section 132**).

Accomplice.—Illustration (b) to section 114 says that the court may presume that an accomplice is unworthy of credit unless he is corroborated in material particulars. Section 133 provides that an accomplice shall be a competent witness against an accused, and a conviction is not illegal merely because it proceeds upon the uncorroborated testimony of an accomplice (**section 133**). A Judge has to keep in mind the practical rule of caution that an accomplice is unworthy of credit unless corroborated in material particulars and he has also to mention this fact in his judgment. In England, there is jury trial and, therefore, the Judge has to give the warning to the jury. In sexual offences the need for this warning has been abolished. See Comment under section 133 on this topic.

Chapter X.—Examination of witnesses.—The order of production and examination of witnesses is regulated by the Civil and Criminal Procedure Codes or by the discretion of the court (**section 135**). The Judge may ask how a particular fact is relevant and admit the evidence if he thinks the fact would be relevant. If the relevancy of a fact depends on the proof of some other fact, such latter fact must be proved first unless the party undertakes to prove it subsequently and the court is satisfied with such undertaking (**section 136**).

The examination of a witness by the party who calls him is called examination-in-chief. The examination of a witness by the adverse party is called cross-examination.

The examination of a witness subsequent to the cross-examination by the party who called him, is called re-examination (**section 137**).

Witnesses are first examined-in-chief, then cross-examined, and then re-examined. The examination and cross-examination must relate to relevant facts, but the cross-examination need not be confined to the facts to which the witness testified on his examination-in-chief. The re-examination must be directed to the explanation of matters referred to in cross-examination. If any new matter is introduced in re-examination, the adverse party may further cross-examine upon that matter (**section 138**). A party must be given a fair chance to cross-examine the witness procedure cannot take away the right of a party to cross-examine the other side.

A person summoned to produce a document does not become a witness and cannot be cross-examined unless he is called as a witness (**section 139**).

Witnesses to character may be cross-examined and re-examined (**section 140**).

The court may permit the person who calls a witness to put any questions to him, which might be put in cross-examination by the adverse party (**section 154**). This is only allowed if the witness proves to be a "hostile witness," i.e., one who from the manner in which he gives evidence shows that he is not desirous of telling the truth to the court.

Leading questions.—Any question suggesting the answer which the person putting it wishes or expects to receive is called a leading question (**section 141**). Such questions must not, if objected to by the adverse party, be asked in an examination-in-chief or in a re-examination, except with the permission of the court (**section 142**).

The court will permit such questions—

(1) as to matters which are (i) introductory, or (ii) undisputed, or (iii) already sufficiently proved (**section 142**), or

(2) in cross-examination (**section 143**).

The prosecution cannot put leading questions on the material part of the evidence which the witness intends to give against the accused. Such leading questions offend the right of the accused to fair trial enshrined in Article 21 of the Constitution. It is not a curable irregularity. *Varkey Joseph v State of Kerala*, AIR 1993 SC 1992 : 1993 Supp (3) SCC 745 : 1993 Cr LJ 2010.

Evidence as to matters in writing.—Section 144 enables the parties to put in force the provisions of sections 91 and 92. Any witness may be asked whether any (a) contract, (b) grant or (c) other disposition of property, as to which he is giving evidence, was not in writing, and if he says that it was, the adverse party may object to such evidence being given until the document is produced or facts proved for the admission of secondary evidence. The same principle applies if a witness is about to make any statement as to the contents of a document, which, in the opinion of the court, ought to be produced (**section 144**).

A witness may be cross-examined as to previous statements made by him and reduced into writing, without such writing being shown to him or proved; but, if it is intended to contradict him by the writing, his attention must, before the writing can be proved, be called to those parts of it which are to be used for the purpose of contradicting him (**section 145**).

Questions lawful in cross-examination.—When a witness is cross-examined he may be asked any questions which tend—

(1) to test his veracity;

(2) to discover who he is and what is his position in life; or

(3) to shake his credit by injuring his character, although the answer to such questions might criminate him or expose him to a penalty or forfeiture

Provided that in a prosecution for an offence under section 376, 376A, section 376AB, section 376B, section 376C, section 376D, section 376DA, section 376DB or section 376E of the Indian Penal Code or for attempt to commit any such offence, where the question of consent is an issue, it shall not be permissible to adduce evidence or to put questions in the cross-examination of the victim as to the general immoral character, or previous sexual experience, of such victim with any person for proving such consent or the quality of consent. (**section 146**).

Questions as to character.—Where the question put to a witness is on a matter relevant to the inquiry, the court may compel the witness to answer the question notwithstanding the fact that the answer may involve him into some liability. section 147 read with section 132. If a question in cross-examination is irrelevant, except in so far as it affects the credit of the witness by injuring his character, the court may compel the witness to answer it or warn him that he is not obliged to answer it. The court in deciding whether a particular question is proper or not will have regard to the following considerations:—

(1) Such questions are proper if the imputation conveyed by them would seriously affect the opinion of the court as to the credibility of the witness.

(2) Such questions are *improper*—

- (i) If the imputation which they convey relates to matters so remote in time, or such character, that it would not affect, or affect in a slight degree, the opinion of the court as to the credibility of the witness;
- (ii) If there is a great disproportion between the importance of the imputations made against the witness's character and the importance of his evidence (**section 148**).

Such questions ought not to be asked unless the person asking it has reasonable grounds for thinking that the imputation which it conveys is well founded (**section 149**). If the court thinks that any question was asked without reasonable grounds, it may, if it was asked by any barrister, attorney, pleader, or vakil, report his conduct to the High Court or other authority to which he is subordinate (**section 150**).

The court may draw from the witness's refusal to answer, the inference that the answer if given would be unfavourable (**section 148**).

Questions that will be forbidden by the Court.—The court will forbid,

(1) any question which it regards as indecent or scandalous unless it refers to facts in issue or to matters necessary to be known in order to determine the facts in issue (**section 151**);

(2) any question which appears to the court (i) to be intended to insult or annoy, or (ii) to be offensive in form (**section 152**).

Answers to questions as to character cannot be contradicted.—When a witness answers any question which is relevant in so far as it shakes his credit, no evidence can be given to contradict him; but if he answers falsely he may be charged with giving false evidence (**section 153**). Evidence, however, may be given (i) of a previous conviction if a witness denies it, or (ii) of facts tending to impeach his impartiality if he denies them (**section 153, Exceptions**).

Hostile witness.—When a witness turns hostile to the very party who called him, such party may, with the permission of the court, put him such questions as might have been asked in cross-examination by the opposite party (**section 154**). The court is not precluded from taking into account the statements of a hostile witness altogether and it is not necessary to discard the same *in toto*. His statements can be relied upon partly.

Impeaching the credit of witness.—The credit of a witness may be impeached by the adverse party, or, with the consent of the court, by the party who calls him in the following ways:—

(1) By the evidence of persons who testify that they believe him to be unworthy of credit.

(2) By proof that the witness has been bribed, or has accepted the offer of a bribe, or has received any other corrupt inducement to give evidence.

(3) By proof of former statements inconsistent with any part of his evidence which is liable to be contradicted.

(4) When a man is prosecuted for rape or attempt to ravish, it may be shown that the prosecutrix was of generally immoral character (**section 155**).

Evidence in corroboration.—When a witness whom it is intended to corroborate gives evidence of a relevant fact—

(i) he may be questioned as to the circumstances which he observed at or near the time or place at which such relevant fact occurred (**section 156**).

(ii) any former statement made by such witness relating to the same fact at or about the time when the fact took place, or before any authority competent to investigate the fact, may be proved (**section 157**).

When a statement relevant under section 32 or section 33 is proved, evidence may be given—

(1) to contradict or corroborate it, or

(2) to impeach or confirm the credit of the person by whom it was made, as if he had been called as a witness and had denied upon cross-examination the truth of the matter suggested (**section 158**).

Refreshing memory.—A witness may refresh his memory by referring to—

(1) any writing made by himself—

(i) at the time of the transaction concerning which he is questioned, or

(ii) so soon afterwards that the transaction was fresh in his memory;

(2) any such writing made by another person and read by the witness and known by him to be correct, while his memory was still fresh;

(3) professional treatises if he is an expert.

A witness may, with the court's permission, refer to a copy of any document to which he might refer if it were produced, provided there is sufficient reason for the non-production of the original (**section 159**). He may also testify to facts mentioned in any such document, although he has no recollection of them, if he is sure that the facts were correctly recorded in the document (**section 160**). Any document to refresh memory must be shown to the adverse party, who may, if he pleases, cross-examine the witness upon it (**section 161**).

Production of document by witness.—A witness summoned to produce a document must, if it is in his possession or power, bring it to Court, notwithstanding any objection which there may be to its production or admissibility. The validity of such objection will be decided by the court. The court may inspect the document unless it refers to matters of State or take evidence to determine its admissibility (**section 162**).

Notice to produce document.—Notice to produce a document is necessary, except in the six cases provided in section 66, in order to make secondary evidence of its contents admissible. When a party gives notice to produce a document, and it is produced and inspected by the party calling for its production, he is bound to give it as evidence if the party producing it requires him to do so (**section 163**). If a party refuses to produce a document after notice, he cannot use it as evidence (i) without the consent of the other party, or (ii) the order of the court (**section 164**).

Court's power to put questions.—The Judge may, in order to ascertain relevant facts,

(1) ask any question (a) at any time, (b) of any witness or parties, (c) about relevant or irrelevant facts—though the judgment must be based on relevant facts only;

(2) order the production of any document or thing.

The parties cannot object to this course, nor can they cross-examine a witness upon any answer given in reply.

The Judge, however, cannot

(1) compel a witness to answer a question or produce a document which such witness would be entitled to refuse to answer or to produce under sections 121 to 132 at the instance of the adverse party;

(2) ask any question as to credit which it would be improper for any other person to ask under section 148 or section 149;

(3) dispense with primary evidence of any document, except where secondary evidence is admissible (**section 165**).

Power of jury to put questions.—A juror or assessor may put any question to a witness, through or by leave of the Judge, which the Judge might put and which he considers proper (**section 166**).

Chapter XI.—Improper admission or rejection of evidence.—The improper admission or rejection of evidence is not a ground—

(1) for a reversal of the judgment, or

(2) for a new trial of the case,

if the court thinks

(i) that independently of the evidence admitted, there was sufficient evidence to justify the decision, or

(ii) that if the rejected evidence had been received it ought not to have varied the decision (**section 167**).

Subject Index

A